S0-ARA-709

1996 Florida Statistical Abstract

Thirtieth Edition

Susan S. Floyd, Editor
Gayle H. Thompson, Managing Editor
Dorothy A. Evans, Publications Production Specialist

Bureau of Economic and Business Research
College of Business Administration

Order books from Bureau of Economic and Business Research
College of Business Administration
221 Matherly Hall, Post Office Box 117145
Gainesville, Florida 32611-7145
phone (352) 392-0171
fax (352) 392-4739
email: bebr@bebr.cba.ufl.edu
http://www.cba.ufl.edu/bebr/

ISBN 0-930885-10-4

Printed in the United States of America on acid-free paper

Cover photograph "Venus Kisses the Moon," January 1995, Newnan's Lake, Gainesville, Florida.
Courtesy of John Moran/The Gainesville Sun

CONTENTS

PREFACE

Since 1967 the *Florida Statistical Abstract* has provided a comprehensive collection of the latest statistics available on the social, economic and political organization of Florida. This thirtieth edition continues the tradition. Most of the data is at the county level, although the *Abstract* also includes information about Florida Metropolitan Statistical Areas, cities, planning districts, and other substate units along with comparisons of Florida with other Sunbelt and other populous states and the United States as a whole. This volume contains a selection of data collected by public and private entities. Agencies of the State of Florida and the Federal Government contribute the majority of the data.

Every effort is made to publish the most up-to-date figures possible; however, these data cover a wide range of activities reported for different time periods so uniformity is impossible. Statistics in this edition are generally for the most recent year or period available by the summer of 1996. Each table title states the time period for data shown in the table and exceptions are footnoted. Sources are given at the bottom of each table. Usually more statistical detail and a more comprehensive discussion of methods and definitions than can be included in the *Abstract* are in the source. Data not available in publications at the time of printing are identified in the source notes as "unpublished data," "prepublication release," and/or with an address on the Internet. Some data are available both in print and on line or CD-ROM.

Recent budget cutbacks on the federal and state levels have forced the reduction of published data. Please refer to the Appendix at the back of the book for discussion on source availability.

Each year all tables are reviewed: new tables of current interest are added, continuing series are updated or revised to reflect changes in source definitions or methods, and less timely data are eliminated. Some tables of "benchmark" data, although not timely, are repeated. The reader is encouraged to use tables in earlier editions.

Organization of the *Florida Statistical Abstract*. The *Abstract* is organized around five divisions, each of which is subdivided into sections. Table numbers correspond to the section numbers. The first division (Sections 1.00 through 7.00) generally includes tables presenting data on characteristics of the population: demographics, housing, education, income, employment, and welfare. Except for Section 8.00, which presents data on physical geography and the environment, the next three divisions (Sections 9.00 through 23.00) refer primarily to establishments engaged in economic, social, and political activities.

Establishments are classified in most sources according to the Standard Industrial Classification (SIC) system. Major industry divisions are assigned two-digit codes 01 through 99; subdivisions are classified by three- and four-digit codes. (See the Glossary, "Industrial Classification System, Standard," for more discussion and employment Table 6.03 for a two-digit industry listing.)

The last division of the *Abstract* contains tables of a comparative nature: economic and social trends. Time series showing the fluctuations of major economic indicators such as prices and employment are included in Section 24.00. Selected statistics of the economic, social, and physical environments of Florida, other Sunbelt and other populous states and the United States comprise Section 25.00.

Changes in this edition. This year marks the first year of a streamlined production process. To achieve the goal of a more efficient process involving less staff, some style changes were necessary. While reverting to previous style in some cases, we also made new changes that we trust will enhance the volume.

As we move further into the nineties and closer to the turn of the century, the demand for data from the 1990 decennial censuses has lessened. Much of the data from the 1990 censuses of population and housing has been phased out of this volume to make room for more timely statistics throughout the volume. Tables showing recently released statistics from the 1992 economic censuses have been added as new tables or retained. The user is referred to the Index of Census Tables at the back of this book for a listing of recent census tables that have appeared in previous *Abstracts. The 1990 Census Handbook: Florida* is also available for the user who is in need of detailed decennial census data. Ordering information is located at the back of the book. Some of the new tables in this edition include new state and county Hispanic population estimates, net migration by state of exchange, homeownership rates, deaths by leading cause, occupational distribution of white and minority employees, top 100 occupations and industry growth trends, historical banking data, boating and personal watercraft accidents, general acute-care hospital data, and voting-age population projections for the upcoming elections.

***Abstract* diskettes**. *Abstract* tables are available on microcomputer diskette. To order diskettes please contact the Bureau of Economic and Business Research, 221 Matherly Hall, P. O. Box 117145, Gainesville, Florida, 32611-7145, (352) 392-0171, or e-mail bebr@bebr.cba.ufl.edu.

Bureau of Economic and Business Research. The Bureau's mission is twofold: (1) to produce, collect, analyze, and disseminate economic and demographic data on Florida; and (2) conduct applied research and publish findings on topics relating to the state's ongoing economic growth and development. The Bureau's activities are organized around four research programs: forecasting, population, survey, and policy studies.

Acknowledgments. As we reflect over the past thirty years of *Abstract* production, we bid farewell to former editor Ann Pierce, who retired after seventeen years of service to the University of Florida and to the BEBR. Ann served as editor of the last two editions of the *Abstract*. She was extremely encouraging when "passing the torch" to this editor who, despite involvement in the production of twenty-one previous volumes, still suffers from occasional bouts of uncertainty. Ann assisted with this year's cover selection process and prepared the cover layout before she left and before the production of this volume began. When last we spoke, she was thoroughly enjoying her retirement and the opportunities to visit with her children and travel. We wish her every happiness in her richly-deserved retirement.

This edition benefited from the advice the BEBR's Associate Director, John F. (Dick) Scoggins, who serves as chairperson of the *1996 Abstract* Advisory Board and of two outside reviewers. Dr. John R. Dunkle and Dr. Joann Mossa, professor and assistant professor of geography at the University of Florida, who reviewed the data on geography and the environment. Their participation in our continuing efforts to make the *Abstract* more valuable to users is greatly appreciated.

The *Abstract* cover photograph was taken by John Moran of the Gainesville Sun. His willingness to work with us and to offer his artistic input was invaluable in the selection process.

As mentioned earlier, the *Abstract* production process has undergone some rather radical changes. Key personnel in the production of the *1996 Abstract* are Gayle Thompson, managing editor; and her student statistical assistants, Francis Vennemann, Jr., Bradley Taylor, and Philip Briggs. Gayle and staff were completely responsible for table layout and design, data entry and proofing, quality control, and final print of the tables. In addition to his other duties, Brad assisted with final proofing of the text portions of the volume and with revisions made in the Census Index. Due to changes in equipment as well as process, Gayle also had the task of converting each table individually into its current format—an extremely time-consuming undertaking. The results of these changes are a much more efficient process, higher quality-control maintenance, and a publication that can get into the hands of the user in a more timely fashion. Dorothy Evans, publications production specialist, was responsible for the preparation of the section dividers and maps and for the conversion of all text material and the index. It is they who bear the greatest responsibility and deserve the greatest credit for this publication.

Many other members of the Bureau also contributed to this volume. Carol McLarty assisted with the cover layout and design and provided data from the BEBR Data Base. Along with production and equipment changes, this edition is the first to be marketed and distributed directly by the BEBR. Carol is responsible for marketing the volume, and Pamela Middleton is in charge of distribution. Carol and Janet Rose assisted with the publication bid processes. June Nogle provided data from the BEBR Population Program. Ken Mease supplied data from the BEBR monthly Florida Economic and Consumer Survey. Scott Cody provided computer support for building permit data. Janet Rose ordered sources, Robyn Richards assisted in their collection and both, along with Janet Fletcher and Pamela Middleton, helped with promotional mailings. Ken Sturrock and Chris McCarty were instrumental in providing computer support in our conversion to new and unfamiliar equipment.

We are always pleased to receive suggestions from users for improving the coverage and presentation of data in the *Florida Statistical Abstract*.

Susan S. Floyd
Editor

Gainesville, Florida
August 1996

Counties and Metropolitan Statistical Areas
Effective December 31, 1992 to present

Daytona Beach MSA
  Flagler County
  Volusia County

Ft. Lauderdale PMSA*
  Broward County

Ft. Myers-Cape Coral MSA
  Lee County

Ft. Pierce-Port St. Lucie MSA
  Martin County
  St. Lucie County

Ft. Walton Beach MSA
  Okaloosa County

Gainesville MSA
  Alachua County

Jacksonville MSA
  Clay County
  Duval County
  Nassau County
  St. Johns County

Lakeland-Winter Haven MSA
  Polk County

Melbourne-Titusville-
Palm Bay MSA
  Brevard County

Miami PMSA*
  Dade County

Naples MSA
  Collier County

Ocala MSA
  Marion County

Orlando MSA
  Lake County
  Orange County
  Osceola County
  Seminole County

Panama City MSA
  Bay County

Pensacola MSA
  Escambia County
  Santa Rosa County

Punta Gorda MSA
  Charlotte County

Sarasota-Bradenton MSA
  Manatee County
  Sarasota County

Tallahassee MSA
  Gadsden County
  Leon County

Tampa-St. Petersburg-
Clearwater MSA
  Hernando County
  Hillsborough County
  Pasco County
  Pinellas County

West Palm Beach-Boca Raton MSA
  Palm Beach County

* Miami-Ft. Lauderdale CMSA

Counties and County Seats

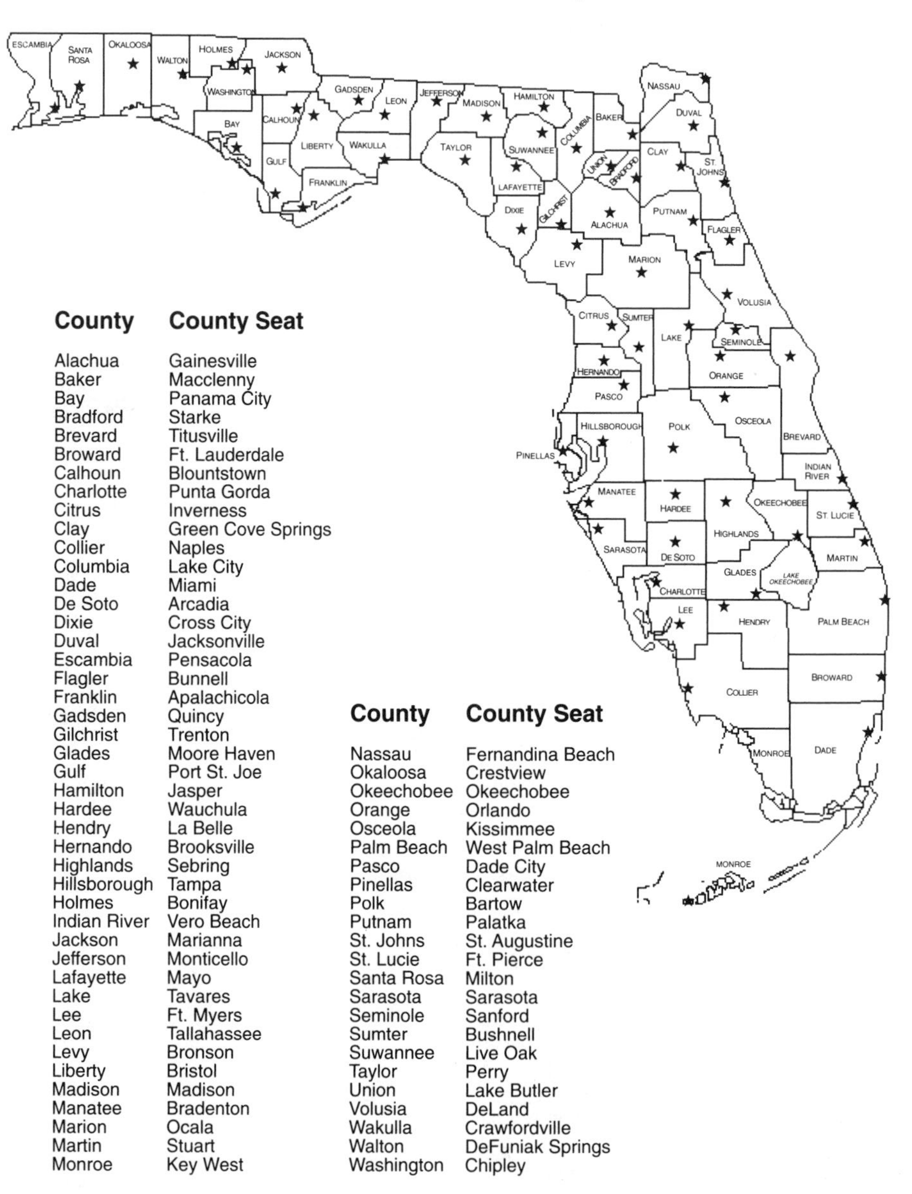

County	County Seat
Alachua	Gainesville
Baker	Macclenny
Bay	Panama City
Bradford	Starke
Brevard	Titusville
Broward	Ft. Lauderdale
Calhoun	Blountstown
Charlotte	Punta Gorda
Citrus	Inverness
Clay	Green Cove Springs
Collier	Naples
Columbia	Lake City
Dade	Miami
De Soto	Arcadia
Dixie	Cross City
Duval	Jacksonville
Escambia	Pensacola
Flagler	Bunnell
Franklin	Apalachicola
Gadsden	Quincy
Gilchrist	Trenton
Glades	Moore Haven
Gulf	Port St. Joe
Hamilton	Jasper
Hardee	Wauchula
Hendry	La Belle
Hernando	Brooksville
Highlands	Sebring
Hillsborough	Tampa
Holmes	Bonifay
Indian River	Vero Beach
Jackson	Marianna
Jefferson	Monticello
Lafayette	Mayo
Lake	Tavares
Lee	Ft. Myers
Leon	Tallahassee
Levy	Bronson
Liberty	Bristol
Madison	Madison
Manatee	Bradenton
Marion	Ocala
Martin	Stuart
Monroe	Key West

County	County Seat
Nassau	Fernandina Beach
Okaloosa	Crestview
Okeechobee	Okeechobee
Orange	Orlando
Osceola	Kissimmee
Palm Beach	West Palm Beach
Pasco	Dade City
Pinellas	Clearwater
Polk	Bartow
Putnam	Palatka
St. Johns	St. Augustine
St. Lucie	Ft. Pierce
Santa Rosa	Milton
Sarasota	Sarasota
Seminole	Sanford
Sumter	Bushnell
Suwannee	Live Oak
Taylor	Perry
Union	Lake Butler
Volusia	DeLand
Wakulla	Crawfordville
Walton	DeFuniak Springs
Washington	Chipley

Population

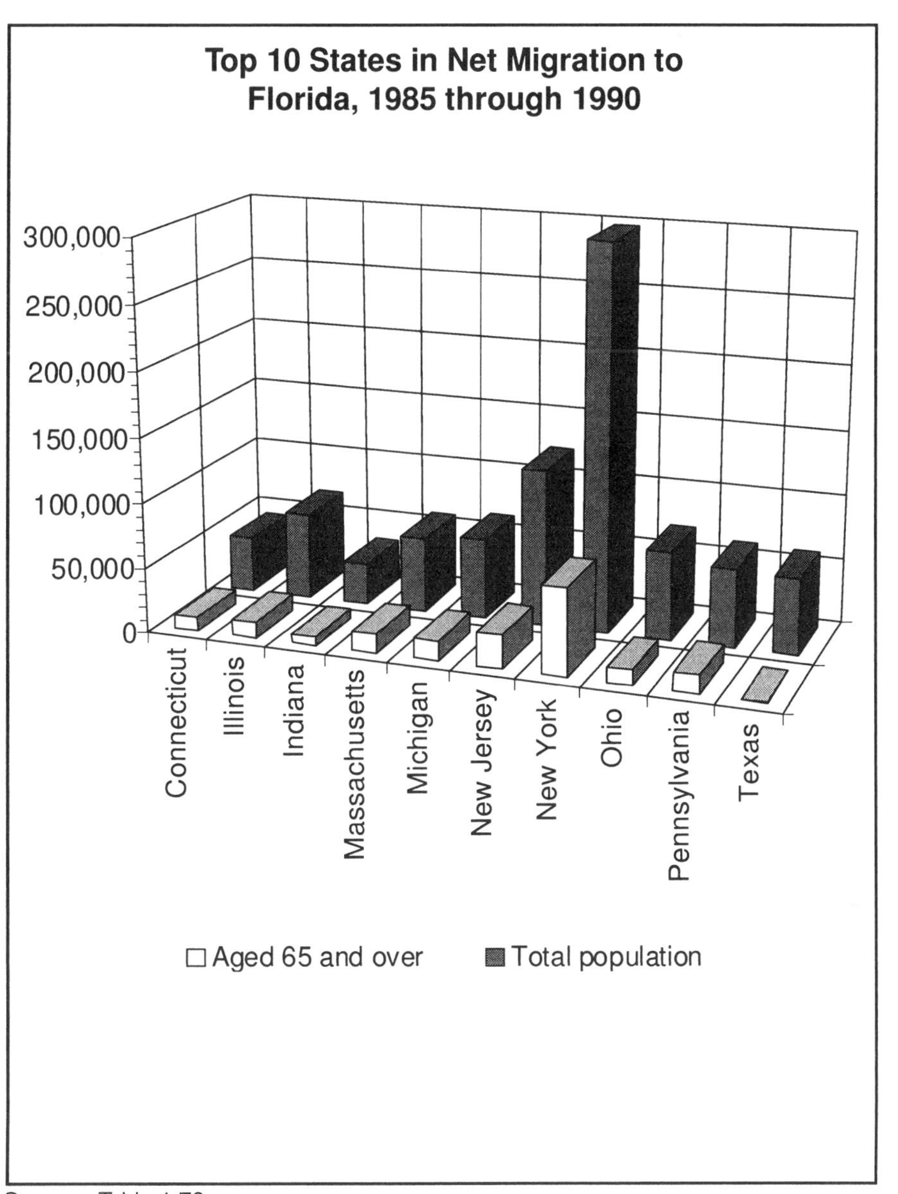

Source: Table 1.73

SECTION 1.00
POPULATION

TABLES LISTED BY MAJOR HEADINGS

SECTION 1.00
POPULATION
(Continued)

TABLES LISTED BY MAJOR HEADINGS

HEADING PAGE

Table 1.10. CENSUS COUNTS: TOTAL, URBAN, AND RURAL POPULATION IN FLORIDA, CENSUS YEARS 1830 TO 1990

Census year and date	Total population Number	Change from preceding census Number	Change from preceding census Percentage	Urban population Number	Urban population Percentage of total	Rural population Number	Rural population Percentage of total
Previous urban definition 1/							
1830 (June 1)	34,730	(X)	(X)	0	0.0	34,730	100.0
1840 (June 1)	54,477	19,747	56.9	0	0.0	54,477	100.0
1850 (June 1)	87,445	32,968	60.5	0	0.0	87,445	100.0
1860 (June 1)	140,424	52,979	60.6	5,708	4.1	134,716	95.9
1870 (June 1)	187,748	47,324	33.7	15,275	8.1	172,473	91.9
1880 (June 1)	269,493	81,745	43.5	26,947	10.0	242,546	90.0
1890 (June 1)	391,422	121,929	45.2	77,358	19.8	314,064	80.2
1900 (June 1)	528,542	137,120	35.0	107,031	20.3	421,511	79.7
1910 (April 15)	752,619	224,077	42.4	219,080	29.1	533,539	70.9
1920 (January 1)	968,470	215,851	28.7	353,515	36.5	614,955	63.5
1930 (April 1)	1,468,211	499,741	51.6	759,778	51.7	708,433	48.3
1940 (April 1)	1,897,414	429,203	29.2	1,045,791	55.1	851,623	44.9
1950 (April 1)	2,771,305	873,891	46.1	1,566,788	56.5	1,204,517	43.5
1960 (April 1)	4,951,560	2,180,255	78.7	3,077,989	62.2	1,873,571	37.8
Current urban definition 2/							
1950 (April 1)	2,771,305	873,891	46.1	1,813,890	65.5	957,415	34.5
1960 (April 1)	4,951,560	2,180,255	78.7	3,661,383	73.9	1,290,177	26.1
1970 (April 1)	6,791,418	1,839,858	37.2	5,544,551	81.6	1,244,892	18.3
1980 (April 1)	9,746,324	2,954,906	43.5	8,212,385	84.3	1,533,939	15.7
1990 (April 1)	12,937,926	3,191,602	32.8	10,970,445	84.8	1,967,481	15.2

(X) Not applicable.

1/ Figures have been adjusted to constitute a substantially consistent series based on incorporated places of 2,500 or more persons with additional areas defined as urban under special rules.

2/ The current urban definition defines the urban population as all persons living in urbanized areas and in places of 2,500 or more persons outside urbanized areas. An urbanized area comprises an incorporated place and adjacent densely settled surrounding area that together have a minimum population of 50,000. Population not classified as urban constitutes the rural population. Rural classification need not imply farm residence or a sparsely settled area because a small city is rural as long as it is outside an urbanized area and has fewer than 2,500 persons.

Source: U.S., Department of Commerce, Bureau of the Census, *1990 Census of Population: General Population Characteristics, Florida,* 1990 CP-1-11, and previous census editions.

Table 1.12. STATES: CENSUS COUNTS, APRIL 1, 1990, AND ESTIMATES, JULY 1, 1995 IN FLORIDA, OTHER STATES, AND THE UNITED STATES

State	Census April 1 1990 (1,000)	Esti- mates July 1 1995 (1,000)	Per- centage change 1990 to 1995
Florida	12,938	14,166	9.5
Alabama	4,040	4,253	5.3
Alaska	550	604	9.7
Arizona	3,665	4,218	15.1
Arkansas	2,351	2,484	5.7
California	29,758	31,589	6.2
Colorado	3,294	3,747	13.7
Connecticut	3,287	3,275	-0.4
Delaware	666	717	7.7
District of Columbia	607	554	-8.7
Georgia	6,478	7,201	11.2
Hawaii	1,108	1,187	7.1
Idaho	1,007	1,163	15.5
Illinois	11,431	11,830	3.5
Indiana	5,544	5,803	4.7
Iowa	2,777	2,842	2.3
Kansas	2,478	2,565	3.5
Kentucky	3,687	3,860	4.7
Louisiana	4,220	4,342	2.9
Maine	1,228	1,241	1.1
Maryland	4,781	5,042	5.5
Massachusett	6,016	6,074	0.9
Michigan	9,295	9,549	2.7
Minnesota	4,376	4,610	5.3
Mississippi	2,575	2,697	4.7
Missouri	5,117	5,324	4.0
Montana	799	870	8.9
Nebraska	1,578	1,637	3.7
Nevada	1,202	1,530	27.3
New Hampshire	1,109	1,148	3.5
New Jersey	7,730	7,945	2.8
New Mexico	1,515	1,685	11.2
New York	17,991	18,136	0.8
North Carolina	6,632	7,195	8.5
North Dakota	639	641	0.4
Ohio	10,847	11,151	2.8
Oklahoma	3,146	3,278	4.2
Oregon	2,842	3,141	10.5
Pennsylvania	11,883	12,072	1.6
Rhode Island	1,003	990	-1.4
South Carolina	3,486	3,673	5.4
South Dakota	696	729	4.7
Tennessee	4,877	5,256	7.8
Texas	16,986	18,724	10.2
Utah	1,723	1,951	13.3
Vermont	563	585	3.9
Virginia	6,189	6,618	6.9
Washington	4,867	5,431	11.6
West Virginia	1,793	1,828	1.9
Wisconsin	4,892	5,123	4.7
Wyoming	454	480	5.9
United States	248,718	262,755	5.6

Note: Includes persons in the Armed Forces residing in each state. Some data may be revised.

Source: U.S., Department of Commerce, Bureau of the Census, Population Division, the Internet at <http://www.census.gov/>.

Table 1.19. COUNTIES: CENSUS COUNTS IN THE STATE AND COUNTIES OF FLORIDA, 1940 THROUGH 1990

County	1940	1950	1960	1970	1980	1990	Percentage change 1940-1950	1950-1960	1960-1970	1970-1980	1980-1990
Florida	1,897,414	2,771,305	4,951,560	6,791,418	9,746,961	12,938,071	46.1	78.7	37.2	43.5	32.7
Alachua	38,607	57,026	74,074	104,764	151,369	181,596	47.7	29.9	41.4	44.5	20.0
Baker	6,510	6,313	7,363	9,242	15,289	18,486	-3.0	16.6	25.5	65.4	20.9
Bay	20,686	42,689	67,131	75,283	97,740	126,994	106.4	57.3	12.1	29.8	29.9
Bradford	8,717	11,457	12,446	14,625	20,023	22,515	31.4	8.6	17.5	36.9	12.4
Brevard	16,142	23,653	111,435	230,006	272,959	398,978	46.5	371.1	106.4	18.7	46.2
Broward	39,794	83,933	333,946	620,100	1,018,257	1,255,531	110.9	297.9	85.7	64.2	23.3
Calhoun	8,218	7,922	7,422	7,624	9,294	11,011	-3.6	-6.3	2.7	21.9	18.5
Charlotte	3,663	4,286	12,594	27,559	58,460	110,975	17.0	193.8	118.8	112.1	89.8
Citrus	5,846	6,111	9,268	19,196	54,703	93,513	4.5	51.7	107.1	185.0	70.9
Clay	6,468	14,323	19,535	32,059	67,052	105,986	121.4	36.4	64.1	109.2	58.1
Collier	5,102	6,488	15,753	38,040	85,971	152,099	27.2	142.8	141.5	126.0	76.9
Columbia	16,859	18,216	20,077	25,250	35,399	42,613	8.0	10.2	25.8	40.2	20.4
Dade	267,739	495,084	935,047	1,267,792	1,625,509	1,937,194	84.9	88.9	35.6	28.2	19.2
De Soto	7,792	9,242	11,683	13,060	19,039	23,865	18.6	26.4	11.8	45.8	25.3
Dixie	7,018	3,928	4,479	5,480	7,751	10,585	-44.0	14.0	22.3	41.4	36.6
Duval	210,143	304,029	455,411	528,865	571,003	672,971	44.7	49.8	16.1	8.0	17.9
Escambia	74,667	112,706	173,829	205,334	233,794	262,798	50.9	54.2	18.1	13.9	12.4
Flagler	3,008	3,367	4,566	4,454	10,913	28,701	11.9	35.6	-2.5	145.0	163.0
Franklin	5,991	5,814	6,576	7,065	7,661	8,967	-3.0	13.1	7.4	8.4	17.0
Gadsden	31,450	36,457	41,989	39,184	41,674	41,116	15.9	15.2	-6.7	6.4	-1.3
Gilchrist	4,250	3,499	2,868	3,551	5,767	9,667	-17.7	-18.0	23.8	62.4	67.6
Glades	2,745	2,199	2,950	3,669	5,992	7,591	-19.9	34.2	24.4	63.3	26.7
Gulf	6,951	7,460	9,937	10,096	10,658	11,504	7.3	33.2	1.6	5.6	7.9

Continued . . .

Table 1.19. COUNTIES: CENSUS COUNTS IN THE STATE AND COUNTIES OF FLORIDA, 1940 THROUGH 1990 (Continued)

County	1940	1950	1960	1970	1980	1990	Percentage change 1940-1950	1950-1960	1960-1970	1970-1980	1980-1990
Hamilton	9,778	8,981	7,705	7,787	8,761	10,930	-8.2	-14.2	1.1	12.5	24.8
Hardee	10,158	10,073	12,370	14,889	20,357	19,499	-0.8	22.8	20.4	36.7	-4.2
Hendry	5,237	6,051	8,119	11,859	18,599	25,773	15.5	34.2	46.1	56.8	38.6
Hernando	5,641	6,693	11,205	17,004	44,469	101,115	18.6	67.4	51.8	161.5	127.4
Highlands	9,246	13,636	21,338	29,507	47,526	68,432	47.5	56.5	38.3	61.1	44.0
Hillsborough	180,148	249,894	397,788	490,265	646,939	834,054	38.7	59.2	23.2	32.0	28.9
Holmes	15,447	13,988	10,844	10,720	14,723	15,778	-9.4	-22.5	-1.1	37.3	7.2
Indian River	8,957	11,872	25,309	35,992	59,896	90,208	32.5	113.2	42.2	66.4	50.6
Jackson	34,428	34,645	36,208	34,434	39,154	41,375	0.6	4.5	-4.9	13.7	5.7
Jefferson	12,032	10,413	9,543	8,778	10,703	11,296	-13.5	-8.4	-8.0	21.9	5.5
Lafayette	4,405	3,440	2,889	2,892	4,035	5,578	-21.9	-16.0	0.1	39.5	38.2
Lake	27,255	36,340	57,383	69,305	104,870	152,104	33.3	57.9	20.8	51.3	45.0
Lee	17,488	23,404	54,539	105,216	205,266	335,113	33.8	133.0	92.9	95.1	63.3
Leon	31,646	51,590	74,225	103,047	148,655	192,493	63.0	43.9	38.8	44.3	29.5
Levy	12,550	10,637	10,364	12,756	19,870	25,912	-15.2	-2.6	23.1	55.8	30.4
Liberty	3,752	3,182	3,138	3,379	4,260	5,569	-15.2	-1.4	7.7	26.1	30.7
Madison	16,190	14,197	14,154	13,481	14,894	16,569	-12.3	-0.3	-4.8	10.5	11.2
Manatee	26,098	34,704	69,168	97,115	148,445	211,707	33.0	99.3	40.4	52.9	42.6
Marion	31,243	38,187	51,616	69,030	122,488	194,835	22.2	35.2	33.7	77.4	59.1
Martin	6,295	7,807	16,932	28,035	64,014	100,900	24.0	116.9	65.6	128.3	57.6
Monroe	14,078	29,957	47,921	52,586	63,188	78,024	112.8	60.0	9.7	20.2	23.5
Nassau	10,826	12,811	17,189	20,626	32,894	43,941	18.3	34.2	20.0	59.5	33.6
Okaloosa	12,900	27,533	61,175	88,187	109,920	143,777	113.4	122.2	44.2	24.6	30.8
Okeechobee	3,000	3,454	6,424	11,233	20,264	29,627	15.1	86.0	74.9	80.4	46.2

Continued . . .

Table 1.19. COUNTIES: CENSUS COUNTS IN THE STATE AND COUNTIES OF FLORIDA, 1940 THROUGH 1990 (Continued)

County	1940	1950	1960	1970	1980	1990	Percentage change 1940-1950	1950-1960	1960-1970	1970-1980	1980-1990
Orange	70,074	114,950	263,540	344,311	470,865	677,491	64.0	129.3	30.6	36.8	43.9
Osceola	10,119	11,406	19,029	25,267	49,287	107,728	12.7	66.8	32.8	95.1	118.6
Palm Beach	79,989	114,688	228,106	348,993	576,758	863,503	43.4	98.9	53.0	65.3	49.7
Pasco	13,981	20,529	36,785	75,955	193,661	281,131	46.8	79.2	106.5	155.0	45.2
Pinellas	91,852	159,249	374,665	522,329	728,531	851,659	73.4	135.3	39.4	39.5	16.9
Polk	86,665	123,997	195,139	228,515	321,652	405,382	43.1	57.4	17.1	40.8	26.0
Putnam	18,698	23,615	32,212	36,424	50,549	65,070	26.3	36.4	13.1	38.8	28.7
St. Johns	20,012	24,998	30,034	31,035	51,303	83,829	24.9	20.1	3.3	65.3	63.4
St. Lucie	11,871	20,180	39,294	50,836	87,182	150,171	70.0	94.7	29.4	71.5	72.3
Santa Rosa	16,085	18,554	29,547	37,741	55,988	81,608	15.3	59.2	27.7	48.3	45.8
Sarasota	16,106	28,827	76,895	120,413	202,251	277,776	79.0	166.7	56.6	68.0	37.3
Seminole	22,304	26,883	54,947	83,692	179,752	287,521	20.5	104.4	52.3	114.8	60.0
Sumter	11,041	11,330	11,869	14,839	24,272	31,577	2.6	4.8	25.0	63.6	30.1
Suwannee	17,073	16,986	14,961	15,559	22,287	26,780	-0.5	-11.9	4.0	43.2	20.2
Taylor	11,565	10,416	13,168	13,641	16,532	17,111	-9.9	26.4	3.6	21.2	3.5
Union	7,094	8,906	6,043	8,112	10,166	10,252	25.5	-32.1	34.2	25.3	0.8
Volusia	53,710	74,229	125,319	169,487	258,762	370,737	38.2	68.8	35.2	52.7	43.3
Wakulla	5,463	5,258	5,257	6,308	10,887	14,202	-3.8	0.0	20.0	72.6	30.4
Walton	14,246	14,725	15,576	16,087	21,300	27,759	3.4	5.8	3.3	32.4	30.3
Washington	12,302	11,888	11,249	11,453	14,509	16,919	-3.4	-5.4	1.8	26.7	16.6

Source: University of Florida, Bureau of Economic and Business Research, *The Urbanization of Florida's Population: An Historical Perspective of County Growth, 1830-1970,* and *Florida Estimates of Population, April 1, 1995.* Data from U.S. Bureau of the Census.

Table 1.20. COUNTIES: CENSUS COUNTS, APRIL 1, 1980 AND 1990, AND ESTIMATES, APRIL 1, 1986 THROUGH 1995 IN THE STATE AND COUNTIES OF FLORIDA

(in thousands, rounded to hundreds)

County	Census		Estimates								
	1980	1990	1986	1987	1988	1989	1991	1992	1993	1994	1995
Florida	9,747.0	12,938.1	11,654.1	12,000.2	12,327.6	12,650.9	13,196.0	13,424.4	13,608.6	13,878.9	14,149.3
Alachua	151.4	181.6	171.5	173.9	176.1	179.1	183.8	186.2	190.7	193.9	198.3
Baker	15.3	18.5	17.2	17.5	17.8	18.1	18.9	19.2	19.5	19.7	20.3
Bay	97.7	127.0	120.1	122.5	124.4	125.8	128.6	131.3	134.1	136.3	139.2
Bradford	20.0	22.5	22.3	22.8	23.0	23.0	22.7	23.1	23.3	24.2	24.3
Brevard	273.0	399.0	349.7	363.0	376.3	388.4	409.4	417.7	427.0	436.3	445.0
Broward	1,018.3	1,255.5	1,147.9	1,176.8	1,206.7	1,232.5	1,278.4	1,294.1	1,317.5	1,340.2	1,364.2
Calhoun	9.3	11.0	9.7	9.8	10.1	10.8	11.2	11.8	11.5	11.6	12.0
Charlotte	58.5	111.0	85.7	91.4	97.0	103.2	115.6	118.7	121.7	124.9	127.6
Citrus	54.7	93.5	77.5	81.7	85.9	90.4	95.9	98.6	100.8	102.8	105.5
Clay	67.1	106.0	89.7	95.7	98.5	103.0	108.2	113.4	114.9	117.8	120.9
Collier	86.0	152.1	122.0	127.7	135.3	143.7	161.6	168.5	174.7	180.5	186.5
Columbia	35.4	42.6	39.6	40.4	41.1	41.9	43.5	45.2	46.4	48.9	50.4
Dade	1,625.5	1,937.2	1,815.6	1,846.8	1,879.1	1,908.9	1,961.7	1,982.9	1,951.1	1,990.4	2,013.8
De Soto	19.0	23.9	22.0	22.4	22.9	23.5	24.5	24.8	25.5	26.3	26.6
Dixie	7.8	10.6	9.4	9.6	9.8	10.2	10.5	10.9	11.8	12.2	12.4
Duval	571.0	673.0	633.7	645.9	656.4	663.4	681.6	693.5	701.6	710.6	718.4
Escambia	233.8	262.8	256.9	259.0	260.4	261.6	265.1	267.8	272.1	277.1	282.7
Flagler	10.9	28.7	18.5	20.5	23.1	26.0	30.5	32.0	33.5	35.3	37.0
Franklin	7.7	9.0	8.6	8.6	8.7	8.8	9.2	9.4	9.8	10.0	10.2
Gadsden	41.7	41.1	41.3	41.4	41.4	41.1	42.2	42.5	43.2	44.9	44.7
Gilchrist	5.8	9.7	7.7	7.9	8.5	9.1	10.0	10.2	10.7	11.5	11.9
Glades	6.0	7.6	6.9	7.1	7.2	7.3	7.9	8.1	8.3	8.4	8.6
Gulf	10.7	11.5	11.1	11.2	11.2	11.3	11.6	11.7	12.4	13.3	13.3

See footnote at end of table.

Continued . . .

Table 1.20. COUNTIES: CENSUS COUNTS, APRIL 1, 1980 AND 1990, AND ESTIMATES, APRIL 1, 1986 THROUGH 1995 IN THE STATE AND COUNTIES OF FLORIDA (Continued)

(in thousands, rounded to hundreds)

County	Census		Estimates								
	1980	1990	1986	1987	1988	1989	1991	1992	1993	1994	1995
Hamilton	8.8	10.9	9.4	9.5	10.1	10.6	11.0	11.5	11.6	11.9	12.5
Hardee	20.4	19.5	20.1	20.0	19.9	19.7	19.8	21.1	22.0	22.5	22.9
Hendry	18.6	25.8	23.3	24.0	24.8	25.3	27.2	27.8	28.1	28.7	29.5
Hernando	44.5	101.1	76.5	83.4	90.5	95.5	104.4	108.1	111.7	114.9	117.9
Highlands	47.5	68.4	59.4	62.1	64.3	66.4	70.6	72.2	73.2	75.9	77.3
Hillsborough	646.9	834.1	769.2	792.2	809.5	822.6	843.2	854.0	866.1	879.1	892.9
Holmes	14.7	15.8	15.1	15.1	15.2	15.5	16.0	16.2	16.3	16.9	17.4
Indian River	59.9	90.2	77.7	80.2	83.7	86.8	92.4	94.1	95.6	97.4	100.3
Jackson	39.2	41.4	40.6	41.2	41.2	41.2	41.6	42.6	44.4	45.4	46.6
Jefferson	10.7	11.3	11.1	11.2	11.2	11.3	12.0	12.3	13.0	13.1	13.5
Lafayette	4.0	5.6	4.7	5.1	5.2	5.4	5.7	5.6	5.6	5.8	6.5
Lake	104.9	152.1	131.2	137.2	141.0	146.5	157.1	162.6	167.2	171.2	176.9
Lee	205.3	335.1	286.7	300.6	312.3	325.4	344.0	350.8	357.6	367.4	376.7
Leon	148.7	192.5	169.7	174.4	178.9	187.5	198.3	202.6	206.3	212.1	217.5
Levy	19.9	25.9	23.3	23.8	24.5	25.3	26.7	27.5	28.2	29.1	29.8
Liberty	4.3	5.6	4.6	4.6	4.7	4.7	5.6	5.5	5.7	6.5	6.9
Madison	14.9	16.6	15.3	15.4	15.4	15.8	16.5	17.0	17.3	17.8	18.3
Manatee	148.4	211.7	186.1	193.5	199.7	205.7	215.1	219.3	223.5	228.3	233.2
Marion	122.5	194.8	167.1	174.2	180.9	188.1	200.3	206.6	212.0	217.9	224.6
Martin	64.0	100.9	84.2	88.3	92.0	96.2	103.1	105.0	106.8	110.2	112.0
Monroe	63.2	78.0	71.4	73.1	75.5	76.8	79.5	81.0	81.8	82.3	83.4
Nassau	32.9	43.9	39.8	41.2	42.1	43.5	45.0	45.5	46.5	47.4	49.1
Okaloosa	109.9	143.8	134.9	137.5	139.8	141.6	146.1	150.0	154.5	158.3	162.7
Okeechobee	20.3	29.6	26.1	27.3	28.1	28.9	30.2	31.1	31.8	32.3	32.9

See footnote at end of table.

Continued . . .

Table 1.20. COUNTIES: CENSUS COUNTS, APRIL 1, 1980 AND 1990, AND ESTIMATES, APRIL 1, 1986 THROUGH 1995 IN THE STATE AND COUNTIES OF FLORIDA (Continued)

(in thousands, rounded to hundreds)

County	Census		Estimates								
	1980	1990	1986	1987	1988	1989	1991	1992	1993	1994	1995
Orange	470.9	677.5	577.9	602.8	622.3	652.4	701.3	712.6	727.8	740.2	759.0
Osceola	49.3	107.7	82.2	87.6	95.2	101.0	114.4	119.8	125.7	131.1	136.6
Palm Beach	576.8	863.5	753.7	784.8	817.5	841.5	883.0	897.0	918.2	937.2	962.8
Pasco	193.7	281.1	249.1	258.2	267.0	274.4	285.4	290.3	294.0	298.9	305.6
Pinellas	728.5	851.7	814.4	825.7	834.0	844.6	855.8	860.7	865.0	870.7	876.2
Polk	321.7	405.4	374.1	383.0	391.6	399.0	414.7	420.9	429.9	437.2	443.2
Putnam	50.5	65.1	59.5	61.0	62.3	63.9	66.0	67.8	67.6	69.0	69.5
St. Johns	51.3	83.8	72.1	74.2	78.3	82.0	86.1	88.4	91.2	94.8	98.2
St. Lucie	87.2	150.2	122.9	129.5	136.3	144.1	155.1	158.9	163.2	166.8	171.2
Santa Rosa	56.0	81.6	70.2	73.3	75.6	79.1	83.9	88.0	90.3	93.8	96.1
Sarasota	202.3	277.8	251.1	258.1	264.3	271.4	283.1	287.2	290.6	296.0	301.5
Seminole	179.8	287.5	238.1	251.4	264.7	277.3	298.1	305.9	310.9	316.6	324.1
Sumter	24.3	31.6	28.6	29.3	29.8	30.9	32.0	33.1	33.8	35.2	36.5
Suwannee	22.3	26.8	25.0	25.3	25.7	26.3	27.4	27.6	28.6	29.3	30.5
Taylor	16.5	17.1	17.1	17.2	17.2	17.2	17.4	17.4	17.4	17.5	18.3
Union	10.2	10.3	10.4	10.6	10.1	10.3	10.6	11.4	12.0	12.5	12.6
Volusia	258.8	370.7	321.1	333.6	347.6	360.2	376.7	384.0	390.1	396.6	403.0
Wakulla	10.9	14.2	12.9	13.2	13.5	13.8	14.4	14.7	15.4	16.4	17.0
Walton	21.3	27.8	25.5	26.2	26.6	27.1	29.2	29.7	30.6	31.9	33.4
Washington	14.5	16.9	15.8	16.3	16.5	16.8	17.2	17.4	17.6	18.1	19.0

Note: These are revised intercensal estimates that incorporate the effects of 1990 census counts, all revisions to 1980 census counts, and any changes that may have occurred in the underlying base data. Estimates reflect changes to Dade and Broward counties as a result of Hurricane Andrew in August 1992.

Source: University of Florida, Bureau of Economic and Business Research, Population Program, *Special Population Reports,* May 1991, and *Florida Estimates of Population, April 1, 1995.* Census data from U.S. Bureau of the Census.

Table 1.31. COUNTIES AND CITIES: CENSUS COUNTS, APRIL 1, 1990, AND ESTIMATES APRIL 1, 1995, IN THE STATE, COUNTIES, AND MUNICIPALITIES OF FLORIDA

Area	Census 1990	Estimates 1995
Florida	12,938,071	14,149,317
Incorporated	6,415,302	6,889,514
Unincorporated	6,522,769	7,259,803
Alachua	181,596	198,261
Alachua	4,547	5,612
Archer	1,372	1,427
Gainesville	85,075	96,051
Hawthorne	1,305	1,381
High Springs	3,144	3,477
LaCrosse	122	113
Micanopy	626	647
Newberry	1,644	2,135
Waldo	1,017	1,047
Unincorporated	82,744	86,371
Baker	18,486	20,275
Glen St. Mary	480	467
Macclenny	3,966	4,201
Unincorporated	14,040	15,607
Bay	126,994	139,173
Callaway	12,253	13,879
Cedar Grove	1,479	1,648
Lynn Haven	9,298	10,590
Mexico Beach	992	1,009
Panama City	34,396	36,706
Panama City Beach	4,051	4,583
Parker	4,598	4,926
Springfield	8,719	9,389
Unincorporated	51,208	56,443
Bradford	22,515	24,336
Brooker	312	312
Hampton	296	311
Lawtey	676	686
Starke	5,226	5,142
Unincorporated	16,005	17,885
Brevard	398,978	444,992
Cape Canaveral	8,014	8,399
Cocoa	17,722	17,942
Cocoa Beach	12,123	12,713
Indialantic	2,844	2,940
Indian Harbour Beach	6,933	7,498
Malabar	1,977	2,313
Melbourne	60,034	66,350
Melbourne Beach	3,078	3,190
Melbourne Village	591	608
Palm Bay	62,543	73,137
Palm Shores	210	484

Area	Census 1990	Estimates 1995
Brevard (Continued)		
Rockledge	16,023	18,125
Satellite Beach	9,889	10,105
Titusville	39,394	41,495
West Melbourne	8,399	9,023
Unincorporated	149,204	170,670
Broward	1,255,531	1,364,168
Coconut Creek	27,269	33,388
Cooper City	21,335	27,398
Coral Springs	78,864	93,439
Dania	13,183	17,201
Davie	47,143	54,611
Deerfield Beach	46,997	48,393
Ft. Lauderdale	149,238	149,491
Hallandale	30,997	31,489
Hillsboro Beach	1,748	1,758
Hollywood	121,720	125,342
Lauderdale-by-the-Sea	2,990	3,003
Lauderdale Lakes	27,341	27,845
Lauderhill	49,015	50,022
Lazy Lake Village	33	40
Lighthouse Point	10,378	10,421
Margate	42,985	47,279
Miramar	40,663	44,412
North Lauderdale	26,473	27,237
Oakland Park	26,326	28,095
Parkland	3,773	8,491
Pembroke Park	4,933	4,911
Pembroke Pines	65,566	87,948
Plantation	66,814	75,184
Pompano Beach	72,411	73,950
Sea Ranch Lakes	619	614
Sunrise	65,683	73,456
Tamarac	44,822	48,758
Wilton Manors	11,804	11,868
Unincorporated	154,408	158,124
Calhoun	11,011	11,988
Altha	497	558
Blountstown	2,404	2,465
Unincorporated	8,110	8,965
Charlotte	110,975	127,646
Punta Gorda	10,637	11,978
Unincorporated	100,338	115,668
Citrus	93,513	105,468
Crystal River	4,050	4,123
Inverness	5,797	6,644
Unincorporated	83,666	94,701

See footnotes at end of table.

Continued . . .

Table 1.31. COUNTIES AND CITIES: CENSUS COUNTS, APRIL 1, 1990, AND ESTIMATES APRIL 1, 1995, IN THE STATE, COUNTIES, AND MUNICIPALITIES OF FLORIDA (Continued)

Area	Census 1990	Estimates 1995
Clay	105,986	120,896
Green Cove Springs	4,497	4,847
Keystone Heights	1,315	1,333
Orange Park	9,488	9,514
Penney Farms	609	638
Unincorporated	90,077	104,564
Collier	152,099	186,504
Everglades	321	543
Naples	19,505	20,605
Unincorporated	132,273	165,356
Columbia	42,613	50,387
Ft. White	468	560
Lake City	9,626	10,055
Unincorporated	32,519	39,772
Dade	1,937,194	2,013,821
Bal Harbour	3,045	3,087
Bay Harbor Islands	4,703	4,717
Biscayne Park	3,068	3,068
Coral Gables	40,091	40,950
El Portal	2,457	2,500
Florida City	5,978	4,898
Golden Beach	774	831
Hialeah	188,008	203,911
Hialeah Gardens	7,727	11,305
Homestead	26,694	23,190
Indian Creek Village	44	52
Islandia	13	13
Key Biscayne 1/	0	8,892
Medley	663	868
Miami	358,648	365,498
Miami Beach	92,639	91,775
Miami Shores	10,084	10,149
Miami Springs	13,268	13,353
North Bay	5,383	5,861
North Miami	50,001	50,758
North Miami Beach	35,361	36,171
Opa-Locka	15,283	16,160
South Miami	10,404	10,527
Surfside	4,108	4,270
Sweetwater	13,909	14,060
Virginia Gardens	2,212	2,272
West Miami	5,727	5,837
Unincorporated	1,036,902	1,078,848
De Soto	23,865	26,640
Arcadia	6,488	6,617
Unincorporated	17,377	20,023

Area	Census 1990	Estimates 1995
Dixie	10,585	12,416
Cross City	2,041	2,033
Horseshoe Beach	252	186
Unincorporated	8,292	10,197
Duval	672,971	718,355
Atlantic Beach	11,636	12,802
Baldwin	1,450	1,546
Jacksonville Beach	17,839	19,866
Neptune Beach	6,816	7,423
Jacksonville (Duval)	635,230	676,718
Escambia	262,798	282,742
Century	1,989	2,046
Pensacola	59,198	60,373
Unincorporated	201,611	220,323
Flagler	28,701	36,997
Beverly Beach	314	322
Bunnell	1,873	2,087
Flagler Beach	3,818	4,175
Marineland (part)	21	12
Unincorporated	22,675	30,401
Franklin	8,967	10,236
Apalachicola	2,602	2,796
Carrabelle	1,200	1,358
Unincorporated	5,165	6,082
Gadsden	41,116	44,734
Chattahoochee	4,382	4,259
Greensboro	586	580
Gretna	1,981	2,298
Havana	1,717	1,858
Midway	976	1,110
Quincy	7,452	7,351
Unincorporated	24,022	27,278
Gilchrist	9,667	11,888
Bell	267	286
Fanning Springs (part)	230	231
Trenton	1,287	1,354
Unincorporated	7,883	10,017
Glades	7,591	8,551
Moore Haven	1,432	1,558
Unincorporated	6,159	6,993
Gulf	11,504	13,271
Port St. Joe	4,044	4,134

See footnotes at end of table.

Continued . . .

Table 1.31. COUNTIES AND CITIES: CENSUS COUNTS, APRIL 1, 1990, AND ESTIMATES APRIL 1, 1995, IN THE STATE, COUNTIES, AND MUNICIPALITIES OF FLORIDA (Continued)

Area	Census 1990	Estimates 1995
Gulf (Continued)		
Wewahitchka	1,779	1,821
Unincorporated	5,681	7,316
Hamilton	10,930	12,487
Jasper	2,099	2,075
Jennings	712	801
White Springs	704	823
Unincorporated	7,415	8,788
Hardee	19,499	22,885
Bowling Green	1,836	1,962
Wauchula	3,243	3,632
Zolfo Springs	1,219	1,264
Unincorporated	13,201	16,027
Hendry	25,773	29,497
Clewiston	6,085	6,357
La Belle	2,703	3,095
Unincorporated	16,985	20,045
Hernando	101,115	117,895
Brooksville	7,589	7,814
Weeki Wachee	11	7
Unincorporated	93,515	110,074
Highlands	68,432	77,270
Avon Park	8,078	8,144
Lake Placid	1,158	1,345
Sebring	8,841	8,949
Unincorporated	50,355	58,832
Hillsborough	834,054	892,874
Plant City	22,754	25,465
Tampa	280,015	285,153
Temple Terrace	16,444	18,724
Unincorporated	514,841	563,532
Holmes	15,778	17,385
Bonifay	2,612	2,751
Esto	253	314
Noma	207	222
Ponce de Leon	406	450
Westville	257	283
Unincorporated	12,043	13,365
Indian River	90,208	100,261
Fellsmere	2,179	2,354
Indian River Shores	2,278	2,599
Orchid	10	25
Sebastian	10,248	13,488
Indian River (Continued)		
Vero Beach	17,350	17,681
Unincorporated	58,143	64,114
Jackson	41,375	46,577
Alford	482	522
Bascom	90	96
Campbellton	202	244
Cottondale	900	995
Graceville	2,675	2,696
Grand Ridge	536	608
Greenwood	474	502
Jacob City	261	308
Malone	765	2,136
Marianna	6,292	6,226
Sneads	1,746	2,044
Unincorporated	26,952	30,200
Jefferson	11,296	13,509
Monticello	2,603	2,896
Unincorporated	8,693	10,613
Lafayette	5,578	6,516
Mayo	917	936
Unincorporated	4,661	5,580
Lake	152,104	176,931
Astatula	981	1,162
Clermont	6,910	7,233
Eustis	12,856	13,971
Fruitland Park	2,715	2,935
Groveland	2,300	2,391
Howey-in-the-Hills	724	787
Lady Lake	8,071	12,045
Leesburg	14,783	15,014
Mascotte	1,761	2,297
Minneola	1,515	2,182
Montverde	890	1,097
Mount Dora	7,316	8,251
Tavares	7,383	8,078
Umatilla	2,350	2,406
Unincorporated	81,549	97,082
Lee	335,113	376,702
Cape Coral	74,991	85,807
Ft. Myers	44,947	46,474
Sanibel	5,468	5,753
Unincorporated	209,707	238,668
Leon	192,493	217,533
Tallahassee	124,773	137,057
Unincorporated	67,720	80,476

See footnotes at end of table.

Continued . . .

Table 1.31. COUNTIES AND CITIES: CENSUS COUNTS, APRIL 1, 1990, AND ESTIMATES APRIL 1, 1995, IN THE STATE, COUNTIES, AND MUNICIPALITIES OF FLORIDA (Continued)

Area	Census 1990	Estimates 1995
Levy	25,912	29,843
Bronson	875	857
Cedar Key	668	704
Chiefland	1,917	1,929
Fanning Springs (part)	263	291
Inglis	1,241	1,282
Otter Creek	136	124
Williston	2,168	2,258
Yankeetown	635	617
Unincorporated	18,009	21,781
Liberty	5,569	6,873
Bristol	937	1,027
Unincorporated	4,632	5,846
Madison	16,569	18,344
Greenville	950	1,023
Lee	306	314
Madison	3,345	3,420
Unincorporated	11,968	13,587
Manatee	211,707	233,160
Anna Maria	1,744	1,840
Bradenton	43,769	47,679
Bradenton Beach	1,657	1,673
Holmes Beach	4,810	5,025
Longboat Key (part)	2,544	2,647
Palmetto	9,268	9,747
Unincorporated	147,915	164,549
Marion	194,835	224,612
Belleview	2,678	3,287
Dunnellon	1,639	1,795
McIntosh	411	423
Ocala	42,045	43,207
Reddick	554	570
Unincorporated	147,508	175,330
Martin	100,900	112,036
Jupiter Island	549	581
Ocean Breeze Park	519	515
Sewall's Point	1,588	1,707
Stuart	11,936	13,435
Unincorporated	86,308	95,798
Monroe	78,024	83,401
Key Colony Beach	977	1,049
Key West	24,832	26,842
Layton	183	200
Unincorporated	52,032	55,310
Nassau	43,941	49,127
Callahan	946	985
Fernandina Beach	8,765	9,673
Hilliard	2,276	2,492
Unincorporated	31,954	35,977
Okaloosa	143,777	162,707
Cinco Bayou	386	390
Crestview	9,886	12,155
Destin	8,090	9,381
Ft. Walton Beach	21,407	22,003
Laurel Hill	543	584
Mary Esther	4,139	4,347
Niceville	10,509	11,575
Shalimar	341	612
Valparaiso	6,316	6,534
Unincorporated	82,160	95,126
Okeechobee	29,627	32,855
Okeechobee	4,943	5,069
Unincorporated	24,684	27,786
Orange	677,491	758,962
Apopka	13,611	18,449
Bay Lake	19	24
Belle Isle	5,272	5,591
Eatonville	2,505	2,489
Edgewood	1,062	1,137
Lake Buena Vista	1,776	23
Maitland	8,932	9,525
Oakland	700	755
Ocoee	12,778	18,578
Orlando	164,674	170,307
Windermere	1,371	1,692
Winter Garden	9,863	12,098
Winter Park	22,623	24,570
Unincorporated	432,305	493,724
Osceola	107,728	136,627
Kissimmee	30,337	37,177
St. Cloud	13,005	15,829
Unincorporated	64,386	83,621
Palm Beach	863,503	962,802
Atlantis	1,653	1,691
Belle Glade	16,177	17,006
Boca Raton	61,486	66,760
Boynton Beach	46,284	49,085
Briny Breezes	400	395
Cloud Lake	121	119
Delray Beach	47,184	50,195

See footnotes at end of table.

Continued . . .

Table 1.31. COUNTIES AND CITIES: CENSUS COUNTS, APRIL 1, 1990, AND ESTIMATES APRIL 1, 1995, IN THE STATE, COUNTIES, AND MUNICIPALITIES OF FLORIDA (Continued)

Area	Census 1990	Estimates 1995
Palm Beach (Continued)		
Glen Ridge	207	217
Golf Village	184	195
Golfview	153	151
Greenacres City	18,683	23,296
Gulf Stream	690	712
Haverhill	1,058	1,192
Highland Beach	3,209	3,251
Hypoluxo	807	1,129
Juno Beach	2,172	2,539
Jupiter	24,907	29,046
Jupiter Inlet Colony	405	405
Lake Clarke Shores	3,364	3,646
Lake Park	6,704	6,919
Lake Worth	28,564	29,167
Lantana	8,392	8,429
Manalapan	312	328
Mangonia Park	1,453	1,382
North Palm Beach	11,343	11,844
Ocean Ridge	1,570	1,605
Pahokee	6,822	6,944
Palm Beach	9,814	9,856
Palm Beach Gardens	22,990	31,011
Palm Beach Shores	1,035	1,036
Palm Springs	9,763	9,825
Riviera Beach	27,646	27,634
Royal Palm Beach	15,532	17,196
South Bay	3,558	4,042
South Palm Beach	1,480	1,495
Tequesta Village	4,499	4,592
West Palm Beach	67,764	76,418
Unincorporated	405,118	462,049
Pasco	281,131	305,576
Dade City	5,633	5,932
New Port Richey	14,044	14,390
Port Richey	2,521	2,658
St. Leo	1,009	714
San Antonio	776	838
Zephyrhills	8,220	8,694
Unincorporated	248,928	272,350
Pinellas	851,659	876,200
Belleair	3,963	4,043
Belleair Beach	2,070	2,104
Belleair Bluffs	2,234	2,221
Belleair Shore	60	60
Clearwater	98,784	101,162
Dunedin	34,027	34,988
Gulfport	11,709	11,876
Indian Rocks Beach	3,963	4,178
Pinellas (Continued)		
Indian Shores	1,405	1,473
Kenneth City	4,345	4,345
Largo	65,910	67,465
Madeira Beach	4,225	4,250
North Redington Beach	1,135	1,154
Oldsmar	8,361	8,925
Pinellas Park	43,571	44,176
Redington Beach	1,626	1,607
Redington Shores	2,366	2,420
Safety Harbor	15,120	16,135
St. Petersburg	240,318	241,563
St. Petersburg Beach	9,200	9,459
Seminole	9,251	9,709
South Pasadena	5,644	5,860
Tarpon Springs	17,874	19,146
Treasure Island	7,266	7,357
Unincorporated	257,232	270,524
Polk	405,382	443,153
Auburndale	8,846	9,267
Bartow	14,716	14,927
Davenport	1,529	1,769
Dundee	2,335	2,525
Eagle Lake	1,758	1,889
Ft. Meade	4,993	5,517
Frostproof	2,875	2,905
Haines City	11,683	12,601
Highland Park	155	157
Hillcrest Heights	221	235
Lake Alfred	3,622	3,716
Lake Hamilton	1,128	1,121
Lake Wales	9,670	9,894
Lakeland	70,576	74,626
Mulberry	2,988	3,327
Polk City	1,439	1,615
Winter Haven	24,725	25,409
Unincorporated	242,123	271,653
Putnam	65,070	69,516
Crescent City	1,859	1,843
Interlachen	1,160	1,376
Palatka	10,444	10,705
Pomona Park	726	758
Welaka	533	575
Unincorporated	50,348	54,259
St. Johns	83,829	98,188
Hastings	595	655
Marineland (part)	0	0
St. Augustine	11,695	12,090

See footnotes at end of table.

Continued . . .

Table 1.31. COUNTIES AND CITIES: CENSUS COUNTS, APRIL 1, 1990, AND ESTIMATES APRIL 1, 1995, IN THE STATE, COUNTIES, AND MUNICIPALITIES OF FLORIDA (Continued)

Area	Census 1990	Estimates 1995
St. Johns (Cont.)		
St. Augustine Beach	3,657	4,024
Unincorporated	67,882	81,419
St. Lucie	150,171	171,160
Ft. Pierce	36,830	37,029
Port St. Lucie	55,761	71,776
St. Lucie Village	584	601
Unincorporated	56,996	61,754
Santa Rosa	81,608	96,091
Gulf Breeze	5,530	5,922
Jay	666	689
Milton	7,216	7,511
Unincorporated	68,196	81,969
Sarasota	277,776	301,528
Longboat Key (part)	3,393	3,806
North Port	11,973	15,161
Sarasota	50,897	51,143
Venice	17,052	18,450
Unincorporated	194,461	212,968
Seminole	287,521	324,130
Altamonte Springs	35,167	37,917
Casselberry	18,849	24,144
Lake Mary	5,929	7,251
Longwood	13,316	13,602
Oviedo	11,114	17,910
Sanford	32,387	35,311
Winter Springs	22,151	25,673
Unincorporated	148,608	162,322
Sumter	31,577	36,456
Bushnell	1,998	2,273
Center Hill	735	758
Coleman	857	854
Webster	746	832
Wildwood	3,560	3,950
Unincorporated	23,681	27,789
Suwannee	26,780	30,534
Branford	670	670
Live Oak	6,332	6,481
Unincorporated	19,778	23,383
Taylor	17,111	18,322
Perry	7,151	7,259
Unincorporated	9,960	11,063
Union	10,252	12,647
Lake Butler	2,116	2,121
Raiford	198	262
Worthington Springs	178	178
Unincorporated	7,760	10,086
Volusia	370,737	402,970
Daytona Beach	61,991	63,306
Daytona Beach Shores	2,197	2,680
DeBary 1/	0	11,336
DeLand	16,622	17,973
Edgewater	15,351	17,484
Holly Hill	11,141	11,539
Lake Helen	2,344	2,438
New Smyrna Beach	16,549	18,393
Oak Hill	917	1,070
Orange City	5,347	6,117
Ormond Beach	29,721	31,539
Pierson	2,988	1,230
Ponce Inlet	1,704	2,120
Port Orange	35,399	39,750
South Daytona	12,488	12,889
Unincorporated	155,978	163,106
Wakulla	14,202	17,005
St. Marks	307	297
Sopchoppy	367	389
Unincorporated	13,528	16,319
Walton	27,759	33,415
DeFuniak Springs	5,200	5,384
Freeport	843	952
Paxton	600	605
Unincorporated	21,116	26,474
Washington	16,919	19,010
Caryville	631	579
Chipley	3,866	4,111
Ebro	255	257
Vernon	778	860
Wausau	313	322
Unincorporated	11,076	12,881

1/ Not incorporated in 1990.

Note: Census counts include all adjustments made through September 30, 1995. Estimates reflect changes to Dade and Broward counties as a result of Hurricane Andrew in August 1992.

Source: University of Florida, Bureau of Economic and Business Research, Population Program, *Florida Estimates of Population, April 1, 1995*. Census data from U.S. Bureau of the Census.

Table 1.34. AGE, RACE, AND SEX: CENSUS COUNTS, APRIL 1, 1990, AND ESTIMATES, APRIL 1, 1995, BY AGE, RACE, AND SEX IN FLORIDA

Age	All races Total	All races Male	All races Female	White Total	White Male	White Female	Black 1/ Total	Black 1/ Male	Black 1/ Female
Census, 1990									
All ages	12,937,926	6,261,770	6,676,156	10,971,995	5,323,424	5,648,571	1,772,356	845,923	926,433
0-14	2,428,671	1,243,364	1,185,307	1,860,162	955,468	904,694	523,856	265,194	258,662
15-24	1,682,627	859,036	823,591	1,343,380	691,738	651,642	305,932	150,087	155,845
25-44	3,920,704	1,954,702	1,966,002	3,290,085	1,658,800	1,631,285	555,627	261,562	294,065
45-64	2,549,998	1,201,564	1,348,434	2,259,374	1,068,506	1,190,868	258,632	118,670	139,962
65-69	737,129	331,267	405,862	689,346	310,846	378,500	44,214	18,850	25,364
70-74	627,699	279,758	347,941	592,046	265,200	326,846	33,373	13,561	19,812
75-79	483,532	204,877	278,655	456,675	194,660	262,015	25,375	9,572	15,803
80-84	302,099	118,468	183,631	286,770	112,991	173,779	14,592	5,145	9,447
85 and over	205,467	68,734	136,733	194,157	65,215	128,942	10,755	3,282	7,473
Estimates, 1995									
All ages	14,149,317	6,872,344	7,276,973	11,856,392	5,765,310	6,091,082	2,042,645	986,586	1,056,059
0-14	2,746,617	1,404,145	1,342,472	2,064,455	1,057,760	1,006,695	621,667	315,541	306,126
15-24	1,696,836	872,298	824,538	1,321,336	680,952	640,384	334,817	169,850	164,967
25-44	4,127,110	2,065,798	2,061,312	3,413,478	1,723,550	1,689,928	620,528	298,915	321,613
45-64	2,938,456	1,396,666	1,541,790	2,575,876	1,232,932	1,342,944	318,354	144,097	174,257
65-69	741,499	338,816	402,683	687,711	315,698	372,013	49,154	21,077	28,077
70-74	716,503	319,418	397,085	674,386	302,029	372,357	38,953	16,001	22,952
75-79	551,263	237,722	313,541	522,077	226,484	295,593	27,234	10,392	16,842
80-84	376,352	149,773	226,579	356,952	142,924	214,028	18,247	6,346	11,901
85 and over	254,681	87,708	166,973	240,121	82,981	157,140	13,691	4,367	9,324

1/ "Black" reflects the self-identification of respondents in the 1990 census.

Note: Data for age and race categories have been modified by the U.S. Bureau of the Census to account for misreporting. As a result, these numbers may differ from those found in other publications.

Source: University of Florida, Bureau of Economic and Business Research, Population Program, *Florida Population Studies,* July 1996, Volume 29, No. 3. Bulletin No. 115, and unpublished data.

Table 1.35. AGE AND SEX: ESTIMATES BY SEX AND AGE GROUP AND MEDIAN AGE IN THE STATE AND COUNTIES OF FLORIDA
APRIL 1, 1995

County	Total	Sex		Age						
		Male	Female	0-14	15-24	25-44	45-64	65 and over	18 and over	Median 1/
Florida	14,149,317	6,872,344	7,276,973	2,746,617	1,696,836	4,127,110	2,938,456	2,640,298	10,948,741	37.8
Alachua	198,261	97,902	100,359	37,612	49,615	62,187	30,158	18,689	154,471	28.5
Baker	20,275	10,703	9,572	4,713	3,392	6,647	3,783	1,740	14,511	31.7
Bay	139,173	68,510	70,663	30,396	18,553	42,902	29,363	17,959	103,470	34.9
Bradford	24,336	13,652	10,684	4,661	3,536	8,076	4,901	3,162	18,725	34.6
Brevard	444,992	218,837	226,155	85,042	49,527	132,761	97,467	80,195	345,985	38.3
Broward	1,364,168	655,561	708,607	256,363	137,955	422,287	275,818	271,745	1,068,979	38.7
Calhoun	11,988	6,369	5,619	2,276	1,866	3,718	2,385	1,743	9,213	35.1
Charlotte	127,646	61,518	66,128	16,970	10,676	26,574	30,554	42,872	107,361	52.2
Citrus	105,468	50,360	55,108	14,874	8,525	21,210	25,742	35,117	87,669	51.9
Clay	120,896	59,685	61,211	28,377	16,717	38,417	26,127	11,258	86,953	33.7
Collier	186,504	91,570	94,934	33,209	17,459	48,692	42,483	44,661	148,203	42.5
Columbia	50,387	25,673	24,714	11,471	6,988	14,510	10,624	6,794	36,716	34.9
Dade	2,013,821	971,352	1,042,469	439,291	257,334	613,015	422,599	281,582	1,503,054	35.1
De Soto	26,640	14,341	12,299	5,231	3,487	7,558	5,210	5,154	20,432	37.2
Dixie	12,416	6,454	5,962	2,453	1,640	3,220	2,924	2,179	9,507	38.0
Duval	718,355	351,112	367,243	167,733	99,274	238,441	132,921	79,986	526,156	32.6
Escambia	282,742	138,315	144,427	61,300	41,913	86,920	56,599	36,010	211,082	33.4
Flagler	36,997	17,742	19,255	5,552	3,397	8,055	9,346	10,647	30,364	48.4
Franklin	10,236	5,129	5,107	1,790	1,196	2,531	2,772	1,947	8,082	41.9
Gadsden	44,734	22,160	22,574	10,983	6,717	13,547	8,404	5,083	31,791	32.2
Gilchrist	11,888	6,343	5,545	2,334	2,446	3,038	2,483	1,587	9,004	33.1
Glades	8,551	4,268	4,283	1,601	1,075	2,084	2,011	1,780	6,590	40.7

See footnotes at end of table.

Continued . . .

Table 1.35. AGE AND SEX: ESTIMATES BY SEX AND AGE GROUP AND MEDIAN AGE IN THE STATE AND COUNTIES OF FLORIDA APRIL 1, 1995 (Continued)

County	Total	Sex		Age						
		Male	Female	0-14	15-24	25-44	45-64	65 and over	18 and over	Median 1/
Gulf	13,271	7,129	6,142	2,437	1,868	4,070	2,969	1,927	10,262	35.9
Hamilton	12,487	6,709	5,778	2,586	2,195	3,906	2,375	1,425	9,238	32.5
Hardee	22,885	12,210	10,675	5,278	3,414	6,421	4,230	3,542	16,613	32.9
Hendry	29,497	15,028	14,469	8,179	4,556	8,223	5,317	3,222	19,951	30.0
Hernando	117,895	56,454	61,441	18,003	10,236	23,829	27,799	38,028	96,574	50.3
Highlands	77,270	36,607	40,663	12,055	6,733	14,331	16,261	27,890	62,986	53.0
Hillsborough	892,874	436,025	456,849	190,703	115,928	289,441	180,396	116,406	671,845	34.7
Holmes	17,385	9,095	8,290	3,189	2,709	4,882	3,838	2,767	13,460	36.4
Indian River	100,261	48,318	51,943	16,613	9,335	24,082	21,431	28,800	80,783	45.1
Jackson	46,577	24,452	22,125	8,503	8,041	13,928	9,543	6,562	36,102	34.3
Jefferson	13,509	6,060	7,449	2,871	1,895	4,028	2,796	1,919	10,055	35.2
Lafayette	6,516	3,775	2,741	1,210	1,101	2,267	1,218	720	5,044	32.4
Lake	176,931	84,811	92,120	30,006	16,213	39,973	39,752	50,987	141,961	46.2
Lee	376,702	181,997	194,705	64,753	35,603	96,290	84,989	95,067	301,579	43.3
Leon	217,533	104,661	112,872	40,201	55,274	67,376	37,027	17,655	169,283	29.2
Levy	29,843	14,320	15,523	5,755	3,472	7,282	6,865	6,469	22,987	40.9
Liberty	6,873	4,025	2,848	1,245	1,038	2,451	1,412	727	5,358	34.2
Madison	18,344	9,571	8,773	4,147	2,805	5,561	3,338	2,493	13,439	32.7
Manatee	233,160	110,932	122,228	39,436	21,998	58,154	48,809	64,763	187,427	44.0
Marion	224,612	108,053	116,559	41,542	23,677	53,995	49,980	55,418	175,643	42.5
Martin	112,036	54,815	57,221	17,426	9,940	28,815	24,477	31,378	91,669	44.9
Monroe	83,401	42,689	40,712	13,456	7,596	28,400	20,663	13,286	68,090	39.9
Nassau	49,127	24,303	24,824	10,973	6,614	14,904	11,319	5,317	36,020	35.1
Okaloosa	162,707	81,591	81,116	37,099	21,986	55,215	31,880	16,527	119,662	33.0

See footnotes at end of table.

Continued . . .

Table 1.35. AGE AND SEX: ESTIMATES BY SEX AND AGE GROUP AND MEDIAN AGE IN THE STATE AND COUNTIES OF FLORIDA APRIL 1, 1995 (Continued)

County	Total	Sex		Age						
		Male	Female	0-14	15-24	25-44	45-64	65 and over	18 and over	Median 1/
Okeechobee	32,855	16,589	16,266	7,587	4,184	8,052	6,862	6,170	23,926	36.9
Orange	758,962	376,452	382,510	161,976	114,086	261,348	139,681	81,871	571,732	32.5
Osceola	136,627	67,029	69,598	29,665	17,972	41,896	28,465	18,629	102,006	35.2
Palm Beach	962,802	462,964	499,838	173,414	91,926	269,586	196,628	231,248	763,221	41.0
Pasco	305,576	145,053	160,523	46,539	27,751	67,032	64,097	100,157	250,950	48.4
Pinellas	876,200	413,471	462,729	138,986	83,815	239,396	190,427	223,576	713,925	43.1
Polk	443,153	214,897	228,256	89,801	53,507	117,032	93,004	89,809	337,926	38.4
Putnam	69,516	33,856	35,660	14,561	8,411	17,449	15,397	13,698	52,219	38.9
St. Johns	98,188	47,811	50,377	17,757	12,080	28,815	22,242	17,294	77,154	38.9
St. Lucie	171,160	83,396	87,764	32,827	18,000	45,854	36,313	38,166	132,763	40.1
Santa Rosa	96,091	47,854	48,237	21,285	12,448	31,650	20,632	10,076	70,933	34.1
Sarasota	301,528	141,823	159,705	40,983	24,040	68,379	69,132	98,994	253,538	49.9
Seminole	324,130	159,080	165,050	67,860	41,528	111,591	69,310	33,841	243,706	34.9
Sumter	36,456	18,685	17,771	6,577	4,439	8,857	8,210	8,373	28,603	41.0
Suwannee	30,534	14,822	15,712	6,109	4,343	7,528	7,041	5,513	22,997	38.4
Taylor	18,322	9,205	9,117	4,176	2,552	5,147	3,804	2,643	13,365	34.4
Union	12,647	8,270	4,377	2,157	1,914	5,256	2,337	983	10,042	33.3
Volusia	402,970	195,157	207,813	69,047	46,927	109,194	85,389	92,413	322,365	40.7
Wakulla	17,005	8,340	8,665	3,723	2,434	4,949	3,812	2,087	12,461	36.2
Walton	33,415	16,922	16,493	5,938	4,216	8,969	8,109	6,183	26,170	39.5
Washington	19,010	9,482	9,528	3,751	2,748	4,916	4,206	3,389	14,390	37.2

1/ Estimates based on Bureau of the Census modified age, race, and sex data.
Note: Detail may not add to totals because of rounding.

Source: University of Florida, Bureau of Economic and Business Research, Population Program, *Florida Population Studies*, July 1996, Volume 29, No. 3. Bulletin No. 115, and unpublished data.

Table 1.36. HISPANIC POPULATION: ESTIMATES BY SEX AND AGE GROUP IN THE STATE AND COUNTIES OF FLORIDA
APRIL 1, 1995

		Sex		Age				
County	Total	Male	Female	0-14	15-24	25-44	45-64	65 and over
Florida	2,014,681	1,005,710	1,008,971	443,229	292,897	682,099	366,240	230,216
Alachua	7,966	4,080	3,886	1,363	3,029	2,528	677	369
Baker	216	153	63	29	23	104	42	18
Bay	2,651	1,366	1,285	659	481	881	440	190
Bradford	480	358	122	55	52	245	99	29
Brevard	18,298	9,237	9,061	4,570	2,809	6,133	3,161	1,625
Broward	170,656	85,289	85,367	39,442	25,393	65,635	27,551	12,635
Calhoun	227	134	93	57	33	104	29	4
Charlotte	3,738	1,986	1,752	760	644	1,107	686	541
Citrus	2,539	1,192	1,347	463	270	484	676	646
Clay	4,320	2,133	2,187	1,252	725	1,487	627	229
Collier	26,129	14,492	11,637	7,801	4,722	8,808	3,524	1,274
Columbia	888	429	459	239	156	259	124	110
Dade	1,126,929	548,323	578,606	217,057	148,331	374,391	227,929	159,221
De Soto	4,308	2,852	1,456	1,308	852	1,720	320	108
Dixie	114	77	37	22	23	50	16	3
Duval	21,765	11,211	10,554	5,953	3,223	8,242	2,939	1,408
Escambia	6,052	3,068	2,984	1,537	949	2,172	927	467
Flagler	2,119	1,005	1,114	495	347	497	459	321
Franklin	69	30	39	17	10	21	13	8
Gadsden	1,073	622	451	378	171	394	89	41
Gilchrist	226	155	71	28	51	85	44	18
Glades	985	569	416	326	172	313	123	51

See footnotes at end of table.

Continued . . .

Table 1.36. HISPANIC POPULATION: ESTIMATES BY SEX AND AGE GROUP IN THE STATE AND COUNTIES OF FLORIDA
APRIL 1, 1995 (Continued)

County	Total	Sex		Age				
		Male	Female	0-14	15-24	25-44	45-64	65 and over
Gulf	256	207	49	28	42	135	36	15
Hamilton	459	300	159	125	88	179	61	6
Hardee	5,471	3,080	2,391	1,925	1,134	1,628	586	198
Hendry	7,988	4,456	3,532	2,685	1,435	2,618	883	367
Hernando	4,468	2,224	2,244	1,048	568	1,127	1,029	696
Highlands	4,394	2,277	2,117	1,353	712	1,274	608	447
Hillsborough	131,305	66,613	64,692	31,039	20,297	42,728	22,403	14,838
Holmes	240	165	75	45	40	109	33	13
Indian River	3,662	2,040	1,622	1,091	576	1,209	486	300
Jackson	1,394	1,081	313	91	166	794	296	47
Jefferson	279	218	61	25	43	152	49	10
Lafayette	316	271	45	31	37	192	48	8
Lake	5,826	3,015	2,811	1,692	916	1,819	953	446
Lee	22,213	11,763	10,450	6,317	4,008	7,125	3,179	1,584
Leon	7,034	3,932	3,102	1,123	2,377	2,598	709	227
Levy	649	301	348	155	110	167	126	91
Liberty	179	158	21	10	20	123	24	2
Madison	298	236	62	57	39	162	25	15
Manatee	13,555	7,385	6,170	4,559	2,525	4,399	1,441	631
Marion	10,182	5,122	5,060	2,631	1,378	3,063	1,894	1,216
Martin	7,025	4,008	3,017	2,203	1,143	2,558	743	378
Monroe	11,084	5,701	5,383	2,382	1,307	3,655	2,334	1,406
Nassau	607	301	306	188	88	186	99	46
Okaloosa	5,608	3,009	2,599	1,533	804	2,190	824	257

See footnotes at end of table.

Continued . . .

Table 1.36. HISPANIC POPULATION: ESTIMATES BY SEX AND AGE GROUP IN THE STATE AND COUNTIES OF FLORIDA
APRIL 1, 1995 (Continued)

County	Total	Sex		Age				
		Male	Female	0-14	15-24	25-44	45-64	65 and over
Okeechobee	4,763	2,802	1,961	1,858	918	1,568	328	91
Orange	101,522	50,557	50,965	26,106	17,703	36,451	15,014	6,248
Osceola	23,778	11,912	11,866	6,504	4,594	7,462	3,899	1,319
Palm Beach	95,282	50,048	45,234	24,177	14,394	34,458	15,377	6,876
Pasco	14,999	7,663	7,336	4,242	2,273	4,260	2,567	1,657
Pinellas	28,262	14,114	14,148	6,100	4,155	9,649	4,959	3,399
Polk	21,036	11,224	9,812	7,297	3,687	6,051	2,651	1,350
Putnam	2,079	1,073	1,006	741	327	543	277	191
St. Johns	2,916	1,432	1,484	703	368	934	571	340
St. Lucie	10,107	5,483	4,624	2,755	1,662	3,376	1,377	937
Santa Rosa	1,730	885	845	533	277	608	223	89
Sarasota	8,579	4,385	4,194	1,927	1,216	2,791	1,610	1,035
Seminole	28,056	13,898	14,158	6,994	4,591	10,090	4,446	1,935
Sumter	1,053	644	409	333	190	357	120	53
Suwannee	927	521	406	235	171	288	142	91
Taylor	280	173	107	50	55	129	30	16
Union	376	302	74	39	40	225	60	12
Volusia	21,851	11,489	10,362	6,277	3,821	6,742	3,069	1,942
Wakulla	89	47	42	25	4	26	25	9
Walton	521	275	246	125	93	149	99	55
Washington	235	159	76	61	39	92	32	11

Note: Detail may not add to totals because of rounding.

Source: University of Florida, Bureau of Economic and Business Research, Population Program, *Special Population Reports: Hispanic Population Estimates by Age and Sex for Florida and Its Counties, April 1, 1995*. August 1996.

Table 1.37. PERSONS AGED 65 AND OVER: CENSUS COUNTS, APRIL 1, 1990, AND ESTIMATES, APRIL 1, 1995, BY AGE IN THE STATE AND COUNTIES OF FLORIDA

County	65-69 Census 1990	65-69 Estimates 1995	70-74 Census 1990	70-74 Estimates 1995	75-79 Census 1990	75-79 Estimates 1995	80-84 Census 1990	80-84 Estimates 1995	85 and over Census 1990	85 and over Estimates 1995	Percentage aged 65 and over 1990	Percentage aged 65 and over 1995
Florida	737,129	741,499	627,699	716,503	483,532	551,263	302,099	376,352	205,467	254,681	18.2	18.7
Alachua	5,652	5,616	4,256	5,139	3,176	3,593	2,064	2,437	1,594	1,904	9.2	9.4
Baker	475	594	391	448	284	322	181	222	119	154	7.8	8.6
Bay	5,673	6,103	4,040	5,003	2,799	3,380	1,611	2,137	1,019	1,336	11.9	12.9
Bradford	962	946	689	904	501	607	344	396	228	309	12.1	13.0
Brevard	24,416	24,969	18,598	23,798	12,108	16,390	6,697	9,356	4,265	5,682	16.6	18.0
Broward	66,625	63,490	66,832	67,082	61,690	60,696	39,750	48,880	24,398	31,597	20.7	19.9
Calhoun	481	469	374	462	342	338	237	264	158	210	14.5	14.5
Charlotte	12,517	12,613	10,563	12,349	7,375	9,063	4,281	5,547	2,570	3,300	33.6	33.6
Citrus	10,174	10,789	8,313	10,008	5,785	7,360	3,066	4,397	1,807	2,563	31.2	33.3
Clay	3,225	3,577	2,248	3,120	1,628	2,031	994	1,376	846	1,154	8.4	9.3
Collier	11,975	13,725	9,810	12,922	6,649	9,162	3,894	5,660	2,128	3,192	22.7	23.9
Columbia	2,063	2,155	1,533	1,985	1,047	1,322	597	798	380	534	13.2	13.5
Dade	80,679	82,361	64,600	70,644	55,537	53,659	38,461	42,186	29,145	32,732	13.9	14.0
De Soto	1,495	1,502	1,323	1,526	934	1,094	523	630	317	402	19.2	19.3
Dixie	612	799	406	617	278	383	139	247	97	133	14.5	17.5
Duval	25,010	24,871	18,494	21,667	13,599	15,702	8,314	10,476	5,985	7,270	10.6	11.1
Escambia	11,247	11,083	8,189	10,217	5,770	6,959	3,450	4,571	2,488	3,180	11.9	12.7
Flagler	3,275	3,866	2,180	3,313	1,048	1,944	482	954	303	570	25.4	28.8
Franklin	492	646	449	464	291	407	192	234	164	196	17.7	19.0
Gadsden	1,574	1,494	1,353	1,322	1,069	1,025	647	680	509	562	12.5	11.4
Gilchrist	482	536	384	463	202	313	136	150	113	125	13.6	13.3
Glades	549	575	424	513	296	378	120	213	79	101	19.3	20.8

Continued . . .

Table 1.37. PERSONS AGED 65 AND OVER: CENSUS COUNTS, APRIL 1, 1990, AND ESTIMATES, APRIL 1, 1995, BY AGE IN THE STATE AND COUNTIES OF FLORIDA (Continued)

County	65-69		70-74		75-79		80-84		85 and over		Percentage aged 65 and over	
	Census 1990	Estimates 1995	Census 1990	Estimates 1995	Census 1990	Estimates 1995	Census 1990	Estimates 1995	Census 1990	Estimates 1995	1990	1995
Gulf	601	599	449	526	338	376	224	246	136	180	15.2	14.5
Hamilton	376	470	324	334	271	279	171	202	100	140	11.4	11.4
Hardee	1,028	1,075	792	1,022	558	679	353	458	214	308	15.1	15.5
Hendry	1,023	1,051	712	882	540	596	323	416	203	277	10.9	10.9
Hernando	11,953	12,201	9,332	11,615	5,635	7,855	2,508	4,096	1,522	2,261	30.6	32.3
Highlands	7,403	7,628	6,572	8,328	4,654	5,990	2,557	3,858	1,558	2,086	33.2	36.1
Hillsborough	34,478	35,012	27,070	32,023	19,750	23,294	11,931	15,319	8,217	10,758	12.2	13.0
Holmes	804	816	629	761	501	513	330	395	216	282	15.7	15.9
Indian River	8,260	8,197	7,086	8,554	4,676	6,274	2,787	3,573	1,642	2,202	27.1	28.7
Jackson	1,841	1,848	1,548	1,608	1,310	1,318	887	996	568	792	14.9	14.1
Jefferson	516	567	416	505	335	392	226	255	175	200	14.8	14.2
Lafayette	227	231	167	205	109	141	74	89	38	54	11.0	11.0
Lake	13,461	14,458	11,212	14,827	8,506	10,594	5,248	6,879	3,239	4,229	27.4	28.8
Lee	27,822	28,432	23,435	27,206	16,350	19,870	9,343	12,362	5,648	7,197	24.6	25.2
Leon	5,325	5,584	4,246	4,691	2,910	3,677	1,880	2,186	1,340	1,517	8.2	8.1
Levy	1,758	2,003	1,415	1,863	904	1,389	513	758	296	456	18.8	21.7
Liberty	197	250	176	179	123	146	75	90	50	62	11.2	10.6
Madison	662	696	603	618	490	512	336	370	228	297	14.0	13.6
Manatee	17,136	16,548	15,799	17,378	12,396	14,013	8,090	9,748	5,761	7,076	28.0	27.8
Marion	15,556	17,082	12,415	16,548	8,170	11,643	4,222	6,396	2,534	3,749	22.0	24.7
Martin	8,985	8,702	7,772	8,921	5,600	6,891	3,267	4,215	1,898	2,649	27.3	28.0
Monroe	4,665	4,394	3,475	3,840	2,285	2,670	1,251	1,591	671	791	15.8	15.9

Continued . . .

Table 1.37. PERSONS AGED 65 AND OVER: CENSUS COUNTS, APRIL 1, 1990, AND ESTIMATES, APRIL 1, 1995, BY AGE IN THE STATE AND COUNTIES OF FLORIDA (Continued)

County	65-69		70-74		75-79		80-84		85 and over		Percentage aged 65 and over	
	Census 1990	Estimates 1995	Census 1990	Estimates 1995	Census 1990	Estimates 1995	Census 1990	Estimates 1995	Census 1990	Estimates 1995	1990	1995
Nassau	1,612	1,882	1,220	1,421	837	985	489	614	285	415	10.1	10.8
Okaloosa	5,345	5,705	3,615	4,847	2,151	3,101	1,215	1,675	916	1,199	9.2	10.2
Okeechobee	1,763	1,996	1,364	1,867	906	1,220	448	677	262	410	16.0	18.8
Orange	25,045	25,859	18,745	22,669	13,071	15,957	8,238	10,288	6,419	7,098	10.6	10.8
Osceola	4,886	5,706	4,028	4,829	2,811	3,897	1,678	2,333	1,436	1,864	13.8	13.6
Palm Beach	58,699	57,917	57,252	61,466	46,390	51,902	28,697	37,080	17,932	22,883	24.2	24.0
Pasco	27,031	25,257	26,172	27,750	19,440	23,414	11,358	15,276	6,501	8,460	32.2	32.8
Pinellas	59,240	54,140	55,480	56,991	46,573	48,072	33,313	35,578	26,278	28,795	25.9	25.5
Polk	25,097	26,392	20,281	25,342	14,753	18,167	8,810	11,700	5,746	8,208	18.4	0.0
Putnam	4,303	4,443	3,211	4,023	2,172	2,636	1,198	1,591	730	1,005	17.8	19.7
St. Johns	4,964	5,492	3,709	4,885	2,475	3,458	1,413	2,053	1,131	1,406	16.3	17.6
St. Lucie	11,312	11,800	9,133	11,271	6,088	8,169	2,989	4,567	1,762	2,359	20.8	22.3
Santa Rosa	3,037	3,617	1,956	2,911	1,412	1,706	753	1,129	559	713	9.5	10.5
Sarasota	25,967	25,285	23,807	26,790	18,835	21,721	12,058	14,833	8,471	10,365	32.1	32.8
Seminole	10,357	10,677	7,697	9,275	5,482	6,541	3,509	4,169	2,515	3,179	10.3	10.4
Sumter	2,540	2,573	2,056	2,524	1,339	1,685	717	1,004	382	587	22.3	23.0
Suwannee	1,400	1,599	1,080	1,463	893	1,044	639	776	477	631	16.8	18.1
Taylor	769	858	615	716	459	515	269	358	164	196	13.3	14.4
Union	279	316	216	284	131	189	76	113	62	81	7.5	7.8
Volusia	26,578	25,639	22,608	25,625	16,707	19,422	10,369	12,700	7,735	9,027	22.7	22.9
Wakulla	573	684	404	563	328	387	194	276	137	177	11.5	12.3
Walton	1,678	2,110	1,173	1,705	850	1,136	500	749	338	483	16.4	18.5
Washington	924	929	783	886	610	699	393	504	263	371	17.6	17.8

Source: University of Florida, Bureau of Economic and Business Research, Population Program, unpublished data. Census data from U.S. Bureau of the Census.

Table 1.38. AGE AND SEX PROJECTIONS: CENSUS COUNTS, APRIL 1, 1990, AND PROJECTIONS, APRIL 1, 2000, 2005, AND 2010, BY AGE AND SEX IN FLORIDA

Age	Census 1990	Projections 2000	2005	2010
Total	12,937,926	15,415,135	16,630,799	17,824,739
0-4	873,022	980,222	999,217	1,058,176
5-9	809,306	1,025,662	1,011,575	1,028,316
10-14	746,343	954,731	1,078,787	1,062,673
15-19	803,784	923,373	1,019,879	1,140,187
15-17	455,160	523,604	579,036	648,444
18-19	348,624	399,769	440,843	491,743
20-24	878,843	900,470	1,021,342	1,112,793
25-29	1,055,071	911,599	909,280	1,024,174
30-34	1,062,261	968,282	947,629	942,866
35-39	951,453	1,143,584	1,019,365	995,634
40-44	851,919	1,174,697	1,208,406	1,080,297
45-49	690,756	1,072,363	1,242,221	1,277,532
50-54	591,849	963,609	1,138,534	1,312,698
55-59	586,872	802,142	1,042,915	1,226,501
60-64	680,521	725,146	896,449	1,153,530
65-69	737,129	729,206	799,316	976,736
70-74	627,699	736,949	726,305	789,562
75-79	483,532	643,297	666,257	652,803
80-84	302,099	438,746	515,936	531,897
85 and over	205,467	321,057	387,386	458,364
Male	6,261,770	7,499,168	8,094,363	8,673,123
0-4	447,221	499,915	509,599	539,666
5-9	414,103	522,722	515,583	524,096
10-14	382,040	489,111	551,144	542,881
15-19	412,795	472,917	522,000	582,047
15-17	234,171	268,771	296,973	331,737
18-19	178,624	204,146	225,027	250,310
20-24	446,241	464,639	526,390	572,640
25-29	532,167	469,428	467,157	525,251
30-34	531,382	490,203	481,844	478,376
35-39	471,494	569,194	507,533	497,114
40-44	419,659	578,599	595,258	531,918
45-49	335,721	523,410	604,773	622,367
50-54	282,812	463,307	546,468	629,089
55-59	274,786	375,913	491,112	576,505
60-64	308,245	334,120	414,944	535,786
65-69	331,267	339,139	373,402	457,167
70-74	279,758	335,473	338,058	368,205
75-79	204,877	279,414	296,969	296,896
80-84	118,468	178,470	212,288	224,723
85 and over	68,734	113,194	139,841	168,396

See footnote at end of table.

Continued . . .

Table 1.38. AGE AND SEX PROJECTIONS: CENSUS COUNTS, APRIL 1, 1990, AND PROJECTIONS, APRIL 1, 2000, 2005, AND 2010, BY AGE AND SEX IN FLORIDA (Continued)

Age	Census 1990	Projections 2000	2005	2010
Female	6,676,156	7,915,967	8,536,436	9,151,616
0-4	425,801	480,307	489,618	518,510
5-9	395,203	502,940	495,992	504,220
10-14	364,303	465,620	527,643	519,792
15-19	390,989	450,456	497,879	558,140
15-17	220,989	254,833	282,063	316,707
18-19	170,000	195,623	215,816	241,433
20-24	432,602	435,831	494,952	540,153
25-29	522,904	442,171	442,123	498,923
30-34	530,879	478,079	465,785	464,490
35-39	479,959	574,390	511,832	498,520
40-44	432,260	596,098	613,148	548,379
45-49	355,035	548,953	637,448	655,165
50-54	309,037	500,302	592,066	683,609
55-59	312,086	426,229	551,803	649,996
60-64	372,276	391,026	481,505	617,744
65-69	405,862	390,067	425,914	519,569
70-74	347,941	401,476	388,247	421,357
75-79	278,655	363,883	369,288	355,907
80-84	183,631	260,276	303,648	307,174
85 and over	136,733	207,863	247,545	289,968

Note: Medium projections are shown. High and low projections are available from the Bureau of Economic and Business Research, University of Florida.

Source: University of Florida, Bureau of Economic and Business Research, Population Program, unpublished data. Census data from U.S. Bureau of the Census.

Table 1.39. MEDIAN AGE: CENSUS, APRIL 1, 1990, AND PROJECTIONS, APRIL 1 2000, 2005, AND 2010, IN THE STATE AND COUNTIES OF FLORIDA

County	Census 1990	Projections 2000	2005	2010	County	Census 1990	Projections 2000	2005	2010
Florida	36.3	39.5	41.1	41.9	Lafayette	32.0	32.8	33.3	33.9
					Lake	44.6	42.9	42.1	39.8
Alachua	28.2	29.1	29.2	29.2	Lee	42.0	45.2	47.4	49.5
Baker	30.2	31.7	32.0	32.7	Leon	28.8	30.0	30.7	31.1
Bay	33.2	36.7	37.9	38.3	Levy	38.4	39.5	39.1	38.0
Bradford	33.6	33.6	33.4	33.4	Liberty	32.5	34.1	33.7	34.0
Brevard	36.1	41.1	43.5	45.7	Madison	32.2	32.9	33.0	33.5
Broward	37.6	40.5	42.0	43.2	Manatee	42.9	45.5	47.4	49.4
Calhoun	33.4	34.5	34.4	34.8	Marion	40.0	40.5	40.4	38.9
Charlotte	53.7	50.0	48.5	46.9	Martin	44.3	44.1	44.3	43.6
Citrus	50.8	48.5	47.3	45.6	Monroe	38.8	43.3	45.7	47.5
Clay	32.0	35.5	36.3	37.2	Nassau	33.3	36.2	36.6	37.0
Collier	40.6	41.0	41.3	40.4	Okaloosa	31.3	36.0	37.7	38.8
Columbia	33.6	35.1	34.7	35.1	Okeechobee	34.3	34.0	33.3	32.5
Dade	34.2	36.6	37.6	38.2	Orange	31.4	35.1	36.2	36.9
De Soto	36.4	35.2	34.8	34.0	Osceola	33.6	36.4	37.2	37.5
Dixie	36.8	35.1	33.8	33.0	Palm Beach	39.8	43.0	45.0	46.8
Duval	31.4	34.9	35.8	36.2	Pasco	47.9	48.5	49.9	51.7
Escambia	32.3	35.2	36.2	36.6	Pinellas	42.1	44.8	46.7	48.5
Flagler	46.4	46.7	46.6	45.3	Polk	36.4	40.8	42.9	44.8
Franklin	38.9	38.8	38.6	37.8	Putnam	37.2	37.7	36.7	35.7
Gadsden	31.8	30.7	30.9	31.1	St. Johns	36.9	40.1	41.2	41.4
Gilchrist	33.5	33.5	33.7	34.2	St. Lucie	37.7	39.5	40.0	38.5
Glades	40.0	39.0	38.2	37.4	Santa Rosa	32.4	36.4	37.6	38.1
Gulf	35.6	35.6	35.5	35.8	Sarasota	48.9	51.5	53.4	55.4
Hamilton	30.8	31.5	32.1	32.9	Seminole	33.2	37.3	39.3	40.9
Hardee	32.7	32.2	31.9	31.8	Sumter	40.1	37.5	36.8	36.0
Hendry	30.3	28.9	28.7	28.2	Suwannee	36.5	37.4	36.9	37.2
Hernando	49.4	47.9	46.7	44.8	Taylor	33.5	34.0	33.7	33.7
Highlands	51.4	45.2	42.8	38.7	Union	31.2	32.9	32.9	33.3
Hillsborough	33.0	37.3	39.1	40.3	Volusia	39.3	43.0	45.1	47.2
Holmes	35.5	36.6	36.8	37.5	Wakulla	34.2	35.8	35.5	36.1
Indian River	43.8	43.7	43.6	42.5	Walton	37.7	39.7	40.3	39.7
Jackson	34.3	34.4	34.9	36.2	Washington	37.2	36.5	36.5	36.8
Jefferson	33.8	33.4	33.0	33.3					

Note: Projections are based on Bureau of the Census modified age, race, and sex data.

Source: University of Florida, Bureau of Economic and Business Research, Population Program, unpublished data. Census data from U.S., Department of Commerce, Bureau of the Census, *1990 Census of Population: General Population Characteristics, Florida*.

Table 1.40. MALE AND FEMALE PROJECTIONS: PROJECTIONS, APRIL 1, 2000, 2005, AND 2010, BY SEX IN THE STATE AND COUNTIES OF FLORIDA

County	2000			2005			2010		
	Total	Male	Female	Total	Male	Female	Total	Male	Female
Florida	15,415,135	7,499,168	7,915,967	16,630,799	8,094,363	8,536,436	17,824,739	8,673,123	9,151,616
Alachua	212,997	105,554	107,443	226,500	112,423	114,077	239,803	119,080	120,723
Baker	22,005	11,740	10,265	23,402	12,461	10,941	24,797	13,154	11,643
Bay	150,099	73,739	76,360	160,803	78,865	81,938	171,302	83,844	87,458
Bradford	25,402	14,334	11,068	26,300	14,780	11,520	27,095	15,169	11,926
Brevard	492,802	241,370	251,432	539,495	263,616	275,879	585,397	285,455	299,942
Broward	1,465,601	706,001	759,600	1,564,001	755,168	808,833	1,660,301	802,349	857,952
Calhoun	12,599	6,703	5,896	13,099	6,953	6,146	13,598	7,199	6,399
Charlotte	147,404	71,098	76,306	166,698	80,491	86,207	185,798	89,794	96,004
Citrus	119,599	57,062	62,537	133,401	63,739	69,662	147,202	70,431	76,771
Clay	136,198	67,126	69,072	151,203	74,381	76,822	165,900	81,405	84,495
Collier	220,102	108,145	111,957	251,902	123,339	128,563	283,496	138,460	145,036
Columbia	55,101	27,924	27,177	59,802	30,181	29,621	64,399	32,370	32,029
Dade	2,129,202	1,030,098	1,099,104	2,241,202	1,086,167	1,155,035	2,350,705	1,139,449	1,211,256
De Soto	30,196	16,580	13,616	32,502	17,634	14,868	34,701	18,653	16,048
Dixie	13,999	7,305	6,694	15,404	8,007	7,397	16,802	8,696	8,106
Duval	760,901	371,696	389,205	802,199	391,757	410,442	842,503	411,122	431,381
Escambia	302,390	150,014	152,376	316,604	157,330	159,274	329,699	163,663	166,036
Flagler	45,594	21,822	23,772	54,302	25,975	28,327	62,898	30,074	32,824
Franklin	11,100	5,597	5,503	11,797	5,919	5,878	12,501	6,242	6,259
Gadsden	47,197	23,742	23,455	48,601	24,442	24,159	50,099	25,164	24,935
Gilchrist	13,901	7,387	6,514	15,701	8,263	7,438	17,500	9,129	8,371
Glades	10,169	5,408	4,761	10,966	5,770	5,196	11,663	6,086	5,577

Continued . . .

Table 1.40. MALE AND FEMALE PROJECTIONS: PROJECTIONS, APRIL 1, 2000, 2005, AND 2010, BY SEX IN THE STATE AND COUNTIES OF FLORIDA (Continued)

County	2000			2005			2010		
	Total	Male	Female	Total	Male	Female	Total	Male	Female
Gulf	15,203	8,783	6,420	15,699	9,009	6,690	16,095	9,190	6,905
Hamilton	14,500	8,269	6,231	15,404	8,707	6,697	16,196	9,082	7,114
Hardee	23,598	12,507	11,091	24,301	12,795	11,506	24,902	13,044	11,858
Hendry	32,706	16,698	16,008	35,702	18,187	17,515	38,596	19,613	18,983
Hernando	138,601	66,308	72,293	159,001	76,165	82,836	179,300	86,014	93,286
Highlands	85,895	40,678	45,217	94,401	44,809	49,592	102,703	48,900	53,803
Hillsborough	955,598	466,577	489,021	1,016,501	496,057	520,444	1,076,099	524,481	551,618
Holmes	18,002	9,462	8,540	18,600	9,762	8,838	19,100	10,002	9,098
Indian River	111,301	53,538	57,763	122,000	58,707	63,293	132,597	63,870	68,727
Jackson	48,498	25,671	22,827	50,201	26,631	23,570	51,797	27,494	24,303
Jefferson	14,302	6,388	7,914	15,101	6,781	8,320	15,799	7,116	8,683
Lafayette	7,503	4,450	3,053	8,004	4,677	3,327	8,500	4,904	3,596
Lake	199,698	95,698	104,000	222,000	106,465	115,535	244,097	117,151	126,946
Lee	422,503	204,003	218,500	467,299	225,733	241,566	511,404	247,085	264,319
Leon	236,997	114,226	122,771	255,698	123,316	132,382	274,203	132,177	142,026
Levy	32,799	15,745	17,054	36,003	17,302	18,701	39,101	18,800	20,301
Liberty	7,495	4,379	3,116	8,001	4,630	3,371	8,503	4,870	3,633
Madison	19,096	9,942	9,154	19,899	10,342	9,557	20,596	10,682	9,914
Manatee	256,097	122,276	133,821	278,500	133,457	145,043	300,403	144,308	156,095
Marion	253,901	121,964	131,937	282,602	135,739	146,863	311,099	149,455	161,644
Martin	125,201	61,243	63,958	137,700	67,312	70,388	149,996	73,309	76,687
Monroe	88,900	44,749	44,151	94,300	46,976	47,324	99,597	49,254	50,343
Nassau	53,897	26,606	27,291	58,502	28,824	29,678	63,003	30,964	32,039
Okaloosa	178,198	88,770	89,428	193,395	95,918	97,477	208,202	102,878	105,324

Continued . . .

Table 1.40. MALE AND FEMALE PROJECTIONS: PROJECTIONS, APRIL 1, 2000, 2005, AND 2010, BY SEX IN THE STATE AND COUNTIES OF FLORIDA (Continued)

County	2000 Total	2000 Male	2000 Female	2005 Total	2005 Male	2005 Female	2010 Total	2010 Male	2010 Female
Okeechobee	37,445	19,226	18,219	40,846	20,781	20,065	44,246	22,361	21,885
Orange	846,203	416,991	429,212	934,298	459,287	475,011	1,021,401	500,850	520,551
Osceola	163,900	80,351	83,549	190,905	93,487	97,418	217,798	106,438	111,360
Palm Beach	1,067,899	514,005	553,894	1,170,301	564,334	605,967	1,271,098	613,666	657,432
Pasco	334,800	159,213	175,587	363,199	173,360	189,839	391,002	187,269	203,733
Pinellas	907,298	431,172	476,126	937,698	448,116	489,582	967,803	464,145	503,658
Polk	477,802	231,448	246,354	511,400	247,639	263,761	544,303	263,409	280,894
Putnam	74,500	36,197	38,303	79,199	38,438	40,761	83,799	40,617	43,182
St. Johns	111,797	54,432	57,365	125,300	60,972	64,328	138,602	67,368	71,234
St. Lucie	194,798	94,608	100,190	218,099	105,801	112,298	241,100	116,854	124,246
Santa Rosa	110,402	55,424	54,978	123,203	61,554	61,649	135,801	67,527	68,274
Sarasota	326,801	154,231	172,570	351,302	166,493	184,809	375,100	178,415	196,685
Seminole	365,696	179,461	186,235	406,402	199,239	207,163	446,696	218,565	228,131
Sumter	43,699	23,739	19,960	47,595	25,549	22,046	51,396	27,351	24,045
Suwannee	33,398	16,220	17,178	36,197	17,575	18,622	38,998	18,908	20,090
Taylor	19,304	9,973	9,331	19,603	10,115	9,488	19,999	10,296	9,703
Union	13,398	8,627	4,771	14,201	9,005	5,196	14,899	9,323	5,576
Volusia	442,397	214,258	228,139	480,800	233,085	247,715	518,499	251,422	267,077
Wakulla	20,254	10,507	9,747	22,452	11,564	10,888	24,455	12,520	11,935
Walton	37,296	18,924	18,372	40,803	20,588	20,215	44,198	22,185	22,013
Washington	21,001	10,786	10,215	22,298	11,419	10,879	23,499	12,003	11,496

Source: University of Florida, Bureau of Economic and Business Research, Population Program, *Florida Population Studies*, July 1996, Volume 29, No. 3. Bulletin No. 115.

Table 1.41. AGE PROJECTIONS: PROJECTIONS, APRIL 1, 2000, 2005, AND 2010, BY AGE IN THE STATE AND COUNTIES OF FLORIDA

County	2000			2005			2010		
	0-24	25-64	65 and over	0-24	25-64	65 and over	0-24	25-64	65 and over
Florida	4,784,458	7,761,422	2,869,255	5,130,800	8,404,799	3,095,200	5,402,145	9,013,232	3,409,362
Alachua	93,483	99,457	20,057	99,315	105,887	21,298	104,240	112,228	23,335
Baker	8,539	11,433	2,033	8,890	12,244	2,268	9,205	13,054	2,538
Bay	51,934	77,819	20,346	55,132	83,060	22,611	57,820	88,391	25,091
Bradford	8,284	13,713	3,405	8,417	14,289	3,594	8,544	14,684	3,867
Brevard	146,868	253,768	92,166	158,923	278,209	102,363	167,952	302,946	114,499
Broward	426,467	761,439	277,695	458,072	819,233	286,696	480,768	871,443	308,090
Calhoun	4,148	6,600	1,851	4,161	6,948	1,990	4,192	7,265	2,141
Charlotte	31,778	67,569	48,057	35,454	78,166	53,078	38,268	87,779	59,751
Citrus	25,415	54,038	40,146	27,222	61,321	44,858	28,570	67,981	50,651
Clay	49,443	72,825	13,930	53,807	80,347	17,049	57,332	87,499	21,069
Collier	59,225	107,425	53,452	67,216	122,605	62,081	74,203	136,778	72,515
Columbia	20,028	27,374	7,699	21,607	29,601	8,594	22,876	31,803	9,720
Dade	737,584	1,095,917	295,701	780,831	1,147,550	312,821	812,238	1,203,757	334,710
De Soto	9,840	14,617	5,739	10,754	15,557	6,191	11,589	16,357	6,755
Dixie	4,465	6,807	2,727	4,808	7,411	3,185	5,123	8,007	3,672
Duval	281,789	393,723	85,389	299,231	413,013	89,955	313,087	432,958	96,458
Escambia	110,136	152,979	39,275	115,312	159,408	41,884	118,926	166,073	44,700
Flagler	10,541	21,366	13,687	12,063	25,513	16,726	13,338	29,472	20,088
Franklin	2,961	5,912	2,227	2,966	6,263	2,568	2,991	6,512	2,998
Gadsden	17,835	23,971	5,391	17,939	24,869	5,793	18,034	25,719	6,346
Gilchrist	5,457	6,581	1,863	6,082	7,522	2,097	6,656	8,418	2,426
Glades	3,044	5,163	1,962	3,227	5,621	2,118	3,363	6,013	2,287

Continued . . .

Table 1.41. AGE PROJECTIONS: PROJECTIONS, APRIL 1, 2000, 2005, AND 2010, BY AGE IN THE STATE AND COUNTIES OF FLORIDA (Continued)

County	2000			2005			2010		
	0-24	25-64	65 and over	0-24	25-64	65 and over	0-24	25-64	65 and over
Gulf	4,641	8,498	2,064	4,742	8,801	2,156	4,818	9,013	2,264
Hamilton	5,187	7,750	1,563	5,305	8,377	1,722	5,415	8,831	1,950
Hardee	8,893	11,059	3,646	9,167	11,365	3,769	9,408	11,548	3,946
Hendry	14,120	15,083	3,503	15,561	16,310	3,831	16,881	17,473	4,242
Hernando	32,387	61,912	44,302	36,351	72,289	50,361	39,373	81,839	58,088
Highlands	20,513	33,800	31,582	22,252	37,533	34,616	23,786	41,150	37,767
Hillsborough	323,108	503,913	128,577	341,601	534,002	140,898	356,002	562,799	157,298
Holmes	5,799	9,288	2,915	5,819	9,677	3,104	5,834	9,973	3,293
Indian River	28,393	50,643	32,265	30,893	56,155	34,952	32,956	61,319	38,322
Jackson	16,101	25,721	6,676	16,152	27,184	6,865	16,236	28,222	7,339
Jefferson	4,799	7,428	2,075	4,864	7,963	2,274	4,929	8,327	2,543
Lafayette	2,540	4,131	832	2,687	4,410	907	2,821	4,711	968
Lake	50,642	90,418	58,638	55,266	101,189	65,545	59,247	111,294	73,556
Lee	110,795	206,749	104,959	120,856	231,710	114,733	128,770	254,402	128,232
Leon	101,971	115,772	19,254	108,651	126,117	20,930	114,674	135,538	23,991
Levy	9,675	15,606	7,518	10,280	17,214	8,509	10,805	18,685	9,611
Liberty	2,424	4,286	785	2,576	4,603	822	2,722	4,881	900
Madison	7,120	9,489	2,487	7,441	9,935	2,523	7,698	10,323	2,575
Manatee	66,696	120,346	69,055	71,819	133,607	73,074	75,781	145,221	79,401
Marion	71,592	117,146	65,163	77,962	130,805	73,835	83,578	143,754	83,767
Martin	30,563	60,127	34,511	33,669	66,808	37,223	36,164	72,825	41,007
Monroe	22,545	52,633	13,722	24,041	56,054	14,205	25,015	59,180	15,402
Nassau	18,756	29,080	6,061	19,957	31,658	6,887	21,064	33,913	8,026
Okaloosa	64,127	94,307	19,764	69,449	101,693	22,253	73,689	109,767	24,746

Continued . . .

Table 1.41. AGE PROJECTIONS: PROJECTIONS, APRIL 1, 2000, 2005, AND 2010, BY AGE IN THE STATE AND COUNTIES OF FLORIDA (Continued)

County	2000			2005			2010		
	0-24	25-64	65 and over	0-24	25-64	65 and over	0-24	25-64	65 and over
Okeechobee	13,047	17,083	7,315	14,187	18,436	8,223	15,232	19,712	9,302
Orange	304,793	449,196	92,214	337,636	493,948	102,714	365,009	539,447	116,945
Osceola	56,047	85,489	22,364	64,262	100,118	26,525	71,634	114,014	32,150
Palm Beach	295,334	523,320	249,245	323,579	578,457	268,265	345,894	628,796	296,408
Pasco	79,991	147,409	107,400	85,631	163,849	113,719	89,659	178,132	123,211
Pinellas	229,159	454,227	223,912	235,427	476,907	225,364	237,826	495,610	234,367
Polk	149,701	227,783	100,318	157,683	244,367	109,350	164,161	259,946	120,196
Putnam	23,949	35,426	15,125	24,975	38,039	16,185	25,783	40,445	17,571
St. Johns	32,564	59,470	19,763	35,456	67,414	22,430	37,979	74,437	26,186
St. Lucie	55,964	94,903	43,931	61,047	107,857	49,195	65,265	120,045	55,790
Santa Rosa	37,267	60,535	12,600	40,547	67,209	15,447	43,384	73,629	18,788
Sarasota	68,803	151,463	106,535	72,423	165,239	113,640	74,691	176,780	123,629
Seminole	120,039	206,943	38,714	130,833	231,105	44,464	139,954	253,544	53,198
Sumter	13,183	21,042	9,474	14,336	22,878	10,381	15,331	24,547	11,518
Suwannee	10,853	16,241	6,304	11,348	17,753	7,096	11,842	19,123	8,033
Taylor	6,903	9,494	2,907	6,970	9,567	3,066	7,034	9,766	3,199
Union	4,054	8,159	1,185	4,150	8,681	1,370	4,201	9,102	1,596
Volusia	125,337	217,414	99,646	135,129	239,092	106,579	142,468	259,170	116,861
Wakulla	6,943	10,918	2,393	7,517	12,185	2,750	8,020	13,224	3,211
Walton	10,804	18,950	7,542	11,389	20,666	8,748	11,935	22,199	10,064
Washington	7,072	10,276	3,653	7,485	10,936	3,877	7,862	11,439	4,198

Source: University of Florida, Bureau of Economic and Business Research, Population Program, *Florida Population Studies*, July 1996, Volume 29, No. 3. Bulletin No. 115.

Table 1.42. PERSONS AGED 65 AND OVER: PROJECTIONS BY AGE IN THE STATE AND COUNTIES OF FLORIDA
APRIL 1, 2000, 2005, AND 2010

County	2000			2005			2010		
	65-74	75-84	85 and over	65-74	75-84	85 and over	65-74	75-84	85 and over
Florida	1,466,155	1,082,043	321,057	1,525,621	1,182,193	387,386	1,766,298	1,184,700	458,364
Alachua	10,576	7,191	2,290	10,662	7,943	2,693	12,256	7,868	3,211
Baker	1,215	625	193	1,292	742	234	1,416	846	276
Bay	11,784	6,812	1,750	12,575	7,858	2,178	14,089	8,311	2,691
Bradford	1,790	1,240	375	1,777	1,366	451	1,989	1,327	551
Brevard	50,476	33,953	7,737	53,082	38,918	10,363	60,860	40,231	13,408
Broward	125,929	111,932	39,834	129,004	112,972	44,720	150,662	108,854	48,574
Calhoun	923	678	250	981	734	275	1,100	722	319
Charlotte	25,582	18,102	4,373	27,067	20,377	5,634	31,948	20,821	6,982
Citrus	21,539	14,899	3,708	22,682	17,174	5,002	26,633	17,632	6,386
Clay	7,814	4,538	1,578	9,454	5,542	2,053	12,011	6,358	2,700
Collier	29,104	19,755	4,593	31,979	23,781	6,321	38,564	25,606	8,345
Columbia	4,316	2,678	705	4,669	3,031	894	5,434	3,160	1,126
Dade	154,897	103,201	37,603	159,707	112,339	40,775	176,384	112,930	45,396
De Soto	3,109	2,112	518	3,165	2,367	659	3,565	2,382	808
Dixie	1,652	874	201	1,787	1,126	272	2,036	1,269	367
Duval	45,440	30,879	9,070	45,510	33,572	10,873	50,829	32,760	12,869
Escambia	21,047	14,148	4,080	21,394	15,494	4,996	23,262	15,339	6,099
Flagler	8,049	4,646	992	8,998	6,098	1,630	10,857	6,783	2,448
Franklin	1,266	733	228	1,443	839	286	1,751	930	317
Gadsden	2,807	1,900	684	2,986	1,989	818	3,437	1,980	929
Gilchrist	1,107	614	142	1,198	709	190	1,404	781	241
Glades	1,075	732	155	1,098	811	209	1,238	790	259

Continued . . .

Table 1.42. PERSONS AGED 65 AND OVER: PROJECTIONS BY AGE IN THE STATE AND COUNTIES OF FLORIDA
APRIL 1, 2000, 2005, AND 2010 (Continued)

County	2000			2005			2010		
	65-74	75-84	85 and over	65-74	75-84	85 and over	65-74	75-84	85 and over
Gulf	1,147	705	212	1,176	742	238	1,255	739	270
Hamilton	897	493	173	962	565	195	1,127	615	208
Hardee	1,886	1,370	390	1,801	1,499	469	2,027	1,353	566
Hendry	1,947	1,196	360	2,066	1,336	429	2,382	1,344	516
Hernando	24,626	16,174	3,502	26,382	18,951	5,028	31,803	19,600	6,685
Highlands	16,035	12,565	2,982	16,425	14,236	3,955	18,566	14,174	5,027
Hillsborough	68,049	46,511	14,017	71,822	51,692	17,384	83,881	52,316	21,101
Holmes	1,566	1,009	340	1,641	1,087	376	1,784	1,078	431
Indian River	16,732	12,621	2,912	16,991	14,093	3,868	19,370	14,080	4,872
Jackson	3,422	2,318	936	3,524	2,327	1,014	3,966	2,304	1,069
Jefferson	1,103	753	219	1,189	836	249	1,396	860	287
Lafayette	480	284	68	512	310	85	529	334	105
Lake	30,665	22,449	5,524	32,477	26,100	6,968	37,729	26,981	8,846
Lee	56,234	39,201	9,524	58,854	43,789	12,090	69,296	44,173	14,763
Leon	10,628	6,863	1,763	11,312	7,482	2,136	13,786	7,731	2,474
Levy	3,995	2,878	645	4,194	3,393	922	4,893	3,502	1,216
Liberty	476	238	71	481	260	81	529	288	83
Madison	1,249	897	341	1,231	921	371	1,314	872	389
Manatee	33,136	27,157	8,762	33,763	28,834	10,477	39,110	28,132	12,159
Marion	35,140	24,576	5,447	37,102	29,142	7,591	43,605	30,110	10,052
Martin	17,410	13,540	3,561	17,808	14,834	4,581	20,670	14,730	5,607
Monroe	7,817	4,912	993	7,850	5,148	1,207	9,038	4,951	1,413
Nassau	3,621	1,894	546	3,976	2,236	675	4,779	2,435	812
Okaloosa	11,687	6,490	1,587	12,470	7,633	2,150	13,452	8,440	2,854

Continued . . .

Table 1.42. PERSONS AGED 65 AND OVER: PROJECTIONS BY AGE IN THE STATE AND COUNTIES OF FLORIDA
APRIL 1, 2000, 2005, AND 2010 (Continued)

County	2000			2005			2010		
	65-74	75-84	85 and over	65-74	75-84	85 and over	65-74	75-84	85 and over
Okeechobee	4,109	2,603	603	4,248	3,152	823	4,931	3,279	1,092
Orange	50,813	32,712	8,689	54,586	37,372	10,756	64,659	39,014	13,272
Osceola	11,982	7,908	2,474	13,891	9,342	3,292	17,593	10,428	4,129
Palm Beach	118,974	100,397	29,874	124,752	107,174	36,339	147,613	106,546	42,249
Pasco	50,989	44,951	11,460	51,859	47,188	14,672	60,205	45,695	17,311
Pinellas	103,644	88,403	31,865	102,161	88,442	34,761	114,106	82,712	37,549
Polk	52,125	37,134	11,059	53,266	42,016	14,068	60,708	42,015	17,473
Putnam	8,463	5,308	1,354	8,447	6,019	1,719	9,430	5,987	2,154
St. Johns	10,538	7,344	1,881	11,164	8,756	2,510	13,970	8,949	3,267
St. Lucie	23,892	16,592	3,447	25,306	19,111	4,778	29,940	19,654	6,196
Santa Rosa	7,695	3,914	991	9,079	5,095	1,273	11,049	5,979	1,760
Sarasota	51,140	42,477	12,918	52,581	45,447	15,612	60,830	44,475	18,324
Seminole	21,521	13,203	3,990	24,440	15,093	4,931	30,952	16,203	6,043
Sumter	5,241	3,395	838	5,485	3,797	1,099	6,294	3,843	1,381
Suwannee	3,278	2,252	774	3,523	2,659	914	4,100	2,810	1,123
Taylor	1,657	1,002	248	1,651	1,127	288	1,692	1,172	335
Union	679	393	113	756	457	157	885	510	201
Volusia	50,551	37,953	11,142	52,086	40,958	13,535	60,311	40,453	16,097
Wakulla	1,330	831	232	1,462	1,006	282	1,792	1,059	360
Walton	4,291	2,565	686	4,533	3,290	925	5,154	3,652	1,258
Washington	1,798	1,370	485	1,826	1,464	587	2,072	1,443	683

Source: University of Florida, Bureau of Economic and Business Research, Population Program, unpublished data.

Table 1.43. RACE PROJECTIONS: ESTIMATES, APRIL 1, 1995, AND PROJECTIONS, APRIL 1, 2000, 2005, AND 2010, BY RACE IN THE STATE AND COUNTIES OF FLORIDA

(rounded to thousands)

County	Estimates, 1995			Projections 2000			Projections 2005			Projections 2010		
	Total	White	Black	Total	White	Black	Total	White	Black	Total	White	Black
Florida	14,149	11,856	2,043	15,415	12,777	2,323	16,631	13,648	2,596	17,825	14,484	2,877
Alachua	198	156	37	213	167	40	227	176	43	240	185	46
Baker	20	17	3	22	19	3	23	20	3	25	21	3
Bay	139	119	16	150	128	18	161	136	20	171	143	22
Bradford	24	19	5	25	19	6	26	20	6	27	20	6
Brevard	445	399	37	493	439	43	539	478	49	585	515	56
Broward	1,364	1,095	242	1,466	1,143	287	1,564	1,187	332	1,660	1,229	376
Calhoun	12	10	2	13	10	2	13	10	2	14	11	3
Charlotte	128	120	6	147	138	7	167	155	9	186	172	11
Citrus	105	102	3	120	115	3	133	129	4	147	142	4
Clay	121	111	7	136	123	9	151	136	11	166	147	13
Collier	187	175	10	220	205	13	252	234	15	283	262	18
Columbia	50	41	9	55	45	10	60	49	10	64	52	11
Dade	2,014	1,531	445	2,129	1,588	494	2,241	1,642	541	2,351	1,693	589
De Soto	27	21	5	30	24	6	33	25	6	35	27	7
Dixie	12	11	1	14	12	1	15	14	2	17	15	2
Duval	718	517	183	761	537	201	802	555	219	843	571	238
Escambia	283	216	58	302	229	63	317	238	67	330	245	71
Flagler	37	33	3	46	40	4	54	48	6	63	55	7
Franklin	10	9	2	11	9	2	12	9	2	13	10	2
Gadsden	45	19	25	47	20	26	49	21	26	50	22	27
Gilchrist	12	11	1	14	12	1	16	14	2	18	15	2
Glades	9	7	1	10	8	2	11	8	2	12	9	2

Continued . . .

Table 1.43. RACE PROJECTIONS: ESTIMATES, APRIL 1, 1995, AND PROJECTIONS, APRIL 1, 2000, 2005, AND 2010, BY RACE IN THE STATE AND COUNTIES OF FLORIDA (Continued)

(rounded to thousands)

County	Estimates, 1995			Projections 2000			Projections 2005			Projections 2010		
	Total	White	Black	Total	White	Black	Total	White	Black	Total	White	Black
Gulf	13	10	3	15	11	4	16	11	4	16	12	4
Hamilton	12	8	5	15	9	6	15	9	6	16	10	6
Hardee	23	20	2	24	21	3	24	21	3	25	21	3
Hendry	29	23	5	33	25	6	36	27	7	39	29	8
Hernando	118	112	5	139	131	6	159	150	7	179	169	9
Highlands	77	68	8	86	75	9	94	82	11	103	89	12
Hillsborough	893	750	125	956	795	140	1,017	836	155	1,076	875	171
Holmes	17	16	1	18	16	1	19	17	1	19	17	2
Indian River	100	91	8	111	101	9	122	110	10	133	120	11
Jackson	47	34	12	48	35	12	50	37	12	52	38	12
Jefferson	14	8	6	14	9	6	15	9	6	16	10	6
Lafayette	7	5	1	8	6	2	8	6	2	9	6	2
Lake	177	159	17	200	179	19	222	199	21	244	217	24
Lee	377	347	26	423	387	31	467	426	36	511	464	41
Leon	218	160	53	237	174	58	256	186	63	274	198	69
Levy	30	26	4	33	29	4	36	31	4	39	34	4
Liberty	7	5	1	7	6	2	8	6	2	9	6	2
Madison	18	11	8	19	11	8	20	11	8	21	12	9
Manatee	233	212	19	256	231	22	279	250	25	300	268	28
Marion	225	194	29	254	219	32	283	242	37	311	265	42
Martin	112	103	8	125	114	10	138	124	12	150	134	14
Monroe	83	77	5	89	82	6	94	86	6	100	91	7
Nassau	49	44	5	54	49	5	59	53	5	63	57	5
Okaloosa	163	141	16	178	153	18	193	164	21	208	175	24

Continued . . .

Table 1.43. RACE PROJECTIONS: ESTIMATES, APRIL 1, 1995, AND PROJECTIONS, APRIL 1, 2000, 2005, AND 2010, BY RACE IN THE STATE AND COUNTIES OF FLORIDA (Continued)

(rounded to thousands)

County	Estimates, 1995			Projections 2000			Projections 2005			Projections 2010		
	Total	White	Black	Total	White	Black	Total	White	Black	Total	White	Black
Okeechobee	33	30	2	37	34	3	41	36	4	44	39	4
Orange	759	604	133	846	654	163	934	703	194	1,021	750	226
Osceola	137	123	10	164	146	13	191	167	17	218	189	21
Palm Beach	963	822	128	1,068	902	148	1,170	979	169	1,271	1,053	191
Pasco	306	295	7	335	321	10	363	346	12	391	371	14
Pinellas	876	791	72	907	814	78	938	836	83	968	859	89
Polk	443	379	59	478	408	64	511	435	69	544	461	75
Putnam	70	57	12	75	61	12	79	65	13	84	69	13
St. Johns	98	89	8	112	102	9	125	114	10	139	126	11
St. Lucie	171	143	27	195	163	29	218	183	33	241	202	36
Santa Rosa	96	89	4	110	101	6	123	113	7	136	124	8
Sarasota	302	285	14	327	307	17	351	328	19	375	349	22
Seminole	324	287	30	366	320	36	406	351	43	447	381	51
Sumter	36	29	7	44	33	10	48	36	11	51	38	12
Suwannee	31	26	4	33	29	4	36	32	4	39	34	4
Taylor	18	14	4	19	15	4	20	15	4	20	15	4
Union	13	9	3	13	9	4	14	10	4	15	10	4
Volusia	403	360	38	442	393	43	481	425	49	518	455	54
Wakulla	17	15	2	20	17	3	22	19	3	24	20	4
Walton	33	30	2	37	34	3	41	37	3	44	41	3
Washington	19	16	3	21	17	4	22	18	4	23	19	4

Source: University of Florida, Bureau of Economic and Business Research, Population Program, *Florida Population Studies,* July 1996, Volume 29, No. 3. Bulletin No. 115.

Table 1.65. METROPOLITAN AREAS: CENSUS COUNTS APRIL 1, 1980 AND 1990, AND ESTIMATES, APRIL 1, 1995, IN THE STATE AND METROPOLITAN AREAS OF FLORIDA

Metropolitan area	Census 1980	Census 1990	Estimates 1995	Percentage change 1980-1990	Percentage change 1990-1995
Florida	9,746,961	12,938,071	14,149,317	32.7	9.4
Metropolitan areas, total	9,038,653	12,023,514	13,119,253	33.0	9.1
Daytona Beach	269,675	399,438	439,967	48.1	10.1
Flagler County	10,913	28,701	36,997	163.0	28.9
Volusia County	258,762	370,737	402,970	43.3	8.7
Ft. Lauderdale	1,018,257	1,255,531	1,364,168	23.3	8.7
Ft. Myers-Cape Coral	205,266	335,113	376,702	63.3	12.4
Ft. Pierce-Port St. Lucie	151,196	251,071	283,196	66.1	12.8
Martin County	64,014	100,900	112,036	57.6	11.0
St. Lucie County	87,182	150,171	171,160	72.3	14.0
Ft. Walton Beach	109,920	143,777	162,707	30.8	13.2
Gainesville	151,369	181,596	198,261	20.0	9.2
Jacksonville	722,252	906,727	986,566	25.5	8.8
Clay County	67,052	105,986	120,896	58.1	14.1
Duval County	571,003	672,971	718,355	17.9	6.7
Nassau County	32,894	43,941	49,127	33.6	11.8
St. Johns County	51,303	83,829	98,188	63.4	17.1
Lakeland-Winter Haven	321,652	405,382	443,153	26.0	9.3
Melbourne-Titusville-Palm Bay	272,959	398,978	444,992	46.2	11.5
Miami	1,625,509	1,937,194	2,013,821	19.2	4.0
Naples	85,971	152,099	186,504	76.9	22.6
Ocala	122,488	194,835	224,612	59.1	15.3
Orlando	804,774	1,224,844	1,396,650	52.2	14.0
Lake County	104,870	152,104	176,931	45.0	16.3
Orange County	470,865	677,491	758,962	43.9	12.0
Osceola County	49,287	107,728	136,627	118.6	26.8
Seminole County	179,752	287,521	324,130	60.0	12.7
Panama City	97,740	126,994	139,173	29.9	9.6
Pensacola	289,782	344,406	378,833	18.9	10.0
Escambia County	233,794	262,798	282,742	12.4	7.6
Santa Rosa County	55,988	81,608	96,091	45.8	17.7
Punta Gorda	58,460	110,975	127,646	89.8	15.0
Sarasota-Bradenton	350,696	489,483	534,688	39.6	9.2
Manatee County	148,445	211,707	233,160	42.6	10.1
Sarasota County	202,251	277,776	301,528	37.3	8.6
Tallahassee	190,329	233,609	262,267	22.7	12.3
Gadsden County	41,674	41,116	44,734	-1.3	8.8
Leon County	148,655	192,493	217,533	29.5	13.0
Tampa-St. Petersburg-Clearwater	1,613,600	2,067,959	2,192,545	28.2	6.0
Hernando County	44,469	101,115	117,895	127.4	16.6
Hillsborough County	646,939	834,054	892,874	28.9	7.1
Pasco County	193,661	281,131	305,576	45.2	8.7
Pinellas County	728,531	851,659	876,200	16.9	2.9
West Palm Beach-Boca Raton	576,758	863,503	962,802	49.7	11.5

Note: Data are for Metropolitan Statistical Areas (MSAs) and for Primary Metropolitan Statistical Areas (PMSAs) based on 1992 MSA designations. See Glossary for definitions and map at the front of the book for area boundaries. Estimates reflect changes to Dade and Broward counties as a result of Hurricane Andrew in August 1992.

Source: University of Florida, Bureau of Economic and Business Research, Population Program, *Florida Estimates of Population, April 1, 1995.* Census data from U.S. Bureau of the Census.

Table 1.66. PLANNING DISTRICTS: CENSUS COUNTS, APRIL 1, 1990, AND ESTIMATES APRIL 1, 1995, IN THE STATE, COMPREHENSIVE PLANNING DISTRICTS, AND COUNTIES OF FLORIDA

District and county	Census 1990	Estimates 1995	Percentage change 1990 to 1995	District and county	Census 1990	Estimates 1995	Percentage change 1990 to 1995
Florida	12,938,071	14,149,317	9.4	District 5	446,952	514,274	15.1
				Citrus	93,513	105,468	12.8
District 1	675,633	750,523	11.1	Hernando	101,115	117,895	16.6
Bay	126,994	139,173	9.6	Levy	25,912	29,843	15.2
Escambia	262,798	282,742	7.6	Marion	194,835	224,612	15.3
Holmes	15,778	17,385	10.2	Sumter	31,577	36,456	15.5
Okaloosa	143,777	162,707	13.2	District 6	1,994,559	2,244,612	12.5
Santa Rosa	81,608	96,091	17.7	Brevard	398,978	444,992	11.5
Walton	27,759	33,415	20.4	Lake	152,104	176,931	16.3
Washington	16,919	19,010	12.4	Orange	677,491	758,962	12.0
District 2	337,533	381,726	13.1	Osceola	107,728	136,627	26.8
Calhoun	11,011	11,988	8.9	Seminole	287,521	324,130	12.7
Franklin	8,967	10,236	14.2	Volusia	370,737	402,970	8.7
Gadsden	41,116	44,734	8.8	District 7	546,805	602,803	10.2
Gulf	11,504	13,271	15.4	De Soto	23,865	26,640	11.6
Jackson	41,375	46,577	12.6	Hardee	19,499	22,885	17.4
Jefferson	11,296	13,509	19.6	Highlands	68,432	77,270	12.9
Leon	192,493	217,533	13.0	Okeechobee	29,627	32,855	10.9
Liberty	5,569	6,873	23.4	Polk	405,382	443,153	9.3
Wakulla	14,202	17,005	19.7	District 8	2,178,551	2,307,810	5.9
District 3	354,196	396,138	11.8	Hillsborough	834,054	892,874	7.1
Alachua	181,596	198,261	9.2	Manatee	211,707	233,160	10.1
Bradford	22,515	24,336	8.1	Pasco	281,131	305,576	8.7
Columbia	42,613	50,387	18.2	Pinellas	851,659	876,200	2.9
Dixie	10,585	12,416	17.3	District 9	909,327	1,030,428	13.3
Gilchrist	9,667	11,888	23.0	Charlotte	110,975	127,646	15.0
Hamilton	10,930	12,487	14.2	Collier	152,099	186,504	22.6
Lafayette	5,578	6,516	16.8	Glades	7,591	8,551	12.6
Madison	16,569	18,344	10.7	Hendry	25,773	29,497	14.4
Suwannee	26,780	30,534	14.0	Lee	335,113	376,702	12.4
Taylor	17,111	18,322	7.1	Sarasota	277,776	301,528	8.6
Union	10,252	12,647	23.4	District 10	1,204,782	1,346,259	11.7
District 4	1,018,984	1,113,354	9.3	Indian River	90,208	100,261	11.1
Baker	18,486	20,275	9.7	Martin	100,900	112,036	11.0
Clay	105,986	120,896	14.1	Palm Beach	863,503	962,802	11.5
Duval	672,971	718,355	6.7	St. Lucie	150,171	171,160	14.0
Flagler	28,701	36,997	28.9	District 11	3,270,749	3,461,390	5.8
Nassau	43,941	49,127	11.8	Broward	1,255,531	1,364,168	8.7
Putnam	65,070	69,516	6.8	Dade	1,937,194	2,013,821	4.0
St. Johns	83,829	98,188	17.1	Monroe	78,024	83,401	6.9

Note: Data are for planning district boundaries as defined in May 1984. See map. Estimates reflect changes to Dade and Broward counties as a result of Hurricane Andrew in August 1992.

Source: University of Florida, Bureau of Economic and Business Research, Population Program, *Florida Estimates of Population, April 1, 1995*. Census data from U.S. Bureau of the Census.

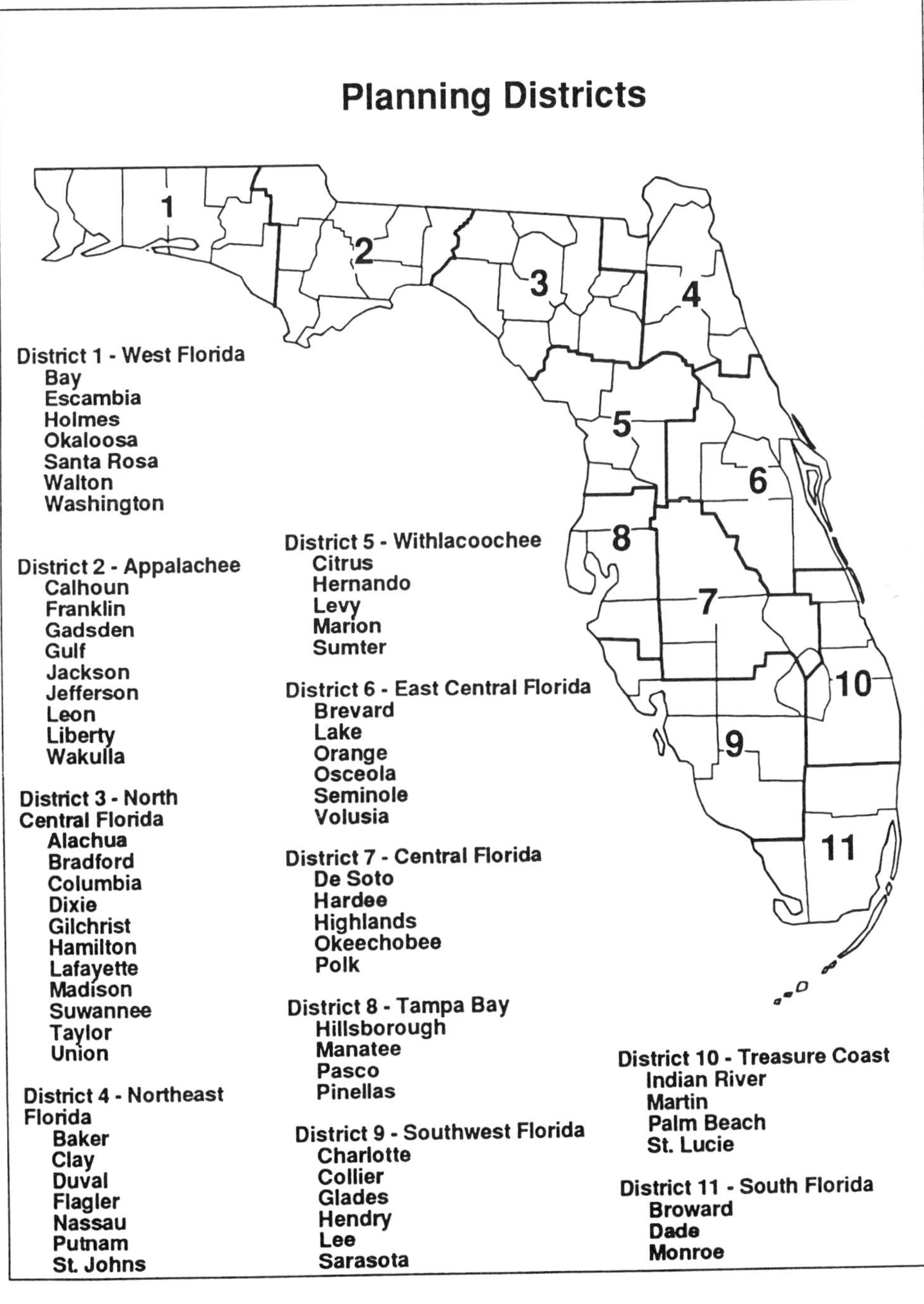
Planning Districts
1
2
3
4
5
6
7
8
9
10
11
District 1 - West Florida
Bay
Escambia
Holmes
Okaloosa
Santa Rosa
Walton
Washington
District 2 - Appalachee
Calhoun
Franklin
Gadsden
Gulf
Jackson
Jefferson
Leon
Liberty
Wakulla
District 3 - North Central Florida
Alachua
Bradford
Columbia
Dixie
Gilchrist
Hamilton
Lafayette
Madison
Suwannee
Taylor
Union
District 4 - Northeast Florida
Baker
Clay
Duval
Flagler
Nassau
Putnam
St. Johns
District 5 - Withlacoochee
Citrus
Hernando
Levy
Marion
Sumter
District 6 - East Central Florida
Brevard
Lake
Orange
Osceola
Seminole
Volusia
District 7 - Central Florida
De Soto
Hardee
Highlands
Okeechobee
Polk
District 8 - Tampa Bay
Hillsborough
Manatee
Pasco
Pinellas
District 9 - Southwest Florida
Charlotte
Collier
Glades
Hendry
Lee
Sarasota
District 10 - Treasure Coast
Indian River
Martin
Palm Beach
St. Lucie
District 11 - South Florida
Broward
Dade
Monroe

Table 1.67. HRS DISTRICTS: CENSUS COUNTS, APRIL 1, 1990, AND ESTIMATES APRIL 1, 1995, IN THE STATE, DEPARTMENT OF HEALTH AND REHABILITATIVE SERVICES (HRS) DISTRICTS AND COUNTIES OF FLORIDA

District and county	Census 1990	Estimates 1995	Percentage change 1990 to 1995
Florida	12,938,071	14,149,317	9.4
District 1	515,942	574,955	58.9
Escambia	262,798	282,742	7.6
Okaloosa	143,777	162,707	13.2
Santa Rosa	81,608	96,091	17.7
Walton	27,759	33,415	20.4
District 2	530,904	593,960	185.4
Bay	126,994	139,173	9.6
Calhoun	11,011	11,988	8.9
Franklin	8,967	10,236	14.2
Gadsden	41,116	44,734	8.8
Gulf	11,504	13,271	15.4
Holmes	15,778	17,385	10.2
Jackson	41,375	46,577	12.6
Jefferson	11,296	13,509	19.6
Leon	192,493	217,533	13.0
Liberty	5,569	6,873	23.4
Madison	16,569	18,344	10.7
Taylor	17,111	18,322	7.1
Wakulla	14,202	17,005	19.7
Washington	16,919	19,010	12.4
District 3	411,498	458,831	166.2
Alachua	181,596	198,261	9.2
Bradford	22,515	24,336	8.1
Columbia	42,613	50,387	18.2
Dixie	10,585	12,416	17.3
Gilchrist	9,667	11,888	23.0
Hamilton	10,930	12,487	14.2
Lafayette	5,578	6,516	16.8
Levy	25,912	29,843	15.2
Putnam	65,070	69,516	6.8
Suwannee	26,780	30,534	14.0
Union	10,252	12,647	23.4
District 4	925,213	1,006,841	59.4
Baker	18,486	20,275	9.7
Clay	105,986	120,896	14.1
Duval	672,971	718,355	6.7
Nassau	43,941	49,127	11.8
St. Johns	83,829	98,188	17.1
District 5	1,132,790	1,181,776	11.6
Pasco	281,131	305,576	8.7
Pinellas	851,659	876,200	2.9
District 6	1,045,761	1,126,034	17.2
Hillsborough	834,054	892,874	7.1
Manatee	211,707	233,160	10.1
District 7	1,471,718	1,664,711	63.1
Brevard	398,978	444,992	11.5
Orange	677,491	758,962	12.0
Osceola	107,728	136,627	26.8
Seminole	287,521	324,130	12.7
District 8	933,192	1,057,068	97.3
Charlotte	110,975	127,646	15.0
Collier	152,099	186,504	22.6
De Soto	23,865	26,640	11.6
Glades	7,591	8,551	12.6
Hendry	25,773	29,497	14.4
Lee	335,113	376,702	12.4
Sarasota	277,776	301,528	8.6
District 9	863,503	962,802	11.5
Palm Beach	863,503	962,802	11.5
District 10	1,255,531	1,364,168	8.7
Broward	1,255,531	1,364,168	8.7
District 11	2,015,218	2,097,222	10.8
Dade	1,937,194	2,013,821	4.0
Monroe	78,024	83,401	6.9
District 12	399,438	439,967	37.6
Flagler	28,701	36,997	28.9
Volusia	370,737	402,970	8.7
District 13	573,144	661,362	76.4
Citrus	93,513	105,468	12.8
Hernando	101,115	117,895	16.6
Lake	152,104	176,931	16.3
Marion	194,835	224,612	15.3
Sumter	31,577	36,456	15.5
District 14	493,313	543,308	39.6
Hardee	19,499	22,885	17.4
Highlands	68,432	77,270	12.9
Polk	405,382	443,153	9.3
District 15	370,906	416,312	47.1
Indian River	90,208	100,261	11.1
Martin	100,900	112,036	11.0
Okeechobee	29,627	32,855	10.9
St. Lucie	150,171	171,160	14.0

Note: See map of districts in Section 7.00. Estimates reflect changes to Dade and Broward counties as a result of Hurricane Andrew in August 1992.

Source: University of Florida, Bureau of Economic and Business Research, Population Program, *Florida Estimates of Population, April 1, 1995*. Census data from U.S. Bureau of the Census.

Table 1.69. POPULOUS CITIES: CENSUS COUNTS, APRIL 1, 1980 AND 1990, AND ESTIMATES APRIL 1, 1995, IN THE 1995 MOST POPULOUS CITIES OF FLORIDA

City	Total population Census 1980	Total population Census 1990	Total population Estimates 1995	Rank 1980	Rank 1990	Rank 1995	Percentage change 1990 to 1995
Jacksonville (Duval)	540,920	635,230	676,718	1	1	1	6.5
Miami	346,865	358,648	365,498	2	2	2	1.9
Tampa	271,577	280,015	285,153	3	3	3	1.8
St. Petersburg	238,647	240,318	241,563	4	4	4	0.5
Hialeah	145,254	188,008	203,911	6	5	5	8.5
Orlando	128,291	164,674	170,307	7	6	6	3.4
Ft. Lauderdale	153,279	149,238	149,491	5	7	7	0.2
Tallahassee	81,548	124,773	137,057	11	8	8	9.8
Hollywood	121,323	121,720	125,342	8	9	9	3.0
Clearwater	85,170	98,784	101,162	10	10	10	2.4
Gainesville	81,371	85,075	96,051	12	12	11	12.9
Coral Springs	37,349	78,864	93,439	27	13	12	18.5
Miami Beach	96,298	92,639	91,775	9	11	13	-0.9
Pembroke Pines	35,776	65,566	87,948	34	21	14	34.1
Cape Coral	32,103	74,991	85,807	41	14	15	14.4
West Palm Beach	63,305	67,764	76,418	13	17	16	12.8
Plantation	48,501	66,814	75,184	20	18	17	12.5
Lakeland	47,406	70,576	74,626	21	16	18	5.7
Pompano Beach	52,618	72,411	73,950	17	15	19	2.1
Sunrise	39,681	65,683	73,456	25	20	20	11.8
Palm Bay	18,560	62,543	73,137	61	22	21	16.9
Port St. Lucie	14,690	55,761	71,776	72	27	22	28.7
Largo	57,958	65,910	67,465	14	19	23	2.4
Boca Raton	49,447	61,486	66,760	18	24	24	8.6
Melbourne	46,536	60,034	66,350	22	25	25	10.5
Daytona Beach	54,176	61,991	63,306	16	23	26	2.1
Pensacola	57,619	59,198	60,373	15	26	27	2.0
Davie	20,515	47,143	54,611	58	32	28	15.8
Sarasota	48,868	50,897	51,143	19	28	29	0.5
North Miami	42,566	50,001	50,758	24	29	30	1.5
Delray Beach	34,329	47,184	50,195	36	31	31	6.4
Lauderhill	37,271	49,015	50,022	28	30	32	2.1
Boynton Beach	35,624	46,284	49,085	35	34	33	6.1
Tamarac	29,376	44,822	48,758	45	36	34	8.8
Deerfield Beach	39,193	46,997	48,393	26	33	35	3.0

Note: Data are for the 35 most populous cities in the state. Changes in city populations include the effects of annexations. Estimates reflect changes to Dade and Broward counties as a result of Hurricane Andrew in August 1992.

Source: University of Florida, Bureau of Economic and Business Research, Population Program, *Florida Estimates of Population, April 1, 1995*. Census data from U.S. Bureau of the Census.

Table 1.72. COMPONENTS OF CHANGE: COMPONENTS OF POPULATION CHANGE IN THE STATE AND COUNTIES OF FLORIDA, APRIL 1, 1990 TO APRIL 1, 1995

County	Total population: Census April 1 1990	Total population: Estimates April 1 1995	Population change 1990 to 1995	Components of change 1/: Natural increase: Number	Natural increase: Percentage	Net migration: Number	Net migration: Percentage
Florida	12,938,071	14,149,317	1,211,246	265,992	22.0	945,254	78.0
Alachua	181,596	198,261	16,665	5,903	35.4	10,762	64.6
Baker	18,486	20,275	1,789	771	43.1	1,018	56.9
Bay	126,994	139,173	12,179	4,640	38.1	7,539	61.9
Bradford	22,515	24,336	1,821	438	24.1	1,383	75.9
Brevard	398,978	444,992	46,014	8,186	17.8	37,828	82.2
Broward	1,255,531	1,364,168	108,637	19,401	17.9	89,236	82.1
Calhoun	11,011	11,988	977	14	1.4	963	98.6
Charlotte	110,975	127,646	16,671	-3,344	0.0	20,015	100.0
Citrus	93,513	105,468	11,955	-2,725	0.0	14,680	100.0
Clay	105,986	120,896	14,910	4,223	28.3	10,687	71.7
Collier	152,099	186,504	34,405	4,176	12.1	30,229	87.9
Columbia	42,613	50,387	7,774	1,104	14.2	6,670	85.8
Dade	1,937,194	2,013,821	76,627	74,141	96.8	2,486	3.2
De Soto	23,865	26,640	2,775	673	24.3	2,102	75.7
Dixie	10,585	12,416	1,831	250	13.7	1,581	86.3
Duval	672,971	718,355	45,384	32,296	71.2	13,088	28.8
Escambia	262,798	282,742	19,944	9,282	46.5	10,662	53.5
Flagler	28,701	36,997	8,296	-297	0.0	8,593	100.0
Franklin	8,967	10,236	1,269	42	3.3	1,227	96.7
Gadsden	41,116	44,734	3,618	1,967	54.4	1,651	45.6
Gilchrist	9,667	11,888	2,221	150	6.8	2,071	93.2
Glades	7,591	8,551	960	87	9.1	873	90.9
Gulf	11,504	13,271	1,767	112	6.3	1,655	93.7
Hamilton	10,930	12,487	1,557	309	19.8	1,248	80.2
Hardee	19,499	22,885	3,386	1,310	38.7	2,076	61.3
Hendry	25,773	29,497	3,724	1,889	50.7	1,835	49.3
Hernando	101,115	117,895	16,780	-2,591	0.0	19,371	100.0
Highlands	68,432	77,270	8,838	-1,265	0.0	10,103	100.0
Hillsborough	834,054	892,874	58,820	31,768	54.0	27,052	46.0
Holmes	15,778	17,385	1,607	134	8.3	1,473	91.7
Indian River	90,208	100,261	10,053	-715	0.0	10,768	100.0
Jackson	41,375	46,577	5,202	554	10.6	4,648	89.4
Jefferson	11,296	13,509	2,213	294	13.3	1,919	86.7
Lafayette	5,578	6,516	938	151	16.1	787	83.9
Lake	152,104	176,931	24,827	-836	0.0	25,663	100.0
Lee	335,113	376,702	41,589	1,773	4.3	39,816	95.7

See footnotes at end of table.

Continued . . .

Table 1.72. COMPONENTS OF CHANGE: COMPONENTS OF POPULATION CHANGE IN THE STATE AND COUNTIES OF FLORIDA, APRIL 1, 1990 TO APRIL 1, 1995 (Continued)

County	Total population: Census April 1 1990	Total population: Estimates April 1 1995	Population change 1990 to 1995	Components of change 1/ Natural increase: Number	Natural increase: Percentage	Net migration: Number	Net migration: Percentage
Leon	192,493	217,533	25,040	7,451	29.8	17,589	70.2
Levy	25,912	29,843	3,931	151	3.8	3,780	96.2
Liberty	5,569	6,873	1,304	178	13.7	1,126	86.3
Madison	16,569	18,344	1,775	417	23.5	1,358	76.5
Manatee	211,707	233,160	21,453	-394	0.0	21,847	100.0
Marion	194,835	224,612	29,777	1,425	4.8	28,352	95.2
Martin	100,900	112,036	11,136	-295	0.0	11,431	100.0
Monroe	78,024	83,401	5,377	1,465	27.2	3,912	72.8
Nassau	43,941	49,127	5,186	1,772	34.2	3,414	65.8
Okaloosa	143,777	162,707	18,930	7,297	38.5	11,633	61.5
Okeechobee	29,627	32,855	3,228	1,278	39.6	1,950	60.4
Orange	677,491	758,962	81,471	33,537	41.2	47,934	58.8
Osceola	107,728	136,627	28,899	4,720	16.3	24,179	83.7
Palm Beach	863,503	962,802	99,299	9,101	9.2	90,198	90.8
Pasco	281,131	305,576	24,445	-6,388	0.0	30,833	100.0
Pinellas	851,659	876,200	24,541	-13,358	0.0	37,899	100.0
Polk	405,382	443,153	37,771	9,541	25.3	28,230	74.7
Putnam	65,070	69,516	4,446	1,080	24.3	3,366	75.7
St. Johns	83,829	98,188	14,359	1,406	9.8	12,953	90.2
St. Lucie	150,171	171,160	20,989	3,337	15.9	17,652	84.1
Santa Rosa	81,608	96,091	14,483	3,646	25.2	10,837	74.8
Sarasota	277,776	301,528	23,752	-7,922	0.0	31,674	100.0
Seminole	287,521	324,130	36,609	11,910	32.5	24,699	67.5
Sumter	31,577	36,456	4,879	238	4.9	4,641	95.1
Suwannee	26,780	30,534	3,754	40	1.1	3,714	98.9
Taylor	17,111	18,322	1,211	422	34.8	789	65.2
Union	10,252	12,647	2,395	119	5.0	2,276	95.0
Volusia	370,737	402,970	32,233	-1,405	0.0	33,638	100.0
Wakulla	14,202	17,005	2,803	401	14.3	2,402	85.7
Walton	27,759	33,415	5,656	369	6.5	5,287	93.5
Washington	16,919	19,010	2,091	188	9.0	1,903	91.0

1/ Natural increase is calculated as the difference between the number of births and the number of deaths; net migration is calculated as the difference between total population change and natural increase.

Note: Vital statistics data for persons of unreported residence are included only in the entries for the state. For this reason, natural increase and net migration columns may not add to their state totals. Estimates reflect changes to Dade and Broward counties as a result of Hurricane Andrew in August 1992.

Source: University of Florida, Bureau of Economic and Business Research, Population Program, *Florida Estimates of Population, April 1, 1995*. Census data from U.S. Bureau of the Census.

Table 1.73. MIGRATION: NET MIGRATION OF THE TOTAL POPULATION AND OF PERSONS AGED 65 AND OVER BY STATE OF EXCHANGE WITH FLORIDA 1985 THROUGH 1990

State	Total popu-lation	Aged 65 and over Total	Aged 65 and over Per-cent-age	State	Total popu-lation	Aged 65 and over Total	Aged 65 and over Per-cent-age
Alabama	5,151	1,108	21.5	Montana	1,736	-45	-2.6
Alaska	1,429	6	0.4	Nebraska	4,203	245	5.8
Arizona	75	-1,122	-1,496.0	Nevada	-775	-358	46.2
Arkansas	3,506	114	3.3	New Hampshire	11,127	2,970	26.7
California	23,174	3,041	13.1	New Jersey	120,962	26,130	21.6
Colorado	9,277	-210	-2.3	New Mexico	2,571	-10	-0.4
Connecticut	42,608	10,484	24.6	New York	297,081	67,343	22.7
Delaware	2,628	934	35.5	North Carolina	-17,224	-1,899	11.0
District of Columbia	2,238	470	21.0	North Dakota	1,895	19	1.0
				Ohio	68,332	11,953	17.5
Georgia	-27,182	-510	1.9	Oklahoma	10,530	186	1.8
Hawaii	3,015	201	6.7	Oregon	-278	-291	104.7
Idaho	800	46	5.8	Pennsylvania	60,603	14,421	23.8
Illinois	66,910	12,525	18.7	Rhode Island	10,189	2,254	22.1
Indiana	31,927	6,513	20.4	South Carolina	-3,536	-76	2.1
Iowa	9,017	977	10.8	South Dakota	1,380	67	4.9
Kansas	4,218	223	5.3	Tennessee	-1,844	-301	16.3
Kentucky	12,138	1,233	10.2	Texas	58,576	432	0.7
Louisiana	29,392	724	2.5	Utah	1,357	-87	-6.4
Maine	7,140	2,499	35.0	Vermont	3,162	1,067	33.7
Maryland	20,755	5,323	25.6	Virginia	11,788	4,070	34.5
Massachusetts	57,645	14,880	25.8	Washington	-192	-252	131.3
Michigan	61,951	15,560	25.1	West Virginia	12,220	1,300	10.6
Minnesota	8,804	1,485	16.9	Wisconsin	20,090	4,467	22.2
Mississippi	8,496	84	1.0	Wyoming	1,588	32	2.0
Missouri	11,029	1,441	13.1				

Note: Based on U.S. Bureau of the Census age, race, and sex data.

Source: University of Florida, Bureau of Economic and Business Research, unpublished data.

Table 1.74. MIGRATION: MIGRATION FLOWS IN THE STATE AND COUNTIES OF FLORIDA, 1990 THROUGH 1993

County	Net migration				In-migration				Out-migration			
	1990	1991	1992	1993	1990	1991	1992	1993	1990	1991	1992	1993
Florida 1/	146,006	99,683	94,230	108,462	496,943	436,574	428,329	429,374	350,937	336,891	334,099	320,912
Alachua	1,345	1,239	276	556	11,950	11,865	11,320	11,176	10,605	10,626	11,044	10,620
Baker	187	142	211	54	986	977	1,037	936	799	835	826	882
Bay	1,436	2,136	2,073	1,179	9,870	10,967	11,470	9,384	8,434	8,831	9,397	8,205
Bradford	195	28	130	-78	1,244	1,169	1,163	1,123	1,049	1,141	1,033	1,201
Brevard	8,486	6,884	7,343	4,595	27,328	25,807	26,557	23,749	18,842	18,923	19,214	19,154
Broward	14,955	11,825	22,377	16,337	70,225	67,150	76,319	75,028	55,270	55,325	53,942	58,691
Calhoun	125	101	52	147	514	582	516	584	389	481	464	437
Charlotte	4,661	3,050	3,210	3,214	10,266	8,944	8,887	8,985	5,605	5,894	5,677	5,771
Citrus	3,084	2,907	2,515	2,775	7,714	7,275	7,879	7,004	4,630	4,368	5,364	4,229
Clay	1,865	2,314	1,643	1,841	12,107	12,285	12,082	11,895	10,242	9,971	10,439	10,054
Collier	4,580	2,937	3,707	4,043	13,984	13,299	13,512	13,827	9,404	10,362	9,805	9,784
Columbia	368	272	515	879	2,654	2,620	2,798	2,945	2,286	2,348	2,283	2,066
Dade	-8,214	-9,036	-36,814	-15,360	50,080	49,396	46,199	46,606	58,294	58,432	83,013	61,966
De Soto	173	-43	-58	43	1,716	1,759	1,747	1,752	1,543	1,802	1,805	1,709
Dixie	197	163	162	271	794	725	717	751	597	562	555	480
Duval	5,319	2,961	1,797	-2,063	46,049	44,745	44,966	38,968	40,730	41,784	43,169	41,031
Escambia	1,198	131	-441	-863	19,238	19,073	18,757	16,059	18,040	18,942	19,198	16,922
Flagler	1,582	1,584	1,619	1,619	3,193	3,109	3,145	3,208	1,611	1,525	1,526	1,589
Franklin	120	71	124	70	499	499	503	470	379	428	379	400
Gadsden	290	-81	145	-76	2,105	1,921	2,165	2,064	1,815	2,002	2,020	2,140
Gilchrist	222	238	333	255	745	783	893	850	523	545	560	595
Glades	-65	-49	-106	134	547	512	513	697	612	561	619	563
Gulf	11	95	323	54	623	621	888	683	612	526	565	629
Hamilton	39	83	39	11	584	554	572	602	545	471	533	591

See footnotes at end of table.

Continued . . .

Table 1.74. MIGRATION: MIGRATION FLOWS IN THE STATE AND COUNTIES OF FLORIDA, 1990 THROUGH 1993 (Continued)

County	Net migration				In-migration				Out-migration			
	1990	1991	1992	1993	1990	1991	1992	1993	1990	1991	1992	1993
Hardee	143	-231	-244	-316	1,648	1,675	1,597	1,491	1,505	1,906	1,841	1,807
Hendry	798	47	77	24	3,058	2,828	3,006	2,783	2,260	2,781	2,929	2,759
Hernando	3,852	3,512	3,635	3,477	9,208	8,725	8,643	8,501	5,356	5,213	5,008	5,024
Highlands	1,365	1,019	1,666	1,347	5,036	5,127	5,482	5,196	3,671	4,108	3,816	3,849
Hillsborough	401	1,521	-218	-1,476	47,445	48,795	47,512	45,410	47,044	47,274	47,730	46,886
Holmes	46	289	159	203	881	1,038	1,019	1,028	835	749	860	825
Indian River	1,347	1,123	683	1,494	6,250	5,827	5,520	5,762	4,903	4,704	4,837	4,268
Jackson	141	555	253	5	1,993	2,342	2,149	2,000	1,852	1,787	1,896	1,995
Jefferson	97	75	17	93	683	675	655	667	586	600	638	574
Lafayette	13	60	-14	46	275	306	308	306	262	246	322	260
Lake	4,414	3,746	4,347	4,962	12,919	11,993	12,404	12,856	8,505	8,247	8,057	7,894
Lee	7,204	4,204	4,685	6,749	24,307	21,703	21,129	22,238	17,103	17,499	16,444	15,489
Leon	2,246	1,888	2,028	1,220	12,566	12,207	13,153	12,698	10,320	10,319	11,125	11,478
Levy	343	372	496	583	1,945	1,887	2,107	1,992	1,602	1,515	1,611	1,409
Liberty	44	23	113	129	271	283	319	326	227	260	206	197
Madison	38	-42	148	87	683	671	711	720	645	713	563	633
Manatee	3,785	2,994	3,702	3,268	16,996	16,536	17,056	16,490	13,211	13,542	13,354	13,222
Marion	4,761	3,868	4,657	5,452	14,218	13,051	14,387	14,048	9,457	9,183	9,730	8,596
Martin	1,950	942	1,931	1,957	8,479	7,657	8,309	8,372	6,529	6,715	6,378	6,415
Monroe	290	190	1,556	-509	7,249	7,294	8,400	6,985	6,959	7,104	6,844	7,494
Nassau	717	946	943	697	3,418	3,712	3,638	3,599	2,701	2,766	2,695	2,902
Okaloosa	1,014	3,128	2,536	1,055	13,840	16,779	17,209	13,241	12,826	13,651	14,673	12,186
Okeechobee	412	-130	231	-342	2,581	2,339	2,532	2,291	2,175	2,469	2,301	2,633
Orange	5,038	2,762	4,196	2,025	56,712	54,805	54,331	51,843	51,674	52,043	50,135	49,818

See footnotes at end of table.

Continued . . .

Table 1.74. MIGRATION: MIGRATION FLOWS IN THE STATE AND COUNTIES OF FLORIDA, 1990 THROUGH 1993 (Continued)

County	Net migration				In-migration				Out-migration			
	1990	1991	1992	1993	1990	1991	1992	1993	1990	1991	1992	1993
Osceola	3,822	1,800	2,578	1,535	12,438	11,255	11,675	11,217	8,616	9,455	9,097	9,682
Palm Beach	12,139	10,905	14,251	15,031	51,478	49,418	50,739	53,062	39,339	38,513	36,488	38,031
Pasco	5,125	4,262	5,736	6,369	20,588	19,931	20,290	20,864	15,463	15,669	14,554	14,495
Pinellas	8,897	4,925	4,146	5,616	48,937	45,935	43,852	43,358	40,040	41,010	39,706	37,742
Polk	3,354	3,589	1,648	4,325	22,576	22,394	20,708	21,403	19,222	18,805	19,060	17,078
Putnam	617	270	530	408	3,556	3,302	3,206	3,048	2,939	3,032	2,676	2,640
St. Johns	1,944	1,603	2,710	2,030	7,467	7,349	8,126	7,980	5,523	5,746	5,416	5,950
St. Lucie	3,478	2,907	2,484	2,469	12,299	11,802	11,237	11,120	8,821	8,895	8,753	8,651
Santa Rosa	2,661	3,140	3,018	2,683	8,753	9,773	9,764	9,350	6,092	6,633	6,746	6,667
Sarasota	5,462	3,259	3,771	4,924	19,736	18,048	17,608	18,460	14,274	14,789	13,837	13,536
Seminole	5,966	3,943	3,450	3,451	30,037	28,685	28,363	28,457	24,071	24,742	24,913	25,006
Sumter	401	377	304	571	2,187	2,124	2,014	2,065	1,786	1,747	1,710	1,494
Suwannee	602	423	533	460	1,849	1,700	1,770	1,801	1,247	1,277	1,237	1,341
Taylor	88	-168	-109	-55	888	681	706	707	800	849	815	762
Union	-7	53	108	23	491	528	590	544	498	475	482	521
Volusia	7,684	5,981	6,138	5,532	25,149	23,187	22,546	21,764	17,465	17,206	16,408	16,232
Wakulla	350	389	440	425	1,180	1,275	1,312	1,362	830	886	872	937
Walton	608	538	697	744	2,044	2,094	2,251	2,230	1,436	1,556	1,554	1,486
Washington	197	65	286	199	1,057	1,057	1,193	1,139	860	992	907	940

1/ County flow data will not add to state flow data due to the method in which the data are aggregated.

Note: Data are based on individual income tax returns filed by citizens and resident aliens with the IRS. Only returns for which the social security number matches from one year to the next are used. Data are affected by births, deaths, marriages, reporting error, and changes in tax filing status. IRS migration data tends to understate activity in Florida due to its large elderly population and foreign immigration.

Source: U.S., Department of the Treasury, Internal Revenue Service, unpublished data.

Table 1.75. COUNTY RANKINGS AND DENSITY: ESTIMATES, RANK, PERCENTAGE DISTRIBUTION LAND AREA, AND DENSITY IN THE STATE AND COUNTIES OF FLORIDA
APRIL 1, 1995

County	Estimates			Land area 1/ (square miles)	Density	
	Number	Rank in state	Percentage of state		Persons per square mile	Rank in state
Florida	14,149,317	(X)	100.00	53,937.2	262	(X)
Alachua	198,261	19	1.40	874.3	227	20
Baker	20,275	51	0.14	585.3	35	50
Bay	139,173	24	0.98	763.7	182	26
Bradford	24,336	49	0.17	293.2	83	37
Brevard	444,992	8	3.14	1,018.5	437	11
Broward	1,364,168	2	9.64	1,208.9	1,128	2
Calhoun	11,988	62	0.08	567.4	21	61
Charlotte	127,646	26	0.90	693.7	184	25
Citrus	105,468	30	0.75	583.6	181	27
Clay	120,896	27	0.85	601.1	201	22
Collier	186,504	20	1.32	2,025.5	92	34
Columbia	50,387	37	0.36	797.2	63	42
Dade	2,013,821	1	14.23	1,944.5	1,036	4
De Soto	26,640	48	0.19	637.3	42	47
Dixie	12,416	61	0.09	704.1	18	63
Duval	718,355	7	5.08	773.9	928	5
Escambia	282,742	15	2.00	663.6	426	12
Flagler	36,997	41	0.26	485.0	76	38
Franklin	10,236	64	0.07	534.0	19	62
Gadsden	44,734	40	0.32	516.2	87	35
Gilchrist	11,888	63	0.08	348.9	34	51
Glades	8,551	65	0.06	773.5	11	66
Gulf	13,271	58	0.09	565.1	23	59
Hamilton	12,487	60	0.09	514.9	24	58
Hardee	22,885	50	0.16	637.4	36	49
Hendry	29,497	47	0.21	1,152.7	26	57
Hernando	117,895	28	0.83	478.3	247	18
Highlands	77,270	35	0.55	1,028.5	75	40
Hillsborough	892,874	4	6.31	1,051.0	850	6
Holmes	17,385	55	0.12	482.6	36	48
Indian River	100,261	31	0.71	503.3	199	23
Jackson	46,577	39	0.33	915.8	51	44
Jefferson	13,509	57	0.10	597.8	23	60
Lafayette	6,516	67	0.05	542.8	12	65
Lake	176,931	21	1.25	953.1	186	24
Lee	376,702	11	2.66	803.6	469	10

See footnotes at end of table.

Continued . . .

Table 1.75. COUNTY RANKINGS AND DENSITY: ESTIMATES, RANK, PERCENTAGE DISTRIBUTION LAND AREA, AND DENSITY IN THE STATE AND COUNTIES OF FLORIDA APRIL 1, 1995 (Continued)

County	Estimates Number	Estimates Rank in state	Estimates Percentage of state	Land area 1/ (square miles)	Density Persons per square mile	Density Rank in state
Leon	217,533	18	1.54	666.8	326	15
Levy	29,843	46	0.21	1,118.4	27	55
Liberty	6,873	66	0.05	835.9	8	67
Madison	18,344	53	0.13	692.0	27	56
Manatee	233,160	16	1.65	741.2	315	16
Marion	224,612	17	1.59	1,579.0	142	30
Martin	112,036	29	0.79	555.7	202	21
Monroe	83,401	34	0.59	997.3	84	36
Nassau	49,127	38	0.35	651.6	75	39
Okaloosa	162,707	23	1.15	935.8	174	28
Okeechobee	32,855	44	0.23	774.3	42	46
Orange	758,962	6	5.36	907.6	836	7
Osceola	136,627	25	0.97	1,322.0	103	31
Palm Beach	962,802	3	6.80	1,974.2	473	9
Pasco	305,576	13	2.16	745.0	410	13
Pinellas	876,200	5	6.19	280.2	3,129	1
Polk	443,153	9	3.13	1,874.9	236	19
Putnam	69,516	36	0.49	722.2	96	32
St. Johns	98,188	32	0.69	609.0	161	29
St. Lucie	171,160	22	1.21	572.5	299	17
Santa Rosa	96,091	33	0.68	1,015.8	95	33
Sarasota	301,528	14	2.13	571.8	527	8
Seminole	324,130	12	2.29	308.2	1,052	3
Sumter	36,456	42	0.26	545.7	67	41
Suwannee	30,534	45	0.22	687.7	44	45
Taylor	18,322	54	0.13	1,042.0	18	64
Union	12,647	59	0.09	240.3	53	43
Volusia	402,970	10	2.85	1,105.9	364	14
Wakulla	17,005	56	0.12	606.7	28	54
Walton	33,415	43	0.24	1,057.7	32	53
Washington	19,010	52	0.13	579.9	33	52

(X) Not applicable.

1/ Land area figures as provided by the Geography division of the U.S. Bureau of the Census represent the total area in the counties in 1990 and are not adjusted for lands which cannot be developed (government-owned parks or reserves) or are uninhabitable (swamps or marshes).

Note: Estimates reflect changes to Dade and Broward counties as a result of Hurricane Andrew in August 1992.

Source: University of Florida, Bureau of Economic and Business Research, Population Program, *Florida Estimates of Population, April 1, 1995*. Census data from U.S. Bureau of the Census.

Table 1.80. INSTITUTIONAL POPULATION: ESTIMATED NUMBER OF INMATES AND PATIENTS RESIDING IN FEDERAL AND STATE GOVERNMENT-OPERATED INSTITUTIONS AND CONSIDERED NONRESIDENTS OF THE LOCAL AREA FOR REVENUE-SHARING PURPOSES IN THE STATE, COUNTIES, AND MUNICIPALITIES OF FLORIDA, APRIL 1, 1995

County or city	Total
Florida	78,964
Incorporated	15,257
Unincorporated	63,707
Alachua	2,018
Gainesville	1,532
Unincorporated	486
Baker	1,741
Bay	138
Panama City	71
Unincorporated	67
Bradford	3,726
Brevard	1,506
Titusville	58
Unincorporated	1,448
Broward	1,579
Davie	3
Ft. Lauderdale	88
Pembroke Pines	486
Pompano Beach	71
Unincorporated	931
Calhoun	1,151
Charlotte	1,232
Punta Gorda	16
Unincorporated	1,216
Clay	11
Green Cove Springs	2
Orange Park	2
Unincorporated	7
Collier	60
Columbia	1,846
Lake City	485
Unincorporated	1,361
Dade	6,372
Homestead	2
Miami	3,114
North Miami	244
Opa-Locka	19
South Miami	5
Unincorporated	2,988
De Soto	1,759
Dixie	1,088
Duval (Jacksonville)	503
Escambia	2,163
Pensacola	118
Unincorporated	2,045
Franklin	271
Carrabelle	35
Unincorporated	236
Gadsden	2,089
Chatahoochee	1,634
Gretna	119
Quincy	336
Gilchrist	871
Gulf	1,193
Hamilton	1,293
Hardee	1,455
Hendry	1,265
Hernando	519
Highlands	74
Hillsborough	1,420
Tampa	985
Unincorporated	435
Holmes	1,279
Indian River	228
Jackson	5,188
Malone	1,386
Marianna	128
Unincorporated	3,674
Jefferson	898
Lafayette	990
Lake	790
Lee	751
Cape Coral	30
Ft. Myers	145
Unincorporated	576
Leon	1,989
Tallahassee	1,809
Unincorporated	180
Levy	260
Liberty	1,314
Madison	1,430
Madison	32
Unincorporated	1,398
Manatee	208
Bradenton	136
Palmetto	24
Unincorporated	48
Marion	2,580
Ocala	89
Unincorporated	2,491
Martin	1,470
Stuart	54
Unincorporated	1,416
Monroe	51
Nassau	33
Fernandina Beach	9
Unincorporated	24

See footnote at end of table.

Continued . . .

Table 1.80. INSTITUTIONAL POPULATION: ESTIMATED NUMBER OF INMATES AND PATIENTS RESIDING IN FEDERAL AND STATE GOVERNMENT-OPERATED INSTITUTIONS AND CONSIDERED NONRESIDENTS OF THE LOCAL AREA FOR REVENUE-SHARING PURPOSES IN THE STATE, COUNTIES, AND MUNICIPALITIES OF FLORIDA, APRIL 1, 1995 (Continued)

County or city	Total
Okaloosa	1,806
Okeechobee	157
Orange	2,749
Eatonville	84
Orlando	90
Winter Park	37
Unincorporated	2,538
Osceola	197
Palm Beach	1,940
Boca Raton	4
Lantana	108
West Palm Beach	277
Unincorporated	1,551
Pasco	799
San Antonio	35
Unincorporated	764
Pinellas	1,390
Clearwater	29
Pinellas Park	25
St. Petersburg	290
Unincorporated	1,046
Polk	2,951
Bartow	229
Unincorporated	2,722
Putnam	430
St. Johns	2
Hastings	2
St. Lucie	157
Ft. Pierce	79
Unincorporated	78
Santa Rosa	272
Milton	29
Unincorporated	243
Sarasota	22
Sarasota	6
Unincorporated	16
Seminole	176
Casselberry	6
Sanford	42
Unincorporated	128
Sumter	1,223
Taylor	546
Union	3,964
Raiford	20
Unincorporated	3,944
Volusia	1,762
Daytona Beach	48
Holly Hill	8
Unincorporated	1,706
Walton	1,072
De Funiak Springs	39
Unincorporated	1,033
Washington	547

Note: Unless city data are specified separately for a county, county data are for unincorporated areas.

Source: University of Florida, Bureau of Economic and Business Research, Population Program, *Florida Estimates of Population, April 1, 1995.*

Table 1.83. PLANNING DISTRICTS: ESTIMATES, APRIL 1, 1995, AND PROJECTIONS SPECIFIED YEARS APRIL 1, 2000 THROUGH 2020, IN THE STATE AND COMPREHENSIVE PLANNING DISTRICTS OF FLORIDA

(in thousands, rounded to hundreds)

District	Estimates 1995	Projections 2000	2005	2010	2015	2020
Florida	14,149.3					
Low		14,700.4	15,391.1	16,087.6	16,825.5	17,595.7
Medium		15,414.9	16,630.3	17,825.0	19,036.6	20,254.8
High		16,093.7	17,834.6	19,526.7	21,209.6	22,871.9
District 1	750.5					
Low		765.3	767.8	760.8	745.6	722.5
Medium		817.3	875.6	931.7	988.9	1,046.3
High		879.1	1,005.6	1,139.3	1,282.1	1,434.2
District 2	381.7					
Low		376.5	368.9	356.3	337.7	315.2
Medium		413.7	440.7	467.1	491.9	516.9
High		454.9	521.8	593.6	667.8	746.5
District 3	396.1					
Low		395.1	390.5	381.4	366.1	346.7
Medium		428.6	457.0	484.8	511.0	536.9
High		466.5	533.6	605.0	678.5	757.0
District 4	1,113.4					
Low		1,123.2	1,125.3	1,113.2	1,088.0	1,048.8
Medium		1,204.9	1,294.1	1,381.5	1,470.7	1,560.1
High		1,302.3	1,497.2	1,706.3	1,931.2	2,171.8
District 5	514.3					
Low		529.9	541.6	540.6	527.2	500.6
Medium		588.9	658.9	728.4	799.2	871.1
High		660.0	803.3	960.6	1,133.4	1,322.0
District 6	2,244.6					
Low		2,273.8	2,304.9	2,288.8	2,228.3	2,121.3
Medium		2,510.7	2,773.9	3,033.9	3,299.4	3,567.2
High		2,793.7	3,345.5	3,946.0	4,602.3	5,313.2
District 7	602.8					
Low		613.8	617.6	614.2	604.3	587.4
Medium		655.0	703.5	750.9	798.9	847.2
High		704.7	808.2	918.2	1,035.8	1,160.8
District 8	2,307.8					
Low		2,294.7	2,269.7	2,223.1	2,156.9	2,070.1
Medium		2,453.8	2,595.9	2,735.3	2,876.8	3,018.7
High		2,638.2	2,977.5	3,337.1	3,720.2	4,126.0
District 9	1,030.4					
Low		1,051.4	1,067.3	1,060.4	1,031.8	980.5
Medium		1,159.7	1,283.9	1,406.1	1,531.0	1,657.2
High		1,289.7	1,548.3	1,830.4	2,139.5	2,475.2
District 10	1,346.3					
Low		1,361.0	1,375.3	1,363.1	1,326.5	1,264.2
Medium		1,499.2	1,648.1	1,794.8	1,944.4	2,095.5
High		1,663.5	1,979.0	2,320.9	2,693.2	3,095.2
District 11	3,461.4					
Low		3,480.8	3,468.6	3,426.4	3,357.2	3,259.8
Medium		3,683.7	3,899.5	4,110.6	4,324.1	4,537.5
High		3,925.1	4,414.6	4,930.6	5,477.6	6,054.0

Note: See footnote on Table 1.84.

Source: University of Florida, Bureau of Economic and Business Research, Population Program, *Florida Population Studies,* February 1996, Volume 29, No. 2. Bulletin No. 114.

Table 1.84. PROJECTIONS: ESTIMATES, APRIL 1, 1995, AND PROJECTIONS SPECIFIED YEARS APRIL 1, 2000 THROUGH 2020, IN THE STATE AND COUNTIES OF FLORIDA

County	Estimates 1995	Projections 2000	2005	2010	2015	2020
Florida	14,149.3					
Low		14,700.4	15,391.1	16,087.6	16,825.5	17,595.7
Medium		15,414.9	16,630.3	17,825.0	19,036.6	20,254.8
High		16,093.7	17,834.6	19,526.7	21,209.6	22,871.9
Alachua	198.3					
Low		201.2	201.3	199.6	194.7	188.2
Medium		213.0	226.5	239.8	251.2	262.5
High		226.8	256.2	287.2	317.6	349.6
Baker	20.3					
Low		19.9	19.4	18.7	17.7	16.5
Medium		22.0	23.4	24.8	26.2	27.6
High		24.3	28.0	31.8	35.9	40.3
Bay	139.2					
Low		141.9	143.3	143.3	141.8	138.9
Medium		150.1	160.8	171.3	181.9	192.5
High		160.1	182.4	206.2	231.3	258.0
Bradford	24.3					
Low		23.0	21.7	20.2	18.6	16.9
Medium		25.4	26.3	27.1	27.9	28.7
High		28.1	31.2	34.4	37.8	41.4
Brevard	445.0					
Low		447.3	449.8	444.1	430.7	409.2
Medium		492.8	539.5	585.4	632.1	679.2
High		546.6	647.3	756.1	874.4	1,001.9
Broward	1,364.2					
Low		1,385.9	1,393.2	1,386.8	1,368.2	1,336.6
Medium		1,465.6	1,564.0	1,660.3	1,757.7	1,855.0
High		1,562.8	1,773.2	1,995.7	2,232.3	2,482.3
Calhoun	12.0					
Low		11.3	10.8	10.1	9.4	8.6
Medium		12.6	13.1	13.6	14.1	14.6
High		13.9	15.5	17.3	19.1	21.1
Charlotte	127.6					
Low		128.2	129.5	126.7	119.9	108.9
Medium		147.4	166.7	185.8	205.5	225.5
High		169.9	211.3	257.3	308.3	364.4
Citrus	105.5					
Low		108.7	111.6	112.2	110.5	106.4
Medium		119.6	133.4	147.2	161.2	175.4
High		132.9	160.7	191.0	224.2	260.4
Clay	120.9					
Low		123.8	126.3	126.3	123.9	118.8
Medium		136.2	151.2	165.9	181.1	196.3
High		151.3	181.8	215.1	251.5	290.9
Collier	186.5					
Low		191.7	196.1	193.8	184.8	168.9
Medium		220.1	251.9	283.5	315.9	348.7
High		254.1	320.0	393.4	475.2	565.4

See footnote at end of table.

Continued . . .

Table 1.84. PROJECTIONS: ESTIMATES, APRIL 1, 1995, AND PROJECTIONS SPECIFIED YEARS APRIL 1, 2000 THROUGH 2020, IN THE STATE AND COUNTIES OF FLORIDA (Continued)

County	Estimates 1995	Projections 2000	2005	2010	2015	2020
Columbia	50.4					
Low		49.9	49.8	48.8	46.9	44.3
Medium		55.1	59.8	64.4	69.1	73.7
High		61.0	71.6	83.1	95.3	108.4
Dade	2,013.8					
Low		2,010.8	1,991.5	1,956.5	1,907.5	1,843.9
Medium		2,129.2	2,241.2	2,350.7	2,461.5	2,572.3
High		2,267.5	2,534.6	2,815.4	3,112.3	3,424.5
De Soto	26.6					
Low		28.6	29.0	29.0	28.8	28.3
Medium		30.2	32.5	34.7	36.9	39.2
High		32.2	36.9	41.8	47.0	52.5
Dixie	12.4					
Low		12.1	11.9	11.4	10.5	9.4
Medium		14.0	15.4	16.8	18.2	19.6
High		16.1	19.4	23.1	27.1	31.5
Duval	718.4					
Low		718.7	713.0	701.5	684.9	662.9
Medium		760.9	802.2	842.5	883.4	924.2
High		810.4	907.4	1,009.5	1,117.5	1,231.1
Escambia	282.7					
Low		285.2	280.8	273.8	265.1	254.8
Medium		302.3	316.5	329.6	343.0	356.4
High		321.6	357.4	393.9	432.5	473.1
Flagler	37.0					
Low		39.9	42.5	43.3	42.4	39.5
Medium		45.6	54.3	62.9	71.8	80.8
High		52.9	69.4	88.0	108.9	132.3
Franklin	10.2					
Low		10.0	9.8	9.4	8.9	8.3
Medium		11.1	11.8	12.5	13.2	13.9
High		12.2	14.0	16.0	18.1	20.3
Gadsden	44.7					
Low		44.4	43.0	41.5	39.7	37.7
Medium		47.2	48.6	50.1	51.6	53.1
High		50.1	54.8	59.7	64.8	70.1
Gilchrist	11.9					
Low		11.5	11.2	10.5	9.3	7.6
Medium		13.9	15.7	17.5	19.3	21.2
High		16.5	20.8	25.7	31.0	37.0
Glades	8.6					
Low		8.8	8.4	7.9	7.2	6.3
Medium		10.2	11.0	11.7	12.5	13.3
High		11.7	13.8	16.0	18.5	21.1
Gulf	13.3					
Low		13.7	12.9	12.1	11.1	10.1
Medium		15.2	15.7	16.1	16.6	17.1
High		16.7	18.6	20.5	22.6	24.7

See footnote at end of table. Continued . . .

Table 1.84. PROJECTIONS: ESTIMATES, APRIL 1, 1995, AND PROJECTIONS SPECIFIED YEARS APRIL 1, 2000 THROUGH 2020, IN THE STATE AND COUNTIES OF FLORIDA (Continued)

County	Estimates 1995	Projections 2000	2005	2010	2015	2020
Hamilton	12.5					
Low		12.5	11.8	10.9	9.8	8.5
Medium		14.5	15.4	16.2	17.1	17.9
High		16.6	19.3	22.1	25.1	28.3
Hardee	22.9					
Low		21.3	20.0	18.6	17.1	15.5
Medium		23.6	24.3	24.9	25.6	26.3
High		26.0	28.8	31.7	34.7	37.8
Hendry	29.5					
Low		29.6	29.7	29.2	28.3	26.8
Medium		32.7	35.7	38.6	41.5	44.5
High		36.2	42.8	49.8	57.4	65.6
Hernando	117.9					
Low		120.7	123.8	122.6	117.2	107.3
Medium		138.6	159.0	179.3	200.1	221.4
High		160.0	202.0	248.9	301.3	359.2
Highlands	77.3					
Low		78.0	78.7	78.0	75.9	72.2
Medium		85.9	94.4	102.7	111.2	119.8
High		95.3	113.3	132.8	154.0	176.9
Hillsborough	892.9					
Low		903.4	905.0	898.1	883.7	861.2
Medium		955.6	1,016.5	1,076.1	1,136.4	1,196.6
High		1,018.7	1,151.8	1,292.4	1,441.7	1,599.4
Holmes	17.4					
Low		16.3	15.3	14.3	13.1	11.9
Medium		18.0	18.6	19.1	19.6	20.2
High		19.9	22.0	24.3	26.6	29.1
Indian River	100.3					
Low		101.0	101.8	100.6	97.7	92.9
Medium		111.3	122.0	132.6	143.3	154.2
High		123.4	146.4	171.3	198.4	227.5
Jackson	46.6					
Low		45.7	44.4	42.9	41.2	39.3
Medium		48.5	50.2	51.8	53.5	55.1
High		51.6	56.5	61.7	67.2	72.9
Jefferson	13.5					
Low		13.0	12.5	11.9	11.1	10.3
Medium		14.3	15.1	15.8	16.5	17.3
High		15.8	17.9	20.2	22.6	25.1
Lafayette	6.5					
Low		6.5	6.2	5.7	5.2	4.6
Medium		7.5	8.0	8.5	9.1	9.6
High		8.6	10.1	11.7	13.4	15.2
Lake	176.9					
Low		181.5	185.6	185.8	182.4	175.2
Medium		199.7	222.0	244.1	266.6	289.3
High		221.8	267.1	316.4	370.4	428.9

See footnote at end of table.

Continued . . .

Table 1.84. PROJECTIONS: ESTIMATES, APRIL 1, 1995, AND PROJECTIONS SPECIFIED YEARS APRIL 1, 2000 THROUGH 2020, IN THE STATE AND COUNTIES OF FLORIDA (Continued)

County	Estimates 1995	Projections 2000	2005	2010	2015	2020
Lee	376.7					
Low		383.8	390.3	389.0	380.3	363.9
Medium		422.5	467.3	511.4	556.5	602.0
High		469.1	561.7	662.3	772.1	891.0
Leon	217.5					
Low		214.6	212.4	206.8	196.7	183.8
Medium		237.0	255.7	274.2	290.8	307.5
High		262.3	305.6	352.1	399.5	449.9
Levy	29.8					
Low		30.1	30.2	29.9	29.0	27.5
Medium		33.1	36.3	39.4	42.5	45.7
High		36.7	43.5	50.9	58.8	67.4
Liberty	6.9					
Low		6.2	5.7	5.0	4.2	3.3
Medium		7.5	8.0	8.5	9.0	9.5
High		8.9	10.5	12.3	14.2	16.3
Madison	18.3					
Low		17.2	16.4	15.5	14.4	13.1
Medium		19.1	19.9	20.6	21.4	22.2
High		21.1	23.6	26.3	29.1	32.1
Manatee	233.2					
Low		232.3	231.9	227.5	219.4	207.4
Medium		256.1	278.5	300.4	322.7	345.1
High		283.9	333.7	387.4	445.4	507.8
Marion	224.6					
Low		230.8	236.4	237.0	232.9	223.8
Medium		253.9	282.6	311.1	340.2	369.5
High		282.0	340.1	403.5	472.8	548.0
Martin	112.0					
Low		113.6	114.9	114.0	111.0	105.8
Medium		125.2	137.7	150.0	162.6	175.4
High		138.9	165.4	194.0	225.3	259.1
Monroe	83.4					
Low		84.1	83.9	83.1	81.5	79.3
Medium		88.9	94.3	99.6	104.9	110.2
High		94.8	106.8	119.5	133.0	147.2
Nassau	49.1					
Low		48.8	48.7	47.7	45.9	43.3
Medium		53.9	58.5	63.0	67.5	72.1
High		59.7	70.0	81.2	93.2	106.1
Okaloosa	162.7					
Low		168.7	172.8	174.6	174.5	172.5
Medium		178.2	193.4	208.2	223.1	238.1
High		190.3	219.9	251.3	284.8	320.4
Okeechobee	32.9					
Low		34.0	34.1	33.6	32.5	30.8
Medium		37.5	40.9	44.3	47.7	51.1
High		41.6	49.1	57.2	65.9	75.4

See footnote at end of table. Continued . . .

Table 1.84. PROJECTIONS: ESTIMATES, APRIL 1, 1995, AND PROJECTIONS SPECIFIED YEARS APRIL 1, 2000 THROUGH 2020, IN THE STATE AND COUNTIES OF FLORIDA (Continued)

County	Estimates 1995	Projections 2000	2005	2010	2015	2020
Orange	759.0					
Low		768.5	780.2	776.6	758.5	725.1
Medium		846.2	934.3	1,021.4	1,110.4	1,200.0
High		939.3	1,122.8	1,322.3	1,539.9	1,775.3
Osceola	136.6					
Low		143.0	149.1	149.5	144.2	133.1
Medium		163.9	190.9	217.8	245.5	273.5
High		189.5	243.2	303.5	370.9	445.5
Palm Beach	962.8					
Low		969.2	976.0	964.6	936.3	890.3
Medium		1,067.9	1,170.3	1,271.1	1,373.8	1,477.2
High		1,184.6	1,404.5	1,642.4	1,900.9	2,179.7
Pasco	305.6					
Low		303.6	302.4	296.0	284.9	268.9
Medium		334.8	363.2	391.0	419.3	447.7
High		371.0	435.1	504.0	578.5	658.3
Pinellas	876.2					
Low		855.4	830.4	801.5	768.9	732.6
Medium		907.3	937.7	967.8	998.4	1,029.3
High		964.6	1,056.9	1,153.3	1,254.6	1,360.5
Polk	443.2					
Low		451.9	455.8	455.0	450.0	440.6
Medium		477.8	511.4	544.3	577.5	610.8
High		509.6	580.1	654.7	734.2	818.2
Putnam	69.5					
Low		70.4	70.5	70.0	68.8	67.1
Medium		74.5	79.2	83.8	88.5	93.2
High		79.4	89.7	100.7	112.3	124.6
St. Johns	98.2					
Low		101.7	104.9	105.7	104.4	100.7
Medium		111.8	125.3	138.6	152.2	165.9
High		124.3	150.9	180.0	211.9	246.5
St. Lucie	171.2					
Low		177.2	182.6	183.9	181.5	175.2
Medium		194.8	218.1	241.1	264.7	288.7
High		216.6	262.7	313.2	368.6	428.9
Santa Rosa	96.1					
Low		100.4	103.1	103.5	101.9	98.1
Medium		110.4	123.2	135.8	148.8	161.8
High		122.7	148.3	176.3	206.9	240.1
Sarasota	301.5					
Low		309.3	313.3	313.8	311.3	305.7
Medium		326.8	351.3	375.1	399.1	423.2
High		348.7	398.7	451.6	508.0	567.7
Seminole	324.1					
Low		332.3	339.8	340.1	333.9	320.8
Medium		365.7	406.4	446.7	487.9	529.7
High		406.1	488.9	579.1	678.0	785.3

See footnote at end of table.

Continued . . .

Table 1.84. PROJECTIONS: ESTIMATES, APRIL 1, 1995, AND PROJECTIONS SPECIFIED YEARS APRIL 1, 2000 THROUGH 2020, IN THE STATE AND COUNTIES OF FLORIDA (Continued)

County	Estimates 1995	Projections 2000	2005	2010	2015	2020
Sumter	36.5					
Low		39.6	39.6	38.9	37.6	35.6
Medium		43.7	47.6	51.4	55.2	59.1
High		48.4	57.0	66.3	76.3	87.0
Suwannee	30.5					
Low		31.6	32.3	32.7	32.6	32.2
Medium		33.4	36.2	39.0	41.7	44.5
High		35.6	41.2	47.0	53.3	59.9
Taylor	18.3					
Low		17.4	16.2	14.9	13.6	12.2
Medium		19.3	19.6	20.0	20.4	20.7
High		21.2	23.3	25.3	27.5	29.8
Union	12.6					
Low		12.2	11.7	11.2	10.5	9.7
Medium		13.4	14.2	14.9	15.6	16.3
High		14.9	16.9	19.1	21.3	23.8
Volusia	403.0					
Low		401.2	400.4	392.7	378.6	357.9
Medium		442.4	480.8	518.5	556.9	595.5
High		490.4	576.2	668.6	768.7	876.3
Wakulla	17.0					
Low		17.6	17.4	16.6	15.4	13.8
Medium		20.3	22.5	24.5	26.6	28.8
High		23.4	28.4	33.8	39.7	46.1
Walton	33.4					
Low		33.8	34.0	33.6	32.5	30.8
Medium		37.3	40.8	44.2	47.7	51.2
High		41.3	49.0	57.1	66.0	75.5
Washington	19.0					
Low		19.0	18.5	17.7	16.7	15.5
Medium		21.0	22.3	23.5	24.8	26.1
High		23.2	26.6	30.2	34.0	38.0

Note: The medium projection is the one we believe is most likely to provide an accurate forecast of future population. The high and low projections indicate the range in which future populations are likely to fall. They do not represent absolute limits to growth; for any county, the future population may be above the high projection or below the low projection. If future distributions of errors are similar to past distributions, however, future populations will fall between high and low projections in approximately two-thirds of Florida's counties. Adjustments have been made to account for the effects of Hurricane Andrew on Dade county. For a detailed description of projection methodology, see the source.

Source: University of Florida, Bureau of Economic and Business Research, Population Program, *Florida Population Studies,* February 1996, Volume 29, No. 2. Bulletin No. 114.

Table 1.87. VETERANS: ESTIMATED NUMBER OF VETERANS IN CIVIL LIFE BY PERIOD OF SERVICE IN FLORIDA AND THE UNITED STATES, JULY 1, 1994

(rounded to thousands)

Area	Total veterans	War veterans						Peacetime veterans		
		Total	World War I	World War II	Korea 1/	Vietnam 1/	Persian Gulf 1/	Between Korea and Vietnam	Post-Vietnam	Other
Florida	1,715	1,351	2	638	236	420	55	152	200	12
United States	26,365	20,327	18	7,770	3,798	7,713	1,027	2,842	3,031	165

1/ No prior wartime service.
Source: U.S., Department of Veterans Affairs, *Annual Report of the Secretary of Veterans Affairs, Fiscal Year, 1994*.

Table 1.89. IMMIGRANTS: NEW ARRIVALS BY PORT OF ENTRY IN FLORIDA AND IN THE UNITED STATES, FISCAL YEARS 1994 AND 1995

Port of entry	1994	1995	Port of entry	1994	1995
Florida	44,364	36,668	Florida (Continued)		
			Port Everglades	133	404
Jacksonville	8	6	Tampa	181	129
Key West	1	0	West Palm Beach	25	34
Miami	42,642	35,090			
Orlando	1,373	1,005	United States	490,429	380,291
Port Canaveral	1	0			

Note: Excludes legal immigrants admitted under "residency since 1982" and special agricultural workers. Data are for fiscal years ending September 30.

Table 1.90. IMMIGRANTS: NUMBER ADMITTED BY SPECIFIED COUNTRY OF BIRTH AND RESIDENCE IN FLORIDA AND THE UNITED STATES, FISCAL YEAR 1995

Country of birth	Florida	United States	Country of birth	Florida	United States
Total 1/	62,023	720,461	Jamaica	4,261	16,398
Canada	1,620	12,932	Mexico	1,922	89,932
Colombia	2,819	10,838	Nicaragua	2,042	4,408
Cuba	15,112	17,937	Peru	1,607	8,066
Dominican Republic	2,090	38,512	Philippines	1,806	50,984
Haiti	5,869	14,021	United Kingdom	1,508	12,326
Honduras	1,236	5,496	Venezuela	1,115	2,627
India	1,141	34,748	Vietnam	1,194	41,752

1/ Only admissions of 1,000 or more immigrants to Florida are shown separately by country of birth, therefore totals include other countries not shown separately.
Note: Data are for fiscal year ending September 30 and includes legalized aliens.
Source for Tables 1.89 and 1.90: U.S., Immigration and Naturalization Service, Statistics Division, unpublished data.

Table 1.91. IMMIGRANTS: NUMBER ADMITTED BY COUNTRY OF BIRTH AND INTENDED RESIDENCE IN THE METROPOLITAN AREAS OF FLORIDA, FISCAL YEAR 1995

County of birth	Daytona Beach	Ft. Lauderdale	Ft. Myers-Cape Coral	Ft. Pierce-Port St. Lucie	Gainesville	Jacksonville	Lakeland-Winter Haven	Melbourne-Titusville-Palm Bay	Miami	Naples
Total 1/	626	8,373	552	507	303	1,528	497	592	30,935	605
Canada	63	324	41	24	20	34	25	32	148	51
Colombia	8	501	15	5	5	18	4	9	1,726	14
Cuba	12	340	7	6	6	31	20	6	13,670	64
Dominican Republic	10	280	18	5	7	14	12	6	1,352	6
Haiti	5	1,274	40	97	6	129	77	3	2,329	142
Honduras	4	69	9	5	3	10	6	8	924	3
India	56	156	7	19	28	56	29	32	143	5
Jamaica	28	1,538	25	31	4	36	53	40	1,352	10
Mexico	84	64	67	129	1	23	76	7	214	96
Nicaragua	3	55	0	1	3	7	0	3	1,855	1
Peru	5	263	11	7	5	5	1	7	1,043	13
Philippines	36	123	20	9	12	255	13	51	480	12
United Kingdom	34	190	35	24	10	60	17	36	152	26
Vietnam	13	78	8	11	11	76	17	18	16	3

County of birth	Ocala	Orlando	Panama City	Pensacola	Punta Gorda	Sarasota-Bradenton	Tallahassee	Tampa-St. Petersburg-Clearwater	West Palm Beach-Boca Raton
Total 1/	195	4,806	162	278	193	730	269	4,379	4,942
Canada	21	137	5	11	33	83	3	290	183
Colombia	8	183	1	1	6	12	1	94	186
Cuba	3	96	2	0	2	17	0	442	239
Dominican Republic	1	175	0	0	0	5	2	90	88
Haiti	1	442	0	0	17	22	3	131	1,111
Honduras	1	37	0	2	2	16	0	50	74
India	24	175	16	10	1	11	27	188	134
Jamaica	7	337	0	2	17	8	9	152	524
Mexico	11	248	3	7	4	81	7	264	183
Nicaragua	1	30	1	2	0	3	2	18	47
Peru	1	88	1	0	1	4	0	77	64
Philippines	8	219	20	49	23	25	12	205	123
United Kingdom	6	300	16	25	15	58	17	195	206
Vietnam	5	311	32	57	1	13	11	421	67

1/ Only admissions of 1,000 or more immigrants to Florida are shown separately by country of birth, therefore totals include other countries not shown separately.

Note: Data are for fiscal year ending September 30 and includes legalized aliens.

Source: U.S., Immigration and Naturalization Service, Statistics Division, unpublished data.

HOUSING

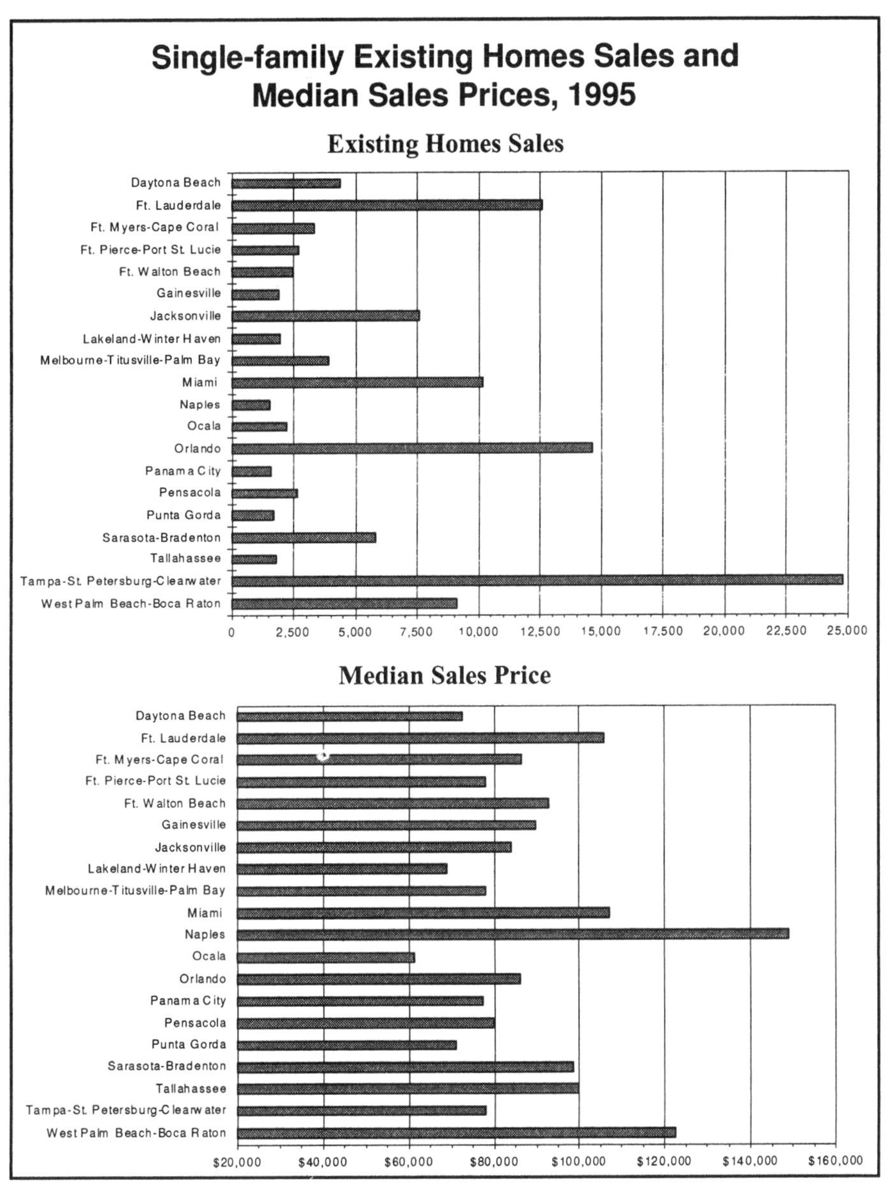

Single-family Existing Homes Sales and Median Sales Prices, 1995
Existing Homes Sales
Daytona Beach
Ft. Lauderdale
Ft. Myers-Cape Coral
Ft. Pierce-Port St. Lucie
Ft. Walton Beach
Gainesville
Jacksonville
Lakeland-Winter Haven
Melbourne-Titusville-Palm Bay
Miami
Naples
Ocala
Orlando
Panama City
Pensacola
Punta Gorda
Sarasota-Bradenton
Tallahassee
Tampa-St. Petersburg-Clearwater
West Palm Beach-Boca Raton
0
2,500
5,000
7,500
10,000
12,500
15,000
17,500
20,000
22,500
25,000
Median Sales Price
Daytona Beach
Ft. Lauderdale
Ft. Myers-Cape Coral
Ft. Pierce-Port St. Lucie
Ft. Walton Beach
Gainesville
Jacksonville
Lakeland-Winter Haven
Melbourne-Titusville-Palm Bay
Miami
Naples
Ocala
Orlando
Panama City
Pensacola
Punta Gorda
Sarasota-Bradenton
Tallahassee
Tampa-St. Petersburg-Clearwater
West Palm Beach-Boca Raton
$20,000
$40,000
$60,000
$80,000
$100,000
$120,000
$140,000
$160,000

Source: Table 2.21

SECTION 2.00
HOUSING

TABLES LISTED BY MAJOR HEADINGS

Table 2.01. STATES: ESTIMATES OF HOUSING UNITS AND HOUSEHOLDS IN FLORIDA, OTHER STATES, AND THE UNITED STATES, JULY 1, 1994

(in thousands)

State	Total housing units	Households Total	Households Persons in--	State	Total housing units	Households Total	Households Persons in--
Florida	6,594	5,456	13,656	Missouri	2,285	2,008	5,133
				Montana	371	325	832
Alabama	1,742	1,583	4,126	Nebraska	685	614	1,575
Alaska	248	208	586	Nevada	618	560	1,433
Arizona	1,783	1,503	3,995	New Hampshire	519	424	1,106
Arkansas	1,031	927	2,395	New Jersey	3,139	2,845	7,740
California	11,679	10,850	30,676	New Mexico	668	587	1,624
Colorado	1,552	1,417	3,576	New York	7,269	6,669	17,620
Connecticut	1,352	1,222	3,177	North Carolina	3,053	2,679	6,840
Delaware	312	264	685	North Dakota	285	241	614
District of				Ohio	4,518	4,190	10,838
Columbia	276	237	529	Oklahoma	1,423	1,236	3,163
Georgia	2,850	2,581	6,880	Oregon	1,288	1,195	3,021
Hawaii	421	381	1,142	Pennsylvania	5,050	4,551	11,704
Idaho	451	405	1,111	Rhode Island	423	374	960
Illinois	4,629	4,308	11,470	South Carolina	1,534	1,337	3,552
Indiana	2,363	2,161	5,593	South Dakota	308	265	696
Iowa	1,179	1,082	2,731	Tennessee	2,133	1,966	5,046
Kansas	1,082	966	2,473	Texas	7,318	6,539	17,984
Kentucky	1,571	1,440	3,724	Utah	642	599	1,878
Louisiana	1,732	1,543	4,198	Vermont	278	220	559
Maine	608	474	1,204	Virginia	2,668	2,439	6,350
Maryland	2,009	1,831	4,891	Washington	2,217	2,042	5,222
Massachusetts	2,526	2,265	5,824	West Virginia	793	705	1,785
Michigan	4,005	3,502	9,285	Wisconsin	2,174	1,890	4,948
Minnesota	1,945	1,711	4,451	Wyoming	207	178	465
Mississippi	1,037	949	2,598	United States	106,842	95,946	253,664

Note: Detail may not add to totals because of rounding. See Glossary for definition of household.

Source: U.S., Department of Commerce, Bureau of the Census the Internet at <http://www.census/gov/>.

Table 2.02. STATES: HOMEOWNERSHIP RATES IN THE STATE AND SPECIFIED METROPOLITAN STATISTICAL AREAS (MSAS) OF FLORIDA AND IN OTHER STATES AND THE UNITED STATES, 1993, 1994, AND 1995

State and MSA	1993	1994	1995	State and MSA	1993	1994	1995
Florida	65.5	65.7	66.6	Minnesota	65.8	68.9	73.3
Ft. Lauderdale MSA	69.4	69.0	68.8	Mississippi	69.7	69.2	71.1
Jacksonville MSA	61.7	63.9	66.6	Missouri	66.4	68.4	69.4
Miami MSA	51.6	51.4	50.9	Montana	69.7	68.8	68.7
Orlando MSA	60.2	59.6	61.7	Nebraska	67.7	68.0	67.1
Tampa-St. Petersburg-				Nevada	55.8	55.8	58.6
Clearwater MSA	66.9	66.0	68.1	New Hampshire	65.4	65.1	66.0
Alabama	70.2	68.5	70.1	New Jersey	64.5	64.1	64.9
Alaska	55.4	58.8	60.9	New Mexico	69.1	66.8	67.0
Arizona	69.1	67.7	62.9	New York	52.8	52.5	52.7
Arkansas	70.5	68.1	67.2	North Carolina	68.8	68.7	70.1
California	56.0	55.5	55.4	North Dakota	62.7	63.3	67.3
Colorado	61.8	62.9	64.6	Ohio	68.5	67.4	67.9
Connecticut	64.5	63.8	68.2	Oklahoma	70.3	68.5	69.8
Delaware	74.1	70.5	71.7	Oregon	63.8	63.9	63.2
District of Columbia	35.7	37.8	39.2	Pennsylvania	72.0	71.8	71.5
Georgia	66.5	63.4	66.6	Rhode Island	57.6	56.5	57.9
Hawaii	52.8	52.3	50.2	South Carolina	71.1	72.0	71.3
Idaho	72.1	70.7	72.0	South Dakota	65.6	66.4	67.5
Illinois	61.8	64.2	66.4	Tennessee	64.1	65.2	67.0
Indiana	68.7	68.4	71.0	Texas	58.7	59.7	61.4
Iowa	68.2	70.1	71.4	Utah	68.9	69.3	71.5
Kansas	68.9	69.0	67.5	Vermont	68.5	69.4	70.4
Kentucky	68.8	70.6	71.2	Virginia	68.5	69.3	68.1
Louisiana	65.4	65.8	65.3	Washington	63.1	62.4	61.6
Maine	71.9	72.6	76.7	West Virginia	73.3	73.7	73.1
Maryland	65.5	64.1	65.8	Wisconsin	65.7	64.2	67.5
Massachusetts	60.7	60.6	60.2	Wyoming	67.1	65.8	69.0
Michigan	72.3	72.0	72.2	United States	64.0	64.0	64.7

Note: Data are based on the American Housing Survey (AHS) conducted by the Bureau of the Census. Homeownership rates are computed by dividing the number of households that are owners by the total number of households.

Source: U.S., Department of Commerce, Bureau of the Census, *Housing Vacancy Survey: Annual Statistics, 1995.* Data from the Internet at <http://www.census.gov/>.

Table 2.05. HOUSEHOLDS AND AVERAGE HOUSEHOLD SIZE: ESTIMATES IN THE STATE AND COUNTIES OF FLORIDA, APRIL 1, 1995

County	Households Estimates	Households Percentage 1/	Average household size Estimates	Average household size Percentage 1/	County	Households Estimates	Households Percentage 1/	Average household size Estimates	Average household size Percentage 1/
Florida	5,613,616	9.3	2.46	0.0	Lafayette	1,971	14.5	2.74	0.0
					Lake	74,150	16.6	2.34	-0.4
Alachua	78,132	9.6	2.39	-0.4	Lee	157,694	12.5	2.35	0.0
Baker	6,157	10.9	2.98	-0.7	Leon	84,697	13.2	2.42	-0.4
Bay	53,992	10.3	2.53	-0.4	Levy	11,636	15.4	2.51	-0.4
Bradford	7,647	6.3	2.68	0.0	Liberty	2,038	19.5	2.69	0.0
Brevard	179,963	11.5	2.43	0.0	Madison	6,040	9.4	2.75	0.0
Broward	575,626	8.9	2.34	-0.4	Manatee	100,238	10.1	2.29	0.0
Calhoun	4,032	6.3	2.63	-0.4	Marion	90,313	15.5	2.44	0.0
Charlotte	55,946	15.5	2.23	0.0	Martin	47,863	11.3	2.28	0.0
Citrus	45,775	12.8	2.27	0.0	Monroe	35,899	6.9	2.24	0.0
Clay	41,930	14.4	2.85	-0.3	Nassau	18,146	12.1	2.68	0.0
Collier	75,898	23.0	2.40	-0.4	Okaloosa	60,226	13.0	2.60	0.0
Columbia	18,001	15.3	2.66	-0.4	Okeechobee	11,394	11.6	2.74	-0.4
Dade	717,062	3.6	2.76	0.4	Orange	288,731	13.3	2.56	0.0
De Soto	9,198	11.9	2.62	0.0	Osceola	49,675	26.9	2.68	0.0
Dixie	4,425	13.0	2.56	0.0	Palm Beach	405,665	11.0	2.33	0.4
Duval	274,838	6.8	2.54	0.0	Pasco	132,178	8.6	2.26	0.0
Escambia	105,365	6.9	2.57	0.0	Pinellas	391,107	2.8	2.18	0.0
Flagler	15,319	28.9	2.40	0.0	Polk	170,775	9.5	2.53	0.0
Franklin	4,043	11.4	2.41	-0.4	Putnam	26,849	7.1	2.54	-0.4
Gadsden	14,601	8.9	2.89	-0.3	St. Johns	39,266	17.5	2.43	-0.4
Gilchrist	4,001	21.8	2.65	0.0	St. Lucie	66,289	13.9	2.54	0.0
Glades	3,257	12.9	2.56	-0.4	Santa Rosa	35,254	17.9	2.68	0.0
Gulf	4,631	7.1	2.56	0.0	Sarasota	135,944	8.3	2.18	0.0
Hamilton	3,900	11.8	2.81	0.0	Seminole	121,562	12.9	2.64	0.0
Hardee	7,056	10.4	2.94	-0.3	Sumter	14,042	15.9	2.46	0.0
Hendry	9,474	12.8	2.98	-0.3	Suwannee	11,461	14.2	2.61	0.0
Hernando	49,128	16.1	2.37	0.0	Taylor	6,662	4.1	2.66	-0.4
Highlands	33,388	13.0	2.28	0.0	Union	2,982	12.2	2.91	0.0
Hillsborough	347,880	7.1	2.51	0.0	Volusia	166,698	8.7	2.33	0.0
Holmes	6,221	7.3	2.56	0.0	Wakulla	6,250	20.0	2.69	-0.4
Indian River	42,371	11.3	2.33	0.0	Walton	13,147	16.4	2.44	0.0
Jackson	15,973	10.4	2.55	-0.4	Washington	7,090	10.0	2.55	0.0
Jefferson	4,454	11.9	2.78	-0.4					

1/ Percentage change 1990 to 1995.

Note: The occurrence of Hurricane Andrew in August 1992 created significant problems in south Florida for the usual estimation methodology. The hurricane destroyed thousands of housing units and forced many residents to move to other locations. In order to obtain information on these population movements, a series of sample surveys in Dade and Broward counties were conducted. The household estimates on this table incorporate the results of those surveys.

Source: University of Florida, Bureau of Economic and Business Research, Population Program, *Florida Population Studies,* January 1996, Volume 29, No. 1. Bulletin No. 113.

Table 2.10. HOUSE PURCHASE PRICE: COST OF A HOUSE IN THE STATE AND COUNTIES OF FLORIDA, 1994 AND 1995

(in dollars)

County	1994	1995 A/	County	1994	1995 A/
Alachua	87,622	83,789	Lake	95,122	90,181
Baker	77,977	75,133	Lee	107,660	96,397
Bay	81,345	80,301	Leon	87,144	81,981
Bradford	80,304	78,232	Levy	80,841	74,902
Brevard	100,769	84,370	Liberty	75,376	68,587
Broward	107,170	109,359	Madison	75,336	68,886
Calhoun	70,616	68,197	Manatee	103,662	90,527
Charlotte	85,480	91,147	Marion	79,583	75,760
Citrus	83,786	79,140	Martin	104,277	95,671
Clay	89,052	86,010	Monroe	144,710	141,640
Collier	112,135	108,953	Nassau	88,419	85,552
Columbia	77,420	75,198	Okaloosa	86,881	84,075
Dade	120,199	114,667	Okeechobee	90,331	85,079
De Soto	80,876	74,401	Orange	96,065	93,559
Dixie	78,546	72,136	Osceola	92,383	87,032
Duval	90,599	87,014	Palm Beach	107,507	101,611
Escambia	80,395	77,487	Pasco	86,119	76,809
Flagler	88,948	87,345	Pinellas	105,258	103,808
Franklin	91,756	81,769	Polk	92,936	89,362
Gadsden	76,801	72,157	Putnam	83,545	80,882
Gilchrist	84,707	76,405	St. Johns	95,809	94,315
Glades	93,039	87,624	St. Lucie	92,437	80,531
Gulf	79,261	76,338	Santa Rosa	79,933	77,517
Hamilton	75,164	68,699	Sarasota	107,053	101,531
Hardee	81,217	75,037	Seminole	92,108	91,695
Hendry	84,157	81,971	Sumter	86,609	81,029
Hernando	91,063	82,543	Suwannee	74,901	69,222
Highlands	84,516	78,359	Taylor	76,824	70,029
Hillsborough	102,742	101,298	Union	79,790	70,660
Holmes	73,013	70,667	Volusia	93,463	85,601
Indian River	98,793	90,712	Wakulla	79,259	77,535
Jackson	73,013	69,807	Walton	82,060	80,599
Jefferson	76,023	69,805	Washington	74,799	70,193
Lafayette	74,890	69,914			

A/ Prices reflect a decrease in the cost of construction as reported by the Florida Department of Revenue.

Note: Data represent the cost of a house as measured by the Florida Price Level Index (FPLI) and are based on a sample of records for those single-family residential properties eligible for homestead exemption and which are between 1,200 and 1,600 square feet. The goal of this method is to provide data on homes that would fit on an "average" lot, eliminate upper and lower income levels, and guard against weekend homes and part-time residents. Excludes mobile homes. See discussion of FPLI on Table 24.80.

Source: State of Florida, Department of Education, Office of Education Budget and Management, unpublished data.

Table 2.20. HOMES FOR THE AGING: HOMES, RESIDENTIAL UNITS, AND BEDS FOR HOMES WHICH ARE MEMBERS OF THE FLORIDA ASSOCIATION OF HOMES FOR THE AGING (FAHA) IN THE STATE, FAHA DISTRICTS, AND CITIES OF FLORIDA, 1995

District and city	Homes	Residential units	Nursing beds
Florida	246	39,469	8,768
District 1	44	6,642	1,519
Atlantic Beach	1	346	42
Crestview	1	70	0
Dowling Park	1	341	161
Gainesville	1	97	0
Jacksonville	21	2,878	752
Jacksonville Beach	1	199	0
Keystone Heights	1	94	0
Lake City	1	150	0
Marianna	2	124	60
Milton	1	0	120
Monticello	1	0	97
Ocala	1	161	0
Palatka	1	76	0
Panama City	1	216	0
Penney Farms	1	291	40
Pensacola	2	482	106
Ponte Vedra Beach	1	258	30
St. Augustine	1	0	51
Shalimar	1	379	0
Tallahassee	3	480	60
District 2	30	4,706	1,301
Apopka	1	32	0
Davenport	1	70	60
Eustis	1	45	0
Fern Park	1	176	0
Lake Alfred	1	0	31
Lakeland	1	389	60
Leesburg	1	0	120
Longwood	1	241	60
Maitland	1	102	39
Mount Dora	2	322	120
Orlando	12	2,001	600
Sanford	1	158	0
Tavares	1	146	30
Winter Haven	1	68	0
Winter Park	4	956	181
District 3	16	2,752	307
Largo	1	400	0
Pinellas Park	2	195	0
St. Petersburg	12	1,977	307
South Pasadena	1	180	0
District 4	19	2,971	250
Lakeland	3	468	0
Lake Wales	1	0	100
Plant City	1	75	0
Tampa	13	2,229	150
Winter Haven	1	199	0
District 5	28	5,364	1,181
Bradenton	3	544	93
Cape Coral	1	221	60
Ft. Myers	3	1,335	280
Grove City	1	100	0
Lehigh Acres	1	80	0
Naples	2	684	169
North Ft. Myers	1	80	0
Port Charlotte	3	147	104
Sarasota	8	1,217	295
Sebring	3	505	120
Venice	2	451	60
District 6	28	3,167	1,145
Florida City	1	30	0
Hialeah	4	285	0
Miami	17	2,238	664
Miami Beach	2	351	0
Miami Springs	1	50	269
North Miami	1	0	212
Opa-Locka	1	113	0
Sweetwater	1	100	0
District 7	43	8,524	1,729
Boca Raton	5	1,400	240
Coral Springs	1	432	0
Deerfield Beach	2	388	0
Delray Beach	3	926	244
Ft. Lauderdale	2	363	0
Hallandale	1	120	0
Hollywood	1	376	0
Jensen Beach	1	99	0
Juno Beach	1	291	60
Lake Worth	2	261	60
Palm City	1	168	42
Pembroke Pines	1	0	85
Plantation	1	328	60
Pompano Beach	3	844	184
Port St. Lucie	1	98	30
West Palm Beach	6	630	430
District 8	10	1,650	294
Cocoa	1	150	0
Melbourne	3	510	0
Merritt Island	1	158	96
Palm Bay	1	66	0
Vero Beach	2	620	84
Viera	1	0	114
West Melbourne	1	146	0
District 9	15	1,866	562
Belleair	1	0	126
Brooksville	2	88	180
Clearwater	6	659	116

See footnote at end of table.

Continued . . .

Table 2.20. HOMES FOR THE AGING: HOMES, RESIDENTIAL UNITS, AND BEDS FOR HOMES WHICH ARE MEMBERS OF THE FLORIDA ASSOCIATION OF HOMES FOR THE AGING (FAHA) IN THE STATE, FAHA DISTRICTS, AND CITIES OF FLORIDA, 1995 (Continued)

District and city	Homes	Residential units	Nursing beds	District and city	Homes	Residential units	Nursing beds
District 9 (Cont.)				District 9 (Cont.)			
Dade City	1	0	120	Tarpon Springs	1	90	0
Dunedin	1	386	100	Zephyrhills	1	48	0
Hudson	1	70	0	District 11	13	1,827	480
Lecanto	1	48	0	Daytona Beach	6	474	240
New Port Richey	1	135	0	DeLand	3	468	60
Palm Harbor	2	639	140	Holly Hill	2	343	60
Port Richey	1	80	0	Orange City	1	470	120
Spring Hill	1	217	0	Port Orange	1	72	0

Note: Includes personal care units, cluster homes, adult congregate living facility units and/or assisted living units. Excludes homes in construction.

Source: Florida Association of Homes for the Aging, *1995 Directory of Members*.

Table 2.21. HOME SALES: SALES AND MEDIAN SALES PRICE OF EXISTING SINGLE-FAMILY HOMES IN SPECIFIED METROPOLITAN STATISTICAL AREAS (MSAS) OF FLORIDA, 1994 AND 1995

MSA	Number of homes sold 1994	Number of homes sold 1995	Number of homes sold Percentage change	Median sales price 1994 (dollars)	Median sales price 1995 (dollars)	Median sales price Percentage change
Florida 1/	120,817	121,533	0.6	86,200	87,900	2.0
Daytona Beach 1/	4,413	4,381	-0.7	71,400	72,500	1.5
Ft. Lauderdale	13,291	12,597	-5.2	103,300	105,900	2.5
Ft. Myers-Cape Coral 1/	3,457	3,335	-3.5	86,500	86,600	0.1
Ft. Pierce-Port St. Lucie	2,561	2,685	4.8	80,200	78,100	-2.6
Ft. Walton Beach	2,435	2,493	2.4	86,800	92,800	6.9
Gainesville	1,909	1,890	-1.0	84,600	89,900	6.3
Jacksonville 1/	7,317	7,591	3.7	83,500	84,000	0.6
Lakeland-Winter Haven 1/	1,909	1,960	2.7	69,100	69,000	-0.1
Melbourne-Titusville-Palm Bay	4,167	3,890	-6.6	75,800	78,000	2.9
Miami 1/	11,240	10,172	-9.5	102,600	107,100	4.4
Naples	1,609	1,515	-5.8	144,700	149,100	3.0
Ocala	2,177	2,206	1.3	59,200	61,200	3.4
Orlando	13,030	14,649	12.4	87,700	86,300	-1.6
Panama City	1,564	1,603	2.5	68,900	77,300	12.2
Pensacola 1/	2,829	2,638	-6.8	76,400	79,800	4.5
Punta Gorda	1,751	1,701	-2.9	69,900	71,000	1.6
Sarasota-Bradenton 1/	5,916	5,820	-1.6	94,200	98,700	4.8
Tallahassee	2,016	1,806	-10.4	97,800	99,800	2.0
Tampa-St. Petersburg-Clearwater	23,620	24,811	5.0	75,300	78,100	3.7
West Palm Beach-Boca Raton	8,989	9,114	1.4	117,400	122,700	4.5

1/ Due to periodic unavailability of data, figures are adjusted for comparison purposes.

Source: Florida Association of Realtors and University of Florida, Real Estate Research Center, unpublished data.

Table 2.30. PUBLIC LODGING: LICENSED LODGINGS, APARTMENTS, ROOMING HOUSES, RENTAL CONDOMINIUMS, AND TRANSIENT APARTMENTS IN THE STATE AND COUNTIES OF FLORIDA, FISCAL YEAR 1995-96

County	Total licensed lodgings 1/		Apartment buildings		Rooming houses		Rental condominiums		Transient apartment buildings 2/	
	Number	Units	Number	Units	Number	Units	Number	Units	Number	Units
Florida	30,401	1,231,386	17,451	806,886	637	8,198	5,981	64,449	1,677	17,494
Alachua	405	23,801	343	20,028	7	73	0	0	2	116
Baker	5	166	2	59	0	0	0	0	0	0
Bay	610	18,547	111	4,492	2	14	286	4,820	4	126
Bradford	28	770	12	367	1	2	0	0	1	4
Brevard	555	29,075	343	18,659	8	81	40	1,473	53	676
Broward	3,763	132,247	2,776	98,759	34	313	43	1,461	377	4,241
Calhoun	4	111	2	88	0	0	0	0	0	0
Charlotte	137	3,126	24	798	1	2	63	835	22	228
Citrus	75	1,986	33	814	4	37	2	127	11	89
Clay	55	5,297	40	4,376	4	38	1	30	2	14
Collier	260	15,655	108	6,568	2	35	66	3,633	8	79
Columbia	85	3,122	46	1,076	2	14	0	0	4	72
Dade	6,857	224,791	6,172	173,840	131	1,557	44	2,041	9	90
De Soto	22	424	13	262	3	25	0	0	0	0
Dixie	13	188	1	32	1	9	0	0	1	7
Duval	788	72,311	643	60,966	28	319	5	40	2	27
Escambia	450	16,177	101	9,716	4	9	270	1,076	4	38
Flagler	43	1,041	9	139	4	37	10	173	3	5
Franklin	280	952	5	131	1	9	255	392	1	8
Gadsden	29	825	14	633	2	13	5	25	0	0
Gilchrist	5	95	1	60	2	6	0	0	1	1
Glades	16	238	2	33	0	0	1	8	2	8

See footnotes at end of table.

Continued . . .

Table 2.30. PUBLIC LODGING: LICENSED LODGINGS, APARTMENTS, ROOMING HOUSES, RENTAL CONDOMINIUMS, AND TRANSIENT APARTMENTS IN THE STATE AND COUNTIES OF FLORIDA, FISCAL YEAR 1995-96 (Continued)

County	Total licensed lodgings 1/		Apartment buildings		Rooming houses		Rental condominiums		Transient apartment buildings 2/	
	Number	Units	Number	Units	Number	Units	Number	Units	Number	Units
Gulf	146	594	3	113	1	12	130	357	2	15
Hamilton	17	539	7	148	0	0	0	0	1	20
Hardee	19	346	10	227	1	10	0	0	5	64
Hendry	34	690	19	319	0	0	1	14	0	0
Hernando	39	1,528	21	898	2	24	1	1	1	10
Highlands	135	3,436	67	1,495	6	44	4	212	32	504
Hillsborough	969	92,791	776	77,413	26	337	1	237	24	311
Holmes	10	286	5	93	0	0	0	0	0	0
Indian River	140	4,000	71	1,842	3	32	25	384	5	55
Jackson	34	1,224	22	667	0	0	1	10	0	0
Jefferson	20	425	10	240	5	16	0	0	1	22
Lafayette	4	70	1	36	2	26	0	0	0	0
Lake	228	6,528	112	4,111	16	137	34	143	16	146
Lee	582	25,604	237	12,160	3	18	130	5,525	51	349
Leon	382	24,710	317	18,812	7	991	1	40	2	13
Levy	52	807	11	278	4	38	8	132	6	30
Liberty	1	13	0	0	0	0	0	0	0	0
Madison	14	465	10	322	1	5	0	0	0	0
Manatee	507	14,977	143	9,952	10	67	155	1,286	128	602
Marion	198	7,872	107	4,373	6	46	1	14	11	46
Martin	113	3,529	69	1,835	4	56	9	181	5	211
Monroe	602	13,286	89	1,775	35	364	97	2,080	186	957
Nassau	78	2,882	17	682	9	60	24	1,038	2	6
Okaloosa	318	11,935	104	3,626	1	24	153	3,826	4	177

See footnotes at end of table.

Continued . . .

Table 2.30. PUBLIC LODGING: LICENSED LODGINGS, APARTMENTS, ROOMING HOUSES, RENTAL CONDOMINIUMS, AND TRANSIENT APARTMENTS IN THE STATE AND COUNTIES OF FLORIDA, FISCAL YEAR 1995-96 (Continued)

County	Total licensed lodgings 1/		Apartment buildings		Rooming houses		Rental condominiums		Transient apartment buildings 2/	
	Number	Units	Number	Units	Number	Units	Number	Units	Number	Units
Okeechobee	23	572	6	136	1	14	0	0	5	60
Orange	1,270	138,578	654	73,922	38	465	333	5,571	42	799
Osceola	2,659	35,518	85	8,245	11	133	2,415	6,038	20	681
Palm Beach	1,385	63,276	993	44,887	56	1,017	20	825	100	1,442
Pasco	190	9,010	104	6,297	3	41	35	771	10	84
Pinellas	2,147	85,560	1,321	59,701	33	485	114	4,960	269	2,253
Polk	1,053	22,773	327	13,169	29	513	513	1,585	64	1,113
Putnam	52	1,380	18	760	8	50	1	23	3	25
St. Johns	210	9,082	52	2,965	29	185	44	1,768	8	47
St. Lucie	143	4,652	62	1,763	2	26	14	494	26	218
Santa Rosa	140	2,297	36	1,233	0	0	93	346	0	0
Sarasota	579	16,593	222	8,140	10	89	166	3,456	94	893
Seminole	173	27,935	137	25,076	4	29	0	0	2	10
Sumter	28	958	14	377	3	9	0	0	3	20
Suwannee	25	588	9	244	1	2	0	0	5	20
Taylor	38	791	7	282	2	2	0	0	4	29
Union	3	84	2	80	1	4	0	0	0	0
Volusia	850	37,484	360	15,909	17	211	108	3,840	31	421
Wakulla	8	165	0	0	0	0	2	25	0	0
Walton	289	4,404	10	345	6	23	256	3,132	2	12
Washington	9	204	3	42	0	0	1	1	0	0

1/ Includes hotels and motels shown separately in Table 19.60.
2/ Apartments which rent for six months or less.

Source: State of Florida, Department of Business and Professional Regulation, Division of Hotels and Restaurants, *Master File Statistics: Public Lodging and Food Service Establishments,* Fiscal Year 1995-96.

Table 2.36. MOBILE HOME AND RECREATIONAL VEHICLE TAGS: NUMBER SOLD IN THE STATE AND COUNTIES OF FLORIDA, FISCAL YEAR 1994-95

County	Mobile homes 1/	Real property 2/	Recreational vehicles	County	Mobile homes 1/	Real property 2/	Recreational vehicles
Florida	508,610	34,935	197,757	Lake	18,276	1,108	6,539
				Lee	32,049	712	7,108
Alachua	3,153	492	2,132	Leon	7,992	615	2,111
Baker	399	295	459	Levy	940	1,445	826
Bay	3,644	688	2,854	Liberty	185	64	91
Bradford	735	148	587	Madison	1,073	246	245
Brevard	12,621	599	8,510	Manatee	24,134	872	5,321
Broward	20,536	154	7,905	Marion	13,128	1,511	6,068
Calhoun	148	153	113	Martin	5,152	299	2,320
Charlotte	8,853	199	2,929	Monroe	1,637	173	2,537
Citrus	4,024	798	3,281	Nassau	1,551	594	978
Clay	1,380	839	1,986	Okaloosa	2,390	812	2,326
Collier	6,070	273	2,910	Okeechobee	2,027	296	2,083
Columbia	1,473	894	889	Orange	15,526	357	7,786
Dade	11,393	130	7,015	Osceola	6,963	460	2,686
De Soto	1,774	121	1,316	Palm Beach	16,780	344	6,633
Dixie	166	314	324	Pasco	26,716	1,494	11,634
Duval	17,414	1,057	7,367	Pinellas	52,773	1,776	11,587
Escambia	3,758	604	4,089	Polk	41,240	2,039	11,126
Flagler	1,013	211	970	Putnam	1,605	904	1,902
Franklin	106	85	190	St. Johns	1,814	630	1,915
Gadsden	774	408	304	St. Lucie	14,844	258	2,723
Gilchrist	638	386	306	Santa Rosa	1,518	548	2,174
Glades	399	128	214	Sarasota	19,955	1,326	5,626
Gulf	128	118	240	Seminole	3,991	444	3,110
Hamilton	372	204	177	Sumter	2,357	386	1,787
Hardee	638	199	993	Suwannee	2,380	763	671
Hendry	2,593	323	881	Taylor	505	251	431
Hernando	4,828	495	2,614	Union	300	114	133
Highlands	10,006	281	3,359	Volusia	23,610	425	7,265
Hillsborough	32,447	991	10,848	Wakulla	423	405	427
Holmes	522	318	193	Walton	613	391	442
Indian River	9,475	40	1,796	Washington	454	216	259
Jackson	1,501	386	657	Office agency	388	117	181
Jefferson	252	128	172	Refunds	0	0	15
Lafayette	88	81	111				

1/ Includes military mobile homes.
2/ Tags sold to mobile home owners who also own the land on which the mobile home stands. A real property tag is bought only once, not annually.

Source: State of Florida, Department of Highway Safety and Motor Vehicles, *Revenue Report, July 1, 1994 through June 30, 1995.*

VITAL STATISTICS AND HEALTH

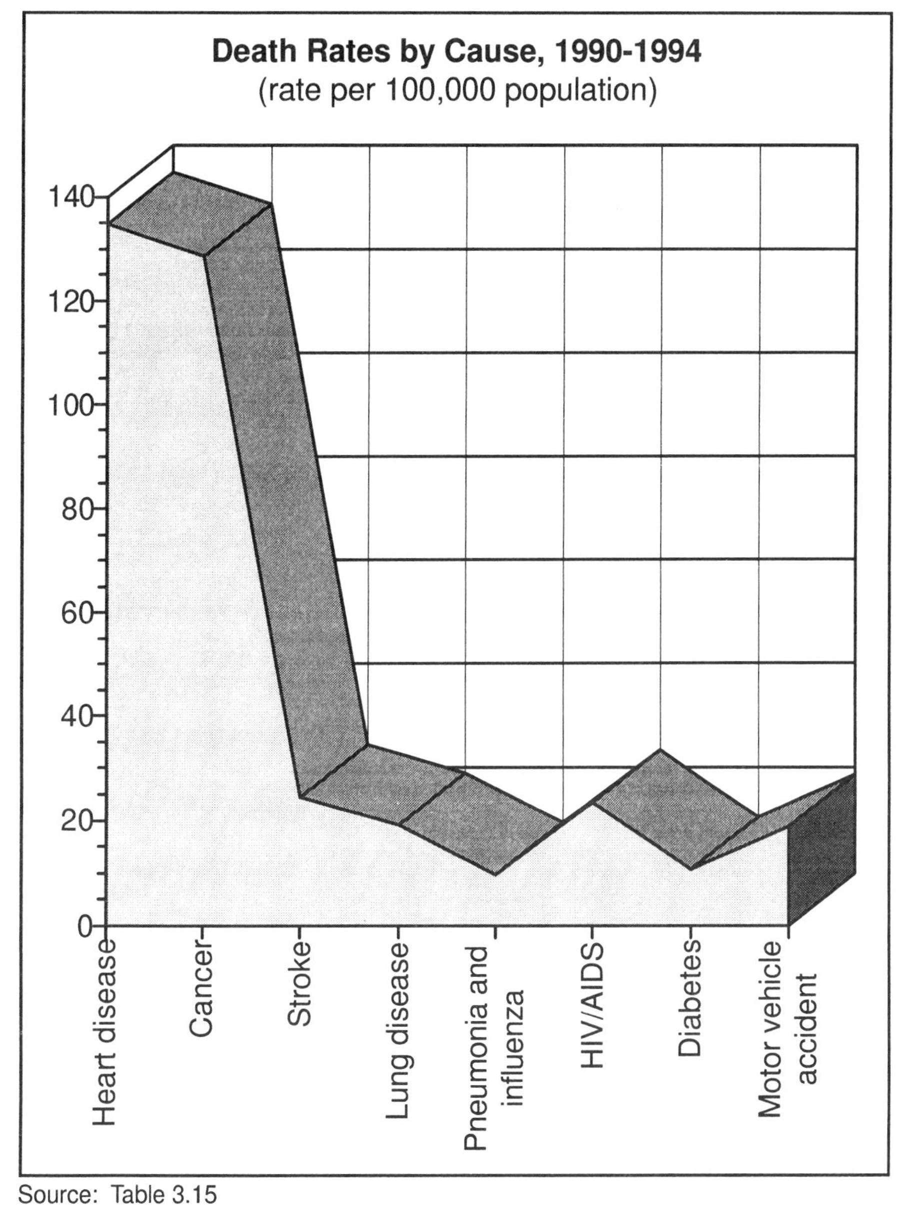

Source: Table 3.15

SECTION 3.00
VITAL STATISTICS AND HEALTH

TABLES LISTED BY MAJOR HEADINGS

Table 3.01. BIRTH AND DEATH RATES: RESIDENT LIVE BIRTH AND DEATH RATES BY RACE IN FLORIDA AND THE UNITED STATES, 1985 THROUGH 1995

	Birth rates 1/						Death rates 1/					
	Total		White		Nonwhite		Total		White		Nonwhite	
Year	Florida	U.S.	Florida	U.S.	Florida	U.S.	Florida	U.S.	Florida	U.S.	Florida	U.S.
1985	14.4	15.8	12.7	14.8	24.5	21.4	10.4	8.7	11.1	9.0	7.8	7.4
1986	14.3	15.6	12.6	14.6	23.9	21.4	10.5	8.7	11.0	9.0	7.6	7.5
1987	14.5	15.7	12.8	14.6	24.3	21.7	10.5	8.7	10.9	9.0	7.9	7.5
1988	14.8	15.9	13.1	14.8	24.9	22.5	10.5	8.8	11.0	9.1	7.8	7.6
1989	15.2	16.3	13.4	15.1	24.9	23.1	10.3	8.7	10.8	8.9	7.6	7.5
1990	15.1	16.7	13.4	15.5	24.3	19.0	10.1	8.6	10.6	8.9	7.2	5.8
1991	14.6	16.3	12.9	15.4	23.9	20.6	10.2	8.6	10.7	8.9	7.3	7.1
1992	14.2	15.9	12.6	15.0	23.2	20.5	10.3	8.5	10.8	8.8	7.3	7.2
1993	14.1	15.5	12.5	14.7	22.6	19.8	10.6	8.8	11.1	9.1	7.6	7.4
1994	13.7	15.3	12.2	(NA)	21.6	(NA)	10.5	8.8	11.1	9.1	7.5	7.4
1995	13.3	15.0	12.0	(NA)	19.8	(NA)	10.7	8.8	11.3	(NA)	7.4	(NA)

(NA) Not available.
1/ Per 1,000 population.
Note: Rates are based on July 1 population estimates for noncensus years. Some data are revised; some 1994 or 1995 data are preliminary.
Source: U.S., Department of Commerce, Bureau of the Census, *Statistical Abstract of the United States, 1996,* annual editions and State of Florida, Department of Health and Rehabilitative Services, Public Health Statistics Section, Office of Vital Statistics, *Florida Vital Statistics, 1995,* and previous editions.

Table 3.02. BIRTHS: NUMBER OF RESIDENT LIVE BIRTHS BY AGE OF MOTHER IN FLORIDA 1990 THROUGH 1995

Age of mother	1990	1991	1992	1993	1994	1995 A/
All ages	199,146	193,717	191,530	192,453	190,546	188,535
Less than 13	(NA)	(NA)	(NA)	(NA)	24	20
13	(NA)	(NA)	(NA)	(NA)	132	128
14	(NA)	(NA)	(NA)	(NA)	594	588
15	1,661	1,559	1,598	1,635	1,646	1,583
16	3,148	3,125	3,035	3,228	3,341	3,236
17	5,193	5,087	4,910	4,856	5,151	5,166
18	7,544	7,240	6,874	6,833	6,753	6,971
19	9,663	9,255	8,758	8,455	8,524	8,112
20-24	53,128	51,544	50,703	50,420	48,540	46,865
25-29	60,340	56,974	55,097	53,612	51,017	49,649
30-34	40,926	40,442	41,043	42,545	43,423	43,689
35-39	14,389	15,216	16,013	17,166	18,053	19,020
40 years and over	2,283	2,433	2,684	2,891	3,295	3,472
Age not stated	111	86	74	40	53	36
Less than 19 years, number	18,306	17,767	17,158	17,324	17,641	17,692
Percentage of total	9.2	9.2	9.0	9.0	9.3	9.4

(NA) Not available.
A/ Provisional.
Source: State of Florida, Department of Health and Rehabilitative Services, Public Health Statistics Section, Office of Vital Statistics, *Florida Vital Statistics, 1995,* and previous editions.

Table 3.05. BIRTHS TO UNWED MOTHERS: RESIDENT LIVE BIRTHS AND BIRTHS TO UNWED MOTHERS BY AGE AND RACE OF THE MOTHER IN THE STATE AND COUNTIES OF FLORIDA, 1995

County	Total resident live births	Births to unwed mothers					
		Number 1/	Percentage of total	Age of mother		Race of mother	
				Under 20	20 and over	White 2/	Nonwhite
Florida	188,535	67,422	35.8	20,438	46,972	29,742	29,742
Alachua	2,444	907	37.1	279	628	555	555
Baker	308	102	33.1	33	69	42	42
Bay	1,997	644	32.2	226	417	215	215
Bradford	270	106	39.3	44	62	47	47
Brevard	4,908	1,422	29.0	481	941	460	460
Broward	20,059	6,569	32.7	1,665	4,904	3,701	3,701
Calhoun	137	42	30.7	12	30	8	8
Charlotte	932	282	30.3	78	204	35	35
Citrus	850	276	32.5	84	192	34	34
Clay	1,647	378	23.0	135	243	80	80
Collier	2,478	867	35.0	269	598	201	201
Columbia	660	278	42.1	115	163	118	118
Dade	32,089	13,179	41.1	3,064	10,108	6,732	6,732
De Soto	381	157	41.2	52	105	43	43
Dixie	160	62	38.8	17	45	17	17
Duval	11,541	4,044	35.0	1,350	2,693	2,481	2,481
Escambia	3,830	1,522	39.7	547	975	901	901
Flagler	322	107	33.2	37	70	34	34
Franklin	94	39	41.5	17	22	10	10
Gadsden	640	387	60.5	151	236	304	304
Gilchrist	150	53	35.3	22	31	4	4
Glades	63	26	41.3	13	13	9	9
Gulf	125	42	33.6	12	30	19	19
Hamilton	148	67	45.3	30	37	46	46
Hardee	444	165	37.2	74	91	23	23
Hendry	608	246	40.5	83	163	85	85
Hernando	1,028	347	33.8	130	217	54	54
Highlands	828	333	40.2	130	203	136	136
Hillsborough	13,499	4,919	36.4	1,589	3,329	1,988	1,988
Holmes	187	61	32.6	20	41	8	8
Indian River	959	350	36.5	114	236	141	141
Jackson	473	158	33.4	56	102	93	93
Jefferson	158	68	43.0	20	48	54	54
Lafayette	66	21	31.8	11	10	4	4
Lake	2,027	724	35.7	267	457	221	221

See footnotes at end of table. Continued . . .

Table 3.05. BIRTHS TO UNWED MOTHERS: RESIDENT LIVE BIRTHS AND BIRTHS TO UNWED MOTHERS BY AGE AND RACE OF THE MOTHER IN THE STATE AND COUNTIES OF FLORIDA, 1995 (Continued)

County	Total resident live births	Births to unwed mothers					
		Number 1/	Percentage of total	Age of mother		Race of mother	
				Under 20	20 and over	White 2/	Nonwhite
Lee	4,270	1,585	37.1	576	1,009	448	448
Leon	2,785	975	35.0	288	687	692	692
Levy	346	130	37.6	42	88	52	52
Liberty	58	21	36.2	6	15	8	8
Madison	182	93	51.1	35	58	74	74
Manatee	2,834	1,081	38.1	372	709	316	316
Marion	2,670	1,039	38.9	350	689	406	406
Martin	1,100	374	34.0	93	281	122	122
Monroe	830	266	32.0	57	209	56	56
Nassau	696	207	29.7	76	131	58	58
Okaloosa	2,450	558	22.8	202	356	177	177
Okeechobee	496	193	38.9	72	121	34	34
Orange	11,639	4,119	35.4	1,329	2,790	1,891	1,891
Osceola	2,009	659	32.8	205	454	103	103
Palm Beach	12,281	4,086	33.3	1,145	2,941	2,012	2,012
Pasco	3,339	1,070	32.0	347	723	100	100
Pinellas	9,237	3,278	35.5	954	2,322	1,209	1,209
Polk	6,145	2,563	41.7	982	1,581	960	960
Putnam	941	442	47.0	176	266	205	205
St. Johns	1,158	330	28.5	121	209	119	119
St. Lucie	2,110	856	40.6	266	590	438	438
Santa Rosa	1,361	318	23.4	128	190	37	37
Sarasota	2,505	746	29.8	226	520	203	203
Seminole	4,374	1,215	27.8	399	816	400	400
Sumter	424	173	40.8	63	110	61	61
Suwannee	352	130	36.9	46	84	54	54
Taylor	213	83	39.0	31	52	28	28
Union	129	35	27.1	16	19	19	19
Volusia	4,301	1,579	36.7	516	1,063	481	481
Wakulla	208	68	32.7	32	36	23	23
Walton	358	119	33.2	34	85	26	26
Washington	224	81	36.2	26	55	27	27

1/ Includes data for mothers whose age was not stated.
2/ Persons designating "Hispanic" as a race were counted as white.

Source: State of Florida, Department of Health and Rehabilitative Services, Public Health Statistics Section, Office of Vital Statistics, *Florida Vital Statistics, 1995.*

Table 3.06. BIRTHS TO TEENAGERS: NUMBER, PERCENTAGE, AND RATE BY RACE OF THE MOTHER IN THE STATE AND COUNTIES OF FLORIDA, 1995

	Births to mothers under age 20				Teenage birth rate to mothers aged 15-19	
	White		Nonwhite			
County	Number	As a percentage of all white births	Number	As a percentage of all nonwhite births	White A/	Non-white B/
Florida	15,771	11.1	10,020	21.5	51.7	104.3
Alachua	130	8.1	206	24.6	18.2	85.4
Baker	50	20.2	8	13.6	71.9	74.1
Bay	237	14.5	86	24.2	66.1	100.7
Bradford	44	21.5	21	32.3	78.2	131.6
Brevard	407	9.8	186	24.9	39.7	100.6
Broward	847	6.2	1,063	16.4	37.6	104.2
Calhoun	24	20.5	2	10.0	72.1	27.8
Charlotte	100	11.6	10	13.7	41.1	37.6
Citrus	100	12.7	12	19.7	46.0	74.3
Clay	175	11.9	31	17.1	43.7	74.2
Collier	302	14.0	64	20.2	76.8	171.9
Columbia	108	21.2	53	35.1	77.9	132.6
Dade	1,922	8.8	1,825	17.9	45.8	93.5
De Soto	57	17.3	19	36.5	99.5	109.8
Dixie	21	14.8	4	22.2	64.2	148.1
Duval	819	11.0	897	22.1	56.8	114.7
Escambia	318	12.9	353	25.9	47.3	121.1
Flagler	32	12.1	14	24.1	44.1	87.8
Franklin	18	23.1	4	25.0	74.2	61.5
Gadsden	42	17.3	123	31.0	100.5	99.0
Gilchrist	35	24.5	2	33.3	102.7	60.6
Glades	14	29.2	3	20.0	78.7	35.3
Gulf	20	19.4	6	27.3	61.0	47.2
Hamilton	22	24.2	20	35.1	69.9	86.0
Hardee	102	24.7	9	29.0	143.1	119.4
Hendry	100	20.2	26	23.2	135.2	84.2
Hernando	148	15.5	24	33.8	60.9	95.0
Highlands	128	19.9	53	28.8	95.0	119.5
Hillsborough	1,319	12.7	702	22.8	62.7	118.9
Holmes	42	23.6	3	33.3	85.9	83.3
Indian River	90	11.7	56	29.9	46.1	120.1
Jackson	61	17.5	35	28.2	55.4	75.8
Jefferson	14	16.3	15	20.8	63.9	61.7
Lafayette	11	18.3	2	33.3	69.6	62.5
Lake	267	15.7	91	28.3	80.5	124.6

See footnotes at end of table.

Continued . . .

Table 3.06. BIRTHS TO TEENAGERS: NUMBER, PERCENTAGE, AND RATE BY RACE OF THE MOTHER IN THE STATE AND COUNTIES OF FLORIDA, 1995 (Continued)

	Births to mothers under age 20				Teenage birth rate to mothers aged 15-19	
	White		Nonwhite			
County	Number	As a percentage of all white births	Number	As a percentage of all nonwhite births	White A/	Nonwhite B/
Lee	500	13.7	206	33.2	66.8	156.8
Leon	122	7.1	226	21.4	15.5	50.2
Levy	40	14.4	17	25.0	55.2	101.4
Liberty	4	8.5	2	18.2	24.0	58.8
Madison	18	20.2	27	29.0	61.9	90.6
Manatee	351	14.7	122	27.2	76.9	151.1
Marion	303	14.7	165	27.4	62.9	138.4
Martin	82	9.0	37	19.3	39.6	111.5
Monroe	67	9.1	17	19.1	47.7	98.8
Nassau	90	14.5	15	20.0	59.1	71.1
Okaloosa	247	12.1	89	22.0	59.1	98.5
Okeechobee	100	22.0	14	34.1	102.1	116.7
Orange	926	10.9	680	21.4	50.9	101.3
Osceola	241	13.6	40	17.2	63.2	65.8
Palm Beach	676	7.5	663	20.6	40.0	120.2
Pasco	463	14.6	39	23.1	72.5	88.6
Pinellas	707	9.5	408	23.0	42.6	113.9
Polk	870	18.1	383	28.8	83.5	140.8
Putnam	151	22.0	85	33.2	95.4	145.1
St. Johns	112	11.4	53	30.1	43.2	144.5
St. Lucie	178	12.0	146	23.6	52.4	118.0
Santa Rosa	170	13.5	15	15.2	59.9	54.9
Sarasota	196	8.8	93	33.2	38.2	127.2
Seminole	313	8.5	159	23.1	36.3	99.9
Sumter	63	18.9	21	23.3	82.1	79.7
Suwannee	50	18.1	22	29.3	54.6	118.0
Taylor	35	19.8	13	36.1	76.1	85.0
Union	18	17.6	8	29.6	78.9	137.9
Volusia	428	12.0	202	27.8	47.3	103.6
Wakulla	36	20.3	9	29.0	72.4	83.3
Walton	51	15.8	8	22.2	56.4	78.4
Washington	37	20.2	8	19.5	74.3	47.9

A/ Per 1,000 female white population aged 15-19.
B/ Per 1,000 female nonwhite population aged 15-19.
Note: Resident live births. Persons designating "Hispanic" as a race were counted as white.

Source: State of Florida, Department of Health and Rehabilitative Services, Public Health Statistics Section, Office of Vital Statistics, *Florida Vital Statistics, 1995.*

Table 3.07. ABORTIONS: REPORTED TERMINATIONS OF PREGNANCY IN FLORIDA 1984 THROUGH 1995

Year	Induced abortions 2/	Resident live births	Total known pregnancies 1/ Number	Total known pregnancies 1/ Rate per 100 women aged 15-44	Abortion rate per 100 pregnancies
1984	50,507	155,344	207,442	9.0	24.5
1985	53,011	163,732	218,315	9.2	24.3
1986	50,262	167,628	219,491	9.0	22.9
1987	52,697	175,072	229,387	9.0	23.0
1988	65,153	183,998	250,889	9.5	26.0
1989	62,626	192,887	257,315	9.5	24.3
1990	66,073	199,146	267,030	9.7	24.7
1991	71,254	193,717	266,663	9.6	26.7
1992	69,285	191,530	262,313	9.3	26.4
1993	70,069	192,453	263,969	9.3	26.5
1994	73,394	190,546	265,459	9.3	27.6
1995	74,749	188,535	264,815	9.0	28.2

(NA) Not available.

1/ Includes induced abortions, total resident births, and total reported resident fetal deaths.

2/ Abortions have been legal in Florida since April 1972.

Note: Some data may be revised.

Source: State of Florida, Department of Health and Rehabilitative Services, Public Health Statistics Section, Office of Vital Statistics, *Florida Vital Statistics, 1995,* previous editions, and unpublished data.

Table 3.08. INFANT DEATHS: NUMBER AND RATE OF RESIDENT INFANT DEATHS BY RACE IN FLORIDA, 1984 THROUGH 1995

Year	Number of deaths Total 1/	Number of deaths White 2/	Number of deaths Nonwhite	Mortality rate per 1,000 live births Total 1/	Mortality rate per 1,000 live births White 2/	Mortality rate per 1,000 live births Nonwhite
1984	1,681	984	696	10.9	8.5	17.8
1985	1,846	1,128	718	11.3	9.1	17.8
1986	1,837	1,097	739	11.0	8.7	18.0
1987	1,844	1,039	802	10.5	7.9	18.6
1988	1,949	1,167	782	10.6	8.5	17.0
1989	1,899	1,141	756	9.8	7.9	15.8
1990	1,909	1,121	786	9.6	7.5	16.0
1991	1,726	966	758	8.9	6.7	15.6
1992	1,685	987	695	8.8	6.9	14.4
1993	1,654	951	699	8.6	6.6	14.5
1994	1,540	927	611	8.1	6.5	12.9
1995	1,402	840	562	7.4	5.9	12.1

1/ Unknown race included in total only.

2/ Persons designating "Hispanic" as a race were counted as white.

Note: Infants are considered to be less than one year. Some data may be revised.

Source: State of Florida, Department of Health and Rehabilitative Services, Public Health Statistics Section, Office of Vital Statistics, *Florida Vital Statistics, 1995,* and previous editions.

Table 3.09. BIRTHS AND DEATHS: NUMBER OF RESIDENT LIVE BIRTHS AND DEATHS 1994 AND 1995, AND NUMBER BY RACE, 1995, IN THE STATE AND COUNTIES OF FLORIDA

County	Number of births 1994	Number of births, 1995 Total 1/	White 2/	Nonwhite	Number of deaths 1994	Number of deaths, 1995 Total 1/	White 2/	Nonwhite
Florida	190,546	188,535	141,848	46,555	146,869	151,619	134,232	17,356
Alachua	2,481	2,444	1,605	839	1,350	1,360	1,032	327
Baker	274	308	248	59	140	155	136	19
Bay	1,955	1,997	1,639	356	1,187	1,248	1,116	132
Bradford	313	270	205	65	252	252	216	36
Brevard	5,221	4,908	4,154	748	4,148	4,274	4,008	265
Broward	19,488	20,059	13,580	6,467	15,519	15,804	14,078	1,722
Calhoun	135	137	117	20	144	132	118	13
Charlotte	1,010	932	859	73	1,798	1,950	1,892	57
Citrus	873	850	789	61	1,581	1,727	1,694	33
Clay	1,613	1,647	1,466	181	794	886	833	53
Collier	2,473	2,478	2,159	317	1,733	1,780	1,708	70
Columbia	639	660	509	151	460	496	406	89
Dade	32,913	32,089	21,837	10,179	18,313	19,181	15,528	3,646
De Soto	395	381	329	52	284	311	266	45
Dixie	129	160	142	18	106	124	119	5
Duval	11,655	11,541	7,474	4,065	6,158	6,261	4,542	1,717
Escambia	4,029	3,830	2,468	1,361	2,534	2,466	1,959	506
Flagler	280	322	264	58	411	455	410	45
Franklin	105	94	78	16	119	136	114	22
Gadsden	682	640	243	397	456	440	184	256
Gilchrist	151	150	143	6	120	115	111	4
Glades	83	63	48	15	92	114	100	14
Gulf	130	125	103	22	147	143	108	35
Hamilton	140	148	91	57	100	120	90	30
Hardee	409	444	413	31	182	202	184	18
Hendry	579	608	496	112	244	255	202	53
Hernando	973	1,028	957	71	1,689	1,718	1,676	42
Highlands	826	828	644	184	1,170	1,266	1,183	83
Hillsborough	13,690	13,499	10,417	3,073	7,937	8,060	7,005	1,053
Holmes	218	187	178	9	204	198	190	8
Indian River	937	959	772	187	1,280	1,281	1,204	77
Jackson	532	473	349	124	455	475	350	125
Jefferson	136	158	86	72	130	140	80	60
Lafayette	58	66	60	6	43	47	44	3
Lake	2,000	2,027	1,706	321	2,277	2,485	2,329	156
Lee	4,311	4,270	3,645	621	4,285	4,480	4,253	227

See footnotes at end of table.

Continued . . .

Table 3.09. BIRTHS AND DEATHS: NUMBER OF RESIDENT LIVE BIRTHS AND DEATHS 1994 AND 1995, AND NUMBER BY RACE, 1995, IN THE STATE AND COUNTIES OF FLORIDA (Continued)

County	Number of births 1994	Number of births, 1995 Total 1/	White 2/	Non-white	Number of deaths 1994	Number of deaths, 1995 Total 1/	White 2/	Non-white
Leon	2,835	2,785	1,726	1,058	1,199	1,312	961	351
Levy	344	346	278	68	353	365	336	29
Liberty	65	58	47	11	48	52	49	3
Madison	223	182	89	93	181	184	113	71
Manatee	2,722	2,834	2,385	449	3,073	3,142	2,943	199
Marion	2,619	2,670	2,068	602	2,646	2,866	2,571	295
Martin	1,137	1,100	908	192	1,412	1,475	1,404	71
Monroe	914	830	740	89	719	724	666	57
Nassau	649	696	620	75	417	410	359	51
Okaloosa	2,433	2,450	2,044	405	1,043	1,165	1,090	75
Okeechobee	478	496	455	41	315	346	319	27
Orange	11,967	11,639	8,460	3,177	5,356	5,599	4,678	918
Osceola	1,995	2,009	1,777	232	1,082	1,191	1,124	66
Palm Beach	12,758	12,281	9,056	3,218	11,443	11,742	10,556	1,185
Pasco	3,214	3,339	3,169	169	4,597	4,814	4,756	58
Pinellas	9,355	9,237	7,463	1,772	12,644	12,381	11,694	686
Polk	6,198	6,145	4,813	1,331	4,681	4,818	4,249	569
Putnam	894	941	685	256	784	816	676	140
St. Johns	1,053	1,158	982	176	913	952	859	93
St. Lucie	2,212	2,110	1,489	619	1,907	2,047	1,740	307
Santa Rosa	1,308	1,361	1,262	99	671	661	639	22
Sarasota	2,555	2,505	2,225	280	4,430	4,479	4,331	148
Seminole	4,475	4,374	3,687	687	2,209	2,210	1,957	253
Sumter	397	424	334	90	482	506	446	60
Suwannee	353	352	277	75	375	371	330	41
Taylor	229	213	177	36	166	217	165	52
Union	112	129	102	27	151	188	132	56
Volusia	4,429	4,301	3,575	726	5,072	5,359	5,008	350
Wakulla	190	208	177	31	129	156	132	24
Walton	382	358	322	36	314	322	297	25
Washington	215	224	183	41	215	212	184	28

1/ Unknown race included in total only.
2/ Persons designating "Hispanic" as a race were counted as white.
Note: Data are for births and deaths occurring to residents of the specified area regardless of place of occurrence.

Source: State of Florida, Department of Health and Rehabilitative Services, Public Health Statistics Section, Office of Vital Statistics, *Florida Vital Statistics, 1995,* and previous edition.

Table 3.10. BIRTH AND DEATH RATES: RESIDENT LIVE BIRTH AND DEATH RATES BY RACE IN THE STATE AND COUNTIES OF FLORIDA, 1995

County	Birth rate			Death rate		
	Total	White 1/	Non-white	Total	White 1/	Non-white
Florida	13.3	12.0	19.8	10.7	11.3	7.4
Alachua	12.3	10.3	19.4	6.8	6.6	7.6
Baker	15.1	14.6	17.4	7.6	8.0	5.6
Bay	14.3	13.6	18.3	8.9	9.3	6.8
Bradford	11.1	11.0	11.3	10.3	11.6	6.3
Brevard	11.0	10.3	16.3	9.6	10.0	5.8
Broward	14.7	12.5	23.1	11.5	12.9	6.2
Calhoun	11.4	11.8	9.6	11.0	11.9	6.2
Charlotte	7.2	7.0	11.9	15.2	15.4	9.3
Citrus	8.0	7.7	17.0	16.3	16.5	9.2
Clay	13.5	13.1	19.3	7.3	7.4	5.6
Collier	13.2	12.2	27.6	9.5	9.7	6.1
Columbia	13.0	12.7	14.3	9.8	10.1	8.4
Dade	15.9	14.3	20.8	9.5	10.1	7.5
De Soto	14.2	15.4	9.5	11.6	12.5	8.2
Dixie	12.8	12.8	13.0	9.9	10.7	3.6
Duval	16.0	14.6	19.6	8.7	8.9	8.3
Escambia	13.5	11.6	19.4	8.7	9.2	7.2
Flagler	8.6	7.9	15.4	12.2	12.2	11.9
Franklin	9.2	9.0	10.2	13.3	13.1	14.1
Gadsden	14.3	13.8	14.6	9.8	10.4	9.4
Gilchrist	12.5	13.2	5.2	9.6	10.2	3.5
Glades	7.3	6.9	8.8	13.2	14.5	8.2
Gulf	9.4	10.1	6.9	10.7	10.6	11.0
Hamilton	11.8	12.2	11.1	9.6	12.1	5.9
Hardee	19.4	20.0	13.9	8.8	8.9	8.1
Hendry	20.5	21.2	18.0	8.6	8.6	8.5
Hernando	8.6	8.5	12.0	14.4	14.8	7.1
Highlands	10.7	9.5	18.8	16.3	17.4	8.5
Hillsborough	15.1	13.9	20.9	9.0	9.4	7.2
Holmes	10.7	11.1	6.3	11.4	11.9	5.6
Indian River	9.5	8.5	18.2	12.7	13.3	7.5
Jackson	10.1	10.5	9.3	10.2	10.5	9.3
Jefferson	11.7	11.9	11.5	10.3	11.0	9.6
Lafayette	10.1	11.2	5.1	7.2	8.2	2.6
Lake	11.4	10.8	16.2	14.0	14.7	7.9
Lee	11.3	10.5	20.4	11.8	12.2	7.5

See footnotes at end of table.

Continued . . .

Table 3.10. BIRTH AND DEATH RATES: RESIDENT LIVE BIRTH AND DEATH RATES BY RACE IN THE STATE AND COUNTIES OF FLORIDA, 1995 (Continued)

County	Birth rate			Death rate		
	Total	White 1/	Non-white	Total	White 1/	Non-white
Leon	12.8	10.8	18.0	6.0	6.0	6.0
Levy	11.5	10.8	16.0	12.2	13.1	6.8
Liberty	8.4	8.5	8.0	7.5	8.9	2.2
Madison	9.9	8.6	11.5	10.0	11.0	8.8
Manatee	12.1	11.2	20.7	13.4	13.8	9.2
Marion	11.8	10.7	18.3	12.7	13.3	9.0
Martin	9.8	8.8	20.9	13.1	13.6	7.7
Monroe	9.9	9.5	15.2	8.7	8.6	9.7
Nassau	14.1	14.1	13.7	8.3	8.2	9.3
Okaloosa	15.0	14.3	19.4	7.1	7.7	3.6
Okeechobee	15.0	15.0	15.5	10.5	10.5	10.2
Orange	15.3	14.1	19.7	7.3	7.8	5.7
Osceola	14.6	14.0	21.3	8.6	8.8	6.1
Palm Beach	12.7	11.0	22.1	12.1	12.8	8.1
Pasco	10.9	10.7	17.2	15.7	16.0	5.9
Pinellas	10.5	9.5	20.0	14.1	14.8	7.7
Polk	13.8	12.7	20.0	10.8	11.2	8.5
Putnam	13.5	12.3	18.2	11.7	12.1	10.0
St. Johns	11.7	11.1	17.6	9.6	9.7	9.3
St. Lucie	12.2	10.7	18.8	11.9	12.5	9.3
Santa Rosa	14.1	13.9	15.8	6.8	7.1	3.5
Sarasota	8.3	7.8	16.9	14.8	15.1	8.9
Seminole	13.4	12.8	18.1	6.8	6.8	6.7
Sumter	11.5	11.3	12.4	13.8	15.1	8.3
Suwannee	11.5	10.8	15.3	12.1	12.8	8.4
Taylor	11.6	12.3	9.0	11.8	11.5	13.0
Union	10.2	11.2	7.6	14.8	14.5	15.7
Volusia	10.6	9.9	16.9	13.2	13.8	8.2
Wakulla	12.1	12.1	12.7	9.1	9.0	9.8
Walton	10.7	10.8	9.7	9.6	9.9	6.8
Washington	11.7	11.9	11.0	11.1	12.0	7.5

1/ Persons designating "Hispanic" as a race were counted as white.
Note: Rates per 1,000 population July 1, 1995. Data are for births and deaths occurring to residents of the specified area regardless of place of occurrence.

Source: State of Florida, Department of Health and Rehabilitative Services, Public Health Statistics Section, Office of Vital Statistics, *Florida Vital Statistics, 1995*.

Table 3.15. DEATHS: DEATH RATES BY LEADING CAUSE IN THE STATE, LOCAL HEALTH COUNCILS DISTRICTS, AND COUNTIES OF FLORIDA, 1990 TO 1994

(rate per 100,000 population)

District and county	All causes 1/	Heart dis-ease	Cancer	Stroke	Lung dis-ease	Pneu-monia and influ-enza	HIV/ AIDS	Dia-betes	Motor Vehi-cle acci-dent
Florida	497.4	134.8	128.7	24.4	19.1	9.6	23.5	10.7	18.9
Northwest--1	543.0	156.2	140.8	29.9	23.6	11.9	9.5	13.5	18.7
Escambia	572.3	153.2	148.5	34.9	24.5	10.5	15.0	15.1	16.8
Okaloosa	505.3	159.7	137.8	19.9	23.9	13.2	3.9	11.4	14.1
Santa Rosa	516.5	154.1	127.7	30.5	23.3	12.6	4.2	12.7	29.1
Walton	559.0	173.3	129.2	26.6	18.2	15.7	6.4	12.1	30.7
Big Bend--2	552.0	143.9	140.0	29.5	26.9	11.5	9.9	14.7	22.6
Bay	543.5	136.6	143.1	24.3	32.1	13.2	11.3	11.7	16.0
Calhoun	644.7	173.1	143.0	31.2	38.9	12.1	3.6	21.0	33.0
Franklin	576.1	150.4	139.6	35.0	25.4	15.9	3.8	24.6	18.8
Gadsden	654.6	167.5	155.5	39.9	21.1	14.5	12.8	25.2	40.0
Gulf	626.6	168.1	154.5	39.0	28.8	11.1	0.0	14.4	35.1
Holmes	625.8	197.7	141.5	22.8	33.9	9.7	6.4	16.7	46.1
Jackson	574.4	165.9	131.0	27.5	24.3	10.9	5.9	13.7	33.4
Jefferson	581.6	134.5	140.3	44.4	21.5	14.3	13.4	16.2	50.9
Leon	488.3	115.5	131.6	31.2	21.9	8.0	11.9	13.0	15.0
Liberty	539.0	174.0	126.9	20.0	32.3	13.4	3.3	12.3	17.7
Madison	599.2	177.4	138.7	38.4	14.1	14.9	5.5	16.5	29.3
Taylor	643.7	171.7	166.7	32.7	37.2	11.3	4.3	25.1	27.5
Wakulla	574.3	144.0	177.5	20.6	26.6	9.0	9.8	17.5	40.3
Washington	597.1	169.1	130.4	23.1	36.6	17.9	7.1	10.0	33.8
North Central--3	517.5	138.8	136.8	27.9	21.5	8.6	13.1	11.9	26.6
Alachua	539.0	117.2	138.2	32.3	20.6	11.6	15.6	17.4	17.1
Bradford	655.8	157.2	170.8	36.8	36.4	12.7	14.3	21.2	30.0
Citrus	468.2	138.9	132.7	21.9	18.3	8.4	6.1	8.6	27.8
Columbia	597.0	167.2	140.8	31.2	38.6	8.4	6.9	15.7	30.5
Dixie	591.8	144.4	152.0	37.3	32.2	11.7	1.8	14.1	48.7
Gilchrist	626.8	162.7	154.4	39.3	31.9	8.4	5.5	16.9	40.2
Hamilton	586.4	158.7	166.3	27.3	14.9	22.6	7.3	12.9	18.7
Hernando	464.9	131.8	133.4	20.5	16.3	7.9	9.5	10.5	24.6
Lafayette	505.2	123.2	112.7	39.5	28.3	3.3	2.8	14.3	28.9
Lake	481.1	132.2	132.6	26.5	19.3	8.1	8.8	9.8	25.6
Levy	582.3	139.8	153.3	28.3	23.2	11.8	4.6	17.0	26.5
Marion	511.9	140.4	135.7	34.0	20.0	6.2	10.3	12.2	30.8
Putnam	602.5	147.6	148.1	24.7	29.6	12.8	8.3	13.8	42.1
Sumter	548.6	179.7	129.0	27.8	19.3	9.4	12.6	9.8	34.7
Suwannee	674.7	173.7	153.0	38.1	46.6	11.5	15.2	16.8	46.3
Union	916.0	178.0	216.2	27.7	35.0	18.6	206.1	10.1	29.5
Northeast Central--4	542.8	149.6	141.6	27.3	24.1	12.1	13.4	12.7	18.1
Baker	636.2	166.9	163.7	38.8	52.1	20.6	4.2	15.3	16.9
Clay	520.0	158.7	142.2	25.3	25.9	11.7	6.0	10.5	15.7
Duval	595.6	160.5	150.7	31.2	26.8	14.4	16.6	14.8	16.1
Flagler	446.1	119.1	120.2	14.8	15.5	4.9	12.0	10.6	24.5
Nassau	601.7	164.8	155.6	29.6	30.2	17.2	3.7	16.3	34.6
St. Johns	497.7	121.9	141.8	24.2	19.5	10.3	8.0	8.9	20.6
Volusia	503.7	145.4	132.5	25.3	21.7	10.2	12.7	11.6	20.5

See footnotes at end of table. Continued . . .

Table 3.15. DEATHS: DEATH RATES BY LEADING CAUSE IN THE STATE, LOCAL HEALTH COUNCILS DISTRICTS, AND COUNTIES OF FLORIDA, 1990 TO 1994 (Continued)

(rate per 100,000 population)

District and county	All causes 1/	Heart disease	Cancer	Stroke	Lung disease	Pneumonia and influenza	HIV/ AIDS	Diabetes	Motor Vehicle accident
Suncoast--5	483.7	133.1	126.6	24.7	19.1	9.0	16.3	9.2	15.6
Pasco	476.1	131.6	128.5	20.5	19.3	9.0	9.5	9.8	22.9
Pinellas	487.2	134.1	126.3	26.2	19.0	9.0	18.3	8.9	13.4
West Central--6	515.7	142.0	131.4	25.8	22.9	9.9	18.6	11.6	22.7
Hardee	543.3	153.2	122.8	24.3	31.1	13.8	7.2	12.4	35.9
Highlands	500.1	125.5	128.7	25.2	22.7	10.7	11.8	12.2	32.9
Hillsborough	554.2	151.8	141.8	28.5	26.0	11.4	21.3	13.2	21.3
Manatee	449.5	123.6	124.1	22.8	18.3	7.3	17.2	6.8	17.6
Polk	513.9	145.5	125.1	24.7	21.2	10.0	14.7	12.9	26.7
East Central--7	469.2	129.2	131.2	22.4	21.6	10.7	15.1	10.8	15.2
Brevard	463.5	123.2	137.0	21.2	22.2	10.6	10.9	9.8	16.9
Orange	489.7	134.8	132.7	24.4	21.0	11.2	20.4	10.9	14.8
Osceola	452.2	132.0	113.2	19.9	23.6	10.0	11.4	12.7	23.5
Seminole	444.9	127.8	127.1	21.6	21.5	9.7	9.9	11.2	11.3
Southwest--8	437.1	113.1	116.1	20.4	15.5	9.2	16.5	8.3	23.7
Charlotte	411.9	115.7	117.6	18.2	13.2	14.8	9.9	10.5	20.1
Collier	398.3	93.4	109.7	16.8	15.0	6.9	15.5	7.0	27.0
De Soto	551.8	136.2	141.9	22.9	25.2	13.8	5.9	11.3	31.6
Glades	503.7	128.3	119.8	22.9	16.1	5.7	1.6	10.3	75.6
Hendry	613.6	180.3	125.2	23.7	18.4	8.7	22.1	21.3	53.2
Lee	447.9	121.5	120.0	18.5	16.1	8.3	20.5	8.7	24.0
Sarasota	426.5	107.6	111.9	24.3	15.3	8.7	15.0	6.6	16.3
Treasure Coast--9	464.2	123.6	124.5	22.2	15.3	7.6	28.5	7.8	19.7
Indian River	431.3	109.3	127.8	28.0	18.0	7.2	9.0	4.9	22.0
Martin	439.5	113.1	132.3	21.3	18.0	6.7	12.9	5.0	18.7
Okeechobee	562.2	159.4	144.0	20.0	27.6	16.2	9.0	9.1	41.6
Palm Beach	461.0	121.7	120.7	21.6	14.1	7.7	33.2	8.5	18.5
St. Lucie	498.7	143.4	135.2	22.4	16.5	7.2	25.8	8.0	20.8
Broward Regional--10	502.6	136.0	129.9	23.2	16.6	6.9	42.5	10.5	14.8
Broward	502.6	136.0	129.9	23.2	16.6	6.9	42.5	10.5	14.8
South--11	526.1	141.6	120.3	23.9	15.3	11.7	44.3	12.7	16.9
Dade	528.5	143.6	120.0	24.0	15.3	11.8	44.3	12.9	16.8
Monroe	470.7	95.3	125.8	21.6	14.4	8.9	44.1	6.9	18.5

HIV/AIDS Human Immunodeficiency Virus/Acquired Immunodeficiency Syndrome.

1/ Includes causes not shown separately.

Note: Rates are per 1,000 persons and are based on Office of the Governor July 1, 1992, population estimates printed January 11, 1995. Local health councils were established in 1982 by the legislature to serve 11 planning districts throughout the state. These councils are responsible for establishing and maintaining the district health plans.

Source: State of Florida, Agency for Health Care Administration, *Florida 1996 Health Data SourceBook*. Compiled by Local Health Councils of Florida.

Table 3.17. DEATHS: NUMBER OF RESIDENT DEATHS BY CAUSE IN FLORIDA 1993, 1994, AND 1995

Cause of death and international list number	1993	1994	1995
All causes	145,068	146,869	151,619
Intestinal infectious diseases, 001-009	42	33	49
Tuberculosis, 010-018	115	112	83
Meningococcal infection, 036	18	23	26
Septicemia, 038	813	784	779
Human immunodeficiency virus (HIV), 042-044	3,492	4,142	4,336
Herpes zoster and simplex, 053-054	20	17	9
Viral hepatitis, 070	187	237	270
Syphilis, 090-097	4	6	8
Mycoses, 110-118	116	122	148
Late effects--tuberculosis, 137	2	10	12
Other infectious and parasitic diseases, 020-139	290	293	258
Malignant neoplasm (cancer), 140-208	35,593	36,145	36,866
Neoplasm not specified malignant, 210-239	437	418	475
Diabetes mellitus, 250	3,251	3,328	3,652
Nutritional deficiencies, 260-269	163	144	170
Anemias, 280-285	286	263	290
Alcohol psychosis, dependence, abuse, 291, 303, 305.0	436	415	378
Meningitis, 320-322	31	35	39
Parkinson's disease, 332	648	597	800
Motor neurone disease, 335.2	222	258	288
Major cardiovascular diseases, 390-448	61,264	61,242	62,829
Phlebitis and thrombophlebitis, 451	94	81	94
Venous embolism and thrombosis, 452-453	25	18	25
Other circulatory diseases, 454-459	139	125	141
Pneumonia and influenza, 480-487	3,659	3,751	3,810
Chronic obstructive pulmonary disease, 490-496	7,069	7,110	7,455
Pulmonary fibrosis and other alveular pneumopathy, 515-516	497	560	568
Ulcer of stomach and duodenum, 531-533	398	382	387
Hernia and intestinal obstruction, 550-553, 560	320	309	309
Diverticula of intestine, 562	215	225	209
Chronic liver disease and cirrhosis, 571	1,758	1,881	1,829
Cholelithiasis, other gallbladder diseases, 574-575	170	154	175
Diseases of pancreas, 577	188	201	190
Nephritis, nephrosis, renal failure, 580-589	1,014	1,006	1,071
Infections of kidney, 590	51	58	48
Maternal causes, 630-676	18	17	18
Congenital anomalies, 740-759	669	661	630
Perinatal conditions, 760-779	766	753	653
Symptoms, signs, ill-defined condition, 780-799	2,189	2,112	2,543
All other diseases, 240-739	9,771	10,424	11,022
Unintentional injury (accident), E800-E949	5,065	4,971	5,259
Suicide, E950-E959	2,107	2,062	2,139
Homicide and legal intervention, E960-E978	1,372	1,307	1,209
All other external causes, E980-E999	84	77	70

Source: State of Florida, Department of Health and Rehabilitative Services, Public Health Statistics Section, Office of Vital Statistics, *Florida Vital Statistics, 1995,* and previous editions.

Table 3.18. DEATHS: NUMBER OF RESIDENT DEATHS AND DEATH RATES BY LEADING CAUSE AND BY RACE IN FLORIDA, 1995

Cause	Number of deaths			Death rate 1/		
	Total 2/	White 3/	Non-white	Total 2/	White 3/	Non-white
Heart disease	49,326	44,974	4,342	347.1	379.4	184.3
Malignant neoplasm (cancer)	36,866	33,476	3,387	259.4	282.4	143.8
Cerebrovascular disease (stroke)	9,821	8,661	1,158	69.1	73.1	49.2
Chronic obstructive pulmonary disease (COPD)	7,455	7,040	414	52.5	59.4	17.6
Unintentional injury (accident)	5,259	4,462	794	37.0	37.6	33.7
Human Immunodeficiency Virus (HIV)	4,336	2,316	2,020	30.5	19.5	85.8
Pneumonia and influenza	3,810	3,399	410	26.8	28.7	17.4
Diabetes mellitus	3,652	2,977	675	25.7	25.1	28.7
Suicide	2,139	1,998	141	15.1	16.9	6.0
Chronic liver disease and cirrhosis	1,829	1,663	165	12.9	14.0	7.0
Homicide and legal intervention	1,209	652	557	8.5	5.5	23.6

1/ Rate per 100,000 population July 1, 1995.
2/ Unknown race included in total only.
3/ Persons designating "Hispanic" as a race were counted as white.
Note: Data are for deaths occurring to residents of Florida regardless of the state of occurrence.

Table 3.19. DEATHS: RESIDENT ACCIDENT AND SUICIDE DEATHS AND DEATH RATES BY RACE AND SEX IN FLORIDA, 1991 THROUGH 1995

Year	Number of deaths					Death rate 1/				
	Total 3/	White 2/		Nonwhite		Total 3/	White 2/		Nonwhite	
		Male	Female	Male	Female		Male	Female	Male	Female
					Unintentional injury (accident)					
1991	4,720	2,641	1,298	566	204	35.6	48.7	22.6	57.0	18.8
1992	4,834	2,669	1,424	499	237	35.9	48.3	24.3	50.0	21.8
1993	5,065	2,766	1,494	554	238	36.9	49.2	25.1	54.2	21.4
1994	4,971	2,763	1,408	577	204	35.6	48.4	23.3	55.0	17.9
1995	5,259	2,942	1,520	566	228	37.0	51.1	24.9	50.1	18.0
					Suicide					
1991	2,086	1,537	423	106	16	15.7	28.3	7.3	10.7	1.5
1992	2,015	1,481	414	97	22	15.0	26.8	7.1	9.7	2.0
1993	2,107	1,498	474	110	22	15.4	26.7	8.0	10.8	2.0
1994	2,062	1,528	392	109	27	14.8	26.8	6.5	10.4	2.4
1995	2,139	1,589	408	114	27	15.1	27.6	6.7	10.1	2.1

1/ Rate per 100,000 population July 1, 1995.
2/ Persons designating "Hispanic" as a race were counted as white.
3/ Unknown race included in total only.

Source for Tables 3.18 and 3.19: State of Florida, Department of Health and Rehabilitative Services, Public Health Statistics Section, Office of Vital Statistics, *Florida Vital Statistics, 1995.*

Table 3.20. CHILD SAFETY: CHILD AND TEEN DEATHS, 1992, AND VERIFIED MALTREATMENTS AND RUNAWAYS, 1992-93, IN THE STATE AND COUNTIES OF FLORIDA

County	1992			1992-93				
	Child deaths 3/	Teen violent deaths 2/		Number of verified maltreatments in reports closed 1/				Run-aways 5/
		Number	Rate 4/	Total	Abuse	Neglect	Threat-ened harm	
Florida	781	493	6.2	130,801	43,998	60,530	26,273	59,327
Alachua	16	10	5.5	1,405	415	673	317	700
Baker	1	3	18.6	216	91	87	38	10
Bay	6	6	6.7	2,477	751	1,175	551	625
Bradford	0	1	6.6	463	126	261	76	68
Brevard	22	11	4.6	4,919	1,478	2,229	1,212	1,602
Broward	64	39	5.9	8,909	3,224	3,674	2,011	4,508
Calhoun	1	0	0.0	165	39	89	37	3
Charlotte	3	1	2.1	435	164	153	118	342
Citrus	1	1	2.2	849	326	368	155	315
Clay	15	4	4.7	1,442	535	606	301	450
Collier	11	11	13.2	1,255	480	563	212	761
Columbia	6	4	11.8	797	276	367	154	146
Dade	113	80	6.4	12,737	4,230	6,295	2,212	6,674
De Soto	3	2	12.8	359	123	149	87	66
Dixie	2	1	14.5	162	46	75	41	5
Duval	51	28	6.2	7,975	2,772	3,942	1,261	3,728
Escambia	17	10	5.1	3,137	979	1,525	633	1,807
Flagler	0	0	0.0	212	99	58	55	58
Franklin	0	2	31.3	176	43	88	45	2
Gadsden	4	2	6.0	1,059	229	644	186	25
Gilchrist	2	0	0.0	131	71	39	21	25
Glades	1	1	18.8	52	28	16	8	14
Gulf	1	0	0.0	90	27	49	14	5
Hamilton	2	1	9.9	117	28	71	18	6
Hardee	3	5	30.7	386	134	185	67	120
Hendry	2	3	13.9	251	88	126	37	141
Hernando	4	4	7.0	927	323	406	198	329
Highlands	8	4	11.2	917	323	431	163	231
Hillsborough	46	36	6.5	13,062	3,829	6,649	2,584	6,005
Holmes	0	5	40.6	455	93	249	113	14
Indian River	5	2	4.1	635	241	301	93	325
Jackson	1	5	14.1	588	196	306	86	52
Jefferson	1	1	10.4	132	47	57	28	6
Lafayette	0	0	0.0	75	35	27	13	0
Lake	13	3	3.5	1,929	630	856	443	484
Lee	29	16	9.2	2,349	913	1,016	420	1,549
Leon	14	10	5.1	1,637	580	679	378	1,272
Levy	3	1	5.9	476	156	212	108	72

See footnotes at end of table. Continued . . .

Table 3.20. CHILD SAFETY: CHILD AND TEEN DEATHS, 1992, AND VERIFIED MALTREATMENTS AND RUNAWAYS, 1992-93, IN THE STATE AND COUNTIES OF FLORIDA (Continued)

	1992			1992-93				
				Number of verified maltreatments in reports closed 1/				
	Child deaths	Teen violent deaths 2/						
County	3/	Number	Rate 4/	Total	Abuse	Neglect	Threat-ened harm	Run-aways 5/
Liberty	1	0	0.0	124	51	58	15	1
Madison	0	1	7.7	113	44	52	17	5
Manatee	9	5	4.7	2,526	836	1,191	499	950
Marion	8	14	12.1	1,927	619	873	435	634
Martin	3	0	0.0	531	203	210	118	242
Monroe	3	2	6.0	807	209	425	173	143
Nassau	7	2	6.1	461	209	171	81	84
Okaloosa	6	7	6.9	2,345	846	924	575	796
Okeechobee	1	3	13.3	372	171	138	63	107
Orange	50	19	3.8	9,477	3,121	4,372	1,984	4,237
Osceola	8	8	9.9	938	400	342	196	790
Palm Beach	54	23	5.3	6,603	2,364	3,199	1,040	3,375
Pasco	9	7	5.1	2,113	747	882	484	1,381
Pinellas	38	30	7.2	7,768	2,670	3,528	1,570	5,539
Polk	38	20	7.4	7,100	2,301	3,309	1,490	2,445
Putnam	6	5	11.1	1,258	449	579	230	256
St. Johns	4	6	10.7	761	298	317	146	289
St. Lucie	14	3	3.4	1,753	665	800	288	660
Santa Rosa	6	5	8.3	1,096	338	373	385	398
Sarasota	7	1	0.8	1,632	581	690	361	1,078
Seminole	14	4	1.9	2,387	952	928	507	1,329
Sumter	0	1	4.8	214	95	87	32	88
Suwannee	2	2	9.4	237	82	92	63	79
Taylor	3	0	0.0	249	80	129	40	24
Union	0	0	0.0	98	30	48	20	5
Volusia	15	10	4.5	3,621	1,182	1,699	740	1,766
Wakulla	2	0	0.0	225	84	94	47	55
Walton	0	1	5.2	383	108	182	93	17
Washington	2	1	7.7	324	95	142	87	9

1/ A maltreatment is defined as the act of treating badly, roughly, unkindly, or abusively. A "verified" finding is used where a preponderance of the credible evidence results in a determination that the specific injury or harm was the result of abuse or neglect.
2/ Deaths from homicides, suicides, and accidents to teens aged 15-19 years.
3/ Deaths from all causes to children aged 1-14 years.
4/ Per 10,000 population aged 15-19 years.
5/ As reported by the Florida Network of Youth and Family Services.

Source: University of South Florida, Florida Mental Health Institute, and State of Florida, Center for Children and Youth, *Key Facts About the Children, A Report on the Status of Florida's Children: Volume V, The 1994 Florida Kids Count Data Book,* (copyright).

Table 3.28. ACQUIRED IMMUNODEFICIENCY SYNDROME (AIDS): ADULT CASES OF AIDS, 1995 AND CUMULATIVE CASES, JANUARY 1, 1980 THROUGH DECEMBER 31, 1995 IN THE STATE AND COUNTIES OF FLORIDA

County	Number of cases		Cumulative cases 1980-95		County	Number of cases		Cumulative cases 1980-95	
	Diag- nosed	Re- port- ed 1/	Number 2/	Rate per 100,000 popula- tion 3/		Diag- nosed	Re- port- ed 1/	Number 2/	Rate per 100,000 popula- tion 3/
Florida	5,434	8,077		0.0	Lake	15	25	130	88.5
					Lee	76	114	943	302.3
Alachua	22	59	313	194.8	Leon	44	61	359	202.4
Baker	1	2	13	83.5	Levy	3	3	20	83.0
Bay	25	32	187	171.9	Liberty	0	0	3	53.3
Bradford	1	1	13	66.1	Madison	1	1	18	126.8
Brevard	92	145	796	221.1	Manatee	50	82	432	223.0
Broward	798	1,220	7,985	720.8	Marion	21	42	254	138.7
Calhoun	0	0	4	41.2	Martin	21	42	173	182.9
Charlotte	16	28	122	110.2	Monroe	56	92	778	1112.3
Citrus	6	10	60	66.2	Nassau	10	16	48	125.8
Clay	2	5	97	104.8	Okaloosa	17	21	122	97.1
Collier	48	60	438	285.7	Okeechobee	3	4	37	146.4
Columbia	4	15	50	128.5	Orange	296	517	2,743	459.5
Dade	1,667	2,249	15,740	999.7	Osceola	30	55	229	214.1
De Soto	5	9	31	144.8	Palm Beach	599	830	4,581	580.3
Dixie	0	1	6	60.2	Pasco	36	44	334	128.9
Duval	238	385	2,600	472.2	Pinellas	215	324	2,093	283.9
Escambia	64	95	604	272.8	Polk	63	102	707	200.1
Flagler	5	7	39	124.0	Putnam	6	11	80	145.6
Franklin	0	1	7	82.9	St. Johns	11	24	156	194.0
Gadsden	9	12	63	186.7	St. Lucie	60	153	640	462.7
Gilchrist	0	0	3	31.4	Santa Rosa	5	6	54	72.2
Glades	1	2	10	143.9	Sarasota	43	77	506	194.2
Gulf	1	2	5	46.2	Seminole	51	90	466	181.8
Hamilton	0	1	6	60.6	Sumter	2	5	18	60.2
Hardee	1	2	32	181.7	Suwannee	6	9	32	131.0
Hendry	7	9	70	328.4	Taylor	1	3	16	113.1
Hernando	5	8	86	86.1	Union	1	2	6	57.2
Highlands	14	17	83	127.3	Volusia	65	91	635	190.2
Hillsborough	325	421	2,961	421.7	Wakulla	4	4	17	128.0
Holmes	2	2	9	63.4	Walton	2	4	22	80.1
Indian River	12	29	113	135.1	Washington	1	2	10	65.5
Jackson	6	7	31	81.4					
Jefferson	1	2	16	150.4	Unknown	0	0	8	(X)
Lafayette	0	0	3	56.5	DOC	242	383	1,829	(X)

DOC Department of Corrections.
(X) Not applicable.
1/ Includes diagnosed cases from earlier years not previously reported. See Appendix for further discussion.
2/ Excludes 1,114 diagnosed and reported pediatric (under age 13) cases of AIDS.
3/ Based on April 1, 1995 population estimates for persons aged 15 and over.

Source: State of Florida, Department of Health and Rehabilitative Services, State Health Office, *The Florida AIDS, STD, and TB Monthly Surveillance Report,* January 1996.

Table 3.32. MARRIAGES AND DISSOLUTIONS OF MARRIAGE: NUMBER PERFORMED OR GRANTED IN THE STATE AND COUNTIES OF FLORIDA, 1994 AND 1995

County	Marriages 1/ 1994	Marriages 1/ 1995	Dissolutions of marriage 2/ 1994	Dissolutions of marriage 2/ 1995	County	Marriages 1/ 1994	Marriages 1/ 1995	Dissolutions of marriage 2/ 1994	Dissolutions of marriage 2/ 1995
Florida	142,895	145,090	81,628	78,416	Lafayette	70	85	30	51
					Lake	1,512	1,476	999	974
Alachua	1,892	1,950	1,020	966	Lee	3,379	3,328	2,022	1,953
Baker	317	281	132	132	Leon	2,268	2,293	1,169	1,061
Bay	2,096	2,036	1,254	1,203	Levy	272	268	184	162
Bradford	313	324	177	177	Liberty	43	64	21	34
Brevard	3,911	3,844	2,566	2,266	Madison	191	177	93	86
Broward	12,471	12,660	6,801	5,172	Manatee	1,909	1,842	1,011	977
Calhoun	139	116	61	104	Marion	1,988	2,137	1,453	1,518
Charlotte	1,003	934	536	570	Martin	934	963	589	518
Citrus	829	852	551	552	Monroe	1,864	1,948	492	499
Clay	1,410	1,378	768	782	Nassau	570	645	368	340
Collier	1,835	1,893	883	930	Okaloosa	2,351	2,122	1,289	1,286
Columbia	613	618	419	339	Okeechobee	377	361	197	201
Dade	23,690	24,998	11,429	12,034	Orange	8,899	9,300	4,709	4,493
De Soto	245	243	147	132	Osceola	2,694	3,113	941	937
Dixie	125	135	75	76	Palm Beach	7,950	8,060	4,585	4,301
Duval	7,270	7,281	5,492	4,539	Pasco	2,336	2,251	1,544	1,488
Escambia	3,829	3,663	1,813	1,877	Pinellas	7,762	7,879	4,606	4,789
Flagler	292	279	129	154	Polk	4,064	4,141	2,959	2,813
Franklin	116	136	76	71	Putnam	675	679	461	417
Gadsden	349	397	200	196	St. Johns	1,301	1,329	496	556
Gilchrist	138	131	57	68	St. Lucie	1,369	1,282	918	964
Glades	45	48	25	13	Santa Rosa	909	886	606	620
Gulf	160	128	75	75	Sarasota	2,595	2,586	1,928	1,844
Hamilton	136	138	77	63	Seminole	2,995	2,824	1,705	1,700
Hardee	250	216	140	125	Sumter	323	305	174	229
Hendry	462	459	205	166	Suwannee	288	294	188	201
Hernando	885	844	524	472	Taylor	197	208	145	124
Highlands	639	642	382	368	Union	118	95	51	61
Hillsborough	9,017	9,175	5,458	5,613	Volusia	3,469	3,649	2,375	2,254
Holmes	328	333	162	139	Wakulla	191	199	115	82
Indian River	836	861	560	558	Walton	411	395	277	210
Jackson	549	473	318	331	Washington	256	249	109	130
Jefferson	175	191	307	280					

1/ State total may include a few marriages performed out of state but recorded in Florida.
2/ Includes divorces and annulments.
Source: State of Florida, Department of Health and Rehabilitative Services, Public Health Statistics Section, Office of Vital Statistics, *Florida Vital Statistics, 1995,* and previous edition.

EDUCATION

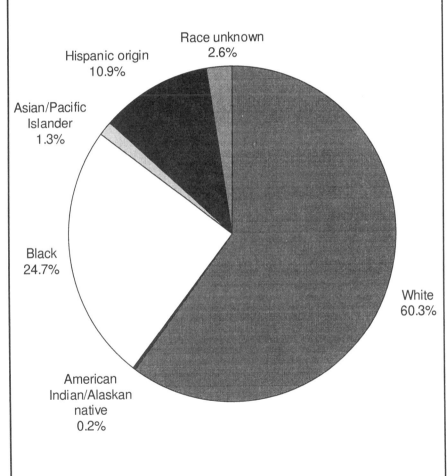

Membership in Exceptional Student Programs by Race or Hispanic origin Fall 1995

Race unknown 2.6%

Hispanic origin 10.9%

Asian/Pacific Islander 1.3%

Black 24.7%

White 60.3%

American Indian/Alaskan native 0.2%

Source: Table 4.03

SECTION 4.00
EDUCATION

TABLES LISTED BY MAJOR HEADINGS

Table 4.02. ELEMENTARY AND SECONDARY SCHOOLS: SPECIFIED STUDENT DATA IN FLORIDA, 1991-92 THROUGH 1994-95

Item	1991-92	1992-93	1993-94	1994-95	Percentage change since 1991-92
Student membership 1/	1,930,719	1,981,731	2,041,714	2,109,052	9.24
Prekindergarten	26,918	31,490	35,681	46,433	72.50
Kindergarten	161,590	161,720	167,142	172,004	6.44
Grade 1	169,986	167,609	169,055	175,026	2.96
Grade 2	164,655	169,417	168,310	169,557	2.98
Grade 3	162,599	165,863	170,876	170,567	4.90
Grade 4	159,190	164,432	168,505	173,194	8.80
Grade 5	153,254	160,342	166,156	170,309	11.13
Grade 6	148,573	155,943	163,451	169,018	13.76
Grade 7	144,600	150,821	157,890	165,490	14.45
Grade 8	135,263	142,381	149,034	155,814	15.19
Grade 9	152,004	154,399	164,988	172,850	13.71
Grade 10	134,984	138,850	140,284	147,925	9.59
Grade 11	116,996	117,538	119,696	120,030	2.59
Grade 12	100,107	100,926	100,646	100,835	0.73
Graduates (standard diplomas)	91,489	89,428	88,032	(NA)	(NA)
Exceptional student membership	296,179	311,468	329,201	350,658	18.39
Educable mentally handicapped	18,062	19,289	21,041	22,862	26.58
Trainable mentally handicapped	6,899	7,078	7,338	7,524	9.06
Speech/language and hearing	73,345	76,014	78,929	82,199	12.07
Emotionally handicapped	20,497	21,803	23,098	24,020	17.19
Specific learning disability	95,826	102,380	109,557	115,816	20.86
Gifted	65,749	67,847	70,874	78,558	19.48
Profoundly handicapped	8,336	9,074	9,726	10,466	25.55
Other exceptionalities	7,465	7,983	8,638	9,213	23.42
Disciplinary actions					
Out-of-school suspensions	159,586	177,894	184,424	(NA)	(NA)
In-school suspensions	147,709	173,033	200,547	(NA)	(NA)
Referrals to dropout prevention for disciplinary reasons	43,913	56,475	62,828	(NA)	(NA)
Corporal punishment	24,198	20,315	14,731	(NA)	(NA)
Expulsions	841	953	740	(NA)	(NA)
Referrals to court/juvenile authorities	5,839	3,386	3,219	(NA)	(NA)
Nonpromotions	67,481	77,640	82,440	(NA)	(NA)
Dropouts K-12	22,964	24,943	28,299	(NA)	(NA)

(NA) Not available.
1/ Based on fall membership survey.
Note: Data are for public schools only.

Source: State of Florida, Department of Education, Division of Administration, *Profiles of Florida School Districts, 1994-95, Student and Staff Data.* EIAS Series 96-14.

Table 4.03. ELEMENTARY AND SECONDARY SCHOOLS: MEMBERSHIP IN EXCEPTIONAL STUDENT PROGRAMS BY RACE OR HISPANIC ORIGIN IN FLORIDA, FALL 1995

Program	Total exceptional membership		Race				
	Number	As a percentage of all students	White	Black	Asian/ Pacific Islander	American Indian/ Alaskan native	Hispanic origin 1/
Total	368,710	17.0	A/ 222,413	A/ 91,064	A/ 4,947	A/ 780	A/ 40,099
Educable mentally handicapped	24,670	1.2	8,679	13,417	134	39	2,401
Trainable mentally handicapped	7,719	0.4	3,628	2,821	95	7	1,168
Specific learning disability	122,493	5.8	74,168	30,782	572	252	16,719
Emotionally handicapped	24,666	1.2	13,436	9,111	58	49	2,012
Speech/language and hearing	85,232	4.0	51,915	24,058	795	205	8,259
Profoundly handicapped	11,192	0.5	5,774	3,945	102	21	1,350
Gifted	83,331	4.0	64,813	6,930	3,191	207	8,190
Other exceptionalities 2/	9,407	0.4	(NA)	(NA)	(NA)	(NA)	(NA)

(NA) Not available.
A/ Does not include other exceptionalities.
1/ Persons of Hispanic origin may be of any race. However, these data are not distributed by race.
2/ Includes physically and visually handicapped, physical and occupational therapy, and hospital/homebound students.
Note: Data were obtained from the Florida DOE Student Information Data Base, Survey 2, as of January 4, 1996 and are for public schools only.

Source: State of Florida, Department of Education, Division of Administration, *Statistical Brief: Membership in Programs for Exceptional Students, Fall 1995*. Series 96-17B.

Table 4.05. ELEMENTARY AND SECONDARY SCHOOLS: SPECIFIED CHARACTERISTICS IN FLORIDA, 1979-80 THROUGH 1994-95

School year	Resident population 1/ Total	Resident population 1/ Aged 5-17	Fall member-ship 2/	Public high school graduates 3/	Instruc-tional personnel
1979-80	9,245,231	1,800,331	1,502,846	87,826	84,623
1980-81	9,739,992	1,876,269	1,508,125	88,755	87,891
1981-82	10,375,332	1,998,658	1,485,593	89,199	88,912
1982-83	10,591,701	2,040,338	1,482,270	86,871	89,898
1983-84	10,891,701	1,724,795	1,492,366	85,908	90,348
1984-85	10,930,389	1,752,422	1,520,975	81,140	94,048
1985-86	11,287,932	1,675,790	1,559,507	81,508	97,139
1986-87	11,549,831	1,667,636	1,603,033	83,692	100,498
1987-88	12,043,618	1,688,627	1,664,563	90,792	104,848
1988-89	12,417,608	1,695,383	1,720,927	92,449	109,865
1989-90	13,152,691	1,700,468	1,789,925	90,790	114,501
1990-91	12,937,926	2,016,641	1,861,671	89,494	119,123
1991-92	13,195,952	2,057,688	1,930,719	93,368	121,185
1992-93	13,424,416	2,100,608	1,981,731	91,423	118,713
1993-94	13,608,627	2,135,410	2,041,714	90,034	124,027
1994-95	14,149,317	2,207,525	2,109,052	(NA)	129,223

School year	Average teacher salary 4/ (dollars)	Number of schools	Assessed valuation of property ($1,000)	Total expenditure all purposes ($1,000)	Current expense per pupil 5/ (dollars)
1979-80	14,149.02	2,302	147,170,490	3,316,050	1,832
1980-81	15,404.90	2,345	147,965,109	3,755,837	2,058
1981-82	16,779.52	2,347	193,536,278	4,133,541	2,283
1982-83	18,351.76	2,350	226,683,285	4,521,420	2,463
1983-84	19,449.12	2,284	243,385,858	4,950,393	2,676
1984-85	20,836.47	2,304	266,774,135	5,461,194	2,964
1985-86	22,250.08	2,296	323,579,927	6,103,747	3,205
1986-87	23,733.76	2,400	353,683,447	6,909,814	3,423
1987-88	25,198.00	2,438	378,703,589	7,643,660	3,679
1988-89	26,974.00	2,485	411,786,114	8,793,842	3,964
1989-90	28,803.00	2,591	414,018,411	10,125,835	4,248
1990-91	30,555.00	2,694	449,979,199	11,308,952	4,475
1991-92	31,067.00	2,730	475,960,538	11,745,293	4,439
1992-93	31,174.00	2,784	479,892,429	11,750,331	4,525
1993-94	31,948.00	2,867	488,458,004	12,780,952	4,724
1994-95	32,600.00	2,946	(NA)	(NA)	(NA)

(NA) Not available.

1/ Population figures for noncensus years are mid-year estimates as of April 1; 1985-86 through 1989-90 population breakdowns are for aged 15-24. Population figures as of 1992-93 are from the University of Florida, Bureau of Economic and Business Research, Population Program and are unpublished.

2/ Based on fall membership survey.

3/ Regular day school only; excludes state/university schools and adult programs. Includes standard and special diplomas.

4/ A professional paid on the instructional salary schedule negotiated by a Florida school district.

5/ Based on full-time equivalent student count.

Note: Data are for public schools only.

Source: State of Florida, Department of Education, *Profiles of Florida School Districts, 1994-95, Student and Staff Data,* and *Profiles of Florida School Districts, 1993-94, Financial Data Statistical Report.*

Table 4.06. ELEMENTARY AND SECONDARY SCHOOLS: ENROLLMENT IN KINDERGARTEN THROUGH GRADE TWELVE IN THE STATE AND COUNTIES OF FLORIDA 1985-86 THROUGH 1994-95

School year	Total enrollment	Public schools Enrollment	Public schools Percentage of total	Nonpublic schools 1/ Enrollment	Nonpublic schools 1/ Percentage of total
1985-86	1,764,340	1,559,507	88.39	204,833	11.61
1986-87	1,806,075	1,603,033	88.76	203,042	11.24
1987-88	1,861,904	1,658,624	89.08	203,380	10.92
1988-89	1,910,310	1,712,613	89.65	197,695	10.35
1989-90	1,973,333	1,775,529	89.98	197,804	10.02
1990-91	2,035,145	1,841,206	90.47	193,939	9.53
1991-92	2,097,761	1,902,563	90.69	195,198	9.31
1992-93	2,150,377	1,950,114	90.69	200,263	9.31
1993-94	2,227,240	2,005,970	90.06	221,270	9.93
1994-95	2,298,752	2,064,884	89.82	233,868	10.17

1/ Private (nonpublic) elementary and secondary schools in Florida are not licensed, approved, accredited, or regulated by the state but they are required to make their existence known to the Department of Education and respond to an annual survey. See Glossary under Private school for definition.

Note: Based on DOE survey taken during the school year. Data may differ slightly from data based on fall surveys as shown in other *Abstract* tables.

Source: State of Florida, Department of Education, Division of Administration, *Statistical Brief: Florida's Nonpublic Schools, 1994-95*. Series 96-6B.

Table 4.07. ELEMENTARY AND SECONDARY SCHOOLS: CHANGE IN MEMBERSHIP IN PREKINDERGARTEN THROUGH GRADE TWELVE IN THE STATE AND COUNTIES OF FLORIDA, FALL 1991 TO FALL 1995

County	Number	Percentage	County	Number	Percentage	County	Number	Percentage
Florida	245,335	12.71	Glades	128	13.14	Nassau	800	9.11
			Gulf	45	2.01	Okaloosa	2,342	8.64
Alachua	1,962	7.21	Hamilton	48	2.08	Okeechobee	548	9.28
Baker	312	7.22	Hardee	907	20.66	Orange	16,401	15.38
Bay	2,562	11.30	Hendry	953	15.59	Osceola	4,925	23.74
Bradford	-67	-1.60	Hernando	1,968	14.66	Palm Beach	21,449	19.36
Brevard	6,747	11.46	Highlands	1,257	13.23	Pasco	6,253	17.60
Broward	38,239	22.48	Hillsborough	15,777	12.38	Pinellas	7,995	8.30
Calhoun	130	6.05	Holmes	325	9.46	Polk	5,963	8.92
Charlotte	2,008	14.78	Indian River	1,627	13.51	Putnam	575	4.65
Citrus	1,787	14.71	Jackson	123	1.56	St. Johns	2,857	22.78
Clay	2,430	10.83	Jefferson	-12	-0.56	St. Lucie	4,288	18.84
Collier	4,521	20.69	Lafayette	-57	-5.14	Santa Rosa	3,499	21.49
Columbia	785	9.40	Lake	2,979	13.64	Sarasota	2,212	7.67
Dade	29,215	9.59	Lee	6,646	15.00	Seminole	3,763	7.40
De Soto	477	11.83	Leon	2,947	10.38	Sumter	480	9.08
Dixie	330	16.98	Levy	822	16.73	Suwannee	209	3.81
Duval	7,946	6.85	Liberty	86	7.44	Taylor	294	8.18
Escambia	1,111	2.52	Madison	170	5.21	Union	252	13.01
Flagler	1,113	26.20	Manatee	4,381	15.98	Volusia	6,688	13.35
Franklin	80	4.92	Marion	5,069	16.64	Wakulla	764	21.79
Gadsden	333	3.99	Martin	2,168	17.77	Walton	613	13.27
Gilchrist	546	27.55	Monroe	1,111	13.23	Washington	130	4.27

Source: State of Florida, Department of Education, Division of Administration, *Statistical Brief: Membership in Florida Public Schools, Fall 1995*. Series 96-16B.

Table 4.20. ELEMENTARY AND SECONDARY SCHOOLS: PUPIL MEMBERSHIP IN PREKINDERGARTEN THROUGH GRADE TWELVE BY RACE OR HISPANIC ORIGIN IN THE STATE AND COUNTIES OF FLORIDA, FALL 1995

		Percentage of membership				
		Race				
County	Total	White	Black	Asian/ Pacific Islander	American Indian/ Alaskan native	Hispanic origin 1/
Florida	2,175,233	57.49	25.25	1.76	0.22	15.28
Alachua	29,166	57.66	36.91	2.20	0.15	3.08
Baker	4,635	82.29	17.35	0.17	0.06	0.13
Bay	25,228	80.94	15.25	2.28	0.27	1.27
Bradford	4,113	76.27	22.34	0.63	0.12	0.63
Brevard	65,619	79.81	14.64	1.82	0.25	3.48
Broward	208,354	48.99	34.87	2.53	0.26	13.35
Calhoun	2,279	82.05	16.32	0.35	0.13	1.14
Charlotte	15,593	87.00	8.61	1.25	0.20	2.94
Citrus	13,934	91.59	4.71	1.09	0.19	2.42
Clay	24,875	86.64	9.05	1.89	0.17	2.26
Collier	26,376	64.37	10.96	0.43	0.44	23.81
Columbia	9,137	72.64	24.63	0.71	0.23	1.79
Dade	333,831	14.20	33.82	1.31	0.08	50.60
De Soto	4,508	61.98	21.98	0.53	0.20	15.31
Dixie	2,274	88.35	11.17	0.04	0.00	0.44
Duval	123,905	54.78	39.88	2.66	0.14	2.54
Escambia	45,215	61.10	34.35	2.88	0.54	1.13
Flagler	5,361	78.36	14.96	1.62	0.22	4.83
Franklin	1,706	80.13	18.70	0.41	0.12	0.64
Gadsden	8,674	8.75	85.21	0.09	0.03	5.91
Gilchrist	2,528	93.59	5.50	0.04	0.08	0.79
Glades	1,102	49.27	29.31	0.09	1.45	19.87
Gulf	2,279	78.98	20.14	0.31	0.18	0.39
Hamilton	2,360	45.89	50.34	0.13	0.08	3.56
Hardee	5,298	47.13	8.87	0.13	0.15	43.71
Hendry	7,064	45.14	19.97	0.58	0.52	33.78
Hernando	15,393	86.60	7.95	0.78	0.12	4.56
Highlands	10,758	65.20	21.61	0.70	0.47	12.02
Hillsborough	143,192	57.04	23.96	1.91	0.33	16.76
Holmes	3,759	95.93	3.19	0.24	0.13	0.51
Indian River	13,669	74.74	18.36	0.65	0.20	6.05
Jackson	7,991	65.10	33.29	0.25	0.24	1.13
Jefferson	2,126	30.71	68.81	0.19	0.05	0.24
Lafayette	1,052	84.51	11.98	0.00	0.00	3.52
Lake	24,827	75.66	18.17	0.79	0.18	5.20
Lee	50,945	71.99	15.86	1.03	0.20	10.93

See footnotes at end of table. Continued . . .

Table 4.20. ELEMENTARY AND SECONDARY SCHOOLS: PUPIL MEMBERSHIP IN PREKINDERGARTEN THROUGH GRADE TWELVE BY RACE OR HISPANIC ORIGIN IN THE STATE AND COUNTIES OF FLORIDA, FALL 1995 (Continued)

		Percentage of membership				
		Race				
County	Total	White	Black	Asian/ Pacific Islander	American Indian/ Alaskan native	Hispanic origin 1/
Leon	31,332	58.98	37.79	1.53	0.11	1.59
Levy	5,736	78.94	18.57	0.33	0.12	2.04
Liberty	1,242	84.22	12.32	0.16	0.08	3.22
Madison	3,434	40.16	58.94	0.09	0.03	0.79
Manatee	31,803	71.01	17.68	0.76	0.11	10.45
Marion	35,527	71.89	22.09	0.64	0.19	5.18
Martin	14,369	77.24	12.95	0.82	0.10	8.89
Monroe	9,508	73.34	9.54	1.06	0.23	15.83
Nassau	9,579	86.63	12.19	0.35	0.13	0.70
Okaloosa	29,454	80.49	12.74	3.36	0.41	3.00
Okeechobee	6,456	70.83	8.66	0.54	1.86	18.11
Orange	123,064	52.36	27.93	3.31	0.28	16.12
Osceola	25,670	60.59	9.98	2.60	0.18	26.66
Palm Beach	132,215	55.05	29.09	1.95	0.31	13.60
Pasco	41,791	88.99	4.02	1.12	0.19	5.68
Pinellas	104,331	75.70	18.88	2.55	0.15	2.72
Polk	72,807	68.19	23.24	0.83	0.16	7.58
Putnam	12,935	64.31	28.38	0.57	0.17	6.56
St. Johns	15,396	85.26	12.11	0.77	0.14	1.73
St. Lucie	27,045	60.58	31.34	0.90	0.22	6.96
Santa Rosa	19,779	91.79	5.30	1.33	0.42	1.15
Sarasota	31,035	83.76	10.80	1.29	0.14	4.00
Seminole	54,599	72.36	14.65	2.77	0.20	10.01
Sumter	5,767	68.51	27.21	0.40	0.31	3.57
Suwannee	5,690	78.42	19.19	0.23	0.07	2.09
Taylor	3,889	72.02	26.69	0.26	0.39	0.64
Union	2,189	79.12	19.42	0.46	0.05	0.96
Volusia	56,788	75.93	16.21	0.97	0.20	6.68
Wakulla	4,270	85.62	13.61	0.30	0.26	0.21
Walton	5,233	85.82	11.35	0.94	0.54	1.36
Washington	3,174	78.92	19.06	0.76	0.54	0.72

1/ Persons of Hispanic origin may be of any race. However, these data are not distributed by race.

Note: Data were obtained from the Florida DOE Student Information Data Base, Survey 2, as of January 4, 1996 and are for public schools only.

Source: State of Florida, Department of Education, Division of Administration, *Statistical Brief: Membership in Florida Public Schools, Fall 1995.* Series 96-16B.

Table 4.23. SECONDARY SCHOOLS: DISTRIBUTION OF DROPOUTS BY SPECIFIED RACE OR HISPANIC ORIGIN IN THE STATE AND COUNTIES OF FLORIDA
1993-94

County	Total	Percentage distribution 1/ Race White	Black	Hispanic origin 2/
Florida	28,299	47.04	31.30	20.45
Alachua	520	41.92	54.62	1.92
Baker	64	68.75	29.69	0.00
Bay	253	81.42	17.00	0.00
Bradford	78	61.54	37.18	1.28
Brevard	387	70.28	24.81	2.84
Broward	3,011	46.53	37.00	14.81
Calhoun	21	95.24	4.76	0.00
Charlotte	214	91.59	6.54	1.40
Citrus	193	92.75	5.70	1.04
Clay	226	75.22	18.14	4.87
Collier	394	46.45	13.96	38.83
Columbia	138	63.04	34.06	0.72
Dade	6,833	11.24	36.95	51.30
De Soto	43	48.84	27.91	23.26
Dixie	43	97.67	0.00	2.33
Duval	1,415	53.43	41.06	2.33
Escambia	198	49.49	48.48	1.01
Flagler	15	86.67	6.67	6.67
Franklin	8	50.00	50.00	0.00
Gadsden	153	13.73	84.31	1.96
Gilchrist	23	95.65	4.35	0.00
Glades	24	62.50	12.50	20.83
Gulf	11	45.45	36.36	18.18
Hamilton	49	40.82	55.10	4.08
Hardee	90	36.67	10.00	53.33
Hendry	104	40.38	20.19	35.58
Hernando	184	80.98	15.22	3.80
Highlands	177	65.54	20.90	12.99
Hillsborough	984	56.20	26.12	16.36
Holmes	32	96.88	3.13	0.00
Indian River	127	70.08	23.62	6.30
Jackson	69	75.36	24.64	0.00
Jefferson	18	16.67	83.33	0.00
Lafayette	20	90.00	10.00	0.00
Lake	423	76.83	18.91	4.02
Lee	695	61.73	23.74	13.81
Leon	307	42.35	57.33	0.00
Levy	88	64.77	29.55	5.68
Liberty	3	100.00	0.00	0.00
Madison	76	28.95	69.74	1.32
Manatee	363	58.40	24.79	15.70
Marion	389	70.95	24.42	4.37
Martin	127	73.23	19.69	6.30
Monroe	213	62.91	12.68	22.54
Nassau	79	87.34	12.66	0.00
Okaloosa	279	71.68	21.15	3.58
Okeechobee	137	58.39	10.95	28.47
Orange	1,184	46.03	32.52	19.59
Osceola	310	59.03	11.29	28.39
Palm Beach	1,878	44.36	34.88	19.49
Pasco	487	87.68	5.54	5.95
Pinellas	1,450	66.90	28.62	1.93
Polk	982	64.05	26.48	8.86
Putnam	196	64.80	32.14	2.55
St. Johns	267	65.92	31.46	1.87
St. Lucie	369	54.47	38.48	5.96
Santa Rosa	121	87.60	9.09	1.65
Sarasota	326	66.87	25.46	6.75
Seminole	477	62.89	22.43	12.79
Sumter	93	70.97	24.73	3.23
Suwannee	57	77.19	19.30	3.51
Taylor	68	64.71	29.41	4.41
Union	11	90.91	9.09	0.00
Volusia	610	68.03	22.95	8.03
Wakulla	28	85.71	14.29	0.00
Walton	45	93.33	6.67	0.00
Washington	26	73.08	26.92	0.00
Dozier School	16	56.25	43.75	0.00

1/ Does not include other races. Distribution may not add to 100 percent.
2/ Persons of Hispanic origin may be of any race. However, these data are not distributed by race.
Note: A dropout is a student over the age of compulsory school attendance (16) who meets one or more of the criteria set forth by the Department of Education. Data are for public schools only. Some data are revised. See Glossary for definition.

Source: State of Florida, Department of Education, Division of Public Schools, Bureau of Information and Accountability Services, unpublished data.

Table 4.26. NONPUBLIC ELEMENTARY AND SECONDARY SCHOOLS: PUPIL MEMBERSHIP IN THE STATE AND COUNTIES OF FLORIDA, 1994-95

County	Membership K-12	Percentage change 1993-94 to 1994-95	As a percentage of total K-12 membership	County	Membership K-12	Percentage change 1993-94 to 1994-95	As a percentage of total K-12 membership
Florida	233,868	5.69	10.17	Lafayette	0	0.00	0.00
				Lake	1,714	-9.36	6.86
Alachua	1,991	10.12	6.71	Lee	4,765	10.56	9.02
Baker	0	0.00	0.00	Leon	4,144	6.69	12.30
Bay	1,542	9.75	5.98	Levy	50	-19.35	0.92
Bradford	4	-20.00	0.10	Liberty	0	0.00	0.00
Brevard	7,179	9.54	10.15	Madison	207	65.60	6.15
Broward	26,206	5.31	11.87	Manatee	2,486	5.88	7.61
Calhoun	0	0.00	0.00	Marion	3,591	-5.03	9.80
Charlotte	646	-0.62	4.21	Martin	1,578	4.99	10.55
Citrus	535	15.80	3.87	Monroe	544	3.03	5.61
Clay	2,207	0.41	8.56	Nassau	319	7.77	3.34
Collier	2,016	7.92	7.67	Okaloosa	1,319	26.10	4.40
Columbia	365	23.73	4.00	Okeechobee	212	5.47	3.40
Dade	49,466	4.26	13.58	Orange	15,885	7.48	11.97
De Soto	37	37.04	0.87	Osceola	1,018	51.94	4.10
Dixie	0	0.00	0.00	Palm Beach	18,581	7.99	12.93
Duval	16,357	8.23	12.12	Pasco	1,659	8.93	4.08
Escambia	5,209	1.07	10.70	Pinellas	14,391	1.93	12.53
Flagler	0	0.00	0.00	Polk	4,830	9.13	6.45
Franklin	107	50.70	6.44	Putnam	657	14.66	5.01
Gadsden	721	3.89	8.26	St. Johns	1,167	6.97	7.49
Gilchrist	325	23.11	12.53	St. Lucie	1,958	-0.91	7.10
Glades	0	0.00	0.00	Santa Rosa	292	2.82	1.55
Gulf	141	(X)	6.18	Sarasota	4,179	7.71	12.30
Hamilton	0	0.00	0.00	Seminole	5,986	6.80	10.27
Hardee	69	64.29	1.54	Sumter	89	111.90	1.61
Hendry	236	29.67	3.48	Suwannee	299	10.74	5.21
Hernando	894	19.04	5.76	Taylor	16	-44.83	0.45
Highlands	489	-3.74	4.56	Union	0	0.00	0.00
Hillsborough	18,302	1.46	11.89	Volusia	4,610	9.92	7.79
Holmes	0	0.00	0.00	Wakulla	25	(X)	0.63
Indian River	1,622	11.86	11.18	Walton	66	13.79	1.31
Jackson	203	19.41	2.56	Washington	0	0.00	0.00
Jefferson	362	0.28	15.35				

K-12 Kindergarten through grade 12; no prekindergarten.
(X) Not applicable.
Note: See Glossary under Private school for definition of nonpublic schools.
Source: State of Florida, Department of Education, Division of Administration, *Statistical Brief: Florida's Nonpublic Schools, 1994-95.* Series 96-6B.

Table 4.27. ELEMENTARY AND SECONDARY SCHOOLS: NUMBER AND PUPIL MEMBERSHIP IN THE STATE AND COUNTIES OF FLORIDA, 1994-95

County	Number of schools	Membership 1/ Total	Membership 1/ Percentage change from 1993-94	County	Number of schools	Membership 1/ Total	Membership 1/ Percentage change from 1993-94
Florida 2/	2,946	2,062,619	2.8	Lake	47	23,277	4.0
				Lee	75	48,073	3.6
Alachua	45	27,694	1.2	Leon	46	29,552	2.1
Baker	8	4,485	1.4	Levy	15	5,383	4.7
Bay	35	24,248	3.6	Liberty	5	1,110	1.8
Bradford	10	3,995	-0.8	Madison	9	3,159	-0.9
Brevard	100	63,541	2.7	Manatee	67	30,174	4.1
Broward	192	194,614	4.5	Marion	49	33,069	3.9
Calhoun	7	2,184	1.5	Martin	31	13,385	4.3
Charlotte	22	14,704	3.1	Monroe	17	9,159	4.9
Citrus	19	13,293	3.2	Nassau	18	9,241	2.6
Clay	28	23,561	3.1	Okaloosa	37	28,662	0.5
Collier	37	24,281	4.5	Okeechobee	14	6,022	1.4
Columbia	14	8,755	2.4	Orange	165	116,817	3.5
Dade	350	314,853	2.5	Osceola	30	23,820	4.4
De Soto	13	4,230	3.1	Palm Beach	161	125,084	4.1
Dixie	6	2,160	3.6	Pasco	52	38,961	4.2
Duval	157	118,652	1.1	Pinellas	146	100,460	1.9
Escambia	70	43,480	0.1	Polk	112	70,099	2.0
Flagler	9	4,889	4.7	Putnam	22	12,468	0.3
Franklin	7	1,554	-0.6	St. Johns	26	14,417	6.1
Gadsden	23	8,010	0.5	St. Lucie	34	25,631	3.5
Gilchrist	7	2,268	7.4	Santa Rosa	30	18,513	4.7
Glades	8	1,014	6.1	Sarasota	38	29,785	1.3
Gulf	7	2,141	0.1	Seminole	55	52,305	1.0
Hamilton	10	2,276	2.1	Sumter	13	5,451	2.1
Hardee	11	4,426	-9.3	Suwannee	8	5,445	0.8
Hendry	15	6,553	3.7	Taylor	9	3,544	1.1
Hernando	19	14,614	3.0	Union	5	2,033	2.4
Highlands	16	10,234	4.8	Volusia	76	54,606	2.8
Hillsborough	187	135,589	2.5	Wakulla	6	3,915	3.4
Holmes	8	3,618	1.1	Walton	11	4,990	4.6
Indian River	22	12,884	4.4	Washington	10	3,044	-0.1
Jackson	19	7,740	0.1	Deaf/Blind	10	612	6.3
Jefferson	7	1,997	0.5	Dozier School	3	258	0.4
Lafayette	5	983	-1.1				

1/ Based on kindergarten through grade 12 fall membership survey.
2/ Detail may not add to total due to receipt of reports not distributed by county.
Note: Data are for public schools only.

Source: State of Florida, Department of Education, Division of Administration, *Profiles of Florida School Districts, 1994-95, Student and Staff Data.* EIAS Series 96-14.

Table 4.28. ELEMENTARY AND SECONDARY SCHOOLS: PUPIL PARTICIPATION IN THE FREE AND REDUCED SCHOOL LUNCH PROGRAMS BY RACE OR HISPANIC ORIGIN IN THE STATE AND COUNTIES OF FLORIDA, 1995-96

County	Free lunch							Reduced lunch						
		Race							Race					
	Total 1/	White	Percentage	Black	Percentage	Hispanic origin 2/	Percentage	Total 1/	White	Percentage	Black	Percentage	Hispanic origin 2/	Percentage
Florida	808,417	263,885	12.13	350,809	16.12	182,243	8.37	141,179	80,400	3.69	32,282	1.48	25,315	1.16
Alachua	11,295	3,212	11.01	7,552	25.89	334	1.15	1,630	865	2.97	677	2.32	51	0.17
Baker	1,691	1,093	23.58	596	12.86	2	0.04	273	218	4.70	55	1.19	0	0.00
Bay	8,731	5,857	23.22	2,433	9.64	132	0.52	2,527	2,042	8.09	370	1.47	59	0.23
Bradford	1,699	1,044	25.35	623	15.13	17	0.41	288	206	5.00	82	1.99	0	0.00
Brevard	15,970	9,230	14.07	5,563	8.48	902	1.37	3,713	2,875	4.38	512	0.78	227	0.35
Broward	65,832	11,946	5.73	41,870	20.10	10,700	5.14	12,602	4,258	2.04	4,992	2.40	2,926	1.40
Calhoun	891	587	25.76	287	12.59	14	0.61	155	134	5.88	21	0.92	0	0.00
Charlotte	4,762	3,496	22.42	925	5.93	275	1.76	1,794	1,592	10.21	126	0.81	49	0.31
Citrus	5,071	4,467	32.06	420	3.01	145	1.04	986	918	6.59	33	0.24	26	0.19
Clay	4,244	2,951	11.86	1,024	4.12	193	0.78	1,584	1,234	4.96	224	0.90	86	0.35
Collier	8,884	2,598	9.85	1,994	7.56	4,217	15.99	1,419	913	3.46	110	0.42	379	1.44
Columbia	4,128	2,370	25.94	1,650	18.06	89	0.97	589	410	4.49	165	1.81	11	0.12
Dade	176,617	8,658	2.59	74,045	22.18	92,593	27.74	18,390	2,000	0.60	4,129	1.24	12,005	3.60
De Soto	2,378	1,059	23.49	747	16.57	560	12.42	395	256	5.68	91	2.02	48	1.06
Dixie	1,173	973	42.84	194	8.54	5	0.22	165	149	6.56	16	0.70	0	0.00
Duval	47,420	14,038	11.33	31,210	25.19	1,331	1.07	9,845	5,031	4.06	4,068	3.28	419	0.34
Escambia	20,646	8,155	18.04	11,534	25.51	235	0.52	4,239	2,760	6.10	1,203	2.66	85	0.19
Flagler	1,718	1,026	19.14	543	10.13	114	2.13	431	325	6.06	57	1.06	44	0.82
Franklin	865	608	35.62	252	14.76	5	0.29	149	122	7.15	25	1.46	2	0.12
Gadsden	5,810	286	3.30	5,109	58.90	409	4.72	529	52	0.60	469	5.41	8	0.09
Gilchrist	1,055	934	36.93	104	4.11	17	0.67	206	199	7.87	5	0.20	2	0.08
Glades	505	163	14.79	176	15.97	157	14.25	67	37	3.36	22	2.00	8	0.73
Gulf	910	606	26.59	294	12.90	6	0.26	172	119	5.22	52	2.28	0	0.00

See footnotes at end of table.

Continued . . .

Table 4.28. ELEMENTARY AND SECONDARY SCHOOLS: PUPIL PARTICIPATION IN THE FREE AND REDUCED SCHOOL LUNCH PROGRAMS BY RACE OR HISPANIC ORIGIN IN THE STATE AND COUNTIES OF FLORIDA, 1995-96 (Continued)

County	Free lunch Total 1/	Free lunch Race White	Per-cent-age	Black	Per-cent-age	His-panic ori-gin 2/	Per-cent-age	Reduced lunch Total 1/	Reduced lunch Race White	Per-cent-age	Black	Per-cent-age	His-panic ori-gin 2/	Per-cent-age
Hamilton	1,258	322	13.64	865	36.65	70	2.97	169	71	3.01	95	4.03	3	0.13
Hardee	1,895	583	10.95	246	4.62	1,061	19.92	242	138	2.59	19	0.36	85	1.60
Hendry	3,509	852	12.06	890	12.60	1,751	24.79	340	181	2.56	57	0.81	96	1.36
Hernando	5,483	4,202	27.30	841	5.46	395	2.57	1,266	1,113	7.23	96	0.62	50	0.32
Highlands	4,957	2,073	19.27	1,825	16.96	1,018	9.46	875	664	6.17	125	1.16	82	0.76
Hillsborough	59,443	18,747	13.09	24,473	17.09	15,216	10.63	9,831	5,421	3.79	2,398	1.67	1,804	1.26
Holmes	1,786	1,691	44.99	81	2.15	10	0.27	422	414	11.01	4	0.11	3	0.08
Indian River	4,746	2,294	16.79	1,795	13.14	630	4.61	908	712	5.21	159	1.16	33	0.24
Jackson	3,373	1,580	19.77	1,732	21.67	47	0.59	743	464	5.81	268	3.35	8	0.10
Jefferson	1,343	253	11.90	1,084	50.99	3	0.14	151	60	2.82	91	4.28	0	0.00
Lafayette	416	298	28.33	88	8.37	30	2.85	75	62	5.89	8	0.76	5	0.48
Lake	8,655	4,660	18.77	3,083	12.42	852	3.43	1,518	1,083	4.36	315	1.27	98	0.39
Lee	17,779	8,027	15.76	5,863	11.51	3,744	7.35	4,492	3,352	6.58	537	1.05	544	1.07
Leon	6,948	1,391	4.44	5,373	17.15	107	0.34	1,101	447	1.43	596	1.90	35	0.11
Levy	2,795	1,892	33.00	812	14.16	79	1.38	480	392	6.84	80	1.40	8	0.14
Liberty	521	382	30.76	108	8.70	31	2.50	89	72	5.80	14	1.13	3	0.24
Madison	2,049	442	12.87	1,585	46.16	22	0.64	247	125	3.64	121	3.52	1	0.03
Manatee	11,428	4,737	14.89	4,002	12.58	2,635	8.28	2,512	1,888	5.94	386	1.21	201	0.63
Marion	15,158	8,412	23.68	5,481	15.43	1,176	3.31	2,740	2,012	5.66	583	1.64	129	0.36
Martin	3,658	1,557	10.84	1,247	8.68	834	5.80	631	482	3.35	96	0.67	47	0.33
Monroe	2,717	1,207	12.69	557	5.86	925	9.73	538	365	3.84	74	0.78	82	0.86
Nassau	2,344	1,622	16.93	678	7.08	27	0.28	666	564	5.89	88	0.92	9	0.09
Okaloosa	6,429	4,251	14.43	1,775	6.03	223	0.76	2,681	2,045	6.94	370	1.26	140	0.48
Okeechobee	2,986	1,593	24.67	385	5.96	965	14.95	485	403	6.24	38	0.59	36	0.56
Orange	40,188	10,522	8.54	18,300	14.86	10,246	8.32	6,561	3,031	2.46	1,531	1.24	1,751	1.42

See footnotes at end of table.

Continued . . .

Table 4.28. ELEMENTARY AND SECONDARY SCHOOLS: PUPIL PARTICIPATION IN THE FREE AND REDUCED SCHOOL LUNCH PROGRAMS BY RACE OR HISPANIC ORIGIN IN THE STATE AND COUNTIES OF FLORIDA, 1995-96 (Continued)

County	Free lunch							Reduced lunch						
		Race							Race					
	Total 1/	White	Percentage	Black	Percentage	Hispanic origin 2/	Percentage	Total 1/	White	Percentage	Black	Percentage	Hispanic origin 2/	Percentage
Osceola	8,481	3,110	12.12	1,323	5.15	3,856	15.02	2,326	1,210	4.71	222	0.86	827	3.22
Palm Beach	40,235	8,136	6.15	22,787	17.23	8,719	6.59	5,031	2,443	1.85	1,431	1.08	988	0.75
Pasco	14,856	11,950	28.59	1,190	2.85	1,558	3.73	3,524	3,194	7.64	104	0.25	182	0.44
Pinellas	31,620	15,844	15.19	13,166	12.62	1,502	1.44	6,784	5,034	4.82	1,241	1.19	233	0.22
Polk	32,077	15,265	20.97	12,303	16.90	4,275	5.87	5,684	4,100	5.63	1,206	1.66	327	0.45
Putnam	7,053	3,366	26.02	2,861	22.12	768	5.94	854	645	4.99	195	1.51	9	0.07
St. Johns	3,028	1,833	11.91	1,105	7.18	76	0.49	711	556	3.61	134	0.87	17	0.11
St. Lucie	11,590	4,122	15.24	6,134	22.68	1,226	4.53	2,043	1,508	5.58	405	1.50	105	0.39
Santa Rosa	4,874	4,168	21.09	571	2.89	66	0.33	1,248	1,096	5.55	87	0.44	20	0.10
Sarasota	7,863	4,602	14.83	2,390	7.70	768	2.47	2,398	2,038	6.57	213	0.69	102	0.33
Seminole	10,940	4,397	8.05	4,221	7.73	2,106	3.86	2,789	1,650	3.02	523	0.96	517	0.95
Sumter	3,117	1,632	28.30	1,282	22.23	180	3.12	455	365	6.30	83	1.44	1	0.02
Suwannee	2,144	1,324	23.27	727	12.78	87	1.53	316	267	4.69	47	0.83	2	0.04
Taylor	1,754	989	25.43	750	19.29	10	0.26	215	154	3.96	57	1.47	0	0.00
Union	764	452	20.65	292	13.34	17	0.78	151	114	5.21	35	1.60	2	0.09
Volusia	18,886	10,170	17.91	6,115	10.77	2,413	4.25	3,751	2,917	5.14	506	0.89	289	0.51
Wakulla	1,270	859	20.12	395	9.25	3	0.07	289	240	5.62	48	1.12	0	0.00
Walton	2,334	1,805	34.49	455	8.69	47	0.90	436	394	7.53	31	0.59	3	0.06
Washington	1,372	914	28.80	428	13.48	17	0.54	263	199	6.27	61	1.92	3	0.09

1/ Includes other races not shown separately.
2/ Persons of Hispanic origin may be of any race. However, these data are not distributed by race.
Note: Data were obtained from the Florida DOE Student Information Data Base, Survey 2 as of February 2, 1996 and are for public schools only. The percentage of students participating in these programs is shown as a percentage of total pupil membership.

Source: State of Florida, Department of Education, Division of Public Schools, Bureau of Information and Accountability Services, unpublished data.

Table 4.50. HIGHER EDUCATION: ENROLLMENT IN SELECTED COLLEGES AND UNIVERSITIES IN SPECIFIED CITIES AND COUNTIES OF FLORIDA ACADEMIC YEAR 1994-95

School 1/	City	County	Enrollment 2/
Art Institute of Ft. Lauderdale	Ft. Lauderdale	Broward	1,802
ATI Health Education Center	Miami	Dade	175
Barry University	Miami	Dade	6,850
Barry University/Brevard County branch	Merritt Island	Brevard	279
Bethune Cookman College	Daytona Beach	Volusia	2,210
Brevard Community College	Cocoa	Brevard	14,425
Broward Community College	Ft. Lauderdale	Broward	25,714
Caribbean Center for Advanced Studies/ Miami Institute of Psychology	Miami	Dade	427
Central Florida Community College	Ocala	Marion	5,919
Chipola Junior College	Marianna	Jackson	2,684
Clearwater Christian College	Clearwater	Pinellas	452
Daytona Beach Community College	Daytona Beach	Volusia	11,654
Eckerd College	St. Petersburg	Pinellas	1,391
Edison Community College	Ft. Myers	Lee	9,933
Edward Waters College	Jacksonville	Duval	786
Embry-Riddle Aeronautical University	Daytona Beach	Volusia	11,210
Flagler Career Institute	Jacksonville	Duval	200
Flagler College	St. Augustine	St. Johns	1,389
Florida Agricultural and Mechanical University	Tallahassee	Leon	9,876
Florida Atlantic University	Boca Raton	Palm Beach	15,769
Florida Baptist Theological College	Graceville	Jackson	490
Florida Bible College	Kissimmee	Osceola	104
Florida Christian College Inc.	Kissimmee	Osceola	160
Florida College	Temple Terrace	Hillsborough	404
Florida Community College at Jacksonville	Jacksonville	Duval	21,228
Florida Institute of Technology	Melbourne	Brevard	4,983
Florida Institute of Traditional Chinese Medicine	Pinellas Park	Pinellas	56
Florida International University	Miami	Dade	24,321
Florida Keys Community College	Key West	Monroe	2,120
Florida Memorial College	Miami	Dade	1,579
Florida Southern College	Lakeland	Polk	2,417
Florida State University	Tallahassee	Leon	28,575
Ft. Lauderdale College	Ft. Lauderdale	Broward	454
Gulf Coast Community	Panama City	Bay	5,872
Hillsborough Community College	Tampa	Hillsborough	21,497
Hobe Sound Bible College	Hobe Sound	Martin	166
Indian River Community College	Ft. Pierce	St. Lucie	12,071
International Academy of Merchandising and Design	Tampa	Hillsborough	375
International College	Naples	Collier	514

See footnotes at end of table.

Continued . . .

Table 4.50. HIGHER EDUCATION: ENROLLMENT IN SELECTED COLLEGES AND UNIVERSITIES IN SPECIFIED CITIES AND COUNTIES OF FLORIDA ACADEMIC YEAR 1994-95 (Continued)

School 1/	City	County	Enroll-ment 2/
International College	Ft. Myers	lee	(NA)
International Fine Arts College	Miami	Dade	647
ITT Technical Institute	Tampa	Hillsborough	689
ITT Technical Institute	Maitland	Orange	634
Jacksonville University	Jacksonville	Duval	2,406
Johnson and Wales University/ Florida campus	North Miami	Dade	(NA)
Jones College Jacksonville	Jacksonville	Duval	674
Jones College/Miami campus	Miami	Dade	(NA)
Keiser College of Technology	Ft. Lauderdale	Broward	872
Keiser College/Melbourne	Melbourne	Brevard	373
Keiser College/Tallahassee	Tallahassee	Leon	(NA)
Lake City Community College	Lake City	Columbia	2,652
Lake-Sumter Community College	Leesburg	Lake	2,658
Lynn University	Boca Raton	Palm Beach	1,333
Manatee Community College	Bradenton	Manatee	8,056
Miami-Dade Community College	Miami	Dade	48,232
National Education Center-Bauder College campus	Ft. Lauderdale	Broward	604
National Education Center-Bauder College campus	Miami	Dade	354
National Education Center-Tampa Technical Institute	Tampa	Hillsborough	1,042
New England Institute of Technology/ Palm Beach	West Palm Beach	Palm Beach	300
New York Institute of Technology/ Florida campus	Boca Raton	Palm Beach	(NA)
North Florida Junior College	Madison	Madison	1,144
Nova Southeastern University	Ft. Lauderdale	Broward	11,049
Okaloosa-Walton Community College	Niceville	Okaloosa	6,162
Orlando College	Orlando	Orange	838
Orlando College South	Orlando	Orange	734
Palm Beach Atlantic College	West Palm Beach	Palm Beach	1,867
Palm Beach Community College	Lake Worth	Palm Beach	18,586
Pasco-Hernando Community College	Dade City	Pasco	5,335
Pensacola Junior College	Pensacola	Escambia	11,788
Phillips Junior College/Daytona Beach	Daytona Beach	Volusia	247
Phillips Junior College/Melbourne	Melbourne	Brevard	277
Polk Community College	Winter Haven	Polk	5,815
Prospect Hall School of Business	Hollywood	Broward	178
Ringling School of Art and Design	Sarasota	Sarasota	771
Rollins College	Winter Park	Orange	3,361
Rollins College/Brevard campus	West Melbourne	Brevard	(NA)
St. John Vianney College Seminary	Miami	Dade	53

See footnotes at end of table. Continued . . .

Table 4.50. HIGHER EDUCATION: ENROLLMENT IN SELECTED COLLEGES AND UNIVERSITIES IN SPECIFIED CITIES AND COUNTIES OF FLORIDA ACADEMIC YEAR 1994-95 (Continued)

School 1/	City	County	Enroll-ment 2/
St. Johns River Community College	Palatka	Putnam	3,250
St. Leo College	St. Leo	Pasco	7,131
St. Petersburg Junior College	St. Petersburg	Pinellas	22,799
St. Thomas University	Miami	Dade	2,792
St. Vincent of De Paul Regional Seminary	Boynton Beach	Palm Beach	90
Santa Fe Community College	Gainesville	Alachua	12,438
Sarasota County Technical Institute	Sarasota	Sarasota	1,980
Seminole Community College	Sanford	Seminole	8,446
South Florida Community College	Avon Park	Highlands	2,582
Southeastern College Assemblies of God	Lakeland	Polk	1,144
Spurgeon Baptist Bible College	Mulberry	Polk	32
Stetson University	DeLand	Volusia	2,955
Tallahassee Community	Tallahassee	Leon	9,390
Talmudic College of Florida	Tampa	Hillsborough	44
Tampa College	Tampa	Hillsborough	1,077
Tampa College/Brandon	Tampa	Hillsborough	940
Tampa College/Lakeland	Lakeland	Polk	700
Tampa College/Pinellas	Clearwater	Pinellas	974
The University of West Florida	Pensacola	Escambia	7,750
Trinity College at Miami	Miami	Dade	338
Trinity College of Florida	New Port Richey	Pasco	189
University of Central Florida	Orlando	Orange	23,692
University of Florida	Gainesville	Alachua	37,324
University of Miami	Coral Gables	Dade	13,842
University of North Florida	Jacksonville	Duval	9,382
University of Sarasota	Sarasota	Sarasota	359
University of South Florida	Tampa	Hillsborough	34,768
University of Tampa	Tampa	Hillsborough	2,377
Valencia Community College	Orlando	Orange	22,593
Ward Stone College	Miami	Dade	(NA)
Warner Southern College	Lake Wales	Polk	531
Webber College	Babson Park	Polk	437

(NA) Not available.

1/ Includes institutions accredited at the college level by an agency recognized by the U.S. Secretary of Education.

2/ Includes undergraduate, graduate, first-professional, and unclassified students, both full- and part-time.

Source: U.S., Department of Education, National Center for Education Statistics, Office of Educational Research and Improvement, *1995 Directory of Postsecondary Institutions: Volume I, 4-Year and 2-Year Institutions.*

Table 4.53. HIGHER EDUCATION: ENROLLMENT IN THE UNIVERSITIES OF THE STATE UNIVERSITY SYSTEM OF FLORIDA BY LEVEL, SEX, RACE OR HISPANIC ORIGIN AND STATUS, FALL 1994

Sex and race	Educational and general		Health and medical center 1/		IFAS	
	Under-graduate	Graduate	Under-graduate	Graduate	Under-graduate	Graduate
			Part-time 2/			
Total	55,255	15,101	307	1,172	274	201
Sex						
Female	31,328	8,257	260	762	130	86
Male	23,896	6,844	47	410	144	115
Not reported	31	0	0	0	0	0
Race						
Asian	1,887	427	13	73	8	10
Black	5,162	890	19	48	16	2
American Indian or Alaskan native	129	32	1	11	1	0
White	38,275	11,435	255	936	225	133
Other	636	951	2	32	6	51
Not reported	571	2	1	1	1	0
Hispanic origin 3/	8,595	1,364	16	71	17	5
			Full-time 4/			
Total	105,937	14,855	1,082	1,819	1,490	438
Sex						
Female	56,427	7,151	789	969	685	152
Male	49,502	7,704	293	850	805	286
Not reported	8	0	0	0	0	0
Race						
Asian	4,290	416	63	122	80	8
Black	15,593	1,263	41	94	120	9
American Indian or Alaskan native	284	46	6	7	5	1
White	70,291	9,956	898	1,370	1,142	198
Other	2,606	2,206	6	108	26	203
Not reported	81	15	1	2	3	1
Hispanic origin 3/	12,792	953	67	116	114	18

IFAS Institute of Food and Agriculture Science.

1/ Includes veterinary medicine.

2/ Includes undergraduates enrolled for fewer than 12 hours and graduate students enrolled for fewer than 9 hours.

3/ Persons of Hispanic origin may be of any race. However, these data are not distributed by race.

4/ Includes undergraduates enrolled for 12 or more hours and graduate students enrolled for 9 or more hours.

Note: Unclassified students are counted as undergraduates. Data are from the student data course file enrollment report, Fall 1993. Staff and senior citizen waivers are excluded.

Source: State of Florida, State University System, Board of Regents, *Fact Book, 1994-95*.

Table 4.54. HIGHER EDUCATION: ENROLLMENT IN THE UNIVERSITIES OF THE STATE UNIVERSITY SYSTEM OF FLORIDA, FALL 1987 THROUGH 1994

University	1987	1988	1989	1990
Educational and general, total	146,967	153,093	163,155	170,548
University of Florida	31,151	31,370	31,481	31,569
Florida State University	23,485	25,555	27,582	28,054
Florida A & M University	5,743	6,247	7,182	8,030
University of South Florida	28,392	28,621	30,255	30,691
Florida Atlantic University	11,082	11,361	11,629	13,004
University of West Florida	6,645	7,017	7,631	7,842
University of Central Florida	17,398	18,158	20,084	21,376
Florida International University	16,313	17,703	19,767	22,122
University of North Florida	6,758	7,061	7,544	7,860
Special units, total 1/	4,828	4,926	5,156	5,412
University of Florida				
Institute of Food and Agriculture Science	1,349	1,354	1,453	1,620
Health and Medical Center	2,599	2,642	2,747	2,759
University of South Florida				
Medical Center	880	930	956	1,033

University	1991	1992	1993	1994
Educational and general, total	176,077	176,762	182,579	191,148
University of Florida	32,159	31,922	32,578	32,827
Florida State University	28,093	27,810	27,951	28,794
Florida A & M University	8,801	9,049	9,378	9,650
University of South Florida	31,771	32,467	32,773	33,614
Florida Atlantic University	14,264	14,822	15,760	17,367
University of West Florida	7,943	7,386	7,564	7,716
University of Central Florida	21,267	21,682	23,531	25,363
Florida International University	23,275	22,597	23,832	26,040
University of North Florida	8,504	9,027	9,212	9,777
Special units, total 1/	5,812	6,134	6,349	6,783
University of Florida				
Institute of Food and Agriculture Science	1,748	1,971	2,141	2,403
Health and Medical Center	2,932	2,961	2,965	3,087
University of South Florida				
Medical Center	1,132	1,202	1,243	1,293

1/ Includes medical professionals.

Note: Data are from the student data course file enrollment reports. Staff and senior citizen waivers are excluded.

Source: State of Florida, State University System, Board of Regents, *Fact Book, 1993-94*.

Table 4.60. PUBLIC COMMUNITY COLLEGES: COLLEGE LEVEL HEADCOUNT ENROLLMENT BY OBJECTIVE STATUS AND INSTITUTION IN FLORIDA, 1994-95

Community college	Total	Advanced and professional	Vocational (credit)	Other objectives: Adult general	Other objectives: Special classification 1/	Other objectives: Lifelong learning
Total	1,014,396	197,503	281,224	161,053	360,280	14,336
Brevard	49,887	10,817	24,335	3,435	9,982	1,318
Broward	60,691	14,032	7,272	10,143	27,640	1,604
Central Florida	21,708	2,115	8,137	2,500	6,778	2,178
Chipola	5,768	1,721	2,811	763	473	0
Daytona Beach	40,425	6,975	12,101	12,468	7,010	1,871
Edison	33,488	5,462	6,594	2,609	18,272	551
Florida Community College at Jacksonville	96,938	7,982	44,665	27,557	16,734	0
Florida Keys	5,521	855	1,311	355	2,958	42
Gulf Coast	23,316	4,824	10,604	1,763	6,115	10
Hillsborough	44,786	14,625	11,547	6,080	12,534	0
Indian River	54,969	2,667	10,431	12,785	29,062	24
Lake City	11,241	1,304	5,923	1,734	2,260	20
Lake Sumter	8,195	1,265	1,834	820	4,002	274
Manatee	22,658	4,624	6,724	1,824	9,347	139
Miami-Dade	131,878	24,024	22,527	19,405	65,922	0
North Florida	3,556	822	1,117	665	952	0
Okaloosa-Walton	20,766	3,992	1,682	3,263	11,829	0
Palm Beach	55,320	7,451	19,970	4,904	22,093	902
Pasco-Hernando	14,787	4,977	6,492	1,291	1,447	580
Pensacola	34,932	7,350	6,314	6,571	13,262	1,435
Polk	28,762	3,273	10,223	1,902	12,484	880
St. Johns River	9,280	3,691	767	1,708	3,114	0
St. Petersburg	74,788	15,414	22,158	7,689	28,567	960
Santa Fe	34,355	11,487	2,789	4,078	16,001	0
Seminole	39,410	5,523	12,035	8,793	12,326	733
South Florida	14,418	1,486	3,879	4,852	4,201	0
Tallahassee	18,066	7,675	1,337	2,790	6,247	17
Valencia	54,487	21,070	15,645	8,306	8,668	798

1/ Students awaiting enrollment in limited access programs, students enrolled in apprenticeship courses, students who are enrolled in courses related to employment, as general freshmen or for other personal objectives.
Note: There may be some duplication between major program areas.

Source: State of Florida, Department of Education, Division of Community Colleges, *Report for the Florida Community College System: The Fact Book,* April 1996.

Table 4.61. PUBLIC COMMUNITY COLLEGES: TRANSFER STUDENTS FROM FLORIDA COMMUNITY COLLEGES TO FLORIDA UNIVERSITIES BY SEX AND UNIVERSITY, FALL 1993 AND 1994

Institution	1993 Total	1993 Male	1993 Female	1994 Total	1994 Male	1994 Female
State University System, total	73,021	32,361	40,660	76,636	33,732	42,897
Florida Agricultural and Mechanical University	1,299	596	703	1,341	620	721
Florida Atlantic University	7,369	2,962	4,407	7,826	3,119	4,707
Florida International University	11,223	4,600	6,623	11,677	4,848	6,829
Florida State University	11,386	5,256	6,130	11,716	5,320	6,396
University of Central Florida	14,104	6,575	7,529	14,747	6,784	7,963
University of Florida	6,927	3,808	3,119	7,523	4,106	3,417
University of North Florida	4,471	1,840	2,631	4,674	1,956	2,718
University of South Florida	13,052	5,442	7,610	13,718	5,615	8,096
University of West Florida	3,190	1,282	1,908	3,414	1,364	2,050

Table 4.62. PUBLIC COMMUNITY COLLEGES: TRANSFER STUDENTS FROM FLORIDA COMMUNITY COLLEGES TO FLORIDA UNIVERSITIES BY RACE OR HISPANIC ORIGIN AND UNIVERSITY, FALL 1994

Institution	Total	Race: White	Race: Black	Race: American Indian	Race: Asian	Race: Other 1/	Hispanic origin 2/
State University System, total	76,636	55,701	6,243	250	2,484	1,219	10,739
Florida Agricultural and Mechanical University	1,341	359	851	1	41	18	71
Florida Atlantic University	7,826	5,813	755	20	305	170	763
Florida International University	11,677	3,188	1,425	13	307	396	6,348
Florida State University	11,716	9,872	841	42	245	50	666
University of Central Florida	14,747	11,778	824	60	605	263	1,217
University of Florida	7,523	6,188	270	32	298	175	560
University of North Florida	4,674	3,971	352	16	181	17	137
University of South Florida	13,718	11,535	714	32	401	121	915
University of West Florida	3,414	2,997	211	34	101	9	62

1/ Includes students classified as nonresident aliens and unclassified students.
2/ Persons of Hispanic origin may be of any race. However, these data are not distributed by race.

Source for Tables 4.61 and 4.62: State of Florida, Department of Education, State Board of Community Colleges, *Articulation Report,* March 1996.

Table 4.76. TESTING: PERCENTAGE OF STUDENTS PASSING THE HIGH SCHOOL COMPETENCY TEST (HSCT) IN THE STATE AND COUNTIES OF FLORIDA, OCTOBER 1994 AND 1995

County	Communi-cations		Mathe-matics	
	1994	1995	1994	1995
Florida	89	89	78	77
Alachua	92	94	84	83
Baker	83	85	72	65
Bay	90	92	78	77
Bradford	81	93	62	66
Brevard	95	94	86	85
Broward	86	86	78	74
Calhoun	92	94	86	86
Charlotte	91	93	83	84
Citrus	96	95	90	85
Clay	90	90	80	79
Collier	89	89	84	81
Columbia	93	93	78	79
Dade	79	80	66	66
De Soto	87	86	73	73
Dixie	89	98	66	81
Duval	90	89	75	69
Escambia	92	92	79	76
Flagler	88	94	74	81
Franklin	86	95	76	78
Gadsden	79	77	52	53
Gilchrist	82	92	70	67
Glades	95	89	66	69
Gulf	90	93	75	88
Hamilton	77	89	55	73
Hardee	84	88	73	72
Hendry	87	85	65	66
Hernando	94	96	86	81
Highlands	94	94	83	80
Hillsborough	95	94	88	87
Holmes	89	89	78	73
Indian River	89	92	77	77
Jackson	91	92	79	77
Jefferson	79	85	57	68
Lafayette	94	83	70	62
Lake	91	91	81	78
Lee	87	87	74	72
Leon	93	93	81	80
Levy	94	93	82	79
Liberty	83	93	67	79
Madison	86	91	67	59
Manatee	88	90	76	79
Marion	88	89	77	75
Martin	94	93	87	81
Monroe	91	88	80	78
Nassau	91	94	75	76
Okaloosa	94	95	86	84
Okeechobee	90	94	73	78
Orange	88	91	76	79
Osceola	90	90	76	70
Palm Beach	89	89	82	79
Pasco	92	92	83	80
Pinellas	93	93	85	84
Polk	92	91	80	78
Putnam	84	88	72	67
St. Johns	92	92	83	81
St. Lucie	88	89	77	70
Santa Rosa	92	91	83	81
Sarasota	92	91	84	84
Seminole	92	92	85	84
Sumter	88	86	64	66
Suwannee	90	91	78	76
Taylor	85	92	74	75
Union	89	91	75	72
Volusia	93	93	83	79
Wakulla	98	91	90	80
Walton	94	92	78	80
Washington	93	91	84	83
Developmental 1/	93	93	85	80

1/ Developmental research schools funded through and administered by the state university system.

Note: Data are for public school students in grade 11. The High School Competency Test (HSCT) measures the application of basic skills to everyday life situations. Minimum student performance skills were established in the basic areas of reading and writing (communications) and mathematics. Passing both the communications section and the mathematics section of the HSCT is a requirement for high school graduation in Florida.

Source: State of Florida, Department of Education, Division of Public Schools, *High School Competency Test (HSCT): State, District, and School Report of Statewide Assessment Results*, October 1995, and previous edition.

Table 4.77. TESTING: MEDIAN NATIONAL PERCENTILE RANK OF STUDENTS TAKING THE GRADE TEN ASSESSMENT TEST (GTAT) IN THE STATE STATE AND COUNTIES OF FLORIDA, APRIL 1995 AND 1996

County	Reading comprehension		Mathematics		County	Reading comprehension		Mathematics	
	1995	1996	1995	1996		1995	1996	1995	1996
Florida	50	47	51	54	Lafayette	36	42	36	50
					Lake	53	49	54	54
Alachua	61	53	58	57	Lee	53	47	54	54
Baker	42	40	43	38	Leon	56	53	54	61
Bay	56	55	58	57	Levy	50	40	51	45
Bradford	42	37	43	41	Liberty	49	49	67	57
Brevard	58	55	61	61	Madison	37	35	38	30
Broward	45	45	51	50	Manatee	50	49	54	57
Calhoun	53	47	63	50	Marion	50	45	51	50
Charlotte	56	53	58	57	Martin	58	53	58	57
Citrus	53	58	58	57	Monroe	48	53	46	57
Clay	56	55	61	61	Nassau	53	53	54	54
Collier	53	49	61	61	Okaloosa	58	58	61	61
Columbia	45	45	51	45	Okeechobee	42	33	38	38
Dade	35	31	38	38	Orange	42	45	43	45
De Soto	41	40	46	45	Osceola	48	40	51	45
Dixie	45	35	43	41	Palm Beach	53	49	58	57
Duval	50	49	54	54	Pasco	53	53	54	57
Escambia	45	42	51	45	Pinellas	56	53	58	54
Flagler	58	55	58	54	Polk	48	47	54	54
Franklin	49	35	58	38	Putnam	45	40	43	41
Gadsden	20	22	26	23	St. Johns	58	58	61	57
Gilchrist	44	53	46	57	St. Lucie	40	45	46	45
Glades	40	41	49	40	Santa Rosa	58	53	58	57
Gulf	45	51	51	50	Sarasota	61	62	64	65
Hamilton	28	31	34	30	Seminole	58	58	64	65
Hardee	35	40	43	41	Sumter	45	45	46	45
Hendry	35	35	38	38	Suwannee	45	45	51	50
Hernando	58	55	58	57	Taylor	42	45	51	45
Highlands	50	47	54	54	Union	37	40	38	38
Hillsborough	53	49	58	57	Volusia	53	53	54	54
Holmes	48	47	54	54	Wakulla	48	55	54	59
Indian River	53	55	54	54	Walton	48	47	46	50
Jackson	50	45	51	45	Washington	53	49	58	45
Jefferson	28	31	30	26					

Note: The Grade Ten Assessment Test (GTAT), is a standardized, norm-referenced achievement test that measures the performance levels of Florida's public schools tenth grade students in the subject areas of reading comprehension and mathematics. It was established in response to changes in the law by the 1990 Legislature. Scores derived from a national sample of students are norms that permit the test user to compare performance of Florida students with that of the nationally representative group. The national percentile rank (NPR) score indicates the percentage of students in the national norm group whose scores fell below a student's raw score.

Source: State of Florida, Department of Education, Division of Public Schools, *Grade Ten Assessment Test (GTAT) State, District, and School Report: Florida Statewide Assessment Program,* April 1996 and previous edition.

Table 4.78. TESTING: AVERAGE SCORES FOR STUDENTS TAKING THE FLORIDA WRITING ASSESSMENT TEST IN THE STATE AND COUNTIES OF FLORIDA, 1995

County	Grade 4	Grade 8	Grade 10	County	Grade 4	Grade 8	Grade 10
Florida	2.4	3.1	3.3	Leon	2.5	3.2	3.5
				Levy	2.2	2.8	3.3
Alachua	2.4	3.3	3.6	Liberty	2.5	3.1	3.5
Baker	2.3	2.6	3.0	Madison	1.9	2.9	3.2
Bay	2.3	3.3	3.2	Manatee	2.3	2.9	3.2
Bradford	2.7	3.2	3.4	Marion	2.2	2.9	2.9
Brevard	2.5	3.2	3.5	Martin	2.5	3.1	3.7
Broward	2.4	3.0	3.2	Monroe	2.3	3.2	3.0
Calhoun	2.5	3.2	3.5	Nassau	2.5	3.1	3.4
Charlotte	2.7	3.3	3.6	Okaloosa	2.7	3.3	3.7
Citrus	2.3	3.1	3.2	Okeechobee	2.2	2.5	3.1
Clay	2.4	2.8	3.0	Orange	2.3	2.9	3.1
Collier	2.5	3.0	3.4	Osceola	2.5	3.2	3.2
Columbia	2.4	2.7	3.0	Palm Beach	2.2	3.0	3.3
Dade	2.4	3.0	3.1	Pasco	2.3	3.1	3.3
De Soto	2.1	2.7	2.6	Pinellas	2.8	3.4	3.6
Dixie	2.1	2.4	2.9	Polk	2.3	2.9	3.4
Duval	2.3	3.1	3.3	Putnam	2.4	3.0	3.1
Escambia	2.4	2.8	3.0	St. Johns	2.6	3.0	3.4
Flagler	2.5	3.6	3.3	St. Lucie	2.4	3.0	3.2
Franklin	2.3	2.6	3.0	Santa Rosa	2.5	3.0	3.1
Gadsden	1.9	2.3	2.7	Sarasota	2.5	3.0	3.4
Gilchrist	2.3	2.7	3.1	Seminole	2.7	3.3	3.5
Glades	2.2	2.8	2.2	Sumter	2.1	2.9	3.1
Gulf	2.1	2.9	3.1	Suwannee	2.3	2.9	3.1
Hamilton	2.2	2.3	2.9	Taylor	2.2	2.5	3.3
Hardee	2.0	2.5	2.9	Union	2.4	3.1	2.8
Hendry	2.2	2.9	2.9	Volusia	2.3	3.1	3.3
Hernando	2.3	2.8	3.1	Wakulla	2.4	3.5	3.4
Highlands	2.2	2.8	3.0	Walton	2.4	3.3	3.1
Hillsborough	2.4	3.2	3.6	Washington	2.1	3.0	3.3
Holmes	2.2	3.1	2.9	A.D. Henderson	3.1	3.3	(NA)
Indian River	2.5	3.0	3.0	FSU Developmental	2.4	3.0	3.5
Jackson	2.5	2.9	3.4	Florida A & M			
Jefferson	2.1	2.3	3.3	University			
Lafayette	1.8	2.5	3.1	High	3.0	2.2	2.6
Lake	2.4	2.8	3.3	P.K. Yonge			
Lee	2.4	2.9	3.3	Developmental	2.3	3.8	3.8

(NA) Not available.

Note: The Florida Writing Assessment Program is given to public elementary and secondary students in grades 4, 8, and 10 and is designed to assess higher-order skills and to measure students' proficiency in writing responses to assigned topics within a designated tested period. It was established in response to changes in the law made by the 1990 legislature. Student writings are scored by trained readers considering four elements: focus, organization, support, and conventions. Scores range from U (unscorable) to 6.

Source: State of Florida, Department of Education, Division of Public Schools, unpublished data.

Table 4.81. HIGH SCHOOL GRADUATES: NONPUBLIC HIGH SCHOOL GRADUATES, 1995, AND GRADUATES CONTINUING EDUCATION BY TYPE OF POST-SECONDARY INSTITUTION ENTERED, 1995-96, IN THE STATE AND COUNTIES OF FLORIDA

County	Total graduates 1995 A/	Graduates continuing education: Total	Graduates entering--: Florida community colleges: Public	Florida community colleges: Private	Florida colleges and universities: Public	Florida colleges and universities: Private	Out-of-state colleges and universities	Technical trade and other: In-state	Technical trade and other: Out-of-state
Florida	9,713	8,334	2,180	72	2,231	945	2,759	109	38
Alachua	48	42	11	0	3	3	24	0	1
Baker	0	0	0	0	0	0	0	0	0
Bay	43	18	12	0	0	2	4	0	0
Bradford	0	0	0	0	0	0	0	0	0
Brevard	213	192	62	0	39	39	52	0	0
Broward	1,402	1,254	297	2	342	135	452	22	4
Calhoun	0	0	0	0	0	0	0	0	0
Charlotte	0	1	0	0	1	0	0	0	0
Citrus	4	2	1	0	0	1	0	0	0
Clay	142	78	15	0	15	9	35	1	3
Collier	49	48	17	0	12	4	13	1	1
Columbia	11	7	7	0	0	0	0	0	0
Dade	2,444	2,274	576	9	742	253	671	12	11
De Soto	0	0	0	0	0	0	0	0	0
Dixie	0	0	0	0	0	0	0	0	0
Duval	728	598	130	1	165	66	227	9	0
Escambia	185	135	40	2	27	26	40	0	0
Flagler	0	0	0	0	0	0	0	0	0
Franklin	0	0	0	0	0	0	0	0	0
Gadsden	35	27	12	0	4	0	11	0	0
Gilchrist	11	16	6	5	1	4	0	0	0
Glades	0	0	0	0	0	0	0	0	0
Gulf	5	4	2	0	0	2	0	0	0
Hamilton	0	0	0	0	0	0	0	0	0
Hardee	1	2	0	0	0	1	1	0	0
Hendry	0	0	0	0	0	0	0	0	0
Hernando	20	19	12	0	3	4	0	0	0
Highlands	14	7	4	0	0	1	2	0	0
Hillsborough	684	587	77	2	211	62	230	5	0
Holmes	0	0	0	0	0	0	0	0	0
Indian River	71	69	4	0	19	13	33	0	0
Jackson	8	5	4	0	0	1	0	0	0
Jefferson	29	18	13	0	3	0	2	0	0
Lafayette	0	0	0	0	0	0	0	0	0
Lake	63	46	9	6	12	2	17	0	0

See footnotes at end of table.

Continued . . .

Table 4.81. HIGH SCHOOL GRADUATES: NONPUBLIC HIGH SCHOOL GRADUATES, 1995, AND GRADUATES CONTINUING EDUCATION BY TYPE OF POST-SECONDARY INSTITUTION ENTERED, 1995-96, IN THE STATE AND COUNTIES OF FLORIDA (Continued)

County	Total graduates 1995 A/	Graduates continuing education: Total	Graduates entering-- Florida community colleges: Public	Florida community colleges: Private	Florida colleges and universities: Public	Florida colleges and universities: Private	Out-of-state colleges and universities	Technical trade and other: In-state	Technical trade and other: Out-of-state
Lee	248	199	77	0	51	23	45	3	0
Leon	142	117	41	2	31	10	31	2	0
Levy	1	1	1	0	0	0	0	0	0
Liberty	0	0	0	0	0	0	0	0	0
Madison	0	0	0	0	0	0	0	0	0
Manatee	171	96	27	4	13	9	39	4	0
Marion	122	54	22	0	5	4	23	0	0
Martin	18	16	4	0	0	9	3	0	0
Monroe	10	11	5	0	2	2	2	0	0
Nassau	5	4	3	0	0	1	0	0	0
Okaloosa	15	13	5	0	0	3	5	0	0
Okeechobee	0	0	0	0	0	0	0	0	0
Orange	479	420	129	2	123	33	127	4	2
Osceola	16	9	4	0	0	1	2	2	0
Palm Beach	775	716	169	20	181	71	251	16	8
Pasco	13	9	5	0	0	3	1	0	0
Pinellas	498	477	139	1	116	56	157	6	2
Polk	167	144	44	1	11	29	54	3	2
Putnam	10	5	2	0	0	1	1	1	0
St. Johns	77	61	18	3	14	5	8	12	1
St. Lucie	130	106	46	1	32	13	13	1	0
Santa Rosa	22	19	3	0	0	0	16	0	0
Sarasota	147	130	35	1	23	9	60	1	1
Seminole	285	144	40	10	6	13	72	1	2
Sumter	3	1	0	0	0	1	0	0	0
Suwannee	9	7	2	0	0	2	1	2	0
Taylor	0	0	0	0	0	0	0	0	0
Union	0	0	0	0	0	0	0	0	0
Volusia	140	126	48	0	24	19	34	1	0
Wakulla	0	0	0	0	0	0	0	0	0
Walton	0	0	0	0	0	0	0	0	0
Washington	0	0	0	0	0	0	0	0	0

A/ Includes standard and special diploma graduates.

Note: See Glossary under Private school for definition of nonpublic schools. Data are based on a survey and are unaudited.

Source: State of Florida, Department of Education, Division of Administration, *Statistical Brief: Florida's Nonpublic Schools, 1994-95*. Series 96-6B.

Table 4.82. HIGH SCHOOL GRADUATES: GRADUATES, 1995, AND GRADUATES CONTINUING EDUCATION BY TYPE OF POST-SECONDARY INSTITUTION ENTERED, 1995-96 IN THE STATE AND COUNTIES OF FLORIDA

County	Total diploma graduates 1995 A/	Graduates continuing education: Total: Number	Total: Percentage	Graduates entering--: Florida community colleges: Public	Florida community colleges: Private	Florida colleges and universities: Public	Florida colleges and universities: Private	Non-Florida college or university	Technical trade and other: In-state	Technical trade and other: Out-of-state
Florida	91,883	59,768	65.1	28,863	550	15,511	3,096	7,607	3,281	860
Alachua	1,162	885	76.2	472	6	220	27	132	21	7
Baker	206	138	67.0	100	0	20	2	10	6	0
Bay	1,079	512	47.5	324	2	77	15	76	15	3
Bradford	169	96	56.8	73	0	7	0	12	4	0
Brevard	2,964	2,087	70.4	1,147	16	432	120	261	47	64
Broward	8,081	5,614	69.5	2,223	26	1,813	431	725	330	66
Calhoun	131	53	40.5	42	0	1	1	5	3	1
Charlotte	802	357	44.5	134	1	92	26	53	44	7
Citrus	664	395	59.5	212	3	84	30	43	19	4
Clay	1,197	656	54.8	333	3	171	24	76	45	4
Collier	964	615	63.8	264	5	158	38	112	31	7
Columbia	338	143	42.3	81	1	30	7	15	8	1
Dade	14,386	10,435	72.5	5,479	60	2,529	660	1,047	578	82
De Soto	149	95	63.8	36	0	20	4	6	29	0
Dixie	71	(NA)	(NA)	(NA)	(NA)	(NA)	(NA)	(NA)	(NA)	(NA)
Duval	4,586	3,015	65.7	1,339	0	995	214	391	76	0
Escambia	2,183	1,663	76.2	651	25	485	24	380	62	36
Flagler	238	154	64.7	73	0	37	8	28	3	5
Franklin	66	21	31.8	14	0	4	0	2	1	0
Gadsden	320	15	4.7	2	1	10	0	1	1	0
Gilchrist	111	56	50.5	8	0	43	0	3	2	0
Glades	42	33	78.6	11	0	6	0	7	6	3
Gulf	157	108	68.8	61	0	19	2	10	12	4
Hamilton	136	89	65.4	47	11	1	3	22	4	1
Hardee	163	145	89.0	89	2	18	7	21	5	3
Hendry	304	193	63.5	123	1	23	7	16	21	2
Hernando	679	525	77.3	275	6	111	22	63	39	9
Highlands	357	282	79.0	179	3	51	9	27	9	4
Hillsborough	5,828	3,825	65.6	1,339	42	1,463	194	448	314	25
Holmes	197	128	65.0	41	24	14	3	22	23	1
Indian River	512	436	85.2	243	5	70	25	58	4	31
Jackson	437	180	41.2	130	1	6	4	19	20	0
Jefferson	100	82	82.0	10	0	30	0	0	42	0
Lafayette	49	42	85.7	21	1	12	2	1	2	3
Lake	1,048	712	67.9	381	1	139	38	52	80	21
Lee	2,096	1,300	62.0	623	3	331	55	186	92	10
Leon	1,282	918	71.6	433	28	293	20	121	15	8
Levy	213	62	29.1	44	0	4	1	8	5	0
Liberty	60	47	78.3	29	2	2	0	4	6	4

See footnotes at end of table.

Continued . . .

Table 4.82. HIGH SCHOOL GRADUATES: GRADUATES, 1995, AND GRADUATES CONTINUING EDUCATION BY TYPE OF POST-SECONDARY INSTITUTION ENTERED, 1995-96 IN THE STATE AND COUNTIES OF FLORIDA (Continued)

County	Total diploma graduates 1995 A/	Graduates continuing education: Total: Number	Total: Percentage	Graduates entering--: Florida community colleges: Public	Florida community colleges: Private	Florida colleges and universities: Public	Florida colleges and universities: Private	Non-Florida college or university	Technical trade and other: In-state	Technical trade and other: Out-of-state
Madison	130	86	66.2	52	0	16	2	11	5	0
Manatee	1,116	756	67.7	371	0	208	26	96	46	9
Marion	1,430	885	61.9	590	2	154	33	77	19	10
Martin	605	361	59.7	159	15	112	2	65	5	3
Monroe	356	297	83.4	163	3	63	12	34	14	8
Nassau	403	219	54.3	97	5	62	6	25	23	1
Okaloosa	1,716	1,188	69.2	558	10	244	20	294	37	25
Okeechobee	234	127	54.3	84	1	17	6	10	4	5
Orange	5,243	3,522	67.2	1,675	112	879	149	467	32	208
Osceola	1,204	875	72.7	471	7	152	42	90	94	19
Palm Beach	5,540	2,619	47.3	1,100	15	825	127	341	189	22
Pasco	1,764	1,271	72.1	692	17	271	60	106	110	15
Pinellas	4,652	3,259	70.1	1,632	3	855	165	430	163	11
Polk	3,040	2,043	67.2	1,036	16	389	151	223	193	35
Putnam	486	72	14.8	38	0	14	0	5	14	1
St. Johns	644	450	69.9	174	6	154	18	67	26	5
St. Lucie	948	6	0.6	4	1	0	0	0	1	0
Santa Rosa	893	759	85.0	366	23	182	9	146	23	10
Sarasota	1,517	1,089	71.8	470	0	269	64	200	79	7
Seminole	2,539	1,219	48.0	552	16	371	61	175	32	12
Sumter	225	165	73.3	91	4	24	9	12	24	1
Suwannee	294	242	82.3	161	0	27	4	10	37	3
Taylor	147	92	62.6	56	1	12	0	5	11	7
Union	79	58	73.4	46	1	6	1	2	2	0
Volusia	2,543	1,659	65.2	951	8	335	98	212	41	14
Wakulla	176	105	59.7	58	2	18	4	4	16	3
Walton	266	141	53.0	71	3	24	3	25	9	6
Washington	166	91	54.8	59	0	7	1	12	8	4

A/ Includes standard and special diploma graduates.

Note: Data were obtained from the Florida DOE Student Information Data Base, Survey 5, as of November 14, 1995 and are for public schools only. Because some high schools do not have a formal follow-up program for graduates, it was necessary for the principal or guidance counselor to prepare estimates for some of the items included. Figures include twelfth grade graduates from adult centers and exceptional and gifted schools.

Source: State of Florida, Department of Education, Division of Administration, *Statistical Brief: Florida Public High School Graduates, 1994-95 School Year.* Series 96-13B.

Table 4.83. HIGH SCHOOL GRADUATES: GRADUATES RECEIVING STANDARD DIPLOMAS BY SEX AND BY RACE OR HISPANIC ORIGIN IN THE STATE AND COUNTIES OF FLORIDA, 1994-95

County	Total		Race: White		Race: Black		Race: Asian or Pacific Islander		Race: American Indian, Eskimo, or Aleut		Hispanic origin 1/	
	Male	Female	Male	Female	Male	Female	Male	Female	Male	Female	Male	Female
Florida	42,232	47,601	26,895	28,920	8,034	10,467	1,196	1,262	85	86	6,022	6,866
Alachua	525	609	355	402	133	172	17	17	0	1	20	17
Baker	81	119	68	107	12	11	1	1	0	0	0	0
Bay	539	539	420	418	81	84	22	30	1	2	15	5
Bradford	76	87	52	73	24	13	0	0	0	0	0	1
Brevard	1,392	1,513	1,158	1,237	142	160	40	55	6	3	46	58
Broward	3,655	4,270	2,040	2,272	1,018	1,365	138	125	6	8	453	500
Calhoun	65	62	49	49	14	11	1	1	0	0	1	1
Charlotte	401	390	345	328	32	38	6	6	0	0	18	18
Citrus	316	333	293	312	9	10	8	2	2	1	4	8
Clay	580	602	511	527	36	44	18	17	0	1	15	13
Collier	454	486	328	365	47	36	3	5	0	0	76	80
Columbia	158	173	127	124	29	39	1	6	0	0	1	4
Dade	6,583	7,582	1,139	1,204	1,932	2,489	131	118	6	3	3,375	3,768
De Soto	62	81	47	54	11	18	0	2	0	0	4	7
Dixie	32	36	29	33	3	3	0	0	0	0	0	0
Duval	1,858	2,491	1,132	1,454	602	882	85	81	1	5	38	69
Escambia	975	1,122	670	734	238	314	59	61	3	6	5	7
Flagler	116	120	94	89	10	22	5	4	1	0	6	5
Franklin	30	36	25	27	5	9	0	0	0	0	0	0
Gadsden	128	190	21	16	104	171	0	0	0	0	3	3
Gilchrist	56	53	54	51	2	1	0	0	0	0	0	1
Glades	18	20	11	11	3	3	0	0	1	1	3	5
Gulf	73	81	56	58	15	22	0	0	1	0	1	1
Hamilton	66	57	36	29	30	28	0	0	0	0	0	0

See footnotes at end of table.

Continued . . .

Table 4.83. HIGH SCHOOL GRADUATES: GRADUATES RECEIVING STANDARD DIPLOMAS BY SEX AND BY RACE OR HISPANIC ORIGIN IN THE STATE AND COUNTIES OF FLORIDA, 1994-95 (Continued)

County	Total		Race: White		Race: Black		Race: Asian or Pacific Islander		Race: American Indian, Eskimo, or Aleut		Hispanic origin 1/	
	Male	Female	Male	Female	Male	Female	Male	Female	Male	Female	Male	Female
Hardee	80	80	51	50	5	12	0	3	1	0	23	15
Hendry	140	151	86	83	22	32	0	3	0	2	32	31
Hernando	310	360	275	312	18	23	3	3	1	1	13	21
Highlands	159	171	111	101	32	45	2	1	0	1	14	23
Hillsborough	2,724	3,018	1,835	1,884	425	543	92	100	6	12	366	479
Holmes	89	100	86	98	2	1	0	0	0	0	1	1
Indian River	237	261	194	213	30	39	5	2	0	0	8	7
Jackson	210	213	157	137	50	71	0	3	1	0	2	2
Jefferson	45	53	11	18	34	35	0	0	0	0	0	0
Lafayette	22	23	16	20	6	3	0	0	0	0	0	0
Lake	463	518	379	405	57	92	5	4	2	0	20	17
Lee	974	1,074	772	861	120	112	13	11	3	0	66	90
Leon	568	669	398	436	146	201	13	20	1	0	10	12
Levy	107	94	86	68	15	23	2	1	1	0	3	2
Liberty	35	25	34	19	1	5	0	1	0	0	0	0
Madison	70	54	33	33	37	21	0	0	0	0	0	0
Manatee	532	531	424	429	78	66	6	8	0	1	24	27
Marion	626	766	479	563	110	150	7	10	2	0	28	43
Martin	306	294	264	239	21	29	9	7	0	0	12	19
Monroe	168	177	118	131	15	13	2	3	1	0	32	30
Nassau	180	217	161	183	18	31	0	1	1	0	0	2
Okaloosa	838	855	679	692	83	100	46	30	2	4	28	29
Okeechobee	114	109	91	88	11	8	1	1	1	1	10	11
Orange	2,378	2,753	1,379	1,488	449	601	144	162	9	8	397	494
Osceola	539	642	343	404	41	52	15	24	2	3	138	159
Palm Beach	2,587	2,897	1,661	1,701	571	790	60	79	7	5	288	322

See footnotes at end of table.

Continued . . .

Table 4.83. HIGH SCHOOL GRADUATES: GRADUATES RECEIVING STANDARD DIPLOMAS BY SEX AND BY RACE OR HISPANIC ORIGIN IN THE STATE AND COUNTIES OF FLORIDA, 1994-95 (Continued)

County	Total		Race: White		Race: Black		Race: Asian or Pacific Islander		Race: American Indian, Eskimo, or Aleut		Hispanic origin 1/	
	Male	Female	Male	Female	Male	Female	Male	Female	Male	Female	Male	Female
Pasco	840	896	764	808	28	31	10	17	0	0	38	40
Pinellas	2,119	2,438	1,785	1,943	186	333	92	90	3	2	53	70
Polk	1,385	1,555	1,024	1,127	263	318	24	23	3	5	71	82
Putnam	229	249	165	175	53	66	3	4	1	0	7	4
St. Johns	297	332	260	277	32	44	1	4	0	1	4	6
St. Lucie	429	513	282	326	119	154	5	7	3	2	20	24
Santa Rosa	417	457	384	419	9	18	12	13	2	4	10	3
Sarasota	699	780	629	690	44	50	7	15	0	1	19	24
Seminole	1,248	1,264	962	947	107	151	59	45	2	1	118	120
Sumter	104	111	73	89	27	16	0	2	1	0	3	4
Suwannee	144	141	114	122	28	17	1	1	0	0	1	1
Taylor	73	74	54	55	17	18	1	1	1	0	0	0
Union	36	43	32	37	3	5	0	0	0	0	1	1
Volusia	1,166	1,314	921	1,049	149	161	18	27	0	0	78	77
Wakulla	92	76	75	59	17	15	0	2	0	0	0	0
Walton	124	128	112	106	10	17	2	2	0	1	0	2
Washington	90	73	76	61	13	10	1	1	0	0	0	1

1/ Persons of Hispanic origin may be of any race. However, these data are not distributed by race.

Note: Standard diplomas are awarded to students who have mastered eleventh grade minimum student performance standards, passed both sections of the High School Competency Test (HSCT or SSAT II), successfully completed the minimum number of academic credits, and successfully completed any other requirements prescribed by state or the local school board. Also includes differentiated diplomas awarded in lieu of the standard diplomas to those students exceeding the prescribed minimums. Data are for public schools only.

Source: State of Florida, Department of Education, Division of Administration, *Statistical Brief: Florida Public High School Graduates, 1994-95 School Year.* Series 96-13B.

INCOME AND WEALTH

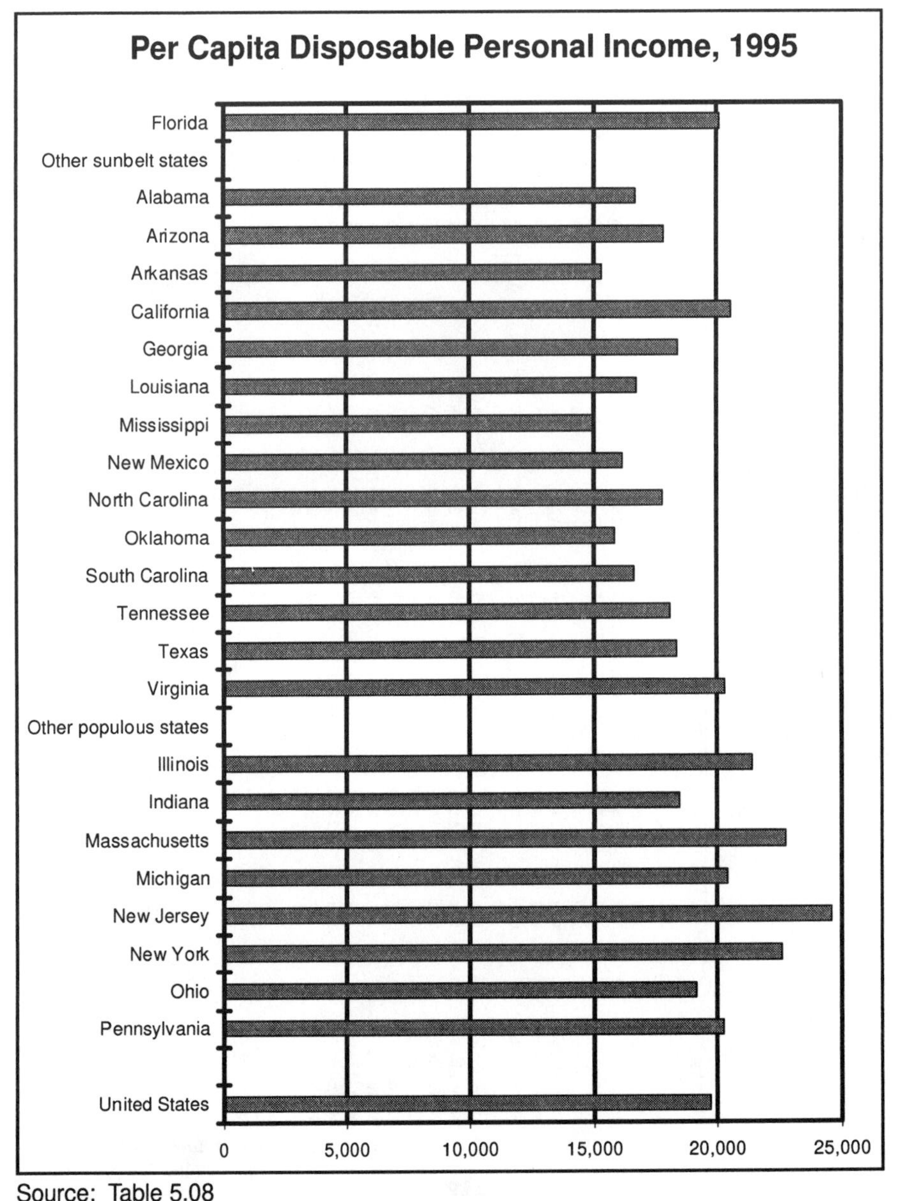
Per Capita Disposable Personal Income, 1995
Florida
Other sunbelt states
Alabama
Arizona
Arkansas
California
Georgia
Louisiana
Mississippi
New Mexico
North Carolina
Oklahoma
South Carolina
Tennessee
Texas
Virginia
Other populous states
Illinois
Indiana
Massachusetts
Michigan
New Jersey
New York
Ohio
Pennsylvania
United States
0
5,000
10,000
15,000
20,000
25,000
Source: Table 5.08

SECTION 5.00
INCOME AND WEALTH

TABLES LISTED BY MAJOR HEADINGS

SECTION 5.00
INCOME AND WEALTH
(Continued)

TABLES LISTED BY MAJOR HEADINGS

HEADING PAGE

Table 5.01. INDIVIDUAL INCOME TAXES: RETURNS, SPECIFIED INCOME, DEDUCTION, AND TAX ITEMS IN FLORIDA AND THE UNITED STATES, 1994

(amounts in thousands of dollars, except where indicated)

Item	Florida	United States
All returns	6,381,121	116,466,422
Number of exemptions 1/	13,945,049	253,599,141
Adjusted gross income (less deficit)	203,882,131	3,898,339,504
Salaries and wages, number of returns	5,148,589	99,140,184
Amount	139,862,427	3,007,825,837
Interest income, number of returns	3,344,345	65,281,203
Amount	10,205,258	127,874,649
Dividends, number of returns	1,479,210	25,227,237
Amount	7,430,295	83,381,186
Net capital gain (less loss), number of returns	986,330	14,612,522
Amount	11,549,951	134,868,594
Taxable pensions and annuities, number of returns	1,150,410	17,839,983
Amount	15,056,851	205,209,213
Unemployment compensation, number of returns	318,328	8,408,793
Amount	740,408	20,290,940
Number of sole proprietorship returns	888,818	16,163,963
Number of farm returns (Schedule F) 2/	33,613	1,902,182
Total itemized deductions, number of returns	1,504,168	33,643,511
Amount	21,480,947	510,244,012
Average (whole dollars)	14,281	15,166
Medical and dental expense, number of returns	394,791	5,724,044
Amount	2,456,038	33,485,961
Taxes paid deductions, number of returns	1,419,142	33,103,513
Amount	4,212,015	179,299,684
Interest paid deductions, number of returns	1,295,686	28,108,744
Amount	9,796,655	201,053,937
Contributions, number of returns	1,296,847	29,869,514
Amount	3,494,811	69,448,089
Taxable income, number of returns	4,938,358	92,585,422
Amount	139,440,226	2,589,783,742
Total tax liability, number of returns	5,109,365	95,199,899
Amount	31,427,206	564,526,097
Average (whole dollars)	6,151	5,930
Earned income credit, number of returns	1,233,475	19,424,837
Amount	1,351,562	21,390,289
Excess earned income credit 3/		
Number of returns	958,502	14,996,537
Amount	1,060,197	16,824,565
Overpayment, number of returns	4,421,439	81,999,738
Amount	5,388,349	98,833,826
Tax due at time of filing, number of returns	1,498,255	27,427,136
Amount	3,904,568	60,538,533

1/ Includes exemptions for age and blindness.

2/ Excludes those farm returns which also included a nonfarm sole proprietorship bus iness schedule(s). These returns are included with the "number of sole proprietorship returns."

3/ Represents the refundable portion of the credit and equals the amount in excess of total tax liability, including any advance earned income credit payments for those returns which had such an excess.

Note: Data are estimates based on samples and are preliminary.

Source: U.S., Department of the Treasury, Internal Revenue Service, *Statistics of Income: SOI Bulletin,* Spring 1996.

Table 5.02. INDIVIDUAL INCOME TAXES: RETURNS, ADJUSTED GROSS INCOME, EXEMPTIONS AND INCOME TAX IN FLORIDA AND THE UNITED STATES, 1984 THROUGH 1994

	Number (1,000)				Amount ($1,000,000)			
	Returns		Exemptions 1/		Adjusted gross income 2/		Total income tax	
Year	Florida	United States	Florida	United States	Florida	United States	Florida	United States
1984	4,906	(NA)	11,595	(NA)	101,265	(NA)	15,842	(NA)
1985	5,113	101,660	12,030	244,180	110,593	2,305,951	17,310	325,710
1986	5,301	(NA)	12,413	(NA)	123,771	(NA)	20,901	(NA)
1987	5,533	106,996	12,473	217,495	140,279	2,773,824	20,737	369,203
1988	5,760	109,708	12,559	221,884	159,547	3,083,020	23,849	412,870
1989	5,971	112,136	12,973	223,756	169,688	3,256,358	25,035	432,940
1990	6,141	113,717	13,390	227,549	176,297	3,405,427	25,643	447,127
1991	6,250	114,730	13,721	231,297	177,889	3,464,534	25,504	448,430
1992	6,239	113,605	13,702	230,547	187,754	3,629,130	27,732	476,239
1993	6,282	115,061	13,840	253,489	193,995	3,720,611	29,539	532,213
1994	6,381	116,466	13,945	253,599	203,882	3,898,340	31,427	564,526

(NA) Not available.
1/ Includes exemptions for age and blindness.
2/ Less deficit. Starting 1987, data are not comparable to earlier years because of major changes in the law.
Note: Includes taxable and nontaxable returns. All figures are estimates based on samples. Some data are revised. 1994 data are preliminary.

Source: U.S., Department of the Treasury, Internal Revenue Service, *Statistics of Income: SOI Bulletin,* Spring 1996, and previous editions.

Table 5.03. HOUSEHOLD INCOME: PERCENTAGE DISTRIBUTION OF ANNUAL INCOME BY INCOME CATEGORY AND HOUSEHOLD SIZE IN FLORIDA, 1995

Income category	Total house-holds	Household size 1	2	3	4	5	6 or more
Total	100.00	23.12	33.49	17.97	16.01	6.35	3.07
Less than $10,000	4.74	2.49	1.11	0.66	0.30	0.07	0.11
$10,000 to $14,999	5.98	2.61	1.51	0.93	0.67	0.19	0.07
$15,000 to $19,999	9.49	3.01	2.90	1.68	1.01	0.54	0.36
$20,000 to $24,999	10.05	3.23	3.22	1.33	1.30	0.57	0.39
$25,000 to $34,999	21.04	4.94	7.54	3.65	2.97	1.35	0.57
$35,000 to $44,999	15.32	2.99	5.15	2.82	2.78	1.04	0.54
$45,000 or more	33.38	3.85	12.06	6.89	6.97	2.59	1.02

Note: Distribution of household income is based on telephone surveys with sample size of approximately 1,000 Florida households. The surveys are conducted throughout the year and the monthly results have been pooled to develop the annual frequency distributions.

Source: University of Florida, Bureau of Economic and Business Research, Survey Program, unpublished data.

Table 5.05. PERSONAL INCOME: TOTAL AND PER CAPITA AMOUNTS IN FLORIDA, OTHER SUNBELT STATES, OTHER POPULOUS STATES, AND THE UNITED STATES 1993 THROUGH 1995

State	Total personal income ($1,000,000)				Per capita personal income (amounts in dollars)			
							1995	
	1993	1994	1995	Percentage change 1994-1995	1993	1994	Amount	Rank among states
			Sunbelt states					
Florida	285,395	302,093	324,616	7.5	20,795	21,654	22,916	20
Alabama	71,506	75,621	79,876	5.6	17,104	17,925	18,781	41
Arizona	71,774	78,050	86,133	10.4	18,194	19,153	20,421	35
Arkansas	38,766	41,248	43,289	4.9	15,980	16,818	17,429	49
California	683,449	702,568	748,629	6.6	21,893	22,353	23,699	12
Georgia	132,830	142,501	153,218	7.5	19,244	20,198	21,278	28
Louisiana	71,026	76,009	81,753	7.6	16,555	17,615	18,827	39
Mississippi	38,844	42,152	44,587	5.8	14,713	15,791	16,531	50
New Mexico	26,326	28,152	30,431	8.1	16,295	17,025	18,055	47
North Carolina	130,128	138,401	148,252	7.1	18,719	19,579	20,604	33
Oklahoma	55,092	57,349	59,498	3.7	17,041	17,602	18,152	46
South Carolina	61,266	64,898	69,013	6.3	16,877	17,713	18,788	40
Tennessee	94,033	100,637	107,098	6.4	18,458	19,446	20,376	36
Texas	342,826	362,398	386,719	6.7	19,023	19,719	20,654	32
Virginia	140,140	147,415	156,174	5.9	21,650	22,503	23,597	14
			Other populous states					
Illinois	263,318	277,424	292,946	5.6	22,533	23,607	24,763	8
Indiana	109,657	116,547	123,457	5.9	19,219	20,261	21,273	29
Massachusetts	146,898	154,705	163,950	6.0	24,410	25,608	26,994	3
Michigan	194,873	210,559	224,896	6.8	20,599	22,172	23,551	15
New Jersey	210,886	219,268	229,286	4.6	26,834	27,741	28,858	2
New York	451,036	467,511	485,713	3.9	24,844	25,726	26,782	4
Ohio	218,238	231,843	245,542	5.9	19,730	20,882	22,021	21
Pennsylvania	256,408	267,501	281,021	5.1	21,314	22,195	23,279	18
United States	5,364,300	5,649,010	5,987,536	6.0	20,809	21,699	22,788	(X)

(X) Not applicable.
Note: Data for 1993 and 1994 are revised; 1995 are preliminary.

Source: U.S., Department of Commerce, Bureau of Economic Analysis, *Survey of Current Business,* May 1996.

Table 5.08. DISPOSABLE PERSONAL INCOME: TOTAL AND PER CAPITA AMOUNTS IN FLORIDA OTHER SUNBELT STATES, OTHER POPULOUS STATES, AND THE UNITED STATES 1990 THROUGH 1995

State	Total disposable personal income ($1,000,000)						Percentage change 1994-1995
	1990	1991	1992	1993	1994	1995	
			Sunbelt states				
Florida	215,305	226,437	234,871	251,835	265,482	284,358	7.1
Alabama	53,564	56,628	61,040	63,845	67,320	70,843	5.2
Arizona	52,753	55,036	59,087	63,261	68,518	75,290	9.9
Arkansas	28,816	30,530	33,075	34,469	36,538	38,122	4.3
California	528,976	550,934	585,345	596,611	612,107	649,480	6.1
Georgia	96,897	102,482	110,109	115,793	123,791	132,528	7.1
Louisiana	53,686	57,042	60,539	63,502	67,797	72,625	7.1
Mississippi	29,597	31,397	33,626	35,355	38,228	40,318	5.5
New Mexico	19,238	20,519	22,011	23,644	25,254	27,210	7.7
North Carolina	94,761	99,380	106,724	113,259	119,931	127,871	6.6
Oklahoma	41,832	43,730	46,586	48,490	50,321	51,874	3.1
South Carolina	46,645	48,882	51,929	54,442	57,572	61,038	6.0
Tennessee	70,020	73,635	79,822	84,185	89,756	95,160	6.0
Texas	252,052	268,981	290,416	306,203	322,803	343,256	6.3
Virginia	104,895	109,582	116,343	121,884	127,443	134,271	5.4
			Other populous states				
Illinois	199,341	206,301	220,284	229,047	240,299	252,812	5.2
Indiana	81,308	84,684	91,600	95,895	101,536	107,006	5.4
Massachusetts	113,899	116,467	120,381	124,806	130,816	138,258	5.7
Michigan	147,448	152,652	162,829	169,981	182,907	194,745	6.5
New Jersey	161,396	165,777	175,431	181,034	186,704	195,090	4.5
New York	337,229	350,565	372,283	382,206	394,824	409,925	3.8
Ohio	165,624	171,697	183,249	190,935	202,028	213,234	5.5
Pennsylvania	195,284	205,137	216,006	224,448	233,436	244,582	4.8
United States	4,033,622	4,218,270	4,490,484	4,678,976	4,908,045	5,183,825	5.6

See footnotes at end of table.

Continued . . .

Table 5.08. DISPOSABLE PERSONAL INCOME: TOTAL AND PER CAPITA AMOUNTS IN FLORIDA OTHER SUNBELT STATES, OTHER POPULOUS STATES, AND THE UNITED STATES 1990 THROUGH 1995 (Continued)

State	Per capita disposable personal income (in dollars)						Rank among states
	1990	1991	1992	1993	1994	1995	1995
			Sunbelt states				
Florida	16,538	17,040	17,385	18,350	19,030	20,074	18
Alabama	13,231	13,856	14,776	15,271	15,957	16,657	40
Arizona	14,340	14,689	15,405	16,036	16,814	17,850	35
Arkansas	12,240	12,875	13,807	14,209	14,897	15,349	49
California	17,688	18,113	18,937	19,111	19,475	20,560	12
Georgia	14,893	15,471	16,277	16,776	17,546	18,404	28
Louisiana	12,730	13,449	14,167	14,801	15,712	16,725	39
Mississippi	11,484	12,105	12,868	13,391	14,321	14,948	50
New Mexico	12,658	13,260	13,923	14,634	15,273	16,145	44
North Carolina	14,236	14,719	15,609	16,292	16,966	17,772	36
Oklahoma	13,293	13,805	14,530	14,999	15,445	15,827	47
South Carolina	13,331	13,741	14,443	14,998	15,713	16,617	42
Tennessee	14,317	14,876	15,898	16,525	17,343	18,105	34
Texas	14,787	15,509	16,438	16,990	17,564	18,332	31
Virginia	16,881	17,430	18,208	18,830	19,454	20,288	15
			Other populous states				
Illinois	17,412	17,900	18,973	19,600	20,448	21,371	9
Indiana	14,637	15,113	16,206	16,807	17,652	18,438	27
Massachusetts	18,925	19,406	20,066	20,739	21,654	22,764	3
Michigan	15,836	16,291	17,279	17,968	19,260	20,393	13
New Jersey	20,852	21,343	22,454	23,035	23,622	24,554	2
New York	18,733	19,432	20,574	21,053	21,726	22,603	4
Ohio	15,248	15,706	16,652	17,261	18,197	19,123	22
Pennsylvania	16,416	17,170	18,015	18,657	19,368	20,260	17
United States	16,173	16,730	17,608	18,151	18,852	19,729	(X)

(X) Not applicable.

Note: Disposable personal income is equal to total personal income less personal tax and nontax payments. Personal taxes are tax payments by persons (except personal contributions to social insurance) and include income, estate and gift, and personal property taxes. Nontaxes include passport fees, fines and penalties, donations, and tuitions and fees paid to government schools and hospitals. 1990 through 1994 data are revised; 1995 data are preliminary.

Source: U.S., Department of Commerce, Bureau of Economic Analysis, *Survey of Current Business,* May 1996.

Table 5.09. PERSONAL INCOME: TOTAL AMOUNT ON A PLACE-OF-RESIDENCE BASIS IN THE UNITED STATES AND IN THE STATE AND COUNTIES OF FLORIDA, 1985 THROUGH 1994

(in millions, rounded to hundred thousands of dollars)

County	1985	1986	1987	1988	1989	1990	1991	1992	1993	1994
United States 1/	3,368,069	3,579,783	3,789,297	4,061,806	4,366,135	4,655,420	4,841,078	5,138,091	5,365,006	5,648,263
Florida	160,983.3	175,286.6	189,557.7	205,126.6	228,024.4	244,604.4	255,028.7	265,729.6	285,248.1	302,099.0
Alachua	1,953.8	2,107.7	2,281.7	2,461.4	2,705.1	2,930.5	3,107.3	3,309.6	3,528.9	3,747.5
Baker	156.6	169.1	183.2	198.7	212.4	231.8	245.3	262.4	278.5	293.9
Bay	1,324.5	1,438.7	1,517.6	1,616.4	1,741.9	1,908.9	2,054.9	2,190.9	2,359.9	2,495.9
Bradford	188.1	200.0	209.0	223.0	238.5	252.6	265.8	286.1	303.0	318.0
Brevard	4,759.7	5,108.3	5,500.6	5,955.0	6,641.0	7,103.9	7,502.0	7,957.7	8,306.3	8,677.9
Broward	19,292.8	20,770.7	22,324.9	23,943.6	26,513.2	28,114.5	28,762.1	30,062.7	32,207.3	34,167.9
Calhoun	72.4	78.4	86.3	97.1	103.3	116.1	121.8	129.2	136.5	146.1
Charlotte	1,105.0	1,249.9	1,377.8	1,524.5	1,792.5	1,945.1	2,014.4	2,117.2	2,241.4	2,400.5
Citrus	858.6	949.8	1,034.3	1,112.8	1,254.6	1,366.8	1,428.8	1,495.6	1,569.4	1,672.6
Clay	1,166.4	1,288.1	1,409.1	1,525.2	1,645.6	1,786.1	1,875.4	1,982.7	2,107.6	2,238.7
Collier	2,128.6	2,447.3	2,806.2	3,338.7	3,827.7	4,209.0	4,429.8	4,720.5	5,118.9	5,452.5
Columbia	387.6	412.5	437.8	479.1	522.0	554.9	585.2	625.5	670.6	719.3
Dade	24,624.6	26,114.5	28,039.9	29,719.2	32,550.5	34,273.5	35,183.1	33,600.6	38,552.8	40,530.0
De Soto	205.9	226.2	248.3	279.8	304.7	326.5	360.9	369.4	389.3	410.1
Dixie	72.0	77.6	85.8	94.6	106.5	113.6	113.3	121.3	121.1	141.5
Duval	8,395.4	9,041.4	9,713.8	10,345.2	11,219.8	12,038.2	12,514.4	13,177.0	13,859.4	14,553.8
Escambia	2,900.0	3,104.8	3,275.2	3,433.3	3,677.9	3,952.5	4,143.8	4,416.4	4,597.2	4,800.2
Flagler	215.6	251.2	294.5	342.3	376.3	420.0	447.7	493.6	545.3	594.1
Franklin	75.3	84.3	87.9	96.2	105.0	115.1	121.4	128.5	139.5	152.0
Gadsden	333.8	361.4	388.0	419.5	453.2	483.4	514.6	556.4	586.3	617.9
Gilchrist	72.6	77.9	82.4	90.6	99.9	111.3	120.7	130.4	140.8	149.7

See footnotes at end of table.

Continued . . .

Table 5.09. PERSONAL INCOME: TOTAL AMOUNT ON A PLACE-OF-RESIDENCE BASIS IN THE UNITED STATES AND IN THE STATE AND COUNTIES OF FLORIDA, 1985 THROUGH 1994 (Continued)

(in millions, rounded to hundred thousands of dollars)

County	1985	1986	1987	1988	1989	1990	1991	1992	1993	1994
Glades	56.6	61.2	65.7	76.6	85.3	93.6	102.3	106.3	112.9	111.7
Gulf	105.6	114.0	117.5	124.7	132.5	141.8	150.1	161.4	175.1	187.6
Hamilton	81.1	85.0	91.8	100.7	114.1	123.3	125.5	135.1	135.7	141.5
Hardee	201.1	208.7	226.2	269.4	287.1	295.2	311.5	314.0	318.0	338.1
Hendry	280.8	294.3	328.2	370.0	402.0	402.8	462.7	475.2	498.5	505.7
Hernando	812.5	932.4	1,046.1	1,208.3	1,358.5	1,476.9	1,551.4	1,639.3	1,737.7	1,872.7
Highlands	699.4	780.8	835.2	918.0	1,021.0	1,065.9	1,131.5	1,158.8	1,228.6	1,296.7
Hillsborough	9,633.6	10,433.9	11,238.5	12,152.6	13,294.7	14,214.2	14,878.7	15,760.6	16,611.5	17,632.0
Holmes	122.8	131.5	134.6	146.3	159.9	168.3	181.7	193.8	204.4	215.2
Indian River	1,277.9	1,425.9	1,590.7	1,812.3	2,088.6	2,275.2	2,395.1	2,495.9	2,599.0	2,772.5
Jackson	357.7	373.1	404.8	440.3	475.6	519.7	562.6	606.5	635.2	665.0
Jefferson	96.8	104.0	111.5	121.1	131.4	145.1	155.9	165.8	177.4	185.2
Lafayette	46.0	49.9	50.1	52.9	61.6	66.2	68.4	74.2	75.2	79.4
Lake	1,658.0	1,822.8	1,961.6	2,062.9	2,340.1	2,499.5	2,607.7	2,812.1	2,979.2	3,170.5
Lee	3,894.2	4,375.5	4,845.9	5,283.9	6,108.8	6,562.5	6,790.6	7,185.1	7,628.9	8,103.2
Leon	1,954.0	2,187.5	2,409.0	2,653.0	2,946.8	3,235.2	3,426.7	3,642.0	3,912.8	4,191.0
Levy	211.2	228.3	242.8	265.3	286.8	305.7	327.8	348.2	369.3	396.7
Liberty	40.8	44.6	48.1	52.0	60.0	67.6	71.3	77.1	83.5	89.8
Madison	131.9	141.5	147.4	157.4	169.4	183.4	193.8	205.8	215.1	223.6
Manatee	2,610.3	2,865.6	3,073.4	3,306.5	3,818.8	4,066.0	4,289.5	4,575.9	4,862.3	5,194.2
Marion	1,778.7	1,995.4	2,197.5	2,376.8	2,646.0	2,855.3	2,977.9	3,245.4	3,414.8	3,655.1
Martin	1,540.7	1,720.5	1,922.6	2,185.3	2,565.5	2,897.1	3,000.7	3,134.5	3,320.0	3,491.4
Monroe	986.0	1,121.7	1,236.2	1,344.7	1,549.6	1,673.4	1,735.2	1,794.0	1,976.6	2,068.3
Nassau	506.8	571.6	601.8	642.1	711.7	770.9	831.8	893.9	968.0	1,035.4

See footnotes at end of table.

Continued . . .

Table 5.09. PERSONAL INCOME: TOTAL AMOUNT ON A PLACE-OF-RESIDENCE BASIS IN THE UNITED STATES AND IN THE STATE AND COUNTIES OF FLORIDA, 1985 THROUGH 1994 (Continued)

(in millions, rounded to hundred thousands of dollars)

County	1985	1986	1987	1988	1989	1990	1991	1992	1993	1994
Okaloosa	1,538.1	1,679.6	1,838.3	1,984.0	2,158.7	2,332.5	2,508.4	2,716.5	2,914.8	3,048.8
Okeechobee	251.2	281.8	299.0	325.6	359.3	383.0	400.0	416.0	443.2	463.6
Orange	7,833.5	8,593.4	9,357.2	10,206.0	11,286.8	12,137.8	12,731.4	13,480.7	14,317.8	15,108.5
Osceola	908.2	1,029.4	1,157.1	1,296.0	1,450.0	1,584.9	1,676.4	1,818.2	1,939.0	2,049.8
Palm Beach	14,554.7	16,193.7	17,959.2	19,777.9	22,400.3	25,319.5	27,016.2	28,548.9	30,415.4	31,994.1
Pasco	2,845.5	3,117.8	3,315.2	3,577.7	3,866.6	4,074.5	4,247.6	4,430.7	4,666.1	5,051.2
Pinellas	12,753.3	13,731.7	14,348.6	15,101.4	16,927.4	17,525.1	17,961.5	18,753.7	20,215.3	21,503.0
Polk	4,271.7	4,589.1	4,959.4	5,429.3	5,969.6	6,229.1	6,488.6	6,821.1	7,114.5	7,661.2
Putnam	555.1	606.0	636.9	683.5	717.4	764.2	813.0	887.2	943.7	978.6
St. Johns	984.2	1,116.1	1,262.4	1,439.9	1,651.0	1,847.6	1,973.7	2,164.1	2,349.1	2,519.9
St. Lucie	1,342.2	1,492.1	1,651.5	1,916.9	2,147.4	2,279.8	2,402.0	2,488.0	2,633.9	2,788.4
Santa Rosa	774.1	843.8	922.3	1,002.1	1,094.8	1,221.1	1,336.8	1,455.1	1,570.4	1,695.0
Sarasota	4,569.4	5,085.4	5,497.7	5,914.7	6,936.0	7,376.5	7,561.7	7,921.6	8,298.6	8,831.9
Seminole	3,237.3	3,616.7	3,975.7	4,492.1	4,984.7	5,422.9	5,693.7	6,095.2	6,565.9	7,062.4
Sumter	253.6	277.5	296.6	317.9	352.9	371.3	401.3	430.4	457.5	487.0
Suwannee	231.3	255.9	262.9	295.2	331.0	353.6	369.8	394.1	413.4	436.8
Taylor	170.6	183.9	186.2	199.2	210.5	220.8	226.2	241.6	236.9	268.2
Union	68.8	70.7	76.7	82.0	88.3	93.1	98.9	104.9	109.8	115.3
Volusia	3,994.8	4,376.7	4,701.0	5,069.8	5,531.8	5,892.6	6,096.1	6,384.6	6,729.9	7,154.9
Wakulla	112.4	127.4	136.0	153.9	171.9	189.2	204.7	218.4	238.4	258.5
Walton	224.0	245.5	254.7	277.5	303.5	333.7	369.0	400.1	439.1	470.8
Washington	135.4	142.7	151.3	165.1	177.5	193.0	208.7	223.9	235.9	248.5

1/ United States numbers are rounded to millions of dollars.
Note: Some data are revised.
Source: U.S., Department of Commerce, Bureau of Economic Analysis, Regional Economic Information System, CD-ROM, June 1996.

Table 5.10. PERSONAL INCOME: PER CAPITA AMOUNTS ON A PLACE-OF-RESIDENCE BASIS IN THE UNITED STATES AND IN THE STATE AND COUNTIES OF FLORIDA, 1984 THROUGH 1994

(rounded to dollars)

County	1984	1985	1986	1987	1988	1989	1990	1991	1992	1993	1994
United States	13,332	14,155	14,906	15,638	16,610	17,690	18,666	19,201	20,147	20,812	21,696
Florida	13,325	14,218	15,041	15,796	16,640	18,024	18,906	19,326	19,795	20,961	21,767
Alachua	10,653	11,545	12,290	13,122	13,981	15,107	16,138	16,908	17,774	18,509	19,329
Baker	8,728	9,251	9,819	10,439	11,166	11,703	12,537	12,975	13,693	14,262	14,916
Bay	10,867	11,371	11,976	12,386	12,993	13,845	15,031	15,982	16,680	17,603	18,313
Bradford	7,931	8,323	8,950	9,151	9,679	10,361	11,218	11,684	12,408	12,998	13,136
Brevard	13,359	14,216	14,606	15,152	15,824	17,099	17,805	18,326	19,049	19,451	19,888
Broward	16,168	17,152	18,094	18,970	19,842	21,512	22,393	22,499	23,231	24,446	25,494
Calhoun	7,074	7,542	8,073	8,804	9,569	9,561	10,542	10,858	10,920	11,888	12,633
Charlotte	12,692	13,690	14,582	15,078	15,721	17,371	17,527	17,432	17,839	18,418	19,222
Citrus	10,503	11,815	12,250	12,661	12,957	13,871	14,616	14,896	15,164	15,565	16,263
Clay	12,785	13,561	14,365	14,721	15,480	15,973	16,852	17,334	17,487	18,340	19,008
Collier	17,117	18,370	20,067	21,969	24,675	26,628	27,672	27,412	28,012	29,307	30,201
Columbia	9,563	9,954	10,409	10,842	11,662	12,446	13,021	13,442	13,842	14,444	14,710
Dade	13,060	13,762	14,383	15,183	15,815	17,052	17,692	17,935	16,945	19,759	20,362
De Soto	8,747	9,591	10,301	11,070	12,223	12,952	13,680	14,712	14,877	15,291	15,618
Dixie	7,245	7,850	8,267	8,983	9,606	10,429	10,729	10,758	11,096	10,252	11,648
Duval	12,720	13,561	14,267	15,039	15,761	16,912	17,888	18,359	18,999	19,754	20,481
Escambia	10,936	11,449	12,084	12,647	13,182	14,059	15,040	15,630	16,492	16,896	17,325
Flagler	11,628	12,703	13,611	14,345	14,816	14,481	14,632	14,695	15,424	16,256	16,832
Franklin	7,769	8,845	9,813	10,186	11,025	11,925	12,834	13,164	13,713	14,272	15,203
Gadsden	7,584	8,054	8,746	9,373	10,125	11,031	11,756	12,195	13,101	13,561	13,776
Gilchrist	9,175	9,744	10,099	10,404	10,626	10,961	11,510	12,085	12,787	13,129	12,992
Glades	8,232	8,361	8,837	9,299	10,699	11,655	12,324	12,908	13,065	13,651	13,357

See footnote at end of table.

Continued . . .

Table 5.10. PERSONAL INCOME: PER CAPITA AMOUNTS ON A PLACE-OF-RESIDENCE BASIS IN THE UNITED STATES AND IN THE STATE AND COUNTIES OF FLORIDA, 1984 THROUGH 1994 (Continued)

(rounded to dollars)

County	1984	1985	1986	1987	1988	1989	1990	1991	1992	1993	1994
Gulf	9,209	9,576	10,256	10,496	11,096	11,750	12,329	12,967	13,797	14,127	14,142
Hamilton	8,504	8,792	9,091	9,636	10,003	10,731	11,277	11,410	11,716	11,690	11,872
Hardee	8,885	9,965	10,377	11,293	13,564	14,607	15,140	15,721	14,911	14,430	15,056
Hendry	12,087	12,519	12,640	13,673	14,921	15,905	15,629	16,993	17,068	17,764	17,630
Hernando	10,544	11,578	12,192	12,545	13,345	14,220	14,606	14,861	15,163	15,558	16,303
Highlands	11,020	12,156	13,142	13,459	14,280	15,377	15,576	16,026	16,059	16,783	17,094
Hillsborough	12,121	12,889	13,564	14,186	15,013	16,161	17,042	17,645	18,455	19,179	20,058
Holmes	7,802	8,167	8,736	8,941	9,616	10,291	10,669	11,354	11,974	12,513	12,714
Indian River	15,193	17,047	18,356	19,833	21,664	24,059	25,222	25,913	26,526	27,175	28,461
Jackson	8,172	8,797	9,183	9,822	10,691	11,540	12,560	13,532	14,245	14,311	14,641
Jefferson	8,136	8,739	9,352	9,970	10,765	11,649	12,841	12,998	13,442	13,662	14,156
Lafayette	10,176	10,147	10,632	9,893	10,090	11,470	11,864	12,048	13,271	13,425	13,635
Lake	12,382	13,108	13,889	14,297	14,635	15,975	16,433	16,603	17,297	17,822	18,523
Lee	13,098	14,228	15,263	16,119	16,918	18,775	19,583	19,738	20,481	21,337	22,055
Leon	10,960	11,705	12,891	13,811	14,832	15,719	16,807	17,283	17,979	18,966	19,759
Levy	8,606	9,355	9,815	10,197	10,819	11,350	11,798	12,286	12,680	13,077	13,627
Liberty	8,521	9,001	9,777	10,380	11,017	12,695	12,141	12,687	14,009	14,598	13,740
Madison	8,128	8,636	9,247	9,603	10,225	10,745	11,069	11,738	12,083	12,419	12,584
Manatee	13,717	14,495	15,396	15,881	16,560	18,564	19,206	19,939	20,865	21,754	22,753
Marion	10,382	11,190	11,943	12,616	13,142	14,069	14,655	14,866	15,706	16,106	16,777
Martin	17,209	19,052	20,433	21,770	23,766	26,664	28,712	29,109	29,844	31,092	31,675
Monroe	12,583	14,097	15,716	16,903	17,820	20,183	21,448	21,817	22,157	24,174	25,146
Nassau	11,924	13,142	14,369	14,618	15,248	16,363	17,545	18,503	19,626	20,840	21,856
Okaloosa	11,179	11,777	12,448	13,365	14,190	15,243	16,223	17,170	18,111	18,865	19,257
Okeechobee	8,966	10,104	10,795	10,938	11,606	12,419	12,928	13,259	13,374	13,954	14,343

See footnote at end of table.

Continued . . .

Table 5.10. PERSONAL INCOME: PER CAPITA AMOUNTS ON A PLACE-OF-RESIDENCE BASIS IN THE UNITED STATES AND IN THE STATE AND COUNTIES OF FLORIDA, 1984 THROUGH 1994 (Continued)

(rounded to dollars)

County	1984	1985	1986	1987	1988	1989	1990	1991	1992	1993	1994
Orange	13,230	14,078	14,870	15,522	16,400	17,301	17,916	18,154	18,917	19,673	20,412
Osceola	11,217	11,733	12,520	13,216	13,613	14,361	14,712	14,652	15,182	15,429	15,634
Palm Beach	18,403	20,122	21,485	22,883	24,192	26,620	29,322	30,594	31,828	33,124	34,138
Pasco	11,261	11,978	12,517	12,838	13,401	14,093	14,493	14,883	15,264	15,873	16,902
Pinellas	15,027	15,916	16,861	17,378	18,108	20,041	20,578	20,989	21,788	23,372	24,696
Polk	11,039	11,702	12,268	12,948	13,863	14,961	15,366	15,646	16,207	16,547	17,523
Putnam	8,962	9,618	10,191	10,439	10,976	11,223	11,744	12,318	13,095	13,955	14,187
St. Johns	13,500	14,436	15,473	17,014	18,383	20,131	22,040	22,919	24,476	25,759	26,593
St. Lucie	10,917	11,525	12,141	12,757	14,067	14,903	15,181	15,484	15,654	16,140	16,716
Santa Rosa	10,921	11,497	12,018	12,589	13,250	13,842	14,963	15,927	16,537	17,399	18,068
Sarasota	17,229	18,716	20,249	21,300	22,380	25,556	26,556	26,707	27,582	28,556	29,837
Seminole	13,546	14,305	15,188	15,813	16,973	17,974	18,861	19,103	19,927	21,120	22,310
Sumter	8,568	9,181	9,690	10,135	10,649	11,403	11,757	12,534	13,021	13,529	13,838
Suwannee	9,153	9,461	10,234	10,379	11,485	12,561	13,203	13,508	14,299	14,456	14,908
Taylor	9,582	10,003	10,742	10,843	11,590	12,268	12,905	13,040	13,864	13,637	15,357
Union	6,245	6,494	6,769	7,251	8,144	8,533	9,083	9,319	9,168	9,128	9,197
Volusia	12,083	12,953	13,632	14,090	14,584	15,359	15,894	16,183	16,627	17,253	18,039
Wakulla	8,223	8,886	9,874	10,322	11,385	12,467	13,325	14,170	14,900	15,482	15,721
Walton	8,490	8,949	9,644	9,736	10,429	11,191	12,020	12,626	13,476	14,363	14,777
Washington	8,340	8,702	9,008	9,298	10,003	10,583	11,405	12,114	12,844	13,436	13,720

Note: These data were derived by dividing each type of income by the total population of the area, not just the segment of the population receiving that particular type of income. Per capita is computed using Bureau of Economic and Business Research Florida Estimates of Population for intercensal years and Bureau of the Census data for 1990. United States per capita computed by the Bureau of Economic Analysis.

Source: U.S., Department of Commerce, Bureau of Economic Analysis, Regional Economic Information System, CD-ROM, June 1996.

Table 5.11. PERSONAL INCOME: TOTAL AND PER CAPITA AMOUNTS ON A PLACE-OF-RESIDENCE BASIS IN THE STATE AND METROPOLITAN AREAS OF FLORIDA, 1992, 1993, AND 1994

Metropolitan area	Total personal income ($1,000,000)			Per capita personal income (dollars)		
	1992	1993	1994	1992	1993	1994
Florida	265,729.6	285,248.1	302,099.0	19,795	20,961	21,767
Daytona Beach	6,878.2	7,275.1	7,748.9	16,535	17,174	17,941
Flagler County	493.6	545.3	594.1	15,424	16,256	16,832
Volusia County	6,384.6	6,729.9	7,154.9	16,627	17,253	18,039
Ft. Lauderdale	30,062.7	32,207.3	34,167.9	23,231	24,446	25,494
Ft. Myers-Cape Coral	7,185.1	7,628.9	8,103.2	20,481	21,337	22,055
Ft. Pierce-Port St. Lucie	5,622.6	5,953.9	6,279.8	21,300	22,054	22,668
Martin County	3,134.5	3,320.0	3,491.4	29,844	31,092	31,675
St. Lucie County	2,488.0	2,633.9	2,788.4	15,654	16,140	16,716
Ft. Walton Beach	2,716.5	2,914.8	3,048.8	18,111	18,865	19,257
Gainesville	3,309.6	3,528.9	3,747.5	17,774	18,509	19,329
Jacksonville	18,217.6	19,284.2	20,347.8	19,362	20,210	20,966
Clay County	1,982.7	2,107.6	2,238.7	17,487	18,340	19,008
Duval County	13,177.0	13,859.4	14,553.8	18,999	19,754	20,481
Nassau County	893.9	968.0	1,035.4	19,626	20,840	21,856
St. Johns County	2,164.1	2,349.1	2,519.9	24,476	25,759	26,593
Lakeland-Winter Haven	6,821.1	7,114.5	7,661.2	16,207	16,547	17,523
Melbourne-Titusville-Palm Bay	7,957.7	8,306.3	8,677.9	19,049	19,451	19,888
Miami	33,600.6	38,552.8	40,530.0	16,945	19,759	20,362
Naples	4,720.5	5,118.9	5,452.5	28,012	29,307	30,201
Ocala	3,245.4	3,414.8	3,655.1	15,706	16,106	16,777
Orlando	24,206.2	25,801.8	27,391.2	18,608	19,378	20,155
Lake County	2,812.1	2,979.2	3,170.5	17,297	17,822	18,523
Orange County	13,480.7	14,317.8	15,108.5	18,917	19,673	20,412
Osceola County	1,818.2	1,939.0	2,049.8	15,182	15,429	15,634
Seminole County	6,095.2	6,565.9	7,062.4	19,927	21,120	22,310
Panama City	2,190.9	2,359.9	2,495.9	16,680	17,603	18,313
Pensacola	5,871.5	6,167.6	6,495.3	16,503	17,022	17,513
Escambia County	4,416.4	4,597.2	4,800.2	16,492	16,896	17,325
Santa Rosa County	1,455.1	1,570.4	1,695.0	16,537	17,399	18,068
Punta Gorda	2,117.2	2,241.4	2,400.5	17,839	18,418	19,222
Sarasota-Bradenton	12,497.5	13,160.9	14,026.1	24,673	25,599	26,753
Manatee County	4,575.9	4,862.3	5,194.2	20,865	21,754	22,753
Sarasota County	7,921.6	8,298.6	8,831.9	27,582	28,556	29,837
Tallahassee	4,198.4	4,499.1	4,808.9	17,133	18,030	18,714
Gadsden County	556.4	586.3	617.9	13,101	13,561	13,776
Leon County	3,642.0	3,912.8	4,191.0	17,979	18,966	19,759
Tampa-St. Petersburg-Clearwater	40,584.3	43,230.5	46,058.9	19,206	20,232	21,289
Hernando County	1,639.3	1,737.7	1,872.7	15,163	15,558	16,303
Hillsborough County	15,760.6	16,611.5	17,632.0	18,455	19,179	20,058
Pasco County	4,430.7	4,666.1	5,051.2	15,264	15,873	16,902
Pinellas County	18,753.7	20,215.3	21,503.0	21,788	23,372	24,696
West Palm Beach-Boca Raton	28,548.9	30,415.4	31,994.1	31,828	33,124	34,138

Note: Data for Metropolitan Statistical Areas (MSAs) and Primary Metropolitan Statistical Areas (PMSAs) based on 1992 MSA designations. See Glossary for definitions and map at the front of the book for area boundaries. Data for 1992 and 1993 are revised. See footnote on per capita computation on Table 5.10.

Source: U.S., Department of Commerce, Bureau of Economic Analysis, Regional Economic Information System, CD-ROM, June 1996.

Table 5.12. PERSONAL INCOME: PER CAPITA AMOUNTS BY TYPE IN THE UNITED STATES AND IN THE STATE AND COUNTIES OF FLORIDA, 1993 AND 1994

(rounded to dollars)

County	1993						1994					
			Transfer payments						Transfer payments			
	Total personal income	Nonfarm personal income	Income maintenance 1/	Unemployment insurance	Retirement and other	Dividends interest and rent 2/	Total personal income	Nonfarm personal income	Income maintenance 1/	Unemployment insurance	Retirement and other	Dividends interest and rent 2/
United States	20,812	20,616	336	134	1,707	3,272	21,696	21,496	346	91	1,781	3,413
Florida	20,961	20,740	289	91	2,046	4,962	21,767	21,591	294	60	2,115	5,185
Alachua	18,509	18,400	315	55	1,392	2,667	19,329	19,255	326	34	1,438	2,831
Baker	14,262	13,624	366	88	1,338	1,158	14,916	14,309	372	47	1,469	1,237
Bay	17,603	17,598	299	113	2,345	2,522	18,313	18,309	313	72	2,482	2,667
Bradford	12,998	12,767	403	58	1,571	1,201	13,136	12,989	419	31	1,644	1,236
Brevard	19,451	19,426	197	107	2,632	3,378	19,888	19,868	205	70	2,771	3,519
Broward	24,446	24,426	209	119	1,995	6,267	25,494	25,480	214	80	2,031	6,542
Calhoun	11,888	11,617	538	75	1,575	1,175	12,633	12,386	548	47	1,678	1,248
Charlotte	18,418	18,308	120	45	3,466	6,518	19,222	19,139	126	29	3,620	6,740
Citrus	15,565	15,558	217	98	3,124	4,563	16,263	16,261	227	64	3,223	4,821
Clay	18,340	18,309	146	62	1,920	1,856	19,008	18,986	148	37	2,037	1,932
Collier	29,307	28,361	170	70	2,274	13,556	30,201	29,562	175	47	2,394	13,948
Columbia	14,444	14,291	444	95	1,835	1,716	14,710	14,605	451	57	1,873	1,747
Dade	19,759	19,636	518	117	1,228	3,413	20,362	20,281	513	84	1,244	3,598
De Soto	15,291	13,536	385	76	1,869	3,116	15,618	14,017	412	40	1,919	3,203
Dixie	10,252	10,143	542	72	1,976	523	11,648	11,595	557	45	2,121	1,492
Duval	19,754	19,738	341	71	1,743	2,413	20,481	20,466	350	46	1,802	2,553
Escambia	16,896	16,877	383	50	2,406	2,156	17,325	17,311	397	32	2,477	2,252
Flagler	16,256	15,960	198	66	3,490	3,512	16,832	16,647	198	37	3,777	3,543
Franklin	14,272	14,272	546	37	2,078	2,345	15,203	15,203	540	27	2,175	2,515
Gadsden	13,561	12,834	677	61	1,473	1,346	13,776	13,117	688	35	1,483	1,390
Gilchrist	13,129	12,315	324	47	1,796	1,434	12,992	12,451	316	25	1,823	1,434
Glades	13,651	10,714	284	110	1,392	2,196	13,357	11,058	313	71	1,388	2,339
Gulf	14,127	14,127	447	85	2,086	1,785	14,142	14,142	443	48	2,222	1,776

See footnotes at end of table.

Continued . . .

Table 5.12. PERSONAL INCOME: PER CAPITA AMOUNTS BY TYPE IN THE UNITED STATES AND IN THE STATE AND COUNTIES OF FLORIDA, 1993 AND 1994 (Continued)

(rounded to dollars)

County	1993 Total personal income	1993 Nonfarm personal income	1993 Transfer payments: Income maintenance 1/	1993 Transfer payments: Unemployment insurance	1993 Transfer payments: Retirement and other	1993 Dividends interest and rent 2/	1994 Total personal income	1994 Nonfarm personal income	1994 Transfer payments: Income maintenance 1/	1994 Transfer payments: Unemployment insurance	1994 Transfer payments: Retirement and other	1994 Dividends interest and rent 2/
Hamilton	11,690	10,709	491	76	1,399	947	11,872	11,132	506	32	1,469	1,024
Hardee	14,430	12,219	552	132	1,298	1,924	15,056	12,964	577	88	1,399	2,005
Hendry	17,764	13,699	404	173	1,280	2,100	17,630	14,153	421	132	1,336	2,195
Hernando	15,558	15,483	205	62	3,248	3,875	16,303	16,245	210	43	3,384	4,084
Highlands	16,783	15,529	279	87	2,938	4,675	17,094	16,033	286	56	3,023	4,796
Hillsborough	19,179	18,966	331	98	1,653	2,523	20,058	19,886	333	59	1,703	2,655
Holmes	12,513	11,813	533	44	1,987	1,184	12,714	12,167	545	30	1,981	1,218
Indian River	27,175	26,404	164	114	2,927	12,587	28,461	27,659	168	77	3,011	13,111
Jackson	14,311	13,970	395	57	1,706	1,456	14,641	14,379	415	37	1,750	1,519
Jefferson	13,662	13,302	550	31	1,576	1,980	14,156	13,924	576	22	1,696	2,095
Lafayette	13,425	10,087	386	46	1,614	1,245	13,635	10,593	363	25	1,579	1,316
Lake	17,822	17,510	236	82	2,927	4,588	18,523	18,245	251	55	3,114	4,816
Lee	21,337	21,101	177	57	2,541	6,984	22,055	21,873	176	36	2,601	7,219
Leon	18,966	18,957	256	39	1,242	2,335	19,759	19,752	251	26	1,303	2,439
Levy	13,077	12,685	392	56	2,050	2,173	13,627	13,340	403	35	2,186	2,331
Liberty	14,598	14,490	394	20	1,607	956	13,740	13,683	364	12	1,595	896
Madison	12,419	11,972	608	49	1,436	1,339	12,584	12,322	595	29	1,423	1,391
Manatee	21,754	21,059	208	55	2,541	6,351	22,753	22,262	214	34	2,618	6,631
Marion	16,106	15,917	308	69	2,566	3,381	16,777	16,627	321	44	2,740	3,522
Martin	31,092	30,438	163	102	2,748	14,612	31,675	30,979	167	66	2,850	15,018
Monroe	24,174	24,174	187	39	1,706	8,701	25,146	25,146	196	25	1,756	9,212
Nassau	20,840	20,531	240	72	1,805	3,329	21,856	21,559	240	47	2,001	3,484
Okaloosa	18,865	18,851	182	70	2,836	2,999	19,257	19,249	187	42	2,984	3,118
Okeechobee	13,954	12,090	332	86	1,852	2,139	14,343	12,679	322	64	1,926	2,242
Orange	19,673	19,435	273	74	1,561	2,615	20,412	20,206	283	49	1,603	2,745
Osceola	15,429	15,238	222	76	1,529	1,681	15,634	15,495	235	49	1,601	1,719

See footnotes at end of table.

Continued . . .

Table 5.12. PERSONAL INCOME: PER CAPITA AMOUNTS BY TYPE IN THE UNITED STATES AND IN THE STATE AND COUNTIES OF FLORIDA, 1993 AND 1994 (Continued)

(rounded to dollars)

County	1993						1994					
			Transfer payments						Transfer payments			
	Total personal income	Nonfarm personal income	Income maintenance 1/	Unemployment insurance	Retirement and other	Dividends interest and rent 2/	Total personal income	Nonfarm personal income	Income maintenance 1/	Unemployment insurance	Retirement and other	Dividends interest and rent 2/
Palm Beach	33,124	32,420	190	131	2,365	13,923	34,138	33,676	193	89	2,464	14,453
Pasco	15,873	15,786	207	70	2,655	3,408	16,902	16,828	217	44	2,694	3,602
Pinellas	23,372	23,364	203	81	2,663	6,375	24,696	24,688	216	50	2,706	6,735
Polk	16,547	16,212	309	105	1,947	2,956	17,523	17,161	316	65	2,047	3,106
Putnam	13,955	13,721	486	79	2,166	1,755	14,187	13,980	502	48	2,248	1,843
St. Johns	25,759	25,618	222	70	2,204	6,169	26,593	26,481	216	45	2,278	6,313
St. Lucie	16,140	15,680	306	158	2,256	3,431	16,716	16,208	310	118	2,357	3,574
Santa Rosa	17,399	17,208	240	52	2,035	2,138	18,068	17,854	235	34	2,202	2,194
Sarasota	28,556	28,508	132	54	3,123	12,141	29,837	29,800	138	34	3,236	12,674
Seminole	21,120	21,066	173	79	1,552	2,707	22,310	22,265	183	53	1,608	2,834
Sumter	13,529	13,055	423	56	2,987	2,009	13,838	13,503	439	36	3,138	2,062
Suwannee	14,456	13,596	415	71	2,037	2,103	14,908	14,245	423	37	2,156	2,184
Taylor	13,637	13,570	511	147	1,851	913	15,357	15,326	545	79	1,997	1,584
Union	9,128	8,904	222	28	926	858	9,197	9,064	228	15	963	879
Volusia	17,253	17,126	228	80	2,461	4,207	18,039	17,911	237	52	2,543	4,423
Wakulla	15,482	15,453	360	30	1,450	1,660	15,721	15,711	362	21	1,450	1,679
Walton	14,363	14,219	353	53	2,703	1,918	14,777	14,661	365	35	2,837	1,962
Washington	13,436	13,183	493	95	2,085	1,452	13,720	13,558	491	57	2,049	1,502

1/ Includes supplemental security income payments, payments to families with dependent children (AFDC), general assistance payments, food stamp payments, and other assistance payments, including emergency assistance.

2/ Includes the capital consumption adjustment for rental income of persons.

Note: These data were derived by dividing each type of income by the total population of the area, not just the segment of the population receiving that particular type of income. Per capita is computed using Bureau of Economic and Business Research *Florida Estimates of Population* for 1993 and 1994, respectively. United States data computed using Bureau of the Census data.

Source: U.S., Department of Commerce, Bureau of Economic Analysis, Regional Economic Information System, CD-ROM, June 1996.

Table 5.13. DERIVATION OF PERSONAL INCOME: DERIVATION ON A PLACE-OF-RESIDENCE BASIS IN THE STATE AND METROPOLITAN AREAS OF FLORIDA, 1994

(in millions of dollars)

Metropolitan Statistical Area (MSA) 1/	Total earnings by place of work	Less personal contributions for social insurance	Plus residence adjustment	Plus dividends interest and rent	Plus transfer payments	Personal income by place of residence
Florida	185,237	11,285	690	71,958	55,500	302,099
Daytona Beach	3,709	247	496	1,879	1,912	7,749
Flagler County	216	16	98	125	170	594
Volusia County	3,492	231	398	1,754	1,742	7,155
Ft. Lauderdale	18,746	1,164	2,391	8,768	5,428	34,168
Ft. Myers-Cape Coral	4,171	268	-17	2,652	1,566	8,103
Ft. Pierce-Port St. Lucie	2,778	176	287	2,252	1,139	6,280
Martin County	1,326	86	116	1,655	480	3,491
St. Lucie County	1,452	90	171	596	659	2,788
Ft. Walton Beach	2,071	120	-109	494	713	3,049
Gainesville	2,854	135	-215	549	694	3,747
Jacksonville	15,038	902	-27	2,805	3,433	20,348
Clay County	768	47	929	228	362	2,239
Duval County	12,947	773	-1,968	1,814	2,534	14,554
Nassau County	457	26	268	165	171	1,035
St. Johns County	867	55	744	598	366	2,520
Lakeland-Winter Haven	5,019	309	15	1,358	1,578	7,661
Melbourne-Titusville-Palm Bay	5,675	354	6	1,535	1,816	8,678
Miami	31,110	1,829	-3,612	7,162	7,700	40,530
Naples	2,433	152	21	2,518	632	5,453
Ocala	1,889	126	196	767	930	3,655
Orlando	21,227	1,279	-838	3,978	4,302	27,391
Lake County	1,358	96	268	824	817	3,170
Orange County	15,409	911	-3,683	2,032	2,262	15,108
Osceola County	1,173	71	348	225	375	2,050
Seminole County	3,288	201	2,230	897	848	7,062
Panama City	1,652	96	-20	363	596	2,496
Pensacola	4,233	248	114	830	1,566	6,495
Escambia County	3,570	209	-420	624	1,234	4,800
Santa Rosa County	663	39	534	206	332	1,695
Punta Gorda	892	66	63	842	670	2,400
Sarasota-Bradenton	6,220	420	414	5,265	2,547	14,026
Manatee County	2,615	168	245	1,514	989	5,194
Sarasota County	3,605	252	169	3,751	1,558	8,832
Tallahassee	3,866	166	-221	580	750	4,809
Gadsden County	323	14	54	62	193	618
Leon County	3,544	151	-275	517	556	4,191
Tampa-St. Petersburg-Clearwater	29,004	1,843	-178	9,744	9,332	46,059
Hernando County	665	53	231	469	561	1,873
Hillsborough County	15,131	893	-1,901	2,334	2,961	17,632
Pasco County	1,792	139	928	1,077	1,394	5,051
Pinellas County	11,417	758	564	5,864	4,416	21,503
West Palm Beach-Boca Raton	14,395	897	997	13,545	3,954	31,994

1/ Based on 1992 MSA designations.

Note: See Table 5.14 for derivation of personal income notes. See Glossary for MSA definitions and map at the front of the book for area boundaries.

Source: U.S., Department of Commerce, Bureau of Economic Analysis, Regional Economic Information System, CD-ROM, June 1996.

Table 5.14. DERIVATION OF PERSONAL INCOME: DERIVATION ON A PLACE-OF-RESIDENCE BASIS IN THE UNITED STATES AND IN THE STATE AND COUNTIES OF FLORIDA 1993 AND 1994

(rounded to millions of dollars)

County	Total earn- ings by place of work 1/	Less personal contri- butions for social insurance	Plus resi- dence adjust- ment 2/	Plus dividends interest and rent 3/	Plus transfer payments	Personal income by place of residence
			1993 A/			
United States	3,869,403	260,684	-828	843,362	913,753	5,365,006
Florida	175,170	10,373	662	67,521	55,500	285,248
Alachua	2,688	123	-200	508	694	3,529
Baker	125	5	70	23	70	278
Bay	1,571	89	-18	338	596	2,360
Bradford	144	7	55	28	88	303
Brevard	5,500	335	-2	1,442	1,816	8,306
Broward	17,549	1,065	2,341	8,257	5,428	32,207
Calhoun	67	4	15	13	48	136
Charlotte	826	60	61	793	670	2,241
Citrus	644	49	34	460	506	1,569
Clay	728	44	873	213	362	2,108
Collier	2,307	137	-3	2,368	632	5,119
Columbia	387	21	50	80	186	671
Dade	29,816	1,713	-3,488	6,659	7,700	38,553
De Soto	213	9	4	79	108	389
Dixie	64	4	11	6	48	121
Duval	12,323	719	-1,836	1,693	2,534	13,859
Escambia	3,433	194	-395	587	1,234	4,597
Flagler	198	14	91	118	170	545
Franklin	63	4	13	23	48	140
Gadsden	315	13	44	58	193	586
Gilchrist	55	2	32	15	45	141
Glades	49	2	26	18	23	113
Gulf	110	6	-5	22	60	175
Hamilton	121	6	-32	11	44	136
Hardee	190	8	24	42	75	318
Hendry	360	14	12	59	86	498
Hernando	614	47	216	433	561	1,738
Highlands	578	36	-6	342	375	1,229
Hillsborough	14,135	812	-1,726	2,185	2,961	16,611
Holmes	80	4	37	19	76	204
Indian River	1,030	66	-3	1,204	459	2,599
Jackson	350	17	26	65	226	635

See footnotes at end of table.

Continued . . .

Table 5.14. DERIVATION OF PERSONAL INCOME: DERIVATION ON A PLACE-OF-RESIDENCE BASIS IN THE UNITED STATES AND IN THE STATE AND COUNTIES OF FLORIDA 1993 AND 1994 (Continued)

(rounded to millions of dollars)

County	Total earn- ings by place of work 1/	Less personal contri- butions for social insurance	Plus resi- dence adjust- ment 2/	Plus dividends interest and rent 3/	Plus transfer payments	Personal income by place of residence
		1993 A/ (Continued)				
Jefferson	71	4	40	26	48	177
Lafayette	43	1	10	7	17	75
Lake	1,272	87	275	767	817	2,979
Lee	3,893	243	8	2,497	1,566	7,629
Leon	3,291	137	-246	482	556	3,913
Levy	146	9	60	61	121	369
Liberty	40	2	11	5	32	84
Madison	114	6	16	23	71	215
Manatee	2,370	146	290	1,419	989	4,862
Marion	1,764	114	191	717	930	3,415
Martin	1,319	84	76	1,560	480	3,320
Monroe	1,013	59	63	711	260	1,977
Nassau	432	24	249	155	171	968
Okaloosa	1,980	111	-86	463	713	2,915
Okeechobee	245	12	27	68	122	443
Orange	14,598	840	-3,491	1,903	2,262	14,318
Osceola	1,089	64	358	211	375	1,939
Palm Beach	13,802	826	950	12,785	3,954	30,415
Pasco	1,646	125	821	1,002	1,394	4,666
Pinellas	10,686	692	510	5,514	4,416	20,215
Polk	4,629	279	6	1,271	1,578	7,114
Putnam	503	30	78	119	291	944
St. Johns	806	50	688	563	366	2,349
St. Lucie	1,356	82	179	560	659	2,634
Santa Rosa	631	37	481	193	332	1,570
Sarasota	3,423	232	124	3,528	1,558	8,299
Seminole	3,029	181	2,072	842	848	6,566
Sumter	184	12	52	68	179	457
Suwannee	215	12	31	60	129	413
Taylor	170	10	-10	16	76	237
Union	95	3	-17	10	27	110
Volusia	3,280	208	377	1,641	1,742	6,730
Wakulla	81	5	89	26	51	238
Walton	206	12	44	59	155	439
Washington	116	6	13	25	91	236

See footnotes at end of table.

Continued . . .

Table 5.14. DERIVATION OF PERSONAL INCOME: DERIVATION ON A PLACE-OF-RESIDENCE BASIS IN THE UNITED STATES AND IN THE STATE AND COUNTIES OF FLORIDA 1993 AND 1994 (Continued)

(rounded to millions of dollars)

County	Total earn-ings by place of work 1/	Less personal contri-butions for social insurance	Plus resi-dence adjust-ment 2/	Plus dividends interest and rent 3/	Plus transfer payments	Personal income by place of residence
			1994			
United States	4,084,922	280,836	-857	888,434	956,600	5,648,263
Florida	185,237	11,285	690	71,958	55,500	302,099
Alachua	2,854	135	-215	549	694	3,747
Baker	131	5	73	24	70	294
Bay	1,652	96	-20	363	596	2,496
Bradford	149	7	58	30	88	318
Brevard	5,675	354	6	1,535	1,816	8,678
Broward	18,746	1,164	2,391	8,768	5,428	34,168
Calhoun	73	4	15	14	48	146
Charlotte	892	66	63	842	670	2,400
Citrus	685	54	39	496	506	1,673
Clay	768	47	929	228	362	2,239
Collier	2,433	152	21	2,518	632	5,453
Columbia	420	23	51	85	186	719
Dade	31,110	1,829	-3,612	7,162	7,700	40,530
De Soto	223	10	5	84	108	410
Dixie	69	4	11	18	48	142
Duval	12,947	773	-1,968	1,814	2,534	14,554
Escambia	3,570	209	-420	624	1,234	4,800
Flagler	216	16	98	125	170	594
Franklin	69	4	14	25	48	152
Gadsden	323	14	54	62	193	618
Gilchrist	56	3	35	17	45	150
Glades	46	2	26	20	23	112
Gulf	116	7	-5	24	60	188
Hamilton	125	6	-33	12	44	141
Hardee	204	9	24	45	75	338
Hendry	357	15	14	63	86	506
Hernando	665	53	231	469	561	1,873
Highlands	606	40	-7	364	375	1,297
Hillsborough	15,131	893	-1,901	2,334	2,961	17,632
Holmes	85	5	38	21	76	215
Indian River	1,119	73	-9	1,277	459	2,773
Jackson	360	18	29	69	226	665
Jefferson	68	4	45	27	48	185
Lafayette	46	1	10	8	17	79
Lake	1,358	96	268	824	817	3,170
Lee	4,171	268	-17	2,652	1,566	8,103
Leon	3,544	151	-275	517	556	4,191

See footnotes at end of table.

Continued . . .

Table 5.14. DERIVATION OF PERSONAL INCOME: DERIVATION ON A PLACE-OF-RESIDENCE BASIS IN THE UNITED STATES AND IN THE STATE AND COUNTIES OF FLORIDA 1993 AND 1994 (Continued)

(rounded to millions of dollars)

County	Total earn- ings by place of work 1/	Less personal contri- butions for social insurance	Plus resi- dence adjust- ment 2/	Plus dividends interest and rent 3/	Plus transfer payments	Personal income by place of residence
			1994 (Continued)			
Levy	155	10	63	68	121	397
Liberty	42	2	12	6	32	90
Madison	117	7	17	25	71	224
Manatee	2,615	168	245	1,514	989	5,194
Marion	1,889	126	196	767	930	3,655
Martin	1,326	86	116	1,655	480	3,491
Monroe	1,045	61	67	758	260	2,068
Nassau	457	26	268	165	171	1,035
Okaloosa	2,071	120	-109	494	713	3,049
Okeechobee	255	14	28	72	122	464
Orange	15,409	911	-3,683	2,032	2,262	15,108
Osceola	1,173	71	348	225	375	2,050
Palm Beach	14,395	897	997	13,545	3,954	31,994
Pasco	1,792	139	928	1,077	1,394	5,051
Pinellas	11,417	758	564	5,864	4,416	21,503
Polk	5,019	309	15	1,358	1,578	7,661
Putnam	502	31	89	127	291	979
St. Johns	867	55	744	598	366	2,520
St. Lucie	1,452	90	171	596	659	2,788
Santa Rosa	663	39	534	206	332	1,695
Sarasota	3,605	252	169	3,751	1,558	8,832
Seminole	3,288	201	2,230	897	848	7,062
Sumter	192	13	56	73	179	487
Suwannee	224	14	33	64	129	437
Taylor	188	12	-12	28	76	268
Union	99	3	-18	11	27	115
Volusia	3,492	231	398	1,754	1,742	7,155
Wakulla	85	5	100	28	51	258
Walton	221	13	45	63	155	471
Washington	124	7	14	27	91	249

A/ Revised.
1/ Consists of wage and salary disbursements, other labor income, and proprietors' income.
2/ An estimate of the net gain or loss to an area because of commuting from place of residence to place of work. Some persons earn income in the area in which they live; others earn income outside that area. United States includes adjustments for border workers, U.S. residents commuting outside U.S. borders less income of foreign residents commuting inside U.S. borders, plus certain Caribbean seasonal workers.
3/ Includes the capital consumption adjustment for rental income of persons.

Source: U.S., Department of Commerce, Bureau of Economic Analysis, Regional Economic Information System, CD-ROM, June 1996.

Table 5.20. EARNED INCOME: TOTAL EARNINGS ON A PLACE-OF-WORK BASIS AND PERCENTAGE DISTRIBUTION BY TYPE AND MAJOR INDUSTRIAL SOURCE IN FLORIDA, OTHER SUNBELT STATES, OTHER POPULOUS STATES AND THE UNITED STATES, 1994

Item	Florida	Other sunbelt states										
		Alabama	Arizona	Arkansas	California	Georgia	Louisiana	Mississippi	New Mexico	North Carolina	Oklahoma	South Carolina
Earnings by place of work ($1,000,000)	185,225	54,330	54,162	29,696	518,094	108,980	53,246	29,191	20,020	105,412	39,679	47,098
	Percentage distribution by type of income											
Wage and salary disbursements	80.4	79.5	81.3	75.9	76.4	80.1	78.3	78.0	79.7	79.6	75.9	81.2
Other labor income	8.7	9.8	9.0	9.8	9.4	9.6	9.5	9.8	9.3	9.4	9.4	9.6
Proprietors' income	10.9	10.7	9.7	14.3	14.2	10.3	12.1	12.2	11.0	11.0	14.7	9.2
	Percentage distribution by industrial source of income											
Farm	1.3	2.2	1.2	4.6	1.4	1.8	1.0	2.4	2.1	2.8	2.8	1.0
Agricultural services 1/	1.1	0.7	0.9	0.9	1.0	0.5	0.6	0.7	0.6	0.6	0.7	0.6
Mining	0.2	1.1	1.1	0.5	0.4	0.3	4.6	0.7	3.5	0.1	5.0	0.1
Construction	5.8	5.3	6.6	5.0	5.4	4.9	6.6	5.2	6.5	5.6	4.6	6.3
Manufacturing	9.4	22.7	14.3	24.0	15.6	17.5	14.7	24.4	7.8	25.8	14.9	26.6
Transportation, communications, and public utilities	6.6	6.6	6.1	8.1	5.9	9.2	8.0	6.4	6.2	6.3	8.1	5.6
Wholesale trade	6.4	5.6	5.9	5.2	6.1	8.6	5.5	4.8	4.3	6.1	5.0	4.4
Retail trade	12.0	9.8	11.6	11.4	9.8	9.7	9.6	10.3	11.4	10.1	10.4	11.4
Finance, insurance, and real estate	8.0	4.7	7.3	4.4	6.9	6.7	5.0	4.4	4.3	5.3	5.1	4.5
Services	33.1	21.8	27.9	20.3	31.6	24.5	26.4	21.3	27.2	20.5	23.3	20.2
Government	16.2	19.4	17.1	15.6	15.9	16.2	17.8	19.4	26.1	16.8	20.2	19.2

See footnotes at end of table.

Continued . . .

Table 5.20. EARNED INCOME: TOTAL EARNINGS ON A PLACE-OF-WORK BASIS AND PERCENTAGE DISTRIBUTION BY TYPE AND MAJOR INDUSTRIAL SOURCE IN FLORIDA, OTHER SUNBELT STATES, OTHER POPULOUS STATES AND THE UNITED STATES, 1994

Item	Other sunbelt states (Continued)			Other populous states								United States
	Tennessee	Texas	Virginia	Illinois	Indiana	Massachusetts	Michigan	New Jersey	New York	Ohio	Pennsylvania	
Earnings by place of work ($1,000,000)	76,674	275,665	103,679	205,735	85,711	114,275	153,257	149,156	339,420	168,645	183,516	4,085,669
	Percentage distribution by type of income											
Wage and salary disbursements	78.5	76.6	83.0	79.8	80.4	81.3	81.6	81.4	79.8	80.8	78.3	79.1
Other labor income	9.6	8.8	8.8	9.6	10.5	9.3	11.1	9.2	8.4	9.6	10.1	9.3
Proprietors' income	12.0	14.6	8.2	10.6	9.2	9.3	7.3	9.3	11.7	9.6	11.6	11.6
	Percentage distribution by industrial source of income											
Farm	0.9	1.3	0.6	0.9	1.1	0.2	0.3	0.2	0.2	0.8	0.5	1.3
Agricultural services 1/	0.4	0.6	0.5	0.5	0.5	0.5	0.4	0.4	0.3	0.4	0.5	0.7
Mining	0.3	4.2	0.6	0.4	0.4	0.1	0.3	0.1	0.1	0.4	0.6	0.9
Construction	5.4	5.6	5.9	5.5	6.0	4.1	4.6	4.5	3.6	5.1	5.5	5.3
Manufacturing	23.6	15.2	13.8	20.4	31.5	18.2	33.0	16.7	12.9	28.3	21.3	18.3
Transportation, communications, and public utilities	7.0	8.6	6.5	7.4	6.4	5.1	5.0	8.1	5.9	5.6	7.0	6.7
Wholesale trade	6.5	6.8	5.3	7.5	5.6	6.7	6.0	8.7	6.0	6.3	5.8	6.2
Retail trade	10.7	9.8	9.2	8.7	9.6	9.0	8.8	8.6	7.1	9.6	9.7	9.6
Finance, insurance, and real estate	5.3	6.1	6.1	8.9	5.2	9.0	4.9	7.8	16.6	5.7	6.9	7.4
Services	25.8	26.2	27.2	27.0	20.8	34.8	23.2	29.9	31.7	24.3	29.1	27.6
Government	14.2	15.7	24.2	12.8	12.9	12.4	13.3	14.9	15.6	13.5	13.2	16.0

1/ Includes forestry, fisheries, and other.

Note: Data differ from figures on other income tables because of revisions made after publication of these numbers. Data reflect the losses from damage caused by the Northridge earthquake in California.

Source: U.S., Department of Commerce, Bureau of Economic Analysis, *Survey of Current Business,* August 1995.

Table 5.21. PERSONAL INCOME: AMOUNTS BY MAJOR SOURCE IN THE METROPOLITAN AND NONMETROPOLITAN AREAS OF FLORIDA THE SOUTHEAST, AND THE UNITED STATES, 1993 AND 1994

(rounded to millions of dollars)

Item	Florida			Southeast			United States		
	Total	Metro-politan areas	Non-metro-politan areas	Total	Metro-politan areas	Non-metro-politan areas	Total	Metro-politan areas	Non-metro-politan areas
	Income by place of residence, 1993 A/								
Total personal income	285,248	269,177	16,071	1,157,405	884,070	273,335	5,365,006	4,524,575	840,431
Derivation of personal income									
Total earnings by place of work	175,170	167,298	7,871	808,494	637,214	171,279	3,869,403	3,345,487	523,916
Less: Personal contributions for social insurance	10,373	9,928	445	51,249	40,062	11,188	260,684	225,877	34,807
Plus: Adjustment for residence	662	-208	870	5,947	-5,308	11,255	-828	-35,215	34,387
Equals: Net earnings by place of residence	165,459	157,163	8,296	763,191	591,844	171,347	3,607,891	3,084,394	523,497
Plus: Dividends, interest, and rent	67,521	63,726	3,795	185,454	148,657	36,797	843,362	712,653	130,709
Plus: Transfer payments	52,268	48,288	3,980	208,761	143,569	65,192	913,753	727,528	186,225
	Earnings by place of work, 1993 A/								
Components of earnings									
Wages and salaries	141,015	135,284	5,731	648,790	518,671	130,119	3,072,687	2,684,208	388,479
Other labor income	14,907	14,263	644	74,585	57,980	16,605	354,994	306,272	48,722
Proprietors' income 1/	19,247	17,752	1,496	85,118	60,563	24,555	441,722	355,007	86,715
Farm	2,194	1,694	500	10,744	4,009	6,735	37,432	14,083	23,349
Nonfarm	17,053	16,058	995	74,374	56,553	17,821	404,290	340,924	63,366

See footnotes at end of table.

Continued . . .

Table 5.21. PERSONAL INCOME: AMOUNTS BY MAJOR SOURCE IN THE METROPOLITAN AND NONMETROPOLITAN AREAS OF FLORIDA THE SOUTHEAST, AND THE UNITED STATES, 1993 AND 1994

(rounded to millions of dollars)

Item	Florida			Southeast			United States		
	Total	Metro-politan areas	Non-metro-politan areas	Total	Metro-politan areas	Non-metro-politan areas	Total	Metro-politan areas	Non-metro-politan areas
	Earnings by place of work, 1993 A/ (Continued)								
Earnings by industry									
Farm	3,003	2,357	646	13,484	5,304	8,179	50,636	21,182	29,454
Nonfarm									
Private	143,213	137,782	5,431	648,381	516,889	131,493	3,187,422	2,793,414	394,008
Agricultural services 2/	1,909	B/ 1,541	B/ 279	5,339	(D)	(D)	24,574	18,481	6,093
Mining	303	B/ 260	(D)	7,757	B/ 3,347	B/ 4,086	35,170	21,729	13,441
Construction	9,920	9,407	B/ 493	43,974	B/ 35,222	B/ 8,548	197,563	169,442	28,121
Manufacturing	16,816	16,009	807	148,150	B/ 99,429	B/ 48,720	709,563	588,295	121,268
Nondurable goods	6,417	5,930	(D)	74,317	B/ 47,731	B/ 25,606	281,692	228,018	53,674
Durable goods	10,399	10,079	B/ 304	73,833	B/ 51,518	B/ 21,441	427,871	360,277	67,594
Transportation 3/	11,543	11,085	B/ 448	57,179	B/ 47,215	B/ 9,025	257,262	224,008	33,254
Wholesale trade	11,053	B/ 10,795	B/ 223	49,251	B/ 42,887	B/ 6,148	240,601	219,879	20,722
Retail trade	20,854	19,845	1,009	83,927	B/ 65,900	B/ 17,900	368,127	311,282	56,845
Finance, insurance, and real estate	14,176	13,872	B/ 303	48,720	B/ 43,599	B/ 5,064	296,428	279,299	17,129
Services	56,640	54,858	1,782	204,084	B/ 174,538	B/ 27,823	1,058,134	960,998	97,136
Government 4/	28,954	27,159	1,795	146,629	115,021	31,607	631,345	530,890	100,455
Federal, civilian	5,027	4,838	190	30,954	27,030	3,924	128,128	114,418	13,710
Federal, military	2,955	2,857	98	18,835	15,960	2,875	49,420	42,281	7,139
State and local	20,971	19,465	1,507	96,840	72,032	24,809	453,797	374,191	79,606

See footnotes at end of table.

Continued . . .

Table 5.21. PERSONAL INCOME: AMOUNTS BY MAJOR SOURCE IN THE METROPOLITAN AND NONMETROPOLITAN AREAS OF FLORIDA THE SOUTHEAST, AND THE UNITED STATES, 1993 AND 1994

(rounded to millions of dollars)

Item	Florida			Southeast			United States		
	Total	Metro-politan areas	Non-metro-politan areas	Total	Metro-politan areas	Non-metro-politan areas	Total	Metro-politan areas	Non-metro-politan areas
	Income by place of residence, 1994								
Total personal income	302,099	285,091	17,008	1,230,171	938,297	291,874	5,648,263	4,754,997	893,266
Derivation of personal income									
Total earnings by place of work	185,237	176,982	8,254	862,079	677,699	184,379	4,084,922	3,524,280	560,642
Less: Personal contributions for social insurance	11,285	10,798	487	55,726	43,510	12,217	280,836	242,901	37,935
Plus: Adjustment for residence	690	-237	927	6,069	-5,826	11,895	-857	-37,293	36,436
Equals: Net earnings by place of residence	174,642	165,947	8,695	812,421	628,363	184,057	3,803,229	3,244,086	559,143
Plus: Dividends, interest, and rent	71,958	67,887	4,071	197,144	157,945	39,200	888,434	749,608	138,826
Plus: Transfer payments	55,500	51,258	4,242	220,606	151,989	68,617	956,600	761,302	195,298
	Earnings by place of work, 1994								
Components of earnings									
Wages and salaries	149,027	142,988	6,039	688,639	549,925	138,714	3,230,515	2,817,592	412,923
Other labor income	16,092	15,395	696	80,752	62,699	18,053	381,000	328,157	52,843
Proprietors' income 1/	20,118	18,599	1,519	92,687	65,075	27,612	473,407	378,530	94,877
Farm	1,664	1,236	428	11,952	3,802	8,150	38,749	12,880	25,869
Nonfarm	18,454	17,363	1,091	80,735	61,273	19,462	434,658	365,651	69,007

See footnotes at end of table.

Continued . . .

Table 5.21. PERSONAL INCOME: AMOUNTS BY MAJOR SOURCE IN THE METROPOLITAN AND NONMETROPOLITAN AREAS OF FLORIDA THE SOUTHEAST, AND THE UNITED STATES, 1993 AND 1994

(rounded to millions of dollars)

Item	Florida			Southeast			United States		
	Total	Metro-politan areas	Non-metro-politan areas	Total	Metro-politan areas	Non-metro-politan areas	Total	Metro-politan areas	Non-metro-politan areas
	Earnings by place of work, 1994 (Continued)								
Earnings by industry									
Farm	2,446	1,877	570	14,528	5,034	9,494	52,046	20,016	32,030
Nonfarm	182,790	175,106	7,685	847,551	672,665	174,886	4,032,876	3,504,263	528,613
Private	152,752	146,932	5,820	694,768	553,067	141,701	3,378,062	2,954,371	423,691
Agricultural services 2/	2,068	B/ 1,667	B/ 303	5,893	B/ 3,711	(D)	26,804	20,140	6,664
Mining	297	B/ 250	(D)	8,197	B/ 3,480	B/ 4,388	36,349	22,326	14,023
Construction	10,756	10,210	B/ 513	48,620	B/ 38,989	B/ 9,442	218,117	186,893	31,224
Manufacturing	17,475	16,618	857	157,059	B/ 105,010	B/ 52,044	747,326	617,130	130,196
Nondurable goods	6,648	6,146	(D)	77,498	B/ 49,777	B/ 26,725	293,036	236,635	56,401
Durable goods	10,828	10,472	B/ 337	79,561	B/ 55,045	B/ 23,435	454,290	380,495	73,795
Transportation 3/	12,170	11,691	B/ 468	60,923	B/ 50,171	B/ 9,737	272,608	237,083	35,525
Wholesale trade	11,815	B/ 11,527	B/ 255	52,600	B/ 45,740	B/ 6,637	254,791	232,687	22,104
Retail trade	22,167	21,102	1,064	90,355	B/ 70,945	B/ 19,274	392,234	331,106	61,128
Finance, insurance, and real estate	14,764	14,445	B/ 318	50,937	B/ 45,548	B/ 5,345	302,857	284,879	17,978
Services	61,239	59,304	B/ 1,894	220,183	B/ 188,266	B/ 30,329	1,126,976	1,022,126	104,850
Government 4/	30,039	28,174	1,865	152,783	119,598	33,185	654,814	549,893	104,921
Federal, civilian	5,071	4,874	197	31,827	27,732	4,095	131,382	117,167	14,215
Federal, military	2,770	2,691	78	18,419	15,573	2,846	47,921	41,014	6,907
State and local	22,198	20,609	1,590	102,537	76,294	26,243	475,511	391,711	83,800

(D) Data withheld to avoid disclosure of information about individual firms.

A/ Revised. B/ This estimate constitutes the major portion of the true estimate.

1/ Includes the inventory valuation and capital consumption adjustments. 2/ Includes forestry, fisheries, and other. "Other" includes wages and salaries of U.S. residents employed by foreign embassies, consulates, and international organizations in the United States. 3/ Includes communications and public utilities. 4/ Includes government enterprises.

Note: See Table 5.14 for derivation of personal income notes.

Source: U.S., Department of Commerce, Bureau of Economic Analysis, Regional Economic Information System, CD-ROM, June 1996.

Table 5.23. PERSONAL INCOME: AMOUNTS BY MAJOR SOURCE IN FLORIDA, FOURTH QUARTER 1994 THROUGH FOURTH QUARTER 1995

(in millions of dollars)

Item	Fourth quarter 1994	1995 First quarter	1995 Second quarter	1995 Third quarter	1995 Fourth quarter
Total personal income 1/	310,632	318,347	322,146	326,941	331,029
Derivation of total personal income					
Total earnings by place of work	189,106	193,344	194,845	198,015	200,845
Less personal contributions for social insurance	11,528	11,916	11,994	12,170	12,309
Plus adjustment for residence	705	715	713	722	727
Equals net earnings by place of residence	178,283	182,143	183,564	186,567	189,263
Plus dividends, interest, and rent 2/	75,736	77,956	79,448	80,446	81,138
Plus transfer payments	56,613	58,248	59,135	59,928	60,628
State unemployment benefits	720	660	653	708	714
Other transfer payments	55,893	57,588	58,481	59,220	59,914
Components of earnings 1/					
Wages and salaries	152,035	155,504	156,616	159,243	161,463
Other labor income	16,457	16,971	17,164	17,328	17,533
Proprietors' income 3/	20,614	20,869	21,065	21,443	21,848
Farm	1,719	1,546	1,589	1,758	2,039
Nonfarm	18,895	19,322	19,476	19,686	19,809
Earnings by industry 1/					
Farm	2,480	2,309	2,361	2,540	2,832
Nonfarm	186,625	191,035	192,484	195,475	198,013
Private	156,813	159,277	162,122	164,178	166,413
Agricultural services, forestry, and fisheries, and other 4/	2,182	2,178	2,121	2,113	2,153
Mining	295	334	351	335	337
Construction	10,971	11,579	11,404	11,282	11,382
Manufacturing	17,695	17,139	17,764	17,614	17,480
Nondurable goods	6,763	6,708	6,710	6,745	6,675
Durable goods	10,932	10,431	11,054	10,869	10,805
Transportation, communications, and public utilities	12,735	12,676	12,991	12,779	12,926
Wholesale trade	12,156	12,638	12,656	12,848	13,039
Retail trade	22,803	22,673	23,304	23,738	24,239
Finance, insurance, and real estate	15,117	15,243	15,532	15,919	16,151
Services	62,861	64,817	66,000	67,550	68,707
Government and government enterprises	29,812	31,757	30,361	31,297	31,600
Federal, civilian	5,016	5,072	5,067	5,116	5,188
Federal, military	2,647	2,589	2,571	2,586	2,676
State and local	22,150	24,097	22,724	23,595	23,736

1/ Income by place of residence; earnings by place of work.
2/ Includes capital consumption adjustment for rental income of persons.
3/ Includes the inventory valuation and capital consumption adjustments.
4/ Includes wages and salaries of U.S. residents employed by foreign embassies, consulates, and international organizations in the United States.

Note: Seasonally adjusted at annual rates. Data reported in April 1996. See Table 5.14 for derivation of personal income notes.

Source: U.S., Department of Commerce, Bureau of Economic Analysis, Regional Economic Information System, CD-ROM, June 1996.

Table 5.26. EARNED INCOME: TOTAL EARNINGS ON A PLACE-OF-WORK BASIS BY MAJOR TYPE OF INCOME IN THE UNITED STATES AND IN THE STATE AND COUNTIES OF FLORIDA, 1993 AND 1994

(in thousands of dollars)

County	Total earnings	Wage and salary disbursements	Other labor income	Proprietors' income Total 1/	Proprietors' income Farm	Proprietors' income Nonfarm
			1993 A/			
United States 2/	3,869,403	3,072,687	354,994	441,722	37,432	404,290
Florida	175,169,736	141,015,058	14,907,477	19,247,201	2,193,996	17,053,205
Alachua	2,687,648	2,197,605	243,582	246,461	17,571	228,890
Baker	125,072	89,974	11,682	23,416	9,754	13,662
Bay	1,571,245	1,293,357	123,947	153,941	499	153,442
Bradford	144,460	113,698	13,053	17,709	5,253	12,456
Brevard	5,499,912	4,611,234	496,734	391,944	6,267	385,677
Broward	17,548,790	14,371,068	1,488,563	1,689,159	15,047	1,674,112
Calhoun	66,617	46,540	5,329	14,748	2,145	12,603
Charlotte	826,161	600,692	63,599	161,870	8,888	152,982
Citrus	644,262	493,616	59,102	91,544	640	90,904
Clay	728,489	554,167	59,047	115,275	704	114,571
Collier	2,307,170	1,671,333	160,703	475,134	109,147	365,987
Columbia	386,521	306,924	36,056	43,541	6,442	37,099
Dade	29,816,160	24,410,715	2,581,689	2,823,756	175,915	2,647,841
De Soto	213,484	137,820	15,695	59,969	37,332	22,637
Dixie	63,982	46,685	5,411	11,886	1,269	10,617
Duval	12,323,434	10,418,548	1,051,311	853,575	6,728	846,847
Escambia	3,432,552	2,911,153	295,424	225,975	4,044	221,931
Flagler	198,065	158,825	18,137	21,103	8,830	12,273
Franklin	62,519	43,423	4,960	14,136	0	14,136
Gadsden	314,990	248,818	28,972	37,200	17,331	19,869
Gilchrist	54,734	36,713	4,293	13,728	6,299	7,429
Glades	48,815	20,648	2,519	25,648	20,181	5,467
Gulf	110,026	90,212	12,248	7,566	0	7,566
Hamilton	121,130	93,609	12,851	14,670	9,800	4,870
Hardee	189,622	115,491	12,468	61,663	38,629	23,034
Hendry	359,574	227,500	23,159	108,915	76,532	32,383
Hernando	613,645	466,261	51,181	96,203	6,733	89,470
Highlands	578,292	381,596	42,925	153,771	72,844	80,927
Hillsborough	14,135,409	11,754,132	1,247,636	1,133,641	128,656	1,004,985
Holmes	80,439	52,520	6,329	21,590	11,016	10,574
Indian River	1,030,020	751,622	74,854	203,544	58,549	144,995
Jackson	350,308	270,448	32,568	47,292	13,682	33,610

See footnotes at end of table. Continued . . .

Table 5.26. EARNED INCOME: TOTAL EARNINGS ON A PLACE-OF-WORK BASIS BY MAJOR TYPE OF INCOME IN THE UNITED STATES AND IN THE STATE AND COUNTIES OF FLORIDA, 1993 AND 1994 (Continued)

(in thousands of dollars)

County	Total earnings	Wage and salary disbursements	Other labor income	Proprietors' income Total 1/	Proprietors' income Farm	Proprietors' income Nonfarm
		1993 A/ (Continued)				
Jefferson	70,527	52,654	6,315	11,558	2,004	9,554
Lafayette	42,775	18,962	2,303	21,510	17,503	4,007
Lake	1,272,054	968,733	108,619	194,702	28,437	166,265
Lee	3,892,595	2,958,674	312,792	621,129	61,337	559,792
Leon	3,291,046	2,775,885	284,832	230,329	550	229,779
Levy	145,873	105,160	11,730	28,983	6,980	22,003
Liberty	39,615	29,032	3,666	6,917	617	6,300
Madison	114,292	84,914	10,976	18,402	6,672	11,730
Manatee	2,370,025	1,811,422	197,514	361,089	119,466	241,623
Marion	1,763,654	1,370,925	166,530	226,199	25,339	200,860
Martin	1,319,353	982,964	101,098	235,291	56,460	178,831
Monroe	1,013,430	765,428	72,147	175,855	0	175,855
Nassau	431,621	332,049	36,686	62,886	9,957	52,929
Okaloosa	1,980,389	1,693,573	133,670	153,146	1,716	151,430
Okeechobee	245,046	156,434	15,532	73,080	39,005	34,075
Orange	14,597,828	12,110,535	1,300,395	1,186,898	114,158	1,072,740
Osceola	1,088,546	811,644	88,369	188,533	18,113	170,420
Palm Beach	13,801,820	10,514,078	1,106,808	2,180,934	492,282	1,688,652
Pasco	1,646,038	1,268,949	139,513	237,576	16,896	220,680
Pinellas	10,685,960	8,653,240	927,437	1,105,283	3,641	1,101,642
Polk	4,629,223	3,598,153	407,230	623,840	108,614	515,226
Putnam	502,557	412,890	49,511	40,156	11,596	28,560
St. Johns	805,961	610,208	66,307	129,446	8,377	121,069
St. Lucie	1,356,082	1,029,096	112,351	214,635	61,860	152,775
Santa Rosa	631,483	478,589	47,663	105,231	16,491	88,740
Sarasota	3,422,791	2,679,112	276,634	467,045	10,432	456,613
Seminole	3,028,675	2,346,839	255,169	426,667	8,477	418,190
Sumter	184,162	125,668	15,077	43,417	13,421	29,996
Suwannee	215,450	142,624	16,895	55,931	20,067	35,864
Taylor	169,930	140,045	18,524	11,361	1,113	10,248
Union	94,636	77,339	8,918	8,379	2,591	5,788
Volusia	3,279,660	2,621,047	283,023	375,590	24,959	350,631
Wakulla	80,823	58,847	7,797	14,179	426	13,753
Walton	206,179	153,054	18,722	34,403	4,169	30,234
Washington	116,090	89,345	10,697	16,048	3,543	12,505

See footnotes at end of table. Continued . . .

Table 5.26. EARNED INCOME: TOTAL EARNINGS ON A PLACE-OF-WORK BASIS BY MAJOR TYPE OF INCOME IN THE UNITED STATES AND IN THE STATE AND COUNTIES OF FLORIDA, 1993 AND 1994 (Continued)

(in thousands of dollars)

County	Total earnings	Wage and salary disbursements	Other labor income	Proprietors' income Total 1/	Farm	Nonfarm
			1994			
United States 2/	4,084,922	3,230,515	381,000	473,407	38,749	434,658
Florida	185,236,774	149,026,678	16,091,696	20,118,400	1,664,321	18,454,079
Alachua	2,853,968	2,328,478	265,000	260,490	10,223	250,267
Baker	131,473	94,776	12,630	24,067	9,090	14,977
Bay	1,652,445	1,349,032	134,523	168,890	357	168,533
Bradford	149,219	118,084	13,980	17,155	3,405	13,750
Brevard	5,674,615	4,724,813	526,573	423,229	4,638	418,591
Broward	18,745,712	15,323,675	1,606,267	1,815,770	9,588	1,806,182
Calhoun	72,572	50,938	5,918	15,716	1,886	13,830
Charlotte	891,628	649,718	69,525	172,385	6,606	165,779
Citrus	685,232	520,893	63,732	100,607	109	100,498
Clay	767,800	579,326	63,159	125,315	283	125,032
Collier	2,433,158	1,796,148	176,941	460,069	67,687	392,382
Columbia	419,833	334,682	40,083	45,068	4,476	40,592
Dade	31,109,868	25,414,786	2,748,278	2,946,804	94,186	2,852,618
De Soto	223,068	147,351	16,508	59,209	34,270	24,939
Dixie	68,540	48,949	5,872	13,719	607	13,112
Duval	12,947,470	10,893,050	1,129,598	924,822	6,099	918,723
Escambia	3,569,988	3,011,783	313,797	244,408	2,773	241,635
Flagler	216,323	176,653	20,866	18,804	5,639	13,165
Franklin	69,427	48,360	5,614	15,453	0	15,453
Gadsden	322,853	256,936	30,384	35,533	13,679	21,854
Gilchrist	55,914	38,599	4,699	12,616	4,093	8,523
Glades	45,507	21,548	2,735	21,224	15,221	6,003
Gulf	115,666	94,235	13,185	8,246	0	8,246
Hamilton	124,503	98,217	14,008	12,278	6,877	5,401
Hardee	203,700	128,043	14,056	61,601	36,952	24,649
Hendry	357,253	230,452	24,882	101,919	65,976	35,943
Hernando	664,535	504,880	56,838	102,817	5,180	97,637
Highlands	605,946	410,148	46,000	149,798	60,997	88,801
Hillsborough	15,130,516	12,580,353	1,362,908	1,187,255	97,307	1,089,948
Holmes	85,455	57,988	7,111	20,356	8,807	11,549
Indian River	1,119,403	815,763	83,386	220,254	63,783	156,471
Jackson	359,967	278,566	34,235	47,166	10,448	36,718
Jefferson	67,996	50,776	6,389	10,831	562	10,269
Lafayette	45,719	21,637	2,757	21,325	16,465	4,860

See footnotes at end of table.

Continued . . .

Table 5.26. EARNED INCOME: TOTAL EARNINGS ON A PLACE-OF-WORK BASIS BY MAJOR TYPE OF INCOME IN THE UNITED STATES AND IN THE STATE AND COUNTIES OF FLORIDA, 1993 AND 1994 (Continued)

(in thousands of dollars)

County	Total earnings	Wage and salary dis- bursements	Other labor income	Proprietors' income Total 1/	Proprietors' income Farm	Proprietors' income Nonfarm
		1994 (Continued)				
Lake	1,357,502	1,032,273	117,842	207,387	24,864	182,523
Lee	4,170,853	3,182,016	339,578	649,259	44,782	604,477
Leon	3,543,565	2,981,448	312,420	249,697	-53	249,750
Levy	155,060	113,626	12,864	28,570	3,897	24,673
Liberty	42,430	31,149	3,983	7,298	372	6,926
Madison	117,189	89,208	11,867	16,114	3,446	12,668
Manatee	2,614,501	2,047,679	226,735	340,087	79,182	260,905
Marion	1,888,630	1,471,972	179,376	237,282	17,057	220,225
Martin	1,326,452	970,980	103,474	251,998	63,387	188,611
Monroe	1,044,824	778,351	76,526	189,947	0	189,947
Nassau	456,577	349,427	39,644	67,506	9,660	57,846
Okaloosa	2,070,586	1,757,016	147,363	166,207	911	165,296
Okeechobee	254,770	166,102	17,025	71,643	34,482	37,161
Orange	15,408,560	12,751,930	1,396,794	1,259,836	94,827	1,165,009
Osceola	1,173,207	879,070	96,521	197,616	12,399	185,217
Palm Beach	14,395,382	11,108,879	1,193,827	2,092,676	291,390	1,801,286
Pasco	1,792,040	1,382,439	154,335	255,266	13,245	242,021
Pinellas	11,417,121	9,215,061	1,007,545	1,194,515	3,650	1,190,865
Polk	5,019,438	3,887,790	447,216	684,432	121,099	563,333
Putnam	501,809	409,282	50,370	42,157	10,042	32,115
St. Johns	866,623	655,252	73,912	137,459	6,070	131,389
St. Lucie	1,451,649	1,091,289	121,805	238,555	71,057	167,498
Santa Rosa	663,159	495,046	51,777	116,336	19,220	97,116
Sarasota	3,605,372	2,813,054	293,484	498,834	7,665	491,169
Seminole	3,287,915	2,547,013	279,375	461,527	6,682	454,845
Sumter	191,654	133,242	16,311	42,101	9,361	32,740
Suwannee	224,400	151,371	18,636	54,393	15,005	39,388
Taylor	187,689	153,931	20,760	12,998	491	12,507
Union	99,009	81,549	9,653	7,807	1,458	6,349
Volusia	3,492,267	2,778,476	307,569	406,222	24,652	381,570
Wakulla	84,557	61,159	8,307	15,091	164	14,927
Walton	221,110	163,992	20,625	36,493	3,448	33,045
Washington	123,602	95,970	11,740	15,892	2,140	13,752

A/ Revised.
1/ Includes the inventory valuation and capital consumption adjustments.
2/ United States numbers are rounded to millions of dollars.

Source: U.S., Department of Commerce, Bureau of Economic Analysis, Regional Economic Information System, CD-ROM, June 1996.

Table 5.30. EARNED INCOME: TOTAL, FARM, AND NONFARM EARNINGS ON A PLACE-OF-WORK BASIS IN THE UNITED STATES AND IN THE STATE AND COUNTIES OF FLORIDA, 1993 AND 1994

(in thousands of dollars)

County	Total earnings	Farm income	Nonfarm					
					Government and government enterprises			
						Federal		State
			Total	Private 1/	Total	Civilian	Military	and local
1993 A/								
United States 2/	3,869,403	50,636	3,818,767	3,187,422	631,345	128,128	49,420	453,797
Florida	175,169,736	3,002,985	172,166,751	143,212,913	28,953,838	5,027,112	2,955,239	20,971,487
Alachua	2,687,648	20,826	2,666,822	1,692,563	974,259	129,211	8,520	836,528
Baker	125,072	12,455	112,617	53,237	59,380	2,259	375	56,746
Bay	1,571,245	669	1,570,576	1,055,564	515,012	137,538	175,417	202,057
Bradford	144,460	5,401	139,059	81,633	57,426	1,441	445	55,540
Brevard	5,499,912	10,588	5,489,324	4,602,417	886,907	274,485	135,336	477,086
Broward	17,548,790	25,806	17,522,984	15,115,779	2,407,205	291,549	31,756	2,083,900
Calhoun	66,617	3,113	63,504	43,188	20,316	1,279	219	18,818
Charlotte	826,161	13,414	812,747	690,607	122,140	9,074	2,367	110,699
Citrus	644,262	736	643,526	551,632	91,894	6,575	1,950	83,369
Clay	728,489	3,551	724,938	607,748	117,190	11,924	2,213	103,053
Collier	2,307,170	165,324	2,141,846	1,915,488	226,358	21,989	3,296	201,073
Columbia	386,521	7,096	379,425	253,874	125,551	39,551	889	85,111
Dade	29,816,160	240,876	29,575,284	25,117,746	4,457,538	867,554	102,907	3,487,077
De Soto	213,484	44,682	168,802	101,252	67,550	1,741	470	65,339
Dixie	63,982	1,297	62,685	40,323	22,362	1,022	218	21,122
Duval	12,323,434	11,233	12,312,201	9,857,976	2,454,225	625,625	819,546	1,009,054
Escambia	3,432,552	5,402	3,427,150	2,376,850	1,050,300	385,391	292,990	371,919
Flagler	198,065	9,926	188,139	153,356	34,783	3,323	688	30,772
Franklin	62,519	0	62,519	47,142	15,377	1,220	181	13,976
Gadsden	314,990	31,434	283,556	154,907	128,649	4,258	997	123,394
Gilchrist	54,734	8,731	46,003	24,398	21,605	798	213	20,594

See footnotes at end of table.

Continued . . .

Table 5.30. EARNED INCOME: TOTAL, FARM, AND NONFARM EARNINGS ON A PLACE-OF-WORK BASIS IN THE UNITED STATES AND IN THE STATE AND COUNTIES OF FLORIDA, 1993 AND 1994 (Continued)

(in thousands of dollars)

County	Total earnings	Farm income	Nonfarm					
					Government and government enterprises			
						Federal		State
			Total	Private 1/	Total	Civilian	Military	and local
1993 A/ (Continued)								
Glades	48,815	24,293	24,522	16,978	7,544	403	142	6,999
Gulf	110,026	0	110,026	86,534	23,492	745	229	22,518
Hamilton	121,130	11,386	109,744	79,356	30,388	921	217	29,250
Hardee	189,622	48,713	140,909	102,439	38,470	1,732	385	36,353
Hendry	359,574	114,061	245,513	192,021	53,492	3,370	537	49,585
Hernando	613,645	8,360	605,285	486,743	118,542	9,192	2,204	107,146
Highlands	578,292	91,817	486,475	398,120	88,355	11,476	2,980	73,899
Hillsborough	14,135,409	184,631	13,950,778	11,773,498	2,177,280	472,967	234,052	1,470,261
Holmes	80,439	11,432	69,007	42,582	26,425	1,780	317	24,328
Indian River	1,030,020	73,746	956,274	821,499	134,775	13,940	1,802	119,033
Jackson	350,308	15,121	335,187	197,232	137,955	20,305	1,449	116,201
Jefferson	70,527	4,673	65,854	44,312	21,542	1,119	226	20,197
Lafayette	42,775	18,706	24,069	12,065	12,004	492	110	11,402
Lake	1,272,054	52,030	1,220,024	1,037,371	182,653	17,286	5,378	159,989
Lee	3,892,595	84,170	3,808,425	3,209,944	598,481	64,613	7,867	526,001
Leon	3,291,046	1,908	3,289,138	1,927,335	1,361,803	71,779	10,736	1,279,288
Levy	145,873	11,086	134,787	98,421	36,366	2,461	1,174	32,731
Liberty	39,615	619	38,996	24,373	14,623	1,410	112	13,101
Madison	114,292	7,740	106,552	74,577	31,975	1,567	326	30,082
Manatee	2,370,025	155,529	2,214,496	1,935,196	279,300	39,030	4,983	235,287
Marion	1,763,654	39,933	1,723,721	1,425,055	298,666	22,009	4,121	272,536
Martin	1,319,353	69,876	1,249,477	1,119,819	129,658	10,705	2,278	116,675
Monroe	1,013,430	0	1,013,430	770,673	242,757	47,879	77,102	117,776

See footnotes at end of table.

Continued . . .

Table 5.30. EARNED INCOME: TOTAL, FARM, AND NONFARM EARNINGS ON A PLACE-OF-WORK BASIS IN THE UNITED STATES AND IN THE STATE AND COUNTIES OF FLORIDA, 1993 AND 1994 (Continued)

(in thousands of dollars)

County	Total earnings	Farm income	Nonfarm		Government and government enterprises			
						Federal		State
			Total	Private 1/	Total	Civilian	Military	and local
			1993 A/ (Continued)					
Nassau	431,621	14,380	417,241	319,116	98,125	43,924	926	53,275
Okaloosa	1,980,389	2,075	1,978,314	1,089,967	888,347	233,049	488,757	166,541
Okeechobee	245,046	59,186	185,860	148,862	36,998	2,548	589	33,861
Orange	14,597,828	173,052	14,424,776	12,560,056	1,864,720	353,292	340,124	1,171,304
Osceola	1,088,546	23,958	1,064,588	906,524	158,064	9,437	2,356	146,271
Palm Beach	13,801,820	646,668	13,155,152	11,631,649	1,523,503	178,129	20,336	1,325,038
Pasco	1,646,038	25,475	1,620,563	1,353,156	267,407	21,420	5,655	240,332
Pinellas	10,685,960	6,849	10,679,111	9,400,254	1,278,857	275,147	48,643	955,067
Polk	4,629,223	144,054	4,485,169	3,863,521	621,648	54,827	8,438	558,383
Putnam	502,557	15,827	486,730	377,923	108,807	5,633	1,297	101,877
St. Johns	805,961	12,820	793,141	668,066	125,075	12,901	2,534	109,640
St. Lucie	1,356,082	75,015	1,281,067	1,050,800	230,267	20,235	4,836	205,196
Santa Rosa	631,483	17,224	614,259	436,175	178,084	25,328	65,152	87,604
Sarasota	3,422,791	14,019	3,408,772	2,988,787	419,985	36,850	5,838	377,297
Seminole	3,028,675	16,669	3,012,006	2,650,731	361,275	51,960	6,048	303,267
Sumter	184,162	16,019	168,143	124,489	43,654	3,513	626	39,515
Suwannee	215,450	24,574	190,876	153,333	37,543	3,569	554	33,420
Taylor	169,930	1,162	168,768	142,608	26,160	1,365	330	24,465
Union	94,636	2,700	91,936	38,033	53,903	719	203	52,981
Volusia	3,279,660	49,565	3,230,095	2,607,149	622,946	51,526	9,565	561,855
Wakulla	80,823	449	80,374	59,702	20,672	2,119	309	18,244
Walton	206,179	4,419	201,760	158,426	43,334	2,887	2,062	38,385
Washington	116,090	4,436	111,654	69,763	41,891	1,746	341	39,804

See footnotes at end of table.

Continued . . .

Table 5.30. EARNED INCOME: TOTAL, FARM, AND NONFARM EARNINGS ON A PLACE-OF-WORK BASIS IN THE UNITED STATES AND IN THE STATE AND COUNTIES OF FLORIDA, 1993 AND 1994 (Continued)

(in thousands of dollars)

			Nonfarm					
					Government and government enterprises			
						Federal		State
County	Total earnings	Farm income	Total	Private 1/	Total	Civilian	Military	and local
			1994					
United States 2/	4,084,922	52,046	4,032,876	3,378,062	654,814	131,382	47,921	475,511
Florida	185,236,774	2,446,408	182,790,366	152,751,811	30,038,555	5,070,565	2,769,843	22,198,147
Alachua	2,853,968	14,391	2,839,577	1,825,993	1,013,584	137,582	7,924	868,078
Baker	131,473	11,959	119,514	61,880	57,634	2,398	376	54,860
Bay	1,652,445	548	1,651,897	1,136,771	515,126	127,112	172,958	215,056
Bradford	149,219	3,558	145,661	85,632	60,029	1,416	442	58,171
Brevard	5,674,615	8,876	5,665,739	4,746,531	919,208	282,663	128,410	508,135
Broward	18,745,712	19,735	18,725,977	16,141,630	2,584,347	313,921	35,326	2,235,100
Calhoun	72,572	2,852	69,720	47,006	22,714	1,400	221	21,093
Charlotte	891,628	10,291	881,337	751,204	130,133	9,488	2,481	118,164
Citrus	685,232	221	685,011	588,918	96,093	7,004	1,980	87,109
Clay	767,800	2,559	765,241	644,404	120,837	12,286	2,274	106,277
Collier	2,433,158	115,484	2,317,674	2,078,284	239,390	23,538	3,367	212,485
Columbia	419,833	5,112	414,721	281,965	132,756	40,589	915	91,252
Dade	31,109,868	160,989	30,948,879	26,237,075	4,711,804	874,665	100,450	3,736,689
De Soto	223,068	42,047	181,021	111,180	69,841	1,862	471	67,508
Dixie	68,540	639	67,901	44,362	23,539	984	223	22,332
Duval	12,947,470	10,933	12,936,537	10,472,137	2,464,400	645,056	783,030	1,036,314
Escambia	3,569,988	3,815	3,566,173	2,555,725	1,010,448	335,766	283,252	391,430
Flagler	216,323	6,537	209,786	171,832	37,954	3,468	723	33,763
Franklin	69,427	0	69,427	53,612	15,815	1,279	184	14,352
Gadsden	322,853	29,571	293,282	160,816	132,466	4,436	926	127,104
Gilchrist	55,914	6,239	49,675	26,449	23,226	843	221	22,162

See footnotes at end of table.

Continued . . .

Table 5.30. EARNED INCOME: TOTAL, FARM, AND NONFARM EARNINGS ON A PLACE-OF-WORK BASIS IN THE UNITED STATES AND IN THE STATE AND COUNTIES OF FLORIDA, 1993 AND 1994 (Continued)

(in thousands of dollars)

County	Total earnings	Farm income	Nonfarm Total	Nonfarm Private 1/	Government and government enterprises Total	Federal Civilian	Federal Military	State and local
			1994 (Continued)					
Glades	45,507	19,239	26,268	18,149	8,119	455	144	7,520
Gulf	115,666	0	115,666	89,708	25,958	806	230	24,922
Hamilton	124,503	8,823	115,680	83,152	32,528	1,024	217	31,287
Hardee	203,700	46,974	156,726	115,440	41,286	1,855	382	39,049
Hendry	357,253	99,740	257,513	200,411	57,102	3,937	539	52,626
Hernando	664,535	6,651	657,884	529,838	128,046	9,935	2,238	115,873
Highlands	605,946	80,505	525,441	432,080	93,361	11,074	1,405	80,882
Hillsborough	15,130,516	151,197	14,979,319	12,760,028	2,219,291	474,478	187,088	1,557,725
Holmes	85,455	9,259	76,196	46,637	29,559	1,860	320	27,379
Indian River	1,119,403	78,175	1,041,228	901,074	140,154	14,580	1,819	123,755
Jackson	359,967	11,867	348,100	207,136	140,964	21,238	1,528	118,198
Jefferson	67,996	3,031	64,965	42,786	22,179	1,165	227	20,787
Lafayette	45,719	17,722	27,997	14,754	13,243	540	110	12,593
Lake	1,357,502	47,577	1,309,925	1,116,107	193,818	18,782	5,397	169,639
Lee	4,170,853	66,703	4,104,150	3,466,966	637,184	69,627	8,009	559,548
Leon	3,543,565	1,368	3,542,197	2,100,633	1,441,564	76,055	10,719	1,354,790
Levy	155,060	8,363	146,697	107,827	38,870	2,570	1,123	35,177
Liberty	42,430	374	42,056	25,551	16,505	1,496	114	14,895
Madison	117,189	4,652	112,537	78,632	33,905	1,618	327	31,960
Manatee	2,614,501	112,267	2,502,234	2,204,274	297,960	42,322	4,954	250,684
Marion	1,888,630	32,728	1,855,902	1,533,402	322,500	23,226	4,238	295,036
Martin	1,326,452	76,631	1,249,821	1,111,586	138,235	11,187	2,304	124,744
Monroe	1,044,824	0	1,044,824	811,668	233,156	48,994	58,509	125,653
Nassau	456,577	14,066	442,511	337,095	105,416	46,397	943	58,076

See footnotes at end of table.

Continued . . .

Table 5.30. EARNED INCOME: TOTAL, FARM, AND NONFARM EARNINGS ON A PLACE-OF-WORK BASIS IN THE UNITED STATES AND IN THE STATE AND COUNTIES OF FLORIDA, 1993 AND 1994 (Continued)

(in thousands of dollars)

County	Total earnings	Farm income	Nonfarm Total	Nonfarm Private 1/	Government and government enterprises Total	Federal Civilian	Federal Military	State and local
			1994 (Continued)					
Okaloosa	2,070,586	1,340	2,069,246	1,207,362	861,884	197,090	488,602	176,192
Okeechobee	254,770	53,790	200,980	161,639	39,341	2,705	581	36,055
Orange	15,408,560	152,520	15,256,040	13,410,403	1,845,637	348,346	279,958	1,217,333
Osceola	1,173,207	18,334	1,154,873	984,797	170,076	10,259	2,397	157,420
Palm Beach	14,395,382	433,062	13,962,320	12,336,625	1,625,695	193,579	20,634	1,411,482
Pasco	1,792,040	22,001	1,770,039	1,478,753	291,286	23,069	5,697	262,520
Pinellas	11,417,121	6,515	11,410,606	10,062,492	1,348,114	290,262	48,687	1,009,165
Polk	5,019,438	158,422	4,861,016	4,201,007	660,009	58,070	8,537	593,402
Putnam	501,809	14,304	487,505	372,286	115,219	5,710	1,305	108,204
St. Johns	866,623	10,599	856,024	721,783	134,241	13,487	2,524	118,230
St. Lucie	1,451,649	84,768	1,366,881	1,119,918	246,963	21,661	5,074	220,228
Santa Rosa	663,159	20,050	643,109	463,753	179,356	26,097	60,995	92,264
Sarasota	3,605,372	10,956	3,594,416	3,145,935	448,481	39,441	5,866	403,174
Seminole	3,287,915	14,278	3,273,637	2,880,238	393,399	56,919	6,154	330,326
Sumter	191,654	11,806	179,848	132,829	47,019	3,883	634	42,502
Suwannee	224,400	19,421	204,979	164,825	40,154	3,906	562	35,686
Taylor	187,689	543	187,146	160,050	27,096	1,450	329	25,317
Union	99,009	1,667	97,342	40,928	56,414	726	204	55,484
Volusia	3,492,267	50,976	3,441,291	2,836,238	605,053	53,626	9,291	542,136
Wakulla	84,557	180	84,377	62,396	21,981	2,377	316	19,288
Walton	221,110	3,684	217,426	172,230	45,196	3,019	2,114	40,063
Washington	123,602	2,924	120,678	76,984	43,694	1,906	344	41,444

A/ Revised.
1/ See Table 5.34 for private nonfarm income by industrial source.
2/ In millions of dollars.
Source: U.S., Department of Commerce, Bureau of Economic Analysis, Regional Economic Information System, CD-ROM, June 1996.

Table 5.33. EARNED INCOME: PRIVATE NONFARM EARNINGS ON A PLACE-OF-WORK BASIS BY INDUSTRIAL SOURCE IN FLORIDA
1989 THROUGH 1994

(in thousands of dollars)

Item	1989	1990	1991	1992	1993	1994	Percentage change 1/
Agricultural services, forestry, fisheries, and other 2/	1,345,161	1,554,031	1,689,255	1,770,883	1,908,932	2,068,437	53.8
Agricultural services	1,234,689	1,423,685	1,563,382	1,668,306	1,804,300	1,954,475	58.3
Forestry	29,641	31,537	31,147	35,106	36,940	38,143	28.7
Fisheries	78,824	96,541	92,297	64,951	64,856	72,749	-7.7
Other 2/	2,007	2,268	2,429	2,520	2,836	3,070	53.0
Mining	308,077	300,975	309,212	315,601	303,182	296,900	-3.6
Coal mining	(D)	(D)	(D)	-149	(D)	A/	(X)
Oil and gas extraction	21,234	25,194	38,555	60,406	44,516	43,357	104.2
Metal mining	(D)	(D)	(D)	16,787	(D)	18,288	(X)
Nonmetallic minerals, except fuels	264,658	254,834	247,275	238,557	242,412	235,250	-11.1
Construction	10,246,727	10,190,972	9,035,019	8,966,871	9,919,543	10,756,365	5.0
General building contractors	2,524,354	2,420,462	2,054,708	2,086,803	2,336,429	2,411,358	-4.5
Heavy construction contractors	1,332,019	1,315,108	1,167,698	1,194,535	1,204,057	1,358,934	2.0
Special trade contractors	6,390,354	6,455,402	5,812,613	5,685,533	6,379,057	6,986,073	9.3
Manufacturing	15,269,923	15,627,625	15,789,450	16,489,224	16,815,925	17,475,332	14.4
Nondurable goods	5,600,172	5,824,482	5,966,471	6,273,761	6,416,561	6,647,658	18.7
Food and kindred products	1,287,347	1,361,255	1,383,332	1,411,004	1,462,878	1,489,174	15.7
Textile mill products	77,899	83,049	99,047	99,063	98,454	98,156	26.0
Apparel and other textile products	508,292	517,083	540,204	576,222	583,114	576,690	13.5
Paper and allied products	518,605	514,867	522,953	581,857	597,900	620,395	19.6
Printing and publishing	1,747,579	1,826,512	1,862,472	1,932,755	2,004,410	2,104,038	20.4
Chemicals and allied products	854,098	876,972	920,171	989,158	958,263	1,006,256	17.8
Petroleum and coal products	58,389	58,388	59,000	63,016	70,537	72,623	24.4
Tobacco products	37,021	37,983	30,594	32,026	34,929	37,601	1.6

See footnotes at end of table.

Continued . . .

Table 5.33. EARNED INCOME: PRIVATE NONFARM EARNINGS ON A PLACE-OF-WORK BASIS BY INDUSTRIAL SOURCE IN FLORIDA 1989 THROUGH 1994 (Continued)

(in thousands of dollars)

Item	1989	1990	1991	1992	1993	1994	Percentage change 1/
Manufacturing (Continued)							
Nondurable goods (Continued)							
Rubber and miscellaneous plastics products	472,081	508,717	510,579	549,210	569,607	603,879	27.9
Leather and leather products	38,861	39,656	38,119	39,450	36,469	38,846	0.0
Durable goods	9,669,751	9,803,143	9,822,979	10,215,463	10,399,364	10,827,674	12.0
Lumber and wood products	571,255	524,688	477,083	487,291	546,345	593,325	3.9
Furniture and fixtures	294,611	286,310	276,080	282,181	309,311	317,124	7.6
Primary metal industries	165,026	177,729	179,582	181,355	185,633	207,330	25.6
Fabricated metal products	907,391	919,422	882,673	857,130	904,693	961,303	5.9
Machinery and computer equipment	1,478,640	1,499,697	1,581,697	1,600,156	1,580,198	1,656,178	12.0
Electric equipment, except computer equipment	1,971,932	2,038,016	2,134,341	2,340,388	2,462,599	2,595,622	31.6
Transportation equipment, excluding motor vehicles	2,175,102	2,193,626	2,154,411	2,185,109	2,013,447	1,954,448	-10.1
Motor vehicles and equipment	168,506	182,337	171,948	219,875	233,906	236,571	40.4
Stone, clay, and glass products	694,701	665,934	589,433	587,143	643,361	704,107	1.4
Instruments and related products	1,036,142	1,106,234	1,165,037	1,259,091	1,269,587	1,333,786	28.7
Miscellaneous manufacturing industries	206,445	209,150	210,694	215,744	250,284	267,880	29.8
Transportation, communications, and public utilities	8,810,575	9,610,658	10,015,291	10,727,608	11,542,662	12,170,366	38.1
Railroad transportation	314,942	332,260	368,000	401,145	437,266	458,625	45.6
Trucking and warehousing	1,839,225	1,875,860	1,886,802	2,008,256	2,174,515	2,368,495	28.8
Water transportation	411,978	476,692	548,004	581,331	592,576	637,441	54.7
Other transportation	2,253,842	2,615,760	2,617,001	2,704,468	3,026,105	3,236,189	43.6
Local and interurban passenger transit	308,641	344,401	382,198	429,990	452,936	483,823	56.8
Transportation by air	1,385,445	1,694,671	1,600,848	1,529,551	1,741,661	1,824,649	31.7
Pipelines, except natural gas	2,309	2,323	2,886	3,430	3,732	5,299	129.5
Transportation services	557,447	574,365	631,069	741,497	827,776	922,418	65.5

See footnotes at end of table.

Continued . . .

Table 5.33. EARNED INCOME: PRIVATE NONFARM EARNINGS ON A PLACE-OF-WORK BASIS BY INDUSTRIAL SOURCE IN FLORIDA 1989 THROUGH 1994 (Continued)

(in thousands of dollars)

Item	1989	1990	1991	1992	1993	1994	Percentage change 1/
Transportation, communications, and public utilities (Continued)							
Communications	2,447,041	2,627,401	2,795,614	3,089,768	3,345,525	3,590,977	46.7
Electric, gas, and sanitary services	1,543,547	1,682,685	1,799,870	1,942,640	1,966,675	1,878,639	21.7
Wholesale trade	9,051,401	9,572,102	9,769,255	10,584,211	11,052,595	11,814,646	30.5
Retail trade	17,642,854	18,422,398	18,579,035	19,619,992	20,853,783	22,166,731	25.6
Building materials and garden equipment	926,975	895,028	865,234	918,750	1,031,136	1,085,755	17.1
General merchandise store	1,830,059	1,921,554	1,939,417	2,061,013	2,176,194	2,288,823	25.1
Food stores	2,800,804	2,965,166	3,134,739	3,240,481	3,328,019	3,512,466	25.4
Automotive dealers and service stations	3,039,540	3,015,216	3,005,814	3,185,430	3,625,746	3,930,084	29.3
Apparel and accessory stores	802,337	863,132	951,431	980,462	951,255	982,502	22.5
Home furniture and furnishings stores	1,298,886	1,338,733	1,207,184	1,184,692	1,299,021	1,406,009	8.2
Eating and drinking places	4,279,561	4,549,467	4,686,234	4,995,719	5,298,485	5,675,107	32.6
Miscellaneous retail	2,664,692	2,874,102	2,788,982	3,053,445	3,143,927	3,285,985	23.3
Finance, insurance, and real estate	11,076,101	11,532,910	11,992,601	13,333,706	14,175,899	14,763,571	33.3
Depository and nondepository credit institutions	3,624,644	3,753,739	3,754,424	3,999,544	4,239,734	4,473,267	23.4
Other finance, insurance, and real estate	7,451,457	7,779,171	8,238,177	9,334,162	9,936,165	10,290,304	38.1
Security and commodity brokers and services	1,041,363	1,091,436	1,254,314	1,638,453	1,919,105	1,858,532	78.5
Insurance carriers	1,911,763	2,109,502	2,273,623	2,458,025	2,605,789	2,805,026	46.7
Insurance agents, brokers, and services	1,452,054	1,641,924	1,715,439	1,825,856	1,965,829	2,084,775	43.6
Real estate	2,673,432	2,505,620	2,503,253	2,785,855	2,903,102	2,956,086	10.6
Holding and other investment companies	372,845	430,689	491,548	625,973	542,340	585,885	57.1

See footnotes at end of table.

Continued . . .

Table 5.33. EARNED INCOME: PRIVATE NONFARM EARNINGS ON A PLACE-OF-WORK BASIS BY INDUSTRIAL SOURCE IN FLORIDA 1989 THROUGH 1994 (Continued)

(in thousands of dollars)

Item	1989	1990	1991	1992	1993	1994	Percentage change 1/
Services	40,378,374	44,798,331	47,589,513	52,207,586	56,640,392	61,239,463	51.7
Hotels and other lodging places	2,539,372	2,594,818	2,610,449	2,733,052	2,971,309	3,048,529	20.1
Personal services	1,478,359	1,543,083	1,563,567	1,670,746	1,804,895	1,906,937	29.0
Private households	559,959	589,873	577,946	643,106	684,043	745,741	33.2
Business services	6,213,414	7,271,013	7,529,128	8,536,192	10,019,377	11,254,508	81.1
Auto repair, services, and parking	1,323,899	1,353,095	1,436,933	1,507,003	1,656,501	1,735,396	31.1
Miscellaneous repair services	714,274	746,964	681,363	704,303	788,943	821,786	15.1
Amusement and recreation services	2,141,763	2,555,062	2,858,348	3,255,616	3,450,927	3,716,072	73.5
Motion pictures	227,226	240,829	282,004	304,501	358,495	374,252	64.7
Health services	13,507,985	15,327,509	16,856,368	18,427,917	19,696,332	21,386,156	58.3
Legal services	3,252,906	3,557,439	3,718,451	4,085,248	4,219,365	4,471,512	37.5
Educational services	1,014,657	1,062,416	1,209,689	1,286,068	1,351,368	1,484,529	46.3
Social services	990,384	1,130,013	1,271,795	1,421,313	1,559,684	1,711,856	72.8
Museums, botanical, zoological gardens	31,786	34,949	41,344	44,761	48,685	54,125	70.3
Membership organizations	1,436,840	1,541,416	1,552,499	1,669,561	1,747,366	1,770,389	23.2
Engineering and management services	4,775,504	5,079,144	5,237,044	5,749,560	6,110,006	6,585,059	37.9
Miscellaneous services	170,046	170,708	162,585	168,639	173,096	172,616	1.5
Government and government enterprises	22,536,491	25,060,092	26,747,886	27,762,999	28,953,838	30,038,555	33.3
Federal, civilian	3,799,796	4,227,234	4,458,302	4,812,494	5,027,112	5,070,565	33.4
Military	2,705,304	2,902,674	3,092,483	3,211,816	2,955,239	2,769,843	2.4
State and local	16,031,391	17,930,184	19,197,101	19,738,689	20,971,487	22,198,147	38.5

(D) Data withheld to avoid disclosure of information about individual industries. (X) Not applicable.

A/ Less than $50,000. Estimates are included in totals.

1/ Percentage change 1989 to 1994.

2/ Includes wages and salaries of U.S. residents employed by foreign embassies, consulates and international organizations in the United States.

Note: Some data are revised.

Source: U.S., Department of Commerce, Bureau of Economic Analysis, Regional Economic Information System, CD-ROM, June 1996.

Table 5.34. EARNED INCOME: PRIVATE NONFARM EARNINGS ON A PLACE-OF-WORK BASIS BY MAJOR INDUSTRIAL SOURCE IN THE UNITED STATES AND IN THE STATE AND COUNTIES OF FLORIDA, 1993 AND 1994

(in thousands of dollars)

County	Total private nonfarm earnings	Agri-culture ser-vices 1/	Manufac-turing	Mining	Construc-tion	Wholesale trade	Retail trade	Finance insurance and real estate	Trans-porta-tion 2/	Services
					1993 A/					
United States 3/	3,187,422	24,574	709,563	35,170	197,563	240,601	368,127	296,428	257,262	1,058,134
Florida 3/	143,213	1,909	16,816	303	9,920	11,053	20,854	14,176	11,543	56,640
Alachua	1,692,563	(D)	162,643	(D)	131,494	63,343	277,906	126,780	68,656	843,103
Baker	53,237	264	8,164	0	3,289	1,838	13,307	2,410	10,398	13,567
Bay	1,055,564	6,581	94,126	170	104,020	70,374	223,237	78,012	80,049	398,995
Bradford	81,633	880	9,310	(D)	7,189	(D)	15,672	3,000	6,433	23,775
Brevard	4,602,417	32,234	1,270,553	2,962	278,830	128,748	542,220	181,509	177,353	1,988,008
Broward	15,115,779	124,932	1,522,717	8,751	1,066,947	1,332,913	2,309,766	1,677,962	1,084,029	5,987,762
Calhoun	43,188	5,170	6,718	0	4,848	2,486	8,477	1,125	2,300	12,064
Charlotte	690,607	10,525	23,418	1,375	94,595	16,497	143,834	49,058	33,512	317,793
Citrus	551,632	5,581	20,258	926	66,121	12,423	95,440	32,122	111,961	206,800
Clay	607,748	11,864	44,086	8,505	62,629	24,985	148,772	27,985	48,813	230,109
Collier	1,915,488	89,395	69,968	5,366	240,715	70,639	331,985	233,033	68,088	806,299
Columbia	253,874	1,742	37,704	282	25,994	24,047	53,164	12,587	20,780	77,574
Dade	25,117,746	136,412	2,302,187	22,536	1,248,506	2,711,605	3,160,870	2,664,110	2,976,780	9,894,740
De Soto	101,252	23,470	2,480	176	10,200	3,995	20,556	3,701	5,575	31,099
Dixie	40,323	1,758	13,350	(D)	5,309	(D)	7,760	183	1,484	7,465
Duval	9,857,976	(D)	1,063,665	(D)	627,913	919,011	1,202,125	1,662,816	1,157,595	3,158,081
Escambia	2,376,850	12,701	360,475	3,294	214,092	152,679	364,247	133,453	195,469	940,440
Flagler	153,356	2,656	33,518	2,039	10,223	1,704	23,267	24,800	6,246	48,903
Franklin	47,142	3,259	3,160	B/	3,078	4,383	8,045	2,223	5,443	17,542
Gadsden	154,907	7,565	32,585	(D)	14,128	(D)	26,974	6,618	9,940	33,687

See footnotes at end of table.

Continued . . .

Table 5.34. EARNED INCOME: PRIVATE NONFARM EARNINGS ON A PLACE-OF-WORK BASIS BY MAJOR INDUSTRIAL SOURCE IN THE UNITED STATES AND IN THE STATE AND COUNTIES OF FLORIDA, 1993 AND 1994 (Continued)

(in thousands of dollars)

County	Total private nonfarm earnings	Agri-culture ser-vices 1/	Manufac-turing	Mining	Construc-tion	Wholesale trade	Retail trade	Finance insurance and real estate	Trans-porta-tion 2/	Services
				1993 A/ (Continued)						
Gilchrist	24,398	1,537	4,084	0	2,530	1,756	3,364	1,222	2,713	7,192
Glades	16,978	3,881	377	(D)	1,147	809	2,301	(D)	3,504	3,741
Gulf	86,534	656	42,730	0	8,961	408	8,117	2,441	11,964	11,257
Hamilton	79,356	683	57,188	0	1,708	341	5,853	561	5,583	7,439
Hardee	102,439	21,392	7,920	(D)	(D)	8,902	17,017	6,033	5,889	23,152
Hendry	192,021	49,546	41,228	(D)	11,296	5,768	25,906	6,878	(D)	39,651
Hernando	486,743	8,978	37,969	9,827	44,637	15,841	95,943	32,104	39,395	202,049
Highlands	398,120	34,266	35,905	1,016	37,847	16,212	79,955	26,675	23,475	142,769
Hillsborough	11,773,498	91,983	1,168,593	728	653,237	1,448,362	1,418,168	1,375,129	1,072,678	4,544,620
Holmes	42,582	345	9,442	B/	3,468	1,504	9,240	1,579	2,869	14,116
Indian River	821,499	72,445	58,082	2,166	78,928	35,386	138,476	77,993	19,878	338,145
Jackson	197,232	4,349	37,784	881	11,197	24,824	45,684	12,445	12,938	47,130
Jefferson	44,312	4,114	5,978	0	4,277	1,304	6,934	2,982	5,628	13,095
Lafayette	12,065	1,708	3,228	0	735	803	1,983	(D)	(D)	2,689
Lake	1,037,371	28,606	124,073	7,708	112,098	36,948	173,045	72,988	82,570	399,335
Lee	3,209,944	46,374	163,428	3,489	398,742	153,371	589,959	302,171	215,620	1,336,790
Leon	1,927,335	11,853	97,628	824	139,320	110,310	328,831	162,268	116,982	959,319
Levy	98,421	(D)	7,147	(D)	16,619	3,705	22,904	5,752	10,129	23,770
Liberty	24,373	448	8,760	0	3,733	B/	2,406	437	3,596	4,953
Madison	74,577	1,548	30,491	0	1,658	3,025	11,800	2,030	4,252	19,773
Manatee	1,935,196	42,140	339,179	1,903	101,842	73,572	281,646	100,741	58,212	935,961
Marion	1,425,055	25,181	296,554	3,447	115,672	117,949	270,370	92,273	71,326	432,283
Martin	1,119,819	33,868	101,690	1,289	102,572	36,209	169,947	174,308	74,895	425,041
Monroe	770,673	15,434	14,283	1,545	62,320	22,791	189,116	49,443	54,999	360,742

See footnotes at end of table.

Continued . . .

Table 5.34. EARNED INCOME: PRIVATE NONFARM EARNINGS ON A PLACE-OF-WORK BASIS BY MAJOR INDUSTRIAL SOURCE IN THE UNITED STATES AND IN THE STATE AND COUNTIES OF FLORIDA, 1993 AND 1994 (Continued)

(in thousands of dollars)

County	Total private nonfarm earnings	Agri-culture ser-vices 1/	Manufac-turing	Mining	Construc-tion	Wholesale trade	Retail trade	Finance insurance and real estate	Trans-porta-tion 2/	Services
				1993 A/ (Continued)						
Nassau	319,116	12,800	86,521	B/	32,181	10,002	50,489	12,752	23,560	90,807
Okaloosa	1,089,967	7,693	106,063	1,129	85,047	30,657	224,158	86,378	60,952	487,890
Okeechobee	148,862	10,513	6,753	B/	14,688	7,503	31,360	7,137	10,241	60,644
Orange	12,560,056	110,289	1,451,038	5,218	736,718	1,004,396	1,484,069	1,122,486	1,162,289	5,483,553
Osceola	906,524	11,268	80,748	171	76,840	43,067	191,033	52,018	20,698	430,681
Palm Beach	11,631,649	226,353	1,559,540	7,012	778,851	741,752	1,577,847	1,344,119	661,813	4,734,362
Pasco	1,353,156	25,518	108,043	1,269	130,797	46,842	268,284	89,603	100,667	582,133
Pinellas	9,400,254	71,978	1,491,794	2,676	574,308	587,356	1,444,159	907,941	471,603	3,848,439
Polk	3,863,521	158,841	633,732	142,131	259,497	257,229	673,177	243,548	270,511	1,224,855
Putnam	377,923	3,428	132,791	3,801	54,836	8,299	54,613	12,925	23,876	83,354
St. Johns	668,066	8,124	87,731	207	45,458	41,772	118,193	35,945	30,645	299,991
St. Lucie	1,050,800	90,363	67,855	1,007	104,866	56,801	170,712	68,986	127,633	362,577
Santa Rosa	436,175	6,068	71,027	10,891	52,714	13,982	64,126	15,373	36,875	165,119
Sarasota	2,988,787	29,994	253,508	2,264	255,031	138,984	503,459	319,431	136,808	1,349,308
Seminole	2,650,731	34,391	334,710	1,619	292,519	201,720	459,128	211,745	205,746	909,153
Sumter	124,489	2,102	17,649	2,496	7,888	8,259	26,035	4,396	24,738	30,926
Suwannee	153,333	(D)	31,131	(D)	12,632	9,683	32,703	6,737	15,194	37,750
Taylor	142,608	1,726	75,214	(D)	(D)	3,935	17,181	4,925	4,575	23,184
Union	38,033	1,248	10,913	(D)	2,746	(D)	3,731	1,097	8,331	9,529
Volusia	2,607,149	23,674	367,411	69	220,342	135,696	533,036	183,651	137,048	1,006,222
Wakulla	59,702	1,589	22,209	0	5,738	2,456	8,869	2,380	3,080	13,381
Walton	158,426	3,161	25,963	1,269	15,953	4,111	30,689	7,809	13,054	56,417
Washington	69,763	861	18,755	0	5,814	2,481	10,143	1,628	12,782	17,299

See footnotes at end of table.

Continued . . .

Table 5.34. EARNED INCOME: PRIVATE NONFARM EARNINGS ON A PLACE-OF-WORK BASIS BY MAJOR INDUSTRIAL SOURCE IN THE UNITED STATES AND IN THE STATE AND COUNTIES OF FLORIDA, 1993 AND 1994 (Continued)

(in thousands of dollars)

County	Total private nonfarm earnings	Agri-culture ser-vices 1/	Manufac-turing	Mining	Construc-tion	Wholesale trade	Retail trade	Finance insurance and real estate	Trans-porta-tion 2/	Services
					1994					
United States 3/	3,378,062	26,804	747,326	36,349	218,117	254,791	392,234	302,857	272,608	1,126,976
Florida 3/	152,752	2,068	17,475	297	10,756	11,815	22,167	14,764	12,170	61,239
Alachua	1,825,993	(D)	176,599	(D)	146,036	64,942	305,841	140,933	74,643	896,319
Baker	61,880	317	9,247	0	(D)	3,142	14,637	2,626	10,949	(D)
Bay	1,136,771	7,240	101,332	175	124,924	73,025	243,300	79,211	84,439	423,125
Bradford	85,632	934	10,289	(D)	8,158	(D)	17,103	2,779	6,701	24,790
Brevard	4,746,531	33,574	1,304,532	2,821	307,600	142,611	574,026	188,979	179,008	2,013,380
Broward	16,141,630	136,364	1,624,178	9,178	1,163,280	1,411,582	2,493,269	1,730,326	1,145,621	6,427,832
Calhoun	47,006	5,680	7,202	0	5,129	2,605	9,410	1,284	2,261	13,435
Charlotte	751,204	11,504	24,474	1,368	99,867	18,592	156,605	50,387	36,174	352,233
Citrus	588,918	6,881	28,883	910	68,387	14,104	102,660	32,144	112,974	221,975
Clay	644,404	12,396	42,740	8,647	70,034	24,860	154,681	28,364	51,832	250,850
Collier	2,078,284	96,703	82,642	5,421	270,263	81,390	361,542	225,002	69,727	885,594
Columbia	281,965	2,000	40,024	306	30,765	27,811	57,166	13,651	20,766	89,476
Dade	26,237,075	143,593	2,349,003	21,660	1,229,424	2,821,259	3,251,235	2,803,760	3,129,021	10,488,120
De Soto	111,180	27,525	2,496	B/	10,429	4,982	21,529	3,749	5,795	34,652
Dixie	44,362	1,818	14,339	(D)	5,949	(D)	8,725	906	1,614	7,553
Duval	10,472,137	(D)	1,086,692	(D)	678,389	939,459	1,206,452	1,811,178	1,208,259	3,467,842
Escambia	2,555,725	14,168	374,816	3,501	236,640	156,980	391,410	133,450	208,990	1,035,770
Flagler	171,832	2,876	38,516	2,055	11,247	1,864	26,894	24,896	6,787	56,697
Franklin	53,612	3,655	3,506	B/	3,446	5,529	8,930	2,846	6,023	19,666
Gadsden	160,816	8,281	32,840	(D)	15,332	(D)	30,312	6,722	10,632	34,403
Gilchrist	26,449	1,779	5,012	0	2,795	1,513	3,492	1,368	2,895	7,595
Glades	18,149	4,242	140	(D)	1,781	859	2,548	(D)	3,397	4,098

See footnotes at end of table.

Continued . . .

Table 5.34. EARNED INCOME: PRIVATE NONFARM EARNINGS ON A PLACE-OF-WORK BASIS BY MAJOR INDUSTRIAL SOURCE IN THE UNITED STATES AND IN THE STATE AND COUNTIES OF FLORIDA, 1993 AND 1994 (Continued)

(in thousands of dollars)

County	Total private nonfarm earnings	Agri-culture ser-vices 1/	Manufac-turing	Mining	Construc-tion	Wholesale trade	Retail trade	Finance insurance and real estate	Trans-porta-tion 2/	Services
1994 (Continued)										
Gulf	89,708	708	43,335	0	8,323	402	8,380	2,764	12,903	12,893
Hamilton	83,152	739	59,786	0	1,497	351	6,139	459	6,331	7,850
Hardee	115,440	26,317	7,540	(D)	(D)	9,043	18,125	6,293	6,209	26,079
Hendry	200,411	51,242	45,300	(D)	11,631	6,398	27,234	6,910	(D)	39,147
Hernando	529,838	9,279	41,703	9,675	49,953	18,515	106,199	34,971	41,585	217,958
Highlands	432,080	38,824	37,200	1,108	42,831	14,263	82,240	26,754	25,705	163,155
Hillsborough	12,760,028	99,600	1,209,537	786	727,445	1,514,493	1,546,211	1,471,739	1,161,630	5,028,587
Holmes	46,637	390	9,803	B/	4,282	1,702	9,701	1,542	3,003	16,194
Indian River	901,074	76,767	66,795	2,364	91,070	49,211	148,059	76,530	22,134	368,144
Jackson	207,136	4,668	37,775	855	13,055	27,887	45,529	14,549	13,937	48,881
Jefferson	42,786	2,234	5,723	0	3,476	1,351	7,127	3,062	5,243	14,570
Lafayette	14,754	2,022	4,463	0	872	1,245	2,237	(D)	(D)	2,790
Lake	1,116,107	30,566	131,141	8,038	120,126	40,941	188,032	74,955	90,942	431,366
Lee	3,466,966	51,168	177,542	3,856	441,268	181,016	637,949	300,309	216,468	1,457,390
Leon	2,100,633	14,651	107,539	939	153,715	121,136	358,281	173,180	122,253	1,048,939
Levy	107,827	(D)	8,021	(D)	18,185	4,766	24,600	6,327	10,660	26,157
Liberty	25,551	501	8,947	0	4,008	B/	2,405	479	3,870	5,298
Madison	78,632	1,459	31,147	0	1,653	3,140	12,120	2,058	4,707	22,348
Manatee	2,204,274	47,251	391,975	1,112	119,503	80,245	308,061	106,636	61,444	1,088,047
Marion	1,533,402	27,195	303,955	3,567	129,855	131,956	290,072	95,018	84,897	466,887
Martin	1,111,586	38,214	98,737	1,302	104,093	47,272	181,558	118,382	73,673	448,355
Monroe	811,668	17,074	14,344	1,642	65,807	25,356	195,625	53,058	57,150	381,612
Nassau	337,095	13,147	92,068	B/	33,854	10,706	52,127	12,850	24,330	98,009
Okaloosa	1,207,362	8,477	117,824	1,293	97,311	31,202	250,499	96,415	62,520	541,821
Okeechobee	161,639	11,621	6,466	B/	14,806	11,365	32,529	9,846	9,795	65,185
Orange	13,410,403	113,392	1,432,548	5,537	819,447	1,093,140	1,598,855	1,151,570	1,231,534	5,964,380

See footnotes at end of table.

Continued . . .

Table 5.34. EARNED INCOME: PRIVATE NONFARM EARNINGS ON A PLACE-OF-WORK BASIS BY MAJOR INDUSTRIAL SOURCE IN THE UNITED STATES AND IN THE STATE AND COUNTIES OF FLORIDA, 1993 AND 1994 (Continued)

(in thousands of dollars)

County	Total private nonfarm earnings	Agri-culture ser-vices 1/	Manufac-turing	Mining	Construc-tion	Wholesale trade	Retail trade	Finance insurance and real estate	Trans-porta-tion 2/	Services
				1994 (Continued)						
Osceola	984,797	12,284	82,579	179	83,041	45,003	197,719	62,953	21,858	479,181
Palm Beach	12,336,625	247,570	1,584,622	6,328	851,625	835,373	1,674,647	1,390,481	685,117	5,060,862
Pasco	1,478,753	29,326	107,524	1,400	158,477	49,573	282,914	89,714	112,806	647,019
Pinellas	10,062,492	77,476	1,547,194	3,227	618,282	667,455	1,499,770	935,675	503,876	4,209,537
Polk	4,201,007	172,018	693,739	133,782	299,608	278,747	746,285	252,222	300,026	1,324,580
Putnam	372,286	3,066	137,242	4,393	35,609	9,199	55,690	13,880	23,478	89,729
St. Johns	721,783	8,952	90,321	254	49,843	46,669	131,375	37,477	32,884	324,008
St. Lucie	1,119,918	94,920	76,905	1,083	114,097	58,009	178,863	70,664	135,437	389,940
Santa Rosa	463,753	7,039	73,346	9,100	59,617	14,900	68,145	16,956	40,136	174,514
Sarasota	3,145,935	33,998	274,394	2,373	270,081	144,872	540,520	323,858	134,121	1,421,718
Seminole	2,880,238	37,836	345,443	1,572	322,940	230,076	507,307	213,294	216,255	1,005,515
Sumter	132,829	2,304	18,518	2,380	9,126	7,636	26,922	4,694	28,061	33,188
Suwannee	164,825	(D)	32,977	(D)	15,538	8,354	36,258	7,324	15,249	41,040
Taylor	160,050	1,745	79,793	1,532	(D)	3,979	19,028	5,899	4,972	(D)
Union	40,928	1,232	10,957	(D)	3,553	(D)	3,937	1,085	9,484	10,084
Volusia	2,836,238	25,881	399,461	68	232,383	149,032	561,530	192,273	132,252	1,143,358
Wakulla	62,396	1,760	21,185	0	6,453	2,185	9,233	2,880	3,827	14,873
Walton	172,230	3,322	27,821	1,152	17,713	3,938	32,274	8,423	14,412	63,175
Washington	76,984	(D)	20,595	(D)	6,767	2,344	12,653	1,680	13,494	18,498

(D) Data withheld to avoid disclosure of information about individual industries.
A/ Revised.
B/ Less than $50,000. Estimates are included in totals.
1/ Includes forestry, fisheries, and other.
2/ Includes communications and public utilities.
3/ United States and Florida numbers are rounded to millions of dollars.
Source: U.S., Department of Commerce, Bureau of Economic Analysis, Regional Economic Information System, CD-ROM, June 1996.

Table 5.38. TRANSFER PAYMENTS: AMOUNTS BY TYPE IN FLORIDA, 1993 AND 1994

(in thousands of dollars)

Type of transfer payment	1993 A/	1994
Total personal income by place of residence	285,248,059	302,099,041
Total transfer payments	52,268,156	55,499,689
Percentage of personal income	18.32	18.37
Government payments to individuals	50,447,206	53,583,126
Retirement and disability insurance benefit payments	27,848,274	29,353,081
Old age, survivors, and disability insurance	20,423,097	21,555,549
Railroad retirement and disability	398,169	406,866
Federal civilian employee retirement	2,645,648	2,736,638
Military retirement	2,774,133	2,881,646
State and local government employee retirement	1,318,655	1,455,071
Workers' compensation (federal and state)	226,009	249,046
Other government disability insurance and retirement 1/	62,563	68,265
Medical payments 2/	15,588,137	17,452,199
Income maintenance benefit payments	3,931,099	4,082,591
Supplemental Security Income (SSI)	1,068,299	1,179,529
Aid to Families with Dependent Children (AFDC)	884,836	852,598
Food stamps	1,328,883	1,323,564
Other income maintenance 3/	649,081	726,900
Unemployment insurance benefit payments	1,243,518	839,415
State unemployment insurance compensation	1,185,165	805,888
Unemployment Compensation for Federal Civilian Employees (UCFE)	9,358	8,803
Unemployment Compensation for Railroad Employees	1,244	1,084
Unemployment Compensation for Veterans (UCX)	46,939	23,174
Other unemployment compensation 4/	812	466
Veterans' benefit payments	1,454,002	1,491,368
Veterans' pensions and compensation	1,259,349	1,265,634
Educational assistance to veterans, dependents, and survivors 5/	58,354	64,327
Veterans' life insurance benefit	130,708	157,802
Other assistance to veterans 6/	5,591	3,605
Federal education and training assistance payments (excluding veterans) 7/	366,061	345,800
Other payments to individuals 8/	16,115	18,672
Payments to nonprofit institutions	1,060,149	1,136,790
Federal government payments	306,514	329,218
State and local government payments 9/	433,859	465,472
Business payments	319,776	342,100
Business payments to individuals 10/	760,801	779,773

A/ Revised. 1/ Includes temporary disability and black lung payments. 2/ Medicare, medical vendor, and CHAMPUS payments. 3/ Includes general, emergency, refugee, and energy assistance, foster home care payments and earned-income tax credits. 4/ Includes trade readjustment, public service employment benefit, and transitional benefit payments. 5/ Includes veterans' readjustment benefit payments and educational assistance to spouses and children of disabled or deceased veterans. 6/ Includes payments to paraplegics, transportation payments for disabled veterans, and veterans' aid and bonuses. 7/ Includes federal fellowship and Job Corps payments, basic educational opportunity grants, and loan interest subsidies. 8/ Includes Bureau of Indian Affairs and education exchange payments, compensation of survivors of public safety officers, crime victims, Japanese interment, natural disasters, and other special payments. 9/ Foster home care supervised by private agency, educational assistance to nonprofit institutions and other payments to nonprofit institutions. 10/ Personal injury payments to individuals other than employees and other business transfer payments.

Source: U.S., Department of Commerce, Bureau of Economic Analysis, Regional Economic Information System, CD-ROM, June 1996.

Table 5.39. TRANSFER PAYMENTS: TOTAL AMOUNTS IN THE UNITED STATES AND IN THE STATE AND COUNTIES OF FLORIDA, 1992, 1993, AND 1994

(amounts in thousands of dollars)

County	1992 A/ Amount	1992 A/ As a percentage of total personal income	1993 A/ Amount	1993 A/ As a percentage of total personal income	1994 Amount	1994 As a percentage of total personal income
United States	858,474,000	16.7	913,753,000	17.0	956,600,000	16.9
Florida	48,933,417	18.4	52,268,156	18.3	55,499,689	18.4
Alachua	606,011	18.3	655,644	18.6	694,458	18.5
Baker	59,362	22.6	65,203	23.4	70,243	23.9
Bay	517,578	23.6	557,807	23.6	595,861	23.9
Bradford	75,763	26.5	81,973	27.1	88,320	27.8
Brevard	1,583,325	19.9	1,701,491	20.5	1,815,953	20.9
Broward	4,806,597	16.0	5,125,120	15.9	5,427,764	15.9
Calhoun	42,139	32.6	44,721	32.8	47,661	32.6
Charlotte	579,891	27.4	620,899	27.7	670,190	27.9
Citrus	455,508	30.5	480,160	30.6	506,400	30.3
Clay	311,875	15.7	336,869	16.0	362,051	16.2
Collier	536,528	11.4	583,792	11.4	631,973	11.6
Columbia	160,182	25.6	174,942	26.1	186,469	25.9
Dade	6,917,601	20.6	7,278,612	18.9	7,699,501	19.0
De Soto	94,246	25.5	101,319	26.0	108,211	26.4
Dixie	39,664	32.7	43,985	36.3	47,644	33.7
Duval	2,267,333	17.2	2,398,139	17.3	2,533,705	17.4
Escambia	1,093,585	24.8	1,167,730	25.4	1,234,484	25.7
Flagler	133,659	27.1	151,919	27.9	170,367	28.7
Franklin	40,536	31.6	44,425	31.8	47,732	31.4
Gadsden	168,262	30.2	182,433	31.1	193,416	31.3
Gilchrist	37,087	28.4	41,409	29.4	44,773	29.9
Glades	21,276	20.0	21,838	19.3	22,630	20.3
Gulf	50,678	31.4	54,322	31.0	59,866	31.9
Hamilton	38,875	28.8	41,439	30.5	44,178	31.2
Hardee	65,550	20.9	69,839	22.0	74,980	22.2
Hendry	75,990	16.0	81,390	16.3	86,151	17.0
Hernando	486,573	29.7	522,386	30.1	560,657	29.9
Highlands	325,527	28.1	350,494	28.5	374,770	28.9
Hillsborough	2,636,254	16.7	2,828,475	17.0	2,961,297	16.8
Holmes	67,626	34.9	72,126	35.3	76,227	35.4
Indian River	410,149	16.4	433,990	16.7	458,665	16.5
Jackson	193,514	31.9	211,316	33.3	225,531	33.9
Jefferson	41,666	25.1	44,903	25.3	48,361	26.1
Lafayette	16,493	22.2	16,889	22.5	17,414	21.9
Lake	693,538	24.7	752,190	25.2	817,227	25.8

See footnote at end of table.

Continued . . .

Table 5.39. TRANSFER PAYMENTS: TOTAL AMOUNTS IN THE UNITED STATES AND IN THE STATE AND COUNTIES OF FLORIDA, 1992, 1993, AND 1994 (Continued)

(amounts in thousands of dollars)

County	1992 A/ Amount	1992 A/ As a percentage of total personal income	1993 A/ Amount	1993 A/ As a percentage of total personal income	1994 Amount	1994 As a percentage of total personal income
Lee	1,370,184	19.1	1,474,315	19.3	1,565,708	19.3
Leon	478,666	13.1	522,339	13.3	556,239	13.3
Levy	103,288	29.7	111,254	30.1	120,572	30.4
Liberty	25,902	33.6	29,166	34.9	31,926	35.5
Madison	63,386	30.8	67,969	31.6	70,825	31.7
Manatee	867,952	19.0	928,551	19.1	988,997	19.0
Marion	796,732	24.5	857,591	25.1	929,642	25.4
Martin	414,147	13.2	448,174	13.5	480,128	13.8
Monroe	226,624	12.6	247,182	12.5	260,286	12.6
Nassau	141,210	15.8	156,951	16.2	171,405	16.6
Okaloosa	617,871	22.7	667,457	22.9	713,442	23.4
Okeechobee	108,196	26.0	115,429	26.0	122,469	26.4
Orange	1,994,035	14.8	2,148,011	15.0	2,262,358	15.0
Osceola	320,977	17.7	345,300	17.8	374,686	18.3
Palm Beach	3,457,170	12.1	3,705,134	12.2	3,953,600	12.4
Pasco	1,249,930	28.2	1,322,038	28.3	1,394,146	27.6
Pinellas	3,962,035	21.1	4,196,939	20.8	4,415,949	20.5
Polk	1,392,674	20.4	1,487,463	20.9	1,578,280	20.6
Putnam	260,459	29.4	274,382	29.1	291,042	29.7
St. Johns	312,597	14.4	342,229	14.6	366,043	14.5
St. Lucie	584,998	23.5	621,091	23.6	659,367	23.6
Santa Rosa	276,669	19.0	301,261	19.2	331,657	19.6
Sarasota	1,362,936	17.2	1,455,145	17.5	1,557,680	17.6
Seminole	748,541	12.3	804,321	12.3	847,835	12.0
Sumter	151,627	35.2	164,814	36.0	179,270	36.8
Suwannee	111,855	28.4	119,567	28.9	128,549	29.4
Taylor	66,053	27.3	71,378	30.1	76,383	28.5
Union	23,684	22.6	24,841	22.6	26,884	23.3
Volusia	1,538,918	24.1	1,640,315	24.4	1,741,800	24.3
Wakulla	43,967	20.1	47,693	20.0	51,206	19.8
Walton	129,357	32.3	142,598	32.5	155,165	33.0
Washington	80,336	35.9	87,069	36.9	91,020	36.6

A/ Revised.

Source: U.S., Department of Commerce, Bureau of Economic Analysis, Regional Economic Information System, CD-ROM, June 1996.

Table 5.41. MILITARY RETIREES: PERSONS RECEIVING MILITARY RETIREMENT INCOME AND AMOUNT OF MONTHLY PAYMENT IN FLORIDA, SEPTEMBER 30, 1994 AND 1995

Branch and type of service	Total 1/		Paid by Department of Defense		Monthly payment ($1,000)	
	1994	1995	1994	1995	1994	1995
Total	165,455	170,625	151,830	156,171	222,698	233,495
Army	41,105	42,468	36,866	37,854	53,144	55,475
Navy	53,605	55,461	49,211	50,883	69,945	74,003
Marine Corps	7,183	7,394	6,165	6,336	9,569	10,047
Air Force	63,562	65,302	59,588	61,098	90,041	93,969
Coast Guard	3,472	3,600	3,311	3,429	5,254	5,544
Officers	53,585	54,221	52,202	52,688	114,073	118,272
Nondisabled and reserve	48,798	49,544	47,828	48,448	105,682	109,934
Disabled	4,787	4,677	4,374	4,240	8,391	8,338
Enlisted	111,870	116,404	99,628	103,483	108,625	115,222
Nondisabled and reserve	98,348	102,570	92,418	96,237	103,589	110,106
Disabled	13,522	13,834	7,210	7,246	5,036	5,116

1/ Includes retirees whose monthly payment is zero or less after survivor benefit deductions and/or other offsets such as Veterans Administration payments, dual compensation, pay cap limitations from civil service employment, and refusal of retired pay.

Note: The monthly amount of payment is before deductions for withholding taxes and allotments, but after deductions for survivor benefits, waivers to obtain benefits from the Veterans Administration, dual compensation, and other adjustments.

Table 5.42. MILITARY RETIREES: SURVIVING FAMILIES RECEIVING RETIREMENT PAYMENTS AND AMOUNT OF MONTHLY PAYMENT IN FLORIDA, SEPTEMBER 30 1993, 1994, AND 1995

Branch of service	Total			Monthly payment received (dollars)		
	1993	1994	1995	1993	1994	1995
Total	18,686	19,874	20,830	11,494,086	12,474,413	13,373,789
Army	6,806	7,197	7,394	4,298,119	4,652,584	4,871,992
Navy	5,537	5,865	6,179	3,183,154	3,401,022	3,674,082
Marine Corps	542	600	654	342,645	392,298	437,784
Air Force	5,801	6,212	6,603	3,670,168	4,028,509	4,389,931

Note: Data are for families receiving payments under the Retired Servicemen's Family Protection Plan or the Survivor Benefit Plan.

Source for Tables 5.41 and 5.42: U.S., Department of Defense, Office of the Actuary *DOD Statistical Report on the Military Retirement System, Fiscal Year 1995,* and previous editions.

Table 5.46. POVERTY THRESHOLDS: AVERAGE POVERTY THRESHOLDS FOR A FAMILY OF FOUR AND THE ANNUAL CONSUMER PRICE INDEX IN THE UNITED STATES, 1982 THROUGH 1995

Year	Average threshold (dollars)	Consumer Price Index (1982-84=100)	Year	Average threshold (dollars)	Consumer Price Index (1982-84=100)
1982	9,862	96.5	1989	12,674	124.0
1983	10,178	99.6	1990	13,359	130.7
1984	10,609	103.9	1991	13,924	136.2
1985	10,989	107.6	1992	14,335	140.3
1986	11,203	109.6	1993	14,763	144.5
1987	11,611	113.6	1994	15,141	148.2
1988	12,092	118.3	1995 A/	15,570	152.4

A/ Preliminary.
Note: See Glossary under Poverty status for definition of poverty thresholds.

Source: U.S., Department of Commerce, Bureau of the Census, *Statistical Abstract of the United States, 1995,* previous editions, and the Internet at <http://www.census.gov/>, U.S., Department of Commerce, Bureau of Economic Analysis, *Survey of Current* Business, May 1994, and previous editions, and U.S., Department of Commerce, Bureau of Labor Statistics, the Internet at <http://stats.bls.gov:80/>.

Table 5.47. POVERTY THRESHOLDS: POVERTY LEVEL BASED ON MONEY INCOME BY SIZE OF FAMILY IN THE UNITED STATES, 1992 THROUGH 1995

(in dollars)

Size of family unit	1992	1993	1994	1995 A/
1 person (unrelated individual)	7,143	7,363	7,547	7,761
Under 65 years	7,299	7,518	7,710	7,929
65 years and over	6,729	6,930	7,108	7,309
2 persons	9,137	9,414	9,661	9,935
Householder under 65 years	9,443	9,728	9,976	10,259
Householder 65 years and over	8,487	8,740	8,967	9,221
3 persons	11,186	11,522	11,821	12,156
4 persons	14,335	14,763	15,141	15,570
5 persons	16,952	17,449	17,900	18,407
6 persons	19,137	19,718	20,235	20,808
7 persons	21,594	22,383	22,923	23,573
8 persons	24,053	24,838	25,427	26,148
9 persons or more	28,745	29,529	30,300	31,159

A/ Preliminary.
Note: See Glossary under Poverty status for definition of poverty thresholds. Some data may be revised.

Source: U.S., Department of Commerce, Bureau of the Census, *Current Population Reports: Consumer Income,* Series P60-188 and the Internet at <http://www.census.gov/>.

LABOR FORCE, EMPLOYMENT, AND EARNINGS

Job Patterns for Minorities and Women in Private Industry, 1994

All minorities

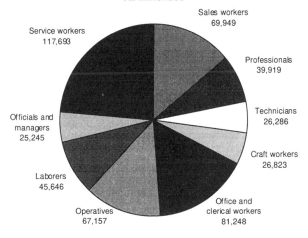

Sales workers
69,949

Professionals
39,919

Technicians
26,286

Craft workers
26,823

Office and
clerical workers
81,248

Operatives
67,157

Laborers
45,646

Officials and
managers
25,245

Service workers
117,693

All women

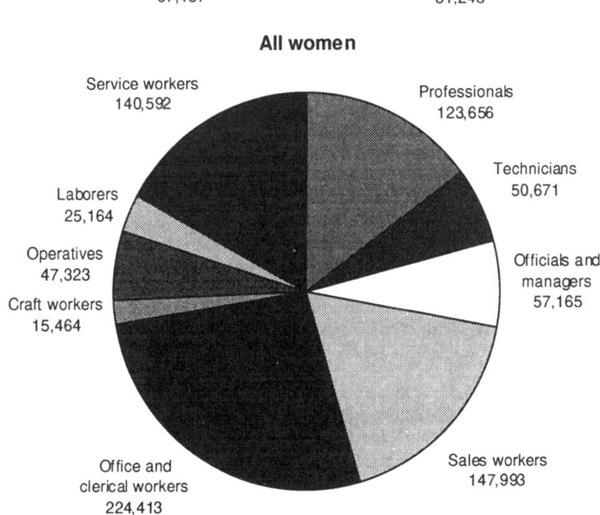

Source: Table 6.20

SECTION 6.00
LABOR FORCE, EMPLOYMENT, AND EARNINGS

TABLES LISTED BY MAJOR HEADINGS

Table 6.01. NONAGRICULTURAL EMPLOYMENT: EMPLOYMENT BY INDUSTRIAL CLASSIFICATION IN FLORIDA, 1957 THROUGH 1995

(in thousands)

Year	Total	Mining	Construction	Manufacturing	Transportation and public utilities 1/	Wholesale and retail trade	Finance insurance and real estate	Services	Government
1957	1,152.7	7.8	122.7	176.1	94.6	313.3	64.6	187.8	185.8
1958	1,185.6	7.7	127.7	180.3	94.4	313.1	70.0	197.2	195.2
1959	1,273.0	7.8	134.6	199.9	97.6	333.4	76.9	215.2	207.6
1960	1,320.6	8.2	124.7	207.5	100.2	349.7	82.1	227.7	220.5
1961	1,333.9	8.3	112.4	211.8	99.8	350.9	84.6	233.8	232.3
1962	1,387.8	8.2	112.7	223.1	99.4	365.0	87.4	244.6	247.4
1963	1,447.4	8.5	120.2	229.3	100.7	375.1	90.8	260.3	262.5
1964	1,526.5	9.2	130.1	237.9	106.0	395.0	93.7	275.9	278.7
1965	1,619.1	9.6	138.8	252.6	109.9	417.7	97.4	291.9	301.2
1966	1,726.8	9.7	137.1	276.1	116.8	443.1	101.7	316.1	326.2
1967	1,816.4	8.9	131.7	293.8	127.1	466.3	106.2	340.1	342.3
1968	1,932.3	8.4	143.6	311.4	135.1	491.5	112.6	367.9	361.8
1969	2,069.9	7.8	169.2	329.2	145.4	521.3	123.0	396.1	377.9
1970	2,152.1	8.3	175.7	322.5	154.5	545.8	131.3	416.2	397.8
1971	2,276.4	8.9	186.8	322.7	161.7	583.5	143.8	449.9	419.1
1972	2,513.1	8.8	230.1	351.3	173.5	643.5	162.4	505.6	437.9
1973	2,778.6	9.2	290.2	380.6	186.7	703.2	182.6	556.2	469.9
1974	2,863.8	9.9	276.1	375.9	189.8	727.6	192.5	581.5	510.5
1075	2,746.4	9.4	182.5	339.4	182.9	713.6	188.3	584.3	546.0
1976	2,784.3	8.8	166.7	354.0	181.4	730.8	191.3	608.5	542.8
1977	2,933.2	9.1	178.9	380.9	185.1	771.0	202.5	640.0	565.7
1978	3,180.6	9.5	209.5	415.5	194.2	836.9	219.3	693.9	601.8
1979	3,381.2	10.1	241.4	443.6	208.5	889.5	235.0	752.6	600.5
1980	3,576.2	11.0	263.9	456.4	220.8	939.8	254.2	811.3	618.8
1981	3,736.0	11.3	283.1	472.2	229.8	984.2	274.3	861.0	620.1
1982	3,761.9	9.6	256.6	456.7	229.9	995.0	276.6	905.0	632.5
1983	3,905.4	9.6	268.8	464.3	231.4	1,034.5	283.2	974.3	639.3
1984	4,204.2	10.2	318.3	501.9	241.1	1,118.0	299.5	1,065.7	649.5
1985	4,410.0	10.1	334.3	514.4	243.0	1,184.8	319.2	1,129.8	674.4
1986	4,599.4	9.3	339.5	517.2	247.4	1,238.8	339.7	1,205.6	701.9
1987	4,848.1	8.7	341.5	531.0	254.8	1,316.7	359.3	1,304.4	731.8
1988	5,066.6	9.1	346.3	539.6	260.8	1,378.8	365.1	1,393.9	773.0
1989	5,260.9	9.2	340.2	537.9	266.4	1,432.6	370.3	1,504.3	800.1
1990	5,387.4	8.9	323.2	522.1	278.4	1,444.4	370.7	1,593.0	846.7
1991	5,294.3	8.2	276.9	492.8	274.9	1,402.6	358.2	1,621.5	859.3
1992	5,358.7	7.1	266.5	482.9	275.8	1,411.7	351.9	1,692.7	870.1
1993	5,571.4	6.3	285.3	485.2	287.1	1,456.3	360.3	1,809.2	881.6
1994	5,799.4	6.8	296.0	484.0	296.3	1,507.2	375.6	1,922.9	910.6
1995	6,000.4	6.9	303.6	482.4	303.4	1,548.0	376.4	2,056.1	923.6

1/ Includes communications except U.S. Postal Service.

Note: Benchmark 1994, not seasonally adjusted. Data for some years have been revised.

Source: U.S., Department of Labor, Bureau of Labor Statistics, *Employment and Earnings*, May issues, and the Internet at <http://stats.bls.gov/>.

Table 6.02. EMPLOYMENT AND EARNINGS: NUMBER OF JOBS AND PROPRIETORS AND AVERAGE EARNINGS PER JOB IN THE UNITED STATES AND IN THE STATE AND COUNTIES OF FLORIDA, 1993 AND 1994

County	Total employment 1/ Wage and salary jobs	Number of proprietors Non-farm 2/	Farm	Average earnings per job (dollars) Total	Wage and salary	Per non-farm pro-prietor
		1993 A/				
United States	118,828,000	19,857,500	2,132,000	27,478	25,858	20,360
Florida	6,023,409	1,042,643	37,170	24,661	23,411	16,356
Alachua	104,297	15,576	1,266	22,186	21,071	14,695
Baker	5,182	933	231	19,709	17,363	14,643
Bay	63,496	10,892	88	21,097	20,369	14,088
Bradford	6,166	1,016	361	19,152	18,440	12,260
Brevard	177,031	32,025	515	26,244	26,048	12,043
Broward	572,025	101,725	363	26,032	25,123	16,457
Calhoun	2,789	660	170	18,408	16,687	19,095
Charlotte	31,078	10,284	209	19,873	19,329	14,876
Citrus	24,650	7,736	357	19,676	20,025	11,751
Clay	29,874	8,057	245	19,082	18,550	14,220
Collier	80,023	20,200	241	22,965	20,886	18,118
Columbia	15,865	2,629	572	20,273	19,346	14,111
Dade	950,224	138,667	1,460	27,345	25,689	19,095
De Soto	8,728	1,416	704	19,680	15,791	15,987
Dixie	2,610	928	124	17,472	17,887	11,441
Duval	412,224	54,049	439	26,405	25,274	15,668
Escambia	127,372	15,880	530	23,873	22,856	13,976
Flagler	8,383	750	107	21,436	18,946	16,364
Franklin	2,710	1,310	0	15,552	16,023	10,791
Gadsden	14,137	1,625	358	19,540	17,600	12,227
Gilchrist	2,083	626	375	17,748	17,625	11,867
Glades	1,367	414	194	24,716	15,105	13,205
Gulf	3,994	699	0	23,445	22,587	10,824
Hamilton	4,029	441	286	25,469	23,234	11,043
Hardee	7,697	1,448	1,210	18,312	15,005	15,907
Hendry	13,296	1,850	418	23,103	17,110	17,504
Hernando	24,019	7,604	432	19,144	19,412	11,766
Highlands	22,413	5,306	735	20,324	17,026	15,252
Hillsborough	483,566	63,105	2,819	25,725	24,307	15,926
Holmes	3,272	931	606	16,727	16,051	11,358
Indian River	36,147	7,581	536	23,270	20,793	19,126
Jackson	15,109	2,274	1,010	19,046	17,900	14,780
Jefferson	3,229	826	318	16,128	16,307	11,567

See footnotes at end of table. Continued . . .

Table 6.02. EMPLOYMENT AND EARNINGS: NUMBER OF JOBS AND PROPRIETORS AND AVERAGE EARNINGS PER JOB IN THE UNITED STATES AND IN THE STATE AND COUNTIES OF FLORIDA, 1993 AND 1994 (Continued)

County	Total employment 1/ Wage and salary jobs	Number of proprietors Non-farm 2/	Farm	Average earnings per job (dollars) Total	Wage and salary	Per non-farm pro-prietor
		1993 A/ (Continued)				
Lafayette	1,150	253	298	25,147	16,489	15,838
Lake	50,760	11,167	1,255	20,133	19,085	14,889
Lee	138,138	34,962	423	22,433	21,418	16,011
Leon	126,315	16,252	310	23,034	21,976	14,139
Levy	6,363	1,999	585	16,304	16,527	11,007
Liberty	1,580	291	86	20,243	18,375	21,649
Madison	4,889	861	507	18,266	17,368	13,624
Manatee	95,028	17,969	772	20,832	19,062	13,447
Marion	70,701	14,724	1,765	20,228	19,390	13,642
Martin	42,179	9,285	307	25,484	23,305	19,260
Monroe	36,721	9,911	0	21,733	20,844	17,743
Nassau	14,607	3,202	338	23,785	22,732	16,530
Okaloosa	77,013	12,137	351	22,127	21,991	12,477
Okeechobee	9,086	2,121	376	21,156	17,217	16,066
Orange	496,859	59,420	1,043	26,193	24,374	18,054
Osceola	43,963	5,212	519	21,905	18,462	32,698
Palm Beach	406,971	82,480	702	28,158	25,835	20,473
Pasco	66,224	15,312	1,026	19,937	19,161	14,412
Pinellas	375,474	75,180	150	23,704	23,046	14,653
Polk	167,797	29,859	2,739	23,100	21,443	17,255
Putnam	19,555	1,689	424	23,194	21,114	16,909
St. Johns	31,573	7,859	162	20,356	19,327	15,405
St. Lucie	50,416	11,342	514	21,777	20,412	13,470
Santa Rosa	23,011	7,390	471	20,455	20,798	12,008
Sarasota	125,443	29,079	344	22,102	21,357	15,703
Seminole	103,615	29,386	388	22,706	22,650	14,231
Sumter	6,906	1,989	732	19,130	18,197	15,081
Suwannee	8,650	2,002	1,061	18,394	16,488	17,914
Taylor	6,425	914	169	22,633	21,797	11,212
Union	4,041	454	221	20,067	19,139	12,749
Volusia	135,699	23,582	934	20,470	19,315	14,869
Wakulla	3,115	1,487	90	17,226	18,891	9,249
Walton	9,110	2,324	454	17,343	16,801	13,009
Washington	4,947	1,086	375	18,116	18,060	11,515

See footnotes at end of table. Continued . . .

Table 6.02. EMPLOYMENT AND EARNINGS: NUMBER OF JOBS AND PROPRIETORS AND AVERAGE EARNINGS PER JOB IN THE UNITED STATES AND IN THE STATE AND COUNTIES OF FLORIDA, 1993 AND 1994 (Continued)

County	Total employment 1/			Average earnings per job (dollars)		
	Wage and salary jobs	Number of proprietors				
		Non-farm 2/	Farm	Total	Wage and salary	Per non-farm pro-prietor
		1994				
United States	122,049,000	20,234,500	2,107,000	28,291	26,469	21,481
Florida	6,261,506	1,063,605	37,177	25,160	23,800	17,351
Alachua	109,274	15,884	1,266	22,575	21,309	15,756
Baker	5,452	955	231	19,806	17,384	15,683
Bay	64,787	11,134	88	21,740	20,823	15,137
Bradford	6,292	1,043	361	19,389	18,767	13,183
Brevard	179,493	32,698	515	26,678	26,323	12,802
Broward	607,150	103,666	363	26,359	25,239	17,423
Calhoun	3,010	680	170	18,801	16,923	20,338
Charlotte	32,649	10,494	209	20,567	19,900	15,798
Citrus	25,632	7,913	357	20,212	20,322	12,700
Clay	30,813	8,238	245	19,539	18,801	15,177
Collier	82,990	20,557	241	23,444	21,643	19,088
Columbia	16,635	2,683	572	21,108	20,119	15,129
Dade	970,588	141,421	1,460	27,940	26,185	20,171
De Soto	9,112	1,450	704	19,800	16,171	17,199
Dixie	2,674	959	124	18,243	18,306	13,673
Duval	426,067	55,135	439	26,882	25,567	16,663
Escambia	129,805	16,224	530	24,359	23,202	14,894
Flagler	9,187	767	107	21,501	19,229	17,164
Franklin	2,893	1,359	0	16,328	16,716	11,371
Gadsden	14,425	1,665	358	19,629	17,812	13,126
Gilchrist	2,147	643	375	17,666	17,978	13,255
Glades	1,453	423	194	21,984	14,830	14,191
Gulf	4,061	715	0	24,218	23,205	11,533
Hamilton	4,205	452	286	25,188	23,357	11,949
Hardee	8,510	1,495	1,210	18,163	15,046	16,488
Hendry	14,066	1,906	418	21,797	16,384	18,858
Hernando	25,715	7,766	432	19,595	19,634	12,572
Highlands	24,009	5,427	735	20,084	17,083	16,363
Hillsborough	509,525	64,381	2,822	26,235	24,690	16,930
Holmes	3,517	955	606	16,828	16,488	12,093
Indian River	37,655	7,731	536	24,376	21,664	20,239
Jackson	15,094	2,330	1,010	19,527	18,455	15,759
Jefferson	3,128	847	318	15,839	16,233	12,124
Lafayette	1,285	259	298	24,820	16,838	18,764

See footnotes at end of table. Continued . . .

Table 6.02. EMPLOYMENT AND EARNINGS: NUMBER OF JOBS AND PROPRIETORS AND AVERAGE EARNINGS PER JOB IN THE UNITED STATES AND IN THE STATE AND COUNTIES OF FLORIDA, 1993 AND 1994 (Continued)

County	Total employment 1/ Wage and salary jobs	Number of proprietors Non-farm 2/	Farm	Average earnings per job (dollars) Total	Wage and salary	Per non-farm pro-prietor
		1994 (Continued)				
Lake	53,359	11,407	1,255	20,562	19,346	16,001
Lee	145,885	35,596	423	22,929	21,812	16,982
Leon	132,074	16,536	310	23,795	22,574	15,103
Levy	6,804	2,050	585	16,428	16,700	12,036
Liberty	1,647	301	86	20,860	18,913	23,010
Madison	5,093	882	507	18,079	17,516	14,363
Manatee	106,700	18,345	772	20,780	19,191	14,222
Marion	73,075	15,048	1,765	21,011	20,143	14,635
Martin	43,060	9,461	307	25,109	22,549	19,936
Monroe	36,621	10,163	0	22,333	21,254	18,690
Nassau	15,004	3,285	339	24,510	23,289	17,609
Okaloosa	81,212	12,393	351	22,038	21,635	13,338
Okeechobee	9,356	2,173	376	21,400	17,754	17,101
Orange	512,874	60,534	1,043	26,823	24,864	19,246
Osceola	45,224	5,322	519	22,975	19,438	34,802
Palm Beach	424,346	83,929	702	28,283	26,179	21,462
Pasco	69,614	15,650	1,027	20,767	19,859	15,465
Pinellas	387,816	76,697	150	24,571	23,761	15,527
Polk	175,079	30,529	2,739	24,092	22,206	18,452
Putnam	19,787	1,729	424	22,872	20,684	18,574
St. Johns	33,092	8,025	162	20,994	19,801	16,372
St. Lucie	51,569	11,588	514	22,799	21,162	14,454
Santa Rosa	23,753	7,564	472	20,861	20,841	12,839
Sarasota	130,371	29,608	345	22,488	21,577	16,589
Seminole	110,175	29,939	388	23,401	23,118	15,192
Sumter	7,034	2,040	732	19,545	18,943	16,049
Suwannee	8,991	2,055	1,061	18,535	16,836	19,167
Taylor	6,613	935	169	24,321	23,277	13,376
Union	4,164	466	221	20,410	19,584	13,624
Volusia	139,821	24,088	934	21,185	19,872	15,841
Wakulla	3,184	1,528	90	17,609	19,208	9,769
Walton	9,595	2,373	454	17,800	17,091	13,925
Washington	5,216	1,111	375	18,443	18,399	12,378

A/ Revised.
1/ Full- and part-time jobs.
2/ Includes limited partners.

Source: U.S., Department of Commerce, Bureau of Economic Analysis, Regional Economic Information System, CD-ROM, June 1996.

Table 6.03. EMPLOYMENT: AVERAGE MONTHLY PRIVATE EMPLOYMENT COVERED BY UNEMPLOYMENT COMPENSATION LAW BY INDUSTRY IN FLORIDA, 1994 AND 1995

SIC code	Industry	1994	1995
01-99	All industries	4,923,510	5,107,953
01-09	Agriculture, forestry, and fishing	157,544	152,424
01	Agricultural production--crops	64,280	61,215
02	Agricultural production--livestock and animal specialties	6,876	6,325
07	Agricultural services	83,972	83,023
08	Forestry	931	924
09	Fishing, hunting, and trapping	1,485	938
10-14	Mining	6,224	6,427
13	Oil and gas extraction	415	414
14	Nonmetallic minerals, except fuels	5,655	5,869
15-17	Construction	296,005	303,870
15	Building--general contractors and builders	67,550	68,520
16	Heavy construction other than building construction--contractors	39,620	40,760
17	Special trade contractors	188,836	194,591
20-39	Manufacturing	484,253	481,699
20	Food and kindred products	42,936	41,648
21	Tobacco products	936	1,257
22	Textile mill products	3,875	4,066
23	Apparel and other finished products made from fabrics and similar materials	30,170	27,567
24	Lumber and wood products, except furniture	21,068	21,261
25	Furniture and fixtures	12,205	12,220
26	Paper and allied products	14,282	14,487
27	Printing, publishing, and allied industries	64,746	63,792
28	Chemicals and allied products	21,172	21,323
29	Petroleum refining and related industries	1,727	1,553
30	Rubber and miscellaneous plastics products	20,371	20,584
31	Leather and leather products	2,530	2,877
32	Stone, clay, glass, and concrete products	21,001	21,468
33	Primary metal industries	5,289	5,744
34	Fabricated metal products, except machinery and transportation equipment	30,361	30,020
35	Industrial and commercial machinery and computer equipment	39,776	38,101
36	Electronic and other electrical equipment and components, except computer equipment	59,587	61,063
37	Transportation equipment	48,003	49,474
38	Measuring, analyzing, and controlling instruments; photographic, medical, and optical goods; watches and clocks	34,531	34,022
39	Miscellaneous manufacturing industries	9,689	9,173
40-49	Transportation, communications, and public utilities	288,191	295,747
41	Passenger transportation	13,631	13,103
42	Motor freight transportation and warehousing	67,832	67,440
44	Water transportation	20,149	20,452
45	Transportation by air	49,238	54,504
46	Pipelines, except natural gas	130	134
47	Transportation services	28,623	31,510
48	Telecommunications	71,908	73,212

See footnotes at end of table.   Continued . . .

Table 6.03. EMPLOYMENT: AVERAGE MONTHLY PRIVATE EMPLOYMENT COVERED BY UNEMPLOYMENT COMPENSATION LAW BY INDUSTRY IN FLORIDA, 1994 AND 1995 (Continued)

SIC code	Industry	1994	1995
40-49	Transportation, communications, and public utilities (Continued)		
49	Electric, gas, and sanitary services	36,680	35,394
50-51	Wholesale trade	305,351	318,669
50	Wholesale trade--durable goods	174,485	184,299
51	Wholesale trade--nondurable goods	130,866	134,371
52-59	Retail trade	1,201,773	1,228,508
52	Building materials, hardware, garden supply, and mobile home dealers	46,652	46,092
53	General merchandise stores	142,719	146,295
54	Food stores	219,438	228,667
55	Automotive dealers and gasoline service stations	117,040	120,209
56	Apparel and accessory stores	67,388	67,637
57	Furniture and home furnishings stores	56,211	58,999
58	Eating and drinking places	414,823	420,144
59	Miscellaneous retail	137,502	140,467
60-67	Finance, insurance, and real estate	372,984	372,560
60	Depository institutions	97,236	94,732
61	Nondeposit credit institutions	35,162	34,838
62	Security and commodity brokers, dealers, exchanges, and services	23,261	23,875
63	Insurance carriers	65,738	65,716
64	Insurance agents, brokers, and service	41,582	43,161
65	Real estate	100,959	100,859
67	Holding and other investment offices	9,046	9,380
70-89	Services	1,796,211	1,915,292
70	Hotels, rooming houses, camps, and other lodging places	136,059	137,513
72	Personal services	67,035	67,427
73	Business services	447,178	517,215
75	Automotive repair services, and parking	59,803	60,813
76	Miscellaneous repair services	22,934	24,131
78	Motion pictures	17,527	17,849
79	Amusement and recreation services	116,802	122,431
80	Health services	514,220	538,142
81	Legal services	58,652	59,069
82	Educational services	46,129	47,657
83	Social services	106,402	109,083
84	Museums, art galleries, botanical and zoological gardens	3,082	3,256
86	Membership organizations	46,344	48,897
87	Engineering, accounting, research, management and related services	135,046	143,437
88	Private households	17,405	16,761
89	Services, NEC	1,593	1,612
99	Nonclassifiable establishments	14,974	32,755

NEC Not elsewhere classified.

Note: Private employment. Data for 1994 are revised and data for 1995 are preliminary. Detail may not add to totals due to disclosure editing and/or rounding. See Tables 23.70, 23.71, 23.72, 23.73, and 23.74 for public employment data.

Source: State of Florida, Department of Labor and Employment Security, Bureau of Labor Market Information, "Employment and Wages" (ES-202), unpublished data.

Table 6.04. EMPLOYMENT AND PAYROLL: AVERAGE MONTHLY PRIVATE REPORTING UNITS EMPLOYMENT, AND PAYROLL COVERED BY UNEMPLOYMENT COMPENSATION LAW FOR ALL INDUSTRIES IN THE STATE AND COUNTIES OF FLORIDA 1994 AND 1995

County	Number of reporting units	Number of employees	Payroll ($1,000)	County	Number of reporting units	Number of employees	Payroll ($1,000)
			All industries, 1994 A/ (SIC codes 01-99)				
Florida	377,614	4,923,510	9,566,423	Lake	3,486	41,886	66,852
				Lee	9,864	115,226	202,627
Alachua	4,667	65,611	109,723	Leon	5,682	73,758	129,067
Baker	269	2,715	3,501	Levy	524	4,755	6,224
Bay	3,656	43,372	66,430	Liberty	81	827	1,230
Bradford	325	3,408	4,876	Madison	319	3,437	4,671
Brevard	9,716	140,686	304,465	Manatee	4,529	68,370	113,773
Broward	42,609	474,703	990,674	Marion	4,632	55,945	92,623
Calhoun	212	1,895	2,363	Martin	3,686	34,199	65,139
Charlotte	2,471	25,688	41,143	Monroe	3,224	26,876	42,329
Citrus	1,952	20,128	33,998	Nassau	983	11,086	19,546
Clay	2,184	24,295	36,404	Okaloosa	3,931	48,038	72,625
Collier	6,509	70,836	123,351	Okeechobee	676	7,280	10,711
Columbia	971	10,890	16,662	Orange	21,945	422,567	854,629
Dade	64,767	767,726	1,638,063	Osceola	2,539	36,085	54,878
De Soto	500	5,291	6,687	Palm Beach	30,998	342,098	749,792
Dixie	204	1,539	2,148	Pasco	5,034	53,688	86,511
Duval	18,085	318,249	651,172	Pinellas	23,248	320,756	622,042
Escambia	6,108	91,008	161,101	Polk	8,743	138,357	254,897
Flagler	672	6,937	11,141	Putnam	1,037	14,187	23,972
Franklin	277	2,046	2,578	St. Johns	2,436	25,793	40,337
Gadsden	594	8,135	11,202	St. Lucie	3,335	38,914	66,642
Gilchrist	138	1,096	1,370	Santa Rosa	1,570	16,136	25,267
Glades	86	661	1,017	Sarasota	9,780	107,916	187,203
Gulf	218	2,693	5,475	Seminole	8,001	89,919	170,427
Hamilton	163	2,666	5,445	Sumter	467	4,462	6,261
Hardee	534	6,120	7,329	Suwannee	514	6,947	9,113
Hendry	569	10,827	15,168	Taylor	421	5,027	10,361
Hernando	1,867	19,178	29,975	Union	124	1,694	2,333
Highlands	1,651	18,474	25,827	Volusia	9,245	108,698	173,121
Hillsborough	23,204	409,114	815,907	Wakulla	236	2,021	3,234
Holmes	217	2,071	2,422	Walton	572	7,117	9,338
Indian River	3,128	30,204	53,436	Washington	286	3,128	4,301
Jackson	722	8,334	11,783	Multicounty 1/	5,885	85,920	185,943
Jefferson	241	1,963	2,452	Out-of-state 2/	19	1,160	2,335
Lafayette	86	678	784				

See footnotes at end of table. Continued . . .

Table 6.04. EMPLOYMENT AND PAYROLL: AVERAGE MONTHLY PRIVATE REPORTING UNITS EMPLOYMENT, AND PAYROLL COVERED BY UNEMPLOYMENT COMPENSATION LAW FOR ALL INDUSTRIES IN THE STATE AND COUNTIES OF FLORIDA 1994 AND 1995 (Continued)

County	Number of reporting units	Number of employees	Payroll ($1,000)	County	Number of reporting units	Number of employees	Payroll ($1,000)
		All industries, 1995 B/ (SIC codes 01-99)					
Florida	379,745	5,107,953	10,254,587	Lake	3,525	44,617	72,528
				Lee	9,779	119,742	213,944
Alachua	4,680	67,812	117,057	Leon	5,687	77,414	140,224
Baker	253	2,705	3,502	Levy	501	5,126	6,851
Bay	3,635	44,353	70,247	Liberty	80	902	1,377
Bradford	322	3,717	5,621	Madison	310	3,708	5,278
Brevard	9,696	139,957	309,307	Manatee	4,579	74,000	124,090
Broward	42,985	490,111	1,056,861	Marion	4,650	57,989	99,611
Calhoun	219	1,924	2,470	Martin	3,679	36,174	70,699
Charlotte	2,364	26,031	43,664	Monroe	3,256	28,036	45,683
Citrus	1,889	20,011	34,593	Nassau	996	11,398	20,585
Clay	2,193	25,180	38,944	Okaloosa	4,050	50,647	78,762
Collier	6,601	72,330	133,298	Okeechobee	673	7,257	11,119
Columbia	976	11,724	18,304	Orange	22,213	439,965	919,009
Dade	64,623	781,199	1,726,410	Osceola	2,552	37,573	58,655
De Soto	495	5,771	7,189	Palm Beach	31,466	348,894	802,267
Dixie	183	1,535	2,193	Pasco	5,044	54,911	91,175
Duval	18,168	332,743	706,466	Pinellas	23,225	331,530	669,444
Escambia	6,034	94,581	172,423	Polk	8,673	141,146	270,193
Flagler	700	7,638	12,729	Putnam	1,062	14,901	26,652
Franklin	271	2,137	2,726	St. Johns	2,525	26,589	44,874
Gadsden	592	8,116	11,668	St. Lucie	3,254	39,051	68,919
Gilchrist	142	1,163	1,580	Santa Rosa	1,583	16,810	26,868
Glades	89	661	1,132	Sarasota	9,821	105,549	197,549
Gulf	211	2,746	5,729	Seminole	8,209	93,904	185,603
Hamilton	167	2,916	6,272	Sumter	471	4,576	6,717
Hardee	522	5,990	7,638	Suwannee	512	7,309	9,789
Hendry	577	11,495	16,531	Taylor	386	5,050	10,086
Hernando	1,868	19,665	31,695	Union	124	1,633	2,292
Highlands	1,663	18,723	26,711	Volusia	9,247	113,611	186,944
Hillsborough	23,338	426,736	884,384	Wakulla	223	2,150	3,315
Holmes	214	2,035	2,457	Walton	570	7,183	9,826
Indian River	3,148	31,374	56,241	Washington	289	3,367	4,722
Jackson	708	8,351	12,106	Multicounty 1/	6,678	120,445	235,616
Jefferson	233	1,935	2,537	Out-of-state 2/	21	748	1,897
Lafayette	83	691	739				

A/ Revised.
B/ Preliminary.
1/ Reporting units without a fixed location within the state or of unknown county location.
2/ Employment based in Florida, but working out of the state or country.
Note: Private employment. Data are preliminary. Detail may not add to totals due to disclosure editing and/or rounding. See Tables 23.70, 23.71, 23.72, 23.73, and 23.74 for public employment data.

Source: State of Florida, Department of Labor and Employment Security, Bureau of Labor Market Information, "Employment and Wages" (ES-202), unpublished data.

Table 6.05. EMPLOYMENT: AVERAGE MONTHLY PRIVATE EMPLOYMENT COVERED BY UNEMPLOYMENT COMPENSATION LAW BY MAJOR INDUSTRY GROUP IN THE STATE AND COUNTIES OF FLORIDA, 1994 AND 1995

County	All industries (01-99)	Agriculture forestry and fishing (01-09)	Mining (10-14)	Construction (15-17)	Manufacturing (20-39)	Transportation communications and public utilities (40-49)	Wholesale trade (50-51)	Retail trade (52-59)	Finance insurance and real estate (60-67)	Services (70-89)	Other (99)
					1994 A/						
Florida	4,923,510	157,544	6,224	296,005	484,253	288,191	305,351	1,201,773	372,984	1,796,211	14,974
Alachua	65,611	1,225	(NA)	3,749	5,527	1,889	1,908	20,295	4,386	26,495	109
Baker	2,715	(NA)	(NA)	133	323	181	61	955	108	597	(NA)
Bay	43,372	247	(NA)	3,183	2,850	2,308	2,216	15,522	3,131	13,822	(NA)
Bradford	3,408	27	(NA)	203	381	152	332	1,198	113	981	(NA)
Brevard	140,686	1,836	36	8,740	28,383	4,698	4,158	34,533	5,584	52,451	268
Broward	474,703	5,812	211	31,764	41,892	26,860	32,653	124,979	41,236	166,733	2,563
Calhoun	1,895	(NA)	(NA)	162	279	42	121	535	61	526	(NA)
Charlotte	25,688	622	(NA)	2,134	875	954	586	8,794	1,496	10,155	(NA)
Citrus	20,128	274	(NA)	1,994	1,057	1,914	431	6,274	1,054	7,059	(NA)
Clay	24,295	661	165	1,988	1,466	1,048	686	9,702	902	7,620	59
Collier	70,836	11,697	54	6,924	2,195	1,913	1,790	18,298	4,670	23,115	180
Columbia	10,890	139	(NA)	875	1,447	525	843	3,436	512	3,093	20
Dade	767,726	12,266	(NA)	35,392	79,589	73,713	70,272	164,339	65,855	262,346	3,522
De Soto	5,291	2,263	(NA)	167	92	150	190	1,232	156	1,034	(NA)
Dixie	1,539	(NA)	(NA)	136	484	66	(NA)	482	42	183	(NA)
Duval	318,249	2,746	(NA)	19,649	28,094	27,130	22,538	66,865	45,652	104,941	467
Escambia	91,008	729	96	7,328	8,910	5,195	4,971	23,989	4,453	35,223	114
Flagler	6,937	256	(NA)	441	1,311	178	67	1,930	622	2,095	(NA)
Franklin	2,046	45	(NA)	58	130	115	168	600	131	789	(NA)
Gadsden	8,135	1,988	(NA)	419	1,304	226	504	1,987	243	1,281	(NA)
Gilchrist	1,096	224	(NA)	35	152	32	77	190	57	325	(NA)
Glades	661	256	(NA)	(NA)	(NA)	(NA)	7	152	15	81	(NA)

See footnotes at end of table.

Continued . . .

Table 6.05. EMPLOYMENT: AVERAGE MONTHLY PRIVATE EMPLOYMENT COVERED BY UNEMPLOYMENT COMPENSATION LAW BY MAJOR INDUSTRY GROUP IN THE STATE AND COUNTIES OF FLORIDA, 1994 AND 1995 (Continued)

County	All industries (01-99)	Agriculture forestry and fishing (01-09)	Mining (10-14)	Construction (15-17)	Manufacturing (20-39)	Transportation communications and public utilities (40-49)	Wholesale trade (50-51)	Retail trade (52-59)	Finance insurance and real estate (60-67)	Services (70-89)	Other (99)
					1994 A/ (Continued)						
Gulf	2,693	36	(NA)	(NA)	1,088	291	(NA)	447	120	484	(NA)
Hamilton	2,666	(NA)	(NA)	59	(NA)	97	(NA)	345	17	320	(NA)
Hardee	6,120	2,968	(NA)	263	240	123	291	943	228	953	(NA)
Hendry	10,827	5,979	(NA)	232	1,119	(NA)	184	1,416	307	1,203	(NA)
Hernando	19,178	347	316	1,427	1,294	986	522	6,428	1,106	6,720	33
Highlands	18,474	3,534	(NA)	1,104	1,315	616	526	4,901	932	5,480	(NA)
Hillsborough	409,114	11,835	(NA)	20,845	36,979	25,904	33,949	81,544	37,794	159,444	804
Holmes	2,071	(NA)	(NA)	(NA)	596	55	69	561	54	609	(NA)
Indian River	30,204	4,058	(NA)	2,552	1,881	625	741	7,738	1,965	10,522	113
Jackson	8,334	233	(NA)	412	1,619	280	1,149	2,590	464	1,536	(NA)
Jefferson	1,963	269	(NA)	(NA)	237	120	59	453	110	601	(NA)
Lafayette	678	246	(NA)	21	(NA)	19	41	105	(NA)	74	(NA)
Lake	41,886	3,341	261	2,950	4,357	2,266	1,273	10,873	2,804	13,683	(NA)
Lee	115,226	4,544	(NA)	11,333	5,609	6,129	4,670	33,880	7,970	40,764	242
Leon	73,758	769	(NA)	4,537	3,435	3,101	3,091	23,950	4,799	29,942	114
Levy	4,755	544	(NA)	558	292	270	221	1,551	280	900	29
Liberty	827	(NA)	(NA)	(NA)	265	80	(NA)	129	(NA)	222	(NA)
Madison	3,437	(NA)	(NA)	48	1,217	110	143	789	86	873	(NA)
Manatee	68,370	5,159	(NA)	2,812	11,244	1,624	2,225	16,992	2,965	25,207	137
Marion	55,945	2,054	106	3,595	10,090	2,148	4,179	16,830	3,168	13,701	76
Martin	34,199	2,219	(NA)	2,648	2,506	1,764	959	9,967	2,281	11,758	100
Monroe	26,876	418	(NA)	1,921	535	1,626	650	10,180	1,417	9,998	111
Nassau	11,086	592	(NA)	867	1,864	484	293	3,242	403	3,306	34
Okaloosa	48,038	371	(NA)	3,387	3,893	1,845	1,110	16,203	3,652	17,457	116

See footnotes at end of table.

Continued . . .

Table 6.05. EMPLOYMENT: AVERAGE MONTHLY PRIVATE EMPLOYMENT COVERED BY UNEMPLOYMENT COMPENSATION LAW BY MAJOR INDUSTRY GROUP IN THE STATE AND COUNTIES OF FLORIDA, 1994 AND 1995 (Continued)

County	All industries (01-99)	Agriculture forestry and fishing (01-09)	Mining (10-14)	Construction (15-17)	Manufacturing (20-39)	Transportation communications and public utilities (40-49)	Wholesale trade (50-51)	Retail trade (52-59)	Finance insurance and real estate (60-67)	Services (70-89)	Other (99)
					1994 A/ (Continued)						
Okeechobee	7,280	2,028	(NA)	383	204	191	410	2,013	232	1,795	24
Orange	422,567	8,965	115	21,875	33,865	29,848	26,165	81,958	29,260	189,811	707
Osceola	36,085	681	(NA)	2,367	1,761	787	1,429	12,659	2,617	13,721	63
Palm Beach	342,098	18,886	22	21,432	29,929	14,722	16,603	85,926	26,731	126,470	1,377
Pasco	53,688	2,221	40	3,932	3,929	2,533	1,614	17,467	2,928	18,920	104
Pinellas	320,756	2,818	(NA)	17,026	44,447	12,070	16,644	80,071	23,064	123,822	768
Polk	138,357	11,052	2,827	7,481	20,506	7,891	7,861	35,245	7,424	37,867	(NA)
Putnam	14,187	746	78	(NA)	3,552	480	338	3,793	515	3,444	(NA)
St. Johns	25,793	884	(NA)	1,251	2,957	632	1,229	8,073	1,108	9,566	80
St. Lucie	38,914	5,370	29	2,787	2,697	2,689	1,689	10,105	2,242	11,240	68
Santa Rosa	16,136	315	131	1,598	2,327	968	405	4,237	653	5,433	69
Sarasota	107,916	1,527	(NA)	6,827	7,865	3,545	3,722	29,377	7,612	47,099	297
Seminole	89,919	1,822	(NA)	8,108	9,968	4,593	5,554	27,605	5,315	26,654	295
Sumter	4,462	299	77	196	531	404	257	1,624	201	864	(NA)
Suwannee	6,947	(NA)	(NA)	436	(NA)	369	300	1,750	272	1,520	(NA)
Taylor	5,027	91	46	(NA)	1,851	119	137	1,236	228	795	(NA)
Union	1,694	(NA)	(NA)	(NA)	513	304	(NA)	200	(NA)	412	(NA)
Volusia	108,698	4,059	(NA)	6,532	11,888	3,430	4,416	33,376	5,612	39,196	189
Wakulla	2,021	(NA)	(NA)	146	624	82	39	534	114	433	(NA)
Walton	7,117	190	(NA)	428	1,252	401	157	1,905	328	2,425	(NA)
Washington	3,128	82	(NA)	217	906	263	105	786	68	689	(NA)
Multicounty 1/	85,920	(NA)	(NA)	3,578	937	1,597	15,215	3,252	2,971	(NA)	931
Out-of-state 2/	1,160	(NA)	(NA)	(NA)	(NA)	(NA)	(NA)	(NA)	(NA)	(NA)	(NA)

See footnotes at end of table.

Continued . . .

Table 6.05. EMPLOYMENT: AVERAGE MONTHLY PRIVATE EMPLOYMENT COVERED BY UNEMPLOYMENT COMPENSATION LAW BY MAJOR INDUSTRY GROUP IN THE STATE AND COUNTIES OF FLORIDA, 1994 AND 1995 (Continued)

County	All industries (01-99)	Agriculture forestry and fishing (01-09)	Mining (10-14)	Construction (15-17)	Manufacturing (20-39)	Transportation communications and public utilities (40-49)	Wholesale trade (50-51)	Retail trade (52-59)	Finance insurance and real estate (60-67)	Services (70-89)	Other (99)
					1995 B/						
Florida	5,107,953	152,424	6,427	303,870	481,699	295,747	318,669	1,228,508	372,560	1,915,292	32,755
Alachua	67,812	1,205	(NA)	3,949	5,449	2,082	2,124	21,091	4,366	27,301	219
Baker	2,705	327	(NA)	152	255	170	71	986	106	625	13
Bay	44,353	225	(NA)	3,450	2,859	2,220	2,198	16,029	2,975	14,238	158
Bradford	3,717	32	(NA)	284	402	164	333	1,353	105	1,032	14
Brevard	139,957	1,703	37	8,475	26,924	4,434	4,519	34,582	5,518	53,183	582
Broward	490,111	5,666	167	32,269	41,550	28,493	34,174	128,080	40,016	175,162	4,536
Calhoun	1,924	130	(NA)	186	292	41	149	551	63	501	11
Charlotte	26,031	581	(NA)	2,066	891	1,011	538	8,836	1,486	10,516	74
Citrus	20,011	256	34	1,682	1,219	1,826	423	6,196	1,048	7,277	50
Clay	25,180	670	184	2,069	1,527	941	705	10,206	818	7,944	117
Collier	72,330	10,683	35	7,206	2,299	2,027	1,973	18,795	4,466	24,451	395
Columbia	11,724	145	(NA)	968	1,599	500	846	3,910	505	3,228	24
Dade	781,199	11,806	374	35,804	76,706	76,319	72,807	163,741	66,186	270,604	6,853
De Soto	5,771	2,661	(NA)	168	94	161	191	1,250	165	1,073	(NA)
Dixie	1,535	(NA)	(NA)	132	521	64	60	445	46	180	(NA)
Duval	332,743	2,821	192	20,594	28,797	27,692	22,725	69,869	45,674	113,074	1,305
Escambia	94,581	728	85	7,912	8,668	5,295	5,047	24,615	4,603	37,481	149
Flagler	7,638	299	(NA)	442	1,540	221	119	2,050	614	2,302	46
Franklin	2,137	29	(NA)	82	130	118	174	594	142	846	20
Gadsden	8,116	1,879	(NA)	428	1,331	241	476	1,934	245	1,378	28
Gilchrist	1,163	230	(NA)	28	155	(NA)	72	213	56	371	(NA)
Glades	661	237	(NA)	24	4	82	7	174	14	95	(NA)
Gulf	2,746	31	(NA)	193	1,048	282	14	451	128	593	(NA)

See footnotes at end of table.

Continued . . .

Table 6.05. EMPLOYMENT: AVERAGE MONTHLY PRIVATE EMPLOYMENT COVERED BY UNEMPLOYMENT COMPENSATION LAW BY MAJOR INDUSTRY GROUP IN THE STATE AND COUNTIES OF FLORIDA, 1994 AND 1995 (Continued)

County	All industries (01-99)	Agriculture forestry and fishing (01-09)	Mining (10-14)	Construction (15-17)	Manufacturing (20-39)	Transportation communications and public utilities (40-49)	Wholesale trade (50-51)	Retail trade (52-59)	Finance insurance and real estate (60-67)	Services (70-89)	Other (99)
1995 B/ (Continued)											
Hamilton	2,916	(NA)	(NA)	61	1,548	91	21	386	19	424	(NA)
Hardee	5,990	2,687	(NA)	306	238	117	321	955	232	995	(NA)
Hendry	11,495	6,413	(NA)	254	1,113	434	195	1,520	270	1,233	21
Hernando	19,665	294	323	1,367	1,248	924	590	6,818	1,130	6,906	67
Highlands	18,723	3,523	(NA)	1,051	1,358	623	529	5,154	851	5,567	38
Hillsborough	426,736	11,652	(NA)	22,191	35,891	26,506	34,332	84,732	38,008	171,169	2,243
Holmes	2,035	(NA)	(NA)	84	489	60	73	560	56	694	(NA)
Indian River	31,374	3,862	(NA)	2,586	2,113	651	935	8,299	1,656	11,134	130
Jackson	8,351	204	(NA)	399	1,859	297	762	2,721	463	1,588	28
Jefferson	1,935	248	(NA)	129	215	109	61	449	119	588	20
Lafayette	691	249	(NA)	32	151	23	52	104	(NA)	60	(NA)
Lake	44,617	3,178	289	3,234	4,316	2,124	1,416	11,284	2,915	15,632	230
Lee	119,742	4,447	(NA)	10,754	6,114	6,386	4,930	35,478	8,125	42,893	525
Leon	77,414	841	(NA)	4,634	3,506	3,286	3,296	24,912	4,848	31,860	202
Levy	5,126	527	(NA)	543	351	278	184	1,860	266	979	29
Liberty	902	(NA)	(NA)	(NA)	276	100	(NA)	131	(NA)	229	(NA)
Madison	3,708	151	(NA)	45	1,281	116	151	834	81	1,011	38
Manatee	74,000	5,447	(NA)	3,295	11,575	1,517	2,272	17,250	2,893	29,412	334
Marion	57,989	2,066	96	3,787	10,366	2,451	4,337	17,102	3,057	14,573	155
Martin	36,174	2,258	(NA)	3,135	2,532	1,761	988	10,168	2,291	12,839	200
Monroe	28,036	406	(NA)	2,052	511	1,673	673	10,321	1,440	10,652	290
Nassau	11,398	627	(NA)	925	1,927	456	269	3,281	384	3,461	69
Okaloosa	50,647	422	(NA)	3,715	4,041	1,861	1,154	16,788	3,797	18,679	189
Okeechobee	7,257	1,780	(NA)	368	171	196	444	2,118	233	1,899	50
Orange	439,965	8,627	107	22,470	33,723	29,821	27,550	84,727	29,520	201,308	2,113
Osceola	37,573	703	(NA)	2,244	1,777	738	1,532	13,538	2,412	14,485	144

See footnotes at end of table.

Continued . . .

Table 6.05. EMPLOYMENT: AVERAGE MONTHLY PRIVATE EMPLOYMENT COVERED BY UNEMPLOYMENT COMPENSATION LAW BY MAJOR INDUSTRY GROUP IN THE STATE AND COUNTIES OF FLORIDA, 1994 AND 1995 (Continued)

County	All industries (01-99)	Agriculture forestry and fishing (01-09)	Mining (10-14)	Construction (15-17)	Manufacturing (20-39)	Transportation communications and public utilities (40-49)	Wholesale trade (50-51)	Retail trade (52-59)	Finance insurance and real estate (60-67)	Services (70-89)	Other (99)
					1995 B/ (Continued)						
Palm Beach	348,894	17,118	23	23,034	29,066	14,598	17,764	85,396	26,324	132,263	3,309
Pasco	54,911	2,196	39	3,746	3,864	2,505	1,666	17,654	2,895	20,136	210
Pinellas	331,530	2,729	25	16,841	44,845	12,565	18,690	78,592	22,869	132,336	2,039
Polk	141,146	10,011	3,067	7,782	21,460	8,171	7,454	36,888	7,503	38,372	439
Putnam	14,901	762	80	1,847	3,625	458	381	3,762	526	3,378	83
St. Johns	26,589	918	(NA)	1,348	3,003	520	1,273	8,342	1,154	9,871	148
St. Lucie	39,051	5,507	29	2,489	2,535	2,757	1,723	10,197	2,183	11,447	185
Santa Rosa	16,810	352	153	1,767	2,364	1,045	413	4,406	679	5,559	73
Sarasota	105,549	1,459	(NA)	6,643	8,294	3,603	4,005	29,699	7,648	43,598	556
Seminole	93,904	1,800	(NA)	8,463	9,594	4,826	6,226	28,850	5,766	27,666	709
Sumter	4,576	242	70	192	561	460	293	1,680	202	862	17
Suwannee	7,309	595	(NA)	426	(NA)	345	344	1,870	284	1,610	16
Taylor	5,050	93	44	(NA)	1,817	111	183	1,282	226	813	21
Union	1,633	55	(NA)	82	416	333	42	207	(NA)	429	(NA)
Volusia	113,611	3,861	(NA)	6,856	11,908	3,494	4,858	34,314	5,803	42,070	449
Wakulla	2,150	39	(NA)	181	616	97	36	628	112	422	20
Walton	7,183	171	(NA)	426	1,098	415	173	1,956	336	2,536	51
Washington	3,367	70	(NA)	273	923	296	94	928	67	686	23
Multicounty 1/	120,445	(NA)	(NA)	2,665	946	2,141	16,241	4,270	3,490	86,952	2,603
Out-of-state 2/	748	(NA)	(NA)	(NA)	(NA)	(NA)	(NA)	(NA)	(NA)	(NA)	(NA)

(NA) Not available.

A/ Revised. B/ Preliminary. 1/ Reporting units without a fixed or known location within the state. 2/ Employment based in Florida, but working out of the state or country.

Note: Private employment. Detail may not add to totals due to disclosure editing and/or rounding. See Tables 23.70, 23.71, 23.72, 23.73, and 23.74 for public employment data.

Source: State of Florida, Department of Labor and Employment Security, Bureau of Labor Market Information, "Employment and Wages" (ES-202), unpublished data.

Table 6.09. LABOR FORCE PARTICIPATION: LABOR FORCE STATUS OF THE POPULATION 16 YEARS OLD AND OVER BY SEX, RACE AND HISPANIC ORIGIN, AND MARITAL STATUS IN FLORIDA AND THE UNITED STATES, ANNUAL AVERAGES 1993

Area and population group	Civilian noninstitutional population (1,000)	Civilian labor force Number (1,000)	Civilian labor force Percentage of population	Employment Number (1,000)	Employment Percentage of population	Unemployment Number (1,000)	Unemployment Rate	Unemployment Error range of rate 1/
Florida								
Total	10,688	6,628	62.0	6,166	57.7	462	7.0	6.7-7.3
Men	5,062	3,567	70.5	3,315	65.5	252	7.1	6.6-7.5
Women	5,626	3,061	54.4	2,851	50.7	209	6.8	6.4-7.3
Both sexes, 16-19 years	618	311	50.4	248	40.2	63	20.3	18.3-22.4
White	9,069	5,577	61.5	5,239	57.8	337	6.0	5.7-6.4
Men	4,321	3,049	70.6	2,859	66.2	190	6.2	5.8-6.7
Women	4,748	2,527	53.2	2,380	50.1	147	5.8	5.3-6.3
Black	1,425	924	64.8	807	56.7	116	12.6	11.5-13.7
Men	654	452	69.0	395	60.4	57	12.5	10.9-14.1
Women	770	472	61.2	412	53.5	60	12.6	11.1-14.2
Hispanic origin 2/	1,463	948	64.8	866	59.2	82	8.7	7.7-9.6
Men	709	565	79.7	518	73.0	48	8.4	7.2-9.6
Women	754	383	50.8	348	46.2	35	9.1	7.6-10.6
Single 3/	2,352	1,687	71.7	1,491	63.4	196	11.6	10.8-12.4
Married 4/	6,015	3,706	61.6	3,533	58.7	174	4.7	4.3-5.1
Other marital status 5/	2,322	1,234	53.2	1,142	49.2	92	7.5	6.7-8.3
United States								
Total	193,550	128,040	66.2	119,306	61.6	8,734	6.8	6.7-6.9
Men	92,620	69,633	75.2	64,700	69.9	4,932	7.1	7.0-7.2
Women	100,930	58,407	57.9	54,606	54.1	3,801	6.5	6.4-6.6
Both sexes, 16-19 years	13,255	6,826	51.5	5,530	41.7	1,296	19.0	18.4-19.5
White	163,921	109,359	66.7	102,812	62.7	6,547	6.0	5.9-6.1
Men	79,080	60,150	76.1	56,397	71.3	3,753	6.2	6.1-6.4
Women	84,841	49,208	58.0	46,415	54.7	2,793	5.7	5.5-5.8
Black	22,329	13,943	62.4	12,146	54.4	1,796	12.9	12.5-13.3
Men	10,078	6,911	68.6	5,957	59.1	954	13.8	13.2-14.4
Women	12,251	7,031	57.4	6,189	50.5	842	12.0	11.4-12.5
Hispanic origin 2/	15,753	10,377	65.9	9,272	58.9	1,104	10.6	10.2-11.0
Men	7,825	6,256	79.9	5,603	71.6	653	10.4	9.9-10.9
Women	7,928	4,120	52.0	3,669	46.3	451	10.9	10.3-11.6
Single 3/	47,667	33,670	70.6	29,836	62.6	3,834	11.4	11.2-11.6
Married 4/	109,187	74,725	68.4	71,381	65.4	3,343	4.5	4.4-4.6
Other marital status 5/	36,696	19,645	53.5	18,089	49.3	1,557	7.9	7.7-8.2

1/ If repeated samples were drawn from the same population and an error range constructed around each sample estimate, in 9 out of 10 cases the true value based on a complete census of the population would be contained within these error ranges.

2/ Persons of Hispanic origin may be of any race.

3/ Never married.

4/ Spouse present.

5/ Includes divorced, widowed, separated, and married, with spouse absent.

Source: U.S., Department of Labor, Bureau of Labor Statistics, *Geographic Profile of Employment and Unemployment, 1993.*

Table 6.10. LABOR FORCE PARTICIPATION: FULL- AND PART-TIME STATUS AND AVERAGE HOURS OF WORK OF EMPLOYED AND UNEMPLOYED PERSONS SEEKING WORK BY SEX, AGE, AND RACE AND HISPANIC ORIGIN IN FLORIDA, ANNUAL AVERAGES 1992 AND 1993

(in thousands)

Population group	Employed: Full-time: Total	Full-time: Full-time schedules 1/	Full-time: Part-time usually full-time 2/	Part-time: Total	Part-time: Voluntary 1/	Part-time: Part-time usually part-time 2/	Average hours: Total	Average hours: Full-time schedules 3/	Unemployed: Seeking full-time work	Unemployed: Seeking part-time work
1992										
Total	5,004	4,852	151	1,014	773	240	39.5	47.1	433	103
Men	2,819	2,725	94	391	281	110	41.9	48.1	245	40
Women	2,185	2,127	57	623	492	131	36.7	45.8	187	63
Both sexes, 16-19 years	80	75	6	157	132	25	26.0	45.0	35	44
White	4,206	4,090	116	857	677	179	39.8	47.5	316	79
Black	711	680	31	136	80	56	37.6	45.0	108	22
Hispanic origin 4/	687	657	30	129	81	48	38.7	45.1	74	18
1993										
Total	5,168	5,043	125	998	797	201	40.0	47.1	372	89
Men	2,930	2,850	80	385	299	86	42.4	48.2	211	41
Women	2,238	2,193	45	613	498	115	37.3	45.6	161	48
Both sexes, 16-19 years	90	86	4	158	134	24	26.0	44.1	29	35
White	4,399	4,303	96	841	685	156	40.4	47.4	268	69
Black	676	648	28	131	91	40	37.9	45.0	98	18
Hispanic origin 4/	730	707	22	136	99	37	39.1	44.5	68	14

1/ Employed persons with a job but not at work are distributed according to whether they usually work full- or part-time.
2/ Due to economic reasons.
3/ Persons who worked 35 hours or more during the survey week.
4/ Persons of Hispanic origin may be of any race.
Source: U.S., Department of Labor, Bureau of Labor Statistics, *Geographic Profile of Employment and Unemployment, 1993,* and previous edition.

Table 6.11. LABOR FORCE: ESTIMATES BY EMPLOYMENT STATUS IN THE UNITED STATES AND IN THE STATE AND COUNTIES OF FLORIDA, 1993, 1994, AND 1995

County	1993 A/				1994 B/				1995 B/			
	Labor force	Employ-ment	Unemployment		Labor force	Employ-ment	Unemployment		Labor force	Employ-ment	Unemployment	
			Number	Rate			Number	Rate			Number	Rate
United States 1/	128,040	119,306	8,734	6.8	131,056	123,060	7,996	6.1	132,304	124,900	7,404	5.6
Florida	6,654,000	6,191,000	463,000	7.0	6,824,000	6,376,000	448,000	6.6	6,830,000	6,455,000	375,000	5.5
Alachua	97,831	93,694	4,137	4.2	100,917	97,139	3,778	3.7	100,035	97,184	2,851	2.9
Baker	8,931	8,197	734	8.2	9,449	8,886	563	6.0	8,668	8,206	462	5.3
Bay	63,639	57,874	5,765	9.1	63,818	58,379	5,439	8.5	62,985	58,803	4,182	6.6
Bradford	9,437	8,821	616	6.5	9,354	8,874	480	5.1	9,301	8,951	350	3.8
Brevard	207,183	191,868	15,315	7.4	207,600	192,769	14,831	7.1	200,861	187,722	13,139	6.5
Broward	694,829	647,651	47,178	6.8	713,544	667,364	46,180	6.5	719,043	678,033	41,010	5.7
Calhoun	4,404	4,089	315	7.2	4,565	4,265	300	6.6	4,536	4,326	210	4.6
Charlotte	43,981	41,080	2,901	6.6	44,701	41,997	2,704	6.0	43,986	41,917	2,069	4.7
Citrus	33,621	30,737	2,884	8.6	34,646	31,896	2,750	7.9	34,136	31,804	2,332	6.8
Clay	56,573	53,748	2,825	5.0	57,869	55,362	2,507	4.3	60,916	59,033	1,883	3.1
Collier	78,640	72,100	6,540	8.3	80,129	73,704	6,425	8.0	81,500	75,839	5,661	6.9
Columbia	21,576	19,567	2,009	9.3	21,741	19,931	1,810	8.3	21,990	20,734	1,256	5.7
Dade	1,022,175	943,106	79,069	7.7	1,039,186	956,198	82,988	8.0	1,032,583	957,048	75,535	7.3
De Soto	9,803	8,852	951	9.7	9,512	8,774	738	7.8	9,710	9,057	653	6.7
Dixie	3,897	3,559	338	8.7	3,892	3,579	313	8.0	4,043	3,709	334	8.3
Duval	355,946	335,952	19,994	5.6	364,928	346,043	18,885	5.2	365,509	351,572	13,937	3.8
Escambia	122,068	115,595	6,473	5.3	124,670	118,312	6,358	5.1	121,039	115,932	5,107	4.2
Flagler	13,015	12,220	795	6.1	13,187	12,530	657	5.0	14,143	13,651	492	3.5
Franklin	4,494	4,303	191	4.3	4,739	4,532	207	4.4	4,832	4,627	205	4.2
Gadsden	18,797	17,501	1,296	6.9	19,085	17,902	1,183	6.2	18,827	18,029	798	4.2
Gilchrist	4,175	3,919	256	6.1	4,165	3,961	204	4.9	4,214	4,061	153	3.6
Glades	3,411	3,055	356	10.4	3,453	3,122	331	9.6	3,426	3,096	330	9.6

See footnotes at end of table.

Continued . . .

Table 6.11. LABOR FORCE: ESTIMATES BY EMPLOYMENT STATUS IN THE UNITED STATES AND IN THE STATE AND COUNTIES OF FLORIDA, 1993, 1994, AND 1995 (Continued)

County	1993 A/ Labor force	1993 A/ Employ-ment	1993 A/ Unemployment Number	1993 A/ Unemployment Rate	1994 B/ Labor force	1994 B/ Employ-ment	1994 B/ Unemployment Number	1994 B/ Unemployment Rate	1995 B/ Labor force	1995 B/ Employ-ment	1995 B/ Unemployment Number	1995 B/ Unemployment Rate
Gulf	5,669	5,251	418	7.4	5,439	5,080	359	6.6	5,779	5,458	321	5.6
Hamilton	3,664	3,123	541	14.8	3,379	3,044	335	9.9	3,502	3,261	241	6.9
Hardee	9,922	8,480	1,442	14.5	9,806	8,388	1,418	14.5	11,159	9,723	1,436	12.9
Hendry	15,171	13,059	2,112	13.9	15,713	13,345	2,368	15.1	15,702	13,309	2,393	15.2
Hernando	38,465	35,586	2,879	7.5	40,184	37,198	2,986	7.4	41,718	39,458	2,260	5.4
Highlands	26,664	23,994	2,670	10.0	26,447	23,853	2,594	9.8	27,669	25,279	2,390	8.6
Hillsborough	471,625	441,482	30,143	6.4	487,826	461,488	26,338	5.4	489,853	468,599	21,254	4.3
Holmes	6,394	5,912	482	7.5	6,687	6,199	488	7.3	6,896	6,422	474	6.9
Indian River	39,017	34,859	4,158	10.7	39,270	35,128	4,142	10.5	41,172	37,151	4,021	9.8
Jackson	19,645	18,244	1,401	7.1	19,485	18,070	1,415	7.3	18,866	17,852	1,014	5.4
Jefferson	5,588	5,310	278	5.0	5,396	5,107	289	5.4	5,238	4,988	250	4.8
Lafayette	2,330	2,175	155	6.7	2,439	2,313	126	5.2	2,635	2,545	90	3.4
Lake	68,583	63,864	4,719	6.9	71,383	66,638	4,745	6.6	73,711	69,734	3,977	5.4
Lee	161,543	151,975	9,568	5.9	167,034	158,240	8,794	5.3	170,063	162,995	7,068	4.2
Leon	118,899	114,236	4,663	3.9	121,659	116,849	4,810	4.0	123,663	120,240	3,423	2.8
Levy	11,341	10,590	751	6.6	11,846	11,147	699	5.9	11,994	11,417	577	4.8
Liberty	2,264	2,162	102	4.5	2,329	2,231	98	4.2	2,408	2,354	54	2.2
Madison	6,822	6,363	459	6.7	6,919	6,525	394	5.7	7,242	6,947	295	4.1
Manatee	96,591	91,207	5,384	5.6	100,412	95,455	4,957	4.9	99,370	95,377	3,993	4.0
Marion	88,640	81,613	7,027	7.9	89,549	83,053	6,496	7.3	88,351	83,561	4,790	5.4
Martin	44,585	40,485	4,100	9.2	44,916	41,007	3,909	8.7	44,435	40,970	3,465	7.8
Monroe	42,588	40,825	1,763	4.1	42,497	40,877	1,620	3.8	43,369	42,190	1,179	2.7
Nassau	23,626	22,157	1,469	6.2	24,219	22,823	1,396	5.8	25,342	24,311	1,031	4.1
Okaloosa	70,247	65,898	4,349	6.2	72,892	68,898	3,994	5.5	76,357	73,075	3,282	4.3
Okeechobee	14,957	13,471	1,486	9.9	15,046	13,416	1,630	10.8	14,974	13,465	1,509	10.1

See footnotes at end of table.

Continued . . .

Table 6.11. LABOR FORCE: ESTIMATES BY EMPLOYMENT STATUS IN THE UNITED STATES AND IN THE STATE AND COUNTIES OF FLORIDA, 1993, 1994, AND 1995 (Continued)

County	1993 A/				1994 B/				1995 B/			
	Labor force	Employ-ment	Unemployment		Labor force	Employ-ment	Unemployment		Labor force	Employ-ment	Unemployment	
			Number	Rate			Number	Rate			Number	Rate
Orange	410,216	384,758	25,458	6.2	426,155	401,471	24,684	5.8	422,112	403,167	18,945	4.5
Osceola	64,508	60,349	4,159	6.4	67,004	62,971	4,033	6.0	68,035	64,743	3,292	4.8
Palm Beach	442,680	404,673	38,007	8.6	456,173	418,300	37,873	8.3	451,190	418,765	32,425	7.2
Pasco	111,231	102,728	8,503	7.6	115,151	107,383	7,768	6.7	118,553	112,470	6,083	5.1
Pinellas	424,997	399,263	25,734	6.1	440,258	417,355	22,903	5.2	440,030	422,104	17,926	4.1
Polk	194,799	176,620	18,179	9.3	199,491	183,007	16,484	8.3	196,632	182,519	14,113	7.2
Putnam	29,447	27,206	2,241	7.6	28,628	26,625	2,003	7.0	29,667	28,154	1,513	5.1
St. Johns	46,271	43,397	2,874	6.2	47,484	44,701	2,783	5.9	51,014	49,223	1,791	3.5
St. Lucie	71,333	62,459	8,874	12.4	73,032	63,264	9,768	13.4	72,536	63,435	9,101	12.5
Santa Rosa	42,078	39,948	2,130	5.1	43,060	40,886	2,174	5.0	45,622	43,702	1,920	4.2
Sarasota	124,634	118,030	6,604	5.3	129,481	123,528	5,953	4.6	127,250	122,908	4,342	3.4
Seminole	179,875	169,452	10,423	5.8	186,908	176,813	10,095	5.4	187,294	179,723	7,571	4.0
Sumter	11,950	11,103	847	7.1	11,965	11,135	830	6.9	12,280	11,598	682	5.6
Suwannee	12,318	11,176	1,142	9.3	12,148	11,281	867	7.1	12,839	12,184	655	5.1
Taylor	7,595	6,492	1,103	14.5	7,385	6,537	848	11.5	7,533	6,806	727	9.7
Union	3,877	3,674	203	5.2	3,857	3,694	163	4.2	4,110	3,932	178	4.3
Volusia	172,941	161,362	11,579	6.7	176,467	165,452	11,015	6.2	173,277	164,918	8,359	4.8
Wakulla	8,675	8,283	392	4.5	8,990	8,567	423	4.7	8,877	8,497	380	4.3
Walton	13,816	13,014	802	5.8	14,424	13,626	798	5.5	14,460	13,824	636	4.4
Washington	7,777	7,134	643	8.3	7,838	7,265	573	7.3	8,687	8,153	534	6.1

A/ Benchmark 1994.
B/ Benchmark 1995.
1/ United States numbers are rounded to thousands. Data are from U.S., Department of Labor, Bureau of Labor Statistics.

Note: Civilian labor force. Data are generated for federal fund allocations. Caution is urged when using these data for short-term economic analysis. Detail may not add to totals because of rounding.

Source: State of Florida, Department of Labor and Employment Security, Bureau of Labor Market Information, *Labor Force Summary: 1995 Annual Averages,* and previous editions.

Table 6.12. LABOR FORCE: ESTIMATES BY EMPLOYMENT STATUS IN THE STATE, METROPOLITAN STATISTICAL AREAS (MSAS) AND SELECTED CITIES OF FLORIDA, 1994 AND 1995

MSA or city 1/	1994				1995			
	Labor force	Employ-ment	Unemployment		Labor force	Employ-ment	Unemployment	
			Number	Rate			Number	Rate
Florida	6,824,000	6,376,000	448,000	6.6	6,830,000	6,455,000	375,000	5.5
Daytona Beach MSA	189,654	177,982	11,672	6.2	187,420	178,570	8,850	4.7
Ft. Lauderdale MSA	713,544	667,364	46,180	6.5	719,043	678,033	41,010	5.7
Ft. Myers-Cape Coral MSA	167,034	158,240	8,794	5.3	170,063	162,995	7,068	4.2
Ft. Pierce-Port St. Lucie MSA	117,949	104,271	13,678	11.6	116,971	104,405	12,566	10.7
Ft. Walton Beach MSA	72,892	68,898	3,994	5.5	76,357	73,075	3,282	4.3
Gainesville MSA	100,917	97,139	3,778	3.7	100,035	97,184	2,851	2.9
Jacksonville MSA	494,500	468,928	25,572	5.2	502,782	484,139	18,643	3.7
Lakeland-Winter Haven MSA	199,491	183,007	16,484	8.3	196,632	182,519	14,113	7.2
Melbourne-Titusville-Palm Bay MSA	207,600	192,769	14,831	7.1	200,861	187,722	13,139	6.5
Miami MSA	1,039,186	956,198	82,988	8.0	1,032,583	957,048	75,535	7.3
Naples MSA	80,129	73,704	6,425	8.0	81,500	75,839	5,661	6.9
Ocala MSA	89,549	83,053	6,496	7.3	88,351	83,561	4,790	5.4
Orlando MSA	751,450	707,893	43,557	5.8	751,153	717,367	33,786	4.5
Panama City MSA	63,818	58,379	5,439	8.5	62,985	58,803	4,182	6.6
Pensacola MSA	167,731	159,198	8,533	5.1	166,660	159,634	7,026	4.2
Punta Gorda MSA	44,701	41,997	2,704	6.0	43,986	41,917	2,069	4.7
Sarasota-Bradenton MSA	229,893	218,983	10,910	4.7	226,620	218,285	8,335	3.7
Tallahassee MSA	140,744	134,751	5,993	4.3	142,489	138,268	4,221	3.0
Tampa-St. Petersburg-Clearwater MSA	1,083,419	1,023,425	59,994	5.5	1,090,153	1,042,630	47,523	4.4
West Palm Beach-Boca Raton MSA	456,173	418,300	37,873	8.3	451,190	418,765	32,425	7.2
Altamonte Springs	26,153	24,790	1,363	5.2	26,220	25,198	1,022	3.9
Boca Raton	34,670	32,807	1,863	5.4	34,439	32,844	1,595	4.6
Boynton Beach	23,112	21,152	1,960	8.5	22,853	21,175	1,678	7.3
Bradenton	20,871	19,686	1,185	5.7	20,624	19,670	954	4.6
Cape Carol	38,101	36,137	1,964	5.2	38,801	37,223	1,578	4.1
Clearwater	52,204	49,326	2,878	5.5	52,139	49,887	2,252	4.3
Coconut Creek	13,899	12,853	1,046	7.5	13,988	13,059	929	6.6
Cooper City	7,008	6,760	248	3.5	13,191	12,782	409	3.1
Coral Gables	23,010	22,043	967	4.2	22,943	22,063	880	3.8

See footnotes at end of table.

Continued . . .

Table 6.12. LABOR FORCE: ESTIMATES BY EMPLOYMENT STATUS IN THE STATE, METROPOLITAN STATISTICAL AREAS (MSAS) AND SELECTED CITIES OF FLORIDA, 1994 AND 1995 (Continued)

MSA or city 1/	1994 Labor force	1994 Employment	1994 Unemployment Number	1994 Unemployment Rate	1995 Labor force	1995 Employment	1995 Unemployment Number	1995 Unemployment Rate
Coral Springs	48,630	46,354	2,276	4.7	49,116	47,095	2,021	4.1
Davie	30,586	28,856	1,730	5.7	30,853	29,317	1,536	5.0
Daytona Beach	30,982	28,429	2,553	8.2	30,275	28,338	1,937	6.4
Deerfield Beach	23,230	21,882	1,348	5.8	23,428	22,231	1,197	5.1
Delray Beach	23,873	21,141	2,732	11.4	23,504	21,165	2,339	10.0
Dunedin	16,661	15,916	745	4.5	16,680	16,097	583	3.5
Ft. Lauderdale	88,011	80,918	7,093	8.1	88,510	82,211	6,299	7.1
Ft. Myers	24,367	22,578	1,789	7.3	24,693	23,256	1,437	5.8
Ft. Pierce	17,755	13,920	3,835	21.6	17,530	13,957	3,573	20.4
Gainesville	45,897	43,856	2,041	4.4	45,418	43,877	1,541	3.4
Hallandale	12,210	11,135	1,075	8.8	12,267	11,313	954	7.8
Hialeah	103,827	95,170	8,657	8.3	103,134	95,254	7,880	7.6
Hollywood	67,756	62,793	4,963	7.3	68,204	63,797	4,407	6.5
Jacksonville	342,320	324,261	18,059	5.3	342,769	329,442	13,327	3.9
Jupiter	15,001	14,121	880	5.9	14,891	14,137	754	5.1
Key West	13,683	13,161	522	3.8	13,963	13,583	380	2.7
Kissimmee	21,363	19,870	1,493	7.0	21,648	20,429	1,219	5.6
Lake Worth	15,503	14,099	1,404	9.1	15,316	14,114	1,202	7.8
Lakeland	34,747	32,114	2,633	7.6	34,283	32,029	2,254	6.6
Largo	32,963	31,481	1,482	4.5	32,999	31,839	1,160	3.5
Lauderdale Lakes	13,363	12,158	1,205	9.0	13,423	12,353	1,070	8.0
Lauderhill	27,518	25,670	1,848	6.7	27,721	26,080	1,641	5.9
Margate	22,712	21,257	1,455	6.4	22,889	21,597	1,292	5.6
Melbourne	31,629	29,047	2,582	8.2	30,573	28,286	2,287	7.5
Miami	181,379	160,576	20,803	11.5	179,654	160,719	18,935	10.5
Miami Beach	44,262	40,150	4,112	9.3	43,928	40,186	3,742	8.5
Miramar	25,236	23,768	1,468	5.8	25,453	24,149	1,304	5.1
North Lauderdale	17,384	16,324	1,060	6.1	17,526	16,585	941	5.4
North Miami	28,588	26,135	2,453	8.6	28,391	26,158	2,233	7.9
North Miami Beach	18,598	17,376	1,222	6.6	18,504	17,392	1,112	6.0
Oakland Park	18,018	17,013	1,005	5.6	18,178	17,285	893	4.9
Ocala	20,719	19,127	1,592	7.7	20,418	19,244	1,174	5.7

See footnotes at end of table.

Continued . . .

Table 6.12. LABOR FORCE: ESTIMATES BY EMPLOYMENT STATUS IN THE STATE, METROPOLITAN STATISTICAL AREAS (MSAS) AND SELECTED CITIES OF FLORIDA, 1994 AND 1995 (Continued)

MSA or city 1/	1994				1995			
	Labor force	Employ-ment	Unemployment Number	Unemployment Rate	Labor force	Employ-ment	Unemployment Number	Unemployment Rate
Orlando	100,212	94,005	6,207	6.2	99,166	94,402	4,764	4.8
Ormond Beach	14,227	13,602	625	4.4	14,032	13,558	474	3.4
Palm Bay	33,874	31,367	2,507	7.4	32,767	30,546	2,221	6.8
Palm Beach Gardens	13,870	13,285	585	4.2	13,801	13,300	501	3.6
Panama City	17,241	15,489	1,752	10.2	16,949	15,602	1,347	7.9
Pembroke Pines	37,560	35,954	1,606	4.3	37,954	36,528	1,426	3.8
Pensacola	27,840	26,289	1,551	5.6	27,006	25,760	1,246	4.6
Pinellas Park	23,063	21,954	1,109	4.8	23,071	22,203	868	3.8
Plantation	42,390	40,378	2,012	4.7	42,811	41,024	1,787	4.2
Plant City	(NA)	(NA)	(NA)	(NA)	12,037	11,521	516	4.3
Pompano Beach	38,424	35,485	2,939	7.6	38,662	36,052	2,610	6.8
Port Orange	17,932	17,080	852	4.8	17,671	17,025	646	3.7
Port St. Lucie	28,779	25,767	3,012	10.5	28,643	25,837	2,806	9.8
Riviera Beach	14,874	12,754	2,120	14.3	14,583	12,768	1,815	12.4
St. Petersburg	127,285	119,657	7,628	6.0	126,989	121,018	5,971	4.7
Sanford	18,593	17,335	1,258	6.8	18,563	17,620	943	5.1
Sarasota	27,006	25,474	1,532	5.7	26,463	25,346	1,117	4.2
Sunrise	35,321	33,237	2,084	5.9	35,619	33,768	1,851	5.2
Tallahassee	77,915	74,095	3,820	4.9	78,964	76,245	2,719	3.4
Tamarac	19,544	18,170	1,374	7.0	19,680	18,460	1,220	6.2
Tampa	155,776	145,358	10,418	6.7	156,005	147,598	8,407	5.4
Titusville	20,616	19,160	1,456	7.1	19,948	18,659	1,289	6.5
West Palm Beach	40,350	36,154	4,196	10.4	39,786	36,194	3,592	9.0
Winter Haven	11570	10694	876	7.6	11416	10666	750	6.6
Winter Springs	(NA)	(NA)	(NA)	(NA)	14,357	13,862	495	3.4

(NA) Not available.

1/ Metropolitan Statistical Areas (MSAs) and Primary Metropolitan Statistical Areas (PMSAs) based on 1992 MSA designations and cities with a population of 25,000 or more in 1995.

Note: Civilian labor force.

Source: State of Florida, Department of Labor and Employment Security, Bureau of Labor Market Information, *Labor Force Summary: 1995 Annual Averages,* and previous edition.

Table 6.20. OCCUPATIONS: PRIVATE INDUSTRY EMPLOYMENT, PARTICIPATION RATE, AND OCCUPATIONAL DISTRIBUTION OF WHITE AND MINORITY EMPLOYEES BY SEX AND BY OCCUPATION IN FLORIDA, 1994

Occupation	All		White		Minority 1/	
	Male	Female	Male	Female	Male	Female
	Number employed (1,000)					
Total	845,469	832,441	599,848	578,096	245,621	254,345
Officials and managers	110,977	57,165	95,645	47,252	15,332	9,913
Professionals	95,977	123,656	80,605	99,109	15,372	24,547
Technicians	52,711	50,671	40,140	36,956	12,571	13,715
Sales workers	122,052	147,993	90,464	109,632	31,588	38,361
Office and clerical workers	49,761	224,413	33,676	159,250	16,085	65,163
Craft workers	100,406	15,464	78,006	11,041	22,400	4,423
Operatives	116,384	47,323	72,010	24,540	44,374	22,783
Laborers	69,590	25,164	36,728	12,380	32,862	12,784
Service workers	127,611	140,592	72,574	77,936	55,037	62,656
	Participation rate (percentage)					
Total	50.4	49.6	35.7	34.5	14.6	15.2
Officials and managers	66.0	34.0	56.9	28.1	9.1	5.9
Professionals	43.7	56.3	36.7	45.1	7.0	11.2
Technicians	51.0	49.0	38.8	35.7	12.2	13.3
Sales workers	45.2	54.8	33.5	40.6	11.7	14.2
Office and clerical workers	18.1	81.9	12.3	58.1	5.9	23.8
Craft workers	86.7	13.3	67.3	9.5	19.3	3.8
Operatives	71.1	28.9	44.0	15.0	27.1	13.9
Laborers	73.4	26.6	38.8	13.1	34.7	13.5
Service workers	47.6	52.4	27.1	29.1	20.5	23.4
	Occupational distribution (percentage)					
Total	100.0	100.0	100.0	100.0	100.0	100.0
Officials and managers	13.1	6.9	15.9	8.2	6.2	3.9
Professionals	11.4	14.9	13.4	17.1	6.3	9.7
Technicians	6.2	6.1	6.7	6.4	5.1	5.4
Sales workers	14.4	17.8	15.1	19.0	12.9	15.1
Office and clerical workers	5.9	27.0	5.6	27.5	6.5	25.6
Craft workers	11.9	1.9	13.0	1.9	9.1	1.7
Operatives	13.8	5.7	12.0	4.2	18.1	9.0
Laborers	8.2	3.0	6.1	2.1	13.4	5.0
Service workers	15.1	16.9	12.1	13.5	22.4	24.6

1/ Includes Black, Asian or Pacific Islander, American Indian, Eskimo, or Aleut, and persons of Hispanic origin.

Note: Private industry data, based on 1987 standard industrial classification (SIC) codes, from the 1994 Equal Employment Opportunity employer information report (EEO-1). Includes private employers with 100 or more employees, or 50 or more employees and: 1) have a federal contract or first-tier subcontract worth $50,000 or more, or 2) act as depositories of federal funds in any amount, or 3) act as issuing and paying agents for U.S. Savings Bonds and Notes. EEO-1 businesses account for 48.9 percent of all private U.S. employment.

Source: U.S., Equal Employment Opportunity Commission, *Job Patterns for Minorities and Women in Private Industry, 1994.*

Table 6.25. OCCUPATIONS: EMPLOYMENT ESTIMATES, 1994, PROJECTIONS, 2005, AND AVERAGE ANNUAL JOB OPENINGS FOR MAJOR OCCUPATIONAL CATEGORIES IN THE STATE OF FLORIDA

Occupation	Estimates 1994	Projections 2005	Change: Number	Change: Percentage	Average annual openings: Total	Average annual openings: Due to growth	Average annual openings: Due to separations
<u>All occupations, total</u>	6,527,347	8,170,109	1,642,762	25.17	294,227	149,337	144,890
Executive, administrative, and managerial	435,711	555,987	120,276	27.60	20,195	10,934	9,261
Professional, paraprofessional, and technical	1,250,851	1,645,525	394,674	31.55	59,940	35,873	24,067
Management support	197,776	249,205	51,429	26.00	8,449	4,673	3,776
Engineers and related occupations	114,957	141,824	26,867	23.37	4,896	2,440	2,456
Computer and mathematical	45,206	69,944	24,738	54.72	3,121	2,247	874
Social scientists, recreation, and religion	79,879	110,469	30,590	38.30	4,363	2,783	1,580
Law and related occupations	56,187	69,982	13,795	24.55	1,967	1,253	714
Teachers, librarians, and counselors	285,334	377,957	92,623	32.46	14,417	8,419	5,998
Health practitioners, and technicians	336,616	450,960	114,344	33.97	16,248	10,394	5,854
Marketing and sales	916,702	1,151,239	234,537	25.58	46,607	21,322	25,285
Administrative support and clerical	1,171,806	1,404,031	232,225	19.82	44,002	21,108	22,894
Secretarial and general office	652,668	784,935	132,267	20.27	24,628	12,023	12,605
Service	1,194,829	1,568,692	373,863	31.29	64,051	33,991	30,060
First line supervisor	54,413	68,191	13,778	25.32	2,710	1,253	1,457
Protective	153,324	213,276	59,952	39.10	9,761	5,450	4,311
Food and beverage	518,746	664,889	146,143	28.17	28,939	13,286	15,653
Health	132,623	194,473	61,850	46.64	7,970	5,623	2,347
Cleaning and building	189,065	234,324	45,259	23.94	7,478	4,116	3,362
Personal service	136,019	179,822	43,803	32.20	6,681	3,983	2,698
Agriculture, forestry, and fishing	261,950	297,807	35,857	13.69	8,227	3,258	4,969
Production, construction, operators, maintenance, and related workers	1,295,498	1,546,828	251,330	19.40	51,205	22,851	28,354
Mechanics, installers, and repairers	255,212	308,556	53,344	20.90	10,712	4,848	5,864
Construction trades and extraction	199,213	230,355	31,142	15.63	6,915	2,830	4,085
Operators, fabricators, and laborers	676,620	816,869	140,249	20.73	27,824	12,754	15,070

Source: State of Florida, Department of Labor and Employment Security, Bureau of Labor Market Information, *Florida Industry and Occupational Employment Projections, 1994-2005, Statewide.*

Table 6.26. OCCUPATIONS: EMPLOYMENT ESTIMATES, 1994, AND PROJECTIONS, 2005, OF THE FASTEST-GROWING OCCUPATIONS IN THE STATE OF FLORIDA

Occupation	Estimates 1994	Projections 2005	Percentage change
Systems analyst	17,911	32,235	79.97
Home health aide	25,846	45,475	75.95
Computer engineer	8,392	14,368	71.21
Physical, corrective therapy assistant	3,936	6,497	65.07
Residential counselor	4,063	6,602	62.49
Physical therapist	5,762	9,335	62.01
Correction officer and jailer	25,400	40,924	61.12
Personal home care aide	3,928	6,296	60.29
Human services worker	5,455	8,742	60.26
Medical assistant	12,424	19,859	59.84
Medical records technician	4,814	7,532	56.46
Data processing equipment repairer	3,920	6,002	53.11
Teacher, special education	19,854	29,214	47.14
Adjustment clerk	19,592	28,801	47.00
Radiologic technologist	7,840	11,415	45.60
Amusement and recreation attendant	14,003	20,237	44.52
Emergency medical technician	6,928	9,970	43.91
Social worker, medical and psychiatric	10,442	14,915	42.84
Sheriff and deputy sheriff	9,833	13,979	42.16
Teacher's aide and educational assistant	15,452	21,898	41.72
Tax preparer	5,607	7,941	41.63
Police patrol officer	15,553	21,951	41.14
Management analyst	16,103	22,508	39.78
Designer, except interior designer	10,231	14,294	39.71
Medicine and health service manager	9,374	13,070	39.43
Food service and lodging manager	35,250	49,050	39.15
Medical secretary	14,811	20,579	38.94
Taxi driver and chauffeur	8,482	11,783	38.92
Flight attendant	5,270	7,320	38.90
Baker, bread and pastry	10,951	15,184	38.65
Paralegal	6,414	8,850	37.98
Dental assistant	10,568	14,554	37.72
Dental hygienist	6,874	9,465	37.69
Teacher, preschool and kindergarten	24,940	34,267	37.40
Social worker, except medical and psychiatric	20,560	28,244	37.37
Guard	60,289	82,777	37.30
Hand packer and packager	58,546	80,309	37.17
Instructor, nonvocational education	8,964	12,267	36.85
Nursery worker	7,841	10,728	36.82
Teacher's aide, paraprofessional	25,010	34,181	36.67
Physician	30,432	41,512	36.41
Lawn maintenance worker	15,661	21,286	35.92
Artist and commercial artist	12,391	16,815	35.70
Receptionist, information clerk	63,915	86,614	35.51
Bill and account collector	16,103	21,783	35.27
Personnel, training, labor relations specialist	19,229	25,874	34.56
Child care worker	50,675	68,172	34.53
Nursing aide and orderly	65,797	88,454	34.43
Waiter and waitress	140,551	188,871	34.38
Instructor and coach, sports	7,876	10,580	34.33
Sales agent, business services	12,877	17,286	34.24
Engineering, math, natural sciences manager	12,611	16,878	33.84
Recreation worker	10,186	13,626	33.77

See footnote at end of table.

Continued . . .

Table 6.26. OCCUPATIONS: EMPLOYMENT ESTIMATES, 1994, AND PROJECTIONS, 2005, OF THE FASTEST-GROWING OCCUPATIONS IN THE STATE OF FLORIDA (Continued)

Occupation	Estimates 1994	Projections 2005	Percentage change
Personnel, training, labor relations manager	6,517	8,716	33.74
Fire fighter	12,666	16,935	33.70
Counselor	8,288	11,065	33.51
Teacher, vocational education	10,426	13,917	33.48
Securities, financial service sales	17,646	23,520	33.29
Teacher, secondary school	65,267	86,836	33.05
Computer programmer	15,535	20,643	32.88
Registered nurse	114,244	151,782	32.86
Pharmacy technician	6,341	8,420	32.79
Marketing, advertising, public relations manager	17,323	22,903	32.21
Licensed practical nurse	50,188	66,217	31.94
Bus driver	9,564	12,613	31.88
Clergy	16,240	21,387	31.69
Insurance adjuster, investigator	8,558	11,262	31.60
Food preparation worker	71,071	93,283	31.25
Music director, singer, and related	8,319	10,917	31.23
Musician, instrumental	9,340	12,250	31.16
Welfare eligibility worker	8,492	11,104	30.76
Animal caretaker, except farm	11,923	15,508	30.07
Customer service representative, utilities	9,961	12,936	29.87
Counter and rental clerk	22,266	28,906	29.82
Grader and sorter, agricultural products	10,941	14,159	29.41
First line supervisor, clerical	65,124	84,224	29.33
Cook, restaurant	47,544	61,477	29.31
Graduate assistant, teaching	8,954	11,573	29.25
Financial manager	37,845	48,916	29.25
Administrative service manager	15,839	20,436	29.02
Laundry, drycleaning machine operator	11,103	14,308	28.87
Cashier	181,892	234,302	28.81
Host and hostess, restaurant, lounge	17,218	22,142	28.60
Dispatcher, except police, fire, ambulance	7,859	10,107	28.60
Accountant and auditor	45,118	57,850	28.22
Order clerk, materials, service	13,813	17,704	28.17
Heating, A/C, refrigeration mechanic	18,697	23,875	27.69
Cook, fast food	35,685	45,467	27.41
Vehicle, equipment cleaner	16,344	20,808	27.31
Cook, short order	15,397	19,599	27.29
Pharmacist	10,276	13,070	27.19
Telemarketer, door-to-door sales, street vendor	30,469	38,726	27.10
Bus driver, school	14,943	18,968	26.94
Sales representative, scientific products, except retail	35,495	44,990	26.75
Medical/clinical laboratory technologist	9,059	11,469	26.60
Bus, truck, diesel engine mechanic	10,114	12,797	26.53
Education administrator	16,268	20,568	26.43
Hotel desk clerk	10,741	13,576	26.39
Loan officer and counselor	9,487	11,977	26.25
First line supervisor, sales	140,782	177,305	25.94

Note: Occupations are ranked based upon the anticipated rate of growth between 1994 and 2005. Only occupations with a minimum total change of 2,000 jobs are included.

Source: State of Florida, Department of Labor and Employment Security, Bureau of Labor Market Information, *Florida Industry and Occupational Employment Projections, 1994-2005, Statewide.*

Table 6.30. EMPLOYERS: NAME AND LOCATION OF CORPORATE HEADQUARTERS OF THE 50 LARGEST PRIVATE EMPLOYERS IN FLORIDA, FEBRUARY 2, 1995

Firm and headquarters location	Number of employees
Barnett Banks, Inc.--Jacksonville, FL	A/
Columbia/HCA Healthcare Corp.--Miami Lakes, FL	A/
Walt Disney World Co.--Lake Buena Vista, FL	A/
Eckerd Corp.--Largo, FL	A/
Kelly Services, Inc.--Troy, MI	A/
K Mart Corp.--Troy, MI	A/
Olsten Corp.--Westbury, NY	A/
Publix Super Markets, Inc.--Lakeland, FL	A/
Sears, Roebuck and Co.--Chicago, IL	A/
Southern Bell Telephone and Telegraph Co.--Atlanta, GA	A/
The Staff Leasing Group--Bradenton, FL	A/
Wal-Mart Stores, Inc.--Bentonville, AR	A/
Winn Dixie Stores, Inc.--Jacksonville, FL	A/
American Telephone & Telegraph Co.--New York, NY	B/
Burdine's Inc.--Miami, FL	B/
First Union National Bank of Florida--Jacksonville, FL	B/
Florida Power & Light Co.-- Juno Beach, FL	B/
General Mills Restaurants, Inc.--Orlando, FL	B/
Payroll Transfers, Inc.--Tampa, FL	B/
United Parcel Service of America, Inc.--Atlanta, GA	B/
The Vincam Group, Inc.--Coral Gables, FL	B/
Albertson's, Inc.--Boise, ID	C/
America Airlines, Inc.--Dallas/Ft. Worth Airport, TX	C/
Anheuser-Busch Companies, Inc.--St. Louis, MO	C/
Beverly Enterprises--Fort Smith, AR	C/
GTE Florida, Inc.--Tampa, FL	C/
Harris Corporation--Melbourne, FL	C/
The Home Depot, Inc.--Atlanta, GA	C/
Kash-N-Karry Food Stores, Inc.--Tampa, FL	C/
Martin Marietta Corp.--Bethesda, MD	C/
J. C. Penney Co., Inc.-Dallas, TX	C/
Sun Bank, N.A.--Orlando, FL	C/
Walgreen Co.--Deerfield, IL	C/
American Express Co.--New York, NY	D/
Blue Cross/Blue Shield of Florida, Inc.--Jacksonville, FL	D/
Brinker International, Inc.--Dallas, TX	D/
Delta Air Lines, Inc.--Atlanta, GA	D/
Employee Services, Inc.--Bradenton, FL	D/
Food Lion, Inc.--Salisbury, NC	D/
Morrison Restaurants, Inc.--Mobile, AL	D/
Motorola, Inc.--Schaumberg, IL	D/
Nationsbank of Florida, N.A.--Tampa, FL	D/
The Prudential Insurance Co. of America--Newark, NJ	D/
Scotty's, Inc.--Winter Haven, FL	D/
Staff Management Systems, Inc.--Tampa, FL	D/
Staffing Concepts International, Inc.--Tampa, FL	D/
Steak & Ale of Florida--Dallas, TX	D/
Target Stores--Minneapolis, MN	
United Technologies Corp.--Hartford, CT	D/
United Telephone Company of Florida--Altamonte Springs, FL	D/

A/ 15,001 and over. B/ 10,001-15,000. C/ 7,501-10,000. D/ 5,000-7,500.

Note: Employers are listed alphabetically within employment size ranges. Employment estimates do not include out-of-state employees in cases where the employer also has operations outside of Florida. Employees of franchise operations are not included in corporate totals. Hospitals and universities are excluded. Employment estimates for help supply services employers include the total number of help available for supplying temporary or continuing help.

Source: State of Florida, Department of Commerce, Bureau of Economic Analysis, *Florida Facts: Florida's Fifty Largest Private Employers,* February 2, 1995.

Table 6.35. EMPLOYMENT AND WAGES: AVERAGE MONTHLY EMPLOYMENT AND WAGES BY MAJOR INDUSTRY DIVISION IN PRIVATE UNITED STATES AND FOREIGN-OWNED ESTABLISHMENTS IN FLORIDA AND THE UNITED STATES, FOURTH QUARTER 1991

Industry	All establishments				Foreign-owned establishments				
	Average monthly employment	Average monthly wages	Percentage change 1990-91		Average monthly employment	Percentage of total employment	Average monthly wages	Percentage change 1990-91	
			Employment	Wages				Employment	Wages
Florida, total 1/	4,484,359	1,924	-2.0	4.5	206,602	4.6	2,071	4.8	7.8
Agriculture, forestry, and fisheries	161,616	1,140	0.3	5.2	2,168	1.3	2,058	-8.2	13.5
Mining	8,150	2,636	(D)	(D)	1,705	20.9	2,872	(D)	(D)
Construction	271,243	2,005	-12.0	1.3	5,766	2.1	2,617	-1.0	-1.2
Manufacturing	490,331	2,391	-3.6	6.1	38,357	7.8	2,671	0.5	7.8
Transportation, communications, and public utilities	266,560	2,432	-2.0	4.9	11,103	4.2	2,316	4.2	10.3
Wholesale trade	288,947	2,674	-1.1	2.8	25,430	8.8	3,206	11.3	6.4
Retail trade	1,120,224	1,149	-3.0	4.2	68,332	6.1	1,329	4.0	10.6
Finance, insurance, and real estate	351,191	2,412	-3.7	7.6	11,159	3.2	3,032	9.4	4.3
Services	1,513,728	2,067	0.9	4.0	42,453	2.8	1,618	7.2	6.3
United States, total 1/	89,539,583	2,172	-1.9	4.2	4,824,461	5.4	2,672	1.9	5.1
Agriculture, forestry, and fisheries	1,454,470	1,320	1.1	2.3	23,320	1.6	1,891	-3.7	11.5
Mining	674,321	3,514	-6.7	6.5	106,614	15.8	4,153	-5.9	9.4
Construction	4,635,186	2,411	-7.6	1.3	92,859	2.0	3,359	8.8	6.6
Manufacturing	18,366,678	2,662	-3.1	5.1	1,914,392	10.4	2,933	2.2	3.9
Transportation, communications, and public utilities	5,507,841	2,689	-1.0	4.5	225,644	4.1	2,865	-1.5	7.3
Wholesale trade	6,075,156	2,857	-2.6	3.8	495,387	8.2	3,570	0.0	6.9
Retail trade	19,611,490	1,143	-1.7	3.7	928,994	4.7	1,305	1.9	4.8
Finance, insurance, and real estate	6,490,043	2,801	-1.1	6.2	360,993	5.6	3,963	10.6	6.8
Services	26,585,024	2,145	-0.4	4.1	673,312	2.5	2,089	0.0	1.0

(D) Data withheld to avoid disclosure of information about individual firms.
1/ Includes data for nonclassifiable establishments not shown separately.
Source: U.S., Department of Commerce, Bureau of the Census, *News*. Release of December 15, 1994.

Table 6.40. INDUSTRY GROWTH TRENDS: EMPLOYMENT ESTIMATES, 1994, AND PROJECTIONS, 2005, OF THE FASTEST-GROWING INDUSTRIES AND INDUSTRIES GAINING THE MOST NEW GROWTH IN THE STATE OF FLORIDA

SIC code	Industry	Estimates 1994	Projections 2005	Change Number	Change Percentage
	Fastest-growing industries 1/				
83	Social services	121,679	180,777	59,098	48.57
87	Engineering and management services	134,185	193,245	59,060	44.01
73	Business services	452,812	648,519	195,707	43.22
80	Health services	515,030	717,509	202,479	39.31
41	Local and interurban transit	13,677	18,899	5,222	38.18
54	Food stores	219,582	296,888	77,306	35.21
62	Security and commodity brokers	23,254	31,145	7,891	33.93
61	Nondepository institutions	35,214	47,095	11,881	33.74
84	Museum and botanical and zoological gardens	3,087	4,105	1,018	32.98
07	Agricultural services	137,464	182,499	45,035	32.76
79	Amusement and recreation services	116,985	152,944	35,959	30.74
82	Educational services	62,924	81,590	18,666	29.66
58	Eating and drinking places	415,233	536,048	120,815	29.10
93	Local government	592,350	762,882	170,532	28.79
75	Auto repair services and parking	59,923	77,000	17,077	28.50
42	Trucking and warehousing	67,067	85,929	18,862	28.12
57	Furniture and homefurnishings stores	56,437	71,778	15,341	27.18
45	Transportation by air	49,536	62,919	13,383	27.02
86	Membership organizations	105,699	134,002	28,303	26.78
51	Wholesale trade, nondurable goods	131,114	165,536	34,422	26.25
	Industries gaining the most new jobs				
80	Health services	515,030	717,509	202,479	39.31
73	Business services	452,812	648,519	195,707	43.22
93	Local government	592,350	762,882	170,532	28.79
58	Eating and drinking places	415,233	536,048	120,815	29.10
54	Food stores	219,582	296,888	77,306	35.21
83	Social services	121,679	180,777	59,098	48.57
87	Engineering and management services	134,185	193,245	59,060	44.01
92	State government	193,218	242,032	48,814	25.26
07	Agricultural services	137,464	182,499	45,035	32.76
79	Amusement and recreation services	116,985	152,944	35,959	30.74
51	Wholesale trade, nondurable goods	131,114	165,536	34,422	26.25
59	Miscellaneous retail stores	137,837	172,154	34,317	24.90
50	Wholesale trade, durable goods	174,531	208,446	33,915	19.43
70	Hotels and other lodging places	140,253	174,014	33,761	24.07
53	General merchandise stores	142,524	170,930	28,406	19.93
86	Membership organizations	105,699	134,002	28,303	26.78
17	Special trade contractors	188,892	215,385	26,493	14.03
55	Auto dealers and service stations	117,008	137,104	20,096	17.17
42	Trucking and warehousing	67,067	85,929	18,862	28.12
82	Educational services	62,924	81,590	18,666	29.66

1/ Industries with a minimum total change of 1,000 jobs.

Source: State of Florida, Department of Labor and Employment Security, Bureau of Labor Market Information, *Florida Industry and Occupational Employment Projections, 1994-2005, Statewide.*

Table 6.57. AVERAGE ANNUAL PAY: PAY OF EMPLOYEES COVERED BY STATE AND FEDERAL UNEMPLOYMENT INSURANCE PROGRAMS IN THE UNITED STATES AND IN THE STATE AND METROPOLITAN AREAS OF FLORIDA, 1993 AND 1994

Industry or metropolitan area	1993 (dollars)	1994 (dollars)	Percentage change 1993-94	Ranking of MSAs in the U.S. By 1994 level	Ranking of MSAs in the U.S. By percentage change 1993-94
United States	25,934	26,494	2.2	(X)	(X)
Florida				(X)	(X)
Private industry 1/	22,918	23,309	1.7	(X)	(X)
Agriculture, forestry, and fishing	(NA)	(NA)	(NA)	(X)	(X)
Mining	35,462	36,087	1.8	(X)	(X)
Construction	23,485	24,236	3.2	(X)	(X)
Manufacturing	29,149	30,095	3.2	(X)	(X)
Transportation, communications, and public utilities	30,997	31,474	1.5	(X)	(X)
Wholesale trade	31,901	32,682	2.4	(X)	(X)
Retail trade	14,365	14,694	2.3	(X)	(X)
Finance, insurance, and real estate	31,190	31,097	-0.3	(X)	(X)
Services	23,016	23,304	1.3	(X)	(X)
Government	27,116	27,315	0.7	(X)	(X)
Daytona Beach	19,397	19,910	2.6	292	151
Ft. Lauderdale	25,365	25,838	1.9	89	213
Ft. Myers-Cape Coral	21,472	21,821	1.6	239	241
Ft. Pierce-Port St. Lucie	22,247	22,277	0.1	222	300
Ft. Walton Beach	19,600	19,333	-1.4	301	309
Gainesville	21,151	21,314	0.8	260	282
Jacksonville	24,443	24,324	-0.5	138	304
Lakeland-Winter Haven	21,609	22,378	3.6	213	56
Melbourne-Titusville-Palm Bay	26,104	26,334	0.9	80	277
Miami	26,026	26,493	1.8	70	223
Naples	20,672	21,564	4.3	247	25
Ocala	19,531	20,288	3.9	285	45
Orlando	23,187	23,632	1.9	166	213
Panama City	19,353	19,865	2.6	294	151
Pensacola	21,789	22,084	1.4	230	248
Punta Gorda	19,560	20,049	2.5	289	168
Sarasota-Bradenton	21,101	21,287	0.9	261	277
Tallahassee	21,706	22,275	2.6	223	151
Tampa-St. Petersburg-Clearwater	23,300	23,776	2.0	155	208
West Palm Beach-Boca Raton	26,339	26,624	1.1	64	267

(X) Not applicable. (NA) Not available.

1/ Includes industries not listed separately.

Note: Some 1993 data are revised. 1994 data are preliminary. Data are for Metropolitan Statistical Areas (MSAs) and Primary Metropolitan Statistical Areas (PMSAs) defined as of December 31, 1992 and are not comparable to data in previous *Abstracts*. See Glossary for definitions and map at the front of the book for area boundaries.

Source: U.S., Department of Labor, Bureau of Labor Statistics, *News: Average Annual Pay by State and Industry, 1994*, release of September 19, 1995, and *News: Average Annual Pay Levels in Metropolitan Areas, 1994*, release of October 27, 1995.

SOCIAL INSURANCE AND WELFARE

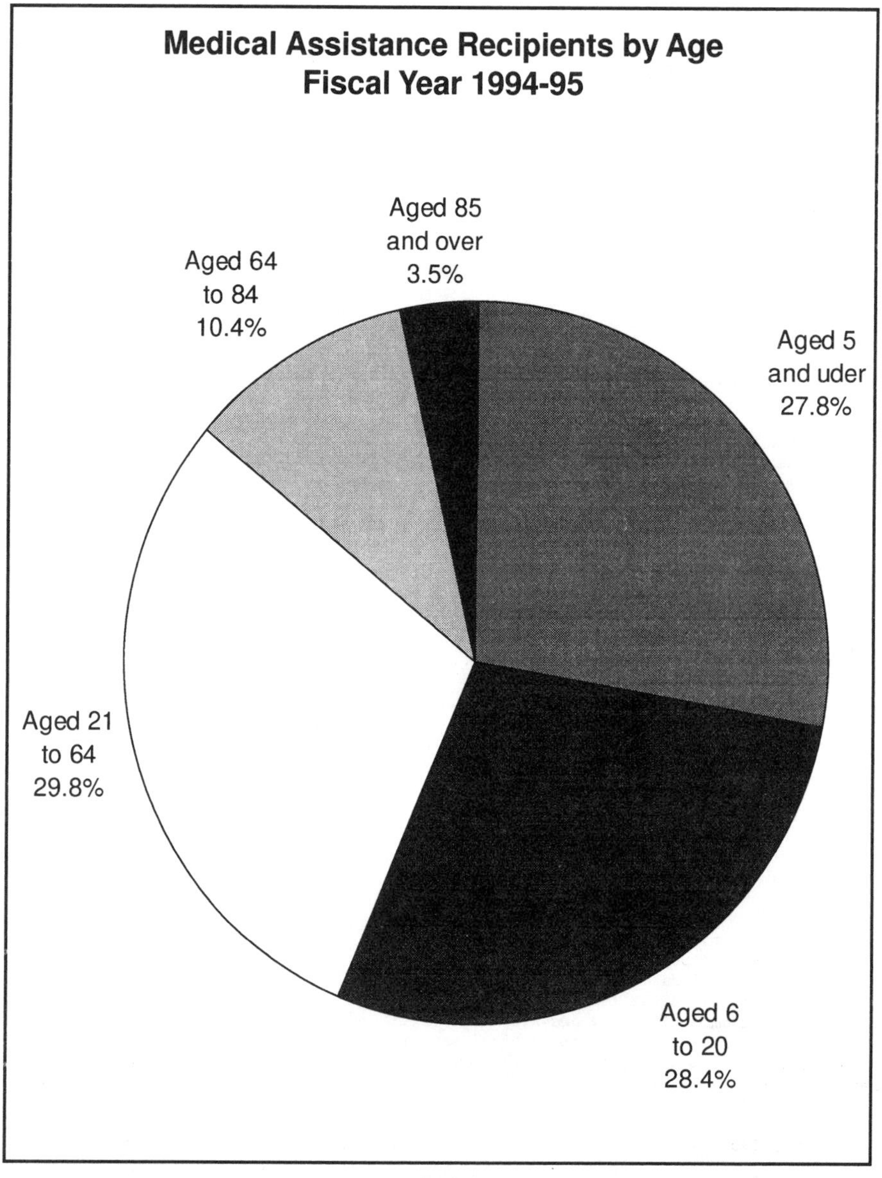

Source: Table 7.16

SECTION 7.00
SOCIAL INSURANCE AND WELFARE

TABLES LISTED BY MAJOR HEADINGS

Table 7.03. MEDICARE: ENROLLMENT IN HOSPITAL AND/OR MEDICAL INSURANCE BY METROPOLITAN/NONMETROPOLITAN RESIDENCE IN FLORIDA, 1994 AND 1995

Item	Total enrollment		Persons aged 65 and over		Disability benefi-ciaries 1/	
	1994	1995	1994	1995	1994	1995
Florida, total	2,582,602	2,627,511	2,367,420	2,395,890	215,182	231,621
Metropolitan counties 2/	2,286,501	2,324,246	2,098,013	2,121,535	188,488	202,711
With central city	2,028,562	2,060,192	1,863,837	1,883,343	164,725	176,849
Without central city	257,939	264,054	234,176	238,192	23,763	25,862
Nonmetropolitan counties	293,510	301,254	266,979	272,505	26,531	28,749

1/ Persons under age 65 entitled to cash disability benefits for at least 24 consecutive months and also those eligible solely on the basis of end-stage renal disease.
2/ Counties included in Metropolitan Statistical Areas (MSAs).

Table 7.04. MEDICARE: ENROLLMENT, JULY 1, AND BENEFIT PAYMENTS, FOR CALENDAR YEAR OF PERSONS AGED 65 AND OVER IN FLORIDA, 1982 THROUGH 1995

Year	Hospital and/or medical insurance		Hospital insurance		Supplementary medical insurance	
	Enroll-ment (1,000)	Benefit payments ($1,000)	Enroll-ment (1,000)	Benefit payments ($1,000)	Enroll-ment (1,000)	Benefit payments ($1,000)
1982	1,680	2,934,263	1,648	1,898,732	1,651	1,035,531
1983	1,736	3,411,057	1,704	2,178,642	1,709	1,232,415
1984	1,791	4,296,524	1,757	2,775,313	1,765	1,521,211
1985	1,856	5,040,418	1,820	3,267,584	1,829	1,772,834
1986	1,921	5,394,033	1,881	3,347,974	1,893	2,046,059
1987	2,135	5,720,000	2,092	3,275,000	2,095	2,445,000
1988	2,114	5,517,000	2,070	2,869,000	2,072	2,648,000
1989	2,174	6,470,000	2,165	3,340,000	2,129	3,130,000
1990	2,174	6,960,000	2,165	3,565,000	2,129	3,394,000
1991	2,230	7,440,000	2,221	3,742,000	2,183	3,698,000
1992	2,273	8,247,006	2,265	4,789,953	2,228	3,457,053
1993	2,322	(NA)	2,313	(NA)	2,275	(NA)
1994	2,367	(NA)	2,359	(NA)	2,318	(NA)
1995	2,396	(NA)	2,385	(NA)	2,344	(NA)

(NA) Not available.
Note: Geographic classification is based on the address to which the enrollee's cash benefit check is being mailed or the mailing address recorded in the health insurance master file. Data from 1985 are estimated.

Source for Tables 7.03 and 7.04: U.S., Department of Health and Human Services, Health Care Financing Administration, unpublished data.

Table 7.12. SOCIAL SECURITY: NUMBER OF BENEFICIARIES AND AMOUNT OF BENEFITS IN CURRENT-PAYMENT STATUS BY TYPE OF BENEFICIARY IN THE STATE AND COUNTIES OF FLORIDA, DECEMBER 1994

Residence of beneficiary	Total	Retired workers 1/	Disabled workers	Wives and husbands	Children	Widows and widowers 2/
			Number of beneficiaries			
Florida	2,934,435	1,990,871	215,262	218,715	184,695	324,892
Alachua	25,420	14,990	2,460	1,775	3,135	3,060
Baker	2,760	1,345	460	170	445	340
Bay	23,605	14,015	2,315	2,005	2,065	3,205
Bradford	2,850	1,620	305	205	325	395
Brevard	96,355	64,920	7,455	8,005	5,550	10,425
Broward	283,800	198,715	17,355	18,080	14,835	34,815
Calhoun	2,180	1,145	245	185	250	355
Charlotte	46,205	34,785	2,280	3,725	1,485	3,930
Citrus	38,210	27,995	2,350	3,035	1,560	3,270
Clay	15,900	9,525	1,590	1,280	1,620	1,885
Collier	45,920	32,625	2,045	5,065	1,700	4,485
Columbia	9,210	5,275	1,085	695	1,000	1,155
Dade	293,085	194,150	23,425	21,105	23,030	31,375
De Soto	5,815	3,730	610	410	505	560
Dixie	2,660	1,465	370	210	315	300
Duval	99,260	59,130	9,950	6,540	10,090	13,550
Escambia	45,555	26,235	4,410	4,265	4,205	6,440
Flagler	12,870	9,665	775	965	560	905
Franklin	2,590	1,595	270	180	205	340
Gadsden	8,165	4,335	1,170	415	1,335	910
Gilchrist	2,270	1,265	280	190	235	300
Glades	1,735	1,175	155	130	110	165
Gulf	2,625	1,455	255	265	220	430
Hamilton	2,025	1,040	265	140	290	290
Hardee	3,825	2,270	360	295	455	445
Hendry	4,350	2,545	400	310	570	525
Hernando	44,275	32,550	2,855	3,420	2,075	3,375
Highlands	27,190	19,955	1,450	2,195	1,215	2,375
Hillsborough	143,225	88,075	15,200	9,880	12,965	17,105
Holmes	3,840	1,995	450	350	395	650
Indian River	31,445	22,715	1,505	2,895	1,180	3,150
Jackson	9,080	4,915	945	690	1,170	1,360
Jefferson	2,455	1,425	235	160	265	370
Lafayette	950	540	105	80	90	135
Lake	55,250	40,250	3,295	4,215	2,220	5,270
Lee	102,855	74,340	5,675	8,255	4,970	9,615
Leon	22,715	14,145	1,800	1,570	2,325	2,875
Levy	7,610	4,730	770	610	640	860
Liberty	995	490	150	75	130	150
Madison	3,220	1,795	375	245	345	460
Manatee	64,635	46,225	3,615	5,000	2,740	7,055
Marion	66,890	46,695	5,110	5,040	4,075	5,970
Martin	33,725	24,585	1,535	3,115	1,100	3,390
Monroe	12,820	8,890	965	1,070	570	1,325
Nassau	7,570	4,250	865	645	800	1,010
Okaloosa	22,560	13,750	1,915	2,175	1,830	2,890
Okeechobee	6,575	3,980	715	485	620	775

See footnotes at end of table. Continued . . .

Table 7.12. SOCIAL SECURITY: NUMBER OF BENEFICIARIES AND AMOUNT OF BENEFITS IN CURRENT-PAYMENT STATUS BY TYPE OF BENEFICIARY IN THE STATE AND COUNTIES OF FLORIDA, DECEMBER 1994 (Continued)

Residence of beneficiary	Total	Retired workers 1/	Disabled workers	Wives and husbands	Children	Widows and widowers 2/
		Number of beneficiaries (Continued)				
Orange	106,760	65,485	11,210	7,465	10,350	12,250
Osceola	22,110	13,630	2,365	1,490	2,365	2,260
Palm Beach	244,325	178,725	11,045	18,465	9,845	26,245
Pasco	101,340	73,140	6,840	7,160	4,430	9,770
Pinellas	231,930	163,660	14,900	15,385	9,770	28,215
Polk	97,225	64,565	8,240	7,050	6,895	10,475
Putnam	16,525	9,860	1,875	1,280	1,610	1,900
St. Johns	20,165	13,320	1,495	1,720	1,370	2,260
St. Lucie	44,255	30,785	3,510	3,125	2,840	3,995
Santa Rosa	14,280	8,145	1,520	1,395	1,450	1,770
Sarasota	99,650	73,520	4,145	8,535	2,740	10,710
Seminole	44,920	28,300	4,020	3,365	4,010	5,225
Sumter	9,670	6,355	920	690	690	1,015
Suwannee	6,815	3,915	775	510	680	935
Taylor	3,720	2,070	415	280	395	560
Union	1,265	670	150	90	185	170
Volusia	107,690	74,125	8,305	7,795	6,005	11,460
Wakulla	2,220	1,290	220	155	270	285
Walton	6,345	3,750	685	550	560	800
Washington	3,940	2,180	440	340	400	580
Unknown	150	80	20	15	20	15
		Amount of monthly cash benefits ($1,000)				
Florida	1,882,692	1,385,150	143,664	76,951	62,112	214,815
Alachua	15,332	10,142	1,569	625	1,101	1,895
Baker	1,535	854	294	47	153	188
Bay	13,691	8,944	1,497	637	691	1,923
Bradford	1,569	987	197	59	106	220
Brevard	61,596	44,822	5,218	2,754	1,949	6,852
Broward	195,469	146,851	11,906	6,624	5,300	24,787
Calhoun	1,138	671	157	51	75	184
Charlotte	30,642	24,376	1,713	1,325	528	2,700
Citrus	24,592	19,135	1,724	1,039	541	2,151
Clay	9,489	6,231	1,101	421	578	1,159
Collier	32,388	24,878	1,468	2,075	614	3,353
Columbia	5,074	3,229	693	207	295	651
Dade	173,633	125,590	14,020	6,860	7,445	19,718
De Soto	3,475	2,464	382	132	151	347
Dixie	1,462	904	239	63	92	165
Duval	60,125	39,584	6,405	2,276	3,452	8,406
Escambia	25,770	16,467	2,843	1,337	1,363	3,760
Flagler	8,729	6,942	610	349	204	625
Franklin	1,459	983	172	56	60	188
Gadsden	4,079	2,481	646	117	359	477
Gilchrist	1,284	782	203	54	76	169
Glades	1,066	777	112	40	38	99
Gulf	1,588	984	173	91	74	267
Hamilton	1,049	615	166	39	83	146

See footnotes at end of table. Continued . . .

Table 7.12. SOCIAL SECURITY: NUMBER OF BENEFICIARIES AND AMOUNT OF BENEFITS IN CURRENT-PAYMENT STATUS BY TYPE OF BENEFICIARY IN THE STATE AND COUNTIES OF FLORIDA, DECEMBER 1994 (Continued)

Residence of beneficiary	Total	Retired workers 1/	Disabled workers	Wives and husbands	Children	Widows and widowers 2/
	Amount of monthly cash benefits ($1,000) (Continued)					
Hardee	2,109	1,434	209	89	129	248
Hendry	2,565	1,716	253	102	177	317
Hernando	28,785	22,475	2,194	1,171	690	2,254
Highlands	17,128	13,484	977	745	363	1,561
Hillsborough	88,082	59,706	9,826	3,393	4,290	10,867
Holmes	1,912	1,119	279	90	106	318
Indian River	21,317	16,492	1,045	1,113	418	2,249
Jackson	4,700	2,885	581	188	359	687
Jefferson	1,280	836	140	46	80	179
Lafayette	525	338	66	23	26	71
Lake	35,378	27,523	2,240	1,459	702	3,454
Lee	68,370	52,918	4,036	3,001	1,741	6,675
Leon	14,175	9,832	1,134	577	801	1,832
Levy	4,508	3,066	538	189	203	513
Liberty	527	299	92	22	39	74
Madison	1,649	1,044	222	64	91	227
Manatee	42,575	32,558	2,463	1,827	936	4,791
Marion	41,927	31,621	3,511	1,688	1,295	3,811
Martin	23,377	18,244	1,089	1,212	379	2,452
Monroe	8,187	6,062	671	380	215	860
Nassau	4,735	2,953	620	230	292	639
Okaloosa	12,883	8,618	1,240	683	640	1,701
Okeechobee	3,911	2,625	480	150	181	475
Orange	65,773	44,827	7,215	2,550	3,370	7,811
Osceola	13,394	9,148	1,606	463	758	1,419
Palm Beach	176,349	138,124	7,744	7,492	3,513	19,477
Pasco	64,936	49,702	4,894	2,399	1,484	6,456
Pinellas	150,755	113,082	9,972	5,440	3,445	18,817
Polk	60,767	43,913	5,396	2,452	2,255	6,751
Putnam	9,659	6,430	1,221	396	472	1,141
St. Johns	13,022	9,383	999	637	492	1,511
St. Lucie	28,615	21,546	2,391	1,090	901	2,687
Santa Rosa	8,305	5,278	1,049	438	512	1,029
Sarasota	68,212	53,324	2,928	3,249	1,026	7,684
Seminole	28,346	19,614	2,732	1,156	1,395	3,450
Sumter	5,752	4,124	608	214	200	606
Suwannee	3,786	2,396	516	149	204	519
Taylor	2,141	1,327	282	86	124	322
Union	671	404	97	26	53	90
Volusia	68,500	50,578	5,726	2,678	2,044	7,475
Wakulla	1,229	803	142	46	84	154
Walton	3,465	2,262	447	158	169	428
Washington	2,092	1,300	277	96	119	301
Unknown	86	53	11	5	8	9

1/ Includes "special age 72" beneficiaries.
2/ Includes nondisabled and disabled widows and widowers, widowed mothers and fathers, and parents.
Note: Detail may not add to totals because of rounding.
Source: U.S., Department of Health and Human Services, Social Security Administration, *OASDI Beneficiaries by State and County, December 1994.*

Table 7.14. SOCIAL SECURITY: AVERAGE MONTHLY BENEFITS OF BENEFICIARIES AGED 65 AND OVER IN THE STATE AND COUNTIES OF FLORIDA, DECEMBER 1994

(in dollars)

County	All beneficiaries	Retired workers	County	All beneficiaries	Retired workers
Florida	641.59	695.75	Lafayette	552.63	625.93
			Lake	640.33	683.80
Alachua	603.15	676.58	Lee	664.72	711.84
Baker	556.16	634.94	Leon	624.04	695.09
Bay	580.00	638.17	Levy	592.38	648.20
Bradford	550.53	609.26	Liberty	529.65	610.20
Brevard	639.26	690.42	Madison	512.11	581.62
Broward	688.76	739.00	Manatee	658.70	704.34
Calhoun	522.02	586.03	Marion	626.81	677.18
Charlotte	663.17	700.76	Martin	693.17	742.08
Citrus	643.60	683.51	Monroe	638.61	681.89
Clay	596.79	654.17	Nassau	625.50	694.82
Collier	705.31	762.54	Okaloosa	571.05	626.76
Columbia	550.92	612.13	Okeechobee	594.83	659.55
Dade	592.43	646.87	Orange	616.08	684.54
De Soto	597.59	660.59	Osceola	605.79	671.17
Dixie	549.62	617.06	Palm Beach	721.78	772.83
Duval	605.73	669.44	Pasco	640.77	679.55
Escambia	565.69	627.67	Pinellas	650.00	690.96
Flagler	678.24	718.26	Polk	625.01	680.14
Franklin	563.32	616.30	Putnam	584.51	652.13
Gadsden	499.57	572.32	St. Johns	645.77	704.43
Gilchrist	565.64	618.18	St. Lucie	646.59	699.89
Glades	614.41	661.28	Santa Rosa	581.58	648.00
Gulf	604.95	676.29	Sarasota	684.52	725.30
Hamilton	518.02	591.35	Seminole	631.03	693.07
Hardee	551.37	631.72	Sumter	594.83	648.94
Hendry	589.66	674.26	Suwannee	555.54	612.01
Hernando	650.14	690.48	Taylor	575.54	641.06
Highlands	629.94	675.72	Union	530.43	602.99
Hillsborough	614.99	677.90	Volusia	636.09	682.33
Holmes	497.92	560.90	Wakulla	553.60	622.48
Indian River	677.91	726.04	Walton	546.10	603.20
Jackson	517.62	586.98	Washington	530.96	596.33
Jefferson	521.38	586.67			

Source: U.S., Department of Health and Human Services, Social Security Administration, *OASDI Beneficiaries by State and County, December 1994.*

Table 7.15. PUBLIC ASSISTANCE: DIRECT ASSISTANCE PAYMENTS, CALENDAR YEARS 1991 THROUGH 1994, AND MEDICAL ASSISTANCE PAYMENTS, FISCAL YEARS 1991-92 THROUGH 1994-95, BY PROGRAM IN FLORIDA

(rounded to thousands of dollars)

Type of assistance	1991	1992	1993	1994
Direct assistance, total	1,329,535	1,603,925	1,904,745	1,995,811
Basic Supplemental Security Income (SSI)	750,603	911,480	1,049,339	1,160,442
Old-Age Assistance (OAA)	216,716	236,640	255,228	271,391
Aid to the Blind (AB)	11,032	11,511	12,095	12,437
Aid to the Disabled (AD)	522,855	663,329	782,016	876,614
SSI State Supplementation 1/	18,872	18,836	18,535	18,608
Aid to Families with Dependent Children (AFDC)	560,060	673,609	836,871	816,761
	1991-92	1992-93	1993-94	1994-95
Medical assistance, total 2/	3,518,403	4,131,306	4,754,229	4,802,304
Aid to the Blind	14,066	13,557	15,849	15,945
Aid to the Disabled	1,160,110	1,339,888	1,615,261	1,785,254
Aid to Families with Dependent Children	1,213,336	1,441,465	1,700,996	1,385,984
Old-Age Assistance	1,074,314	1,263,255	1,429,508	1,551,516

1/ Payments to persons eligible for state benefits but not eligible under federal requirements.

2/ Federal fiscal year ending September 30. Excludes "other."

Source: U.S., Department of Health and Human Services, Social Security Administration, *Social Security Bulletin: Annual Statistical Supplement, 1996,* prepublication release and previous editions, and State of Florida, Agency for Health Care Administration, unpublished data.

Table 7.16. MEDICAL ASSISTANCE: NUMBER OF RECIPIENTS BY AGE OF RECIPIENT IN FLORIDA, FISCAL YEAR 1994-95

Type of service	Total	Aged 5 and under	Aged 6 to 20	Aged 21 to 64	Aged 65 to 84	Aged 85 and over
Unduplicated total	1,735,141	483,064	493,175	517,696	180,899	60,307
Inpatient hospital	260,409	42,673	38,264	119,963	42,913	16,596
Mental hospital--aged	259	0	0	47	194	18
Intermediate care facilities	49,443	5	225	6,710	20,361	22,142
Skilled nursing facilities	61,654	40	80	5,704	27,670	28,160
Physician	1,333,994	402,754	373,697	406,723	118,532	32,288
Dental	339,475	81,498	188,171	38,186	21,780	9,840
Other practitioners	191,755	17,585	34,910	79,985	43,009	16,266
Outpatient hospital	672,683	180,283	149,916	239,623	80,799	22,062
Clinic	124,745	23,165	37,871	51,361	10,302	2,046
Home health	81,896	19,352	10,919	35,401	11,976	4,248
Family planning	123,824	208	39,084	84,217	258	57
Lab and X-ray	816,469	213,092	194,763	317,525	68,347	22,742
Prescribed drugs	1,111,466	314,258	251,303	344,194	151,617	50,094
Early and periodic screening	211,273	166,977	44,191	103	0	2
Rural health clinic	90,029	33,719	26,506	25,236	3,780	788
Other care	574,416	107,986	136,042	197,015	95,743	37,630

Note: Data are for fiscal year ending September 30.

Source: State of Florida, Agency for Health Care Administration, unpublished data.

Table 7.18. PUBLIC ASSISTANCE: AID TO FAMILIES WITH DEPENDENT CHILDREN (AFDC) PAYMENTS AND AVERAGE MONTHLY CASES IN THE STATE, DEPARTMENT OF HEALTH AND REHABILITATIVE SERVICES (HRS) DISTRICTS, AND COUNTIES OF FLORIDA, FISCAL YEAR 1994-95

District and county	Total		Regular		Unemployed parent	
	Amount (dollars)	Average monthly cases	Amount (dollars)	Average monthly cases	Amount (dollars)	Average monthly cases
Florida	723,843,738	234,487	709,753,349	230,662	14,090,389	3,825
District 1	29,914,285	9,813	29,060,545	9,576	853,740	237
Escambia	20,147,058	6,481	19,637,352	6,342	509,706	139
Okaloosa	4,191,205	1,445	4,085,434	1,416	105,771	29
Santa Rosa	3,942,046	1,336	3,770,662	1,286	171,384	50
Walton	1,633,976	551	1,567,097	532	66,879	19
District 2	35,712,849	11,908	34,724,663	11,637	988,186	271
Bay	6,980,897	2,304	6,841,487	2,265	139,410	39
Calhoun	1,093,241	354	1,022,654	335	70,587	19
Franklin	450,718	158	442,485	156	8,233	2
Gadsden	5,311,491	1,771	5,229,718	1,747	81,773	24
Gulf	860,355	288	810,388	274	49,967	14
Holmes	1,417,404	478	1,268,428	439	148,976	39
Jackson	2,557,713	874	2,463,789	846	93,924	28
Jefferson	1,174,576	389	1,153,282	384	21,294	5
Leon	10,412,895	3,473	10,252,152	3,431	160,743	42
Liberty	340,979	112	334,859	110	6,120	2
Madison	1,372,094	456	1,338,902	447	33,192	9
Taylor	1,533,745	505	1,487,669	493	46,076	12
Wakulla	991,991	335	940,824	319	51,167	16
Washington	1,214,750	411	1,138,026	391	76,724	20
District 3	32,930,628	10,596	32,028,751	10,356	901,877	240
Alachua	13,230,629	4,211	12,936,595	4,132	294,034	79
Bradford	2,118,279	696	2,035,971	674	82,308	22
Columbia	3,919,061	1,296	3,800,961	1,260	118,100	36
Dixie	1,005,023	328	978,027	321	26,996	7
Gilchrist	604,311	200	590,653	195	13,658	5
Hamilton	1,107,816	355	1,095,855	351	11,961	4
Lafayette 1/	0	0	0	0	0	0
Levy	2,024,858	665	1,936,667	644	88,191	21
Putnam	6,634,948	2,094	6,416,351	2,041	218,597	53
Suwannee	2,285,702	751	2,237,670	738	48,032	13
Union 2/	0	0	0	0	0	0
District 4	54,996,851	17,934	54,445,302	17,781	551,549	153
Baker	1,407,765	466	1,354,731	451	53,034	15
Clay	2,593,855	887	2,572,565	881	21,290	6
Duval	46,222,750	14,930	45,836,412	14,823	386,338	107
Nassau	1,810,543	649	1,773,371	638	37,172	11
St. Johns	2,961,938	1,002	2,908,223	988	53,715	14
District 5	45,587,221	14,911	44,200,889	14,541	1,386,332	370
Pasco	11,229,319	3,707	10,735,121	3,573	494,198	134
Pinellas	34,357,902	11,204	33,465,768	10,968	892,134	236
District 6	64,978,369	20,618	64,123,182	20,402	855,187	216
Hillsborough	56,188,781	17,762	55,491,918	17,588	696,863	174
Manatee	8,789,587	2,856	8,631,263	2,814	158,324	42

See footnote at end of table.   Continued . . .

Health and Rehabilitative Services Districts
Effective July 1, 1993

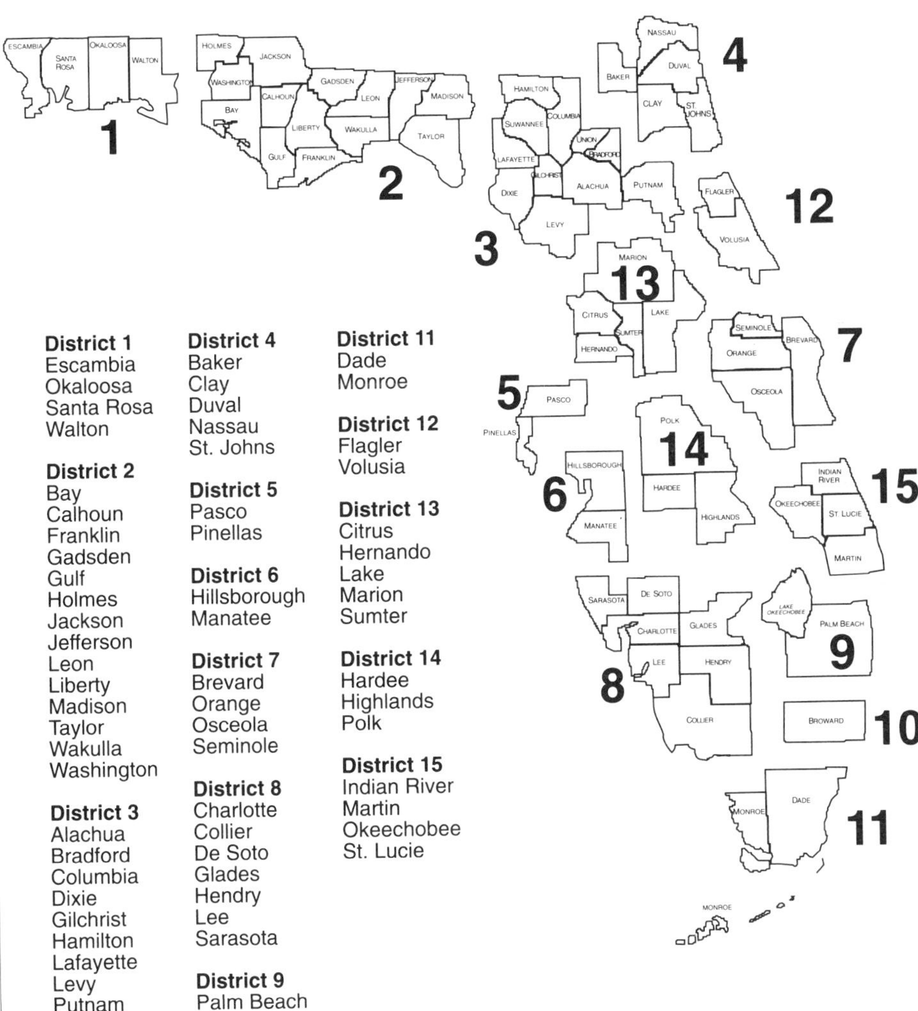

District 1
Escambia
Okaloosa
Santa Rosa
Walton

District 2
Bay
Calhoun
Franklin
Gadsden
Gulf
Holmes
Jackson
Jefferson
Leon
Liberty
Madison
Taylor
Wakulla
Washington

District 3
Alachua
Bradford
Columbia
Dixie
Gilchrist
Hamilton
Lafayette
Levy
Putnam
Suwannee
Union

District 4
Baker
Clay
Duval
Nassau
St. Johns

District 5
Pasco
Pinellas

District 6
Hillsborough
Manatee

District 7
Brevard
Orange
Osceola
Seminole

District 8
Charlotte
Collier
De Soto
Glades
Hendry
Lee
Sarasota

District 9
Palm Beach

District 10
Broward

District 11
Dade
Monroe

District 12
Flagler
Volusia

District 13
Citrus
Hernando
Lake
Marion
Sumter

District 14
Hardee
Highlands
Polk

District 15
Indian River
Martin
Okeechobee
St. Lucie

Table 7.18. PUBLIC ASSISTANCE: AID TO FAMILIES WITH DEPENDENT CHILDREN (AFDC) PAYMENTS AND AVERAGE MONTHLY CASES IN THE STATE, DEPARTMENT OF HEALTH AND REHABILITATIVE SERVICES (HRS) DISTRICTS, AND COUNTIES OF FLORIDA, FISCAL YEAR 1994-95 (Continued)

District and county	Total		Regular		Unemployed parent	
	Amount (dollars)	Average monthly cases	Amount (dollars)	Average monthly cases	Amount (dollars)	Average monthly cases
District 7	72,527,385	23,568	70,740,728	23,085	1,786,657	483
Brevard	15,895,151	5,268	15,315,901	5,108	579,250	160
Orange	38,758,020	12,450	38,237,392	12,306	520,628	144
Osceola	6,920,531	2,289	6,597,968	2,204	322,563	85
Seminole	10,953,684	3,561	10,589,468	3,467	364,216	94
District 8	29,133,679	9,560	28,603,702	9,423	529,977	137
Charlotte	2,322,066	791	2,245,033	771	77,033	20
Collier	5,076,937	1,671	5,026,846	1,658	50,091	13
De Soto	1,938,127	612	1,879,445	598	58,682	14
Glades 3/	0	0	0	0	0	0
Hendry	3,092,038	949	3,015,329	931	76,709	18
Lee	10,817,512	3,535	10,651,000	3,491	166,512	44
Sarasota	5,887,000	2,002	5,786,050	1,974	100,950	28
District 9	33,794,055	10,827	33,100,168	10,641	693,887	186
Palm Beach	33,794,055	10,827	33,100,168	10,641	693,887	186
District 10	55,199,816	17,964	54,583,724	17,793	616,092	171
Broward	55,199,816	17,964	54,583,724	17,793	616,092	171
District 11	169,554,291	54,239	167,444,482	53,642	2,109,809	597
Dade	167,160,542	53,425	165,073,507	52,835	2,087,035	590
Monroe	2,393,749	814	2,370,975	807	22,774	7
District 12	18,621,084	6,268	18,017,321	6,103	603,763	165
Flagler	1,547,128	525	1,439,856	497	107,272	28
Volusia	17,073,956	5,743	16,577,465	5,606	496,491	137
District 13	33,117,531	10,859	31,787,905	10,497	1,329,626	362
Citrus	4,165,195	1,395	3,918,001	1,329	247,194	66
Hernando	4,984,167	1,643	4,687,663	1,561	296,504	82
Lake	8,502,049	2,779	8,184,142	2,690	317,907	89
Marion	12,947,198	4,212	12,566,714	4,110	380,484	102
Sumter	2,518,922	830	2,431,385	807	87,537	23
District 14	31,339,546	10,098	30,817,986	9,957	521,560	141
Hardee	1,912,602	608	1,908,714	607	3,888	1
Highlands	3,507,998	1,149	3,470,480	1,138	37,518	11
Polk	25,918,946	8,341	25,438,792	8,212	480,154	129
District 15	16,436,149	5,324	16,074,002	5,228	362,147	96
Indian River	2,592,892	861	2,536,159	846	56,733	15
Martin	3,026,711	979	2,931,521	955	95,190	24
Okeechobee	1,554,202	529	1,517,447	519	36,755	10
St. Lucie	9,262,344	2,955	9,088,875	2,908	173,469	47

1/ Payments issued by Suwannee County.
2/ Payments issued by Bradford County.
3/ Payments issued by Hendry County.
Note: Detail may not add to total because of rounding.

Source: State of Florida, Department of Health and Rehabilitative Services, unpublished data.

Table 7.19. PUBLIC ASSISTANCE: RECIPIENTS OF SUPPLEMENTAL SECURITY INCOME AND AMOUNT OF PAYMENTS IN THE STATE AND COUNTIES OF FLORIDA
DECEMBER 1994 AND DECEMBER 1995

	Beneficiaries							
		Reason for eligibility						
		Adults			Children			
County	Total	Aged	Blind	Disabled	Blind	Disabled	Aged 65 and over	Payments ($1,000)
				December 1994				
Florida	317,038	96,622	2,966	166,160	315	50,975	129,948	104,001
Alachua	4,414	707	73	2,720	3	911	1,119	1,445
Baker	409	79	7	239	2	82	126	124
Bay	3,112	622	34	1,936	7	513	958	918
Bradford	648	137	9	403	1	98	230	196
Brevard	6,151	1,102	42	3,343	6	1,658	1,426	2,045
Broward	20,660	5,845	177	10,952	13	3,673	7,379	6,679
Calhoun	484	137	8	299	0	40	226	142
Charlotte	1,175	265	21	682	2	205	340	362
Citrus	1,235	259	12	785	2	177	358	331
Clay	989	178	12	561	1	237	256	306
Collier	1,649	429	20	906	0	294	587	523
Columbia	1,790	348	19	1,142	2	279	549	581
Dade	102,125	50,910	697	43,574	46	6,898	65,821	34,438
De Soto	659	152	7	356	3	141	202	214
Dixie	403	69	4	289	0	41	118	149
Duval	16,430	3,230	162	9,165	21	3,852	4,747	5,519
Escambia	7,657	1,347	95	4,709	19	1,487	2,087	2,635
Flagler	383	94	4	172	1	112	129	128
Franklin	407	123	5	227	1	51	189	121
Gadsden	2,576	589	26	1,434	2	525	903	734
Gilchrist	303	82	3	167	0	51	122	89
Glades	137	37	1	68	2	29	50	45
Gulf	332	79	2	231	0	20	141	92
Hamilton	570	175	7	324	0	64	250	175
Hardee	794	192	6	481	2	113	266	228
Hendry	529	126	7	276	0	120	179	157
Hernando	1,452	255	20	883	6	288	346	474
Highlands	1,709	330	17	941	5	416	469	550
Hillsborough	22,225	4,733	203	12,701	26	4,562	6,685	7,467
Holmes	764	252	12	434	0	66	376	206
Indian River	1,190	217	8	684	4	277	319	378
Jackson	2,061	619	14	1,205	3	220	917	581
Jefferson	620	221	6	305	1	87	300	178
Lafayette	164	41	1	104	0	18	59	46

Continued . . .

Table 7.19. PUBLIC ASSISTANCE: RECIPIENTS OF SUPPLEMENTAL SECURITY INCOME AND AMOUNT OF PAYMENTS IN THE STATE AND COUNTIES OF FLORIDA DECEMBER 1994 AND DECEMBER 1995 (Continued)

	Beneficiaries							
		Reason for eligibility						
		Adults			Children			
County	Total	Aged	Blind	Dis-abled	Blind	Dis-abled	Aged 65 and over	Payments ($1,000)
		December 1994 (Continued)						
Lake	3,106	623	23	1,713	3	744	874	947
Lee	4,642	771	58	2,873	8	932	1,100	1,479
Leon	3,434	739	65	1,948	8	674	1,072	1,055
Levy	780	189	6	462	0	123	287	229
Liberty	231	50	8	152	1	20	87	51
Madison	1,050	254	17	578	1	200	384	336
Manatee	3,018	524	33	1,734	5	722	742	1,014
Marion	5,003	929	58	2,909	3	1,104	1,359	1,595
Martin	1,189	232	11	635	2	309	319	383
Monroe	997	331	13	572	0	81	441	321
Nassau	698	135	7	452	1	103	210	237
Okaloosa	2,175	393	23	1,415	3	341	639	660
Okeechobee	761	136	10	439	0	176	202	251
Orange	15,695	3,161	148	8,523	15	3,848	4,366	5,447
Osceola	1,588	363	11	863	0	351	489	533
Palm Beach	11,549	3,130	128	5,879	17	2,395	4,036	3,779
Pasco	4,366	731	30	2,802	5	798	1,033	1,355
Pinellas	12,746	2,631	166	7,576	17	2,356	3,599	3,967
Polk	10,054	1,754	78	5,596	7	2,619	2,528	3,325
Putnam	2,327	423	27	1,450	4	423	630	758
St. Johns	1,564	317	26	924	5	292	448	457
St. Lucie	3,735	519	24	2,072	1	1,119	725	1,277
Santa Rosa	1,237	240	20	799	2	176	379	388
Sarasota	2,737	605	30	1,644	3	455	768	825
Seminole	3,720	830	30	1,986	6	868	1,140	1,171
Sumter	1,137	233	11	615	0	278	324	357
Suwannee	945	290	11	550	1	93	406	261
Taylor	680	154	1	385	0	140	243	224
Union	265	68	2	163	0	32	105	74
Volusia	6,884	1,245	118	4,214	12	1,295	1,774	2,202
Wakulla	362	95	6	207	0	54	144	103
Walton	797	226	10	490	1	70	345	217
Washington	809	211	12	515	2	69	365	260
Unknown	551	109	4	327	1	110	156	202

Continued . . .

Table 7.19. PUBLIC ASSISTANCE: RECIPIENTS OF SUPPLEMENTAL SECURITY INCOME AND AMOUNT OF PAYMENTS IN THE STATE AND COUNTIES OF FLORIDA DECEMBER 1994 AND DECEMBER 1995 (Continued)

County	Beneficiaries							Payments ($1,000)
		Reason for eligibility						
		Adults			Children		Aged	
	Total	Aged	Blind	Disabled	Blind	Disabled	65 and over	
				December 1995				
Florida	338,244	99,038	2,944	177,661	311	58,290	133,458	115,203
Alachua	4,511	665	74	2,776	3	993	1,065	1,464
Baker	437	76	5	262	1	93	122	149
Bay	3,239	600	33	2,029	6	571	968	1,071
Bradford	687	127	10	443	0	107	227	221
Brevard	6,675	1,109	42	3,688	7	1,829	1,469	2,307
Broward	22,346	6,220	183	11,750	16	4,177	7,872	7,545
Calhoun	464	118	8	293	0	45	209	147
Charlotte	1,245	281	16	716	2	230	361	395
Citrus	1,346	276	13	831	0	226	385	391
Clay	1,051	180	12	600	2	257	264	342
Collier	1,758	433	20	964	2	339	605	565
Columbia	1,876	330	17	1,212	2	315	536	623
Dade	108,002	53,116	732	46,069	46	8,039	68,423	37,378
De Soto	692	146	7	386	2	151	199	216
Dixie	454	77	4	309	1	63	129	165
Duval	17,356	3,178	164	9,656	15	4,343	4,713	6,048
Escambia	7,965	1,299	91	4,936	20	1,619	2,034	2,767
Flagler	410	89	5	195	0	121	125	137
Franklin	432	123	4	243	1	61	186	147
Gadsden	2,681	558	25	1,514	1	583	879	798
Gilchrist	322	82	5	189	0	46	127	101
Glades	127	31	1	65	2	28	42	39
Gulf	350	84	2	231	1	32	148	127
Hamilton	563	160	5	322	0	76	230	189
Hardee	823	189	6	506	3	119	265	240
Hendry	574	131	6	297	2	138	184	201
Hernando	1,581	262	21	983	4	311	366	550
Highlands	1,827	347	16	985	4	475	488	641
Hillsborough	23,681	4,725	207	13,642	25	5,082	6,770	8,411
Holmes	768	242	10	445	0	71	361	253
Indian River	1,243	213	7	720	4	299	320	376
Jackson	2,085	584	13	1,247	2	239	883	666
Jefferson	655	209	4	347	0	95	298	205
Lafayette	184	39	1	122	0	22	61	64

Continued . . .

Table 7.19. PUBLIC ASSISTANCE: RECIPIENTS OF SUPPLEMENTAL SECURITY INCOME AND AMOUNT OF PAYMENTS IN THE STATE AND COUNTIES OF FLORIDA DECEMBER 1994 AND DECEMBER 1995 (Continued)

	Beneficiaries							
		Reason for eligibility						
		Adults			Children			
County	Total	Aged	Blind	Disabled	Blind	Disabled	Aged 65 and over	Payments ($1,000)
	December 1995 (Continued)							
Lake	3,332	593	21	1,881	4	833	848	1,135
Lee	5,136	788	57	3,163	10	1,118	1,137	1,708
Leon	3,610	730	71	2,051	9	749	1,074	1,185
Levy	828	194	5	486	0	143	288	244
Liberty	234	43	4	165	1	21	75	71
Madison	1,110	241	13	638	1	217	375	375
Manatee	3,244	510	31	1,876	4	823	735	1,075
Marion	5,296	908	51	3,074	4	1,259	1,349	1,788
Martin	1,277	232	9	683	2	351	316	410
Monroe	1,058	323	13	626	0	96	437	366
Nassau	694	126	6	439	2	121	196	210
Okaloosa	2,310	387	19	1,498	4	402	637	801
Okeechobee	805	137	11	474	0	183	212	269
Orange	17,657	3,271	146	9,528	17	4,695	4,526	6,255
Osceola	1,738	379	14	934	1	410	521	594
Palm Beach	12,342	3,226	122	6,295	17	2,682	4,177	4,083
Pasco	4,877	763	29	3,177	4	904	1,058	1,656
Pinellas	13,759	2,613	159	8,200	17	2,770	3,632	4,549
Polk	10,899	1,744	79	6,001	6	3,069	2,545	3,727
Putnam	2,443	389	28	1,554	5	467	619	824
St. Johns	1,631	310	25	949	5	342	434	491
St. Lucie	4,005	539	23	2,211	1	1,231	758	1,453
Santa Rosa	1,321	253	18	848	2	200	392	416
Sarasota	2,957	640	30	1,783	3	501	806	927
Seminole	4,054	840	34	2,151	3	1,026	1,149	1,417
Sumter	1,253	226	9	670	0	348	318	416
Suwannee	1,004	277	10	612	1	104	405	273
Taylor	682	140	1	391	1	149	225	262
Union	264	70	2	163	0	29	98	75
Volusia	7,350	1,221	108	4,499	11	1,511	1,785	2,401
Wakulla	408	98	5	231	0	74	142	115
Walton	829	217	10	526	1	75	351	240
Washington	825	194	11	546	1	73	345	258
Unknown	602	117	1	365	0	119	179	194

Source: U.S., Department of Health and Human Services, Social Security Administration, *SSI Recipients by State and County,* December 1995, and previous edition.

Table 7.20. MEDICAID: RECIPIENTS AND EXPENDITURE IN THE STATE AND COUNTIES OF FLORIDA, FISCAL YEAR 1994-95

County	Recipients	Expenditure (dollars)	County	Recipients	Expenditure (dollars)
Florida	A/ 1,915,606	5,243,598,635	Lafayette	1,010	1,878,571
Other states 1/	17	48,712	Lake	24,585	55,665,946
Alachua	29,437	112,855,164	Lee	39,541	121,839,882
Baker	3,945	6,746,168	Leon	23,811	61,528,548
Bay	21,751	59,821,276	Levy	5,990	13,285,642
Bradford	4,619	14,152,562	Liberty	1,158	5,599,430
Brevard	46,018	113,895,852	Madison	4,008	10,064,153
Broward	150,684	371,259,256	Manatee	27,259	61,483,516
Calhoun	2,895	7,914,794	Marion	36,033	75,133,062
Charlotte	11,035	32,801,921	Martin	10,542	27,884,048
Citrus	13,339	32,647,935	Monroe	7,227	21,912,702
Clay	9,820	15,243,841	Nassau	5,953	11,233,203
Collier	20,937	39,328,631	Okaloosa	14,276	41,085,235
Columbia	10,628	27,355,105	Okeechobee	6,110	13,669,429
Dade	414,110	1,221,683,703	Orange	106,691	273,878,437
De Soto	6,199	14,966,288	Osceola	21,553	44,553,163
Dixie	3,040	4,694,381	Palm Beach	96,821	280,123,523
Duval	109,774	292,324,804	Pasco	39,640	89,080,522
Escambia	47,872	119,973,428	Pinellas	99,729	335,463,463
Flagler	4,195	7,418,432	Polk	72,788	152,190,508
Franklin	1,874	7,396,439	Putnam	16,158	34,660,852
Gadsden	12,295	30,196,644	St. Johns	11,538	31,031,806
Gilchrist	2,292	6,971,765	St. Lucie	23,037	64,936,103
Glades	169	681,304	Santa Rosa	31,503	24,214,915
Gulf	2,537	6,148,841	Sarasota	10,881	71,338,699
Hamilton	2,608	5,706,948	Seminole	27,430	68,608,563
Hardee	7,019	12,737,874	Sumter	6,899	13,533,975
Hendry	8,704	15,910,164	Suwannee	5,983	17,279,131
Hernando	14,343	32,522,493	Taylor	3,994	9,948,630
Highlands	11,446	28,837,395	Union	1,569	2,611,528
Hillsborough	142,919	319,645,986	Volusia	52,016	137,781,553
Holmes	4,776	11,487,699	Wakulla	2,756	7,509,923
Indian River	8,927	18,293,598	Walton	5,851	13,753,446
Jackson	7,980	38,002,077	Washington	4,372	11,414,431
Jefferson	2,941	7,750,611			

A/ Unduplicated total.
1/ Florida residents receiving treatment in Alabama or Georgia.
Note: A person may receive aid and be counted as a recipient in more than one county, therefore detail will not add to the state total.

Source: State of Florida, Agency for Health Care Administration, unpublished data.

Table 7.21. MEDICAID: PERSONS ELIGIBLE FOR MEDICAID, ALL AGES AND AGED 65 AND OVER, IN THE STATE, LOCAL HEALTH COUNCILS DISTRICTS AND COUNTIES OF FLORIDA, 1995

District and county	Total	Aged 65 and over Number	Aged 65 and over Percentage
Florida	1,561,469	244,509	15.7
Northwest--1	65,024	7,990	12.3
Escambia	40,245	4,437	11.0
Okaloosa	11,541	1,698	14.7
Santa Rosa	8,636	1,042	12.1
Walton	4,602	813	17.7
Big Bend--2	79,418	12,887	16.2
Bay	17,676	2,471	14.0
Calhoun	2,312	502	21.7
Franklin	1,407	371	26.4
Gadsden	10,517	1,536	14.6
Gulf	1,992	361	18.1
Holmes	3,739	819	21.9
Jackson	6,800	1,613	23.7
Jefferson	2,442	539	22.1
Leon	19,453	2,204	11.3
Liberty	891	151	16.9
Madison	3,308	687	20.8
Taylor	3,285	545	16.6
Wakulla	2,163	342	15.8
Washington	3,433	746	21.7
North Central--3	141,566	18,689	13.2
Alachua	24,703	2,396	9.7
Bradford	3,582	575	16.1
Citrus	10,258	1,717	16.7
Columbia	8,455	1,188	14.1
Dixie	2,201	268	12.2
Gilchrist	1,571	291	18.5
Hamilton	2,260	421	18.6
Hernando	10,917	1,322	12.1
Lafayette	807	98	12.1
Lake	19,245	2,668	13.9
Levy	4,541	738	16.3
Marion	28,649	3,676	12.8
Putnam	13,168	1,516	11.5
Sumter	5,537	719	13.0
Suwannee	4,466	941	21.1
Union	1,206	155	12.9
Northeast Central--4	146,999	18,714	12.7
Baker	2,796	216	7.7
Clay	6,431	561	8.7
Northeast Central--4 (Continued)			
Duval	83,993	10,664	12.7
Flagler	1,793	323	18.0
Nassau	4,019	431	10.7
St. Johns	7,637	1,211	15.9
Volusia	40,330	5,308	13.2
Suncoast--5	102,669	16,716	16.3
Pasco	27,569	3,746	13.6
Pinellas	75,100	12,970	17.3
West Central--6	201,273	24,008	11.9
Hardee	5,230	525	10.0
Highlands	8,506	1,210	14.2
Hillsborough	111,818	13,396	12.0
Manatee	19,872	2,343	11.8
Polk	55,847	6,534	11.7
East Central--7	156,657	18,650	11.9
Brevard	35,919	4,196	11.7
Orange	82,183	9,809	11.9
Osceola	15,548	1,919	12.3
Seminole	23,007	2,726	11.8
Southwest--8	77,291	10,702	13.8
Charlotte	7,534	1,410	18.7
Collier	14,531	1,451	10.0
De Soto	4,211	481	11.4
Glades	142	44	31.0
Hendry	5,960	553	9.3
Lee	28,263	3,581	12.7
Sarasota	16,650	3,182	19.1
Treasure Coast--9	110,858	14,347	12.9
Indian River	6,633	1,014	15.3
Martin	7,617	1,111	14.6
Okeechobee	3,998	526	13.2
Palm Beach	72,624	9,710	13.4
St. Lucie	19,986	1,986	9.9
Broward Regional--10	111,757	13,705	12.3
Broward	111,757	13,705	12.3
South--11	367,957	88,101	23.9
Dade	362,338	87,123	24.0
Monroe	5,619	978	17.4

Note: Local health councils were established in 1982 by the legislature to serve 11 planning districts throughout the state. These councils are responsible for establishing and maintaining the district health plans.

Source: State of Florida, Agency for Health Care Administration, *Florida 1996 Health Data SourceBook*. Compiled by Local Health Councils of Florida.

Table 7.22. FOOD STAMPS: RECIPIENTS AND BENEFITS IN THE STATE AND COUNTIES OF FLORIDA, DECEMBER 1995

County	Recipients: Total	Recipients: Receiving public assistance	Benefits in food stamps ($1,000)
Florida	1,401,472	634,147	111,222
Alachua	21,835	10,880	1,708
Baker	2,853	1,239	211
Bay	16,450	6,197	1,217
Bradford	3,764	1,527	284
Brevard	32,734	13,039	2,566
Broward	94,414	44,721	7,910
Calhoun	1,916	784	138
Charlotte	6,127	1,870	444
Citrus	10,184	3,430	763
Clay	5,073	1,955	394
Collier	12,537	3,830	985
Columbia	7,969	3,347	608
Dade	357,540	177,432	29,315
De Soto	4,277	1,479	319
Dixie	2,272	868	160
Duval	69,746	36,485	5,640
Escambia	35,471	16,142	2,606
Flagler	2,964	1,292	224
Franklin	945	381	69
Gadsden	9,976	4,161	697
Gilchrist	1,366	517	97
Glades 1/	(X)	(X)	(X)
Gulf	1,900	720	139
Hamilton	1,842	848	133
Hardee	5,077	1,588	394
Hendry 1/	6,091	2,260	462
Hernando	10,666	4,114	818
Highlands	7,315	3,097	556
Hillsborough	96,644	46,771	7,864
Holmes	3,799	1,302	257
Indian River	5,437	2,085	423
Jackson	5,179	2,150	352
Jefferson	2,318	961	160
Lafayette	739	276	51
Lake	16,348	6,792	1,217
Lee	23,269	9,159	1,771
Leon	18,230	8,614	1,488
Levy	4,225	1,709	302
Liberty	709	254	47
Madison	2,580	1,173	166
Manatee	16,765	6,219	1,333
Marion	27,253	11,267	1,985
Martin	6,093	2,443	500
Monroe	4,805	1,787	398
Nassau	3,056	1,101	233
Okaloosa	9,631	3,580	698
Okeechobee	3,163	1,125	230
Orange	71,190	32,121	5,613
Osceola	14,883	5,777	1,200
Palm Beach	60,191	26,177	4,908
Pasco	24,957	9,717	1,928
Pinellas	61,921	28,231	4,952
Polk	51,241	23,098	4,091
Putnam	12,560	5,436	927
St. Johns	6,250	2,448	488
St. Lucie	17,217	7,663	1,350
Santa Rosa	7,236	2,879	534
Sarasota	12,753	4,615	967
Seminole	19,473	8,622	1,549
Sumter	5,990	2,414	417
Suwannee	3,937	1,669	291
Taylor	3,219	1,264	222
Union	1,159	553	87
Volusia	34,882	15,005	2,752
Wakulla	1,839	769	132
Walton	3,906	1,520	273
Washington	3,121	1,198	211

(X) Not applicable.

1/ No food stamp issuance office located in Glades County. Food stamp activities are handled in Hendry County.

Note: Figures represent regular participation. Issuance includes duplicate mail issuance. Data shown in previous *Abstracts* were cumulative and should not be compared with these data.

Source: State of Florida, Department of Health and Rehabilitative Services, Office of Economic Services, *Florida Food Stamp Program Participation Statistics for State Fiscal Year 1995-1996*.

Table 7.56. AVERAGE WEEKLY WAGES: AMOUNT RECEIVED BY PERSONS COVERED BY UNEMPLOYMENT COMPENSATION LAW IN FLORIDA, 1957 THROUGH 1995

(in dollars)

Year	Average weekly wages 1/	Year	Average weekly wages 1/	Year	Average weekly wages 1/
1957	71.22	1970	129.33	1983	288.34
1958	74.43	1971	131.97	1984	306.55
1959	78.28	1972	138.02	1985	314.88
1960	80.89	1973	143.30	1986	329.60
1961	82.64	1974	155.82	1987	344.32
1962	85.50	1975	167.02	1988	362.41
1963	88.23	1976	175.27	1989	382.00
1964	92.54	1977	185.69	1990	392.18
1965	96.34	1978	195.01	1991	408.82
1966	100.25	1979	210.73	1992	424.66
1967	104.80	1980	227.97	1993	443.95
1968	111.71	1981	252.92	1994	453.38
1969	122.57	1982	271.25	1995	465.23

1/ Data prior to 1972 do not include state, local, or federal government figures. Beginning in 1972 state data were included, and beginning in 1974 local data were included. Does not include federal data after 1974. Data are for fiscal years from 1971 to date; data are for calendar years prior to 1971.

Note: In 1972 and 1978 changes were made extending coverage of workers.

Table 7.57. UNEMPLOYMENT INSURANCE: CONTRIBUTIONS AND DISBURSEMENTS FOR UNEMPLOYMENT INSURANCE IN FLORIDA, 1957 THROUGH 1995

(rounded to thousands of dollars)

Year	Contributions deposits 1/	Total disbursements 2/	Year	Contributions deposits 1/	Total disbursements 2/	Year	Contributions deposits 1/	Total disbursements 2/
1957	19,005	13,941	1970	48,594	37,306	1983	451,459	406,075
1958	20,118	28,559	1971	57,425	49,704	1984	526,691	279,457
1959	36,721	22,484	1972	71,799	45,441	1985	514,281	277,463
1960	34,766	31,925	1973	85,861	44,962	1986	478,859	315,337
1961	41,970	43,830	1974	99,304	117,453	1987	469,296	285,736
1962	52,392	33,201	1975	263,243	496,688	1988	468,348	304,930
1963	45,079	29,652	1976	342,166	407,060	1989	480,211	355,749
1964	45,956	24,492	1977	360,650	271,917	1990	461,103	488,961
1965	45,160	20,273	1978	424,988	136,723	1991	560,898	897,263
1966	40,720	17,410	1979	389,370	135,457	1992	1,275,490	1,512,423
1967	37,029	20,639	1980	321,578	197,981	1993	1,259,207	1,199,657
1968	34,094	22,343	1981	305,028	206,012	1994	927,283	801,120
1969	42,145	20,875	1982	326,706	379,067	1995	694,134	632,215

1/ Includes interest, reimbursable interstate and state and local government benefits.

2/ Includes payable interstate benefits.

Source for Tables 7.56 and 7.57: State of Florida, Department of Labor and Employment Security, Division of Employment Security, *Historical Series of Unemployment Insurance Statistical Data, 1937-1979*, and State of Florida, Department of Labor and Employment Security, Division of Unemployment Compensation, unpublished data.

Table 7.58. UNEMPLOYMENT INSURANCE: SPECIFIED DATA FOR FLORIDA 1991, 1992, and 1993

Item	1991	1992	1993
Covered employment			
Average monthly number of workers (1,000)	5,185	5,243	5,463
Total payroll ($1,000,000)	112,764	119,900	127,151
Insured unemployment as percentage of covered employment	2.3	2.4	2.2
Number of first payments	352,661	339,288	276,244
Average weekly benefit for total unemployment			
Amount (dollars)	157.69	158.01	167.16
Percentage of average weekly wages	37.7	36.4	37.3
Weeks compensated for all unemployment (1,000)	5,297	(NA)	(NA)
Average weekly insured unemployment	(NA)	126,952	122,519
Average actual duration (weeks)	15.0	16.3	15.2
Claimants exhausting benefits			
Number (1,000)	158	191	148
Percentage of first payments	49.6	54.0	51.0
Contributions collected ($1,000,000)	305.3	468.7	618.3
Benefits paid ($1,000,000)	822.5	860.7	697.0
Funds available for benefits at end of year ($1,000,000)	1,624.4	(NA)	(NA)
Average employer contribution rate 1/	1.0	1.5	1.8

(NA) Not available.

1/ As a percentage of taxable payroll. The standard contribution rate for most states is 2.7 percent.

Source: U.S., Department of Health and Human Services, Social Security Administration, *Social Security Bulletin: Annual Statistical Supplement, 1995,* and previous editions.

Table 7.59. WORKERS' COMPENSATION: ESTIMATES OF PAYMENTS BY TYPE OF INSURANCE IN FLORIDA, 1991, 1992, AND 1993

(in thousands of dollars)

Item	1991	1992	1993
Total	1,960,860	1,860,758	1,704,939
Insurance losses paid by private insurance carriers 1/	1,225,860	1,163,280	1,065,867
State and federal fund disbursements 2/	0	0	0
Self-insurance payments 3/	735,000	697,478	639,072
Percentage change in total payments from previous year	-0.8	-5.1	-8.4

1/ Net cash and medical benefits paid during the calendar year by private insurance carriers under standard workers' compensation policies. Data primarily from A.M. Best Company.

2/ Net cash and medical benefits paid by state funds compiled from state reports (published and unpublished).

3/ Cash and medical benefits paid by self-insurers, plus the value of medical benefits paid by employers carrying workers' compensation policies that do not include standard medical coverage. Estimated from available state data.

Source: U.S., Department of Health and Human Services, Social Security Administration, *Social Security Bulletin,* Summer 1994.

Table 7.60. WORKERS' COMPENSATION: NUMBER OF INJURIES AND PAYMENTS IN THE STATE AND COUNTIES OF FLORIDA, 1995

County	Work injuries	Payments (dollars) Total	Medical	Indemnity	Settlement
Florida	70,648	342,983,081	205,458,018	118,209,749	19,315,314
Alachua	796	3,249,879	1,813,840	1,215,939	220,100
Baker	95	472,511	277,413	157,718	37,380
Bay	639	2,876,734	1,859,280	883,547	133,907
Bradford	92	339,731	214,994	123,738	1,000
Brevard	2,069	9,238,154	5,271,310	3,552,187	414,657
Broward	5,958	33,330,067	20,485,426	10,791,300	2,053,341
Calhoun	32	180,439	125,006	52,433	3,000
Charlotte	491	2,575,033	1,584,601	853,209	137,223
Citrus	372	1,571,893	928,661	627,231	16,000
Clay	364	1,584,601	922,547	598,082	63,972
Collier	1,279	6,756,877	4,025,926	2,357,463	373,488
Columbia	128	631,826	379,077	214,999	37,750
Dade	9,108	44,538,594	26,705,542	15,084,645	2,748,406
De Soto	159	1,084,518	719,094	253,175	112,250
Dixie	36	326,020	194,316	131,704	0
Duval	3,725	19,890,575	12,181,007	6,925,139	784,430
Escambia	1,065	4,366,800	2,557,597	1,688,137	121,066
Flagler	174	931,995	560,424	330,171	41,400
Franklin	36	182,805	109,812	72,994	0
Gadsden	243	831,905	443,095	321,811	67,000
Gilchrist	41	141,334	70,742	65,392	5,200
Glades	32	218,827	138,922	64,905	15,000
Gulf	53	613,834	483,649	130,185	0
Hamilton	56	299,457	183,547	102,410	13,500
Hardee	158	847,346	511,986	216,262	119,098
Hendry	307	1,465,733	854,444	482,694	128,595
Hernando	505	2,317,702	1,360,549	786,644	170,509
Highlands	349	1,892,046	1,147,083	561,763	183,200
Hillsborough	4,389	19,672,304	11,758,742	6,953,522	960,039
Holmes	45	180,451	125,593	42,321	12,537
Indian River	563	3,723,281	2,133,774	1,202,466	387,041
Jackson	210	883,329	550,155	310,674	22,500
Jefferson	27	198,550	99,839	92,967	5,745
Lafayette	25	128,417	95,364	32,303	750
Lake	733	3,345,294	2,085,047	1,164,146	96,100
Lee	1,793	8,180,605	5,175,037	2,800,559	205,009

See footnote at end of table.		Continued . . .

Table 7.60. WORKERS' COMPENSATION: NUMBER OF INJURIES AND PAYMENTS IN THE STATE AND COUNTIES OF FLORIDA, 1995 (Continued)

County	Work injuries	Payments (dollars)			
		Total	Medical	Indemnity	Settlement
Leon	825	3,233,366	1,898,255	1,251,061	84,050
Levy	114	684,846	447,053	226,043	11,750
Liberty	33	140,654	89,423	51,231	0
Madison	80	282,218	185,317	96,901	0
Manatee	945	3,564,115	2,101,272	1,265,119	197,725
Marion	1,117	5,211,728	3,008,557	1,830,896	372,275
Martin	629	3,789,902	2,133,452	1,390,129	266,321
Monroe	458	2,559,415	1,567,158	934,977	57,280
Nassau	193	947,639	519,761	336,678	91,200
Okaloosa	663	2,982,735	1,764,148	1,063,070	155,517
Okeechobee	208	909,074	562,278	281,096	65,700
Orange	5,833	27,129,672	15,732,173	9,201,934	2,195,565
Osceola	582	2,270,467	1,244,800	813,648	212,019
Palm Beach	4,698	25,393,733	14,741,233	9,274,964	1,377,536
Pasco	1,012	4,806,916	2,945,998	1,632,390	228,528
Pinellas	3,408	15,418,088	9,574,516	5,314,486	529,086
Polk	1,888	9,268,403	5,449,592	3,249,282	569,528
Putnam	268	1,712,777	1,149,986	510,648	52,143
St. Johns	372	1,659,954	947,337	624,316	88,300
St. Lucie	794	4,630,874	2,898,076	1,536,851	195,947
Santa Rosa	283	1,707,750	1,142,282	500,147	65,321
Sarasota	1,457	5,825,948	3,529,115	2,052,958	243,876
Seminole	1,154	4,977,826	2,890,823	1,595,175	491,828
Sumter	127	562,401	350,117	195,034	17,250
Suwannee	123	806,033	560,288	204,245	41,500
Taylor	94	992,618	779,264	207,122	6,232
Union	70	384,880	184,071	151,808	49,000
Volusia	1,612	8,002,168	4,797,894	2,702,544	501,729
Wakulla	57	249,708	114,371	90,937	44,400
Walton	138	715,187	467,568	222,619	25,000
Washington	61	441,125	185,162	105,963	150,000
Out-of-state	651	4,579,266	2,301,363	2,008,151	269,752
Unknown	4,554	18,072,126	11,061,871	6,042,490	967,764

Note: Injuries are reported on a place-of-occurrence basis.

Source: State of Florida, Department of Labor and Employment Security, Division of Workers' Compensation, Workers' Compensation Research and Education Unit, *1995 Report on Occupational Injuries.*

Table 7.61. WORKERS' COMPENSATION: NUMBER OF WORK INJURIES BY ACCIDENT TYPE AND BY INDUSTRY IN FLORIDA, 1995

Industry 1/	Total	Struck by or caught in	Slips/ falls	Cut	Motor Vehi- cle	Strain/ sprain	Strik- ing against	Other 2/
Total	70,648	9,326	18,317	3,824	3,565	25,178	2,684	7,754
Agriculture, forestry, and fishing	3,284	482	885	283	198	842	165	429
Mining	96	12	22	7	10	29	3	13
Construction	8,760	1,349	2,389	696	319	2,831	328	848
Building construction, general contractors	1,592	248	500	151	34	485	57	117
Construction, special trade contractors	6,005	826	1,656	494	213	1,981	223	612
Manufacturing	6,497	1,158	1,196	559	205	2,262	246	871
Food and kindred products	822	117	183	55	39	306	28	94
Transportation, communications, and public utilities	4,798	651	958	129	387	2,051	194	428
Motor freight transportation and warehousing	2,223	293	446	56	203	982	80	163
Wholesale and retail trade	14,747	1,863	4,298	988	568	5,019	498	1,513
Wholesale trade	3,159	539	719	127	176	1,158	126	314
Food stores	2,720	371	684	237	30	1,065	81	252
Eating and drinking places	3,973	309	1,733	392	96	809	118	516
Finance, insurance, and real estate	2,308	245	619	68	123	881	75	297
Real estate	1,181	151	348	54	35	436	53	104
Services	16,859	1,922	4,491	665	857	6,471	630	1,823
Business services	5,208	712	1,374	319	310	1,678	218	597
Health services	4,410	359	1,050	57	244	2,179	122	399
Government	9,311	1,100	2,424	248	706	3,347	410	1,076
Establishments, NEC	3,988	544	1,035	181	192	1,445	135	456

NEC Not elsewhere classified.
1/ Major industry group totals include data for industries not shown separately.
2/ Includes burn or scald and contact with injuries and injuries reported with no accident type given.

Source: State of Florida, Department of Labor and Employment Security, Division of Workers' Compensation, Workers' Compensation Research and Education Unit, *1995 Report on Occupational Injuries*.

PHYSICAL GEOGRAPHY AND ENVIRONMENT

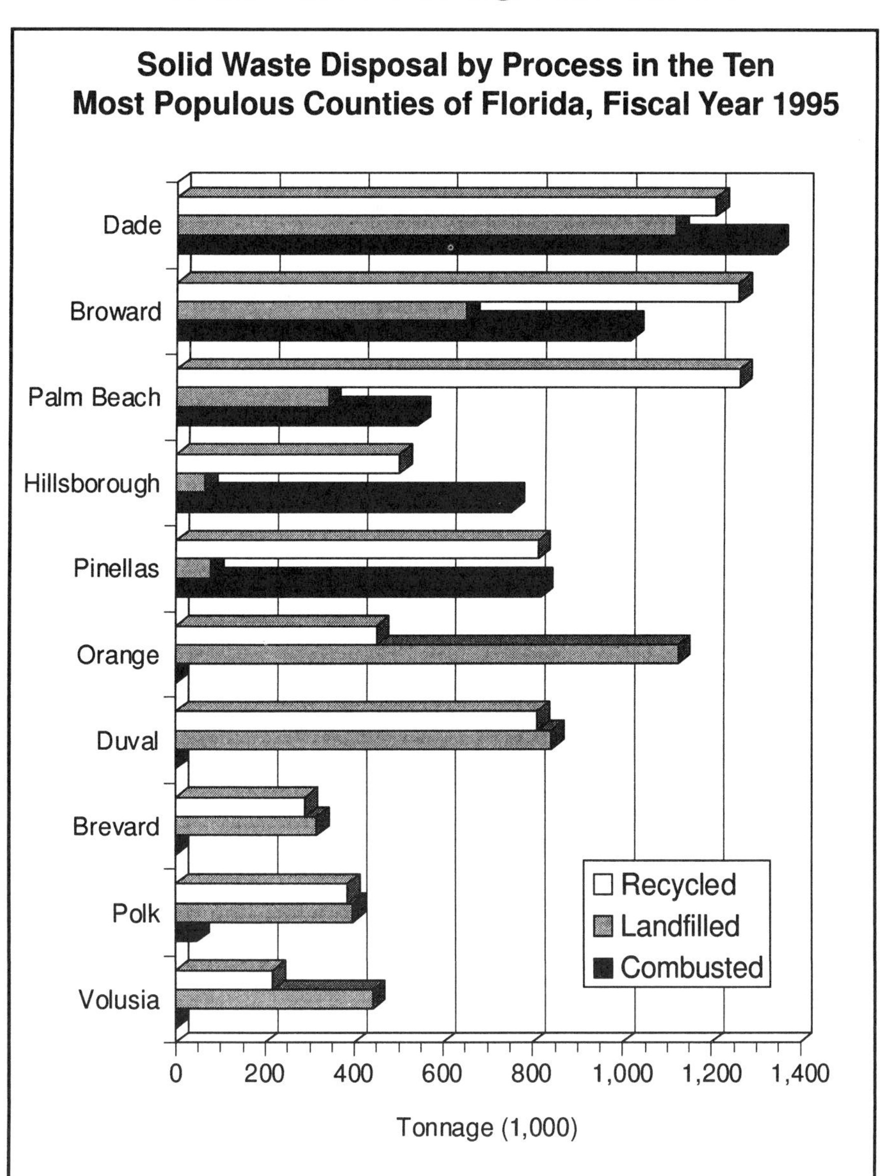

Source: Table 8.15

SECTION 8.00
PHYSICAL GEOGRAPHY AND ENVIRONMENT

TABLES LISTED BY MAJOR HEADINGS

Table 8.01. GEOGRAPHY: LAND AND WATER AREAS, COASTLINE, AND ELEVATIONS OF FLORIDA OTHER SUNBELT STATES, OTHER POPULOUS STATES, AND THE UNITED STATES, 1990

State	Area (square miles)			Coastline (statute miles)		Elevation (feet)		
	Total	Land 1/	Water 2/	General coast-line 3/	Tidal shore-line 4/	High-est	Low-est	Ap-prox-imate mean
			Sunbelt states					
Florida	59,928	53,937	5,991	1,350	8,426	345	A/	100
Alabama	52,237	50,750	1,486	53	607	2,405	A/	500
Arizona	114,006	113,642	364	0	0	12,633	70	4,100
Arkansas	53,182	52,075	1,107	0	0	2,753	55	650
California	158,869	155,973	2,895	840	3,427	14,494	-282	2,900
Georgia	58,977	57,919	1,058	100	2,344	4,784	A/	600
Louisiana	49,651	43,566	6,085	397	7,721	535	-8	100
Mississippi	48,286	46,914	1,372	44	359	806	A/	300
New Mexico	121,598	121,364	234	0	0	13,161	2,842	5,700
North Carolina	52,672	48,718	3,954	301	3,375	6,684	A/	700
Oklahoma	69,903	68,679	1,224	0	0	4,973	289	1,300
South Carolina	31,189	30,111	1,078	187	2,876	3,560	A/	350
Tennessee	42,146	41,219	926	0	0	6,643	178	900
Texas	267,277	261,914	5,363	367	3,359	8,749	A/	1,700
Virginia	42,326	39,598	2,729	112	3,315	5,729	A/	950
			Other populous states					
Illinois	57,918	55,593	2,325	0	0	1,235	279	600
Indiana	36,420	35,870	550	0	0	1,257	320	700
Massachusetts	9,241	7,838	1,403	192	1,519	3,487	A/	500
Michigan	96,705	56,809	39,895	0	0	1,979	571	900
New Jersey	8,215	7,419	796	130	1,792	1,803	A/	250
New York	53,989	47,224	6,766	127	1,850	5,344	A/	1,000
Ohio	44,828	40,953	3,875	0	0	1,549	455	850
Pennsylvania	46,058	44,820	1,239	0	89	3,213	A/	1,100
United States	3,717,796	3,536,278	181,518	12,383	88,633	20,320	-282	2,500

A/ Sea level.

1/ Dry land and land temporarily or partially covered by water, as marshland and swamps.

2/ Includes inland and coastal waters. In 1990, inland water was defined as lakes, reservoirs, ponds and rivers, canals, estuaries, and bays from the point downstream at which they are narrower than one nautical mile to the point upstream where they appear as a single line feature on the Census Bureau's TIGER File. Coastal water is within embayments separated from territorial waters by 1 to 24 nautical miles. Excludes territorial waters (waters between the 3-mile limit and the shoreline).

3/ Figures are lengths of general outline of seacoast. Unit of measure is 30 minutes of latitude on charts at approximate scale of 1:1,200,000.

4/ Figures are lengths of shoreline of outer coast, offshore islands, sounds, bays, rivers, and creeks to the head of tidewater, and were obtained in 1961.

Note: Some data are revised.

Source: U.S., Department of Commerce, Bureau of the Census, *Statistical Abstract of the United States, 1996,* U.S., Department of Commerce, Geography Division, unpublished data, and U.S., Department of Commerce, National Oceanic and Atmospheric Administration, unpublished data.

Table 8.03. LAND AND WATER AREA: AREA OF THE STATE AND COUNTIES OF FLORIDA, APRIL 1, 1990

(square miles)

County	Total 1/	Land area	Water area 1/ Total	Inland	Coastal	Terri-torial
Florida	65,758.1	53,937.0	11,821.1	4,682.9	1,308.1	5,830.0
Alachua	969.2	874.3	94.9	94.9	0.0	0.0
Baker	588.9	585.3	3.7	3.7	0.0	0.0
Bay	1,033.4	763.7	269.6	118.9	0.0	150.7
Bradford	300.1	293.2	6.9	6.9	0.0	0.0
Brevard	1,557.3	1,018.5	538.8	276.0	0.0	262.8
Broward	1,319.7	1,208.9	110.9	12.7	0.0	98.2
Calhoun	574.4	567.4	7.0	7.0	0.0	0.0
Charlotte	859.3	693.7	165.6	122.4	0.0	43.2
Citrus	773.2	583.6	189.6	79.8	0.0	109.8
Clay	643.7	601.1	42.6	42.6	0.0	0.0
Collier	2,305.1	2,025.5	279.6	91.0	0.0	188.7
Columbia	801.1	797.2	4.0	4.0	0.0	0.0
Dade	2,429.6	1,944.5	485.1	76.8	199.8	208.5
De Soto	639.6	637.3	2.2	2.2	0.0	0.0
Dixie	863.7	704.1	159.7	20.4	0.0	139.2
Duval	918.3	773.9	144.4	75.7	0.0	68.8
Escambia	893.9	663.6	230.3	88.1	0.0	142.2
Flagler	570.8	485.0	85.8	22.6	0.0	63.1
Franklin	1,026.5	534.0	492.5	32.1	198.9	261.5
Gadsden	528.5	516.2	12.4	12.4	0.0	0.0
Gilchrist	355.5	348.9	6.6	6.6	0.0	0.0
Glades	986.2	773.5	212.7	212.7	0.0	0.0
Gulf	755.8	565.1	190.7	17.9	65.3	107.6
Hamilton	519.4	514.9	4.5	4.5	0.0	0.0
Hardee	638.4	637.4	1.0	1.0	0.0	0.0
Hendry	1,189.9	1,152.7	37.2	37.2	0.0	0.0
Hernando	589.1	478.3	110.8	23.7	0.0	87.1
Highlands	1,106.4	1,028.5	77.9	77.9	0.0	0.0
Hillsborough	1,266.4	1,051.0	215.3	39.7	155.9	19.8
Holmes	488.8	482.6	6.2	6.2	0.0	0.0
Indian River	617.0	503.3	113.7	36.8	0.0	76.9
Jackson	954.7	915.8	38.9	38.9	0.0	0.0
Jefferson	636.7	597.8	38.9	15.4	0.0	23.5
Lafayette	548.0	542.8	5.1	5.1	0.0	0.0
Lake	1,156.5	953.1	203.4	203.4	0.0	0.0
Lee	1,212.0	803.6	408.4	236.5	6.1	165.9

See footnote at end of table.

Continued . . .

Table 8.03. LAND AND WATER AREA: AREA OF THE STATE AND COUNTIES OF FLORIDA, APRIL 1, 1990 (Continued)

(square miles)

County	Total 1/	Land area	Water area 1/ Total	Inland	Coastal	Terri-torial
Leon	701.8	666.8	35.0	35.0	0.0	0.0
Levy	1,412.4	1,118.4	294.0	46.9	0.0	247.1
Liberty	843.2	835.9	7.3	7.3	0.0	0.0
Madison	715.9	692.0	23.9	23.9	0.0	0.0
Manatee	892.8	741.2	151.6	55.2	46.7	49.8
Marion	1,663.1	1,579.0	84.1	84.1	0.0	0.0
Martin	752.9	555.7	197.2	121.4	0.0	75.8
Monroe	3,737.4	997.3	2,740.2	406.8	540.6	1,792.8
Nassau	725.9	651.6	74.3	18.5	0.0	55.7
Okaloosa	1,082.1	935.8	146.3	59.8	0.0	86.5
Okeechobee	892.0	774.3	117.7	117.7	0.0	0.0
Orange	1,004.3	907.6	96.7	96.7	0.0	0.0
Osceola	1,506.5	1,322.0	184.5	184.5	0.0	0.0
Palm Beach	2,386.5	1,974.2	412.3	256.3	0.0	156.0
Pasco	868.0	745.0	123.0	23.1	0.0	99.9
Pinellas	607.8	280.2	327.6	65.4	94.9	167.3
Polk	2,010.2	1,874.9	135.3	135.3	0.0	0.0
Putnam	827.2	722.2	105.1	105.1	0.0	0.0
St. Johns	821.5	609.0	212.4	64.0	0.0	148.4
St. Lucie	688.1	572.5	115.6	43.3	0.0	72.3
Santa Rosa	1,155.3	1,015.8	139.5	128.7	0.0	10.8
Sarasota	725.3	571.8	153.5	34.2	0.0	119.3
Seminole	344.9	308.2	36.7	36.7	0.0	0.0
Sumter	580.4	545.7	34.7	34.7	0.0	0.0
Suwannee	691.9	687.7	4.3	4.3	0.0	0.0
Taylor	1,232.1	1,042.0	190.1	13.5	0.0	176.6
Union	249.7	240.3	9.4	9.4	0.0	0.0
Volusia	1,432.5	1,105.9	326.6	159.0	0.0	167.7
Wakulla	735.8	606.7	129.1	32.9	0.0	96.2
Walton	1,238.1	1,057.7	180.5	90.1	0.0	90.3
Washington	615.8	579.9	36.0	36.0	0.0	0.0

1/ Water area measurement figures in the 1990 census data reflect all water, including inland, coastal, territorial, new reservoirs, and other man-made lakes. Measurement figures reported in previous censuses were only for inland water; the total water area of the state has increased substantially. See note on Table 8.01 for definitions of inland, coastal, and territorial waters.

Source: U.S., Department of Commerce, Bureau of the Census, Geography Division, unpublished data.

Table 8.15. SOLID WASTE: TONNAGE BY DISPOSAL PROCESS AND PER CAPITA AMOUNT IN THE STATE AND COUNTIES OF FLORIDA FISCAL YEARS 1994 AND 1995

County	Disposal process 1/ Recycled		Landfilled		Combusted		Per capita tons 2/	
	1994	1995	1994	1995	1994	1995	1994	1995
Florida	8,607.8	9,714.7	9,661.9	9,214.5	5,291.3	5,382.6	1.70	1.72
Alachua	96.1	119.8	150.0	135.7	1.1	0.0	1.28	1.29
Baker	2.2	3.7	14.1	15.4	0.0	0.0	0.83	0.94
Bay	48.2	41.9	34.7	17.2	156.3	146.5	1.75	1.48
Bradford	2.0	4.9	15.9	14.4	0.0	0.0	0.74	0.79
Brevard	276.8	290.7	309.4	317.2	0.0	0.0	1.34	1.37
Broward	1,021.6	1,260.3	417.1	652.6	996.6	1,016.5	1.82	2.15
Calhoun	1.6	1.7	0.3	0.2	4.3	4.8	0.53	0.55
Charlotte	66.1	80.0	86.6	89.5	0.0	0.0	1.22	1.33
Citrus	47.3	65.6	120.4	141.5	0.0	0.0	1.63	1.96
Clay	35.8	32.8	81.6	77.9	0.0	0.0	1.00	0.92
Collier	145.2	123.5	189.1	160.5	0.0	0.0	1.85	1.52
Columbia	2.8	3.4	48.7	43.9	0.0	0.0	1.05	0.94
Dade	1,134.2	1,207.8	1,191.4	1,116.9	1,357.8	1,342.4	1.85	1.82
De Soto	3.9	3.5	16.8	15.7	0.0	0.6	0.79	0.74
Dixie	1.1	0.5	6.6	7.9	0.0	0.0	0.63	0.67
Duval	635.1	810.9	814.3	843.4	0.0	0.0	2.04	2.30
Escambia	126.5	94.7	316.0	299.9	0.0	0.0	1.60	1.40
Flagler	6.9	8.2	23.0	26.2	0.0	0.0	0.85	0.93
Franklin	0.8	0.8	1.4	1.6	6.7	8.4	0.88	1.05
Gadsden	11.5	13.5	29.1	31.4	0.0	0.0	0.91	1.00
Gilchrist	0.3	0.4	3.7	4.3	0.0	0.0	0.35	0.39
Glades	1.8	1.5	5.1	7.6	0.0	0.0	0.83	1.07
Gulf	2.8	3.7	5.5	10.1	5.7	6.5	1.06	1.53
Hamilton	0.4	1.7	7.7	6.8	0.0	0.0	0.68	0.68
Hardee	5.1	3.4	15.4	18.6	0.0	0.0	0.91	0.96
Hendry	4.7	2.3	27.1	10.3	0.0	22.3	1.11	1.18
Hernando	35.0	38.0	29.1	30.3	48.9	50.4	0.98	1.01
Highlands	34.2	39.1	70.6	69.5	0.0	0.0	1.38	1.41
Hillsborough	495.8	501.9	77.7	63.5	736.6	752.5	1.49	1.48
Holmes	0.4	0.4	7.6	7.6	0.0	0.0	0.47	0.46
Indian River	28.1	46.1	108.5	124.7	1.2	0.9	1.41	1.71
Jackson	3.5	1.2	26.1	26.8	0.0	0.0	0.65	0.60
Jefferson	1.0	1.2	8.5	8.3	0.0	0.0	0.72	0.70
Lafayette	0.4	0.4	1.3	1.8	0.0	0.0	0.29	0.35
Lake	59.8	36.2	13.7	22.6	129.0	128.6	1.18	1.06
Lee	217.0	191.0	378.0	77.9	0.0	190.2	1.62	1.22

See footnotes at end of table. Continued . . .

Table 8.15. SOLID WASTE: TONNAGE BY DISPOSAL PROCESS AND PER CAPITA AMOUNT IN THE STATE AND COUNTIES OF FLORIDA FISCAL YEARS 1994 AND 1995 (Continued)

County	Disposal process 1/						Per capita tons 2/	
	Recycled		Landfilled		Combusted			
	1994	1995	1994	1995	1994	1995	1994	1995
Leon	172.5	142.4	225.1	238.1	0.0	0.0	1.87	1.75
Levy	2.8	4.1	11.6	14.7	0.0	0.0	0.49	0.63
Liberty	0.3	1.1	1.1	3.1	1.8	0.0	0.49	0.61
Madison	2.0	2.4	14.1	14.1	0.0	0.0	0.91	0.90
Manatee	214.2	141.7	315.5	298.1	0.0	0.0	2.32	1.89
Marion	65.6	153.3	189.0	173.2	0.0	0.0	1.17	1.45
Martin	65.2	65.1	136.3	138.0	0.0	0.0	1.83	1.81
Monroe	46.1	39.4	100.6	68.0	40.9	33.2	2.28	1.69
Nassau	6.1	7.5	36.5	36.6	0.0	0.0	0.90	0.90
Okaloosa	54.5	62.6	136.8	128.2	0.0	0.0	1.21	1.17
Okeechobee	11.0	10.9	33.2	37.6	0.0	0.0	1.37	1.48
Orange	408.0	450.7	1,045.0	1,125.3	0.0	0.0	1.96	2.08
Osceola	53.7	60.3	150.1	124.4	0.0	0.0	1.55	1.35
Palm Beach	826.3	1,261.1	475.0	341.2	515.2	542.3	1.94	2.23
Pasco	106.4	127.7	13.5	17.1	233.6	240.3	1.18	1.26
Pinellas	810.3	812.3	285.2	78.1	998.2	818.0	2.40	1.95
Polk	420.0	386.3	414.7	396.4	33.7	46.8	1.99	1.87
Putnam	22.7	25.4	52.5	54.0	0.0	0.0	1.09	1.14
St. Johns	26.1	28.1	101.7	103.7	0.0	0.0	1.35	1.34
St. Lucie	138.0	161.7	159.0	156.4	0.0	0.0	1.78	1.86
Santa Rosa	6.2	12.3	73.0	68.0	0.9	1.1	0.86	0.85
Sarasota	240.5	311.3	221.4	246.0	0.0	0.0	1.56	1.85
Seminole	138.3	161.0	319.1	316.6	0.0	0.0	1.45	1.47
Sumter	6.8	14.4	9.6	21.1	14.2	19.4	0.87	1.50
Suwannee	4.5	5.7	27.4	26.1	0.4	0.3	1.10	1.05
Taylor	1.8	1.9	11.6	12.1	0.0	0.0	0.77	0.77
Union	2.7	2.1	9.3	6.1	0.0	0.0	0.96	0.65
Volusia	193.3	217.1	410.6	442.3	0.1	0.1	1.52	1.64
Wakulla	2.4	4.2	5.7	2.9	5.1	6.8	0.80	0.82
Walton	2.4	3.0	21.4	21.2	0.0	0.0	0.75	0.72
Washington	0.6	1.0	4.5	6.3	3.0	3.7	0.45	0.58

1/ In thousand tons, rounded to hundreds.
2/ Based on April 1, 1994 and 1995 population estimates prepared by the Bureau of Economic and Business Research, University of Florida.
Note: Detail may not add to totals because of rounding.

Source: State of Florida, Department of Environmental Protection, Division of Waste Management, Bureau of Solid and Hazardous Waste, *Solid Waste Management in Florida,* March 1996.

Table 8.39. WATER USE: FRESHWATER WITHDRAWALS BY CATEGORY OF USE AND BY WATER MANAGEMENT DISTRICT IN FLORIDA, 1990

(in millions of gallons per day)

Category	Northwest Florida	St. Johns River	South Florida	Southwest Florida	Suwannee River
Total	686	1,479	3,461	1,572	335
Public supply	158	444	856	453	14
Domestic self-supplied	32	86	89	68	25
Commercial/industrial	106	136	144	283	100
Agricultural irrigation	83	600	2,349	689	85
Thermoelectric power generation	307	213	23	79	111

Note: Values may not be identical to the data reported or published by the water management districts due to differences in data collection procedures and categories used or revisions in reported values. Detail may not add to totals because of rounding.

Source: U.S., Department of the Interior, Geological Survey in cooperation with the Florida Department of Environmental Regulation and the 5 water management districts, *Water Withdrawals, Use, and Trends in Florida, 1990: U.S. Geological Survey Water-Resources Investigations Report* 92-4140.

Table 8.40. WATER USE: FRESHWATER WITHDRAWALS BY CATEGORY OF USE IN FLORIDA 1970, 1975, 1980, 1985, AND 1990

(in millions of gallons per day)

Disposition	1970	1975	1980	1985	1990
Total	6,011	6,864	7,298	6,258	7,531
Public supply	883	1,146	1,361	1,660	1,925
Domestic self-supplied	165	203	251	259	299
Commercial/industrial	927	940	781	709	770
Agricultural irrigation	2,349	2,880	3,057	2,979	3,805
Thermoelectric power generation	1,687	1,695	1,848	651	732

Source: U.S., Department of the Interior, Geological Survey, *Water Withdrawals, Use, and Trends in Florida, 1985: U.S., Geological Survey Water-Resources Investigations Report* 88-4103, and *Water Withdrawals in Florida During 1990, With Trends from 1950 to 1990: U.S. Geological Survey Open-File Report* 92-80.

Water Management Districts

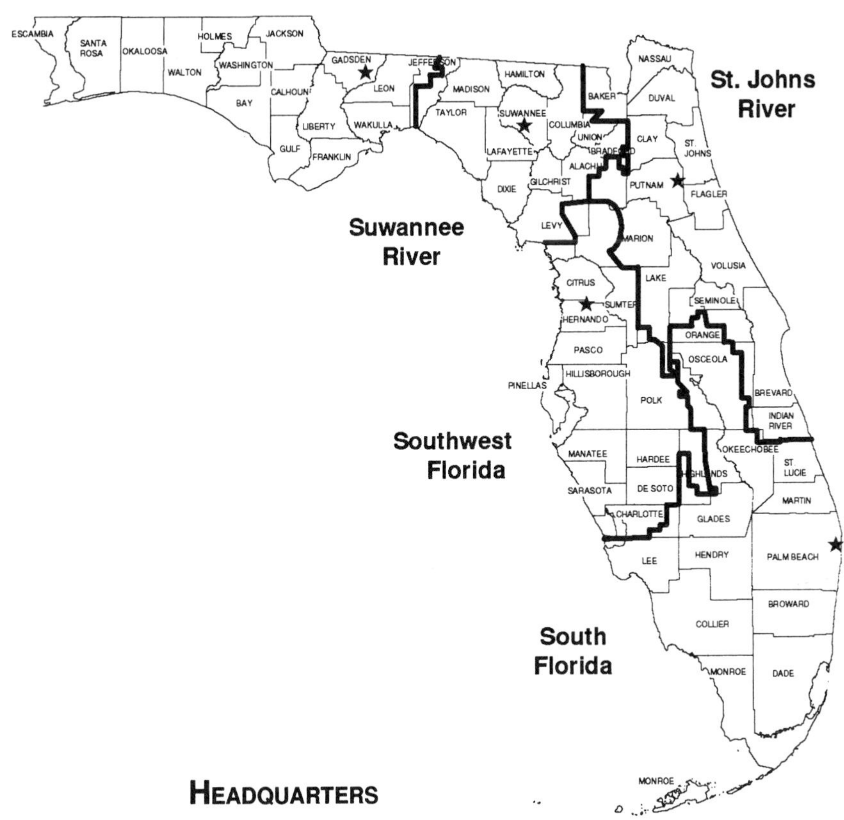

Headquarters

District	City	County
Northwest Florida	Havana	Gadsden
Suwannee River	Live Oak	Suwannee
St. Johns River	Palatka	Putnam
Southwest Florida	Brooksville	Hernando
South Florida	West Palm Beach	Palm Beach

Table 8.41. WATER USE: WATER WITHDRAWALS BY SOURCE IN THE STATE AND COUNTIES OF FLORIDA, 1990

(in millions of gallons per day)

County	Total	Ground			Surface		
		Total	Fresh	Saline	Total	Fresh	Saline
Florida	17,897.92	4,714.00	4,664.72	49.28	13,183.92	2,867.06	10,316.86
Alachua	52.48	52.12	52.12	0.00	0.36	0.36	0.00
Baker	10.07	7.87	7.87	0.00	2.20	2.20	0.00
Bay	285.86	16.02	16.02	0.00	269.84	42.16	227.68
Bradford	9.02	8.96	8.96	0.00	0.06	0.06	0.00
Brevard	1,195.89	117.85	117.85	0.00	1,078.04	26.64	1,051.40
Broward	1,292.09	244.78	244.78	0.00	1,047.31	21.75	1,025.56
Calhoun	2.38	1.88	1.88	0.00	0.50	0.50	0.00
Charlotte	50.67	43.95	43.95	0.00	6.72	6.72	0.00
Citrus	1,481.36	25.55	25.55	0.00	1,455.81	0.27	1,455.54
Clay	25.64	25.20	25.20	0.00	0.44	0.44	0.00
Collier	213.79	195.30	195.30	0.00	18.49	18.49	0.00
Columbia	11.38	11.15	11.15	0.00	0.23	0.23	0.00
Dade	576.15	531.53	526.60	4.93	44.62	14.37	30.25
De Soto	121.97	102.05	102.05	0.00	19.92	19.92	0.00
Dixie	5.87	5.87	5.87	0.00	0.00	0.00	0.00
Duval	512.47	152.98	152.98	0.00	359.49	1.40	358.09
Escambia	292.17	82.26	82.26	0.00	209.91	209.91	0.00
Flagler	14.67	13.47	13.47	0.00	1.20	1.20	0.00
Franklin	2.67	2.56	2.56	0.00	0.11	0.11	0.00
Gadsden	18.51	9.53	9.53	0.00	8.98	8.98	0.00
Gilchrist	11.06	11.06	11.06	0.00	0.00	0.00	0.00
Glades	81.71	19.16	19.16	0.00	62.55	62.55	0.00
Gulf	56.43	7.11	7.11	0.00	49.32	38.06	11.26
Hamilton	50.60	50.60	50.60	0.00	0.00	0.00	0.00
Hardee	66.55	60.60	60.60	0.00	5.95	5.95	0.00
Hendry	492.96	174.45	174.45	0.00	318.51	318.51	0.00
Hernando	45.83	45.48	45.48	0.00	0.35	0.35	0.00
Highlands	141.47	129.35	129.35	0.00	12.12	12.12	0.00
Hillsborough	2,304.94	179.73	179.73	0.00	2,125.21	88.94	2,036.27
Holmes	6.76	5.60	5.60	0.00	1.16	1.16	0.00
Indian River	328.35	72.85	72.85	0.00	255.50	117.53	137.97
Jackson	141.50	30.13	30.13	0.00	111.37	111.37	0.00
Jefferson	12.10	10.29	10.29	0.00	1.81	1.81	0.00
Lafayette	9.64	9.10	9.10	0.00	0.54	0.54	0.00
Lake	97.03	84.35	84.35	0.00	12.68	12.68	0.00
Lee	572.93	123.05	123.05	0.00	449.88	38.25	411.63

See footnote at end of table. Continued . . .

Table 8.41. WATER USE: WATER WITHDRAWALS BY SOURCE IN THE STATE AND COUNTIES OF FLORIDA, 1990 (Continued)

(in millions of gallons per day)

County	Total	Ground			Surface		
		Total	Fresh	Saline	Total	Fresh	Saline
Leon	39.49	39.00	39.00	0.00	0.49	0.49	0.00
Levy	24.56	21.52	21.52	0.00	3.04	3.04	0.00
Liberty	3.72	3.72	3.72	0.00	0.00	0.00	0.00
Madison	7.46	7.19	7.19	0.00	0.27	0.27	0.00
Manatee	141.84	96.53	96.53	0.00	45.31	45.31	0.00
Marion	51.07	49.20	49.20	0.00	1.87	1.87	0.00
Martin	209.61	55.71	55.71	0.00	153.90	153.90	0.00
Monroe	45.64	45.64	1.29	44.35	0.00	0.00	0.00
Nassau	44.77	42.77	42.77	0.00	2.00	0.60	1.40
Okaloosa	31.59	31.59	31.59	0.00	0.00	0.00	0.00
Okeechobee	44.26	38.90	38.90	0.00	5.36	5.36	0.00
Orange	282.34	220.87	220.87	0.00	61.47	61.47	0.00
Osceola	76.84	63.44	63.44	0.00	13.40	13.40	0.00
Palm Beach	1,419.08	201.04	201.04	0.00	1,218.04	795.80	422.24
Pasco	1,465.90	138.71	138.71	0.00	1,327.19	2.38	1,324.81
Pinellas	563.97	48.10	48.10	0.00	515.87	1.35	514.52
Polk	437.50	353.67	353.67	0.00	83.83	83.83	0.00
Putnam	80.24	61.43	61.43	0.00	18.81	18.81	0.00
St. Johns	52.65	51.26	51.26	0.00	1.39	1.39	0.00
St. Lucie	1,510.94	83.84	83.84	0.00	1,427.10	170.66	1,256.44
Santa Rosa	23.83	23.54	23.54	0.00	0.29	0.29	0.00
Sarasota	62.67	59.49	59.49	0.00	3.18	3.18	0.00
Seminole	67.37	65.57	65.57	0.00	1.80	1.80	0.00
Sumter	73.60	73.13	73.13	0.00	0.47	0.47	0.00
Suwannee	141.76	32.30	32.30	0.00	109.46	109.46	0.00
Taylor	50.66	49.38	49.38	0.00	1.28	1.28	0.00
Union	5.05	4.37	4.37	0.00	0.68	0.68	0.00
Volusia	277.64	74.43	74.43	0.00	203.21	203.21	0.00
Wakulla	54.49	2.69	2.69	0.00	51.80	0.00	51.80
Walton	9.05	7.93	7.93	0.00	1.12	1.12	0.00
Washington	3.36	3.25	3.25	0.00	0.11	0.11	0.00

Note: Values may not be identical to the data reported or published by the water management districts due to differences in data collection procedures and categories used or revisions in reported values.

Source: U.S., Department of the Interior, Geological Survey in cooperation with the Florida Department of Environmental Regulation and the 5 water management districts, *Water Withdrawals, Use, and Trends in Florida, 1990: U.S. Geological Survey Water-Resources Investigations Report* 92-4140.

Table 8.42. WATER USE: PUBLIC SUPPLY WATER WITHDRAWALS AND WATER USE BY TYPE OF USE IN THE STATE AND COUNTIES OF FLORIDA, 1990

(in millions of gallons per day)

County	Population served	Water use Total	Residential/ domestic	Commercial/ institutional	Industrial	Utility 1/	Other 2/
Florida	11,228,059	1,925.15	1,248.82	282.09	182.69	172.77	38.78
Alachua	142,104	22.95	14.75	4.05	1.63	2.30	0.22
Baker	4,102	0.81	0.61	0.08	0.04	0.08	0.00
Bay	103,672	47.18	15.74	3.09	23.64	4.71	0.00
Bradford	7,333	1.61	0.82	0.25	0.38	0.12	0.04
Brevard	363,066	51.31	30.89	7.65	7.13	3.85	1.79
Broward	1,195,865	192.53	132.25	28.14	15.45	14.44	2.25
Calhoun	3,304	0.53	0.24	0.10	0.15	0.04	0.00
Charlotte	99,870	15.17	11.08	1.50	0.31	2.12	0.16
Citrus	46,314	8.65	6.14	1.17	0.37	0.87	0.10
Clay	75,297	11.11	8.38	1.39	0.40	0.83	0.11
Collier	122,450	36.71	27.41	4.09	0.78	3.67	0.76
Columbia	15,336	2.93	1.16	0.62	0.93	0.22	0.00
Dade	1,875,160	325.62	212.36	44.33	30.00	32.42	6.51
De Soto	7,341	0.84	0.44	0.20	0.14	0.06	0.00
Dixie	4,555	0.66	0.52	0.06	0.04	0.04	0.00
Duval	619,196	96.32	59.85	16.96	10.29	7.22	2.00
Escambia	239,571	37.78	27.56	4.96	2.06	2.83	0.37
Flagler	19,329	3.85	2.70	0.36	0.37	0.39	0.03
Franklin	8,021	1.63	1.31	0.11	0.06	0.12	0.03
Gadsden	25,928	3.42	2.03	0.29	0.85	0.25	0.00
Gilchrist	1,656	0.27	0.17	0.04	0.03	0.02	0.01
Glades	3,085	0.40	0.28	0.03	0.06	0.03	0.00
Gulf	9,079	1.26	0.84	0.11	0.24	0.06	0.01
Hamilton	5,101	0.97	0.62	0.22	0.06	0.07	0.00
Hardee	8,302	1.43	1.14	0.15	0.04	0.10	0.00
Hendry	16,649	3.60	1.69	0.24	1.40	0.27	0.00
Hernando	90,403	14.97	12.43	1.07	0.35	1.12	0.00
Highlands	51,441	8.30	6.24	0.74	0.29	0.62	0.41
Hillsborough	816,641	125.19	78.46	20.40	12.97	9.39	3.97
Holmes	5,118	1.10	0.65	0.18	0.19	0.08	0.00
Indian River	53,734	13.17	9.03	1.67	0.76	1.58	0.13
Jackson	15,758	2.38	1.42	0.38	0.41	0.17	0.00
Jefferson	4,620	0.72	0.46	0.08	0.12	0.05	0.01
Lafayette	1,140	0.18	0.07	0.03	0.07	0.01	0.00
Lake	103,785	20.67	15.69	2.13	1.09	1.55	0.21
Lee	281,489	42.75	29.12	7.10	1.75	4.27	0.51

See footnotes at end of table.

Continued . . .

Table 8.42. WATER USE: PUBLIC SUPPLY WATER WITHDRAWALS AND WATER USE BY TYPE OF USE IN THE STATE AND COUNTIES OF FLORIDA, 1990 (Continued)

(in millions of gallons per day)

		Water use					
County	Population served	Total	Resi-dential/ domestic	Commer-cial/ insti-tutional	Indus-trial	Utility 1/	Other 2/
Leon	156,581	25.02	15.91	5.87	1.11	1.88	0.25
Levy	10,453	1.58	1.11	0.22	0.14	0.11	0.00
Liberty	2,010	0.26	0.15	0.03	0.06	0.02	0.00
Madison	5,943	1.43	0.46	0.26	0.60	0.11	0.00
Manatee	211,105	27.84	20.13	3.48	0.93	1.53	1.77
Marion	89,903	16.47	9.23	2.93	2.99	1.24	0.08
Martin	61,863	13.66	8.46	1.95	1.06	1.37	0.82
Monroe	78,024	12.07	6.64	2.64	0.22	1.81	0.76
Nassau	22,014	3.85	2.45	0.78	0.29	0.29	0.04
Okaloosa	126,641	20.92	14.94	2.63	1.36	1.57	0.42
Okeechobee	17,035	2.09	1.37	0.32	0.11	0.29	0.00
Orange	653,739	137.77	87.55	24.43	12.71	10.33	2.75
Osceola	79,625	12.08	6.72	3.25	0.71	0.91	0.49
Palm Beach	764,425	164.65	112.83	22.52	9.59	16.47	3.24
Pasco	201,609	26.07	19.60	3.27	1.03	1.97	0.20
Pinellas	837,617	118.20	68.92	20.30	14.61	11.82	2.55
Polk	300,574	65.52	41.55	7.62	5.90	6.55	3.90
Putnam	22,543	3.15	1.87	0.59	0.38	0.31	0.00
St. Johns	66,138	8.39	5.67	1.56	0.49	0.63	0.04
St. Lucie	83,500	14.39	9.32	2.00	0.92	1.44	0.71
Santa Rosa	77,355	10.57	8.38	0.98	0.37	0.79	0.05
Sarasota	248,778	34.23	16.39	6.63	3.88	7.33	0.00
Seminole	270,791	50.79	38.40	4.71	3.38	3.80	0.50
Sumter	12,252	1.90	1.15	0.35	0.25	0.14	0.01
Suwannee	8,445	1.36	0.83	0.28	0.15	0.10	0.00
Taylor	10,100	1.42	0.73	0.22	0.36	0.11	0.00
Union	2,116	0.63	0.21	0.30	0.07	0.05	0.00
Volusia	321,635	44.21	29.06	7.57	3.76	3.32	0.50
Wakulla	7,395	0.77	0.57	0.09	0.06	0.05	0.00
Walton	24,990	3.71	2.93	0.21	0.13	0.37	0.07
Washington	7,045	1.18	0.74	0.13	0.22	0.09	0.00

1/ Water used for fire fighting, system flushing, and water lost to leakage.
2/ Includes water used for power generation, heating and cooling systems, and urban irrigation.
Note: Public supply refers to municipal or other private water utilities which serve the public.

Source: U.S., Department of the Interior, Geological Survey in cooperation with the Florida Department of Environmental Regulation and the 5 water management districts, *Water Withdrawals, Use, and Trends in Florida, 1990: U.S. Geological Survey Water-Resources Investigations Report* 92-4140.

Table 8.43. WATER USE: WATER DISCHARGED FROM WASTEWATER TREATMENT FACILITIES BY TYPE OF FACILITY IN THE STATE AND COUNTIES OF FLORIDA, 1990

(in millions of gallons per day)

County	Total	Domes-tic	Indus-trial	County	Total	Domes-tic	Indus-trial
Florida	1,764.83	1,382.55	382.28	Lafayette	0.12	0.12	0.00
				Lake	8.55	7.99	0.56
Alachua	13.41	13.39	0.02	Lee	32.11	32.11	0.00
Baker	0.81	0.81	0.00	Leon	16.37	16.37	0.00
Bay	33.28	33.28	0.00	Levy	0.54	0.54	0.00
Bradford	5.55	2.02	3.53	Liberty	0.11	0.11	0.00
Brevard	41.63	41.63	0.00	Madison	0.63	0.63	0.00
Broward	169.87	169.87	0.00	Manatee	33.50	23.99	9.51
Calhoun	0.50	0.50	0.00	Marion	6.83	6.83	0.00
Charlotte	5.38	5.38	0.00	Martin	4.76	4.49	0.27
Citrus	2.57	2.57	0.00	Monroe	9.45	9.45	0.00
Clay	10.03	6.90	3.13	Nassau	25.69	2.37	23.32
Collier	19.17	19.17	0.00	Okaloosa	14.70	14.70	0.00
Columbia	1.69	1.69	0.00	Okeechobee	0.38	0.38	0.00
Dade	282.72	282.72	0.00	Orange	91.67	91.67	0.00
De Soto	1.10	1.10	0.00	Osceola	10.22	10.22	0.00
Dixie	0.26	0.26	0.00	Palm Beach	89.10	87.92	1.18
Duval	75.49	66.62	8.87	Pasco	26.05	15.88	10.17
Escambia	60.10	18.45	41.65	Pinellas	124.18	124.18	0.00
Flagler	2.86	2.86	0.00	Polk	146.33	25.23	121.10
Franklin	1.01	1.01	0.00	Putnam	39.69	2.47	37.22
Gadsden	5.03	1.96	3.07	St. Johns	5.07	5.07	0.00
Gilchrist	0.23	0.23	0.00	St. Lucie	9.00	9.00	0.00
Glades	0.05	0.05	0.00	Santa Rosa	6.01	2.80	3.21
Gulf	43.29	32.04	11.25	Sarasota	19.96	19.96	0.00
Hamilton	17.33	0.68	16.65	Seminole	29.74	29.74	0.00
Hardee	1.11	1.11	0.00	Sumter	0.84	0.84	0.00
Hendry	10.69	2.14	8.55	Suwannee	1.46	0.78	0.68
Hernando	9.86	4.71	5.15	Taylor	54.69	0.79	53.90
Highlands	2.44	2.44	0.00	Union	0.43	0.43	0.00
Hillsborough	97.12	79.43	17.69	Volusia	29.88	29.82	0.06
Holmes	0.66	0.66	0.00	Wakulla	0.61	0.10	0.51
Indian River	4.80	4.55	0.25	Walton	2.43	1.65	0.78
Jackson	2.40	2.40	0.00	Washington	0.74	0.74	0.00
Jefferson	0.55	0.55	0.00				

Note: Discharge is to both surface and ground.

Source: U.S., Department of the Interior, Geological Survey in cooperation with the Florida Department of Environmental Regulation, *Water Withdrawals, Use, and Trends in Florida, 1990: U.S. Geological Survey Water-Resources Investigations Report* 92-4140.

National Weather Station Offices

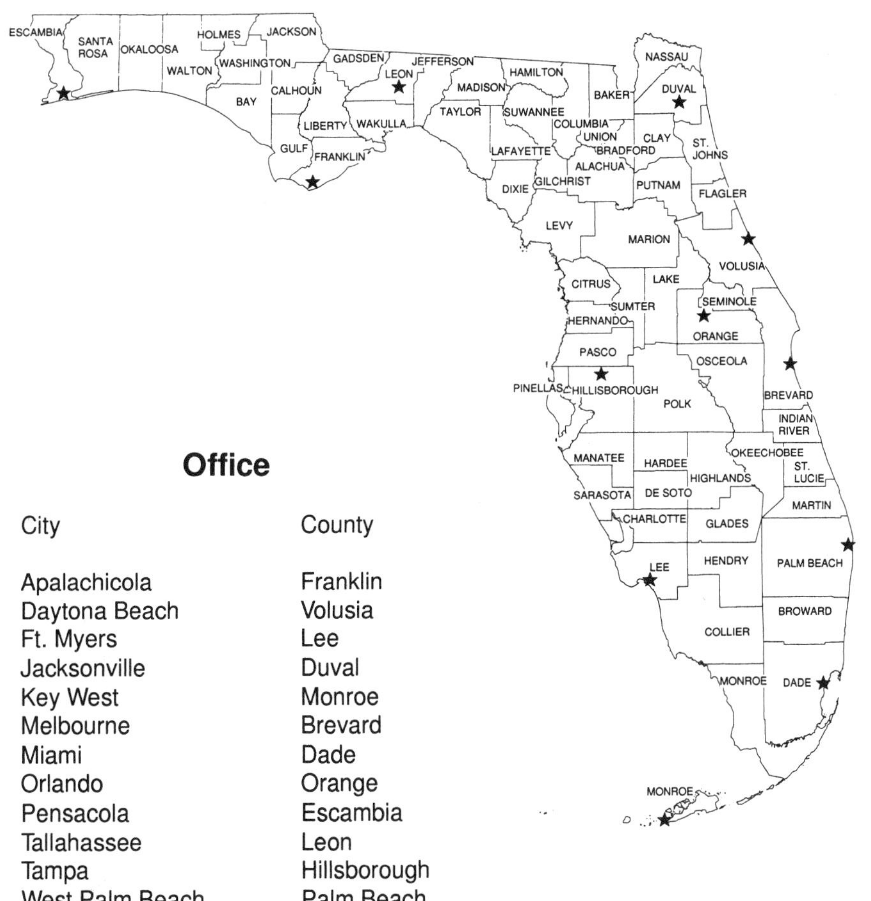

Office

City	County
Apalachicola	Franklin
Daytona Beach	Volusia
Ft. Myers	Lee
Jacksonville	Duval
Key West	Monroe
Melbourne	Brevard
Miami	Dade
Orlando	Orange
Pensacola	Escambia
Tallahassee	Leon
Tampa	Hillsborough
West Palm Beach	Palm Beach

Table 8.70. CLIMATE: TEMPERATURE CHARACTERISTICS AND TOTAL PRECIPITATION AT NATIONAL WEATHER STATION OFFICES IN FLORIDA BY MONTH, 1995

(temperature in degrees Fahrenheit)

Station and characteristics	January	February	March	April	May	June	July	August	September	October	November	December
Apalachicola												
Temperature												
Average maximum	63.7	66.5	71.7	76.7	86.2	87.7	92.1	91.6	88.3	82.1	70.2	61.1
Average minimum	42.5	47.3	55.5	58.9	68.1	71.1	75.0	76.1	71.9	64.8	48.8	42.7
Heating degree days	367	227	93	24	0	0	0	0	0	14	195	408
Cooling degree days	5	7	58	116	381	438	584	592	459	282	36	10
Days with maximum 90 degrees or more	0	0	0	0	3	7	25	23	7	1	0	0
Days with minimum 32 degrees or less	5	4	0	0	0	0	0	0	0	0	0	8
Precipitation (inches)	3.4	2.1	3.8	3.5	4.5	9.4	4.5	8.0	0.7	3.2	7.5	2.5
Pensacola												
Temperature												
Average maximum	62.5	66.9	70.8	76.6	85.4	89.9	(NA)	92.9	(NA)	(NA)	68.1	61.7
Average minimum	44.3	46.9	54.6	57.6	68.0	71.1	(NA)	76.1	(NA)	(NA)	46.5	42.7
Heating degree days	352	228	121	29	0	0	(NA)	0	(NA)	(NA)	240	418
Cooling degree days	1	9	61	100	370	473	(NA)	605	(NA)	(NA)	19	31
Days with maximum 90 degrees or more	0	0	0	0	3	20	(NA)	25	(NA)	(NA)	0	0
Days with minimum 32 degrees or less	5	3	0	0	0	0	(NA)	0	(NA)	(NA)	0	12
Precipitation (inches)	5.6	4.1	8.9	8.5	6.5	2.7	(NA)	(NA)	(NA)	(NA)	13.3	5.5
Tallahassee												
Temperature												
Average maximum	63.5	67.6	75.6	81.4	89.2	89.8	94.5	93.5	88.7	81.1	68.9	62.0
Average minimum	38.0	42.5	52.4	53.0	62.9	67.7	72.2	73.4	69.4	60.9	42.9	39.1
Heating degree days	435	282	84	36	1	0	0	0	0	31	294	451
Cooling degree days	1	10	62	110	351	423	576	581	430	223	28	10
Days with maximum 90 degrees or more	0	0	0	1	18	17	30	28	14	0	0	0
Days with minimum 32 degrees or less	10	9	1	0	0	0	0	0	0	0	5	12
Precipitation (inches)	3.3	2.6	5.6	2.1	4.0	7.6	9.6	2.7	3.7	3.9	3.4	3.8

See footnotes at end of table.

Continued . . .

Table 8.70. CLIMATE: TEMPERATURE CHARACTERISTICS AND TOTAL PRECIPITATION AT NATIONAL WEATHER STATION OFFICES IN FLORIDA BY MONTH, 1995 (Continued)

(temperature in degrees Fahrenheit)

Station and characteristics	January	February	March	April	May	June	July	August	September	October	November	December
Jacksonville												
Temperature												
Average maximum	64.0	67.0	74.3	81.5	88.9	89.5	93.9	89.0	85.3	81.7	69.8	63.6
Average minimum	41.7	43.1	51.9	54.6	63.8	68.8	71.7	74.0	69.9	64.0	45.8	42.3
Heating degree days	369	289	103	40	0	0	0	0	0	22	249	371
Cooling degree days	2	19	51	138	356	434	557	521	386	274	39	6
Days with maximum 90 degrees or more	0	0	0	5	12	15	27	13	5	2	0	0
Days with minimum 32 degrees or less	2	5	0	0	0	0	0	0	0	0	0	8
Precipitation (inches)	1.9	2.1	3.7	1.8	1.8	5.4	9.5	9.9	5.4	3.5	3.2	2.2
Daytona Beach												
Temperature												
Average maximum	66.9	70.1	74.9	79.9	88.9	87.0	89.6	88.2	86.8	83.0	73.5	67.8
Average minimum	46.0	47.2	57.1	60.7	69.1	71.0	72.7	74.3	72.2	69.7	52.0	48.3
Heating degree days	269	200	41	16	0	0	0	0	0	3	135	239
Cooling degree days	12	29	81	182	442	426	507	511	441	365	74	32
Days with maximum 90 degrees or more	0	0	0	3	15	10	17	10	4	1	0	0
Days with minimum 32 degrees or less	0	4	0	0	0	0	0	0	0	0	0	5
Precipitation (inches)	1.5	1.4	2.0	1.3	1.3	6.6	6.6	10.7	14.1	4.0	1.4	3.4
Orlando												
Temperature												
Average maximum	68.6	72.0	78.1	82.4	90.5	88.2	91.3	90.6	90.7	85.0	76.3	70.8
Average minimum	48.9	50.1	58.3	62.7	69.8	71.6	73.4	75.4	73.4	69.6	54.9	51.1
Heating degree days	205	153	24	5	0	0	0	0	0	0	76	191
Cooling degree days	19	52	132	241	476	455	546	567	518	391	103	74
Days with maximum 90 degrees or more	0	0	0	4	23	12	24	21	21	4	0	0
Days with minimum 32 degrees or less	0	1	0	0	0	0	0	0	0	0	0	1
Precipitation (inches)	1.5	1.1	2.1	0.8	4.2	8.2	5.1	9.5	3.6	4.4	1.7	0.8

See footnotes at end of table.

Continued . . .

Table 8.70. CLIMATE: TEMPERATURE CHARACTERISTICS AND TOTAL PRECIPITATION AT NATIONAL WEATHER STATION OFFICES IN FLORIDA BY MONTH, 1995 (Continued)

(temperature in degrees Fahrenheit)

Station and characteristics	January	February	March	April	May	June	July	August	September	October	November	December
Melbourne												
Temperature												
Average maximum	70.0	72.4	78.2	81.3	88.9	88.0	90.0	89.6	89.2	84.6	77.3	71.3
Average minimum	48.3	50.0	59.0	62.2	69.2	71.1	72.6	74.7	72.5	71.1	55.9	51.2
Heating degree days	195	148	17	3	0	0	0	0	0	0	59	177
Cooling degree days	21	49	132	213	441	446	513	541	483	405	112	68
Days with maximum 90 degrees or more	0	0	0	1	11	10	18	16	11	1	0	0
Days with minimum 32 degrees or less	0	2	0	0	0	0	0	0	0	0	0	2
Precipitation (inches)	2.6	2.0	2.8	3.1	4.6	8.7	7.9	19.1	7.9	10.5	0.7	0.8
Tampa												
Temperature												
Average maximum	68.5	72.1	78.6	83.1	91.5	88.1	90.9	89.9	88.9	85.3	75.1	70.2
Average minimum	49.1	50.7	58.7	63.9	72.0	72.3	75.0	76.7	75.1	70.3	55.3	51.7
Heating degree days	200	151	23	1	0	0	0	0	0	0	83	180
Cooling degree days	15	59	145	264	526	464	561	574	518	405	95	63
Days with maximum 90 degrees or more	0	0	0	1	24	11	22	20	13	6	0	0
Days with minimum 32 degrees or less	0	1	0	0	0	0	0	0	0	0	0	0
Precipitation (inches)	3.5	2.0	2.0	1.5	1.7	9.8	10.1	13.8	2.8	4.7	1.2	1.0
Ft. Myers												
Temperature												
Average maximum	73.0	75.1	81.4	84.5	91.7	89.4	91.5	91.5	91.0	(NA)	(NA)	(NA)
Average minimum	53.4	54.5	61.5	65.9	72.2	74.0	75.2	77.1	75.1	(NA)	(NA)	(NA)
Heating degree days	97	91	5	0	0	0	0	0	0	(NA)	(NA)	(NA)
Cooling degree days	50	91	215	312	535	510	574	604	550	(NA)	(NA)	(NA)
Days with maximum 90 degrees or more	0	0	0	0	24	13	23	23	22	(NA)	(NA)	(NA)
Days with minimum 32 degrees or less	0	0	0	0	0	0	0	0	0	(NA)	(NA)	(NA)
Precipitation (inches)	3.1	1.4	0.9	5.3	1.4	14.0	12.1	13.9	9.6	(NA)	(NA)	(NA)

See footnotes at end of table.

Continued . . .

Table 8.70. CLIMATE: TEMPERATURE CHARACTERISTICS AND TOTAL PRECIPITATION AT NATIONAL WEATHER STATION OFFICES IN FLORIDA BY MONTH, 1995 (Continued)

(temperature in degrees Fahrenheit)

Station and characteristics	January	February	March	April	May	June	July	August	September	October	November	December
Miami												
Temperature												
Average maximum	75.2	76.0	80.7	84.4	88.7	87.7	91.0	90.6	90.1	86.6	81.1	75.4
Average minimum	59.4	59.8	66.3	70.5	75.5	75.8	78.0	77.8	77.1	76.4	66.4	60.9
Heating degree days	39	51	1	0	0	0	0	0	0	0	3	77
Cooling degree days	119	138	274	377	537	509	612	602	565	519	272	178
Days with maximum 90 degrees or more	0	0	0	2	9	9	23	20	20	3	0	0
Days with minimum 32 degrees or less	0	0	0	0	0	0	0	0	0	0	0	0
Precipitation (inches)	3.1	1.4	4.6	3.7	2.9	20.3	6.4	13.1	10.4	9.9	2.5	0.9
West Palm Beach												
Temperature												
Average maximum	73.2	74.7	80.0	83.6	88.6	87.6	89.1	89.5	88.8	86.1	79.1	74.1
Average minimum	55.2	55.4	64.1	67.8	72.9	74.1	75.4	76.0	76.0	75.0	62.3	57.3
Heating degree days	91	93	3	0	0	0	0	0	0	0	16	115
Cooling degree days	74	102	228	330	499	483	542	558	528	490	196	141
Days with maximum 90 degrees or more	0	0	2	1	11	9	17	18	10	4	0	0
Days with minimum 32 degrees or less	0	0	0	0	0	0	0	0	0	0	0	0
Precipitation (inches)	3.9	1.1	2.4	3.9	0.8	7.8	6.9	20.1	7.5	11.5	1.5	1.6
Key West												
Temperature												
Average maximum	74.6	75.6	79.5	83.3	88.3	88.5	90.3	90.8	90.0	86.5	79.8	74.1
Average minimum	63.6	63.1	68.2	73.5	78.7	77.8	79.2	79.7	78.3	77.0	70.9	64.2
Heating degree days	15	24	0	0	0	0	0	0	0	0	0	37
Cooling degree days	147	152	283	409	583	551	618	638	580	526	318	170
Days with maximum 90 degrees or more	0	0	0	0	6	12	24	22	19	3	0	0
Days with minimum 32 degrees or less	0	0	0	0	0	0	0	0	0	0	0	0
Precipitation (inches)	4.2	0.1	1.9	2.2	0.7	7.9	2.9	2.9	4.4	8.7	T	2.9

T Trace (NA) Not available.

Note: Degree day totals are the sums of the negative (heating) or positive (cooling) departures of average daily temperatures from 65 degrees Fahrenheit.

Source: U.S., Department of Commerce, National Oceanic and Atmospheric Administration, National Environmental Satellite, Data and Information Service, *Climatological Data: Florida,* 1995 monthly reports.

Table 8.74. CLIMATE: CHARACTERISTICS FOR JACKSONVILLE, MIAMI, LOS ANGELES, ATLANTA CHICAGO, AND NEW YORK, SPECIFIED DATES THROUGH 1994

Characteristic	Jackson-ville Florida	Miami Florida	Los Angeles Cali-fornia	Atlanta Georgia	Chicago Illinois	New York New York 1/
Normal temperature 2/						
January average	52.4	67.2	56.8	41.0	21.0	31.5
July average	81.6	82.6	69.1	78.8	73.2	76.8
Annual average	68.0	75.9	63.0	61.3	49.0	54.7
January normal high	64.2	75.2	65.7	50.4	29.0	37.6
July normal high	91.4	89.0	75.3	88.0	83.7	85.2
Annual average high	78.9	82.8	70.4	71.2	58.6	62.3
January normal low	40.5	59.2	47.8	31.5	12.9	25.3
July normal low	71.9	76.2	62.8	69.5	62.6	68.4
Annual average low	57.1	69.0	55.5	51.3	39.5	47.1
Extreme temperatures 3/						
Highest temperature of record	105	98	110	105	104	106
Lowest temperature of record	7	30	23	-8	-27	-15
Length of record (years)	53	52	59	46	36	126
Normal annual precipitation 2/ (inches)	51.32	55.91	12.01	50.77	35.82	47.25
Average number of days precipitation 0.01 or more 3/	116	130	35	115	126	121
Length of record (years)	53	52	59	60	36	125
Average total snow and ice pellets 3/ (inches)	T	0.0	T	2.0	38.5	28.4
Length of record (years)	53	52	59	60	36	126
Average annual percentage of possible sunshine 3/ 4/	61	68	72	59	52	64
Length of record (years)	46	45	59	60	36	42
Average annual wind speed 3/ (MPH)	7.9	9.3	7.5	9.1	10.4	9.4
Length of record (years)	45	45	46	56	36	58
Heating and cooling degree days 2/ 5/						
Heating degree days	1,434	200	1,458	2,991	6,536	4,805
Cooling degree days	2,551	4,198	727	1,667	752	1,096
Average relative humidity 3/						
Length of record	58	30	35	34	36	61
Annual (percentage)						
Morning	88	84	79	82	80	72
Afternoon	56	61	64	56	60	56

T Trace. MPH Miles per hour.

1/ City office data.

2/ Based on 1961-90 period of record.

3/ Record through 1994.

4/ Percentage of days that are either clear or partly cloudy.

5/ Degree day normals are used to determine relative estimates of heating requirements for buildings. Each day that the average temperature for a day is below 65 degrees F. produces one heating degree day and each day it is above 65 degrees F. produces one cooling degree day.

Note: All temperatures are in degrees Fahrenheit.

Source: U.S., Department of Commerce, Bureau of the Census, *Statistical Abstract of the United States, 1996*. Data from U.S. National Oceanic and Atmospheric Administration.

Table 8.76. HURRICANES: AREA OF LANDFALL, NAME, YEAR, FORCE CATEGORY, AND RANK OF THE FIFTEEN DEADLIEST HURRICANES IN THE UNITED STATES, 1900 THROUGH 1995

Area of landfall/name	Year	Force category 1/	Deaths Number	Deaths Rank
Galveston, Texas/(NA)	1900	4	6,000	1
Lake Okeechobee, Florida/(NA)	1928	4	1,836	2
Florida Keys; S. Texas/(NA)	1919	4	600	3
New England/(NA)	1938	3	600	4
Florida Keys/(NA)	1935	5	408	5
S.W. Louisiana; N. Texas/Audrey	1957	4	390	6
N.E. United States/(NA)	1944	3	390	7
Grand Isle, Louisiana/(NA)	1909	4	350	8
New Orleans, Louisiana/(NA)	1915	4	275	9
Galveston, Texas/(NA)	1915	4	275	10
Mississippi; Louisiana/Camille	1969	5	256	11
Miami, Florida/(NA)	1926	4	243	12
N.E. United States/Diane	1955	1	184	13
S.E. Florida/(NA)	1906	2	164	14
Mississippi; Alabama; Pensacola, Florida/(NA)	1906	3	134	15

(NA) Not available.

1/ Assigned based on the Saffir/Simpson scale. Ratings are 1-5 and a "5" indicates central pressure less than 920 millibars or winds greater than 155 mph or storm surge higher than 18 feet and damage classified as catastrophic.

Table 8.77. HURRICANES: AREA OF LANDFALL, NAME, YEAR, FORCE CATEGORY, AND RANK OF THE TEN COSTLIEST HURRICANES IN THE UNITED STATES, 1900 THROUGH 1995

Area of landfall/name	Year	Force category 1/	Value of damage 2/ Amount ($1,000)	Value of damage 2/ Rank
Florida; Louisiana/Andrew	1992	4	25,000,000	1
South Carolina/Hugo	1989	4	7,155,120	2
Florida; Louisiana/Betsy	1965	3	6,461,303	3
N.E. United States/Agnes	1972	1	6,418,143	4
Mississippi; Alabama/Camille	1969	5	5,242,380	5
N.E. United States/Diane	1955	1	4,199,645	6
New England/(NA)	1938	3	3,593,853	7
Alabama; Mississippi/Frederic	1979	3	3,502,942	8
Florida/Opal	1995	4	A/ 3,000,000	9
N. Texas/Alicia	1983	3	2,391,854	10

(NA) Not available.

A/ Preliminary estimate.

1/ Assigned based on the Saffir/Simpson scale. Ratings are 1-5 and a "5" indicates central pressure less than 920 millibars or winds greater than 155 mph or storm surge higher than 18 feet and damage classified as catastrophic.

2/ Adjusted to 1990 dollars on basis of U.S. Department of Commerce composite construction cost indexes.

Source for Tables 8.76 and 8.77: U.S., Department of Commerce, National Oceanic and Atmospheric Administration, *The Deadliest, Costliest, and Most Intense United States Hurricanes of this Century*. NOAA Technical Memorandum NWS NHC-31, and National Climatic Data Center, *1995 Atlantic Tropical Storms,* Technical Report 96-01.

Table 8.80. AIR POLLUTION: PARTICULATE MATTER (PM) CONCENTRATIONS IN SPECIFIED CITIES OF FLORIDA, 1995

Area 1/	Site Address	PM10 concentration (UG/M^3) 2nd highest 24-hour value 2/	Annual arith-metic mean 3/
Alachua County			
Gainesville	721 NW 6th Street	37	20
Bay County			
Panama City	Cherry Street & Henderson Avenue S.T.P.	58	24
Brevard County			
Merritt Island	2575 N Courtenay Parkway	27	16
Titusville	611 Singleton Avenue	30	16
Broward County			
Davie	U of F AG RSCH, 3205 SW 70th Avenue	29	15
Ft. Lauderdale	N.W. Corner of Lincoln Park	48	20
Hollywood	12701 Plunkett Street	31	15
Margate	6300 NW 18th Street	27	16
Pembroke Pines	11251 Taft Street	36	15
Plantation	Mirror Lake Elementary School, 1200 NW 72	27	14
Pompano Beach	Pompano Beach Water Plant, 301 North	31	17
Tamarac	7601 N University Drive	28	15
Collier County			
Naples	E Naples Fire Dept, SR 858	34	16
Dade County			
Homestead	Fire Station 325 NW 2nd Street	49	29
Miami	FS, NW 12th Avenue & 20th Street	40	25
Duval County			
Jacksonville	1070 E Adams St.	61	29
Escambia County			
Cantonment	St. Regis Golf Course	54	23
Pensacola	Ellyson Industrial Park	45	21
Gulf County			
Port St. Joe	Water Plant on Kenny's Mill Road	47	22
Hamilton County			
White Springs	County Road 137	48	23
Hendry County			
Clewiston	Delta Ranch on SR 832	48	22
Hernando County			
Brooksville	14843 Buczak Road	36	19
Ridge Manor	6223 Kettering Road	36	17
Spring Hill	Forest Oaks Boulevard	39	18
Hillsborough County			
Brandon	2829 S. Kingsway Avenue	39	21
County	Gardinier Park, HWY 41 N	39	22
Gibsonton	ICWU Building, Highway 41 North Gibsonton	77	31
Tampa	5012 Causeway Boulevard	52	27
Lee County			
Ft. Myers	Ft. Myers Water Treatment Plant	30	16
Manatee County			
Bradenton	End of Piney Point Road	40	18
County	Holland House 100 yards east of US 41	32	18
Palmetto	Police Station, 1115 10th Street W	40	19
Martin County			
Indiantown	SR 710 at Calkins	34	17

See footnotes at end of table.

Continued . . .

Table 8.80. AIR POLLUTION: PARTICULATE MATTER (PM) CONCENTRATIONS IN SPECIFIED CITIES OF FLORIDA, 1995 (Continued)

Area 1/	Site Address	PM10 concentration (UG/M³) 2nd highest 24-hour value 2/	PM10 concentration (UG/M³) Annual arithmetic mean 3/
Nassau County			
Fernandina Beach	WWTP 5th St. N of Lime Avenue	43	24
Orange County			
Orlando	2401 W 33rd Street	41	25
Winter Park	Lake Isle Estates	34	18
Zellwood	Zellwood Elementary School	33	17
Palm Beach County			
Belle Glade	P O Box 484	88	29
Canal Point	US 98 1.8 miles south of Hatton	60	26
Delray Beach	345 S Congress	37	19
Pahokee	Pahokee Water Treatment Plant	35	19
Palm Beach Gardens	3188 PGA Boulevard	34	17
South Bay	Sunshine Sod Company	37	21
West Palm Beach	3730 Belvedere Road	32	18
Pinellas County			
Largo	1301 Ulmerton Road	49	23
St. Petersburg	1313 19th Street North	40	23
Tarpon Springs	Brooker Creek Park	43	19
Polk County			
Auburndale	300 E. Bridgers Avenue	40	20
Lakeland	1501 W. Bella Vista St.	36	17
Mulberry	Mulberry High School, NE 4th Circle	35	21
Putnam County			
Palatka	100 feet west of Comfort intersection	39	22
St. Johns County			
St. Augustine	30 Pellicer Lane, City Warehouse	44	24
Sarasota County			
Sarasota	1642 12th Street (Reverse Osmosis Plant)	43	22
Venice	448 East Venice Avenue	45	25
Seminole County			
Altamonte Springs	2150 Sand Lake Road	34	18
Sanford	City Hall 2nd Story N Park Avenue	32	16
Volusia County			
Daytona Beach	1185-A Dunn Avenue	38	21
Holly Hill	1200 Center Avenue	35	19

UG/M³ Micrograms per cubic meter.

1/ Source includes more sites than could be reported here. Major cities in each county are reported. If more than one site was available, the one with the highest annual arithmetic mean is reported. 2/ Florida standard is 150 UG/M³, not to be exceeded more than once per year. 3/ Florida standard is 50 UG/M³.

Note: Particulate describes airborne solid or liquid particles of about 0.1 to 50 microns in diameter (1 micron = 0.0001 centimeter). PM consists of sulfate, nitrate, and acidic particles formed by oxidation of the pollutant gases sulfur dioxide and nitrogen dioxide; of soot and organic particles released in forest fires and other low-temperature combustion processes; of lead-containing particles emitted from motor vehicles; of products of industrial processes and high temperature fuel combustion; of local soil; and of airborne sea salt. PM10 is a subset of particulate matter and refers to airborne particles that are 10 microns or less in size.

Source: State of Florida, Department of Environmental Protection, Division of Air Resources Management, *Comparison of Air Quality Data with the National Ambient Air Quality Standards, 1995.*

AGRICULTURE

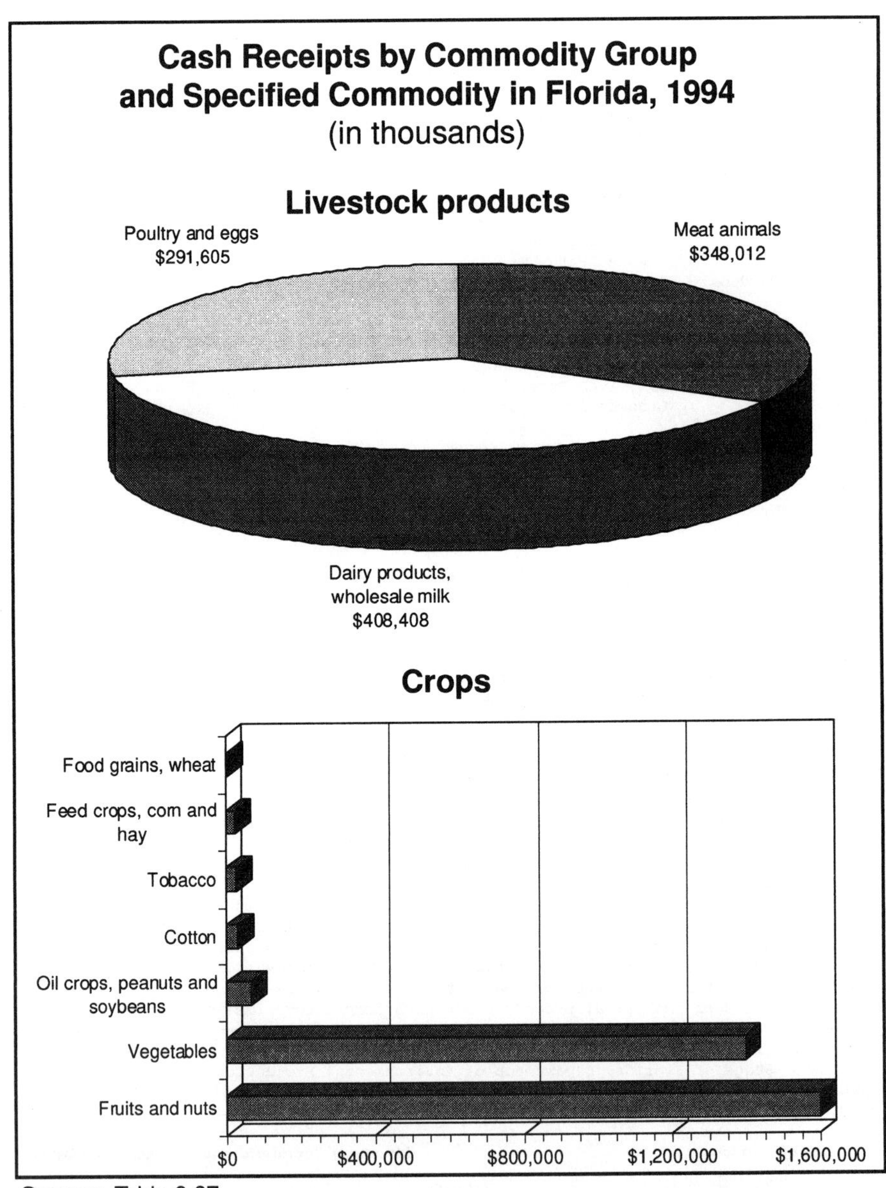

Cash Receipts by Commodity Group
and Specified Commodity in Florida, 1994
(in thousands)
Livestock products
Poultry and eggs
$291,605
Meat animals
$348,012
Dairy products,
wholesale milk
$408,408
Crops
Food grains, wheat
Feed crops, corn and hay
Tobacco
Cotton
Oil crops, peanuts and soybeans
Vegetables
Fruits and nuts
$0
$400,000
$800,000
$1,200,000
$1,600,000

Source: Table 9.37

SECTION 9.00
AGRICULTURE

TABLES LISTED BY MAJOR HEADINGS

HEADING PAGE

SECTION 9.00
AGRICULTURE
(Continued)

TABLES LISTED BY MAJOR HEADINGS

Table 9.04. VETERINARIANS: LICENSED DOCTORS OF VETERINARY MEDICINE IN THE STATE AND COUNTIES OF FLORIDA, JUNE 6, 1995

Location of licensee	Doctors of veterinary medicine	Location of licensee	Doctors of veterinary medicine
Total 1/	5,505	Jefferson	7
NonFlorida	2,502	Lafayette	1
Unknown	0	Lake	34
Alachua	187	Lee	86
Baker	1	Leon	53
Bay	28	Levy	11
Bradford	6	Liberty	0
Brevard	80	Madison	4
Broward	292	Manatee	28
Calhoun	1	Marion	120
Charlotte	17	Martin	33
Citrus	16	Monroe	32
Clay	30	Nassau	9
Collier	34	Okaloosa	36
Columbia	8	Okeechobee	8
Dade	324	Orange	135
De Soto	5	Osceola	18
Dixie	2	Palm Beach	243
Duval	132	Pasco	52
Escambia	53	Pinellas	181
Flagler	6	Polk	69
Franklin	3	Putnam	15
Gadsden	6	St. Johns	27
Gilchrist	3	St. Lucie	21
Glades	0	Santa Rosa	18
Gulf	2	Sarasota	81
Hamilton	1	Seminole	72
Hardee	5	Sumter	9
Hendry	6	Suwannee	13
Hernando	16	Taylor	3
Highlands	13	Union	0
Hillsborough	193	Volusia	67
Holmes	1	Wakulla	3
Indian River	27	Walton	6
Jackson	4	Washington	6

1/ Total includes all active, involuntary inactive, and voluntary inactive licensed persons.

Source: State of Florida, Department of Business and Professional Regulation, unpublished data.

Table 9.10. EMPLOYMENT: ESTIMATES OF AVERAGE MONTHLY EMPLOYMENT OF FARM PROPRIETORS AND WAGE AND SALARY WORKERS IN THE UNITED STATES AND IN THE STATE AND COUNTIES OF FLORIDA, 1993 AND 1994

County	1993 A/			1994		
		Farm wage and salary employees			Farm wage and salary employees	
	Farm proprie-tors	Number	As a per-centage of all wage and salary employees	Farm proprie-tors	Number	As a per-centage of all wage and salary employees
United States	2,132,000	914,000	0.77	2,107,000	894,000	0.73
Florida	37,170	60,369	1.00	37,177	63,555	1.02
Alachua	1,266	269	0.26	1,266	374	0.34
Baker	231	261	5.04	231	295	5.41
Bay	88	14	0.02	88	16	0.02
Bradford	361	6	0.10	361	5	0.08
Brevard	515	267	0.15	515	305	0.17
Broward	363	680	0.12	363	697	0.11
Calhoun	170	76	2.72	170	112	3.72
Charlotte	209	235	0.76	209	210	0.64
Citrus	357	3	0.01	357	4	0.02
Clay	245	202	0.68	245	180	0.58
Collier	241	8,011	10.01	241	6,811	8.21
Columbia	572	50	0.32	572	46	0.28
Dade	1,460	4,802	0.51	1,460	5,444	0.56
De Soto	704	504	5.77	704	593	6.51
Dixie	124	0	0.00	124	0	0.00
Duval	439	278	0.07	439	341	0.08
Escambia	530	210	0.16	530	162	0.12
Flagler	107	70	0.84	107	73	0.79
Franklin	0	0	0.00	0	0	0.00
Gadsden	358	1,308	9.25	358	1,494	10.36
Gilchrist	375	138	6.63	375	163	7.59
Glades	194	202	14.78	194	219	15.07
Gulf	0	0	0.00	0	0	0.00
Hamilton	286	196	4.86	286	259	6.16
Hardee	1,210	840	10.91	1,210	920	10.81
Hendry	418	2,350	17.67	418	2,562	18.21
Hernando	432	103	0.43	432	98	0.38
Highlands	735	1,157	5.16	735	1,335	5.56
Hillsborough	2,819	5,608	1.16	2,822	6,325	1.24
Holmes	606	27	0.83	606	33	0.94
Indian River	536	828	2.29	536	888	2.36
Jackson	1,010	120	0.79	1,010	139	0.92
Jefferson	318	205	6.35	318	200	6.39
Lafayette	298	113	9.83	298	136	10.58

See footnote at end of table.

Continued . . .

Table 9.10. EMPLOYMENT: ESTIMATES OF AVERAGE MONTHLY EMPLOYMENT OF FARM PROPRIETORS AND WAGE AND SALARY WORKERS IN THE UNITED STATES AND IN THE STATE AND COUNTIES OF FLORIDA, 1993 AND 1994 (Continued)

County	1993 A/ Farm proprie- tors	1993 A/ Farm wage and salary employees Number	1993 A/ Farm wage and salary employees As a per- centage of all wage and salary employees	1994 Farm proprie- tors	1994 Farm wage and salary employees Number	1994 Farm wage and salary employees As a per- centage of all wage and salary employees
Lake	1,255	1,567	3.09	1,255	1,650	3.09
Lee	423	2,096	1.52	423	2,224	1.52
Leon	310	113	0.09	310	127	0.10
Levy	585	272	4.27	585	318	4.67
Liberty	86	0	0.00	86	0	0.00
Madison	507	85	1.74	507	103	2.02
Manatee	772	2,676	2.82	772	2,931	2.75
Marion	1,765	983	1.39	1,765	1,083	1.48
Martin	307	863	2.05	307	896	2.08
Monroe	0	0	0.00	0	0	0.00
Nassau	338	194	1.33	339	206	1.37
Okaloosa	351	30	0.04	351	37	0.05
Okeechobee	376	1,111	12.23	376	1,158	12.38
Orange	1,043	3,715	0.75	1,043	3,924	0.77
Osceola	519	330	0.75	519	347	0.77
Palm Beach	702	8,665	2.13	702	8,571	2.02
Pasco	1,026	666	1.01	1,027	760	1.09
Pinellas	150	179	0.05	150	170	0.04
Polk	2,739	2,342	1.40	2,739	2,691	1.54
Putnam	424	431	2.20	424	496	2.51
St. Johns	162	267	0.85	162	347	1.05
St. Lucie	514	726	1.44	514	791	1.53
Santa Rosa	471	53	0.23	472	68	0.29
Sarasota	344	274	0.22	345	252	0.19
Seminole	388	402	0.39	388	416	0.38
Sumter	732	193	2.79	732	191	2.72
Suwannee	1,061	451	5.21	1,061	469	5.22
Taylor	169	3	0.05	169	4	0.06
Union	221	7	0.17	221	17	0.41
Volusia	934	2,462	1.81	934	2,797	2.00
Wakulla	90	1	0.03	90	0	0.00
Walton	454	14	0.15	454	12	0.13
Washington	375	65	1.31	375	60	1.15

A/ Revised.

Source: U.S., Department of Commerce, Bureau of Economic Analysis, Regional Economic Information System, CD-ROM, June 1996.

Table 9.15. PRODUCTION AND SERVICES: AVERAGE MONTHLY PRIVATE REPORTING UNITS EMPLOYMENT, AND PAYROLL COVERED BY UNEMPLOYMENT COMPENSATION LAW IN THE STATE AND COUNTIES OF FLORIDA, 1995

County	Number of re-porting units	Number of em-ployees	Payroll ($1,000)	County	Number of re-porting units	Number of em-ployees	Payroll ($1,000)
			Agriculture production--crops (SIC code 01)				
Florida	2,475	61,215	77,306	Lee	39	2,336	2,389
				Leon	10	114	138
Alachua	26	271	277	Levy	11	55	82
Baker	4	303	294	Madison	9	64	42
Brevard	21	181	224	Manatee	66	3,462	3,595
Broward	58	723	1,016	Marion	22	203	235
Calhoun	4	89	109	Martin	37	1,032	1,507
Charlotte	16	203	371	Monroe	3	12	14
Collier	81	7,177	5,585	Okeechobee	17	458	876
Dade	314	5,805	7,557	Orange	184	4,178	6,611
De Soto	40	583	769	Osceola	29	267	421
Duval	11	322	505	Palm Beach	269	8,309	14,460
Flagler	9	105	120	Pasco	37	409	391
Gadsden	21	1,625	1,848	Pinellas	12	164	293
Gilchrist	3	12	14	Polk	166	2,465	3,614
Glades	9	126	267	Putnam	37	539	485
Hardee	61	744	795	St. Johns	47	371	528
Hendry	52	2,624	4,132	St. Lucie	37	792	1,290
Hernando	5	13	10	Santa Rosa	9	71	79
Highlands	79	1,134	1,757	Sarasota	18	237	346
Hillsborough	238	6,393	5,358	Seminole	26	380	761
Indian River	41	874	1,490	Sumter	10	148	190
Jackson	7	112	94	Suwannee	16	362	318
Jefferson	10	160	194	Volusia	136	2,785	2,714
Lafayette	3	12	6	Walton	3	18	21
Lake	85	1,590	2,224	Washington	3	7	4
			Agriculture production--livestock (SIC code 02)				
Florida	589	6,325	9,327	Highlands	22	288	410
				Hillsborough	42	489	709
Alachua	17	123	169	Indian River	5	48	86
Baker	3	11	10	Jackson	7	28	29
Brevard	9	135	230	Jefferson	5	45	36
Broward	10	71	121	Lafayette	16	140	114
Clay	7	174	241	Lake	11	243	353
Collier	5	26	37	Lee	3	3	9
Columbia	4	37	33	Leon	5	21	24
Dade	15	52	92	Levy	12	311	512
De Soto	11	87	128	Madison	4	44	56
Duval	7	75	106	Manatee	15	137	176
Gilchrist	7	171	245	Marion	89	971	1,472
Glades	5	99	161	Martin	6	44	91
Hardee	23	205	312	Monroe	4	60	116
Hendry	9	29	40	Nassau	7	58	76
Hernando	8	47	62	Okeechobee	35	712	1,143

See footnote at end of table. Continued . . .

Table 9.15. PRODUCTION AND SERVICES: AVERAGE MONTHLY PRIVATE REPORTING UNITS EMPLOYMENT, AND PAYROLL COVERED BY UNEMPLOYMENT COMPENSATION LAW IN THE STATE AND COUNTIES OF FLORIDA, 1995 (Continued)

County	Number of re-porting units	Number of em-ployees	Payroll ($1,000)	County	Number of re-porting units	Number of em-ployees	Payroll ($1,000)
	Agriculture production--livestock (SIC code 02) (Continued)						
Orange	7	22	26	Sarasota	5	33	42
Osceola	13	114	181	Sumter	8	36	43
Palm Beach	16	103	135	Suwannee	18	154	168
Pasco	27	403	584	Volusia	9	94	146
Polk	24	201	301	Washington	4	32	40
St. Lucie	8	34	75				
	Agriculture services (SIC code 07)						
Florida	8,461	83,023	102,059	Leon	100	673	821
				Levy	20	141	178
Alachua	95	781	946	Madison	4	16	25
Baker	4	11	5	Manatee	151	1,837	2,004
Bay	40	191	256	Marion	142	886	1,151
Bradford	8	26	31	Martin	122	1,169	1,526
Brevard	231	1,338	1,648	Monroe	53	227	298
Broward	799	4,849	7,273	Nassau	17	101	135
Calhoun	3	12	9	Okaloosa	76	358	402
Charlotte	61	334	458	Okeechobee	27	599	619
Citrus	42	234	260	Orange	485	4,415	6,346
Clay	64	440	550	Osceola	57	322	411
Collier	284	3,461	3,774	Palm Beach	876	8,684	11,757
Columbia	17	93	102	Pasco	151	1,352	1,521
Dade	656	5,937	7,462	Pinellas	450	2,493	3,486
De Soto	69	1,983	1,969	Polk	404	7,327	8,268
Duval	345	2,299	3,202	Putnam	29	190	179
Escambia	93	569	691	St. Johns	56	533	499
Flagler	29	194	188	St. Lucie	196	4,666	5,416
Gadsden	14	228	265	Santa Rosa	45	260	335
Hardee	98	1,722	1,340	Sarasota	242	1,168	1,681
Hendry	71	3,761	3,693	Seminole	207	1,404	1,898
Hernando	53	221	284	Sumter	11	59	58
Highlands	125	2,091	2,009	Suwannee	14	75	92
Hillsborough	468	4,678	5,142	Taylor	5	21	28
Indian River	190	2,936	4,170	Union	4	22	27
Jackson	16	53	69	Volusia	209	939	1,066
Jefferson	7	24	28	Wakulla	4	30	36
Lake	129	1,340	1,581	Walton	12	151	190
Lee	249	1,863	2,404	Washington	5	15	17

Note: Private employment. Three-digit classifications of these two-digit groups are listed in Table 9.27. Data are preliminary. Only counties for which data are disclosed are shown. Detail may not add to totals due to disclosure editing and/or rounding. See Tables in 23.70, 23.71, 23.72, 23.73, and 23.74 for public employment data.

Source: State of Florida, Department of Labor and Employment Security, Bureau of Labor Market Information, "Employment and Wages" (ES-202), unpublished data.

Table 9.21. LABOR AND PROPRIETORS' INCOME: FARM LABOR AND EXPENSE IN FLORIDA 1991 THROUGH 1994

(in thousands of dollars)

Item	1991	1992	1993	1994
Cash receipts from marketing	6,255,658	6,240,830	6,182,915	6,081,642
Total livestock and products	1,267,124	1,252,377	1,307,106	1,279,296
Total crops	4,988,534	4,988,453	4,875,809	4,802,346
Other income	197,393	202,231	278,712	196,920
Government payments	40,786	53,085	110,680	58,637
Imputed income and rent received 1/	156,607	149,146	168,032	138,283
Production expenses	3,849,938	3,703,538	4,070,561	4,162,488
Feed purchased	273,104	263,052	290,671	287,335
Livestock purchased	154,134	141,351	163,512	149,918
Seed purchased	188,764	172,661	181,718	182,009
Fertilizer and lime purchased	551,012	529,149	579,750	571,410
Petroleum products purchased	126,693	112,393	113,133	104,957
Hired farm labor 2/	1,064,644	1,035,319	1,143,153	1,168,465
All other production expenses 3/	1,491,587	1,449,613	1,598,624	1,698,394
Value of inventory change	28,902	4,975	16,930	27,902
Livestock	22,052	-3,215	24,828	19,175
Crops	6,850	8,190	-7,898	8,727
Derivation of farm labor and proprietors' income:				
Total cash receipts and other income	6,453,051	6,443,061	6,461,627	6,278,562
Less: Total production expenses	3,849,938	3,703,538	4,070,561	4,162,488
Realized net income	2,603,113	2,739,523	2,391,066	2,116,074
Plus: Value of inventory change	28,902	4,975	16,930	27,902
Total net income including corporate farms	2,632,015	2,744,498	2,407,996	2,143,976
Less: Corporate farms	254,968	685,268	214,001	479,658
Plus: Statistical Adjustment	A/	A/	A/	A/
Total net farm proprietors' income	2,377,056	2,059,244	2,193,996	1,664,321
Plus: Farm wages and perquisites	673,964	655,218	743,402	707,912
Plus: Farm other labor income	60,219	57,478	65,587	74,175
Total farm labor and proprietors' income	3,111,239	2,771,940	3,002,985	2,446,408

A/ Less than $50,000. Estimates are included in totals.

1/ Includes imputed income such as gross rental value of dwellings and value of home consumption and other farm-related income components such as machine hire and custom work income, rental income, and income from forest products.

2/ Consists of hired workers' cash wages, social security, perquisites, and contract labor, machine hire and custom work expenses.

3/ Includes repair and operation of machinery; depreciation, interest, rent and taxes; and other miscellaneous expenses, including agricultural chemicals.

Note: Data for 1991 through 1993 may be revised.

Source: U.S., Department of Commerce, Bureau of Economic Analysis, Regional Economic Information System, CD-ROM, June 1996.

Table 9.22. LABOR AND PROPRIETORS' INCOME: DERIVATION OF FARM LABOR AND PROPRIETORS' INCOME IN THE UNITED STATES AND IN THE STATE AND COUNTIES OF FLORIDA, 1993 AND 1994

(in thousands of dollars)

County	Cash receipts from marketings	Plus other income 1/	Less production expenses	Plus value of inventory change	Total net farm income	Less corporate farm income	Total net farm proprietors' income 2/	Plus farm wages	Plus farm other labor income	Total farm labor and proprietors' income
				1993 A/						
United States 3/	189,418	27,663	171,706	-6,297	39,077	1,645	37,432	12,207	997	50,636
Florida	6,182,915	278,712	4,070,561	16,930	2,407,996	214,001	2,193,996	743,402	65,587	3,002,985
Alachua	46,741	7,596	36,811	360	17,886	316	17,571	2,862	393	20,826
Baker	26,190	2,091	18,336	61	10,006	252	9,754	2,406	295	12,455
Bay	1,863	458	1,825	B/	500	B/	499	139	B/	669
Bradford	18,235	2,149	15,121	96	5,359	106	5,253	89	59	5,401
Brevard	29,926	1,888	25,678	440	6,576	309	6,267	3,902	419	10,588
Broward	58,503	2,947	45,062	266	16,654	1,607	15,047	9,677	1,082	25,806
Calhoun	10,042	1,860	9,564	-154	2,184	B/	2,145	860	108	3,113
Charlotte	26,245	1,967	18,974	396	9,634	746	8,888	4,270	256	13,414
Citrus	7,950	601	7,945	54	660	B/	640	B/	59	736
Clay	26,716	1,574	27,665	122	747	B/	704	2,591	256	3,551
Collier	226,252	3,172	117,112	193	112,505	3,358	109,147	54,320	1,857	165,324
Columbia	20,322	2,524	16,302	B/	6,539	97	6,442	532	122	7,096
Dade	355,562	66,627	232,500	160	189,849	13,934	175,915	60,387	4,574	240,876
De Soto	101,935	2,860	67,625	1,023	38,193	861	37,332	6,697	653	44,682
Dixie	2,281	729	1,790	51	1,271	B/	1,269	B/	B/	1,297
Duval	27,808	1,016	21,861	80	7,043	315	6,728	4,147	358	11,233
Escambia	13,306	7,344	15,802	-786	4,062	B/	4,044	1,246	112	5,402
Flagler	18,623	1,424	11,311	116	8,852	B/	8,830	958	138	9,926
Franklin	0	0	0	0	0	0	0	0	0	0
Gadsden	57,455	1,883	41,321	B/	17,996	665	17,331	13,400	703	31,434
Gilchrist	21,379	2,285	17,325	267	6,606	307	6,299	2,226	206	8,731

See footnotes at end of table.

Continued . . .

Table 9.22. LABOR AND PROPRIETORS' INCOME: DERIVATION OF FARM LABOR AND PROPRIETORS' INCOME IN THE UNITED STATES AND IN THE STATE AND COUNTIES OF FLORIDA, 1993 AND 1994 (Continued)

(in thousands of dollars)

County	Cash receipts from marketings	Plus other income 1/	Less production expenses	Plus value of inventory change	Total net farm income	Less corporate farm income	Total net farm proprietors' income 2/	Plus farm wages	Plus farm other labor income	Total farm labor and proprietors' income
				1993 A/ (Continued)						
Glades	50,646	3,231	32,391	895	22,381	2,200	20,181	3,638	474	24,293
Gulf	0	0	0	0	0	0	0	0	0	0
Hamilton	18,768	3,704	12,329	-281	9,862	62	9,800	1,488	98	11,386
Hardee	129,537	5,768	96,105	1,135	40,335	1,706	38,629	9,172	912	48,713
Hendry	232,804	4,989	151,852	1,328	87,269	10,737	76,532	35,866	1,663	114,061
Hernando	31,462	1,177	25,887	271	7,023	290	6,733	1,371	256	8,360
Highlands	190,322	4,528	115,488	1,395	80,757	7,913	72,844	17,512	1,461	91,817
Hillsborough	332,546	9,906	206,874	1,008	136,586	7,930	128,656	51,893	4,082	184,631
Holmes	34,159	3,305	26,420	B/	11,036	B/	11,016	288	128	11,432
Indian River	195,124	3,360	134,916	280	63,848	5,299	58,549	13,725	1,472	73,746
Jackson	61,272	8,860	55,438	-884	13,810	128	13,682	1,075	364	15,121
Jefferson	21,307	3,203	22,458	B/	2,038	B/	2,004	2,305	364	4,673
Lafayette	48,421	1,461	32,332	199	17,749	246	17,503	1,028	175	18,706
Lake	108,876	4,915	84,178	289	29,902	1,465	28,437	21,679	1,914	52,030
Lee	132,952	1,882	72,291	174	62,717	1,380	61,337	20,531	2,302	84,170
Leon	5,100	2,518	7,023	B/	589	B/	550	1,264	94	1,908
Levy	24,415	3,642	21,103	174	7,128	148	6,980	3,932	174	11,086
Liberty	1,115	345	833	B/	640	B/	617	0	B/	619
Madison	28,412	3,826	25,326	-119	6,793	121	6,672	784	284	7,740
Manatee	261,299	3,877	134,981	844	131,039	11,573	119,466	33,590	2,473	155,529
Marion	123,188	7,451	104,523	462	26,578	1,239	25,339	13,135	1,459	39,933
Martin	179,637	3,114	122,889	419	60,281	3,821	56,460	11,890	1,526	69,876
Monroe	0	0	0	0	0	0	0	0	0	0

See footnotes at end of table.

Continued . . .

Table 9.22. LABOR AND PROPRIETORS' INCOME: DERIVATION OF FARM LABOR AND PROPRIETORS' INCOME IN THE UNITED STATES AND IN THE STATE AND COUNTIES OF FLORIDA, 1993 AND 1994 (Continued)

(in thousands of dollars)

County	Cash receipts from marketings	Plus other income 1/	Less production expenses	Plus value of inventory change	Total net farm income	Less corporate farm income	Total net farm proprietors' income 2/	Plus farm wages	Plus farm other labor income	Total farm labor and proprietors' income
1993 A/ (Continued)										
Nassau	26,591	787	17,375	105	10,108	151	9,957	4,271	152	14,380
Okaloosa	5,536	2,990	6,711	-92	1,723	B/	1,716	325	B/	2,075
Okeechobee	144,678	2,119	106,572	2,066	42,291	3,286	39,005	18,974	1,207	59,186
Orange	296,689	4,787	179,109	191	122,558	8,400	114,158	54,078	4,816	173,052
Osceola	78,010	3,901	62,908	1,255	20,258	2,145	18,113	5,051	794	23,958
Palm Beach	1,242,885	12,915	667,040	131	588,891	96,609	492,282	139,233	15,153	646,668
Pasco	73,225	3,699	59,854	525	17,595	699	16,896	7,973	606	25,475
Pinellas	12,256	985	9,569	B/	3,664	B/	3,641	2,942	266	6,849
Polk	353,081	13,693	251,671	1,262	116,365	7,751	108,614	32,463	2,977	144,054
Putnam	35,467	1,711	25,253	128	12,053	457	11,596	3,841	390	15,827
St. Johns	44,761	1,367	37,951	481	8,658	281	8,377	3,978	465	12,820
St. Lucie	218,995	4,480	150,667	407	73,215	11,355	61,860	11,320	1,835	75,015
Santa Rosa	29,937	7,377	19,614	-1,019	16,681	190	16,491	585	148	17,224
Sarasota	24,475	2,229	16,092	283	10,895	463	10,432	3,370	217	14,019
Seminole	29,444	1,065	21,799	106	8,816	339	8,477	7,621	571	16,669
Sumter	44,290	2,129	32,615	619	14,423	1,002	13,421	2,283	315	16,019
Suwannee	78,256	5,408	63,449	65	20,280	213	20,067	4,131	376	24,574
Taylor	3,648	394	2,986	82	1,138	B/	1,113	B/	B/	1,162
Union	10,908	1,015	9,448	128	2,603	B/	2,591	55	54	2,700
Volusia	85,129	3,103	62,645	162	25,749	790	24,959	22,993	1,613	49,565
Wakulla	1,537	343	1,442	B/	427	B/	426	B/	B/	449
Walton	21,958	2,303	19,665	-191	4,405	236	4,169	168	82	4,419
Washington	12,463	1,855	10,559	B/	3,717	174	3,543	788	105	4,436

See footnotes at end of table.

Continued . . .

Table 9.22. LABOR AND PROPRIETORS' INCOME: DERIVATION OF FARM LABOR AND PROPRIETORS' INCOME IN THE UNITED STATES AND IN THE STATE AND COUNTIES OF FLORIDA, 1993 AND 1994 (Continued)

(in thousands of dollars)

County	Cash receipts from marketings	Plus other income 1/	Less production expenses	Plus value of inventory change	Total net farm income	Less corporate farm income	Total net farm proprietors' income 2/	Plus farm wages	Plus farm other labor income	Total farm labor and proprietors' income
					1994					
United States 3/	186,549	22,095	177,234	11,448	42,858	4,109	38,749	12,177	1,120	52,046
Florida	6,081,642	196,920	4,162,488	27,902	2,143,976	479,658	1,664,321	707,912	74,175	2,446,408
Alachua	44,236	4,304	38,463	647	10,724	501	10,223	3,722	446	14,391
Baker	27,005	1,419	18,778	83	9,729	639	9,090	2,538	331	11,959
Bay	1,912	315	1,883	B/	358	B/	357	155	B/	548
Bradford	17,552	1,195	15,308	151	3,590	185	3,405	86	67	3,558
Brevard	30,447	1,526	26,957	340	5,356	718	4,638	3,772	466	8,876
Broward	58,166	1,467	46,887	197	12,943	3,355	9,588	8,917	1,230	19,735
Calhoun	10,284	1,189	9,905	418	1,986	100	1,886	846	120	2,852
Charlotte	26,721	1,213	19,908	308	8,334	1,728	6,606	3,392	293	10,291
Citrus	7,634	580	8,265	174	123	B/	109	B/	67	221
Clay	26,661	1,303	27,725	166	405	122	283	1,987	289	2,559
Collier	193,979	2,398	123,139	138	73,376	5,689	67,687	45,733	2,064	115,484
Columbia	19,576	1,632	16,840	292	4,660	184	4,476	498	138	5,112
Dade	336,965	23,645	244,193	61	116,478	22,292	94,186	61,600	5,203	160,989
De Soto	104,484	2,538	71,367	812	36,467	2,197	34,270	7,048	729	42,047
Dixie	2,115	329	1,883	B/	609	B/	607	B/	B/	639
Duval	28,300	924	22,480	179	6,923	824	6,099	4,420	414	10,933
Escambia	13,859	4,341	16,630	1,238	2,808	B/	2,773	912	130	3,815
Flagler	16,418	979	11,808	87	5,676	B/	5,639	742	156	6,537
Franklin	0	0	0	0	0	0	0	0	0	0
Gadsden	57,257	1,391	43,573	100	15,175	1,496	13,679	15,102	790	29,571
Gilchrist	20,844	1,466	18,012	374	4,672	579	4,093	1,912	234	6,239
Glades	50,586	2,769	33,585	705	20,475	5,254	15,221	3,480	538	19,239

See footnotes at end of table.

Continued . . .

Table 9.22. LABOR AND PROPRIETORS' INCOME: DERIVATION OF FARM LABOR AND PROPRIETORS' INCOME IN THE UNITED STATES AND IN THE STATE AND COUNTIES OF FLORIDA, 1993 AND 1994 (Continued)

(in thousands of dollars)

County	Cash receipts from marketings	Plus other income 1/	Less production expenses	Plus value of inventory change	Total net farm income	Less corporate farm income	Total net farm proprietors' income 2/	Plus farm wages	Plus farm other labor income	Total farm labor and proprietors' income
					1994 (Continued)					
Gulf	0	0	0	0	0	0	0	0	0	0
Hamilton	17,238	2,392	12,801	163	6,992	115	6,877	1,837	109	8,823
Hardee	132,306	4,696	96,772	966	41,196	4,244	36,952	8,990	1,032	46,974
Hendry	232,290	4,360	145,767	1,009	91,892	25,916	65,976	31,919	1,845	99,740
Hernando	30,590	968	26,129	390	5,819	639	5,180	1,180	291	6,651
Highlands	199,307	4,021	122,163	1,178	82,343	21,346	60,997	17,858	1,650	80,505
Hillsborough	320,281	8,119	214,640	982	114,742	17,435	97,307	49,207	4,683	151,197
Holmes	33,225	2,123	26,834	336	8,850	B/	8,807	303	149	9,259
Indian River	204,213	3,146	129,334	220	78,245	14,462	63,783	12,780	1,612	78,175
Jackson	60,535	6,326	57,760	1,623	10,724	276	10,448	1,007	412	11,867
Jefferson	21,508	2,112	23,314	291	597	B/	562	2,055	414	3,031
Lafayette	48,431	1,150	32,838	335	17,078	613	16,465	1,059	198	17,722
Lake	109,706	6,862	88,250	367	28,685	3,821	24,864	20,502	2,211	47,577
Lee	120,593	1,735	74,974	147	47,501	2,719	44,782	19,350	2,571	66,703
Leon	5,354	1,822	7,430	125	-129	-76	-53	1,311	110	1,368
Levy	22,791	2,645	21,780	471	4,127	230	3,897	4,268	198	8,363
Liberty	1,032	218	865	B/	409	B/	372	0	B/	374
Madison	26,342	2,641	25,631	268	3,620	174	3,446	883	323	4,652
Manatee	239,463	3,953	141,443	740	102,713	23,531	79,182	30,296	2,789	112,267
Marion	119,997	7,023	108,228	762	19,554	2,497	17,057	14,006	1,665	32,728
Martin	187,174	3,004	116,873	348	73,653	10,266	63,387	11,530	1,714	76,631
Monroe	0	0	0	0	0	0	0	0	0	0
Nassau	26,877	734	17,768	204	10,047	387	9,660	4,231	175	14,066
Okaloosa	5,467	2,099	7,024	379	921	B/	911	388	B/	1,340
Okeechobee	149,681	2,329	110,198	1,606	43,418	8,936	34,482	17,949	1,359	53,790
Orange	295,585	7,153	187,364	178	115,552	20,725	94,827	52,246	5,447	152,520

See footnotes at end of table.

Continued . . .

Table 9.22. LABOR AND PROPRIETORS' INCOME: DERIVATION OF FARM LABOR AND PROPRIETORS' INCOME IN THE UNITED STATES AND IN THE STATE AND COUNTIES OF FLORIDA, 1993 AND 1994 (Continued)

(in thousands of dollars)

County	Cash receipts from marketings	Plus other income 1/	Less production expenses	Plus value of inventory change	Total net farm income	Less corporate farm income	Total net farm proprietors' income 2/	Plus farm wages	Plus farm other labor income	Total farm labor and proprietors' income
					1994 (Continued)					
Osceola	78,621	3,869	66,013	1,032	17,509	5,110	12,399	5,035	900	18,334
Palm Beach	1,174,355	11,961	689,119	121	497,318	205,931	291,390	124,511	17,161	433,062
Pasco	72,141	3,674	61,624	640	14,831	1,586	13,245	8,065	691	22,001
Pinellas	13,059	682	10,030	B/	3,714	64	3,650	2,565	300	6,515
Polk	371,734	11,265	241,803	1,158	142,354	21,255	121,099	33,975	3,348	158,422
Putnam	36,033	1,374	26,372	127	11,162	1,120	10,042	3,819	443	14,304
St. Johns	45,196	961	39,534	58	6,681	611	6,070	4,003	526	10,599
St. Lucie	243,860	4,438	145,879	297	102,716	31,659	71,057	11,669	2,042	84,768
Santa Rosa	34,638	3,389	20,312	2,089	19,804	584	19,220	657	173	20,050
Sarasota	23,538	1,743	16,949	293	8,625	960	7,665	3,043	248	10,956
Seminole	28,722	1,432	22,828	127	7,453	771	6,682	6,941	655	14,278
Sumter	41,624	2,634	33,425	629	11,462	2,101	9,361	2,094	351	11,806
Suwannee	75,657	3,604	64,524	700	15,437	432	15,005	3,995	421	19,421
Taylor	3,216	314	3,083	75	522	B/	491	B/	B/	543
Union	10,237	720	9,652	171	1,476	B/	1,458	147	62	1,667
Volusia	88,871	3,047	65,306	237	26,849	2,197	24,652	24,489	1,835	50,976
Wakulla	1,485	190	1,514	B/	165	B/	164	B/	B/	180
Walton	21,713	1,790	19,804	334	4,033	585	3,448	142	94	3,684
Washington	11,955	1,279	10,948	163	2,449	309	2,140	662	122	2,924

A/ Revised.
B/ Less than $50,000. Estimates are included in totals.
1/ Includes government payments, imputed income, and rent received.
2/ Includes statistical adjustment.
3/ United States numbers are rounded to millions of dollars.
Note: See also tables in Section 5.00.
Source: U.S., Department of Commerce, Bureau of Economic Analysis, Regional Economic Information System, CD-ROM, June 1996.

Table 9.25. INCOME: ESTIMATED CASH RECEIPTS FROM FARM MARKETINGS BY SPECIFIED COMMODITY IN THE UNITED STATES AND LEADING STATES IN RANK ORDER, 1993

(in millions of dollars)

Commodity and state	Cash receipts	Commodity and state	Cash receipts	Commodity and state	Cash receipts
All commodities		All livestock 1/		All crops	
United States	175,052	United States	90,555	United States	84,497
California	19,850	Texas	8,342	California	14,604
Texas	12,617	Nebraska	5,842	Illinois	5,835
Iowa	10,001	Iowa	5,829	Florida	4,548
Nebraska	8,909	California	5,246	Texas	4,275
Illinois	8,082	Kansas	4,870	Iowa	4,173
Kansas	7,363	Wisconsin	4,164	Indiana	3,186
Minnesota	6,574	Minnesota	3,774	Nebraska	3,067
Florida	5,750	North Carolina	3,201	Washington	3,013
North Carolina	5,457	Arkansas	2,902	Minnesota	2,800
Wisconsin	5,250	Colorado	2,879	Ohio	2,720
Greenhouse 2/ (7)		Tobacco (12)		Potatoes (14)	
United States	9,293	United States	2,949	United States	2,320
California	1,903	North Carolina	1,030	Idaho	554
Florida	1,018	Kentucky	919	Washington	433
Texas	701	Tennessee	266	California	181
Ohio	476	South Carolina	186	Florida	128
Michigan	376	Virginia	181	Wisconsin	118
Oregon	364	Georgia	157	Oregon	114
North Carolina	337	Ohio	39	Colorado	106
Pennsylvania	309	Indiana	33	Michigan	94
Oklahoma	275	Florida	31	Maine	93
New York	271	Pennsylvania	24	North Dakota	92
Tomatoes (16)		Lettuce (17)		Peanuts (22)	
United States	1,696	United States	1,474	United States	1,004
California	796	California	1,141	Georgia	425
Florida	(D)	Arizona	260	Texas	156
Ohio	50	Florida	26	Alabama	145
South Carolina	(D)	Colorado	11	North Carolina	91
Virginia	35	New Jersey	11	Florida	57
Georgia	25	New Mexico	7	Virginia	52
Michigan	24	Ohio	7	Oklahoma	51
New Jersey	(D)	New York	4	New Mexico	19
Tennessee	19	Washington	3	South Carolina	7
Indiana	18	Michigan	2	Arizona	1
Oranges (19)		Sugarcane (24)			
United States	1,337	United States	850		
Florida	867	Florida	439		
California	461	Louisiana	225		
Arizona	8	Hawaii	151		
Texas	3	Texas	35		

(D) Data withheld to avoid disclosure of information about individual producers.
1/ Includes poultry and products. 2/ Includes nursery.
Note: Commodities listed are among 25 leading commodities ranked by value of farm marketings. The number after the commodity name indicates rank order in cash receipts in the United States. Receipts include commodity credit corporation loans.
Source: U.S., Department of Agriculture, Economic Research Service, *Economic Indicators of the Farm Sector: State Financial Summary, 1993.*

Table 9.26. INCOME: CASH RECEIPTS BY COMMODITY AND COMMODITY GROUP IN FLORIDA 1992 THROUGH 1994

Commodity	1992 A/ Cash receipts ($1,000)	1992 A/ Percentage of total	1993 A/ Cash receipts ($1,000)	1993 A/ Percentage of total	1994 B/ Cash receipts ($1,000)	1994 B/ Percentage of total
Cash receipts 1/	6,139,084	100.00	6,069,496	100.00	5,977,970	100.00
Crops	4,973,210	81.01	4,858,365	80.05	4,786,346	80.07
Citrus	1,354,915	22.07	1,344,274	22.15	1,465,419	24.51
Grapefruit	309,473	5.04	251,166	4.14	256,997	4.30
K-early citrus fruit	1,375	0.02	1,037	0.02	318	0.01
Lemons	2,637	0.04	2,879	0.05	2,675	0.04
Limes	11,213	0.18	3,151	0.05	2,092	0.03
Oranges	946,785	15.42	1,008,026	16.61	1,121,264	18.76
Tangelos	14,994	0.24	14,428	0.24	20,087	0.34
Tangerines	48,459	0.79	51,129	0.84	49,632	0.83
Temples	19,979	0.33	12,458	0.21	12,354	0.21
Other fruits and nuts	141,267	2.30	137,631	2.27	134,535	2.25
Avocados	7,701	0.13	3,608	0.06	12,320	0.21
Mangos	4,280	0.07	950	0.02	1,500	0.03
Pecans	3,770	0.06	3,460	0.06	1,600	0.03
Strawberries	108,864	1.77	121,313	2.00	101,425	1.70
Blueberries	3,752	0.06	1,300	0.02	5,690	0.10
Other	12,900	0.21	7,000	0.12	12,000	0.20
Vegetables and melons	1,756,993	28.62	1,688,676	27.82	1,397,380	23.38
Cabbage	31,084	0.51	42,585	0.70	29,689	0.50
Carrots	20,228	0.33	25,551	0.42	10,808	0.18
Celery	39,110	0.64	58,670	0.97	21,571	0.36
Cucumbers	86,097	1.40	80,010	1.32	57,572	0.96
Eggplant	17,410	0.28	13,075	0.22	15,606	0.26
Escarole	7,000	0.11	7,611	0.13	4,995	0.08
Green peppers	209,630	3.41	215,939	3.56	215,853	3.61
Lettuce	18,128	0.30	26,770	0.44	12,548	0.21
Potatoes	92,359	1.50	128,194	2.11	118,905	1.99
Radishes	21,578	0.35	36,961	0.61	25,888	0.43
Snap beans	71,599	1.17	71,086	1.17	53,754	0.90
Squash	45,850	0.75	38,170	0.63	43,216	0.72
Sweet corn	73,149	1.19	102,588	1.69	99,347	1.66
Tomatoes	822,299	13.39	607,704	10.01	428,696	7.17
Watermelons	66,150	1.08	66,600	1.10	57,868	0.97
Other	135,322	2.20	167,162	2.75	201,064	3.36
Field crops	651,969	10.62	628,516	10.36	656,537	10.98
Corn	11,117	0.18	12,094	0.20	11,045	0.18
Cotton	20,502	0.33	23,393	0.39	31,590	0.53
Hay	13,389	0.22	10,801	0.18	14,025	0.23
Peanuts	57,886	0.94	57,684	0.95	58,302	0.98
Soybeans	7,375	0.12	8,091	0.13	7,490	0.13
Sugarcane	471,096	7.67	442,738	7.29	462,367	7.73
Tobacco	31,729	0.52	30,638	0.50	27,248	0.46
Wheat	2,349	0.04	2,268	0.04	1,717	0.03
Other	36,526	0.59	40,809	0.67	42,753	0.72
Foliage and floriculture	552,694	9.00	542,655	8.94	610,552	10.21
Other crops and products	515,372	8.39	516,613	8.51	521,923	8.73
Livestock and products	1,165,874	18.99	1,211,131	19.95	1,191,624	19.93
Milk	401,700	6.54	385,503	6.35	408,408	6.83
Cattle and calves	349,447	5.69	362,495	5.97	335,837	5.62

See footnotes at end of table. Continued . . .

Table 9.26. INCOME: CASH RECEIPTS BY COMMODITY AND COMMODITY GROUP IN FLORIDA 1992 THROUGH 1994 (Continued)

Commodity	1992 A/ Cash receipts ($1,000)	1992 A/ Percentage of total	1993 A/ Cash receipts ($1,000)	1993 A/ Percentage of total	1994 B/ Cash receipts ($1,000)	1994 B/ Percentage of total
Livestock and products (Cont.)						
Poultry and eggs	259,678	4.2	298,831	4.9	291,605	4.9
Broilers	164,856	2.7	187,714	3.1	191,151	3.2
Eggs	91,104	1.5	106,838	1.8	98,348	1.6
Other	3,718	0.1	4,279	0.1	2,106	0.0
Catfish	1,719	0.0	364	0.0	280	0.0
Hogs	13,126	0.2	15,106	0.2	11,899	0.2
Honey	12,126	0.2	11,300	0.2	8,887	0.1
Sheep and lambs, wool	55	0.0	82	0.0	288	0.0
Other	128,023	2.1	137,450	2.3	134,420	2.2

A/ Revised. B/ Preliminary.
1/ Farm marketings. Includes additional receipts not published.
Source: State of Florida, Department of Agriculture and Consumer Services, Florida Agricultural Statistics Service, *Florida Agriculture: Cash Receipts, 1994,* release of September 8, 1995.

Table 9.27. PRODUCTION AND SERVICES: AVERAGE MONTHLY PRIVATE REPORTING UNITS EMPLOYMENT, AND PAYROLL COVERED BY UNEMPLOYMENT COMPENSATION LAW BY INDUSTRY IN FLORIDA, 1995

SIC code	Industry	Number of reporting units	Number of employees	Payroll ($1,000)
01	Agricultural production--crops	2,475	61,215	77,306
011	Cash grains	14	149	204
013	Field crops, except cash grains	215	4,595	10,446
016	Vegetables and melons	372	19,312	17,511
017	Fruits and tree nuts	675	11,851	16,061
018	Horticultural specialties	1,180	24,804	32,347
019	General farms, primarily crop	19	504	737
02	Agricultural production--livestock	589	6,325	9,327
021	Livestock, except dairy, and poultry	221	1,320	2,038
024	Dairy farms	164	2,661	3,884
025	Poultry and eggs	30	818	1,133
027	Animal specialties	166	1,473	2,211
029	General farms, primarily animal	9	54	61
07	Agricultural services	8,461	83,023	102,059
071	Soil preparation services	32	145	215
072	Crop services	347	10,792	13,835
074	Veterinary services	1,355	10,490	16,490
075	Animal services, except veterinary	538	1,864	2,120
076	Farm labor and management services	860	28,184	26,011
078	Landscape and horticultural services	5,330	31,549	43,388

Note: Private employment. Detail may not add to totals due to disclosure editing and/or rounding. See Tables 23.70, 23.71, 23.72, 23.73, and 23.74 for public employment data.
Source: State of Florida, Department of Labor and Employment Security, Bureau of Labor Market Information, "Employment and Wages" (ES-202), unpublished data.

Table 9.34. FARMS: SPECIFIED CHARACTERISTICS OF FARMS IN FLORIDA 1987 AND 1992

Item	All farms 1987	All farms 1992	All farms Percentage change	Farms with sales of $10,000 or more 1987	Farms with sales of $10,000 or more 1992	Farms with sales of $10,000 or more Percentage change
Number of farms	36,556	35,204	-3.7	14,667	14,945	1.9
By size						
1 to 9 acres	7,300	7,664	5.0	1,968	2,185	11.0
10 to 49 acres	13,346	12,692	-4.9	3,919	4,074	4.0
50 to 179 acres	8,379	7,738	-7.7	3,274	3,309	1.1
180 to 499 acres	4,255	4,011	-5.7	2,706	2,683	-0.8
500 to 999 acres	1,598	1,451	-9.2	1,279	1,195	-6.6
1,000 to 1,999 acres	789	776	-1.6	708	689	-2.7
2,000 acres or more	889	872	-1.9	813	810	-0.4
With irrigated land	11,981	13,500	12.7	7,788	8,265	6.1
By SIC code						
Cash grains (011)	635	449	-29.3	236	166	-29.7
Field crops, except cash grains (013)	2,218	2,106	-5.0	1,203	1,257	4.5
Vegetables and melons (016)	1,511	1,483	-1.9	1,057	1,110	5.0
Fruits and tree nuts (017)	8,388	8,853	5.5	4,007	3,838	-4.2
Horticultural specialties (018)	4,096	4,942	20.7	2,849	3,483	22.3
General farms, primarily crop (019)	434	394	-9.2	219	206	-5.9
Livestock, except dairy, poultry, and animal specialties (021)	14,738	12,811	-13.1	3,296	3,295	0.0
Dairy farms (024)	358	372	3.9	358	337	-5.9
Poultry and eggs (025)	746	618	-17.2	629	502	-20.2
Animal specialties (27)	3,170	2,807	-11.5	798	731	-8.4
General farms, primarily livestock (29)	234	369	57.7	15	20	33.3
Selected farm production expenses 1/ ($1,000)						
Livestock and poultry purchased	148,405	131,497	-11.4	(NA)	123,668	(X)
Feed for livestock and poultry	336,690	382,945	13.7	322,471	369,869	14.7
Commercial fertilizer	209,617	283,424	35.2	198,090	268,075	35.3
Petroleum products	104,591	128,168	22.5	96,529	120,122	24.4
Hired farm labor	721,540	937,571	29.9	716,905	932,283	30.0
Interest expense	191,913	219,234	14.2	(NA)	207,581	(X)
Agricultural chemicals 2/	227,063	320,675	41.2	218,474	311,910	42.8
Livestock and poultry inventory						
Cattle and calves						
Farms	17,321	15,522	-10.4	5,403	5,474	1.3
Number	1,879,124	1,783,968	-5.1	1,609,538	1,553,165	-3.5

See footnotes at end of table.

Continued . . .

Table 9.34. FARMS: SPECIFIED CHARACTERISTICS OF FARMS IN FLORIDA 1987 AND 1992 (Continued)

Item	All farms 1987	All farms 1992	All farms Percentage change	Farms with sales of $10,000 or more 1987	Farms with sales of $10,000 or more 1992	Farms with sales of $10,000 or more Percentage change
Livestock/poultry inventory (Continued)						
Cattle and calves (Continued)						
Beef cows						
Farms	14,672	13,423	-8.5	4,653	4,785	2.8
Number	995,250	962,527	-3.3	835,048	827,655	-0.9
Milk cows						
Farms	1,073	877	-18.3	503	487	-3.2
Number	176,993	171,675	-3.0	175,647	170,852	-2.7
Chickens 3/						
Farms	2,275	1,454	-36.1	(NA)	(NA)	(X)
Number	12,964,760	10,802,573	-16.7	(NA)	(NA)	(X)
Crops harvested 4/						
Corn						
Farms	2,088	1,548	-25.9	1,079	905	-16.1
Acres	95,874	86,407	-9.9	82,973	76,488	-7.8
Soybeans						
Farms	708	415	-41.4	575	351	-39.0
Acres	89,938	49,072	45.4	86,038	47,215	-45.1
Sugarcane						
Farms	138	139	0.7	(NA)	(NA)	(X)
Acres	403,014	431,677	7.1	(NA)	(NA)	(X)
Hay						
Farms	5,643	4,892	-13.3	2,589	2,527	-2.4
Acres	280,639	270,404	-3.6	219,396	218,675	-0.3
Vegetables						
Farms	2,053	1,988	-3.2	1,456	1,532	5.2
Acres	311,659	299,867	-3.8	308,960	297,934	-3.6
Orchards						
Farms	9,965	10,258	2.9	4,669	4,539	-2.8
Acres	762,068	914,642	20.0	693,903	834,170	20.2

SIC Standard Industrial Classification. See Glossary.
(NA) Not available.
(X) Not applicable.
1/ Data are based on a sample of farms. In current dollars and unadjusted.
2/ Excludes the cost of lime.
3/ Three months old or older.
4/ Corn for grain or seed; soybeans for beans; sugarcane for sugar; hay includes alfalfa, and other tame, small grain, wild, grass silage, green chop, etc.; vegetables harvested for sale; vegetable acreage is counted only once even when it is replanted.

Note: Livestock and poultry inventories are as of December 31. Crop and livestock production, sales, and expense data are for the calendar year, except for a few crops for which the production and calendar years overlap. The agriculture census is on a 5-year cycle collecting data for years ending in 2 or 7.

Source: U.S., Department of Commerce, Bureau of the Census, *1992 Census of Agriculture: State and County Data, Florida*. AC92-A-9.

Table 9.35. FARMS: NUMBER, LAND IN FARMS, AND VALUE OF LAND AND BUILDINGS IN THE STATE AND COUNTIES OF FLORIDA, 1987 AND 1992

County	Number of farms		Land in farms (acres) Total		Average size of farm		Average estimated market value of land and buildings per farm 1/ (dollars)	
	1987	1992	1987	1992	1987	1992	1987	1992
Florida	36,556	35,204	11,194,090	10,766,077	306	306	543,830	619,265
Alachua	1,161	1,089	192,255	191,140	166	176	284,184	275,767
Baker	220	193	27,937	24,489	127	127	177,109	227,722
Bay	85	63	11,448	9,135	135	145	161,306	220,367
Bradford	349	315	41,178	36,230	118	115	190,212	202,625
Brevard	495	496	165,082	199,724	333	403	423,756	562,655
Broward	448	393	35,909	23,735	80	60	395,098	315,376
Calhoun	159	132	48,166	43,314	303	328	298,088	355,378
Charlotte	197	214	214,364	227,202	1,088	1,062	1,143,893	1,310,837
Citrus	331	288	74,264	70,672	224	245	280,141	449,229
Clay	244	210	83,994	86,026	344	410	580,689	884,620
Collier	224	254	332,177	301,977	1,483	1,189	1,755,839	2,305,229
Columbia	535	523	98,620	96,968	184	185	209,752	234,203
Dade	1,623	1,891	83,061	83,681	51	44	342,513	389,694
De Soto	654	804	351,402	334,623	537	416	721,087	848,575
Dixie	114	106	56,416	31,693	495	299	388,298	227,346
Duval	434	378	41,766	40,039	96	106	248,028	307,468
Escambia	502	454	65,426	57,179	130	126	194,191	166,769
Flagler	104	93	83,332	52,259	801	562	712,875	797,013
Franklin	6	6	(D)	(D)	(D)	(D)	(D)	49,979
Gadsden	348	333	62,114	57,853	178	174	243,289	322,888
Gilchrist	336	329	87,500	70,987	260	216	414,080	317,870
Glades	194	206	222,232	369,965	1,146	1,796	1,054,114	1,243,443
Gulf	35	27	33,644	14,203	961	526	564,314	733,567
Hamilton	256	224	73,603	69,405	288	310	244,828	251,658
Hardee	1,130	1,169	303,892	327,611	269	280	493,415	569,627
Hendry	396	389	545,111	529,835	1,377	1,362	2,215,972	2,539,049
Hernando	431	411	66,167	61,019	154	148	296,826	339,864
Highlands	735	652	413,381	483,835	562	742	871,313	1,532,899
Hillsborough	2,754	2,760	287,951	265,443	105	96	325,425	364,794
Holmes	572	523	86,701	86,706	152	166	118,550	141,788
Indian River	539	447	195,671	174,673	363	391	1,189,302	1,400,034
Jackson	910	808	269,663	244,185	296	302	256,502	247,068
Jefferson	296	297	130,376	118,352	440	398	433,835	575,501
Lafayette	273	252	94,847	95,833	347	380	255,901	373,438

See footnotes at end of table. Continued . . .

Table 9.35. FARMS: NUMBER, LAND IN FARMS, AND VALUE OF LAND AND BUILDINGS IN THE STATE AND COUNTIES OF FLORIDA, 1987 AND 1992 (Continued)

County	Number of farms		Land in farms (acres) Total		Average size of farm		Average estimated market value of land and buildings per farm 1/ (dollars)	
	1987	1992	1987	1992	1987	1992	1987	1992
Lake	1,285	1,320	232,657	199,098	181	151	447,166	480,005
Lee	415	517	132,665	106,721	320	206	633,500	606,292
Leon	302	263	101,885	100,764	337	383	452,103	666,946
Levy	540	473	179,608	190,553	333	403	383,861	374,647
Liberty	80	71	17,507	11,738	219	165	121,675	186,451
Madison	482	481	132,173	132,208	274	275	208,608	212,290
Manatee	766	728	329,388	299,699	430	412	759,265	796,187
Marion	1,707	1,654	311,074	296,242	182	179	475,794	448,675
Martin	316	305	231,522	190,788	733	626	1,882,291	1,863,414
Monroe	16	15	27	32	2	2	(D)	173,818
Nassau	317	277	48,999	44,962	155	162	245,448	250,847
Okaloosa	322	315	62,662	56,704	195	180	274,201	232,732
Okeechobee	400	418	384,169	351,885	960	842	1,003,723	1,264,286
Orange	1,125	990	161,900	138,418	144	140	489,619	541,725
Osceola	503	499	787,046	716,542	1,565	1,436	1,639,801	1,492,793
Palm Beach	975	924	659,438	637,934	676	690	2,202,349	2,417,525
Pasco	1,011	922	218,953	221,232	217	240	478,293	506,609
Pinellas	166	124	8,549	4,123	52	33	220,491	227,337
Polk	2,638	2,294	602,461	611,336	228	266	569,292	676,596
Putnam	421	400	106,993	105,621	254	264	347,653	352,198
St. Johns	172	166	49,414	48,839	287	294	486,269	558,362
St. Lucie	522	539	297,433	300,622	570	558	1,597,356	1,667,942
Santa Rosa	435	430	81,667	79,270	188	184	223,359	202,461
Sarasota	352	328	166,766	151,242	474	461	624,344	878,490
Seminole	390	352	59,933	59,642	154	169	360,221	476,796
Sumter	705	720	253,897	253,330	360	352	347,387	489,501
Suwannee	985	932	182,409	161,936	185	174	221,691	232,428
Taylor	158	125	77,346	(D)	490	(D)	255,975	353,773
Union	205	175	67,317	48,280	328	276	386,156	355,457
Volusia	920	978	192,768	138,208	210	141	346,207	382,517
Wakulla	87	83	(D)	8,679	(D)	105	(D)	149,612
Walton	430	383	104,239	96,730	242	253	154,098	228,124
Washington	318	274	61,647	45,214	194	165	124,191	143,811

(D) Data withheld to avoid disclosure of information about individual farms.
1/ Data are based on a sample of farms.
Note: The agriculture census is on a 5-year cycle collecting data for years ending in 2 and 7.

Source: U.S., Department of Commerce, Bureau of the Census, *1992 Census of Agriculture: State and County Data, Florida.* AC92-A-9.

Table 9.36. FARMS: LAND IN FARMS BY USE IN THE STATE AND COUNTIES OF FLORIDA, 1992

(in acres)

County	Total land in farms	Land according to use: Cropland Total	Cropland Harvested	Woodland 1/	Pastureland 2/	Other 3/	Irrigated land
Florida	10,766,077	3,841,505	2,400,704	1,922,035	4,456,686	545,851	1,782,680
Alachua	191,140	79,607	29,566	40,604	63,430	7,499	7,371
Baker	24,489	8,820	3,002	12,246	1,969	1,454	456
Bay	9,135	2,829	634	5,342	(D)	(D)	309
Bradford	36,230	14,185	4,447	9,815	10,473	1,757	553
Brevard	199,724	35,435	21,081	38,164	117,465	8,660	24,958
Broward	23,735	(D)	4,398	(D)	12,803	1,858	3,388
Calhoun	43,314	30,422	20,725	9,285	2,709	898	1,148
Charlotte	227,202	35,622	21,927	24,646	160,603	6,331	17,882
Citrus	70,672	15,057	4,904	14,377	30,517	10,721	658
Clay	86,026	6,818	3,042	59,604	17,108	2,496	1,293
Collier	301,977	87,628	65,021	72,485	114,537	27,327	64,611
Columbia	96,968	49,628	14,402	31,903	11,456	3,981	2,597
Dade	83,681	68,795	61,342	1,892	9,619	3,375	52,363
De Soto	334,623	89,670	62,250	21,213	210,951	12,789	58,806
Dixie	31,693	8,412	1,805	4,709	17,733	839	990
Duval	40,039	13,056	5,474	17,628	5,270	4,085	1,203
Escambia	57,179	38,720	29,986	12,718	2,529	3,212	641
Flagler	52,259	8,818	5,277	31,745	10,791	905	4,744
Franklin	(D)	(D)	0	(D)	0	(D)	0
Gadsden	57,853	22,244	9,387	28,477	2,997	4,135	3,378
Gilchrist	70,987	43,487	19,366	14,463	11,378	1,659	6,440
Glades	369,965	43,236	27,856	28,477	287,709	10,543	60,239
Gulf	14,203	6,382	1,875	2,074	3,672	2,075	(D)
Hamilton	69,405	32,639	11,805	20,888	12,257	3,621	3,591
Hardee	327,611	99,729	61,233	28,176	186,603	13,103	53,777
Hendry	529,835	195,139	178,124	63,679	222,952	48,065	178,504
Hernando	61,019	22,726	6,730	10,994	25,939	1,360	521
Highlands	483,835	118,077	80,883	72,729	285,005	8,024	83,301
Hillsborough	265,443	104,125	60,092	41,765	102,220	17,333	45,709
Holmes	86,706	40,690	17,202	26,921	12,949	6,146	421
Indian River	174,673	86,343	76,610	24,031	56,776	7,523	77,493
Jackson	244,185	151,053	80,035	60,704	21,657	10,771	13,365
Jefferson	118,352	37,031	16,669	59,579	11,414	10,328	4,257
Lafayette	95,833	25,383	7,917	21,359	47,014	2,077	3,198
Lake	199,098	95,428	39,843	24,481	56,037	23,152	24,373
Lee	106,721	29,990	19,673	12,477	58,212	6,042	17,114

See footnotes at end of table.

Continued . . .

Table 9.36. FARMS: LAND IN FARMS BY USE IN THE STATE AND COUNTIES OF FLORIDA, 1992 (Continued)

(in acres)

County	Total land in farms	Land according to use: Cropland Total	Cropland Harvested	Woodland 1/	Pastureland 2/	Other 3/	Irrigated land
Leon	100,764	19,769	7,881	63,363	11,378	6,254	2,781
Levy	190,553	70,593	24,494	49,460	63,629	6,871	9,895
Liberty	11,738	2,014	638	7,480	1,754	490	(D)
Madison	132,208	58,083	25,666	51,156	13,607	9,362	2,686
Manatee	299,699	109,143	61,950	61,002	113,797	15,757	54,568
Marion	296,242	114,134	40,290	74,302	90,059	17,747	5,217
Martin	190,788	79,264	66,727	16,228	77,902	17,394	58,742
Monroe	32	(D)	17	0	(D)	(D)	10
Nassau	44,962	13,490	4,541	22,808	6,708	1,956	33
Okaloosa	56,704	21,978	9,731	18,444	14,303	1,979	1,778
Okeechobee	351,885	72,717	30,509	14,192	247,552	17,424	27,662
Orange	138,418	50,507	33,697	51,898	26,043	9,970	25,249
Osceola	716,542	63,060	26,074	38,486	596,209	18,787	14,474
Palm Beach	637,934	578,699	510,263	12,475	16,373	30,387	422,966
Pasco	221,232	65,105	27,267	43,381	96,886	15,860	11,024
Pinellas	4,123	1,888	706	610	1,374	251	288
Polk	611,336	201,621	125,944	65,830	322,637	21,248	116,734
Putnam	105,621	23,655	13,337	54,709	22,258	4,999	9,560
St. Johns	48,839	28,658	25,190	9,583	8,715	1,883	24,208
St. Lucie	300,622	136,715	122,471	20,477	130,746	12,684	138,133
Santa Rosa	79,270	57,747	42,462	15,819	2,999	2,705	337
Sarasota	151,242	25,290	7,832	11,743	110,626	3,583	5,207
Seminole	59,642	9,542	4,499	12,867	29,512	7,721	3,155
Sumter	253,330	62,382	27,905	50,523	131,057	9,368	3,974
Suwannee	161,936	96,048	40,934	40,342	17,784	7,762	12,869
Taylor	(D)	(D)	1,237	49,039	20,488	1,657	433
Union	48,280	13,076	3,626	28,280	5,668	1,256	470
Volusia	138,208	25,068	13,583	43,719	59,443	9,978	8,460
Wakulla	8,679	3,623	1,103	3,896	655	505	(D)
Walton	96,730	51,080	12,310	27,369	6,663	11,618	989
Washington	45,214	24,704	13,237	12,263	4,543	3,704	179

(D) Data withheld to avoid disclosure of information about individual farms.
1/ Includes woodland pasture.
2/ Pastureland and rangeland other than cropland and woodland pasture.
3/ Land in house lots, ponds, roads, wasteland, etc.
Note: Because data for selected items are collected from a sample of operators, the results are subject to sampling variability. The agriculture census is on a 5-year cycle collecting data for years ending in 2 or 7.

Source: U.S., Department of Commerce, Bureau of the Census, *1992 Census of Agriculture: State and County Data, Florida.* AC92-A-9.

Table 9.37. INCOME: CASH RECEIPTS BY COMMODITY GROUP AND SPECIFIED COMMODITY IN FLORIDA, 1990 THROUGH 1994

(in thousands of dollars)

Commodity 1/	1990	1991	1992	1993	1994
All commodities	5,701,555	6,144,385	6,139,084	6,069,496	5,977,970
Livestock and products	1,258,961	1,171,626	1,165,874	1,211,131	1,191,624
Meat animals	409,407	380,784	362,616	377,674	348,012
Cattle and calves	388,849	363,351	349,447	362,495	335,837
Hogs	20,558	17,304	13,126	15,106	11,899
Dairy products, wholesale milk	421,007	372,947	401,700	385,503	408,408
Poultry and eggs	288,758	277,068	259,678	298,831	291,605
Broilers	152,012	151,704	164,856	187,714	191,151
Farm chickens	2,486	3,764	3,028	3,569	1,406
Chicken eggs	133,610	120,930	91,104	106,838	98,348
Crops	4,442,594	4,972,759	4,973,210	4,858,365	4,786,346
Food grains, wheat	5,178	1,837	2,349	2,268	1,717
Feed crops, corn	11,416	9,645	11,117	12,094	11,045
Hay	4,920	9,929	13,389	10,801	14,025
Cotton	15,512	18,718	20,502	23,393	31,590
Tobacco	32,020	26,392	31,729	30,638	27,248
Oil crops, peanuts	70,200	73,551	57,886	57,684	58,302
Soybeans	10,904	6,949	7,375	8,091	7,490
Vegetables	1,238,950	1,558,786	1,756,993	1,688,676	1,397,380
Potatoes	139,914	164,885	92,359	128,194	118,905
Beans, fresh snap	40,948	50,495	71,271	70,517	52,185
Carrots	17,604	22,563	20,228	25,551	10,808
Corn, sweet	94,848	91,674	73,149	102,588	99,347
Cucumbers, fresh	61,873	78,489	78,747	72,072	46,860
Eggplant, all	13,537	12,974	17,410	13,075	15,606
Escarole	7,945	10,633	7,000	7,611	4,995
Lettuce	18,747	18,913	18,128	26,770	12,548
Peppers, green	111,246	173,628	209,630	215,939	215,853
Tomatoes, fresh	414,528	570,801	821,805	607,464	428,455
Radishes	28,497	35,269	21,578	36,961	25,888
Squash	36,598	50,221	45,850	38,170	43,216
Watermelons	64,350	80,767	66,150	66,600	57,868
Fruits and nuts	1,582,584	1,711,450	1,496,182	1,481,905	1,599,954
Grapefruit	271,702	346,753	309,473	251,166	256,997
Lemons	2,767	5,072	2,637	2,879	2,675
Limes	28,286	26,901	11,213	3,151	2,092
Oranges	1,112,885	1,135,126	966,764	1,020,484	1,133,618
Tangelos	23,266	24,088	14,994	14,428	20,087
Tangerines, processed	4,357	4,108	3,434	2,966	4,636
Avocados	12,812	13,455	7,701	3,608	12,320
Mangos	4,725	6,150	4,280	950	1,500
Strawberries	75,324	84,876	108,864	121,313	101,425
Blueberries	3,720	2,719	3,752	1,300	5,690
Pecans	3,480	3,325	3,770	3,460	1,600

1/ Totals include data for "other" categories not shown separately.
Note: Data are estimates. Value of sales for some individual commodities may be understated; balance is included in "other."
Source: U.S., Department of Agriculture, the Internet at <http://usda.mannlib.cornell.edu:70/>.

Table 9.38. INCOME: MARKET VALUE OF AGRICULTURAL PRODUCTS SOLD IN THE STATE AND COUNTIES OF FLORIDA, 1992

(in thousands of dollars, except where indicated)

County	All products Total	All products Average per farm (dollars)	Crops 1/	Livestock poultry and their products
Florida	5,266,033	149,586	4,197,420	1,068,613
Alachua	39,680	36,437	24,219	15,461
Baker	27,816	144,127	11,760	16,056
Bay	831	13,197	716	115
Bradford	16,900	53,652	1,914	14,986
Brevard	35,136	70,838	20,834	14,302
Broward	34,742	88,403	26,982	7,760
Calhoun	15,159	114,843	13,534	1,625
Charlotte	37,903	177,117	31,928	5,975
Citrus	5,561	19,308	2,504	3,056
Clay	33,967	161,747	1,932	32,035
Collier	260,740	1,026,536	254,916	5,825
Columbia	20,636	39,457	8,728	11,908
Dade	356,967	188,772	352,988	3,979
De Soto	128,656	160,020	113,091	15,565
Dixie	2,678	25,263	1,299	1,379
Duval	22,443	59,373	6,868	15,575
Escambia	15,653	34,479	8,812	6,841
Flagler	10,129	108,911	8,809	1,320
Franklin	79	13,161	0	79
Gadsden	71,048	213,357	66,088	4,960
Gilchrist	28,218	85,770	6,943	21,276
Glades	56,706	275,270	32,584	24,121
Gulf	(D)	(D)	(D)	152
Hamilton	14,445	64,488	9,078	5,368
Hardee	127,720	109,255	95,257	32,462
Hendry	273,308	702,590	254,368	18,939
Hernando	18,675	45,439	2,210	16,465
Highlands	185,929	285,168	152,296	33,633
Hillsborough	259,221	93,921	188,542	70,680
Holmes	31,327	59,898	5,646	25,680
Indian River	145,065	324,530	139,807	5,258
Jackson	52,626	65,132	34,299	18,327
Jefferson	21,046	70,861	10,202	10,844
Lafayette	43,709	173,449	4,214	39,495

See footnotes at end of table. Continued . . .

Table 9.38. INCOME: MARKET VALUE OF AGRICULTURAL PRODUCTS SOLD IN THE STATE AND COUNTIES OF FLORIDA, 1992 (Continued)

(in thousands of dollars, except where indicated)

County	All products Total	All products Average per farm (dollars)	Crops 1/	Livestock poultry and their products
Lake	90,258	68,378	72,082	18,177
Lee	81,553	157,742	78,932	2,620
Leon	3,843	14,613	1,663	2,180
Levy	42,558	89,975	10,384	32,175
Liberty	647	9,114	(D)	(D)
Madison	19,888	41,348	6,584	13,304
Manatee	209,865	288,277	187,741	22,124
Marion	64,074	38,739	17,688	46,387
Martin	155,038	508,320	136,964	18,073
Monroe	(D)	(D)	286	(D)
Nassau	27,816	100,418	770	27,046
Okaloosa	6,213	19,725	2,758	3,456
Okeechobee	133,235	318,743	23,706	109,528
Orange	207,782	209,881	204,286	3,496
Osceola	53,197	106,607	30,647	22,550
Palm Beach	891,196	964,497	884,066	7,130
Pasco	62,193	67,455	21,511	40,683
Pinellas	11,460	92,423	11,228	233
Polk	203,350	88,644	169,614	33,737
Putnam	33,318	83,296	27,916	5,402
St. Johns	45,831	276,089	44,285	1,546
St. Lucie	207,123	384,273	194,784	12,339
Santa Rosa	21,460	49,907	19,291	2,169
Sarasota	18,903	57,631	13,026	5,877
Seminole	20,399	57,951	18,199	2,200
Sumter	36,892	51,239	15,270	21,622
Suwannee	93,048	99,837	27,044	66,004
Taylor	2,630	21,042	699	1,931
Union	8,144	46,536	2,708	5,436
Volusia	78,882	80,656	71,537	7,345
Wakulla	1,516	18,261	426	1,090
Walton	22,256	58,108	3,275	18,981
Washington	10,994	40,123	3,464	7,529

(D) Data withheld to avoid disclosure of information about individual farms.
1/ Includes nursery and greenhouse products.
Note: The agriculture census is on a 5-year cycle collecting data for years ending in 2 and 7.

Source: U.S., Department of Commerce, Bureau of the Census, *1992 Census of Agriculture: State and County Data, Florida*. AC92-A-9.

Table 9.39. FARM OPERATORS: NUMBER OF OPERATORS BY PRINCIPAL OCCUPATION AGE, AND RACE AND HISPANIC ORIGIN AND NUMBER OF FARMS AND ACRES OPERATED BY FEMALES IN THE STATE AND COUNTIES OF FLORIDA, 1992

County	Total	Principal occupation		Average age (years)	Non-white	His-panic ori-gin 1/	Female operators	
		Farming	Other				Number of farms	Land in farms (acres)
Florida	35,204	16,557	18,647	55.3	1,126	928	4,851	748,592
Alachua	1,089	482	607	54.0	77	13	178	11,736
Baker	193	80	113	54.8	6	0	11	702
Bay	63	15	48	55.2	0	0	8	264
Bradford	315	112	203	56.2	5	6	43	2,651
Brevard	496	173	323	56.7	14	10	73	5,442
Broward	393	202	191	52.6	19	26	80	1,213
Calhoun	132	71	61	56.5	4	0	9	1,997
Charlotte	214	93	121	57.3	0	0	23	11,865
Citrus	288	121	167	57.3	3	4	47	4,719
Clay	210	86	124	56.9	3	3	27	1,459
Collier	254	143	111	50.2	7	7	23	(D)
Columbia	523	214	309	55.6	28	5	69	8,912
Dade	1,891	943	948	53.2	179	403	205	2,294
De Soto	804	345	459	57.1	10	8	107	9,096
Dixie	106	34	72	57.7	0	0	11	2,197
Duval	378	168	210	57.2	7	5	50	7,335
Escambia	454	185	269	55.2	16	0	33	2,778
Flagler	93	41	52	50.9	0	0	7	123
Franklin	6	1	5	52.7	0	0	0	0
Gadsden	333	127	206	57.1	23	4	31	4,343
Gilchrist	329	171	158	54.0	3	3	47	8,817
Glades	206	113	93	56.3	6	5	19	13,077
Gulf	27	7	20	55.6	0	0	0	0
Hamilton	224	109	115	53.3	19	0	19	6,148
Hardee	1,169	537	632	57.1	7	15	165	29,262
Hendry	389	221	168	55.3	9	17	38	26,347
Hernando	411	166	245	55.1	15	14	69	3,723
Highlands	652	320	332	54.4	9	6	92	58,986
Hillsborough	2,760	1,268	1,492	56.6	80	94	443	17,144
Holmes	523	248	275	54.5	6	0	45	6,041
Indian River	447	244	203	55.9	5	6	65	2,676
Jackson	808	443	365	55.2	79	4	47	9,463
Jefferson	297	119	178	56.6	28	0	28	16,565
Lafayette	252	128	124	52.8	0	0	26	3,389
Lake	1,320	601	719	55.3	23	13	183	20,099
Lee	517	230	287	53.0	4	6	71	4,547

See footnotes at end of table.

Continued . . .

Table 9.39. FARM OPERATORS: NUMBER OF OPERATORS BY PRINCIPAL OCCUPATION AGE, AND RACE AND HISPANIC ORIGIN AND NUMBER OF FARMS AND ACRES OPERATED BY FEMALES IN THE STATE AND COUNTIES OF FLORIDA, 1992 (Continued)

County	Total	Principal occupation		Average age (years)	Non-white	His-panic ori-gin 1/	Female operators	
		Farming	Other				Number of farms	Land in farms (acres)
Leon	263	84	179	56.3	30	0	34	22,955
Levy	473	228	245	54.8	10	5	75	9,974
Liberty	71	23	48	57.4	0	0	7	3,720
Madison	481	224	257	56.8	24	0	67	13,238
Manatee	728	362	366	55.3	7	7	109	21,561
Marion	1,654	817	837	55.2	82	43	328	31,708
Martin	305	147	158	55.0	7	7	35	17,111
Monroe	15	6	9	54.7	0	0	7	9
Nassau	277	116	161	55.1	0	0	28	3,744
Okaloosa	315	138	177	56.4	3	3	26	2,301
Okeechobee	418	192	226	52.8	4	14	50	21,630
Orange	990	510	480	55.1	48	9	172	16,853
Osceola	499	240	259	55.6	8	0	80	49,098
Palm Beach	924	555	369	51.4	34	54	139	8,502
Pasco	922	405	517	56.6	10	24	144	22,443
Pinellas	124	51	73	54.1	0	0	38	715
Polk	2,294	959	1,335	56.8	35	18	358	36,862
Putnam	400	188	212	54.8	12	3	64	11,348
St. Johns	166	107	59	52.7	4	3	17	5,051
St. Lucie	539	285	254	53.6	3	4	53	8,290
Santa Rosa	430	220	210	55.0	0	0	27	1,344
Sarasota	328	133	195	54.1	0	4	57	22,654
Seminole	352	186	166	55.3	21	6	62	7,250
Sumter	720	347	373	56.1	22	11	130	23,786
Suwannee	932	509	423	55.7	25	10	100	17,722
Taylor	125	50	75	58.2	0	0	8	(D)
Union	175	78	97	57.1	0	0	18	1,098
Volusia	978	495	483	53.8	13	9	160	8,798
Wakulla	83	30	53	54.5	4	0	13	283
Walton	383	178	205	56.0	11	0	39	30,653
Washington	274	133	141	57.3	3	0	14	1,061
Other	0	0	0	0.0	12	17	0	0

(D) Data withheld to avoid disclosure of information about individual farms.
1/ Persons of Hispanic origin may be of any race.
Note: The agriculture census is on a 5-year cycle collecting data for years ending in 2 and 7.

Source: U.S., Department of Commerce, Bureau of the Census, *1992 Census of Agriculture: State and County Data, Florida*. AC92-A-9.

Table 9.42. INCOME: CASH RECEIPTS FROM FARMING AND VALUE OF HOME AGRICULTURAL COMMODITY CONSUMPTION IN FLORIDA, OTHER AGRICULTURAL STATES AND THE UNITED STATES, 1994

(in thousands of dollars)

State	Total: Amount	Total: Rank among states	Cash receipts from farming: Total	Cash receipts from farming: Marketings	Cash receipts from farming: Government payments	Value of commodities consumed on farms 1/
Florida	6,039,978	9	6,036,607	5,977,970	58,637	3,371
California	20,530,754	1	20,510,845	20,238,064	272,781	19,909
Texas	13,437,840	2	13,415,451	12,552,238	863,213	22,389
Iowa	10,834,208	3	10,816,883	10,084,316	732,567	17,325
Nebraska	8,920,366	4	8,909,654	8,561,321	348,333	10,712
Illinois	8,544,358	5	8,525,955	8,222,796	303,159	18,403
Kansas	8,170,778	6	8,155,009	7,687,299	467,710	15,769
Minnesota	7,166,253	7	7,144,648	6,522,323	622,325	21,605
North Carolina	6,460,857	8	6,446,785	6,369,139	77,646	14,072
Wisconsin	5,641,178	10	5,620,672	5,384,188	236,484	20,506
Arkansas	5,584,478	11	5,578,375	5,275,623	302,752	6,103
Indiana	4,989,539	12	4,974,614	4,837,594	137,020	14,925
Washington	4,885,786	13	4,873,336	4,720,482	152,854	12,450
Georgia	4,863,342	14	4,855,510	4,715,685	139,825	7,832
Missouri	4,816,920	15	4,791,606	4,524,209	267,397	25,314
United States	188,029,882	(X)	187,547,728	179,666,692	7,881,036	482,154

(X) Not applicable.
1/ Value of farm products consumed directly in farm households where produced.

Source: U.S., Department of Agriculture, *Agricultural Statistics, 1995.*

Table 9.43. TAXES: AMOUNT LEVIED ON FARM REAL ESTATE IN FLORIDA AND THE UNITED STATES, 1991, 1992, AND 1993

Item	Florida 1991	Florida 1992	Florida 1993	United States 1/ 1991	United States 1/ 1992	United States 1/ 1993
Total taxes levied ($1,000,000)	130.2	143.8	140.7	4,743.3	4,869.2	5,023.3
Taxes per acre Amount (dollars)	13.36	14.75	14.71	5.61	5.80	5.98
Taxes per $100 of full value (dollars)	0.63	0.72	0.71	0.82	0.84	0.85

1/ Excludes Alaska.

Source: U.S., Department of Agriculture, *Agricultural Statistics, 1995*, and previous edition.

Table 9.45. LAND: TOTAL FARM ACREAGE, 1990, AND ACREAGE OWNED BY NONRESIDENT ALIENS, 1993, IN THE STATE AND COUNTIES OF FLORIDA

County	Estimated total farmland acreage 1/	Acreage foreign-owned 2/			
		Reported value 3/ ($1,000)	Amount	As a percentage of total farmland	County total as a percentage of state total
Florida	24,300,104	1,150,294	620,835	2.55	100.00
Alachua	519,000	6,825	12,064	2.32	1.94
Baker	301,528	0	0	0.00	0.00
Bay	410,490	0	0	0.00	0.00
Bradford	173,000	0	0	0.00	0.00
Brevard	478,050	12,621	5,900	1.23	0.95
Broward	28,670	20,423	1,932	6.74	0.31
Calhoun	343,710	2,239	2,397	0.70	0.39
Charlotte	268,170	14,858	7,210	2.69	1.16
Citrus	178,310	1,010	973	0.55	0.16
Clay	368,000	10,500	7,088	1.93	1.14
Collier	576,400	24,268	11,746	2.04	1.89
Columbia	534,065	1,986	4,505	0.84	0.73
Dade	85,306	197,546	18,741	21.97	3.02
De Soto	354,000	9,345	4,816	1.36	0.78
Dixie	278,725	157	157	0.06	0.03
Duval	301,900	0	0	0.00	0.00
Escambia	308,207	401	249	0.08	0.04
Flagler	310,100	0	0	0.00	0.00
Franklin	310,000	17,107	37,026	11.94	5.96
Gadsden	261,800	2,608	5,699	2.18	0.92
Gilchrist	216,560	1,792	9,279	4.28	1.49
Glades	443,500	6,931	5,907	1.33	0.95
Gulf	363,000	256	311	0.09	0.05
Hamilton	333,219	1,286	2,532	0.76	0.41
Hardee	326,302	11,158	4,679	1.43	0.75
Hendry	734,000	23,652	12,368	1.69	1.99
Hernando	216,299	0	0	0.00	0.00
Highlands	600,549	9,838	4,753	0.79	0.77
Hillsborough	530,000	20,047	12,057	2.27	1.94
Holmes	343,300	0	0	0.00	0.00
Indian River	210,161	60,753	26,507	12.61	4.27
Jackson	576,000	6,278	7,129	1.24	1.15
Jefferson	346,072	1,373	3,488	1.01	0.56
Lafayette	337,868	0	0	0.00	0.00
Lake	515,245	31,577	13,366	2.59	2.15
Lee	244,484	36,081	8,295	3.39	1.34
Leon	304,350	323	162	0.05	0.03
Levy	646,185	2,562	10,061	1.56	1.62
Liberty	268,375	393	850	0.32	0.14
Madison	417,961	16	80	0.02	0.01

See footnotes at end of table. Continued . . .

Table 9.45. LAND: TOTAL FARM ACREAGE, 1990, AND ACREAGE OWNED BY NONRESIDENT ALIENS, 1993, IN THE STATE AND COUNTIES OF FLORIDA (Continued)

County	Estimated total farmland acreage 1/	Acreage foreign-owned 2/ Reported value 3/ ($1,000)	Amount	As a percentage of total farmland	County total as a percentage of state total
Manatee	329,388	30,439	9,643	2.93	1.55
Marion	575,000	48,729	17,277	3.00	2.78
Martin	278,000	56,832	31,975	11.50	5.15
Monroe	0	0	0	(X)	0.00
Nassau	351,800	1,009	315	0.09	0.05
Okaloosa	208,069	23,950	21,718	10.44	3.50
Okeechobee	465,500	18,262	16,541	3.55	2.66
Orange	323,984	136,439	26,840	8.28	4.32
Osceola	802,100	70,315	17,571	2.19	2.83
Palm Beach	569,135	110,683	139,755	24.56	22.51
Pasco	324,755	7,742	2,491	0.77	0.40
Pinellas	47,000	900	55	0.12	0.01
Polk	851,600	54,822	29,791	3.50	4.80
Putnam	330,670	849	1,829	0.55	0.29
St. Johns	340,000	1,488	1,156	0.34	0.19
St. Lucie	294,158	7,709	11,878	4.04	1.91
Santa Rosa	550,080	1,089	1,263	0.23	0.20
Sarasota	166,766	1,077	513	0.31	0.08
Seminole	116,200	16,965	2,087	1.80	0.34
Sumter	595,000	5,871	4,257	0.72	0.69
Suwannee	441,600	5,374	5,431	1.23	0.87
Taylor	296,800	3	20	0.01	A/
Union	149,932	0	0	0.00	0.00
Volusia	529,360	11,661	8,321	1.57	1.34
Wakulla	160,472	56	61	0.04	0.01
Walton	505,222	1,820	27,720	5.49	4.46
Washington	334,652	0	0	0.00	0.00

(X) Not applicable.
A/ Less than 0.005 percent.
1/ Land currently used for agricultural, forestry, or timber production or, if idle, land used for such purposes within the last five years.
2/ A foreign investor is defined as any nonresident alien, any corporation incorporated outside the U.S., or any U.S. corporation with 5 percent or more foreign interest. A foreign investor holding more than 5 percent or more interest in any agricultural lands must disclose such holdings.
3/ Reported value is purchase price or nonpurchase price (estimated value) at time of acquisition.
Note: Data were compiled by the U.S. Department of Agriculture, Agricultural Stabilization and Conservation Service from disclosure forms filed under the Agriculture Foreign Investment Disclosure Act of 1978. Detail may not add to total because of rounding.

Source: U.S., Department of Agriculture, Agricultural Stabilization and Conservation Service, *Foreign Ownership of U.S. Agricultural Land Through December 31, 1993,* and unpublished data.

Table 9.51. CITRUS: ESTIMATED PRODUCTION AND VALUE OF CITRUS BY TYPE IN FLORIDA CROP YEARS 1990-91 THROUGH 1994-95

Type of citrus	1990-91	1991-92	1992-93	1993-94	1994-95 A/
	Production (1,000 boxes)				
All citrus	205,660	191,815	251,540	235,760	270,920
Oranges	151,600	139,800	186,600	174,400	205,400
Early and midseason	87,500	83,400	114,300	107,300	119,700
Late (Valencia)	64,100	56,400	72,300	67,100	85,700
Grapefruit	45,100	42,400	55,150	51,050	55,700
Seedy	1,600	1,200	1,750	1,050	1,300
White seedless	21,700	19,100	25,700	24,500	25,700
Colored seedless	21,800	22,100	27,700	25,500	28,700
Other citrus	8,960	9,615	9,790	10,310	9,820
Temples	2,500	2,350	2,500	2,250	2,550
Tangelos	2,650	2,600	3,050	3,350	3,150
Tangerines 1/	850	1,330	1,400	2,370	2,350
Honey tangerines	1,100	1,270	1,400	1,730	1,200
K-early citrus	160	165	185	210	120
Limes	1,450	1,600	B/ 1,000	200	230
Lemons 2/	250	300	255	200	220
	Value of production ($1,000)				
All citrus	1,236,126	1,208,944	855,812	916,959	820,597
Oranges	892,675	828,749	649,713	713,312	682,657
Early and midseason	471,049	453,501	369,438	403,802	315,415
Late (Valencia)	421,626	375,248	280,275	309,510	367,242
Grapefruit	255,328	280,629	146,432	144,316	82,518
Seedy	6,288	5,484	3,290	1,869	1,885
White seedless	99,622	123,337	56,973	69,693	45,849
Colored seedless	149,418	151,808	86,169	72,754	34,784
Other citrus	88,123	99,566	59,667	59,331	55,422
Temples	15,786	15,289	7,475	6,136	6,482
Tangelos	16,203	18,618	10,092	7,976	4,224
Tangerines 1/	13,468	24,453	20,070	23,172	17,688
Honey tangerines	19,881	22,344	18,433	17,131	23,182
K-early citrus	799	489	1,015	377	180
Limes	20,289	14,589	B/ 1,017	2,541	1,989
Lemons 2/	1,697	3,784	1,565	1,998	1,677

A/ Preliminary.
B/ Hurricane Andrew August 1992.
1/ Excludes honey tangerines. Fallglo tangerines not included prior to 1993-94.
2/ Florida lemons bloom and harvest during the calendar year; data are for the years 1990 through 1994.
Note: Some data may be revised.

Source: State of Florida, Department of Agriculture and Consumer Services, Florida Agricultural Statistics Service, *Florida Agricultural Statistics: Citrus Summary, 1994-95.*

Table 9.52. ORANGES AND GRAPEFRUIT: BEARING ACREAGE, PRODUCTION, AND YIELD PER ACRE IN FLORIDA, OTHER CITRUS STATES, AND THE UNITED STATES, CROP YEARS 1988-89 THROUGH 1994-95

State and year	Oranges: Bearing acreage (1,000 acres)	Oranges: Production (1,000 tons)	Oranges: Yield per acre (tons)	Grapefruit: Bearing acreage (1,000 acres)	Grapefruit: Production (1,000 tons)	Grapefruit: Yield per acre (tons)
Florida						
1988-89	388.7	6,597	17.0	106.9	2,327	21.8
1989-90	399.5	4,959	12.4	103.0	1,517	14.7
1990-91	420.9	6,822	16.2	104.2	1,916	18.4
1991-92	444.4	6,291	14.2	104.7	1,802	17.2
1992-93	489.2	8,397	17.2	111.9	2,344	20.9
1993-94	510.8	7,848	15.4	118.3	2,170	18.3
1994-95 A/	562.8	9,243	16.4	127.3	2,367	18.6
Arizona						
1988-89	10.4	64	6.2	6.5	62	9.5
1989-90	10.2	59	5.8	6.4	71	11.1
1990-91	9.9	66	6.7	6.2	77	12.4
1991-92	10.4	89	8.6	5.9	89	15.1
1992-93	10.6	69	6.5	5.9	69	11.7
1993-94	10.6	72	6.8	5.9	B/ 59	10.0
1994-95 A/	10.4	40	3.8	5.6	47	10.0
California						
1988-89	177.6	2,209	12.4	19.9	263	13.2
1989-90	175.1	2,676	15.3	19.2	310	16.1
1990-91	178.4	960	5.4	18.3	263	14.4
1991-92	181.8	2,528	13.9	18.5	330	17.8
1992-93	184.0	2,505	13.6	17.8	303	17.0
1993-94	185.0	2,385	12.9	18.0	B/ 312	17.3
1994-95 A/	191.0	2,288	12.0	18.4	312	17.0
Texas						
1988-89	12.0	79	6.6	16.9	192	11.4
1989-90	13.0	51	3.9	18.7	80	4.3
1990-91	3.5	0	0.0	4.5	0	0.0
1991-92	3.5	1	0.3	7.5	3	0.4
1992-93	4.4	21	4.8	10.1	75	7.4
1993-94	5.5	24	4.4	12.8	120	9.4
1994-95 A/	7.0	45	6.4	15.0	186	12.4
United States						
1988-89	588.7	8,949	15.2	150.2	2,844	18.9
1989-90	597.8	7,745	13.0	147.3	1,978	13.4
1990-91	612.7	7,848	12.8	133.2	2,256	16.9
1991-92	640.1	8,909	13.9	136.6	2,224	16.3
1992-93	688.2	10,992	16.0	145.7	2,791	19.2
1993-94	711.9	10,329	14.5	155.0	2,661	17.2
1994-95 A/	771.2	11,616	15.1	166.3	2,912	17.5

A/ Preliminary.
B/ Box weight for California Desert and Arizona grapefruit changed in 1993-94.
Note: Some data may be revised.
Source: State of Florida, Department of Agriculture and Consumer Services, Florida Agricultural Statistics Service, *Florida Agricultural Statistics: Citrus Summary, 1994-95.*

Table 9.53. ORANGES AND GRAPEFRUIT: SEASON AVERAGE ON-TREE PRICES PER BOX AND VALUE OF PRODUCTION IN FLORIDA AND THE UNITED STATES, CROP YEARS 1987-88 THROUGH 1994-95

Crop year	Season average price (in dollars per box)			Value of production (in thousands of dollars)		
	Total	Fresh use	Processing	Total	Fresh use	Processing
			Oranges 1/			
Florida						
1987-88	7.58	7.96	7.56	1,046,700	75,749	970,951
1988-89	7.41	7.61	7.40	1,086,319	64,628	1,021,691
1989-90	6.21	10.31	5.98	684,226	61,053	623,173
1990-91	5.89	8.46	5.66	892,675	105,289	787,386
1991-92	5.93	8.52	5.69	828,749	98,404	730,345
1992-93	3.48	3.81	3.46	649,713	40,877	608,836
1993-94	4.09	5.98	3.98	713,312	59,162	654,150
1994-95 A/	3.32	4.86	3.24	682,657	50,784	631,873
United States						
1987-88	7.18	8.41	6.78	1,424,847	450,588	974,259
1988-89	7.08	8.21	6.76	1,470,582	426,433	1,044,149
1989-90	6.13	8.49	5.25	1,128,626	463,303	665,323
1990-91	6.78	14.84	5.29	1,239,979	462,185	777,794
1991-92	5.52	8.06	4.72	1,146,430	439,856	706,574
1992-93	3.88	6.92	3.03	1,005,498	433,663	571,835
1993-94	4.40	7.67	3.48	1,067,237	448,181	619,056
1994-95 A/	3.75	7.69	2.84	1,024,023	434,383	589,640
			Grapefruit			
Florida						
1987-88	5.57	6.85	4.61	299,887	158,213	141,674
1988-89	4.45	6.03	3.24	243,874	144,068	99,806
1989-90	5.65	10.00	3.06	201,756	133,413	68,343
1990-91	5.66	8.83	2.08	255,328	211,244	44,084
1991-92	6.62	8.69	4.20	280,629	198,391	82,238
1992-93	2.66	4.86	1.06	146,432	112,476	33,956
1993-94	2.83	5.52	0.71	144,316	124,167	20,149
1994-95 A/	1.48	4.52	-0.54	82,518	100,697	-18,179
United States						
1987-88	5.43	6.84	4.16	370,452	226,968	143,484
1988-89	4.41	6.05	2.84	305,644	210,151	95,493
1989-90	5.86	10.00	2.53	291,150	227,152	63,998
1990-91	5.55	8.74	1.65	306,652	268,479	38,173
1991-92	6.20	8.34	3.44	336,939	258,803	78,136
1992-93	2.75	5.10	0.77	188,014	162,415	25,599
1993-94	2.97	5.63	0.50	194,160	179,341	14,819
1994-95 A/	1.86	4.84	-0.59	137,534	161,112	-23,578

A/ Preliminary.
1/ Includes early, midseason, and late type (Valencia) oranges.
Note: Charges for picking, hauling, and packing are deducted from the weighted average of prices obtained from all segments of the citrus industry to arrive at the final on-tree price received by producers. United States data include Arizona, California, Florida, and Texas. Some data may be revised.
Source: State of Florida, Department of Agriculture and Consumer Services, Florida Agricultural Statistics Service, *Florida Agricultural Statistics: Citrus Summary, 1994-95.*

Table 9.54. CITRUS: ESTIMATED PRODUCTION OF PRINCIPAL TYPES OF CITRUS IN THE STATE AND COUNTIES OF FLORIDA, CROP YEAR 1994-95

(in 1,000 boxes)

Area and county	Total 1/	Oranges: All oranges	Oranges: Early and mid-season	Oranges: Valencias	All grape-fruit	Spe-cialty fruit 2/
Florida	270,470	205,400	119,700	85,700	55,700	9,370
District						
Indian River	60,954	21,900	10,700	11,200	37,600	1,454
Northern	11,469	9,723	7,813	1,910	412	1,334
Central	57,917	48,302	25,473	22,829	6,557	3,058
Western	66,842	62,842	43,349	19,493	2,535	1,465
Southern	73,288	62,633	32,365	30,268	8,596	2,059
County						
Brevard	2,911	2,074	1,152	922	777	60
Charlotte	4,784	3,991	2,142	1,849	622	171
Collier	10,963	9,531	4,575	4,956	1,219	213
De Soto	24,682	23,679	13,646	10,033	574	429
Glades	3,077	2,931	1,990	941	114	32
Hardee	21,436	20,507	15,824	4,683	450	479
Hendry	31,318	26,507	13,255	13,252	3,944	867
Highlands	22,226	19,060	7,749	11,311	1,910	1,256
Hillsborough	10,927	10,187	8,090	2,097	485	255
Indian River	21,687	6,734	3,621	3,113	14,582	371
Lake	4,783	3,637	3,017	620	259	887
Lee	3,656	3,330	1,705	1,625	275	51
Manatee	8,885	7,866	5,430	2,436	784	235
Martin	15,349	12,603	5,541	7,062	2,390	356
Okeechobee	3,201	2,645	1,832	813	484	72
Orange	2,608	2,293	1,609	684	58	257
Osceola	5,532	4,655	3,276	1,379	603	274
Palm Beach	4,187	2,620	1,654	966	1,211	356
Pasco	3,157	2,980	2,448	532	76	101
Polk	30,620	24,954	14,748	10,206	4,107	1,559
St. Lucie	32,389	11,025	5,205	5,820	20,436	928
Sarasota	839	558	337	221	222	59
Seminole	274	240	187	53	2	32
Volusia	341	257	196	61	75	9
Other 3/	638	536	471	65	41	61

1/ Does not include lemon and lime production.
2/ Includes tangelos, temples, tangerines, and K-early citrus.
3/ Includes Broward, Citrus, Hernando, Marion, Pinellas, and Putnam counties.
Note: Citrus districts are based on citrus marketings/production areas. Several counties are in more than one district.

Source: State of Florida, Department of Agriculture and Consumer Services, Florida Agricultural Statistics Service, *Florida Agricultural Statistics: Citrus Summary, 1994-95.*

Table 9.55. CITRUS: ACREAGE BY TYPE OF FRUIT IN THE STATE AND SPECIFIED COUNTIES OF FLORIDA, JANUARY 1, 1994

County	Total	Oranges: All oranges 1/	Oranges: Early and mid-season	Oranges: Valencias	All grape-fruit 1/	Specialty fruit 2/
Florida	854,692	653,370	333,507	300,704	146,915	54,407
Brevard	11,663	8,644	5,115	3,413	2,251	768
Broward	246	205	47	110	31	10
Charlotte	19,995	14,781	6,619	7,895	3,655	1,559
Citrus	233	194	170	13	25	14
Collier	36,534	31,043	14,305	16,738	4,165	1,326
Dade 3/	2,618	0	0	0	0	2,618
De Soto	62,407	58,734	28,985	29,333	1,495	2,178
Glades	9,270	8,690	5,250	3,336	341	239
Hardee	54,211	50,378	35,273	14,166	1,112	2,721
Hendry	98,604	83,463	34,012	46,273	10,528	4,613
Hernando	1,109	1,023	919	14	25	61
Highlands	74,035	64,318	23,451	39,997	4,735	4,982
Hillsborough	27,739	25,397	18,100	6,016	1,058	1,284
Indian River	69,240	29,837	15,404	13,604	37,036	2,367
Lake	21,053	15,865	11,822	2,181	1,224	3,964
Lee	12,238	9,903	4,422	5,444	1,260	1,076
Manatee	23,940	20,756	13,261	7,442	2,068	1,115
Marion	1,138	884	836	25	52	202
Martin	48,221	40,780	15,045	24,316	5,847	1,594
Okeechobee	11,270	9,129	5,856	3,237	1,686	455
Orange	10,402	8,683	5,807	2,600	308	1,411
Osceola	15,654	13,067	8,745	4,134	1,563	1,024
Palm Beach	12,885	7,612	4,334	3,086	2,751	2,522
Pasco	11,555	10,655	8,702	1,597	314	586
Pinellas	248	162	82	68	58	28
Polk	104,007	85,354	43,529	36,347	9,562	9,091
Putnam	122	93	73	12	0	29
St. Lucie	108,448	49,587	20,634	27,946	53,053	5,808
Sarasota	2,516	1,767	872	895	489	260
Seminole	1,462	1,179	929	200	32	251
Volusia	1,453	1,153	874	266	191	109
Other 4/	176	34	34	0	0	142

1/ Includes unidentified variety acreage.
2/ Includes limes and lemons.
3/ Surveyed as of October 1994. Reflected in the state total.
4/ Includes Flagler and Sumter counties.

Source: State of Florida, Department of Agriculture and Consumer Services, Florida Agricultural Statistics Service, *Florida Agricultural Statistics: Citrus Summary, 1994-95.*

Table 9.56. ORANGE JUICE SALES: GALLONS SOLD AND CONSUMER RETAIL DOLLARS SPENT IN UNITED STATES FOOD STORES, 1982 THROUGH 1995

Season 1/	Total: Amount	Total: Percentage change from previous year	Chilled orange juice 2/	Canned single strength	Frozen concentrated orange juice
	Reconstituted gallons (rounded to millions)				
1982	804	-0.5	295	25	484
1983	863	7.3	346	23	494
1984	856	-0.8	378	20	457
1985	817	-4.6	373	18	426
1986	884	8.2	437	17	430
1987 A/	701	(X)	358	9	334
1988	667	-4.9	356	9	302
1989	690	3.5	392	9	289
1990	628	-9.0	363	8	256
1991	701	11.5	412	8	280
1992	689	-1.7	417	8	263
1993	748	8.5	480	9	260
1994	740	-1.0	494	8	238
1995	745	0.6	517	8	220
	Consumer retail dollars (rounded to millions)				
1982	2,498	3.9	1,020	96	1,382
1983	2,628	5.2	1,156	91	1,381
1984	2,993	13.9	1,418	91	1,483
1985	3,102	3.6	1,512	88	1,502
1986	2,871	-7.4	1,550	77	1,244
1987 A/	2,081	(X)	1,145	41	895
1988	2,394	15.0	1,386	42	963
1989	2,568	7.3	1,589	42	935
1990	2,684	4.5	1,695	42	944
1991	2,570	-4.2	1,693	40	835
1992	2,645	2.9	1,790	40	812
1993	2,505	-5.3	1,773	37	694
1994	2,503	-0.1	1,823	35	646
1995	2,561	2.3	1,933	32	596

(X) Not applicable.
A/ Data not comparable to previous years due to changes in data collection methods.
1/ December of the previous year through November of the present year.
2/ Includes glass and plastic containers and cartons.
Note: Data for 1982-86 come from an audit of 1,300 food stores throughout the United States and relate to the retail market only. Data for 1987-95 come from scanner supermarkets doing over $4 million in retail sales annually. Sales from these stores are estimated to represent 73 percent of total retail sales. Some data may be revised.

Source: State of Florida, Department of Citrus, *Market Research Report: A.C. Nielsen Retail Food Index, Annual Summary, 1986,* and previous editions and *Market Research Report: Nielsen Scantrack, Annual Summary, 1993,* previous editions, and unpublished data.

Table 9.62. FIELD CROPS: ACREAGE HARVESTED, PRODUCTION, YIELD, AND VALUE OF PRODUCTION IN FLORIDA, CROP YEARS 1993 AND 1994

Crop	Harvested acres (1,000) 1993	Harvested acres (1,000) 1994	Unit	Production Total (1,000) 1993	Production Total (1,000) 1994	Yield per acre 1993	Yield per acre 1994	Value ($1,000) 1993	Value ($1,000) 1994
Corn 1/	100	80	Bu.	6,500	6,800	65	85	16,575	16,320
Cotton	54	68	2/	78	104	696	735	20,673	36,077
Cottonseed	(X)	(X)	Tons	27	33	(X)	(X)	2,727	2,640
Hay, all	250	240	Tons	650	744	3	3	55,250	67,704
Peanuts 3/	84	84	Lbs.	194,880	207,480	2,320	2,470	57,684	58,302
Potatoes	42	46	Cwt.	7,760	9,992	181	215	128,945	119,967
Soybeans 4/	50	42	Bu.	1,250	1,302	25	31	7,938	7,031
Sugarcane 5/	444	444	Tons	15,152	14,937	34	34	441,165	457,072
Tobacco, flue-cured 14	7	7	Lbs.	18,673	16,575	2,630	2,550	30,586	27,349
Wheat	25	15	Bu.	825	630	33	42	2,228	1,764

(X) Not applicable.
1/ Harvested for grain.
2/ Production in 480 net weight bales. Yield in pounds.
3/ Harvested for dry nuts.
4/ Harvested for beans.
5/ For sugar and seed.
Note: Data for 1993 may be revised. All 1994 estimates are preliminary.

Table 9.63. CORN: ACREAGE HARVESTED FOR GRAIN AND BUSHELS PRODUCED IN THE STATE CROP-REPORTING DISTRICTS, AND SPECIFIED COUNTIES OF FLORIDA, 1994

District and county	Acres harvested	Production (1,000 bushels)
Florida	80,000	6,800
District 1--West	45,800	4,088
Calhoun	1,500	128
Escambia	6,400	608
Gadsden	1,100	90
Holmes	2,500	200
Jackson	17,800	1,635
Jefferson	4,200	357
Leon	1,100	90
Okaloosa	1,500	150
Santa Rosa	1,700	145
Walton	3,200	269
Washington	3,600	320
District 1--West (Cont.)		
Other counties	1,200	96
District 3--North	20,900	1,681
Columbia	2,900	200
Hamilton	6,700	724
Madison	4,800	330
Suwannee	3,800	251
Other counties	2,700	176
District 5--Central	9,800	713
Alachua	3,000	213
Gilchrist	600	41
Levy	3,300	241
Other counties	2,900	218
District 8--South	3,500	318

Note: See accompanying map for counties in crop-reporting districts. Data are preliminary.

Source for Tables 9.62 and 9.63: State of Florida, Department of Agriculture and Consumer Services, Florida Agricultural Statistics Service, *Florida Agricultural Statistics: Field Crops Summary, 1994.*

Crop-reporting Districts

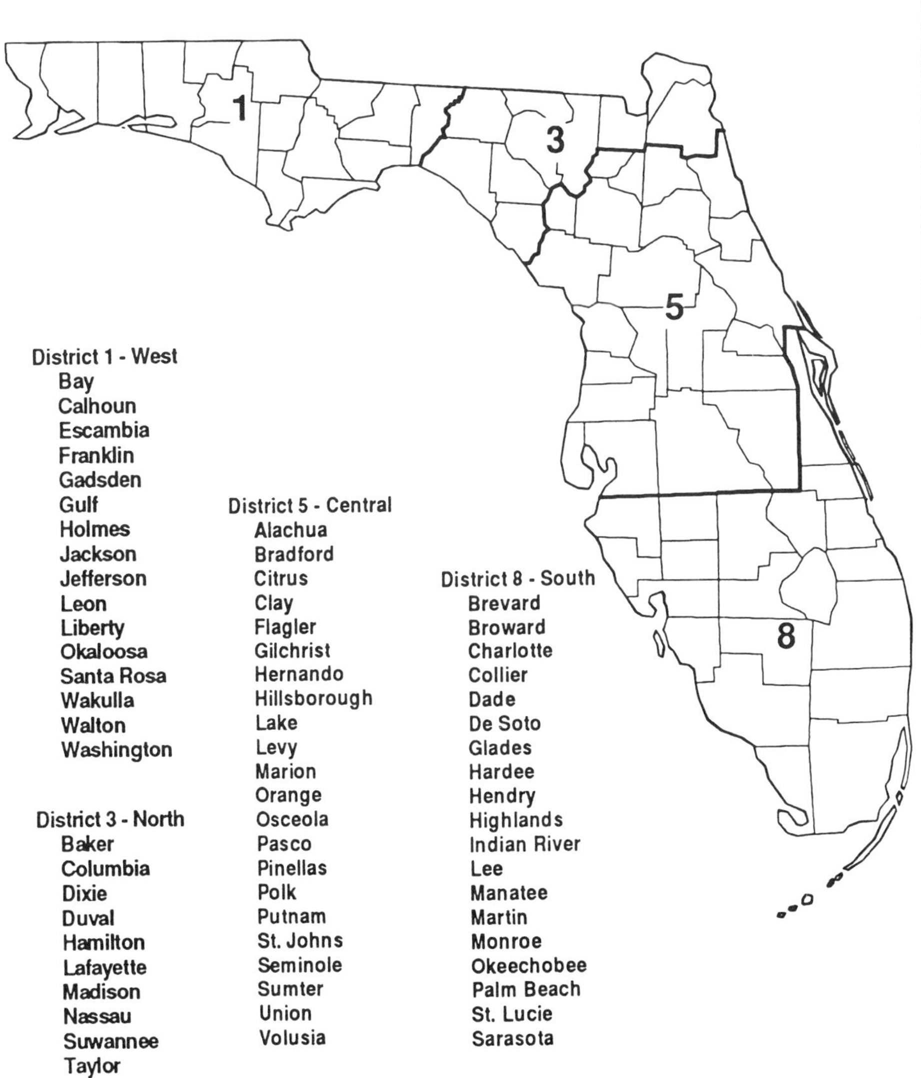
1
3
5
8
District 1 - West
Bay
Calhoun
Escambia
Franklin
Gadsden
Gulf
Holmes
Jackson
Jefferson
Leon
Liberty
Okaloosa
Santa Rosa
Wakulla
Walton
Washington
District 3 - North
Baker
Columbia
Dixie
Duval
Hamilton
Lafayette
Madison
Nassau
Suwannee
Taylor
District 5 - Central
Alachua
Bradford
Citrus
Clay
Flagler
Gilchrist
Hernando
Hillsborough
Lake
Levy
Marion
Orange
Osceola
Pasco
Pinellas
Polk
Putnam
St. Johns
Seminole
Sumter
Union
Volusia
District 8 - South
Brevard
Broward
Charlotte
Collier
Dade
De Soto
Glades
Hardee
Hendry
Highlands
Indian River
Lee
Manatee
Martin
Monroe
Okeechobee
Palm Beach
St. Lucie
Sarasota

Table 9.64. PEANUTS: ACREAGE HARVESTED AND PRODUCTION IN THE STATE, CROP-REPORTING DISTRICTS, AND SPECIFIED COUNTIES OF FLORIDA, 1994

District and county	Acres harvested	Production (1,000 pounds)	District and county	Acres harvested	Production (1,000 pounds)
Florida	84,000	207,480	District 3--North	7,200	20,614
			Columbia	1,600	3,869
District 1--West	67,600	159,134	Madison	900	2,146
Calhoun	3,500	7,540	Suwannee	4,400	13,639
Gadsden	700	1,337	Other counties	300	960
Holmes	5,800	8,959			
Jackson	35,300	82,453	District 5--Central	9,200	27,732
Jefferson	1,000	2,400	Alachua	1,600	4,713
Leon	400	804	Gilchrist	400	990
Okaloosa	800	2,104	Levy	4,600	14,099
Santa Rosa	12,500	39,695	Marion	2,500	7,680
Walton	5,000	9,073	Other counties	100	250
Washington	2,000	3,353			
Other counties	600	1,416			

Note: See accompanying map for counties in crop-reporting districts. Data are preliminary.

Table 9.65. SOYBEANS: ACREAGE HARVESTED FOR BEANS AND BUSHELS PRODUCED IN THE STATE, CROP-REPORTING DISTRICTS, AND SPECIFIED COUNTIES OF FLORIDA, 1994

District and county	Acres harvested	Production (1,000 pounds)	District and county	Acres harvested	Production (1,000 pounds)
Florida	42,000	1,302	District 1--West (Cont.)		
			Walton	2,100	61
District 1--West	37,000	1,183	Washington	1,300	42
Calhoun	6,000	174	Other counties	800	22
Escambia	5,800	219			
Gadsden	1,000	28	District 3--North	3,500	82
Holmes	1,600	48	Madison	2,300	55
Jackson	11,400	365	Suwannee	1,000	23
Jefferson	1,800	50	Other counties	200	4
Okaloosa	1,000	31			
Santa Rosa	4,200	143	Other	1,500	37

Note: See accompanying map for counties in crop-reporting districts. Data are preliminary.

Source for Tables 9.64 and 9.65: State of Florida, Department of Agriculture and Consumer Services, Florida Agricultural Statistics Service, *Florida Agricultural Statistics: Field Crops Summary, 1994.*

Table 9.66. COTTON: ACREAGE HARVESTED AND PRODUCTION IN THE STATE, CROP-REPORTING DISTRICTS, AND SPECIFIED COUNTIES OF FLORIDA, 1994

District and county	Acres harvested	Production (tons)	District and county	Acres harvested	Production (tons)
Florida	68,000	104,100	District 1 (Cont.)		
			Santa Rosa	23,150	38,200
District 1	64,050	99,400	Walton	1,250	2,000
Calhoun	4,050	6,000	Other counties	1,700	2,000
Escambia	12,600	21,200			
Holmes	1,250	1,700	Districts 3 and 5	3,950	4,700
Jackson	15,600	21,200	Columbia	1,050	1,100
Jefferson	1,250	1,800	Suwannee	1,150	1,400
Okaloosa	3,200	5,300	Other counties	1,750	2,200

Note: Data are preliminary. See accompanying map for counties in crop-reporting districts.

Table 9.67. SUGARCANE: ACREAGE HARVESTED AND PRODUCTION IN THE STATE CROP-REPORTING DISTRICTS, AND SPECIFIED COUNTIES OF FLORIDA, 1994

County	Acres harvested	Production (tons)	County	Acres harvested	Production (tons)
Florida	423,000	14,216,000	Hendry	73,000	2,440,000
			Martin	12,000	395,000
Glades	19,000	610,000	Palm Beach	319,000	10,771,000

Note: Data are preliminary. See accompanying map for counties in crop-reporting districts.

Table 9.68. TOBACCO: ACREAGE HARVESTED AND PRODUCTION OF FLUE-CURED TOBACCO IN THE STATE, CROP-REPORTING DISTRICTS, AND SPECIFIED COUNTIES OF FLORIDA, 1994

District and county	Acres harvested	Production (tons)	District and county	Acres harvested	Production (tons)
Florida	6,500	16,575,000	District 3 (Cont.)		
			Madison	800	1,699,000
District 1--West	330	664,000	Suwannee	1,580	4,307,000
Gadsden	110	196,000	Taylor	110	285,000
Jefferson	130	277,000	Other counties	70	194,000
Other counties	90	191,000	District 5--Central	1,370	3,327,000
District 3--North	4,800	12,584,000	Alachua	860	2,120,000
Baker	110	219,000	Bradford	90	220,000
Columbia	660	1,883,000	Gilchrist	150	393,000
Hamilton	990	2,503,000	Union	190	451,000
Lafayette	480	1,494,000	Other counties	80	143,000

Note: Data are preliminary. See accompanying map for counties in crop-reporting districts.

Source for Tables 9.66, 9.67, and 9.68: State of Florida, Department of Agriculture and Consumer Services, Florida Agricultural Statistics Service, *Florida Agricultural Statistics: Field Crops Summary, 1994.*

Table 9.69. POTATOES: ACREAGE HARVESTED IN THE STATE AND SPECIFIED COUNTIES OF FLORIDA, 1989 THROUGH 1994

(in acres)

County or season	1989	1990	1991	1992	1993	1994
Florida	42,600	44,700	43,000	40,100	41,900	46,400
Winter	7,600	7,700	7,600	8,100	8,400	7,800
Spring	35,000	37,000	35,400	32,000	33,500	38,600
Dade	5,100	4,800	4,800	4,900	4,700	4,300
Flagler	3,000	3,100	2,500	1,975	2,500	2,600
Putnam	4,500	4,900	4,200	4,800	4,900	5,400
St. Johns	20,500	20,700	20,300	18,225	18,600	21,000
Other counties	9,500	11,200	11,200	10,200	11,200	13,100

Note: 1994 data are preliminary.

Source: State of Florida, Department of Agriculture and Consumer Services, Florida Agricultural Statistics Service, *Florida Agricultural Statistics: Field Crops Summary, 1994.*

Table 9.70. CROPS: ACREAGE PLANTED AND HARVESTED, PRODUCTION, AND VALUE OF CROPS IN FLORIDA, CROP YEAR 1994-95

Crop	Acreage planted	Acreage harvested	Production (1,000 CWT)	Total value ($1,000)
All crops, total	379,150	356,800	66,640	1,479,951
Vegetables, total	208,050	194,000	34,992	971,690
Snap beans 1/	33,000	30,500	1,268	50,597
Cabbage	7,400	7,000	1,915	17,388
Carrots 1/	7,800	5,600	728	15,361
Sweet corn	39,600	36,900	4,835	105,311
Cucumbers 1/	13,800	13,200	3,114	42,610
Eggplant	2,350	2,300	495	13,500
Escarole	2,000	1,600	250	11,057
Bell peppers	21,400	20,300	4,406	188,938
Radishes	19,200	15,700	603	23,873
Squash	12,500	11,900	1,320	41,686
Tomatoes	49,000	49,000	16,060	461,369
Other 2/	81,300	79,600	12,736	238,800
Watermelons	37,000	33,000	8,250	61,793
Potatoes	46,800	42,900	A/ 8,957	A/ 84,010
Strawberries	6,000	6,000	1,680	118,608
Blueberries	0	1,300	25	5,050

CWT Hundred weight.

A/ Production sold.

1/ Fresh and processing.

2/ Fresh and processing vegetables and cantaloupes.

Source: State of Florida, Department of Agriculture and Consumer Services, Florida Agricultural Statistics Service, *Florida Agricultural Statistics: Vegetable Summary, 1994-95.*

Table 9.72. LIVESTOCK: CASH RECEIPTS FROM MARKETINGS IN FLORIDA 1989 THROUGH 1995

(in thousands of dollars, except where indicated)

Year	Total livestock and products Amount	Total livestock and products Percentage of total farm cash receipts	Cattle and calves	Hogs	Milk	Chickens and eggs	Honey
1989	1,218,705	19	359,986	19,010	387,960	308,032	7,200
1990	1,258,961	22	383,791	20,558	421,007	288,108	10,032
1991	1,171,626	19	363,351	17,304	372,947	276,398	9,898
1992	1,165,874	19	349,447	13,126	401,700	258,988	12,126
1993	1,211,131	20	362,495	15,106	385,503	298,121	11,300
1994	1,191,420	20	335,836	12,399	408,408	290,905	9,080
1995	1,108,331	20	289,802	11,581	363,528	314,537	12,461

Note: Data are for calendar year, except for hogs, chickens and eggs, and honey which report for a marketing year of December through November. Value of eggs is for total production including consumption on farms where produced. Data do not include government payments. Some data are revised.

Table 9.73. LIVESTOCK INVENTORY: NUMBER ON FARMS IN FLORIDA, LEADING STATE, AND THE UNITED STATES, 1995 OR 1996

(numbers in thousands)

Type of livestock	Florida Rank among states	Florida Number	Leading state Name	Leading state Number	United States
Cattle and calves 1/	15	1,990	Texas	15,000	103,819
Beef cows 1/	10	1,105	Texas	5,900	35,333
Hogs 2/	29	85	Iowa	14,300	59,694

1/ January 1, 1996. 2/ December 1, 1995.

Table 9.74. HONEY: PRODUCTION AND VALUE IN FLORIDA AND THE UNITED STATES 1992 THROUGH 1995

Year	Florida Number of colonies (1,000)	Florida Production (1,000 pounds)	Florida Value ($1,000)	United States Number of colonies (1,000)	United States Production (1,000 pounds)	United States Value ($1,000)
1992	220	22,880	12,126	3,030	220,584	121,321
1993	200	22,600	11,300	2,876	230,655	124,323
1994	230	19,320	9,080	2,770	217,168	114,665
1995	230	19,780	12,461	2,647	210,437	135,521

Note: Some data may be revised.

Source for Tables 9.72, 9.73, and 9.74: State of Florida, Department of Agriculture and Consumer Services, Florida Agricultural Statistics Service, *Florida Agricultural Statistics: Livestock, Dairy, and Poultry Summary, 1995.*

Table 9.86. DAIRY PRODUCTION: NUMBER OF MILK COWS AND ANNUAL MILK PRODUCTION IN FLORIDA, OTHER LEADING PRODUCTION STATES, AND THE UNITED STATES, 1995

State	Milk cows 2/ (1,000)	Production 1/ Total milk (1,000,000 pounds)	Rank among states	Per milk cow (pounds)
Florida	162	2,381	16	14,698
California	1,254	25,327	1	20,197
Wisconsin	1,490	22,942	2	15,397
New York	703	11,643	3	16,562
Pennsylvania	642	10,600	4	16,511
Minnesota	599	9,442	5	15,763
Texas	401	6,113	6	15,244
Michigan	326	5,565	7	17,071
Washington	266	5,302	8	19,932
Ohio	289	4,600	9	15,917
Idaho	232	4,210	10	18,147
Iowa	251	4,038	11	16,088
New Mexico	191	3,623	12	18,969
Missouri	190	2,690	13	14,158
Illinois	163	2,545	14	15,613
Vermont	157	2,538	15	16,166
United States	9,461	115,644	(X)	16,451

(X) Not applicable.
1/ Excludes milk sucked by calves.
2/ Average number on farms during year, excluding heifers not yet fresh.

Table 9.87. CHICKEN AND EGGS: CASH RECEIPTS IN FLORIDA, MARKETING YEARS 1988 THROUGH 1995

(in thousands of dollars)

Year	Total	Broilers	Eggs 1/	Other chickens 2/
1988	253,789	156,585	94,461	2,400
1989	308,032	181,636	123,078	3,318
1990	288,108	152,012	133,610	2,486
1991	276,371	151,704	120,903	3,764
1992	258,988	164,856	91,104	3,028
1993	298,121	187,714	106,838	3,569
1994	290,905	191,151	98,348	1,406
1995	314,537	218,361	95,158	1,018

1/ Total production, including consumption on farms where produced.
2/ Value of sales.
Note: Data are for marketing years beginning December 1 and ending November 30. Some data may be revised.

Source for Tables 9.86 and 9.87: State of Florida, Department of Agriculture and Consumer Services, Florida Agricultural Statistics Service, *Florida Agricultural Statistics: Livestock, Dairy, and Poultry Summary, 1995.*

FORESTRY, FISHERIES, AND MINERALS

Mineral Industries Establishments and Employees in Florida, Census Years 1972 Through 1992

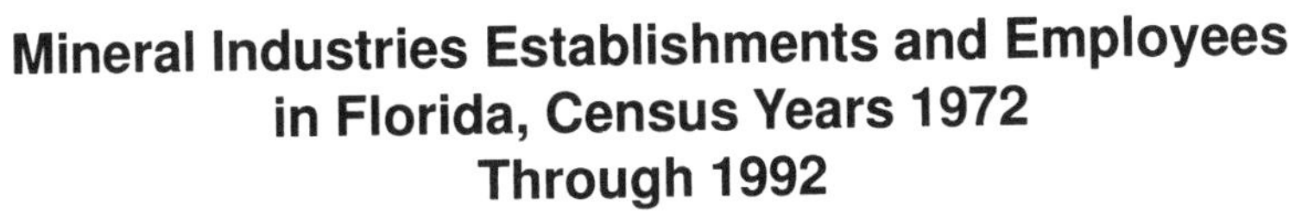

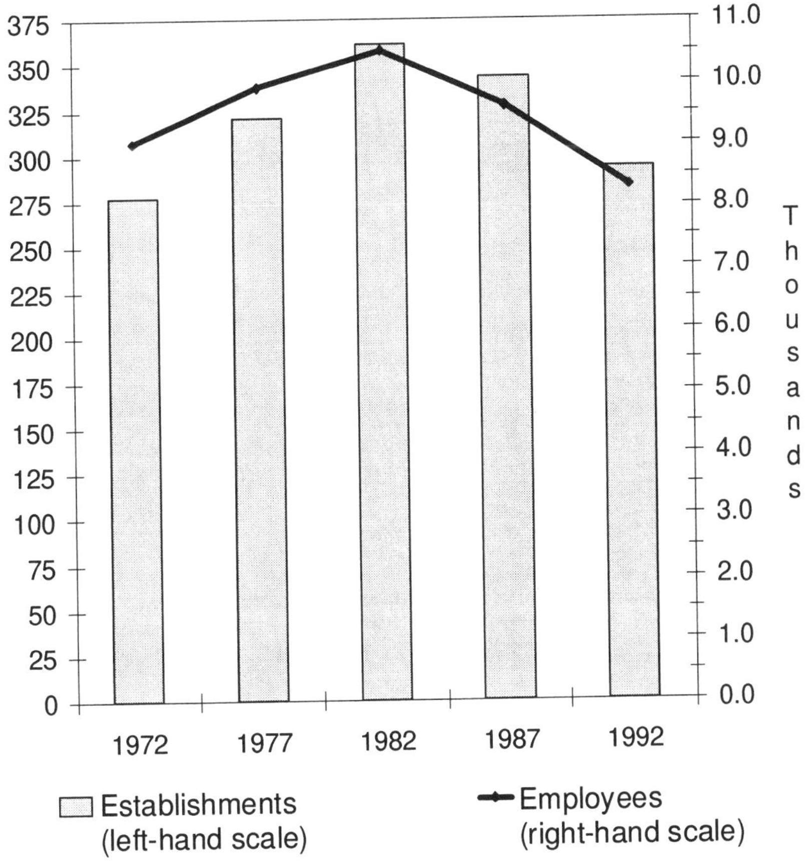

Source: Table 10.60

SECTION 10.00
FORESTRY, FISHERIES, AND MINERALS

TABLES LISTED BY MAJOR HEADINGS

Table 10.07. FOREST PRODUCTS: HARVEST BY PRODUCT AND BY SPECIES GROUP IN THE STATE AND COUNTIES OF FLORIDA, 1993

County	Softwood				Hardwood			
	Saw logs (MBF)	Veneer logs (MBF)	Pulp-wood 1/ (Cords)	Other pro-ducts 2/ (MCF)	Saw logs (MBF)	Veneer logs (MBF)	Pulp-wood 3/ (Cords)	Other pro-ducts 2/ (MCF)
Florida	767,185	145,387	3,545,975	29,155	25,581	9,352	524,109	2,917
Alachua	17,567	11,387	136,593	119	356	0	11,809	73
Baker	33,508	5,693	96,459	383	0	112	6,823	0
Bay	21,600	0	160,486	79	1,484	0	15,196	0
Bradford	44,928	5,693	79,446	86	0	0	15,612	0
Brevard	13	0	13,631	0	0	0	5	0
Broward	0	0	0	0	0	0	0	0
Calhoun	24,511	0	97,365	310	2,738	333	16,870	0
Charlotte	0	0	1,190	0	0	0	0	0
Citrus	409	0	17,285	297	0	140	5,588	24
Clay	26,430	5,693	63,888	153	0	0	5,286	0
Collier	26	0	201	0	0	0	0	0
Columbia	37,238	5,693	121,832	1,901	6	630	7,881	697
Dade	0	0	0	0	0	0	0	0
De Soto	324	0	14,374	397	0	0	0	0
Dixie	38,279	5,693	116,269	864	2,128	630	39,544	0
Duval	12,935	5,693	79,511	819	259	0	5,211	0
Escambia	20,358	5,250	68,865	9	1	0	16,095	0
Flagler	23,692	5,693	80,021	870	0	0	10,216	0
Franklin	0	0	91,008	0	0	0	1,846	0
Gadsden	4,317	13,294	61,414	48	2,177	1,111	11,674	59
Gilchrist	12,764	5,693	47,025	443	0	420	4,626	73
Glades	0	0	38,739	0	0	0	0	0
Gulf	6,862	0	48,741	46	1,939	0	456	0
Hamilton	10,675	0	59,476	3,601	0	0	8,487	0
Hardee	0	0	6,689	82	0	0	0	0
Hendry	0	0	12,448	0	0	0	0	0
Hernando	2,870	0	14,908	54	350	0	3,222	0
Highlands	0	0	4,457	617	0	0	0	0
Hillsborough	546	0	3,542	83	0	868	353	0
Holmes	19,361	6,361	26,262	113	2	0	14,047	0
Indian River	0	0	2,220	0	0	0	0	0
Jackson	34,637	11,024	49,890	369	1,141	0	36,973	0
Jefferson	14,852	1,714	33,675	169	1,563	260	11,776	568
Lafayette	14,993	5,693	41,652	425	0	210	4,800	0
Lake	2,207	0	16,676	791	0	280	1,540	0
Lee	0	0	1,309	0	0	0	0	0

See footnotes at end of table.

Continued . . .

Table 10.07. FOREST PRODUCTS: HARVEST BY PRODUCT AND BY SPECIES GROUP IN THE STATE AND COUNTIES OF FLORIDA, 1993 (Continued)

County	Softwood				Hardwood			
	Saw logs (MBF)	Veneer logs (MBF)	Pulp-wood 1/ (Cords)	Other pro-ducts 2/ (MCF)	Saw logs (MBF)	Veneer logs (MBF)	Pulp-wood 3/ (Cords)	Other pro-ducts 2/ (MCF)
Leon	8,483	4,570	42,478	10	1,517	260	23,640	20
Levy	28,770	5,693	86,512	725	1,875	840	20,758	36
Liberty	7,061	0	75,728	209	2,425	0	11,166	0
Madison	13,598	0	50,467	537	0	642	24,343	619
Manatee	85	0	147	0	0	0	0	0
Marion	29,011	5,693	107,804	1,018	2,649	140	16,531	36
Martin	0	0	28	0	0	0	0	0
Monroe	0	0	7	0	0	0	0	0
Nassau	32,412	0	134,029	903	19	0	18,145	0
Okaloosa	12,214	0	91,656	93	0	0	15,653	0
Okeechobee	0	0	0	428	0	0	0	0
Orange	163	0	3,935	0	0	0	0	0
Osceola	3,041	0	3,683	6,431	0	168	68	0
Palm Beach	0	0	9	0	0	0	0	0
Pasco	5,393	0	12,099	1,356	0	588	2,387	0
Pinellas	0	0	20	0	0	0	0	0
Polk	5,401	0	7,207	1,269	0	0	0	0
Putnam	18,635	5,693	64,814	160	166	140	10,799	0
St. Johns	18,393	5,693	92,795	273	18	0	13,958	0
St. Lucie	0	0	1,766	0	0	0	0	0
Santa Rosa	15,680	5,250	188,527	252	0	0	22,015	0
Sarasota	2,136	0	4,818	0	0	0	0	0
Seminole	463	0	13,985	91	0	0	0	0
Sumter	2,720	0	29,097	406	0	84	5,405	0
Suwannee	22,266	5,693	75,552	141	0	420	8,504	0
Taylor	44,898	0	516,673	826	1,736	796	27,481	697
Union	11,141	5,693	41,802	102	0	0	5,234	0
Volusia	4,478	0	59,079	372	0	280	7,096	0
Wakulla	8,453	1,142	21,942	143	0	0	437	15
Walton	29,307	0	65,906	174	2	0	8,656	0
Washington	17,081	0	45,863	108	1,030	0	25,897	0

MBF Thousand board feet.
MCF Thousand cubic feet.
1/ Includes 150,986 roundwood that was delivered to nonpulp mills, chipped and then sold to pulp mills as residues.
2/ Includes composite board, poles/piling, post and other industrial.
3/ Includes 15,047 roundwood that was delivered to nonpulp mills, chipped and then sold to pulp mills as residues.

Source: State of Florida, Department of Agriculture and Consumer Services, Division of Forestry, unpublished data.

Table 10.25. NATIONAL FOREST LAND: GROSS AND NET AREA OF NATIONAL FOREST AND OTHER LAND ADMINISTERED BY THE FOREST SERVICE IN FLORIDA AND THE UNITED STATES AS OF SEPTEMBER 30, 1995

(in acres)

Unit name and area	Gross area within unit boundaries	National forest system lands	Other lands within unit boundaries
Total	1,255,420	1,107,724	147,696
Apalachicola National Forest	632,890	565,465	67,425
National wilderness areas	32,692	(X)	(X)
Bradwell Bay 1/	24,602	(X)	(X)
Mud Swamp/New River	8,090	(X)	(X)
Choctawhatchee National Forest	1,152	1,152	0
Ocala National Forest	430,446	383,224	47,222
National wilderness areas	28,147	(X)	(X)
Alexander Springs	7,941	(X)	(X)
Billies Bay	3,092	(X)	(X)
Juniper Prairie	14,281	(X)	(X)
Little Lake George	2,833	(X)	(X)
National game refuge, Ocala	79,735	(X)	(X)
Osceola National Forest	190,932	157,883	33,049
National wilderness area, Big Gum Swamp	13,660	(X)	(X)
United States	231,745,585	191,614,904	40,130,681

(X) Not applicable.
1/ Protected under the Clean Air Act.

Table 10.26. NATIONAL FOREST LAND: NET AREA OF LAND ADMINISTERED BY THE NATIONAL FOREST SERVICE IN THE STATE AND COUNTIES OF FLORIDA AND THE UNITED STATES AS OF SEPTEMBER 30, 1995

County	National forest area	Acres
Total	(X)	1,146,671
Baker	Nekoosa Purchase Units	26
	Osceola National Forest	79,409
	Pinhook Purchase Units	23,193
Columbia	Nekoosa Purchase Units	78
	Osceola National Forest	78,474
	Pinhook Purchase Units	11,597
Franklin	Apalachicola National Forest	21,816
	Tates Hell-New River Purchase Units	976
Lake	Ocala National Forest	84,110
Leon	Apalachicola National Forest	104,490
Liberty	Apalachicola National Forest	267,298
	Tates Hell-New River Purchase Units	3,077
Marion	Ocala National Forest	275,502
Okaloosa	Choctawhatchee National Forest	523
Putnam	Ocala National Forest	23,612
Santa Rosa	Choctawhatchee National Forest	108
Wakulla	Apalachicola National Forest	171,861
Walton	Choctawhatchee National Forest	521
United States	(X)	191,614,904

(X) Not applicable.
Source for Tables 10.25 and 10.26: U.S., Department of Agriculture, Forest Service, *Land Areas of the National Forest System as of September 30, 1995.*

Table 10.34. FORESTRY: AVERAGE MONTHLY PRIVATE REPORTING UNITS, EMPLOYMENT AND PAYROLL COVERED BY UNEMPLOYMENT COMPENSATION LAW IN THE STATE AND COUNTIES OF FLORIDA, 1995

County	Number of reporting units	Number of employees	Payroll ($1,000)	County	Number of reporting units	Number of employees	Payroll ($1,000)
			Forestry (SIC code 08)				
Florida	121	924	2,090	Lee	4	41	71
				Leon	5	31	44
Alachua	4	30	58	Levy	4	17	39
Calhoun	7	29	50	Nassau	7	241	748
Gadsden	5	25	43	Taylor	5	54	121
Jackson	3	11	23				

Note: Private employment. For a list of three-digit code industries included see Table 10.35. Data are preliminary. Only counties for which data are disclosed are shown. Detail may not add to totals due to disclosure editing and/or rounding. See Tables 23.70, 23.71, 23.72, 23.73, and 23.74 for public employment data.

Table 10.35. FORESTRY AND FISHING INDUSTRIES: AVERAGE MONTHLY PRIVATE REPORTING UNITS, EMPLOYMENT, AND PAYROLL COVERED BY UNEMPLOYMENT COMPENSATION LAW BY INDUSTRY IN FLORIDA, 1995

SIC code	Industry	Number of reporting units	Number of employees	Payroll ($1,000)
08	Forestry	121	924	2,090
081	Timber tracts	58	395	868
083	Forest products	10	82	97
085	Forestry services	53	448	1,124
09	Fishing, hunting, and trapping	395	938	1,719
091	Commercial fishing	374	850	1,592
092	Fish hatcheries and preserves	9	29	44
097	Hunting and trapping, and game propagation	13	60	82

Note: Private employment. Data are preliminary. Detail may not add to totals due to disclosure editing and/or rounding. See Tables 23.70, 23.71, 23.72, 23.73, and 23.74 for public employment data.

Source for Tables 10.34 and 10.35: State of Florida, Department of Labor and Employment Security, Bureau of Labor Market Information, "Employment and Wages" (ES-202), unpublished data.

Table 10.36. FISHERIES: NUMBER OF PROCESSING AND WHOLESALING PLANTS AND AVERAGE ANNUAL EMPLOYMENT IN FLORIDA, GEOGRAPHIC AREAS, OTHER MAJOR PRODUCTION STATES AND THE UNITED STATES, 1993

Area	Number of plants Total	Number of plants Processing	Number of plants Wholesale	Average annual employment Total	Average annual employment Processing	Average annual employment Wholesale
Area						
South Atlantic and Gulf	1,750	590	1,160	17,929	13,495	4,434
New England	891	221	670	7,792	4,743	3,049
Mid-Atlantic	509	159	350	8,517	5,635	2,882
Pacific	1,242	538	704	24,402	21,709	2,693
Inland States	94	58	36	1,425	1,201	224
State						
Florida	466	147	319	4,576	2,870	1,706
Maine	341	63	278	2,256	1,381	875
Massachusetts	390	111	279	4,021	2,464	1,557
North Carolina	222	79	143	2,166	1,577	589
Washington	262	130	132	4,497	4,054	443
California	565	166	399	7,326	5,381	1,945
Alaska	321	191	130	10,778	10,564	214
United States 1/	4,567	1,597	2,970	69,269	55,672	13,597

1/ Includes American Samoa, Hawaii, and Puerto Rico.

Source: U.S., Department of Commerce, National Oceanic and Atmospheric Administration, National Marine Fisheries Service, *Fisheries of the United States, 1995*

Table 10.37. FISHING, HUNTING, AND TRAPPING: AVERAGE MONTHLY PRIVATE REPORTING UNITS, EMPLOYMENT, AND PAYROLL COVERED BY UNEMPLOYMENT COMPENSATION LAW IN THE STATE AND COUNTIES OF FLORIDA, 1995

County	Number of reporting units	Number of employees	Payroll ($1,000)	County	Number of reporting units	Number of employees	Payroll ($1,000)
Fishing, hunting, and trapping (SIC code 09)							
Florida	395	938	1,719	Hillsborough	17	77	216
				Lee	72	205	380
Bay	9	14	23	Monroe	36	107	188
Brevard	15	48	70	Nassau	10	24	44
Broward	7	9	13	Okaloosa	9	21	44
Charlotte	10	14	24	Pasco	9	22	46
Citrus	10	14	23	Pinellas	29	69	115
Duval	30	74	143	Polk	3	13	21
Escambia	7	14	13	St. Lucie	11	16	34
Franklin	13	19	24	Volusia	12	19	20

Note: Private employment. For a list of three-digit code industries included see Table 10.35. Data are preliminary. Only counties for which data are disclosed are shown. Detail may not add to totals due to disclosure editing and/or rounding. See Tables 23.70, 23.71, 23.72, 23.73, and 23.74 for public employment data.

Source: State of Florida, Department of Labor and Employment Security, Bureau of Labor Market Information, "Employment and Wages" (ES-202), unpublished data.

Table 10.40. FISH AND SHELLFISH: QUANTITY OF LANDINGS BY TYPE OF SPECIES AND TRIPS IN THE STATE AND SPECIFIED COUNTIES OF FLORIDA, 1995

Area and county	Landings 1/ (pounds) Total	Fish	Shellfish 2/	Trips 3/
Florida	128,282,147	63,583,437	64,698,710	387,238
East coast	37,225,680	19,762,763	17,462,917	171,260
West coast	90,512,759	43,575,135	46,937,624	215,380
Inland/out of state 4/	543,708	245,539	298,169	598
Bay	5,247,257	4,070,281	1,176,976	8,522
Brevard	11,765,914	3,711,503	8,054,411	90,084
Broward	1,623,049	1,299,943	323,106	4,169
Charlotte	1,873,696	893,239	980,457	8,590
Citrus	2,890,254	1,039,969	1,850,285	10,907
Clay	13,831	0	13,831	31
Collier	3,993,844	1,502,581	2,491,263	11,042
Dade	2,102,457	780,494	1,321,963	13,138
Dixie	1,544,858	480,454	1,064,404	5,193
Duval	4,522,001	1,910,550	2,611,451	10,077
Escambia	1,723,979	1,007,218	716,761	3,404
Flagler	34,011	4,537	29,474	98
Franklin	5,325,726	1,529,580	3,796,146	18,519
Gulf	5,368,817	4,049,482	1,319,335	1,341
Hernando	390,419	19,420	370,999	3,571
Hillsborough	2,975,928	624,715	2,351,213	3,717
Indian River	1,728,493	1,609,284	119,209	11,168
Jefferson	457	402	55	2
Lee	9,843,245	2,738,526	7,104,719	26,475
Levy	1,401,146	354,467	1,046,679	4,719
Manatee	4,325,175	3,772,108	553,067	3,881
Martin	2,322,302	2,273,322	48,980	4,993
Monroe	22,849,686	7,753,559	15,096,127	70,571
Nassau	1,596,708	85,060	1,511,648	3,095
Okaloosa	3,301,866	3,021,699	280,167	3,390
Palm Beach	1,794,412	1,711,906	82,506	9,635
Pasco	1,225,781	455,105	770,676	3,892
Pinellas	11,426,526	7,757,544	3,668,982	15,907
Putnam	155,603	7,358	148,245	1,114
St. Johns	1,440,258	377,565	1,062,693	5,820
St. Lucie	4,838,192	3,424,411	1,413,781	7,196
Santa Rosa	1,079,578	834,911	244,667	2,649
Sarasota	282,628	207,343	75,285	982
Taylor	824,549	614,693	209,856	2,587
Volusia	3,288,449	2,566,830	721,619	10,642
Wakulla	2,568,184	835,765	1,732,419	5,027
Walton	49,160	12,074	37,086	492

1/ Based on whole weight of species with some exceptions, e.g., stone crabs, sponges.
2/ Includes clams, conch, crabs, lobster, octopus, oysters, scallops, shrimp, sponges, and squid.
3/ Only successful trips of fishermen.
4/ Landings from seafood dealers residing in inland counties or out-of-state who bought Florida produced seafood.
Note: Landings are recorded in county where products first crossed the shore. Data are preliminary.
Source: State of Florida, Department of Natural Resources, Marine Fisheries Information System, unpublished data.

Table 10.60. MINERAL INDUSTRIES: ESTABLISHMENTS, EMPLOYMENT, PAYROLL VALUE ADDED BY MINING, AND CAPITAL EXPENDITURE IN FLORIDA CENSUS YEARS 1972 THROUGH 1992

Year	Number of establishments		All employees		Value added by mining (million dollars)	Capital expenditure 1/ (million dollars)
	Total	With 20 employees or more	Number (1,000)	Payroll (million dollars)		
1972	277	72	9.0	81.1	297.5	107.8
1977	321	69	9.9	132.4	1,038.9	100.3
1982	361	(NA)	10.5	216.0	1,860.4	321.9
1987	343	78	9.6	231.9	1,027.4	166.5
1992	293	61	8.3	260.5	979.9	130.8

(NA) Not available.
1/ New and used capital expenditure.
Note: The minerals industries census is on a 5-year cycle collecting data for years ending in 2 and 7.

Table 10.61. MINERAL INDUSTRIES: CHARACTERISTICS OF MINERAL INDUSTRIES IN FLORIDA, 1992

(in millions of dollars, except where indicated)

Item	1992
Establishments during year (number)	293
0-4 employees	147
5-9 employees	52
10-19 employees	33
20-49 employees	31
50-99 employees	11
100-249 employees	14
250-499 employees	2
500-999 employees	2
1,000-2,499 employees	1
All employees	
Average for the year (1,000)	8.3
Production, development, and exploration workers (1,000)	6.3
Payroll	260.5
Supplemental labor costs not included in payroll	67.0
Value added by mining	979.9
Inventories, beginning of year	288.4
Inventories, end of year	315.4
Cost of supplies	699.4
Cost of purchased communications services	2.4
Value of shipments and receipts	1,548.6
Capital expenditure during year (except land and mineral rights)	130.8
New	82.0
Used	46.3
Rental payments during year	8.7
Expensed mineral exploration, development, land, and rights 1/	57.4

1/ Excludes mining services industries and natural gas liquids industries and data data for mineral land and rights for the crude petroleum and natural gas industries.
Note: The minerals industries census is on a 5-year cycle collecting data for years ending in 2 and 7.
Source for Tables 10.60 and 10.61: U.S., Department of Commerce, Bureau of the Census, *1992 Census of Mineral Industries: South Atlantic States.* Geographic Area Series MIC92-A-10.

Table 10.71. NONFUEL MINERAL PRODUCTION: QUANTITY AND VALUE IN FLORIDA 1993 THROUGH 1995

(quantity in thousand metric tons; value in millions of dollars)

Mineral	1993 Quantity	1993 Value	1994 Quantity	1994 Value	1995 Quantity	1995 Value
Total	(X)	1,310	(X)	1,370	(X)	1,390
Cement: Masonry	351	27	400	35	393	34
Portland	4,190	211	3,370	228	2,970	200
Clays 1/	407	53	430	55	363	55
Peat	219	4	206	3	(D)	(D)
Sand and gravel: Construction	22,800	73	16,600	61	15,800	59
Industrial	504	6	540	6	591	6
Stone (crushed) 2/	64,900	313	67,000	343	66,500	343
Combined value 3/	(X)	624	(X)	639	(X)	689

(X) Not applicable.
(D) Data withheld to avoid disclosure of information about individual companies.
1/ Excludes certain clays; included with "Combined value."
2/ Excludes certain stones in 1994; included with "Combined value."
3/ Includes minerals not listed separately and values indicated by symbol (D).
Note: Production as measured by mine shipments, sales, or marketable production (including consumption by producers). Some data are estimated. 1995 data are preliminary.
Source: U.S., Department of the Interior, Bureau of Mines, *Mineral Industry Surveys: Florida 1994 Annual Estimates,* and U.S., Department of the Interior, U.S. Geological Survey, unpublished data.

Table 10.72. MINING: AVERAGE MONTHLY PRIVATE REPORTING UNITS, EMPLOYMENT AND PAYROLL COVERED BY UNEMPLOYMENT COMPENSATION LAW BY INDUSTRY IN FLORIDA, 1995

SIC code	Industry	Number of reporting units	Number of employees	Payroll ($1,000)
	Mining	198	6,427	20,068
13	Oil and gas extraction	55	414	1,847
131	Crude petroleum and natural gas	15	153	1,043
138	Oil and gas fields services	40	261	804
14	Nonmetallic minerals, except fuels	136	5,869	17,659
141	Dimension stone	4	43	78
142	Crushed and broken stone, including riprap	39	1,541	4,286
144	Sand and gravel	40	713	1,772
145	Clay, ceramic, and refractory minerals	4	225	551
147	Chemical and fertilizer mineral mining	12	2,940	10,050
148	Nonmetallic minerals services, except fuels	6	32	65
149	Miscellaneous nonmetallic minerals, except fuels	32	375	856

Note: Private employment. Detail may not add to totals due to disclosure editing and/or rounding. See Tables 23.70, 23.71, 23.72, 23.73, and 23.74 for public employment data.
Source: State of Florida, Department of Labor and Employment Security, Bureau of Labor Market Information, "Employment and Wages" (ES-202), unpublished data.

Table 10.84. PHOSPHATE ROCK PRODUCTION: SALES OR USE BY PRODUCERS BY TYPE OF USE AND BY REGION IN THE UNITED STATES, CROP YEARS 1992-93 AND 1993-94

(in thousand metric tons)

Region	Year ending June 30, 1993				Year ending June 30, 1994			
	Domestic 1/				Domestic 1/			
	Total	Agri-cultural	Indus-trial	Ex-port 2/	Total	Agri-cultural	Indus-trial	Ex-port 2/
Florida and North Carolina								
Rock	32,696	32,160	536	3,066	32,734	32,643	92	3,136
P205 content	9,819	9,642	177	985	9,819	9,789	30	994
Idaho, Montana, and Utah								
Rock	6,095	2,354	3,741	79	6,047	1,685	4,361	44
P205 content	1,708	723	985	24	1,693	549	1,144	13

1/ Includes rock converted to products and exported.
2/ Exports reported to Bureau of Mines by companies.

Table 10.85. PHOSPHATE ROCK PRODUCTION: PRODUCTION AND SALES BY REGION IN THE UNITED STATES, CROP YEARS 1992-93 AND 1993-94

Item	Year ending June 30, 1993				Year ending June 30, 1994			
	Thousand metric tons		Value 1/		Thousand metric tons		Value 1/	
	Rock	P205 content	Total (million dollars)	Average per ton (dollars)	Rock	P205 content	Total (million dollars)	Average per ton (dollars)
Mine production	134,559	19,138	(NA)	(NA)	122,016	20,430	(NA)	(NA)
Florida and North Carolina	126,144	16,997	(NA)	NA)	112,133	17,979	(NA)	NA)
Idaho, Montana, and Utah	8,415	2,141	(NA)	(NA)	9,883	2,451	(NA)	(NA)
Marketable production	41,203	12,608	902	21.88	37,570	11,087	750	19.96
Florida and North Carolina	35,773	10,807	811	22.68	30,963	9,254	634	20.48
Idaho, Montana, and Utah	5,430	1,801	90	16.64	6,607	1,833	116	17.49
Sold or used by producers	41,936	12,536	917	21.87	41,961	12,519	838	19.96
Florida and North Carolina	35,762	10,804	813	22.72	35,871	10,813	733	20.43
Idaho, Montana, and Utah	6,174	1,732	105	16.93	6,090	1,706	105	17.16

(NA) Not available.
1/ Calculated value based on weighted sold or used value.
Note: Detail may not add to totals because of rounding or revisions made to totals only.

Source for Tables 10.84 and 10.85: U.S., Department of the Interior, Bureau of Mines, *Mineral Industry Surveys: Marketable Phosphate Rock, 1994 Crop Year,* and previous edition.

CONSTRUCTION

Single-family Construction Starts, 1995

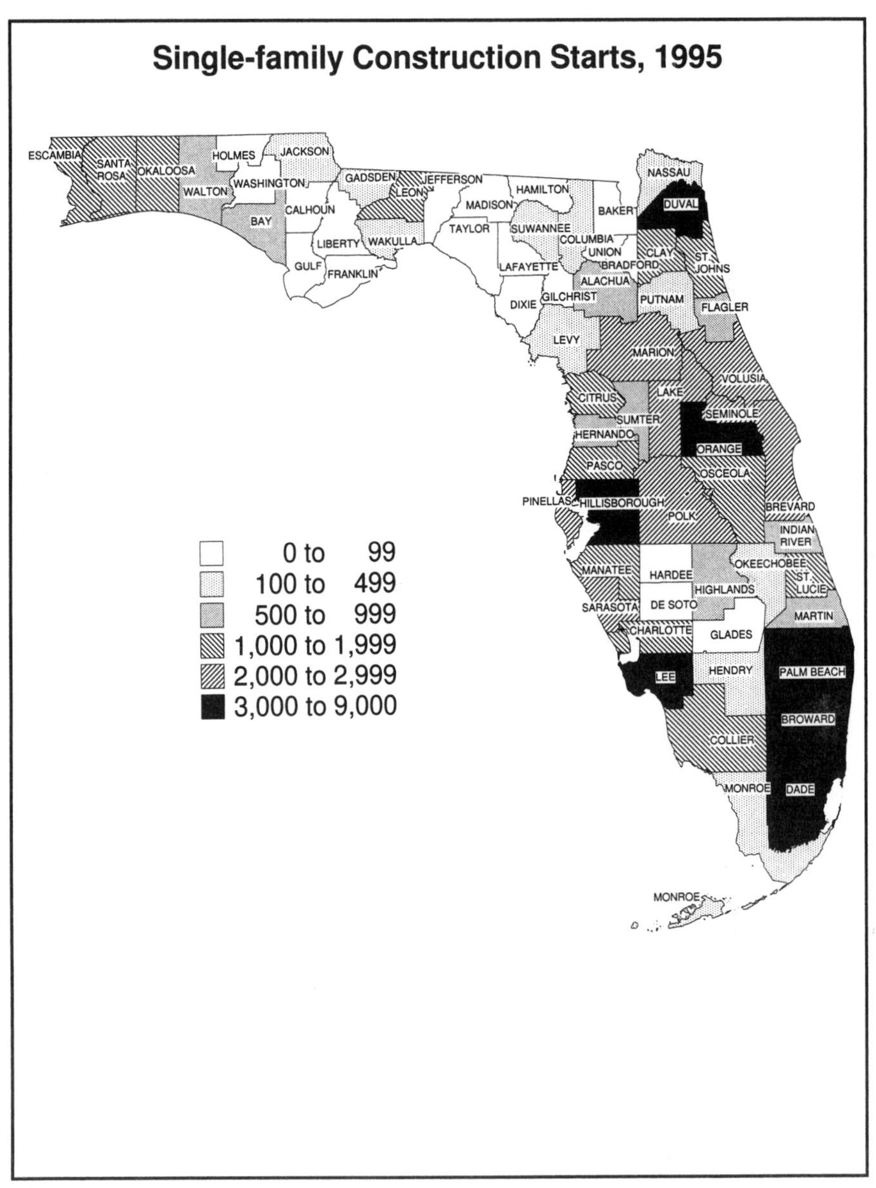

Source: Table 11.05

SECTION 11.00
CONSTRUCTION

TABLES LISTED BY MAJOR HEADINGS

Table 11.03. CONSTRUCTION CONTRACTS: VALUE IN FLORIDA AND THE UNITED STATES 1987 THROUGH 1995

(in millions of dollars)

Year	Florida	United States	Year	Florida	United States
1987	19,447	258,090	1993	19,117	271,529
1988	19,587	260,752	1994	22,140	296,212
1989	21,090	271,300	1995		
1990	16,975	246,022	Total 1/	21,570	303,790
1991	15,401	230,923	Residential	10,868	127,890
1992	16,744	252,191	Nonresidential	6,938	112,395

1/ Includes nonbuildings.
Note: Includes new structures/additions/major alterations to existing structures. Some data are revised.
Source: U.S., Department of Commerce, Bureau of the Census, *Statistical Abstract of the United States, 1996*. Data from F.W. Dodge Division.

Table 11.04. BUILDING PERMIT ACTIVITY: NUMBER OF PRIVATE RESIDENTIAL HOUSING UNITS AUTHORIZED BY BUILDING PERMITS IN FLORIDA, OTHER SUNBELT STATES OTHER POPULOUS STATES, AND THE UNITED STATES, 1991 THROUGH 1994

State	1991	1992	1993	1994
Florida	95,308	102,022	115,103	128,228
Other sunbelt states				
Alabama 1/	11,277	13,905	16,105	15,636
Arizona	23,521	31,793	38,656	51,205
Arkansas 1/	6,881	7,934	9,962	12,215
California	105,956	97,781	84,341	96,511
Georgia 1/	37,580	44,566	53,874	58,958
Louisiana 1/	7,182	9,750	11,226	14,056
Mississippi 1/	5,160	6,321	8,116	10,441
New Mexico	6,057	7,240	8,874	11,582
North Carolina 1/	39,034	48,158	53,281	61,366
Oklahoma 1/	5,918	7,678	8,673	9,520
South Carolina	18,712	20,221	21,060	24,016
Tennessee 1/	19,265	23,319	26,984	29,579
Texas 1/	51,866	64,235	77,754	95,019
Virginia	33,706	40,205	44,963	47,189
Other populous states				
Illinois	32,846	40,430	44,742	48,683
Indiana	23,936	28,739	30,803	33,916
Massachusetts	12,672	16,411	17,460	17,996
Michigan	33,806	37,026	39,755	46,663
New Jersey	14,856	19,072	25,188	25,373
New York	28,580	29,851	28,604	28,019
Ohio 1/	35,810	42,610	44,235	47,170
Pennsylvania	34,608	38,282	40,126	37,271
United States	948,794	1,094,933	1,199,063	1,374,636

1/ Percentage of population in permit-issuing places is less than 90.
Note: Data are from a national sample of 17,000 permit-issuing places 1991 through 1993 and 19,000 in 1994, a universe which accounts for approximately 92 percent of new residential construction. Some data may be revised. See also Table 24.20.
Source: U.S., Department of Commerce, International Trade Administration, *Construction Review, Spring 1995*.

Table 11.05. CONSTRUCTION ACTIVITY: SINGLE- AND MULTIFAMILY HOUSING UNITS PERMITTED AND CONSTRUCTION STARTS IN THE STATE AND COUNTIES OF FLORIDA, 1993, 1994, AND 1995

County	Single-family housing units						Multifamily housing units					
	Permitted			Construction starts			Permitted			Construction starts		
	1993	1994	1995 A/	1993	1994	1995 A/	1993	1994	1995 A/	1993	1994	1995 A/
Florida	91,252	96,283	84,921	89,785	94,397	87,241	23,838	32,354	37,778	16,752	30,272	32,678
Alachua	962	1,062	930	948	1,038	955	521	520	1,188	280	526	802
Baker	72	93	76	72	86	81	0	0	0	0	0	0
Bay	1,080	984	776	1,051	990	822	294	35	231	170	98	209
Bradford	70	75	66	68	69	75	0	0	0	0	0	0
Brevard	3,716	3,622	2,653	3,700	3,554	2,797	233	385	188	174	364	154
Broward	9,808	10,667	8,454	9,470	10,310	9,000	3,156	5,061	4,786	1,881	4,978	4,128
Calhoun	43	30	50	43	30	51	0	0	0	0	0	0
Charlotte	1,366	1,331	967	1,377	1,315	1,023	109	255	34	98	203	87
Citrus	1,195	1,219	1,066	1,184	1,177	1,112	85	8	11	60	27	16
Clay	1,061	1,341	1,163	1,032	1,317	1,192	24	0	404	12	9	143
Collier	1,702	1,964	1,966	1,687	1,897	1,994	1,957	2,358	2,402	1,465	2,075	2,333
Columbia	227	252	257	229	242	260	4	9	2	5	6	1
Dade	5,793	6,080	7,376	5,802	5,979	6,737	3,233	5,231	5,945	2,549	4,373	5,627
De Soto	68	74	76	69	73	77	29	4	46	15	11	45
Dixie	41	43	29	41	46	30	0	0	0	0	0	0
Duval	4,325	3,991	3,473	4,325	3,911	3,584	297	1,182	880	222	1,227	798
Escambia	1,358	1,407	1,310	1,348	1,394	1,306	58	100	516	55	74	330
Flagler	771	855	807	741	838	831	29	61	21	22	38	33
Franklin	93	99	94	95	96	97	0	0	0	1	0	0
Gadsden	132	150	125	130	145	128	79	6	2	62	13	4
Gilchrist	59	61	55	59	53	59	0	0	0	0	0	0

See footnotes at end of table.

Continued . . .

Table 11.05. CONSTRUCTION ACTIVITY: SINGLE- AND MULTIFAMILY HOUSING UNITS PERMITTED AND CONSTRUCTION STARTS IN THE STATE AND COUNTIES OF FLORIDA, 1993, 1994, AND 1995 (Continued)

County	Single-family housing units						Multifamily housing units					
	Permitted			Construction starts			Permitted			Construction starts		
	1993	1994	1995 A/	1993	1994	1995 A/	1993	1994	1995 A/	1993	1994	1995 A/
Glades	28	23	26	28	24	29	0	0	0	0	0	0
Gulf	69	80	92	68	81	93	0	0	0	0	0	0
Hamilton	17	45	28	19	27	46	0	0	0	0	4	0
Hardee	48	39	36	45	39	38	4	0	2	2	0	2
Hendry	135	153	132	140	150	138	4	8	3	1	9	1
Hernando	1,351	1,192	935	1,302	1,227	978	73	60	24	54	66	28
Highlands	590	679	537	580	658	565	147	105	92	113	109	90
Hillsborough	4,484	5,208	4,664	4,414	5,073	4,831	695	2,340	2,466	617	1,749	2,363
Holmes	52	61	53	51	58	56	8	0	8	5	0	4
Indian River	859	1,041	840	848	999	883	95	158	169	81	148	136
Jackson	117	130	119	118	125	125	58	27	40	40	25	28
Jefferson	54	62	44	54	59	46	0	0	0	0	0	0
Lafayette	37	20	20	35	22	21	0	0	0	0	0	0
Lake	2,400	2,157	2,069	2,284	2,219	2,152	163	307	211	121	204	319
Lee	3,672	3,736	3,094	3,559	3,693	3,225	1,656	1,580	1,648	1,242	1,524	1,484
Leon	1,621	1,615	1,555	1,602	1,610	1,565	402	482	1,167	306	457	761
Levy	154	143	136	151	144	140	6	36	8	1	34	5
Liberty	10	22	17	10	20	19	0	0	0	0	0	0
Madison	46	53	46	46	51	48	0	0	0	0	0	0
Manatee	1,551	1,917	1,603	1,504	1,873	1,656	239	272	767	238	222	561
Marion	2,281	2,290	2,034	2,220	2,258	2,114	92	26	189	49	63	84
Martin	789	825	854	770	775	909	523	373	310	373	376	315
Monroe	284	286	377	300	286	374	114	69	147	70	98	151
Nassau	359	456	457	357	444	460	24	9	232	24	24	103

See footnotes at end of table.

Continued . . .

Table 11.05. CONSTRUCTION ACTIVITY: SINGLE- AND MULTIFAMILY HOUSING UNITS PERMITTED AND CONSTRUCTION STARTS IN THE STATE AND COUNTIES OF FLORIDA, 1993, 1994, AND 1995 (Continued)

County	Single-family housing units						Multifamily housing units					
	Permitted			Construction starts			Permitted			Construction starts		
	1993	1994	1995 A/	1993	1994	1995 A/	1993	1994	1995 A/	1993	1994	1995 A/
Okaloosa	1,577	1,637	1,079	1,576	1,627	1,117	240	708	757	207	531	691
Okeechobee	124	111	99	122	109	103	2	5	2	2	7	1
Orange	5,835	6,121	5,264	5,847	6,044	5,477	2,440	3,055	4,465	995	3,664	3,906
Osceola	1,858	1,670	1,548	1,866	1,657	1,604	1,260	238	94	1,033	463	82
Palm Beach	7,029	8,587	7,480	6,899	8,289	7,689	1,861	3,060	3,103	1,503	2,221	2,848
Pasco	2,098	2,177	1,790	2,056	2,131	1,848	123	239	267	87	211	235
Pinellas	2,398	2,420	2,122	2,403	2,393	2,197	1,241	1,123	1,428	970	1,188	1,137
Polk	2,587	2,573	2,190	2,486	2,588	2,263	68	111	122	51	111	102
Putnam	195	159	133	196	162	135	2	86	4	4	54	34
St. Johns	1,272	1,389	1,410	1,251	1,333	1,445	146	193	569	111	161	291
St. Lucie	1,436	1,486	1,268	1,431	1,426	1,336	358	566	511	254	492	435
Santa Rosa	1,514	1,715	998	1,482	1,690	1,047	4	51	62	3	31	65
Sarasota	2,260	2,238	2,069	2,196	2,216	2,155	568	729	515	440	628	502
Seminole	2,423	2,406	2,070	2,362	2,375	2,126	258	700	292	83	850	131
Sumter	497	703	858	457	683	866	0	0	0	0	0	0
Suwannee	122	147	144	124	140	147	0	18	0	0	16	0
Taylor	50	46	44	49	45	46	0	0	0	0	0	0
Union	27	43	52	24	41	52	0	0	0	0	0	0
Volusia	2,276	2,189	1,974	2,275	2,153	2,051	599	304	814	403	398	584
Wakulla	143	140	151	140	137	147	12	0	0	7	0	0
Walton	502	600	552	489	593	578	210	75	599	172	82	457
Washington	79	93	89	78	90	90	35	26	35	19	30	32

A/ Preliminary.
Note: Permit data compiled by BEBR based on data from the U.S. Bureau of the Census.

Source: University of Florida, Bureau of Economic and Business Research, unpublished data.

Table 11.15. BUILDING PERMIT ACTIVITY: VALUE REPORTED ON BUILDING PERMITS AND NEW HOUSING UNITS AUTHORIZED BY BUILDING PERMITS IN THE STATE, COUNTIES MUNICIPALITIES, AND UNINCORPORATED AREAS OF FLORIDA, 1995

(values rounded to thousands of dollars)

Area 1/	Total value	Value of all housekeeping residential 2/	Number of housekeeping units Single-family	Number of housekeeping units Multi-family	Value of nonresidential 3/	Value of additions and alterations
Florida	17,002,857	10,848,752	84,877	39,010	3,414,956	2,739,150
Alachua	182,462	111,475	920	944	42,334	28,654
Alachua	12,196	6,193	85	2	5,254	749
Archer	84	77	1	0	3	4
Gainesville	47,031	22,030	215	224	11,189	13,812
Hawthorne	528	134	2	0	305	89
High Springs	1,825	885	14	0	642	297
Micanopy	477	217	4	0	0	260
Newberry	1,922	1,503	25	0	145	273
Waldo	145	106	2	0	7	31
County office	118,256	80,329	572	718	24,788	13,139
Baker	9,393	4,591	82	0	2,169	2,633
Macclenny	4,207	1,227	23	0	1,318	1,661
County office	5,186	3,363	59	0	851	971
Bay	121,244	55,332	810	234	26,544	39,368
Lynn Haven	20,290	13,819	134	0	5,119	1,352
Panama City Beach	28,834	11,843	138	98	2,575	14,416
County office	72,120	29,670	538	136	18,850	23,600
Bradford	5,409	3,687	66	0	342	1,380
Hampton	(NA)	(NA)	(NA)	(NA)	(NA)	(NA)
County office	5,409	3,687	66	0	342	1,380
Brevard	407,365	278,134	2,553	241	82,095	47,137
Cape Canaveral	3,402	1,486	13	2	1,818	98
Cocoa	4,685	584	8	0	1,706	2,395
Cocoa Beach	2,536	170	1	0	565	1,800
Indialantic	2,475	1,094	8	0	884	497
Indian Harbour Beach	7,842	5,337	37	0	1,958	547
Malabar	1,881	1,114	10	0	276	492
Melbourne	58,443	33,885	366	2	10,215	14,342
Melbourne Beach	1,021	708	5	0	0	313
Melbourne Village	1,145	283	3	0	793	69
Palm Bay	71,967	49,214	524	0	12,491	10,262
Palm Shores	999	999	15	0	0	0
Rockledge	22,281	16,724	138	60	5,253	304
Satellite Beach	2,627	873	3	6	0	1,754
Titusville	11,949	4,713	44	0	2,962	4,273
West Melbourne	10,407	6,523	71	0	2,759	1,125
County office	203,706	154,427	1,307	171	40,414	8,865
Broward	1,743,540	1,159,764	8,470	4,693	293,527	290,249
Coconut Creek	40,364	30,215	312	0	9,202	948
Cooper City	4,029	3,265	52	0	0	764
Coral Springs	235,339	189,807	1,190	909	34,623	10,909
Dania	13,223	8,267	39	146	3,140	1,816
Davie	124,062	68,113	462	356	40,918	15,032
Deerfield Beach	38,316	5,639	35	80	10,726	21,951

See footnotes at end of table. Continued . . .

Table 11.15. BUILDING PERMIT ACTIVITY: VALUE REPORTED ON BUILDING PERMITS AND NEW HOUSING UNITS AUTHORIZED BY BUILDING PERMITS IN THE STATE, COUNTIES MUNICIPALITIES, AND UNINCORPORATED AREAS OF FLORIDA, 1995 (Continued)

(values rounded to thousands of dollars)

Area 1/	Total value	Value of all house-keeping residen-tial 2/	Number of housekeeping units Single-family	Multi-family	Value of non-residen-tial 3/	Value of additions and alter-ations
Broward (Continued)						
Ft. Lauderdale	120,254	12,281	50	16	73,311	34,662
Hallandale	6,445	1,886	18	4	1,688	2,871
Hillsboro Beach	5,266	5,266	1	12	0	0
Hollywood	112,559	47,431	181	722	20,177	44,952
Lauderdale-by-the-sea	1,827	0	0	0	985	842
Lauderdale Lakes	1,583	900	3	0	0	683
Lauderhill	41,530	7,369	55	0	476	33,684
Lighthouse Point	3,427	1,083	5	0	0	2,344
Margate	34,717	20,168	185	118	4,415	10,133
Miramar	128,356	115,129	1,016	384	11,724	1,504
North Lauderdale	4,741	3,701	51	0	428	612
Oakland Park	4,803	1,467	13	6	2,193	1,143
Parkland	54,644	52,459	315	20	1,747	437
Pembroke Park	500	0	0	0	500	0
Pembroke Pines	241,442	214,051	1,608	799	17,954	9,437
Plantation	76,090	43,587	400	175	22,173	10,329
Pompano Beach	28,422	10,824	48	208	8,178	9,421
Sea Ranch Lakes	1,121	227	1	0	50	844
Sunrise	34,509	18,516	101	226	9,966	6,027
Tamarac	45,079	36,787	335	404	4,788	3,505
Wilton Manor	472	195	1	0	12	266
County office	340,420	261,130	1,993	108	14,154	65,135
Calhoun	5,709	3,408	49	0	1,843	458
Blountstown	580	157	4	0	241	182
County office	5,129	3,251	45	0	1,602	276
Charlotte	129,229	97,042	941	32	19,575	12,612
Punta Gorda	23,175	16,937	160	2	2,632	3,606
County office	106,055	80,106	781	30	16,942	9,006
Citrus	97,091	63,058	1,066	11	20,308	13,726
Crystal River	3,540	1,430	7	5	857	1,253
Inverness	6,879	3,099	72	0	2,073	1,708
County office	86,671	58,529	987	6	17,378	10,765
Clay	150,824	121,273	1,195	203	22,001	7,551
Green Cove Springs	4,937	4,391	42	0	220	326
Orange Park	2,379	548	6	0	198	1,633
Penney Farms	442	135	2	0	200	107
County office	143,066	116,199	1,145	203	21,383	5,484
Collier	628,664	501,797	1,956	2,300	72,734	54,133
Everglades	219	0	0	0	60	159
Naples	88,396	41,007	37	118	25,380	22,008
County office	540,049	460,789	1,919	2,182	47,294	31,965
Columbia	27,237	20,224	266	0	4,924	2,089
Lake City	4,427	1,322	31	0	1,016	2,089
County office	22,810	18,902	235	0	3,908	0

See footnotes at end of table. Continued . . .

Table 11.15. BUILDING PERMIT ACTIVITY: VALUE REPORTED ON BUILDING PERMITS AND NEW HOUSING UNITS AUTHORIZED BY BUILDING PERMITS IN THE STATE, COUNTIES MUNICIPALITIES, AND UNINCORPORATED AREAS OF FLORIDA, 1995 (Continued)

(values rounded to thousands of dollars)

Area 1/	Total value	Value of all house-keeping residential 2/	Number of housekeeping units: Single-family	Number of housekeeping units: Multi-family	Value of non-residential 3/	Value of additions and alterations
Dade	1,938,625	1,213,966	7,364	7,425	248,868	475,791
Bal Harbour	1,135	275	2	0	43	817
Bay Harbor Islands	1,989	1,800	0	12	0	189
Biscayne Park	103	0	0	0	27	76
Coral Gables	90,481	51,111	50	256	3,429	35,941
El Portal	841	0	0	0	0	841
Florida City	13,000	10,393	41	197	2,585	22
Golden Beach	2,622	1,840	4	0	93	689
Hialeah	68,884	39,412	258	359	8,267	21,205
Hialeah Gardens	8,814	8,324	208	0	449	42
Homestead	27,126	4,117	46	49	311	22,699
Indian Creek Village	862	500	1	0	0	362
Islandia	(NA)	(NA)	(NA)	(NA)	(NA)	(NA)
Medley	6,867	0	0	0	5,719	1,147
Miami	187,454	133,547	60	1,284	11,893	42,015
Miami Beach	244,648	201,535	4	1,976	5,050	38,063
Miami Shores	2,132	114	1	0	1,417	602
Miami Springs	2,852	214	3	0	271	2,367
North Bay	107	0	0	0	0	107
North Miami	5,261	995	2	6	1,361	2,906
North Miami Beach	9,784	215	2	0	2,779	6,790
Opa-Locka	945	570	8	20	5	370
South Miami	1,160	903	8	4	0	257
Surfside	534	456	5	0	0	77
Sweetwater	1,091	178	1	4	0	914
Virginia Gardens	96	75	0	2	0	21
County office	1,259,838	757,394	6,660	3,256	205,170	297,274
De Soto	13,455	7,589	76	46	4,146	1,720
County office	13,455	7,589	76	46	4,146	1,720
Dixie	5,018	1,799	29	0	1,714	1,505
Horseshoe Beach	218	110	2	0	62	46
County office	4,800	1,689	27	0	1,652	1,459
Duval	716,465	373,670	3,490	858	208,949	133,846
Atlantic Beach	11,037	8,646	77	18	377	2,014
Baldwin	319	60	1	0	0	259
Jacksonville 4/	662,456	346,263	3,269	791	187,552	128,641
Jacksonville Beach	38,554	16,435	124	45	20,656	1,463
Neptune Beach	4,099	2,267	19	4	364	1,469
Escambia	225,104	124,861	1,376	518	55,969	44,274
Pensacola	34,318	9,252	87	8	6,043	19,023
County office	190,786	115,609	1,289	510	49,926	25,251
Flagler	74,996	57,108	821	19	14,740	3,148
Beverly Beach	172	142	2	0	0	30
Bunnell	602	369	6	2	102	131
Flagler Beach	3,740	3,303	39	0	114	323
Marineland	0	0	0	0	0	0

See footnotes at end of table. Continued . . .

Table 11.15. BUILDING PERMIT ACTIVITY: VALUE REPORTED ON BUILDING PERMITS AND NEW HOUSING UNITS AUTHORIZED BY BUILDING PERMITS IN THE STATE, COUNTIES MUNICIPALITIES, AND UNINCORPORATED AREAS OF FLORIDA, 1995 (Continued)

(values rounded to thousands of dollars)

Area 1/	Total value	Value of all housekeeping residential 2/	Number of housekeeping units: Single-family	Number of housekeeping units: Multi-family	Value of nonresidential 3/	Value of additions and alterations
Flagler (Continued)						
County office	70,482	53,294	774	17	14,524	2,664
Franklin	21,374	15,544	123	0	2,674	3,156
Apalachicola	3,544	1,797	29	0	258	1,488
County office	17,830	13,747	94	0	2,415	1,668
Gadsden	17,470	11,360	126	2	1,640	4,470
Quincy	3,420	1,113	14	2	449	1,857
County office	14,051	10,247	112	0	1,191	2,613
Gilchrist	4,109	3,768	55	0	341	0
County office	4,109	3,768	55	0	341	0
Glades	4,176	2,084	30	0	859	1,233
Moore Haven	744	152	4	0	442	149
County office	3,432	1,932	26	0	416	1,084
Gulf	8,656	6,883	92	0	954	819
County office	8,656	6,883	92	0	954	819
Hamilton	2,344	1,591	28	0	172	581
County office	2,344	1,591	28	0	172	581
Hardee	8,610	2,290	30	0	4,417	1,903
Wauchula	932	162	4	0	357	413
County office	7,678	2,128	26	0	4,060	1,490
Hendry	18,191	6,613	103	0	7,237	4,341
Clewiston	2,980	362	3	0	82	2,537
La Belle	2,545	1,663	32	0	765	117
County office	12,665	4,588	68	0	6,390	1,687
Hernando	122,278	82,706	935	16	26,617	12,955
Brooksville	1,771	682	10	0	155	934
Weeki Wachee	0	0	0	0	0	0
County office	120,507	82,024	925	16	26,462	12,021
Highlands	56,825	35,685	537	92	11,153	9,987
Avon Park	1,278	646	6	8	52	580
Sebring	3,593	446	5	2	2,157	990
County office	51,954	34,592	526	82	8,944	8,418
Hillsborough	890,004	528,927	4,664	2,466	184,536	176,540
Plant City	32,174	18,399	247	0	6,558	7,218
Tampa	219,262	90,939	683	332	46,399	81,923
Temple Terrace	25,887	25,033	10	352	10	844
County office	612,680	394,556	3,724	1,782	131,569	86,556
Holmes	5,858	3,427	53	8	1,196	1,235
County office	5,858	3,427	53	8	1,196	1,235
Indian River	201,956	134,561	782	331	44,181	23,213
Fellsmere	871	359	8	0	2	510
Indian River Shores	19,854	16,955	45	0	665	2,234
Orchid	3,141	3,007	9	0	128	6
Sebastian	16,498	13,721	183	6	1,974	804
Vero Beach	13,171	2,681	13	16	2,706	7,783

See footnotes at end of table. Continued . . .

Table 11.15. BUILDING PERMIT ACTIVITY: VALUE REPORTED ON BUILDING PERMITS AND NEW HOUSING UNITS AUTHORIZED BY BUILDING PERMITS IN THE STATE, COUNTIES MUNICIPALITIES, AND UNINCORPORATED AREAS OF FLORIDA, 1995 (Continued)

(values rounded to thousands of dollars)

Area 1/	Total value	Value of all house-keeping residen-tial 2/	Number of housekeeping units: Single-family	Number of housekeeping units: Multi-family	Value of non-residen-tial 3/	Value of additions and alter-ations
Indian River (Continued)						
County office	148,420	97,839	524	309	38,706	11,875
Jackson	15,941	8,034	119	40	4,678	3,229
County office	15,941	8,034	119	40	4,678	3,229
Jefferson	9,322	4,398	43	0	4,428	496
County office	9,322	4,398	43	0	4,428	496
Lafayette	2,164	1,318	20	0	468	378
Mayo	498	116	2	0	243	139
County office	1,666	1,202	18	0	225	239
Lake	247,674	164,991	2,113	158	44,976	37,708
Eustis	14,661	9,808	92	9	3,239	1,614
Fruitland Park	605	269	5	0	253	82
Lady Lake	10,522	3,783	47	0	3,218	3,521
Leesburg	16,452	4,700	28	46	3,172	8,580
Mascotte	2,406	1,968	45	0	90	348
Mount Dora	16,627	11,115	112	6	4,975	538
Tavares	7,309	4,280	59	4	2,484	545
Umatilla	880	288	6	0	157	435
County office	178,212	128,781	1,719	93	27,388	22,043
Lee	710,258	509,667	3,028	1,974	123,415	77,176
Cape Coral	71,775	48,603	872	66	19,808	3,364
Ft. Myers	27,692	3,130	19	15	10,212	14,350
Sanibel	27,098	20,743	65	12	2,364	3,991
County office	583,692	437,190	2,072	1,881	91,030	55,472
Leon	290,940	213,942	1,596	1,157	45,427	31,570
Tallahassee	194,509	131,584	864	1,142	36,379	26,545
County office	96,431	82,358	732	15	9,048	5,025
Levy	24,890	12,367	140	14	8,287	4,236
Cedar Key	3,687	3,617	24	12	0	70
Chiefland	1,670	225	5	2	1,374	72
Fanning Springs	110	110	4	0	0	0
Williston	3,178	245	4	0	2,906	27
County office	16,244	8,170	103	0	4,007	4,067
Liberty	1,967	1,279	16	0	633	55
County office	1,967	1,279	16	0	633	55
Madison	4,347	2,654	45	0	816	877
Madison	702	208	6	0	67	426
County office	3,645	2,446	39	0	749	450
Manatee	265,795	171,425	1,605	767	59,081	35,289
Anna Maria	3,594	2,273	17	0	128	1,193
Bradenton	29,953	12,472	102	209	10,405	7,077
Bradenton Beach	1,766	266	1	2	647	853
Holmes Beach	5,777	3,726	18	22	881	1,169
Palmetto	11,647	9,467	49	122	109	2,071
County office	213,057	143,221	1,418	412	46,911	22,925

See footnotes at end of table. Continued . . .

Table 11.15. BUILDING PERMIT ACTIVITY: VALUE REPORTED ON BUILDING PERMITS AND NEW HOUSING UNITS AUTHORIZED BY BUILDING PERMITS IN THE STATE, COUNTIES MUNICIPALITIES, AND UNINCORPORATED AREAS OF FLORIDA, 1995 (Continued)

(values rounded to thousands of dollars)

Area 1/	Total value	Value of all housekeeping residential 2/	Number of housekeeping units: Single-family	Number of housekeeping units: Multi-family	Value of nonresidential 3/	Value of additions and alterations
Marion	221,642	132,310	2,033	189	52,603	36,730
Belleview	593	120	2	0	440	33
Dunnellon 5/	2,112	631	8	0	244	1,236
McIntosh	10	0	0	0	0	10
Ocala	64,447	16,023	116	163	30,568	17,856
County office	154,480	115,536	1,907	26	21,350	17,594
Martin	242,091	196,294	850	272	31,564	14,233
Jupiter Island	8,585	4,686	4	0	358	3,540
Ocean Breeze Park	0	0	0	0	0	0
Sewall's Point	3,205	2,027	8	0	200	978
Stuart	9,625	1,358	14	0	3,052	5,215
County office	220,676	188,223	824	272	27,954	4,499
Monroe	101,409	39,657	406	135	21,133	40,619
Key Colony Beach	1,978	1,320	13	0	253	405
Key West	24,818	14,328	95	133	10,200	291
Layton	438	388	2	0	50	0
County office	74,175	23,622	296	2	10,630	39,923
Nassau	83,296	52,866	464	232	24,568	5,862
Callahan	2,786	265	6	0	2,454	67
Fernandina Beach	12,467	8,990	96	2	658	2,819
Hilliard	616	417	7	0	76	124
County office	67,426	43,194	355	230	21,380	2,852
Okaloosa	191,721	128,034	1,046	642	35,719	27,968
Crestview	9,780	6,382	114	0	2,144	1,254
Destin	78,353	67,323	183	510	7,932	3,098
Ft. Walton Beach	6,393	1,272	14	24	2,995	2,126
Mary Esther	2,161	839	16	0	554	768
Niceville	7,058	4,263	57	0	1,127	1,669
Valparaiso	3,340	1,806	26	0	929	605
County office	84,634	46,148	636	108	20,038	18,448
Okeechobee	6,900	6,357	79	4	324	220
County office	6,900	6,357	79	4	324	220
Orange	1,493,154	704,173	5,250	4,465	564,490	224,490
Apopka	26,408	19,270	336	16	3,707	3,431
Bay Lake	46,967	0	0	0	32,138	14,830
Eatonville	431	327	9	0	0	104
Edgewood	3,599	2,806	14	0	338	455
Lake Buena Vista	7,369	0	0	0	3,607	3,763
Maitland	10,695	8,841	49	0	160	1,694
Oakland	898	545	8	0	179	174
Ocoee	101,846	27,410	312	0	73,831	604
Orlando	362,953	112,421	487	1,340	127,576	122,957
Winter Garden	10,302	7,382	97	0	2,108	812
Winter Park	26,597	11,191	86	2	4,204	11,201
County office	895,088	513,978	3,852	3,107	316,644	64,466

See footnotes at end of table. Continued . . .

Table 11.15. BUILDING PERMIT ACTIVITY: VALUE REPORTED ON BUILDING PERMITS AND NEW HOUSING UNITS AUTHORIZED BY BUILDING PERMITS IN THE STATE, COUNTIES MUNICIPALITIES, AND UNINCORPORATED AREAS OF FLORIDA, 1995 (Continued)

(values rounded to thousands of dollars)

Area 1/	Total value	Value of all housekeeping residential 2/	Number of housekeeping units: Single-family	Number of housekeeping units: Multi-family	Value of nonresidential 3/	Value of additions and alterations
Osceola	242,006	176,032	1,559	159	52,734	13,241
Kissimmee	46,487	35,000	410	50	7,683	3,804
St. Cloud	21,643	11,506	139	2	8,317	1,820
County office	173,877	129,526	1,010	107	36,735	7,616
Palm Beach	1,469,810	1,012,052	7,473	3,108	212,080	245,678
Atlantis	8,403	428	1	0	6,095	1,880
Belle Glade	4,232	722	8	2	1,799	1,711
Boca Raton	173,233	76,364	338	306	35,297	61,572
Boynton Beach	60,296	51,876	366	381	2,685	5,735
Briny Breezes	0	0	0	0	0	0
Cloud Lake	0	0	0	0	0	0
Delray Beach	44,209	30,658	156	228	4,392	9,159
Glen Ridge	10	0	0	0	0	10
Golf Village	1,280	806	2	0	0	474
Golfview	450	0	0	0	450	0
Greenacres City	19,653	17,686	183	30	877	1,091
Haverhill	67	0	0	0	0	67
Highland Beach	9,212	8,417	14	0	212	584
Hypoluxo	1,267	386	0	7	0	882
Jupiter	993	980	4	0	0	14
Jupiter Inlet Colony	54,627	35,908	186	12	13,103	5,615
Lake Clarke Shores	55	0	0	0	0	55
Lake Park	1,283	0	0	0	1,143	140
Lake Worth	8,655	1,098	16	0	224	7,333
Lantana	3,458	1,116	10	0	382	1,960
Manalapan	7,206	980	2	0	0	6,226
Mangonia Park	839	45	1	0	319	475
North Palm Beach	19,891	18,474	23	140	251	1,166
Ocean Ridge	2,178	1,410	4	0	238	530
Pahokee	833	406	9	0	0	427
Palm Beach	174,750	119,252	404	355	47,125	8,373
Palm Beach Gardens	276	0	0	0	0	276
Palm Beach Shores	44,695	10,707	14	0	672	33,316
Palm Springs	297	0	0	0	141	156
Riviera Beach	18,321	11,667	122	73	4,506	2,148
Royal Palm Beach Village	21,709	18,930	212	0	2,212	567
South Bay	603	420	8	0	140	43
South Palm Beach	635	0	0	0	0	635
Tequesta Village	8,856	6,523	12	21	169	2,165
West Palm Beach	98,805	55,309	346	303	6,801	36,695
County office	678,531	541,485	5,032	1,250	82,847	54,199
Pasco	212,927	139,123	1,786	267	52,571	21,233
Dade City	1,611	512	11	0	633	465
New Port Richey	5,396	1,190	14	0	3,215	991
Port Richey	671	456	4	0	55	161

See footnotes at end of table.

Continued . . .

Table 11.15. BUILDING PERMIT ACTIVITY: VALUE REPORTED ON BUILDING PERMITS AND NEW HOUSING UNITS AUTHORIZED BY BUILDING PERMITS IN THE STATE, COUNTIES MUNICIPALITIES, AND UNINCORPORATED AREAS OF FLORIDA, 1995 (Continued)

(values rounded to thousands of dollars)

Area 1/	Total value	Value of all house-keeping residen-tial 2/	Number of housekeeping units Single-family	Multi-family	Value of non-residen-tial 3/	Value of additions and alter-ations
Pasco (Continued)						
San Antonio	1,060	1,020	16	0	36	3
Zephyrhills	13,201	4,995	90	2	6,727	1,479
County office	190,989	130,950	1,651	265	41,904	18,134
Pinellas	691,569	398,973	2,139	1,450	126,883	165,713
Belleair	1,252	502	2	0	215	535
Belleair Beach	5,588	3,928	11	0	39	1,621
Clearwater	122,307	40,745	160	165	36,466	45,096
Dunedin	11,854	5,030	35	0	3,077	3,747
Gulfport	5,608	4,096	19	0	1,053	459
Indian Rocks Beach	2,526	1,604	13	8	459	462
Indian Shores	1,503	1,439	13	0	0	64
Kenneth City	263	0	0	0	0	263
Largo	20,391	4,518	57	0	11,141	4,732
North Redington Beach	657	225	1	0	57	375
Oldsmar	13,650	8,790	79	70	3,236	1,625
Pinellas Park	19,463	4,015	40	24	6,560	8,887
Redington Beach	1,444	1,202	3	0	0	242
Redington Shores	609	367	4	0	53	189
Safety Harbor	19,205	6,644	56	0	767	11,793
St. Petersburg	8,912	5,865	1	192	613	2,435
St. Pete Beach	5,287	180	1	0	3,679	1,429
Seminole	88,569	32,524	182	114	13,658	42,387
South Pasadena	13,052	7,997	19	94	34	5,020
Tarpon Springs	18,057	12,430	124	0	951	4,676
Treasure Island	4,077	1,166	7	0	475	2,436
County office	327,296	255,707	1,312	783	44,350	27,240
Polk	379,671	161,592	2,187	179	147,022	71,057
Auburndale	11,570	5,262	36	61	5,563	746
Bartow	8,833	1,589	20	2	894	6,349
Davenport	800	369	6	0	340	91
Dundee	2,225	1,353	24	0	625	248
Eagle Lake	346	119	3	0	100	127
Ft. Meade	465	251	5	0	96	118
Frostproof	1,187	60	1	0	339	788
Haines City	9,698	4,592	65	4	2,017	3,088
Lake Alfred	952	526	10	0	93	333
Lake Hamilton	332	158	1	2	30	144
Lake Wales	9,547	1,929	35	3	4,700	2,919
Lakeland	80,125	12,644	135	43	37,963	29,518
Mulberry	1,360	0	0	0	1,077	283
Polk City	312	256	3	0	33	23
Winter Haven	57,474	6,056	88	24	45,833	5,585
County office	194,445	126,429	1,755	40	47,318	20,697
Putnam	27,277	10,805	136	0	6,486	9,986
Palatka	8,005	790	10	0	3,375	3,840

See footnotes at end of table.

Continued . . .

Table 11.15. BUILDING PERMIT ACTIVITY: VALUE REPORTED ON BUILDING PERMITS AND NEW HOUSING UNITS AUTHORIZED BY BUILDING PERMITS IN THE STATE, COUNTIES MUNICIPALITIES, AND UNINCORPORATED AREAS OF FLORIDA, 1995 (Continued)

(values rounded to thousands of dollars)

Area 1/	Total value	Value of all housekeeping residential 2/	Number of housekeeping units Single-family	Multi-family	Value of nonresidential 3/	Value of additions and alterations
Putnam (Continued)						
Welaka	261	0	0	0	236	25
County office	19,011	10,015	126	0	2,875	6,121
St. Johns	301,827	249,210	1,418	569	25,956	26,661
St. Augustine	10,041	2,502	32	0	3,184	4,356
St. Augustine Beach	6,052	5,635	50	4	151	266
County office	285,735	241,074	1,336	565	22,622	22,040
St. Lucie	201,223	150,517	1,265	474	30,244	20,463
Ft. Pierce	5,369	1,360	19	0	3,269	740
Port St. Lucie	125,969	101,758	909	363	8,289	15,921
St. Lucie Village	123	0	0	0	0	123
County office	69,763	47,398	337	111	18,686	3,679
Santa Rosa	131,213	97,740	998	62	31,326	2,147
County office 6/	131,213	97,740	998	62	31,326	2,147
Sarasota	441,473	289,483	2,083	557	72,998	78,992
Longboat Key	35,053	20,295	42	62	2,169	12,589
North Port Charlotte	48,083	45,766	394	0	1,431	886
Sarasota	46,382	10,810	70	12	11,003	24,569
Venice	25,535	11,033	96	15	8,233	6,269
County office	286,421	201,579	1,481	468	50,163	34,679
Seminole	462,165	313,385	2,067	292	114,286	34,493
Altamonte Springs	29,657	7,609	97	12	15,121	6,927
Casselberry	5,031	2,771	37	0	942	1,318
Lake Mary	23,201	18,601	159	0	3,770	830
Longwood	7,983	522	7	0	2,702	4,759
Oviedo	82,581	73,838	458	6	6,652	2,092
Sanford	29,650	5,588	83	4	23,392	670
Winter Springs	47,741	45,620	302	0	1,287	833
County office	236,321	158,837	924	270	60,419	17,065
Sumter	76,796	71,331	858	0	2,433	3,032
Bushnell	1,073	807	16	0	99	168
Wildwood	2,288	1,332	26	0	765	191
County office	73,434	69,193	816	0	1,570	2,672
Suwannee	14,593	10,777	144	0	2,440	1,375
Live Oak	1,544	446	8	0	459	638
County office	13,049	10,331	136	0	1,981	737
Taylor	3,747	1,693	31	0	1,268	786
Perry	990	301	7	0	486	203
County office	2,757	1,393	24	0	782	583
Union	4,479	3,714	52	0	475	290
County office	4,479	3,714	52	0	475	290
Volusia	432,041	250,973	1,947	806	83,458	97,610
Daytona Beach	89,712	22,819	55	322	30,126	36,768
Daytona Beach Shores	15,827	15,263	0	110	0	564
DeLand	27,584	9,974	74	70	11,943	5,667
Edgewater	11,108	7,286	82	0	1,198	2,624

See footnotes at end of table. Continued . . .

Table 11.15. BUILDING PERMIT ACTIVITY: VALUE REPORTED ON BUILDING PERMITS AND NEW HOUSING UNITS AUTHORIZED BY BUILDING PERMITS IN THE STATE, COUNTIES MUNICIPALITIES, AND UNINCORPORATED AREAS OF FLORIDA, 1995 (Continued)

(values rounded to thousands of dollars)

Area 1/	Total value	Value of all housekeeping residential 2/	Number of housekeeping units: Single-family	Number of housekeeping units: Multifamily	Value of nonresidential 3/	Value of additions and alterations
Volusia (Continued)						
Holly Hill	2,366	461	10	0	674	1,232
Lake Helen	881	642	10	0	103	136
New Smyrna Beach	32,764	8,421	72	46	4,745	19,597
Oak Hill	512	396	6	0	3	114
Orange City	12,530	2,575	20	30	9,209	746
Ormond Beach	41,730	26,624	176	0	8,842	6,264
Pierson	459	124	1	0	97	238
Ponce Inlet	26,383	25,953	17	154	153	278
Port Orange	37,070	30,528	296	0	4,615	1,927
South Daytona	4,567	2,839	35	0	930	798
County office	128,548	97,070	1,093	74	10,822	20,657
Wakulla	16,758	12,047	151	0	2,874	1,838
County office	16,758	12,047	151	0	2,874	1,838
Walton	125,159	110,133	552	599	13,463	1,563
DeFuniak Springs	1,475	553	6	0	567	355
County office	123,685	109,580	546	599	12,896	1,209
Washington	10,932	5,189	90	0	4,592	1,151
County office	10,932	5,189	90	0	4,592	1,151

(NA) Not available.

1/ County office data includes permitting for unincorporated areas and occasionally may include incorporated areas in the same county not shown separately. The definition is more service-based than geographical.

2/ Includes single-family and multifamily units. Excludes mobile homes.

3/ Includes offices, stores, schools, religious buildings, industrial and institutional buildings, other nonresidential structures, and nonhousekeeping residential buildings such as hotels, motels, cabins, and other transient accommodations.

4/ Includes unincorporated Duval County.

5/ Included in county office beginning in October.

6/ Includes unincorporated Navarre Beach located entirely in Escambia County.

Note: Data are based on voluntary reports from local building officials processed by the Bureau of the Census by the 12th working day of the month. Data may also include estimates for nonreports. Value figures are estimated on a cost-per-foot basis by each jurisdiction and may not be comparable to other locations.

Source: University of Florida, Bureau of Economic and Business Research, *Building Permit Activity in Florida, Calendar Year 1995.*

Table 11.20. EMPLOYMENT: AVERAGE MONTHLY PRIVATE REPORTING UNITS, EMPLOYMENT AND PAYROLL COVERED BY UNEMPLOYMENT COMPENSATION LAW BY CONSTRUCTION INDUSTRY IN FLORIDA, 1995

SIC code	Industry	Number of reporting units	Number of employees	Payroll ($1,000)
	Construction	34,850	303,870	636,709
15	Building--general contractors and operative builders	9,411	68,520	160,536
152	General building contractors--residential	7,568	40,345	89,675
153	Operative builders	132	1,850	4,946
154	General building contractors--nonresidential	1,711	26,324	65,916
16	Heavy construction other than building--contractors	1,837	40,760	98,280
161	Highway and street, except elevated highways	332	11,627	26,733
162	Heavy construction, except highway and street	1,505	29,133	71,548
17	Special trade contractors	23,603	194,591	377,892
171	Plumbing, heating, and air-conditioning	4,531	43,666	90,566
172	Painting and paper hanging	2,058	10,431	17,745
173	Electrical work	4,071	42,389	86,614
174	Masonry, stonework, tile setting, and plastering	3,225	26,650	47,851
175	Carpentry and floor work	2,245	11,185	19,759
176	Roofing, siding, and sheet metal work	1,799	15,341	26,723
177	Concrete work	1,617	15,095	26,549
178	Water well drilling	235	1,241	2,440
179	Miscellaneous special trade contractors	3,822	28,594	59,644

Note: Private employment. Detail may not add to totals due to disclosure editing and/or rounding. See Tables 23.70, 23.71, 23.72, 23.73, and 23.74 for public employment data.

Source: State of Florida, Department of Labor and Employment Security, Bureau of Labor Market Information, "Employment and Wages" (ES-202), unpublished data.

Table 11.21. EMPLOYMENT: AVERAGE MONTHLY PRIVATE REPORTING UNITS, EMPLOYMENT AND PAYROLL COVERED BY UNEMPLOYMENT COMPENSATION LAW IN THE STATE AND COUNTIES OF FLORIDA, 1995

County	Number of re- porting units	Number of em- ployees	Payroll ($1,000)	County	Number of re- porting units	Number of em- ployees	Payroll ($1,000)
			Construction (SIC codes 15-17)				
Florida	34,850	303,870	636,709	Jefferson	22	129	208
				Lafayette	6	32	46
Alachua	397	3,949	7,634	Lake	399	3,234	6,228
Baker	28	152	203	Lee	1,284	10,754	22,262
Bay	399	3,450	6,326	Leon	565	4,634	8,863
Bradford	27	284	507	Levy	43	543	1,040
Brevard	1,067	8,475	16,436	Madison	19	45	55
Broward	3,752	32,269	73,314	Manatee	409	3,295	6,989
Calhoun	23	186	283	Marion	491	3,787	6,337
Charlotte	352	2,066	3,649	Martin	428	3,135	6,661
Citrus	244	1,682	2,591	Monroe	339	2,052	3,981
Clay	282	2,069	3,591	Nassau	125	925	1,668
Collier	812	7,206	15,512	Okaloosa	482	3,715	6,024
Columbia	114	968	1,797	Okeechobee	77	368	545
Dade	3,985	35,804	78,092	Orange	1,971	22,470	48,843
De Soto	42	168	271	Osceola	232	2,244	4,392
Dixie	17	132	222	Palm Beach	2,908	23,034	51,468
Duval	1,683	20,594	45,499	Pasco	649	3,746	6,184
Escambia	630	7,912	15,601	Pinellas	1,865	16,841	34,859
Flagler	109	442	699	Polk	823	7,782	16,444
Franklin	22	82	124	Putnam	120	1,847	3,534
Gadsden	59	428	680	St. Johns	249	1,348	2,352
Gilchrist	20	28	31	St. Lucie	410	2,489	4,450
Glades	8	24	49	Santa Rosa	240	1,767	2,904
Gulf	22	193	498	Sarasota	1,087	6,643	13,679
Hamilton	21	61	74	Seminole	888	8,463	19,010
Hardee	31	306	411	Sumter	46	192	272
Hendry	46	254	439	Suwannee	52	426	832
Hernando	307	1,367	2,289	Union	8	82	130
Highlands	208	1,051	1,607	Volusia	1,005	6,856	12,341
Hillsborough	1,841	22,191	50,607	Wakulla	35	181	261
Holmes	15	84	120	Walton	78	426	596
Indian River	403	2,586	4,713	Washington	34	273	454
Jackson	55	399	515	Multicounty 1/	407	2,665	7,131

1/ Reporting units without a fixed location within the state or of unknown county location.

Note: Construction includes general contractors and operative builders (SIC code 15), heavy construction contractors (SIC code 16), and special trade contractors (SIC code 17). Private employment. Data are preliminary. Only counties for which data are disclosed are shown. Detail may not add to totals due to disclosure editing and/or rounding. See Tables 23.70, 23.71, 23.72, 23.73, and 23.74 for public employment data.

Source: State of Florida, Department of Labor and Employment Security, Bureau of Labor Market Information, "Employment and Wages" (ES-202), unpublished data.

Table 11.22. BUILDING MATERIALS, HARDWARE, GARDEN SUPPLY, AND MOBILE HOME DEALERS AVERAGE MONTHLY PRIVATE REPORTING UNITS, EMPLOYMENT, AND PAYROLL COVERED BY UNEMPLOYMENT COMPENSATION LAW IN THE STATE AND COUNTIES OF FLORIDA, 1995

County	Number of reporting units	Number of employees	Payroll ($1,000)	County	Number of reporting units	Number of employees	Payroll ($1,000)
	Building materials, hardware, garden supply, and mobile home dealers (SIC code 52)						
Florida	3,476	46,092	77,947	Jackson	15	87	131
				Jefferson	6	42	59
Alachua	47	751	1,086	Lake	66	785	1,145
Baker	5	21	22	Lee	106	1,820	3,198
Bay	52	642	919	Leon	60	1,032	1,814
Bradford	8	42	64	Levy	12	66	91
Brevard	120	1,459	2,120	Madison	7	31	29
Broward	279	3,535	7,114	Manatee	45	575	910
Calhoun	5	39	57	Marion	93	1,026	1,694
Charlotte	35	429	695	Martin	35	653	1,082
Citrus	39	365	474	Monroe	41	470	772
Clay	27	282	487	Nassau	14	127	191
Collier	57	848	1,529	Okaloosa	63	720	1,063
Columbia	24	233	383	Okeechobee	10	110	140
Dade	363	5,502	9,416	Osceola	22	438	688
De Soto	8	50	74	Pasco	66	770	1,165
Dixie	5	33	37	Polk	115	2,080	3,712
Duval	162	2,635	4,423	Putnam	27	245	318
Escambia	91	1,290	2,095	St. Johns	32	278	434
Flagler	10	63	91	St. Lucie	38	375	648
Franklin	4	31	47	Santa Rosa	31	184	212
Gadsden	7	73	74	Sarasota	104	1,291	2,110
Gilchrist	4	33	43	Seminole	72	1,126	1,927
Gulf	8	51	56	Sumter	9	36	32
Hardee	6	57	77	Suwannee	12	140	225
Hendry	13	121	211	Taylor	8	50	65
Hernando	23	232	272	Volusia	109	1,405	2,004
Highlands	19	161	193	Wakulla	5	16	13
Hillsborough	185	2,601	5,201	Walton	14	120	139
Holmes	3	13	14	Washington	7	44	61
Indian River	39	309	516	Multicounty 1/	13	94	353

1/ Reporting units without a fixed location within the state or of unknown county location.

Note: Private employment. For a list of three-digit code industries included see Table 11.20. Data are preliminary. Only counties for which data are disclosed are shown. Detail may not add to totals due to disclosure editing and/or rounding. See Tables in 23.70, 23.71, 23.72, 23.73, and 23.74 for public employment data.

Source: State of Florida, Department of Labor and Employment Security, Bureau of Labor Market Information, "Employment and Wages" (ES-202), unpublished data.

Table 11.25. MOBILE HOMES: SHIPMENTS OF MOBILE HOMES TO FLORIDA, SELECTED STATES AND THE UNITED STATES, 1990 THROUGH 1994

State 1/	1990	1991	1992	1993	1994 A/
Florida	17,297	14,416	19,948	17,148	17,805
Alabama	8,297	6,782	8,965	11,394	15,263
Arizona	3,047	2,721	3,470	4,654	6,258
Arkansas	2,557	3,065	3,626	5,122	6,516
California	9,706	6,022	4,865	3,763	4,088
Colorado	596	783	1,485	2,535	3,930
Georgia	10,160	8,963	10,822	13,525	18,121
Idaho	820	1,089	1,696	2,779	3,712
Illinois	2,856	2,504	2,965	3,727	4,226
Indiana	6,274	5,364	6,303	7,100	8,196
Iowa	1,588	1,557	1,973	2,307	2,598
Kansas	1,266	1,459	1,726	2,150	2,872
Kentucky	6,207	6,230	8,126	10,505	10,344
Louisiana	1,460	1,772	3,565	5,088	6,784
Michigan	9,356	8,288	8,979	9,322	10,059
Minnesota	1,615	1,545	1,831	2,309	2,611
Mississippi	3,704	3,705	4,560	6,681	8,380
Missouri	3,994	3,715	5,117	6,381	9,015
Nevada	2,386	1,747	1,688	1,661	2,087
New Mexico	1,784	1,953	3,346	4,879	5,681
New York	5,998	4,945	5,405	5,336	5,225
North Carolina	16,897	15,858	19,985	24,561	28,275
Ohio	6,048	5,744	6,270	6,909	7,504
Oklahoma	674	765	1,744	2,629	3,877
Oregon	4,905	4,720	5,103	6,454	7,597
Pennsylvania	6,639	5,761	6,152	6,546	7,267
South Carolina	11,090	8,489	10,464	13,484	15,326
Tennessee	6,941	6,803	9,224	11,691	13,422
Texas	4,374	4,988	10,369	18,439	26,339
Virginia	5,452	4,786	5,248	6,267	6,974
Washington	5,645	5,353	5,964	6,849	7,332
West Virginia	2,778	2,751	3,057	3,584	4,471
Wisconsin	2,766	2,523	3,109	3,624	4,041
United States	188,251	170,900	210,453	254,265	303,903

A/ Preliminary.
1/ States with 1994 shipments of 2,000 or more are listed.
Note: Shipment figures are based on reports submitted by manufacturers on the number of mobile homes actually shipped during the survey month. Shipments to dealers may not be placed for residential uses in the month as they are shipped. The number of mobile "homes" used for nonresidential purposes is not known. These shipment statistics are produced by the National Conference of States on Building Codes and Standards, Inc. See Glossary for definition of mobile home.
Source: U.S., Department of Commerce, Bureau of the Census, *Current Construction Reports: Housing Units Authorized by Building Permits, February 1995,* and previous editions.

Table 11.42. PRODUCER PRICES: INDEX OF PRODUCER PRICES OF MATERIALS USED IN CONSTRUCTION BY SPECIFIED GROUP AND COMMODITY IN THE UNITED STATES, ANNUAL AVERAGES 1992 THROUGH 1995

(1982 = 100, except where indicated)

Group and commodity	1992	1993	1994	1995	Percentage change annual 1994 to 1995
All construction materials	122.5	128.6	133.8	138.9	3.8
Softwood lumber	148.6	193.0	198.1	178.9	-9.7
Hardwood lumber	140.7	163.3	168.3	167.0	-0.8
General millwork	146.3	158.5	163.6	165.5	1.2
Prefabricated structural members	132.7	159.7	169.3	163.5	-3.4
Softwood plywood	147.2	169.7	176.7	188.2	6.5
Hardwood plywood	106.9	115.4	122.3	122.1	-0.2
Particleboard, platen-type 1/	121.1	139.3	155.8	155.7	-0.1
Fabricated hardboard products 2/	100.7	107.1	109.6	112.6	2.7
Prefabricated wood buildings and components 3/	122.8	132.5	141.6	147.8	4.4
Mobile homes	121.7	127.8	137.0	145.9	6.5
Construction machinery and equipment	128.7	132.0	133.7	136.6	2.2
Prepared paint	131.6	133.2	135.3	142.1	5.0
Builders hardware	141.4	144.9	148.0	153.2	3.5
Plastic construction products					
Group index 4/	112.7	116.6	122.9	134.2	9.2
Plumbing products	94.0	101.8	111.1	120.7	8.6
Plastic pipe and fittings 1/	90.1	98.2	108.9	119.7	9.9
Lighting fixtures					
Residential	136.4	137.8	139.5	143.2	2.7
Commercial and industrial	131.8	132.4	133.7	138.9	3.9
Welded wire for concrete reinforcement	101.3	104.5	108.7	108.1	-0.6
Concrete reinforcing bars 5/	100.1	104.4	115.0	116.1	1.0
Roofing steel	106.3	107.0	109.6	119.1	8.7
Building wire and cable 1/	145.6	131.2	148.9	165.5	11.1
Metal door sash and trim	135.0	136.6	142.0	156.4	10.1
Metal moulding, trim, and storefronts 6/	163.9	169.0	(NA)	(NA)	(NA)
Steel fencing and fence gates 5/	117.0	116.3	110.6	123.9	12.0
Cast iron pressure and soil pipe and fittings	138.2	141.4	137.7	156.7	13.8
Steel for buildings	115.5	118.4	122.3	127.2	4.0
Steel for bridges	108.7	101.3	94.4	68.9	-27.0
Architectural and ornamental metalwork 7/	117.7	119.5	113.0	127.9	13.2
Prefab metal buildings 8/	112.3	117.0	113.1	130.4	15.3
Heating equipment					
Group index 4/	137.3	140.4	142.5	147.5	3.5
Steam and hot water	138.0	138.9	138.6	141.6	2.2
Warm air furnaces and attachments	134.8	137.3	138.0	141.3	2.4
Water heaters, domestic	127.9	133.4	137.9	146.1	5.9
Heating stoves, domestic	118.4	118.2	120.2	124.2	3.3
Unitary air conditioners including heat pumps	115.9	115.0	115.5	118.9	2.9

See footnotes at end of table.

Continued . . .

Table 11.42. PRODUCER PRICES: INDEX OF PRODUCER PRICES OF MATERIALS USED IN CONSTRUCTION BY SPECIFIED GROUP AND COMMODITY IN THE UNITED STATES, ANNUAL AVERAGES 1992 THROUGH 1995 (Continued)

(1982 = 100, except where indicated)

Group and commodity	1992	1993	1994	1995	Percentage change annual 1994 to 1995
Plumbing fixtures and brass fittings					
Group index	153.1	155.9	159.6	166.0	4.0
Vitreous china fixtures	127.6	127.0	128.9	131.9	2.3
Brass fittings	167.7	172.3	177.3	185.1	4.4
Metal fixtures 9/	120.7	121.4	123.4	128.2	3.9
Hard-surfaced floor coverings	142.0	145.2	147.5	153.2	3.9
Soft-surfaced floor coverings	117.4	116.7	118.1	119.5	1.2
Concrete ingredients					
Group index 4/	119.4	123.4	128.7	134.6	4.6
Sand, gravel, and crushed stone	130.6	134.0	137.9	142.3	3.2
Portland cement	106.3	111.7	119.5	128.0	7.1
Concrete products					
Group index 4/	117.2	120.2	124.6	129.5	3.9
Building block	130.7	132.8	136.0	141.0	3.7
Concrete pipe	114.3	114.9	117.2	121.9	4.0
Ready mixed concrete	115.3	118.8	123.8	129.1	4.3
Precast concrete	128.6	130.1	133.2	136.4	2.4
Prestressed concrete	100.4	102.6	108.9	112.2	3.0
Structural clay products					
Group index 4/	132.0	135.1	138.3	141.4	2.2
Brick and structural clay tile 3/	118.0	122.0	125.6	128.9	2.6
Ceramic floor and wall tile	132.6	133.5	135.5	138.0	1.8
Gypsum products					
Group index 4/	99.9	108.3	136.1	154.5	13.5
Wallboard 1/2 inch	87.3	97.0	112.4	(NA)	(NA)
Type X wallboard	94.8	103.1	131.4	(NA)	(NA)
Cut stone and stone products 3/	128.1	129.6	130.7	133.0	1.8
Prepared asphalt roofing	94.3	94.9	92.9	97.8	5.3
Sheet, plate, and float glass	94.1	96.6	106.9	115.1	7.7
Insulation materials	102.3	105.8	112.0	118.8	6.1
Paving mixtures and blocks	100.2	102.0	103.3	105.9	2.5

(NA) Not available.
1/ December 1982 = 100.
2/ June 1984 = 100.
3/ December 1984 = 100.
4/ Includes items not shown separately.
5/ June 1982 = 100.
6/ June 1983 = 100.
7/ December 1983 = 100.
8/ December 1987 = 100.
9/ January 1987 = 100.
Note: Some data may be revised.

Source: U.S., Department of Commerce, International Trade Administration, *Construction Review,* Fall and Winter 1995-96.

Manufacturing

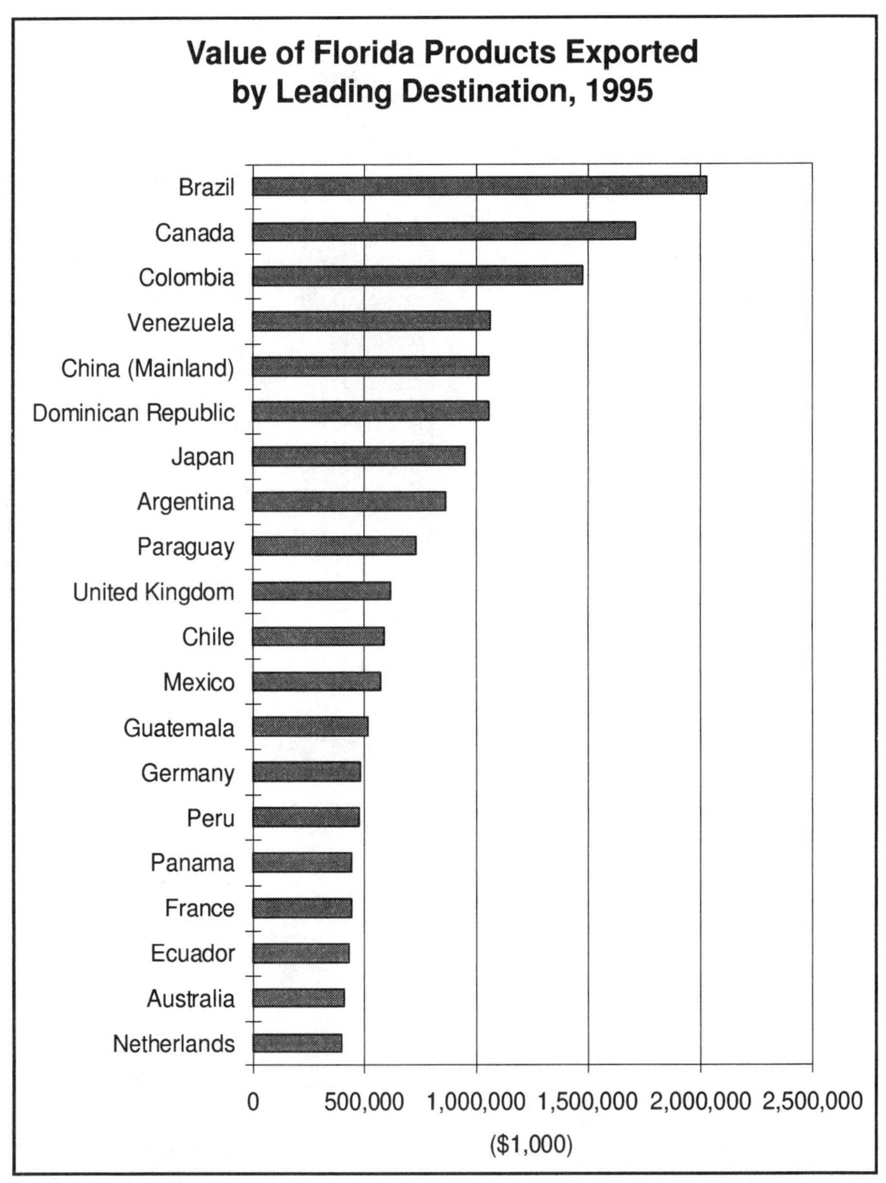

Value of Florida Products Exported
by Leading Destination, 1995
Brazil
Canada
Colombia
Venezuela
China (Mainland)
Dominican Republic
Japan
Argentina
Paraguay
United Kingdom
Chile
Mexico
Guatemala
Germany
Peru
Panama
France
Ecuador
Australia
Netherlands
0
500,000
1,000,000
1,500,000
2,000,000
2,500,000
($1,000)

Source: Table 12.87

SECTION 12.00
MANUFACTURING

TABLES LISTED BY MAJOR HEADINGS

SECTION 12.00
MANUFACTURING
(Continued)

TABLES LISTED BY MAJOR HEADINGS

Table 12.01. MANUFACTURING: CHARACTERISTICS IN THE STATE AND SELECTED CONSOLIDATED METROPOLITAN STATISTICAL AREAS (CMSAS), PRIMARY METROPOLITAN STATISTICAL AREAS (PMSAS), AND METROPOLITAN STATISTICAL AREAS (MSAS) OF FLORIDA SPECIFIED YEARS 1987 THROUGH 1992

Year and source 2/	Number of establishments 1/ Total	Number of establishments 1/ With 20 employees or more	All employees Number (1,000)	All employees Payroll (million dollars)	All employees Percentage of U.S. total	Value added by manufacture (million dollars)	New capital expenditure (million dollars)
Florida							
1987--census	15,603	4,046	499.3	10,954.0	2.63	27,574.2	1,910.7
1989--ASM	(NA)	(NA)	496.6	11,880.9	2.61	28,844.4	1,887.3
1990--ASM	(NA)	(NA)	497.9	12,381.5	2.64	29,792.7	1,866.9
1991--ASM	(NA)	(NA)	473.1	12,201.3	2.62	29,054.7	1,791.9
1992--census	16,382	3,758	472.4	12,991.0	2.59	32,634.4	2,111.5
Miami-Ft. Lauderdale CMSA 3/							
1987--census	5,185	1,338	132.6	2,504.3	0.70	5,700.2	254.0
1992--census	5,215	1,185	122.1	3,047.6	0.67	7,130.4	337.2
Ft. Lauderdale PMSA							
1987--census 4/	1,790	397	43.3	936.0	0.23	2,138.3	122.0
1992--census	1,879	370	41.8	1,236.3	0.23	2,888.4	133.9
Miami PMSA							
1987--census 5/	3,395	941	89.3	1,568.4	0.47	3,561.9	132.0
1992--census	3,336	815	80.3	1,811.3	0.44	4,242.0	203.3
Orlando MSA							
1987--census	1,249	358	51.9	1,302.9	0.27	3,197.8	203.4
1992--census	1,574	390	53.3	1,661.5	0.29	3,754.2	195.2
Tampa-St. Petersburg-Clearwater MSA							
1987--census	2,546	681	84.5	1,834.5	0.45	4,139.8	279.1
1992--census	2,583	639	83.7	2,330.5	0.46	5,164.9	315.5

(NA) Not available.

1/ Includes establishments with payroll at any time during the year.

2/ Data for the years 1987 and 1992 are from the Census of Manufactures. Data for Annual Survey of Manufactures (ASM) years are estimates based on a representative sample of establishments canvassed annually and may differ from results of a complete canvas of all establishments.

3/ Consists of Dade and Broward counties.

4/ Ft. Lauderdale-Hollywood-Pompano Beach PMSA.

5/ Miami-Hialeah PMSA.

Note: Data are reported for metropolitan areas with 40,000 manufacturing employees or more in 1992. The manufactures census is on a 5-year cycle collecting data for years ending in 2 and 7. See Glossary for definitions of metropolitan areas and maps at the front of the book for area boundaries.

Source: U.S., Department of Commerce, Bureau of the Census, *1992 Census of Manufactures: Florida*. Geographic Area Series M92-A-10, and *1991 Annual Survey of Manufactures*. Geographic Area Series M91(AS)-3.

Table 12.06. MANUFACTURING: ESTABLISHMENTS, EMPLOYMENT, VALUE ADDED BY MANUFACTURE, VALUE OF SHIPMENTS, AND NEW CAPITAL EXPENDITURE IN THE STATE AND COUNTIES OF FLORIDA, 1992

(in millions of dollars, except where indicated)

County	Establishments 1/ (number)	All employees 1/ Number (1,000)	All employees 1/ Payroll	Value added by manufacture	Value of shipments 2/	New capital expenditure
Florida	16,382	472.4	12,991.0	32,634.4	64,274.7	2,111.5
Alachua	174	5.3	132.2	323.9	691.1	33.7
Baker	15	0.3	6.1	19.2	73.1	0.6
Bay	132	3.3	87.0	235.9	565.7	26.5
Bradford	23	0.5	8.4	20.9	35.4	1.8
Brevard	425	22.3	853.5	1,789.5	2,792.4	65.1
Broward	1,879	41.8	1,236.3	2,888.4	4,822.6	133.9
Calhoun	29	0.2	3.6	9.6	22.4	0.5
Charlotte	72	0.6	11.1	19.4	39.9	0.8
Citrus	58	0.9	15.6	37.1	68.4	2.5
Clay	82	1.4	33.0	79.5	211.0	14.7
Collier	177	2.2	52.2	107.4	188.0	9.4
Columbia	49	1.2	25.5	50.7	133.0	2.3
Dade	3,336	80.3	1,811.3	4,242.0	7,650.5	203.3
De Soto	8	0.2	3.6	15.6	20.3	0.1
Dixie	25	0.4	8.0	16.1	46.4	0.6
Duval	755	27.8	780.0	2,595.5	5,236.4	290.9
Escambia	244	8.7	287.3	866.8	1,893.8	71.2
Flagler	35	1.1	22.3	59.0	133.8	2.1
Franklin	11	0.1	1.5	2.7	6.6	0.3
Gadsden	46	1.5	28.0	84.8	156.7	3.7
Gilchrist	8	0.1	0.9	2.0	4.9	0.1
Glades	5	A/	0.4	0.8	1.6	A/
Gulf	16	(D)	(D)	(D)	(D)	(D)
Hamilton	7	(D)	(D)	(D)	(D)	(D)
Hardee	13	0.2	3.4	6.4	27.0	0.4
Hendry	21	0.9	27.2	128.2	429.9	15.1
Hernando	77	1.1	21.8	80.5	146.4	2.3
Highlands	58	1.1	24.4	61.1	161.8	4.7
Hillsborough	1,002	36.5	951.1	2,178.0	4,983.5	152.3
Holmes	28	0.4	5.7	13.7	21.4	0.6
Indian River	113	1.5	38.1	87.8	173.4	2.9
Jackson	33	1.9	32.5	60.9	171.4	5.5
Jefferson	14	0.2	3.5	6.3	11.1	0.5
Lafayette	7	0.1	1.2	2.6	5.3	0.3
Lake	161	3.8	83.3	196.0	686.6	8.0
Lee	352	5.6	119.1	298.8	535.6	13.1

See footnotes at end of table. Continued . . .

Table 12.06. MANUFACTURING: ESTABLISHMENTS, EMPLOYMENT, VALUE ADDED BY MANUFACTURE, VALUE OF SHIPMENTS, AND NEW CAPITAL EXPENDITURE IN THE STATE AND COUNTIES OF FLORIDA, 1992 (Continued)

(in millions of dollars, except where indicated)

County	Establishments 1/ (number)	All employees 1/ Number (1,000)	All employees 1/ Payroll	Value added by manufacture	Value of shipments 2/	New capital expenditure
Leon	130	2.8	60.2	131.4	222.5	7.5
Levy	33	0.3	6.5	14.8	33.5	1.1
Liberty	21	0.2	3.1	7.7	24.5	0.6
Madison	38	1.2	21.9	81.1	296.3	9.2
Manatee	219	8.1	211.1	749.7	1,761.4	23.1
Marion	234	8.6	194.9	651.3	1,579.5	16.1
Martin	158	3.0	79.8	173.9	368.6	5.2
Monroe	84	0.4	8.2	19.8	37.0	1.0
Nassau	66	2.2	74.1	274.7	802.0	(D)
Okaloosa	136	4.2	80.9	201.4	365.5	7.0
Okeechobee	23	0.3	5.0	13.6	59.6	0.4
Orange	920	36.9	1,228.9	2,818.5	5,007.4	153.9
Osceola	75	2.0	75.6	125.1	240.3	6.1
Palm Beach	1,003	30.5	1,056.5	3,320.5	5,524.1	133.2
Pasco	170	3.5	77.0	168.1	570.2	17.7
Pinellas	1,334	42.6	1,280.6	2,738.3	4,447.4	143.1
Polk	508	20.0	522.5	1,481.1	4,340.4	247.7
Putnam	66	3.0	83.0	230.9	578.7	8.3
St. Johns	72	1.8	37.4	85.9	169.2	(D)
St. Lucie	121	2.2	45.2	137.0	388.9	15.9
Santa Rosa	63	2.1	41.6	109.8	254.9	8.4
Sarasota	423	10.2	252.1	582.5	963.1	28.2
Seminole	418	10.5	273.7	614.6	1,269.8	27.2
Sumter	29	0.7	15.7	34.2	148.4	1.8
Suwannee	29	1.3	21.7	12.7	117.5	(D)
Taylor	35	2.0	59.5	242.1	450.7	(D)
Union	11	0.6	8.6	23.2	44.4	0.8
Volusia	413	12.1	304.2	691.1	1,265.3	33.6
Wakulla	11	(D)	(D)	(D)	(D)	(D)
Walton	23	1.2	18.2	28.5	105.9	1.2
Washington	26	0.9	13.9	37.6	83.4	4.8

(D) Data withheld to avoid disclosure of information about individual companies.

A/ Less than 500 employees or $500,000.

1/ Includes establishments with payroll at anytime during the year.

2/ The total value of shipments may include extensive duplication arising from shipments between establishments in the same industry classification.

Note: The manufactures census is on a 5-year cycle collecting data for years ending in 2 and 7.

Source: U.S., Department of Commerce, Bureau of the Census, *1992 Census of Manufactures: Florida*. Geographic Area Series M92-A-10.

Table 12.50. EMPLOYMENT: AVERAGE MONTHLY PRIVATE REPORTING UNITS, EMPLOYMENT AND PAYROLL COVERED BY UNEMPLOYMENT COMPENSATION LAW BY MANUFACTURING INDUSTRY IN FLORIDA, 1994 AND 1995

SIC code	Industry	Number of reporting units	Number of employees	Payroll ($1,000)
	1994 A/			
	Manufacturing	15,923	484,253	1,214,900
20	Food and kindred products	693	42,936	103,557
201	Meat products	74	6,029	10,118
202	Dairy products	34	2,047	5,069
203	Canned, frozen, and preserved fruits, vegetables, and food specialties	108	11,301	28,289
204	Grain mill products	61	843	2,032
205	Bakery products	102	6,016	13,466
206	Sugar and confectionery products	33	3,058	9,483
207	Fats and oils	8	205	450
208	Beverages	68	7,217	22,714
209	Miscellaneous food preparations and kindred products	205	6,221	11,935
21	Tobacco products	23	936	2,151
212	Cigars	20	905	2,037
22	Textile mill products	206	3,875	7,568
221	Broadwoven fabric mills, cotton	24	226	317
222	Broadwoven fabric mills, manmade fiber and silk	8	24	29
224	Narrow fabrics and other smallwares mills--cotton, wool, silk, and manmade fiber	14	376	917
225	Knitting mills	22	1,017	1,825
226	Dyeing and finishing textiles, except wool fabrics and knit goods	88	1,220	1,973
227	Carpets and rugs	10	91	163
228	Yarn and thread mills	9	107	138
229	Miscellaneous textile goods	31	811	2,202
23	Apparel and other fabricated textile products	1,271	30,170	41,060
231	Men's and boys' suits, coats, and overcoats	7	459	578
232	Men's and boys' furnishings, work clothing, and allied garments	111	6,131	9,608
233	Women's, misses', and juniors' outerwear	468	9,756	11,380
234	Women's, misses', children's, and infants' undergarments	17	1,663	1,775
235	Hats, caps, and millinery	17	532	656
236	Girls', children's, and infants' outerwear	44	1,390	1,856
238	Miscellaneous apparel and accessories	44	1,284	1,724
239	Miscellaneous fabricated textile products	562	8,955	13,483
24	Lumber and wood products, except furniture	1,134	21,068	39,081
241	Logging	353	2,621	5,003
242	Sawmills and planing mills	85	2,782	5,349

See footnotes at end of table.

Continued . . .

Table 12.50. EMPLOYMENT: AVERAGE MONTHLY PRIVATE REPORTING UNITS, EMPLOYMENT AND PAYROLL COVERED BY UNEMPLOYMENT COMPENSATION LAW BY MANUFACTURING INDUSTRY IN FLORIDA, 1994 AND 1995 (Continued)

SIC code	Industry	Number of reporting units	Number of employees	Payroll ($1,000)
	1994 A/ (Continued)			
24	Lumber and wood products, except furniture (Continued)			
243	Millwork, veneer, plywood, and structural wood members	492	9,546	17,364
244	Wood containers	54	988	1,563
245	Wood buildings and mobile homes	27	3,069	6,249
249	Miscellaneous wood products	124	2,062	3,554
25	Furniture and fixtures	564	12,205	20,635
251	Household furniture	305	6,624	10,362
252	Office furniture	37	599	989
253	Public building and related furniture	23	740	1,304
254	Partitions, shelving, lockers, and office and store fixtures	77	1,792	3,505
259	Miscellaneous furniture and fixtures	122	2,450	4,476
26	Paper and allied products	212	14,282	43,967
262	Paper mills	8	1,817	7,119
263	Paperboard mills	14	2,213	7,990
265	Paperboard containers and boxes	84	4,411	11,523
267	Converted paper and paperboard products, except containers and boxes	99	4,979	13,392
27	Printing, publishing, and allied industries	3,574	64,746	145,806
271	Newspapers: publishing, or publishing and printing	324	26,539	58,040
272	Periodicals: publishing, or publishing and printing	438	6,766	16,975
273	Books	148	2,694	7,158
274	Miscellaneous publishing	318	5,371	14,147
275	Commercial printing	2,096	19,058	39,430
276	Manifold business forms	25	1,051	2,567
278	Blankbooks, looseleaf binders, and bookbinding and related work	54	1,353	2,610
279	Service industries for the printing trade	168	1,860	4,761
28	Chemicals and allied products	543	21,172	69,610
281	Industrial inorganic chemicals	48	1,154	5,323
283	Drugs	60	3,223	10,824
284	Soap, detergents, and cleaning preparations; perfumes, cosmetics, and other toilet preparations	134	2,644	6,546
285	Paints, varnishes, lacquers, enamels, and allied products	80	1,493	3,704
286	Industrial organic chemicals	23	1,970	7,345
287	Agricultural chemicals	89	6,670	21,142

See footnotes at end of table. Continued . . .

Table 12.50. EMPLOYMENT: AVERAGE MONTHLY PRIVATE REPORTING UNITS, EMPLOYMENT AND PAYROLL COVERED BY UNEMPLOYMENT COMPENSATION LAW BY MANUFACTURING INDUSTRY IN FLORIDA, 1994 AND 1995 (Continued)

SIC code	Industry	Number of reporting units	Number of employees	Payroll ($1,000)
	1994 A/ (Continued)			
28	Chemicals and allied products (Continued)			
289	Miscellaneous chemical products	64	1,370	4,232
29	Petroleum refining and related industries	63	1,727	4,366
291	Petroleum refining	4	28	68
295	Asphalt paving and roofing materials	49	1,442	3,752
299	Miscellaneous products of petroleum and coal	10	257	546
30	Rubber and miscellaneous plastics products	709	20,371	42,335
302	Rubber and plastics footwear	6	1,457	1,893
305	Gaskets, packing, and sealing devices and rubber and plastics hose and belting	16	1,066	2,260
306	Fabricated rubber products, NEC	57	1,699	3,729
308	Miscellaneous plastics products	627	16,106	34,385
31	Leather and leather products	66	2,530	3,193
314	Footwear, except rubber	16	521	709
316	Luggage	10	276	344
317	Handbags and other personal leather goods	26	694	896
32	Stone, clay, glass, and concrete products	782	21,001	49,436
321	Flat glass	15	208	363
322	Glass and glassware, pressed or blown	15	1,230	3,274
323	Glass products, made of purchased glass	88	1,904	3,330
324	Cement, hydraulic	11	756	2,455
325	Structural clay products	13	722	1,643
326	Pottery and related products	39	236	415
327	Concrete, gypsum, and plaster products	468	14,002	32,881
328	Cut stone and stone products	49	501	965
329	Abrasive, asbestos, and miscellaneous nonmetallic mineral products	84	1,441	4,110
33	Primary metal industries	135	5,289	13,775
331	Steel works, blast furnaces and rolling and finishing mills	35	1,611	5,638
332	Iron and steel foundries	12	561	1,482
334	Secondary smelting and refining of nonferrous metals	10	116	290
335	Rolling, drawing, and extruding of nonferrous metals	37	2,420	5,237
336	Nonferrous foundries (castings)	26	405	738
339	Miscellaneous primary metal products	12	140	349
34	Fabricated metal products, except machinery and transportation equipment	1,250	30,361	66,341
341	Metal cans and shipping containers	15	966	3,855

See footnotes at end of table.

Continued . . .

Table 12.50. EMPLOYMENT: AVERAGE MONTHLY PRIVATE REPORTING UNITS, EMPLOYMENT AND PAYROLL COVERED BY UNEMPLOYMENT COMPENSATION LAW BY MANUFACTURING INDUSTRY IN FLORIDA, 1994 AND 1995 (Continued)

SIC code	Industry	Number of re- porting units	Number of em- ployees	Payroll ($1,000)
	1994 A/ (Continued)			
34	Fabricated metal products, except machinery and transportation equipment (Continued)			
342	Cutlery, handtools, and general hardware	71	1,600	3,488
343	Heating equipment, except electric and warm air; and plumbing fixtures	30	497	1,040
344	Fabricated structural metal products	656	15,615	31,055
345	Screw machine products, and bolts, nuts, screws, rivets, and washers	42	977	2,301
346	Metal forgings and stampings	77	2,280	4,947
347	Coating, engraving, and allied services	151	1,608	3,586
348	Ordnance and accessories, except vehicles and guided missiles	31	1,087	2,816
349	Miscellaneous fabricated metal products	177	5,731	13,253
35	Industrial and commercial machinery and computer equipment	1,597	39,776	117,861
351	Engines and turbines	35	2,499	11,082
352	Farm and garden machinery and equipment	43	1,157	2,533
353	Construction, mining, and materials handling machinery and equipment	116	2,649	6,476
354	Metalworking machinery and equipment	295	4,797	11,913
355	Special industry machinery, except metal-working machinery	106	2,327	6,767
356	General industrial machinery and equipment	159	4,508	11,813
357	Computer and office equipment	98	10,771	43,403
358	Refrigeration and service industry machinery	149	5,557	12,335
359	Miscellaneous industrial and commercial machinery and equipment	598	5,511	11,540
36	Electronic and other electrical equipment and components, except computer equipment	716	59,587	181,221
361	Electric transmission and distribution equipment	34	2,089	5,005
362	Electrical industrial apparatus	54	2,350	6,766
363	Household appliances	14	178	953
364	Electric lighting and wiring equipment	101	3,346	6,144
365	Household audio and video equipment, and audio recordings	41	1,550	3,120
366	Communications equipment	129	20,974	73,640
367	Electronic components and accessories	253	22,014	66,221
369	Miscellaneous electrical machinery, equipment, and supplies	90	7,085	19,371
37	Transportation equipment	1,075	48,003	148,996
371	Motor vehicles and motor vehicle equipment	197	7,324	15,038
372	Aircraft and parts	143	13,369	49,654

See footnotes at end of table. Continued . . .

Table 12.50. EMPLOYMENT: AVERAGE MONTHLY PRIVATE REPORTING UNITS, EMPLOYMENT AND PAYROLL COVERED BY UNEMPLOYMENT COMPENSATION LAW BY MANUFACTURING INDUSTRY IN FLORIDA, 1994 AND 1995 (Continued)

SIC code	Industry	Number of reporting units	Number of employees	Payroll ($1,000)
	1994 A/ (Continued)			
37	Transportation equipment (Continued)			
373	Ship and boat building and repairing	624	13,011	27,730
375	Motorcycles, bicycles, and parts	12	103	147
376	Guided missiles and space vehicles and parts	38	13,050	54,250
379	Miscellaneous transportation equipment	55	770	1,322
38	Measuring, analyzing, and controlling instruments; photographic, medical, and optical goods; watches and clocks	531	34,531	95,544
381	Search, detection, navigation, guidance, aeronautical, and nautical systems, instruments, and equipment	44	9,193	30,769
382	Laboratory apparatus and analytical, optical, measuring, and controlling instruments	153	5,253	12,617
384	Surgical, medical, and dental instruments and supplies	230	13,436	36,612
385	Ophthalmic goods	66	6,252	14,645
386	Photographic equipment and supplies	29	332	771
387	Watches, clocks, clockwork operated devices, and parts	8	66	130
39	Miscellaneous manufacturing industries	782	9,689	18,397
391	Jewelry, silverware, and plated ware	111	1,302	2,688
393	Musical instruments	13	234	421
394	Dolls, toys, games, and sporting and athletic goods	168	1,994	3,319
395	Pens, pencils, and other artists' materials	43	1,039	2,453
396	Costume jewelry, costume novelties, buttons, and miscellaneous notions, except precious metal	34	736	1,354
399	Miscellaneous manufacturing industries	412	4,384	8,162

See footnotes at end of table.

Continued . . .

Table 12.50. EMPLOYMENT: AVERAGE MONTHLY PRIVATE REPORTING UNITS, EMPLOYMENT AND PAYROLL COVERED BY UNEMPLOYMENT COMPENSATION LAW BY MANUFACTURING INDUSTRY IN FLORIDA, 1994 AND 1995 (Continued)

SIC code	Industry	Number of re-porting units	Number of em-ployees	Payroll ($1,000)
	1995 B/			
	Manufacturing	15,104	481,699	1,243,754
20	Food and kindred products	655	41,648	103,539
201	Meat products	70	6,057	10,416
202	Dairy products	32	1,966	5,055
203	Canned, frozen, and preserved fruits, vegetables, and food specialties	109	11,441	28,586
204	Grain mill products	55	766	2,081
205	Bakery products	96	5,707	13,317
206	Sugar and confectionery products	32	2,979	10,040
207	Fats and oils	7	205	476
208	Beverages	62	6,917	22,162
209	Miscellaneous food preparations and kindred products	193	5,610	11,407
21	Tobacco products	21	1,257	3,214
212	Cigars	19	1,236	3,120
22	Textile mill products	191	4,066	7,997
221	Broadwoven fabric mills, cotton	17	181	271
224	Narrow fabrics and other smallwares mills--cotton, wool, silk, and manmade fiber	13	332	886
225	Knitting mills	31	1,234	2,266
226	Dyeing and finishing textiles, except wool fabrics and knit goods	77	1,355	2,272
227	Carpets and rugs	9	45	93
228	Yarn and thread mills	10	116	138
229	Miscellaneous textile goods	28	669	1,725
23	Apparel and other fabricated textile products	1,123	27,567	38,546
231	Men's and boys' suits, coats, and overcoats	7	346	414
232	Men's and boys' furnishings, work clothing, and allied garments	97	5,492	8,813
233	Women's, misses', and juniors' outerwear	348	8,167	10,060
234	Women's, misses', children's, and infants' undergarments	16	1,468	1,633
235	Hats, caps, and millinery	15	476	622
236	Girls', children's, and infants' outerwear	41	1,537	2,129
238	Miscellaneous apparel and accessories	44	1,413	1,813
239	Miscellaneous fabricated textile products	556	8,668	13,063
24	Lumber and wood products, except furniture	1,056	21,261	40,536
241	Logging	330	2,707	5,368
242	Sawmills and planing mills	82	2,757	5,529
243	Millwork, veneer, plywood, and structural wood members	446	9,587	18,023

See footnotes at end of table. Continued . . .

Table 12.50. EMPLOYMENT: AVERAGE MONTHLY PRIVATE REPORTING UNITS, EMPLOYMENT AND PAYROLL COVERED BY UNEMPLOYMENT COMPENSATION LAW BY MANUFACTURING INDUSTRY IN FLORIDA, 1994 AND 1995 (Continued)

SIC code	Industry	Number of reporting units	Number of employees	Payroll ($1,000)
	1995 B/ (Continued)			
24	Lumber and wood products, except furniture (Continued)			
244	Wood containers	50	1,077	1,722
245	Wood buildings and mobile homes	24	3,149	6,347
249	Miscellaneous wood products	125	1,985	3,547
25	Furniture and fixtures	529	12,220	21,827
251	Household furniture	271	6,456	10,805
252	Office furniture	33	567	982
253	Public building and related furniture	16	539	1,039
254	Partitions, shelving, lockers, and office and store fixtures	81	2,026	4,020
259	Miscellaneous furniture and fixtures	127	2,632	4,981
26	Paper and allied products	205	14,487	45,395
262	Paper mills	9	1,932	7,864
263	Paperboard mills	13	2,158	8,008
265	Paperboard containers and boxes	81	4,453	11,916
267	Converted paper and paperboard products, except containers and boxes	96	5,101	14,049
27	Printing, publishing, and allied industries	3,397	63,792	150,246
271	Newspapers: publishing, or publishing and printing	311	26,175	60,616
272	Periodicals: publishing, or publishing and printing	414	6,837	17,654
273	Books	152	2,747	7,661
274	Miscellaneous publishing	302	5,181	14,472
275	Commercial printing	1,990	18,694	39,987
276	Manifold business forms	25	967	2,467
277	Greeting cards	4	49	123
278	Blankbooks, looseleaf binders, and bookbinding and related work	50	1,281	2,472
279	Service industries for the printing trade	151	1,862	4,794
28	Chemicals and allied products	517	21,323	73,276
281	Industrial inorganic chemicals	41	1,070	6,175
282	Plastics materials and synthetic resins, synthetic rubber, cellulosic and other manmade fibers, except glass	41	2,610	11,061
283	Drugs	60	3,242	11,414
284	Soap, detergents, and cleaning preparations; perfumes, cosmetics, and other toilet preparations	128	2,606	6,278
285	Paints, varnishes, lacquers, enamels, and allied products	75	1,422	3,685

See footnotes at end of table.

Continued . . .

Table 12.50. EMPLOYMENT: AVERAGE MONTHLY PRIVATE REPORTING UNITS, EMPLOYMENT AND PAYROLL COVERED BY UNEMPLOYMENT COMPENSATION LAW BY MANUFACTURING INDUSTRY IN FLORIDA, 1994 AND 1995 (Continued)

SIC code	Industry	Number of re- porting units	Number of em- ployees	Payroll ($1,000)
	1995 B/ (Continued)			
28	Chemicals and allied products (Continued)			
286	Industrial organic chemicals	27	2,016	7,594
287	Agricultural chemicals	83	6,854	22,559
289	Miscellaneous chemical products	62	1,505	4,511
29	Petroleum refining and related industries	59	1,553	4,241
291	Petroleum refining	4	14	33
295	Asphalt paving and roofing materials	46	1,280	3,591
299	Miscellaneous products of petroleum and coal	9	259	617
30	Rubber and miscellaneous plastics products	699	20,584	44,168
302	Rubber and plastics footwear	5	1,129	1,490
305	Gaskets, packing, and sealing devices and rubber and plastics hose and belting	15	1,090	2,403
306	Fabricated rubber products, NEC	58	1,966	4,357
308	Miscellaneous plastics products	620	16,359	35,838
31	Leather and leather products	66	2,877	3,688
311	Leather tanning and finishing	5	15	44
313	Boot and shoe cut stock and findings	3	19	50
314	Footwear, except rubber	17	538	764
316	Luggage	11	341	443
317	Handbags and other personal leather goods	25	846	1,050
32	Stone, clay, glass, and concrete products	736	21,468	52,645
321	Flat glass	14	167	351
322	Glass and glassware, pressed or blown	13	1,056	3,255
323	Glass products, made of purchased glass	82	1,952	3,577
324	Cement, hydraulic	14	710	2,307
325	Structural clay products	15	735	1,841
326	Pottery and related products	34	230	346
327	Concrete, gypsum, and plaster products	461	14,838	35,962
328	Cut stone and stone products	39	537	1,064
329	Abrasive, asbestos, and miscellaneous nonmetallic mineral products	66	1,246	3,943
33	Primary metal industries	134	5,744	15,087
331	Steel works, blast furnaces and rolling and finishing mills	34	1,858	6,203
332	Iron and steel foundries	11	602	1,661
334	Secondary smelting and refining of nonferrous metals	6	111	292
335	Rolling, drawing, and extruding of nonferrous metals	44	2,542	5,477
336	Nonferrous foundries (castings)	26	473	1,066
339	Miscellaneous primary metal products	11	158	387

See footnotes at end of table.

Continued . . .

Table 12.50. EMPLOYMENT: AVERAGE MONTHLY PRIVATE REPORTING UNITS, EMPLOYMENT AND PAYROLL COVERED BY UNEMPLOYMENT COMPENSATION LAW BY MANUFACTURING INDUSTRY IN FLORIDA, 1994 AND 1995 (Continued)

SIC code	Industry	Number of re- porting units	Number of em- ployees	Payroll ($1,000)
	1995 B/ (Continued)			
34	Fabricated metal products, except machinery and transportation equipment	1,208	30,020	68,250
341	Metal cans and shipping containers	16	1,084	4,219
342	Cutlery, handtools, and general hardware	73	1,848	4,129
343	Heating equipment, except electric and warm air; and plumbing fixtures	26	260	543
344	Fabricated structural metal products	608	15,066	31,233
345	Screw machine products, and bolts, nuts, screws, rivets, and washers	48	1,109	2,669
346	Metal forgings and stampings	76	2,689	6,293
347	Coating, engraving, and allied services	158	1,781	4,023
348	Ordnance and accessories, except vehicles and guided missiles	28	694	2,041
349	Miscellaneous fabricated metal products	176	5,490	13,100
35	Industrial and commercial machinery and computer equipment	1,523	38,101	111,911
351	Engines and turbines	27	2,415	10,738
352	Farm and garden machinery and equipment	40	1,111	2,440
353	Construction, mining, and materials handling machinery and equipment	109	2,815	7,085
354	Metalworking machinery and equipment	276	4,694	11,903
355	Special industry machinery, except metal-working machinery	109	2,756	7,908
356	General industrial machinery and equipment	160	4,476	12,155
357	Computer and office equipment	85	8,768	34,878
358	Refrigeration and service industry machinery	141	5,712	13,208
359	Miscellaneous industrial and commercial machinery and equipment	578	5,354	11,597
36	Electronic and other electrical equipment and components, except computer equipment	717	61,063	187,300
361	Electric transmission and distribution equipment	35	2,138	5,120
362	Electrical industrial apparatus	58	2,445	7,141
363	Household appliances	15	443	1,524
364	Electric lighting and wiring equipment	106	3,575	6,660
365	Household audio and video equipment, and audio recordings	42	2,036	4,135
366	Communications equipment	127	21,207	76,380
367	Electronic components and accessories	251	21,890	66,974
369	Miscellaneous electrical machinery, equipment, and supplies	85	7,329	19,366
37	Transportation equipment	1,018	49,474	155,296
371	Motor vehicles and motor vehicle equipment	188	7,893	17,389

See footnotes at end of table. Continued . . .

Table 12.50. EMPLOYMENT: AVERAGE MONTHLY PRIVATE REPORTING UNITS, EMPLOYMENT AND PAYROLL COVERED BY UNEMPLOYMENT COMPENSATION LAW BY MANUFACTURING INDUSTRY IN FLORIDA, 1994 AND 1995 (Continued)

SIC code	Industry	Number of re- porting units	Number of em- ployees	Payroll ($1,000)
	1995 B/ (Continued)			
37	Transportation equipment (Continued)			
372	Aircraft and parts	144	14,466	52,708
373	Ship and boat building and repairing	578	13,832	30,440
374	Railroad equipment	8	368	831
375	Motorcycles, bicycles, and parts	13	100	143
376	Guided missiles and space vehicles and parts	37	12,000	52,312
379	Miscellaneous transportation equipment	51	817	1,472
38	Measuring, analyzing, and controlling instruments; photographic, medical, and optical goods; watches and clocks	509	34,022	98,479
381	Search, detection, navigation, guidance, aeronautical, and nautical systems, instruments, and equipment	44	8,689	31,335
382	Laboratory apparatus and analytical, optical, measuring, and controlling instruments	155	5,099	12,743
384	Surgical, medical, and dental instruments and supplies	219	13,930	38,496
385	Ophthalmic goods	63	5,947	15,104
386	Photographic equipment and supplies	21	288	663
387	Watches, clocks, clockwork operated devices, and parts	7	69	137
39	Miscellaneous manufacturing industries	742	9,173	18,112
391	Jewelry, silverware, and plated ware	111	1,099	2,168
393	Musical instruments	10	210	367
394	Dolls, toys, games, and sporting and athletic goods	179	2,187	4,014
395	Pens, pencils, and other artists' materials	40	1,075	2,559
396	Costume jewelry, costume novelties, buttons, and miscellaneous notions, except precious metal	23	632	1,251
399	Miscellaneous manufacturing industries	380	3,971	7,754

A/ Revised.
B/ Preliminary.
Note: Private employment. Detail may not add to totals due to disclosure editing and/or rounding. See Tables 23.70, 23.71, 23.72, 23.73, and 23.74 for public employment data.

Source: State of Florida, Department of Labor and Employment Security, Bureau of Labor Market Information, "Employment and Wages" (ES-202), unpublished data.

Table 12.51. EMPLOYMENT: AVERAGE MONTHLY PRIVATE REPORTING UNITS, EMPLOYMENT AND PAYROLL COVERED BY UNEMPLOYMENT COMPENSATION LAW IN THE STATE AND COUNTIES OF FLORIDA, 1994 AND 1995

County	Number of reporting units	Number of employees	Payroll ($1,000)	County	Number of reporting units	Number of employees	Payroll ($1,000)
			Manufacturing industry, 1994 A/ (SIC codes 20-39)				
Florida	15,923	484,253	1,214,900	Lake	155	4,357	8,556
				Lee	344	5,609	12,167
Alachua	160	5,527	12,407	Leon	134	3,435	7,445
Baker	13	323	583	Levy	34	292	477
Bay	138	2,850	6,786	Liberty	19	265	494
Bradford	27	381	663	Madison	28	1,217	1,994
Brevard	453	28,383	92,209	Manatee	231	11,244	27,200
Broward	1,836	41,892	113,678	Marion	220	10,090	20,837
Calhoun	31	279	453	Martin	139	2,506	6,829
Charlotte	68	875	1,482	Monroe	89	535	920
Citrus	51	1,057	1,749	Nassau	64	1,864	6,126
Clay	82	1,466	2,826	Okaloosa	136	3,893	8,003
Collier	171	2,195	5,340	Okeechobee	20	204	412
Columbia	50	1,447	2,770	Orange	881	33,865	99,962
Dade	3,139	79,589	164,062	Osceola	75	1,761	5,674
De Soto	17	92	176	Palm Beach	920	29,929	111,185
Dixie	22	484	833	Pasco	172	3,929	7,207
Duval	749	28,094	72,712	Pinellas	1,303	44,447	108,893
Escambia	245	8,910	25,660	Polk	489	20,506	48,209
Flagler	40	1,311	2,533	Putnam	69	3,552	9,352
Franklin	15	130	220	St. Johns	78	2,957	6,011
Gadsden	45	1,304	2,283	St. Lucie	123	2,697	5,340
Gilchrist	8	152	233	Santa Rosa	58	2,327	5,029
Gulf	16	1,088	3,048	Sarasota	361	7,865	19,018
Hardee	15	240	346	Seminole	388	9,968	24,138
Hendry	15	1,119	3,009	Sumter	28	531	1,160
Hernando	72	1,294	2,824	Taylor	38	1,851	5,654
Highlands	47	1,315	2,566	Union	14	513	733
Hillsborough	983	36,979	84,325	Volusia	379	11,888	27,929
Holmes	29	596	640	Wakulla	16	624	1,425
Indian River	114	1,881	4,526	Walton	20	1,252	1,896
Jackson	29	1,619	2,648	Washington	29	906	1,330
Jefferson	19	237	349	Multicounty 1/	126	937	2,799

See footnotes at end of table.

Continued . . .

Table 12.51. EMPLOYMENT: AVERAGE MONTHLY PRIVATE REPORTING UNITS, EMPLOYMENT AND PAYROLL COVERED BY UNEMPLOYMENT COMPENSATION LAW IN THE STATE AND COUNTIES OF FLORIDA, 1994 AND 1995 (Continued)

County	Number of reporting units	Number of employees	Payroll ($1,000)	County	Number of reporting units	Number of employees	Payroll ($1,000)
			Manufacturing industry, 1995 B/ (SIC codes 20-39)				
Florida	15,104	481,699	1,243,754	Lafayette	6	151	151
				Lake	148	4,316	8,718
Alachua	151	5,449	12,326	Lee	337	6,114	13,781
Baker	11	255	541	Leon	127	3,506	7,880
Bay	132	2,859	6,808	Levy	35	351	591
Bradford	25	402	784	Liberty	17	276	506
Brevard	441	26,924	88,299	Madison	23	1,281	2,212
Broward	1,747	41,550	117,626	Manatee	229	11,575	27,829
Calhoun	31	292	450	Marion	206	10,366	21,747
Charlotte	66	891	1,586	Martin	138	2,532	7,524
Citrus	47	1,219	2,199	Monroe	78	511	901
Clay	81	1,527	3,059	Nassau	59	1,927	6,347
Collier	166	2,299	5,625	Okaloosa	135	4,041	8,355
Columbia	51	1,599	3,202	Okeechobee	19	171	367
Dade	2,864	76,706	165,954	Orange	847	33,723	103,042
De Soto	17	94	191	Osceola	79	1,777	5,664
Dixie	21	521	896	Palm Beach	873	29,066	107,540
Duval	730	28,797	77,861	Pasco	161	3,864	7,136
Escambia	233	8,668	25,788	Pinellas	1,239	44,845	113,096
Flagler	39	1,540	3,205	Polk	471	21,460	52,946
Franklin	14	130	223	Putnam	70	3,625	9,819
Gadsden	41	1,331	2,479	St. Johns	72	3,003	6,613
Gilchrist	8	155	242	St. Lucie	117	2,535	5,177
Glades	4	4	5	Santa Rosa	57	2,364	5,268
Gulf	14	1,048	3,061	Sarasota	348	8,294	20,473
Hamilton	8	1,548	4,691	Seminole	371	9,594	24,808
Hardee	13	238	353	Sumter	31	561	1,280
Hendry	18	1,113	3,369	Taylor	36	1,817	5,313
Hernando	60	1,248	2,948	Union	15	416	617
Highlands	50	1,358	2,725	Volusia	363	11,908	28,049
Hillsborough	917	35,891	84,708	Wakulla	17	616	1,397
Holmes	26	489	558	Walton	17	1,098	1,761
Indian River	112	2,113	4,958	Washington	27	923	1,397
Jackson	26	1,859	3,071	Multicounty 1/	133	946	2,870
Jefferson	17	215	361				

A/ Revised.
B/ Preliminary.
1/ Reporting units without a fixed location within the state or of unknown county location.

Note: See Table 12.50 for a list of industries. Private employment. Only counties for which data are disclosed are shown. Detail may not add to totals due to disclosure editing and/or rounding. See Tables 23.70, 23.71, 23.72, 23.73, and 23.74 for public employment data.

Source: State of Florida, Department of Labor and Employment Security, Bureau of Labor Market Information, "Employment and Wages" (ES-202), unpublished data.

Table 12.52. FOOD PRODUCTS: AVERAGE MONTHLY PRIVATE REPORTING UNITS, EMPLOYMENT AND PAYROLL COVERED BY UNEMPLOYMENT COMPENSATION LAW IN THE STATE AND COUNTIES OF FLORIDA, 1995

County	Number of re- porting units	Number of em- ployees	Payroll ($1,000)	County	Number of re- porting units	Number of em- ployees	Payroll ($1,000)
			Food and kindred products (SIC code 20)				
Florida	655	41,648	103,539	Lee	15	515	1,311
				Manatee	6	2,890	8,470
Alachua	3	69	49	Marion	10	198	401
Bay	6	64	78	Okaloosa	4	9	10
Brevard	8	69	100	Okeechobee	4	60	162
Broward	40	1,473	3,673	Orange	33	2,913	7,707
Clay	8	237	488	Osceola	6	162	459
Collier	3	15	23	Palm Beach	37	2,824	9,422
Columbia	3	47	88	Pinellas	29	1,000	2,201
Dade	148	5,319	12,988	Polk	42	4,721	11,834
Duval	31	4,157	12,409	St. Lucie	9	565	1,132
Escambia	5	75	155	Sarasota	6	81	136
Franklin	5	69	87	Seminole	12	288	908
Hendry	8	998	3,169	Volusia	11	374	719
Hillsborough	64	5,065	12,308	Wakulla	5	168	107
Lake	15	1,329	3,024				
			Meat products (SIC code 201)				
Florida	70	6,057	10,416	Dade	20	683	1,216
				Hillsborough	4	937	2,717
Broward	4	82	161				
			Canned, frozen, and preserved fruits, vegetables, and food specialties (SIC code 203)				
Florida	109	11,441	28,586	Lake	7	1,163	2,776
				Manatee	4	2,760	8,138
Broward	5	86	152	Orange	6	443	1,189
Dade	18	381	658	Pinellas	5	350	821
Hendry	3	372	919	Polk	18	2,537	6,929
Hillsborough	8	337	762	St. Lucie	5	539	1,077
			Bakery products (SIC code 205)				
Florida	96	5,707	13,317	Hillsborough	14	445	771
				Palm Beach	6	374	924
Broward	7	154	249	Pinellas	4	30	29
Dade	33	1,688	4,249	Polk	4	1,225	2,775
Duval	5	490	1,289	Sarasota	3	76	133

Note: Private employment. For a list of three-digit code industries included see Table 12.50. Data are preliminary. Only counties for which data are disclosed are shown. Detail may not add to totals due to disclosure editing and/or rounding. See Tables 23.70, 23.71, 23.72, 23.73, and 23.74 for public employment data.

Source: State of Florida, Department of Labor and Employment Security, Bureau of Labor Market Information, "Employment and Wages" (ES-202), unpublished data.

Table 12.53. TOBACCO, TEXTILE, AND APPAREL PRODUCTS: AVERAGE MONTHLY PRIVATE REPORTING UNITS, EMPLOYMENT, AND PAYROLL COVERED BY UNEMPLOYMENT COMPENSATION LAW IN THE STATE AND COUNTIES OF FLORIDA, 1995

County	Number of reporting units	Number of employees	Payroll ($1,000)	County	Number of reporting units	Number of employees	Payroll ($1,000)
			Tobacco products (SIC code 21)				
Florida	21	1,257	3,214	Hillsborough	7	546	1,152
Dade	12	128	252				
			Textile mill products (SIC code 22)				
Florida	191	4,066	7,997	Hillsborough	6	11	12
				Lee	4	6	9
Alachua	3	31	37	Nassau	3	9	16
Broward	22	324	826	Orange	7	63	98
Dade	85	2,690	4,946	Palm Beach	7	20	81
Duval	6	92	138	Pinellas	7	59	82
Escambia	5	255	552				
			Apparel and other textile products (SIC code 23)				
Florida	1,123	27,567	38,546	Manatee	12	555	922
				Marion	5	103	157
Brevard	21	162	270	Martin	15	89	147
Broward	134	1,489	2,382	Monroe	6	31	53
Charlotte	4	15	26	Orange	30	217	307
Collier	6	32	46	Palm Beach	46	480	949
Dade	541	14,302	18,607	Pasco	8	98	110
Duval	21	246	358	Pinellas	64	1,234	1,993
Hillsborough	33	2,334	4,193	Polk	14	427	585
Holmes	3	323	280	Sarasota	19	111	153
Indian River	8	87	106	Seminole	17	263	434
Lake	4	30	36	Volusia	13	126	202
Lee	28	262	435	Multicounty 1/	6	8	25
Leon	5	168	245				

1/ Reporting units without a fixed location within the state or of unknown county location.

Note: Private employment. For a list of three-digit code industries included see Table 12.50. Data are preliminary. Only counties for which data are disclosed are shown. Detail may not add to totals due to disclosure editing and/or rounding. See Tables 23.70, 23.71, 23.72, 23.73, and 23.74 for public employment data.

Source: State of Florida, Department of Labor and Employment Security, Bureau of Labor Market Information, "Employment and Wages" (ES-202), unpublished data.

Table 12.57. LUMBER AND WOOD PRODUCTS, EXCEPT FURNITURE: AVERAGE MONTHLY PRIVATE REPORTING UNITS, EMPLOYMENT, AND PAYROLL COVERED BY UNEMPLOYMENT COMPENSATION LAW IN THE STATE AND COUNTIES OF FLORIDA, 1995

County	Number of reporting units	Number of employees	Payroll ($1,000)	County	Number of reporting units	Number of employees	Payroll ($1,000)
	Lumber and wood products, except furniture (SIC code 24)						
Florida	1,056	21,261	40,536	Lee	17	237	441
				Leon	7	80	161
Alachua	10	300	518	Levy	20	196	316
Baker	4	16	24	Liberty	16	268	502
Bay	22	316	606	Madison	16	333	672
Bradford	8	101	246	Manatee	9	327	563
Brevard	18	423	668	Marion	31	1,488	2,888
Broward	50	716	1,579	Martin	4	23	46
Calhoun	24	187	339	Monroe	3	16	21
Charlotte	6	69	85	Nassau	27	202	424
Clay	15	72	134	Okaloosa	16	257	454
Collier	13	110	223	Orange	31	718	1,543
Columbia	22	692	1,285	Osceola	6	123	190
Dade	98	1,709	2,914	Palm Beach	44	706	1,669
Dixie	19	506	881	Pasco	18	259	366
Duval	41	1,082	2,608	Pinellas	42	1,072	2,169
Escambia	25	188	304	Polk	33	2,025	3,824
Flagler	7	177	302	Putnam	27	687	1,636
Franklin	4	38	96	St. Lucie	8	219	408
Gilchrist	3	47	77	Santa Rosa	11	67	89
Gulf	4	26	54	Sarasota	12	185	331
Hardee	6	74	121	Seminole	15	196	411
Hernando	6	123	197	Sumter	8	72	88
Hillsborough	52	1,355	2,365	Taylor	16	364	814
Holmes	16	77	113	Union	11	230	421
Indian River	9	101	168	Volusia	34	485	719
Jackson	9	235	436	Washington	17	147	227
Jefferson	8	107	241				
Lake	19	657	1,141	Multicounty 1/	3	20	87

1/ Reporting units without a fixed location within the state or of unknown county location.

Note: Private employment. For a list of three-digit code industries included see Table 12.50. Data are preliminary. Only counties for which data are disclosed are shown. Detail may not add to totals due to disclosure editing and/or rounding. See Tables 23.70, 23.71, 23.72, 23.73, and 23.74 for public employment data.

Source: State of Florida, Department of Labor and Employment Security, Bureau of Labor Market Information, "Employment and Wages" (ES-202), unpublished data.

Table 12.63. FURNITURE AND FIXTURES AND PAPER AND ALLIED PRODUCTS: AVERAGE MONTHLY PRIVATE REPORTING UNITS, EMPLOYMENT, AND PAYROLL COVERED BY UNEMPLOYMENT COMPENSATION LAW IN THE STATE AND COUNTIES OF FLORIDA, 1995

County	Number of re- porting units	Number of em- ployees	Payroll ($1,000)	County	Number of re- porting units	Number of em- ployees	Payroll ($1,000)
			Furniture and fixtures (SIC code 25)				
Florida	529	12,220	21,827	Manatee	10	320	595
				Marion	7	452	653
Alachua	3	6	3	Martin	3	36	79
Bay	5	36	50	Orange	27	744	1,396
Brevard	7	128	216	Palm Beach	35	360	739
Broward	80	1,906	4,358	Pinellas	29	563	994
Collier	7	127	177	Polk	15	477	686
Dade	180	3,161	5,362	Sarasota	12	204	347
Duval	24	621	1,127	Seminole	15	471	926
Hillsborough	22	668	1,256	Volusia	9	55	74
Lee	8	66	115				
			Household furniture (SIC code 251)				
Florida	271	6,456	10,805	Marion	4	317	472
				Orange	17	551	1,033
Broward	43	570	1,317	Palm Beach	19	284	616
Dade	107	1,531	2,260	Pinellas	9	187	295
Duval	11	216	465	Polk	9	426	615
Hillsborough	8	164	359	Sarasota	6	107	172
Manatee	7	311	583	Seminole	4	79	132
			Paper and allied products (SIC code 26)				
Florida	205	14,487	45,395	Manatee	5	94	215
				Marion	5	128	265
Broward	12	364	1,010	Nassau	3	1,031	3,748
Dade	43	1,881	3,893	Orange	13	592	1,679
Duval	39	2,508	7,499	Pasco	3	90	185
Escambia	5	1,542	6,293	Pinellas	8	348	689
Hillsborough	18	913	2,401	Polk	11	626	1,710
Lee	5	25	506	Sarasota	3	42	84

Note: Private employment. For a list of three-digit code industries included see Table 12.50. Data are preliminary. Only counties for which data are disclosed are shown. Detail may not add to totals due to disclosure editing and/or rounding. See Tables 23.70, 23.71, 23.72, 23.73, and 23.74 for public employment data.

Source: State of Florida, Department of Labor and Employment Security, Bureau of Labor Market Information, "Employment and Wages" (ES-202), unpublished data.

Table 12.64. PRINTING, PUBLISHING, AND ALLIED INDUSTRIES: AVERAGE MONTHLY PRIVATE REPORTING UNITS, EMPLOYMENT, AND PAYROLL COVERED BY UNEMPLOYMENT COMPENSATION LAW IN THE STATE AND COUNTIES OF FLORIDA, 1995

County	Number of re- porting units	Number of em- ployees	Payroll ($1,000)	County	Number of re- porting units	Number of em- ployees	Payroll ($1,000)
	Printing, publishing, and allied industries (SIC code 27)						
Florida	3,397	63,792	150,246	Marion	29	628	1,144
				Martin	33	551	1,175
Alachua	40	826	1,613	Monroe	22	187	322
Bay	18	357	679	Nassau	9	61	126
Brevard	74	1,375	3,208	Okaloosa	25	319	505
Broward	422	5,702	15,631	Okeechobee	4	48	74
Charlotte	19	314	541	Orange	243	5,818	15,864
Clay	20	214	361	Osceola	17	164	302
Collier	47	739	1,815	Palm Beach	238	3,724	10,301
Columbia	5	63	132	Pasco	33	424	708
Dade	618	11,121	31,629	Pinellas	246	6,884	14,689
De Soto	3	22	32	Polk	74	1,190	2,586
Duval	167	3,360	7,534	Putnam	4	131	272
Escambia	58	955	1,709	St. Johns	19	365	595
Flagler	4	27	49	St. Lucie	25	290	486
Hernando	13	106	259	Santa Rosa	11	120	193
Highlands	7	111	159	Sarasota	92	1,431	3,296
Hillsborough	226	8,534	16,899	Seminole	93	699	1,326
Indian River	31	368	899	Sumter	3	15	19
Lake	30	384	660	Taylor	4	23	26
Lee	96	1,272	2,677	Volusia	75	1,546	3,210
Leon	70	1,436	3,069	Wakulla	3	16	22
Manatee	33	562	1,436	Multicounty 1/	37	407	727

1/ Reporting units without a fixed location within the state or of unknown county location.

Note: Private employment. For a list of three-digit code industries included see Table 12.50. Data are preliminary. Only counties for which data are disclosed are shown. Detail may not add to totals due to disclosure editing and/or rounding. See Tables 23.70, 23.71, 23.72, 23.73, and 23.74 for public employment data.

Source: State of Florida, Department of Labor and Employment Security, Bureau of Labor Market Information, "Employment and Wages" (ES-202), unpublished data.

Table 12.67. CHEMICALS AND ALLIED PRODUCTS: AVERAGE MONTHLY PRIVATE REPORTING UNITS, EMPLOYMENT, AND PAYROLL COVERED BY UNEMPLOYMENT COMPENSATION LAW IN THE STATE AND COUNTIES OF FLORIDA, 1995

County	Number of reporting units	Number of employees	Payroll ($1,000)	County	Number of reporting units	Number of employees	Payroll ($1,000)
			Chemicals and allied products (SIC code 28)				
Florida	517	21,323	73,276	Marion	5	117	313
				Martin	4	68	153
Alachua	6	260	724	Orange	31	531	1,703
Brevard	17	277	740	Osceola	3	13	11
Broward	46	688	1,842	Palm Beach	21	718	4,625
Collier	5	15	27	Pinellas	40	1,199	3,273
Dade	84	2,975	9,824	Polk	39	4,065	13,189
Duval	36	1,709	5,918	Putnam	4	25	70
Flagler	3	43	39	Santa Rosa	5	664	2,880
Highlands	3	11	22	Sarasota	8	127	545
Hillsborough	58	2,030	6,989	Seminole	13	155	307
Lake	5	119	241	Volusia	12	555	1,328
Lee	9	157	416				
Manatee	12	217	614	Multicounty 1/	11	208	1,023
			Drugs (SIC code 283)				
Florida	60	3,242	11,414	Duval	3	61	86
				Hillsborough	5	35	164
Broward	8	117	320	Orange	3	28	106
Dade	16	1,940	7,003	Pinellas	7	749	2,263
			Soap, detergents, and cleaning preparations; perfumes, cosmetics, and other toilet preparations (SIC code 284)				
Florida	128	2,606	6,278	Hillsborough	12	294	696
				Orange	7	50	163
Brevard	6	64	110	Palm Beach	7	56	90
Broward	17	271	674	Pinellas	13	132	247
Dade	34	323	610	Polk	4	201	533
Duval	6	722	2,052	Seminole	4	20	33
			Agricultural chemicals (SIC code 287)				
Florida	83	6,854	22,559	Lake	3	88	179
				Manatee	5	87	233
Dade	3	54	126	Orange	5	162	544
Hillsborough	13	1,336	4,781	Polk	20	3,421	11,102

1/ Reporting units without a fixed location within the state or of unknown county location.

Note: Private employment. For a list of three-digit code industries included see Table 12.50. Data are preliminary. Only counties for which data are disclosed are shown. Detail may not add to totals due to disclosure editing and/or rounding. See Tables 23.70, 23.71, 23.72, 23.73, and 23.74 for public employment data.

Source: State of Florida, Department of Labor and Employment Security, Bureau of Labor Market Information, "Employment and Wages" (ES-202), unpublished data.

Table 12.70. PETROLEUM, RUBBER, PLASTICS, AND LEATHER PRODUCTS: AVERAGE MONTHLY PRIVATE REPORTING UNITS, EMPLOYMENT, AND PAYROLL COVERED BY UNEMPLOYMENT COMPENSATION LAW IN THE STATE AND COUNTIES OF FLORIDA, 1995

County	Number of reporting units	Number of employees	Payroll ($1,000)	County	Number of reporting units	Number of employees	Payroll ($1,000)
Petroleum refining and related industries (SIC code 29)							
Florida	59	1,553	4,241	Orange	4	69	154
				Palm Beach	3	15	71
Broward	7	336	1,049	Pinellas	4	42	121
Duval	6	220	583	Polk	5	45	103
Hillsborough	9	371	1,157				
Rubber and miscellaneous plastics products (SIC code 30)							
Florida	699	20,584	44,168	Manatee	9	267	466
				Marion	17	951	2,056
Alachua	9	220	440	Martin	5	44	269
Bay	6	286	602	Okaloosa	5	88	149
Brevard	30	495	854	Orange	45	1,644	3,739
Broward	91	1,940	4,013	Osceola	12	709	3,332
Collier	12	178	364	Palm Beach	29	595	1,015
Dade	107	4,080	7,872	Pinellas	59	2,128	4,435
Duval	34	965	2,317	Polk	38	1,029	1,899
Escambia	9	98	170	St. Johns	4	34	56
Hernando	7	108	144	St. Lucie	9	256	496
Hillsborough	43	1,058	2,320	Sarasota	20	1,254	2,882
Indian River	6	100	167	Seminole	16	392	880
Lake	8	227	479	Volusia	25	614	1,098
Lee	12	224	438				
Leather and leather products (SIC code 31)							
Florida	66	2,877	3,688	Highlands	3	13	16
				Palm Beach	8	62	106
Dade	30	2,104	2,639	Pinellas	6	393	494

Note: Private employment. For a list of three-digit code industries included see Table 12.50. Data are preliminary. Only counties for which data are disclosed are shown. Detail may not add to totals due to disclosure editing and/or rounding. See Tables 23.70, 23.71, 23.72, 23.73, and 23.74 for public employment data.

Source: State of Florida, Department of Labor and Employment Security, Bureau of Labor Market Information, "Employment and Wages" (ES-202), unpublished data.

Table 12.71. STONE, CLAY, GLASS, AND CONCRETE PRODUCTS: AVERAGE MONTHLY PRIVATE REPORTING UNITS, EMPLOYMENT, AND PAYROLL COVERED BY UNEMPLOYMENT COMPENSATION LAW IN THE STATE AND COUNTIES OF FLORIDA, 1995

County	Number of reporting units	Number of employees	Payroll ($1,000)	County	Number of reporting units	Number of employees	Payroll ($1,000)
Stone, clay, glass, and concrete products (SIC code 32)							
Florida	736	21,468	52,645	Lee	28	753	1,614
				Leon	5	111	223
Alachua	11	205	418	Manatee	14	610	1,592
Bay	5	116	263	Marion	16	352	767
Brevard	23	387	796	Martin	9	227	548
Broward	83	1,702	4,206	Monroe	6	74	164
Charlotte	7	120	240	Okaloosa	5	50	89
Citrus	10	166	301	Orange	45	1,492	3,255
Collier	13	321	867	Osceola	7	73	162
Columbia	3	56	114	Palm Beach	47	1,385	4,697
Dade	92	3,039	7,265	Pasco	17	328	644
Duval	35	2,638	5,987	Pinellas	33	615	1,609
Escambia	13	645	1,907	Polk	24	1,159	3,180
Flagler	3	47	93	St. Lucie	11	226	516
Gadsden	6	103	182	Santa Rosa	4	46	144
Hernando	6	274	930	Sarasota	28	553	1,246
Hillsborough	43	1,647	4,516	Seminole	16	277	615
Indian River	10	92	216	Sumter	4	32	56
Lake	13	606	1,300	Volusia	13	409	848
Concrete, gypsum, and plaster products (SIC code 327)							
Florida	461	14,838	35,962	Leon	5	111	223
				Manatee	9	119	270
Alachua	10	179	359	Marion	11	207	463
Bay	3	107	253	Martin	6	145	368
Brevard	11	221	495	Monroe	5	72	162
Broward	38	1,263	3,186	Okaloosa	5	50	89
Charlotte	7	119	238	Orange	30	1,252	2,826
Citrus	7	155	287	Osceola	5	66	145
Collier	8	290	748	Pasco	12	269	568
Dade	49	1,886	4,451	Pinellas	20	534	1,458
Duval	23	1,370	3,269	Polk	15	450	1,140
Escambia	9	234	508	St. Lucie	9	162	398
Flagler	3	47	93	Santa Rosa	4	46	144
Hillsborough	24	1,325	3,704	Sarasota	19	507	1,169
Indian River	4	58	154	Seminole	9	143	338
Lake	11	570	1,228	Sumter	3	28	54
Lee	18	708	1,539	Volusia	10	327	715

Note: Private employment. For a list of three-digit code industries included see Table 12.50. Data are preliminary. Only counties for which data are disclosed are shown. Detail may not add to totals due to disclosure editing and/or rounding. See Tables 23.70, 23.71, 23.72, 23.73, and 23.74 for public employment data.

Source: State of Florida, Department of Labor and Employment Security, Bureau of Labor Market Information, "Employment and Wages" (ES-202), unpublished data.

Table 12.72. FABRICATED METAL PRODUCTS, EXCEPT MACHINERY AND TRANSPORTATION EQUIPMENT: AVERAGE MONTHLY PRIVATE REPORTING UNITS, EMPLOYMENT, AND PAYROLL COVERED BY UNEMPLOYMENT COMPENSATION LAW IN THE STATE AND COUNTIES OF FLORIDA, 1995

County	Number of reporting units	Number of employees	Payroll ($1,000)	County	Number of reporting units	Number of employees	Payroll ($1,000)
		Fabricated metal products, except machinery and transportation equipment (SIC code 34)					
Florida	1,208	30,020	68,250	Leon	9	399	894
				Manatee	26	907	2,148
Alachua	9	541	1,571	Marion	15	1,158	1,827
Bay	10	114	214	Monroe	6	31	77
Brevard	40	782	1,769	Okaloosa	9	114	159
Broward	155	2,611	6,649	Orange	82	1,855	4,553
Charlotte	5	20	50	Osceola	5	48	99
Clay	7	189	434	Palm Beach	66	967	2,154
Collier	12	203	710	Pasco	8	131	261
Dade	182	4,175	7,969	Pinellas	124	3,749	7,818
Duval	67	2,459	6,399	Polk	41	951	2,066
Escambia	23	801	1,457	Putnam	7	187	380
Hernando	7	80	142	St. Lucie	11	209	457
Highlands	9	51	67	Sarasota	31	1,217	3,026
Hillsborough	97	2,983	8,017	Seminole	40	794	1,663
Indian River	10	74	169	Taylor	6	186	306
Lake	7	220	499	Volusia	28	627	1,403
Lee	19	347	733	Multicounty 1/	8	34	111
		Fabricated structural metal products (SIC code 344)					
Florida	608	15,066	31,233	Leon	4	51	105
				Manatee	13	231	581
Alachua	7	157	333	Marion	8	138	235
Bay	6	55	91	Monroe	4	24	70
Brevard	18	248	574	Orange	38	862	2,039
Broward	66	1,405	3,473	Palm Beach	34	645	1,368
Charlotte	3	8	31	Pasco	3	28	60
Collier	7	29	46	Pinellas	53	1,929	3,301
Dade	99	2,438	4,262	Polk	25	705	1,539
Duval	43	1,599	3,456	Putnam	6	184	376
Escambia	13	378	791	St. Lucie	6	111	237
Hernando	5	45	88	Sarasota	13	428	811
Hillsborough	52	1,509	3,680	Seminole	21	531	986
Indian River	5	47	85	Volusia	10	77	134
Lee	9	263	537	Multicounty 1/	5	22	85

1/ Reporting units without a fixed location within the state or of unknown county location.

Note: Private employment. For a list of three-digit code industries included see Table 12.50. Data are preliminary. Only counties for which data are disclosed are shown. Detail may not add to totals due to disclosure editing and/or rounding. See Tables 23.70, 23.71, 23.72, 23.73, and 23.74 for public employment data.

Source: State of Florida, Department of Labor and Employment Security, Bureau of Labor Market Information, "Employment and Wages" (ES-202), unpublished data.

Table 12.74. INDUSTRIAL AND COMMERCIAL MACHINERY AND COMPUTER EQUIPMENT: AVERAGE MONTHLY PRIVATE REPORTING UNITS, EMPLOYMENT, AND PAYROLL COVERED BY UNEMPLOYMENT COMPENSATION LAW IN THE STATE AND COUNTIES OF FLORIDA, 1995

County	Number of reporting units	Number of employees	Payroll ($1,000)	County	Number of reporting units	Number of employees	Payroll ($1,000)
		Industrial and commercial machinery and computer equipment (SIC code 35)					
Florida	1,523	38,101	111,911	Levy	3	4	5
				Manatee	37	942	2,581
Alachua	12	391	1,042	Marion	27	634	1,577
Bay	12	171	415	Martin	9	154	489
Brevard	52	1,782	3,708	Nassau	4	43	73
Broward	185	4,310	13,118	Okaloosa	13	154	312
Charlotte	9	153	347	Okeechobee	4	12	17
Clay	10	171	329	Orange	81	4,279	15,624
Collier	14	175	392	Osceola	8	46	79
Columbia	7	97	251	Palm Beach	84	3,998	18,608
Dade	187	3,195	6,863	Pasco	23	423	976
Duval	84	2,184	5,572	Pinellas	210	5,398	16,832
Escambia	26	283	571	Polk	72	1,982	4,738
Flagler	9	159	471	Putnam	5	44	96
Hendry	6	31	64	St. Johns	10	88	229
Hernando	5	35	109	St. Lucie	14	206	481
Hillsborough	81	1,439	3,498	Sarasota	45	605	1,837
Indian River	9	338	812	Seminole	34	1,055	2,661
Lake	13	140	296	Volusia	48	1,116	2,568
Lee	24	579	1,747	Multicounty 1/	10	19	59
		Computer and office equipment (SIC code 357)					
Florida	85	8,768	34,878	Dade	4	160	437
				Orange	7	611	2,175
Brevard	9	1,291	2,545	Pinellas	16	2,286	8,554
Broward	16	1,132	4,889	Seminole	5	43	111

1/ Reporting units without a fixed location within the state or of unknown county location.

Note: Private employment. For a list of three-digit code industries included see Table 12.50. Data are preliminary. Only counties for which data are disclosed are shown. Detail may not add to totals due to disclosure editing and/or rounding. See Tables 23.70, 23.71, 23.72, 23.73, and 23.74 for public employment data.

Source: State of Florida, Department of Labor and Employment Security, Bureau of Labor Market Information, "Employment and Wages" (ES-202), unpublished data.

Table 12.77. ELECTRONIC AND OTHER ELECTRICAL EQUIPMENT AND COMPONENTS, EXCEPT COMPUTER EQUIPMENT: AVERAGE MONTHLY PRIVATE REPORTING UNITS, EMPLOYMENT AND PAYROLL COVERED BY UNEMPLOYMENT COMPENSATION LAW IN THE STATE AND COUNTIES OF FLORIDA, 1995

County	Number of reporting units	Number of employees	Payroll ($1,000)	County	Number of reporting units	Number of employees	Payroll ($1,000)
Electronic and other electrical equipment and components, except computer equipment (SIC code 36)							
Florida	717	61,063	187,300	Leon	7	874	2,326
				Manatee	13	1,490	3,091
Bay	4	27	62	Marion	8	210	474
Brevard	42	9,768	36,076	Martin	8	154	530
Broward	113	11,346	39,659	Okaloosa	9	559	1,197
Citrus	4	38	41	Orange	53	4,734	13,230
Collier	5	34	112	Pasco	4	16	24
Dade	81	2,095	3,620	Pinellas	90	7,758	21,430
Duval	21	695	1,557	Polk	7	431	897
Flagler	3	364	752	St. Lucie	4	52	131
Hernando	5	390	969	Sarasota	18	1,423	4,081
Hillsborough	35	3,177	8,335	Seminole	44	3,665	10,316
Indian River	3	19	59	Volusia	18	2,431	7,377
Lake	7	72	102	Multicounty 1/	9	13	56
Lee	12	621	1,127				
Communications equipment (SIC code 366)							
Florida	127	21,207	76,380	Hillsborough	10	1,132	3,227
				Leon	5	766	2,135
Brevard	13	985	3,022	Manatee	3	370	1,097
Broward	19	8,814	32,042	Orange	6	332	827
Dade	12	71	167				
Electronic components and accessories (SIC code 367)							
Florida	251	21,890	66,974	Okaloosa	7	551	1,187
				Orange	18	2,153	7,033
Broward	49	1,330	4,122	Pinellas	42	3,240	8,274
Dade	13	430	803	Polk	3	206	246
Hillsborough	10	1,089	2,122	Sarasota	5	199	465
Lake	3	20	22	Seminole	16	683	1,761
Lee	6	464	767	Volusia	9	425	724
Manatee	3	68	88				

1/ Reporting units without a fixed location within the state or of unknown county location.

Note: Private employment. For a list of three-digit code industries included see Table 12.50. Data are preliminary. Only counties for which data are disclosed are shown. Detail may not add to totals due to disclosure editing and/or rounding. See Tables 23.70, 23.71, 23.72, 23.73, and 23.74 for public employment data.

Source: State of Florida, Department of Labor and Employment Security, Bureau of Labor Market Information, "Employment and Wages" (ES-202), unpublished data.

Table 12.83. SHIP AND BOAT BUILDING: AVERAGE MONTHLY PRIVATE REPORTING UNITS EMPLOYMENT, AND PAYROLL COVERED BY UNEMPLOYMENT COMPENSATION LAW IN THE STATE AND COUNTIES OF FLORIDA, 1995

County	Number of reporting units	Number of em- ployees	Payroll ($1,000)	County	Number of reporting units	Number of em- ployees	Payroll ($1,000)
	Ship and boat building and repairing (SIC code 373)						
Florida	578	13,832	30,440	Hillsborough	23	655	1,662
				Lee	22	223	421
Alachua	6	613	1,235	Martin	18	155	381
Bay	19	311	558	Monroe	19	78	146
Brevard	19	1,093	2,572	Okaloosa	6	18	26
Broward	99	1,611	3,820	Orange	11	715	1,511
Charlotte	4	23	37	Pinellas	58	860	1,586
Collier	12	48	91	Polk	7	25	32
Dade	84	1,207	2,650	Putnam	3	58	106
Duval	26	1,093	3,131	St. Lucie	8	226	499
Escambia	13	146	235	Volusia	11	556	1,210

Note: Private employment. For a list of three-digit code industries included see Table 12.50. Data are preliminary. Only counties for which data are disclosed are shown. Detail may not add to totals due to disclosure editing and/or rounding. See Tables 23.70, 23.71, 23.72, 23.73, and 23.74 for public employment data.

Table 12.84. INSTRUMENTS AND RELATED PRODUCTS: AVERAGE MONTHLY PRIVATE REPORTING UNITS, EMPLOYMENT, AND PAYROLL COVERED BY UNEMPLOYMENT COMPENSATION LAW IN THE STATE AND COUNTIES OF FLORIDA, 1995

County	Number of reporting units	Number of em- ployees	Payroll ($1,000)	County	Number of reporting units	Number of em- ployees	Payroll ($1,000)
	Instruments and related products (SIC code 38)						
Florida	509	34,022	98,479	Marion	6	1,090	2,870
				Martin	7	88	295
Alachua	17	194	400	Okaloosa	8	513	1,573
Brevard	27	3,000	11,574	Orange	32	1,037	2,909
Broward	48	1,962	5,777	Palm Beach	40	782	2,646
Citrus	4	23	36	Pasco	5	53	71
Collier	3	27	71	Pinellas	84	8,782	26,056
Dade	72	8,334	23,590	Polk	7	877	1,825
Duval	18	2,095	7,106	St. Lucie	5	127	265
Escambia	9	173	421	Santa Rosa	5	48	119
Hillsborough	19	591	1,564	Sarasota	13	278	634
Lake	4	288	513	Seminole	16	363	783
Lee	9	602	1,393	Volusia	12	1,541	3,511
Leon	3	18	51				
Manatee	9	649	1,398	Multicounty 1/	6	15	70

1/ Reporting units without a fixed location within the state or of unknown county location.

Note: Private employment. For a list of three-digit code industries included see Table 12.50. Data are preliminary. Only counties for which data are disclosed are shown. Detail may not add to totals due to disclosure editing and/or rounding. See Tables 23.70, 23.71, 23.72, 23.73, and 23.74 for public employment data.

Source for Tables 12.83 and 12.84: State of Florida, Department of Labor and Employment Security, Bureau of Labor Market Information, "Employment and Wages" (ES-202), unpublished data.

Table 12.86. TRADE: VALUE OF FLORIDA PRODUCTS EXPORTED BY INDUSTRY IN FLORIDA 1993, 1994, AND 1995

Industry	Value ($1,000) 1993	1994	1995	Percentage change 1993 to 1994	1994 to 1995
Total	18,204,245	20,513,534	23,671,149	12.7	15.4
Industrial machinery, computer equipment	3,460,464	4,012,624	4,657,411	16.0	16.1
Electronic, electric equipment, excluding computer	2,592,132	3,173,170	3,599,897	22.4	13.4
Chemicals and allied products	2,020,228	2,600,922	3,354,043	28.7	29.0
Transportation equipment	2,665,157	2,836,382	2,858,726	6.4	0.8
Instruments and related products	1,238,408	1,332,465	1,563,177	7.6	17.3
Food and kindred products	935,775	1,005,541	1,218,393	7.5	21.2
Paper and allied products	630,274	667,912	1,040,422	6.0	55.8
Apparel and other textile products	873,619	1,023,109	973,212	17.1	-4.9
Agricultural production, crops	515,311	543,937	606,573	5.6	11.5
Fabricated metal products	552,754	521,324	553,211	-5.7	6.1
Rubber and miscellaneous plastics products	389,918	419,663	492,894	7.6	17.4
Primary metal industries	362,725	373,758	464,330	3.0	24.2
Miscellaneous manufacturing industries	348,305	367,425	450,428	5.5	22.6
Textile mill products	317,453	284,136	281,568	-10.5	-0.9
Scrap and waste	89,188	92,143	250,952	3.3	172.3
Printing and publishing	158,446	196,348	185,701	23.9	-5.4
Lumber and wood products	138,176	157,689	169,226	14.1	7.3
Stone, clay, and glass products	174,058	157,643	169,069	-9.4	7.2
Furniture and fixtures	135,871	145,946	161,648	7.4	10.8
Used or second-hand merchandise	123,169	121,222	100,948	-1.6	-16.7
Fishing, hunting, and trapping	68,986	72,663	95,958	5.3	32.1
Leather and leather products	68,680	67,290	92,419	-2.0	37.3
Special classification provisions, NEC	100,424	86,391	83,751	-14.0	-3.1
Petroleum and coal products	67,967	80,797	59,829	18.9	-26.0
Canadian, nonCanadian goods returned to Canada	32,899	50,297	44,620	52.9	-11.3
Agricultural production, livestock	46,484	37,403	42,834	-19.5	14.5
Tobacco manufactures	24,897	32,027	34,346	28.6	7.2
Forestry	54,037	37,203	32,624	-31.2	-12.3
Nonmetallic minerals, except fuels	16,625	13,909	27,961	-16.3	101.0
Metal mining	945	1,392	3,270	47.3	135.0
Oil and gas extraction	832	800	1,590	-3.9	98.7
Bituminous coal and lignite mining	40	3	121	-92.0	3,679.1

NEC Not elsewhere classified.

Source: State of Florida, Department of Commerce, Bureau of Economic Analysis, University of Massachusetts Institute for Social and Economic Research (MISER), unpublished trade data.

Table 12.87. TRADE: VALUE OF FLORIDA PRODUCTS EXPORTED BY SELECTED DESTINATIONS, 1993, 1994, AND 1995

Location 1/	Value ($1,000) 1993	1994	1995	Percentage change 1993 to 1994	1994 to 1995
Total	18,204,245	20,513,534	23,671,149	12.7	15.4
Brazil	842,592	1,412,017	2,027,351	67.6	43.6
Canada	1,618,136	1,568,673	1,710,089	-3.1	9.0
Colombia	1,086,243	1,259,752	1,477,825	16.0	17.3
Venezuela	1,225,297	882,020	1,064,976	-28.0	20.7
China (Mainland)	243,777	694,174	1,059,799	184.8	52.7
Dominican Republic	814,628	996,689	1,058,666	22.3	6.2
Japan	570,337	748,471	951,402	31.2	27.1
Argentina	933,092	1,058,326	866,881	13.4	-18.1
Paraguay	347,145	593,543	730,304	71.0	23.0
United Kingdom	537,441	549,410	617,174	2.2	12.3
Chile	448,446	568,751	588,042	26.8	3.4
Mexico	755,008	844,148	569,707	11.8	-32.5
Guatemala	449,280	480,626	515,603	7.0	7.3
Germany	428,653	380,589	478,999	-11.2	25.9
Peru	290,407	432,257	477,438	48.8	10.5
Panama	446,954	464,860	442,445	4.0	-4.8
France	346,211	351,679	442,108	1.6	25.7
Ecuador	358,281	441,813	432,032	23.3	-2.2
Australia	260,571	346,704	407,309	33.1	17.5
Netherlands	289,829	302,338	396,302	4.3	31.1
Bahamas	422,618	407,553	389,785	-3.6	-4.4
Costa Rica	431,246	405,926	382,410	-5.9	-5.8
Jamaica	299,308	285,093	378,930	-4.7	32.9
Honduras	323,671	386,128	376,921	19.3	-2.4
Spain	229,437	153,414	297,820	-33.1	94.1
Korea, Republic of	187,628	177,082	280,726	-5.6	58.5
Singapore	217,384	196,480	267,605	-9.6	36.2
El Salvador	217,954	240,220	259,014	10.2	7.8
India	188,271	129,885	253,310	-31.0	95.0
Hong Kong	128,452	169,290	250,092	31.8	47.7
Haiti	100,324	84,595	246,423	-15.7	191.3
Italy	196,367	175,722	237,317	-10.5	35.1
Belgium	150,758	148,738	230,807	-1.3	55.2
Netherlands Antilles	206,450	196,427	200,560	-4.9	2.1
China (Taiwan)	125,204	171,204	130,100	36.7	-24.0
Israel	67,405	119,454	127,585	77.2	6.8
Uruguay	90,163	95,018	124,300	5.4	30.8
Saudi Arabia	133,896	111,843	123,355	-16.5	10.3
Trinidad and Tobago	77,535	83,149	120,381	7.2	44.8
Russia	44,543	46,724	117,917	4.9	152.4
Republic of South Africa	53,851	74,187	115,823	37.8	56.1
Switzerland	86,423	80,161	115,206	-7.2	43.7
Cayman Islands	84,150	107,356	113,173	27.6	5.4
Other locations	1,848,877	2,091,044	2,217,133	13.1	6.0

1/ Countries, areas, and agencies receiving an annual value of shipments in 1995 of $100,000,000 or more are shown separately.

Source: State of Florida, Department of Commerce, Bureau of Economic Analysis, University of Massachusetts Institute for Social and Economic Research (MISER), unpublished trade data.

TRANSPORTATION

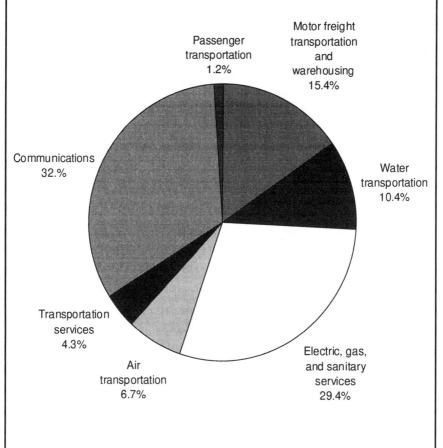

Transportation, Communications, and Public Utilities Revenue by Kind of Business in Florida, 1992

Note: Excludes pipelines.

Source: Table 13.01

SECTION 13.00
TRANSPORTATION

TABLES LISTED BY MAJOR HEADINGS

HEADING PAGE

SECTION 13.00
TRANSPORTATION
(Continued)

TABLES LISTED BY MAJOR HEADINGS

Table 13.01. TRANSPORTATION, COMMUNICATIONS, AND PUBLIC UTILITIES ESTABLISHMENTS, REVENUE, AND ANNUAL PAYROLL BY KIND OF BUSINESS IN FLORIDA, 1992

SIC code	Kind of business	Number of establish- ments	Revenue ($1,000)	Annual payroll ($1,000)
41	Passenger transportation	720	474,152	165,895
411	Local and suburban	353	266,790	101,973
412	Taxicabs	123	57,192	15,353
413	Intercity and rural bus service	30	42,597	18,018
414	Charter bus service	75	81,268	22,378
415	School buses	139	26,305	8,173
417	Bus terminal and service facilities	0	0	0
42	Motor freight transportation and warehousing	4,247	5,927,195	1,540,605
421	Trucking and courier services, except air	3,579	5,550,333	1,461,909
422	Public warehousing and storage	663	(D)	(D)
423	Trucking terminal facilities	5	(D)	(D)
44	Water transportation	980	4,013,806	535,141
441, 2	Deep sea foreign and domestic freight	52	1,071,455	77,612
443, 4	Other water transportation of freight	14	31,094	5,769
448	Water transportation of passengers	200	2,215,908	198,858
449	Services incidental to water transportation	714	695,349	252,902
45 pt.	Air transportation 1/	782	2,576,518	552,906
451 pt.	Scheduled and air courier services 1/	317	1,503,994	272,129
452	Nonscheduled	144	348,528	59,106
458	Airport terminal services	321	723,996	221,671
46	Pipelines, except natural gas	13	27,382	3,856
47	Transportation services	3,953	1,657,528	523,497
472	Arrangement of passenger transportation	2,732	953,208	287,656
473	Freight shipping services	1,069	574,929	190,297
474	Rental of railroad cars	0	0	0
478	Miscellaneous services incidental to transportation	155	129,391	45,544
48	Communications	1,979	12,585,982	2,390,833
481	Telephone	1,216	10,014,974	1,858,007
482	Telegraph	29	24,545	3,690
483	Radio and television broadcasting	448	1,098,434	323,659
484	Cable and other pay television	204	1,365,139	189,399
489	Communication services, NEC	82	82,890	16,078
49	Electric, gas, and sanitary services	718	11,325,998	1,615,058
491	Electric services	178	9,730,288	1,323,847
492	Gas production and distribution	57	402,366	58,818
493	Combination utility services	29	172,307	31,766
494	Water supply	141	134,997	31,948
495	Sanitary services	303	881,254	167,800
496, 7	Miscellaneous utility services	10	4,786	879

NEC Not elsewhere classified.
(D) Data withheld to avoid disclosure of information about individual firms.
1/ Excludes large, certificated passenger carrier reporting to the Office of Airline Statistics.

Source: U.S., Department of Commerce, Bureau of the Census, *1992 Census of Transportation, Communications, and Public Utilities*. Geographic Area Series UC92-A-1 Summary.

Table 13.16. ROADS AND HIGHWAYS: EXISTING MILEAGE OF PUBLIC ROADS AND HIGHWAYS BY JURISDICTION IN FLORIDA, DECEMBER 1991 THROUGH 1994

Jurisdiction	1991	1992	1993	1994
Total	109,374	110,640	112,808	113,478
Rural mileage	61,627	62,003	63,630	65,084
Under state control 1/	7,598	7,592	7,509	6,995
Under local control	54,029	54,305	54,815	56,780
County roads	53,848	54,115	54,616	56,587
Other jurisdictions 2/	181	190	199	193
Under federal control 3/	0	106	1,306	1,309
Urban mileage	47,747	48,637	49,178	48,394
Under state control 1/	4,268	4,278	4,423	4,926
Under local control	43,479	44,359	44,755	43,468
County roads	1,442	1,403	1,861	2,914
Other jurisdictions 2/	42,037	42,956	42,894	40,554

1/ Includes state highway agency, state park, state toll, and other state agency roadways.
2/ Includes mileage not identified by ownership. Contains mainly municipal mileage for urban summaries.
3/ Includes mileage in federal parks, forests, and reservations that are not part of the state and local highway system.

Table 13.17. ROADS AND HIGHWAYS: EXISTING MILEAGE OF PUBLIC ROADS AND HIGHWAYS BY FUNCTIONAL SYSTEM OF HIGHWAY AND BY PAVEMENT CONDITION IN FLORIDA DECEMBER 31, 1994

Function	Total existing mileage	Pavement conditions: Poor	Medi-ocre	Fair	Good	Very good
Total	113,478	(NA)	(NA)	(NA)	(NA)	(NA)
Rural	65,084	(NA)	(NA)	(NA)	(NA)	(NA)
Interstate	953	11	404	232	252	54
Other principal arterial	3,361	247	1,194	868	949	103
Minor arterial	2,785	198	1,089	629	850	19
Major collector	4,671	19	940	2,105	704	903
Minor collector	4,879	(NA)	(NA)	(NA)	(NA)	(NA)
Local	48,435	(NA)	(NA)	(NA)	(NA)	(NA)
Urban	48,394	(NA)	(NA)	(NA)	(NA)	(NA)
Interstate	519	13	238	82	155	31
Other freeways and expressways	404	14	176	92	108	14
Other principal arterial	2,682	379	929	527	798	49
Minor arterial	2,856	77	338	1,016	691	734
Collector	6,147	626	966	2,775	1,096	684
Local	35,786	(NA)	(NA)	(NA)	(NA)	(NA)

(NA) Not available.

Source for Tables 13.16 and 13.17: U.S., Department of Transportation, Federal Highway Administration, *Highway Statistics, 1994,* and previous editions.

Table 13.20. ROADS AND HIGHWAYS: RECEIPTS AND DISBURSEMENTS FOR ROADS AND HIGHWAYS BY ALL UNITS OF GOVERNMENT IN FLORIDA FISCAL YEARS 1990-91 THROUGH 1992-93

(in thousands of dollars)

Item	1990-91	1991-92	1992-93
Total receipts	4,084,783	3,739,425	4,325,929
Bond proceeds, par value 1/	542,133	327,072	524,099
Total current income	3,542,650	3,412,353	3,801,830
Highway-user tax revenue 2/	2,425,901	2,150,937	2,389,815
Federal agencies	786,470	476,513	610,710
State agencies	1,285,161	1,284,409	1,369,634
Local	354,270	390,015	409,471
Road and crossing tolls	245,225	271,632	297,509
Appropriations from general fund	209,553	211,418	330,176
Property taxes	136,038	154,848	82,603
Other imposts	227,232	349,595	430,791
Miscellaneous receipts 3/	298,701	273,923	270,936
Total disbursements 4/	3,266,894	3,858,336	4,346,445
Bond retirement, par value 1/	109,008	153,681	374,748
Total direct expenditure	3,157,886	3,704,655	3,971,697
Capital outlay	1,814,686	2,122,527	2,320,608
State-administered highways	1,141,425	1,440,203	1,675,637
Locally administered roads	670,006	681,642	642,870
Federal roads and unclassified	3,255	682	2,101
Maintenance	588,596	649,505	694,500
State-administered highways	240,188	282,812	311,412
Locally administered roads	347,862	366,381	382,882
Federal roads and unclassified	546	312	206
Administration and miscellaneous	304,447	428,351	376,608
Highway law enforcement and safety	248,868	271,756	309,105
Interest	201,289	232,516	270,876

1/ Excludes short-term notes and refunding bond issues.

2/ Excludes amounts allocated for collection expenses and nonhighway purposes. Revenues are segregated according to the collecting agency. Amounts shown for federal agencies are mostly grants-in-aid payments.

3/ Highway Trust Fund revenues attributable to highway-user taxes that were expended for highways in each state.

4/ Disbursements are classified by system on which expended, rather than by expending agencies; capital outlay on county and other local rural roads includes expenditures from federal, state, and local funds.

Note: This table presents combined summaries of the highway finances of all government agencies in net amounts; duplications that would otherwise have resulted from interfund or intergovernmental transfers have been removed. Data may include estimates.

Source: U.S., Department of Transportation, Federal Highway Administration, *Highway Statistics, 1994,* and previous editions.

Table 13.21. ROAD AND HIGHWAY BRIDGES: NUMBER BY FUNCTIONAL SYSTEM OF HIGHWAY IN FLORIDA AND THE UNITED STATES, 1993 AND 1994

Functional system	Florida 1993	Florida 1994	United States 1993	United States 1994
Total	10,671	10,836	575,719	577,481
Rural	5,884	5,973	458,466	456,806
Interstate	827	830	28,944	28,768
Other principal arterial	1,143	1,312	33,160	35,102
Minor arterial	818	739	44,444	37,514
Major collector	711	683	99,301	98,306
Minor collector	649	665	49,696	49,392
Local	1,736	1,744	202,921	207,724
Urban	4,787	4,863	117,253	120,675
Interstate	944	949	25,223	25,682
Other freeways and expressways	622	713	13,200	13,649
Other principal arterial	1,101	1,021	23,142	23,371
Minor arterial	590	648	18,894	19,782
Collector	448	456	14,059	14,644
Local	1,082	1,076	22,735	23,547

Note: Highway bridges greater than or equal to 20 feet. Because functional system has been estimated or assigned in some cases, data may not be precise.

Source: U.S., Department of Transportation, Federal Highway Administration, *Highway Statistics, 1994,* and previous edition.

Table 13.22. ROADS AND HIGHWAYS: PERCENTAGE DISTRIBUTION OF ANNUAL VEHICLE DISTANCE TRAVELED BY FUNCTIONAL SYSTEM OF HIGHWAY AND BY VEHICLE TYPE IN FLORIDA, 1994

Type of vehicle	Rural: Interstate	Rural: Other major arterial	Rural: Minor arterial	Urban: Interstate	Urban: Other freeways and expressways	Urban: Other principal arterial	Urban: Minor arterial
All motor vehicles	100.0	100.0	100.0	100.0	100.0	100.0	100.0
Passenger cars and other 2-axle, 4-tire vehicles	80.5	86.3	90.2	91.5	95.7	95.0	95.4
Passenger cars	69.6	71.3	75.3	81.6	87.7	84.3	84.9
Motorcycles	0.5	0.7	0.5	0.4	0.4	0.7	0.6
Buses	0.7	0.6	0.5	0.6	0.3	0.5	0.4
Other 2-axle, 4-tire vehicles 1/	10.9	15.0	14.9	9.9	8.0	10.6	10.6
Single unit 2-axle, 6-tire or more and combination trucks	18.3	12.4	8.8	7.5	3.6	3.9	3.6
Single unit 2-axle, 6-tire or more trucks	3.7	4.2	3.8	2.6	2.3	2.2	2.3
Combination trucks							
Single trailer	13.6	7.9	4.8	4.6	1.2	1.6	1.1
Multiple trailer	1.0	0.3	0.2	0.3	0.1	0.1	0.1

1/ Excludes passenger cars. Includes vans, pickup trucks, and sport/utility vehicles.

Source: U.S., Department of Transportation, Federal Highway Administration, *Highway Statistics, 1994.*

Table 13.29. ROADS AND HIGHWAYS: ESTIMATED ANNUAL VEHICLE MILES OF TRAVEL BY FUNCTIONAL SYSTEM OF HIGHWAY IN FLORIDA, 1993 AND 1994

(in millions of miles)

Functional system of highway	Total		Rural		Urban	
	1993 A/	1994	1993 A/	1994	1993 A/	1994
Total	120,467	121,989	34,314	31,727	86,153	90,262
Interstate	22,501	24,001	10,064	9,502	12,437	14,499
Other freeways and expressways	4,402	5,978	0	0	4,402	5,978
Other principal arterial	35,402	37,237	11,331	10,518	24,071	26,719
Minor arterial	19,188	18,512	4,464	4,311	14,724	14,201
Collector	14,779	13,375	5,042	3,860	9,737	9,515
Local	24,195	22,886	3,413	3,536	20,782	19,350

A/ Revised.
Note: Data are estimated highway travel based on traffic counts taken at selected highway locations.

Table 13.30. MOTOR VEHICLE REGISTRATIONS: NUMBER BY TYPE OF VEHICLE IN FLORIDA 1977 THROUGH 1994

(rounded to hundreds, except where indicated)

Year	All motor vehicles 1/	Percentage change from previous year	Automobiles 2/	Buses	Trucks 2/	Motorcycles
1977	6,444.3	6.9	4,978.9	22.7	1,349.3	93.3
1978	7,068.9	9.7	5,738.0	26.1	1,151.8	152.9
1979	7,519.4	6.4	6,011.0	28.2	1,259.7	220.5
1980	7,833.0	4.2	6,196.6	29.3	1,387.6	219.5
1981	8,194.1	4.6	6,484.6	30.4	1,459.1	220.0
1982	8,561.0	4.5	6,753.6	32.2	1,548.8	226.4
1983	9,041.0	5.6	7,113.9	33.3	1,661.3	232.5
1984	9,635.1	6.6	7,552.4	34.4	1,807.4	240.9
1985	10,096.8	4.8	7,849.1	35.8	1,979.9	232.0
1986	10,591.2	4.9	8,263.3	34.2	2,064.0	229.7
1987	10,903.1	2.9	8,521.6	34.8	2,127.1	219.5
1988	11,183.1	2.6	8,713.2	35.5	2,234.9	199.5
1989	11,410.8	2.0	8,972.7	36.2	2,197.9	203.9
1990	11,155.6	-2.2	8,694.9	36.8	2,218.1	205.8
1991	10,176.1	-8.8	7,910.3	37.5	2,032.3	196.0
1992	10,426.1	2.5	8,131.4	38.1	2,062.8	193.7
1993	10,358.4	-0.6	8,072.5	38.8	2,058.3	188.8
1994	10,429.2	0.7	7,519.2	39.6	2,693.0	177.4

1/ Includes motorcycles.
2/ Beginning in 1994, personal passenger vans, passenger minivans, and utility-type vehicles were classified by the source as trucks rather than automobiles. Therefore, caution should be used when making comparisons to earlier years.
Note: Excludes vehicles owned by the military service.
Source for Tables 13.29 and 13.30: U.S., Department of Transportation, Federal Highway Administration, *Highway Statistics, 1994,* and previous editions.

Table 13.32. MOTOR VEHICLE TAGS: TOTAL TAGS AND PASSENGER CAR TAGS SOLD AND REVENUE COLLECTED IN THE STATE AND COUNTIES OF FLORIDA FISCAL YEAR 1994-95

County	Total tags		Passenger car tags		Total revenue ($1,000)
	Number	Percentage change from 1993-94	Number	Percentage change from 1993-94	
Florida 1/	16,980,698	0.8	7,373,932	0.9	387,250
Alachua	220,913	1.7	107,726	3.3	4,231
Baker	23,988	4.0	9,300	2.4	550
Bay	164,354	6.9	81,503	4.4	3,468
Bradford	31,881	9.0	11,079	2.9	620
Brevard	533,128	0.5	266,352	1.6	10,661
Broward	1,367,992	0.5	729,859	-1.8	28,889
Calhoun	10,851	-2.9	4,420	5.9	259
Charlotte	157,509	-0.5	81,069	3.2	3,344
Citrus	132,508	2.3	59,024	2.6	2,744
Clay	150,049	4.4	69,299	3.8	3,013
Collier	236,994	8.9	127,793	8.6	5,588
Columbia	59,613	-2.7	22,347	2.5	1,233
Dade	2,204,356	-3.1	1,164,304	-1.1	51,119
De Soto	34,893	1.3	11,197	4.2	766
Dixie	12,686	2.5	4,219	4.4	314
Duval	838,176	1.6	384,330	1.6	17,011
Escambia	281,857	0.6	151,225	-1.4	6,257
Flagler	48,544	10.1	25,849	8.6	1,044
Franklin	9,491	5.1	4,189	6.3	217
Gadsden	35,279	4.8	16,290	4.6	783
Gilchrist	13,447	6.4	4,563	4.0	313
Glades	6,317	6.8	2,147	4.8	159
Gulf	13,677	7.6	6,141	6.4	322
Hamilton	9,844	7.0	4,047	6.9	220
Hardee	30,207	5.0	9,390	2.0	695
Hendry	40,325	2.8	14,322	1.7	1,075
Hernando	127,230	5.7	65,358	3.6	2,647
Highlands	105,956	3.9	43,251	4.2	2,193
Hillsborough	1,047,780	-3.1	466,364	-1.0	23,629
Holmes	16,951	5.5	6,790	1.5	391
Indian River	133,103	3.1	64,648	2.1	2,723
Jackson	51,786	4.0	20,571	1.8	1,024
Jefferson	12,312	2.5	5,034	2.7	293
Lafayette	5,998	7.7	2,042	3.4	140
Lake	243,423	3.0	96,081	4.7	4,879
Lee	480,054	1.0	223,171	-0.1	10,198
Leon	254,497	6.5	123,296	4.0	4,857
Levy	37,601	9.1	13,512	3.7	926

See footnotes at end of table. Continued . . .

Table 13.32. MOTOR VEHICLE TAGS: TOTAL TAGS AND PASSENGER CAR TAGS SOLD AND REVENUE COLLECTED IN THE STATE AND COUNTIES OF FLORIDA FISCAL YEAR 1994-95 (Continued)

County	Total tags		Passenger car tags		
	Number	Percentage change from 1993-94	Number	Percentage change from 1993-94	Total revenue ($1,000)
Liberty	6,496	4.9	2,146	-0.5	18,209,351
Madison	17,192	6.6	6,814	4.3	386
Manatee	520,676	-3.0	258,370	-3.4	13,066
Marion	300,369	7.4	125,796	5.4	6,287
Martin	160,625	0.9	81,181	2.0	3,451
Monroe	99,607	5.4	46,024	7.5	2,175
Nassau	55,372	3.6	24,249	3.5	1,190
Okaloosa	213,780	0.1	104,145	2.3	4,011
Okeechobee	45,253	3.8	14,509	2.1	1,096
Orange	984,542	4.1	474,951	3.1	22,139
Osceola	171,488	3.2	76,948	5.0	3,208
Palm Beach	944,424	0.4	577,926	-0.7	23,708
Pasco	407,169	2.0	183,194	1.5	8,043
Pinellas	1,011,008	-2.3	500,753	-0.3	19,282
Polk	559,231	2.4	230,379	3.6	12,658
Putnam	79,356	4.9	30,486	2.2	1,623
St. Johns	120,502	6.0	62,397	5.3	2,530
St. Lucie	205,520	2.7	93,922	3.6	4,184
Santa Rosa	110,725	5.0	51,570	6.8	2,265
Sarasota	383,406	1.0	204,094	1.2	7,924
Seminole	421,079	1.6	207,402	3.1	8,092
Sumter	41,678	5.8	15,752	6.5	992
Suwannee	39,982	6.8	12,993	1.9	835
Taylor	22,420	4.1	7,690	5.3	489
Union	10,834	-3.9	3,504	-3.3	285
Volusia	486,810	0.0	228,096	3.3	9,447
Wakulla	17,861	7.5	6,597	7.4	413
Walton	28,052	9.8	12,075	4.0	619
Washington	17,224	2.4	7,113	1.3	380
Office agency	35,219	1.3	10,429	-6.9	1,089
DHSMV 2/	204,169	2.7	0	0.0	208
Motor carrier service	56,992	0.9	0	-100.0	26,258

1/ Details may not add to totals due to reporting practices involving tags outside the computer system and refunds.

2/ Sales made by the Department of Highway Safety and Motor Vehicles district offices.

Note: See Table 2.36 for mobile home and recreational vehicle tag sales.

Source: State of Florida, Department of Highway Safety and Motor Vehicles, *Revenue Report, July 1, 1994 through June 30, 1995.*

Table 13.33. DRIVER LICENSES: NUMBER ISSUED BY TYPE AND BY AGE OF DRIVER IN FLORIDA, JANUARY 1, 1996

Age	Re-strict-ed	Oper-ator	Chauf-feur	Com-mer-cial	Age	Re-strict-ed	Oper-ator	Chauf-feur	Com-mer-cial
Total	270,253	10,365,887	983,528	399,488	45	1,925	172,790	24,430	10,478
					46	1,773	172,254	23,851	10,313
15	42,477	0	0	0	47	1,682	172,127	23,480	10,121
16	32,182	66,441	14	0	48	1,537	180,494	24,038	10,390
17	20,857	102,129	53	0	49	1,523	162,806	21,609	9,499
18	15,083	128,885	370	55	50	1,323	137,639	18,500	8,161
19	12,214	140,436	917	257	51	1,253	137,799	18,219	8,182
20	10,929	153,896	1,723	675	52	1,152	143,939	18,659	8,425
21	10,862	168,868	2,713	1,533	53	1,182	139,410	17,837	7,701
22	10,463	179,648	3,991	2,569	54	1,028	123,732	15,837	7,117
23	7,924	190,135	5,917	4,013	55	1,038	119,079	15,187	6,654
24	6,914	211,886	8,826	5,605	56	935	115,217	14,652	6,171
25	6,202	224,777	12,086	6,802	57	892	115,773	14,133	6,170
26	5,260	215,230	13,963	7,460	58	826	112,296	13,546	5,596
27	5,015	210,598	16,360	8,426	59	763	110,350	12,952	5,320
28	4,685	210,201	18,206	9,029	60	650	110,312	12,349	4,801
29	4,547	216,633	21,010	10,123	61	633	108,650	12,067	4,320
30	4,414	222,563	23,285	11,111	62	576	107,353	11,460	3,685
31	4,437	235,922	26,480	12,182	63	543	114,096	11,679	3,523
32	4,333	235,716	27,990	12,836	64	529	114,536	11,074	3,018
33	4,054	236,286	29,150	13,189	65	540	121,515	11,519	2,723
34	3,480	233,458	29,742	13,756	66	485	120,590	10,692	2,144
35	3,521	230,157	30,441	13,786	67	464	124,535	10,592	1,721
36	3,278	224,506	30,596	13,433	68	428	126,059	10,413	1,422
37	3,108	219,025	30,323	13,245	69	379	123,375	9,344	1,106
38	2,885	218,663	30,340	13,526	70	361	123,087	8,727	854
39	2,746	210,297	29,823	13,463	71	316	123,490	7,947	619
40	2,654	204,112	29,184	12,857	72	270	118,198	6,806	528
41	2,441	198,309	29,083	12,541	73	275	113,356	6,215	388
42	2,298	191,830	27,912	11,938	74	227	113,452	5,757	337
43	2,126	186,385	26,978	11,534	75	184	104,319	4,735	226
44	2,049	180,362	26,031	11,280	76+	1,123	735,905	21,715	551

Note: Data are essentially an inventory of current licenses as of January 1, 1996, according to the records of the Florida Department of Highway Safety and Motor Vehicles. Figures do not include temporary permits.

Source: State of Florida, Department of Highway Safety and Motor Vehicles, Division of Driver Licenses, unpublished data.

Table 13.34. DRIVER LICENSES: NUMBER ISSUED BY COUNTY OF DRIVER'S MAILING ADDRESS AND BY SEX OF LICENSE HOLDER IN THE STATE AND COUNTIES OF FLORIDA JANUARY 1, 1996

County of driver's mailing address	Male	Female	County of driver's mailing address	Male	Female
Florida	6,173,994	5,845,162	Lake	77,628	77,174
			Lee	170,319	164,236
Alachua	79,377	77,813	Leon	82,318	83,775
Baker	6,872	6,757	Levy	11,518	11,069
Bay	63,046	61,091	Liberty	1,927	1,880
Bradford	8,014	7,848	Madison	5,798	5,781
Brevard	200,016	189,751	Manatee	95,964	95,168
Broward	617,034	577,543	Marion	98,603	98,277
Calhoun	3,822	3,865	Martin	53,489	50,764
Charlotte	56,428	56,345	Monroe	47,733	35,735
Citrus	47,513	46,281	Nassau	22,667	21,324
Clay	51,580	50,189	Okaloosa	70,905	68,106
Collier	92,112	82,355	Okeechobee	15,833	13,206
Columbia	17,147	17,368	Orange	340,860	318,752
Dade	857,590	735,153	Osceola	63,046	57,616
De Soto	10,061	8,762	Palm Beach	444,508	425,009
Dixie	4,446	4,190	Pasco	133,546	132,128
Duval	275,124	278,743	Pinellas	373,318	378,610
Escambia	113,487	112,242	Polk	174,888	170,387
Flagler	17,387	16,985	Putnam	24,979	24,005
Franklin	3,789	3,540	St. Johns	43,908	43,402
Gadsden	14,074	14,072	St. Lucie	72,749	69,059
Gilchrist	3,950	3,782	Santa Rosa	42,326	41,167
Glades	2,198	1,840	Sarasota	138,265	141,632
Gulf	4,983	4,868	Seminole	133,836	131,253
Hamilton	3,873	3,890	Sumter	13,708	13,367
Hardee	9,889	7,862	Suwannee	11,971	11,722
Hendry	13,894	10,419	Taylor	6,808	6,807
Hernando	51,966	51,661	Union	3,047	3,019
Highlands	34,063	32,626	Volusia	181,050	173,637
Hillsborough	368,374	355,558	Wakulla	6,265	6,081
Holmes	6,523	6,279	Walton	11,340	10,905
Indian River	48,360	47,478	Washington	7,309	7,183
Jackson	16,030	16,164	Unknown county 1/	24,739	20,490
Jefferson	4,315	4,182	Out-of-state 2/	57,870	33,394
Lafayette	1,619	1,540			

1/ Licenses mailed to addresses which do not permit specification of county. Also includes licenses with incorrect or unknown zip codes.

2/ Licenses mailed to out-of-state addresses.

Note: Data are essentially an inventory of current licenses as of January 1, 1996, according to the records of the Florida Department of Highway Safety and Motor Vehicles. Figures include restricted, operator, chauffeur, and commercial licenses. Figures do not include temporary permits.

Source: State of Florida, Department of Highway Safety and Motor Vehicles, Division of Driver Licenses, unpublished data.

Table 13.35. EMPLOYMENT: AVERAGE MONTHLY PRIVATE REPORTING UNITS, EMPLOYMENT AND PAYROLL COVERED BY UNEMPLOYMENT COMPENSATION LAW BY TRANSPORTATION INDUSTRY IN FLORIDA, 1995

SIC code	Industry	Number of reporting units	Number of employees	Payroll ($1,000)
41	Passenger transportation	737	13,103	20,667
411	Local and suburban passenger transportation	379	7,583	13,045
412	Taxicabs	117	1,483	2,338
413	Intercity and rural bus transportation	34	864	1,458
414	Bus charter service	76	1,979	2,862
415	School buses	122	1,177	947
417	Terminal and service facilities for motor vehicle passenger transportation	9	17	17
42	Motor freight transportation and warehousing	4,799	67,440	145,010
421	Trucking and courier services, except air	4,109	61,875	134,308
422	Public warehousing and storage	681	5,490	10,482
423	Terminal and joint terminal maintenance facilities for motor freight transportation	9	76	220
44	Water transportation	1,047	20,452	48,935
441	Deep sea foreign transportation of freight	30	1,241	4,699
442	Deep sea domestic transportation of freight	17	1,429	4,932
444	Water transportation of freight, NEC	18	625	1,647
448	Water transportation of passengers	119	5,479	13,794
449	Services incidental to water transportation	862	11,679	23,863
45	Air transportation	1,097	54,504	137,787
451	Air transportation, scheduled, and air courier services	396	36,033	103,415
452	Air transportation, nonscheduled	216	4,801	11,493
458	Airports, flying fields, and airport terminal services	485	13,670	22,879
47	Transportation services	4,409	31,510	63,689
472	Arrangement of passenger transportation	2,609	17,094	30,706
473	Arrangement of transportation of freight and cargo	1,606	11,431	28,862
474	Rental of railroad cars	4	60	179
478	Miscellaneous services incidental to transportation	190	2,925	3,941

NEC Not elsewhere classified.

Note: Private employment. Data are preliminary. Detail may not add to totals due to disclosure editing and/or rounding. See Tables 23.70, 23.71, 23.72, 23.73, and 23.74 for public employment data.

Source: State of Florida, Department of Labor and Employment Security, Bureau of Labor Market Information, "Employment and Wages" (ES-202), unpublished data.

Table 13.36. TRANSPORTATION AND PUBLIC UTILITIES: AVERAGE MONTHLY PRIVATE REPORTING UNITS, EMPLOYMENT, AND PAYROLL COVERED BY UNEMPLOYMENT COMPENSATION LAW IN THE STATE AND COUNTIES OF FLORIDA, 1995

County	Number of re- porting units	Number of em- ployees	Payroll ($1,000)	County	Number of re- porting units	Number of em- ployees	Payroll ($1,000)
		Transportation and public utilities (SIC codes 40-49)					
Florida	14,660	295,747	795,059	Lake	123	2,124	5,342
				Lee	367	6,386	14,057
Alachua	118	2,082	5,050	Leon	148	3,286	8,786
Baker	22	170	467	Levy	19	278	569
Bay	154	2,220	5,130	Liberty	14	100	170
Bradford	16	164	479	Madison	17	116	265
Brevard	321	4,434	11,101	Manatee	139	1,517	3,704
Broward	1,494	28,493	76,484	Marion	185	2,451	5,990
Calhoun	7	41	94	Martin	127	1,761	4,957
Charlotte	71	1,011	2,311	Monroe	157	1,673	3,377
Citrus	77	1,826	7,033	Nassau	55	456	1,040
Clay	74	941	2,553	Okaloosa	143	1,861	4,248
Collier	211	2,027	4,705	Okeechobee	29	196	447
Columbia	40	500	1,304	Orange	981	29,821	77,644
Dade	3,299	76,319	217,180	Osceola	101	738	1,326
De Soto	23	161	238	Palm Beach	902	14,598	44,781
Dixie	18	64	76	Pasco	188	2,505	6,632
Duval	908	27,692	68,831	Pinellas	649	12,565	34,265
Escambia	275	5,295	14,038	Polk	398	8,171	18,824
Flagler	23	221	580	Putnam	39	458	1,262
Franklin	21	118	233	St. Johns	75	520	1,120
Gadsden	23	241	550	St. Lucie	121	2,757	9,179
Glades	4	82	195	Santa Rosa	73	1,045	2,572
Gulf	12	282	653	Sarasota	276	3,603	8,945
Hamilton	8	91	275	Seminole	240	4,826	13,973
Hardee	17	117	273	Sumter	29	460	1,152
Hendry	24	434	603	Suwannee	32	345	819
Hernando	67	924	1,964	Taylor	17	111	298
Highlands	61	623	1,381	Union	17	333	551
Hillsborough	884	26,506	76,591	Volusia	285	3,494	8,048
Holmes	11	60	152	Wakulla	16	97	222
Indian River	85	651	1,320	Walton	28	415	916
Jackson	33	297	743	Washington	15	296	832
Jefferson	10	109	295				
Lafayette	5	23	43	Multicounty 1/	240	2,141	5,727

1/ Reporting units without a fixed location within the state or of unknown county location.

Note: See Table 13.35 for a list of industries. Private employment. Only counties for which data are disclosed are shown. Detail may not add to totals due to disclosure editing and/or rounding. See Tables 23.70, 23.71, 23.72, 23.73, and 23.74 for public employment data.

Source: State of Florida, Department of Labor and Employment Security, Bureau of Labor Market Information, "Employment and Wages" (ES-202), unpublished data.

Table 13.37. PASSENGER TRANSPORTATION AND MOTOR FREIGHT TRANSPORTATION AND WAREHOUSING: AVERAGE MONTHLY PRIVATE REPORTING UNITS, EMPLOYMENT AND PAYROLL COVERED BY UNEMPLOYMENT COMPENSATION LAW IN THE STATE AND COUNTIES OF FLORIDA, 1995

County	Number of reporting units	Number of employees	Payroll ($1,000)	County	Number of reporting units	Number of employees	Payroll ($1,000)
Passenger transportation (SIC code 41)							
Florida	737	13,103	20,667	Leon	9	148	210
				Manatee	4	16	24
Alachua	7	62	66	Marion	8	70	76
Brevard	21	296	459	Martin	4	22	36
Broward	68	1,727	2,585	Monroe	9	120	169
Charlotte	7	64	95	Okaloosa	5	17	12
Citrus	3	17	17	Orange	59	2,464	4,061
Clay	3	10	6	Osceola	10	108	124
Collier	9	75	79	Palm Beach	53	721	1,354
Dade	113	1,638	3,427	Pasco	8	100	109
Duval	132	2,009	2,697	Pinellas	36	1,080	1,714
Franklin	4	17	15	Polk	13	163	175
Hernando	9	18	16	St. Lucie	9	104	130
Hillsborough	22	436	623	Sarasota	17	90	107
Indian River	4	11	12	Seminole	7	91	132
Lake	5	144	291	Volusia	18	450	761
Lee	19	172	227				
Motor freight transportation and warehousing (SIC code 42)							
Florida	4,799	67,440	145,010	Hillsborough	335	5,607	12,572
				Holmes	5	10	14
Alachua	48	643	1,264	Indian River	28	137	277
Baker	14	54	87	Jackson	16	52	97
Bay	49	480	888	Lafayette	4	16	21
Brevard	101	1,210	2,655	Lake	49	577	1,143
Broward	424	4,581	9,526	Lee	124	1,037	2,052
Calhoun	6	17	30	Leon	49	841	1,742
Charlotte	19	206	327	Levy	8	60	96
Citrus	36	161	223	Liberty	12	60	81
Clay	32	232	480	Madison	7	15	15
Collier	65	355	661	Manatee	49	559	1,092
Columbia	26	156	323	Marion	107	1,413	3,191
Dade	776	10,707	23,996	Martin	31	798	2,025
De Soto	13	88	121	Monroe	22	239	477
Duval	384	10,941	26,218	Nassau	22	78	171
Escambia	134	1,292	2,349	Okaloosa	39	582	1,036
Flagler	5	22	36	Okeechobee	17	91	177
Franklin	5	12	18	Orange	348	6,787	14,245
Gadsden	10	62	89	Osceola	27	113	151
Gilchrist	4	16	25	Palm Beach	272	2,634	5,646
Gulf	3	17	25	Pasco	84	1,025	2,013
Hamilton	5	75	219	Pinellas	161	1,910	3,602
Hardee	8	19	27	Polk	224	5,813	12,728
Hernando	27	466	877	Putnam	17	120	163
Highlands	22	121	220	St. Johns	22	162	246

See footnotes at end of table.

Continued . . .

Table 13.37. PASSENGER TRANSPORTATION AND MOTOR FREIGHT TRANSPORTATION AND WAREHOUSING: AVERAGE MONTHLY PRIVATE REPORTING UNITS, EMPLOYMENT AND PAYROLL COVERED BY UNEMPLOYMENT COMPENSATION LAW IN THE STATE AND COUNTIES OF FLORIDA, 1995 (Continued)

County	Number of reporting units	Number of employees	Payroll ($1,000)	County	Number of reporting units	Number of employees	Payroll ($1,000)
Motor freight transportation and warehousing (SIC code 42) (Continued)							
St. Lucie	49	384	732	Taylor	5	11	15
Santa Rosa	28	121	220	Union	14	316	528
Sarasota	70	714	1,335	Volusia	103	873	1,590
Seminole	75	833	1,549	Wakulla	6	37	66
Sumter	17	94	179	Walton	9	39	73
Suwannee	18	94	142	Multicounty 1/	80	930	2,223

1/ Reporting units without a fixed location within the state or of unknown county location.

Note: Private employment. For a list of three-digit code industries included see Table 13.35. Data are preliminary. Only counties for which data are disclosed are shown. Detail may not add to totals due to disclosure editing and/or rounding. See Tables 23.70, 23.71, 23.72, 23.73, and 23.74 for public employment data.

Table 13.38. WATER AND AIR TRANSPORTATION AND TRANSPORTATION SERVICES: AVERAGE MONTHLY PRIVATE REPORTING UNITS, EMPLOYMENT, AND PAYROLL COVERED BY COMPENSATION LAW IN THE STATE AND COUNTIES OF FLORIDA, 1995

County	Number of reporting units	Number of employees	Payroll ($1,000)	County	Number of reporting units	Number of employees	Payroll ($1,000)
Water transportation (SIC code 44)							
Florida	1,047	20,452	48,935	Manatee	23	168	368
				Martin	31	137	230
Bay	33	298	556	Monroe	61	548	898
Brevard	31	493	959	Okaloosa	20	86	106
Broward	153	2,362	5,960	Orange	5	24	33
Charlotte	6	47	60	Palm Beach	75	347	692
Citrus	6	45	56	Pasco	7	13	21
Collier	31	266	475	Pinellas	65	530	881
Dade	157	8,008	20,764	Putnam	3	5	4
Dixie	5	22	16	St. Johns	10	44	96
Duval	87	4,030	9,614	St. Lucie	9	66	96
Escambia	23	474	835	Sarasota	15	143	219
Franklin	5	34	46	Seminole	8	79	244
Hendry	3	37	46	Volusia	21	103	149
Hillsborough	55	1,279	4,208	Wakulla	5	33	39
Lake	5	22	32				
Lee	42	282	468	Multicounty 1/	11	28	99

See footnotes at end of table.

Continued . . .

Table 13.38. WATER AND AIR TRANSPORTATION AND TRANSPORTATION SERVICES: AVERAGE MONTHLY PRIVATE REPORTING UNITS, EMPLOYMENT, AND PAYROLL COVERED BY COMPENSATION LAW IN THE STATE AND COUNTIES OF FLORIDA, 1995 (Continued)

County	Number of re-porting units	Number of em-ployees	Payroll ($1,000)	County	Number of re-porting units	Number of em-ployees	Payroll ($1,000)
			Air transportation (SIC code 45)				
Florida	1,097	54,504	137,787	Indian River	9	76	146
				Lee	20	1,361	1,730
Alachua	5	136	351	Manatee	7	77	161
Bay	12	164	278	Osceola	7	64	87
Brevard	19	383	822	Palm Beach	63	1,285	3,067
Broward	147	5,989	14,328	Pasco	5	57	90
Charlotte	5	51	129	St. Lucie	9	323	603
Collier	15	167	470	Santa Rosa	6	312	826
Dade	359	25,389	72,920	Sarasota	17	357	778
Escambia	17	595	1,834	Volusia	25	323	642
Highlands	9	62	112				
Hillsborough	47	5,633	12,726	Multicounty 1/	22	428	694
			Transportation services (SIC code 47)				
Florida	4,409	31,510	63,689	Leon	24	147	255
				Manatee	31	107	145
Alachua	24	132	238	Marion	21	76	118
Bay	22	157	362	Martin	34	130	234
Brevard	86	374	631	Monroe	22	84	117
Broward	483	4,033	8,624	Nassau	12	112	180
Charlotte	17	67	82	Okaloosa	27	122	153
Citrus	9	35	32	Orange	302	2,809	4,696
Clay	16	84	207	Osceola	37	263	380
Collier	57	226	353	Palm Beach	295	1,889	4,575
Dade	1,594	12,142	27,651	Pasco	43	141	179
Duval	147	1,357	3,301	Pinellas	226	1,837	2,665
Escambia	30	132	176	Polk	69	449	942
Flagler	6	23	30	Putnam	6	16	18
Hernando	18	82	102	St. Johns	21	69	132
Highlands	12	25	39	St. Lucie	24	113	149
Hillsborough	230	1,881	3,308	Santa Rosa	11	43	50
Indian River	22	77	114	Sarasota	88	409	735
Jackson	3	5	4	Seminole	85	658	874
Lake	31	150	229	Volusia	70	269	342
Lee	79	285	416	Multicounty 1/	52	156	463

1/ Reporting units without a fixed location within the state or of unknown county location.

Note: Private employment. For a list of three-digit code industries included see Table 13.35. Data are preliminary. Only counties for which data are disclosed are shown. Detail may not add to totals due to disclosure editing and/or rounding. See Tables 23.70, 23.71, 23.72, 23.73, and 23.74 for public employment data.

Source for Tables 13.37 and 13.38: State of Florida, Department of Labor and Employment Security, Bureau of Labor Market Information, "Employment and Wages" (ES-202), unpublished data.

Table 13.40. MOTOR VEHICLE REGISTRATIONS: NUMBER OF OUT-OF-STATE VEHICLES REGISTERED IN FLORIDA BY STATE OF PREVIOUS REGISTRATION 1991 THROUGH 1995

State in 1995 rank order	1991	1992	1993	1994	1995 Number	1995 Percentage of total
Total	335,649	359,198	382,452	403,095	479,275	100.0
New York	37,492	37,940	40,188	44,185	51,013	10.6
Georgia	29,856	31,727	33,314	35,120	45,040	9.4
New Jersey	23,505	23,020	23,357	24,982	27,896	5.8
Alabama	16,377	17,778	18,969	20,695	25,948	5.1
Ohio	16,939	17,418	19,217	19,929	24,341	5.1
Pennsylvania	15,824	16,269	17,836	18,714	23,032	4.8
Michigan	16,365	16,920	18,498	18,825	21,945	4.6
North Carolina	13,259	14,459	15,891	16,896	20,837	4.3
Virginia	13,727	14,747	15,030	16,331	19,998	3.7
Illinois	12,460	13,399	15,107	15,929	18,475	3.9
California	12,357	14,395	15,782	15,525	17,816	4.2
Texas	11,812	14,088	14,388	15,412	17,505	3.7
Massachusetts	14,262	13,777	14,095	13,686	15,232	3.2
Tennessee	8,358	11,401	11,536	10,896	14,221	3.0
South Carolina	7,663	9,254	9,978	10,772	12,677	2.6
Maryland	7,801	9,055	9,211	9,985	11,740	2.4
Indiana	7,677	7,908	9,064	9,471	11,211	2.3
Connecticut	8,518	9,210	9,516	9,545	10,995	2.3
Kentucky	4,490	4,529	4,967	5,239	6,358	1.3
Louisiana	3,934	4,568	5,169	5,220	6,217	1.3
Missouri	4,063	4,333	4,451	4,852	5,608	1.2
Wisconsin	3,603	3,915	4,345	4,567	5,379	1.1
Colorado	3,032	3,212	3,466	3,991	4,941	1.0
New Hampshire	3,997	3,693	4,048	3,983	4,684	1.0
Mississippi	2,833	3,224	3,323	3,897	4,562	1.0
Maine	2,749	2,720	2,948	3,083	3,837	0.7
Minnesota	2,480	2,547	2,983	3,046	3,667	0.8
Arizona	2,110	2,506	2,560	2,753	3,494	0.6
Oklahoma	1,972	2,075	2,414	3,391	3,090	0.6
Rhode Island	2,398	2,433	2,617	2,581	2,971	0.8
West Virginia	2,131	2,366	2,373	2,559	2,872	0.6
Iowa	1,723	1,764	1,986	1,955	2,573	0.5
Washington	1,568	1,753	1,962	2,121	2,523	0.5
Arkansas	1,600	1,763	1,927	2,054	2,315	0.5
Kansas	1,399	1,643	2,001	2,042	2,192	0.5
Other states	10,234	11,793	12,430	12,639	14,559	3.0
Other areas 1/	4,816	5,233	5,134	5,987	7,225	1.5
Special affidavit	265	363	371	237	286	0.1

1/ Includes Canada, Puerto Rico, other Caribbean islands, and other foreign countries.

Source: State of Florida, Department of Highway Safety and Motor Vehicles, Division of Motor Vehicles, unpublished data.

Table 13.41. MOTOR VEHICLE REGISTRATIONS: NUMBER OF OUT-OF-STATE VEHICLES REGISTERED BY COUNTY OF REGISTRATION IN THE STATE AND COUNTIES OF FLORIDA, 1994 AND 1995

County	1994	1995 Number	1995 Percentage of total
Florida	403,095	479,275	100.0
Alachua	4,810	6,103	1.3
Baker	295	381	0.1
Bay	8,106	9,627	2.0
Bradford	408	602	0.1
Brevard	13,901	16,271	3.4
Broward	26,195	27,351	5.7
Calhoun	195	252	0.1
Charlotte	5,313	5,849	1.2
Citrus	3,747	4,371	0.9
Clay	3,796	5,061	1.1
Collier	8,106	9,718	2.0
Columbia	1,189	1,527	0.3
Dade	33,743	41,911	8.7
De Soto	869	859	0.2
Dixie	204	284	0.1
Duval	21,552	25,004	5.2
Escambia	14,730	17,200	3.6
Flagler	2,135	2,624	0.5
Franklin	273	393	0.1
Gadsden	757	1,089	0.2
Gilchrist	197	294	0.1
Glades	149	191	A/
Gulf	354	486	0.1
Hamilton	278	387	0.1
Hardee	579	696	0.1
Hendry	820	1,051	0.2
Hernando	3,637	4,109	0.9
Highlands	2,494	2,933	0.6
Hillsborough	21,950	26,213	5.5
Holmes	748	980	0.2
Indian River	3,191	3,868	0.8
Jackson	1,944	2,295	0.5
Jefferson	344	423	0.1
Lafayette	92	109	A/
Lake	6,066	7,024	1.5
Lee	14,111	16,364	3.4
Leon	6,290	7,920	1.7
Levy	625	798	0.2
Liberty	114	179	A/
Madison	491	611	0.1
Manatee	8,274	11,473	2.4
Marion	7,834	9,669	2.0
Martin	3,771	4,874	1.0
Monroe	3,647	4,655	1.0
Nassau	1,686	2,153	0.4
Okaloosa	10,154	11,814	2.5
Okeechobee	877	1,148	0.2
Orange	23,046	27,357	5.7
Osceola	4,382	5,851	1.2
Palm Beach	24,751	27,934	5.8
Pasco	9,764	11,907	2.5
Pinellas	23,673	27,603	5.8
Polk	12,067	13,943	2.9
Putnam	1,646	1,927	0.4
St. Johns	4,023	4,698	1.0
St. Lucie	5,261	6,433	1.3
Santa Rosa	4,331	5,986	1.2
Sarasota	10,664	12,643	2.6
Seminole	10,712	12,143	2.5
Sumter	958	1,346	0.3
Suwannee	760	978	0.2
Taylor	396	526	0.1
Union	299	213	A/
Volusia	13,551	16,041	3.3
Wakulla	342	480	0.1
Walton	905	1,416	0.3
Washington	523	656	0.1

A/ Less than 0.05 percent.

Source: State of Florida, Department of Highway Safety and Motor Vehicles, Division of Motor Vehicles, unpublished data.

Table 13.45. TRAFFIC STATISTICS: DRIVERS, VEHICLES, MILEAGE, ACCIDENTS, INJURIES AND DEATHS IN FLORIDA, 1985 THROUGH 1995

Year	Licensed drivers	Registered vehicles	Vehicle miles (millions)	Acci- dents 1/	Nonfatal injuries	Deaths	Mileage death rate 2/
1985	9,630,975	10,827,693	88,057	250,412	216,596	2,870	3.3
1986	9,924,110	11,651,253	87,325	242,381	219,352	2,874	3.3
1987	10,241,063	11,738,273	92,865	240,429	215,886	2,891	3.1
1988	10,648,019	11,997,948	105,030	256,543	230,738	3,152	3.0
1989	11,109,288	12,276,272	108,876	252,439	230,060	3,033	2.8
1990	11,612,402	12,465,790	109,997	216,245	214,208	2,951	2.7
1991	12,170,821	A/ 11,184,146	113,484	195,312	195,122	2,523	2.2
1992	B/ 11,550,126	11,205,298	114,000	196,176	205,432	2,480	2.2
1993	11,767,409	11,159,938	119,768	199,039	212,454	2,719	2.3
1994	11,992,578	11,393,982	120,929	206,183	223,458	2,722	2.3
1995	12,019,156	12,062,731	127,800	228,589	233,900	2,847	2.2

A/ Decrease primarily reflects a change in accounting procedures to eliminate double counting of vehicles involved in tag transfers.
B/ Decrease reflects the exclusion of surrendered licenses, disqualified A, B, or C licenses, and licenses expired more than 15 months.
1/ Statutory revisions in 1989 reduced the number of non-injury accidents required to be reported.
2/ The number of deaths per 100 million vehicle miles traveled.
Note: Some data may be revised. See Note on Table 13.47.

Table 13.46. MOTOR VEHICLE ACCIDENTS: NUMBER OF DRIVERS AND PEDESTRIANS ASSIGNED A CONTRIBUTING CAUSE BY TYPE OF CIRCUMSTANCE IN FLORIDA, 1995

Cause of accident	All accidents		Fatal accidents		Injury accidents	
	Number	Percentage of total	Number	Percentage of total	Number	Percentage of total
Total	394,311	100.0	5,570	100.0	291,784	100.0
No improper driving action	195,300	49.5	1,883	33.8	139,452	47.8
Speed too fast	8,442	2.1	554	9.9	6,319	2.2
Failed to yield right of way	44,305	11.2	644	11.6	35,269	12.1
Disregarded stop sign	3,837	1.0	84	1.5	3,037	1.0
Disregarded other traffic control	9,188	2.3	137	2.5	7,368	2.5
Drove left of center	1,875	0.5	163	2.9	1,400	0.5
Improper overtaking	6,520	1.7	93	1.7	4,768	1.6
Followed too closely	6,751	1.7	3	0.1	5,248	1.8
Alcohol, under influence	9,440	2.4	337	6.1	5,051	1.7
Careless driving	67,069	17.0	751	13.5	52,411	18.0
Mechanical defect	2,387	0.6	32	0.6	1,738	0.6
Other	39,197	9.9	889	16.0	29,723	10.2

Note: See Note on Table 13.47.

Source for Tables 13.45 and 13.46: State of Florida, Department of Highway Safety and Motor Vehicles, Office of Management and Planning Services, *Florida Traffic Crash Facts, 1995*.

Table 13.47. MOTOR VEHICLE ACCIDENTS: NUMBER OF ACCIDENTS AND PERSONS INVOLVED BY TYPE OF ACCIDENT IN FLORIDA, 1995

Type of accident	Number of accidents: Total	Fatal	Nonfatal injury	Property damage
Total	228,589	2,586	143,839	82,164
Motor vehicle in transport	158,684	1,128	105,823	51,733
Fixed object	24,933	424	12,431	12,078
Other object	564	4	259	301
Parked motor vehicle	10,690	24	1,252	9,414
Pedestrian	7,379	522	6,695	162
Bicyclist	5,590	122	5,092	376
Moped	80	2	74	4
Overturning	3,781	127	3,002	652
Noncollison	6,436	142	3,986	2,308
Motor vehicle on other roadway	452	1	307	144
Animal	403	1	254	148
Railway train	58	14	20	24
Other and not stated	9,539	75	4,644	4,820

Type of accident	Number of persons: Total killed	Injured: Incapacitating injury	Injured: Non-incapacitating or possible injury	No injury 1/
Total	2,847	31,657	202,243	359,939
Motor vehicle in transport	1,301	21,681	163,693	300,375
Fixed object	470	3,408	13,204	15,666
Other object	5	45	309	783
Parked motor vehicle	24	221	1,415	8,046
Pedestrian	531	1,935	5,410	8,797
Bicyclist	123	982	4,375	6,932
Moped	2	19	62	126
Overturning	133	1,095	3,354	1,755
Noncollison	159	1,165	4,269	4,624
Motor vehicle on other roadway	1	61	475	793
Animal	1	72	258	330
Railway train	19	18	36	130
Other and not stated	78	955	5,383	11,582

1/ Drivers only.

Note: Legally reportable accidents are those involving death, bodily injury, or one or more of the following circumstances: (1) driver leaves the accident scene where death, injury, or property damage has occurred; (2) driver is under the influence of alcohol or drugs; and, (3) a wrecker is required to remove an inoperative vehicle.

Source: State of Florida, Department of Highway Safety and Motor Vehicles, Office of Management and Planning Services, *Florida Traffic Crash Facts, 1995*.

Table 13.48. MOTOR VEHICLE ACCIDENTS: DRIVERS AND MOTOR VEHICLES INVOLVED IN ACCIDENTS BY AGE, SEX, AND RESIDENCE OF DRIVER AND BY TYPE OF MOTOR VEHICLE IN FLORIDA, 1995

Item	All accidents	Fatal accidents	Injury accidents
Drivers involved in accidents, total 1/	365,111	1,615	150,471
Age and sex			
15 and under	3,699	35	2,883
16	7,599	15	3,030
17	9,536	26	3,916
18	10,702	42	4,399
19	9,936	46	4,083
20	9,837	42	4,130
21-24	38,846	155	16,154
25-34	89,944	327	36,724
35-44	72,220	289	29,499
45-54	44,758	162	18,152
55-64	26,711	108	10,761
65-74	21,390	148	8,652
75 and over	15,264	196	6,333
Not stated	4,669	24	1,755
Male	222,204	1,194	81,623
Female	142,243	420	68,830
Not stated	664	1	18
Residence			
County of crash	304,499	1,220	127,094
Resident elsewhere in state	43,176	299	17,509
Nonresident of state	13,897	82	4,928
Foreign	2,587	5	745
Not stated	952	9	195
Vehicles involved in accidents, total	451,443	4,385	288,342
Passenger vehicle	323,509	2,802	216,633
Recreational	370	7	220
Light truck (pickup)	55,584	706	36,167
Medium truck	5,325	96	3,443
Truck (heavy)	2,811	65	1,787
Truck-tractor (all combination)	4,622	162	2,823
Motorcycle	4,884	190	4,289
All terrain vehicle	325	8	257
Moped	414	7	381
Bicycle	7,520	142	6,844
Law enforcement vehicle	2,896	24	1,694
Emergency vehicle	472	5	263
Taxi cab	2,696	18	1,771
School bus	1,019	8	604
Bus	1,283	7	855
Government/military equipment	1,619	10	935
Other	36,094	128	9,376

1/ Includes bicycle drivers.

Note: Legally reportable accidents are those involving death, bodily injury, or one or more of the following circumstances: (1) driver leaves the accident scene where death, injury, or property damage has occurred; (2) driver is under the influence of alcohol or drugs; and, (3) a wrecker is required to remove an inoperative vehicle.

Source: State of Florida, Department of Highway Safety and Motor Vehicles, Office of Management and Planning Services, *Florida Traffic Crash Facts, 1995.*

Table 13.49. MOTOR VEHICLE ACCIDENTS: PERSONS KILLED OR INJURED AND TOTAL ACCIDENTS IN THE STATE AND COUNTIES OF FLORIDA, 1995

County	Reported accidents					Persons killed	Persons injured
		Fatal		Injury			
	Total	Number	Per-centage	Number	Per-centage		
Florida 1/	228,589	2,586	1.13	143,839	62.92	2,847	233,900
Alachua	3,414	29	0.85	2,137	62.60	31	3,303
Baker	226	5	2.21	161	71.24	5	260
Bay	2,085	29	1.39	1,365	65.47	33	2,170
Bradford	369	7	1.90	210	56.91	7	352
Brevard	4,650	76	1.63	3,206	68.95	87	5,332
Broward	25,958	199	0.77	15,899	61.25	210	25,308
Calhoun	102	2	1.96	81	79.41	3	127
Charlotte	1,358	20	1.47	844	62.15	23	1,427
Citrus	1,060	32	3.02	779	73.49	35	1,388
Clay	1,006	18	1.79	664	66.00	20	1,110
Collier	2,392	44	1.84	1,472	61.54	49	2,435
Columbia	575	14	2.43	444	77.22	14	737
Dade	43,233	301	0.70	24,480	56.62	333	40,357
De Soto	315	11	3.49	238	75.56	12	379
Dixie	145	2	1.38	115	79.31	2	203
Duval	13,053	111	0.85	7,565	57.96	117	11,810
Escambia	3,985	44	1.10	2,769	69.49	47	4,486
Flagler	360	10	2.78	262	72.78	11	461
Franklin	108	2	1.85	75	69.44	2	126
Gadsden	607	10	1.65	394	64.91	14	716
Gilchrist	90	3	3.33	73	81.11	3	111
Glades	93	5	5.38	65	69.89	6	114
Gulf	88	2	2.27	61	69.32	2	99
Hamilton	126	7	5.56	85	67.46	8	149
Hardee	266	8	3.01	180	67.67	8	347
Hendry	330	16	4.85	241	73.03	18	474
Hernando	993	15	1.51	803	80.87	17	1,352
Highlands	769	26	3.38	553	71.91	30	1,011
Hillsborough	21,071	178	0.84	12,531	59.47	203	19,981
Holmes	151	6	3.97	122	80.79	8	222
Indian River	1,191	23	1.93	738	61.96	25	1,239
Jackson	458	10	2.18	345	75.33	12	648
Jefferson	178	6	3.37	144	80.90	6	245
Lafayette	46	0	0.00	40	86.96	0	64
Lake	1,677	39	2.33	1,143	68.16	44	1,865
Lee	7,170	69	0.96	4,503	62.80	70	7,146

See footnotes at end of table. Continued . . .

Table 13.49. MOTOR VEHICLE ACCIDENTS: PERSONS KILLED OR INJURED AND TOTAL ACCIDENTS IN THE STATE AND COUNTIES OF FLORIDA, 1995 (Continued)

County	Reported accidents					Persons killed	Persons injured
	Total	Fatal		Injury			
		Number	Per-centage	Number	Per-centage		
Leon	4,921	38	0.77	2,576	52.35	40	4,066
Levy	303	5	1.65	224	73.93	5	371
Liberty	64	1	1.56	45	70.31	1	99
Madison	217	13	5.99	167	76.96	17	298
Manatee	3,190	48	1.50	1,971	61.79	51	3,129
Marion	2,967	68	2.29	2,273	76.61	79	3,936
Martin	1,455	22	1.51	940	64.60	26	1,533
Monroe	1,123	20	1.78	770	68.57	22	1,191
Nassau	401	16	3.99	274	68.33	18	472
Okaloosa	1,671	23	1.38	1,198	71.69	28	2,002
Okeechobee	365	5	1.37	258	70.68	6	425
Orange	12,870	129	1.00	9,115	70.82	144	15,047
Osceola	1,865	36	1.93	1,265	67.83	40	2,302
Palm Beach	14,929	184	1.23	9,638	64.56	200	15,411
Pasco	3,344	61	1.82	2,468	73.80	67	4,178
Pinellas	11,919	117	0.98	8,214	68.92	122	13,074
Polk	6,735	114	1.69	4,269	63.39	129	7,176
Putnam	869	20	2.30	553	63.64	21	907
St. Johns	1,297	18	1.39	878	67.69	20	1,421
St. Lucie	2,200	35	1.59	1,480	67.27	40	2,553
Santa Rosa	1,036	24	2.32	752	72.59	27	1,369
Sarasota	3,856	45	1.17	2,361	61.23	46	3,626
Seminole	3,326	33	0.99	2,150	64.64	40	3,361
Sumter	394	7	1.78	286	72.59	8	526
Suwannee	296	14	4.73	199	67.23	15	360
Taylor	271	9	3.32	163	60.15	9	307
Union	87	1	1.15	63	72.41	1	105
Volusia	6,016	74	1.23	3,853	64.05	80	5,962
Wakulla	194	7	3.61	139	71.65	7	230
Walton	384	12	3.13	283	73.70	14	505
Washington	182	8	4.40	144	79.12	9	288

1/ Includes data not distributed by county.

Note: Legally reportable accidents are those involving death, bodily injury, or one or more of the following circumstances: (1) driver leaves the accident scene where death, injury, or property damage has occurred; (2) driver is under the influence of alcohol or drugs; and, (3) a wrecker is required to remove an inoperative vehicle.

Source: State of Florida, Department of Highway Safety and Motor Vehicles, Office of Management and Planning Services, *Florida Traffic Crash Facts, 1995.*

Table 13.50. ALCOHOL-RELATED MOTOR VEHICLE ACCIDENTS AND FATALITIES: NUMBER PERCENTAGE OF TOTAL, AND ACCIDENTS PER 100,000 POPULATION IN THE STATE AND COUNTIES OF FLORIDA, 1995

County	Alcohol-related accidents			Alcohol-related fatalities	
	Total	As a percentage of all accidents	Per 100,000 population	Total	As a percentage of all fatalities
Florida 1/	24,873	10.88	175.8	1,073	37.69
Alachua	342	10.02	172.5	15	48.39
Baker	45	19.91	221.9	5	100.00
Bay	404	19.38	290.3	20	60.61
Bradford	68	18.43	279.4	3	42.86
Brevard	776	16.69	174.4	36	41.38
Broward	2,291	8.83	167.9	55	26.19
Calhoun	22	21.57	183.5	3	100.00
Charlotte	165	12.15	129.3	8	34.78
Citrus	186	17.55	176.4	10	28.57
Clay	170	16.90	140.6	11	55.00
Collier	371	15.51	198.9	16	32.65
Columbia	111	19.30	220.3	3	21.43
Dade	2,577	5.96	128.0	82	24.62
De Soto	60	19.05	225.2	4	33.33
Dixie	29	20.00	233.6	1	50.00
Duval	1,231	9.43	171.4	34	29.06
Escambia	669	16.79	236.6	22	46.81
Flagler	65	18.06	175.7	3	27.27
Franklin	27	25.00	263.8	2	100.00
Gadsden	117	19.28	261.5	11	78.57
Gilchrist	20	22.22	168.2	1	33.33
Glades	23	24.73	269.0	5	83.33
Gulf	25	28.41	188.4	1	50.00
Hamilton	28	22.22	224.2	5	62.50
Hardee	34	12.78	148.6	4	50.00
Hendry	68	20.61	230.5	8	44.44
Hernando	143	14.40	121.3	5	29.41
Highlands	102	13.26	132.0	7	23.33
Hillsborough	2,070	9.82	231.8	71	34.98
Holmes	25	16.56	143.8	2	25.00
Indian River	165	13.85	164.6	15	60.00
Jackson	74	16.16	158.9	7	58.33
Jefferson	29	16.29	214.7	1	16.67
Lafayette	12	26.09	184.2	0	0.00
Lake	249	14.85	140.7	11	25.00

See footnotes at end of table. Continued . . .

Table 13.50. ALCOHOL-RELATED MOTOR VEHICLE ACCIDENTS AND FATALITIES: NUMBER PERCENTAGE OF TOTAL, AND ACCIDENTS PER 100,000 POPULATION IN THE STATE AND COUNTIES OF FLORIDA, 1995 (Continued)

County	Alcohol-related accidents			Alcohol-related fatalities	
	Total	As a percentage of all accidents	Per 100,000 population	Total	As a percentage of all fatalities
Lee	926	12.91	245.8	33	47.14
Leon	497	10.10	228.5	16	40.00
Levy	55	18.15	184.3	4	80.00
Liberty	19	29.69	276.4	1	100.00
Madison	31	14.29	169.0	4	23.53
Manatee	469	14.70	201.1	15	29.41
Marion	346	11.66	154.0	35	44.30
Martin	268	18.42	239.2	12	46.15
Monroe	232	20.66	278.2	13	59.09
Nassau	82	20.45	166.9	8	44.44
Okaloosa	328	19.63	201.6	12	42.86
Okeechobee	80	21.92	243.5	5	83.33
Orange	1,402	10.89	184.7	55	38.19
Osceola	235	12.60	172.0	25	62.50
Palm Beach	1,575	10.55	163.6	66	33.00
Pasco	417	12.47	136.5	29	43.28
Pinellas	1,504	12.62	171.7	41	33.61
Polk	721	10.71	162.7	53	41.09
Putnam	177	20.37	254.6	13	61.90
St. Johns	218	16.81	222.0	9	45.00
St. Lucie	282	12.82	164.8	17	42.50
Santa Rosa	182	17.57	189.4	15	55.56
Sarasota	551	14.29	182.7	21	45.65
Seminole	357	10.73	110.1	18	45.00
Sumter	50	12.69	137.2	3	37.50
Suwannee	56	18.92	183.4	7	46.67
Taylor	59	21.77	322.0	7	77.78
Union	17	19.54	134.4	0	0.00
Volusia	770	12.80	191.1	35	43.75
Wakulla	55	28.35	323.4	7	100.00
Walton	81	21.09	242.4	4	28.57
Washington	23	12.64	121.0	3	33.33

1/ Includes data not distributed by county.

Note: Legally reportable accidents are those involving death, bodily injury, or one or more of the following circumstances: (1) driver leaves the accident scene where death, injury, or property damage has occurred; (2) driver is under the influence of alcohol or drugs; and, (3) a wrecker is required to remove an inoperative vehicle.

Source: State of Florida, Department of Highway Safety and Motor Vehicles, Office of Management and Planning Services, *Florida Traffic Crash Facts, 1995*.

Table 13.60. RAILROADS: MILES OF TRACK AND PERCENTAGE OF STATE SYSTEM BY RAILROAD COMPANY IN FLORIDA, 1994

Company	Tracks (in miles)	Percent- age of state system	Company	Tracks (in miles)	Percent- age of state system
Total	2,988	100.0	Florida Northern	27	0.9
Apalachicola Northern	96	3.2	Florida West Coast	29	1.0
Atlanta and St. Andrews Bay	72	2.4	Georgia Southern and Florida 2/	92	3.1
Burlington Northern	44	1.5	Live Oak, Perry, and South Georgia 2/	52	1.7
CSX Transportation 1/	A/ 1,778	59.5	Seminole Gulf	119	4.0
Florida Central	66	2.2	South Central Florida	101	3.4
Florida East Coast	442	14.8	Terminal Companies	30	1.0
Florida Midland	40	1.3			

A/ Includes the Southeast Florida Rail Corridor owned by the State of Florida between West Palm Beach and Miami.

1/ Amtrak operates in Florida but owns no trackage in the state other than yard and terminal tracks. It operates mainly over CSXT main tracks. It also operates over trackage owned by the State of Florida between West Palm Beach and Miami (81 miles).

2/ Wholly owned subsidiaries of the Norfolk Southern Railway Company.

Source: State of Florida, Department of Transportation, Office of Planning, *1994 Florida Rail System Plan.*

Table 13.70. PORT ACTIVITY: TONNAGE HANDLED IN SPECIFIED PORTS IN FLORIDA FISCAL YEAR 1994-95 OR CALENDAR YEAR 1995

Port and type of cargo	Short tons	Port and type of cargo	Short tons
Canaveral (fiscal year 1994-95), total	3,266,581	Miami (fiscal year 1994-95), total	5,840,815
Exports	1,038,655	Exports	2,778,368
Imports	2,227,926	Imports	3,062,447
Everglades (calendar year 1995), total	20,681,673	Palm Beach (fiscal year 1994-95), total	889,125
Exports	2,620,999	Exports	789,852
Imports	7,014,861	Imports	99,273
Domestic	10,046,964	Panama City (calendar year 1995), total	458,705
Bunker	998,849	Exports	247,904
Ft. Pierce (calendar year 1995), total	141,180	Imports	82,073
Exports	31,168	Domestic	128,729
Imports	110,020	Pensacola (fiscal year 1994-95), total	668,749
Jacksonville 1/ (fiscal year 1994-95), total JPA terminals	5,691,440	Exports	548,171
General cargo exports	2,765,606	Imports	120,578
General cargo imports	2,925,834	Tampa (fiscal year 1994-95), total	51,358,647
Containerized cargo	3,363,991	Exports	13,441,403
Bulk cargo and other	2,327,449	Imports	5,992,772
Manatee (fiscal year 1994-95), total	4,354,759	Domestic	31,924,472
Exports	1,382,261		
Imports	2,972,498		

1/ Tonnage passing through facilities owned by the Jacksonville Port Authority only; therefore they differ from movements into and out of the Port of Jacksonville.

Source: Data are reported in annual or cumulative monthly reports of each port authority.

Table 13.73. EXPORTS AND IMPORTS: VALUE OF SHIPMENTS HANDLED BY CUSTOMS DISTRICTS IN FLORIDA 1990 THROUGH 1995

(amounts in millions of dollars)

Trade area and item	1990	1991	1992	1993	1994	1995
Annual trade, total	30,583	33,702	38,161	39,877	45,937	52,113
Percentage change from previous year	8.27	10.20	13.23	4.50	15.20	13.45
Customs District 52 (Miami)	19,144	21,639	25,666	27,893	31,109	36,067
Percentage change from previous year	10.08	13.03	18.61	8.68	11.53	15.94
Customs District 18 (Tampa)	11,440	12,063	12,496	11,984	14,828	16,047
Percentage change from previous year	5.37	5.45	3.59	-4.10	23.73	8.22
Exports, total	15,518	18,626	21,276	21,820	25,074	29,433
Percentage change from previous year	7.51	20.03	14.23	2.56	14.91	17.38
Customs District 52 (Miami)	11,187	13,377	16,031	17,113	19,468	22,748
Percentage change from previous year	7.26	19.58	19.84	6.75	13.76	16.85
Percentage of Florida exports	72.09	71.82	75.35	78.43	77.64	77.29
Customs District 18 (Tampa)	4,332	5,249	5,246	4,707	5,606	6,685
Percentage change from previous year	8.18	21.17	-0.06	-10.27	19.10	19.25
Percentage of Florida exports	27.92	28.18	24.65	21.57	22.36	22.71
Imports, total	15,065	15,076	16,885	18,057	20,863	22,681
Percentage change from previous year	9.05	0.07	12.00	6.94	15.54	8.71
Customs District 52 (Miami)	7,957	8,262	9,635	10,780	11,641	13,319
Percentage change from previous year	14.31	3.83	16.62	11.88	7.99	14.41
Percentage of Florida exports	52.82	54.80	57.06	59.70	55.80	58.72
Customs District 18 (Tampa)	7,108	6,814	7,250	7,277	9,222	9,362
Percentage change from previous year	3.71	-4.14	6.40	0.37	26.73	1.52
Percentage of Florida exports	47.18	45.20	42.94	40.30	44.20	41.28

Note: Represents all shipments regardless of state of origin or destination.

Source: State of Florida, Department of Commerce, Bureau of Economic Analysis, *Florida International Trade Update.* Release of April 5, 1996.

Table 13.74. EXPORTS AND IMPORTS: LEADING DESTINATIONS AND VALUE OF MERCHANDISE EXPORTED AND LEADING SOURCES AND VALUE OF MERCHANDISE IMPORTED THROUGH FLORIDA CUSTOMS DISTRICTS, 1995

(in dollars)

Export destination	Value	Import source	Value
Total	29,432,710,350	Total	22,680,747,152
Brazil	4,168,803,205	Japan	4,373,834,900
Colombia	2,433,387,586	Dominican Republic	1,290,021,151
Venezuela	2,203,075,286	Germany	1,273,829,372
Argentina	1,781,023,898	Colombia	1,199,275,906
Dominican Republic	1,467,569,149	Brazil	873,459,889
Chile	1,033,367,344	China (Mainland)	855,058,417
China (Mainland)	875,531,899	Honduras	844,744,613
Jamaica	846,488,906	United Kingdom	753,426,715
Paraguay	817,852,674	Costa Rica	732,830,039
Costa Rica	806,713,069	Venezuela	723,096,747
Other	12,998,897,334	Other	9,761,169,403

Note: Data based on information from the U.S. Department of Commerce, Bureau of the Census Trade Data.

Table 13.75. EXPORTS AND IMPORTS: LEADING TYPES AND VALUE OF MERCHANDISE EXPORTED AND IMPORTED THROUGH FLORIDA CUSTOMS DISTRICTS, 1995

(in dollars)

Commodity exported	Value	Commodity imported	Value
Total	29,432,710,350	Total	22,680,747,152
Fertilizers	1,902,523,114	Passenger vehicles	4,795,167,169
Office machines parts/ accessories	1,407,821,822	Men's/boys' trousers	838,286,953
Passenger vehicles	1,191,753,337	Special trans- actions	671,195,389
Transmission apparatus	710,208,543	Frozen crustaceans	508,081,905
I/O devices	466,428,202	Coffee	417,523,010
Tractor parts/accessories	464,549,551	T-shirts	413,228,380
Civil engineering parts/ accessories	460,568,068	Cut flowers	397,017,831
Aircraft parts/accessories	435,777,367	Men's/boys' shirts	395,470,115
Telecommunication parts/ accessories	415,627,655	Inorganic bases	387,138,597
Data processing units	410,936,592	Kerosene	370,068,696
Other	21,566,516,099	Other	13,487,569,107

Note: Data based on information from the U.S. Department of Commerce, Bureau of the Census Trade Data.

Source for Tables 13.74 and 13.75: State of Florida, Department of Commerce, Bureau of Economic Analysis, *Florida International Trade Update*. Release of April 5, 1996.

Table 13.90. AIRPORT ACTIVITY: OPERATIONS AT AIRPORTS WITH FEDERAL AVIATION ADMINISTRATION (FAA)-OPERATED TRAFFIC CONTROL TOWERS IN FLORIDA
FISCAL YEAR 1994-95

Location and type of operation	Total operations 1/	Air carrier 2/	Air taxi 3/	General aviation 4/	Military
Florida	4,685,134	969,252	694,636	2,900,926	120,320
Itinerant	3,499,361	969,252	694,636	1,755,285	80,188
Local	1,185,773	0	0	1,145,641	40,132
Craig Field Jacksonville	111,048	0	8,782	93,151	9,115
Itinerant	72,058	0	8,782	58,527	4,749
Local	38,990	0	0	34,624	4,366
Daytona Beach	254,442	8,958	6,445	238,271	768
Itinerant	209,891	8,958	6,445	193,844	644
Local	44,551	0	0	44,427	124
Ft. Lauderdale	238,108	106,133	60,692	70,389	894
Itinerant	236,481	106,133	60,692	68,762	894
Local	1,627	0	0	1,627	0
Ft. Lauderdale Executive	234,675	0	7,721	226,657	297
Itinerant	187,336	0	7,721	179,326	289
Local	47,339	0	0	47,331	8
Ft. Myers Page Field	96,549	0	4,612	91,441	496
Itinerant	61,799	0	4,612	56,851	336
Local	34,750	0	0	34,590	160
Ft. Myers Regional	67,026	39,492	17,766	9,119	649
Itinerant	66,153	39,492	17,766	8,489	406
Local	873	0	0	630	243
Ft. Pierce	149,906	20	2,350	147,440	96
Itinerant	78,350	20	2,350	75,886	94
Local	71,556	0	0	71,554	2
Gainesville	75,841	2,618	15,038	54,124	4,061
Itinerant	55,818	2,618	15,038	36,553	1,609
Local	20,023	0	0	17,571	2,452
Hollywood	129,955	0	0	129,480	475
Itinerant	49,036	0	0	48,632	404
Local	80,919	0	0	80,848	71
Jacksonville International	142,786	55,610	37,799	27,715	21,662
Itinerant	128,930	55,610	37,799	22,399	13,122
Local	13,856	0	0	5,316	8,540
Key West	92,903	0	33,266	56,608	3,029
Itinerant	74,563	0	33,266	38,916	2,381
Local	18,340	0	0	17,692	648
Lakeland	173,584	0	186	169,578	3,820
Itinerant	87,409	0	186	85,472	1,751
Local	86,175	0	0	84,106	2,069

See footnotes at end of table.

Continued . . .

Table 13.90. AIRPORT ACTIVITY: OPERATIONS AT AIRPORTS WITH FEDERAL AVIATION ADMINISTRATION (FAA)-OPERATED TRAFFIC CONTROL TOWERS IN FLORIDA FISCAL YEAR 1994-95 (Continued)

Location and type of operation	Total operations 1/	Air carrier 2/	Air taxi 3/	General aviation 4/	Military
Melbourne	151,403	6,476	9,103	134,994	830
Itinerant	93,640	6,476	9,103	77,231	830
Local	57,763	0	0	57,763	0
Miami International	576,609	328,209	168,461	72,810	7,129
Itinerant	576,609	328,209	168,461	72,810	7,129
Local	0	0	0	0	0
Naples	19,806	0	3,825	15,956	25
Itinerant	14,120	0	3,825	10,272	23
Local	5,686	0	0	5,684	2
Opa-Locka	188,902	11	7,847	168,629	12,415
Itinerant	108,332	11	7,847	92,422	8,052
Local	80,570	0	0	76,207	4,363
Orlando Executive	164,652	0	17,192	146,184	1,276
Itinerant	119,755	0	17,192	101,469	1,094
Local	44,897	0	0	44,715	182
Orlando International	343,609	189,766	115,581	30,644	7,618
Itinerant	343,609	189,766	115,581	30,644	7,618
Local	0	0	0	0	0
Panama City-Bay County	100,471	2,866	20,974	71,154	5,477
Itinerant	60,869	2,866	20,974	34,635	2,394
Local	39,602	0	0	36,519	3,083
Pensacola	119,795	14,330	35,674	47,045	22,746
Itinerant	97,499	14,330	35,674	30,483	17,012
Local	22,296	0	0	16,562	5,734
Pompano Beach Airpark	135,886	16	3,466	132,253	151
Itinerant	43,570	16	3,466	40,085	3
Local	92,316	0	0	92,168	148
Sanford	256,302	797	273	254,422	810
Itinerant	87,863	797	273	86,328	465
Local	168,439	0	0	168,094	345
Sarasota-Bradenton	145,886	17,199	18,453	107,737	2,497
Itinerant	121,384	17,199	18,453	83,437	2,295
Local	24,502	0	0	24,300	202
St. Petersburg-Clearwater	186,700	13,514	6,370	145,981	20,835
Itinerant	99,543	13,514	6,370	72,387	7,272
Local	87,157	0	0	73,594	13,563
St. Petersburg Whitt	121,950	0	5,111	115,406	1,433
Itinerant	51,020	0	5,111	45,418	491
Local	70,930	0	0	69,988	942

See footnotes at end of table. Continued . . .

Table 13.90. AIRPORT ACTIVITY: OPERATIONS AT AIRPORTS WITH FEDERAL AVIATION ADMINISTRATION (FAA)-OPERATED TRAFFIC CONTROL TOWERS IN FLORIDA FISCAL YEAR 1994-95 (Continued)

Location and type of operation	Total operations 1/	Air carrier 2/	Air taxi 3/	General aviation 4/	Military
Stuart/Witham Field	72,277	0	1,105	70,523	649
Itinerant	41,228	0	1,105	39,498	625
Local	31,049	0	0	31,025	24
Tallahassee	119,993	14,736	36,211	63,596	5,450
Itinerant	96,587	14,736	36,211	42,078	3,562
Local	23,406	0	0	21,518	1,888
Tamiami	199,657	0	204	198,917	536
Itinerant	81,879	0	204	81,191	484
Local	117,778	0	0	117,726	52
Tampa International	261,617	117,171	100,603	42,227	1,616
Itinerant	261,617	117,171	100,603	42,227	1,616
Local	0	0	0	0	0
Titusville-Cocoa	23,828	0	0	23,432	396
Itinerant	12,299	0	0	12,241	58
Local	11,529	0	0	11,191	338
Vero Beach	204,524	5	1,521	202,738	260
Itinerant	101,577	5	1,521	99,862	189
Local	102,947	0	0	102,876	71
West Palm Beach	205,104	56,809	27,510	119,086	1,699
Itinerant	175,863	56,809	27,510	89,915	1,629
Local	29,241	0	0	29,171	70

1/ An aircraft arrival at or departure from an airport with FAA traffic control.
2/ Air carrier authorized by the Department of Transportation to provide scheduled service over specified routes with limited nonscheduled operations.
3/ Performs at least five round trips per week between two or more points and publishes flight schedules or transports mail.
4/ All operations not classified as an air carrier, air taxi, or military.
Note: Itinerant includes all aircraft arrivals and departures other than local. Local includes aircraft operations which operate in the local traffic pattern or within sight of the tower.

Source: U.S., Department of Transportation, Federal Aviation Administration, *FAA Air Traffic Activity, Fiscal Year 1995,* preliminary data.

Table 13.92. AIRPORT ACTIVITY: ENPLANED REVENUE PASSENGERS AND ENPLANED REVENUE TONS OF FREIGHT AND MAIL CARGO OF CERTIFICATED ROUTE AIR CARRIERS BY COMMUNITY SERVED AND AIRPORT IN FLORIDA, 1994

Community served	Airport 2/	Enplaned passengers 3/	Enplaned cargo tons 1/		
			Total	Freight	Mail
Daytona Beach	Daytona Beach Regional	385,469	333	329	4
Destin	Ft. Walton Beach	0	345	345	0
Ft. Myers	Page Field	0	22	22	0
Ft. Myers	Southwest	1,812,528	6,173	3,246	2,926
Ft. Pierce	Ft. Pierce	0	158	158	0
Gainesville	Gainesville Municipal	134,346	255	251	3
Jacksonville	Craig Municipal	0	110	110	0
Jacksonville	Jacksonville International	1,746,759	16,393	6,490	9,903
Key West	Key West International	8,476	163	162	1
Marathon	Marathon Flight Strip	282	84	84	0
Melbourne	Cape Kennedy Regional	283,066	394	325	69
Miami/Ft. Lauderdale	Dade-Collier	0	2	2	0
Miami/Ft. Lauderdale	Ft. Lauderdale-Hollywood International	4,612,512	60,977	53,461	7,517
Miami/Ft. Lauderdale	Miami International	10,831,532	460,308	432,221	28,087
Orlando	Orlando International	9,166,580	65,173	50,882	14,291
Panama City	Panama City-Bay County	113,946	1,276	502	774
Pensacola	Pensacola Regional	422,365	1,784	733	1,051
Sarasota/Bradenton	Sarasota-Bradenton	778,330	773	584	189
Tallahassee	Tallahassee Municipal	379,674	2,943	2,070	872
Tampa and St. Petersburg/Clearwater	St. Petersburg/Clearwater International	174,367	79	79	0
Tampa and St. Petersburg/Clearwater	Tampa International	5,439,230	48,573	27,554	21,018
Valparaiso	Eglin Air Force Base	149,715	124	124	0
West Palm Beach/Palm Beach	Palm Beach International	2,621,125	9,589	3,827	5,762

1/ Includes originating and transfer tons.
2/ Data are included for only those airports at which aircraft departures were performed in scheduled service in 1994.
3/ Includes all revenue passengers boarding aircraft.
Note: Data are for all services operations of large air carriers (seating capacity of 60 seats or a maximum payload capacity of more than 18,000 pounds) holding a Certificate of Public Convenience and Necessity issued by the U.S. Department of Transportation. Excluded are data for charter only, commuter, intrastate, and foreign-flag air carriers.

Source: U.S., Department of Transportation, Federal Aviation Administration, unpublished data.

Table 13.93. AIRCRAFT PILOTS: ACTIVE AIRCRAFT PILOTS BY TYPE OF CERTIFICATE AND FLIGHT INSTRUCTORS IN THE STATE AND COUNTIES OF FLORIDA
DECEMBER 31, 1995

	Pilots						
			Airplane pilots 1/				
County	Total	Student 2/	Private	Commercial	Airline transport 3/	Miscellaneous 4/	Flight instructors
Florida	45,637	6,536	16,223	10,550	11,541	787	5,969
Alachua	495	100	216	107	55	17	51
Baker	15	0	10	3	2	0	0
Bay	570	79	184	174	123	10	76
Bradford	18	5	8	3	2	0	3
Brevard	2,052	299	825	487	411	30	284
Broward	5,015	603	1,432	1,098	1,808	74	804
Calhoun	20	1	7	9	2	1	2
Charlotte	393	44	155	80	106	8	55
Citrus	243	24	126	55	37	1	26
Clay	584	71	152	144	210	7	59
Collier	915	92	375	168	274	6	109
Columbia	96	19	52	15	10	0	6
Dade	5,254	693	1,302	1,346	1,828	85	629
De Soto	47	4	22	17	4	0	6
Dixie	10	0	4	3	2	1	2
Duval	1,712	285	583	409	392	43	209
Escambia	1,147	130	282	317	385	33	94
Flagler	120	16	41	33	28	2	25
Franklin	28	6	12	4	6	0	2
Gadsden	47	6	27	7	5	2	6
Gilchrist	10	1	5	2	2	0	1
Glades	16	2	6	7	1	0	0
Gulf	18	3	5	7	3	0	0
Hamilton	5	1	2	1	1	0	1
Hardee	43	2	25	11	4	1	1
Hendry	84	24	28	19	12	1	10
Hernando	190	31	93	35	29	2	20
Highlands	200	21	107	45	24	3	26
Hillsborough	2,160	380	875	409	449	47	228
Holmes	13	2	7	3	1	0	1
Indian River	876	117	301	306	146	6	172
Jackson	73	11	33	20	7	2	6
Jefferson	12	4	4	3	1	0	0
Lafayette	6	0	4	0	1	1	0
Lake	523	77	245	112	80	9	60
Lee	1,237	191	524	254	259	9	112

See footnotes at end of table. Continued . . .

Table 13.93. AIRCRAFT PILOTS: ACTIVE AIRCRAFT PILOTS BY TYPE OF CERTIFICATE AND FLIGHT INSTRUCTORS IN THE STATE AND COUNTIES OF FLORIDA DECEMBER 31, 1995 (Continued)

County	Pilots						Flight instructors
			Airplane pilots 1/				
	Total	Student 2/	Private	Commercial	Airline transport 3/	Miscellaneous 4/	
Leon	524	118	210	103	82	11	55
Levy	63	11	30	16	6	0	6
Liberty	5	1	1	1	1	1	0
Madison	20	4	11	3	2	0	3
Manatee	517	68	200	113	128	8	68
Marion	596	80	273	125	112	6	74
Martin	494	59	200	101	130	4	73
Monroe	723	78	249	134	259	3	72
Nassau	242	33	83	61	61	4	31
Okaloosa	937	122	259	255	283	18	112
Okeechobee	97	10	57	19	9	2	5
Orange	2,269	346	820	502	541	60	338
Osceola	318	70	108	67	63	10	58
Palm Beach	3,603	449	1,369	705	1,022	58	456
Pasco	500	80	216	117	70	17	50
Pinellas	2,804	458	1,171	530	599	46	301
Polk	1,026	166	456	235	153	16	152
Putnam	125	25	54	25	17	4	15
St. Johns	677	74	115	224	239	25	55
St. Lucie	1,031	131	470	236	181	13	123
Santa Rosa	1,155	198	423	286	223	25	187
Sarasota	387	53	156	84	88	6	50
Seminole	423	59	198	101	63	2	55
Sumter	43	11	28	2	2	0	3
Suwannee	81	16	36	19	9	1	10
Taylor	18	3	9	5	1	0	2
Union	4	1	2	1	0	0	0
Volusia	2,584	449	892	742	465	36	518
Wakulla	30	6	11	7	6	0	5
Walton	49	6	20	12	10	1	3
Washington	25	3	14	4	3	1	2
Unknown	20	4	3	2	3	8	1

1/ Includes pilots with airplane only certificates and with airplane and helicopter and/or glider certificates.
2/ Category of certificate unknown.
3/ Includes airline transport airplane only and airline transport airplane and helicopter certificates.
4/ Includes helicopter, gyroplane, glider and recreational certificates.

Source: U.S., Department of Transportation, Federal Aviation Administration, Office of Aviation Policy and Plans, *U.S. Civil Airmen Statistics, Calendar Year 1994,* and unpublished data.

COMMUNICATIONS

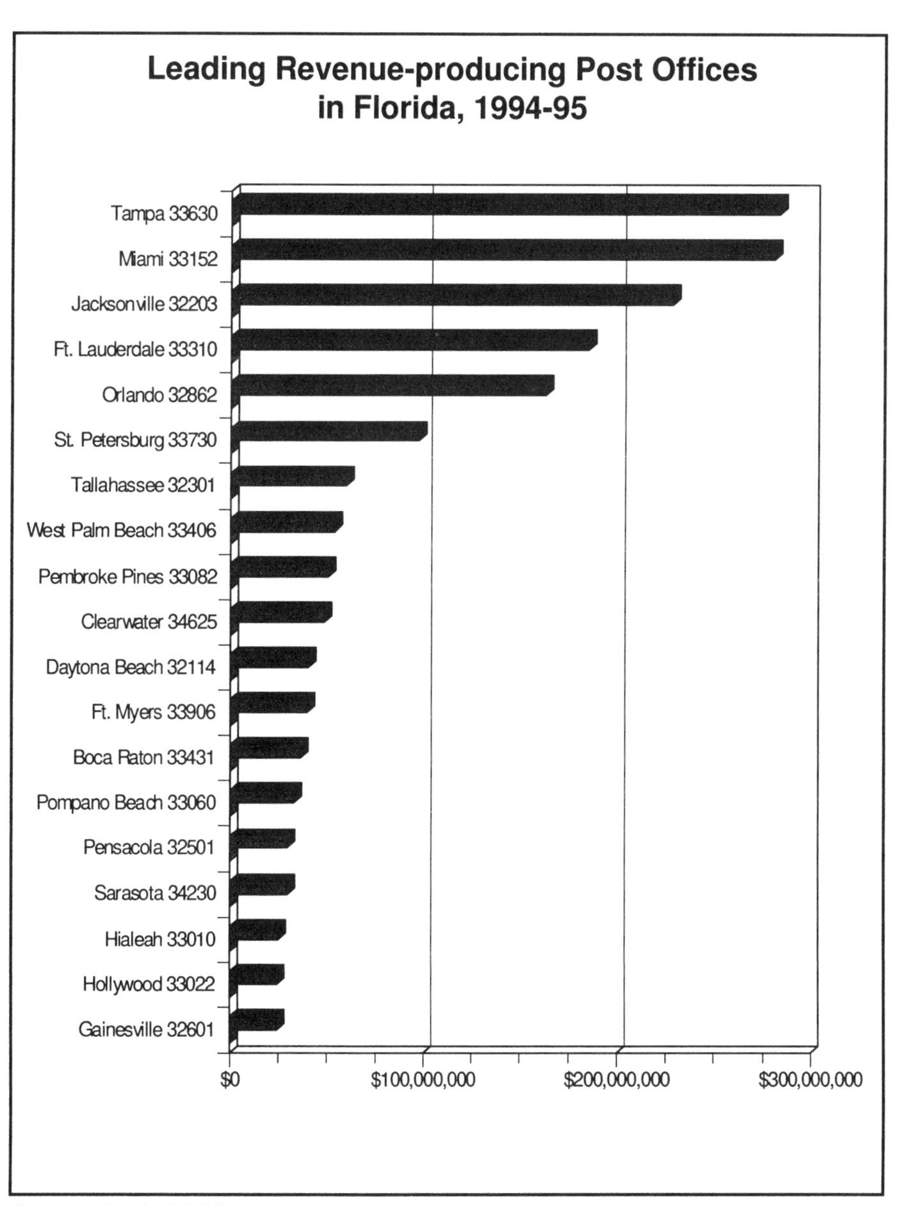

Source: Table 14.33

SECTION 14.00
COMMUNICATONS

TABLES LISTED BY MAJOR HEADINGS

HEADING PAGE

Table 14.33. POST OFFICES: ZIP CODES AND NET POSTAL REVENUE IN THE STATE AND SPECIFIED CITIES OF FLORIDA, FISCAL YEAR 1994-95

First class post office	ZIP code	Net revenue (dollars)	Per-cent-age change from prior year	First class post office	ZIP code	Net revenue (dollars)	Per-cent-age change from prior year
Florida	(X)	2,434,226,129	10.0	Cross City	32628	307,973	7.1
				Crystal River	34429	1,833,461	7.6
Alachua	32615	613,336	10.9	Dade City	33525	2,384,393	5.7
Altamonte Springs	32714	8,957,854	21.0	Dania	33004	2,223,692	5.5
Anna Maria	34216	289,272	-0.3	Davenport	33837	470,453	2.8
Apalachicola	32320	377,535	6.4	Daytona Beach	32114	40,311,942	21.9
Apopka	32703	14,658,667	0.5	DeBary	32713	752,561	15.2
Arcadia	33821	1,274,144	8.9	Deerfield Beach	33441	8,832,234	6.0
Auburndale	33823	1,469,399	12.8	DeFuniak Springs	32433	1,038,772	12.4
Avon Park	33825	1,455,386	9.8	DeLand	32720	5,346,202	26.0
Bartow	33830	2,913,723	7.6	De Leon Springs	32130	393,815	5.8
Bay Pines	33504	771,507	12.2	Delray Beach	33444	9,663,443	4.9
Belle Glade	33430	1,068,783	1.5	Destin	32541	2,765,669	10.4
Belleview	34420	1,200,255	18.1	Dundee	33838	416,868	14.6
Blountstown	32424	482,886	6.2	Dunedin	34698	3,865,419	18.7
Boca Grande	33921	325,524	10.6	Dunnellon	34432	1,059,316	15.1
Boca Raton	33431	36,017,706	9.6	Eagle Lake	33839	344,905	12.4
Bonifay	32425	600,897	2.4	Eaton Park	33840	1,036,165	8.2
Bonita Springs	33923	2,982,591	16.4	Edgewater	32132	1,436,688	15.5
Boynton Beach	33436	6,744,902	15.7	Eglin Air Force Base	32542	953,267	6.3
Bradenton	34205	14,810,997	8.5				
Bradenton Beach	34217	515,888	-27.3	Elfers	34259	1,379,662	7.8
Brandon	33511	7,516,945	30.0	Ellenton	34222	860,605	7.6
Brooksville	34601	9,017,846	12.1	Englewood	34223	2,954,595	8.8
Bunnell	32110	617,993	19.2	Estero	33928	1,041,090	21.5
Bushnell	33513	589,719	5.7	Eustis	32726	1,570,323	6.1
Callahan	32011	485,426	16.3	Fernandina Beach	32834	2,573,676	32.2
Cantonment	32533	620,723	16.1	Flagler Beach	32136	20,623,380	25.0
Cape Canaveral	32920	1,196,179	3.3	Floral City	34436	340,112	20.0
Captiva	33924	326,874	-2.7	Ft. Lauderdale	33310	185,527,104	15.9
Casselberry	32707	6,423,119	15.3	Ft. Meade	33841	320,388	2.9
Chattahoochee	32324	366,858	5.3	Ft. Myers	33906	39,680,174	12.0
Chiefland	32626	792,930	12.3	Ft. Myers Beach	33931	1,632,950	2.2
Chipley	32428	753,343	8.9	Ft. Pierce	34981	11,438,444	8.8
Christmas	32709	294,409	11.7	Ft. Walton Beach	32548	5,735,806	16.3
Clearwater	34625	48,180,068	14.3	Frostproof	33843	487,060	8.7
Clermont	34711	1,480,083	22.0	Fruitland Park	34731	621,198	20.2
Clewiston	33440	938,365	-15.4	Gainesville	32601	24,196,094	3.9
Cocoa	32922	4,391,778	-7.5	Gibsonton	33534	298,242	9.9
Cocoa Beach	32931	1,633,822	4.6	Goldenrod	32733	1,460,640	13.6
Crawfordville	32327	496,789	17.6	Gonzalez	32560	470,565	26.3
Crescent City	32112	954,170	6.2	Gotha	34734	483,214	20.2
Crestview	32536	1,634,768	13.1	Graceville	32440	519,278	12.0

See footnotes at end of table. Continued . . .

Table 14.33. POST OFFICES: ZIP CODES AND NET POSTAL REVENUE IN THE STATE AND SPECIFIED CITIES OF FLORIDA, FISCAL YEAR 1994-95 (Continued)

First class post office	ZIP code	Net revenue (dollars)	Per-cent-age change from prior year	First class post office	ZIP code	Net revenue (dollars)	Per-cent-age change from prior year
Green Cove Springs	32043	1,058,627	15.3	Land O' Lakes	34639	968,087	16.3
Groveland	34736	337,892	9.8	Largo	34640	17,839,526	11.3
Gulf Breeze	32561	2,528,792	17.3	Lecanto	34465	1,261,407	10.2
Haines City	33844	1,597,487	18.6	Leesburg	34748	4,185,187	12.8
Hallandale	33809	4,615,170	8.0	Lehigh Acres	33936	1,590,745	8.3
Havana	32333	452,662	16.6	Live Oak	32060	1,743,883	16.7
Hernando	34442	729,739	22.5	Longboat Key	34228	1,296,625	2.0
Hialeah	33010	24,930,583	5.9	Longwood	32779	8,310,718	19.9
Highland City	33846	475,199	17.8	Loxahatchee	33470	1,181,408	1.7
High Springs	32643	451,418	-1.7	Lutz	33549	1,485,731	4.9
				Lynn Haven	32444	1,219,708	10.8
Hobe Sound	33455	1,331,745	10.0	Macclenny	32063	645,703	14.3
Hollywood	33022	24,374,827	5.7	Madison	32348	766,894	7.1
Homestead	33030	3,489,859	9.3	Maitland	32751	18,453,629	-8.2
Homosassa Springs	34447	1,110,981	15.5	Malabar	32950	431,139	23.7
Immokalee	33934	850,797	4.8	Mango	34262	9,732,412	-23.0
Indian Rocks Beach	34635	1,137,372	7.2	Marathon	33050	1,651,114	6.7
Indiantown	34956	510,509	-1.6	Marco	33937	2,400,219	8.3
Interlachen	32148	296,048	10.9	Marianna	32446	1,705,217	10.1
Inverness	32650	2,691,007	11.7	Mary Esther	32569	1,549,630	14.2
				Melbourne	32901	22,285,562	15.6
				Merritt Island	32952	3,165,081	7.9
Islamorada	33036	631,725	7.0	Miami	33152	280,367,162	2.0
Jacksonville	32203	228,600,152	4.6	Middleburg	32068	938,882	11.5
Jasper	32052	353,085	15.9	Milton	32570	2,781,766	13.6
Jensen Beach	34957	1,952,391	13.2	Mims	32754	385,821	9.7
Jupiter	33458	6,559,618	7.4	Minneola	34755	311,308	(X)
Kathleen	33849	506,049	16.3	Monticello	32344	591,187	4.4
Key Largo	33037	1,651,996	7.2	Mount Dora	32757	2,138,824	7.8
Keystone Heights	32656	1,092,394	9.5	Mulberry	33860	2,314,246	15.3
Key West	33040	5,044,622	8.5	Naples	33940	20,322,528	8.3
Kissimmee	34744	9,266,851	6.9	New Port Richey	34652	4,582,312	6.7
La Belle	33935	896,877	10.3	New Smyrna Beach	32169	2,793,469	6.6
Lady Lake	32159	1,719,688	22.9	Niceville	32578	1,867,185	13.0
Lake Alfred	33858	446,183	11.9	Nokomis	34275	1,398,994	5.6
Lake Butler	32054	367,678	9.5	Ocala	34478	16,992,238	9.6
Lake City	32055	4,795,705	78.4	Ocklawaha	32179	351,270	5.3
Lake Helen	32744	346,100	24.1	Ocoee	34761	1,190,609	12.7
Lakeland	33802	19,437,507	11.3	Odessa	33556	459,008	16.5
Lake Mary	32746	6,080,942	15.8	Okeechobee	34972	1,852,076	10.5
Lake Monroe	32747	354,076	28.1	Oldsmar	34677	1,886,544	15.4
Lake Placid	33852	1,265,461	12.2	Oneco	34264	812,587	5.3
Lake Wales	33853	2,415,130	6.9	Opa-locka	33054	3,072,739	2.5
Lake Worth	33461	10,898,439	7.1	Orange City	32763	3,594,717	10.2

See footnotes at end of table.

Continued . . .

Table 14.33. POST OFFICES: ZIP CODES AND NET POSTAL REVENUE IN THE STATE AND SPECIFIED CITIES OF FLORIDA, FISCAL YEAR 1994-95 (Continued)

First class post office	ZIP code	Net revenue (dollars)	Per-cent-age change from prior year	First class post office	ZIP code	Net revenue (dollars)	Per-cent-age change from prior year
Orange Park	32073	4,878,454	8.6	Sarasota	34230	29,296,199	11.5
Orlando	32862	163,080,888	10.4	Sebastian	32958	1,467,242	9.7
Ormond Beach	32174	5,732,693	17.1	Sebring	33870	3,326,568	6.3
Osprey	34229	1,316,170	16.4	Seffner	33584	1,003,477	11.0
Oviedo	32765	2,359,315	20.1	Shalimar	32579	1,202,604	5.5
Pahokee	33476	319,581	7.6	Sharpes	32959	563,804	21.7
Palatka	32177	2,132,469	11.4	Silver Springs	34488	1,072,910	19.2
Palm Beach	33480	3,156,866	3.5	Starke	32091	878,233	4.3
Palm City	34990	1,770,578	10.6	Stuart	34994	9,941,453	5.4
Palmetto	34221	1,764,541	15.2	Summerfield	34491	318,164	3.0
Palm Harbor	34683	7,355,453	12.6	Summerland Key	33042	974,391	5.7
Panama City	32401	11,703,525	8.6	Sumterville	34267	397,071	14.6
Pembroke Pines	33082	50,054,958	40.9	Tallahassee	32301	59,580,723	10.4
Pensacola	32501	29,813,168	8.3	Tallevast	34270	1,689,246	4.4
Perry	32347	1,098,491	9.9	Tampa	33630	283,561,004	12.1
Pinellas Park	34665	9,850,037	108.7	Tampa	33622	5,645,046	17.2
Placida	33946	407,481	23.1	Tarpon Springs	34689	4,247,904	-0.2
Plant City	33566	2,994,708	0.3	Tavares	32778	1,759,929	11.1
Plymouth	32768	285,638	(X)	Tavernier	33070	1,271,097	26.6
Pompano Beach	33060	33,125,269	8.5	Thonotosassa	33592	427,891	15.8
Ponte Vedra Beach	32082	2,323,630	15.2	Titusville	32780	4,826,655	3.1
Port Richey	34668	5,413,589	8.8	Trenton	32693	376,105	11.9
Port St. Joe	32456	630,710	4.3	Umatilla	32784	588,289	9.5
Port Salerno	34992	877,043	12.1	Valpariso	32580	668,119	5.5
Punta Gorda	33950	9,445,985	7.1	Valrico	33594	1,432,080	7.0
Quincy	32351	3,087,293	9.0	Venice	34285	7,951,290	9.6
Riverview	33569	1,099,505	23.7	Vero Beach	32960	11,254,847	7.9
Rockledge	32955	1,769,176	4.7	Wabasso	32970	1,854,059	0.8
Roseland	32957	426,292	17.3	Wauchula	33873	1,008,689	2.6
				Weirsdale	32195	961,411	19.2
Ruskin	33570	2,552,861	8.7	West Palm Beach	33406	53,643,934	11.2
Safety Harbor	34695	1,666,712	47.0	White Springs	32096	444,572	22.3
St. Augustine	32084	6,180,137	9.6	Wildwood	34785	577,600	21.8
St. Cloud	34769	1,863,828	11.4	Williston	32696	558,231	13.4
St. James City	33956	297,530	10.4	Windermere	34786	1,022,749	42.1
St. Petersburg	33730	97,343,814	14.9	Winter Garden	32787	1,244,615	8.0
Sanford	32771	4,013,861	18.0	Winter Haven	33880	9,515,493	6.1
Sanibel	33957	1,541,549	7.9	Winter Park	32789	12,270,780	7.0
				Yulee	32097	334,001	24.3
Santa Rosa Beach	32459	573,006	19.2	Zephyrhills	33540	2,964,527	14.5

(X) Not applicable.

Note: Data are for first class post offices. Florida totals include revenue from all post offices.

Source: U.S., Postal Service Headquarters, unpublished data.

Table 14.35. EMPLOYMENT: AVERAGE MONTHLY PRIVATE REPORTING UNITS, EMPLOYMENT AND PAYROLL COVERED BY UNEMPLOYMENT COMPENSATION LAW BY INDUSTRY IN FLORIDA, 1995

SIC code	Industry	Number of reporting units	Number of employees	Payroll ($1,000)
27	Printing, publishing, and allied industries	3,397	63,792	150,246
48	Telecommunications	1,839	73,212	249,262
481	Telephone communications	1,121	50,849	184,469
482	Telegraph and other message communications	26	166	1,004
483	Radio and television broadcasting stations	419	12,333	38,713
484	Cable and other pay television services	234	9,531	23,894
489	Communication services, NEC	41	333	1,183

NEC Not elsewhere classified.

Note: Private employment. Data are prelimiary. Detail may not add to totals due to disclosure editing and/or rounding. See Tables in Section 23.00 for public employment data. See Appendix for an explanation of selection of industries included.

Table 14.36. TELECOMMUNICATIONS: AVERAGE MONTHLY PRIVATE REPORTING UNITS EMPLOYMENT, AND PAYROLL COVERED BY UNEMPLOYMENT COMPENSATION LAW IN THE STATE AND COUNTIES OF FLORIDA, 1995

County	Number of reporting units	Number of employees	Payroll ($1,000)	County	Number of reporting units	Number of employees	Payroll ($1,000)
			Telecommunications (SIC code 48)				
Florida	1,839	73,212	249,262	Manatee	17	290	883
Alachua	26	940	2,704	Marion	22	529	1,518
Baker	5	71	215	Martin	9	207	683
Bay	27	757	1,885	Monroe	19	279	739
Brevard	52	1,111	3,649	Nassau	4	44	158
Broward	173	7,279	26,913	Okaloosa	25	530	1,548
Charlotte	8	292	769	Orange	146	10,107	35,793
Clay	5	70	253	Pasco	17	591	2,381
Collier	23	571	1,630	Pinellas	108	3,678	12,368
Columbia	6	186	501	Polk	43	854	2,605
Dade	257	12,558	46,034	Putnam	8	84	243
De Soto	4	43	66	St. Johns	9	126	336
Duval	82	6,410	20,910	St. Lucie	18	796	2,204
Escambia	44	1,462	4,372	Santa Rosa	7	260	829
Flagler	4	27	50	Sarasota	45	1,047	3,066
Gadsden	7	57	148	Seminole	36	2,286	8,442
Hillsborough	141	7,366	27,060	Suwannee	4	90	244
Indian River	12	223	630	Taylor	4	54	124
Jackson	6	48	135	Volusia	35	595	1,777
Lee	58	2,232	6,040	Multicounty 1/	58	378	1,640

1/ Units without a fixed or known location within the state.

Note: Private employment. Data are preliminary. Detail may not add to totals due to disclosure editing and/or rounding. See Tables in Section 23.00 for public employment data.

Source for Tables 14.35 and 14.36: State of Florida, Department of Labor and Employment Security, Bureau of Labor Market Information, "Employment and Wages" (ES-202), unpublished data.

Table 14.37. NEWSPAPER PRINTING AND PUBLISHING, TELEPHONE COMMUNICATIONS, AND RADIO AND TELEVISION BROADCASTING STATIONS: AVERAGE MONTHLY PRIVATE REPORTING UNITS, EMPLOYMENT, AND PAYROLL COVERED BY UNEMPLOYMENT COMPENSATION LAW IN THE STATE AND COUNTIES OF FLORIDA, 1995

County	Number of reporting units	Number of employees	Payroll ($1,000)	County	Number of reporting units	Number of employees	Payroll ($1,000)
	Newspaper printing and publishing (SIC code 271)						
Florida	311	26,175	60,616	Okaloosa	3	219	364
				Osceola	3	98	179
Alachua	5	417	714	Palm Beach	22	1,781	5,310
Broward	25	1,998	6,096	Pasco	4	192	293
Charlotte	4	253	433	Polk	7	574	1,222
Lake	11	302	522	Santa Rosa	3	63	82
Lee	9	847	1,659	Seminole	7	90	146
Monroe	5	106	167	Volusia	8	924	2,006
	Telephone communications (SIC code 481)						
Florida	1,121	50,849	184,469	Indian River	7	88	363
				Orange	103	7,822	28,835
Bay	9	331	1,072	Pinellas	74	2,257	7,811
Broward	121	5,644	21,718	Putnam	4	51	187
Clay	4	65	247	Saint Lucie	7	581	1,737
Duval	57	4,734	16,805	Seminole	27	2,085	7,752
Escambia	26	1,079	3,527	Volusia	13	142	529
Hillsborough	106	5,641	21,316	Multicounty 1/	31	194	1,003
	Radio and television broadcasting stations (SIC code 483)						
Florida	419	12,333	38,713	Martin	3	32	78
				Monroe	11	96	153
Alachua	9	237	457	Okaloosa	11	128	197
Bay	13	301	537	Orange	25	1,123	3,781
Brevard	15	201	356	Pasco	3	47	65
Broward	22	600	2,415	Pinellas	20	798	3,053
Collier	7	120	315	Polk	9	101	202
Dade	44	3,077	11,799	St. Johns	3	26	27
Duval	22	1,048	2,701	St. Lucie	9	167	384
Escambia	14	183	388	Sarasota	10	192	406
Hillsborough	17	1,042	3,606	Seminole	5	151	505
Lee	18	558	1,379	Volusia	14	147	342
Marion	7	124	239				

1/ Reporting units without a fixed location within the state or of unknown county location.

Note: Private employment. Data are preliminary. Only counties for which data are disclosed are shown. Detail may not add to totals due to disclosure editing and/or rounding. See Tables 23.70, 23.71, 23.72, 23.73, and 23.74 for public employment data.

Source: State of Florida, Department of Labor and Employment Security, Bureau of Labor Market Information, "Employment and Wages" (ES-202), unpublished data.

Table 14.60. TELEPHONE COMPANIES: SPECIFIED CHARACTERISTICS OF COMPANIES IN FLORIDA, DECEMBER 1995

Companies and headquarters	Number of exchanges	Florida access lines 1/ Total number	Percentage of state total	Annual growth rate (percentage)
Florida	282	9,256,947	100.00	4.69
ALLTEL Florida, Inc. Live Oak	27	68,638	0.74	3.36
BellSouth Telecommunications Company Miami	101	5,384,687	58.17	4.80
Central Telephone Company of Florida Tallahassee	35	356,943	3.86	5.08
Florala Telephone Company Florala, Alabama	2	2,079	0.02	2.57
Frontier Communications of the South Atmore, Alabama	2	3,761	0.04	3.72
GTE Florida, Inc. Tampa	24	2,016,976	21.80	4.15
Gulf Telephone Company Perry	2	8,654	0.09	1.91
Indiantown Telephone System, Inc. Indiantown	1	3,265	0.04	7.12
Northeast Florida Telephone Company Macclenny	2	7,144	0.08	5.26
Quincy Telephone Company Quincy	3	12,464	0.13	5.95
St. Joseph Telephone and Telegraph Company Port St. Joe	13	27,024	0.29	3.19
United Telephone Company of Florida Altamonte Springs	69	1,353,466	14.62	4.95
Vista-United Telecommunications Lake Buena Vista	1	11,846	0.13	16.86

1/ An access line is the line going to a home or building for the main telephone located there.

Note: Telephone companies listed above have headquarters in Florida, except as specified. Detail may not add to totals due to rounding.

Source: State of Florida, Public Service Commission, *1995 Annual Report*.

Table 14.61. TELEPHONE COMPANIES: NUMBER OF CALLS AND BILLED ACCESS MINUTES BY TELEPHONE COMPANY IN FLORIDA, 1994

(rounded to thousands)

Company	Local calls	IntraLATA toll calls completed (originating)	InterLATA toll calls completed (originating)			InterLATA billed access minutes (originating and terminating)		
			Total	Interstate	Intrastate	Total	Interstate	Intrastate
Florida	29,992,719	973,906	3,782,434	2,658,707	1,123,727	36,252,653	26,720,799	9,531,854
ALLTEL	179,785	8,601	21,297	12,982	8,315	223,237	122,293	100,945
CENTEL	990,306	9,608	183,005	117,472	65,533	1,389,897	905,240	484,657
Florala 1/	3,434	420	416	310	106	5,162	3,813	1,350
GTE	5,075,153	125,275	837,512	572,738	264,774	7,408,546	5,429,709	1,978,837
Gulf	44,129	1,639	3,223	2,023	1,199	26,368	12,746	13,622
Indiantown	2,333	955	1,381	743	639	10,426	6,119	4,307
Northeast	16,425	603	688	407	281	17,365	10,811	6,554
Quincy 1/	38,928	450	3,882	2,168	1,714	30,898	24,937	5,961
St. Joseph	31,738	4,318	7,573	4,251	3,321	(NA)	(NA)	(NA)
Southern Bell	21,026,785	709,740	2,116,064	1,609,776	506,288	21,230,992	16,044,906	5,186,086
Southland 1/	(NA)	339	482	315	167	3,505	2,553	952
United	2,503,576	110,944	591,263	322,630	268,633	5,805,177	4,076,253	1,728,924
Vista-United	80,127	1,013	15,649	12,891	2,757	101,081	81,420	19,660

LATA Local Access Transport Area.
(NA) Not available.
1/ Florida only.
Note: See Table 14.60 for a complete list of company names and headquarters.

Source: State of Florida, Public Service Commission, Division of Research and Regulatory Review, *Statistics of the Florida Local Exchange Companies, 1994.*

Table 14.62. TELEPHONE RATES: INTRASTATE INTRALATA MESSAGE TOLL SERVICE RATES BY MILEAGE AND BY TELEPHONE COMPANY IN FLORIDA, 1994

(in dollars)

Mileage	Southern Bell 1/ 1st minute	Southern Bell 1/ Additional minutes	ALLTEL 1/ 1st minute	ALLTEL 1/ Additional minutes	Florala 1/ 1st minute	Florala 1/ Additional minutes
Day						
0-10	0.1500	0.0800	0.1500	0.0800	0.1500	0.0800
11-22	0.1800	0.1200	0.1800	0.1200	0.1800	0.1400
23-55	0.1900	0.1900	0.1900	0.1900	0.2500	0.2400
56-124	0.2000	0.2000	0.2000	0.2000	0.2500	0.2400
125-292	0.2000	0.2000	0.5800	0.3900	0.2500	0.2400
Evening						
0-10	0.1050	0.0560	0.1200	0.0640	0.0900	0.0480
11-22	0.1260	0.0840	0.1440	0.0960	0.1080	0.0840
23-55	0.1330	0.1330	0.1520	0.1520	0.1500	0.1440
56-124	0.1400	0.1400	0.1600	0.1600	0.1500	0.1440
125-292	0.1400	0.1400	0.4640	0.3120	0.1500	0.1440
Night/Weekend						
0-10	0.0900	0.0480	0.0900	0.0480	0.0900	0.0480
11-22	0.1080	0.0720	0.1080	0.0720	0.1080	0.0840
23-55	0.1140	0.1140	0.1140	0.1140	0.1500	0.1440
56-124	0.1200	0.1200	0.1200	0.1200	0.1500	0.1440
125-292	0.1200	0.1200	0.3480	0.2340	0.1500	0.1440

Mileage	Gulf 1/ 1st minute	Gulf 1/ Additional minutes	United 1st minute	United Additional minutes	CENTEL 1/ 1st minute	CENTEL 1/ Additional minutes
Day						
0-10	0.1500	0.0800	(NA)	(NA)	0.1700	0.0700
11-22	0.1800	0.1200	0.2400	0.1400	0.1800	0.1400
23-55	0.2100	0.1800	0.2400	0.2100	0.2400	0.2000
56-124	0.2100	0.1800	0.2400	0.2100	0.2400	0.2000
125-292	0.2100	0.1800	0.2400	0.2100	0.2400	0.2000
Evening						
0-10	0.0900	0.0480	(NA)	(NA)	0.1275	0.0525
11-22	0.1080	0.0720	0.1800	0.1050	0.1350	0.1050
23-55	0.1260	0.1080	0.1800	0.1575	0.1800	0.1500
56-124	0.1260	0.1080	0.1800	0.1575	0.1800	0.1500
125-292	0.1260	0.1080	0.1800	0.1575	0.1800	0.1500
Night/Weekend						
0-10	0.0900	0.0480	(NA)	(NA)	0.0850	0.0350
11-22	0.1080	0.0720	0.1200	0.0700	0.0900	0.0700
23-55	0.1260	0.1080	0.1200	0.1050	0.1200	0.1000
56-124	0.1260	0.1080	0.1200	0.1050	0.1200	0.1000
125-292	0.1260	0.1080	0.1200	0.1050	0.1200	0.1000

See footnotes at end of table.

Continued . . .

Table 14.62. TELEPHONE RATES: INTRASTATE INTRALATA MESSAGE TOLL SERVICE RATES BY MILEAGE AND BY TELEPHONE COMPANY IN FLORIDA, 1994 (Continued)

(in dollars)

Mileage	Quincy 1/ 1st minute	Quincy 1/ Additional minutes	Northeast 1st minute	Northeast Additional minutes	GTE 1st minute	GTE Additional minutes
Day						
0-10	0.1600	0.1400	(NA)	(NA)	0.1400	0.0700
11-22	0.1600	0.1400	0.1800	0.1200	0.2100	0.1200
23-55	0.2400	0.2200	0.2400	0.2100	0.2800	0.2100
56-124	0.2400	0.2200	0.2400	0.2100	0.3700	0.2700
125-292	0.2400	0.2200	(NA)	(NA)	(NA)	(NA)
Evening						
0-10	0.1200	0.1050	(NA)	(NA)	0.1050	0.0525
11-22	0.1200	0.1050	0.1080	0.0720	0.1575	0.0900
23-55	0.1800	0.1650	0.1440	0.1260	0.2100	0.1575
56-124	0.1800	0.1650	0.1440	0.1260	0.2775	0.2025
125-292	0.1800	0.1650	(NA)	(NA)	(NA)	(NA)
Night/Weekend						
0-10	0.0800	0.0800	(NA)	(NA)	0.0700	0.0350
11-22	0.1200	0.0700	0.1080	0.0720	0.1050	0.0600
23-55	0.1200	0.1100	0.1440	0.1260	0.1400	0.1050
56-124	0.1200	0.1100	0.1440	0.1260	0.1850	0.1350
125-292	0.1200	0.1100	(NA)	(NA)	(NA)	(NA)

Mileage	Indiantown 1st minute	Indiantown Additional minutes	Southland and St. Joseph 1st minute	Southland and St. Joseph Additional minutes	Vista-United 1st minute	Vista-United Additional minutes
Day						
0-10	(NA)	(NA)	(NA)	(NA)	(NA)	(NA)
11-22	0.1800	0.1200	0.1800	0.1400	0.2500	0.1600
23-55	0.1900	0.1900	0.2500	0.2400	0.2500	0.2400
56-124	0.2000	0.2000	0.2500	0.2400	0.2500	0.2400
125-292	0.2000	0.2000				
Evening						
0-10	(NA)	(NA)	(NA)	(NA)	(NA)	(NA)
11-22	0.1440	0.0960	0.1080	0.0840	0.1875	0.1200
23-55	0.1520	0.1520	0.1500	0.1440	0.1875	0.1800
56-124	0.1600	0.1600	0.1500	0.1440	0.1875	0.1800
125-292	0.1600	0.1600	(NA)	(NA)	(NA)	(NA)
Night/Weekend						
0-10	(NA)	(NA)	(NA)	(NA)	(NA)	(NA)
11-22	0.1080	0.0720	0.1080	0.0840	0.1250	0.0800
23-55	0.1140	0.1140	0.1500	0.1440	0.1250	0.1200
56-124	0.1200	0.1200	0.1500	0.1440	0.1250	0.1200
125-292	0.1200	0.1200	(NA)	(NA)	(NA)	(NA)

LATA Local Access Transport Area.
(NA) Not available.
1/ 1994 rates remain unchanged from 1993.
Note: Intrastate toll messages originate and terminate within the same state. Toll messages are completed calls between stations in different exchanges for which charges are applicable. See Table 14.60 for a complete list of company names and headquarters.
Source: State of Florida, Public Service Commission, Division of Research and Regulatory Review, *Statistics of the Florida Local Exchange Companies, 1994.*

POWER AND ENERGY

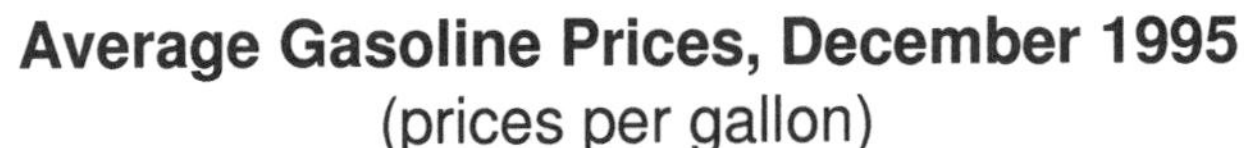

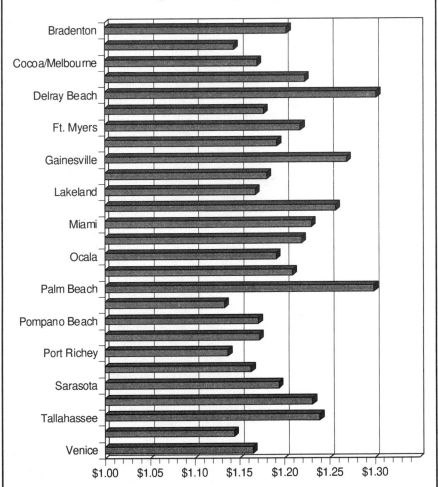

Average Gasoline Prices, December 1995
(prices per gallon)

Bradenton
Cocoa/Melbourne
Delray Beach
Ft. Myers
Gainesville
Lakeland
Miami
Ocala
Palm Beach
Pompano Beach
Port Richey
Sarasota
Tallahassee
Venice

$1.00 $1.05 $1.10 $1.15 $1.20 $1.25 $1.30

Note: Prices are for mid-grade self-service unleaded gasoline.

Source: Table 15.66

SECTION 15.00
POWER AND ENERGY

TABLES LISTED BY MAJOR HEADINGS

Table 15.06. ENERGY CONSUMPTION: AMOUNT CONSUMED BY TYPE OF FUEL IN FLORIDA 1983 THROUGH 1993

(in trillions of British thermal units)

Year	Total	Petro-leum 1/	Natural gas	Coal	Nuclear	Electric inter-state 2/	Hydro-elec-tric
1983	2,388.7	1,426.3	321.0	318.9	161.4	158.6	2.3
1984	2,459.1	1,320.5	318.2	378.7	261.1	178.5	2.2
1985	2,610.5	1,325.5	305.1	472.4	253.7	251.4	2.5
1986	2,693.9	1,509.3	298.9	459.4	238.0	186.1	2.2
1987	2,793.1	1,469.1	313.6	586.6	202.3	219.2	2.3
1988	2,954.4	1,583.7	305.8	611.5	281.4	169.8	2.2
1989	3,026.1	1,585.9	337.2	630.2	224.3	246.0	2.4
1990	3,060.0	1,573.8	342.0	624.3	232.6	285.4	1.8
1991	3,018.1	1,552.0	361.0	642.8	220.3	239.4	2.7
1992	3,066.4	1,577.1	370.3	652.7	268.2	195.7	2.4
1993	3,128.2	1,636.0	354.9	652.2	276.5	206.4	2.2

1/ Includes asphalt, aviation gasoline, jet fuel, distillates, kerosene, lubricants, motor gasoline, residual fuel, and liquefied petroleum gas.

2/ Combines electric sales and energy losses associated with interstate sales. Losses estimated to be 7,088 of the 10,400 British thermal units per kilowatt-hour purchased.

Table 15.07. ENERGY CONSUMPTION: PER CAPITA ENERGY CONSUMPTION BY TYPE OF FUEL IN FLORIDA, 1983 THROUGH 1993

(in millions of British thermal units)

Year	Total	Petro-leum 1/	Natural gas	Coal	Nuclear	Electric inter-state 2/	Hydro-elec-tric
1983	225.5	134.7	30.3	30.1	15.2	15.0	0.2
1984	225.0	120.8	29.1	34.6	23.9	16.3	0.2
1985	231.3	117.4	27.0	41.9	22.5	22.3	0.2
1986	231.1	129.5	25.6	39.4	20.4	16.0	0.2
1987	231.9	122.0	26.0	48.7	16.8	18.2	0.2
1988	237.9	127.5	24.6	49.2	22.7	13.7	0.2
1989	236.5	123.9	26.3	49.2	17.5	19.2	0.2
1990	236.5	121.6	26.4	48.3	18.0	22.1	0.1
1991	228.7	117.6	27.4	48.7	16.7	18.1	0.2
1992	228.4	117.5	27.6	48.6	20.0	14.6	0.2
1993	229.9	120.2	26.1	47.9	20.3	15.2	0.2

1/ Includes asphalt, aviation gasoline, jet fuel, distillates, kerosene, lubricants, motor gasoline, residual fuel, and liquefied petroleum gas.

2/ Combines electric sales and energy losses associated with interstate sales. Losses estimated to be 7,088 of the 10,400 British thermal units per kilowatt-hour purchased.

Note: Per capita is computed using Bureau of the Census data for 1990 and *Florida Estimates of Population* for all other years.

Source for Tables 15.06 and 15.07: U.S., Department of Energy, Energy Information Administration, *State Energy Data Report, 1993: Consumption Estimates,* July 1995. Compiled by State of Florida, Department of Community Affairs.

Table 15.08. ENERGY CONSUMPTION: CONSUMPTION OF RENEWABLE ENERGY BY TYPE IN FLORIDA, 1988 THROUGH 1993

(in trillions of British thermal units)

Type of energy	1988	1989	1990	1991	1992	1993
Total	159.4	167.7	168.7	171.1	180.8	177.2
Direct solar	3.9	4.4	4.8	5.1	5.6	6.0
Biomass energy, total	153.3	160.9	162.1	163.3	172.8	169.1
Wood	116.8	115.9	113.3	109.9	114.1	109.5
Pulp and paper industry	100.2	98.9	95.9	90.7	94.8	89.8
Residential	15.2	15.6	16.0	16.3	16.5	16.8
Electric utility	1.4	1.4	1.4	2.9	2.9	2.9
Crop residues	14.1	14.0	16.5	16.8	16.0	16.5
Alcohol fuels	0.6	0.6	0.7	0.8	0.5	0.6
Municipal solid waste	19.6	28.0	29.8	33.1	39.8	42.6
Hydroelectric energy	2.2	2.4	1.8	2.7	2.4	2.2

Note: Consumption of renewable energy in Florida from wind systems and animal waste is negligible (greater than 0 but less than 0.05 trillion British thermal units) and consumption of geothermal energy is significant, but impossible to measure. Therefore, these data are not included in this table. Detail may not add to totals because of rounding.

Source: State of Florida, Department of Community Affairs, *Florida Energy Data Report, 1970-1992*, and unpublished data.

Table 15.09. CRUDE OIL AND NATURAL GAS: AMOUNT PRODUCED BY FIELD IN FLORIDA 1993 THROUGH 1995

Field	Crude oil (barrels)			Natural gas (1,000 cubic feet)		
	1993	1994	1995	1993	1994	1995
Total	5,604,126	6,095,150	5,681,618	8,055,745	8,514,155	7,171,557
South Florida	1,217,353	1,502,617	1,545,308	173,353	281,703	198,105
Bear Island	97,297	123,877	90,125	23,631	24,453	23,099
Corkscrew	70,189	61,667	47,136	0	0	0
Lake Trafford	0	2,590	0	0	0	0
Lehigh Park	47,235	50,153	43,271	5,636	66,851	6,318
Mid-Felda	38,435	17,074	10,299	0	0	0
Raccoon Point	625,142	891,456	991,719	114,193	162,299	(NA)
Sunniland	0	0	0	0	0	0
Sunoco Felda	0	0	0	0	0	0
Townsend Canal	16,994	2,590	4,816	0	0	0
West Felda	322,061	353,210	357,942	29,893	28,100	(NA)
Northwest Florida	4,386,773	4,592,533	4,136,310	7,882,392	8,232,452	6,973,452
Blackjack Creek	360,943	354,722	301,964	908,051	814,154	738,079
Bluff Springs	0	0	0	0	0	0
Coldwater Creek	9,357	32,699	3,404	956	0	0
Jay	3,954,826	4,159,336	3,810,967	6,960,372	7,410,410	6,230,813
McDavid	0	0	0	0	0	0
McLellan	32,901	24,842	17,238	13,013	7,888	4,560
Mt. Carmel	28,746	20,934	2,737	0	0	0

(NA) Not available.

Note: Data from Florida Geological Survey.

Source: State of Florida, Department of Community Affairs, unpublished data.

Table 15.14. ELECTRIC UTILITY INDUSTRY: SALES, CUSTOMERS, AND COUNTIES SERVED BY PRIVATELY AND PUBLICLY OWNED UTILITIES AND BY RURAL ELECTRIC COOPERATIVES IN FLORIDA, 1994

Utility	Electricity sales to ultimate customers (MWH)	Number of ultimate customers December 1/	Counties served
Investor-owned systems			
Florida Power 2/	27,675,220	1,243,876	Alachua, Bay, Brevard, Citrus, Columbia, Dixie, Flagler, Franklin, Gadsden, Gilchrist, Gulf, Hamilton, Hardee, Hernando, Highlands, Hillsborough, Jefferson, Lafayette, Lake, Leon, Levy, Liberty, Madison, Marion, Orange, Osceola, Pasco, Pinellas, Polk, Seminole, Sumter, Suwannee, Taylor, Volusia, Wakulla
Florida Power and Light	73,607,623	3,422,174	Alachua, Baker, Bradford, Brevard, Broward, Charlotte, Clay, Collier, Columbia, Dade, De Soto, Duval, Flagler, Glades, Hardee, Hendry, Highlands, Indian River, Lee, Manatee, Martin, Monroe, Nassau, Okeechobee, Orange, Osceola, Palm Beach, Putnam, St. Johns, St. Lucie, Sarasota, Seminole, Suwannee, Union, Volusia
Florida Public Utilities	544,923	22,180	Calhoun, Jackson, Liberty, Nassau
Gulf Power	8,165,245	318,572	Bay, Escambia, Holmes, Jackson, Okaloosa, Santa Rosa, Walton, Washington
Tampa Electric	13,931,660	485,699	Hillsborough, Pasco, Pinellas, Polk
Generating municipal systems			
Ft. Pierce	509,710	23,682	St. Lucie
Gainesville	1,359,460	70,119	Alachua
Homestead	237,193	12,164	Dade
Jacksonville	9,221,117	311,002	Duval
Key West	562,262	25,281	Monroe
Kissimmee	803,676	38,911	Osceola
Lake Worth	345,911	24,350	Palm Beach
Lakeland	2,138,509	100,324	Polk
New Smyrna Beach	286,378	20,248	Volusia
Orlando	5,054,684	166,043	Orange
Reedy Creek	845,856	1,062	Orange
St. Cloud	(NA)	(NA)	Osceola
Starke	57,693	2,556	Bradford
Tallahassee	1,954,234	84,243	Leon
Vero Beach	524,333	26,503	Indian River
Wauchula	51,296	2,524	Hardee
Florida Keys	532,809	28,616	Monroe
Seminole 3/	0	0	(X)

See footnotes at end of table.

Continued . . .

Table 15.14. ELECTRIC UTILITY INDUSTRY: SALES, CUSTOMERS, AND COUNTIES SERVED BY PRIVATELY AND PUBLICLY OWNED UTILITIES AND BY RURAL ELECTRIC COOPERATIVES IN FLORIDA, 1994 (Continued)

Utility	Electricity sales to ultimate customers (MWH)	Number of ultimate customers December 1/	Counties served
Nongenerating municipal systems			
Alachua	50,505	2,177	Alachua
Bartow	250,609	10,000	Polk
Blountstown	31,285	1,422	Calhoun
Bushnell	16,471	891	Sumter
Chattahoochee	49,129	1,327	Gadsden
Clewiston	95,484	3,950	Hendry
Ft. Meade	57,693	2,583	Polk
Green Cove Springs	101,014	2,632	Clay
Havana	18,943	1,315	Gadsden
Jacksonville Beach	510,256	25,750	Duval
Leesburg	371,542	17,024	Lake
Moore Haven	(NA)	(NA)	Glades
Mount Dora	73,289	4,766	Lake
Newberry	26,971	873	Alachua
Ocala	976,645	47,924	Marion
Quincy	136,250	4,447	Gadsden
Williston	24,307	1,267	Levy
Nongenerating rural electric cooperatives			
Central Florida	261,584	22,977	Alachua, Dixie, Gilchrist, Levy
Choctawhatchee	369,821	25,493	Holmes, Okaloosa, Santa Rosa, Walton
Clay	1,738,688	110,505	Alachua, Baker, Bradford, Clay, Columbia, Duval, Lake, Levy, Marion, Putnam, Union, Volusia
Escambia River	116,549	7,908	Escambia, Santa Rosa
Glades	207,205	12,762	Glades, Hendry, Highlands, Okeechobee
Gulf Coast	168,373	13,522	Bay, Calhoun, Gulf, Jackson, Walton, Washington
Lee County	2,106,322	128,500	Charlotte, Collier, Hendry, Lee
Okefenokee 4/	104,739	6,914	Baker, Duval, Nassau, Okeechobee
Peace River	256,270	19,718	Brevard, De Soto, Hardee, Highlands, Hillsborough, Indian River, Manatee, Osceola, Polk, Sarasota, Sumter
Sumter	1,011,337	79,922	Citrus, Hernando, Lake, Levy, Marion, Pasco, Sumter
Suwannee Valley	215,873	16,447	Columbia, Hamilton, Lafayette, Suwannee
Talquin	631,149	40,067	Gadsden, Leon, Liberty, Wakulla
Tri-county	146,633	13,027	Dixie, Jefferson, Madison, Taylor
West Florida	260,923	22,091	Calhoun, Holmes, Jackson, Washington

See footnotes at end of table. Continued . . .

Table 15.14. ELECTRIC UTILITY INDUSTRY: SALES, CUSTOMERS, AND COUNTIES SERVED BY PRIVATELY AND PUBLICLY OWNED UTILITIES AND BY RURAL ELECTRIC COOPERATIVES IN FLORIDA, 1994 (Continued)

Utility	Electricity sales to ultimate customers (MWH)	Number of ultimate customers December 1/	Counties served
Nongenerating rural electric cooperatives (Continued)			
Withlacoochee River	2,055,886	135,044	Citrus, Hernando, Pasco, Polk, Sumter

MWH Megawatt-hours (1,000 kilowatt-hours).
(NA) Not available.
(X) Not applicable.
1/ Year-end monthly average.
2/ Beginning in 1994, includes the Sebring municipal system.
3/ Generates only for resale.
4/ Florida customers only.

Source: State of Florida, Public Service Commission, Division of Research and Regulatory Review, *Statistics of the Florida Electric Utility Industry, 1994.*

Table 15.15. ELECTRIC, GAS, AND SANITARY SERVICES: AVERAGE MONTHLY PRIVATE REPORTING UNITS, EMPLOYMENT, AND PAYROLL COVERED BY UNEMPLOYMENT COMPENSATION LAW BY INDUSTRY IN FLORIDA, 1995

SIC code	Industry	Number of reporting units	Number of employees	Payroll ($1,000)
49	Electric, gas, and sanitary services	722	35,394	129,298
491	Electric services	155	24,518	101,860
492	Gas production and distribution	50	2,104	6,175
493	Combination electric and gas, and other utility services	12	58	210
494	Water supply	151	1,556	3,321
495	Sanitary services	346	7,097	17,593
497	Irrigation systems	7	39	68

Note: Private employment. Data are preliminary. Detail may not add to totals due to disclosure editing and/or rounding. See Tables 23.70, 23.71, 23.72, 23.73, and 23.74 for public employment data.

Source: State of Florida, Department of Labor and Employment Security, Bureau of Labor Market Information, "Employment and Wages" (ES-202), unpublished data.

Table 15.16. ELECTRIC, GAS, AND SANITARY SERVICES: AVERAGE MONTHLY PRIVATE REPORTING UNITS, EMPLOYMENT, AND PAYROLL COVERED BY UNEMPLOYMENT COMPENSATION LAW IN THE STATE AND COUNTIES OF FLORIDA, 1995

County	Number of re- porting units	Number of em- ployees	Payroll ($1,000)	County	Number of re- porting units	Number of em- ployees	Payroll ($1,000)
		Electric, gas, and sanitary services (SIC code 49)					
Florida	722	35,394	129,298	Jackson	5	178	491
				Jefferson	3	54	190
Alachua	9	170	426	Lake	11	304	920
Bay	9	355	1,150	Lee	25	1,016	3,126
Brevard	13	568	1,926	Leon	6	195	518
Charlotte	9	284	849	Madison	6	77	194
Clay	11	406	1,290	Manatee	8	301	1,031
Collier	11	360	1,014	Marion	22	287	911
Columbia	4	124	390	Monroe	8	197	597
Dade	43	5,877	22,388	Okaloosa	13	269	756
Dixie	4	9	9	Orange	30	1,198	3,827
Duval	30	537	1,487	Osceola	10	54	149
Flagler	5	137	454	Pasco	24	578	1,839
Gulf	5	103	270	Polk	33	670	1,878
Hernando	5	229	543	Putnam	5	199	792
Highlands	7	89	293	Santa Rosa	18	220	550
Hillsborough	51	4,273	15,974	Seminole	19	640	2,140
Holmes	3	34	91	Sumter	3	241	792
Indian River	4	19	44	Walton	12	168	387
			Sanitary services (SIC code 495)				
Florida	346	7,097	17,593	Lee	9	162	415
				Marion	7	19	28
Alachua	6	99	185	Okaloosa	5	31	45
Bay	6	52	122	Orange	19	210	449
Brevard	8	80	120	Osceola	6	34	71
Charlotte	3	114	284	Pasco	7	37	74
Clay	7	78	190	Polk	16	266	475
Dade	32	1,416	3,388	Santa Rosa	4	23	17
Duval	23	408	1,120	Seminole	11	211	485
Hillsborough	21	680	1,785	Walton	5	48	87

Note: Private employment. For a list of three-digit industries included see Table 15.15. Data are preliminary. Only counties for which data are disclosed are shown. Detail may not add to totals due to disclosure editing and/or rounding. See Tables 23.70, 23.71, 23.72, 23.73, and 23.74 for public employment data.

Source: State of Florida, Department of Labor and Employment Security, Bureau of Labor Market Information, "Employment and Wages" (ES-202), unpublished data.

Table 15.25. ELECTRIC RATES: RESIDENTIAL ELECTRIC RATES CHARGED BY MUNICIPAL, COOPERATIVE, AND INVESTOR-OWNED UTILITIES IN FLORIDA, DECEMBER 31, 1994

(in dollars)

Utility	Minimum bill or customer charge	500 KWH	750 KWH	1,000 KWH	1,500 KWH
Municipal					
Alachua	8.00	49.40	70.10	90.80	132.20
Bartow	5.50	41.12	58.92	76.73	35.00
Blountstown	3.50	33.43	48.39	63.36	93.28
Bushnell	6.75	43.79	62.30	80.82	117.86
Chattahoochee	4.50	41.15	59.48	77.80	114.45
Clewiston	6.50	41.25	58.63	76.00	110.75
Ft. Meade	8.67	50.84	71.93	93.01	135.18
Ft. Pierce	5.35	42.66	61.31	79.96	117.27
Gainesville	4.90	39.40	56.65	74.95	111.55
Green Cove Springs	6.00	46.22	66.32	86.43	126.65
Havana	6.00	48.31	69.47	90.62	132.93
Homestead	5.50	44.00	63.25	82.51	121.01
Jacksonville	5.50	36.70	52.30	67.90	99.10
Jacksonville Beach	4.50	42.00	60.75	79.50	117.00
Key West	4.76	43.86	63.41	82.96	122.06
Kissimmee	4.00	41.88	60.81	79.75	117.63
Lake Worth	2.78	41.07	60.21	79.36	117.64
Lakeland	3.94	39.52	57.31	75.10	110.68
Leesburg	5.00	40.85	58.78	76.70	112.55
Moore Haven	8.50	48.00	67.75	87.50	127.00
Mount Dora	4.94	40.14	57.74	75.34	110.54
New Smyrna Beach	4.75	44.14	63.83	83.52	122.90
Newberry	5.00	43.20	62.29	81.39	119.59
Ocala	7.00	44.68	63.51	82.35	120.03
Orlando	6.00	41.70	59.54	77.39	113.09
Quincy	2.40	41.53	61.09	80.65	119.78
Reedy Creek	2.85	35.90	52.42	68.94	101.99
St. Cloud	7.39	45.28	66.29	87.29	129.30
Starke	6.45	39.00	55.28	71.55	115.10
Tallahassee	4.94	45.65	66.01	86.36	127.07
Vero Beach	7.00	43.66	61.99	80.32	116.98
Wauchula	8.62	44.36	62.22	80.09	115.83
Williston	6.00	45.13	64.70	84.26	123.39

See footnotes at end of table. Continued . . .

Table 15.25. ELECTRIC RATES: RESIDENTIAL ELECTRIC RATES CHARGED BY MUNICIPAL, COOPERATIVE, AND INVESTOR-OWNED UTILITIES IN FLORIDA, DECEMBER 31, 1994 (Continued)

(in dollars)

Utility	Minimum bill or customer charge	500 KWH	750 KWH	1,000 KWH	1,500 KWH
Cooperative					
Central Florida	8.50	44.25	62.13	80.00	115.75
Choctawhatchee	12.32	42.42	57.48	72.53	102.63
Clay	9.00	44.80	62.70	80.60	121.60
Escambia River	7.00	41.40	58.60	75.80	110.20
Florida Keys	6.40	36.66	51.79	66.92	97.18
Glades	10.50	53.50	75.00	96.50	139.50
Gulf Coast	7.00	42.60	60.40	78.20	113.80
Lee County	5.00	42.80	61.70	80.60	118.40
Okefenokee	10.00	46.42	64.62	82.83	119.25
Peace River	10.50	54.75	76.88	99.00	143.25
Sumter	8.37	49.16	69.56	89.95	130.74
Suwannee Valley	8.73	52.76	74.77	96.78	140.81
Talquin	8.00	45.50	64.25	83.00	120.50
Tri-county	8.00	55.34	79.01	102.68	150.03
West Florida	8.00	44.81	63.22	81.62	118.43
Withlacoochee River	9.75	46.37	64.67	82.98	119.60
Investor-owned					
Florida Power	8.85	45.16	63.32	81.47	117.78
Florida Power and Light	5.65	37.02	52.70	70.88	107.25
Florida Public Utilities					
Fernandina Beach division	7.00	38.01	53.52	69.02	100.03
Marianna division	8.30	39.11	54.51	69.91	100.72
Gulf Power 1/	8.07	38.71	54.03	69.35	99.99
Tampa Electric	8.50	44.42	62.38	80.34	116.26

1/ Summer/winter rates in effect. Winter rates are shown.

Note: Cost excludes local taxes. December 1994 fuel costs are included for municipal and cooperative utilities. October 1994 through March 1995 fuel costs are included for investor-owned utilities.

Source: State of Florida, Public Service Commission, Division of Research and Regulatory Review, *Statistics of the Florida Electric Utility Industry, 1994*.

Table 15.26. ELECTRIC RATES: COMMERCIAL AND INDUSTRIAL ELECTRIC RATES CHARGED BY MUNICIPAL, COOPERATIVE, AND INVESTOR-OWNED UTILITIES IN FLORIDA, DECEMBER 31, 1994

(in dollars)

Utility	15,000 KWH	45,000 KWH	150,000 KWH	400,000 KWH	800,000 KWH
Municipal					
Alachua	1,378	3,642	12,088	30,213	60,403
Bartow	1,419	3,651	12,126	29,771	59,523
Blountstown	1,036	3,095	10,299	27,453	54,899
Bushnell	1,385	3,603	11,962	29,597	59,173
Chattahoochee	1,221	3,732	12,440	31,500	63,000
Clewiston	1,273	3,478	11,510	29,435	58,835
Ft. Meade	1,308	4,011	13,161	32,226	64,362
Ft. Pierce	1,299	3,394	11,244	27,966	55,902
Gainesville	1,191	3,176	10,551	23,241	46,421
Green Cove Springs	1,441	3,749	12,440	26,597	53,070
Havana	1,275	3,814	12,699	33,854	67,702
Homestead	1,368	3,706	12,436	31,137	62,310
Jacksonville	1,082	2,715	8,933	20,760	41,320
Jacksonville Beach	1,614	4,171	13,866	34,116	68,216
Key West	1,596	4,260	14,190	35,535	71,065
Kissimmee	1,307	3,209	11,115	25,602	51,162
Lake Worth	1,472	3,864	12,852	31,904	63,796
Lakeland	1,163	3,088	10,465	24,862	49,348
Leesburg	1,343	3,395	11,277	27,377	54,737
Moore Haven	1,515	4,058	13,473	33,923	67,823
Mount Dora	978	2,533	8,410	20,755	41,495
New Smyrna Beach	1,455	3,863	12,799	32,142	64,250
Newberry	1,461	3,603	11,974	28,571	57,127
Ocala	1,169	2,978	9,877	24,137	48,253
Orlando	1,123	2,814	9,344	22,559	45,103
Quincy	1,099	2,900	9,524	24,064	48,308
Reedy Creek	1,055	2,828	9,392	23,647	47,279
St. Cloud	1,447	3,968	13,168	31,793	67,245
Starke	1,316	3,928	13,074	34,849	69,689
Tallahassee	1,348	3,419	11,258	27,538	55,036
Vero Beach	1,217	3,301	10,796	27,476	54,883
Wauchula	1,114	3,562	11,721	29,323	58,581
Williston	1,328	3,575	11,663	29,018	59,929

See footnotes at end of table. Continued . . .

Table 15.26. ELECTRIC RATES: COMMERCIAL AND INDUSTRIAL ELECTRIC RATES CHARGED BY MUNICIPAL, COOPERATIVE, AND INVESTOR-OWNED UTILITIES IN FLORIDA, DECEMBER 31, 1994 (Continued)

(in dollars)

Utility	15,000 KWH	45,000 KWH	150,000 KWH	400,000 KWH	800,000 KWH
Cooperative					
Central Florida	1,288	3,215	10,600	25,350	50,650
Choctawhatchee	1,013	2,644	9,126	20,335	40,170
Clay	1,221	3,273	10,780	27,405	50,103
Escambia River	1,203	3,115	10,290	25,540	51,040
Florida Keys	1,106	3,217	10,845	28,090	56,232
Glades	1,631	4,553	14,575	35,575	70,975
Gulf Coast	1,013	2,714	9,017	22,692	45,372
Lee County	1,134	2,997	10,530	25,455	50,895
Okefenokee	1,230	3,017	9,825	23,932	47,764
Peace River	1,258	3,230	10,650	26,350	52,650
Sumter	1,368	3,527	11,642	28,338	56,626
Suwannee Valley	1,584	4,207	13,929	35,021	70,001
Talquin	1,281	3,198	10,520	23,080	45,860
Tri-county	1,499	3,773	12,343	29,424	58,747
West Florida	1,090	2,719	8,945	21,770	43,490
Withlacoochee River	1,174	3,010	9,976	24,509	48,993
Investor-owned					
Florida Power	971	2,604	8,654	21,792	43,572
Florida Power and Light	995	2,804	9,091	21,503	42,958
Florida Public Utilities					
Fernandina Beach division	932	2,587	8,536	22,108	44,178
Marianna division	886	2,392	7,871	20,116	40,188
Gulf Power 1/	959	2,453	8,973	20,693	41,159
Tampa Electric	1,200	2,974	9,814	23,813	47,371

KWH Kilowatt-hour.
1/ Summer/winter rates in effect. Winter rates are shown.
Note: Cost excludes local taxes. December 1994 fuel costs are included for municipal and cooperative utilities. October 1994 through March 1995 fuel costs are included for investor-owned utilities.

Source: State of Florida, Public Service Commission, Division of Research and Regulatory Review, *Statistics of the Florida Electric Utility Industry, 1994.*

Table 15.27. ELECTRIC UTILITY INDUSTRY: CAPACITY, NET GENERATION, FUEL CONSUMPTION, SALES, PER CAPITA CONSUMPTION, AND REVENUE IN FLORIDA, 1990 THROUGH 1994

Item	1990	1991	1992	1993	1994
Nameplate capacity, total (MW)	37,532	36,979	36,988	38,039	39,084
Conventional steam	27,947	26,968	26,784	27,316	27,263
Internal combustion and gas turbine	5,024	5,138	5,217	5,925	6,234
Combined cycle	596	728	842	652	1,442
Hydroelectric	43	21	21	21	21
Steam, nuclear	3,922	4,124	4,124	4,124	4,124
Net generation, total (GWH)	125,468	134,443	140,060	149,388	152,779
By prime mover					
Conventional steam	99,571	109,226	110,126	119,286	115,196
Internal combustion and gas turbine	1,154	1,223	1,070	2,267	8,537
Combined cycle	2,472	2,836	2,361	0	0
Hydroelectric	176	27	247	225	295
Steam, nuclear	22,095	21,121	26,256	27,610	28,750
By fuel type					
Natural gas	15,920	17,472	17,744	18,064	20,420
Coal	62,110	66,037	58,836	61,000	62,511
Residual	25,907	31,207	28,588	33,985	33,286
Distillate	711	637	10,145	10,885	10,267
Hydroelectric	249	28	54	51	80
Nuclear	20,572	19,062	24,693	25,403	26,216
By type of ownership					
Investor-owned	96,491	101,821	104,776	112,251	117,134
Municipal	28,976	32,622	35,284	37,137	35,645
Fuel consumed for generation					
Natural gas (billion cubic feet)	188	203	137	174	181
Coal (1,000 short tons)	26,250	27,955	31,260	28,954	30,239
Residual (1,000 barrels)	38,814	46,611	43,577	54,347	52,233
Distillate (1,000 barrels)	1,766	1,798	1,472	1,426	1,195
U-235 (trillion BTU)	226	205	268	301	286
Sales to ultimate consumers, total (GWH)	143,303	146,105	149,238	152,219	160,851
Residential	71,035	72,694	73,293	76,843	80,405
Commercial	45,770	46,810	45,879	48,598	51,519
Industrial	22,110	21,672	24,960	22,022	22,057
Other public utilities	4,389	4,929	5,107	4,755	6,870
Per capita consumption 1/ (KWH)					
Sales per capita, total	11,432	11,293	11,309	11,339	(NA)
Residential sales per capita	5,542	5,619	5,554	5,724	(NA)
Kilowatt-hours per capita 2/	10,116	10,391	10,614	11,128	(NA)

See footnotes at end of table.

Continued . . .

Table 15.27. ELECTRIC UTILITY INDUSTRY: CAPACITY, NET GENERATION, FUEL CONSUMPTION, SALES, PER CAPITA CONSUMPTION, AND REVENUE IN FLORIDA, 1990 THROUGH 1994 (Continued)

Item	1990	1991	1992	1993	1994
Revenues per GWH by class of service ($1,000)	70.3	71.5	69.0	72.1	69.0
Residential	77.7	78.9	77.5	79.9	77.8
Commercial	68.2	68.8	64.1	64.3	63.3
Industrial	51.0	52.9	53.6	61.8	55.6
Other	69.2	69.5	65.9	73.7	52.3

MW Megawatt (1,000 kilowatts).
GWH Gigawatt-hours (million kilowatt-hours).
BTU British thermal units.
KWH Kilowatt-hours.
(NA) Not available.
1/ Total sales divided by population.
2/ Net generation divided by population.
Note: Detail may not add to totals because of rounding. Some data are revised.

Source: State of Florida, Public Service Commission, Division of Research and Regulatory Review, *Statistics of the Florida Electric Utility Industry, 1994.*

Table 15.41. NATURAL GAS: TYPICAL NATURAL GAS BILLS FOR RESIDENTIAL SERVICE OF COMPANIES IN FLORIDA, DECEMBER 31, 1995

(amounts in dollars)

Company	Minimum bill	20 therms	30 therms	40 therms	50 therms	100 therms
Chesapeake Utilities Company	6.50	22.66	30.74	38.82	46.90	87.30
City Gas Company of Florida	6.00	21.69	29.53	37.37	45.21	84.43
Florida Public Utilities Company	8.00	22.74	30.12	37.49	44.86	81.72
Indiantown Gas Company	5.00	12.28	15.91	19.55	23.19	41.38
Peoples Gas System, Inc.	7.00	21.79	29.19	36.58	43.98	80.96
Sebring Gas System, Inc.	7.00	22.14	29.71	37.28	44.85	82.69
St. Joe Natural Gas Company	3.00	9.51	12.77	16.03	19.29	35.57
South Florida Natural Gas Company	7.00	22.55	30.32	38.09	45.87	84.73
West Florida Natural Gas Company	7.00	20.65	27.47	34.29	41.11	75.23

1 Therm = 100,000 British thermal units.

Source: State of Florida, Public Service Commission, *1995 Annual Report.*

Table 15.42. NATURAL GAS: PRODUCTION, MOVEMENT, AND CONSUMPTION IN FLORIDA AND THE UNITED STATES, 1993 AND 1994

(quantity in millions of cubic feet)

Item	Florida 1993	Florida 1994	United States 1993	United States 1994
Marketed production 1/	7,085	7,486	19,305,087	19,635,495
Net interstate movements	336,155	359,143	0	0
Net movements across U.S. borders	0	0	2,209,931	2,496,868
Net storage changes 2/	0	0	35,701	302,641
Extraction loss	2,557	1,789	886,455	888,500
Supplemental gas supplies	0	0	118,999	110,826
Balancing item 3/	-3,334	2,713	-413,742	-296,577
Consumption, total	337,349	367,552	20,279,095	20,755,471
Delivered to consumers	331,289	361,428	18,482,847	18,909,587
Lease fuel	476	653	723,118	736,678
Plant fuel	1,241	167	448,822	423,878
Pipeline fuel	4,342	5,304	624,308	685,327

1/ Gross withdrawals from gas and oil wells less gas used for repressuring, nonhydrocarbon gases removed, and quantities vented and flared.
2/ Positive numbers indicate an increase in storage, thus a decrease in supply.
3/ Represents an imbalance between available supplies and consumption.
Note: Some data may be revised.

Source: U.S., Department of Energy, Energy Information Administration, *Natural Gas Annual, 1994,* and previous edition.

Table 15.43. NATURAL GAS: VOLUME CONSUMED, CONSUMERS, AND PRICE OF NATURAL GAS DELIVERED TO CONSUMERS IN FLORIDA AND THE UNITED STATES, 1994

Item	Residential	Commercial	Industrial	Vehicle fuel	Electric utilities
Florida					
Volume consumed (MCF)	13,855	39,935	126,873	68	180,697
Consumers	497,777	47,851	481	(NA)	(NA)
Average price (dollars per thousand cubic feet)	9.98	5.54	3.51	4.36	2.18
United States					
Volume consumed (MCF)	4,847,702	2,895,034	8,177,975	1,730	2,987,146
Consumers	53,393,142	4,537,500	202,953	(NA)	(NA)
Average price (dollars per thousand cubic feet)	6.41	5.44	3.05	4.13	2.28

MCF Million cubic feet.
(NA) Not available.

Source: U.S., Department of Energy, Energy Information Administration, *Natural Gas Annual, 1994.*

Table 15.50. NUCLEAR POWER PLANTS: LOCATION AND CAPACITY OF PLANTS IN OPERATION IN FLORIDA AND THE UNITED STATES, 1993

Location	Plant	Capacity (net MWe)	Utility	Type of reactor	Date operable
Florida 1/	(X)	3,828	(X)	(X)	(X)
Florida City	Turkey Point 3	666	Florida Power and Light	PWR	Nov-72
Florida City	Turkey Point 4	666	Florida Power and Light	PWR	Jun-73
Ft. Pierce	St. Lucie 1	839	Florida Power and Light	PWR	May-76
Ft. Pierce	St. Lucie 2	839	Florida Power and Light	PWR	Jun-83
Red Level	Crystal River 3	818	Florida Power Corp.	PWR	Jan-77
United States 2/	(X)	99,040	(X)	(X)	(X)

MWe Megawatt electrical.
PWR Pressurized-water reactor.
(X) Not applicable.
1/ 5 plants.
2/ 112 plants.

Source: U.S., Department of Commerce, Bureau of the Census, *Statistical Abstract of the United States, 1995*, and McGraw-Hill, Inc., New York, NY, *World Nuclear Performance*, (copyright).

Table 15.51. ENERGY CONSUMPTION: AMOUNT CONSUMED BY SECTOR IN FLORIDA 1979 THROUGH 1993

(in trillions of British thermal units)

Year	Total	Residential	Commercial 1/	Industrial 2/	Transportation 3/
1979	2,373.4	538.1	384.7	518.4	832.2
1980	2,444.3	568.0	384.1	541.7	950.6
1981	2,428.9	576.9	422.7	474.7	954.5
1982	2,322.5	558.0	426.4	401.2	937.0
1983	2,388.7	586.0	460.7	403.8	938.2
1984	2,459.1	611.2	487.7	432.9	927.2
1985	2,610.5	664.2	559.6	435.4	951.2
1986	2,693.9	694.4	589.4	404.1	1,006.0
1987	2,793.1	721.3	612.5	398.8	1,060.5
1988	2,954.4	752.4	640.7	434.9	1,126.4
1989	3,026.0	790.7	667.1	426.6	1,141.7
1990	3,060.0	807.2	690.8	426.3	1,135.6
1991	3,018.1	823.7	699.6	420.7	1,074.1
1992	3,066.4	820.7	695.3	438.0	1,112.4
1993	3,128.2	853.3	701.0	467.8	1,106.1

1/ Includes establishments under SIC codes 15-17, 48-49 (except 491 and part of 493), 50-59, 70-89, and 91-93.
2/ Includes establishments under SIC codes 1-14 and 20-39.
3/ Includes establishments under SIC codes 40-47.

Source: U.S., Department of Energy, Energy Information Administration, *State Energy Data Report, 1993: Consumption Estimates*, July 1995. Compiled by State of Florida, Department of Community Affairs.

Table 15.60. MOTOR FUELS: CONSUMPTION BY USE IN FLORIDA, 1958 THROUGH 1994

(in thousands of gallons)

Year	Total quantity consumed 1/	Nonhighway use 2/	Highway use
1958	1,787,338	243,149	1,525,619
1959	1,933,950	276,033	1,641,576
1960	1,950,650	167,431	1,765,819
1961	1,980,408	160,451	1,800,927
1962	2,071,490	133,801	1,917,987
1963	2,169,084	124,988	2,022,714
1964	2,286,002	112,073	2,160,479
1965	2,409,617	104,646	2,291,031
1966	2,562,586	120,505	2,428,962
1967	2,711,163	135,851	2,561,698
1968	2,959,259	138,496	2,803,754
1969	3,215,457	129,949	3,069,173
1970	3,484,439	153,969	3,312,830
1971	3,771,337	146,210	3,585,727
1972	4,215,995	124,098	4,045,322
1973	4,695,983	126,054	4,494,951
1974	4,510,456	123,058	4,342,185
1975	4,639,217	135,547	4,456,610
1976	4,827,840	136,774	4,650,302
1977	5,023,007	131,635	4,846,201
1978	5,337,604	139,114	5,152,263
1979	5,374,535	142,358	5,171,693
1980	5,293,548	164,430	5,116,312
1981	5,390,545	137,165	5,240,229
1982	5,469,775	139,779	5,317,892
1983	5,723,316	163,810	5,548,590
1984	5,934,391	181,767	5,740,587
1985	6,110,435	254,402	5,843,396
1986	6,394,295	263,337	6,116,961
1987	6,700,629	275,337	6,387,472
1988	6,863,376	281,739	6,530,151
1989	7,034,489	292,036	6,680,708
1990	7,043,054	306,520	6,674,542
1991	6,930,325	319,863	6,549,254
1992	7,163,374	264,516	6,827,210
1993	7,431,207	169,860	7,187,669
1994	7,487,188	178,304	7,308,884

1/ Includes losses allowed for evaporation and handling.
2/ Gasoline. Includes gasohol.
Note: Includes gasoline and all other fuels (except under nonhighway use) under state motor fuel laws.

Source: U.S., Department of Transportation, Federal Highway Administration, *Highway Statistics, 1994,* and previous editions.

Table 15.66. GASOLINE: AVERAGE PRICES IN SELECTED CITIES IN FLORIDA, DECEMBER 1995 AND ANNUALLY IN FLORIDA AND THE UNITED STATES, 1992 THROUGH 1994

(prices in dollars per gallon)

City	Average pump price: Full service unleaded: Regular	Mid-grade	Premium	Self-service unleaded: Regular	Mid-grade	Premium
Bradenton	1.542	1.607	1.702	1.074	1.203	1.288
Brandon	(NA)	(NA)	(NA)	1.026	1.144	1.223
Cocoa/Melbourne	1.443	1.562	1.666	1.091	1.170	1.255
Daytona Beach	1.407	1.504	1.601	1.078	1.223	1.312
Delray Beach	(NA)	(NA)	(NA)	1.153	1.302	1.368
Ft. Lauderdale	1.582	1.661	1.736	1.062	1.177	1.252
Ft. Myers	1.479	1.556	1.647	1.112	1.218	1.308
Ft. Pierce	1.405	1.573	1.677	1.077	1.192	1.295
Gainesville	1.409	1.509	1.609	1.151	1.269	1.361
Jacksonville	1.599	1.699	1.799	1.073	1.181	1.279
Lakeland	1.402	1.497	1.602	1.050	1.168	1.273
Leesburg	1.375	1.479	1.583	1.061	1.257	1.290
Miami	1.426	1.539	1.604	1.164	1.230	1.293
Naples	1.484	1.579	1.679	1.137	1.219	1.329
Ocala	1.437	1.513	1.605	1.067	1.191	1.279
Orlando	1.471	1.565	1.646	1.078	1.209	1.291
Palm Beach	1.545	1.664	1.720	1.160	1.299	1.359
Pensacola	1.524	1.624	1.724	1.028	1.133	1.235
Pompano Beach	1.503	1.614	1.685	1.063	1.171	1.253
Port Charlotte	1.371	1.412	1.557	1.053	1.172	1.270
Port Richey	(NA)	(NA)	(NA)	1.023	1.137	1.217
St. Petersburg	1.504	1.629	1.716	1.018	1.163	1.249
Sarasota	1.646	1.749	1.837	1.068	1.194	1.280
Stuart	(NA)	(NA)	(NA)	1.104	1.231	1.292
Tallahassee	1.454	1.544	1.634	1.129	1.239	1.332
Tampa	1.579	1.679	1.779	1.033	1.144	1.211
Venice	1.634	1.749	1.824	1.058	1.165	1.254

Area and year	Average sales price to end users 1/: Nominal price	Implicit price deflator 2/ (1987 = 1.000)	Constant price (1987 dollars): Amount	Percentage change
Florida				
1992	78.7	1.235	63.7	-7.0
1993	76.5	1.266	60.4	-5.2
1994	72.7	1.293	56.2	-7.0
United States				
1992	78.7	1.235	63.7	-5.9
1993	75.3	1.266	59.5	-6.7
1994	72.9	1.293	56.4	-5.2

(NA) Not available.
1/ Prices are in cents per gallon and exclude all federal, state, and county taxes.
2/ For personal consumption expenditures. Data from U.S. Department of Commerce, Bureau of Economic Analysis.
Note: City data are from AAA Clubs of Florida Survey. Some data may be revised.
Source: State of Florida, Department of Community Affairs, unpublished data, and U.S., Department of Energy, Energy Information Administration, *Petroleum Marketing Annual 1995*, and previous editions.

Table 15.67. GASOLINE: TOTAL AND PER CAPITA GALLONS SOLD IN THE STATE AND COUNTIES OF FLORIDA, 1993 AND 1994

County	Total sales (1,000 gallons) 1993	1994	Percentage change 1993-94	Per capita sales (gallons) 1993	1994	Percentage change 1993-94
Florida	6,356,978	6,493,727	2.2	467.1	467.9	0.2
Alachua	90,301	90,212	-0.1	473.6	465.3	-1.8
Baker	10,943	11,684	6.8	560.4	593.1	5.8
Bay	72,636	75,565	4.0	541.8	554.4	2.3
Bradford	12,830	13,484	5.1	550.4	557.0	1.2
Brevard	204,493	208,627	2.0	478.9	478.1	-0.2
Broward	607,301	638,842	5.2	460.9	476.7	3.4
Calhoun	5,399	5,983	10.8	470.3	517.3	10.0
Charlotte	56,478	62,308	10.3	464.1	498.9	7.5
Citrus	42,026	43,341	3.1	416.8	421.4	1.1
Clay	52,901	54,038	2.1	460.3	458.8	-0.3
Collier	89,458	92,606	3.5	512.2	512.9	0.1
Columbia	36,766	37,837	2.9	791.9	773.8	-2.3
Dade	827,953	804,736	-2.8	424.3	404.3	-4.7
De Soto	10,220	10,314	0.9	401.4	392.8	-2.2
Dixie	8,171	6,986	-14.5	691.9	575.0	-16.9
Duval	333,635	335,471	0.6	475.5	472.1	-0.7
Escambia	126,251	128,883	2.1	464.0	465.2	0.2
Flagler	16,168	18,242	12.8	482.0	516.9	7.2
Franklin	3,379	3,972	17.5	345.7	397.4	15.0
Gadsden	18,784	19,471	3.7	434.4	434.1	-0.1
Gilchrist	2,996	3,414	14.0	279.4	296.2	6.0
Glades	3,836	3,959	3.2	463.9	473.2	2.0
Gulf	5,205	5,535	6.3	420.0	417.3	-0.7
Hamilton	11,290	10,414	-7.8	972.9	873.8	-10.2
Hardee	10,364	10,886	5.0	470.3	484.8	3.1
Hendry	15,710	16,536	5.3	559.9	576.4	3.0
Hernando	47,387	49,695	4.9	424.3	432.6	2.0
Highlands	35,806	35,874	0.2	489.1	472.9	-3.3
Hillsborough	399,221	412,836	3.4	460.9	469.6	1.9
Holmes	8,232	8,756	6.4	504.1	517.3	2.6
Indian River	43,911	46,519	5.9	459.1	477.5	4.0
Jackson	28,461	29,554	3.8	641.2	650.7	1.5
Jefferson	9,897	9,960	0.6	762.0	761.2	-0.1
Lafayette	2,173	2,361	8.7	387.8	405.3	4.5
Lake	75,812	78,976	4.2	453.5	461.4	1.7
Lee	178,340	181,609	1.8	498.8	494.3	-0.9

See footnote at end of table.

Continued . . .

Table 15.67. GASOLINE: TOTAL AND PER CAPITA GALLONS SOLD IN THE STATE AND COUNTIES OF FLORIDA, 1993 AND 1994 (Continued)

County	Total sales (1,000 gallons)			Per capita sales (gallons)		
	1993	1994	Percentage change 1993-94	1993	1994	Percentage change 1993-94
Leon	99,045	105,082	6.1	480.1	495.4	3.2
Levy	16,774	17,560	4.7	594.1	603.2	1.5
Liberty	776	3,120	302.1	135.7	477.2	251.8
Madison	10,266	9,851	-4.0	592.9	554.4	-6.5
Manatee	92,087	97,647	6.0	412.0	427.7	3.8
Marion	118,893	126,329	6.3	560.7	579.9	3.4
Martin	47,909	55,807	16.5	448.7	506.3	12.8
Monroe	45,414	50,054	10.2	555.4	608.5	9.6
Nassau	26,189	25,487	-2.7	563.8	538.0	-4.6
Okaloosa	77,112	84,360	9.4	499.1	532.9	6.8
Okeechobee	20,128	21,317	5.9	633.8	659.5	4.0
Orange	384,646	397,091	3.2	528.5	536.5	1.5
Osceola	75,423	81,486	8.0	600.1	621.5	3.6
Palm Beach	407,703	417,002	2.3	444.0	444.9	0.2
Pasco	114,218	119,170	4.3	388.5	398.8	2.6
Pinellas	329,822	341,021	3.4	381.3	391.7	2.7
Polk	200,641	212,750	6.0	466.7	486.6	4.3
Putnam	29,519	32,034	8.5	436.5	464.4	6.4
St. Johns	51,343	55,049	7.2	563.0	580.9	3.2
St. Lucie	77,091	80,744	4.7	472.4	484.1	2.5
Santa Rosa	40,672	47,504	16.8	450.6	506.4	12.4
Sarasota	124,562	126,101	1.2	428.6	426.0	-0.6
Seminole	121,854	131,972	8.3	392.0	416.9	6.4
Sumter	32,234	31,534	-2.2	953.3	896.1	-6.0
Suwannee	18,135	17,999	-0.7	634.1	614.3	-3.1
Taylor	12,271	12,799	4.3	706.3	733.0	3.8
Union	3,565	3,919	9.9	296.3	312.7	5.5
Volusia	174,477	179,925	3.1	447.3	453.6	1.4
Wakulla	6,896	7,526	9.1	447.8	457.8	2.2
Walton	19,906	22,353	12.3	651.2	701.6	7.7
Washington	9,164	9,643	5.2	522.0	532.3	2.0

Note: Includes gasohol. Per capita is computed using Bureau of Economic and Business Business Research *Florida Estimates of Population*. Some data are revised.

Source: State of Florida, Department of Community Affairs, *1994 Florida Motor Gasoline and Diesel Fuel Report,* April 1995, and unpublished data. Data from State of Florida, Department of Revenue.

WHOLESALE AND RETAIL TRADE

Gross Sales by Kind of Business, 1995

(rounded to thousands of dollars)

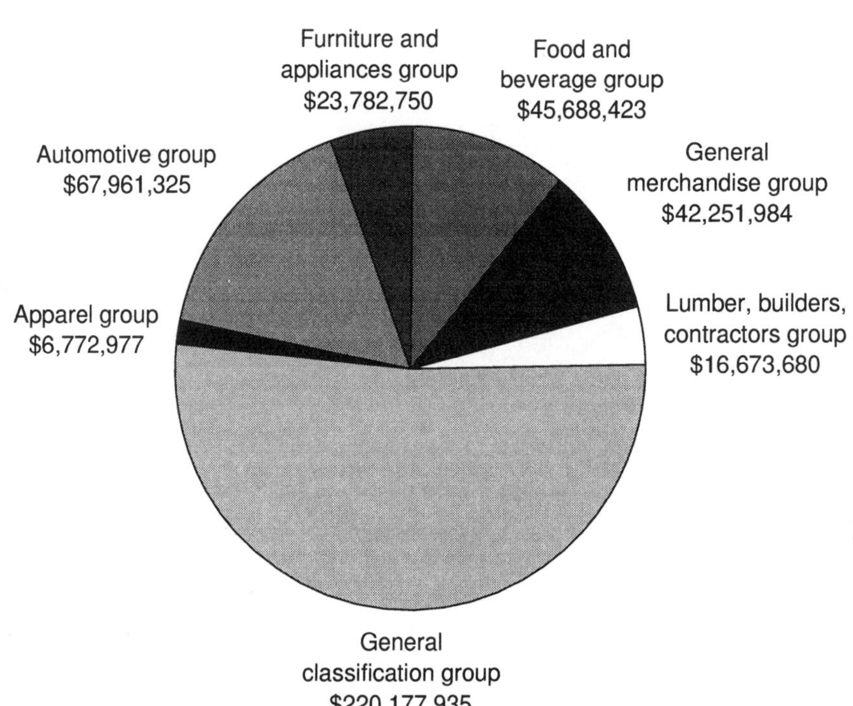

Source: Table 16.81

SECTION 16.00
WHOLESALE AND RETAIL TRADE

TABLES LISTED BY MAJOR HEADINGS

SECTION 16.00
WHOLESALE AND RETAIL TRADE
(Continued)

TABLES LISTED BY MAJOR HEADINGS

HEADING PAGE

Table 16.01. WHOLESALE TRADE: ESTABLISHMENTS, SALES, AND SALES PER ESTABLISHMENT IN FLORIDA, CENSUS YEARS 1967 THROUGH 1992

Census year	Establishments		Sales		Sales per establishment	
	Number	Percentage change	Amount ($1,000)	Percentage change	Amount (dollars)	Percentage change
1967	9,650	8.5	10,302,824	37.6	1,067,650	26.9
1972	13,450	39.4	19,983,912	94.0	1,485,793	39.2
1977	15,409	14.6	34,380,491	72.0	2,231,195	50.2
1982	19,537	26.8	65,614,610	90.8	3,358,479	50.5
1987	25,636	31.2	97,360,044	48.4	3,797,786	13.1
1992	30,137	17.6	132,562,218	36.2	4,398,653	15.8

Note: The wholesale trade census is on a 5-year cycle collecting data for years ending in 2 and 7.

Table 16.02. WHOLESALE TRADE: ESTABLISHMENTS, SALES, AND SALES PER ESTABLISHMENT BY KIND OF BUSINESS IN FLORIDA, 1992

SIC code	Kind of business	Number of establishments	Sales ($1,000)	Sales per establishment (dollars)
	Total	30,137	132,562,218	4,398,653
50	Durable goods	19,725	68,135,799	3,454,286
501	Motor vehicles and automotive parts and supplies	2,902	21,011,402	7,240,318
502	Furniture and home furnishings	1,268	2,263,815	1,785,343
503	Lumber and other construction materials	1,325	4,504,328	3,399,493
504	Sporting, recreational, photographic, and hobby goods, toys, and supplies	3,212	9,993,446	3,111,285
505	Metals and minerals, except petroleum	482	2,244,623	4,656,894
506	Electrical goods	2,672	11,309,423	4,232,568
507	Hardware and plumbing and heating equipment and supplies	1,560	3,226,598	2,068,332
508	Machinery, equipment, and supplies	3,938	8,573,734	2,177,180
509	Miscellaneous durable goods	2,366	5,008,430	2,116,834
51	Nondurable goods	10,412	64,426,419	6,187,708
511	Paper and paper products	1,112	3,887,952	3,496,360
512	Drugs, drug proprietaries, and druggists' sundries	542	5,531,365	10,205,470
513	Apparel, piece goods, and notions	1,217	2,389,730	1,963,624
514	Groceries and related products	2,956	26,713,857	9,037,164
515	Farm-product raw materials	141	1,731,637	12,281,113
516	Chemicals and allied products	782	2,569,769	3,286,150
517	Petroleum and petroleum products	587	8,940,891	15,231,501
518	Beer, wine, and distilled alcoholic beverages	179	3,984,416	22,259,307
519	Miscellaneous nondurable goods	2,896	8,676,802	2,996,133

Note: The wholesale trade census is on a 5-year cycle collecting data for years ending in 2 and 7.

Source for tables 16.01 and 16.02: U.S., Department of Commerce, Bureau of the Census, *1992 Census of Wholesale Trade: Florida,* and previous editions.

Table 16.06. WHOLESALE AND RETAIL TRADE: SALES IN THE STATE AND COUNTIES OF FLORIDA, 1992

(in thousands of dollars)

County	Wholesale trade	Retail trade	County	Wholesale trade	Retail trade
Florida	132,562,218	118,741,770	Lafayette	11,076	8,179
			Lake	742,333	1,085,771
Alachua	493,922	1,525,129	Lee	1,203,415	3,393,129
Baker	20,597	73,257	Leon	805,067	1,721,972
Bay	437,901	1,224,342	Levy	33,793	141,320
Bradford	22,642	114,224	Liberty	2,288	12,677
Brevard	1,161,850	3,915,909	Madison	60,679	64,687
Broward	17,740,357	14,539,331	Manatee	1,115,600	1,580,441
Calhoun	32,676	41,730	Marion	1,309,987	1,552,749
Charlotte	106,716	816,794	Martin	249,237	1,036,012
Citrus	77,310	619,974	Monroe	154,886	821,142
Clay	199,149	811,838	Nassau	75,847	292,388
Collier	545,847	1,783,047	Okaloosa	248,735	1,283,036
Columbia	303,760	388,240	Okeechobee	149,866	199,974
Dade	30,878,059	17,642,481	Orange	18,607,483	7,397,885
De Soto	66,063	125,956	Osceola	799,070	1,133,792
Dixie	5,443	37,284	Palm Beach	6,491,016	9,084,460
Duval	11,327,784	6,015,387	Pasco	315,471	1,762,857
Escambia	1,298,888	2,272,972	Pinellas	4,509,687	8,451,895
Flagler	34,378	147,856	Polk	3,450,660	3,047,387
Franklin	40,591	39,422	Putnam	78,485	340,567
Gadsden	398,886	163,923	St. Johns	343,453	649,153
Gilchrist	8,850	18,746	St. Lucie	656,637	1,132,724
Glades	6,044	13,300	Santa Rosa	89,906	405,117
Gulf	17,567	35,059	Sarasota	854,195	2,921,187
Hamilton	7,396	47,529	Seminole	2,756,110	2,725,323
Hardee	81,901	112,876	Sumter	52,969	162,223
Hendry	55,542	149,486	Suwannee	66,149	158,275
Hernando	96,608	585,906	Taylor	34,230	100,169
Highlands	166,907	646,525	Union	4,691	18,371
Hillsborough	18,935,505	7,686,678	Volusia	988,130	3,048,473
Holmes	9,759	40,405	Wakulla	63,596	42,385
Indian River	1,374,614	781,201	Walton	69,381	169,587
Jackson	162,417	282,640	Washington	30,621	54,907
Jefferson	21,540	42,109			

Source: U.S., Department of Commerce, Bureau of the Census, *1992 Census of Wholesale Trade: Florida,* and *1992 Census of Retail Trade: Florida.*

Table 16.11. RETAIL TRADE: ESTABLISHMENTS, SALES, AND SALES PER ESTABLISHMENT IN FLORIDA, CENSUS YEARS 1948 THROUGH 1992

Census year	Establishments		Retail sales		Sales per establishment	
	Number	Percentage change	Amount ($1,000)	Percentage change	Amount (dollars)	Percentage change
1948	32,513	13.6	2,326,682	278.7	71,562	233.2
1954	41,303	27.0	4,014,417	72.5	97,194	35.8
1958	49,547	20.0	5,839,600	45.5	117,860	21.3
1963	53,293	7.6	7,609,717	30.3	142,790	21.2
1967	58,727	10.2	10,280,334	35.1	175,053	22.6
1972	70,898	20.7	19,430,163	89.0	274,058	56.6
1977	83,013	17.1	31,300,103	61.1	377,051	37.6
1982	88,733	6.9	55,468,945	77.2	625,122	65.8
1987 A/	83,808	(X)	87,925,609	(X)	1,049,131	(X)
1992 A/	87,653	4.6	118,741,770	35.0	1,354,680	29.1

(X) Not applicable.
A/ Establishments with payroll only.
Note: Prior to 1987, establishments represented the number of businesses at the end of the year. Subsequent counts include establishments in business at any time during the year. Therefore caution should be used in comparing these data. The retail trade census is now on a 5-year cycle collecting data for years ending in 2 and 7.

Table 16.12. RETAIL TRADE: ESTABLISHMENTS, SALES, AND ANNUAL PAYROLL BY KIND OF BUSINESS IN FLORIDA, 1992

SIC code	Kind of business	Number of estab-lishments	Sales ($1,000)	Annual payroll Total ($1,000)	Annual payroll Per em-ployee 1/ (dollars)
	Total	87,653	118,741,770	13,275,960	12,044
52	Building materials and garden supplies stores	3,792	5,523,991	613,331	15,190
53	General merchandise stores	1,631	14,096,715	1,441,509	12,497
54	Food stores	9,734	21,195,238	2,159,126	11,476
55	Automotive dealers and gasoline service stations	11,556	37,492,434	2,471,751	(NA)
56	Apparel and accessory stores	9,626	6,506,119	742,788	10,384
57	Furniture and home furnishings stores	7,604	6,148,396	740,917	16,921
58	Eating and drinking places	22,664	12,110,554	3,195,546	8,107
59	Drug, proprietary and miscellaneous retail	21,046	15,668,323	1,910,992	(NA)

(NA) Not available.
1/ Based on number of employees for pay period ending March 12.
Note: The retail trade census is on a 5-year cycle collecting data for years ending in 2 and 7.

Source for Tables 16.11 and 16.12: U.S., Department of Commerce, Bureau of the Census, *1992 Census of Retail Trade: Florida,* and previous editions.

Table 16.43. EMPLOYMENT: AVERAGE MONTHLY PRIVATE REPORTING UNITS, EMPLOYMENT AND PAYROLL COVERED BY UNEMPLOYMENT COMPENSATION LAW BY WHOLESALE AND RETAIL TRADE INDUSTRY IN FLORIDA, 1994 AND 1995

SIC code	Industry	Number of reporting units	Number of employees	Payroll ($1,000)
	1994 A/			
	Wholesale trade	36,045	305,351	832,024
50	Wholesale trade--durable goods	23,287	174,485	494,327
501	Motor vehicles and motor vehicle parts and supplies	2,697	25,233	56,851
502	Furniture and homefurnishings	1,216	6,598	16,994
503	Lumber and other construction materials	1,563	11,923	30,608
504	Professional and commercial equipment and supplies	5,133	42,169	146,102
505	Metals and minerals, except petroleum	419	3,445	10,029
506	Electrical goods	3,210	24,174	72,005
507	Hardware, plumbing and heating equipment and supplies	1,825	14,285	38,386
508	Machinery, equipment, and supplies	4,471	31,414	87,780
509	Miscellaneous durable goods	2,754	15,245	35,573
51	Wholesale trade--nondurable goods	12,758	130,866	337,697
511	Paper and paper products	1,276	15,204	34,716
512	Drugs, drug proprietaries, and druggists' sundries	1,086	11,536	39,918
513	Apparel, piece goods, and notions	1,458	9,409	20,559
514	Groceries and related products	3,578	46,656	113,992
515	Farm-product raw materials	112	1,023	1,639
516	Chemicals and allied products	1,009	6,947	23,144
517	Petroleum and petroleum products	502	6,578	17,954
518	Beer, wine, and distilled alcoholic beverages	253	9,160	29,628
519	Miscellaneous nondurable goods	3,484	24,354	56,146
	Retail trade	78,103	1,201,773	1,469,720
52	Building materials, hardware, garden supply, and mobile home dealers	3,581	46,652	74,196
521	Lumber and other building materials dealers	1,025	30,966	50,679
523	Paint, glass, and wallpaper stores	700	3,585	6,759
525	Hardware stores	776	5,612	7,473
526	Retail nurseries, lawn and garden supply stores	752	4,514	5,720
527	Mobile home dealers	328	1,976	3,565
53	General merchandise stores	1,676	142,719	165,779
531	Department stores	833	125,396	148,149
533	Variety stores	390	6,000	5,708
539	Miscellaneous general merchandise stores	454	11,323	11,922
54	Food stores	8,842	219,438	245,209
541	Grocery stores	6,314	202,105	226,713
542	Meat and fish markets and freezer provisioners	494	3,073	3,837
543	Fruit and vegetable markets	298	2,166	2,749
544	Candy, nut, and confectionery stores	195	1,127	899

See footnotes at end of table. Continued . . .

Table 16.43. EMPLOYMENT: AVERAGE MONTHLY PRIVATE REPORTING UNITS, EMPLOYMENT AND PAYROLL COVERED BY UNEMPLOYMENT COMPENSATION LAW BY WHOLESALE AND RETAIL TRADE INDUSTRY IN FLORIDA, 1994 AND 1995 (Continued)

SIC code	Industry	Number of re- porting units	Number of em- ployees	Payroll ($1,000)
	1994 A/ (Continued)			
	Retail trade (Continued)			
54	Food stores (Continued)			
546	Retail bakeries	940	7,774	7,426
549	Miscellaneous food stores	554	2,943	3,416
55	Automotive dealers and gasoline service stations	9,672	117,040	267,065
551	Motor vehicle dealers (new and used)	1,099	59,493	176,408
552	Motor vehicle dealers (used only)	1,466	6,081	12,117
553	Auto and home supply stores	2,519	19,664	34,143
554	Gasoline service stations	3,549	24,236	28,926
555	Boat dealers	600	3,907	7,608
556	Recreational vehicle dealers	165	1,970	4,554
557	Motorcycle dealers	200	1,379	2,724
559	Automotive dealers, NEC	75	310	585
56	Apparel and accessory stores	7,883	67,388	70,962
561	Men's and boys' clothing and accessory stores	587	3,515	4,740
562	Women's clothing stores	2,428	20,593	19,677
563	Women's accessory and specialty stores	456	3,052	2,946
564	Children's and infants' wear stores	248	1,988	1,914
565	Family clothing stores	1,004	18,023	18,891
566	Shoe stores	1,838	11,732	12,758
569	Miscellaneous apparel and accessory stores	1,323	8,485	10,035
57	Furniture and home furnishings stores	7,881	56,211	97,013
571	Home furniture and furnishings store	4,946	33,518	56,992
572	Household appliance stores	538	3,245	5,900
573	Radio, television, and computer stores	2,397	19,448	34,121
58	Eating and drinking places	20,994	414,823	351,770
59	Miscellaneous retail	17,575	137,502	197,725
591	Drug stores and proprietary stores	1,229	37,223	59,677
592	Liquor stores	771	4,714	4,534
593	Used merchandise stores	1,374	4,925	5,857
594	Miscellaneous shopping goods stores	7,080	45,563	54,084
596	Nonstore retailers	955	13,935	28,527
598	Fuel dealers	359	3,153	5,829
599	Retail stores, NEC	5,808	27,989	39,216

See footnotes at end of table.

Continued . . .

Table 16.43. EMPLOYMENT: AVERAGE MONTHLY PRIVATE REPORTING UNITS, EMPLOYMENT AND PAYROLL COVERED BY UNEMPLOYMENT COMPENSATION LAW BY WHOLESALE AND RETAIL TRADE INDUSTRY IN FLORIDA, 1994 AND 1995 (Continued)

SIC code	Industry	Number of reporting units	Number of employees	Payroll ($1,000)
	1995 B/			
	Wholesale trade	35,863	318,669	907,423
50	Wholesale trade--durable goods	23,182	184,299	543,731
501	Motor vehicles and motor vehicle parts and supplies	2,638	26,015	59,629
502	Furniture and homefurnishings	1,202	6,785	17,777
503	Lumber and other construction materials	1,570	12,574	32,908
504	Professional and commercial equipment and supplies	5,102	45,011	161,424
505	Metals and minerals, except petroleum	414	3,589	11,140
506	Electrical goods	3,189	26,028	81,703
507	Hardware, plumbing and heating equipment and supplies	1,789	14,775	41,550
508	Machinery, equipment, and supplies	4,451	33,040	96,826
509	Miscellaneous durable goods	2,828	16,484	40,773
51	Wholesale trade--nondurable goods	12,681	134,371	363,692
511	Paper and paper products	1,278	16,003	41,727
512	Drugs, drug proprietaries, and druggists' sundries	1,093	12,153	43,395
513	Apparel, piece goods, and notions	1,446	9,198	20,506
514	Groceries and related products	3,467	47,503	121,007
515	Farm-product raw materials	114	920	1,554
516	Chemicals and allied products	1,015	6,969	25,738
517	Petroleum and petroleum products	490	6,335	17,015
518	Beer, wine, and distilled alcoholic beverages	261	9,411	31,384
519	Miscellaneous nondurable goods	3,518	25,880	61,367
	Retail trade	76,806	1,228,508	1,547,498
52	Building materials, hardware, garden supply, and mobile home dealers	3,476	46,092	77,947
521	Lumber and other building materials dealers	1,003	30,448	53,219
523	Paint, glass, and wallpaper stores	686	3,658	7,238
525	Hardware stores	735	5,580	7,707
526	Retail nurseries, lawn and garden supply stores	723	4,408	5,858
527	Mobile home dealers	330	1,998	3,925
53	General merchandise stores	1,672	146,295	173,999
531	Department stores	848	129,432	156,524
533	Variety stores	392	5,609	5,478
539	Miscellaneous general merchandise stores	433	11,254	11,997
54	Food stores	8,818	228,667	257,658
541	Grocery stores	6,253	210,299	237,063
542	Meat and fish markets and freezer provisioners	470	3,189	4,091
543	Fruit and vegetable markets	285	2,085	2,657
544	Candy, nut, and confectionery stores	172	1,081	947
545	Dairy products stores	50	234	176

See footnotes at end of table.

Continued . . .

Table 16.43. EMPLOYMENT: AVERAGE MONTHLY PRIVATE REPORTING UNITS, EMPLOYMENT AND PAYROLL COVERED BY UNEMPLOYMENT COMPENSATION LAW BY WHOLESALE AND RETAIL TRADE INDUSTRY IN FLORIDA, 1994 AND 1995 (Continued)

SIC code	Industry	Number of re- porting units	Number of em- ployees	Payroll ($1,000)
	1995 B/ (Continued)			
	Retail trade (Continued)			
54	Food stores (Continued)			
546	Retail bakeries	963	8,344	8,347
549	Miscellaneous food stores	626	3,436	4,378
55	Automotive dealers and gasoline service stations	9,499	120,209	282,027
551	Motor vehicle dealers (new and used)	1,143	61,695	186,253
552	Motor vehicle dealers (used only)	1,404	5,973	12,233
553	Auto and home supply stores	2,502	20,506	36,838
554	Gasoline service stations	3,434	23,991	29,575
555	Boat dealers	600	4,193	8,339
556	Recreational vehicle dealers	159	1,980	4,805
557	Motorcycle dealers	183	1,462	3,056
559	Automotive dealers, NEC	75	409	927
56	Apparel and accessory stores	7,599	67,637	73,835
561	Men's and boys' clothing and accessory stores	536	3,322	4,779
562	Women's clothing stores	2,320	20,429	19,899
563	Women's accessory and specialty stores	452	3,021	3,127
564	Children's and infants' wear stores	236	1,997	1,855
565	Family clothing stores	946	18,346	19,509
566	Shoe stores	1,825	11,739	13,344
569	Miscellaneous apparel and accessory stores	1,284	8,784	11,322
57	Furniture and home furnishings stores	7,764	58,999	103,505
571	Home furniture and furnishings store	4,784	34,190	59,429
572	Household appliance stores	524	3,173	5,838
573	Radio, television, and computer stores	2,457	21,636	38,238
58	Eating and drinking places	20,802	420,144	366,734
59	Miscellaneous retail	17,176	140,467	211,792
591	Drug stores and proprietary stores	1,154	36,919	61,148
592	Liquor stores	732	4,265	4,538
593	Used merchandise stores	1,391	5,306	6,526
594	Miscellaneous shopping goods stores	6,899	46,212	57,152
596	Nonstore retailers	982	14,686	32,058
598	Fuel dealers	346	3,122	5,986
599	Retail stores, NEC	5,674	29,957	44,386

NEC Not elsewhere classified.
A/ Revised.
B/ Preliminary.
Note: Private employment. Detail may not add to totals due to disclosure editing and/or rounding. See Tables 23.70, 23.71, 23.72, 23.73, and 23.74 for public employment data.

Source: State of Florida, Department of Labor and Employment Security, Bureau of Labor Market Information, "Employment and Wages" (ES-202), unpublished data.

Table 16.44. WHOLESALE TRADE: AVERAGE MONTHLY PRIVATE REPORTING UNITS, EMPLOYMENT AND PAYROLL COVERED BY UNEMPLOYMENT COMPENSATION LAW IN THE STATE AND COUNTIES OF FLORIDA, 1995

County	Number of re-porting units	Number of em-ployees	Payroll ($1,000)	County	Number of re-porting units	Number of em-ployees	Payroll ($1,000)
			Wholesale trade (SIC codes 50-51)				
Florida	35,863	318,669	907,423	Lafayette	7	52	85
				Lake	224	1,416	3,023
Alachua	264	2,124	4,817	Lee	635	4,930	12,246
Baker	12	71	178	Leon	312	3,296	8,676
Bay	228	2,198	4,957	Levy	30	184	244
Bradford	22	333	998	Madison	19	151	179
Brevard	631	4,519	10,608	Manatee	280	2,272	5,707
Broward	4,158	34,174	100,250	Marion	341	4,337	9,244
Calhoun	18	149	201	Martin	200	988	3,120
Charlotte	109	538	1,124	Monroe	136	673	1,535
Citrus	74	423	782	Nassau	52	269	696
Clay	138	705	1,597	Okaloosa	190	1,154	2,300
Collier	341	1,973	5,372	Okeechobee	38	444	765
Columbia	78	846	1,816	Orange	2,295	27,550	79,837
Dade	8,809	72,807	199,700	Osceola	132	1,532	3,514
De Soto	24	191	298	Palm Beach	2,229	17,764	57,716
Dixie	7	60	118	Pasco	273	1,666	3,551
Duval	1,650	22,725	66,258	Pinellas	1,965	18,690	51,430
Escambia	498	5,047	11,249	Polk	742	7,454	17,311
Flagler	36	119	213	Putnam	56	381	672
Franklin	28	174	270	St. Johns	169	1,273	3,215
Gadsden	27	476	1,070	St. Lucie	207	1,723	3,672
Gilchrist	14	72	106	Santa Rosa	108	413	825
Glades	3	7	20	Sarasota	631	4,005	9,991
Gulf	6	14	19	Seminole	983	6,226	17,602
Hamilton	5	21	20	Sumter	28	293	587
Hardee	35	321	614	Suwannee	49	344	627
Hendry	32	195	458	Taylor	21	183	297
Hernando	101	590	1,257	Union	6	42	38
Highlands	75	529	997	Volusia	535	4,858	9,997
Hillsborough	2,681	34,332	108,267	Wakulla	13	36	78
Holmes	14	73	92	Walton	28	173	295
Indian River	166	935	2,947	Washington	15	94	109
Jackson	61	762	1,348				
Jefferson	15	61	103	Multicounty 1/	2,562	16,241	70,082

1/ Reporting units without a fixed location within the state or of unknown county location.

Note: Private employment. For a list of three-digit code industries included see Table 16.43. Data are preliminary. Only counties for which data are disclosed are shown. Detail may not add to totals due to disclosure editing and/or rounding. See Tables 23.70, 23.71, 23.72, 23.73, and 23.74 for public employment data.

Source: State of Florida, Department of Labor and Employment Security, Bureau of Labor Market Information, "Employment and Wages" (ES-202), unpublished data.

Table 16.45. RETAIL TRADE: AVERAGE MONTHLY PRIVATE REPORTING UNITS, EMPLOYMENT AND PAYROLL COVERED BY UNEMPLOYMENT COMPENSATION LAW IN THE STATE AND COUNTIES OF FLORIDA, 1994 AND 1995

County	Number of reporting units	Number of employees	Payroll ($1,000)	County	Number of reporting units	Number of employees	Payroll ($1,000)
			Retail trade, 1994 A/ (SIC codes 52-59)				
Florida	78,103	1,201,773	1,469,720	Lafayette	18	105	85
				Lake	785	10,873	12,068
Alachua	1,096	20,295	19,396	Lee	2,175	33,880	40,974
Baker	92	955	820	Leon	1,140	23,950	23,580
Bay	974	15,522	15,631	Levy	135	1,551	1,382
Bradford	90	1,198	1,067	Liberty	16	129	114
Brevard	2,299	34,533	36,912	Madison	92	789	729
Broward	8,299	124,979	170,408	Manatee	1,044	16,992	19,847
Calhoun	59	535	490	Marion	1,100	16,830	18,922
Charlotte	600	8,794	9,869	Martin	765	9,967	12,376
Citrus	514	6,274	6,638	Monroe	913	10,180	12,061
Clay	574	9,702	10,231	Nassau	260	3,242	3,111
Collier	1,370	18,298	23,496	Okaloosa	1,095	16,203	16,271
Columbia	261	3,436	3,662	Okeechobee	179	2,013	2,042
Dade	12,004	164,339	222,128	Orange	4,308	81,958	104,400
De Soto	107	1,232	1,311	Osceola	710	12,659	13,127
Dixie	58	482	406	Palm Beach	5,799	85,926	112,875
Duval	3,791	66,865	80,091	Pasco	1,168	17,467	18,741
Escambia	1,554	23,989	25,980	Pinellas	4,841	80,071	98,508
Flagler	155	1,930	1,858	Polk	1,967	35,245	48,710
Franklin	71	600	539	Putnam	260	3,793	3,723
Gadsden	162	1,987	1,901	St. Johns	664	8,073	8,021
Gilchrist	34	190	176	St. Lucie	739	10,105	11,692
Glades	20	152	132	Santa Rosa	362	4,237	4,047
Gulf	67	447	398	Sarasota	2,091	29,377	35,890
Hamilton	55	345	311	Seminole	1,537	27,605	31,750
Hardee	100	943	1,010	Sumter	137	1,624	1,446
Hendry	127	1,416	1,442	Suwannee	131	1,750	1,950
Hernando	441	6,428	6,984	Taylor	124	1,236	1,178
Highlands	377	4,901	5,041	Union	24	200	187
Hillsborough	4,312	81,544	100,429	Volusia	2,259	33,376	35,759
Holmes	62	561	496	Wakulla	53	534	430
Indian River	653	7,738	9,344	Walton	195	1,905	1,709
Jackson	224	2,590	2,567	Washington	72	786	693
Jefferson	55	453	369	Multicounty 1/	285	3,252	9,438

See footnotes at end of table.

Continued . . .

Table 16.45. RETAIL TRADE: AVERAGE MONTHLY PRIVATE REPORTING UNITS, EMPLOYMENT AND PAYROLL COVERED BY UNEMPLOYMENT COMPENSATION LAW IN THE STATE AND COUNTIES OF FLORIDA, 1994 AND 1995 (Continued)

County	Number of re- porting units	Number of em- ployees	Payroll ($1,000)	County	Number of re- porting units	Number of em- ployees	Payroll ($1,000)
			Retail trade, 1995 B/ (SIC codes 52-59)				
Florida	76,806	1,228,508	1,547,498	Lafayette	19	104	86
				Lake	790	11,284	12,646
Alachua	1,092	21,091	20,643	Lee	2,113	35,478	43,713
Baker	82	986	852	Leon	1,134	24,912	25,057
Bay	961	16,029	16,806	Levy	138	1,860	1,640
Bradford	86	1,353	1,215	Liberty	15	131	122
Brevard	2,230	34,582	38,275	Madison	87	834	781
Broward	8,072	128,080	177,268	Manatee	1,037	17,250	20,461
Calhoun	60	551	521	Marion	1,106	17,102	19,716
Charlotte	560	8,836	10,287	Martin	740	10,168	12,809
Citrus	505	6,196	6,642	Monroe	898	10,321	12,531
Clay	570	10,206	10,797	Nassau	266	3,281	3,262
Collier	1,378	18,795	24,908	Okaloosa	1,109	16,788	17,789
Columbia	263	3,910	4,122	Okeechobee	178	2,118	2,201
Dade	11,681	163,741	229,673	Orange	4,279	84,727	113,717
De Soto	101	1,250	1,308	Osceola	695	13,538	14,539
Dixie	52	445	374	Palm Beach	5,648	85,396	115,847
Duval	3,776	69,869	86,138	Pasco	1,161	17,654	19,248
Escambia	1,529	24,615	27,350	Pinellas	4,691	78,592	100,625
Flagler	154	2,050	2,035	Polk	1,938	36,888	51,475
Franklin	77	594	540	Putnam	257	3,762	3,981
Gadsden	154	1,934	2,005	St. Johns	668	8,342	8,585
Gilchrist	35	213	199	St. Lucie	716	10,197	12,118
Glades	21	174	146	Santa Rosa	373	4,406	4,137
Gulf	68	451	409	Sarasota	2,053	29,699	37,651
Hamilton	60	386	354	Seminole	1,547	28,850	35,109
Hardee	93	955	1,026	Sumter	142	1,680	1,561
Hendry	124	1,520	1,479	Suwannee	131	1,870	2,024
Hernando	443	6,818	7,375	Taylor	117	1,282	1,261
Highlands	374	5,154	5,314	Union	24	207	192
Hillsborough	4,247	84,732	107,586	Volusia	2,242	34,314	37,978
Holmes	63	560	498	Wakulla	52	628	475
Indian River	655	8,299	10,093	Walton	188	1,956	1,821
Jackson	222	2,721	2,786	Washington	73	928	854
Jefferson	53	449	361	Multicounty 1/	340	4,270	11,825

A/ Revised.
B/ Preliminary.
1/ Reporting units without a fixed location within the state or of unknown county location.
Note: For a list of three-digit code industries included see Table 16.43. Private employment. Only counties for which data are disclosed are shown. Detail may not add to totals due to disclosure editing and/or rounding. See Tables 23.70, 23.71, 23.72, 23.73, and 23.74 for public employment data.

Source: State of Florida, Department of Labor and Employment Security, Bureau of Labor Market Information, "Employment and Wages" (ES-202), unpublished data.

Table 16.46. GENERAL MERCHANDISE STORES: AVERAGE MONTHLY PRIVATE REPORTING UNITS, EMPLOYMENT, AND PAYROLL COVERED BY UNEMPLOYMENT COMPENSATION LAW IN THE STATE AND COUNTIES OF FLORIDA, 1995

County	Number of re- porting units	Number of em- ployees	Payroll ($1,000)	County	Number of re- porting units	Number of em- ployees	Payroll ($1,000)
		General merchandise stores (SIC code 53)					
Florida	1,672	146,295	173,999	Lee	40	4,145	4,841
				Leon	28	3,052	3,348
Alachua	29	3,272	3,202	Madison	3	33	28
Bay	19	2,013	2,127	Manatee	26	1,893	1,963
Brevard	51	4,956	5,199	Marion	27	2,955	3,417
Broward	145	13,686	16,176	Martin	20	1,409	1,515
Calhoun	5	20	19	Monroe	14	690	748
Charlotte	19	1,656	1,810	Nassau	5	278	274
Citrus	12	788	797	Okaloosa	19	2,156	2,170
Clay	16	1,561	1,764	Orange	92	8,502	10,580
Collier	21	1,868	2,265	Osceola	13	995	1,054
Columbia	8	634	645	Palm Beach	90	9,653	12,285
Dade	232	18,257	25,956	Pasco	28	2,456	2,664
Duval	88	9,686	10,588	Pinellas	100	8,710	10,357
Escambia	36	3,436	4,037	Polk	50	5,301	6,101
Flagler	3	260	230	Putnam	9	483	474
Franklin	3	10	8	St. Lucie	19	1,349	1,399
Gulf	5	20	18	Santa Rosa	7	468	460
Hernando	10	908	1,416	Sarasota	34	3,070	3,425
Highlands	11	712	678	Seminole	43	4,159	4,843
Hillsborough	99	9,869	11,609	Suwannee	6	196	182
Holmes	5	15	14	Volusia	43	4,175	4,603
Indian River	13	1,029	1,139	Wakulla	3	14	10
Jackson	10	324	299				
Lake	23	1,565	1,615	Multicounty 1/	15	690	2,783

1/ Reporting units without a fixed location within the state or of unknown county location.

Note: Private employment. For a list of three-digit code industries included see Table 16.43. Data are preliminary. Only counties for which data are disclosed are shown. Detail may not add to totals due to disclosure editing and/or rounding. See Tables 23.70, 23.71, 23.72, 23.73, and 23.74 for public employment data.

Source: State of Florida, Department of Labor and Employment Security, Bureau of Labor Market Information, "Employment and Wages" (ES-202), unpublished data.

Table 16.47. FOOD STORES: AVERAGE MONTHLY PRIVATE REPORTING UNITS EMPLOYMENT, AND PAYROLL COVERED BY UNEMPLOYMENT COMPENSATION LAW IN THE STATE AND COUNTIES OF FLORIDA, 1995

County	Number of re- porting units	Number of em- ployees	Payroll ($1,000)	County	Number of re- porting units	Number of em- ployees	Payroll ($1,000)
			Food stores (SIC code 54)				
Florida	8,818	228,667	257,658	Jefferson	10	148	105
				Lafayette	5	44	44
Alachua	120	3,716	3,397	Lake	113	2,732	2,524
Baker	17	262	222	Lee	207	6,258	6,557
Bay	96	2,774	2,873	Leon	78	3,488	3,119
Bradford	14	393	320	Levy	23	588	432
Brevard	246	6,551	6,256	Liberty	6	45	48
Broward	798	23,200	29,071	Madison	12	202	158
Calhoun	9	173	146	Manatee	117	3,355	3,268
Charlotte	51	1,767	1,731	Martin	76	1,868	2,088
Collier	133	3,883	4,149	Okaloosa	120	2,421	2,512
Dade	1,383	27,129	32,587	Okeechobee	36	607	593
De Soto	21	359	325	Orange	495	13,962	16,731
Dixie	7	126	99	Osceola	92	2,460	2,511
Escambia	178	3,396	3,458	Palm Beach	558	14,782	17,277
Flagler	25	654	635	Polk	270	10,248	16,484
Franklin	12	217	190	St. Johns	77	1,747	1,725
Gadsden	34	539	456	St. Lucie	91	2,203	2,380
Gilchrist	7	83	64	Santa Rosa	64	1,025	844
Glades	9	91	75	Sarasota	172	6,236	7,246
Gulf	17	199	178	Seminole	162	5,662	5,985
Hamilton	14	89	69	Sumter	28	403	367
Hardee	21	299	273	Union	5	91	74
Hendry	25	543	437	Volusia	216	6,577	6,497
Hernando	73	2,016	1,887	Wakulla	10	256	178
Highlands	48	1,255	1,151	Walton	26	356	295
Holmes	12	125	100	Washington	17	197	165
Indian River	73	1,881	2,123				
Jackson	29	376	327	Multicounty 1/	38	606	1,547

1/ Reporting units without a fixed location within the state or of unknown county location.

Note: Private employment. For a list of three-digit code industries included see Table 16.43. Data are preliminary. Only counties for which data are disclosed are shown. Detail may not add to totals due to disclosure editing and/or rounding. See Tables 23.70, 23.71, 23.72, 23.73, and 23.74 for public employment data.

Source: State of Florida, Department of Labor and Employment Security, Bureau of Labor Market Information, "Employment and Wages" (ES-202), unpublished data.

Table 16.48. AUTOMOTIVE DEALERS AND GASOLINE SERVICE STATIONS: AVERAGE MONTHLY PRIVATE REPORTING UNITS, EMPLOYMENT, AND PAYROLL COVERED BY UNEMPLOYMENT COMPENSATION LAW IN THE STATE AND COUNTIES OF FLORIDA, 1995

County	Number of re- porting units	Number of em- ployees	Payroll ($1,000)	County	Number of re- porting units	Number of em- ployees	Payroll ($1,000)
	Automotive dealers and gasoline service stations (SIC code 55)						
Florida	9,499	120,209	282,027	Lafayette	3	8	6
				Lake	112	1,232	2,799
Alachua	129	1,825	3,638	Lee	233	3,334	7,584
Baker	14	115	122	Leon	145	1,740	3,800
Bay	124	1,449	3,041	Levy	23	168	263
Bradford	18	163	236	Madison	28	237	296
Brevard	286	3,281	7,501	Manatee	133	1,530	3,430
Broward	958	13,142	36,201	Marion	172	1,964	3,946
Calhoun	17	94	118	Martin	105	1,144	2,655
Charlotte	74	965	2,290	Monroe	68	522	995
Citrus	79	757	1,568	Nassau	39	367	598
Clay	68	937	2,103	Okaloosa	130	1,541	3,225
Collier	105	1,464	4,040	Okeechobee	36	261	463
Columbia	45	473	902	Orange	543	7,189	17,745
Dade	1,375	15,679	36,605	Osceola	73	1,022	2,314
De Soto	18	224	419	Palm Beach	576	8,166	20,845
Dixie	12	60	72	Pasco	155	1,701	3,661
Duval	496	8,568	19,417	Pinellas	531	7,734	18,857
Escambia	198	2,519	5,237	Polk	306	4,017	9,341
Flagler	17	175	363	Putnam	45	376	718
Franklin	7	31	41	St. Johns	73	723	1,343
Gadsden	29	234	393	St. Lucie	100	1,262	3,110
Gilchrist	6	13	15	Santa Rosa	50	530	934
Glades	4	16	27	Sarasota	208	2,866	7,256
Gulf	8	28	34	Seminole	174	2,346	5,953
Hamilton	22	147	134	Sumter	26	246	328
Hardee	19	138	270	Suwannee	29	270	404
Hendry	19	163	288	Taylor	20	177	296
Hernando	58	606	1,264	Union	8	30	37
Highlands	73	715	1,366	Volusia	320	3,364	7,616
Hillsborough	556	7,888	19,178	Wakulla	9	56	53
Holmes	11	108	114	Walton	26	168	181
Indian River	58	873	1,964	Washington	14	52	49
Jackson	41	630	972				
Jefferson	13	76	60	Multicounty 1/	38	290	897

1/ Reporting units without a fixed location within the state or of unknown county location.

Note: Private employment. For a list of three-digit code industries included see Table 16.43. Data are preliminary. Only counties for which data are disclosed are shown. Detail may not add to totals due to disclosure editing and/or rounding. See Tables 23.70, 23.71, 23.72, 23.73, and 23.74 for public employment data.

Source: State of Florida, Department of Labor and Employment Security, Bureau of Labor Market Information, "Employment and Wages" (ES-202), unpublished data.

Table 16.49. AUTO AND HOME SUPPLY STORES: AVERAGE MONTHLY PRIVATE REPORTING UNITS, EMPLOYMENT, AND PAYROLL COVERED BY UNEMPLOYMENT COMPENSATION LAW IN THE STATE AND COUNTIES OF FLORIDA, 1995

County	Number of reporting units	Number of employees	Payroll ($1,000)	County	Number of reporting units	Number of employees	Payroll ($1,000)
			Auto and home supply stores (SIC code 553)				
Florida	2,502	20,506	36,838	Lee	54	477	820
				Leon	42	331	581
Alachua	34	347	628	Levy	9	30	39
Baker	7	23	33	Madison	4	20	22
Bay	36	267	402	Manatee	31	255	418
Bradford	4	15	16	Marion	52	418	665
Brevard	76	583	947	Martin	25	173	309
Broward	256	1,921	3,781	Monroe	15	112	167
Calhoun	6	34	33	Nassau	12	42	59
Charlotte	23	169	275	Okaloosa	32	226	350
Citrus	21	113	162	Okeechobee	10	69	112
Clay	23	194	312	Orange	137	1,279	2,743
Collier	29	225	398	Osceola	14	198	326
Columbia	9	88	148	Palm Beach	157	1,555	3,299
Dade	388	2,673	4,449	Pasco	35	260	405
De Soto	7	44	58	Pinellas	114	1,050	2,026
Duval	143	1,429	2,667	Polk	75	1,125	2,122
Escambia	54	564	838	Putnam	11	93	138
Flagler	6	45	55	St. Johns	14	55	87
Gadsden	10	45	65	St. Lucie	25	268	489
Gilchrist	4	7	8	Santa Rosa	17	104	140
Gulf	6	22	28	Sarasota	45	368	634
Hamilton	3	7	8	Seminole	47	355	661
Hardee	4	29	45	Sumter	5	26	36
Hendry	6	32	39	Suwannee	6	40	45
Hernando	18	138	202	Taylor	4	31	54
Highlands	21	131	210	Union	3	19	27
Hillsborough	138	1,160	2,059	Volusia	78	652	1,148
Holmes	7	31	41	Walton	7	52	65
Indian River	12	98	175	Washington	6	31	30
Jackson	14	87	118				
Lake	30	193	325	Multicounty 1/	20	63	254

1/ Reporting units without a fixed location within the state or of unknown county location.

Note: Private employment. Data are preliminary. Only counties for which data are disclosed are shown. Detail may not add to totals due to disclosure editing and/or rounding. See Tables 23.70, 23.71, 23.72, 23.73, and 23.74 for public employment data.

Source: State of Florida, Department of Labor and Employment Security, Bureau of Labor Market Information, "Employment and Wages" (ES-202), unpublished data.

Table 16.50. GASOLINE SERVICE STATIONS: AVERAGE MONTHLY PRIVATE REPORTING UNITS, EMPLOYMENT, AND PAYROLL COVERED BY UNEMPLOYMENT COMPENSATION LAW IN THE STATE AND COUNTIES OF FLORIDA, 1995

County	Number of reporting units	Number of employees	Payroll ($1,000)	County	Number of reporting units	Number of employees	Payroll ($1,000)
			Gasoline service stations (SIC code 554)				
Florida	3,434	23,991	29,575	Lee	61	577	677
				Leon	53	424	464
Alachua	47	362	377	Levy	11	67	68
Baker	6	81	66	Madison	21	207	261
Bay	32	325	358	Manatee	36	232	238
Bradford	9	60	47	Marion	57	500	532
Brevard	100	586	640	Martin	30	158	173
Broward	345	2,147	2,736	Monroe	27	159	232
Calhoun	5	10	10	Nassau	19	185	183
Charlotte	22	184	199	Okaloosa	44	360	356
Citrus	22	118	117	Okeechobee	12	76	76
Clay	20	150	133	Orange	189	1,153	1,449
Collier	34	236	313	Osceola	29	194	219
Columbia	20	119	102	Palm Beach	230	1,600	2,056
Dade	552	3,188	4,887	Pasco	50	245	260
De Soto	5	38	39	Pinellas	207	1,320	1,634
Dixie	6	21	18	Polk	113	665	740
Duval	156	2,192	2,742	Putnam	12	52	57
Escambia	55	351	374	St. Johns	31	255	258
Flagler	6	57	74	St. Lucie	31	188	203
Franklin	4	16	19	Santa Rosa	20	199	153
Gadsden	13	96	90	Sarasota	74	469	558
Hamilton	18	135	116	Seminole	50	333	457
Hardee	9	28	32	Sumter	16	174	161
Hendry	9	48	65	Suwannee	14	96	93
Hernando	20	93	75	Taylor	9	65	65
Highlands	19	114	129	Union	4	10	9
Hillsborough	220	1,446	1,926	Volusia	110	582	632
Indian River	24	253	296	Walton	15	94	73
Jackson	18	309	330	Washington	6	14	13
Jefferson	11	72	56				
Lake	30	167	159	Multicounty 1/	11	203	588

1/ Reporting units without a fixed location within the state or of unknown county location.

Note: Private employment. Data are preliminary. Only counties for which data are disclosed are shown. Detail may not add to totals due to disclosure editing and/or rounding. See Tables 23.70, 23.71, 23.72, 23.73, and 23.74 for public employment data.

Source: State of Florida, Department of Labor and Employment Security, Bureau of Labor Market Information, "Employment and Wages" (ES-202), unpublished data.

Table 16.51. APPAREL AND ACCESSORY STORES: AVERAGE MONTHLY PRIVATE REPORTING UNITS, EMPLOYMENT, AND PAYROLL COVERED BY UNEMPLOYMENT COMPENSATION LAW IN THE STATE AND COUNTIES OF FLORIDA, 1995

County	Number of reporting units	Number of employees	Payroll ($1,000)	County	Number of reporting units	Number of employees	Payroll ($1,000)
			Apparel and accessory stores (SIC code 56)				
Florida	7,599	67,637	73,835	Madison	4	19	16
				Manatee	116	1,748	2,281
Alachua	101	851	753	Marion	78	685	580
Baker	5	30	17	Martin	70	449	380
Bay	112	922	723	Monroe	105	478	569
Bradford	6	37	26	Nassau	25	92	75
Brevard	142	1,172	1,321	Okaloosa	130	1,238	1,119
Broward	848	8,489	9,507	Okeechobee	10	97	80
Charlotte	56	425	361	Orange	411	4,657	4,951
Citrus	28	232	188	Osceola	56	614	568
Clay	60	498	388	Palm Beach	642	5,875	7,644
Collier	195	1,464	1,719	Pasco	81	587	468
Columbia	14	95	72	Pinellas	408	3,416	3,411
Dade	1,573	13,745	17,045	Polk	145	1,037	952
De Soto	3	16	14	Putnam	13	60	44
Duval	310	2,987	3,099	St. Johns	72	448	399
Escambia	124	971	848	St. Lucie	60	397	348
Gadsden	7	25	20	Santa Rosa	15	64	44
Hendry	6	32	25	Sarasota	221	1,651	1,665
Hernando	20	146	117	Seminole	144	1,263	1,124
Hillsborough	362	3,384	3,221	Sumter	4	15	15
Indian River	83	468	461	Suwannee	7	33	25
Jackson	20	144	128	Taylor	9	42	37
Lake	43	289	247	Volusia	166	1,382	1,146
Lee	262	2,005	2,227	Walton	16	115	125
Leon	108	1,383	1,101	Washington	3	9	8
Levy	5	30	19	Multicounty 1/	54	1,010	1,883

1/ Reporting units without a fixed location within the state or of unknown county location.

Note: Private employment. For a list of three-digit code industries included see Table 16.43. Data are preliminary. Only counties for which data are disclosed are shown. Detail may not add to totals due to disclosure editing and/or rounding. See Tables 23.70, 23.71, 23.72, 23.73, and 23.74 for public employment data.

Source: State of Florida, Department of Labor and Employment Security, Bureau of Labor Market Information, "Employment and Wages" (ES-202), unpublished data.

Table 16.52. HOME FURNITURE, FURNISHINGS, AND EQUIPMENT STORES: AVERAGE MONTHLY PRIVATE REPORTING UNITS, EMPLOYMENT, AND PAYROLL COVERED BY UNEMPLOYMENT COMPENSATION LAW IN THE STATE AND COUNTIES OF FLORIDA, 1995

County	Number of reporting units	Number of employees	Payroll ($1,000)	County	Number of reporting units	Number of employees	Payroll ($1,000)
	Home furniture, furnishings, and equipment stores (SIC code 57)						
Florida	7,764	58,999	103,505	Lee	241	2,295	4,442
				Leon	118	979	1,391
Alachua	111	781	1,020	Levy	7	20	20
Baker	3	21	31	Madison	7	34	35
Bay	76	467	662	Manatee	109	802	1,231
Bradford	5	59	120	Marion	106	666	997
Brevard	242	1,427	2,164	Martin	92	483	758
Broward	910	7,328	14,622	Monroe	54	225	343
Calhoun	4	25	29	Nassau	14	49	62
Charlotte	65	422	615	Okaloosa	100	705	1,058
Citrus	49	286	349	Okeechobee	11	44	52
Clay	47	378	534	Orange	367	4,037	6,664
Collier	209	1,139	2,008	Osceola	51	247	372
Columbia	23	139	203	Palm Beach	670	4,175	8,460
Dade	1,132	9,442	16,833	Pasco	117	812	1,187
De Soto	6	20	27	Pinellas	454	3,187	5,730
Duval	378	3,032	4,878	Polk	180	2,378	4,732
Escambia	140	1,264	1,796	Putnam	20	119	177
Flagler	12	43	52	St. Johns	50	334	482
Franklin	4	5	5	St. Lucie	86	417	611
Gilchrist	4	11	11	Santa Rosa	35	167	229
Gulf	4	17	19	Sarasota	252	1,555	2,741
Hamilton	3	8	11	Seminole	191	1,357	2,295
Hardee	8	24	28	Sumter	11	109	124
Hendry	4	17	25	Taylor	9	49	92
Hernando	44	215	298	Volusia	210	1,373	2,200
Highlands	37	187	251	Wakulla	3	19	21
Hillsborough	425	3,931	7,681	Walton	14	48	66
Indian River	84	439	686	Washington	5	37	37
Jackson	15	55	59				
Lake	75	408	616	Multicounty 1/	37	134	437

1/ Reporting units without a fixed location within the state or of unknown county location.

Note: Private employment. For a list of three-digit code industries included see Table 16.43. Data are preliminary. Only counties for which data are disclosed are shown. Detail may not add to totals due to disclosure editing and/or rounding. See Tables 23.70, 23.71, 23.72, 23.73, and 23.74 for public employment data.

Source: State of Florida, Department of Labor and Employment Security, Bureau of Labor Market Information, "Employment and Wages" (ES-202), unpublished data.

Table 16.81. GROSS AND TAXABLE SALES: SALES REPORTED TO THE DEPARTMENT OF REVENUE BY KIND OF BUSINESS IN FLORIDA 1994 AND 1995

(rounded to thousands of dollars)

Kind of business		Gross sales		Taxable sales	
Code	Description	1994	1995	1994	1995
	Total	385,110,860	423,309,074	159,956,355	171,551,705
	<u>Food and beverage group</u>	43,657,229	45,688,423	23,464,929	24,529,053
01	Grocery stores	24,819,246	25,563,710	7,816,282	8,072,901
02	Meat markets, poultry	371,589	398,402	11,399	12,719
03	Seafood dealers	165,823	194,716	17,125	17,376
04	Vegetable and fruit markets	212,001	281,177	30,197	34,297
05	Bakeries	287,651	280,136	73,705	70,745
06	Delicatessens	328,087	315,502	135,667	132,148
07	Candy and confectionery	967,574	1,180,500	357,035	390,375
08	Restaurants and lunchrooms	14,596,117	15,509,171	13,265,506	13,998,378
09	Taverns, nightclubs, liquor stores	1,909,142	1,965,109	1,758,013	1,800,113
	<u>Apparel group</u>	6,556,484	6,772,977	5,413,564	5,759,994
10	Clothing stores, alterations	5,447,799	5,716,401	4,600,591	4,827,536
11	Shoe stores	1,064,778	986,194	777,642	880,012
12	Hat shops	43,907	70,382	35,332	52,447
	<u>General merchandise group</u>	37,866,542	42,251,984	24,516,974	26,913,363
13	Department stores	9,631,236	10,916,233	8,571,662	9,536,653
14	Variety stores	8,636,558	10,725,361	6,378,264	7,873,654
15	Drug stores	6,381,635	6,702,069	2,091,620	2,066,091
16	Jewelry, leather, sporting goods	3,416,289	3,815,587	2,221,869	2,324,668
17	Feed, seed, and fertilizer stores	525,026	510,701	105,744	105,131
18	Hardware, paints, machinery	3,429,554	3,584,861	1,735,292	1,825,058
19	Farm implements and supplies	746,510	792,874	335,990	379,424
20	General merchandise stores	4,129,675	4,153,231	2,471,181	2,191,200
21	Second-hand stores	509,156	591,745	308,464	347,748
22	Dry good stores	460,904	459,321	296,888	263,737

See footnotes at end of table.

Continued . . .

Table 16.81. GROSS AND TAXABLE SALES: SALES REPORTED TO THE DEPARTMENT OF REVENUE BY KIND OF BUSINESS IN FLORIDA 1994 AND 1995 (Continued)

(rounded to thousands of dollars)

Kind of business		Gross sales		Taxable sales	
Code	Description	1994	1995	1994	1995
	Automotive group	64,504,180	67,961,325	29,608,913	32,226,988
23	Motor vehicle dealers	46,080,262	48,045,351	22,853,807	25,011,870
24	Auto accessories, tires, parts	4,518,861	4,875,794	2,207,169	2,350,761
25	Filling and service stations	6,347,617	6,201,050	975,231	1,002,354
26	Garages, auto paint and body shops	3,270,393	3,498,552	2,131,146	2,310,250
27	Aircraft dealers	1,878,894	2,520,098	188,085	202,153
28	Motorboat and yacht dealers	2,408,154	2,820,480	1,253,474	1,349,599
	Furniture and appliances group	20,876,602	23,782,750	10,098,469	11,056,609
29	Furniture stores, new and used	4,772,463	5,071,183	3,370,446	3,563,256
30	Household appliances, dinnerware, etc.	1,959,440	2,064,757	1,277,803	1,271,351
31	Store and office equipment	3,844,382	4,278,108	1,693,767	1,999,713
32	Music stores, radios, televisions	10,300,318	12,368,703	3,756,453	4,222,289
	Lumber, builders, contractors group	16,038,165	16,673,680	9,269,058	9,356,248
33	Building contractors	1,646,613	1,820,163	284,081	331,567
34	Heating and air conditioning	1,425,903	1,643,818	479,891	495,523
35	Electrical and plumbing	2,474,225	2,461,326	1,098,622	1,166,353
36	Decorating, painting, papering	980,131	999,734	577,377	587,139
37	Roofing and sheet metal	347,770	380,028	165,054	172,881
38	Lumber and building materials	9,163,523	9,368,611	6,664,033	6,602,785
	General classification group	195,611,656	220,177,935	57,584,448	61,709,451
39	Hotels, apartment houses, etc. 1/	7,927,436	8,598,639	7,239,118	7,768,974
40	Auctioneers and commission dealers	1,869,187	2,059,855	422,499	449,796
41	Barber and beauty shops	1,248,880	1,308,147	547,762	574,837
42	Book stores	805,600	918,957	555,558	616,166
43	Cigar stands and tobacco shops	62,890	78,434	28,964	35,335
44	Florists	465,523	504,874	274,392	284,528
45	Fuel and L.P. gas dealers	4,314,480	4,171,534	414,021	406,605

See footnotes at end of table.

Continued . . .

Table 16.81. GROSS AND TAXABLE SALES: SALES REPORTED TO THE DEPARTMENT OF REVENUE BY KIND OF BUSINESS IN FLORIDA 1994 AND 1995 (Continued)

(rounded to thousands of dollars)

Kind of business		Gross sales		Taxable sales	
Code	Description	1994	1995	1994	1995
	General classification group (Continued)				
46	Funeral directors and monuments	274,060	326,828	87,980	102,530
47	Scrap metal, junk yards	398,170	452,181	37,659	40,017
48	Itinerant vendors	549,748	617,520	247,482	259,008
49	Laundry and cleaning services	534,130	568,681	181,120	196,063
50	Machine shops and foundries	674,908	711,175	178,098	192,335
51	Horse, cattle, pet dealers	2,687,492	2,829,273	1,087,416	1,087,759
52	Photographers, photo and art supplies	1,440,834	1,557,457	825,296	873,112
53	Shoe repair shops	19,844	19,708	16,808	16,120
54	Storage and warehousing	245,246	252,215	129,134	120,266
55	Gift, card, novelty shops	2,250,522	2,382,535	1,613,689	1,690,776
56	Newsstands	145,510	186,379	54,398	56,139
57	Social clubs and associations	682,486	536,830	424,136	425,869
58	Industrial machinery equipment	5,552,226	6,179,096	1,827,975	2,046,732
59	Admissions	3,407,414	3,671,096	3,100,436	3,423,705
60	Holiday season vendors	9,323	13,460	6,918	10,228
61	Rental of tangible property	4,632,410	4,976,807	2,761,949	2,984,691
62	Fabrication, sales of cabinets, etc.	1,778,943	1,880,509	660,825	687,956
63	Manufacturing and mining	30,671,312	34,015,614	3,641,202	3,820,471
64	Bottlers, soft drinks, etc.	929,536	939,164	85,024	70,561
65	Pawn shops	107,671	117,614	84,961	92,101
66	Communications	9,958,349	12,039,981	6,007,442	6,726,352
67	Transportation	388,931	448,788	93,791	85,103
68	Graphic arts and printing	3,952,504	4,357,887	1,429,099	1,535,742
69	Insurance, banking, etc.	691,553	789,323	291,017	311,348
70	Sanitary and industrial supplies	2,673,140	3,222,326	473,146	479,696
71	Packaging materials and paper boxes	1,243,670	1,354,495	109,687	126,555
72	Repair of tangible personal property	2,903,726	3,212,637	938,813	999,207
73	Advertising	1,623,840	1,673,448	266,601	280,485

See footnotes at end of table.

Continued . . .

Table 16.81. GROSS AND TAXABLE SALES: SALES REPORTED TO THE DEPARTMENT OF REVENUE BY KIND OF BUSINESS IN FLORIDA 1994 AND 1995 (Continued)

(rounded to thousands of dollars)

Kind of business		Gross sales		Taxable sales	
Code	Description	1994	1995	1994	1995
	General classification group (Continued)				
74	Top soil, clay, sand, fill dirt	869,568	1,043,218	232,771	265,105
75	Trade stamp redemption centers	76	641	51	220
76	Nurseries and landscaping	1,314,268	1,439,661	393 808	405,491
77	Vending machines	546,238	677,874	291,777	342,598
78	Importing and exporting	11,410,029	13,970,731	158,045	175,233
79	Medical, dental, surgical, optical	3,285,946	5,328,192	453,491	518,466
80	Wholesale dealers	48,554,791	54,047,626	4,398,379	4,493,883
81	Schools and colleges	103,869	111,062	50,683	57,339
82	Office space and commercial rentals	11,808,631	12,578,980	9,417,185	9,902,851
83	Parking lots, boat docking, storage	361,051	389,662	268,741	284,545
84	Utilities, electricity or gas	12,252,692	12,746,460	3,544,944	3,596,336
86	Dual uses of special fuels	147,212	210,026	16,005	16,448
88	Public works, governmental contractor	110,968	127,781	12,548	31,857
90	Flea markets	161,331	199,738	121,641	128,841
91	Fairs, concessions, carnivals	11,891	12,156	7,364	7,008
92	Other professional services	1,078,050	810,205	23,263	24,192
93	Other personal services	2,099,927	3,292,756	1,100,544	1,190,652
94	Other industrial services	449,958	585,063	79,577	80,937
98	Commercial fisherman	14,021	15,834	1,922	2,127
99	Miscellaneous	3,909,647	5,616,802	867,290	1,308,151

1/ Includes sales reported under categories 85 and 89 which are for hotels, rooming houses and apartments.

Note: Data are audited sales reported to the Florida Department of Revenue for the 6 percent regular sales tax, 6 percent use tax, and 3 percent vehicle and farm equipment sales tax. Sales occurred, for the most part, from December 1, 1993, through November 30, 1995. Data are not comparable with retail sales reported by the U.S. Bureau of the Census.

Source: State of Florida, Department of Revenue, unpublished data prepared by the University of Florida, Bureau of Economic and Business Research.

Table 16.82. GROSS AND TAXABLE SALES: SALES REPORTED TO THE DEPARTMENT OF REVENUE IN THE STATE AND COUNTIES OF FLORIDA, 1994 AND 1995

(rounded to thousands of dollars)

County	Gross sales 1994	Gross sales 1995	Taxable sales 1994	Taxable sales 1995
Florida	385,110,860	423,309,074	159,956,355	171,551,705
Alachua	3,244,445	3,570,618	1,871,007	2,032,398
Baker	155,257	160,024	65,153	70,826
Bay	2,733,630	3,068,450	1,633,464	1,760,979
Bradford	247,795	277,775	117,324	130,997
Brevard	8,579,469	9,167,169	3,690,338	3,852,810
Broward	39,529,466	41,699,646	16,818,383	17,894,729
Calhoun	107,680	124,465	46,227	50,934
Charlotte	1,743,988	1,848,271	1,077,869	1,131,357
Citrus	1,143,613	1,238,547	669,197	692,760
Clay	1,695,194	1,908,161	901,101	983,206
Collier	4,422,364	4,806,919	2,756,289	2,987,310
Columbia	853,797	1,044,140	419,898	466,331
Dade	61,346,512	67,940,140	21,046,767	22,119,253
De Soto	259,540	278,253	139,788	146,249
Dixie	123,107	108,989	36,092	36,853
Duval	20,607,034	22,729,671	8,137,570	8,842,822
Escambia	5,739,837	6,002,629	2,560,910	2,795,338
Flagler	437,361	651,699	202,356	250,774
Franklin	89,354	181,385	54,241	60,946
Gadsden	577,473	569,851	163,550	171,740
Gilchrist	61,754	64,924	26,710	27,605
Glades	34,490	42,196	14,923	15,302
Gulf	153,685	162,238	41,731	43,831
Hamilton	93,079	158,752	35,513	41,650
Hardee	233,501	262,078	103,393	118,752
Hendry	626,797	749,718	170,132	183,790
Hernando	2,782,831	3,224,631	616,063	658,016
Highlands	1,062,555	1,090,522	564,793	589,547
Hillsborough	27,539,944	30,544,630	10,924,605	11,733,238
Holmes	101,976	110,449	50,200	53,620
Indian River	1,579,933	1,759,393	869,059	965,110
Jackson	618,138	598,444	276,674	289,906
Jefferson	77,476	81,905	34,199	37,696
Lafayette	39,774	43,467	10,259	10,658
Lake	2,627,793	2,751,042	1,295,809	1,363,801
Lee	7,438,153	7,842,774	4,511,930	4,746,429
Leon	3,945,975	4,349,475	2,236,880	2,415,857
Levy	254,501	289,968	139,034	157,413

See footnotes at end of table.

Continued . . .

Table 16.82. GROSS AND TAXABLE SALES: SALES REPORTED TO THE DEPARTMENT OF REVENUE IN THE STATE AND COUNTIES OF FLORIDA, 1994 AND 1995 (Continued)

(rounded to thousands of dollars)

County	Gross sales		Taxable sales	
	1994	1995	1994	1995
Liberty	53,488	63,558	10,039	11,940
Madison	120,018	130,211	53,614	56,873
Manatee	4,359,668	4,780,536	2,076,181	2,194,532
Marion	4,626,772	4,864,338	1,959,425	2,099,762
Martin	2,410,921	2,767,024	1,340,570	1,443,503
Monroe	2,013,111	2,115,676	1,389,137	1,459,206
Nassau	1,004,807	1,152,528	328,680	352,513
Okaloosa	2,690,900	3,087,901	1,584,552	1,733,666
Okeechobee	448,677	457,095	223,207	236,061
Orange	29,177,073	32,766,347	14,538,353	16,028,827
Osceola	3,278,492	3,690,286	1,540,657	1,740,890
Palm Beach	21,680,940	23,900,981	11,480,822	12,436,455
Pasco	3,529,492	3,823,385	1,909,128	1,993,578
Pinellas	18,678,732	20,545,423	8,591,995	8,953,300
Polk	9,180,703	9,760,546	3,832,755	4,039,131
Putnam	1,388,499	1,456,894	343,712	374,511
St. Johns	1,563,627	1,721,917	902,976	972,844
St. Lucie	2,452,888	2,618,665	1,268,568	1,350,074
Santa Rosa	1,066,872	1,228,344	427,004	470,890
Sarasota	5,998,332	6,430,642	3,359,039	3,531,154
Seminole	6,558,560	7,243,584	3,272,072	3,563,657
Sumter	388,406	428,986	143,002	152,701
Suwannee	333,478	363,289	165,428	179,156
Taylor	289,892	325,743	121,389	129,989
Union	150,445	156,366	26,676	28,699
Volusia	6,657,907	7,275,384	3,552,771	3,750,998
Wakulla	117,083	132,186	45,177	50,418
Walton	455,796	520,785	313,460	366,776
Washington	138,729	163,163	56,472	77,520
Out of state	49,878,732	55,290,564	10,599,466	11,482,068
In/out state 1/	1,508,545	2,543,318	170,598	359,182

1/ Reports that have not yet been allocated to counties.

Note: Data are audited sales reported to the Florida Department of Revenue for the 6 percent regular sales tax, 6 percent use tax, and 3 percent vehicle and farm equipment sales tax. Sales occurred, for the most part, December 1, 1993, through November 30, 1995. Kind of business data for counties are available from the Bureau of Economic and Business Research, University of Florida. Data are not comparable with retail sales reported by the U.S. Bureau of the Census.

Source: State of Florida, Department of Revenue, unpublished data prepared by the University of Florida, Bureau of Economic and Business Research.

FINANCE, INSURANCE, AND REAL ESTATE

Life Insurance and Annuity Payments in Florida, 1994

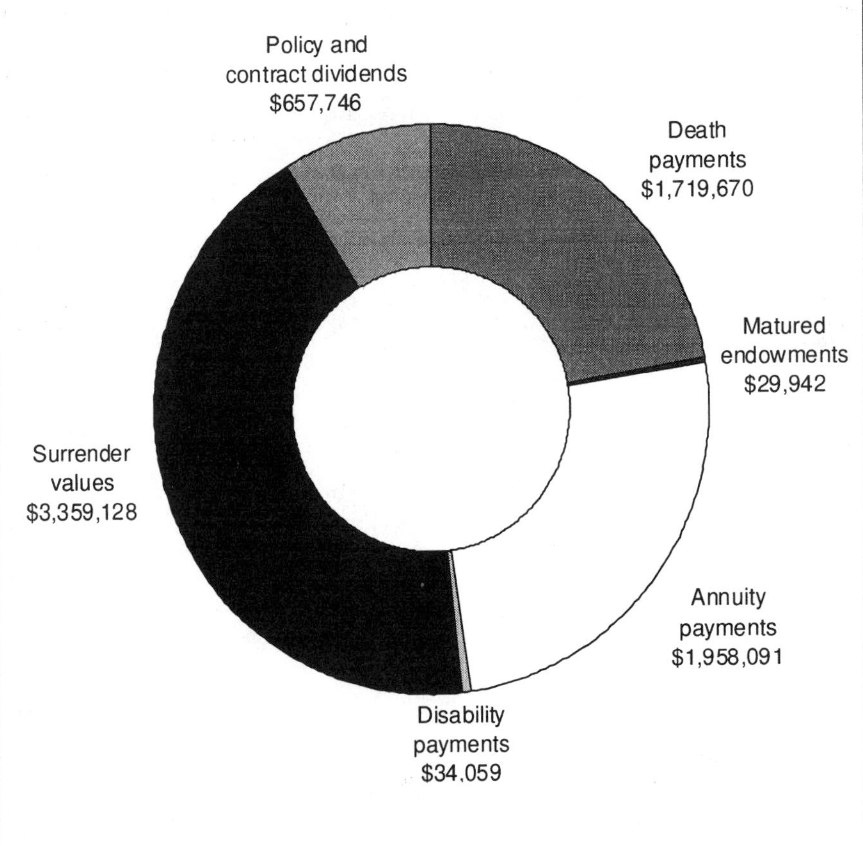

Source: Table 17.60

SECTION 17.00
FINANCE, INSURANCE, AND REAL ESTATE

TABLES LISTED BY MAJOR HEADINGS

SECTION 17.00
FINANCE, INSURANCE, AND REAL ESTATE
(Continued)

TABLES LISTED BY MAJOR HEADINGS

HEADING PAGE

Table 17.07. BANKING OFFICES: NUMBER OF FDIC-INSURED COMMERCIAL BANKS AND TRUST COMPANIES BY CHARTER CLASS AND OFFICE TYPE IN FLORIDA DECEMBER 31, 1994 AND 1995

Charter class	All offices	Banks: Total	Banks: Unit banks	Banks: Banks operating branches	Branches
Total by charter class	3,505	333	69	264	3,172
National	2,040	109	16	93	1,931
State	1,465	224	53	171	1,241
Member of Federal Reserve System	758	73	15	58	685
Nonmember of Federal Reserve System	707	151	38	113	556
Total in operation					
December 31, 1994	4,386	436	(NA)	(NA)	3,950
December 31, 1995	4,246	403	(NA)	(NA)	3,843
Net change during 1995	-140	-33	(NA)	(NA)	-107
Beginning operation in 1995	(NA)	4	(NA)	(NA)	(NA)
Ceasing operation in 1995	(NA)	37	(NA)	(NA)	(NA)
Failed banks	(NA)	0	(NA)	(NA)	(X)
Mergers, absorptions, and consolidations	(NA)	37	(NA)	(NA)	(X)

(NA) Not available.
(X) Not applicable.

Table 17.08. BANKING ACTIVITY: NUMBER OF FDIC-INSURED COMMERCIAL BANKS AND TRUST COMPANIES AND AMOUNT OF ASSETS AND DEPOSITS BY ASSET SIZE IN FLORIDA, DECEMBER 31, 1995

(amounts in millions of dollars)

Size of assets	Number of banks	Assets	Deposits
All banks	333	150,762	125,026
Less than $25 million	15	277	224
$25 to $50 million	74	2,820	2,452
$50 to $100 million	96	6,926	5,950
$100 to $300 million	79	13,160	11,307
$300 to $500 million	16	6,215	5,449
$500 million to $1 billion	28	19,922	16,795
$1 to $3 billion	15	25,593	21,612
$3 to $10 billion	9	39,258	31,439
$10 billion or more	1	36,591	29,798

Note: Asset size of bank determined from domestic and foreign consolidated assets.

Source for Tables 17.07 and 17.08: Federal Deposit Insurance Corporation, Division of Research and Statistics, *Statistics on Banking, 1995*.

Table 17.09. BANKING ACTIVITY: NUMBER OF FDIC-INSURED COMMERCIAL AND SAVINGS BANKS AND BANKING OFFICES AND AMOUNT OF DEPOSITS IN THE STATE AND COUNTIES OF FLORIDA, JUNE 30, 1995

County	Number of banks 1/	Number of banking offices 2/	Amount of deposits ($1,000) Total	IPC	Other 3/
Florida	345	3,491	141,125,384	135,404,484	5,720,893
Alachua	11	47	1,370,661	1,326,741	43,919
Baker	3	4	99,623	90,529	9,094
Bay	7	29	648,331	616,062	32,269
Bradford	3	6	154,258	145,333	8,924
Brevard	11	99	3,039,562	3,014,098	25,464
Broward	38	307	14,946,898	14,741,671	205,227
Calhoun	3	3	74,954	70,476	4,478
Charlotte	11	31	1,229,849	1,221,435	8,414
Citrus	10	32	1,157,855	1,133,580	24,275
Clay	9	24	484,294	470,765	13,529
Collier	15	78	2,892,389	2,841,141	51,248
Columbia	4	11	301,448	281,177	20,271
Dade	61	410	25,154,030	23,758,874	1,395,156
De Soto	4	5	174,216	165,556	8,660
Dixie	2	3	38,259	36,124	2,135
Duval	15	139	7,023,446	6,081,775	941,670
Escambia	15	71	2,155,444	2,010,973	144,471
Flagler	5	8	420,074	404,544	15,530
Franklin	2	7	62,896	59,628	3,268
Gadsden	4	10	195,798	185,820	9,978
Gilchrist	2	4	57,333	53,232	4,101
Glades	2	2	21,404	17,140	4,264
Gulf	2	3	45,128	38,877	6,251
Hamilton	1	1	18,569	18,516	53
Hardee	3	5	236,628	204,543	32,085
Hendry	4	9	185,754	157,773	27,981
Hernando	8	35	1,467,277	1,435,628	31,649
Highlands	7	25	887,112	874,216	12,896
Hillsborough	29	184	8,342,046	7,504,646	837,400
Holmes	3	3	95,073	90,367	4,706
Indian River	10	39	1,494,077	1,468,739	25,338
Jackson	6	14	317,785	293,881	23,904
Jefferson	2	2	78,419	74,615	3,804
Lafayette	1	1	23,438	19,936	3,502
Lake	11	52	1,767,588	1,745,154	22,434
Lee	18	120	3,820,918	3,775,751	45,167

See footnotes at end of table.

Continued . . .

Table 17.09. BANKING ACTIVITY: NUMBER OF FDIC-INSURED COMMERCIAL AND SAVINGS BANKS AND BANKING OFFICES AND AMOUNT OF DEPOSITS IN THE STATE AND COUNTIES OF FLORIDA, JUNE 30, 1995 (Continued)

County	Number of banks 1/	Number of banking offices 2/	Amount of deposits ($1,000) Total	IPC	Other 3/
Leon	12	60	1,866,967	1,686,392	180,574
Levy	3	12	195,934	178,973	16,961
Liberty	1	1	26,660	22,107	4,553
Madison	2	4	83,544	78,276	5,268
Manatee	12	63	2,324,969	2,307,958	17,011
Marion	13	61	2,180,900	2,129,042	51,858
Martin	7	39	1,314,495	1,283,821	30,673
Monroe	8	40	970,558	895,536	75,022
Nassau	5	14	281,667	268,087	13,580
Okaloosa	15	54	1,430,095	1,319,170	110,925
Okeechobee	3	7	221,458	214,160	7,298
Orange	21	166	6,220,363	5,882,185	338,176
Osceola	10	24	772,695	767,228	5,467
Palm Beach	32	247	9,460,152	9,290,079	170,073
Pasco	12	87	3,372,719	3,344,504	28,215
Pinellas	22	255	11,609,444	11,449,990	159,454
Polk	13	105	3,299,864	3,215,707	84,157
Putnam	5	12	298,294	280,409	17,885
St. Johns	10	26	874,675	857,662	17,013
St. Lucie	7	31	1,288,737	1,206,249	82,488
Santa Rosa	8	23	604,539	537,825	66,714
Sarasota	20	116	4,961,909	4,917,847	44,062
Seminole	19	76	2,054,822	2,037,131	17,691
Sumter	3	6	145,151	138,216	6,935
Suwannee	4	6	173,993	168,519	5,474
Taylor	2	4	62,869	55,578	7,291
Union	1	1	31,528	27,109	4,419
Volusia	13	113	4,168,539	4,103,737	64,802
Wakulla	2	3	81,220	73,119	8,101
Walton	5	9	188,771	172,668	16,103
Washington	3	3	75,019	65,884	9,135

IPC Individuals, partnerships, and corporations.

1/ Number of banks in each county includes each bank operating at least one office within the county, regardless of the location of its main office; therefore, a bank operating a branch in a second county would be counted as a bank in each county, but only once in the state total.

2/ Includes each location at which deposit business is transacted.

3/ Transaction, demand, and nontransaction deposits not included under IPC.

Source: Federal Deposit Insurance Corporation, Division of Supervision, *Data Book: Operating Banks and Branches, June 30, 1995.*

Table 17.20. STATE-CHARTERED BANKS AND TRUST COMPANIES: NUMBER, ASSETS CAPITAL ACCOUNTS, LOANS, AND DEPOSITS IN FLORIDA SPECIFIED YEARS 1895 THROUGH 1995

(amounts in thousands of dollars)

Year	Number	Assets	Capital accounts	Loans	Deposits
1895	21	1,692	666	943	974
1900	22	4,510	1,006	2,637	3,408
1905	41	14,338	3,222	9,332	10,291
1910	113	27,599	5,607	17,711	20,884
1915	192	42,656	9,811	26,280	30,527
1920	212	114,374	13,272	71,347	95,349
1925	271	539,101	33,427	309,492	501,553
1930	151	92,928	16,422	38,534	70,235
1935	102	64,276	9,768	13,662	53,552
1940	114	116,169	14,233	31,285	101,545
1945	112	450,838	20,135	36,851	430,256
1950	130	619,824	37,603	128,517	580,607
1955	146	1,138,114	67,726	329,340	1,064,763
1960	181	1,781,837	139,368	711,387	1,620,185
1965	243	2,571,685	216,444	1,139,398	2,541,195
1970	282	5,603,445	425,945	2,668,971	4,996,082
1975	449	11,757,147	989,185	5,860,781	10,346,695
1980	358	22,416,088	1,679,111	10,380,658	17,942,643
1981	321	21,303,799	1,609,024	10,423,906	17,991,930
1982	297	20,912,278	1,570,467	9,978,160	18,175,117
1983	274	22,940,431	1,678,551	11,152,310	20,212,039
1984	256	23,186,313	1,636,747	12,568,673	20,319,366
1985	251	24,160,155	1,627,920	13,372,532	21,321,726
1986	241	28,055,385	1,896,402	16,174,559	24,948,817
1987	246	30,362,358	2,136,083	18,647,857	26,683,250
1988	251	31,658,397	2,264,319	19,950,857	27,831,065
1989	258	32,801,720	2,402,253	21,338,510	29,128,762
1990	261	37,247,099	2,587,920	23,793,358	33,324,544
1991	260	39,051,128	2,852,114	24,076,458	35,021,312
1992	256	41,551,323	3,196,327	25,095,945	37,137,219
1993	248	51,271,342	4,265,301	32,194,235	44,490,477
1994	238	58,803,093	4,783,598	38,780,991	50,081,893
1995	224	58,344,123	5,143,296	38,320,163	49,393,436

Note: Data for 1986 through 1995 excludes nondeposit trust companies and industrial savings banks.

Source: State of Florida, Office of the Comptroller, *Annual Report of the Division of Banking, 1995,* prepublication release.

Table 17.21. STATE-CHARTERED BANKS AND TRUST COMPANIES: NUMBER ASSETS, AND DEPOSITS IN THE STATE AND COUNTIES OF FLORIDA, DECEMBER 31, 1995

(amounts in thousands of dollars)

County	Number	Assets	Deposits	County	Number	Assets	Deposits
Florida	224	58,344,123	49,393,436	Lafayette	1	27,330	23,606
				Lake	4	332,560	293,663
Alachua	4	305,566	273,567	Lee	5	1,287,154	1,065,752
Baker	1	84,563	72,289	Leon	5	1,464,931	1,228,255
Bay	1	135,117	123,805	Levy	3	229,882	204,636
Bradford	1	38,075	32,938	Liberty	1	31,397	27,890
Brevard	3	277,824	253,417	Madison	0	0	0
Broward	11	1,326,767	1,171,984	Manatee	2	160,586	131,375
Calhoun	1	46,639	42,851	Marion	5	940,583	771,768
Charlotte	4	231,867	204,833	Martin	1	28,187	24,105
Citrus	3	371,800	325,959	Monroe	4	757,930	648,722
Clay	1	22,874	20,652	Nassau	2	162,818	133,141
Collier	4	1,152,001	1,018,568	Okaloosa	6	704,939	618,183
Columbia	2	307,479	273,475	Okeechobee	1	198,897	175,581
Dade	24	6,116,499	5,062,241	Orange	6	716,452	610,448
De Soto	1	97,997	81,836	Osceola	1	44,268	40,270
Dixie	0	0	0	Palm Beach	14	4,473,797	3,985,244
Duval	4	1,107,637	960,971	Pasco	2	1,094,658	1,006,278
Escambia	10	2,272,233	1,921,017	Pinellas	14	5,078,173	4,327,707
Flagler	0	0	0	Polk	6	1,957,762	1,681,868
Franklin	2	72,424	65,190	Putnam	1	36,704	33,040
Gadsden	2	127,635	108,140	St. Johns	2	516,492	458,894
Gilchrist	2	66,604	59,363	St. Lucie	1	629,465	564,509
Glades	0	0	0	Santa Rosa	0	0	0
Gulf	1	28,603	26,017	Sarasota	7	3,989,194	3,318,844
Hamilton	0	0	0	Seminole	1	82,660	72,873
Hardee	1	229,518	195,343	Sumter	0	0	0
Hendry	2	179,663	162,546	Suwannee	1	32,229	28,336
Hernando	2	1,229,611	1,076,502	Taylor	1	40,507	36,354
Highlands	2	478,241	414,944	Union	1	48,373	43,187
Hillsborough	18	13,009,199	10,417,315	Volusia	7	2,868,354	2,508,151
Holmes	1	58,972	50,670	Wakulla	2	122,947	113,291
Indian River	2	234,840	208,137	Walton	1	24,132	21,316
Jackson	5	562,440	493,993	Washington	0	0	0
Jefferson	1	88,074	77,586				

Source: State of Florida, Office of the Comptroller, *Annual Report of the Division of Banking, 1995,* prepublication release.

Table 17.23. STATE-CHARTERED BANKS AND TRUST COMPANIES: ASSETS, LIABILITIES INCOME, EXPENSES, AND NUMBER OF BANKS BY ASSET SIZE IN FLORIDA, DECEMBER 31, 1995

(in thousands of dollars, except where indicated)

Item	All banks	Less than 50 million	50-500 million	Over 500 million
Assets	58,344,123	2,310,620	16,870,148	39,163,355
Liabilities	53,200,827	2,053,551	15,298,287	35,848,989
Capital	5,143,296	257,069	1,571,861	3,314,366
Interest income	4,212,550	166,934	1,221,938	2,823,678
Interest expense	1,775,320	66,362	485,570	1,223,388
Gains/losses on securities	2,402	116	705	1,581
Net income 1/	707,409	18,362	184,982	504,065
Number of institutions	224	68	129	27

1/ After taxes and extraordinary items.
Note: Nondeposit trust companies and industrial savings banks are excluded.

Table 17.24. INTERNATIONAL BANKS: NUMBER AND ASSETS OF AGENCIES BY NATION OF ORIGIN IN FLORIDA, DECEMBER 31, 1994 AND 1995

Nation of origin	1994 Number	1994 Assets ($1,000)	1995 Number	1995 Assets ($1,000)
Total	47	11,423,666	46	13,539,796
Argentina	1	111,876	1	77,417
Bolivia	2	51,014	2	74,519
Brazil	4	563,158	4	433,372
Canada	1	531,406	1	546,567
Cayman Islands	1	41,799	1	46,976
Chile	1	23,514	1	68,783
Colombia	1	227,625	1	211,418
Ecuador	2	133,875	2	179,840
England	3	3,479,933	3	3,593,300
France	3	626,994	3	665,498
Germany	1	1,142,170	1	2,203,179
Israel	3	735,184	3	813,745
Jamaica	1	47,540	1	43,104
Japan	3	300,826	3	300,504
Korea	1	73,332	1	110,635
Netherlands	1	630,787	1	857,984
Panama	1	303,181	1	304,148
Peru	1	254,589	1	263,828
Portugal	1	103,294	1	84,254
Spain	8	1,063,730	7	1,470,353
Switzerland	2	589,093	2	829,163
United States	1	38,109	1	38,356
Venezuela	4	350,637	4	322,853

Source for Tables 17.23 and 17.24: State of Florida, Office of the Comptroller, *Annual Report of the Division of Banking, 1995,* prepublication release.

Table 17.30. CREDIT UNIONS: FINANCIAL CONDITION OF STATE-CHARTERED CREDIT UNIONS IN FLORIDA, DECEMBER 31, 1995

(in thousands of dollars, except where indicated)

Item	Amount	Item	Amount
Number of institutions 1/	115	Gross income, total	316,275
Net loans	2,400,817	Operating expense, total	160,697
Assets, total	3,728,429	Cost of funds	113,490
Shares and deposits, total	3,336,160	Net income	39,001
Liabilities and equity, total	3,728,429	Ratio of expense to $100 gross income (dollars)	50.8

1/ Does not include credit unions in liquidation.

Table 17.31. CREDIT UNIONS: ASSETS AND DEPOSITS OF STATE-CHARTERED CREDIT UNIONS IN THE STATE AND COUNTIES OF FLORIDA, DECEMBER 31, 1995

(amounts in thousands of dollars)

County	Number of institu-tions	Assets	Deposits	County	Number of institu-tions	Assets	Deposits
Florida	115	3,728,429	3,336,160	Lee	2	2,425	2,057
				Leon	7	248,382	226,046
Alachua	5	113,434	102,422	Madison	1	1,439	1,111
Bay	1	40,646	35,193	Marion	3	33,315	29,597
Bradford	1	2,899	2,554	Martin	1	6,462	5,391
Brevard	2	710,175	657,330	Nassau	2	12,262	10,403
Broward	8	311,912	284,419	Orange	3	47,859	41,349
Calhoun	1	14,851	13,051	Palm Beach	7	114,382	102,076
Clay	1	5,632	4,939	Pinellas	5	249,507	219,762
Columbia	1	12,243	10,695	Polk	6	40,896	36,086
Dade	10	184,080	161,034	Putnam	1	13,647	11,800
Duval	15	843,078	747,724	St. Johns	1	6,832	6,126
Escambia	5	286,637	252,098	St. Lucie	1	4,436	4,149
Gadsden	1	35,239	30,399	Santa Rosa	2	17,249	14,787
Hillsborough	7	157,546	137,075	Sarasota	3	104,583	94,879
Holmes	1	7,544	6,443	Taylor	1	7,150	6,659
Jackson	2	13,548	10,945	Volusia	3	9,493	8,137
Jefferson	1	3,600	3,257	Washington	1	15,159	12,808
Lake	3	49,887	43,359				

Source for Tables 17.30 and 17.31: State of Florida, Office of the Comptroller, *Annual Report of the Division of Banking, 1995,* prepublication release.

Table 17.33. MORTGAGE ACTIVITY: NUMBER AND VALUE OF NEW AND EXISTING RESIDENTIAL PURCHASE LOANS IN SPECIFIED COUNTIES OF FLORIDA, 1993, 1994, and 1995

County	Number of loans			Value ($1,000,000)		
	1993	1994	1995	1993	1994	1995
Total	217,155	240,123	230,672	18,189	20,924	20,251
Alachua	2,513	2,592	2,564	183	197	189
Brevard	7,785	7,461	6,744	571	565	506
Broward	26,996	32,325	29,958	2,548	3,138	2,946
Charlotte	1,885	2,199	1,999	129	154	141
Citrus	1,090	1,376	1,431	69	71	75
Clay	2,006	2,424	2,405	163	201	212
Collier	4,283	5,212	5,148	454	597	610
Dade	29,704	32,142	30,696	2,694	2,929	2,836
De Soto	174	226	295	10	10	13
Duval	11,068	10,895	10,816	883	897	887
Escambia	3,363	3,731	3,631	238	264	263
Flagler	673	796	710	54	60	55
Hernando	1,361	1,585	1,613	74	93	94
Highlands	762	905	857	39	48	46
Hillsborough	12,668	14,068	14,343	1,073	1,231	1,247
Indian River	1,223	1,504	1,345	119	140	118
Lake	2,414	2,761	2,933	157	185	202
Lee	7,086	8,405	7,555	600	751	677
Leon	3,586	3,762	3,860	294	304	309
Manatee	3,644	4,186	3,961	291	325	319
Marion	2,258	2,481	2,607	135	154	160
Martin	1,758	2,039	1,976	166	203	183
Monroe	1,342	1,679	1,537	163	207	202
Nassau	626	735	790	53	69	72
Okaloosa	3,364	3,256	2,969	272	270	265
Orange	12,803	13,920	13,329	1,137	1,256	1,188
Osceola	3,185	2,638	2,710	179	192	193
Palm Beach	18,537	20,775	19,440	1,888	2,157	2,026
Pasco	4,257	4,752	4,912	251	288	303
Pinellas	14,370	16,235	15,324	1,148	1,281	1,237
Polk	4,592	5,472	5,091	295	357	332
Putnam	387	398	453	21	22	26
St. Johns	1,916	2,242	2,235	196	235	244
St. Lucie	2,508	2,630	2,627	158	174	176
Santa Rosa	1,872	2,168	2,048	143	176	170
Sarasota	5,704	6,047	5,756	256	564	568
Seminole	6,168	6,476	6,168	589	615	587
Sumter	261	423	538	14	24	34
Volusia	6,072	6,227	6,348	405	420	433
Walton	891	975	950	77	99	108

Note: Only counties for which data are collected are shown.
Source: TRW REDI Property Data, Anaheim, CA, unpublished data, (copyright).

Table 17.36. SAVINGS AND LOAN ASSOCIATIONS: NUMBER OF ASSOCIATIONS AND OFFICES AND AMOUNT OF DEPOSITS IN THE STATE AND COUNTIES OF FLORIDA, JUNE 30, 1995

County	Number of asso- cia- tions	Number of associ- ation offices	Depos- its 1/ ($1,000)	County	Number of asso- cia- tions	Number of associ- ation offices	Depos- its 1/ ($1,000)
Florida	198	728	35,953,380	Lafayette	1	1	8,787
				Lake	2	10	372,897
Alachua	0	0	0	Lee	5	25	1,068,517
Baker	0	0	0	Leon	2	3	59,817
Bay	3	13	436,481	Levy	1	3	36,816
Bradford	0	0	0	Liberty	0	0	0
Brevard	4	18	476,326	Madison	1	1	33,697
Broward	17	104	7,062,559	Manatee	8	19	528,855
Calhoun	0	0	0	Marion	1	2	105,006
Charlotte	5	11	509,543	Martin	8	21	498,523
Citrus	3	6	262,438	Monroe	0	0	0
Clay	0	0	0	Nassau	0	0	0
Collier	7	10	262,165	Okaloosa	1	2	54,950
Columbia	1	2	32,804	Okeechobee	2	2	52,969
Dade	19	124	8,303,207	Orange	5	16	815,106
De Soto	1	1	22,359	Osceola	1	5	127,350
Dixie	1	1	9,605	Palm Beach	31	161	7,743,300
Duval	3	3	58,428	Pasco	8	10	647,024
Escambia	1	1	37,085	Pinellas	8	36	1,786,627
Flagler	0	0	0	Polk	3	14	444,200
Franklin	1	1	10,032	Putnam	1	4	141,464
Gadsden	0	0	0	St. Johns	1	1	12,981
Gilchrist	1	1	7,016	St. Lucie	3	12	415,460
Glades	0	0	0	Santa Rosa	0	0	0
Gulf	1	1	40,190	Sarasota	10	27	891,314
Hamilton	1	2	16,349	Seminole	4	11	504,537
Hardee	0	0	0	Sumter	1	1	33,862
Hendry	1	2	54,180	Suwannee	1	2	67,323
Hernando	4	5	266,469	Taylor	1	1	46,085
Highlands	2	4	143,315	Union	0	0	0
Hillsborough	4	8	288,129	Volusia	3	11	801,984
Holmes	0	0	0	Wakulla	0	0	0
Indian River	4	8	343,623	Walton	0	0	0
Jackson	1	1	11,626	Washington	0	0	0
Jefferson	0	0	0				

1/ Includes savings, NOW accounts, and noninterest bearing deposits.

Note: Data are for all SAIF-insured (Savings Associations Insurance Fund) OTS regulated associations and are the result of a survey. Figures indicate the activity of an association within specific counties whether the county offices are home or branch offices, although some institutions with centralized accounting do not have precise data on deposits by office. Detail may not add to totals due to rounding.

Source: U.S., Office of Thrift Supervision, *Summary of Deposits in SAIF-Insured OTS Regulated Associations, Regional Data Book, Southeast Region, June 30, 1995.*

Table 17.38. EMPLOYMENT: AVERAGE MONTHLY PRIVATE REPORTING UNITS, EMPLOYMENT, AND PAYROLL COVERED BY UNEMPLOYMENT COMPENSATION LAW BY FINANCE, INSURANCE AND REAL ESTATE INDUSTRY IN FLORIDA, 1994 AND 1995

SIC code	Industry	Number of reporting units	Number of employees	Payroll ($1,000)
	1994 A/			
	Finance, insurance, and real estate	34,273	372,984	966,681
60	Depository institutions	2,489	97,236	225,563
601	Central reserve depository institutions	3	653	1,663
602	Commercial banks	1,158	66,445	153,782
603	Savings institutions	667	17,385	40,140
606	Credit unions	344	7,649	13,709
608	Foreign banking and branches and agencies of foreign banks	73	2,174	8,724
609	Functions related to depository banking	244	2,930	7,545
61	Nondepository credit institutions	2,630	35,162	94,931
614	Personal credit institutions	864	9,721	26,956
615	Business credit institutions	183	8,282	20,950
616	Mortgage bankers and brokers	1,553	15,992	44,687
62	Security and commodity brokers, dealers, exchanges, and services	1,895	23,261	125,253
621	Security brokers, dealers, flotation companies	1,085	20,634	109,284
622	Commodity contracts brokers and dealers	49	249	1,621
628	Services allied with the exchange of securities or commodities	754	2,364	14,232
63	Insurance carriers	2,197	65,738	186,986
631	Life insurance	615	20,996	56,915
632	Accident and health insurance and medical service plans	223	11,961	33,895
633	Fire, marine, and casualty insurance	622	25,209	77,355
635	Surety insurance	63	408	1,585
636	Title insurance	602	6,618	14,687
637	Pension, health, and welfare funds	61	487	2,324
639	Insurance carriers, NEC	11	59	224
64	Insurance agents, brokers, and service	6,988	41,582	109,242
65	Real estate	16,910	100,959	189,042
651	Real estate operators (except developers) and lessors	6,224	36,252	54,225
653	Real estate agents and managers	9,103	47,929	95,276
654	Title abstract offices	229	1,588	3,194
655	Land subdividers and developers	1,355	15,189	36,347
67	Holding and other investment offices	1,165	9,046	35,663
671	Holding offices	416	5,670	24,466
672	Investment offices	58	303	1,348
673	Trusts	166	989	2,516
679	Miscellaneous investing	526	2,085	7,333

See footnotes at end of table.

Continued . . .

Table 17.38. EMPLOYMENT: AVERAGE MONTHLY PRIVATE REPORTING UNITS, EMPLOYMENT, AND PAYROLL COVERED BY UNEMPLOYMENT COMPENSATION LAW BY FINANCE, INSURANCE AND REAL ESTATE INDUSTRY IN FLORIDA, 1994 AND 1995 (Continued)

SIC code	Industry	Number of reporting units	Number of employees	Payroll ($1,000)
	1995 B/			
	Finance, insurance, and real estate	34,311	372,560	1,022,466
60	Depository institutions	2,789	94,732	233,648
601	Central reserve depository institutions	3	632	1,682
602	Commercial banks	1,546	66,773	162,286
603	Savings institutions	586	13,579	34,308
606	Credit unions	347	8,163	15,131
608	Foreign banking and branches and agencies of foreign banks	69	2,295	10,646
609	Functions related to depository banking	240	3,291	9,594
61	Nondepository credit institutions	2,642	34,838	101,064
611	Federal and federally-sponsored credit agencies	29	1,246	2,560
614	Personal credit institutions	892	10,567	30,306
615	Business credit institutions	187	8,893	24,128
616	Mortgage bankers and brokers	1,535	14,133	44,069
62	Security and commodity brokers, dealers, exchanges, and services	1,888	23,875	138,845
621	Security brokers, dealers, flotation companies	1,072	20,856	117,153
622	Commodity contracts brokers and dealers	52	336	6,670
623	Security and commodity exchanges	4	6	19
628	Services allied with the exchange of securities or commodities	760	2,677	15,003
63	Insurance carriers	2,315	65,716	194,871
631	Life insurance	580	20,412	57,248
632	Accident and health insurance and medical service plans	233	13,875	41,270
633	Fire, marine, and casualty insurance	752	24,661	78,492
635	Surety insurance	69	513	1,992
636	Title insurance	600	5,700	13,481
637	Pension, health, and welfare funds	62	472	2,045
639	Insurance carriers, NEC	20	83	344
64	Insurance agents, brokers, and service	6,989	43,161	118,272
65	Real estate	16,496	100,859	194,990
651	Real estate operators (except developers) and lessors	5,920	35,135	54,739
653	Real estate agents and managers	9,101	49,395	100,836
654	Title abstract offices	220	1,266	2,733
655	Land subdividers and developers	1,255	15,064	36,682
67	Holding and other investment offices	1,193	9,380	40,777
671	Holding offices	423	5,775	27,717
672	Investment offices	94	357	1,761
673	Trusts	147	985	2,619
679	Miscellaneous investing	529	2,263	8,679

NEC Not elsewhere classified. A/ Revised. B/ Preliminary.

Note: Private employment. Detail may not add to totals due to disclosure editing and/or rounding. See Tables 23.70, 23.71, 23.72, 23.73, and 23.74 for public employment data.

Source: State of Florida, Department of Labor and Employment Security, Bureau of Labor Market Information, "Employment and Wages" (ES-202), unpublished data.

Table 17.39. EMPLOYMENT: AVERAGE MONTHLY PRIVATE REPORTING UNITS, EMPLOYMENT AND PAYROLL COVERED BY UNEMPLOYMENT COMPENSATION LAW IN THE STATE AND COUNTIES OF FLORIDA, 1994 AND 1995

County	Number of re- porting units	Number of em- ployees	Payroll ($1,000)	County	Number of re- porting units	Number of em- ployees	Payroll ($1,000)
Finance, insurance, and real estate, 1994 A/ (SIC codes 60-67)							
Florida	34,273	372,984	966,681	Jefferson	16	110	195
				Lake	282	2,804	4,789
Alachua	451	4,386	9,165	Lee	1,032	7,970	18,532
Baker	15	108	166	Leon	586	4,799	11,384
Bay	311	3,131	5,263	Levy	45	280	406
Bradford	26	113	183	Madison	17	86	130
Brevard	791	5,584	12,101	Manatee	405	2,965	6,168
Broward	3,771	41,236	114,394	Marion	396	3,168	6,092
Calhoun	9	61	85	Martin	350	2,281	6,660
Charlotte	227	1,496	3,050	Monroe	251	1,417	3,057
Citrus	170	1,054	1,947	Nassau	65	403	808
Clay	161	902	1,728	Okaloosa	360	3,652	6,347
Collier	711	4,670	13,578	Okeechobee	44	232	642
Columbia	70	512	870	Orange	2,133	29,260	76,088
Dade	5,724	65,855	182,483	Osceola	259	2,617	4,208
De Soto	29	156	245	Palm Beach	3,118	26,731	85,706
Dixie	10	42	49	Pasco	430	2,928	5,683
Duval	1,725	45,652	121,559	Pinellas	2,229	23,064	60,455
Escambia	502	4,453	8,929	Polk	700	7,424	16,149
Flagler	57	622	1,686	Putnam	80	515	935
Franklin	20	131	191	St. Johns	181	1,108	2,213
Gadsden	39	243	443	St. Lucie	264	2,242	4,582
Gilchrist	8	57	91	Santa Rosa	119	653	1,010
Glades	4	15	26	Sarasota	959	7,612	20,328
Gulf	17	120	181	Seminole	729	5,315	13,517
Hamilton	5	17	30	Sumter	30	201	308
Hardee	22	228	421	Suwannee	35	272	440
Hendry	39	307	477	Taylor	20	228	399
Hernando	145	1,106	2,167	Volusia	780	5,612	12,013
Highlands	129	932	1,730	Wakulla	16	114	193
Hillsborough	2,360	37,794	98,588	Walton	47	328	555
Holmes	8	54	101	Washington	18	68	111
Indian River	274	1,965	4,657				
Jackson	58	464	977	Multicounty 1/	384	2,971	8,859

See footnotes at end of table.

Continued . . .

Table 17.39. EMPLOYMENT: AVERAGE MONTHLY PRIVATE REPORTING UNITS, EMPLOYMENT AND PAYROLL COVERED BY UNEMPLOYMENT COMPENSATION LAW IN THE STATE AND COUNTIES OF FLORIDA, 1994 AND 1995 (Continued)

County	Number of re- porting units	Number of em- ployees	Payroll ($1,000)	County	Number of re- porting units	Number of em- ployees	Payroll ($1,000)
Finance, insurance, and real estate, 1995 B/ (SIC codes 60-67)							
Florida	34,311	372,560	1,022,466	Jefferson	17	119	213
				Lake	296	2,915	5,449
Alachua	439	4,366	9,908	Lee	1,017	8,125	20,199
Baker	14	106	175	Leon	576	4,848	12,113
Bay	306	2,975	5,346	Levy	39	266	429
Bradford	24	105	184	Madison	17	81	163
Brevard	797	5,518	12,648	Manatee	433	2,893	6,298
Broward	3,748	40,016	115,625	Marion	396	3,057	7,191
Calhoun	9	63	93	Martin	346	2,291	6,776
Charlotte	228	1,486	3,027	Monroe	243	1,440	3,290
Citrus	177	1,048	2,065	Nassau	69	384	858
Clay	153	818	1,827	Okaloosa	376	3,797	7,085
Collier	707	4,466	14,797	Okeechobee	43	233	871
Columbia	69	505	877	Orange	2,120	29,520	79,988
Dade	5,627	66,186	193,264	Osceola	256	2,412	4,086
De Soto	29	165	266	Palm Beach	3,082	26,324	95,592
Dixie	11	46	57	Pasco	442	2,895	6,000
Duval	1,787	45,674	128,286	Pinellas	2,247	22,869	63,453
Escambia	496	4,603	9,546	Polk	723	7,503	17,074
Flagler	63	614	1,530	Putnam	85	526	984
Franklin	21	142	216	St. Johns	196	1,154	2,735
Gadsden	38	245	440	St. Lucie	266	2,183	4,723
Gilchrist	8	56	104	Santa Rosa	122	679	1,054
Glades	4	14	24	Sarasota	965	7,648	21,650
Gulf	18	128	199	Seminole	739	5,766	14,441
Hamilton	6	19	32	Sumter	26	202	336
Hardee	22	232	460	Suwannee	38	284	472
Hendry	39	270	451	Taylor	20	226	424
Hernando	144	1,130	2,270	Volusia	795	5,803	12,622
Highlands	126	851	1,621	Wakulla	15	112	205
Hillsborough	2,377	38,008	103,933	Walton	52	336	574
Holmes	9	56	103	Washington	18	67	116
Indian River	277	1,656	4,381				
Jackson	56	463	986	Multicounty 1/	405	3,490	10,110

A/ Revised.
B/ Preliminary.
1/ Reporting units without a fixed location within the state or of unknown county location.
Note: Private employment. Only counties for which data are disclosed are shown. Detail may not add to totals due to disclosure editing and/or rounding. See Tables 23.70, 23.71, 23.72, 23.73, and 23.74 for public employment data.

Source: State of Florida, Department of Labor and Employment Security, Bureau of Labor Market Information, "Employment and Wages" (ES-202), unpublished data.

Table 17.40. DEPOSITORY INSTITUTIONS: AVERAGE MONTHLY PRIVATE REPORTING UNITS EMPLOYMENT, AND PAYROLL COVERED BY UNEMPLOYMENT COMPENSATION LAW IN THE STATE AND COUNTIES OF FLORIDA, 1995

County	Number of reporting units	Number of employees	Payroll ($1,000)	County	Number of reporting units	Number of employees	Payroll ($1,000)
			Depository institutions (SIC code 60)				
Florida	2,789	94,732	233,648	Lake	32	1,008	1,991
				Lee	65	2,479	6,355
Alachua	25	927	1,774	Leon	51	1,341	2,857
Baker	3	80	141	Levy	10	168	302
Bay	25	1,074	1,965	Madison	3	48	121
Bradford	5	64	118	Manatee	58	906	1,805
Brevard	58	1,602	3,015	Marion	41	1,159	2,374
Broward	224	9,354	24,448	Martin	37	701	1,836
Calhoun	4	52	75	Monroe	25	608	1,512
Charlotte	24	506	1,025	Nassau	14	172	389
Citrus	27	423	902	Okaloosa	46	1,112	2,137
Clay	8	138	256	Okeechobee	6	133	289
Collier	43	1,240	3,057	Orange	123	5,414	12,308
Columbia	9	219	443	Osceola	20	391	740
Dade	463	20,109	58,649	Palm Beach	219	6,460	18,635
De Soto	5	95	171	Pasco	57	1,033	2,195
Duval	154	9,450	25,030	Pinellas	194	4,967	11,504
Escambia	59	1,506	3,058	Polk	54	1,976	3,819
Flagler	8	85	158	Putnam	15	253	468
Franklin	5	66	108	St. Johns	14	354	773
Gadsden	9	127	251	St. Lucie	21	1,054	2,309
Gilchrist	3	37	76	Santa Rosa	17	259	435
Gulf	4	90	147	Sarasota	81	2,117	4,841
Hardee	3	160	321	Seminole	45	1,182	2,495
Hendry	5	179	339	Suwannee	6	131	258
Hernando	22	536	1,181	Taylor	5	184	358
Highlands	16	356	759	Volusia	60	1,768	3,845
Hillsborough	178	7,624	16,526	Wakulla	3	89	164
Holmes	4	41	83	Walton	9	79	126
Indian River	24	511	1,225	Washington	4	32	54
Jackson	13	244	498	Multicounty 1/	15	33	123

1/ Reporting units without a fixed location within the state or of unknown county location.

Note: Private employment. For a list of three-digit code industries included see Table 17.38. Data are preliminary. Only counties for which data are disclosed are shown. Detail may not add to totals due to disclosure editing and/or rounding. See Tables 23.70, 23.71, 23.72, 23.73, and 23.74 for public employment data.

Source: State of Florida, Department of Labor and Employment Security, Bureau of Labor Market Information, "Employment and Wages" (ES-202), unpublished data.

Table 17.41. NONDEPOSITORY CREDIT INSTITUTIONS: AVERAGE MONTHLY PRIVATE REPORTING UNITS, EMPLOYMENT, AND PAYROLL COVERED BY UNEMPLOYMENT COMPENSATION LAW IN THE STATE AND COUNTIES OF FLORIDA, 1995

County	Number of re- porting units	Number of em- ployees	Payroll ($1,000)	County	Number of re- porting units	Number of em- ployees	Payroll ($1,000)
			Nondepository credit institutions (SIC code 61)				
Florida	2,642	34,838	101,064	Leon	39	278	681
				Manatee	22	132	349
Alachua	34	191	480	Marion	27	117	249
Bay	18	66	156	Martin	15	97	322
Brevard	57	251	697	Monroe	10	22	45
Broward	315	6,356	18,366	Okaloosa	23	106	237
Charlotte	13	52	131	Orange	175	2,108	6,031
Citrus	7	38	88	Osceola	16	54	110
Clay	14	70	167	Palm Beach	191	1,472	5,863
Collier	34	102	320	Pasco	27	80	201
Columbia	7	23	40	Pinellas	164	1,323	3,940
Dade	452	5,487	16,679	Polk	52	221	537
Duval	169	8,997	25,721	Putnam	5	16	35
Escambia	44	532	1,154	St. Johns	10	28	57
Flagler	4	24	61	St. Lucie	21	119	264
Hernando	8	25	59	Santa Rosa	7	21	37
Hillsborough	269	4,426	12,381	Sarasota	62	349	962
Indian River	12	24	41	Seminole	92	628	1,758
Jackson	7	46	109	Volusia	55	254	528
Lake	15	50	94				
Lee	69	298	704	Multicounty 1/	56	277	1,196

1/ Reporting units without a fixed location within the state or of unknown county location.

Note: Private employment. For a list of three-digit code industries included see Table 17.38. Data are preliminary. Only counties for which data are disclosed are shown. Detail may not add to totals due to disclosure editing and/or rounding. See Tables 23.70, 23.71, 23.72, 23.73, and 23.74 for public employment data.

Source: State of Florida, Department of Labor and Employment Security, Bureau of Labor Market Information, "Employment and Wages" (ES-202), unpublished data.

Table 17.43. INSURANCE CARRIERS: AVERAGE MONTHLY PRIVATE REPORTING UNITS EMPLOYMENT, AND PAYROLL COVERED BY UNEMPLOYMENT COMPENSATION LAW IN THE STATE AND COUNTIES OF FLORIDA, 1995

County	Number of reporting units	Number of employees	Payroll ($1,000)	County	Number of reporting units	Number of employees	Payroll ($1,000)
Insurance carriers (SIC code 63)							
Florida	2,315	65,716	194,871	Manatee	20	154	564
				Marion	27	266	790
Alachua	37	1,490	4,321	Martin	13	82	267
Bay	28	303	777	Monroe	6	20	48
Bradford	4	11	23	Okaloosa	22	297	764
Brevard	62	518	1,775	Okeechobee	3	20	438
Broward	233	5,598	16,262	Orange	189	6,402	18,493
Charlotte	17	107	345	Osceola	16	117	283
Citrus	12	90	203	Palm Beach	167	2,364	8,692
Clay	10	116	433	Pasco	26	237	734
Collier	29	203	586	Pinellas	132	3,212	9,702
Columbia	10	140	237	Polk	55	2,021	6,003
Dade	291	9,673	30,991	Putnam	7	37	61
Duval	171	15,093	42,149	St. Johns	14	54	125
Escambia	47	525	1,614	St. Lucie	18	206	623
Hernando	10	81	213	Santa Rosa	4	9	51
Highlands	9	82	198	Sarasota	66	1,027	3,211
Hillsborough	243	11,205	31,582	Seminole	43	597	1,626
Indian River	11	41	170	Suwannee	4	39	75
Jackson	5	78	183	Volusia	51	642	2,046
Lake	12	125	343	Wakulla	3	9	17
Lee	66	715	2,290	Walton	3	13	30
Leon	53	643	2,246				
Levy	3	9	10	Multicounty 1/	43	950	3,087

1/ Reporting units without a fixed location within the state or of unknown county location.

Note: Private employment. For a list of three-digit code industries included see Table 17.38. Data are preliminary. Only counties for which data are disclosed are shown. Detail may not add to totals due to disclosure editing and/or rounding. See Tables 23.70, 23.71, 23.72, 23.73, and 23.74 for public employment data.

Source: State of Florida, Department of Labor and Employment Security, Bureau of Labor Market Information, "Employment and Wages" (ES-202), unpublished data.

Table 17.44. INSURANCE AGENTS, BROKERS, AND SERVICE: AVERAGE MONTHLY PRIVATE REPORTING UNITS, EMPLOYMENT, AND PAYROLL COVERED BY UNEMPLOYMENT COMPENSATION LAW IN THE STATE AND COUNTIES OF FLORIDA, 1995

County	Number of reporting units	Number of employees	Payroll ($1,000)	County	Number of reporting units	Number of employees	Payroll ($1,000)
	Insurance agents, brokers, and service (SIC code 64)						
Florida	6,989	43,161	118,272	Lake	59	228	442
				Lee	192	779	2,078
Alachua	77	320	853	Leon	128	1,056	2,911
Baker	3	10	16	Levy	10	38	60
Bay	56	224	578	Madison	6	20	27
Bradford	5	10	14	Manatee	79	371	906
Brevard	159	706	1,662	Marion	89	369	782
Broward	875	5,256	14,194	Martin	67	312	894
Calhoun	4	10	17	Monroe	25	150	417
Charlotte	35	130	231	Nassau	12	56	96
Citrus	32	130	241	Okaloosa	61	259	577
Clay	32	84	163	Okeechobee	9	41	87
Collier	80	413	1,208	Orange	481	3,596	10,653
Columbia	10	33	57	Osceola	34	146	352
Dade	1,059	7,400	20,668	Palm Beach	573	3,018	9,946
De Soto	9	31	41	Pasco	94	456	773
Duval	413	3,032	8,581	Pinellas	468	2,907	7,808
Escambia	114	512	1,066	Polk	173	1,106	2,547
Flagler	5	35	63	Putnam	23	132	343
Franklin	3	15	28	St. Johns	28	88	217
Gadsden	9	40	81	St. Lucie	63	193	367
Gulf	4	13	26	Santa Rosa	17	53	91
Hardee	8	19	54	Sarasota	184	1,304	4,367
Hendry	10	39	56	Seminole	184	1,525	4,132
Hernando	33	170	302	Sumter	6	23	52
Highlands	24	141	214	Suwannee	12	59	86
Hillsborough	531	4,759	13,281	Taylor	4	9	10
Holmes	3	10	15	Volusia	159	733	1,874
Indian River	53	243	848	Walton	4	8	15
Jackson	13	45	67	Washington	3	13	20
Jefferson	7	28	42	Multicounty 1/	71	241	646

1/ Reporting units without a fixed location within the state or of unknown county location.

Note: Private employment. For a list of three-digit code industries included see Table 17.38. Data are preliminary. Only counties for which data are disclosed are shown. Detail may not add to totals due to disclosure editing and/or rounding. See Tables 23.70, 23.71, 23.72, 23.73, and 23.74 for public employment data.

Source: State of Florida, Department of Labor and Employment Security, Bureau of Labor Market Information, "Employment and Wages" (ES-202), unpublished data.

Table 17.45. REAL ESTATE: AVERAGE MONTHLY PRIVATE REPORTING UNITS, EMPLOYMENT AND PAYROLL COVERED BY UNEMPLOYMENT COMPENSATION LAW IN THE STATE AND COUNTIES OF FLORIDA, 1995

County	Number of re- porting units	Number of em- ployees	Payroll ($1,000)	County	Number of re- porting units	Number of em- ployees	Payroll ($1,000)
			Real estate (SIC code 65)				
Florida	16,496	100,859	194,990	Lee	562	3,430	6,741
				Leon	264	1,163	1,815
Alachua	240	1,251	1,918	Levy	16	52	58
Baker	5	9	7	Madison	6	10	11
Bay	163	1,220	1,530	Manatee	229	1,089	1,674
Bradford	9	16	19	Marion	189	973	1,408
Brevard	411	2,047	3,265	Martin	166	805	1,489
Broward	1,769	9,480	20,629	Monroe	157	594	1,049
Charlotte	119	603	953	Nassau	32	117	223
Citrus	93	337	489	Okaloosa	208	1,878	2,545
Clay	86	398	783	Okeechobee	22	37	53
Collier	450	1,991	5,233	Orange	980	10,009	23,219
Columbia	32	84	94	Osceola	168	1,701	2,584
Dade	2,832	19,500	39,089	Palm Beach	1,448	8,342	18,921
De Soto	12	26	26	Pasco	214	913	1,326
Dixie	6	21	21	Pinellas	1,059	5,736	9,657
Duval	731	5,095	9,908	Polk	335	1,854	2,695
Escambia	203	1,315	1,650	Putnam	34	85	68
Flagler	44	457	1,205	St. Johns	112	546	915
Franklin	11	50	60	St. Lucie	129	541	863
Gadsden	15	51	51	Santa Rosa	74	316	383
Gulf	9	25	25	Sarasota	458	1,808	3,022
Hardee	10	42	60	Seminole	321	1,548	3,126
Hendry	21	43	42	Sumter	16	119	93
Hernando	63	281	342	Suwannee	13	49	36
Highlands	67	241	328	Taylor	7	25	39
Hillsborough	955	6,704	14,032	Volusia	431	2,056	2,951
Indian River	136	663	1,151	Wakulla	6	10	10
Jackson	18	51	129	Walton	31	225	361
Jefferson	4	11	11	Washington	7	15	31
Lake	159	1,405	2,079	Multicounty 1/	127	1,389	2,473

1/ Reporting units without a fixed location within the state or of unknown county location.

Note: Private employment. For a list of three-digit code industries included see Table 17.38. Data are preliminary. Only counties for which data are disclosed are shown. Detail may not add to totals due to disclosure editing and/or rounding. See Tables 23.70, 23.71, 23.72, 23.73, and 23.74 for public employment data.

Source: State of Florida, Department of Labor and Employment Security, Bureau of Labor Market Information, "Employment and Wages" (ES-202), unpublished data.

Table 17.47. REAL ESTATE: HOMEOWNER AND RENTAL VACANCY RATES IN FLORIDA OTHER SUNBELT STATES, OTHER POPULOUS STATES, AND THE UNITED STATES, SPECIFIED YEARS 1990 THROUGH 1995

State	Homeowner vacancy rates					Rental vacancy rates				
	1990	1992	1993	1994	1995	1990	1992	1993	1994	1995
	Sunbelt states									
Florida	2.7	3.0	2.8	2.4	2.1	9.0	8.7	8.3	8.0	7.8
Alabama	1.5	1.3	1.4	1.4	1.5	8.1	6.4	6.8	7.2	8.5
Arizona	2.5	2.1	1.3	1.5	1.9	10.7	9.5	7.4	8.8	7.2
Arkansas	2.5	1.7	0.9	1.2	1.5	7.9	6.9	7.2	6.8	7.4
California	1.8	2.1	1.7	2.0	2.1	6.0	7.5	8.2	7.9	8.5
Georgia	1.8	1.7	1.2	1.8	1.2	9.4	8.9	7.3	9.1	11.3
Louisiana	1.7	1.1	0.9	1.5	0.8	13.1	7.8	7.2	9.4	9.6
Mississippi	1.6	1.0	0.9	0.8	0.9	8.7	7.4	8.0	7.9	13.2
New Mexico	2.4	1.4	0.9	1.1	1.1	13.7	7.8	3.5	5.1	4.8
North Carolina	1.6	1.7	1.3	1.1	1.2	7.2	7.0	5.6	6.1	8.2
Oklahoma	3.1	1.9	1.5	1.7	1.5	14.6	9.7	11.5	8.9	10.3
South Carolina	1.0	1.2	1.1	2.4	2.6	8.4	10.0	10.6	12.3	9.3
Tennessee	2.4	1.1	1.0	1.4	1.5	9.5	6.0	4.6	4.6	5.4
Texas	2.5	1.6	1.9	1.8	1.9	9.7	8.9	8.9	7.9	8.2
Virginia	1.7	2.0	1.7	1.5	1.6	5.8	8.2	7.7	8.9	7.6
	Other populous states									
Illinois	1.3	1.3	1.1	1.2	1.1	6.1	7.0	6.3	6.8	7.4
Indiana	1.5	1.1	0.9	0.7	1.2	5.3	7.0	7.2	5.0	5.2
Massachusetts	1.4	1.0	1.2	1.4	1.2	6.9	8.8	7.8	7.1	6.2
Michigan	1.1	1.2	1.1	0.9	1.3	7.3	7.7	7.9	8.9	8.8
New Jersey	1.8	1.2	1.3	1.2	1.5	5.9	6.9	8.2	7.1	6.6
New York	1.8	1.7	1.7	1.9	1.6	4.9	5.8	5.5	5.9	6.3
Ohio	1.2	1.0	1.0	0.9	1.2	5.5	6.2	7.1	6.8	7.4
Pennsylvania	1.1	1.0	1.0	1.1	1.4	7.2	7.0	7.5	8.0	8.0
United States	1.7	1.5	1.4	1.5	1.5	7.2	7.4	7.3	7.4	7.6

Note: Data are based on a monthly sample survey conducted by the Bureau of the Census. See Glossary for definitions.

Source: U.S., Department of Commerce, Bureau of the Census, *Housing Vacancy Survey: Annual Statistics, 1995*. Data from the Internet at <http://www.census.gov/>.

Table 17.48. REAL ESTATE: LICENSED BROKERS AND SALESPERSONS IN THE STATE AND COUNTIES OF FLORIDA, JUNE 6, 1995

Location of licensee	Brokers	Sales-persons	Location of licensee	Brokers	Sales-persons
Total 1/	67,779	183,900	Jefferson	26	64
NonFlorida	2,418	7,753	Lafayette	6	2
Unknown	122	891	Lake	782	1,920
Alachua	752	1,385	Lee	2,547	7,340
Baker	19	47	Leon	930	2,044
Bay	518	1,346	Levy	111	237
Bradford	49	94	Liberty	2	10
Brevard	1,929	5,556	Madison	22	48
Broward	6,733	21,280	Manatee	901	2,363
Calhoun	15	31	Marion	910	2,210
Charlotte	605	1,832	Martin	872	2,001
Citrus	486	1,267	Monroe	611	1,427
Clay	386	1,157	Nassau	165	418
Collier	1,680	4,916	Okaloosa	857	1,807
Columbia	132	279	Okeechobee	95	213
Dade	8,067	22,282	Orange	3,909	11,042
De Soto	83	190	Osceola	503	1,988
Dixie	30	52	Palm Beach	6,075	17,318
Duval	2,534	5,605	Pasco	896	2,690
Escambia	771	1,793	Pinellas	4,894	11,791
Flagler	196	769	Polk	1,324	2,802
Franklin	50	121	Putnam	165	378
Gadsden	53	136	St. Johns	610	1,531
Gilchrist	33	62	St. Lucie	722	1,864
Glades	16	26	Santa Rosa	345	999
Gulf	31	83	Sarasota	2,381	6,068
Hamilton	11	14	Seminole	1,873	5,073
Hardee	56	111	Sumter	85	209
Hendry	70	174	Suwannee	81	163
Hernando	425	1,422	Taylor	34	44
Highlands	310	685	Union	10	23
Hillsborough	3,548	8,839	Volusia	1,890	5,264
Holmes	30	60	Wakulla	60	132
Indian River	681	1,642	Walton	143	282
Jackson	60	151	Washington	43	84

1/ Total includes all active, involuntary inactive, and voluntary inactive licensed persons.

Source: State of Florida, Department of Business and Professional Regulation, unpublished data.

Table 17.60. LIFE INSURANCE: NUMBER OF COMPANIES, POLICIES IN FORCE, PURCHASES AND AMOUNT OF LIFE INSURANCE, BENEFIT PAYMENTS, PREMIUM RECEIPTS MORTGAGES, AND REAL ESTATE OWNED BY U.S. LIFE INSURANCE COMPANIES IN FLORIDA AND THE UNITED STATES, 1994

Item	Florida	United States
Number of U.S. life insurance companies	31	1,808
Purchases of ordinary life insurance ($1,000,000)	61,251	1,107,216
Insurance in force		
Total		
Policies (1,000)	13,167	228,546
Amount ($1,000,000)	533,397	11,673,621
Ordinary		
Policies (1,000)	6,876	139,632
Amount ($1,000,000)	345,963	6,835,239
Group		
Master policies (1,000)	49	951
Amount ($1,000,000)	175,181	4,608,746
Industrial		
Policies (1,000)	1,534	28,670
Amount ($1,000,000)	1,121	20,145
Credit		
Policies 1/ (1,000)	4,708	59,293
Amount ($1,000,000)	11,132	209,491
Average amount in force 2/ (dollars)	94,800	118,700
Insurance and annuity benefit payments ($1,000)	7,758,636	148,769,831
Death payments	1,719,670	31,706,022
Matured endowments	29,942	555,129
Annuity payments	1,958,091	39,756,663
Disability payments	34,059	646,703
Surrender values	3,359,128	59,625,726
Policy and contract dividends	657,746	16,479,588
Payments to beneficiaries ($1,000), total	1,719,670	31,706,022
Ordinary	1,157,087	18,151,434
Group	470,550	12,152,766
Industrial	23,125	457,219
Credit	68,908	944,603
Premium receipts of companies ($1,000,000)	15,303	309,522
Life	4,234	86,563
Annuity	2,431	44,424
Health	3,979	71,549
Deposit-type funds	4,659	106,986
Mortgages owned by companies ($1,000), total	12,661,745	210,903,454
Farm	1,297,366	9,562,839
Nonfarm	11,364,379	201,340,615
Real estate owned by companies ($1,000), total	4,063,521	52,813,855
Farm	254,804	2,616,206
Nonfarm	3,808,717	50,197,649

1/ Includes group credit certificates.
2/ Average amounts per household. See Glossary for a definition of "household."
Source: American Council of Life Insurance, *1995 Life Insurance Fact Book Update*.

Table 17.61. LIFE INSURANCE: DIRECT WRITINGS, DIRECT LOSSES, AND LIFE INSURANCE IN FORCE IN FLORIDA, 1987 THROUGH 1993

(amounts rounded to thousands of dollars)

Year	Life insurance in force at end of year	Direct writings	Direct losses paid	Losses as a percentage of writings
	All life insurance companies			
1987	322,472,329	5,246,052	2,805,237	53.5
1988	312,711,163	5,633,515	1,290,565	22.9
1989	344,548,493	5,675,962	1,328,876	23.4
1990	355,761,910	7,139,533	4,547,212	63.7
1991	378,564,234	5,561,421	4,939,376	88.8
1992	409,360,123	6,130,141	5,321,483	86.8
1993	445,360,646	6,108,608	3,202,293	52.4
	Florida life insurance companies only			
1987	18,051,822	349,383	86,154	24.7
1988	19,746,098	379,699	96,467	25.4
1989	18,548,502	386,459	97,020	25.1
1990	18,548,502	386,459	97,020	25.1
1991	15,232,004	241,948	116,200	48.0
1992	15,839,284	214,372	159,425	74.4
1993	17,893,604	208,847	91,460	43.8

Note: Includes ordinary, group, industrial, and credit insurance and annuities.

Table 17.62. FRATERNAL INSURANCE SOCIETIES: DIRECT PREMIUMS WRITTEN, BENEFITS PAID, AND INSURANCE IN FORCE IN FLORIDA, 1987 THROUGH 1993

(rounded to thousands of dollars)

Year	Life insurance in force at end of year	Direct premiums written		Direct losses paid	
		Life	Accident and health	Life	Accident and health
1987	3,201,595	63,798	3,887	13,166	3,314
1988	3,552,068	659,886	4,105	14,940	3,693
1989	3,907,921	634,901	4,980	18,414	4,744
1990	4,227,258	77,899	5,950	21,432	3,999
1991	4,580,593	112,686	6,650	30,978	5,546
1992	4,951,219	148,764	7,842	29,627	6,559
1993	5,315,106	141,262	7,536	45,781	5,885

Source for Tables 17.61 and 17.62: State of Florida, Department of Insurance, *Florida Department of Insurance 1994 Annual Report*, and previous editions.

Table 17.72. PROPERTY AND CASUALTY INSURANCE: PREMIUMS WRITTEN AND LOSSES PAID BY PROPERTY AND CASUALTY, TITLE, AND LIFE INSURANCE COMPANIES IN FLORIDA, 1993

(rounded to thousands of dollars)

Line of business	All companies: Direct premiums written	All companies: Direct losses paid	Florida companies: Direct premiums written	Florida companies: Direct losses paid
Total	18,082,950	15,166,278	3,546,563	2,285,036
Fire	144,002	382,566	13,182	7,786
Allied lines	256,187	534,878	62,284	61,398
Multiple peril crop	7,475	8,258	0	0
Farmowners' multiple peril	7,649	12,699	341	1,272
Homeowners' multiple peril	1,240,040	2,377,920	79,686	145,073
Commercial multiple peril	1,002,352	1,646,216	74,158	49,099
Mortgage guaranty	89,266	37,840	A/	0
Ocean marine	85,676	71,831	8,187	4,401
Inland marine	303,268	240,361	42,902	16,655
Financial guaranty	100,819	9,283	1	-821
Medical malpractice	183,695	90,476	53,663	20,603
Earthquake	1,792	2,595	7	0
Accident and health, total	5,584,056	4,009,966	1,695,644	1,303,203
Group	3,367,719	2,486,879	753,639	582,651
Federal employees	432,401	402,890	415,956	385,482
Credit	272,823	177,448	219,566	151,620
Collectively renewable	76,048	47,313	5,680	2,938
Noncancellable	203,112	143,899	1,712	489
Guaranteed renewable	787,601	438,108	130,957	66,973
Nonrenewable for stated reasons only	136,636	102,989	0	0
Other accident only	14,872	7,639	106	109
All other	292,843	202,801	168,028	112,941
Workers' compensation	1,182,204	1,046,797	282,010	101,869
Other liability	710,452	348,779	46,043	11,161
Products liability	52,555	24,205	608	31
Private passenger automobile no-fault, PIP	846,917	603,410	202,435	130,599
Other private passenger automobile liability	2,789,616	1,803,395	408,204	225,469
Commercial automobile no-fault, PIP	21,570	12,351	4,339	3,169
Other commercial automobile liability	683,739	410,051	106,892	45,174
Private passenger automobile physical damage	1,513,602	1,061,201	247,503	134,093
Commercial automobile physical damage	149,136	87,800	21,836	10,936
Aircraft (all perils)	52,878	33,631	0	-42
Fidelity	35,397	22,070	1,438	977
Surety	139,324	33,288	27,911	2,188
Glass	1,950	579	26	3
Burglary and theft	6,077	1,658	502	58
Boiler and machinery	25,629	22,087	99	14
Credit	11,967	3,930	1,660	782
Title	574,048	24,485	149,869	3,505
All other lines	279,614	201,674	15,130	6,381

PIP Personal injury protection.
A/ Less than $500.
Source: State of Florida, Department of Insurance, *Florida Department of Insurance 1994 Annual Report.*

PERSONAL AND BUSINESS SERVICES

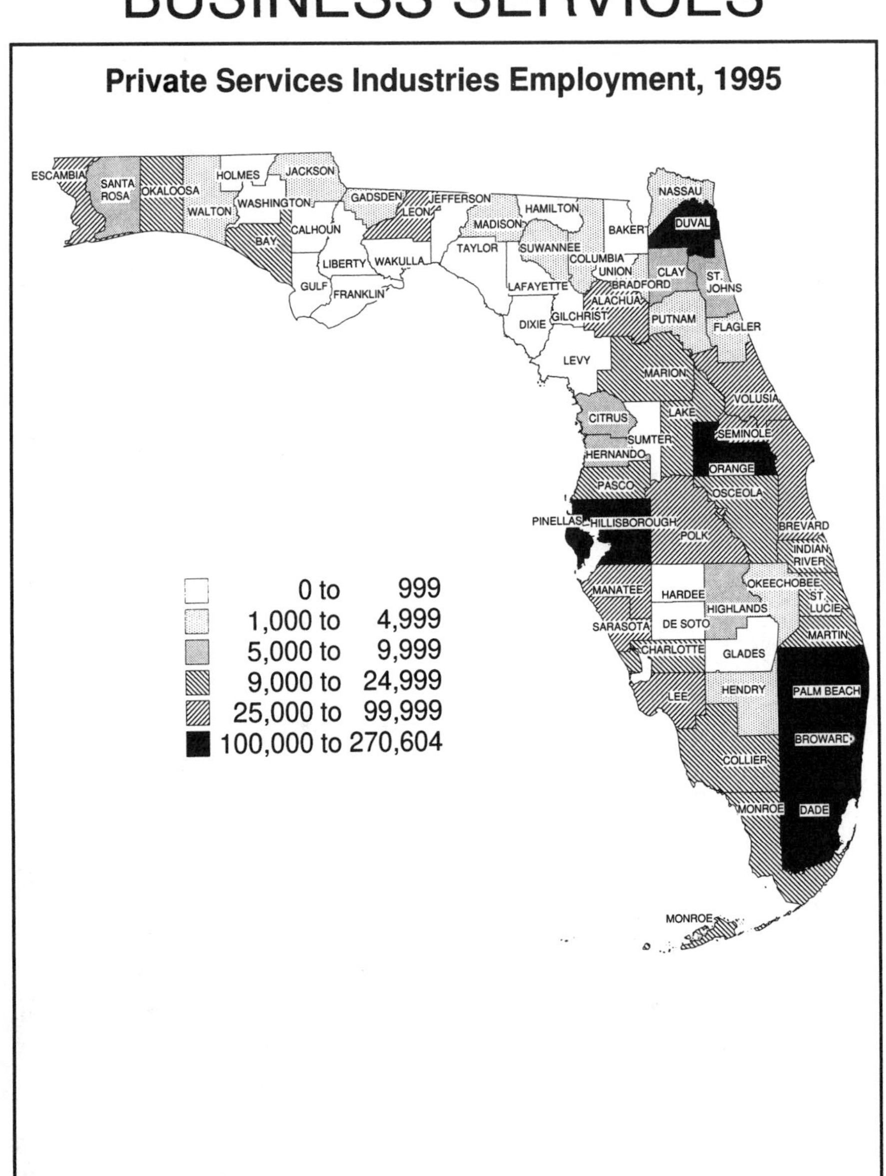

Private Services Industries Employment, 1995

Source: Table 18.28

SECTION 18.00
PERSONAL AND BUSINESS SERVICES

TABLES LISTED BY MAJOR HEADINGS

Table 18.01. AUTOMOTIVE, BUSINESS, AND PROFESSIONAL SERVICES: ESTABLISHMENTS AND RECEIPTS, 1987 AND 1992, AND PAYROLL, 1992, IN FLORIDA

(amounts in thousands of dollars)

SIC code	Kind of business	Number of establishments 1987	Number of establishments 1992	Receipts 1987	Receipts 1992	Receipts Percentage change	Annual payroll 1992
72	Personal services	10,680	11,893	1,596,527	2,339,691	46.5	792,820
73	Business services	16,132	21,521	7,636,598	13,765,193	80.3	5,577,252
75	Automotive repair, services and parking	7,930	9,552	3,230,507	4,473,536	38.5	886,249
76	Miscellaneous repair services	4,398	5,106	1,248,086	1,944,734	55.8	601,332
81	Legal services	8,965	10,871	3,697,540	5,394,019	45.9	2,647,841
871	Engineering, architectural, and surveying services	3,877	4,372	2,251,146	3,126,227	38.9	1,259,478
872	Accounting, auditing and bookkeeping services	4,377	5,661	1,175,297	1,572,668	33.8	682,637
873	Research, development, and testing services (except 8733 noncommercial research organizations	631	663	379,951	736,964	94.0	291,036
874	Management and public relations services	3,678	5,023	2,198,584	3,638,981	65.5	1,636,869

Note: Data are for firms subject to federal income tax. The service industries census is on a 5-year cycle collecting data for years ending in 2 and 7.

Source: U.S., Department of Commerce, Bureau of the Census, *1992 Census of Service Industries: Florida.* SC92-A-10.

Table 18.20. PERSONAL AND HOUSEHOLD SERVICES: AVERAGE MONTHLY PRIVATE REPORTING UNITS, EMPLOYMENT, AND PAYROLL COVERED BY UNEMPLOYMENT COMPENSATION LAW BY INDUSTRY IN FLORIDA, 1995

SIC code	Industry	Number of reporting units	Number of employees	Payroll ($1,000)
72	Personal services	10,654	67,427	79,125
721	Laundry, cleaning, and garment services	3,110	22,961	28,741
722	Photographic studios, portrait	563	3,523	3,860
723	Beauty shops	5,149	27,047	28,309
724	Barber shops	118	334	358
725	Shoe repair shops and shoeshine parlors	144	290	289
726	Funeral service and crematories	412	4,609	8,578
729	Miscellaneous personal services	1,160	8,665	8,991
88	Private households 1/	11,860	16,761	19,878

1/ Private households which employ workers in domestic services such as cooks, maids, sitters, butlers, personal secretaries, gardeners and caretakers, and managers of personal affairs.

Note: Private employment. Data are preliminary. Detail may not add to totals due to disclosure editing and/or rounding. See Tables 23.70, 23.71, 23.72, 23.73, and 23.74 for public employment data.

Table 18.21. BUSINESS SERVICES: AVERAGE MONTHLY PRIVATE REPORTING UNITS EMPLOYMENT, AND PAYROLL COVERED BY UNEMPLOYMENT COMPENSATION LAW BY INDUSTRY IN FLORIDA, 1994 AND 1995

SIC code	Industry	Number of reporting units	Number of employees	Payroll ($1,000)
	1994 A/			
73	Business services	22,342	447,178	656,034
731	Advertising	1,406	9,677	23,840
732	Credit reporting and collection	481	5,383	10,286
733	Mailing, reproduction, and stenographic	1,936	11,767	22,280
734	Services to dwellings and other buildings	4,295	47,333	48,469
735	Miscellaneous equipment rental and leasing	1,893	14,043	31,195
736	Personnel supply services	1,970	240,588	271,998
737	Computer and data processing services	3,433	38,009	129,852
738	Miscellaneous business services	6,928	80,379	118,113
	1995 B/			
73	Business services	22,921	517,215	773,858
731	Advertising	1,420	10,244	26,413
732	Credit reporting and collection	450	5,462	11,031
733	Mailing, reproduction, and stenographic	1,970	13,150	25,375
734	Services to dwellings and other buildings	4,302	48,292	51,408
735	Miscellaneous equipment rental and leasing	1,839	14,510	33,790
736	Personnel supply services	2,020	297,568	340,960
737	Computer and data processing services	3,674	42,212	151,507
738	Miscellaneous business services	7,247	85,778	133,374

A/ Revised.
B/ Preliminary.

Note: Private employment. Detail may not add to totals due to disclosure editing and/or rounding. See Tables 23.70, 23.71, 23.72, 23.73, and 23.74 for public employment data.

Source for Tables 18.20 and 18.21: State of Florida, Department of Labor and Employment Security, Bureau of Labor Market Information, "Employment and Wages" (ES-202), unpublished data.

Table 18.22. AUTOMOTIVE AND MISCELLANEOUS REPAIR SERVICES: AVERAGE MONTHLY PRIVATE REPORTING UNITS, EMPLOYMENT, AND PAYROLL COVERED BY UNEMPLOYMENT COMPENSATION LAW BY INDUSTRY IN FLORIDA, 1995

SIC code	Industry	Number of reporting units	Number of employees	Payroll ($1,000)
75	Automotive repair, services, and parking	9,048	60,813	106,271
751	Automotive rental, no driver	684	18,279	37,277
752	Automobile parking	64	2,003	1,913
753	Automotive repair shops	6,883	30,174	54,746
754	Automotive services, except repair	1,417	10,357	12,335
76	Miscellaneous repair services	4,840	24,131	48,767
762	Electrical repair shops	1,730	9,425	20,020
763	Watch, clock, and jewelry repair	128	340	406
764	Reupholstery and furniture repair	461	1,353	1,792
769	Miscellaneous repair shops and related services	2,521	13,014	26,549

Note: Private employment. Data are preliminary. Detail may not add to totals due to disclosure editing and/or rounding. See Tables 23.70, 23.71, 23.72, 23.73, and 23.74 for public employment data.

Table 18.23. ENGINEERING AND MANAGEMENT SERVICES: AVERAGE MONTHLY PRIVATE REPORTING UNITS, EMPLOYMENT, AND PAYROLL COVERED BY UNEMPLOYMENT COMPENSATION LAW BY INDUSTRY IN FLORIDA, 1995

SIC code	Industry	Number of reporting units	Number of employees	Payroll ($1,000)
87	Engineering, accounting, research, management, and related services	18,624	143,437	438,089
871	Engineering, architectural, and surveying services	3,914	40,271	130,291
872	Accounting, auditing, and bookkeeping services	5,910	33,133	86,024
873	Research, development, and testing services	1,001	13,824	32,307
874	Management and public relations services	7,799	56,209	189,467
89	Miscellaneous services	367	1,612	5,786

Note: Private employment. Data are preliminary. Detail may not add to totals due to disclosure editing and/or rounding. See Tables 23.70, 23.71, 23.72, 23.73, and 23.74 for public employment data.

Source for Tables 18.22 and 18.23: State of Florida, Department of Labor and Employment Security, Bureau of Labor Market Information, "Employment and Wages" (ES-202), unpublished data.

Table 18.28. SERVICES: AVERAGE MONTHLY PRIVATE REPORTING UNITS, EMPLOYMENT AND PAYROLL COVERED BY UNEMPLOYMENT COMPENSATION LAW IN THE STATE AND COUNTIES OF FLORIDA, 1994 AND 1995

County	Number of reporting units	Number of employees	Payroll ($1,000)	County	Number of reporting units	Number of employees	Payroll ($1,000)
			Services, 1994 A/ (SIC codes 70-89)				
Florida	142,361	1,796,211	3,492,099	Lafayette	17	74	91
				Lake	1,226	13,683	22,982
Alachua	1,991	26,495	51,394	Lee	3,393	40,764	77,041
Baker	68	597	730	Leon	2,592	29,942	61,869
Bay	1,332	13,822	22,505	Levy	131	900	1,065
Bradford	105	981	1,218	Liberty	19	222	245
Brevard	3,648	52,451	123,237	Madison	100	873	1,135
Broward	17,151	166,733	346,696	Manatee	1,666	25,207	39,867
Calhoun	53	526	678	Marion	1,583	13,701	23,901
Charlotte	878	10,155	18,606	Martin	1,436	11,758	22,896
Citrus	668	7,059	11,780	Monroe	1,157	9,998	17,127
Clay	754	7,620	12,509	Nassau	301	3,306	4,734
Collier	2,372	23,115	47,199	Okaloosa	1,418	17,457	30,175
Columbia	323	3,093	4,676	Okeechobee	194	1,795	2,993
Dade	24,541	262,346	581,307	Orange	8,227	189,811	364,977
De Soto	130	1,034	1,557	Osceola	883	13,721	21,906
Dixie	41	183	323	Palm Beach	13,207	126,470	270,796
Duval	6,891	104,941	202,618	Pasco	1,818	18,920	35,385
Escambia	2,228	35,223	62,158	Pinellas	9,472	123,822	238,768
Flagler	214	2,095	3,523	Polk	2,859	37,867	68,134
Franklin	63	789	982	Putnam	331	3,444	5,146
Gadsden	195	1,281	1,650	St. Johns	872	9,566	16,617
Gilchrist	33	325	380	St. Lucie	1,119	11,240	21,007
Glades	23	81	85	Santa Rosa	519	5,433	8,460
Gulf	60	484	634	Sarasota	3,935	47,099	77,948
Hamilton	50	320	329	Seminole	2,854	26,654	52,924
Hardee	123	953	1,324	Sumter	132	864	1,036
Hendry	149	1,203	1,638	Suwannee	128	1,520	1,795
Hernando	630	6,720	11,438	Taylor	113	795	1,110
Highlands	504	5,480	8,155	Union	34	412	526
Hillsborough	8,828	159,444	302,558	Volusia	3,490	39,196	64,671
Holmes	70	609	802	Wakulla	64	433	568
Indian River	1,142	10,522	20,121	Walton	152	2,425	3,278
Jackson	213	1,536	2,176	Washington	84	689	761
Jefferson	77	601	666				

See footnotes at end of table.

Continued . . .

Table 18.28. SERVICES: AVERAGE MONTHLY PRIVATE REPORTING UNITS, EMPLOYMENT AND PAYROLL COVERED BY UNEMPLOYMENT COMPENSATION LAW IN THE STATE AND COUNTIES OF FLORIDA, 1994 AND 1995 (Continued)

County	Number of reporting units	Number of employees	Payroll ($1,000)	County	Number of reporting units	Number of employees	Payroll ($1,000)
			Services, 1995 B/ (SIC codes 70-89)				
Florida	142,585	1,915,292	3,832,170	Lafayette	16	60	70
				Lake	1,239	15,632	25,976
Alachua	2,006	27,301	54,858	Lee	3,417	42,893	81,449
Baker	67	625	767	Leon	2,611	31,860	67,445
Bay	1,346	14,238	24,381	Levy	133	979	1,265
Bradford	104	1,032	1,400	Liberty	18	229	249
Brevard	3,698	53,183	128,808	Madison	100	1,011	1,417
Broward	17,085	175,162	380,000	Manatee	1,681	29,412	46,840
Calhoun	52	501	644	Marion	1,601	14,573	26,121
Charlotte	845	10,516	20,624	Martin	1,438	12,839	25,401
Citrus	677	7,277	12,875	Monroe	1,184	10,652	19,050
Clay	767	7,944	13,820	Nassau	301	3,461	5,219
Collier	2,422	24,451	52,066	Okaloosa	1,465	18,679	32,182
Columbia	323	3,228	5,008	Okeechobee	195	1,899	3,213
Dade	24,275	270,604	614,384	Orange	8,257	201,308	399,097
De Soto	131	1,073	1,728	Osceola	878	14,485	23,964
Dixie	42	180	314	Palm Beach	13,315	132,263	296,879
Duval	6,851	113,074	226,535	Pasco	1,843	20,136	39,507
Escambia	2,202	37,481	67,708	Pinellas	9,371	132,336	264,534
Flagler	217	2,302	4,071	Polk	2,803	38,372	72,996
Franklin	65	846	1,063	Putnam	347	3,378	5,389
Gadsden	199	1,378	1,819	St. Johns	927	9,871	18,955
Gilchrist	34	371	496	St. Lucie	1,092	11,447	22,481
Glades	25	95	101	Santa Rosa	510	5,559	8,947
Gulf	60	593	843	Sarasota	3,918	43,598	82,020
Hamilton	46	424	551	Seminole	2,895	27,666	56,871
Hardee	124	995	1,541	Sumter	131	862	1,064
Hendry	151	1,233	1,731	Suwannee	124	1,610	2,006
Hernando	644	6,906	12,427	Taylor	116	813	1,195
Highlands	521	5,567	8,780	Union	35	429	598
Hillsborough	8,867	171,169	337,472	Volusia	3,495	42,070	73,338
Holmes	71	694	915	Wakulla	59	422	603
Indian River	1,154	11,134	21,905	Walton	145	2,536	3,555
Jackson	211	1,588	2,386	Washington	82	686	844
Jefferson	68	588	689	Multicounty 1/	1,499	86,952	117,183

A/ Revised.
B/ Preliminary.
1/ Reporting units without a fixed location within the state or of unknown county location.
Note: Private employment. Only counties for which data are disclosed are shown. Detail may not add to totals due to disclosure editing and/or rounding. See Tables 23.70, 23.71, 23.72, 23.73, and 23.74 for public employment data.

Source: State of Florida, Department of Labor and Employment Security, Bureau of Labor Market Information, "Employment and Wages" (ES-202), unpublished data.

Table 18.30. PERSONAL SERVICES: AVERAGE MONTHLY PRIVATE REPORTING UNITS EMPLOYMENT, AND PAYROLL COVERED BY UNEMPLOYMENT COMPENSATION LAW IN THE STATE AND COUNTIES OF FLORIDA, 1995

County	Number of reporting units	Number of employees	Payroll ($1,000)	County	Number of reporting units	Number of employees	Payroll ($1,000)
			Personal services (SIC code 72)				
Florida	10,654	67,427	79,125	Jefferson	4	23	39
				Lake	97	583	663
Alachua	127	896	865	Lee	269	1,794	2,134
Baker	6	23	16	Leon	153	1,679	2,023
Bay	102	559	565	Levy	8	57	59
Bradford	9	90	100	Madison	7	43	54
Brevard	318	1,864	1,950	Manatee	164	721	758
Broward	1,287	7,520	9,083	Marion	148	878	933
Calhoun	6	26	21	Martin	106	536	659
Charlotte	80	400	415	Monroe	65	205	234
Citrus	73	314	326	Nassau	34	132	142
Clay	83	416	398	Okaloosa	121	713	707
Collier	195	987	1,286	Okeechobee	15	59	61
Columbia	22	122	106	Orange	570	4,372	5,482
Dade	1,661	10,590	12,491	Osceola	81	368	382
De Soto	15	70	55	Palm Beach	904	5,704	7,276
Dixie	3	8	10	Pasco	188	988	908
Duval	563	4,150	4,930	Pinellas	731	4,734	5,807
Escambia	172	1,248	1,260	Polk	242	1,605	1,956
Flagler	21	89	71	Putnam	27	133	127
Franklin	4	8	5	St. Johns	59	344	399
Gadsden	15	68	62	St. Lucie	89	570	573
Glades	3	4	3	Santa Rosa	44	194	167
Gulf	8	14	9	Sarasota	290	1,640	2,038
Hamilton	4	14	13	Seminole	260	1,885	2,100
Hardee	7	33	42	Sumter	8	35	27
Hendry	8	24	23	Suwannee	10	35	48
Hernando	72	365	349	Taylor	13	42	37
Highlands	48	224	194	Volusia	291	1,737	1,708
Hillsborough	571	4,311	5,007	Walton	4	14	12
Holmes	4	30	45	Washington	6	20	18
Indian River	102	427	493				
Jackson	13	66	71	Multicounty 1/	37	593	1,290

1/ Reporting units without a fixed location within the state or of unknown county location.

Note: Private employment. For a list of three-digit code industries included see Table 18.20. Data are preliminary. Only counties for which data are disclosed are shown. Detail may not add to totals due to disclosure editing and/or rounding. See Tables 23.70, 23.71, 23.72, 23.73, and 23.74 for public employment data.

Source: State of Florida, Department of Labor and Employment Security, Bureau of Labor Market Information, "Employment and Wages" (ES-202), unpublished data.

Table 18.35. BUSINESS SERVICES: AVERAGE MONTHLY PRIVATE REPORTING UNITS EMPLOYMENT, AND PAYROLL COVERED BY UNEMPLOYMENT COMPENSATION LAW IN THE STATE AND COUNTIES OF FLORIDA, 1994 AND 1995

County	Number of reporting units	Number of employees	Payroll ($1,000)	County	Number of reporting units	Number of employees	Payroll ($1,000)
			Business services, 1994 A/ (SIC code 73)				
Florida	22,342	447,178	656,034	Madison	8	73	134
				Manatee	216	9,957	11,079
Alachua	209	3,117	3,581	Marion	201	2,026	2,405
Bay	173	1,809	2,118	Martin	202	1,695	2,236
Bradford	5	27	40	Monroe	129	527	793
Brevard	564	7,883	16,568	Nassau	35	113	164
Broward	3,027	39,079	64,238	Okaloosa	211	4,558	6,468
Citrus	81	753	1,171	Okeechobee	22	84	122
Clay	108	994	1,309	Orange	1,555	38,886	57,473
Collier	354	3,320	5,523	Osceola	113	777	942
Columbia	32	182	241	Palm Beach	1,934	22,326	36,232
Dade	3,740	58,711	94,900	Pasco	230	1,908	2,156
De Soto	8	45	69	Pinellas	1,562	29,136	49,351
Duval	1,158	35,055	51,247	Polk	342	6,823	9,097
Escambia	311	9,660	11,400	Putnam	33	310	460
Gadsden	12	19	23	St. Johns	108	665	1,082
Gilchrist	4	12	23	St. Lucie	144	1,063	1,248
Hendry	12	67	88	Santa Rosa	76	896	1,033
Hernando	87	709	838	Sarasota	593	16,296	16,947
Hillsborough	1,682	68,974	100,471	Seminole	634	5,680	11,212
Holmes	7	16	20	Sumter	12	28	33
Indian River	139	1,072	1,758	Suwannee	23	124	140
Jackson	12	104	119	Taylor	16	70	73
Lake	143	2,340	2,501	Volusia	471	5,123	6,786
Lee	509	8,324	9,419	Wakulla	9	29	40
Leon	372	4,937	7,329	Walton	19	120	154
Levy	7	19	27				

See footnotes at end of table.

Continued . . .

Table 18.35. BUSINESS SERVICES: AVERAGE MONTHLY PRIVATE REPORTING UNITS EMPLOYMENT, AND PAYROLL COVERED BY UNEMPLOYMENT COMPENSATION LAW IN THE STATE AND COUNTIES OF FLORIDA, 1994 AND 1995 (Continued)

County	Number of re- porting units	Number of em- ployees	Payroll ($1,000)	County	Number of re- porting units	Number of em- ployees	Payroll ($1,000)
			Business services, 1995 B/ (SIC code 73)				
Florida	22,921	517,215	773,858	Lee	530	9,290	9,818
				Leon	391	5,885	9,247
Alachua	221	3,361	4,196	Levy	8	27	45
Baker	4	9	17	Madison	9	51	114
Bay	177	1,842	2,596	Manatee	219	13,956	16,723
Bradford	6	28	40	Marion	214	2,320	2,859
Brevard	603	8,625	17,632	Martin	203	1,989	2,486
Broward	3,060	42,259	75,507	Monroe	131	548	843
Calhoun	3	9	10	Nassau	37	135	187
Charlotte	111	1,380	1,359	Okaloosa	231	5,184	6,659
Citrus	84	799	1,214	Okeechobee	22	93	134
Clay	113	887	1,400	Orange	1,610	43,589	66,528
Collier	371	3,737	6,264	Osceola	120	1,170	1,597
Columbia	31	170	259	Palm Beach	2,001	24,554	43,054
Dade	3,749	65,195	104,878	Pasco	229	2,094	2,769
De Soto	8	49	74	Pinellas	1,586	34,985	62,080
Duval	1,178	40,544	57,626	Polk	343	7,190	10,457
Escambia	316	11,003	13,725	Putnam	38	408	587
Flagler	28	555	782	St. Johns	125	720	1,176
Franklin	8	77	54	St. Lucie	139	973	1,259
Gadsden	13	24	29	Santa Rosa	80	872	1,035
Gilchrist	4	15	25	Sarasota	585	10,288	13,141
Hardee	5	9	12	Seminole	638	6,260	12,660
Hendry	10	59	83	Sumter	12	38	39
Hernando	93	759	1,012	Suwannee	24	161	165
Highlands	62	638	608	Taylor	17	60	70
Hillsborough	1,743	75,434	114,568	Volusia	491	5,631	7,768
Holmes	7	14	19	Wakulla	7	25	45
Indian River	142	1,210	2,234	Walton	22	126	158
Jackson	16	94	115	Washington	9	46	67
Lake	156	3,416	3,293	Multicounty 1/	523	76,196	90,299

A/ Revised.
B/ Preliminary.
1/ Reporting units without a fixed location within the state or of unknown county location.
Note: Private employment. For a list of three-digit code industries included see Table 18.21. Data are preliminary. Only counties for which data are disclosed are shown. Detail may not add to totals due to disclosure editing and/or rounding. See Tables 23.70, 23.71, 23.72, 23.73, and 23.74 for public employment data.

Source: State of Florida, Department of Labor and Employment Security, Bureau of Labor Market Information, "Employment and Wages" (ES-202), unpublished data.

Table 18.40. AUTOMOTIVE REPAIR, SERVICES, AND PARKING: AVERAGE MONTHLY PRIVATE REPORTING UNITS, EMPLOYMENT, AND PAYROLL COVERED BY UNEMPLOYMENT COMPENSATION LAW IN THE STATE AND COUNTIES OF FLORIDA, 1995

County	Number of re-porting units	Number of em-ployees	Payroll ($1,000)	County	Number of re-porting units	Number of em-ployees	Payroll ($1,000)
	Automotive repair, services, and parking (SIC code 75)						
Florida	9,048	60,813	106,271	Lee	259	1,817	3,127
				Leon	168	1,344	2,055
Alachua	122	737	1,221	Levy	11	31	46
Baker	6	21	32	Madison	12	43	57
Bay	83	458	628	Manatee	98	602	915
Bradford	6	12	21	Marion	129	618	975
Brevard	287	1,460	2,266	Martin	80	310	547
Broward	1,133	8,179	16,482	Monroe	55	213	366
Charlotte	60	186	333	Nassau	21	87	124
Citrus	52	164	239	Okaloosa	124	716	978
Clay	64	377	552	Okeechobee	21	85	117
Collier	118	498	913	Orange	484	6,767	11,510
Columbia	34	99	143	Osceola	62	392	489
Dade	1,374	10,345	20,095	Palm Beach	665	3,914	7,022
De Soto	12	52	73	Pasco	157	738	1,139
Duval	476	3,963	6,810	Pinellas	582	3,138	5,239
Escambia	181	1,242	1,747	Polk	229	1,127	1,903
Flagler	15	60	85	Putnam	29	96	152
Gadsden	15	64	89	St. Johns	50	216	325
Gulf	3	6	8	St. Lucie	108	412	668
Hamilton	5	23	20	Santa Rosa	38	195	331
Hardee	12	31	43	Sarasota	224	1,131	1,664
Hendry	13	30	42	Seminole	164	993	1,593
Hernando	64	187	312	Sumter	18	80	107
Highlands	36	98	122	Suwannee	6	13	18
Hillsborough	573	5,011	8,633	Taylor	9	33	53
Holmes	7	34	51	Volusia	248	1,237	1,699
Indian River	70	281	428	Wakulla	7	20	25
Jackson	21	67	104	Walton	10	46	62
Jefferson	4	10	13				
Lake	105	433	627	Multicounty 1/	21	231	766

1/ Reporting units without a fixed location within the state or of unknown county location.

Note: Private employment. For a list of three-digit code industries included see Table 18.22. Data are preliminary. Only counties for which data are disclosed are shown. Detail may not add to totals due to disclosure editing and/or rounding. See Tables 23.70, 23.71, 23.72, 23.73, and 23.74 for public employment data.

Source: State of Florida, Department of Labor and Employment Security, Bureau of Labor Market Information, "Employment and Wages" (ES-202), unpublished data.

Table 18.51. ENGINEERING, ACCOUNTING, RESEARCH, MANAGEMENT, AND RELATED SERVICES AVERAGE MONTHLY PRIVATE REPORTING UNITS, EMPLOYMENT, AND PAYROLL COVERED BY UNEMPLOYMENT COMPENSATION LAW IN THE STATE AND COUNTIES OF FLORIDA, 1995

County	Number of re- porting units	Number of em- ployees	Payroll ($1,000)	County	Number of re- porting units	Number of em- ployees	Payroll ($1,000)
	Engineering, accounting, research, management, and related services (SIC code 87)						
Florida	18,624	143,437	438,089	Lee	460	3,715	9,115
				Leon	379	3,010	9,240
Alachua	269	2,538	7,048	Levy	14	39	57
Bay	142	1,462	3,663	Madison	7	30	43
Bradford	10	69	169	Manatee	204	788	2,558
Brevard	510	14,687	50,796	Marion	141	580	1,382
Broward	2,272	14,049	44,922	Martin	181	627	1,903
Calhoun	5	11	16	Monroe	126	574	1,771
Charlotte	79	613	1,504	Nassau	40	134	465
Citrus	65	381	952	Okaloosa	200	2,940	9,145
Clay	92	492	1,257	Okeechobee	11	41	77
Collier	323	1,281	5,126	Orange	1,283	13,142	42,176
Columbia	26	118	253	Osceola	74	326	710
Dade	3,118	19,720	67,445	Palm Beach	1,813	8,806	31,285
De Soto	9	21	41	Pasco	161	727	1,391
Dixie	3	13	50	Pinellas	1,174	8,185	21,220
Duval	885	9,020	25,444	Polk	318	1,720	5,525
Escambia	257	2,320	6,284	Putnam	32	88	153
Flagler	25	93	254	St. Johns	122	402	1,799
Franklin	7	13	25	St. Lucie	111	671	1,795
Gulf	8	38	85	Santa Rosa	61	837	1,950
Hardee	16	56	176	Sarasota	504	2,849	7,266
Hendry	14	53	111	Seminole	483	2,200	6,422
Hernando	63	228	477	Sumter	14	36	61
Highlands	33	184	377	Suwannee	10	30	77
Hillsborough	1,297	13,141	41,069	Taylor	7	21	30
Holmes	8	34	50	Volusia	355	1,438	3,396
Indian River	138	560	1,633	Wakulla	8	78	120
Jackson	13	78	146	Walton	12	64	161
Jefferson	9	26	43	Washington	13	46	57
Lake	125	708	1,934	Multicounty 1/	458	6,430	13,388

1/ Reporting units without a fixed location within the state or of unknown county location.

Note: Private employment. For a list of three-digit code industries included see Table 18.23. Data are preliminary. Only counties for which data are disclosed are shown. Detail may not add to totals due to disclosure editing and/or rounding. See Tables 23.70, 23.71, 23.72, 23.73, and 23.74 for public employment data.

Source: State of Florida, Department of Labor and Employment Security, Bureau of Labor Market Information, "Employment and Wages" (ES-202), unpublished data.

Table 18.56. ACCOUNTANTS, ARCHITECTS, AND PROFESSIONAL ENGINEERS: NUMBER LICENSED IN THE STATE AND COUNTIES OF FLORIDA, JUNE 6, 1995

Location of licensee	Accountants	Architects	Professional engineers	Location of licensee	Accountants	Architects	Professional engineers
Total 1/	26,086	9,576	27,487	Jefferson	10	4	9
NonFlorida	4,792	4,829	12,581	Lafayette	2	0	1
Unknown	6	0	0	Lake	119	31	95
Alachua	332	110	483	Lee	402	123	371
Baker	6	1	10	Leon	767	162	650
Bay	112	17	130	Levy	10	1	17
Bradford	13	1	4	Liberty	4	0	2
Brevard	395	64	629	Madison	6	0	3
Broward	2,815	396	1,118	Manatee	209	45	131
Calhoun	6	0	1	Marion	136	30	96
Charlotte	54	12	63	Martin	142	45	200
Citrus	36	10	68	Monroe	62	31	47
Clay	128	20	118	Nassau	19	15	29
Collier	266	82	173	Okaloosa	97	28	96
Columbia	40	1	66	Okeechobee	13	0	6
Dade	3,734	1,173	1,623	Orange	1,590	379	1,261
De Soto	8	0	5	Osceola	64	11	69
Dixie	1	0	0	Palm Beach	1,947	419	1,435
Duval	1,380	272	919	Pasco	127	7	106
Escambia	266	82	243	Pinellas	1,499	272	940
Flagler	19	6	24	Polk	379	51	437
Franklin	5	4	5	Putnam	20	9	36
Gadsden	33	7	15	St. Johns	162	35	106
Gilchrist	2	0	3	St. Lucie	104	17	101
Glades	0	0	0	Santa Rosa	81	10	88
Gulf	2	2	2	Sarasota	464	154	294
Hamilton	3	0	3	Seminole	543	141	538
Hardee	9	0	3	Sumter	4	1	5
Hendry	18	3	13	Suwannee	14	2	11
Hernando	47	8	63	Taylor	10	1	9
Highlands	37	7	22	Union	1	0	1
Hillsborough	1,975	334	1,445	Volusia	365	62	293
Holmes	3	1	5	Wakulla	16	1	14
Indian River	125	41	96	Walton	4	3	12
Jackson	19	2	12	Washington	7	1	33

1/ Total includes all active, involuntary inactive, and voluntary inactive licensed persons.

Source: State of Florida, Department of Business and Professional Regulation, unpublished data.

Operators with No Instruction Involved in Recreational Boating Accidents by Age in Florida, 1995

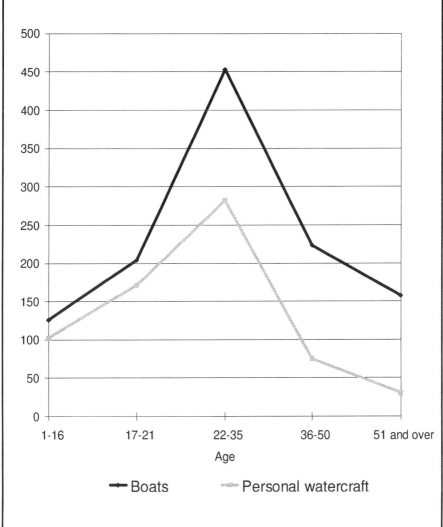

500
450
400
350
300
250
200
150
100
50
0

1-16 17-21 22-35 36-50 51 and over

Age

Boats Personal watercraft

Source: Table 19.46

SECTION 19.00
TOURISM AND RECREATION

TABLES LISTED BY MAJOR HEADINGS

HEADING PAGE

Table 19.24. TOURISTS: PERCENTAGE DISTRIBUTION OF VISITORS TRAVELING BY AIR AND AUTOMOBILE TO FLORIDA BY STATE OF ORIGIN AND COUNTY DESTINATION, 1995

State or province of origin	Air Percentage	Air Rank	Automobile Percentage	Automobile Rank	County of destination	Air Percentage	Air Rank	Automobile Percentage	Automobile Rank
New York	12.5	1	4.9	4	Dade	15.2	1	(NA)	(NA)
California	6.1	2	(NA)	(NA)	Broward	14.0	2	4.3	7
New Jersey	5.7	3	(NA)	(NA)	Orange	10.6	3	12.8	1
Pennsylvania	5.7	3	4.1	10	Palm Beach	8.6	4	3.0	10
Illinois	5.4	6	(NA)	(NA)	Pinellas	5.1	6	3.3	9
Texas	5.2	6	4.5	8	Hillsborough	4.3	6	(NA)	(NA)
Massachusetts	5.0	7	(NA)	(NA)	Sarasota	3.8	7	(NA)	(NA)
Ohio	4.3	8	5.7	2	Lee	3.8	8	(NA)	(NA)
Michigan	3.9	9	4.7	5	Bay	3.6	9	12.7	2
Georgia	3.8	10	16.0	1	Brevard	3.4	10	4.7	6
North Carolina	(NA)	(NA)	5.3	3	Volusia	(NA)	(NA)	9.7	3
Tennessee	(NA)	(NA)	4.7	5	Okaloosa	(NA)	(NA)	6.0	4
Alabama	(NA)	(NA)	4.6	7	Duval	(NA)	(NA)	4.8	5
South Carolina	(NA)	(NA)	4.3	9	Osceola	(NA)	(NA)	3.5	8

(NA) Not available.

Note: Data based on approximately 9,500 person-to-person interviews conducted annually with visitors to Florida as they are leaving the state. Individuals must not be residents of Florida and must have been in the state longer than one night and less than 180. Excludes children traveling without an adult, commuters and military personnel on transfer status.

Table 19.25. TOURISTS: INTERNATIONAL TRAVELERS TO FLORIDA AND THE UNITED STATES BY SPECIFIED COUNTRY OR REGION OF ORIGIN, 1993 AND 1994

Country or region 2/	Florida 1/ 1993	Florida 1/ 1994	Florida 1/ Percentage change	United States 1993	United States 1994	United States Percentage change
Canada	2,246,000	1,855,000	-17.4	17,315,000	14,980,000	-13.5
Overseas, total	4,619,256	4,189,459	-9.3	20,253,495	20,866,297	3.0
Western Europe	2,231,128	1,849,321	-17.1	8,397,055	8,251,396	-1.7
Germany	455,046	312,667	-31.3	1,826,757	1,704,811	-6.7
United Kingdom	1,127,739	954,998	-15.3	2,999,301	2,920,975	-2.6
South America	1,124,277	1,135,849	1.0	2,026,391	2,142,827	5.7
Argentina	200,933	179,894	-10.5	387,116	390,109	0.8
Brazil	294,976	334,793	13.6	555,102	661,265	19.1
Venezuela	268,992	262,997	-2.2	444,355	424,161	-4.5
Central America	245,328	230,640	-6.0	544,602	521,540	-4.2
Other countries/regions						
Caribbean	536,177	477,800	-10.9	1,098,110	1,008,214	-8.2
Mexico	230,408	236,518	2.7	1,591,678	1,657,657	4.1

1/ Data are collected through the use of the Immigration and Naturalization Service (INS) I-94 form and are for those travelers whose first intended address was Florida. Data do not necessarily represent "total" international visitors since they may stay at their port of entry or another state prior to visiting Florida.

2/ 150,000 or more travelers to Florida in 1994.

Source for Tables 19.24 and 19.25: State of Florida, Department of Commerce, Office of Tourism Research, *1995 Florida Visitor Study,* and unpublished data.

Table 19.26. TRAFFIC COUNTS: AVERAGE DAILY TRAFFIC ENTERING AND LEAVING FLORIDA AND PASSING OTHER SPECIFIC POINTS, MONTHS OF 1994

Location and direction		January	February	March	April	May	June
I-95 Georgia	N	16,374	18,747	23,461	24,257	20,710	20,612
	S	18,356	19,894	21,010	18,403	17,619	19,447
U.S. 1 Georgia	N	3,835	4,123	4,479	4,503	4,467	4,590
	S	3,822	4,046	4,284	4,252	4,351	4,511
I-75 Georgia	N	11,622	12,383	16,958	17,573	13,676	15,367
	S	12,548	13,367	15,791	13,113	12,055	14,775
U.S. 27 Georgia	N	2,940	3,174	3,299	3,299	3,237	3,356
	S	3,005	3,198	3,333	3,310	3,306	3,367
U.S. 231 Alabama	N	4,039	4,485	5,880	6,141	5,954	6,738
	S	4,505	4,834	6,151	5,679	6,117	7,031
I-275 Tampa 1/	N	27,391	29,284	30,250	29,832	28,728	28,643
	S	27,420	28,728	29,510	28,779	27,958	28,457
I-4 Orlando	E	52,074	56,844	60,136	56,030	54,915	56,211
	W	52,298	56,946	60,190	55,641	54,812	55,927
Turnpike Wildwood	N	13,298	14,897	18,202	18,338	15,561	15,517
	S	14,662	15,632	16,737	14,420	13,260	14,641

Location and direction		July	August	September	October	November	December
I-95 Georgia	N	22,792	20,667	17,076	17,173	18,755	19,398
	S	22,468	21,155	18,086	20,490	21,300	22,955
U.S. 1 Georgia	N	4,756	4,605	4,391	4,312	4,426	4,535
	S	4,705	4,650	4,600	4,550	4,512	4,573
I-75 Georgia	N	15,295	14,376	11,757	12,220	12,977	14,120
	S	14,616	14,420	12,289	13,970	14,704	16,982
U.S. 27 Georgia	N	3,314	3,328	3,444	3,658	3,465	3,536
	S	3,434	3,363	3,550	3,730	3,772	3,620
U.S. 231 Alabama	N	7,680	6,655	5,541	4,856	4,827	5,019
	S	8,279	6,812	5,877	5,403	5,346	5,695
I-275 Tampa 1/	N	27,712	28,027	27,255	27,117	27,075	27,501
	S	27,938	28,366	26,056	27,101	27,217	27,640
I-4 Orlando	E	59,390	57,755	51,960	53,470	51,890	53,331
	W	59,146	57,935	52,025	53,616	52,112	53,628
Turnpike Wildwood	N	15,235	12,294	12,949	13,400	13,900	14,302
	S	13,400	12,250	13,371	15,194	15,938	16,359

1/ Due to changes in reporting, these data are for a different intersection than as shown in previous *Abstracts* and are not comparable to earlier monthly data.

Source: State of Florida, Department of Transportation, Transportation Statistics Office, unpublished data.

Table 19.45. BOATS: NUMBER REGISTERED BY TYPE IN THE STATE AND COUNTIES OF FLORIDA, FISCAL YEAR 1994-95

County	Pleasure boats	Commer- cial boats	County	Pleasure boats	Commer- cial boats
Florida	713,413	34,188	Lafayette	517	13
			Lake	16,163	247
Alachua	8,634	256	Lee	31,201	1,721
Baker	1,487	2	Leon	10,265	161
Bay	14,453	1,487	Levy	2,337	358
Bradford	1,625	31	Liberty	898	14
Brevard	26,836	1,870	Madison	852	4
Broward	41,271	1,901	Manatee	13,898	615
Calhoun	1,107	7	Marion	14,344	342
Charlotte	15,514	827	Martin	12,926	524
Citrus	11,699	911	Monroe	17,520	4,140
Clay	7,869	179	Nassau	3,182	207
Collier	14,897	1,185	Okaloosa	14,064	841
Columbia	3,745	23	Okeechobee	4,530	294
Dade	47,140	1,914	Orange	28,593	301
De Soto	1,637	47	Osceola	6,108	236
Dixie	1,639	383	Palm Beach	31,402	941
Duval	28,023	816	Pasco	16,310	580
Escambia	15,822	479	Pinellas	43,678	1,964
Flagler	2,750	87	Polk	24,349	424
Franklin	1,557	960	Putnam	7,130	392
Gadsden	2,267	65	St. Johns	6,641	322
Gilchrist	1,063	68	St. Lucie	9,470	484
Glades	1,030	168	Santa Rosa	8,418	347
Gulf	1,996	281	Sarasota	16,520	658
Hamilton	653	1	Seminole	15,112	310
Hardee	1,471	12	Sumter	2,585	116
Hendry	2,623	262	Suwannee	2,079	24
Hernando	5,534	211	Taylor	2,584	217
Highlands	7,848	116	Union	539	2
Hillsborough	35,526	866	Volusia	19,667	768
Holmes	1,484	5	Wakulla	3,609	477
Indian River	8,356	530	Walton	2,522	94
Jackson	3,653	51	Washington	1,522	27
Jefferson	669	22			

Source: State of Florida, Department of Highway Safety and Motor Vehicles, Bureau of Vessel Titles and Registrations, *Vessels Registered in Florida, Fiscal Year 1994-95.*

Table 19.46. RECREATIONAL BOATING ACCIDENTS: TOTAL AND NUMBER OF FATAL BOATING ACCIDENTS AND PERSONAL WATERCRAFT ACCIDENTS BY TYPE, OPERATION AND OPERATOR IN FLORIDA, 1995

Item	Boats 1/ Number	Boats 1/ Fatal	Personal water-craft 2/
Accidents, total	1,337	68	503
Type 3/			
Capsizing	68	11	8
Collision with fixed object	238	10	53
Collision with floating object	27	1	3
Collision with vessel	549	9	325
Fallen skier	29	1	4
Falls in boat	54	0	28
Falls overboard	84	20	41
Fire or explosion, fuel related	37	1	3
Fire or explosion, nonfuel	20	0	0
Flooding	60	7	2
Grounding	60	2	8
Hit by boat	29	1	19
Hit by prop	13	0	1
Sinking	40	1	2
Other	29	4	6
Operation at time of accident 4/			
At anchor	81	3	10
Being towed	11	2	0
Commercial fishing	2	0	0
Cruising	1,085	47	548
Docking	56	1	10
Drifting	150	10	75
Fishing	61	13	2
Hunting	0	0	0
Maneuvering	544	12	304
Racing	13	1	9
SCUBA diving	3	0	0
Skiing	60	3	11
Skin diving	4	0	0
Swimming	4	0	1
Tied to dock	187	1	5
Towing	15	1	4
Other commercial	16	2	5
Other	71	5	32
Operators, total	1,821	77	825
Age (years)			
0-16	144	3	110
17-21	240	6	203
22-35	625	22	344
36-50	414	24	104
51 and over	398	22	64
Experience (hours)			
Less than 20	463	13	381
20-100	307	15	189
101-500	329	11	123
500 or more	596	33	93
Data unavailable	126	5	39

See footnotes at end of table.

Continued . . .

Table 19.46. RECREATIONAL BOATING ACCIDENTS: TOTAL AND NUMBER OF FATAL BOATING ACCIDENTS AND PERSONAL WATERCRAFT ACCIDENTS BY TYPE, OPERATION AND OPERATOR IN FLORIDA, 1995 (Continued)

Item	Boats 1/		Personal water-craft 2/
	Number	Fatal	
Operators (Continued)			
With no instruction by age (years)			
All ages	1,163	57	660
1-16	126	2	102
17-21	204	6	171
22-35	453	17	282
36-50	223	15	75
51 and over	157	17	30

1/ Registered recreational vessels.
2/ Accidents involving a small vessel designed to be operated by a person sitting, standing, or kneeling on, or being towed behind the vessel, rather than in the conventional manner of sitting or standing inside the vessel.
3/ Based on first harmful event.
4/ Each accident may contain multiple entries.
Note: A reportable boat accident is any boating accident that results in death, disappearance of any person, injury requiring medical treatment beyond first aid, and/or property damage totaling more than $500.

Table 19.47. RECREATIONAL BOATING ACCIDENTS: REPORTED ACCIDENTS AND PROPERTY DAMAGE RESULTING FROM PERSONAL WATERCRAFT ACCIDENTS IN THE STATE AND COUNTIES OF FLORIDA, 1995

County	Acci-dents	Damages (dol-lars)	County	Acci-dents	Damages (dol-lars)	County	Acci-dents	Damages (dol-lars)
Florida	503	521,568	Gilchrist	1	2,000	Okaloosa	36	21,370
			Hendry	1	500	Orange	17	27,902
Baker	1	650	Hernando	2	2,100	Osceola	1	0
Bay	46	38,885	Highlands	1	2,220	Palm Beach	25	25,267
Brevard	6	8,700	Hillsborough	8	12,800	Pasco	1	700
Broward	39	38,250	Indian River	5	3,150	Pinellas	40	49,025
Charlotte	7	4,700	Jackson	1	0	Polk	8	5,550
Citrus	6	5,750	Lake	4	5,250	St. Johns	4	3,500
Clay	5	4,750	Lee	22	34,865	St. Lucie	4	1,400
Collier	13	15,925	Leon	4	2,650	Santa Rosa	5	4,500
Dade	48	50,200	Manatee	5	3,750	Sarasota	9	7,907
Duval	12	11,050	Marion	4	3,400	Seminole	4	4,050
Escambia	18	8,325	Martin	7	17,070	Volusia	9	11,900
Flagler	1	0	Monroe	66	79,477	Walton	4	0
Franklin	1	600	Nassau	1	1,500	Washington	1	0

Note: A personal water craft is a small vessel designed to be operated by a person sitting, standing, or kneeling on, or being towed behind the vessel, rather than in the conventional manner of sitting or standing inside the vessel.
Source for Tables 19.46 and 19.47: State of Florida, Department of Environmental Protection, Division of Law Enforcement, Office of Waterway Management, *1995 Florida Recreational Boating Accident Report.*

Table 19.48. RECREATIONAL BOATING ACCIDENTS: NUMBER OF VESSELS REGISTERED, REPORTED ACCIDENTS, PERSONS KILLED OR INJURED, AND PROPERTY DAMAGES RESULTING FROM RECREATIONAL BOATING ACCIDENTS IN THE STATE AND COUNTIES OF FLORIDA, 1995

County	Number regis-tered	Reported accidents 1/		Fatalities		Damages (dollars)
		Number	Rate 2/	Number	Rate 2/	
Florida	713,413	1,337	187.40	78	10.93	5,283,469
Alachua	8,634	1	11.58	0	0.00	100
Baker	1,487	1	67.25	0	0.00	650
Bay	14,453	81	560.44	2	13.84	139,835
Bradford	1,625	0	0.00	0	0.00	0
Brevard	26,836	34	126.70	1	3.73	261,665
Broward	41,271	108	261.69	7	16.96	679,025
Calhoun	1,107	2	180.67	2	180.67	0
Charlotte	15,514	16	103.13	1	6.45	16,920
Citrus	11,699	17	145.31	1	8.55	17,250
Clay	7,869	11	139.79	0	0.00	4,850
Collier	14,897	35	234.95	1	6.71	132,475
Columbia	3,745	1	26.70	1	26.70	0
Dade	47,140	91	193.04	2	4.24	363,208
De Soto	1,637	2	122.17	0	0.00	17,050
Dixie	1,639	2	122.03	0	0.00	15,550
Duval	28,023	39	139.17	1	3.57	131,150
Escambia	15,822	36	227.53	3	18.96	58,500
Flagler	2,750	4	145.45	0	0.00	7,600
Franklin	1,557	10	642.26	1	64.23	68,595
Gadsden	2,267	0	0.00	0	0.00	0
Gilchrist	1,063	1	94.07	0	0.00	2,000
Glades	1,030	2	194.17	0	0.00	21,200
Gulf	1,996	6	300.60	4	200.40	800
Hamilton	653	0	0.00	0	0.00	0
Hardee	1,471	0	0.00	0	0.00	0
Hendry	2,623	3	114.37	0	0.00	5,200
Hernando	5,534	8	144.56	1	18.07	12,000
Highlands	7,848	2	25.48	0	0.00	2,700
Hillsborough	35,526	29	81.63	6	16.89	86,800
Holmes	1,484	2	134.77	0	0.00	500
Indian River	8,356	11	131.64	0	0.00	13,800
Jackson	3,653	2	54.75	0	0.00	0
Jefferson	669	0	0.00	0	0.00	0
Lafayette	517	0	0.00	0	0.00	0
Lake	16,163	16	98.99	3	18.56	14,850
Lee	31,201	60	192.30	5	16.03	129,141

See footnote at end of table.

Continued . . .

Table 19.48. RECREATIONAL BOATING ACCIDENTS: NUMBER OF VESSELS REGISTERED, REPORTED ACCIDENTS, PERSONS KILLED OR INJURED, AND PROPERTY DAMAGES RESULTING FROM RECREATIONAL BOATING ACCIDENTS IN THE STATE AND COUNTIES OF FLORIDA, 1995 (Continued)

County	Number registered	Reported accidents 1/		Fatalities		Damages (dollars)
		Number	Rate 2/	Number	Rate 2/	
Leon	10,265	9	87.68	3	29.23	22,650
Levy	2,337	4	171.16	0	0.00	5,450
Liberty	898	1	111.36	0	0.00	300
Madison	852	1	117.37	0	0.00	200
Manatee	13,898	16	115.12	2	14.39	103,570
Marion	14,344	9	62.74	0	0.00	37,900
Martin	12,926	33	255.30	1	7.74	446,987
Monroe	17,520	150	856.16	5	28.54	390,982
Nassau	3,182	8	251.41	1	31.43	10,750
Okaloosa	14,064	78	554.61	3	21.33	136,720
Okeechobee	4,530	3	66.23	2	44.15	100
Orange	28,593	30	104.92	2	6.99	35,602
Osceola	6,108	8	130.98	0	0.00	8,980
Palm Beach	31,402	104	331.19	2	6.37	1,045,648
Pasco	16,310	10	61.31	0	0.00	30,700
Pinellas	43,678	71	162.55	2	4.58	134,875
Polk	24,349	17	69.82	4	16.43	16,750
Putnam	7,130	10	140.25	1	14.03	9,800
St. Johns	6,641	25	376.45	0	0.00	148,450
St. Lucie	9,470	13	137.28	0	0.00	20,910
Santa Rosa	8,418	14	166.31	4	47.52	25,800
Sarasota	16,520	24	145.28	0	0.00	302,232
Seminole	15,112	9	59.56	1	6.62	15,499
Sumter	2,585	1	38.68	0	0.00	5,500
Suwannee	2,079	1	48.10	0	0.00	0
Taylor	2,584	2	77.40	1	38.70	3,250
Union	539	0	0.00	0	0.00	0
Volusia	19,667	37	188.13	0	0.00	80,100
Wakulla	3,609	7	193.96	1	27.71	38,350
Walton	2,522	6	237.91	0	0.00	2,000
Washington	1,522	3	197.11	1	65.70	0

1/ A reportable boat accident is any boating accident that results in death, disappearance of any person, injury requiring medical treatment beyond first aid, and/or property damage totaling more than $500.

2/ Accidents per 100,000 registered vessels.

Source: State of Florida, Department of Environmental Protection, Division of Law Enforcement, Office of Waterway Management, *1995 Florida Recreational Boating Accident Report*.

Table 19.52. STATE PARKS AND AREAS: ATTENDANCE AT PARKS IN THE STATE AND SPECIFIED COUNTIES OF FLORIDA, FISCAL YEARS 1993-94 AND 1994-95

Property designation	County	1993-94	1994-95
Total	(X)	11,805,075	11,762,022
Addison Blockhouse	Volusia	101	0
Alfred B. Maclay Gardens	Leon	50,555	54,010
Amelia Island	Nassau	62,576	58,078
Anastasia	St. Johns	315,682	277,835
Anclote Key	Pasco, Pinellas	92,559	108,379
Bahia Honda	Monroe	369,905	367,990
Barnacle, The	Dade	6,327	11,252
Big Lagoon	Escambia	74,381	87,266
Big Talbot Island	Duval	57,902	47,998
Blackwater River	Santa Rosa	31,541	23,910
Blue Spring	Volusia	355,381	288,143
Bulow Creek	Flagler, Volusia	39,635	42,698
Bulow Plantation Ruins	Flagler	30,126	30,836
Caladesi Island	Pinellas	136,684	106,060
Cape Florida	Dade	275,317	372,230
Cayo Costa	Lee	51,824	50,510
Cedar Key	Levy	20,429	21,610
Collier-Seminole	Collier	59,084	62,207
Constitution Convention	Gulf	1,388	1,052
Coral Reef 1/	Monroe	984,350	950,843
Crystal River	Citrus	22,082	21,126
Curry Hammock	Monroe	0	16,587
Dade Battlefield	Sumter	26,769	31,754
De Leon Springs	Volusia	222,731	208,885
Dead Lakes	Gulf	13,742	13,809
Delnor-Wiggins Pass	Collier	475,147	444,263
Devil's Millhopper	Alachua	47,756	45,604
Don Pedro Island	Charlotte	10,391	8,454
Eden	Walton	47,320	53,185
Egmont Key	Hillsborough	85,404	75,425
Fakahatchee Strand	Collier	65,016	63,696
Falling Waters	Washington	26,393	28,238
Faver-Dykes	St. Johns	22,872	22,529
Flagler Beach	Flagler	69,173	77,556
Florida Caverns	Jackson	115,698	105,951
Forest Capital	Taylor	28,532	26,748
Ft. Clinch	Nassau	161,499	159,969
Ft. Cooper	Citrus	19,280	24,890
Ft. George Island	Duval	17,594	26,251
Ft. Pierce Inlet 1/	St. Lucie	118,628	121,650
Ft. Zachary Taylor	Monroe	235,667	229,999
Gamble Plantation	Manatee	29,714	25,948
Gasparilla Island	Hillsborough	410,925	362,469
Gold Head Branch	Clay	59,111	58,572
Grayton Beach	Walton	68,193	81,768
Green Mound	Volusia	337	0
Guana River	St. Johns	148,424	160,182
Henderson Beach	Okaloosa	70,459	73,096
Highlands Hammock	Hardee	113,041	172,194
Hillsborough River	Hillsborough	130,526	106,797
Homosassa Springs	Citrus	209,614	207,784

See footnotes at end of table. Continued . . .

Table 19.52. STATE PARKS AND AREAS: ATTENDANCE AT PARKS IN THE STATE AND SPECIFIED COUNTIES OF FLORIDA, FISCAL YEARS 1993-94 AND 1994-95 (Continued)

Property designation	County	1993-94	1994-95
Honeymoon Island	Pinellas	452,616	432,794
Hontoon Island	Volusia, Lake	34,362	30,407
Hugh Taylor Birch	Broward	249,343	263,898
Ichetucknee Springs	Columbia, Suwannee	167,135	155,860
Indian Key	Monroe	5,801	6,659
John Gorrie	Franklin	6,002	6,058
Jonathan Dickinson	Martin	119,571	134,930
Key Largo Hammock 2/	Monroe	7,550	5,418
Koreshan	Lee	41,224	42,863
Lake Griffin	Lake	25,466	27,376
Lake Jackson Mounds	Leon	17,322	23,048
Lake Kissimmee	Polk	43,198	44,347
Lake Louisa	Lake	25,369	26,939
Lake Manatee	Manatee	48,528	44,334
Lake Talquin	Gadsden, Leon, Liberty	11,975	10,975
Lignumvitae Key	Monroe	2,421	3,202
Little Manatee River	Hillsborough	23,314	19,462
Little Talbot Island	Duval	120,525	123,714
Lloyd Beach	Broward	636,166	570,307
Long Key	Monroe	80,847	72,973
Lovers Key	Lee	63,059	58,594
Lower Wekiva River	Lake, Seminole	2,052	2,742
MacArthur Beach	Palm Beach	98,629	90,907
Madira Bickel Mound	Manatee	2,686	2,988
Manatee Springs	Levy	127,676	127,729
Marjorie Kinnan Rawlings	Alachua	20,753	21,883
Myakka River	Manatee, Sarasota	241,014	242,904
Natural Bridge Battlefield	Leon	19,794	23,526
North Peninsula	Volusia	26,178	24,508
North Shore	Dade	19,643	7,656
O'Leno	Alachua, Columbia	56,608	60,030
Ochlockonee River	Wakulla	36,385	35,640
Oleta River	Dade	145,207	123,852
Olustee Battlefield	Baker	42,245	43,085
Oscar Scherer	Sarasota	86,539	99,435
Paynes Creek	Hardee	35,152	31,701
Paynes Prairie	Alachua	91,399	99,234
Peacock Springs	Suwannee	10,000	8,948
Perdido Key	Escambia	16,137	25,153
Ponce De Leon Springs	Holmes, Walton	17,601	16,161
Rainbow Springs	Marion	53,500	67,899
Ravine	Putnam	124,699	135,460
Rock Springs Run	Orange	2,317	5,744
Rocky Bayou	Okaloosa	27,388	24,651
St. Andrews 2/	Bay	445,796	479,246
St. George Island	Franklin	213,815	172,624
St. Joseph Peninsula	Gulf	85,575	93,711
St. Lucie Inlet	Martin	24,295	24,560
San Felasco Hammock	Alachua	11,829	13,588
San Marcos de Apalache	Wakulla	18,260	19,063
San Pedro	Monroe	1,432	1,289
Sebastian Inlet	Brevard, Indian River	509,619	524,642
Silver River	Marion	0	11,388

See footnotes at end of table.

Continued . . .

Table 19.52. STATE PARKS AND AREAS: ATTENDANCE AT PARKS IN THE STATE AND SPECIFIED COUNTIES OF FLORIDA, FISCAL YEARS 1993-94 AND 1994-95 (Continued)

Property designation	County	1993-94	1994-95
Spruce Creek	Volusia	942	0
Stephen Foster	Hamilton	63,619	57,753
Sunshine Skyway Fishing Piers	Hillsborough, Pinellas	0	26,970
Suwannee River	Hamilton, Madison, Suwannee	44,002	45,877
Tallahassee/St. Marks	Leon	103,543	184,947
Three Rivers	Jackson	20,923	19,374
Tomoka	Volusia	66,717	50,863
Torreya	Liberty	16,501	18,326
Tosohatchee	Orange	15,339	13,749
Van Fleet	Lake, Polk, Sumter	8,995	7,536
Waccasassa Bay	Levy	31,235	29,585
Wakulla Springs	Wakulla	185,417	167,065
Washington Oaks	Flagler	52,854	52,250
Wekiwa Springs	Orange, Seminole	213,489	195,572
Windley Key	Monroe	541	954
Withlacoochee	Citrus, Pasco, Hernando	34,605	55,280
Ybor City	Hillsborough	25,960	15,255
Yulee Sugar Mill Ruins	Citrus	36,591	36,275

(X) Not applicable.
1/ Beginning in 1993-94, includes Jack Island.
2/ Beginning in 1993-94, includes Shell Island.
Note: Data include areas reporting actual visitor counts from full-time entrance stations and areas reporting estimates of attendance from sample counts. Some parks may have been closed for repairs. Totals may include data from parks that are closed or no longer under the state system.
Source: State of Florida, Department of Environmental Protection, Recreation and Parks Management Information System, unpublished data.

Table 19.53. NATIONAL PARK SYSTEMS: RECREATIONAL VISITS TO NATIONAL PARK SERVICE AREAS IN FLORIDA, 1993 THROUGH 1995

Park, monument, or memorial	County	1993	1994	1995
Florida	(X)	8,058.0	8,082.6	8,055.5
Big Cypress Preserve	Broward, Hendry	234.8	294.3	365.5
Biscayne Park 1/	Dade	20.0	25.1	584.5
Canaveral Seashore	Brevard, Volusia	1,211.5	1,432.9	1,380.4
Castillo de San Marcos Monument	St. Johns	715.8	675.0	643.3
De Soto Memorial	Dade	215.5	250.4	211.5
Everglades Park	Dade	973.7	886.5	820.5
Ft. Caroline Memorial	Duval	129.6	162.0	124.4
Ft. Matanzas Monument	St. Johns	387.9	487.2	451.5
Gulf Islands Seashore 1/ 2/	Escambia, Okaloosa, Santa Rosa	5,456.3	5,069.5	4,520.4
Jefferson National Expansion Memorial 1/	Monroe	2,539.7	2,553.7	3,235.0

(X) Not applicable.
1/ Due to changes in counting procedures, closings, or special events, data may not be comparable to earlier years.
2/ Part located in Mississippi; excluded from total.
Note: Data are in thousands, rounded to hundreds.
Source: U.S., Department of the Interior, National Park Service, *National Park Service Statistical Abstract, 1995,* and previous editions.

Table 19.54. TOURIST DEVELOPMENT TAXES: LOCAL OPTION TAX COLLECTIONS IN THE STATE AND COUNTIES OF FLORIDA, FISCAL YEARS 1993-94 AND 1994-95

(amounts rounded to thousands of dollars)

County	1993-94	1994-95 Amount	1994-95 Percentage change	County	1993-94	1994-95 Amount	1994-95 Percentage change
Florida	163,212	182,268	11.7	Leon	972	1,311	34.9
				Manatee	1,834	1,988	8.4
Alachua	866	950	9.8	Monroe	7,537	8,146	8.1
Bay	2,319	2,541	9.6	Nassau	750	844	12.6
Bradford	39	39	1.3	Okaloosa	1,583	1,718	8.5
Brevard	3,126	3,511	12.3	Okeechobee	76	77	1.1
Broward	10,938	10,942	0.0	Orange	50,416	58,412	15.9
Charlotte	793	955	20.3	Osceola	10,830	12,227	12.9
Citrus	191	176	-8.0	Palm Beach	10,349	12,399	19.8
Clay	129	146	13.6	Pasco	497	570	14.6
Collier	3,881	4,259	9.8	Pinellas	8,768	8,700	-0.8
Columbia	316	257	-18.6	Polk	1,553	2,220	42.9
Dade	14,656	15,560	6.2	Putnam	61	73	18.1
Duval	2,139	3,602	68.4	St. Johns	2,148	2,366	10.2
Escambia	1,946	2,080	6.9	St. Lucie	814	847	4.0
Flagler	160	177	11.0	Santa Rosa	62	68	9.1
Hernando	109	126	15.2	Sarasota	2,747	2,904	5.7
Hillsborough	6,666	7,269	9.1	Seminole	898	1,018	13.3
Indian River	549	650	18.4	Suwannee	40	41	1.0
Jackson	0	0	0.0	Volusia	3,425	3,487	1.8
Lake	422	353	-16.3	Wakulla	0	2	(X)
Lee	7,217	7,709	6.8	Walton	1,389	1,548	11.4

(X) Not applicable.

Note: Data reflect both state- and locally-administered tourist development tax collections.

Source: State of Florida, Department of Revenue, unpublished data.

Table 19.60. TOURIST FACILITIES: HOTELS AND MOTELS BY NUMBER OF UNITS AND FOOD SERVICE ESTABLISHMENTS BY SEATING CAPACITY IN THE STATE AND COUNTIES OF FLORIDA, FISCAL YEAR 1995-96

County	Licensed hotels		Licensed motels		Food service establishments	
	Number	Units	Number	Units	Number of licenses	Seating capacity
Florida	803	132,992	3,852	201,367	35,261	2,928,768
Alachua	5	779	48	2,805	416	34,015
Baker	0	0	3	107	24	1,359
Bay	2	354	205	8,741	506	43,245
Bradford	1	29	13	368	32	1,831
Brevard	13	1,909	98	6,277	975	82,417
Broward	98	14,584	435	12,889	3,519	283,521
Calhoun	0	0	2	23	20	1,460
Charlotte	1	183	26	1,080	291	26,041
Citrus	2	111	23	808	236	16,561
Clay	1	15	7	824	199	16,340
Collier	16	3,152	60	2,188	685	64,943
Columbia	0	0	33	1,960	93	7,548
Dade	278	33,643	223	13,620	5,403	342,569
De Soto	1	10	5	127	38	3,048
Dixie	0	0	10	140	20	1,208
Duval	24	4,105	86	6,854	1,635	125,222
Escambia	8	900	63	4,438	539	45,931
Flagler	2	232	15	455	111	8,080
Franklin	1	31	17	381	46	3,204
Gadsden	0	0	8	154	44	3,257
Gilchrist	0	0	1	28	14	700
Glades	0	0	11	189	21	1,049
Gulf	1	14	9	83	20	1,269
Hamilton	0	0	9	371	16	762
Hardee	0	0	3	45	29	1,371
Hendry	1	59	13	298	53	4,123
Hernando	0	0	14	595	230	16,139
Highlands	5	494	21	687	161	14,173
Hillsborough	31	7,194	111	7,299	1,968	163,497
Holmes	0	0	5	193	15	1,142
Indian River	1	208	35	1,479	243	20,456
Jackson	0	0	11	547	64	3,817
Jefferson	0	0	4	147	27	1,717
Lafayette	0	0	1	8	6	297
Lake	2	135	48	1,856	365	28,639
Lee	18	2,414	143	5,138	1,088	93,948

See footnote at end of table. Continued . . .

Table 19.60. TOURIST FACILITIES: HOTELS AND MOTELS BY NUMBER OF UNITS AND FOOD SERVICE ESTABLISHMENTS BY SEATING CAPACITY IN THE STATE AND COUNTIES OF FLORIDA, FISCAL YEAR 1995-96 (Continued)

County	Licensed hotels		Licensed motels		Food service establishments	
	Number	Units	Number	Units	Number of licenses	Seating capacity
Leon	10	1,356	45	3,498	499	44,516
Levy	0	0	23	329	71	4,180
Liberty	0	0	1	13	4	338
Madison	0	0	3	138	26	1,584
Manatee	2	299	69	2,771	536	46,099
Marion	6	687	67	2,706	450	33,559
Martin	4	336	22	910	334	27,250
Monroe	25	2,066	170	6,044	590	43,726
Nassau	2	461	24	635	120	9,779
Okaloosa	1	44	55	4,238	432	37,984
Okeechobee	0	0	11	362	77	5,379
Orange	78	32,731	125	25,090	2,462	306,397
Osceola	19	4,376	109	16,045	471	52,321
Palm Beach	57	8,904	159	6,201	2,572	233,873
Pasco	0	0	38	1,817	547	42,741
Pinellas	31	4,550	379	13,611	2,188	195,952
Polk	9	673	111	5,720	830	68,983
Putnam	0	0	22	522	116	6,954
St. Johns	6	935	71	3,182	338	23,946
St. Lucie	5	963	34	1,188	356	24,517
Santa Rosa	1	8	10	710	135	8,626
Sarasota	7	719	80	3,296	769	68,269
Seminole	5	651	25	2,169	664	55,870
Sumter	0	0	8	552	93	3,473
Suwannee	0	0	10	322	36	2,237
Taylor	0	0	25	478	36	2,773
Union	0	0	0	0	4	322
Volusia	21	2,250	313	14,853	1,163	98,676
Wakulla	1	28	5	112	38	2,695
Walton	1	400	14	492	123	9,386
Washington	0	0	5	161	29	1,464

Note: Apartment buildings, rooming houses, rental condominiums, transient apartments, and total public lodgings are shown in Table 2.30.

Source: State of Florida, Department of Business and Professional Regulation, Division of Hotels and Restaurants, *Master File Statistics: Public Lodging and Food Service Establishments,* Fiscal Year 1995-96.

Table 19.70. TOURIST- AND RECREATION-RELATED BUSINESSES: GROSS AND TAXABLE SALES AND SALES AND USE TAX COLLECTIONS BY KIND OF BUSINESS IN FLORIDA 1994 AND 1995

(rounded to thousands of dollars)

Kind of business	Gross sales	Taxable sales	Sales and use tax collections
1994			
Candy, sundries, and concessions	967,574	357,035	22,745
Restaurants and lunchrooms	14,596,117	13,265,506	808,591
Bars, nightclubs, and liquor stores	1,909,142	1,758,013	107,941
Sporting goods, pro shops, jewelry, and leather	3,416,289	2,221,869	134,490
Motorboats, yachts, and marine parts	2,408,154	1,253,474	76,204
Music, electronics, and record shops	10,300,318	3,756,453	232,467
Hotels, rooming houses, and trailer parks	7,927,436	7,239,118	441,139
Bookstores	805,600	555,558	33,644
Tobacco shops	62,890	28,964	1,767
Photo and art supplies, photographers, and art galleries	1,440,834	825,296	50,381
Gift, novelty, hobby, and toy stores	2,250,522	1,613,689	97,860
Newsstands	145,510	54,398	3,437
Admissions	3,407,414	3,100,436	205,904
Holiday season vendors	9,323	6,918	421
Rental of amusement machines, houseboats, and horses	4,632,410	2,761,949	171,382
Fairs, concessions, and carnivals	11,891	7,364	448
1995			
Candy, sundries, and concessions	1,180,500	390,375	24,934
Restaurants and lunchrooms	15,509,171	13,998,378	856,570
Bars, nightclubs, and liquor stores	1,965,109	1,800,113	111,242
Sporting goods, pro shops, jewelry, and leather	3,815,587	2,324,668	141,160
Motorboats, yachts, and marine parts	2,820,480	1,349,599	82,531
Music, electronics, and record shops	12,368,703	4,222,289	261,942
Hotels, rooming houses, and trailer parks	8,598,639	7,768,974	475,943
Bookstores	918,957	616,166	37,564
Tobacco shops	78,434	35,335	2,141
Photo and art supplies, photographers, and art galleries	1,557,457	873,112	53,317
Gift, novelty, hobby, and toy stores	2,382,535	1,690,776	103,088
Newsstands	186,379	56,139	3,614
Admissions	3,671,096	3,423,705	228,127
Holiday season vendors	13,460	10,228	627
Rental of amusement machines, houseboats, and horses	4,976,807	2,984,691	184,104
Fairs, concessions, and carnivals	12,156	7,008	423

Note: Audited sales reported for the 6 percent regular sales tax, 6 percent use tax, and 3 percent vehicle and farm equipment sales tax. Sales occurred, for the most part, from December 1, 1993, through November 30, 1995. Kind of business data for counties are available from the Bureau of Economic and Business Research, University of Florida. Data includes all sales in the category. See Table 16.81 for taxable sales for all businesses; see Table 23.43 for tax collections.

Source: State of Florida, Department of Revenue, unpublished data.

Table 19.73. EATING AND DRINKING PLACES: AVERAGE MONTHLY PRIVATE REPORTING UNITS EMPLOYMENT, AND PAYROLL COVERED BY UNEMPLOYMENT COMPENSATION LAW IN THE STATE AND COUNTIES OF FLORIDA, 1994 AND 1995

County	Number of re- porting units	Number of em- ployees	Payroll ($1,000)	County	Number of re- porting units	Number of em- ployees	Payroll ($1,000)
			Eating and drinking places, 1994 A/ (SIC code 58)				
Florida	20,994	414,823	351,770	Lake	197	3,114	2,286
				Lee	574	11,426	9,294
Alachua	309	7,538	5,040	Leon	332	10,306	7,124
Baker	21	266	184	Levy	39	492	308
Bay	292	6,382	4,730	Madison	19	181	98
Bradford	19	420	228	Manatee	283	5,581	4,501
Brevard	706	12,473	8,990	Marion	248	4,882	3,534
Broward	2,363	42,495	38,208	Martin	179	2,737	2,336
Calhoun	9	151	81	Monroe	312	4,585	4,706
Charlotte	156	2,515	1,830	Nassau	69	1,266	993
Citrus	137	1,790	1,140	Okaloosa	301	6,487	4,703
Clay	149	3,273	2,231	Okeechobee	41	522	351
Collier	349	6,073	5,892	Orange	1,188	32,851	33,507
Columbia	52	1,078	700	Osceola	236	6,329	5,243
Dade	2,887	52,497	53,997	Palm Beach	1,612	30,332	27,521
De Soto	26	364	226	Pasco	333	5,552	3,780
Dixie	21	186	101	Pinellas	1,463	27,481	21,727
Duval	1,050	22,597	17,136	Polk	474	8,672	6,865
Escambia	406	8,707	6,303	Putnam	63	921	547
Flagler	53	601	398	St. Johns	192	3,222	2,381
Franklin	26	229	156	St. Lucie	181	3,108	2,227
Gadsden	24	378	217	Santa Rosa	86	1,394	834
Gilchrist	10	38	19	Sarasota	534	9,845	8,168
Gulf	10	103	72	Seminole	405	9,580	7,340
Hardee	21	224	134	Sumter	35	594	384
Hendry	39	446	306	Suwannee	28	493	333
Hernando	128	1,952	1,269	Taylor	28	455	308
Highlands	85	1,263	871	Volusia	686	12,319	9,026
Hillsborough	1,155	30,502	25,340	Wakulla	16	263	189
Holmes	12	221	163	Walton	54	739	545
Indian River	143	2,371	1,876	Washington	12	205	150
Jackson	47	728	450				
Jefferson	8	105	45	Multicounty 1/	50	733	2,018

See footnotes at end of table. Continued . . .

Table 19.73. EATING AND DRINKING PLACES: AVERAGE MONTHLY PRIVATE REPORTING UNITS EMPLOYMENT, AND PAYROLL COVERED BY UNEMPLOYMENT COMPENSATION LAW IN THE STATE AND COUNTIES OF FLORIDA, 1994 AND 1995 (Continued)

County	Number of re- porting units	Number of em- ployees	Payroll ($1,000)	County	Number of re- porting units	Number of em- ployees	Payroll ($1,000)
			Eating and drinking places, 1995 B/ (SIC code 58)				
Florida	20,802	420,144	366,734	Jefferson	9	101	48
				Lafayette	5	23	12
Alachua	302	7,753	5,250	Lake	201	3,325	2,508
Baker	18	299	194	Lee	554	12,057	9,987
Bay	292	6,577	5,027	Leon	337	10,919	7,927
Bradford	18	474	251	Levy	42	554	331
Brevard	669	12,218	9,230	Madison	16	207	119
Broward	2,312	42,814	39,761	Manatee	283	5,403	4,547
Calhoun	10	154	89	Marion	262	4,913	3,629
Charlotte	145	2,433	1,783	Martin	181	2,845	2,406
Citrus	135	1,744	1,147	Monroe	306	4,634	4,832
Clay	146	3,508	2,442	Nassau	75	1,315	1,068
Collier	356	6,225	6,317	Okaloosa	300	6,464	4,750
Columbia	51	1,246	800	Okeechobee	40	590	403
Dade	2,848	51,482	54,532	Orange	1,212	33,886	37,243
De Soto	26	373	237	Osceola	241	6,827	5,834
Dixie	18	168	100	Palm Beach	1,567	29,696	27,808
Duval	1,057	23,173	18,200	Pasco	327	5,449	3,886
Escambia	402	9,131	6,745	Pinellas	1,403	26,118	21,061
Flagler	53	667	452	Polk	479	9,111	6,646
Franklin	29	238	166	Putnam	61	973	624
Gadsden	22	374	215	St. Johns	200	3,384	2,618
Gilchrist	8	40	19	St. Lucie	179	3,204	2,348
Glades	5	51	29	Santa Rosa	84	1,501	866
Gulf	11	94	67	Sarasota	525	9,720	8,366
Hamilton	7	70	39	Seminole	410	9,752	7,750
Hardee	20	217	137	Sumter	36	640	423
Hendry	38	444	301	Suwannee	27	554	333
Hernando	126	2,014	1,324	Taylor	26	466	316
Highlands	82	1,438	958	Volusia	704	12,865	9,866
Hillsborough	1,150	31,529	26,202	Wakulla	17	252	172
Holmes	12	220	161	Walton	54	733	556
Indian River	149	2,391	1,934	Washington	11	219	154
Jackson	47	743	467	Multicounty 1/	66	1,066	2,665

A/ Revised.
B/ Preliminary.
1/ Reporting units without a fixed location within the state or of unknown county location.
Note: Private employment. Only counties for which data are disclosed are shown. Detail may not add to totals due to disclosure editing and/or rounding. See Tables 23.70, 23.71, 23.72, 23.73, and 23.74 for public employment data.

Source: State of Florida, Department of Labor and Employment Security, Bureau of Labor Market Information, "Employment and Wages" (ES-202), unpublished data.

Table 19.75. TOURIST- AND RECREATION-RELATED BUSINESSES: AVERAGE MONTHLY PRIVATE REPORTING UNITS, EMPLOYMENT, AND PAYROLL COVERED BY UNEMPLOYMENT COMPENSATION LAW BY INDUSTRY IN FLORIDA, 1995

SIC code	Industry	Number of reporting units	Number of employees	Payroll ($1,000)
413	Intercity and rural bus transportation	34	864	1,458
414	Bus charter service	76	1,979	2,862
448	Water transportation of passengers	119	5,479	13,794
451	Air transportation, scheduled, and air courier services	396	36,033	103,415
452	Air transportation, nonscheduled	216	4,801	11,493
472	Arrangement of passenger transportation	2,609	17,094	30,706
544	Candy, nut, and confectionery stores	172	1,081	947
555	Boat dealers	600	4,193	8,339
556	Recreational vehicle dealers	159	1,980	4,805
573	Radio, television, consumer electronics, and music stores	2,457	21,636	38,238
581	Eating and drinking places	20,802	420,144	366,734
592	Liquor stores	732	4,265	4,538
594	Miscellaneous shopping goods stores	6,899	46,212	57,152
701	Hotels and motels	2,970	132,855	170,234
703	Camps and recreational vehicle parks	396	2,927	3,302
751	Automotive rental and leasing, without drivers	684	18,279	37,277
783	Motion picture theaters	281	6,338	4,187
784	Video tape rental	767	7,571	11,720
79	Amusement and recreation services	5,181	122,431	202,391
791	Dance studios, schools, and halls	314	1,412	1,337
792	Theatrical producers, orchestras, entertainers	595	6,046	12,405
793	Bowling centers	144	3,067	2,720
794	Commercial sports	546	11,532	39,274
799	Miscellaneous services 1/	3,583	100,375	146,656
841	Museums and art galleries	105	1,828	2,643
842	Arboreta, botanical and zoological gardens	43	1,429	2,105

1/ Includes physical fitness and membership recreation facilities, public golf and driving ranges, coin-operated amusement devices, amusement parks, carnivals, fairs, animal shows, commercial museums and rental of bicycles, motorcycles, pleasure boats, etc.

Note: Private employment. Data are preliminary. Detail may not add to totals due to disclosure editing and/or rounding. See Tables 23.70, 23.71, 23.72, 23.73, and 23.74 for public employment data.

Source: State of Florida, Department of Labor and Employment Security, Bureau of Labor Market Information, "Employment and Wages" (ES-202), unpublished data.

Table 19.76. HOTELS, ROOMING HOUSES, CAMPS, AND LODGING PLACES: AVERAGE MONTHLY PRIVATE REPORTING UNITS, EMPLOYMENT, AND PAYROLL COVERED BY UNEMPLOYMENT COMPENSATION LAW IN THE STATE AND COUNTIES OF FLORIDA, 1995

County	Number of re-porting units	Number of em-ployees	Payroll ($1,000)	County	Number of re-porting units	Number of em-ployees	Payroll ($1,000)
	Hotels, rooming houses, camps, and lodging places (SIC code 70)						
Florida	3,507	137,513	175,926	Lake	126	4,198	5,791
				Leon	62	1,412	1,157
Alachua	65	850	704	Levy	14	62	45
Baker	3	32	17	Manatee	49	637	645
Bay	125	2,487	2,615	Marion	55	1,037	890
Brevard	85	2,510	2,401	Martin	20	743	945
Broward	294	8,957	11,974	Monroe	181	4,723	6,894
Charlotte	22	271	288	Nassau	18	1,510	2,126
Citrus	27	378	346	Okaloosa	45	1,178	1,093
Clay	6	292	284	Okeechobee	15	153	160
Collier	63	3,415	5,223	Orange	197	33,851	46,968
Columbia	26	344	237	Osceola	125	5,146	6,124
Dade	408	17,905	24,431	Palm Beach	145	8,511	13,604
De Soto	6	48	39	Pasco	41	452	457
Duval	104	3,772	3,976	Pinellas	261	7,272	8,805
Escambia	41	867	697	Polk	93	2,273	2,791
Flagler	8	191	178	Putnam	14	152	118
Franklin	15	115	102	St. Johns	78	2,173	2,661
Gadsden	7	35	23	St. Lucie	28	762	668
Glades	7	24	20	Santa Rosa	10	331	315
Hamilton	7	78	45	Sarasota	75	2,546	3,238
Hardee	5	22	17	Seminole	24	690	692
Hendry	10	172	164	Sumter	18	141	104
Hernando	9	152	126	Suwannee	9	61	42
Highlands	23	187	173	Taylor	12	75	49
Hillsborough	108	6,831	7,810	Volusia	205	4,414	3,981
Holmes	4	24	11	Walton	11	1,199	1,717
Indian River	25	667	681				
Lake	39	775	871	Multicounty 1/	10	88	158

1/ Reporting units without a fixed location within the state or of unknown county location.

Note: Private employment. Data are preliminary. Only counties for which data are disclosed are shown. Detail may not add to totals due to disclosure editing and/or rounding. See Tables 23.70, 23.71, 23.72, 23.73, and 23.74 for public employment data.

Source: State of Florida, Department of Labor and Employment Security, Bureau of Labor Market Information, "Employment and Wages" (ES-202), unpublished data.

Table 19.78. AMUSEMENT AND RECREATION SERVICES: AVERAGE MONTHLY PRIVATE REPORTING UNITS, EMPLOYMENT, AND PAYROLL COVERED BY UNEMPLOYMENT COMPENSATION LAW IN THE STATE AND COUNTIES OF FLORIDA, 1995

County	Number of re-porting units	Number of em-ployees	Payroll ($1,000)	County	Number of re-porting units	Number of em-ployees	Payroll ($1,000)
Amusement and recreation services (SIC code 79)							
Florida	5,181	122,431	202,391	Lee	153	2,218	2,707
				Leon	71	728	651
Alachua	51	1,040	1,360	Levy	12	50	43
Bay	105	1,055	1,035	Madison	5	50	77
Brevard	124	1,842	2,046	Manatee	62	1,066	1,554
Broward	666	11,160	17,802	Marion	66	939	1,043
Calhoun	3	15	8	Martin	74	1,582	2,261
Charlotte	38	546	563	Monroe	158	886	1,844
Citrus	33	382	393	Nassau	12	46	37
Clay	35	675	789	Okaloosa	100	739	722
Collier	111	3,038	4,757	Okeechobee	6	63	53
Columbia	13	133	106	Orange	305	40,821	74,433
Dade	603	10,295	24,172	Osceola	52	1,071	1,254
De Soto	7	102	114	Palm Beach	505	10,028	16,217
Duval	177	2,445	2,791	Pasco	74	611	660
Escambia	75	907	814	Pinellas	293	4,618	5,921
Flagler	9	111	113	Polk	89	1,972	2,330
Gadsden	4	16	11	Putnam	8	40	23
Hardee	6	29	29	St. Johns	44	1,107	3,274
Hendry	6	13	13	St. Lucie	37	568	576
Hernando	25	478	437	Santa Rosa	28	214	183
Highlands	19	376	401	Sarasota	163	3,555	5,052
Hillsborough	274	8,075	13,813	Seminole	106	1,674	1,835
Holmes	4	23	24	Suwannee	5	23	14
Indian River	41	1,285	1,903	Taylor	4	13	13
Jackson	8	44	26	Volusia	171	2,532	3,689
Lake	45	462	490	Multicounty 1/	73	237	1,468

1/ Reporting units without a fixed location within the state or of unknown county location.

Note: Private employment. For a list of three-digit code industries included see Table 19.75. Data are preliminary. Only counties for which data are disclosed are shown. Detail may not add to totals due to disclosure editing and/or rounding. See Tables 23.70, 23.71, 23.72, 23.73, and 23.74 for public employment data.

Source: State of Florida, Department of Labor and Employment Security, Bureau of Labor Market Information, "Employment and Wages" (ES-202), unpublished data.

HEALTH, EDUCATION, AND CULTURAL SERVICES

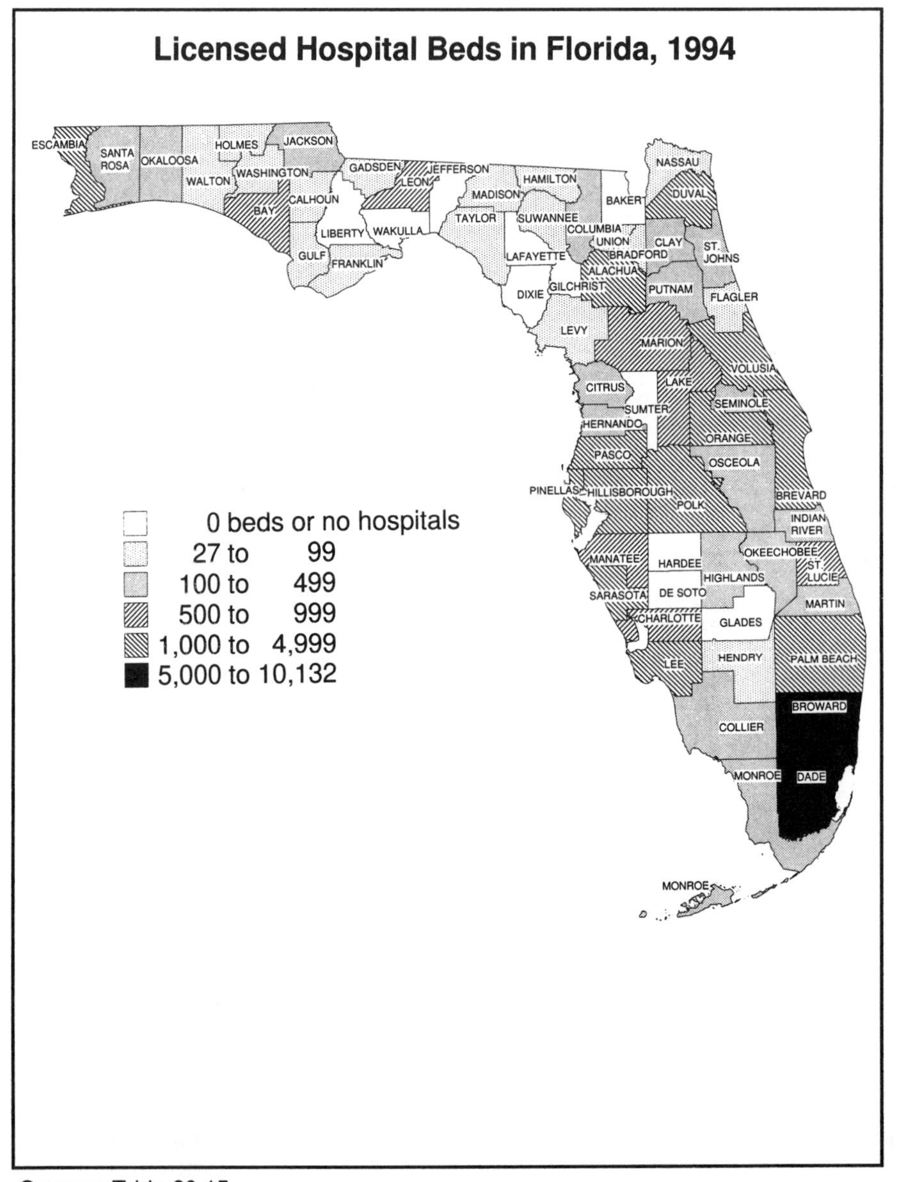

Source: Table 20.15

SECTION 20.00
HEALTH, EDUCATION, AND CULTURAL SERVICES

TABLES LISTED BY MAJOR HEADINGS

SECTION 20.00
HEALTH, EDUCATION, AND CULTURAL SERVICES
(Continued)

TABLES LISTED BY MAJOR HEADINGS

HEADING PAGE

Table 20.01. HEALTH, EDUCATIONAL, AND SOCIAL SERVICES: ESTABLISHMENTS AND RECEIPTS, 1987 AND 1992, AND PAYROLL, 1992, IN FLORIDA

(amounts in thousands of dollars)

SIC code	Kind of business	Number of establishments 1987	Number of establishments 1992	Receipts 1987	Receipts 1992	Receipts Percentage change	Annual payroll 1992
80	Health services	24,048	29,601	12,901,041	23,306,589	80.7	9,632,590
801	Offices and clinics of doctors of medicine	12,533	14,487	6,002,814	10,360,884	72.6	4,942,036
802	Offices and clinics of dentists	4,674	5,374	1,212,130	1,893,179	56.2	735,558
803	Offices and clinics of doctors of osteopathy	610	762	189,828	325,522	71.5	147,644
804	Offices and clinics of other health practitioners	3,243	4,909	608,044	1,239,318	103.8	438,625
805	Nursing and personal care facilities	543	722	932,501	1,906,975	104.5	816,684
806	Hospitals	142	160	2,836,850	4,795,458	69.0	1,564,118
807	Medical and dental labs labs	971	1,294	392,044	874,743	123.1	253,152
808	Home health care services	465	852	284,363	1,141,072	301.3	485,872
809	Miscellaneous health and allied services, NEC	867	1,041	442,467	769,438	73.9	248,901
823, 4, 9	Selected educational services	623	955	324,286	423,789	30.7	132,236
823	Libraries	7	9	905	1,206	33.3	520
824	Vocational schools	219	304	207,430	234,636	13.1	74,185
829	Schools and educational services, NEC	397	642	115,951	187,947	62.1	57,531
83	Social services	2,832	3,797	458,635	824,710	79.8	326,313
835	Child day care services	1,910	2,409	232,856	378,299	62.5	167,498
832, 3, 6, 9	Other social services	922	1,388	225,779	446,411	97.7	158,815
832	Individual and family social services	(NA)	477	(NA)	96,298	(X)	38,019
833	Job training and vocational rehabilitation services	(NA)	128	(NA)	58,756	(X)	25,941
836	Residential care	(NA)	691	(NA)	275,792	(X)	90,559
839	Social services, NEC	(NA)	92	(NA)	15,565	(X)	4,296

NEC Not elsewhere classified.
(NA) Not available.
(X) Not applicable.

Note: Data are for firms subject to federal income tax. The service industries census is on a 5-year cycle collecting data for years ending in 2 and 7.

Source: U.S., Department of Commerce, Bureau of the Census, *1992 Census of Service Industries: Florida*. SC92-A-10.

Table 20.05. EMPLOYMENT: AVERAGE MONTHLY PRIVATE REPORTING UNITS, EMPLOYMENT AND PAYROLL COVERED BY UNEMPLOYMENT COMPENSATION LAW BY INDUSTRY IN FLORIDA, 1994 AND 1995

SIC code	Industry	Units	Em- ployees	Payroll ($1,000)
1994 A/				
80	Health services	29,037	514,220	1,291,558
801	Offices and clinics of doctors of medicine	13,680	99,564	440,417
802	Offices and clinics of dentists	5,254	30,313	72,363
803	Offices and clinics of doctors of osteopathy	699	3,959	13,357
804	Offices of other health practitioners	5,313	26,410	62,196
805	Nursing and personal care facilities	704	73,865	99,630
806	Hospitals	351	202,141	457,976
807	Medical and dental laboratories	1,358	12,577	30,240
808	Home health care services	957	43,914	71,481
809	Miscellaneous health and allied services, NEC	722	21,479	43,898
82	Educational services	1,708	46,129	84,069
821	Elementary and secondary schools	516	16,811	27,031
822	Colleges and universities	123	18,713	40,058
823	Libraries	25	210	268
824	Vocational schools	289	3,326	5,827
829	School and education services, NEC	756	7,069	10,886
83	Social services	5,884	106,402	126,657
832	Individual and family social services	1,262	20,783	28,221
833	Job training and related services	379	10,921	13,435
835	Child day care services	2,409	29,038	25,437
836	Residential care	1,284	36,556	44,878
839	Social services, NEC	550	9,103	14,688
84	Museums, botanical and zoological gardens 1/	147	3,082	4,224
1995 B/				
80	Health services	28,979	538,142	1,399,514
801	Offices and clinics of doctors of medicine	13,493	107,991	482,978
802	Offices and clinics of dentists	5,326	31,470	77,733
803	Offices and clinics of doctors of osteopathy	645	3,948	13,684
804	Offices of other health practitioners	5,335	28,125	68,645
805	Nursing and personal care facilities	732	78,117	114,090
806	Hospitals	386	210,128	492,335
807	Medical and dental laboratories	1,335	12,581	30,789
808	Home health care services	953	44,829	76,565
809	Miscellaneous health and allied services, NEC	777	20,955	42,694
82	Educational services	1,758	47,657	89,072
821	Elementary and secondary schools	529	17,443	28,914
822	Colleges and universities	129	19,291	42,106
823	Libraries	23	231	306
824	Vocational schools	302	3,520	6,591
829	School and education services, NEC	776	7,173	11,154
83	Social services	5,926	109,083	135,069
832	Individual and family social services	1,295	22,507	31,792
833	Job training and related services	379	11,106	14,429
835	Child day care services	2,381	29,152	26,799
836	Residential care	1,306	37,991	47,976
839	Social services, NEC	566	8,328	14,073
84	Museums, botanical and zoological gardens 1/	148	3,256	4,748

NEC Not elsewhere classified.

A/ Revised. B/ Preliminary. 1/ See Table 19.75 for detail.

Note: Private employment. Detail may not add to totals due to disclosure editing and/or rounding. See Tables in Section 23.00 for public employment data.

Source: State of Florida, Department of Labor and Employment Security, Bureau of Labor Market Information, "Employment and Wages" (ES-202), unpublished data.

Table 20.06. OFFICES AND CLINICS OF DOCTORS OF MEDICINE: AVERAGE MONTHLY PRIVATE REPORTING UNITS, EMPLOYMENT, AND PAYROLL COVERED BY UNEMPLOYMENT COMPENSATION LAW IN THE STATE AND AND COUNTIES OF FLORIDA, 1995

County	Number of reporting units	Number of employees	Payroll ($1,000)	County	Number of reporting units	Number of employees	Payroll ($1,000)
	Offices and clinics of doctors of medicine (SIC code 801)						
Florida	13,493	107,991	482,978	Lake	141	1,205	4,330
				Lee	260	2,882	16,675
Alachua	232	1,944	8,462	Leon	176	2,243	9,239
Baker	5	23	54	Levy	8	37	59
Bay	121	1,009	4,727	Manatee	175	1,363	5,925
Bradford	6	53	91	Marion	180	1,322	5,924
Brevard	378	3,133	15,397	Martin	112	808	3,911
Broward	1,502	11,105	51,846	Monroe	65	277	1,189
Charlotte	110	1,021	5,313	Nassau	13	59	204
Citrus	76	508	2,030	Okaloosa	107	899	3,149
Clay	81	607	2,353	Okeechobee	23	96	383
Collier	167	1,056	5,971	Orange	656	7,323	33,833
Columbia	25	164	628	Osceola	99	762	3,155
Dade	2,912	18,117	73,259	Palm Beach	1,142	7,605	41,230
De Soto	14	50	253	Pasco	313	2,218	9,946
Duval	629	7,303	34,171	Pinellas	870	6,862	32,897
Escambia	177	2,795	11,782	Polk	199	3,275	11,162
Flagler	12	104	291	Putnam	40	272	848
Franklin	4	14	53	St. Johns	86	359	1,816
Gadsden	7	33	60	St. Lucie	129	901	3,897
Gilchrist	3	28	66	Santa Rosa	43	300	1,041
Hamilton	3	12	29	Sarasota	388	2,754	13,052
Hardee	13	68	194	Seminole	214	1,662	7,204
Hendry	8	28	52	Sumter	3	67	164
Hernando	81	412	2,233	Suwannee	7	30	60
Highlands	72	329	1,037	Taylor	8	53	130
Hillsborough	928	7,722	32,944	Union	4	29	46
Holmes	7	33	82	Volusia	276	2,591	11,295
Indian River	112	1,101	4,609	Walton	8	43	98
Jackson	19	152	443	Washington	7	31	75
Jefferson	3	19	44	Multicounty 1/	21	401	893

1/ Reporting units without a fixed location within the state or of unknown county location.

Note: Private employment. Data are preliminary. Only counties for which data are disclosed are shown. Detail may not add to totals due to disclosure editing and/or rounding. See Tables 23.70, 23.71, 23.72, 23.73, and 23.74 for public employment data.

Source: State of Florida, Department of Labor and Employment Security, Bureau of Labor Market Information, "Employment and Wages" (ES-202), unpublished data.

Table 20.07. OFFICES AND CLINICS OF DENTISTS: AVERAGE MONTHLY PRIVATE REPORTING UNITS, EMPLOYMENT, AND PAYROLL COVERED BY UNEMPLOYMENT COMPENSATION LAW IN THE STATE AND COUNTIES OF FLORIDA, 1995

County	Number of reporting units	Number of employees	Payroll ($1,000)	County	Number of reporting units	Number of employees	Payroll ($1,000)
	Offices and clinics of dentists (SIC code 802)						
Florida	5,326	31,470	77,733	Lake	55	349	752
				Lee	122	777	2,104
Alachua	81	525	1,169	Leon	67	539	1,421
Bay	40	311	799	Levy	4	32	42
Bradford	5	30	76	Manatee	88	534	1,333
Brevard	151	1,053	2,760	Marion	60	438	930
Broward	620	3,496	9,047	Martin	49	258	741
Calhoun	3	15	27	Monroe	25	133	305
Charlotte	39	247	596	Nassau	11	71	134
Citrus	20	143	327	Okaloosa	65	373	679
Clay	42	308	674	Okeechobee	7	41	71
Collier	87	427	1,127	Orange	301	1,886	5,041
Columbia	13	72	144	Osceola	28	193	469
Dade	871	4,441	10,433	Palm Beach	514	2,744	7,334
De Soto	3	15	19	Pasco	67	431	1,069
Dixie	3	18	28	Pinellas	394	2,473	6,404
Duval	267	1,680	4,006	Polk	109	717	1,835
Escambia	102	635	1,507	Putnam	11	84	166
Flagler	7	56	162	St. Johns	28	174	401
Gadsden	6	35	67	St. Lucie	45	261	616
Gulf	3	14	21	Santa Rosa	23	144	258
Hamilton	3	19	19	Sarasota	172	883	2,190
Hendry	7	41	62	Seminole	116	816	1,813
Hernando	31	248	611	Suwannee	3	27	43
Highlands	22	92	207	Volusia	130	779	1,719
Hillsborough	327	1,964	5,104	Walton	6	26	35
Indian River	45	254	556	Washington	4	13	16
Jackson	8	46	66				

Note: Private employment. Data are preliminary. Only counties for which data are disclosed are shown. Detail may not add to totals due to disclosure editing and/or rounding. See Tables 23.70, 23.71, 23.72, 23.73, and 23.74 for public employment data.

Source: State of Florida, Department of Labor and Employment Security, Bureau of Labor Market Information, "Employment and Wages" (ES-202), unpublished data.

Table 20.11. NURSING AND PERSONAL CARE FACILITIES AND HOSPITALS: AVERAGE MONTHLY PRIVATE REPORTING UNITS, EMPLOYMENT, AND PAYROLL COVERED BY UNEMPLOYMENT COMPENSATION LAW IN THE STATE AND COUNTIES OF FLORIDA, 1995

County	Number of reporting units	Number of employees	Payroll ($1,000)	County	Number of reporting units	Number of employees	Payroll ($1,000)
			Nursing and personal care facilities (SIC code 805)				
Florida	732	78,117	114,090	Manatee	14	1,627	2,218
				Marion	8	854	1,112
Alachua	6	866	1,090	Martin	7	709	1,007
Bay	6	686	876	Monroe	3	267	398
Brevard	20	2,180	3,109	Nassau	3	374	483
Broward	45	5,153	7,708	Okaloosa	11	769	935
Charlotte	8	1,031	1,301	Okeechobee	3	268	353
Citrus	8	1,098	1,428	Orange	34	4,199	6,045
Clay	7	739	1,018	Osceola	9	1,097	1,513
Collier	9	1,101	1,566	Palm Beach	54	6,746	10,717
Columbia	3	268	314	Pasco	16	1,616	2,333
Dade	81	7,649	12,366	Pinellas	88	8,944	13,634
Duval	30	3,089	4,270	Polk	19	2,228	3,065
Escambia	10	1,513	1,899	Putnam	4	336	440
Hernando	4	632	793	St. Johns	9	493	694
Highlands	5	559	669	St. Lucie	6	762	1,154
Hillsborough	29	3,212	4,778	Santa Rosa	4	328	359
Indian River	5	653	820	Sarasota	34	3,269	5,319
Lake	10	1,028	1,365	Seminole	16	1,288	2,036
Lee	14	1,354	1,952	Suwannee	3	597	663
Leon	9	959	1,288	Volusia	29	3,331	4,142
Madison	3	145	168	Multicounty 1/	10	789	2,652
			Hospitals (SIC code 806)				
Florida	386	210,128	492,335	Leon	7	4,333	9,083
				Manatee	10	3,507	7,146
Alachua	5	7,290	17,376	Monroe	4	882	2,075
Brevard	10	5,926	13,512	Okaloosa	5	1,625	3,378
Broward	25	11,581	26,818	Orange	21	16,449	39,723
Charlotte	5	2,595	5,645	Osceola	5	1,466	3,407
Citrus	9	1,318	2,882	Palm Beach	28	15,033	36,867
Dade	47	34,306	90,762	Pasco	13	4,790	10,320
Duval	16	13,793	33,182	Pinellas	35	17,507	38,135
Escambia	5	5,932	12,517	Polk	7	6,438	15,198
Hernando	6	1,868	3,774	St. Lucie	5	2,336	5,550
Highlands	4	1,319	2,671	Santa Rosa	7	880	1,594
Hillsborough	23	15,161	34,395	Sarasota	8	4,270	10,009
Indian River	3	1,976	4,314	Seminole	6	2,660	6,293
Lake	7	2,986	6,049	Volusia	10	5,602	12,445
Lee	8	4,294	9,186				

1/ Reporting units without a fixed location within the state or of unknown county location.

Note: Private employment. Data are preliminary. Only counties for which data are disclosed are shown. Detail may not add to totals due to disclosure editing and/or rounding. See Tables 23.70, 23.71, 23.72, 23.73, and 23.74 for public employment data.

Source: State of Florida, Department of Labor and Employment Security, Bureau of Labor Market Information, "Employment and Wages" (ES-202), unpublished data.

Table 20.14. VETERANS ADMINISTRATION MEDICAL CENTERS (VAMC): INPATIENT AND OUTPATIENT MEDICAL AND DENTAL CARE BY VAMC IN FLORIDA FISCAL YEAR 1994

Item	Bay Pines	Gaines-ville	Lake City	Miami	Tampa
Inpatient medical care					
Hospitals					
Average operating beds 1/ 2/	581	377	270	627	538
Medical 3/	300	153	182	352	291
Surgical	132	134	42	90	128
Psychiatric	149	90	46	185	119
Patients treated 2/ 4/	11,560	9,604	6,059	12,051	12,325
Medical 3/	6,502	3,905	3,883	7,242	6,671
Surgical	3,025	4,292	1,420	2,440	3,722
Psychiatric	2,033	1,407	756	2,369	1,932
Average daily census 5/	398	272	221	443	388
Nursing homes					
Patients treated in VAMC facility	488	224	216	421	506
Patients treated in community home 6/	481	143	59	246	437
Domiciliaries					
Patients treated in VAMC facility	609	0	0	0	0
Outpatient medical care					
Visits to VAMC staff	264,921	183,575	89,620	396,341	372,733
Fee basis care	61,692	0	0	0	0
Inpatient dental care					
Patients treated in VAMC facility	6,117	1,171	15,106	4,017	1,344
Outpatient dental care					
Visits to VAMC staff	9,886	5,772	2,267	9,856	8,164
Fee based cases completed	1,342	0	0	0	0

1/ Based on the number of operating beds at the end of each month for 13 consecutive months (September 1993 through September 1994).

2/ Beds are classified according to their intended use; patients are classified according to the classification of the beds they occupy, rather than on a diagnostic basis.

3/ Medical bed section includes medicine, neurology, intermediate care, spinal cord injury, rehabilitation medicine, and blind rehabilitation.

4/ The number of discharges and deaths during the fiscal year plus the patients remaining on September 30, 1994, plus the number of interhospital transfers.

5/ Number of patient days during the fiscal year divided by the number of days in the fiscal year.

6/ Authorized and paid for by Veterans Administration.

Source: U.S., Department of Veterans Affairs, *Annual Report of the Secretary of Veterans Affairs, Fiscal Year 1994.*

Community Health Purchasing Alliance (CHPA) Regions

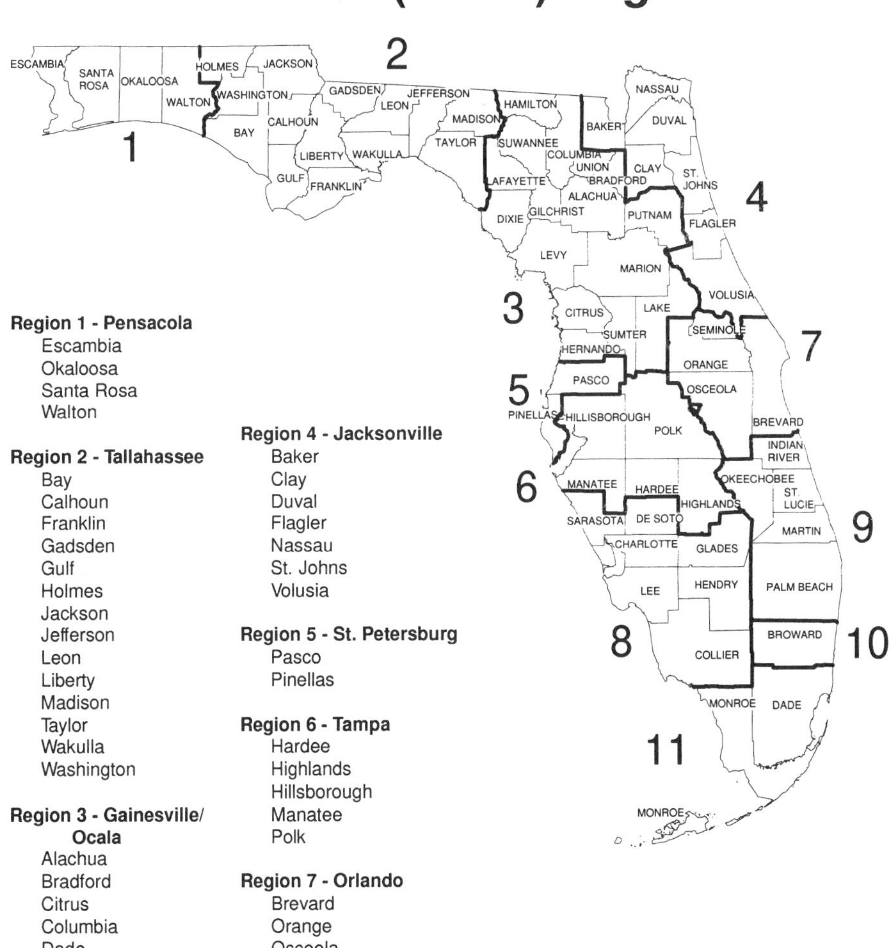

Region 1 - Pensacola
- Escambia
- Okaloosa
- Santa Rosa
- Walton

Region 2 - Tallahassee
- Bay
- Calhoun
- Franklin
- Gadsden
- Gulf
- Holmes
- Jackson
- Jefferson
- Leon
- Liberty
- Madison
- Taylor
- Wakulla
- Washington

Region 3 - Gainesville/ Ocala
- Alachua
- Bradford
- Citrus
- Columbia
- Dade
- Gilchrist
- Hamilton
- Hernando
- Lafayette
- Lake
- Levy
- Marion
- Putnam
- Sumter
- Suwannee
- Union

Region 4 - Jacksonville
- Baker
- Clay
- Duval
- Flagler
- Nassau
- St. Johns
- Volusia

Region 5 - St. Petersburg
- Pasco
- Pinellas

Region 6 - Tampa
- Hardee
- Highlands
- Hillsborough
- Manatee
- Polk

Region 7 - Orlando
- Brevard
- Orange
- Osceola
- Seminole

Region 8 - Sarasota/ Ft. Myers
- Charlotte
- Collier
- De Soto
- Glades
- Hendry
- Lee
- Sarasota

Region 9 - West Palm Beach
- Indian River
- Martin
- Okeechobee
- Palm Beach
- St. Lucie

Region 10 - Ft. Lauderdale
- Broward

Region 11- Miami
- Dade
- Monroe

Table 20.15. HOSPITALS: NUMBER OF GENERAL, SHORT-TERM ACUTE CARE HOSPITALS AND NUMBER OF LICENSED AND ACUTE CARE BEDS IN THE STATE, COMMUNITY HEALTH PURCHASING ALLIANCE (CHPA) REGIONS, AND COUNTIES OF FLORIDA, 1994

CHPA and county 1/	Number of hospitals	Beds	
		Licensed	Acute care
Florida	200	55,384	48,404
CHPA 1	10	2,189	1,774
Escambia	3	1,463	1,116
Okaloosa	3	432	374
Santa Rosa	3	244	234
Walton	1	50	50
CHPA 2	14	2,002	1,758
Bay	2	529	507
Calhoun	1	36	36
Franklin	1	29	29
Gadsden	1	51	51
Gulf	1	45	45
Holmes	1	34	34
Jackson	2	157	157
Leon	2	950	728
Madison	1	42	42
Taylor	1	48	48
Washington	1	81	81
CHPA 3	21	3,672	3,373
Alachua	3	1,349	1,165
Bradford	1	54	54
Citrus	2	299	283
Columbia	2	203	178
Hamilton	1	42	42
Hernando	3	370	370
Lake	3	544	500
Levy	1	40	40
Marion	2	553	553
Putnam	1	161	131
Suwannee	1	30	30
Union	1	27	27
CHPA 4	17	4,590	4,003
Clay	1	224	196
Duval	8	2,833	2,458
Flagler	1	81	81
CHPA 4 (Continued)			
Volusia	7	1,452	1,268
Nassau	1	54	54
St. Johns	1	230	222
CHPA 5	22	5,647	5,001
Pasco	5	1,032	916
Pinellas	17	4,615	4,085
CHPA 6	20	6,543	5,672
Highlands	2	277	260
Hillsborough	10	3,454	3,052
Manatee	2	895	795
Polk	6	1,917	1,565
CHPA 7	13	5,194	4,567
Brevard	4	1,191	1,146
Orange	6	3,402	2,900
Osceola	1	169	169
Seminole	2	432	352
CHPA 8	15	4,349	3,735
Charlotte	3	669	582
Collier	1	434	381
De Soto	1	82	82
Hendry	1	66	66
Lee	5	1,536	1,423
Sarasota	4	1,562	1,201
CHPA 9	21	4,908	4,419
Indian River	2	480	410
Martin	1	336	331
Okeechobee	1	101	101
Palm Beach	15	3,478	3,167
St. Lucie	2	513	410
CHPA 10	18	5,889	5,257
Broward	18	5,889	5,257
CHPA 11	29	10,401	8,845
Dade	26	10,132	8,621
Monroe	3	269	224

1/ CHPA regions are state-chartered, not-for-profit, private purchasing organizations with exclusive territories that were authorized by the 1993 Legislature to assist their members in securing the highest quality health care at the lowest possible price. CHPA membership is voluntary and available primarily to businesses that have 50 or fewer employees. See accompanying map for counties in CHPA regions.

Note: Based on reports from 202 hospitals statewide. Reports include some teaching and specialty hospitals. For the most part, data are for general, short-term acute care hospitals which offer more intensive services than those required for room, board, personal services, and general nursing care. See Glossary for definitions.

Source: State of Florida, Agency for Health Care Administration, *1996 Guide to Hospitals in Florida.*

Table 20.16. HOSPITALS: DISCHARGES OF PATIENTS OF GENERAL, SHORT-TERM ACUTE CARE HOSPITALS BY SERVICE LINE IN THE STATE, COMMUNITY HEALTH PURCHASING ALLIANCE (CHPA) REGIONS, AND COUNTIES OF FLORIDA, 1994

CHPA and county 1/	Total	Cardiology 2/	Gastroenterology	General surgery	Gynecology 3/	Neonatology	Neurology 4/	Oncology	Orthopedics	Other medicine 5/
Florida	1,484,242	291,899	111,460	149,298	224,991	47,686	86,083	48,150	129,702	394,973
CHPA 1	58,143	10,167	4,400	5,756	9,949	2,050	2,895	2,145	5,354	15,427
Escambia	40,081	7,237	2,649	4,260	7,085	1,658	2,051	1,832	3,452	9,857
Okaloosa	11,365	1,806	942	970	2,044	331	517	216	1,234	3,305
Santa Rosa	5,940	948	692	470	769	61	271	97	668	1,964
Walton	757	176	117	56	51	0	56	0	0	301
CHPA 2	52,685	8,792	4,164	4,561	10,128	1,508	3,082	881	4,364	15,205
Bay	17,070	3,113	1,465	1,741	2,578	380	1,032	358	1,608	4,795
Calhoun	396	100	46	0	0	0	37	0	0	213
Franklin	547	97	89	0	0	0	0	0	44	317
Gadsden	588	53	89	0	31	0	31	0	0	384
Gulf	326	86	71	0	0	0	0	0	0	169
Holmes	882	167	96	40	0	0	47	0	0	532
Jackson	3,758	504	374	228	921	54	179	0	304	1,194
Leon	27,126	4,272	1,713	2,445	6,566	1,074	1,645	523	2,408	6,480
Madison	221	46	0	0	0	0	0	0	0	175
Taylor	641	87	110	63	32	0	30	0	0	319
Washington	1,130	267	111	44	0	0	81	0	0	627
CHPA 3	118,058	23,089	9,645	12,495	16,892	2,445	7,061	3,401	10,160	32,870
Alachua	42,378	6,046	2,896	4,488	7,481	1,642	2,374	1,693	4,278	11,480
Bradford	689	168	105	0	0	0	63	0	0	353
Citrus	11,563	2,321	1,147	1,304	1,269	86	727	317	920	3,472
Columbia	4,577	1,007	533	250	487	71	244	32	120	1,833
Hamilton	346	64	49	0	0	0	0	0	0	233
Hernando	13,257	3,247	1,304	1,507	1,120	104	885	255	965	3,870
Lake	17,375	3,265	1,476	1,998	3,025	276	1,131	435	1,390	4,379
Levy	694	244	97	0	0	0	62	0	0	291
Marion	21,260	5,397	1,526	2,621	2,879	193	1,248	594	2,074	4,728

See footnotes at end of table.

Continued . . .

Table 20.16. HOSPITALS: DISCHARGES OF PATIENTS OF GENERAL, SHORT-TERM ACUTE CARE HOSPITALS BY SERVICE LINE IN THE STATE, COMMUNITY HEALTH PURCHASING ALLIANCE (CHPA) REGIONS, AND COUNTIES OF FLORIDA, 1994 (Continued)

CHPA and county 1/	Total	Cardiology 2/	Gastroenterology	General surgery	Gynecology 3/	Neonatology	Neuroogy 4/	Oncology	Orthopedics	Other medicine 5/
CHPA 3 (Continued)										
Putnam	5,384	1,263	427	327	631	73	327	75	326	1,935
Suwannee	179	0	36	0	0	0	0	0	0	143
Union	356	67	49	0	0	0	0	0	87	153
CHPA 4	125,775	25,531	9,900	14,402	10,972	4,013	8,077	3,753	11,597	37,530
Clay	7,809	1,275	599	717	1,803	196	391	122	664	2,042
Duval	74,591	15,049	5,205	8,534	6,359	3,015	4,593	2,427	6,645	22,764
Flagler	1,074	262	133	88	0	0	105	0	123	363
Nassau	1,022	194	106	138	88	57	47	0	65	327
St. Johns	5,935	1,015	805	745	324	90	439	110	358	2,049
Volusia	35,344	7,736	3,052	4,180	2,398	655	2,502	1,094	3,742	9,985
CHPA 5	144,848	31,395	12,150	16,063	15,721	2,996	9,619	3,838	14,837	38,229
Pasco	32,160	9,495	3,210	3,584	657	329	2,211	741	2,815	9,118
Pinellas	112,688	21,900	8,940	12,479	15,064	2,667	7,408	3,097	12,022	29,111
CHPA 6	171,931	28,244	12,186	16,219	32,318	6,434	9,471	6,868	15,524	44,667
Highlands	10,775	1,931	1,091	975	1,194	199	690	285	643	3,767
Hillsborough	92,969	12,568	5,773	8,976	19,904	3,935	5,193	4,030	8,765	23,825
Manatee	21,979	4,671	1,773	2,376	3,283	493	1,333	728	2,260	5,062
Polk	46,208	9,074	3,549	3,892	7,937	1,807	2,255	1,825	3,856	12,013
CHPA 7	170,563	34,194	11,633	16,098	33,994	5,642	8,428	5,265	13,079	42,230
Brevard	44,814	9,645	3,630	4,214	6,772	1,171	2,637	1,336	3,794	11,615
Orange	108,020	21,667	6,727	10,110	22,845	3,916	4,962	3,456	8,169	26,168
Osceola	7,331	1,022	395	650	2,367	275	298	144	374	1,806
Seminole	10,398	1,860	881	1,124	2,010	280	531	329	742	2,641
CHPA 8	113,230	25,416	9,591	12,867	9,095	2,412	7,220	4,301	13,964	28,364
Charlotte	17,082	3,945	1,273	1,797	2,198	321	1,007	573	1,489	4,479

See footnotes at end of table.

Continued . . .

Table 20.16. HOSPITALS: DISCHARGES OF PATIENTS OF GENERAL, SHORT-TERM ACUTE CARE HOSPITALS BY SERVICE LINE IN THE STATE, COMMUNITY HEALTH PURCHASING ALLIANCE (CHPA) REGIONS, AND COUNTIES OF FLORIDA, 1994 (Continued)

CHPA and county 1/	Total	Cardiology 2/	Gastroenterology	General surgery	Gynecology 3/	Neonatology	Neurology 4/	Oncology	Orthopedics	Other medicine 5/
CHPA 8 (Continued)										
Collier	15,059	2,550	1,586	1,626	649	347	1,248	637	2,137	4,279
De Soto	2,407	438	214	191	556	94	131	0	0	783
Hendry	941	189	123	90	0	0	81	0	0	458
Lee	40,136	9,425	3,405	4,718	1,363	1,197	2,516	1,380	5,816	10,316
Sarasota	37,605	8,869	2,990	4,445	4,329	453	2,237	1,711	4,522	8,049
CHPA 9	151,722	30,718	11,315	15,052	23,087	4,904	9,403	5,539	13,697	38,007
Indian River	11,764	2,125	1,055	1,363	1,319	271	872	546	1,271	2,942
Martin	10,885	2,109	976	1,413	423	315	812	677	1,177	2,983
Okeechobee	3,201	790	360	275	58	0	236	44	88	1,350
Palm Beach	110,383	22,844	7,778	10,456	18,832	3,753	6,418	3,833	9,800	26,669
St. Lucie	15,489	2,850	1,146	1,545	2,455	565	1,065	439	1,361	4,063
CHPA 10	142,556	30,699	10,086	13,400	24,129	5,013	7,717	4,472	10,848	36,192
Broward	142,556	30,699	10,086	13,400	24,129	5,013	7,717	4,472	10,848	36,192
CHPA 11	234,731	43,654	16,390	22,385	38,706	10,269	13,110	7,687	16,278	66,252
Dade	228,939	42,860	15,935	21,702	37,752	10,190	12,846	7,534	15,639	64,481
Monroe	5,792	794	455	683	954	79	264	153	639	1,771

1/ CHPA regions are state-chartered, not-for-profit, private puchasing organizations with exclusive territories that were authorized by the 1993 Legislature to assist their members in securing the highest quality health care at the lowest possible price. See accompanying map for counties in CHPA regions.
2/ Includes cardiac surgery.
3/ Includes obstetrics.
4/ Includes neurosurgery.
5/ Includes pediatrics, pulmonary medicine, and urology.
Note: Based on reports from 202 hospitals statewide. Reports include some teaching and specialty hospitals. For the most part, data are for general, short-term acute care hospitals which offer more intensive services than those required for room, board, personal services, and general nursing care. See Glossary for definitions.

Source: State of Florida, Agency for Health Care Administration, *1996 Guide to Hospitals in Florida.*

Table 20.17. HOSPITALS: PEDIATRIC DISCHARGES FROM GENERAL, SHORT-TERM ACUTE CARE HOSPITALS AND AVERAGE CHARGES FOR SERVICES TO PATIENTS AGED 28 DAYS TO 17 YEARS IN THE STATE, COMMUNITY HEALTH PURCHASING ALLIANCE (CHPA) REGIONS, AND COUNTIES OF FLORIDA, 1994

CHPA and county 1/	Pediatric discharges	Average charges (dollars)
Florida	90,795	(X)
CHPA 1	3,718	(X)
Escambia	2,828	A/ 16,700
Okaloosa	565	A/ 11,300
Santa Rosa	293	A/ 5,400
Walton	32	(NA)
CHPA 2	3,323	(X)
Bay	984	11,600
Franklin	33	(NA)
Gadsden	138	3,500
Holmes	54	(NA)
Jackson	247	7,500
Leon	1,758	A/ 5,700
Taylor	62	(NA)
Washington	47	(NA)
CHPA 3	7,544	(X)
Alachua	4,711	21,800
Citrus	194	A/ 6,300
Columbia	404	A/ 3,500
Hamilton	46	(NA)
Hernando	472	A/ 8,500
Lake	651	A/ 9,100
Marion	544	A/ 4,500
Putnam	464	A/ 6,600
Union	58	(NA)
CHPA 4	7,805	(X)
Clay	224	5,400
Duval	5,848	A/ 31,500
St. Johns	256	3,900
Volusia	1,477	A/ 13,900
CHPA 5	6,082	(X)
Pasco	538	A/ 12,500
Pinellas	5,544	A/ 38,800
CHPA 6	10,558	(X)
Highlands	793	9,800
Hillsborough	6,829	A/ 55,000
Manatee	699	A/ 5,500
Polk	2,237	A/ 22,500
CHPA 7	11,478	(X)
Brevard	2,454	17,200
Orange	8,340	27,000
Osceola	396	4,900
Seminole	288	A/ 4,500
CHPA 8	4,615	(X)
Charlotte	1,069	12,500
Collier	915	4,900
De Soto	167	4,500
Hendry	47	(NA)
Lee	1,845	A/ 17,500
Sarasota	572	A/ 4,300
CHPA 9	7,916	(X)
Indian River	215	7,200
Martin	512	4,300
Okeechobee	210	5,500
Palm Beach	6,045	A/ 52,300
St. Lucie	934	10,900
CHPA 10	8,471	(X)
Broward	8,471	A/ 56,800
CHPA 11	19,285	(X)
Dade	18,891	A/ 83,600
Monroe	394	A/ 3,000

(X) Not applicable.
(NA) Not available.
A/ Excludes hospitals treating fewer than 100 pediatric cases.
1/ CHPA regions are state-chartered, not-for-profit, private purchasing organizations with exclusive territories that were authorized by the 1993 Legislature to assist their members in securing the highest quality health care at the lowest possible price. CHPA membership is voluntary and available primarily to businesses that have 50 or fewer employees. See accompanying map for counties in CHPA regions.
Note: Based on reports from 202 hospitals statewide. Reports include some teaching and specialty hospitals. For the most part, data are for general, short-term acute care hospitals which offer more intensive services than those required for room, board, personal services, and general nursing care. See Glossary for definitions.

Source: State of Florida, Agency for Health Care Administration, *1996 Guide to Hospitals in Florida.*

Table 20.25. MANAGED HEALTH CARE: LICENSED HEALTH MAINTENANCE ORGANIZATIONS (HMOS) ENROLLMENT AND RATES BY TYPE OF PLAN IN THE STATE, LOCAL HEALTH COUNCIL DISTRICTS, AND COUNTIES OF FLORIDA, 1995

District and county	All plans		Commercial		Medicaid and prepaid health plans		Medicare	
	Number	Rate	Number	Rate	Number	Rate 1/	Number	Rate
Florida	3,216,684	226.0	2,382,181	232.6	432,754	277.1	401,749	165.4
Northwest--1	75,527	131.6	64,198	143.9	11,325	174.2	4	0.1
Escambia	50,805	180.7	40,248	192.7	10,553	262.2	4	0.1
Okaloosa	8,956	55.1	8,956	66.3	0	0.0	0	0.0
Santa Rosa	15,766	162.0	14,994	189.8	772	89.4	0	0.0
Walton	0	0.0	0	0.0	0	0.0	0	0.0
Big Bend--2	118,790	199.9	107,381	235.5	9,358	117.8	2,051	34.8
Bay	3,285	23.6	3,285	31.1	0	0.0	0	0.0
Calhoun	0	0.0	0	0.0	0	0.0	0	0.0
Franklin	0	0.0	0	0.0	0	0.0	0	0.0
Gadsden	15,814	348.0	11,769	374.6	3,799	361.2	246	70.3
Gulf	0	0.0	0	0.0	0	0.0	0	0.0
Holmes	0	0.0	0	0.0	0	0.0	0	0.0
Jackson	0	0.0	0	0.0	0	0.0	0	0.0
Jefferson	4,015	301.0	3,873	405.2	86	35.2	56	41.8
Leon	86,623	398.8	80,399	444.5	4,632	238.1	1,592	94.5
Liberty	0	0.0	0	0.0	0	0.0	0	0.0
Madison	1,755	97.2	1,347	104.6	408	123.3	0	0.0
Taylor	585	31.9	585	44.8	0	0.0	0	0.0
Wakulla	6,713	393.9	6,123	470.2	433	200.2	157	84.6
Washington	0	0.0	0	0.0	0	0.0	0	0.0
North Central--3	86,148	76.5	43,532	57.8	33,373	235.7	9,243	39.8
Alachua	31,091	157.2	20,659	132.0	8,698	352.1	1,734	104.7
Bradford	2,948	120.0	1,679	90.9	1,017	283.9	252	100.7
Citrus	3,594	33.6	1,659	26.8	893	87.1	1,042	30.1
Columbia	4,000	79.6	2,050	56.9	1,563	184.9	387	66.8
Dixie	748	59.9	184	21.7	455	206.7	109	60.0
Gilchrist	1,394	116.2	974	109.2	269	171.2	151	100.2
Hamilton	310	25.2	309	34.3	0	0.0	1	1.0
Hernando	7,735	64.1	2,844	40.5	3,156	289.1	1,735	43.9
Lafayette	0	0.0	0	0.0	0	0.0	0	0.0
Lake	11,666	65.8	6,216	56.3	5,442	282.8	8	0.2
Levy	3,814	127.2	2,225	111.5	1,144	251.9	445	81.1
Marion	12,037	53.2	1,821	12.3	7,399	258.3	2,817	56.6
Putnam	3,282	46.6	625	13.9	2,632	199.9	25	2.0
Sumter	0	0.0	0	0.0	0	0.0	0	0.0
Suwannee	2,846	95.1	1,881	89.3	428	95.8	537	122.5
Union	683	52.7	406	37.1	277	229.7	0	0.0
Northeast Central--4	398,797	273.5	296,164	267.9	56,814	386.5	45,819	222.8
Baker	9,006	443.8	8,085	507.5	751	268.6	170	108.8
Clay	30,530	249.9	27,236	260.0	2,227	346.3	1,067	97.3
Duval	232,427	321.6	184,653	325.8	38,059	453.1	9,715	135.1
Flagler	5,064	134.7	1,737	70.1	904	504.2	2,423	219.8
Nassau	13,922	286.8	12,066	307.3	896	222.9	960	182.8
St. Johns	9,599	97.5	7,040	94.7	2,183	285.8	376	22.9
Volusia	98,249	240.6	55,347	198.0	11,794	292.4	31,108	351.5

See footnotes at end of table.

Continued . . .

Table 20.25. MANAGED HEALTH CARE: LICENSED HEALTH MAINTENANCE ORGANIZATIONS (HMOS) ENROLLMENT AND RATES BY TYPE OF PLAN IN THE STATE, LOCAL HEALTH COUNCIL DISTRICTS, AND COUNTIES OF FLORIDA, 1995 (Continued)

District and county	All plans		Commercial		Medicaid and prepaid health plans		Medicare	
	Number	Rate	Number	Rate	Number	Rate 1/	Number	Rate
Suncoast--5	273,215	230.0	190,498	244.7	33,312	324.5	49,405	161.1
Pasco	68,016	221.3	40,314	217.8	8,200	297.4	19,502	205.9
Pinellas	205,199	233.1	150,184	253.0	25,112	334.4	29,903	141.2
West Central--6	373,518	222.2	273,033	227.8	74,129	368.3	26,356	93.9
Hardee	341	15.0	341	23.3	0	0.0	0	0.0
Highlands	2,969	38.0	906	20.7	2,062	242.4	1	0.0
Hillsborough	295,651	329.4	226,466	332.6	43,722	391.0	25,463	242.8
Manatee	18,044	76.8	11,742	77.0	5,418	272.6	884	14.1
Polk	56,513	126.4	33,578	109.4	22,927	410.5	8	0.1
East Central--7	330,203	196.7	256,828	194.6	44,782	285.9	28,593	141.4
Brevard	25,457	56.5	15,564	46.3	9,892	275.4	1	0.0
Orange	194,886	256.1	153,597	253.6	24,247	295.0	17,042	232.9
Osceola	35,137	253.4	25,759	245.5	4,577	294.4	4,801	264.5
Seminole	74,723	227.4	61,908	227.0	6,066	263.7	6,749	205.9
Southwest--8	55,132	51.6	37,823	53.8	17,305	223.9	4	0.0
Charlotte	2,914	22.3	1,615	21.1	1,299	172.4	0	0.0
Collier	99	0.5	96	0.7	0	0.0	3	0.1
De Soto	1,218	45.0	2	0.1	1,216	288.8	0	0.0
Glades	139	16.0	10	1.5	129	908.5	0	0.0
Hendry	705	23.8	68	3.3	637	106.9	0	0.0
Lee	28,119	73.9	18,466	71.1	9,652	341.5	1	0.0
Sarasota	21,938	72.3	17,566	92.4	4,372	262.6	0	0.0
Treasure Coast--9	273,751	197.2	186,566	195.5	26,620	240.1	60,565	187.7
Indian River	71	0.7	71	1.1	0	0.0	0	0.0
Martin	5,439	47.7	4,022	53.5	1,408	184.8	9	0.3
Okeechobee	1,399	42.0	876	36.4	522	130.6	1	0.2
Palm Beach	261,523	270.6	178,344	265.3	22,625	311.5	60,554	273.1
St. Lucie	5,319	30.7	3,253	27.9	2,065	103.3	1	0.0
Broward Regional--10	432,981	316.4	307,830	308.1	35,210	315.1	89,941	349.1
Broward	432,981	316.4	307,830	308.1	35,210	315.1	89,941	349.1
South--11	798,622	379.0	618,328	404.7	90,526	246.0	89,768	424.4
Dade	798,118	394.4	617,826	422.0	90,526	249.8	89,766	455.4
Monroe	504	6.0	502	7.9	0	0.0	2	0.1

1/ Based on the total population under age 65 and who are Medicaid eligible (see Table 7.21). Only persons eligible for Medicaid based upon being an Aid to Families with Dependent Children (AFDC) recipient are eligible for the prepaid plans.

Note: Rates are per 1,000 population and are based on Office of the Governor, July 1, 1995, population estimates. Local health councils were established in 1982 by the legislature to serve 11 planning districts throughout the state. These councils are responsible for establishing and maintaining the district health plans.

Source: State of Florida, Agency for Health Care Administration, *Florida 1996 Health Data SourceBook*. Compiled by Local Health Councils of Florida.

Table 20.27. EDUCATIONAL SERVICES: AVERAGE MONTHLY PRIVATE REPORTING UNITS EMPLOYMENT, AND PAYROLL COVERED BY UNEMPLOYMENT COMPENSATION LAW IN THE STATE AND COUNTIES OF FLORIDA, 1994 AND 1995

County	Number of re- porting units	Number of em- ployees	Payroll ($1,000)	County	Number of re- porting units	Number of em- ployees	Payroll ($1,000)
			Educational services, 1994 A/ (SIC code 82)				
Florida	1,708	46,129	84,069	Lee	32	555	760
				Leon	39	440	594
Alachua	33	612	786	Manatee	16	191	274
Bay	12	135	177	Marion	10	193	234
Brevard	49	1,468	2,734	Martin	12	123	191
Broward	181	5,345	9,854	Monroe	12	174	240
Charlotte	10	103	136	Nassau	5	17	25
Citrus	4	35	50	Okaloosa	8	92	114
Clay	10	200	298	Orange	120	2,900	5,513
Collier	20	483	881	Osceola	14	212	246
Dade	299	12,736	26,546	Palm Beach	137	3,005	5,232
Duval	97	2,740	3,884	Pinellas	134	2,506	4,650
Escambia	37	1,268	1,943	Polk	37	1,505	2,257
Highlands	5	95	117	Saint Lucie	8	178	223
Hillsborough	132	2,949	5,201	Sarasota	40	577	1,023
Indian River	10	297	531	Seminole	50	1,124	2,056
Lake	13	276	460	Volusia	43	2,461	5,111
			Vocational schools, 1994 A/ (SIC code 824)				
Florida	289	3,326	5,827	Hillsborough	23	174	338
				Orange	25	316	755
Brevard	7	31	48	Palm Beach	30	160	235
Broward	32	518	969	Pinellas	20	137	287
Dade	57	963	1,515	Volusia	11	105	186
Duval	18	165	210				

See footnotes at end of table.

Continued . . .

Table 20.27. EDUCATIONAL SERVICES: AVERAGE MONTHLY PRIVATE REPORTING UNITS EMPLOYMENT, AND PAYROLL COVERED BY UNEMPLOYMENT COMPENSATION LAW IN THE STATE AND COUNTIES OF FLORIDA, 1994 AND 1995 (Continued)

County	Number of re-porting units	Number of em-ployees	Payroll ($1,000)	County	Number of re-porting units	Number of em-ployees	Payroll ($1,000)
			Educational services, 1995 B/ (SIC code 82)				
Florida	1,758	47,657	89,072	Manatee	18	203	294
				Marion	11	200	233
Alachua	35	621	826	Martin	11	138	213
Bay	13	141	180	Monroe	10	186	270
Brevard	49	1,470	2,804	Nassau	5	14	16
Broward	192	5,731	10,783	Okaloosa	10	90	100
Charlotte	10	99	144	Orange	128	3,093	5,925
Citrus	4	35	50	Osceola	16	187	261
Clay	13	227	355	Palm Beach	140	3,140	5,682
Collier	20	464	874	Pasco	16	445	735
Columbia	4	40	34	Pinellas	137	2,570	5,025
Dade	305	12,888	27,652	Polk	37	1,541	2,414
Duval	98	2,807	4,307	St. Johns	11	317	561
Escambia	36	1,345	2,093	St. Lucie	7	157	207
Hernando	4	105	111	Santa Rosa	5	12	18
Hillsborough	127	2,982	5,470	Sarasota	38	713	1,261
Indian River	12	356	586	Seminole	52	991	1,720
Lake	14	296	468	Volusia	41	2,533	5,299
Lee	35	649	911				
Leon	41	458	621	Multicounty 1/	25	72	187
			Vocational schools, 1995 B/ (SIC code 824)				
Florida	302	3,520	6,591	Lee	8	48	51
				Leon	6	22	29
Alachua	7	127	158	Orange	27	371	914
Bay	4	9	11	Palm Beach	29	170	288
Brevard	8	33	42	Pinellas	23	187	436
Broward	31	536	1,019	Polk	5	105	233
Dade	59	980	1,622	Seminole	12	259	497
Duval	17	193	284	Volusia	11	113	198
Hillsborough	21	153	341	Multicounty 1/	7	21	40

A/ Revised.
B/ Preliminary.
1/ Reporting units without a fixed location within the state or of unknown county location.
Note: Private employment. See Table 20.05 for a list of educational services included. Only counties for which data are disclosed are shown. Detail may not add to totals due to disclosure editing and/or rounding. See tables 23.70, 23.71, 23.72, 23.73, and 23.74 for public employment data.

Source: State of Florida, Department of Labor and Employment Security, Bureau of Labor Market Information, "Employment and Wages" (ES-202), unpublished data.

Table 20.28. SOCIAL SERVICES: AVERAGE MONTHLY PRIVATE EMPLOYMENT COVERED BY UNEMPLOYMENT COMPENSATION LAW BY TYPE OF SOCIAL SERVICE IN THE STATE AND COUNTIES OF FLORIDA, 1995

County	Total (SIC 83)	Individual and family (SIC 832)	Job training and vocational rehabilitation (SIC 833)	Child day care (SIC 835)	Residential care 1/ (SIC 836)	Social services NEC 2/ (SIC 839)
Florida	109,083	22,507	11,106	29,152	37,991	8,328
Alachua	2,043	286	(NA)	660	644	242
Baker	130	(NA)	(NA)	38	(NA)	(NA)
Bay	1,199	327	84	359	406	23
Bradford	117	(NA)	38	48	17	(NA)
Brevard	2,550	526	519	1,019	432	55
Broward	10,022	1,735	702	3,487	3,412	686
Calhoun	73	(NA)	(NA)	(NA)	15	(NA)
Charlotte	539	80	26	206	221	(NA)
Citrus	510	(NA)	(NA)	140	212	(NA)
Clay	810	(NA)	(NA)	226	407	(NA)
Collier	1,410	172	141	382	570	145
Columbia	282	8	(NA)	158	19	(NA)
Dade	13,811	3,075	1,710	3,063	4,414	1,549
De Soto	121	36	(NA)	70	(NA)	(NA)
Dixie	20	9	(NA)	(NA)	(NA)	(NA)
Duval	6,409	2,012	477	1,889	1,759	273
Escambia	3,353	715	192	639	1,499	308
Flagler	136	83	(NA)	10	43	(NA)
Franklin	35	(NA)	(NA)	(NA)	(NA)	(NA)
Gadsden	181	(NA)	(NA)	77	34	63
Gilchrist	9	(NA)	(NA)	(NA)	(NA)	(NA)
Glades	33	(NA)	(NA)	(NA)	(NA)	(NA)
Gulf	66	64	(NA)	(NA)	(NA)	(NA)
Hamilton	22	(NA)	(NA)	(NA)	(NA)	(NA)
Hardee	204	(NA)	(NA)	89	72	(NA)
Hendry	231	(NA)	13	123	75	(NA)
Hernando	478	(NA)	(NA)	69	226	(NA)
Highlands	562	(NA)	61	141	283	(NA)
Hillsborough	7,936	2,061	519	2,246	2,562	548
Holmes	142	(NA)	(NA)	58	(NA)	(NA)
Indian River	776	199	(NA)	234	240	(NA)
Jackson	318	162	(NA)	77	(NA)	(NA)
Jefferson	42	(NA)	(NA)	(NA)	19	(NA)
Lafayette	31	(NA)	(NA)	(NA)	(NA)	(NA)
Lake	1,337	20	53	240	933	(NA)
Lee	3,932	430	294	708	2,328	173
Leon	2,678	743	242	625	770	299
Levy	199	29	(NA)	56	(NA)	(NA)
Liberty	19	(NA)	(NA)	(NA)	(NA)	(NA)
Madison	152	(NA)	(NA)	27	(NA)	(NA)

See footnotes at end of table. Continued . . .

Table 20.28. SOCIAL SERVICES: AVERAGE MONTHLY PRIVATE EMPLOYMENT COVERED BY UNEMPLOYMENT COMPENSATION LAW BY TYPE OF SOCIAL SERVICE IN THE STATE AND COUNTIES OF FLORIDA, 1995 (Continued)

County	Total (SIC 83)	Individual and family (SIC 832)	Job training and vocational rehabilitation (SIC 833)	Child day care (SIC 835)	Residential care 1/ (SIC 836)	Social services NEC 2/ (SIC 839)
Manatee	1,695	496	(NA)	302	697	(NA)
Marion	1,326	280	224	482	331	(NA)
Martin	756	140	(NA)	172	290	(NA)
Monroe	300	109	(NA)	130	(NA)	(NA)
Nassau	387	189	(NA)	43	(NA)	(NA)
Okaloosa	986	165	(NA)	444	315	13
Okeechobee	379	38	(NA)	92	(NA)	(NA)
Orange	6,647	1,353	789	1,798	2,122	585
Osceola	678	159	(NA)	178	36	(NA)
Palm Beach	7,918	1,314	924	2,205	2,271	1,204
Pasco	1,532	490	199	333	490	20
Pinellas	9,607	1,609	1,632	1,927	4,019	421
Polk	2,808	475	401	861	1,011	60
Putnam	449	33	(NA)	94	127	189
St. Johns	1,031	182	(NA)	301	496	(NA)
St. Lucie	1,120	384	40	449	157	90
Santa Rosa	444	123	(NA)	184	136	(NA)
Sarasota	2,155	361	129	325	1,221	119
Seminole	1,733	215	127	848	521	22
Sumter	129	(NA)	(NA)	14	(NA)	(NA)
Suwannee	286	(NA)	(NA)	(NA)	(NA)	(NA)
Taylor	54	(NA)	(NA)	20	(NA)	(NA)
Union	110	(NA)	(NA)	(NA)	(NA)	(NA)
Volusia	3,096	679	(NA)	628	1,389	326
Wakulla	69	39	(NA)	(NA)	(NA)	(NA)
Walton	246	(NA)	(NA)	(NA)	(NA)	(NA)
Washington	129	(NA)	(NA)	28	(NA)	41
Multicounty 3/	103	(NA)	(NA)	(NA)	(NA)	(NA)

NEC Not elsewhere classified.
(NA) Not available.
1/ Residential social and personal care for children, the aged, and other persons with limits on ability for self-care, but where medical care is not a major concern.
2/ Includes establishments primarily engaged in community improvement and social change, such as advocacy groups, fundraising organizations (except contract or fee basis), health and welfare councils, united fund councils, community action agencies, etc.
3/ Reporting units without a fixed location within the state or of unknown county location.
Note: Private employment. Data are preliminary. Detail may not add to totals due to disclosure editing and/or rounding. See Tables 23.70, 23.71, 23.72, 23.73, and 23.74 for public employment data.

Source: State of Florida, Department of Labor and Employment Security, Bureau of Labor Market Information, "Employment and Wages" (ES-202), unpublished data.

Table 20.29. MUSEUMS, ART GALLERIES, BOTANICAL AND ZOOLOGICAL GARDENS: AVERAGE MONTHLY PRIVATE REPORTING UNITS, EMPLOYMENT, AND PAYROLL COVERED BY UNEMPLOYMENT COMPENSATION LAW IN THE STATE AND COUNTIES OF FLORIDA, 1995

County	Number of reporting units	Number of employees	Payroll ($1,000)	County	Number of reporting units	Number of employees	Payroll ($1,000)
Museums, art galleries, botanical and zoological gardens (SIC code 84)							
Florida	148	3,256	4,748	Lee	4	25	22
				Monroe	8	118	174
Bay	4	104	98	Okaloosa	4	46	52
Broward	14	299	438	Orange	11	382	585
Collier	5	50	76	Palm Beach	19	292	499
Dade	12	286	490	Pinellas	9	159	257
Duval	6	226	332	Polk	3	92	122
Escambia	4	51	69	St. Johns	12	258	267
Hillsborough	8	428	706	Sarasota	5	108	140

Note: Private employment. For a list of three-digit industries included see Table 20.05. Data are preliminary. Detail may not add to totals due to disclosure editing and/or rounding. See Tables 23.70, 23.71, 23.72, 23.73, and 23.74 for public employment data.

Table 20.30. MEMBERSHIP ORGANIZATIONS: AVERAGE MONTHLY PRIVATE REPORTING UNITS EMPLOYMENT, AND PAYROLL COVERED BY UNEMPLOYMENT COMPENSATION LAW BY INDUSTRY IN FLORIDA, 1995

SIC code	Industry	Number of reporting units	Number of employees	Payroll ($1,000)
86	Membership organizations	5,969	48,897	74,260
861	Business associations	624	3,771	9,271
862	Professional membership organizations	192	1,676	4,573
863	Labor unions and similar labor organizations	523	3,138	4,964
864	Civic, social, and fraternal organizations	3,762	29,907	38,394
865	Political organizations	45	189	297
866	Religious organizations	540	5,231	6,688
869	Membership organizations, NEC	283	4,986	10,072

NEC Not elsewhere classified.

Note: Private employment. Data are preliminary. Detail may not add to totals due to disclosure editing and/or rounding. See Tables 23.70, 23.71, 23.72, 23.73, and 23.74 for public employment data.

Source for Tables 20.29 and 20.30: State of Florida, Department of Labor and Employment Security, Bureau of Labor Market Information, "Employment and Wages" (ES-202), unpublished data.

Table 20.31. CHURCHES: NUMBER AND MEMBERSHIP OF CHURCHES BY DENOMINATION IN FLORIDA, 1990

Denomination	Churches	Members	Adherents
Florida	8,577	2,651,825	A/ 5,672,756
Advent Christian	35	1,839	A/ 2,285
African Methodist Episcopal Zion	32	6,304	7,983
Allegheny Wesleyan Methodist Connection	1	0	0
American Baptist in the U.S.A.	33	7,805	A/ 9,449
American Carpatho-Russian Orthodox Greek Catholic Diocese of the U.S.A.	2	116	116
Apostolic Christian (Nazarene)	3	72	A/ 85
Apostolic Christian of America	3	116	201
Apostolic Lutheran of America	1	78	154
Armenian Apostolic of America, Eastern Prelacy	1	200	500
Assemblies of God	576	84,077	134,297
Associate Reformed Presbyterian (General Synod)	13	3,074	3,607
Baptist General Conference	20	1,819	A/ 2,212
Baptist Missionary Association of America	11	1,129	A/ 1,420
Beachy Amish Mennonite	1	145	A/ 165
Brethren Church (Ashland, Ohio)	6	395	A/ 457
Brethren in Christ	9	301	377
Catholic	479	(X)	1,598,457
Christian and Missionary Alliance	119	8,083	15,133
Christian Church (Disciples of Christ)	87	16,996	23,725
Christian Churches and Churches of Christ	179	35,695	A/ 43,070
Christian Reformed	16	1,885	2,713
Church of God (Anderson, Indiana)	105	10,326	12,440
Church of God (Cleveland, Tennessee)	479	57,587	A/ 70,108
Church of God (Seventh Day), Denver, Colorado	4	45	86
Church of God in Christ (Mennonite)	1	188	A/ 235
Church of God of Prophecy	125	4,301	A/ 5,276
Church of God of the Mountain Assembly, Inc.	5	213	A/ 258
Church of Jesus Christ of Latter-Day Saints	160	(X)	59,845
Church of the Brethren	16	1,891	A/ 2,276
Church of the Lutheran Brethren of America	2	106	222
Church of the Lutheran Confession	3	109	167
Church of the Nazarene	227	26,323	39,413
Churches of Christ	514	55,123	73,462
Congregational Christian Churches, National Association	10	1,468	A/ 1,746
Congregational Christian Churches (not national)	2	110	A/ 139
Conservative Congregational Christian Conference	1	18	A/ 22
Cumberland Presbyterian	7	937	994
Episcopal	334	114,236	158,595
Estonian Evangelical Lutheran	3	164	A/ 194
Evangelical Congregational	1	57	88
Evangelical Free Church of America	21	1,835	3,331
Evangelical Lutheran Church in America	209	73,121	92,732
Evangelical Lutheran Synod	6	675	858
Evangelical Methodist	2	150	A/ 186
Evangelical Presbyterian	8	2,140	2,271
Free Methodist Church of North America	39	1,940	2,978
Free Will Baptist, National Association, Inc.	77	6,103	A/ 7,527
Friends	25	800	A/ 1,460
Holy Apostolic Catholic Assyrian of the East	0	15	47

See footnotes at end of table.

Continued . . .

Table 20.31. CHURCHES: NUMBER AND MEMBERSHIP OF CHURCHES BY DENOMINATION IN FLORIDA, 1990 (Continued)

Denomination	Churches	Members	Adherents
International Church of the Foursquare Gospel	30	1,843	A/ 2,240
Interstate and Foreign Landmark Missionary Baptists Association	1	89	A/ 111
Jasper and Pleasant Valley Baptists Association	1	50	A/ 58
Latvian Evangelical Lutheran Church in America	2	295	303
Lutheran Church, Missouri Synod	152	52,966	67,645
Lutheran, American Association	1	120	142
Mennonite	31	2,918	4,435
Eastern Pennsylvania Mennonite	1	39	A/ 49
Missionary	10	493	665
Moravian Church in America (Unitas Fratrum), Southern Province	2	596	857
North American Baptist Conference	2	85	A/ 101
Old Order Amish	1	(X)	150
Old Regular Baptists	6	198	A/ 244
Pentecostal Church of God	25	938	1,705
Pentecostal Holiness	87	9,609	A/ 11,815
(Plymouth) Christian Brethren	47	2,918	4,988
Presbyterian Church (U.S.A.)	358	136,910	A/ 165,255
Presbyterian Church in America	94	31,031	35,998
Primitive Baptists Associations	66	1,406	A/ 1,755
Primitive Methodist, U.S.A.	4	107	120
Reformed Church in America	16	2,454	4,350
Reformed Episcopal	2	23	23
Salvation Army	37	4,516	4,880
Seventh-Day Adventists	229	46,968	A/ 57,336
Seventh Day Baptist General Conference	5	233	A/ 278
Southern Baptist Convention	1,741	951,040	A/ 1,167,850
Syrian Orthodox Church of Antioch	2	(X)	1,000
Unitarian Universalist Association	35	4,587	5,506
United Baptists	1	15	A/ 18
United Brethren in Christ	5	298	371
United Church of Christ	112	36,621	A/ 43,854
United Methodist	849	380,963	A/ 462,174
Wesleyan	41	2,498	7,014
Wisconsin Evangelical Lutheran Synod	36	3,924	5,317
Jewish estimate 1/	183	(X)	566,945
Black Baptist estimate 2/	(X)	444,964	A/ 544,592
Independent, charismatic 3/	38	(X)	35,202
Independent, noncharismatic 3/	108	(X)	84,048

(X) Not applicable.

A/ Estimated from known number of communicant, confirmed, full members.

1/ Estimates of client population, rather than institutional adherence, made by some 200 Jewish Federations.

2/ Estimates of black Baptists to the black population using a 3-step estimation procedure based on surveys taken in Georgia, Tennessee, and Oregon.

3/ Based on self-identification as an independent rather than denominational church, and self-classification as either charismatic or noncharismatic.

Note: Excludes churches who did not report adherents or membership. Membership data are for communicant, confirmed, full members.

Source: Glenmary Research Center, Atlanta, GA, *Churches and Church Membership, 1990,* (copyright).

Table 20.33. PHYSICIANS: LICENSED DOCTORS OF MEDICINE AND OSTEOPATHY IN THE STATE AND COUNTIES OF FLORIDA, JUNE 6, 1995

Location of licensee	Doctors of-- Medicine	Doctors of-- Osteopathy	Location of licensee	Doctors of-- Medicine	Doctors of-- Osteopathy
Total 1/	43,116	3,929	Jefferson	5	0
NonFlorida	11,239	1,763	Lafayette	5	0
Unknown	3	1	Lake	227	15
Alachua	1,351	11	Lee	643	99
Baker	15	1	Leon	538	17
Bay	230	12	Levy	20	2
Bradford	12	1	Liberty	3	1
Brevard	769	32	Madison	9	2
Broward	3,175	311	Manatee	393	14
Calhoun	8	0	Marion	303	17
Charlotte	218	19	Martin	242	18
Citrus	142	18	Monroe	148	26
Clay	189	23	Nassau	39	2
Collier	327	14	Okaloosa	263	14
Columbia	79	7	Okeechobee	35	4
Dade	6,703	248	Orange	1,781	113
De Soto	40	0	Osceola	145	11
Dixie	2	4	Palm Beach	2,412	222
Duval	1,898	80	Pasco	403	46
Escambia	654	25	Pinellas	2,036	355
Flagler	34	5	Polk	662	13
Franklin	8	1	Putnam	73	4
Gadsden	46	1	St. Johns	197	8
Gilchrist	3	0	St. Lucie	218	9
Glades	2	0	Santa Rosa	99	7
Gulf	14	2	Sarasota	784	37
Hamilton	6	1	Seminole	508	53
Hardee	16	0	Sumter	9	3
Hendry	19	2	Suwannee	9	0
Hernando	135	9	Taylor	11	2
Highlands	121	4	Union	16	0
Hillsborough	2,450	130	Volusia	635	76
Holmes	6	0	Wakulla	5	1
Indian River	256	10	Walton	14	0
Jackson	44	3	Washington	12	0

1/ Total includes all active, involuntary inactive, and voluntary inactive licensed persons.

Source: State of Florida, Department of Business and Professional Regulation, unpublished data.

Table 20.35. DENTISTS AND DENTAL HYGIENISTS: NUMBER LICENSED IN THE STATE AND COUNTIES OF FLORIDA, JUNE 6, 1995

Location of licensee	Dentists	Dental hygienists	Location of licensee	Dentists	Dental hygienists
Total 1/	10,433	7,700	Jefferson	3	5
NonFlorida	2,347	1,353	Lafayette	2	2
Unknown	1	0	Lake	68	67
Alachua	223	163	Lee	192	150
Baker	4	10	Leon	109	149
Bay	55	60	Levy	4	6
Bradford	7	10	Liberty	1	1
Brevard	236	230	Madison	5	3
Broward	914	740	Manatee	101	92
Calhoun	6	3	Marion	79	110
Charlotte	56	39	Martin	79	77
Citrus	36	35	Monroe	38	32
Clay	67	82	Nassau	13	22
Collier	122	89	Okaloosa	86	84
Columbia	16	20	Okeechobee	9	8
Dade	1,474	591	Orange	413	349
De Soto	6	4	Osceola	39	31
Dixie	3	5	Palm Beach	776	585
Duval	399	352	Pasco	80	73
Escambia	142	152	Pinellas	602	500
Flagler	14	8	Polk	139	134
Franklin	1	2	Putnam	19	22
Gadsden	13	14	St. Johns	45	51
Gilchrist	1	2	St. Lucie	68	68
Glades	0	3	Santa Rosa	33	64
Gulf	5	7	Sarasota	251	162
Hamilton	4	3	Seminole	191	191
Hardee	3	0	Sumter	4	3
Hendry	7	5	Suwannee	7	5
Hernando	37	31	Taylor	3	3
Highlands	35	26	Union	1	3
Hillsborough	459	352	Volusia	178	167
Holmes	2	2	Wakulla	1	3
Indian River	65	55	Walton	11	9
Jackson	17	17	Washington	6	4

1/ Total includes all active, involuntary inactive, and voluntary inactive licensed persons.

Source: State of Florida, Department of Business and Professional Regulation, unpublished data.

Table 20.36. HEALTH PRACTITIONERS: NUMBER LICENSED IN THE STATE AND COUNTIES OF FLORIDA, JUNE 6, 1995

Location of licensee	Chiro-practors	Optome-trists	Podia-trists	Therapists: Occupa-tional	Therapists: Phys-ical	Nursing home adminis-trators	Psy-chol-ogists
Total 1/	4,616	2,147	1,684	5,076	11,493	1,815	2,902
NonFlorida	1,397	600	727	1,207	2,836	278	400
Unknown	0	0	1	1	0	0	0
Alachua	37	16	8	145	225	17	131
Baker	1	1	0	1	0	1	1
Bay	22	17	6	34	75	12	11
Bradford	2	2	0	2	2	4	1
Brevard	110	44	20	144	258	33	86
Broward	490	195	172	425	1,090	138	357
Calhoun	1	1	0	0	0	2	2
Charlotte	23	11	11	39	74	10	10
Citrus	16	12	6	17	45	14	3
Clay	18	17	4	31	48	16	10
Collier	47	19	13	60	110	16	14
Columbia	5	6	0	11	13	4	2
Dade	323	225	167	398	1,082	130	516
De Soto	4	3	0	2	6	2	1
Dixie	0	0	0	0	1	0	0
Duval	95	76	38	166	355	68	98
Escambia	42	24	9	57	160	21	57
Flagler	6	1	1	8	13	2	2
Franklin	3	0	1	0	1	5	0
Gadsden	3	3	1	2	3	5	8
Gilchrist	0	0	0	0	0	1	1
Glades	0	0	0	0	2	0	0
Gulf	2	1	0	1	5	1	0
Hamilton	1	0	0	0	2	2	0
Hardee	2	2	0	4	5	0	1
Hendry	5	2	0	4	9	4	1
Hernando	18	7	5	21	46	10	4
Highlands	11	4	2	14	45	11	2
Hillsborough	177	92	48	275	494	78	246
Holmes	1	0	0	0	4	2	0
Indian River	25	11	5	36	79	13	12
Jackson	4	6	0	3	8	8	4
Jefferson	0	1	0	2	1	2	0

See footnote at end of table. Continued . . .

Table 20.36. HEALTH PRACTITIONERS: NUMBER LICENSED IN THE STATE AND COUNTIES OF FLORIDA, JUNE 6, 1995 (Continued)

Location of licensee	Chiro-practors	Optome-trists	Podia-trists	Therapists: Occupa-tional	Therapists: Phys-ical	Nursing home adminis-trators	Psy-chol-ogists
Lafayette	0	0	0	1	0	0	0
Lake	31	20	4	26	72	20	9
Lee	115	52	28	115	233	36	35
Leon	35	27	5	81	160	17	127
Levy	7	1	0	4	7	2	1
Liberty	1	0	0	0	1	0	0
Madison	1	3	0	1	3	1	1
Manatee	47	21	11	91	137	35	19
Marion	44	19	9	48	103	13	17
Martin	45	19	8	28	60	15	20
Monroe	16	9	1	12	34	7	12
Nassau	6	4	1	6	15	2	2
Okaloosa	21	21	4	30	66	17	18
Okeechobee	5	2	1	1	7	4	0
Orange	150	84	37	204	441	70	90
Osceola	23	7	3	29	54	14	5
Palm Beach	367	131	140	369	710	120	218
Pasco	62	19	9	63	127	33	12
Pinellas	275	115	78	336	947	240	128
Polk	71	38	16	67	170	49	22
Putnam	6	5	0	10	23	1	5
St. Johns	20	13	2	26	93	16	17
St. Lucie	36	9	7	39	77	12	8
Santa Rosa	12	3	0	29	52	11	11
Sarasota	136	45	34	159	308	64	61
Seminole	66	38	23	79	236	28	43
Sumter	3	2	0	1	3	2	1
Suwannee	6	2	0	3	10	4	1
Taylor	3	1	1	0	2	2	0
Union	0	0	0	0	1	0	1
Volusia	104	36	17	104	235	66	35
Wakulla	3	0	0	1	2	1	2
Walton	6	2	0	3	5	1	0
Washington	2	0	0	0	2	2	0

1/ Total includes all active, involuntary inactive, and voluntary inactive licensed persons.

Source: State of Florida, Department of Business and Professional Regulation, unpublished data.

Table 20.37. NURSES: LICENSED REGISTERED AND PRACTICAL NURSES IN THE STATE AND COUNTIES OF FLORIDA, JUNE 6, 1995

Location of licensee	Total registered and practical nurses 1/	Registered nurses	Practical nurses	Location of licensee	Total registered and practical nurses 1/	Registered nurses	Practical nurses
Total	256,574	187,662	68,912	Jefferson	133	74	59
NonFlorida	46,221	38,475	7,746	Lafayette	41	23	18
Unknown	24	15	9	Lake	2,599	1,572	1,027
Alachua	4,585	3,718	867	Lee	6,401	4,616	1,785
Baker	216	159	57	Leon	3,205	2,388	817
Bay	2,338	1,569	769	Levy	345	198	147
Bradford	224	140	84	Liberty	51	20	31
Brevard	6,317	4,833	1,484	Madison	186	83	103
Broward	22,946	16,352	6,594	Manatee	3,687	2,464	1,223
Calhoun	131	61	70	Marion	2,992	2,169	823
Charlotte	2,398	1,585	813	Martin	1,746	1,364	382
Citrus	1,510	973	537	Monroe	1,121	939	182
Clay	1,996	1,511	485	Nassau	531	398	133
Collier	2,689	1,781	908	Okaloosa	2,152	1,501	651
Columbia	753	521	232	Okeechobee	383	205	178
Dade	20,819	15,256	5,563	Orange	10,424	7,373	3,051
De Soto	383	192	191	Osceola	1,452	938	514
Dixie	96	55	41	Palm Beach	14,130	10,814	3,316
Duval	9,726	7,486	2,240	Pasco	4,637	3,021	1,616
Escambia	4,708	3,043	1,665	Pinellas	18,465	13,180	5,285
Flagler	542	414	128	Polk	5,732	3,761	1,971
Franklin	104	49	55	Putnam	807	446	361
Gadsden	464	272	192	St. Johns	1,557	1,113	444
Gilchrist	126	77	49	St. Lucie	2,505	1,748	757
Glades	33	21	12	Santa Rosa	1,840	1,256	584
Gulf	159	75	84	Sarasota	6,496	4,367	2,129
Hamilton	87	41	46	Seminole	5,229	3,934	1,295
Hardee	185	88	97	Sumter	308	160	148
Hendry	255	140	115	Suwannee	477	255	222
Hernando	1,978	1,285	693	Taylor	140	62	78
Highlands	1,169	725	444	Union	115	71	44
Hillsborough	13,458	9,527	3,931	Volusia	6,682	4,614	2,068
Holmes	197	95	102	Wakulla	178	90	88
Indian River	1,664	1,235	429	Walton	307	150	157
Jackson	735	401	334	Washington	284	125	159

1/ Includes active, involuntary inactive, and voluntary inactive licensed registered and practical nurses.

Source: State of Florida, Department of Business and Professional Regulation, unpublished data.

Table 20.38. HEALTH-RELATED RETAILERS: LICENSED DISPENSING OPTICIANS AND PHARMACISTS IN THE STATE AND COUNTIES OF FLORIDA, JUNE 6, 1995

Location of licensee	Dispensing opticians	Phar- macists	Location of licensee	Dispensing opticians	Phar- macists
Total 1/	3,390	19,113	Jefferson	1	13
NonFlorida	243	6,889	Lafayette	0	2
Unknown	0	0	Lake	42	111
Alachua	38	372	Lee	88	320
Baker	0	5	Leon	37	254
Bay	24	114	Levy	4	11
Bradford	3	16	Liberty	0	5
Brevard	97	302	Madison	0	15
Broward	384	1,406	Manatee	47	145
Calhoun	0	15	Marion	58	147
Charlotte	21	86	Martin	20	92
Citrus	20	65	Monroe	13	56
Clay	19	65	Nassau	5	26
Collier	35	144	Okaloosa	16	97
Columbia	5	41	Okeechobee	3	14
Dade	540	1,681	Orange	127	646
De Soto	3	14	Osceola	11	53
Dixie	1	4	Palm Beach	244	908
Duval	106	559	Pasco	70	156
Escambia	42	224	Pinellas	256	977
Flagler	4	18	Polk	77	279
Franklin	0	8	Putnam	9	35
Gadsden	6	36	St. Johns	22	79
Gilchrist	2	2	St. Lucie	38	102
Glades	0	0	Santa Rosa	9	94
Gulf	1	8	Sarasota	88	326
Hamilton	0	6	Seminole	57	344
Hardee	1	8	Sumter	1	3
Hendry	2	13	Suwannee	1	14
Hernando	24	85	Taylor	1	7
Highlands	17	54	Union	1	8
Hillsborough	301	1,035	Volusia	80	347
Holmes	0	14	Wakulla	1	5
Indian River	20	68	Walton	2	19
Jackson	2	34	Washington	0	12

1/ Total includes all active, involuntary inactive, and voluntary inactive licensed persons.

Source: State of Florida, Department of Business and Professional Regulation, unpublished data.

Table 20.39. CLINICAL LAB PERSONNEL: LICENSED LAB DIRECTORS, SUPERVISORS TECHNOLOGISTS, AND TECHNICIANS IN THE STATE AND COUNTIES OF FLORIDA MAY 17, 1996

Location of licensee	Total	Di- rec- tors	Su- per- vi- sors	Tech- nolo- gists	Tech- ni- cians
Total 1/	15,825	225	4,093	8,378	3,129
NonFlorida	1,174	21	239	754	160
Alachua	448	5	123	258	62
Baker	8	0	1	6	1
Bay	86	1	21	50	14
Bradford	11	0	2	5	4
Brevard	540	5	146	309	80
Broward	1,685	23	430	767	465
Calhoun	4	0	3	1	0
Charlotte	94	1	27	52	14
Citrus	102	2	30	57	13
Clay	118	1	39	60	18
Collier	152	5	44	76	27
Columbia	63	1	4	47	11
Dade	2,795	55	577	1,521	642
De Soto	15	0	2	10	3
Dixie	4	0	0	2	2
Duval	866	16	209	478	163
Escambia	275	1	67	166	41
Flagler	22	0	7	12	3
Franklin	3	0	0	2	1
Gadsden	19	1	5	10	3
Gilchrist	3	0	2	1	0
Glades	2	0	0	2	0
Gulf	6	0	3	1	2
Hamilton	5	0	0	5	0
Hardee	11	0	1	2	8
Hendry	12	0	1	7	4
Hernando	87	1	20	43	23
Highlands	52	0	17	23	12
Hillsborough	1,206	19	305	570	312
Holmes	8	0	3	3	2
Indian River	95	2	16	64	13
Jackson	28	1	6	16	5
Jefferson	1	0	0	1	0

Location of licensee	Total	Di- rec- tors	Su- per- vi- sors	Tech- nolo- gists	Tech- ni- cians
Lafayette	1	0	0	1	0
Lake	92	1	32	43	16
Lee	285	1	88	140	56
Leon	187	2	45	116	24
Levy	21	0	9	11	1
Liberty	2	0	0	2	0
Madison	5	0	3	2	0
Manatee	159	2	54	66	37
Marion	135	3	27	70	35
Martin	92	0	26	50	16
Monroe	59	0	18	27	14
Nassau	34	0	4	28	2
Okaloosa	110	0	36	57	17
Okeechobee	26	0	6	15	5
Orange	657	9	185	345	118
Osceola	83	0	16	49	18
Palm Beach	892	11	251	490	140
Pasco	284	2	86	124	72
Pinellas	1,060	14	350	518	178
Polk	305	5	97	154	49
Putnam	35	1	7	24	3
St. Johns	101	1	28	55	17
St. Lucie	180	2	36	112	30
Santa Rosa	102	0	32	51	19
Sarasota	283	2	107	120	54
Seminole	229	3	67	126	33
Sumter	11	0	4	4	3
Suwannee	20	0	3	10	7
Taylor	13	0	2	9	2
Union	4	0	1	2	1
Volusia	335	5	115	167	48
Wakulla	9	0	5	3	1
Walton	9	0	2	4	3
Washington	5	0	1	2	2

1/ Total includes all licensed persons regardless of current status.

Source: State of Florida, Department of Business and Professional Regulation, Board of Clinical Laboratory Personnel, unpublished data.

Table 20.40. PUBLIC LIBRARIES: OPERATING EXPENDITURE AND NUMBER OF VOLUMES IN REGIONS AND COUNTIES OF FLORIDA, FISCAL YEAR 1993-94

Area and library	Total operating expenditure (dollars)	Number of volumes 1/
Regional and multi-county systems		
Central Florida Regional 2/	1,462,151	168,290
Charlotte-Glades	1,851,170	326,781
Jacksonville Public 3/	13,952,508	2,561,664
Northwest Regional 4/	1,472,770	335,461
Panhandle Public 5/	689,103	105,815
Suwannee River Regional 6/	1,035,221	176,693
West Florida Regional 7/	2,262,327	251,554
Wilderness Coast Public 8/	689,288	69,146
County		
Alachua		
Alachua County	4,971,756	631,899
Baker		
Emily Taber Public	60,292	49,293
Bradford		
Bradford County	316,118	(NA)
Brevard		
Brevard County	8,578,032	1,100,463
Broward		
Broward County	27,791,519	5,016,829
Oakland Park	345,045	43,161
Citrus		
Citrus County	1,455,048	108,455
Clay		
Clay County	1,134,961	240,387
Collier		
Collier County	2,764,307	274,442
Columbia		
Columbia County	517,819	102,487
Dade		
Brockway Memorial	216,974	58,936
Hialeah	838,623	208,816
Lafe Allen Memorial	549,574	83,219
Miami-Dade	30,391,495	3,788,140
North Miami	725,279	150,898
De Soto		
De Soto County	141,133	25,844
Flagler		
Flagler County	273,485	48,869
Gadsden		
Gadsden County	477,444	55,516
Hardee		
Hardee County	96,328	36,987
Hendry		
Hendry County	216,835	65,892
Hernando		
Hernando County	1,662,585	168,733
Highlands		
Highlands County	484,697	91,487
Hillsborough		
Bruton Memorial	408,638	81,092
Tampa-Hillsborough	12,271,998	1,961,722
Temple Terrace	438,379	78,530
Indian River		
Indian River	2,067,626	429,582
Lake		
Eustis Memorial	443,384	86,315
Fruitland Park	62,078	17,853
Lake County	1,045,482	150,458
Leesburg	649,700	138,142
Lee		
Lee County	8,874,443	744,932
Sanibel	288,226	36,347
Leon		
Leon County	3,159,886	384,229
Manatee		
Manatee County	3,281,743	502,177
Martin		
Martin County	1,752,422	203,611
Monroe		
Monroe County	1,260,331	185,852
Okaloosa		
Destin	67,868	58,681
Niceville	157,450	27,087
Robert L. F. Sikes	43,725	51,200
Okeechobee		
Okeechobee County	167,872	29,052
Orange		
Maitland	308,695	71,873

See footnotes at end of table. Continued . . .

Table 20.40. PUBLIC LIBRARIES: OPERATING EXPENDITURE AND NUMBER OF VOLUMES IN REGIONS AND COUNTIES OF FLORIDA, FISCAL YEAR 1993-94 (Continued)

Area and library	Total operating expenditure (dollars)	Number of volumes 1/
Orange (Continued)		
Orange County	14,946,168	1,727,454
Winter Park	926,941	176,159
Osceola		
Osceola County	2,687,938	277,263
Palm Beach		
Delray Beach	685,915	83,488
Highland Beach	79,025	9,068
Lake Park	165,747	56,189
Lake Worth	264,835	77,734
North Palm Beach	406,540	44,565
Palm Beach County	14,413,587	757,320
Palm Springs	300,202	43,458
Pasco		
New Port Richey	446,490	60,644
Pasco County	3,765,031	456,428
Zephyrhills	104,284	31,311
Pinellas		
Pinellas	10,364,130	1,719,872
Polk		
Haines City	108,523	37,625
Lake Wales	215,732	38,363
Lakeland	1,006,154	273,397
Latt Maxcy Memorial	90,074	25,684
Polk (Continued)		
Polk City Municipal	8,784	14,220
Winter Haven	385,107	58,134
Putnam		
Putnam County	591,389	76,268
St. Johns		
St. Johns County	1,714,329	154,040
St. Lucie		
St. Lucie County	2,475,587	506,489
Sarasota		
Sarasota County	4,355,561	478,359
Seminole		
Altamonte Springs	180,371	40,451
Seminole County	4,201,317	600,344
Taylor		
Taylor County	205,413	61,718
Union		
Union County	100,360	13,031
Volusia		
Volusia County	6,372,979	1,008,157
Walton		
Walton/DeFuniak	177,957	48,432

(NA) Not available.
1/ Includes volumes of books and bound periodicals.
2/ Serves Levy and Marion counties.
3/ Serves Duval and Nassau counties.
4/ Serves Bay, Gulf, and Liberty counties.
5/ Serves Calhoun, Holmes, Jackson, and Washington counties.
6/ Serves Hamilton, Madison, and Suwannee counties.
7/ Serves Escambia and Santa Rosa counties.
8/ Serves Franklin, Jefferson, and Wakulla counties.

Note: Libraries are omitted if they failed to report to the Division of Library Services or if they failed to meet or are not part of a system which met all of the following criteria: at least 10 hours of public service per week, a book collection of at least 2,000 volumes, at least 200 volumes purchased a year, and expenditure of at least $1,000 per year.

Source: State of Florida, Department of State, Division of Library and Information Services, *1995 Florida Library Directory with Statistics*.

Table 20.56. ELEMENTARY AND SECONDARY SCHOOLS: TOTAL STAFF AND DISTRIBUTION OF ADMINISTRATIVE STAFF IN THE STATE AND COUNTIES OF FLORIDA, FALL 1995

County	Total staff 1/	Administrative staff: Total	Officials administrators managers	Consultants/ supervisors of instruction	Principals	Assistant principals	Community education coordinators	Deans/ curriculum coordinators
Florida	140,703	8,827	1,948	652	2,522	3,055	122	528
Alachua	2,011	136	45	19	39	30	3	0
Baker	280	24	13	0	5	6	0	0
Bay	1,721	91	19	8	33	31	0	0
Bradford	298	26	10	0	8	6	0	2
Brevard	4,281	227	33	1	76	35	0	82
Broward	11,668	697	90	64	190	353	0	0
Calhoun	167	9	4	0	5	0	0	0
Charlotte	1,012	70	25	2	21	22	0	0
Citrus	984	59	20	4	18	17	0	0
Clay	1,514	111	35	6	26	44	0	0
Collier	1,794	116	29	15	31	26	6	9
Columbia	576	34	13	1	10	10	0	0
Dade	20,006	1,248	290	48	314	554	42	0
De Soto	306	23	10	0	5	6	0	2
Dixie	173	18	10	0	4	4	0	0
Duval	7,289	490	115	15	146	62	37	115
Escambia	3,075	218	51	25	61	41	6	34
Flagler	415	31	23	2	5	1	0	0
Franklin	122	11	7	0	4	0	0	0
Gadsden	592	55	14	6	15	6	0	14
Gilchrist	167	17	9	2	4	2	0	0
Glades	78	7	4	0	2	1	0	0
Gulf	169	15	5	1	7	2	0	0
Hamilton	191	20	10	1	6	1	1	1
Hardee	339	29	14	1	6	8	0	0
Hendry	433	38	15	2	11	10	0	0
Hernando	995	54	14	0	14	25	1	0
Highlands	688	48	15	3	14	16	0	0
Hillsborough	10,329	629	94	113	163	170	0	89
Holmes	261	19	7	0	7	5	0	0
Indian River	885	72	35	3	18	12	0	4
Jackson	623	40	14	0	16	10	0	0
Jefferson	159	18	8	2	4	2	1	1
Lafayette	82	8	3	2	2	0	0	1
Lake	1,594	98	13	5	37	28	0	15

See footnotes at end of table. Continued . . .

Table 20.56. ELEMENTARY AND SECONDARY SCHOOLS: TOTAL STAFF AND DISTRIBUTION OF ADMINISTRATIVE STAFF IN THE STATE AND COUNTIES OF FLORIDA, FALL 1995 (Continued)

County	Total staff 1/	Administrative staff Total	Officials administrators managers	Consultants/ supervisors of instruction	Principals	Assistant principals	Community education coordinators	Deans/ curriculum coordinators
Lee	3,280	223	49	16	68	65	0	25
Leon	2,171	144	33	9	46	56	0	0
Levy	393	35	15	1	12	6	1	0
Liberty	89	10	6	0	3	1	0	0
Madison	228	22	6	5	7	1	0	3
Manatee	1,997	122	28	8	36	47	1	2
Marion	2,301	147	30	17	42	37	5	16
Martin	998	72	19	2	19	24	5	3
Monroe	651	52	14	9	12	17	0	0
Nassau	573	43	15	0	16	7	1	4
Okaloosa	1,851	91	19	12	34	20	0	6
Okeechobee	411	32	12	0	8	10	0	2
Orange	8,190	419	62	56	133	166	0	2
Osceola	1,574	107	22	2	28	35	0	20
Palm Beach	8,734	475	63	25	138	249	0	0
Pasco	2,903	201	54	21	46	65	7	8
Pinellas	7,492	461	77	49	133	187	5	10
Polk	4,862	326	57	22	109	138	0	0
Putnam	840	73	22	4	18	18	0	11
St. Johns	1,142	97	25	12	24	27	0	9
St. Lucie	2,183	118	28	4	50	17	0	19
Santa Rosa	1,272	69	13	4	26	26	0	0
Sarasota	1,982	114	38	4	33	39	0	0
Seminole	3,231	163	20	1	47	86	0	9
Sumter	386	27	13	1	9	4	0	0
Suwannee	348	27	13	0	6	8	0	0
Taylor	277	29	12	2	7	2	0	6
Union	146	14	7	1	3	3	0	0
Volusia	4,062	229	26	7	64	132	0	0
Wakulla	271	25	12	1	5	3	0	4
Walton	353	29	10	4	7	8	0	0
Washington	235	25	12	2	6	5	0	0

1/ Administrative and instructional staff.
Note: Data are for public schools only. Does not include special schools.

Source: State of Florida, Department of Education, Division of Public Schools, Bureau of Information and Accountability Services, prepublication release.

Table 20.57. ELEMENTARY AND SECONDARY SCHOOLS: DISTRIBUTION OF INSTRUCTIONAL STAFF IN THE STATE AND COUNTIES OF FLORIDA, FALL 1995

County	Teachers: Elementary 1/	Teachers: Secondary 2/	Teachers: Exceptional student education	Teachers: Other	Guidance counselors	Visiting teachers/ social workers	School psychologists	Librarians/ audiovisual workers	Other 3/
Florida	51,516	43,604	19,122	4,971	4,829	688	913	2,538	3,695
Alachua	658	694	286	14	69	0	14	49	91
Baker	97	107	28	3	9	0	1	6	5
Bay	559	557	307	40	63	3	11	39	51
Bradford	99	103	41	5	8	0	1	9	6
Brevard	1,718	1,240	675	96	135	7	19	87	77
Broward	4,511	3,442	1,252	907	403	98	88	202	68
Calhoun	58	59	22	2	6	0	0	5	6
Charlotte	308	377	141	10	32	3	7	18	46
Citrus	351	327	130	29	33	3	6	18	28
Clay	602	479	212	12	44	3	0	28	23
Collier	676	548	259	25	76	3	18	32	41
Columbia	217	210	72	3	17	1	2	12	8
Dade	7,950	5,527	2,405	1,087	875	99	163	323	329
De Soto	113	103	30	14	7	2	0	5	9
Dixie	65	48	26	2	4	0	0	4	6
Duval	2,936	2,121	1,102	92	204	41	34	140	129
Escambia	1,095	1,083	415	25	97	15	13	63	51
Flagler	120	131	52	30	11	0	2	5	33
Franklin	51	38	16	0	3	0	0	3	0
Gadsden	214	190	61	27	17	3	4	14	7
Gilchrist	54	60	21	3	5	1	1	3	2
Glades	30	29	6	0	2	0	0	2	2
Gulf	58	59	20	2	5	2	2	3	3
Hamilton	62	62	21	4	8	1	1	4	8
Hardee	122	115	32	16	10	0	1	7	7
Hendry	172	127	53	10	15	0	2	9	7
Hernando	358	372	97	6	43	7	6	16	36
Highlands	238	202	108	21	26	4	4	12	25
Hillsborough	4,031	2,808	1,645	211	364	102	77	185	277
Holmes	99	99	24	1	8	0	1	8	2
Indian River	350	259	112	31	21	1	7	9	23
Jackson	208	215	75	23	24	0	2	13	23
Jefferson	47	53	24	4	4	1	0	3	5
Lafayette	31	27	7	3	2	0	0	2	2
Lake	553	489	219	67	61	6	11	34	56
Lee	1,102	1,100	519	55	121	21	28	70	41

See footnotes at end of table.

Continued . . .

Table 20.57. ELEMENTARY AND SECONDARY SCHOOLS: DISTRIBUTION OF INSTRUCTIONAL STAFF IN THE STATE AND COUNTIES OF FLORIDA, FALL 1995 (Continued)

County	Teachers				Guidance counselors	Visiting teachers/ social workers	School psychologists	Librarians/ audio-visual workers	Other 3/
	Elementary 1/	Secondary 2/	Exceptional student education	Other					
Leon	719	651	335	70	80	12	16	43	101
Levy	142	126	52	4	12	2	0	10	10
Liberty	30	31	10	4	1	0	0	3	0
Madison	72	83	34	1	6	0	0	3	7
Manatee	776	617	308	19	66	15	13	39	22
Marion	885	734	289	58	69	15	15	43	46
Martin	305	333	147	47	30	2	6	19	37
Monroe	235	210	92	22	15	4	5	6	10
Nassau	202	195	83	3	21	3	3	15	5
Okaloosa	744	697	153	12	61	2	9	40	42
Okeechobee	163	122	47	12	15	0	3	8	9
Orange	2,713	2,581	1,075	431	264	42	51	124	490
Osceola	499	538	166	79	62	3	11	25	84
Palm Beach	3,021	2,843	1,493	150	254	0	56	119	323
Pasco	943	915	457	49	107	20	19	59	133
Pinellas	2,414	2,382	1,180	278	229	66	55	130	297
Polk	1,916	1,503	540	163	175	7	42	109	81
Putnam	322	251	88	13	34	1	7	20	31
St. Johns	385	434	112	9	41	2	6	21	35
St. Lucie	596	565	187	537	50	6	9	32	83
Santa Rosa	486	459	144	3	42	2	6	26	35
Sarasota	712	621	380	9	43	11	12	15	65
Seminole	1,179	1,178	399	65	110	17	15	52	53
Sumter	134	130	43	12	10	0	1	9	20
Suwannee	130	128	28	6	12	0	0	6	11
Taylor	104	74	36	12	5	2	1	4	10
Union	50	58	15	0	5	0	0	3	1
Volusia	1,442	1,349	620	20	153	27	24	93	105
Wakulla	93	94	36	2	8	0	0	7	6
Walton	123	141	36	0	7	0	1	8	8
Washington	68	101	22	1	10	0	1	5	2

1/ Prekindergarten through grade 6.
2/ Grades 7 through 12.
3/ Nonadministrative/instructional professional staff.
Note: Data are for public schools only. Does not include special schools.

Source: State of Florida, Department of Education, Division of Public Schools, Bureau of Information and Accountability Services, prepublication release.

Table 20.59. ELEMENTARY AND SECONDARY SCHOOLS: NUMBER AND AVERAGE SALARY OF SPECIFIED DISTRICT STAFF PERSONNEL IN THE STATE AND COUNTIES OF FLORIDA, 1995-96

(salaries in dollars)

		Principals						Board members	
	Superin-tendent	High school		Junior high/ middle school		Elementary			
County	salary	Number	Salary	Number	Salary	Number	Salary	Number	Salary
Florida	86,837	324	65,526	427	61,559	1,480	59,519	343	20,513
Alachua	107,000	5	62,412	7	59,095	23	53,805	5	23,161
Baker	84,896	1	56,776	1	54,444	3	54,666	5	16,878
Bay	79,710	3	61,142	7	56,620	19	54,117	5	21,820
Bradford	64,760	1	56,863	1	52,598	5	47,331	5	17,140
Brevard	110,250	10	63,183	15	55,863	51	54,255	5	25,673
Broward	161,500	23	77,466	24	75,378	102	69,970	7	25,699
Calhoun	68,063	1	56,100	1	51,100	1	52,200	5	16,404
Charlotte	96,000	3	68,177	4	60,301	9	61,530	5	21,554
Citrus	76,951	3	60,815	4	58,335	9	56,482	5	20,958
Clay	78,677	4	52,443	5	53,737	16	53,275	5	20,491
Collier	100,487	4	80,002	6	65,402	17	61,124	5	22,851
Columbia	78,409	1	54,157	2	53,032	7	53,170	5	17,716
Dade	220,401	32	81,364	48	76,689	195	75,256	7	27,859
De Soto	62,659	1	55,970	1	51,178	3	50,619	5	16,596
Dixie	93,781	1	55,050	1	47,345	2	50,045	5	16,438
Duval	133,808	16	61,806	22	56,035	100	52,872	7	25,761
Escambia	102,597	8	56,681	12	53,563	38	51,613	5	24,202
Flagler	78,346	1	58,104	1	52,151	3	50,182	5	17,786
Franklin	65,376	1	50,489	0	0	2	50,131	5	16,247
Gadsden	77,721	4	53,516	2	50,824	7	50,026	5	18,343
Gilchrist	66,499	2	52,755	0	0	2	46,852	5	16,337
Glades	63,428	1	44,970	0	0	1	43,930	5	15,994
Gulf	79,004	2	51,550	1	51,077	3	49,500	5	16,503
Hamilton	67,553	1	54,483	1	51,983	3	48,513	5	16,424
Hardee	66,407	1	51,937	1	50,003	4	48,360	5	17,041
Hendry	68,630	2	54,890	2	53,790	5	52,700	5	16,688
Hernando	83,000	3	59,453	3	57,023	8	55,813	5	20,418
Highlands	84,926	3	68,397	3	62,324	8	58,817	5	19,843
Hillsborough	139,993	15	72,648	27	65,194	106	61,890	7	26,373
Holmes	63,155	2	48,690	1	46,425	2	47,185	5	16,716
Indian River	95,000	2	65,672	3	61,350	12	58,714	5	20,854
Jackson	72,093	2	46,950	1	46,000	5	50,960	5	18,390
Jefferson	62,310	1	52,873	1	51,594	1	45,602	5	16,492
Lafayette	62,472	0	0	0	0	1	40,450	4	15,280
Lake	82,271	6	55,604	8	54,229	18	53,912	5	22,632
Lee	91,499	9	64,760	12	66,149	36	53,333	5	25,251

See footnote at end of table. Continued . . .

Table 20.59. ELEMENTARY AND SECONDARY SCHOOLS: NUMBER AND AVERAGE SALARY OF SPECIFIED DISTRICT STAFF PERSONNEL IN THE STATE AND COUNTIES OF FLORIDA, 1995-96 (Continued)

(salaries in dollars)

County	Superin- tendent salary	Principals: High school Number	Principals: High school Salary	Principals: Junior high/ middle school Number	Principals: Junior high/ middle school Salary	Principals: Elementary Number	Principals: Elementary Salary	Board members Number	Board members Salary
Leon	96,114	4	57,398	9	53,944	22	53,761	5	23,444
Levy	65,839	2	47,048	1	49,588	4	44,767	5	17,426
Liberty	60,868	1	49,606	0	0	1	49,606	5	15,506
Madison	63,341	1	47,769	4	45,320	2	47,309	5	16,765
Manatee	110,250	3	64,766	6	61,111	25	57,038	5	22,658
Marion	85,174	6	64,689	7	62,618	25	58,391	0	0
Martin	77,797	3	59,911	4	53,229	9	56,722	5	21,213
Monroe	85,100	3	58,342	1	56,960	8	54,305	5	20,147
Nassau	74,654	3	55,337	3	52,638	9	52,609	5	18,490
Okaloosa	77,888	4	63,402	6	59,711	21	57,245	5	21,377
Okeechobee	79,429	1	64,601	1	56,061	5	55,785	5	17,613
Orange	119,574	12	68,167	23	57,544	87	56,724	7	26,956
Osceola	77,378	4	63,685	7	59,872	14	58,617	5	20,731
Palm Beach	125,000	20	66,660	24	61,561	86	57,611	7	27,722
Pasco	93,530	10	62,234	8	55,920	27	51,510	5	19,612
Pinellas	123,521	16	64,949	22	62,945	78	59,851	7	27,463
Polk	101,981	13	63,070	20	59,045	65	52,658	5	25,778
Putnam	71,589	3	58,831	4	53,665	9	52,823	5	19,528
St. Johns	0	2	60,987	5	55,342	13	54,179	5	20,648
St. Lucie	85,258	5	63,845	7	59,327	18	58,611	5	22,531
Santa Rosa	75,657	5	58,697	5	53,875	14	52,296	5	20,604
Sarasota	97,500	4	71,556	5	67,330	20	65,568	5	24,422
Seminole	112,812	6	71,637	10	63,502	29	61,140	5	24,662
Sumter	78,854	2	58,374	2	53,464	5	51,481	5	17,780
Suwannee	67,908	1	55,285	1	53,626	2	53,626	5	17,437
Taylor	63,273	1	50,810	1	48,837	3	49,175	5	16,747
Union	67,240	0	0	1	48,041	1	48,041	5	16,460
Volusia	103,400	9	67,561	9	58,206	43	57,263	5	25,594
Wakulla	71,082	1	61,810	1	58,020	3	53,975	5	16,688
Walton	66,444	2	54,790	1	54,197	3	51,461	5	17,586
Washington	63,167	2	53,414	1	47,676	2	47,234	5	16,719

Note: Data are for public schools only. The number of months worked varies from district to district. Salaries have not been adjusted for a full 12-month calendar year. Does not include special schools such as university laboratory schools.

Source: State of Florida, Department of Education, Division of Administration, *Statistical Brief: Florida District Staff Salaries of Selected Positions, 1995-96*. Series 97-02B.

Table 20.60. ELEMENTARY AND SECONDARY SCHOOLS: NUMBER AND AVERAGE SALARY OF TEACHERS BY DEGREE ATTAINMENT IN THE STATE AND COUNTIES OF FLORIDA, 1994-95

(salaries in dollars)

County	Total		Bachelor's		Master's		Specialist		Doctorate	
	Number	Average salary	Number	Average salary	Number	Average salary	Number	Average salary	Number	Average salary
Florida	126,264	32,601	76,425	29,834	45,268	36,239	3,273	43,388	1,298	41,512
Alachua	1,821	28,989	718	26,021	945	30,343	114	33,434	44	36,810
Baker	253	28,948	166	27,226	85	32,145	2	36,039	0	0
Bay	1,511	30,772	1,028	29,443	446	33,383	30	35,770	7	38,154
Bradford	264	27,606	174	25,633	82	31,462	5	27,376	3	36,982
Brevard	3,942	31,351	2,360	28,815	1,504	35,006	49	38,405	29	36,193
Broward	10,775	35,771	6,316	33,349	4,093	38,831	245	43,960	121	42,050
Calhoun	152	30,420	96	29,264	53	32,252	1	40,325	2	32,425
Charlotte	938	30,026	524	27,238	391	33,292	15	38,250	8	37,533
Citrus	893	30,091	492	27,241	377	33,443	16	35,924	8	35,718
Clay	1,317	27,532	876	25,924	435	30,701	5	31,795	1	35,600
Collier	1,563	36,629	790	33,151	724	39,928	34	44,323	15	43,191
Columbia	526	29,361	327	27,189	186	32,747	9	34,806	4	37,137
Dade	18,100	37,718	9,426	32,901	6,680	41,608	1,627	47,410	367	47,687
De Soto	272	29,182	198	27,574	67	33,439	4	34,817	3	32,734
Dixie	140	26,767	98	24,853	38	30,494	1	29,536	3	41,136
Duval	6,704	31,906	4,296	29,814	2,312	35,473	58	39,604	38	39,738
Escambia	2,834	30,000	1,578	27,226	1,209	33,388	24	35,865	23	36,181
Flagler	299	29,414	198	28,193	100	31,702	1	42,478	0	0
Franklin	111	27,571	73	25,499	36	31,294	1	36,296	1	36,067
Gadsden	498	27,692	318	26,522	175	29,758	4	30,612	1	26,577
Gilchrist	132	29,380	80	27,927	48	31,681	3	31,026	1	30,221
Glades	68	28,018	47	26,145	21	32,209	0	0	0	0
Gulf	150	28,710	98	27,455	51	31,010	0	0	1	34,462
Hamilton	169	28,012	133	26,977	32	31,121	4	37,569	0	0
Hardee	314	29,864	240	28,597	69	33,989	3	33,197	2	34,523
Hendry	374	29,850	354	29,368	12	38,378	0	0	8	38,371
Hernando	863	27,442	534	25,048	314	31,213	9	34,691	6	32,301
Highlands	609	31,415	413	29,381	190	35,681	3	33,083	3	39,596
Hillsborough	9,287	30,829	5,883	28,315	3,228	34,982	105	39,166	71	37,950
Holmes	220	29,662	133	27,381	85	33,099	1	34,798	1	35,650
Indian River	713	32,220	445	30,721	234	34,522	28	35,539	6	38,084
Jackson	562	26,871	286	24,356	256	29,249	17	32,635	3	30,980
Jefferson	132	29,171	84	27,907	43	31,279	4	33,347	1	28,006
Lafayette	72	25,433	57	24,666	14	28,627	1	24,470	0	0

See footnote at end of table.

Continued . . .

Table 20.60. ELEMENTARY AND SECONDARY SCHOOLS: NUMBER AND AVERAGE SALARY OF TEACHERS BY DEGREE ATTAINMENT IN THE STATE AND COUNTIES OF FLORIDA, 1994-95 (Continued)

(salaries in dollars)

County	Total		Bachelor's		Master's		Specialist		Doctorate	
	Number	Average salary	Number	Average salary	Number	Average salary	Number	Average salary	Number	Average salary
Lake	1,457	29,284	967	27,070	458	33,509	5	37,035	27	35,496
Lee	2,906	32,191	1,725	29,608	1,101	35,688	48	39,660	32	39,871
Leon	1,947	31,379	1,004	29,122	865	33,425	45	38,630	33	36,511
Levy	342	28,846	214	27,386	124	31,258	3	33,192	1	29,256
Liberty	73	29,684	47	28,410	26	31,987	0	0	0	0
Madison	208	29,159	140	27,493	64	32,686	4	31,049	0	0
Manatee	1,788	30,717	1,048	27,846	683	34,361	46	39,808	11	39,997
Marion	2,069	28,772	1,393	27,103	630	31,894	31	36,847	15	35,981
Martin	909	30,042	564	27,773	319	33,289	19	39,420	7	39,428
Monroe	578	33,983	378	32,589	194	36,751	2	34,379	4	31,339
Nassau	516	32,316	322	30,499	189	35,361	3	36,328	2	31,199
Okaloosa	1,753	31,898	1,046	29,748	665	34,833	27	37,630	15	41,405
Okeechobee	371	31,324	259	29,362	106	35,707	6	38,566	0	0
Orange	7,265	30,397	4,439	27,979	2,685	34,039	81	37,006	60	37,346
Osceola	1,374	28,383	909	26,675	444	31,537	8	37,078	13	34,732
Palm Beach	7,963	36,652	4,972	34,234	2,757	40,314	138	45,713	96	43,678
Pasco	2,585	27,924	1,725	26,358	840	31,021	5	29,720	15	33,960
Pinellas	6,825	33,259	4,262	31,209	2,409	36,464	95	39,994	59	39,658
Polk	4,276	28,456	3,440	27,057	803	34,142	26	36,209	7	34,884
Putnam	793	29,031	527	27,336	255	32,374	8	33,483	3	30,900
St. Johns	948	30,040	599	28,318	346	32,968	0	0	3	36,227
St. Lucie	1,484	32,298	959	29,882	485	36,488	28	40,401	12	37,173
Santa Rosa	1,190	29,490	759	27,389	413	33,109	13	34,028	5	37,745
Sarasota	1,797	36,272	892	32,037	873	40,199	9	48,793	23	46,591
Seminole	2,940	32,963	1,705	29,694	1,118	36,983	88	41,982	29	42,792
Sumter	328	30,599	232	28,958	92	34,391	4	38,548	0	0
Suwannee	322	31,553	213	29,668	103	35,048	6	38,466	0	0
Taylor	221	29,861	130	26,951	83	33,702	4	36,361	4	38,250
Union	126	26,478	94	25,427	31	29,736	1	24,300	0	0
Volusia	3,580	30,594	2,136	28,066	1,315	34,054	91	37,432	38	36,558
Wakulla	231	27,327	151	25,987	76	29,645	3	34,595	1	31,635
Walton	307	28,593	218	27,294	87	31,715	1	32,948	1	35,784
Washington	214	28,965	117	26,935	94	31,417	2	29,935	1	34,160

Note: Average salary paid to a professional on the instructional salary schedule negotiated by a Florida school district. Data are for public schools only.

Source: State of Florida, Department of Education, Division of Administration, *Statistical Brief: Teacher Salary, Experience and Degree Level, 1994-95.*

Table 20.62. ELEMENTARY AND SECONDARY SCHOOLS: STUDENT-TEACHER RATIOS AND SPECIFIED PERSONNEL PERCENTAGES AND RATIOS IN THE STATE AND COUNTIES OF FLORIDA, 1994-95

County	FTE students per FTE teacher		Percentage of full-time staff who are--		Ratio of--	
	Elementary 1/	Secondary	Teachers 2/	Administrators	Teacher aides to teachers 2/	Administrators to teachers 2/
Florida	23.69	20.19	49.24	3.72	1:4.71	1:13.23
Alachua	23.48	17.17	43.39	3.67	1:4.16	1:11.83
Baker	26.44	17.95	45.96	5.13	1:3.94	1:8.96
Bay	24.95	18.36	49.92	3.15	1:3.82	1:15.82
Bradford	23.55	16.64	58.21	6.04	1:3.82	1:9.64
Brevard	21.83	21.93	52.22	3.23	1:7.34	1:16.15
Broward	25.97	22.90	53.30	3.56	1:5.93	1:14.98
Calhoun	21.81	15.47	53.01	5.26	1:9.40	1:10.07
Charlotte	24.75	17.88	45.50	3.94	1:4.17	1:11.56
Citrus	22.25	18.23	46.98	3.31	1:5.35	1:14.19
Clay	22.77	22.17	52.18	4.74	1:10.54	1:11.00
Collier	22.41	18.90	46.16	3.56	1:3.16	1:12.95
Columbia	21.94	19.32	45.67	3.39	1:3.46	1:13.47
Dade	22.99	24.50	52.18	4.05	1:5.63	1:12.87
De Soto	22.91	15.92	46.93	3.79	1:3.25	1:12.38
Dixie	20.31	19.59	42.81	5.56	1:3.19	1:7.70
Duval	25.19	21.80	54.03	4.32	1:4.90	1:12.51
Escambia	21.96	17.87	48.50	3.72	1:4.45	1:13.03
Flagler	23.31	17.86	42.95	4.07	1:4.17	1:10.56
Franklin	17.25	17.76	51.49	5.45	1:6.11	1:9.45
Gadsden	20.37	19.83	44.59	5.37	1:2.78	1:8.31
Gilchrist	24.42	19.75	47.39	6.34	1:4.23	1:7.47
Glades	20.24	15.25	48.84	5.43	1:4.84	1:9.00
Gulf	19.28	17.64	48.77	4.91	1:6.04	1:9.92
Hamilton	20.15	15.63	41.48	5.49	1:3.43	1:7.55
Hardee	21.44	15.14	40.44	3.96	1:2.22	1:10.20
Hendry	22.87	23.18	40.28	4.42	1:2.60	1:9.10
Hernando	24.53	19.08	47.94	3.31	1:3.76	1:14.49
Highlands	26.23	22.15	43.28	4.02	1:3.65	1:10.76
Hillsborough	20.07	20.97	48.51	3.55	1:4.14	1:13.68
Holmes	21.33	16.02	50.47	4.44	1:5.02	1:11.36
Indian River	22.38	24.15	47.54	4.99	1:5.46	1:9.52
Jackson	20.90	15.95	47.71	3.76	1:3.82	1:12.68
Jefferson	25.07	17.19	39.67	5.90	1:2.88	1:6.72
Lafayette	16.90	17.65	47.48	5.76	1:6.00	1:8.25
Lake	24.93	20.92	47.54	3.69	1:4.78	1:12.87
Lee	26.68	18.78	49.71	5.04	1:7.87	1:9.86

See footnotes at end of table. Continued . . .

Table 20.62. ELEMENTARY AND SECONDARY SCHOOLS: STUDENT-TEACHER RATIOS AND SPECIFIED PERSONNEL PERCENTAGES AND RATIOS IN THE STATE AND COUNTIES OF FLORIDA, 1994-95 (Continued)

County	FTE students per FTE teacher		Percentage of full-time staff who are--		Ratio of--	
	Elementary 1/	Secondary	Teachers 2/	Administrators	Teacher aides to teachers 2/	Administrators to teachers 2/
Leon	23.74	19.34	45.19	3.55	1:3.65	1:12.74
Levy	22.16	17.85	45.48	4.94	1:3.65	1:9.20
Liberty	20.60	17.57	49.65	6.99	1:7.88	1:7.10
Madison	24.71	15.40	47.20	5.11	1:3.73	1:9.23
Manatee	24.23	18.67	46.44	3.30	1:3.73	1:14.05
Marion	22.08	19.50	45.50	3.33	1:3.27	1:13.64
Martin	24.28	17.00	46.78	4.08	1:4.69	1:11.47
Monroe	22.73	18.88	44.73	2.94	1:4.34	1:15.22
Nassau	27.37	20.11	44.81	4.00	1:4.02	1:11.21
Okaloosa	21.68	17.47	50.47	3.11	1:6.78	1:16.21
Okeechobee	21.17	22.54	43.31	4.20	1:2.42	1:10.30
Orange	26.17	19.79	44.91	2.92	1:4.12	1:15.39
Osceola	27.30	20.20	45.01	3.36	1:3.61	1:13.38
Palm Beach	25.34	18.51	51.08	3.25	1:5.00	1:15.71
Pasco	23.56	18.68	48.15	3.99	1:4.98	1:12.07
Pinellas	24.24	18.11	49.51	3.73	1:4.12	1:13.26
Polk	21.21	19.79	47.82	3.92	1:3.99	1:12.18
Putnam	22.21	17.66	43.64	4.52	1:3.54	1:9.65
St. Johns	24.57	14.51	49.39	5.55	1:6.10	1:8.89
St. Lucie	26.88	18.50	49.19	3.16	1:4.55	1:15.57
Santa Rosa	21.78	17.58	55.88	3.64	1:6.13	1:15.34
Sarasota	26.77	20.97	47.14	3.04	1:5.19	1:15.50
Seminole	25.63	20.04	53.99	3.20	1:6.63	1:16.88
Sumter	24.25	17.63	42.09	3.67	1:2.59	1:11.46
Suwannee	21.63	20.38	46.46	4.09	1:4.83	1:11.34
Taylor	23.02	19.07	41.50	6.07	1:2.69	1:6.83
Union	20.72	19.04	44.19	5.99	1:5.90	1:7.37
Volusia	22.67	17.44	47.73	2.48	1:4.91	1:19.21
Wakulla	25.45	17.37	46.58	5.34	1:4.36	1:8.72
Walton	22.80	16.19	43.91	4.11	1:2.90	1:10.67
Washington	25.47	12.39	45.05	5.86	1:3.92	1:7.69

FTE Full-time equivalent.

1/ Kindergarten through grade 6.

2/ Teachers in grades prekindergarten through grade 12 and exceptional education, primary education specialists, and others including postsecondary vocational instructors and adult education instructors.

Note: Data are for public schools only.

Source: State of Florida, Department of Education, Division of Administration, *Profiles of Florida School Districts, 1994-95, Student and Staff Data.* EIAS Series 96-14.

Table 20.63. ELEMENTARY AND SECONDARY SCHOOLS: ALL FUNDS REVENUE BY MAJOR SOURCE IN THE STATE AND COUNTIES OF FLORIDA, 1993-94

(in thousands of dollars, except where indicated)

County	Total all revenue receipts	Revenue per FTE (dollars)	Revenue receipts from-- Federal sources	State sources	Local sources
Florida 1/	12,104,175	5,464	921,140	6,158,618	5,024,416
Alachua	162,031	5,684	16,982	96,818	48,230
Baker	22,814	4,955	1,901	17,716	3,197
Bay	126,897	5,105	10,780	80,625	35,492
Bradford	21,241	4,982	1,927	15,883	3,432
Brevard	329,273	5,150	20,400	175,034	133,839
Broward	1,220,859	5,538	76,153	617,046	527,660
Calhoun	11,229	4,932	1,211	8,514	1,503
Charlotte	86,698	5,716	4,980	25,766	55,952
Citrus	74,649	5,437	5,085	34,145	35,419
Clay	110,200	4,708	5,987	77,172	27,041
Collier	175,186	6,654	12,984	28,939	133,263
Columbia	48,920	5,532	4,088	36,660	8,172
Dade	2,007,418	5,419	169,912	1,148,156	689,350
De Soto	24,356	5,289	2,609	16,051	5,696
Dixie	11,742	5,478	1,312	8,528	1,902
Duval	620,876	5,178	52,999	355,646	212,231
Escambia	244,241	5,220	26,486	157,916	59,840
Flagler	36,206	6,281	1,618	12,497	22,091
Franklin	8,933	5,487	1,042	5,155	2,736
Gadsden	48,950	5,838	7,800	35,774	5,376
Gilchrist	12,012	5,486	906	9,356	1,750
Glades	6,173	6,230	624	2,604	2,945
Gulf	12,793	5,554	980	7,520	4,293
Hamilton	14,888	6,364	1,431	10,472	2,985
Hardee	28,172	5,434	3,909	16,623	7,640
Hendry	36,798	5,516	4,522	21,236	11,040
Hernando	81,556	5,580	4,355	39,814	37,387
Highlands	58,670	5,584	5,363	31,960	21,347
Hillsborough	802,341	5,434	79,436	455,171	267,734
Holmes	17,894	4,962	1,998	13,950	1,946
Indian River	82,608	6,495	4,666	22,284	55,658
Jackson	44,378	4,947	4,746	34,149	5,483
Jefferson	12,599	5,816	1,397	9,343	1,859
Lafayette	6,051	5,854	571	4,547	934
Lake	125,566	5,296	9,516	70,772	45,279

See footnotes at end of table. Continued . . .

Table 20.63. ELEMENTARY AND SECONDARY SCHOOLS: ALL FUNDS REVENUE BY MAJOR SOURCE IN THE STATE AND COUNTIES OF FLORIDA, 1993-94 (Continued)

(in thousands of dollars, except where indicated)

County	Total all revenue receipts	Revenue per FTE (dollars)	Revenue receipts from-- Federal sources	State sources	Local sources
Lee	295,704	5,895	19,206	88,876	187,622
Leon	188,880	5,782	12,911	112,895	63,075
Levy	28,740	5,414	2,363	19,799	6,578
Liberty	6,474	5,229	624	5,111	738
Madison	17,223	5,369	2,178	12,938	2,107
Manatee	172,717	5,567	12,611	78,772	81,334
Marion	172,120	5,079	14,817	104,383	52,920
Martin	88,837	6,108	4,577	14,660	69,600
Monroe	58,490	6,335	4,252	12,805	41,432
Nassau	46,306	4,941	2,623	26,984	16,699
Okaloosa	138,615	4,730	12,154	91,760	34,701
Okeechobee	33,130	5,409	3,863	21,444	7,823
Orange	665,159	5,233	45,613	296,456	323,090
Osceola	129,756	5,382	6,672	71,637	51,447
Palm Beach	833,540	6,310	49,634	242,005	541,901
Pasco	218,674	5,531	16,079	122,329	80,265
Pinellas	577,723	5,312	38,289	254,575	284,859
Polk	362,093	4,910	33,414	222,261	106,417
Putnam	67,088	5,327	6,823	41,856	18,409
St. Johns	89,147	5,345	5,338	40,562	43,248
St. Lucie	144,383	5,766	12,259	60,077	72,048
Santa Rosa	92,397	4,975	7,006	62,478	22,914
Sarasota	218,146	6,540	11,299	55,986	150,861
Seminole	266,444	5,047	12,028	142,009	112,407
Sumter	27,761	5,056	3,005	19,223	5,533
Suwannee	28,512	4,997	2,617	20,512	5,383
Taylor	20,406	5,319	2,139	12,657	5,610
Union	10,772	5,398	783	8,854	1,135
Volusia	299,782	5,520	19,171	145,707	134,905
Wakulla	20,958	5,277	1,307	16,496	3,154
Walton	27,155	5,634	2,566	11,838	12,751
Washington	21,607	5,464	2,239	16,623	2,745
Eckerd Youth	214	5,209	3	212	0

FTE Full-time equivalent.
1/ Includes special schools.
Note: Data are for public schools only.

Source: State of Florida, Department of Education, Division of Public Schools, *Profiles of Florida School Districts, 1993-94, Financial Data Statistical Report*. EIAS Series 95-21, July 1995.

Table 20.65. ELEMENTARY AND SECONDARY SCHOOLS: ALL FUNDS EXPENDITURE BY MAJOR TYPE IN THE STATE AND COUNTIES OF FLORIDA, 1993-94

(in thousands of dollars, except where indicated)

County	Total expenditure all funds	Total current expenditure	Current expenditure per FTE (dollars)	Capital outlay	Debt service
Florida 1/	12,780,952	10,467,974	4,724	1,765,579	547,399
Alachua	180,366	136,956	4,803	31,543	11,867
Baker	24,437	21,803	4,735	2,406	228
Bay	126,093	117,504	4,727	7,962	623
Bradford	20,358	19,655	4,610	408	296
Brevard	371,008	287,109	4,490	74,142	9,758
Broward	1,278,625	1,012,134	4,591	194,068	72,423
Calhoun	11,094	10,338	4,541	706	50
Charlotte	88,274	73,571	4,851	10,426	4,277
Citrus	76,530	61,632	4,488	14,405	493
Clay	113,871	94,383	4,031	18,028	1,460
Collier	200,181	143,329	5,444	47,808	9,044
Columbia	49,709	38,777	4,385	10,411	521
Dade	2,103,547	1,823,689	4,922	231,962	47,896
De Soto	23,667	22,011	4,779	1,392	264
Dixie	16,364	10,458	4,878	5,760	146
Duval	636,220	537,666	4,484	77,786	20,768
Escambia	262,361	225,278	4,815	29,723	7,360
Flagler	37,421	27,540	4,777	5,949	3,931
Franklin	9,134	8,208	5,041	576	350
Gadsden	50,248	41,147	4,907	8,943	158
Gilchrist	12,069	10,712	4,892	1,051	306
Glades	5,832	5,069	5,115	679	83
Gulf	12,446	11,654	5,059	556	235
Hamilton	14,401	13,330	5,697	896	175
Hardee	28,609	25,612	4,940	2,659	338
Hendry	39,344	32,822	4,919	2,409	4,113
Hernando	89,995	64,815	4,434	15,969	9,211
Highlands	57,469	51,094	4,863	4,625	1,750
Hillsborough	849,312	727,456	4,926	101,449	20,406
Holmes	17,627	16,759	4,646	685	184
Indian River	103,878	65,074	5,116	31,537	7,267
Jackson	43,684	40,191	4,480	2,690	803
Jefferson	11,628	10,821	4,995	739	67
Lafayette	5,726	5,204	5,034	185	337
Lake	121,422	104,097	4,390	15,168	2,157
Lee	391,198	252,574	5,035	118,089	20,536

See footnotes at end of table. Continued . . .

Table 20.65. ELEMENTARY AND SECONDARY SCHOOLS: ALL FUNDS EXPENDITURE BY MAJOR TYPE IN THE STATE AND COUNTIES OF FLORIDA, 1993-94 (Continued)

(in thousands of dollars, except where indicated)

County	Total expenditure all funds	Total current expenditure	Current expenditure per FTE (dollars)	Capital outlay	Debt service
Leon	182,154	149,265	4,569	21,726	11,164
Levy	28,382	26,136	4,924	1,413	833
Liberty	6,182	5,821	4,702	268	93
Madison	18,030	16,330	5,090	1,425	276
Manatee	180,417	143,880	4,637	34,037	2,500
Marion	182,331	150,761	4,449	22,315	9,255
Martin	93,874	75,530	5,192	16,396	1,949
Monroe	64,417	52,472	5,682	6,350	5,595
Nassau	46,876	39,633	4,228	6,777	465
Okaloosa	136,459	123,024	4,197	8,655	4,780
Okeechobee	33,888	29,240	4,774	4,229	420
Orange	718,556	582,345	4,581	84,951	51,260
Osceola	122,705	101,981	4,229	12,789	7,935
Palm Beach	849,471	686,850	5,199	128,260	34,361
Pasco	234,956	181,180	4,581	31,539	22,237
Pinellas	599,335	505,710	4,649	90,053	3,572
Polk	376,009	329,625	4,469	35,988	10,395
Putnam	67,231	59,186	4,699	5,204	2,841
St. Johns	105,794	72,024	4,318	25,755	8,014
St. Lucie	147,533	120,980	4,831	14,256	12,297
Santa Rosa	103,329	80,326	4,325	18,419	4,585
Sarasota	217,585	175,079	5,249	30,192	12,314
Seminole	264,569	220,042	4,167	26,058	18,468
Sumter	29,510	25,783	4,696	3,122	604
Suwannee	28,998	26,898	4,714	1,946	153
Taylor	21,340	16,859	4,394	3,137	1,344
Union	10,504	9,677	4,849	578	250
Volusia	355,651	249,652	4,597	48,042	57,957
Wakulla	20,435	17,245	4,342	2,833	358
Walton	28,644	23,472	4,870	4,005	1,167
Washington	21,410	20,263	5,124	1,068	79
Eckerd Youth	0	229	5,556	0	0

FTE Full-time equivalent.
1/ Includes special schools.
Note: Data are for public schools only.

Source: State of Florida, Department of Education, Division of Public Schools, *Profiles of Florida School Districts, 1993-94, Financial Data Statistical Report.* EIAS Series 95-21, July 1995.

Table 20.67. ELEMENTARY AND SECONDARY SCHOOLS: OPERATING TAX MILLAGE, OPERATING TAX YIELD, ASSESSED VALUE OF NONEXEMPT PROPERTY AND ASSESSED VALUATION PER FTE STUDENT IN THE STATE AND COUNTIES OF FLORIDA, 1993-94

County	Operating tax millage	Operating tax yield ($1,000)	Assessed value of nonexempt property: Amount ($1,000)	Assessed value of nonexempt property: Valuation per FTE student (dollars)
Florida	(X)	3,299,642	488,458,004	178,893
Alachua	7.052	24,342	3,633,420	103,525
Baker	7.080	1,613	239,880	42,794
Bay	7.077	26,349	3,919,119	121,948
Bradford	7.336	2,312	331,807	63,915
Brevard	7.215	91,314	13,322,273	172,657
Broward	7.174	334,458	49,074,521	183,222
Calhoun	6.625	953	151,360	54,593
Charlotte	7.054	40,028	5,973,109	318,489
Citrus	7.115	24,766	3,663,977	216,095
Clay	6.988	17,605	2,651,898	94,079
Collier	6.339	92,216	15,313,053	466,348
Columbia	7.244	4,953	719,754	67,088
Dade	7.283	443,108	64,043,547	143,239
De Soto	6.957	3,869	585,467	102,314
Dixie	7.316	1,232	177,231	68,430
Duval	6.930	127,315	19,338,563	129,930
Escambia	7.447	38,376	5,424,375	89,483
Flagler	6.929	13,510	2,052,425	298,900
Franklin	6.952	2,347	355,373	179,085
Gadsden	6.934	3,230	490,352	47,531
Gilchrist	7.382	1,127	160,656	57,636
Glades	7.380	2,268	323,516	278,729
Gulf	6.996	3,488	524,794	187,344
Hamilton	7.237	2,166	315,081	108,809
Hardee	7.201	4,849	708,802	113,555
Hendry	6.920	7,002	1,065,060	132,048
Hernando	7.084	22,111	3,285,464	187,574
Highlands	7.128	14,547	2,148,265	159,222
Hillsborough	7.254	171,519	24,889,195	133,994
Holmes	6.574	1,047	167,607	39,169
Indian River	6.973	35,813	5,406,246	333,310
Jackson	7.252	3,887	564,209	51,543
Jefferson	6.932	1,303	197,894	72,764
Lafayette	6.922	572	86,941	67,191
Lake	6.938	29,787	4,519,269	154,832
Lee	7.235	133,048	19,357,303	307,098

See footnotes at end of table.

Continued . . .

Table 20.67. ELEMENTARY AND SECONDARY SCHOOLS: OPERATING TAX MILLAGE, OPERATING TAX YIELD, ASSESSED VALUE OF NONEXEMPT PROPERTY AND ASSESSED VALUATION PER FTE STUDENT IN THE STATE AND COUNTIES OF FLORIDA, 1993-94 (Continued)

County	Operating tax millage	Operating tax yield ($1,000)	Assessed value of nonexempt property: Amount ($1,000)	Assessed value of nonexempt property: Valuation per FTE student (dollars)
Leon	6.944	34,353	5,207,567	121,600
Levy	7.325	4,224	606,948	91,867
Liberty	7.488	583	81,927	54,808
Madison	6.943	1,599	242,427	60,841
Manatee	6.950	55,559	8,414,778	213,940
Marion	7.331	34,734	4,987,364	121,414
Martin	7.126	49,331	7,286,982	409,634
Monroe	5.591	34,249	6,448,183	563,442
Nassau	7.051	11,404	1,702,442	152,895
Okaloosa	7.015	24,433	3,666,263	107,369
Okeechobee	6.975	5,197	784,284	101,533
Orange	6.930	216,666	32,910,484	220,531
Osceola	6.940	31,534	4,782,907	163,663
Palm Beach	7.457	363,835	51,358,970	308,270
Pasco	7.128	47,388	6,998,117	141,379
Pinellas	7.082	200,836	29,851,288	213,229
Polk	7.102	74,892	11,100,189	125,001
Putnam	6.999	13,111	1,971,872	130,089
St. Johns	6.943	26,766	4,057,980	206,439
St. Lucie	7.313	48,459	6,975,159	222,784
Santa Rosa	6.935	14,963	2,271,237	102,759
Sarasota	6.938	102,004	15,476,093	347,909
Seminole	6.975	68,021	10,265,343	162,135
Sumter	7.278	3,569	516,136	76,875
Suwannee	7.215	3,305	482,141	70,241
Taylor	6.928	3,779	574,193	122,980
Union	7.302	617	88,984	36,214
Volusia	7.148	82,592	12,162,640	179,384
Wakulla	7.366	1,798	256,927	52,952
Walton	6.857	9,595	1,472,968	256,701
Washington	7.003	1,819	273,404	58,170

FTE Full-time equivalent.
(X) Not applicable.
Note: Data are for public schools only.

Source: State of Florida, Department of Education, Division of Public Schools, *Profiles of Florida School Districts, 1993-94, Financial Data Statistical Report.* EIAS Series 95-21, July 1995.

Table 20.69. ELEMENTARY AND SECONDARY SCHOOLS: EXPENDITURE FOR PUPIL TRANSPORTATION SERVICES IN THE STATE AND COUNTIES OF FLORIDA, 1993-94

(in dollars)

County	1993-94	County	1993-94
Florida	427,224,049	Lafayette	296,583
		Lake	4,477,640
Alachua	5,578,339	Lee	14,491,689
Baker	1,107,551	Leon	5,846,090
Bay	4,498,515	Levy	1,567,979
Bradford	844,250	Liberty	397,534
Brevard	12,789,840	Madison	858,304
Broward	30,518,232	Manatee	5,698,856
Calhoun	409,936	Marion	8,150,651
Charlotte	3,206,292	Martin	3,140,359
Citrus	4,015,150	Monroe	2,454,522
Clay	4,304,096	Nassau	2,521,844
Collier	6,022,908	Okaloosa	4,487,653
Columbia	2,056,030	Okeechobee	1,418,285
Dade	57,548,477	Orange	26,424,927
De Soto	1,016,246	Osceola	3,608,525
Dixie	554,945	Palm Beach	18,268,497
Duval	28,824,963	Pasco	8,483,837
Escambia	9,594,494	Pinellas	16,675,278
Flagler	1,312,749	Polk	11,334,925
Franklin	288,768	Putnam	2,853,647
Gadsden	1,838,532	St. Johns	2,715,246
Gilchrist	516,666	St. Lucie	7,619,363
Glades	219,590	Santa Rosa	4,134,696
Gulf	627,992	Sarasota	9,467,101
Hamilton	604,488	Seminole	10,503,068
Hardee	1,475,618	Sumter	1,400,909
Hendry	1,716,557	Suwannee	1,694,010
Hernando	4,075,823	Taylor	1,002,262
Highlands	2,743,365	Union	472,566
Hillsborough	38,264,448	Volusia	8,178,473
Holmes	862,540	Wakulla	1,043,307
Indian River	3,235,113	Walton	1,376,608
Jackson	1,715,625	Washington	991,192
Jefferson	779,454		

Note: Data are for public schools only. Detail may not add to total due to rounding.

Source: State of Florida, Department of Education, Division of Public Schools, *Profiles of Florida School Districts, 1993-94, Financial Data Statistical Report.* EIAS Series 95-21, July 1995.

Table 20.74. FEDERAL AID: SPECIFIED FEDERAL HEALTH AND EDUCATION PROGRAM EXPENDITURES IN FLORIDA, OTHER SUNBELT STATES, AND THE UNITED STATES, 1994

(in millions of dollars)

State	Total 1/	Compensatory education for the disadvantaged	Medicaid	ETA employment/ training
Florida	8,018	297	1,945	301
Alabama	3,209	125	1,287	97
Arizona	2,996	99	1,103	99
Arkansas	1,966	76	834	63
California	26,219	777	7,861	997
Georgia	5,028	172	2,080	123
Louisiana	5,233	178	3,256	118
Mississippi	2,507	121	1,068	68
New Mexico	1,714	57	531	42
North Carolina	4,862	141	2,098	138
Oklahoma	2,359	78	782	75
South Carolina	2,726	90	1,329	77
Tennessee	3,940	122	1,803	98
Texas	12,669	578	5,386	387
Virginia	3,180	110	1,006	120
United States	214,239	6,819	82,034	6,733

ETA Employment and Training Administration.
1/ Includes other amounts not shown separately.
Source: U.S., Department of Commerce, Bureau of the Census, *Statistical Abstract of the United States, 1995.*

Table 20.75. CULTURE AND THE ARTS: STATE GRANTS TO GROUPS AND INDIVIDUALS IN THE STATE AND SPECIFIED COUNTIES OF FLORIDA, 1995-96

(in dollars)

County	Amount	County	Amount	County	Amount
Florida	21,968,126	Glades	1,200	Nassau	5,887
		Gulf	2,100	Okaloosa	51,711
Alachua	244,174	Hamilton	1,000	Okeechobee	4,800
Bay	88,138	Hernando	2,400	Orange	1,709,224
Bradford	16,800	Highlands	24,791	Osceola	21,208
Brevard	122,116	Hillsborough	1,566,735	Palm Beach	1,371,946
Broward	1,838,301	Holmes	1,800	Pasco	12,260
Calhoun	17,692	Indian River	155,790	Pinellas	1,622,224
Charlotte	17,819	Jackson	9,300	Polk	1,270,105
Citrus	19,000	Jefferson	14,716	Putnam	20,390
Clay	4,423	Lake	12,904	Sarasota	1,386,888
Collier	81,330	Lee	263,982	Seminole	51,659
Dade	5,949,452	Leon	331,057	St. Johns	55,333
De Soto	400	Levy	49,568	St. Lucie	8,471
Duval	1,792,693	Manatee	27,407	Sumter	1,600
Escambia	361,891	Marion	30,602	Suwannee	6,666
Flagler	15,500	Martin	33,796	Volusia	964,743
Gilchrist	800	Monroe	293,891	Walton	9,443

Source: State of Florida, Department of State, Division of Cultural Affairs, *1995-96 Florida Funding for Culture and the Arts.*

GOVERNMENT AND ELECTIONS

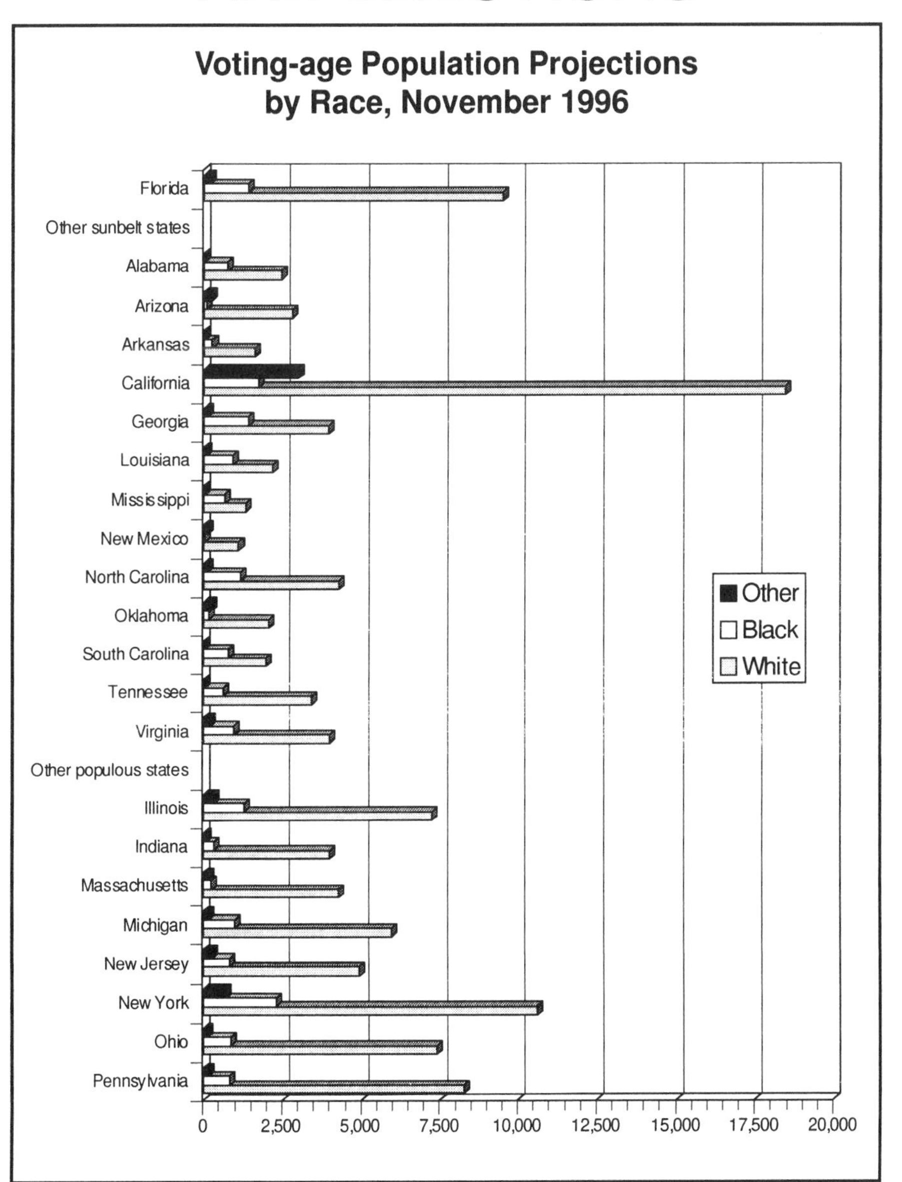

Source: Table 21.23

SECTION 21.00
GOVERNMENT AND ELECTIONS

TABLES LISTED BY MAJOR HEADINGS

Table 21.01. GOVERNMENTAL UNITS: NUMBER BY TYPE IN FLORIDA AND THE UNITED STATES, 1992

Type of unit	Florida	United States
All units	1,014	85,006
Federal government	0	1
State government	1	50
Local government	1,013	84,955
County 1/	66	3,043
Municipal	390	19,279
School districts	95	14,422
Special districts	462	31,555
With property taxing power	224	14,951
Without property taxing power	238	16,604
Single-function	429	29,036
Education services	7	1,800
Education 2/	4	757
Libraries	3	1,043
Social services	45	1,321
Hospitals	29	737
Health	16	584
Transportation	17	1,306
Highways	3	636
Airports	6	435
Other 3/	8	235
Fire protection	53	5,260
Environment and housing	256	12,959
Natural resources 4/	135	6,228
Drainage and flood control	62	2,709
Irrigation	5	792
Soil and water conservation	63	2,428
Other	5	299
Parks and recreation	13	1,156
Housing and community development	105	3,470
Sewerage	3	1,710
Solid waste management	0	395
Utilities	29	3,763
Water supply	17	3,302
Other 5/	12	461
Cemeteries	0	1,628
Industrial development and mortgage credit	5	155
Other single-function districts	17	844
Multiple-function	33	2,519
Natural resources and water supply	3	131
Sewerage and water supply	5	1,344
Other	25	1,044

1/ In 1968, Duval County and the City of Jacksonville consolidated to form one government, designated the City of Jacksonville. Jacksonville is counted as a municipal government, rather than as a county government, in census reporting.
2/ Primarily school building authorities.
3/ Includes parking facilities and water transport and terminals.
4/ Functions within the "natural resources" category overlap.
5/ Includes electric power, gas supply, and transit.
Note: The governments census is on a 5-year cycle collecting data for years ending in 2 and 7.
Source: U.S., Department of Commerce, Bureau of the Census, *1992 Census of Governments, Volume I, No. 1: Governmental Organization.*

Table 21.07. LOCAL GOVERNMENTS AND PUBLIC SCHOOL SYSTEMS: NUMBER OF POLITICAL UNITS AND ELECTED OFFICIALS BY TYPE OF GOVERNMENT IN THE STATE AND COUNTIES OF FLORIDA, 1992

	Political units			Elected officials			
County	Munici-palities	School dis-tricts	Special dis-tricts	County	Munici-palities	School dis-tricts	Special dis-tricts
Florida	390	95	462	842	2,238	396	1,178
Alachua	9	2	4	15	48	5	5
Baker	2	1	3	11	10	6	5
Bay	8	2	6	14	40	6	8
Bradford	4	1	1	10	24	6	0
Brevard	15	2	15	10	84	5	28
Broward	28	2	33	11	158	7	98
Calhoun	2	1	0	12	11	6	0
Charlotte	1	1	5	14	5	5	11
Citrus	2	1	2	10	12	6	6
Clay	4	1	4	19	20	6	7
Collier	2	1	14	7	13	5	40
Columbia	2	2	3	11	10	6	5
Dade	26	2	6	36	145	7	12
De Soto	1	1	4	12	6	6	8
Dixie	2	1	1	11	12	5	5
Duval 1/	5	2	2	(X)	50	7	5
Escambia	2	2	5	12	16	6	10
Flagler	4	1	4	10	23	6	13
Franklin	2	1	7	11	10	6	13
Gadsden	6	1	2	11	36	6	5
Gilchrist	3	1	3	11	18	6	11
Glades	1	1	3	12	7	6	11
Gulf	2	1	2	12	10	6	5
Hamilton	3	1	2	11	16	6	5
Hardee	3	1	2	10	20	6	5
Hendry	2	1	18	10	11	6	43
Hernando	2	1	6	12	8	6	10
Highlands	3	2	6	11	19	6	21
Hillsborough	3	2	12	12	19	7	34
Holmes	5	1	3	12	29	6	0
Indian River	5	1	11	12	26	5	37
Jackson	11	2	5	13	60	6	13
Jefferson	1	1	1	10	9	6	5
Lafayette	1	1	1	13	6	6	5
Lake	14	2	4	10	76	6	3
Lee	3	2	32	10	19	5	132

See footnotes at end of table. Continued . . .

Table 21.07. LOCAL GOVERNMENTS AND PUBLIC SCHOOL SYSTEMS: NUMBER OF POLITICAL UNITS AND ELECTED OFFICIALS BY TYPE OF GOVERNMENT IN THE STATE AND COUNTIES OF FLORIDA, 1992 (Continued)

	Political units			Elected officials			
County	Munici-palities	School dis-tricts	Special dis-tricts	County	Munici-palities	School dis-tricts	Special dis-tricts
Leon	1	2	5	12	5	6	5
Levy	7	1	3	12	39	6	10
Liberty	1	1	0	12	8	6	0
Madison	3	2	2	11	16	6	5
Manatee	6	2	18	21	40	5	36
Marion	5	2	6	10	28	6	5
Martin	4	1	6	9	22	6	15
Monroe	3	2	6	10	16	6	10
Nassau	3	1	4	12	19	6	12
Okaloosa	9	2	12	10	58	6	32
Okeechobee	1	1	3	11	6	5	11
Orange	13	2	15	11	73	7	21
Osceola	2	1	2	10	10	6	5
Palm Beach	37	2	39	14	204	7	104
Pasco	6	2	4	11	31	6	13
Pinellas	24	2	15	66	132	8	19
Polk	17	2	11	10	91	6	17
Putnam	5	2	4	10	28	6	5
St. Johns	3	1	9	14	17	6	38
St. Lucie	3	2	9	10	17	5	26
Santa Rosa	3	1	10	14	21	5	38
Sarasota	3	1	13	10	17	5	59
Seminole	7	2	3	11	37	5	5
Sumter	5	1	1	11	28	6	5
Suwannee	2	1	4	10	14	6	5
Taylor	1	1	1	10	5	6	0
Union	3	1	2	10	17	6	5
Volusia	14	2	13	19	75	5	15
Wakulla	2	1	1	12	10	6	5
Walton	3	1	6	10	20	6	23
Washington	5	1	3	11	48	6	5

(X) Not applicable.
1/ County-type area without any county government.
Note: School districts include community college districts. The governments census is on a 5-year cycle collecting data for years ending in 2 and 7.

Source: U.S., Department of Commerce, Bureau of the Census, *1992 Census of Governments, Volume I, No. 2: Popularly Elected Officials.*

Table 21.23. VOTING-AGE POPULATION: ELECTORAL VOTES AND VOTING-AGE POPULATION PROJECTIONS BY SEX AND BY RACE AND HISPANIC ORIGIN IN FLORIDA, OTHER SUNBELT STATES, OTHER POPULOUS STATES, AND THE UNITED STATES
NOVEMBER 1996

State	Number of electoral votes	Voting-age population (1,000)					
		Total		Race			Hispanic origin 1/
		Male	Female	White	Black	Other	
Sunbelt states							
Florida	25	5,130	5,913	9,487	1,375	201	1,409
Alabama	9	1,526	1,692	2,438	744	37	20
Arizona	8	1,478	1,616	2,795	85	214	602
Arkansas	6	875	985	1,583	253	25	18
California	54	11,357	11,774	18,447	1,716	2,970	6,323
Georgia	13	2,605	2,791	3,937	1,368	91	101
Louisiana	9	1,485	1,653	2,183	902	53	75
Mississippi	7	925	1,036	1,311	632	18	12
New Mexico	5	578	632	1,078	22	111	505
North Carolina	14	2,648	2,851	4,249	1,126	124	69
Oklahoma	8	1,159	1,260	2,044	164	211	69
South Carolina	8	1,325	1,452	1,978	771	28	27
Tennessee	11	1,917	2,104	3,390	589	42	29
Texas	32	6,612	7,011	11,670	1,564	389	3,730
Virginia	13	2,468	2,621	3,992	924	173	133
Other populous states							
Illinois	22	4,217	4,547	7,219	1,245	300	728
Indiana	12	2,097	2,271	3,987	331	51	81
Massachusetts	12	2,210	2,413	4,252	234	137	229
Michigan	18	3,374	3,693	5,956	972	139	159
New Jersey	15	2,867	3,138	4,917	819	269	632
New York	33	6,445	7,135	10,614	2,292	674	1,616
Ohio	21	3,980	4,378	7,387	866	105	112
Pennsylvania	23	4,366	4,831	8,241	814	142	196
United States	538	94,296	102,213	165,225	22,857	8,427	18,609

1/ Persons of Hispanic origin may be of any race.

Source: U.S., Department of Commerce, Bureau of the Census, Population Division, the Internet at <http://www.census.gov/>.

Table 21.24. VOTING-AGE POPULATION: ESTIMATES BY AGE IN FLORIDA, OTHER SUNBELT STATES, OTHER POPULOUS STATES, AND THE UNITED STATES, JULY 1, 1995

	Population		Percentage of persons aged 18 and over			
State	Total (1,000)	Aged 18 and over (1,000)	Aged 18 to 24	Aged 25 to 44	Aged 45 to 64	Aged 65 and over
			Sunbelt states			
Florida	14,166	10,794	10.7	38.5	26.4	24.4
Alabama	4,253	3,173	13.9	40.7	27.9	17.4
Arizona	4,218	3,025	13.1	42.2	26.1	18.5
Arkansas	2,484	1,834	13.6	38.6	28.3	19.6
California	31,589	22,796	13.2	46.7	24.9	15.2
Georgia	7,201	5,277	13.8	45.8	26.8	13.6
Louisiana	4,342	3,103	14.8	42.0	27.3	15.9
Mississippi	2,697	1,935	15.6	40.4	26.9	17.1
New Mexico	1,685	1,185	14.1	42.6	27.8	15.5
North Carolina	7,195	5,396	13.2	42.6	27.4	16.7
Oklahoma	3,278	2,400	13.7	39.6	28.2	18.4
South Carolina	3,673	2,729	14.1	42.3	27.5	16.1
Tennessee	5,256	3,946	13.1	41.8	28.4	16.7
Texas	18,724	13,324	14.5	44.7	26.4	14.4
Virginia	6,618	5,006	13.1	45.0	27.1	14.7
			Other populous states			
Illinois	11,830	8,704	12.8	43.3	26.9	17.1
Indiana	5,803	4,316	13.5	42.1	27.5	17.0
Massachusetts	6,074	4,642	11.6	44.1	25.8	18.5
Michigan	9,549	7,030	13.1	42.9	27.2	16.8
New Jersey	7,945	5,982	11.2	42.7	27.8	18.2
New York	18,136	13,599	12.0	42.7	27.4	17.8
Ohio	11,151	8,291	12.8	41.7	27.5	18.0
Pennsylvania	12,072	9,163	11.7	40.1	27.3	20.9
United States	262,755	194,015	12.9	43.0	26.9	17.3

Note: Includes Armed Forces residing in each state.

Source: U.S., Department of Commerce, Bureau of the Census, Population Division, the Internet at <http://www.census.gov/>.

Table 21.25. VOTING-AGE POPULATION: CENSUS COUNTS, APRIL 1,1990, AND ESTIMATES APRIL 1, 1995, BY SEX AND RACE OF PERSONS AGED 18 AND OVER IN THE STATE AND COUNTIES OF FLORIDA

County	Census 1990	Estimates, 1995 Total	Percentage of total Sex Male	Female	Race White	Black
Florida	10,054,095	10,948,741	47.82	52.18	86.28	12.09
Alachua	141,760	154,471	48.98	51.02	81.39	15.66
Baker	12,810	14,511	53.50	46.50	84.27	14.90
Bay	94,532	103,470	48.58	51.42	87.71	9.75
Bradford	17,087	18,725	57.37	42.63	76.55	22.31
Brevard	311,152	345,985	48.66	51.34	91.26	6.94
Broward	997,360	1,068,979	47.20	52.80	83.74	14.45
Calhoun	8,127	9,213	53.80	46.20	81.56	16.86
Charlotte	93,590	107,361	47.64	52.36	95.05	3.97
Citrus	76,980	87,669	47.04	52.96	97.37	1.96
Clay	75,330	86,953	48.76	51.24	92.60	5.12
Collier	121,474	148,203	48.64	51.36	95.14	4.14
Columbia	30,642	36,716	50.71	49.29	81.81	17.06
Dade	1,465,595	1,503,054	47.23	52.77	79.16	19.02
De Soto	18,143	20,432	54.56	45.44	81.62	17.34
Dixie	7,979	9,507	52.36	47.64	89.26	10.03
Duval	497,830	526,156	48.16	51.84	74.76	22.75
Escambia	196,088	211,082	48.15	51.85	79.76	17.32
Flagler	23,187	30,364	47.41	52.59	90.49	8.14
Franklin	6,807	8,082	49.90	50.10	85.24	13.52
Gadsden	28,845	31,791	48.75	51.25	46.31	52.66
Gilchrist	7,235	9,004	53.45	46.55	90.08	9.24
Glades	5,724	6,590	49.47	50.53	83.72	10.88
Gulf	8,655	10,262	54.19	45.81	77.45	21.45
Hamilton	7,757	9,238	54.51	45.49	64.16	35.07
Hardee	13,759	16,613	53.74	46.26	88.20	10.40
Hendry	17,614	19,951	50.76	49.24	80.35	16.64
Hernando	82,412	96,574	47.24	52.76	95.99	3.34
Highlands	55,510	62,986	46.62	53.38	91.35	7.76
Hillsborough	630,690	671,845	48.02	51.98	86.37	11.79
Holmes	11,836	13,460	52.44	47.56	90.53	7.62
Indian River	72,602	80,783	47.58	52.42	92.72	6.64
Jackson	31,022	36,102	52.76	47.24	73.74	25.21
Jefferson	8,013	10,055	43.03	56.97	60.92	38.17
Lafayette	4,191	5,044	59.87	40.13	80.55	18.32
Lake	121,614	141,961	47.12	52.88	91.95	7.41
Lee	269,118	301,579	47.57	52.43	93.89	5.30

Continued . . .

Table 21.25. VOTING-AGE POPULATION: CENSUS COUNTS, APRIL 1,1990, AND ESTIMATES APRIL 1, 1995, BY SEX AND RACE OF PERSONS AGED 18 AND OVER IN THE STATE AND COUNTIES OF FLORIDA (Continued)

		Estimates, 1995				
			Percentage of total			
	Census		Sex		Race	
County	1990	Total	Male	Female	White	Black
Leon	149,007	169,283	47.29	52.71	75.50	22.60
Levy	19,602	22,987	47.18	52.82	89.18	9.84
Liberty	4,214	5,358	60.66	39.34	75.64	23.29
Madison	11,978	13,439	52.21	47.79	60.48	38.68
Manatee	170,868	187,427	46.67	53.33	92.69	6.47
Marion	151,424	175,643	47.21	52.79	88.61	10.49
Martin	83,024	91,669	48.41	51.59	93.39	5.75
Monroe	64,389	68,090	51.18	48.82	93.83	4.96
Nassau	31,983	36,020	48.80	51.20	90.73	8.59
Okaloosa	106,323	119,662	49.86	50.14	88.29	8.40
Okeechobee	21,521	23,926	49.85	50.15	92.81	6.06
Orange	514,989	571,732	49.23	50.77	82.24	14.96
Osceola	80,433	102,006	48.35	51.65	91.45	6.05
Palm Beach	692,775	763,221	47.28	52.72	88.19	10.55
Pasco	230,665	250,950	46.64	53.36	97.13	1.93
Pinellas	699,455	713,925	46.30	53.70	92.15	6.52
Polk	306,940	337,926	47.58	52.42	87.96	11.08
Putnam	48,414	52,219	47.92	52.08	84.84	14.44
St. Johns	65,007	77,154	47.99	52.01	92.28	6.91
St. Lucie	115,265	132,763	48.04	51.96	86.57	12.51
Santa Rosa	59,385	70,933	49.15	50.85	93.59	4.02
Sarasota	233,828	253,538	46.24	53.76	95.68	3.61
Seminole	214,314	243,706	48.33	51.67	89.75	8.06
Sumter	24,512	28,603	51.19	48.81	83.27	15.87
Suwannee	19,645	22,997	47.57	52.43	87.69	11.62
Taylor	12,272	13,365	50.00	50.00	81.11	17.43
Union	7,616	10,042	68.65	31.35	70.11	28.26
Volusia	297,236	322,365	47.77	52.23	90.74	8.14
Wakulla	10,176	12,461	48.29	51.71	87.86	11.19
Walton	21,139	26,170	50.33	49.67	91.05	6.71
Washington	12,626	14,390	49.57	50.43	83.22	14.23

Source: University of Florida, Bureau of Economic and Business Research, Population Program, *Florida Population Studies,* July 1996, Volume 29, No. 3. Bulletin No. 115.

Table 21.26. VOTING-AGE POPULATION: PROJECTIONS, APRIL 1, 2000, 2005, AND 2010 OF PERSONS AGED 18 AND OVER BY SEX IN THE STATE AND COUNTIES OF FLORIDA

County	2000		2005		2010	
	Male	Female	Male	Female	Male	Female
Florida	5,718,649	6,212,267	6,221,064	6,741,120	6,734,743	7,292,387
Alachua	81,763	84,386	87,405	89,922	93,164	95,755
Baker	8,696	7,366	9,317	7,942	9,889	8,530
Bay	54,244	57,588	58,510	62,289	62,839	67,174
Bradford	11,411	8,316	11,815	8,709	12,180	9,081
Brevard	186,338	198,424	205,887	220,164	225,487	241,993
Broward	540,424	601,393	581,678	642,728	624,281	687,246
Calhoun	5,302	4,552	5,545	4,794	5,769	5,023
Charlotte	59,245	64,905	67,551	73,722	75,987	82,652
Citrus	47,220	53,143	53,432	59,788	59,747	66,524
Clay	48,108	50,824	54,109	57,393	60,049	64,006
Collier	85,123	89,823	97,469	103,762	110,323	118,064
Columbia	20,310	19,976	22,130	21,971	23,906	23,961
Dade	748,955	830,172	794,605	875,797	843,127	927,461
De Soto	12,933	10,217	13,629	11,126	14,368	12,047
Dixie	5,694	5,142	6,266	5,732	6,833	6,322
Duval	266,656	287,922	281,895	304,542	297,831	322,128
Escambia	111,017	115,522	117,099	121,290	122,684	127,312
Flagler	17,865	19,932	21,534	24,053	25,226	28,177
Franklin	4,502	4,455	4,826	4,834	5,142	5,216
Gadsden	16,982	17,070	17,657	17,700	18,414	18,460
Gilchrist	5,616	4,928	6,270	5,632	6,916	6,345
Glades	4,313	3,745	4,616	4,124	4,883	4,453
Gulf	7,172	4,919	7,372	5,125	7,543	5,323
Hamilton	6,525	4,620	6,921	5,019	7,263	5,398
Hardee	9,123	7,953	9,297	8,207	9,482	8,462
Hendry	11,188	10,725	12,127	11,713	13,091	12,760
Hernando	53,834	60,308	62,553	69,808	71,464	79,358
Highlands	32,690	37,517	36,166	41,273	39,726	44,972
Hillsborough	345,497	373,648	370,540	400,594	396,290	429,195
Holmes	7,453	6,656	7,751	6,965	8,003	7,242
Indian River	42,618	47,175	47,025	51,985	51,601	56,850
Jackson	20,246	17,762	21,137	18,443	22,006	19,169
Jefferson	4,657	6,179	4,997	6,558	5,301	6,912
Lafayette	3,637	2,280	3,810	2,496	3,982	2,708
Lake	75,819	84,981	85,087	95,028	94,559	105,279
Lee	161,274	177,763	180,275	198,079	199,564	218,811

Continued . . .

Table 21.26. VOTING-AGE POPULATION: PROJECTIONS, APRIL 1, 2000, 2005, AND 2010 OF PERSONS AGED 18 AND OVER BY SEX IN THE STATE AND COUNTIES OF FLORIDA (Continued)

County	2000		2005		2010	
	Male	Female	Male	Female	Male	Female
Leon	87,880	97,531	95,451	105,670	102,925	113,994
Levy	12,072	13,506	13,424	14,993	14,765	16,452
Liberty	3,553	2,318	3,735	2,512	3,909	2,714
Madison	7,275	6,659	7,594	6,953	7,894	7,246
Manatee	96,712	109,360	106,457	119,132	116,286	129,157
Marion	94,351	105,611	106,162	118,614	118,209	131,769
Martin	49,542	52,724	54,675	58,181	59,893	63,695
Monroe	36,304	36,069	38,232	38,953	40,311	41,770
Nassau	19,374	20,400	21,222	22,404	23,063	24,478
Okaloosa	64,705	66,279	70,442	72,962	76,251	79,700
Okeechobee	14,097	13,493	15,283	14,934	16,517	16,391
Orange	309,669	324,650	342,179	360,949	375,773	398,639
Osceola	59,247	63,420	69,632	74,646	80,190	86,302
Palm Beach	399,303	444,330	441,501	488,324	485,331	534,289
Pasco	128,844	146,733	141,532	159,538	154,445	172,452
Pinellas	344,855	393,642	361,553	406,828	378,804	422,052
Polk	174,249	192,147	188,329	207,323	202,434	222,808
Putnam	26,980	29,442	28,929	31,610	30,878	33,798
St. Johns	42,616	46,104	48,348	52,272	54,039	58,510
St. Lucie	73,132	79,574	82,925	90,330	92,724	101,069
Santa Rosa	41,191	41,517	46,371	47,193	51,532	52,995
Sarasota	127,960	147,465	139,499	158,904	151,182	170,483
Seminole	133,979	142,929	150,698	160,818	167,485	179,296
Sumter	19,040	15,708	20,425	17,383	21,852	19,015
Suwannee	12,211	13,353	13,393	14,618	14,523	15,906
Taylor	7,390	6,865	7,539	7,026	7,722	7,239
Union	7,288	3,525	7,654	3,923	7,953	4,275
Volusia	169,165	184,837	185,545	201,916	202,212	219,610
Wakulla	7,981	7,344	8,838	8,295	9,604	9,164
Walton	14,986	14,658	16,470	16,307	17,913	17,942
Washington	8,248	7,787	8,724	8,302	9,204	8,808

Source: University of Florida, Bureau of Economic and Business Research, Population Program, *Florida Population Studies*, July 1996, Volume 29, No. 3. Bulletin No. 115.

Table 21.30. REGISTERED VOTERS: VOTERS BY PARTY IN THE STATE AND COUNTIES OF FLORIDA, FEBRUARY 13, 1996

County	Total	Democratic		Republican		Other 1/	Number of pre-cincts
		Total	Black	Total	Black		
Florida	7,434,999	3,500,992	654,495	3,078,750	42,556	855,257	5,697
Alachua	96,072	56,285	11,851	28,490	644	11,297	68
Baker	10,760	9,612	1,133	986	11	162	16
Bay	78,404	43,360	5,322	26,805	431	8,239	47
Bradford	11,475	9,044	1,358	1,770	39	661	19
Brevard	262,318	106,282	11,957	127,507	1,021	28,529	156
Broward	747,497	397,249	69,254	257,189	5,354	93,059	618
Calhoun	6,164	5,651	658	432	8	81	13
Charlotte	87,484	31,796	1,643	46,078	202	9,610	63
Citrus	68,380	31,909	904	27,911	50	8,560	29
Clay	63,808	21,513	1,988	34,515	291	7,780	47
Collier	91,257	23,059	1,042	58,145	101	10,053	94
Columbia	25,016	17,227	3,167	6,284	132	1,505	48
Dade	739,950	363,463	134,535	290,548	6,993	85,939	578
De Soto	12,559	8,665	1,289	3,161	50	733	15
Dixie	8,726	7,685	461	812	7	229	11
Duval	347,402	195,885	74,287	120,600	3,711	30,917	280
Escambia	141,315	76,583	20,144	53,657	1,201	11,075	101
Flagler	24,658	10,390	1,620	11,087	132	3,181	24
Franklin	6,925	6,015	668	688	17	222	8
Gadsden	23,280	20,603	11,930	1,976	303	701	16
Gilchrist	6,969	5,497	180	1,134	1	338	10
Glades	5,093	3,828	469	1,027	6	238	13
Gulf	8,758	7,387	1,241	1,114	23	257	14
Hamilton	6,562	6,014	2,062	418	38	130	8
Hardee	9,842	7,853	725	1,637	39	352	11
Hendry	13,488	9,286	1,571	3,346	114	856	22
Hernando	83,258	35,665	1,851	37,871	165	9,722	46
Highlands	46,560	21,663	2,304	20,758	154	4,139	24
Hillsborough	408,406	199,757	38,816	155,999	2,659	52,650	288
Holmes	9,169	8,236	174	733	2	200	16
Indian River	57,729	18,922	2,167	33,642	251	5,165	38
Jackson	23,004	18,869	4,661	3,376	174	759	26
Jefferson	6,640	5,529	2,341	875	40	236	13
Lafayette	3,519	3,324	200	164	2	31	5
Lake	101,351	38,546	3,689	52,683	849	10,122	80
Lee	220,321	76,744	6,248	115,297	663	28,280	142

See footnotes at end of table. Continued . . .

Table 21.30. REGISTERED VOTERS: VOTERS BY PARTY IN THE STATE AND COUNTIES OF FLORIDA, FEBRUARY 13, 1996 (Continued)

County	Total	Democratic		Republican		Other 1/	Number of pre-cincts
		Total	Black	Total	Black		
Leon	126,362	78,428	24,689	33,859	938	14,075	94
Levy	16,495	12,027	1,151	3,530	56	938	21
Liberty	3,303	3,140	353	137	1	26	8
Madison	8,908	7,642	2,894	1,015	97	251	8
Manatee	135,176	50,768	5,804	69,007	410	15,401	126
Marion	125,731	57,939	8,741	54,387	657	13,405	90
Martin	72,031	20,692	1,761	43,037	376	8,302	36
Monroe	47,356	21,459	1,442	19,055	159	6,842	33
Nassau	28,055	16,873	1,739	9,436	65	1,746	17
Okaloosa	90,053	33,089	4,166	47,386	643	9,578	47
Okeechobee	15,752	11,072	797	3,810	55	870	18
Orange	322,945	133,952	31,941	148,507	2,545	40,486	239
Osceola	71,662	31,507	2,311	29,505	269	10,650	62
Palm Beach	561,116	259,776	35,825	221,529	2,767	79,811	479
Pasco	188,480	82,919	1,839	81,712	169	23,849	127
Pinellas	581,488	230,439	30,912	268,556	2,655	82,493	350
Polk	212,557	109,659	18,958	85,086	1,137	17,812	150
Putnam	39,727	26,956	4,434	9,799	301	2,972	55
St. Johns	60,582	25,053	3,081	29,173	164	6,356	46
St. Lucie	113,879	49,925	11,243	47,968	617	15,986	67
Santa Rosa	60,155	29,069	1,471	26,203	134	4,883	34
Sarasota	196,569	61,586	3,957	113,459	548	21,524	136
Seminole	169,427	59,927	8,470	89,725	803	19,775	133
Sumter	20,173	11,930	1,810	6,687	65	1,556	23
Suwannee	18,163	13,690	1,949	3,499	67	974	16
Taylor	10,514	9,023	1,355	1,253	33	238	14
Union	4,992	4,505	642	388	11	99	11
Volusia	226,140	106,832	13,553	93,412	818	25,896	190
Wakulla	11,236	9,033	1,096	1,693	15	510	12
Walton	20,579	13,475	1,023	5,576	62	1,528	33
Washington	11,274	9,211	1,178	1,646	41	417	15

1/ Includes registered Constitutional Party, Socialist Workers, Green, Independence, Independent, Libertarian, Natural Law, Reform, Reform Silly, United States Taxpayers, and those with no party affiliation.

Note: See Table 21.25 for voting-age population.

Source: State of Florida, Department of State, Division of Elections, unpublished data.

Table 21.32. ELECTION RESULTS: VOTES CAST FOR PRESIDENT AND VICE PRESIDENT IN THE GENERAL ELECTION BY PARTY IN THE STATE AND COUNTIES OF FLORIDA, NOVEMBER 3, 1992

County	Clinton and Gore (Democrat)	Bush and Quayle (Republican)	Perot and Stockdale (Independent)	County	Clinton and Gore (Democrat)	Bush and Quayle (Republican)	Perot and Stockdale (Independent)
Florida	2,072,698	2,173,310	1,053,067	Lafayette	866	1,037	612
				Lake	23,199	30,818	15,606
Alachua	37,876	22,806	15,293	Lee	53,656	73,423	38,446
Baker	1,974	3,417	1,315	Leon	47,770	31,964	17,207
Bay	12,830	22,820	9,702	Levy	4,330	3,796	2,784
Bradford	3,040	3,671	1,572	Liberty	820	1,126	617
Brevard	61,070	84,545	49,491	Madison	2,644	2,006	1,174
Broward	276,309	164,782	90,923	Manatee	33,826	42,708	23,282
Calhoun	1,665	1,721	1,176	Marion	30,823	35,438	20,524
Charlotte	22,904	24,302	14,711	Martin	14,778	24,768	13,433
Citrus	15,935	16,402	12,310	Monroe	10,435	9,891	8,306
Clay	10,597	26,313	8,414	Nassau	5,497	9,364	3,251
Collier	18,794	38,447	14,514	Okaloosa	12,003	32,755	16,649
Columbia	5,526	6,489	2,906	Okeechobee	3,418	3,298	2,645
Dade	254,444	235,149	53,957	Orange	82,656	108,738	44,827
De Soto	2,646	3,070	1,687	Osceola	15,009	19,139	11,021
Dixie	1,855	1,401	1,094	Palm Beach	187,840	140,317	76,223
Duval	92,010	123,480	33,335	Pasco	53,125	47,721	34,650
Escambia	32,018	52,775	19,868	Pinellas	160,217	158,733	101,150
Flagler	6,692	6,241	3,387	Polk	51,442	65,952	28,198
Franklin	1,534	1,660	1,143	Putnam	10,707	8,909	5,975
Gadsden	8,478	3,975	1,871	St. Johns	12,284	20,173	7,397
Gilchrist	1,511	1,395	1,090	St. Lucie	23,873	24,397	19,813
Glades	1,305	1,185	878	Santa Rosa	6,526	17,229	8,735
Gulf	1,938	2,650	1,245	Sarasota	54,536	66,831	34,281
Hamilton	1,622	1,402	695	Seminole	35,649	57,085	24,477
Hardee	2,017	2,898	1,498	Sumter	5,027	4,366	2,901
Hendry	2,690	3,279	2,032	Suwannee	3,985	4,571	2,790
Hernando	19,171	17,896	11,845	Taylor	2,568	2,693	1,929
Highlands	11,234	14,497	6,592	Union	1,247	1,543	770
Hillsborough	115,261	130,611	63,037	Volusia	65,213	59,155	30,813
Holmes	1,877	3,196	1,426	Wakulla	2,319	2,586	1,790
Indian River	12,359	19,137	12,375	Walton	3,886	5,719	3,886
Jackson	5,481	6,720	2,447	Washington	2,544	3,694	1,596
Jefferson	2,270	1,506	894	Absentees 1/	1,047	1,529	586

1/ Absentees counted per: Division of Elections Rule 1S-2.013. These votes are included in state totals but not in county detail.
Note: Excludes other candidates.

Source: State of Florida, Department of State, Division of Elections, *1992 Elections: Official General Election Returns, November 3, 1992.*

Table 21.33. ELECTION RESULTS: VOTES CAST FOR UNITED STATES SENATOR, NOVEMBER 3 1992 AND NOVEMBER 8, 1994, AND FOR GOVERNOR AND LIEUTENANT GOVERNOR NOVEMBER 8, 1994, IN THE STATE AND COUNTIES OF FLORIDA

County	United States Senator 1/ 1992 A/ Bob Graham (D)	United States Senator 1/ 1992 A/ Bill Grant (R)	United States Senator 1/ 1994 B/ Connie Mack (R)	United States Senator 1/ 1994 B/ Hugh E. Rodham (D)	Governor/Lieutenant Governor--1994 C/ Lawton Chiles/ Buddy MacKay (D)	Governor/Lieutenant Governor--1994 C/ Jeb Bush/ Tom Feeney (R)
Florida	3,245,565	1,716,505	2,895,200	1,210,577	2,135,008	2,071,068
Alachua	54,950	20,013	35,723	19,740	35,030	21,624
Baker	4,686	2,647	4,010	1,185	1,654	3,600
Bay	21,912	18,390	29,885	7,951	17,816	23,498
Bradford	5,790	2,400	5,124	1,905	2,642	4,470
Brevard	110,461	82,132	121,019	37,177	72,393	82,878
Broward	339,396	107,396	219,370	170,539	261,368	138,333
Calhoun	2,890	1,263	2,515	926	1,811	1,775
Charlotte	36,374	24,664	38,693	12,980	24,159	27,965
Citrus	27,675	17,697	29,884	10,528	20,094	20,633
Clay	23,700	21,165	28,614	5,561	9,986	24,290
Collier	36,387	33,823	47,974	10,688	22,860	36,370
Columbia	9,474	5,564	9,223	3,303	5,288	7,408
Dade	410,593	111,366	245,803	143,047	215,276	198,371
De Soto	5,021	2,655	4,547	1,667	2,856	3,407
Dixie	3,346	1,385	2,080	1,178	2,003	1,981
Duval	136,447	79,864	134,072	50,415	80,945	108,900
Escambia	57,036	43,668	60,370	17,175	33,210	45,261
Flagler	10,081	5,784	9,946	4,891	7,954	7,160
Franklin	2,444	1,408	2,709	1,107	2,636	1,324
Gadsden	10,479	2,328	5,598	5,311	7,751	3,422
Gilchrist	2,990	1,315	2,629	970	1,701	1,922
Glades	2,350	1,057	1,882	819	1,387	1,310
Gulf	3,490	2,231	3,826	1,449	3,060	2,339
Hamilton	2,669	1,040	1,825	976	1,453	1,429
Hardee	4,128	2,208	3,974	1,292	2,695	2,649
Hendry	5,498	2,369	4,325	1,563	2,623	3,308
Hernando	35,310	19,628	34,727	14,653	25,331	24,532
Highlands	18,809	13,074	19,688	6,396	12,323	14,617
Hillsborough	187,254	117,606	168,720	67,109	117,974	124,561
Holmes	3,740	2,494	3,800	1,069	2,134	2,942
Indian River	23,306	20,121	28,263	7,969	16,410	20,630
Jackson	9,582	5,133	8,659	3,756	5,907	6,698
Jefferson	3,631	1,082	2,493	1,566	2,575	1,625
Lafayette	1,749	797	1,599	406	936	1,105
Lake	42,939	25,830	46,359	13,181	29,797	30,394
Lee	88,273	62,413	103,187	30,201	58,785	75,365
Leon	73,399	22,512	47,243	26,194	47,323	27,265
Levy	7,259	3,643	6,304	2,524	4,588	4,322
Liberty	1,703	695	1,352	513	947	985
Madison	4,386	1,626	3,102	1,573	2,564	2,161

See footnotes at end of table. Continued . . .

Table 21.33. ELECTION RESULTS: VOTES CAST FOR UNITED STATES SENATOR, NOVEMBER 3 1992 AND NOVEMBER 8, 1994, AND FOR GOVERNOR AND LIEUTENANT GOVERNOR NOVEMBER 8, 1994, IN THE STATE AND COUNTIES OF FLORIDA
(Continued)

County	United States Senator 1/				Governor/Lieutenant Governor--1994 C/	
	1992 A/		1994 B/			
	Bob Graham (D)	Bill Grant (R)	Connie Mack (R)	Hugh E. Rodham (D)	Lawton Chiles/ Buddy MacKay (D)	Jeb Bush/ Tom Feeney (R)
Manatee	58,568	39,896	60,863	20,263	40,473	41,915
Marion	18,196	10,015	15,518	7,607	13,232	10,086
Martin	52,864	32,390	51,032	17,073	31,345	38,784
Monroe	28,342	22,037	34,986	9,603	20,706	25,239
Nassau	10,934	7,022	11,594	3,512	5,331	9,968
Okaloosa	29,759	30,050	40,330	7,390	16,459	31,459
Okeechobee	6,158	3,141	4,790	2,118	3,492	3,545
Orange	143,024	89,915	128,915	46,223	85,098	92,096
Osceola	26,394	15,923	24,112	8,516	15,292	18,437
Palm Beach	249,191	105,937	195,964	117,166	198,638	125,208
Pasco	78,506	44,296	76,901	30,624	57,597	52,418
Pinellas	243,038	133,047	233,140	83,762	166,858	160,115
Polk	90,339	55,474	91,915	31,248	58,364	65,415
Putnam	18,221	7,009	13,420	6,461	9,658	10,505
St. Johns	19,389	15,966	26,912	4,975	11,726	20,345
St. Lucie	70,688	52,946	96,345	29,277	60,770	67,531
Santa Rosa	65,917	48,229	68,643	19,280	39,324	49,387
Sarasota	22,066	17,065	27,043	7,291	12,791	22,036
Seminole	40,085	22,565	37,992	15,928	27,956	27,436
Sumter	7,337	2,987	7,817	2,785	5,603	5,360
Suwannee	7,414	3,934	7,016	1,907	3,935	5,064
Taylor	4,896	2,162	4,271	1,513	2,979	3,024
Union	2,622	980	2,083	679	791	2,009
Volusia	101,346	49,850	84,804	38,268	66,614	58,632
Wakulla	4,933	1,771	4,417	1,678	3,696	2,492
Walton	7,717	5,207	8,727	2,439	5,067	6,493
Washington	4,748	2,856	4,534	1,538	2,968	3,240
Overseas military absentees	1,266	1,349	0	0	(X)	(X)

(D) Democrat.
(R) Republican.
(X) Not applicable.
A/ Does not include 220 write-in votes.
B/ Does not include 1,039 write-in votes.
C/ Does not include 583 write-in votes.
1/ Absentee ballots counted per: Division of Elections Rule 1S-2.013. These votes are included in state but not in county detail in 1992.

Source: State of Florida, Department of State, Division of Elections, *1994 Elections: Official General Election Returns, November 8, 1994,* and previous edition.

Table 21.35. FEMALE OFFICIALS: WOMEN IN STATE LEGISLATURES IN FLORIDA AND THE UNITED STATES, 1996

Area	Total legislators	Women legislators Number	Percentage of total	Senate	House
Florida	160	31	19.4	6	25
United States	7,424	1,546	20.8	344	1,202

Source: Center for the American Woman and Politics (CAWP), National Information Bank on Women in Public Office, Eagleton Institute of Politics, Rutgers University, (copyright).

Table 21.36. BLACK OFFICIALS: BLACK ELECTED OFFICIALS BY OFFICE IN FLORIDA, THE SOUTH, AND THE UNITED STATES, JANUARY 1992 AND 1993

Office	Florida 1992	Florida 1993	South 1/ 1992	South 1/ 1993	United States 1992	United States 1993
Total	183	200	5,110	5,492	7,517	7,984
U.S. and state legislatures 2/	14	22	280	328	499	561
City and county offices 3/	126	133	3,432	3,675	4,557	4,819
Law enforcement 4/	24	28	474	518	847	922
Education 5/	19	17	924	971	1,614	1,682

1/ Includes Alabama, Arkansas, Delaware, District of Columbia, Florida, Georgia, Kentucky, Louisiana, Maryland, Mississippi, North Carolina, Oklahoma, South Carolina, Tennessee, Texas, Virginia, and West Virginia.
2/ Includes elected state administrators.
3/ County commissioners, councilmen, mayors, vice mayors, aldermen, regional officers and others.
4/ Judges, magistrates, constables, marshals, sheriffs, justices of the peace, and others.
5/ Members of state education agencies, college boards, school boards, and others.
Source: Joint Center for Political and Economic Studies, Washington, DC, *Black Elected Officials: A National Roster,* annual, (copyright).

Table 21.37. HISPANIC OFFICIALS: HISPANIC ELECTED OFFICIALS BY OFFICE IN FLORIDA THE SOUTH, AND THE UNITED STATES, SEPTEMBER 1994

Office	Florida	South	United States
Total	64	2,298	5,459
State executives and legislators, including U.S. representatives	16	61	199
County and municipal officials	33	1,059	2,197
Judicial and law enforcement	12	410	651
Education and school boards	3	768	2,412

Source: U.S., Department of Commerce, Bureau of the Census, *Statistical Abstract of the United States, 1996.*

Table 21.42. COMPOSITION OF CONGRESS AND STATE LEGISLATURES: NUMBER OF UNITED STATES REPRESENTATIVES AND SENATORS AND STATE LEGISLATORS BY PARTY AFFILIATION, SPECIFIED YEARS 1988 THROUGH 1996

Year 1/	Florida				United States			
	Demo-crats	Repub-licans	Demo-crats	Repub-licans	Demo-crats	Repub-licans	Demo-crats	Repub-licans
	U.S. represent-atives		U.S. senators		U.S. represent-atives		U.S. senators	
1989	10	9	1	1	259	174	55	45
1991	9	10	1	1	267	167	56	44
1993	10	13	1	1	258	176	57	43
1994	10	13	1	1	257	176	56	44
1995	8	15	1	1	204	230	47	53
1996	8	15	1	1	197	236	46	53
	State represent-atives		State senators		State represent-atives		State senators	
1988	73	47	23	17	3,277	2,176	1,192	751
1990	74	46	22	18	3,242	2,202	1,186	757
1992	71	49	20	20	3,186	2,223	1,132	799
1994 A/	63	57	19	21	2,817	2,603	1,021	905

A/ Status as of December 7, 1994.

1/ U.S. representative and senator data refer to the beginning of the first session. State legislative data refer to election years.

Note: Excludes vacancies and persons classified as Independents.

Source: U.S., Department of Commerce, Bureau of the Census, *Statistical Abstract of the United States, 1996*. Copyright 1995. The Council of State Governments. Reprinted with permission from *State Elective Officials and the Legislatures,* and 1994 National Conference of State Legislatures, Denver, CO, unpublished data, (copyright).

Table 21.43. APPORTIONMENT: MEMBERSHIP IN THE UNITED STATES HOUSE OF REPRESENTATIVES FOR FLORIDA AND THE UNITED STATES 1840 THROUGH 1990

Census of--	Florida	United States	Census of--	Florida	United States
1840	A/ 1	232	1930	5	435
1850	1	237	1940	6	435
1860	1	243	1950	8	437
1870	2	293	1960	12	435
1880	2	332	1970	15	435
1890	2	357	1980	19	435
1900	3	391	1990	23	435
1910	4	435			

A/ Assigned after apportionment.

Note: Total membership includes representatives assigned to newly admitted states after the apportionment acts. Population figures used for apportionment purposes are those determined for states by each decennial census.

Source: U.S., Department of Commerce, Bureau of the Census, *1990 Census Profile: Population Trends and Congressional Apportionment,* No. 1, March 1991.

COURTS AND LAW ENFORCEMENT

Youths Referred for Delinquency in Florida 1990-91 through 1994-95

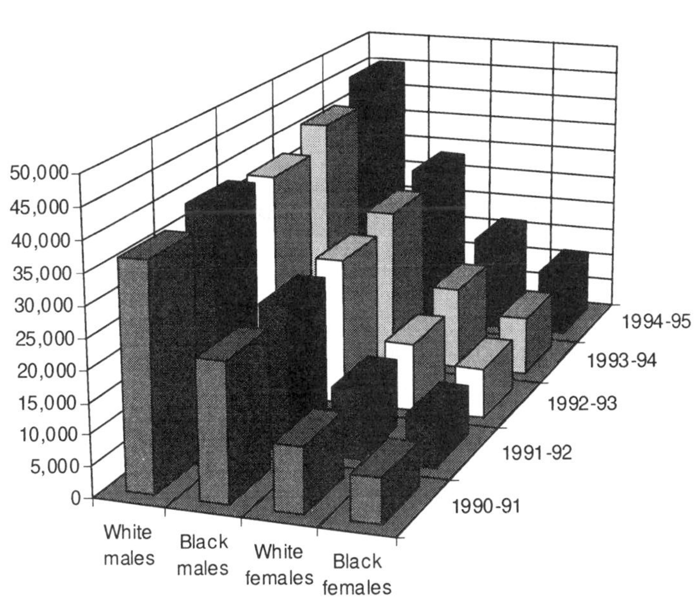

	1990-91	1991-92	1992-93	1993-94	1994-95
While males	36,770	38,902	37,957	41,443	45,251
Black males	22,431	23,831	24,689	26,729	28,265
Other males	264	307	301	365	405
White females	10,523	11,357	11,436	13,931	16,252
Black females	7,203	8,239	8,471	9,886	11,136
Other females	76	89	98	136	178
Unknown	310	387	510	640	788
Total	77,577	83,112	83,462	93,130	102,275

Source: State of Florida, Department of Juvenile Justice, Bureau of Research and Data, *Profile of Delinquency Cases and Youths Referred at Each State of the Juvenile Justice System, 1990-91 through 1994-95*. See Table 22.23 for county breakdowns for current year.

SECTION 22.00
COURTS AND LAW ENFORCEMENT

TABLES LISTED BY MAJOR HEADINGS

HEADING PAGE

SECTION 22.00
COURTS AND LAW ENFORCEMENT
(Continued)

TABLES LISTED BY MAJOR HEADINGS

HEADING PAGE

Table 22.01. CRIMINAL OFFENSES AND RATES: CRIME INDEX OFFENSES BY TYPE OF OFFENSE IN FLORIDA, 1991 THROUGH 1995

Item	Total index offenses 1/	Violent crime: Murder	Violent crime: Forcible sex	Violent crime: Robbery	Violent crime: Aggravated assault	Nonviolent crime: Burglary	Nonviolent crime: Larceny	Nonviolent crime: Motor vehicle theft
Number of index offenses 2/								
1991	1,129,704	1,276	12,390	53,076	91,439	264,749	603,922	102,852
1992	1,112,746	1,191	13,429	48,957	97,560	252,003	594,053	105,553
1993	1,116,567	1,187	13,752	47,742	99,108	245,353	594,793	114,632
1994	1,130,875	1,152	13,413	45,263	98,007	233,006	617,195	122,839
1995	1,078,619	1,030	12,259	42,142	94,777	213,050	605,751	109,610
Percentage change from previous year								
1991	0.6	-8.0	83.6	-1.7	-1.7	-3.8	3.1	1.5
1992	-1.5	-6.7	8.4	-7.8	6.7	-4.8	-1.6	2.6
1993	0.3	-0.3	2.4	-2.5	1.6	-2.6	0.1	8.6
1994	1.3	-2.9	-2.5	-5.2	-1.1	-5.0	3.8	7.2
1995	-4.6	-10.6	-8.6	-6.9	-3.3	-8.6	-1.9	-10.8
Rate per 100,000 population								
1991	8,561.0	9.7	93.9	402.2	692.9	2,006.3	4,576.6	779.4
1992	8,289.0	8.9	100.0	364.7	726.7	1,877.2	4,425.2	786.3
1993	8,204.8	8.7	101.1	350.8	728.3	1,802.9	4,370.7	842.3
1994	8,148.2	8.3	96.6	326.1	706.2	1,678.9	4,447.0	885.1
1995	7,623.1	7.3	86.6	297.8	669.8	1,505.7	4,281.1	774.7
Percentage change from previous year								
1991	0.3	-9.8	80.0	-3.7	-3.6	-5.6	1.1	-0.5
1992	-3.2	-8.2	6.5	-9.3	4.9	-6.4	-3.3	0.9
1993	-1.0	-1.7	1.0	-3.8	0.2	-4.0	-1.2	7.1
1994	-0.7	-4.8	-4.4	-7.0	-3.0	-6.9	1.7	5.1
1995	-6.4	-12.3	-10.4	-8.7	-5.1	-10.3	-3.7	-12.5
Percentage cleared								
1991	22.0	63.9	58.9	24.2	60.1	15.0	19.2	16.4
1992	21.3	67.8	55.6	24.7	59.8	14.5	17.7	15.4
1993	21.0	67.7	55.2	23.8	57.4	14.8	17.6	14.4
1994	21.2	68.8	54.6	24.3	57.8	14.8	18.2	13.8
1995	(NA)	(NA)	(NA)	(NA)	(NA)	(NA)	(NA)	(NA)

(NA) Not available.

1/ The crimes selected for use in the index are chosen based on their serious nature, their frequency of occurrence, and the reliability of reporting from citizens to law enforcement agencies. The Crime Index is used as a basic measure of crime.

2/ Actual offenses known to law enforcement officers, not the number of persons who committed them or number of injuries they caused.

Note: Rates may not add to totals due to rounding.

Source: State of Florida, Department of Law Enforcement, *Crime in Florida: 1995 Annual Report*, previous editions, and unpublished data.

Table 22.02. CRIMINAL OFFENSES AND RATES: CRIME INDEX OFFENSES, CRIME RATES, AND OFFENSES CLEARED IN THE STATE AND COUNTIES OF FLORIDA, 1995

County	Crime index offenses			Crime rate per 100,000 population		Offenses clear-ed 4/ (per-centage)
	Total 1/	Vio-lent 2/	Nonvio-lent 3/	1995	Per-centage change 1994 to 1995	
Florida	1,078,619	150,208	928,411	7,623.2	-6.4	21.5
Alachua	19,190	2,786	16,404	9,679.2	-5.7	22.3
Baker	597	136	461	2,944.5	51.8	20.1
Bay	8,804	898	7,906	6,325.9	-0.6	38.1
Bradford	1,148	134	1,014	4,717.3	-3.1	18.4
Brevard	24,876	3,353	21,523	5,590.2	-11.9	22.0
Broward	113,528	11,819	101,709	8,322.1	-10.4	23.0
Calhoun	71	11	60	592.3	-22.2	56.3
Charlotte	4,112	353	3,759	3,221.4	-6.2	23.6
Citrus	3,025	323	2,702	2,868.2	8.3	34.3
Clay	4,720	651	4,069	3,904.2	-3.7	44.7
Collier	10,157	1,308	8,849	5,446.0	0.9	18.4
Columbia	3,313	545	2,768	6,575.1	0.5	19.2
Dade	251,433	38,659	212,774	12,485.4	-0.9	15.7
De Soto	1,809	306	1,503	6,790.5	0.9	35.4
Dixie	571	77	494	4,598.9	-3.7	16.1
Duval	63,308	9,840	53,468	8,812.9	-8.4	21.5
Escambia	17,776	3,365	14,411	6,287.0	-9.5	29.0
Flagler	1,138	197	941	3,075.9	-6.7	29.5
Franklin	293	11	282	2,862.4	-21.8	5.1
Gadsden	1,878	371	1,507	4,198.1	-16.8	24.3
Gilchrist	124	16	108	1,043.1	-26.2	12.1
Glades	443	67	376	5,180.7	-15.2	11.1
Gulf	301	92	209	2,268.1	28.6	34.6
Hamilton	66	16	50	528.5	-8.7	6.1
Hardee	1,338	175	1,163	5,846.6	3.7	34.5
Hendry	1,156	287	869	3,919.0	-14.5	13.3
Hernando	4,740	663	4,077	4,020.5	-7.7	19.9
Highlands	4,408	566	3,842	5,704.7	5.1	24.5
Hillsborough	81,684	13,227	68,457	9,148.4	-15.8	19.9
Holmes	294	62	232	1,691.1	286.8	22.4
Indian River	5,610	559	5,051	5,596.4	-1.7	25.7
Jackson	1,299	214	1,085	2,788.9	-12.0	36.4
Jefferson	390	123	267	2,887.0	-18.4	38.5
Lafayette	0	0	0	0.0	0.0	0.0
Lake	7,056	1,075	5,981	3,988.0	-4.5	33.3
Lee	20,393	2,429	17,964	5,413.6	-6.5	27.1

See footnotes at end of table. Continued . . .

Table 22.02. CRIMINAL OFFENSES AND RATES: CRIME INDEX OFFENSES, CRIME RATES, AND OFFENSES CLEARED IN THE STATE AND COUNTIES OF FLORIDA, 1995 (Continued)

County	Crime index offenses			Crime rate per 100,000 population		Offenses cleared 4/ (percentage)
	Total 1/	Violent 2/	Nonviolent 3/	1995	Percentage change 1994 to 1995	
Leon	21,015	2,591	18,424	9,660.6	-7.7	27.0
Levy	1,067	133	934	3,575.4	-18.5	20.7
Liberty	36	4	32	523.8	-25.6	30.6
Madison	434	66	368	2,365.9	-5.7	27.6
Manatee	17,322	2,799	14,523	7,309.9	-4.4	21.6
Marion	14,154	2,419	11,735	6,301.5	1.3	39.0
Martin	5,899	797	5,102	5,265.3	2.8	25.5
Monroe	7,056	551	6,505	8,460.3	-5.0	15.2
Nassau	1,990	355	1,635	4,050.7	-1.7	28.6
Okaloosa	5,570	547	5,023	3,423.3	-5.1	25.2
Okeechobee	1,506	225	1,281	4,583.8	-9.3	30.1
Orange	64,602	9,694	54,908	8,512.3	-7.4	23.7
Osceola	9,684	1,179	8,505	7,087.9	-5.8	34.1
Palm Beach	82,954	9,433	73,521	8,615.9	-2.5	16.1
Pasco	12,377	1,372	11,005	4,050.4	-1.9	25.5
Pinellas	56,975	9,241	47,734	6,502.5	-6.4	25.8
Polk	32,561	3,320	29,241	7,347.6	-11.1	17.2
Putnam	5,843	886	4,957	8,405.3	2.5	51.5
St. Johns	3,928	604	3,324	4,000.5	-23.2	31.5
St. Lucie	10,041	1,462	8,579	5,866.4	2.0	24.4
Santa Rosa	4,120	579	3,541	4,287.6	2.3	20.4
Sarasota	17,014	1,833	15,181	5,715.1	-1.6	23.9
Seminole	15,088	1,674	13,414	4,654.9	-16.3	18.8
Sumter	1,343	277	1,066	3,683.9	2.2	30.2
Suwannee	697	78	619	2,282.7	-36.9	28.7
Taylor	907	222	685	4,950.3	-34.8	36.5
Union	60	10	50	474.4	-18.5	53.3
Volusia	21,801	2,877	18,924	5,410.1	-11.6	26.9
Wakulla	512	95	417	3,010.9	11.7	29.3
Walton	604	81	523	1,807.6	6.4	22.8
Washington	410	90	320	2,156.8	7.6	18.8

1/ Actual offenses known to law enforcement officers, not the number of persons who committed them or number of injuries they caused.

2/ Includes murder, forcible sex, robbery, and aggravated assault.

3/ Includes breaking and entering (burglary), larceny, and auto theft.

4/ Clearance of an offense occurs when an offender is identified, charged, and taken into custody, or occasionally when some element beyond law enforcement control precludes formal charges against the offender.

Note: Data are aggregates of offenses reported to municipal, county, and state law enforcement agencies and campus police departments.

Source: State of Florida, Department of Law Enforcement, unpublished data.

Table 22.03. CRIMINAL OFFENSES AND RATES: CRIME INDEX OFFENSES AND CRIME RATES IN THE STATE, COUNTIES, CITIES, AND SPECIFIED AREAS OF FLORIDA, 1995

Area	Number of index offenses 1/	Crime rate per 100,000 population
Florida	1,078,619	7,623.2
Alachua	19,190	9,679.2
Sheriff's office	6,498	7,513.5
Alachua	407	7,252.3
Archer	217	15,206.7
Gainesville	10,003	10,414.3
Hawthorne	223	16,147.7
High Springs	118	3,393.7
Micanopy	58	8,964.5
Newberry	215	10,070.3
Santa Fe Community College	74	(X)
University of Florida	1,331	(X)
Waldo	46	4,393.5
Baker	597	2,944.5
Sheriff's office	597	2,944.5
Bay	8,804	6,325.9
Sheriff's office	3,620	5,147.7
Cedar Grove	62	3,762.1
Florida State University	0	(X)
Lynn Haven	240	2,266.3
Mexico Beach	38	3,766.1
Panama City	3,304	9,001.3
Panama City Beach	1,240	27,056.5
Parker	155	3,146.6
Springfield	145	1,544.4
Bradford	1,148	4,717.3
Sheriff's office	581	3,027.0
Starke	567	11,026.8
Brevard	24,876	5,590.2
Sheriff's office	7,264	3,994.1
Cocoa	1,359	7,574.4
Cocoa Beach	1,127	8,864.9
Indialantic	115	3,911.6
Indian Harbour Beach	180	2,400.6
Melbourne	5,817	8,767.1
Melbourne Airport Authority	5	(X)
Melbourne Beach	96	3,009.4
Melbourne Village Police Department	0	0.0
Palm Bay	4,010	5,482.9
Rockledge	1,156	6,377.9
Brevard (Continued)		
Satellite Beach	429	4,245.4
Titusville	2,872	6,921.3
West Melbourne	445	4,931.8
State agencies	1	(X)
Broward	113,528	8,322.1
Sheriff's office	10,304	6,514.8
Coconut Creek	1,290	3,863.7
Cooper City	724	2,642.5
Coral Springs	4,859	5,200.2
Dania	2,350	13,662.0
Davie	3,413	6,249.7
Deerfield Beach	3,223	6,660.1
Ft. Lauderdale	25,036	16,747.5
Hallandale	2,719	8,634.8
Hillsboro Beach	10	568.8
Hollywood	12,146	9,690.3
Lauderdale Lakes	2,958	10,623.1
Lauderdale-by-the-Sea	288	9,590.4
Lauderhill	3,375	6,747.0
Lighthouse Point	345	3,310.6
Margate	2,519	5,327.9
Miramar	2,981	6,712.1
North Lauderdale	1,570	5,764.2
Oakland Park	4,025	14,326.4
Parkland	188	2,214.1
Pembroke Park	696	14,172.3
Pembroke Pines	4,502	5,118.9
Plantation	6,047	8,042.9
Pompano Beach	8,772	11,862.1
Sea Ranch Lakes	18	2,931.6
Seminole Indian Reservation	491	(X)
Sunrise	5,085	6,922.5
Tamarac	2,330	4,778.7
Wilton Manors	1,167	9,833.2
State agencies	97	(X)
Calhoun	71	592.3
Sheriff's office	0	0.0
Blountstown	71	2,880.3
Charlotte	4,112	3,221.4
Sheriff's office	3,699	3,197.9
Punta Gorda	413	3,448.0
Citrus	3,025	2,868.2
Sheriff's office	2,034	2,147.8

See footnotes at end of table.

Continued . . .

Table 22.03. CRIMINAL OFFENSES AND RATES: CRIME INDEX OFFENSES AND CRIME RATES IN THE STATE, COUNTIES, CITIES, AND SPECIFIED AREAS OF FLORIDA, 1995 (Continued)

Area	Number of index offenses 1/	Crime rate per 100,000 population
Citrus (Continued)		
Crystal River	615	14,916.3
Inverness	376	5,659.2
Clay	4,720	3,904.2
Sheriff's office	3,986	3,741.5
Green Cove Springs	294	6,065.6
Orange Park	440	4,624.8
Collier	10,157	5,446.0
Sheriff's office	8,766	5,283.9
Naples	1,390	6,745.9
State agencies	1	(X)
Columbia	3,313	6,575.1
Sheriff's office	1,838	4,557.2
Lake City	1,475	14,669.3
Dade	251,433	12,485.4
Metro-Dade	130,812	12,125.0
Bal Harbour	130	4,211.2
Bay Harbor Islands	97	2,056.4
Biscayne Park	92	2,998.7
Coral Gables	4,299	10,498.2
El Portal	115	4,600.0
Florida City	167	3,409.6
Florida International University	437	(X)
Golden Beach	18	2,166.1
Hialeah	15,654	7,676.9
Hialeah Gardens	841	7,439.2
Homestead	3,636	15,679.2
Indian Creek Village	5	9,615.4
Key Biscayne Police Department	279	3,137.7
Medley	419	48,271.9
Miami	59,170	16,188.9
Miami Beach	16,897	18,411.3
Miami Shores	993	9,784.2
Miami Springs	1,293	9,683.2
Miccosukee Police Department	49	(X)
North Bay Village	405	6,910.1
North Miami	6,812	13,420.5
North Miami Beach	3,391	9,374.9
Opa-Locka	3,001	18,570.5
South Miami	1,214	11,532.3
Surfside	462	10,819.7
Sweetwater	161	1,145.1
Dade (Continued)		
Virginia Gardens	124	5,457.7
West Miami	396	6,784.3
State agencies	64	(X)
De Soto	1,809	6,790.5
Sheriff's office	962	4,804.5
Arcadia	847	12,800.4
Dixie	571	4,598.9
Sheriff's office	468	4,507.4
Cross City	103	5,066.4
Duval	63,308	8,812.9
Atlantic Beach	0	0.0
Jacksonville	61,129	9,012.6
Jacksonville Airport	33	(X)
Jacksonville Beach	1,605	8,079.1
Neptune Beach	437	5,887.1
University of North Florida	104	(X)
Escambia	17,776	6,287.0
Sheriff's office	13,121	5,900.6
Pensacola	4,584	7,592.8
University of West Florida	68	(X)
State agencies	3	(X)
Flagler	1,138	3,075.9
Sheriff's office	796	2,589.9
Bunnell	196	9,391.5
Flagler Beach	146	3,497.0
Franklin	293	2,862.4
Sheriff's office	293	3,938.2
Apalachicola	0	0.0
Gadsden	1,878	4,198.1
Sheriff's office	999	3,195.2
Chattahoochee	41	962.7
Havana	101	5,436.0
Quincy	737	10,025.8
Gilchrist	124	1,043.1
Sheriff's office	124	1,043.1
Glades	443	5,180.7
Sheriff's office	443	5,180.7

See footnotes at end of table. Continued . . .

Table 22.03. CRIMINAL OFFENSES AND RATES: CRIME INDEX OFFENSES AND CRIME RATES IN THE STATE, COUNTIES, CITIES, AND SPECIFIED AREAS OF FLORIDA, 1995 (Continued)

Area	Number of index offenses 1/	Crime rate per 100,000 population
Gulf	301	2,268.1
Sheriff's office	201	2,199.8
Port St. Joe	99	2,394.8
State agencies	1	(X)
Hamilton	66	528.5
Sheriff's office	0	0.0
Jasper	4	192.8
White Springs	62	7,533.4
Hardee	1,338	5,846.6
Sheriff's office	877	5,472.0
Bowling Green	115	5,861.4
Wauchula	346	9,526.4
Zolfo Springs	0	0.0
Hendry	1,156	3,919.0
Sheriff's office	869	3,755.4
Clewiston	287	4,514.7
Hernando	4,740	4,020.5
Sheriff's office	4,154	3,773.6
Brooksville	586	7,499.4
Highlands	4,408	5,704.7
Sheriff's office	2,309	3,837.0
Avon Park	860	10,559.9
Sebring	1,239	13,845.1
Hillsborough	81,684	9,148.4
Sheriff's office	36,724	6,516.8
Plant City	2,256	8,859.2
Tampa	41,112	14,417.5
Tampa International Airport	363	(X)
Temple Terrace	539	2,878.7
University of South Florida	689	(X)
State agencies	1	(X)
Holmes	294	1,691.1
Sheriff's office	271	1,851.9
Bonifay	23	836.1
Indian River	5,610	5,596.4
Sheriff's office	3,372	5,258.9
Fellsmere	45	1,911.6
Indian River Shores	35	1,346.7
Sebastian	733	5,434.5
Indian River (Continued)		
Vero Beach	1,425	8,059.5
Jackson	1,299	2,788.9
Sheriff's office	939	2,636.8
Graceville	118	4,376.9
Marianna	233	3,742.4
Sneads	7	342.5
State agencies	2	(X)
Jefferson	390	2,887.0
Sheriff's office	279	2,628.9
Monticello	111	3,832.9
Lafayette	0	0.0
Sheriff's office	0	0.0
Lake	7,056	3,988.0
Sheriff's office	3,326	3,348.1
Clermont	377	5,212.2
Eustis	441	3,156.5
Fruitland Park	35	1,192.5
Groveland	82	3,429.5
Howey-in-the-Hills	7	889.5
Lady Lake	176	1,461.2
Leesburg	1,471	9,797.5
Mascotte	50	2,176.8
Minneola	3	137.5
Mount Dora	701	8,495.9
Tavares	266	3,292.9
Umatilla	118	4,904.4
State agencies	3	(X)
Lee	20,393	5,413.6
Sheriff's office	10,158	4,256.1
Cape Coral	3,487	4,063.8
Ft. Myers	6,327	13,614.1
Lee County Port Authority	201	(X)
Sanibel Police Department	210	3,650.3
State agencies	10	(X)
Leon	21,015	9,660.6
Sheriff's office	3,429	4,260.9
Capitol Police	84	(X)
Florida A & M University	443	(X)

See footnotes at end of table.

Continued . . .

Table 22.03. CRIMINAL OFFENSES AND RATES: CRIME INDEX OFFENSES AND CRIME RATES IN THE STATE, COUNTIES, CITIES, AND SPECIFIED AREAS OF FLORIDA, 1995 (Continued)

Area	Number of index offenses 1/	Crime rate per 100,000 population
Leon (Continued)		
Florida State University	447	(X)
Tallahassee	16,611	12,119.8
State agencies	1	(X)
Levy	1,067	3,575.4
Sheriff's office	473	1,843.6
Chiefland	322	16,692.6
Williston	272	12,046.1
Liberty	36	523.8
Sheriff's office	36	523.8
Madison	434	2,365.9
Sheriff's office	274	1,836.0
Madison	160	4,678.4
Manatee	17,322	7,309.9
Sheriff's office	11,601	6,972.2
Bradenton	4,281	8,978.8
Bradenton Beach	97	5,798.0
Holmes Beach	367	7,303.5
Longboat Key	131	2,030.1
Palmetto	843	8,648.8
State agencies	2	(X)
Marion	14,154	6,301.5
Sheriff's office	7,058	4,002.9
Belleview	106	3,224.8
Dunnellon	143	7,966.6
Ocala	6,847	15,847.0
Martin	5,899	5,265.3
Sheriff's office	4,553	4,727.3
Jupiter Island	28	4,819.3
Sewalls Point	26	1,523.1
Stuart	1,292	9,616.7
Monroe	7,056	8,460.3
Sheriff's office	4,005	7,081.1
Key West	3,051	11,366.5
Nassau	1,990	4,050.7
Sheriff's office	1,355	3,434.4
Fernandina Beach	635	6,564.7
Okaloosa	5,570	3,423.3
Sheriff's office	3,411	3,088.6
Okaloosa (Continued)		
Crestview	623	5,125.5
Ft. Walton Beach	1,219	5,540.2
Niceville	281	2,427.6
Okaloosa Air Terminal	0	(X)
Valparaiso	36	551.0
Okeechobee	1,506	4,583.8
Sheriff's office	1,191	4,286.3
Okeechobee	315	6,214.2
Orange	64,602	8,512.3
Sheriff's office	36,923	7,394.0
Apopka	1,921	10,412.5
Eatonville	183	7,352.4
Edgewood	107	9,410.7
Maitland	571	5,994.8
Oakland Police Department	46	6,092.7
Ocoee	1,012	5,447.3
Orlando Police Department	20,750	12,185.6
University of Central Florida	277	(X)
Windermere	24	1,418.4
Winter Garden	902	7,455.8
Winter Park	1,880	7,651.6
State agencies	6	(X)
Osceola	9,684	7,087.9
Sheriff's office	4,612	5,515.4
Kissimmee	4,094	11,012.2
St. Cloud	978	6,178.5
Palm Beach	82,954	8,615.9
Sheriff's office	31,608	6,813.2
Atlantis	55	3,252.5
Belle Glade	2,587	15,212.3
Boca Raton	3,154	4,724.4
Boynton Beach	5,774	11,763.3
Briny Breezes	11	2,784.8
Delray Beach	6,767	13,481.4
Florida Atlantic University	239	(X)
Greenacres City	1,504	6,456.0
Gulf Stream	18	2,528.1
Highland Beach	41	1,261.2
Hypoluxo	93	8,237.4
Juno Beach	68	2,678.2

See footnotes at end of table.

Continued . . .

Table 22.03. CRIMINAL OFFENSES AND RATES: CRIME INDEX OFFENSES AND CRIME RATES IN THE STATE, COUNTIES, CITIES, AND SPECIFIED AREAS OF FLORIDA, 1995 (Continued)

Area	Number of index offenses 1/	Crime rate per 100,000 population
Palm Beach (Continued)		
Jupiter	1,461	5,030.0
Jupiter Inlet Colony	1	246.9
Lake Clarke Shores	78	2,139.3
Lake Park	908	13,123.3
Lake Worth	4,093	14,033.0
Lantana	960	11,389.3
Manalapan	21	6,402.4
Mangonia Park	461	33,357.5
North Palm Beach	543	4,584.6
Ocean Ridge	44	2,741.4
Pahokee	355	5,112.3
Palm Beach	474	4,809.3
Palm Beach County School Board	1,471	(X)
Palm Beach Gardens	2,037	6,568.6
Palm Beach Shores	70	6,756.8
Palm Springs	615	6,259.5
Riviera Beach	4,072	14,735.5
Royal Palm Beach	828	4,815.1
South Bay	258	6,383.0
South Palm Beach	17	1,137.1
Tequesta	136	2,961.7
West Palm Beach	12,086	15,815.6
State agencies	46	(X)
Pasco	12,377	4,050.4
Sheriff's office	9,790	3,574.3
Dade City	911	15,357.4
New Port Richey	894	6,212.6
Port Richey	154	5,793.8
Zephyrhills	628	7,223.4
Pinellas	56,975	6,502.5
Sheriff's office	12,954	4,787.4
Belleair	89	2,201.3
Belleair Beach	17	808.0
Belleair Bluffs	64	2,881.6
Clearwater	7,249	7,165.7
Dunedin	1,380	3,944.2
Gulfport	1,117	9,405.5
Indian Rocks Beach	242	5,792.2
Indian Shores	71	4,820.1
Kenneth City	303	6,973.5
Largo	3,160	4,683.9
Madeira Beach	215	5,058.8
Oldsmar	574	6,431.4
Pinellas County Campus Police	44	(X)
Pinellas (Continued)		
Pinellas Park	3,255	7,368.3
Redington Beach 2/	35	1,267.7
Redington Shores	47	1,942.1
Safety Harbor	656	4,065.7
St. Pete Beach	739	7,812.7
St. Petersburg	22,899	9,479.5
Seminole	414	4,264.1
South Pasadena	211	3,600.7
Tarpon Springs	973	5,082.0
Treasure Island	219	2,976.8
University of South Florida	41	(X)
State agencies	7	(X)
Polk	32,561	7,347.6
Sheriff's office	14,312	5,229.8
Auburndale	1,119	12,075.1
Bartow	1,393	9,332.1
Davenport	26	1,469.8
Dundee	47	1,861.4
Eagle Lake	60	3,176.3
Ft. Meade	213	3,860.8
Frostproof	152	5,232.4
Haines City	1,111	8,816.8
Lake Alfred	211	5,678.1
Lake Hamilton	129	11,507.6
Lake Wales	897	9,066.1
Lakeland	9,941	13,321.1
Mulberry	196	5,891.2
Winter Haven	2,754	10,838.7
Putnam	5,843	8,405.3
Sheriff's office	3,935	6,907.4
Crescent City	119	6,456.9
Palatka	1,789	16,711.8
St. Johns	3,928	4,000.5
Sheriff's office	2,905	3,539.5
Florida School Deaf and Blind	12	(X)
St. Augustine	765	6,327.5
St. Augustine Beach	246	6,113.3
St. Lucie	10,041	5,866.4
Sheriff's office	2,263	3,629.2
Ft. Pierce	5,075	13,705.5
Port St. Lucie	2,701	3,763.1
State agencies	2	(X)

See footnotes at end of table.

Continued . . .

Table 22.03. CRIMINAL OFFENSES AND RATES: CRIME INDEX OFFENSES AND CRIME RATES IN THE STATE, COUNTIES, CITIES, AND SPECIFIED AREAS OF FLORIDA, 1995 (Continued)

Area	Number of index offenses 1/	Crime rate per 100,000 population
Santa Rosa	4,120	4,287.6
Sheriff's office	3,404	4,118.2
Gulf Breeze	241	4,069.6
Milton	474	6,310.7
State agencies	1	(X)
Sarasota	17,014	5,715.1
Sheriff's office	9,778	4,591.3
North Port	403	2,658.1
Sarasota	6,236	12,195.2
University of South Florida	55	(X)
Venice	541	2,932.2
State agencies	1	(X)
Seminole	15,088	4,654.9
Sheriff's office	5,451	3,358.1
Altamonte Springs	2,882	7,600.8
Casselberry	1,310	5,425.8
Lake Mary	102	1,406.7
Longwood	679	4,991.9
Oviedo	728	4,064.8
Sanford	3,114	8,818.8
Winter Springs	821	3,197.9
State agencies	1	(X)
Sumter	1,343	3,683.9
Sheriff's office	964	3,469.0
Bushnell	72	3,167.6
Center Hill	31	4,089.7
Coleman	0	0.0
Webster	34	4,086.5
Wildwood	242	6,126.6
Suwannee	697	2,282.7
Sheriff's office	697	2,282.7
Taylor	907	4,950.3
Sheriff's office	301	2,720.8
Taylor (Continued)		
Perry	606	8,348.3
Union	60	474.4
Sheriff's office	60	474.4
Volusia	21,801	5,410.1
Sheriff's office	6,075	3,458.1
Daytona Beach	7,027	11,100.1
Daytona Beach Regional	0	(X)
Daytona Beach Shores	240	8,955.2
DeLand	2,646	14,722.1
Edgewater	667	3,814.9
Holly Hill	918	7,955.6
Lake Helen	31	1,271.5
New Smyrna Beach	863	4,692.0
Oak Hill	23	2,149.5
Orange City	598	9,776.0
Ormond Beach Police Department	1,298	4,115.5
Ponce Inlet	21	990.6
Port Orange	864	2,173.6
South Daytona	320	2,482.7
Volusia County Beach Management	210	(X)
Wakulla	512	3,010.9
Sheriff's office	512	3,010.9
Walton	604	1,807.6
Sheriff's office	458	1,633.9
DeFuniak Springs	145	2,693.2
State agencies	1	(X)
Washington	410	2,156.8
Sheriff's office	258	1,731.7
Chipley	151	3,673.1
State agencies	1	(X)

(X) Not applicable.

1/ Actual offenses known to enforcement officers. Index offenses include murder, forcible sex, robbery, aggravated assault, burglary, larceny, and auto theft.

2/ Includes North Redington Beach.

Note: The data reflected in this table is by geographic jurisdiction and is not intended to depict an individual law enforcement agency's activity. Sheriff's office totals include the activity occurring within those incorporated jurisdictions who do not report directly to the Uniform Crime Reporting (UCR) program. County totals reflect all UCR activity occurring within that county. State agencies are listed only for counties with state agency activity.

Source: State of Florida, Department of Law Enforcement, unpublished data.

Table 22.04. CRIMINAL OFFENSES: NUMBER OF ARRESTS BY AGE, SEX, RACE, AND OFFENSE IN FLORIDA, 1995

Offense	Age: 17 and under	Age: 18 and over	Sex: Male	Sex: Female	Race: White	Race: Black	Race: Other
Total	106,534	619,706	582,529	143,711	460,723	262,307	2,777
Murder	182	943	1,023	102	546	575	2
Forcible rape	372	1,921	2,268	25	1,304	974	8
Forcible sodomy	98	293	376	15	259	128	2
Forcible fondling	144	694	816	22	595	237	2
Robbery	3,326	6,904	9,308	922	3,907	6,298	18
Aggravated assault	7,094	37,740	35,248	9,586	24,235	20,445	126
Burglary	10,863	15,660	24,327	2,196	16,620	9,815	64
Larceny	31,367	61,853	61,877	31,343	58,372	34,398	438
Motor vehicle theft	4,871	6,537	9,949	1,459	6,164	5,211	28
Manslaughter	11	146	131	26	111	45	1
Kidnap/abduction	47	716	690	73	472	286	4
Arson	295	312	494	113	428	175	3
Simple assault	8,664	54,983	50,465	13,182	42,129	21,200	233
Drug arrests	9,292	78,745	73,386	14,651	48,140	39,658	173
Bribery	2	29	24	7	22	9	0
Embezzlement	82	460	293	249	364	177	1
Fraud	610	8,458	6,189	2,879	6,242	2,799	27
Counterfeit/forgery	284	5,209	3,981	1,512	3,442	2,018	28
Extortion/blackmail	38	257	273	22	175	118	1
Intimidation	1,237	7,899	7,610	1,526	5,479	3,627	27
Prostitution/commercialized sex	103	6,800	3,610	3,293	5,107	1,776	20
Nonforcible sex offenses	267	2,645	2,601	311	2,385	521	6
Stolen property: buy/ receive/possess	823	4,008	4,214	617	2,792	2,013	23
Driving under influence	271	51,447	43,049	8,669	47,124	3,831	705
Destruction/damage/ vandalism	2,483	2,434	4,210	707	3,485	1,408	18
Gambling	90	658	704	44	237	500	11
Weapons violations	1,803	6,084	7,193	694	4,287	3,557	41
Liquor law violations	1,670	21,025	18,824	3,871	18,292	4,211	190
Miscellaneous	20,145	234,846	209,396	45,595	158,008	96,297	577

Note: A person is counted each time he/she is arrested or summoned; therefore, arrest counts do not reflect the specific number of persons arrested since one individual may be arrested several times for the same or different crimes. Arrest data are useful for measuring law enforcement activity and involvement in criminal acts by the age, sex, and race of perpetrators.

Source: State of Florida, Department of Law Enforcement, *Crime in Florida: 1995 Annual Report,* and unpublished data.

Table 22.05. CRIMINAL OFFENSES: NUMBER OF NARCOTIC DRUG ARRESTS FOR SALE AND POSSESSION BY AGE, RACE, SEX, AND RESIDENCY IN FLORIDA, 1995

Classification	Total	Age: 17 and under	Age: 18 and over	Race: White	Race: Black	Race: Other	Sex: Male	Sex: Female	Residency: In-state	Residency: Out-of-state
Sale/manufacture										
Total	18,897	1,649	17,248	7,683	11,182	32	16,140	2,757	18,254	643
Amphetamine	108	3	105	102	6	0	79	29	104	4
Barbiturate	57	8	49	54	3	0	38	19	57	0
Cocaine	13,005	965	12,040	4,028	8,962	15	11,157	1,848	12,639	366
Heroin	223	11	212	133	89	1	193	30	201	22
Hallucinogen	202	46	156	181	19	2	180	22	190	12
Marijuana	4,288	537	3,751	2,374	1,900	14	3,719	569	4,092	196
Opium/derivative	50	1	49	49	1	0	28	22	49	1
Paraphernalia/equipment	44	7	37	28	16	0	30	14	43	1
Synthetic	80	8	72	66	14	0	59	21	77	3
Unknown	444	31	413	360	84	0	375	69	433	11
Other	396	32	364	308	88	0	282	114	369	27
Possession/use										
Total	73,650	8,191	65,459	42,943	30,562	145	61,078	12,572	71,595	2,055
Amphetamine	380	19	361	368	12	0	267	113	369	11
Barbiturate	249	22	227	235	14	0	183	66	242	7
Cocaine	29,882	2,184	27,698	12,321	17,524	37	24,370	5,512	29,263	619
Heroin	376	14	362	257	118	1	306	70	368	8
Hallucinogen	612	146	466	573	36	3	518	94	583	29
Marijuana	32,825	5,075	27,750	23,607	9,130	88	28,628	4,197	31,713	1,112
Opium/derivative	88	9	79	80	8	0	60	28	85	3
Paraphernalia/equipment	8,124	617	7,507	4,510	3,600	14	5,914	2,210	7,905	219
Synthetic	179	15	164	154	25	0	134	45	175	4
Unknown	190	17	173	170	20	0	144	46	178	12
Other	745	73	672	668	75	2	554	191	714	31

Note: Data are for all drug sale and possession arrests, regardless of the offense status as a primary or secondary offense.

Source: State of Florida, Department of Law Enforcement, unpublished data.

Table 22.06. DOMESTIC VIOLENCE: CRIMES BY TYPE OF OFFENSE, 1994 AND 1995, AND ARRESTS BY OFFENSE AND BY AGE AND SEX OF OFFENDER, 1995, IN FLORIDA

Offense	Crimes 1994 Number	Crimes 1994 Rate per 100,000 population 1/	Crimes 1995 Number	Crimes 1995 Rate per 100,000 population 1/	Crimes 1995 As a percentage of all crimes 2/	Percentage change 1994 to 1995
Total	119,930	864.1	131,152	926.9	A/	9.4
Murder	230	1.7	195	1.4	18.9	-15.2
Manslaughter	10	0.1	14	0.1	25.5	40.0
Forcible sex offenses	3,435	24.7	3,129	22.1	25.5	-8.9
Forcible rape	1,667	12.0	1,465	10.4	21.5	-12.1
Forcible sodomy	578	4.2	526	3.7	31.3	-9.0
Forcible fondling	1,190	8.6	1,138	8.0	30.3	-4.4
Aggravated assault	23,765	171.2	25,817	182.5	27.2	8.6
Simple assault	89,583	645.5	98,628	697.1	46.7	10.1
Intimidation	2,808	20.2	3,273	23.1	(NA)	16.6
Arson	99	0.7	96	0.7	2.9	-3.0

Offense	Arrests, 1995 Number	As a percentage of all arrests 2/	Juveniles Male	Juveniles Female	Adults Male	Adults Female
Total	56,931	7.8	3,024	1,628	41,985	10,294
Murder	122	10.8	10	3	89	20
Manslaughter	7	4.5	1	0	3	3
Forcible sex offenses	587	16.7	67	1	517	2
Forcible rape	390	17.0	44	0	346	0
Forcible sodomy	53	13.6	10	0	43	0
Forcible fondling	144	17.2	13	1	128	2
Aggravated assault	15,893	35.4	958	492	10,931	3,512
Simple assault	39,184	61.6	1,869	1,104	29,564	6,647
Intimidation	916	10.0	76	22	729	89
Arson	32	5.3	7	1	14	10
Weapons violations	190	2.4	36	5	138	11

(NA) Not available.

A/ Total number of crimes as represented by the source includes index and mandatory offenses and excludes optional offenses such as intimidation, weapons violations, destruction/damage/vandalism, etc. for which no report to FDLE is required; therefore a comparison of the totals is not valid.

1/ Computed using Bureau of Economic and Business Research Florida Estimates of Population.

2/ As a percentage of all similarly committed crimes or arrests.

Source: State of Florida, Department of Law Enforcement, *Crime in Florida: 1995 Annual Report*.

Table 22.07. DOMESTIC VIOLENCE: VICTIMS AND RELATIONSHIP TO OFFENDER BY AGE AND SEX OF VICTIM AND BY TYPE OF WEAPON USED IN FLORIDA, 1995

Relationship to offender	Total victims	Age and sex of victim: Juveniles: Total	Juveniles: Male	Juveniles: Female	Adults: Total	Adults: Male	Adults: Female
Total	131,152	16,563	6,470	10,093	114,589	28,834	85,755
Spouse	40,768	276	23	253	40,492	8,146	32,346
Ex-spouse	4,715	30	2	28	4,685	1,017	3,668
Parent	7,807	0	0	0	7,807	2,080	5,727
Step-parent	1,234	296	111	185	938	698	240
Brother/sister	8,873	2,920	1,281	1,639	5,953	2,697	3,256
Child	8,343	6,121	2,608	3,513	2,222	761	1,461
Step-child	1,845	1,275	519	756	570	279	291
Child of boy/ girlfriend	661	473	192	281	188	63	125
Other	4,939	1,676	607	1,069	3,263	1,107	2,156
In-laws	1,457	104	39	65	1,353	634	719
Cohabitant	39,968	1,703	418	1,285	38,265	8,776	29,489
Acquaintance	10,542	1,689	670	1,019	8,853	2,576	6,277

Relationship to offender	Type of weapon used: Handgun	Other firearm	Knife	Blunt object	Hands/ fists/ feet	Threat/ intimidation	Other 1/
Total	2,338	1,004	7,659	7,353	104,178	3,458	5,162
Spouse	624	261	1,844	1,506	34,249	1,138	1,146
Ex-spouse	135	30	169	179	3,322	661	219
Parent	78	40	547	553	6,072	245	272
Step-parent	23	12	107	83	885	36	88
Brother/sister	177	77	950	669	6,495	146	359
Child	109	71	291	823	6,000	171	878
Step-child	38	19	69	115	1,405	53	146
Child of boy/ girlfriend	16	7	27	56	492	16	47
Other	153	56	419	405	3,454	119	333
In-laws	59	21	121	106	1,027	58	65
Cohabitant	455	214	2,463	2,034	33,254	526	1,022
Acquaintance	471	196	652	824	7,523	289	587

1/ Includes unknown weapon.

Source: State of Florida, Department of Law Enforcement, *Crime in Florida: 1995 Annual Report*.

Table 22.08. CRIME RATES: PROPERTY AND VIOLENT CRIME RATES IN FLORIDA AND THE UNITED STATES, 1985 THROUGH 1994

(rates per 100,000 population)

Year	Florida			United States		
	All crime	Property crime 1/	Violent crime 2/	All crime	Property crime 1/	Violent crime 2/
1985	7,574.2	6,633.1	941.1	5,206.7	4,650.5	556.2
1986	8,228.4	7,191.9	1,036.5	5,480.4	4,862.6	617.7
1987	8,503.2	7,478.7	1,024.4	5,550.0	4,940.3	609.7
1988 A/	8,937.6	7,819.9	1,117.7	5,664.2	5,027.1	637.2
1989	8,804.5	7,695.1	1,109.4	5,741.0	5,077.9	663.1
1990	8,810.8	7,566.5	1,244.3	5,820.3	5,088.5	731.8
1991	8,547.2	7,362.9	1,184.3	5,897.8	5,139.7	758.1
1992	8,358.2	7,151.0	1,207.2	5,660.2	4,902.7	757.5
1993	8,351.0	7,145.0	1,206.0	5,484.4	4,737.6	746.8
1994	8,250.0	7,103.2	1,146.8	5,374.4	4,658.3	716.0

A/ Data for Florida were unavailable and are estimates.
1/ Includes burglary, larceny-theft, and motor vehicle theft.
2/ Includes murder, forcible rape, robbery, and aggravated assault.
Note: Some data may be revised.
Source: U.S., Department of Justice, Federal Bureau of Investigation, *Crime in the United States, 1994,* and previous editions.

Table 22.09. CAPITAL PUNISHMENT: PRISONERS UNDER SENTENCE OF DEATH BY RACE, SEX, AND HISPANIC ORIGIN IN FLORIDA, THE SOUTH AND THE UNITED STATES, DECEMBER 31, 1993 AND 1994

Item	Florida		South 1/		United States
	Number	Percentage of United States	Number	Percentage of United States	
Prisoners under sentence of death on 12-31-93 A/	325	11.9	1,512	55.4	2,729
Changes during 1994					
Received under death sentence	39	12.8	195	64.1	304
Removed from death row 2/	21	18.8	71	63.4	112
Executed	1	3.2	26	83.9	31
Prisoners under sentence of death on 12-31-94	342	11.8	1,610	55.7	2,890
White	214	13.0	922	56.0	1,645
Black	128	10.7	666	55.6	1,197
Women	4	9.8	21	51.2	41
Hispanic origin 3/	32	14.3	107	47.8	224

A/ Revised.
1/ Includes Alabama, Arkansas, Delaware, Florida, Georgia, Kentucky, Louisiana, Maryland, Mississippi, North Carolina, Oklahoma, South Carolina, Tennessee, Texas, and Virginia.
2/ Excludes executions. Includes suicide, murder, and death by natural causes.
3/ Persons of Hispanic origin may be of any race.

Source: U.S., Department of Justice, Bureau of Justice Statistics, *Bureau of Justice Statistics Bulletin: Capital Punishment, 1994.*

Table 22.10. PRISONERS: NUMBER UNDER JURISDICTION OF STATE OR FEDERAL CORRECTIONAL AUTHORITIES IN FLORIDA AND THE UNITED STATES DECEMBER 31, 1991 THROUGH 1994

Item	1991	1992	1993 A/	1994 B/
Florida				
Total prisoners	46,533	48,302	53,048	57,139
Percentage change from previous year	4.8	3.8	9.8	7.7
Prisoners sentenced to more than a year	46,533	48,285	52,883	57,129
Per 100,000 resident population	346	348	385	406
United States				
Total prisoners	825,619	883,656	970,444	1,053,738
Percentage change from previous year	6.7	7.0	9.8	8.6
Prisoners sentenced to more than a year	789,349	847,271	932,266	1,012,463
Per 100,000 resident population	310	329	351	387

A/ Revised.
B/ Preliminary.
Source: U.S., Department of Justice, Bureau of Justice Statistics, *Bureau of Justice Statistics Bulletin: Prisoners in 1994,* and previous editions.

Table 22.11. POPULATION UNDER CRIMINAL SENTENCE: INCARCERATED OFFENDERS AND OFFENDERS UNDER COMMUNITY SUPERVISION OF THE FLORIDA DEPARTMENT OF CORRECTIONS, JUNE 30, 1991 THROUGH 1995

Item	1991	1992	1993	1994	1995
Under supervision, total	147,912	158,098	180,543	189,718	198,048
Incarcerated offenders	46,233	47,012	50,603	56,052	61,992
White male	17,624	17,460	18,654	21,117	23,658
White female	1,049	966	983	1,175	1,494
Black male	25,123	25,901	28,069	30,818	33,586
Black female	1,614	1,439	1,536	1,714	1,998
Other male	A/ 799	A/ 1,147	A/ 1,242	1,228	1,253
Other female	A/ 24	A/ 99	A/ 119	0	3
Offenders under community supervision	101,679	111,086	129,940	133,666	136,056
Probation	79,467	82,966	91,070	91,236	93,723
Felony	78,481	81,889	88,782	88,717	90,879
Misdemeanor	986	1,077	1,191	1,212	1,362
Administrative	(NA)	(NA)	1,097	1,307	1,482
Parole	2,243	2,596	2,907	2,965	2,838
Pretrial intervention	4,158	4,917	5,441	6,455	7,793
Community control	(NA)	(NA)	14,892	14,926	14,692
Drug offender probation	(NA)	(NA)	3,587	4,808	6,332
Other	15,811	20,607	12,043	13,276	10,678

(NA) Not available.
A/ Includes data not distributed by race.
Source: State of Florida, Department of Corrections, *1994-95 Annual Report: Guidebook to Corrections in Florida,* and previous editions.

Table 22.12. POPULATION UNDER CRIMINAL SENTENCE: INCARCERATED OFFENDERS AND OFFENDERS UNDER COMMUNITY SUPERVISION OF THE FLORIDA DEPARTMENT OF CORRECTIONS BY PRIMARY OFFENSE, JUNE 30, 1995

Primary offense	Incarcerated offenders		Community supervision				
	Total	Admitted 1994-95	Total 1/	Probation 2/	Community control	Control release	Parole
Total	61,992	22,247	136,046	100,045	14,692	7,899	2,838
Murder, manslaughter	9,019	1,259	2,281	1,370	223	36	558
First degree murder	4,102	467	300	108	31	3	145
Second degree murder	3,844	471	702	301	49	0	311
Third degree murder	104	21	87	59	9	0	14
Homicide, other	53	23	287	228	29	5	22
Manslaughter	644	187	582	427	52	17	63
DUI manslaughter	272	90	323	247	53	11	3
Sexual offenses	6,070	1,437	8,311	6,748	1,081	0	195
Capital sexual battery	2,096	412	830	701	86	0	8
Life sexual battery	1,153	130	290	218	34	0	24
First degree sexual battery	1,170	271	1,637	1,321	196	0	61
Other sexual battery	181	14	369	256	33	0	70
Lewd, lascivious behavior	1,470	610	5,185	4,252	732	0	32
Robbery	9,431	2,454	4,768	2,576	693	447	465
Robbery with weapon	5,762	1,362	1,921	959	258	148	331
Robbery without weapon	3,669	1,092	2,847	1,617	435	299	134
Violent personal offenses	6,186	2,569	17,118	13,385	2,058	368	154
Aggravated assault	675	399	4,424	3,611	474	75	40
Aggravated battery	2,209	1,015	5,354	4,091	708	186	46
Assault and battery on law enforcement officers	1,175	472	2,824	2,145	369	1	6
Other battery	62	32	674	572	55	1	14
Aggravated stalking	19	14	278	226	37	3	1
Resisting arrest with violence	404	245	1,829	1,385	215	56	3
Kidnapping	1,300	249	584	432	70	16	33
Arson	197	74	271	197	34	25	5
Abuse of children	105	53	735	605	87	4	6
Other violent offenses	40	16	145	121	9	1	0
Burglary	10,301	4,146	15,948	10,862	2,136	1,703	266
Burglary of structure	2,928	1,384	8,436	5,960	1,071	692	124
Burglary of dwelling	4,449	1,894	4,700	2,943	665	823	77
Armed burglary	1,648	497	776	460	137	122	17
Burglary with assault	1,191	321	832	573	149	39	20
Other burglary offenses	85	50	1,204	926	114	27	28
Theft, forgery, fraud	5,896	3,054	33,847	25,649	3,015	1,718	262
Grand theft	1,485	828	14,401	11,140	1,181	462	117
Grand theft, automobile	1,301	659	2,743	1,901	265	329	27

See footnotes at end of table.

Continued . . .

Table 22.12. POPULATION UNDER CRIMINAL SENTENCE: INCARCERATED OFFENDERS AND OFFENDERS UNDER COMMUNITY SUPERVISION OF THE FLORIDA DEPARTMENT OF CORRECTIONS BY PRIMARY OFFENSE, JUNE 30, 1995 (Continued)

Primary offense	Incarcerated offenders Total	Incarcerated offenders Admitted 1994-95	Community supervision Total 1/	Probation 2/	Community control	Control release	Parole
Theft, forgery, fraud (Continued)							
Petit theft, third conviction	310	109	784	585	85	83	4
Stolen property	1,539	730	3,631	2,546	523	405	30
Forgery, uttering and counterfeiting	707	419	4,472	3,230	452	254	40
Worthless checks	186	122	2,793	2,238	198	71	12
Fraudulent practices	368	187	5,023	4,009	311	114	32
Drugs	11,085	5,616	37,511	26,408	4,028	3,111	709
Sale/purchase/manufacturing	6,018	2,918	15,016	10,105	1,779	1,790	220
Trafficking	2,076	887	2,109	1,471	197	205	161
Possession	2,991	1,811	20,386	14,832	2,052	1,116	328
Weapons, escape	2,674	1,170	5,432	3,916	626	327	61
Escape	1,238	399	521	285	87	86	20
Carry concealed firearm	104	91	2,361	1,802	163	52	9
Possess firearm or any weapon	955	462	1,159	750	198	137	10
Shoot into dwelling or vehicle	262	148	724	556	106	38	3
Other weapons offenses	115	70	667	523	72	14	19
Other offenses	1,246	542	9,379	7,937	738	187	54
Failure to stop after accident	81	59	924	753	103	30	1
DUI, fourth conviction	183	141	1,021	808	144	55	9
Cause injury while DUI	67	48	673	555	100	10	2
Racketeering	91	26	243	206	17	17	2
Criminal procedure violation	561	130	781	616	80	29	7
Arson, other	135	51	535	406	70	24	7
Kidnapping, custody offenses	7	3	123	102	7	2	1
Traffic, other	2	0	136	120	11	1	3
Pollution/hazardous materials	2	3	207	154	11	2	0
Other offenses	117	81	4,736	4,217	195	17	22
Data unavailable	84	0	1,451	1,194	94	2	114

DUI Driving under the influence.
1/ Includes pretrial intervention, conditional release, and other supervision not reported separately.
2/ Includes drug offender probation.

Source: State of Florida, Department of Corrections, *1994-95 Annual Report: The Guidebook to Corrections in Florida.*

Table 22.13. POPULATION UNDER CRIMINAL SENTENCE: INCARCERATED OFFENDERS AND OFFENDERS UNDER COMMUNITY SUPERVISION OF THE FLORIDA DEPARTMENT OF CORRECTIONS BY COUNTY OF COMMITMENT OR SUPERVISION AND BY RACE IN THE STATE AND COUNTIES OF FLORIDA
JUNE 30, 1995

County	Incarcerated offenders				Community supervision 1/			
	Total	White	Black	Other races 2/	Total 3/	White	Black	Other races
Florida	61,992	25,152	35,584	1,256	136,056	84,571	49,286	2,111
Alachua	799	177	620	2	1,860	841	1,014	5
Baker	127	64	60	3	170	119	51	0
Bay	1,049	569	471	9	2,204	1,571	613	20
Bradford	257	122	130	5	422	240	178	4
Brevard	1,494	745	737	12	3,301	2,286	992	23
Broward	6,880	2,444	4,400	36	14,944	8,244	6,552	148
Calhoun	87	33	52	2	128	90	38	0
Charlotte	298	199	93	6	655	566	76	13
Citrus	167	143	23	1	665	593	65	7
Clay	237	137	96	4	701	567	127	7
Collier	472	295	170	7	1,552	1,300	232	20
Columbia	375	156	218	1	954	567	384	3
Dade	8,327	2,805	5,209	313	13,835	6,938	6,332	565
De Soto	228	95	124	9	303	185	114	4
Dixie	120	73	47	0	217	169	46	2
Duval	3,234	914	2,300	20	5,471	2,800	2,625	46
Escambia	1,724	642	1,070	12	4,271	2,314	1,935	22
Flagler	68	32	36	0	290	209	74	7
Franklin	59	36	23	0	136	88	48	0
Gadsden	369	45	323	1	715	140	565	10
Gilchrist	26	21	5	0	101	93	6	2
Glades	29	15	13	1	71	47	22	2
Gulf	57	18	38	1	155	105	50	0
Hamilton	71	22	45	4	200	73	126	1
Hardee	147	74	58	15	316	244	63	9
Hendry	110	42	61	7	295	180	108	7
Hernando	299	188	111	0	983	826	151	6
Highlands	312	138	159	15	608	363	237	8
Hillsborough	6,433	2,497	3,712	224	11,650	7,179	4,256	215
Holmes	70	55	14	1	154	138	16	0
Indian River	416	155	258	3	753	539	205	9
Jackson	344	136	199	9	490	291	199	0
Jefferson	89	14	75	0	145	46	99	0
Lafayette	40	19	20	1	46	40	6	0
Lake	594	267	315	12	1,540	1,056	470	14
Lee	946	418	488	40	2,042	1,429	575	38

See footnotes at end of table. Continued . . .

Table 22.13. POPULATION UNDER CRIMINAL SENTENCE: INCARCERATED OFFENDERS AND OFFENDERS UNDER COMMUNITY SUPERVISION OF THE FLORIDA DEPARTMENT OF CORRECTIONS BY COUNTY OF COMMITMENT OR SUPERVISION AND BY RACE IN THE STATE AND COUNTIES OF FLORIDA JUNE 30, 1995 (Continued)

County	Incarcerated offenders				Community supervision 1/			
	Total	White	Black	Other races 2/	Total 3/	White	Black	Other races
Leon	1,061	224	833	4	2,939	1,233	1,695	11
Levy	60	30	30	0	378	263	111	4
Liberty	38	14	23	1	55	44	11	0
Madison	119	29	89	1	318	98	220	0
Manatee	785	386	377	22	2,393	1,649	728	16
Marion	909	418	485	6	2,958	1,913	1,014	31
Martin	424	162	246	16	742	554	183	5
Monroe	622	390	216	16	1,582	1,269	292	21
Nassau	106	50	54	2	335	265	68	2
Okaloosa	518	225	284	9	1,387	1,016	359	12
Okeechobee	150	79	59	12	382	311	67	4
Orange	3,805	1,419	2,240	146	9,393	5,197	3,987	209
Osceola	376	201	156	19	1,703	1,314	326	63
Palm Beach	2,139	753	1,366	20	6,771	4,265	2,231	275
Pasco	976	782	175	19	2,460	2,300	141	19
Pinellas	4,282	1,929	2,303	50	9,566	6,491	3,009	66
Polk	3,116	1,467	1,598	51	5,120	3,369	1,724	27
Putnam	405	162	240	3	830	480	345	5
St. Johns	368	184	178	6	805	535	265	5
St. Lucie	1,048	298	737	13	1,630	957	663	10
Santa Rosa	219	178	37	4	644	588	52	4
Sarasota	633	320	304	9	1,904	1,460	431	13
Seminole	712	331	364	17	2,849	2,035	775	39
Sumter	175	61	112	2	496	337	157	2
Suwannee	170	70	99	1	434	296	135	3
Taylor	166	57	108	1	388	225	163	0
Union	179	77	99	3	48	28	19	1
Volusia	1,623	774	838	11	4,298	2,982	1,273	43
Wakulla	79	50	28	1	231	176	54	1
Walton	88	49	38	1	371	292	77	2
Washington	83	54	27	2	215	153	61	1
			0					
Interstate	124	88	26	10	2	(NA)	(NA)	(NA)
Data unavailable	80	36	42	2	86	(NA)	(NA)	(NA)

(NA) Not available.

1/ Felony and misdemeanor probation, community control, pretrial intervention, control release, parole, and other supervision.

2/ Males only.

3/ Includes data not distributed by race.

Source: State of Florida, Department of Corrections, *1994-95 Annual Report: The Guidebook to Corrections in Florida,* and unpublished data.

Table 22.15. COUNTY DETENTION FACILITIES: AVERAGE DAILY INMATE POPULATION AND INCARCERATION RATES IN THE STATE AND COUNTIES OF FLORIDA 1993 THROUGH 1995

County	Average daily population 1/					Incarceration rate 2/		
				Percentage change				
	1993	1994	1995	1993-1995	1994-1995	1993	1994	1995
Florida	34,530	37,485	42,760	23.8	14.1	2.5	2.7	3.1
Alachua	437	509	651	49.0	27.9	2.3	2.6	3.4
Baker	71	73	59	-16.9	-19.2	3.7	3.7	3.0
Bay	445	533	512	15.1	-3.9	3.3	3.9	3.8
Bradford	34	41	42	23.5	2.4	1.5	1.7	1.7
Brevard	667	736	790	18.4	7.3	1.6	1.7	1.8
Broward	2,980	3,331	3,546	19.0	6.5	2.3	2.5	2.6
Calhoun	15	15	19	26.7	26.7	1.3	1.3	1.7
Charlotte	147	153	165	12.2	7.8	1.2	1.2	1.3
Citrus	129	163	158	22.5	-3.1	1.3	1.6	1.5
Clay	113	127	142	25.7	11.8	1.0	1.1	1.2
Collier	385	472	513	33.2	8.7	1.0	2.6	2.8
Columbia	177	189	197	11.3	4.2	3.9	3.9	4.0
Dade	5,600	6,439	6,787	21.2	5.4	2.8	3.2	3.4
De Soto	74	80	89	20.3	11.3	2.9	3.0	3.4
Dixie	18	36	54	200.0	50.0	1.6	3.0	4.4
Duval	2,347	2,496	2,518	7.3	0.9	3.4	3.5	3.5
Escambia	1,016	1,123	1,222	20.3	8.8	3.9	4.1	4.4
Flagler	41	50	58	41.5	16.0	1.2	1.4	1.7
Franklin	19	39	70	268.4	79.5	2.0	3.9	7.0
Gadsden	117	134	139	18.8	3.7	2.8	3.0	3.1
Gilchrist	39	30	27	-30.8	-10.0	3.7	2.6	2.3
Glades	25	28	26	4.0	-7.1	3.1	3.4	3.1
Gulf	30	33	30	0.0	-9.1	2.6	2.5	2.3
Hamilton	71	58	80	12.7	37.9	6.2	4.8	6.7
Hardee	83	96	103	24.1	7.3	4.1	4.3	4.6
Hendry	112	105	120	7.1	14.3	4.0	3.7	4.2
Hernando	247	230	257	4.0	11.7	2.2	2.0	2.2
Highlands	171	173	198	15.8	14.5	2.3	2.3	2.6
Hillsborough	2,112	2,150	2,520	19.3	17.2	2.4	2.4	2.9
Holmes	14	22	19	35.7	-13.6	0.9	1.3	1.1
Indian River	274	277	288	5.1	4.0	2.9	2.8	3.0
Jackson	122	149	178	45.9	19.5	2.9	3.3	3.9
Jefferson 3/	17	(X)	12	-29.4	(X)	1.4	(X)	0.9
Lafayette	9	9	13	44.4	44.4	1.5	1.5	2.2
Lake	442	432	469	6.1	8.6	2.7	2.5	2.7
Lee	712	791	887	24.6	12.1	1.4	2.2	2.4
Leon	509	588	732	43.8	24.5	2.5	2.8	3.5
Levy	90	79	81	-10.0	2.5	3.3	2.7	2.8

See footnotes at end of table.

Continued . . .

Table 22.15. COUNTY DETENTION FACILITIES: AVERAGE DAILY INMATE POPULATION AND INCARCERATION RATES IN THE STATE AND COUNTIES OF FLORIDA 1993 THROUGH 1995 (Continued)

	Average daily population 1/					Incarceration rate 2/		
				Percentage change				
County	1993	1994	1995	1993-1995	1994-1995	1993	1994	1995
Liberty	11	8	8	-27.3	0.0	1.9	1.2	1.2
Madison	18	66	75	316.7	13.6	1.1	3.7	4.2
Manatee	618	732	759	22.8	3.7	2.8	3.2	3.3
Marion	869	883	962	10.7	8.9	4.1	4.1	4.4
Martin	300	344	348	16.0	1.2	2.8	3.1	3.2
Monroe	307	385	465	51.5	20.8	3.8	4.7	5.7
Nassau	86	92	105	22.1	14.1	1.9	1.9	2.2
Okaloosa	275	347	371	34.9	6.9	1.8	2.2	2.3
Okeechobee	137	132	164	19.7	24.2	4.3	4.1	5.1
Orange	3,063	3,170	3,198	4.4	0.9	4.2	4.3	4.3
Osceola	323	392	522	61.6	33.2	2.6	3.0	4.0
Palm Beach	1,627	1,745	2,097	28.9	20.2	1.8	1.9	2.2
Pasco	416	426	480	15.4	12.7	1.4	1.4	1.6
Pinellas	1,483	1,521	1,806	21.8	18.7	1.7	1.7	2.1
Polk	1,340	1,277	1,337	-0.2	4.7	3.1	2.9	3.1
Putnam	155	167	188	21.3	12.6	2.3	2.4	2.7
St. Johns	192	209	239	24.5	14.4	2.1	2.2	2.5
St. Lucie	580	652	702	21.0	7.7	3.6	3.9	4.2
Santa Rosa	146	149	149	2.1	0.0	1.6	1.6	1.6
Sarasota	492	562	616	25.2	9.6	1.7	1.9	2.1
Seminole	631	601	667	5.7	11.0	2.0	1.9	2.1
Sumter	97	107	96	-1.0	-10.3	2.9	3.1	2.7
Suwannee	34	43	59	73.5	37.2	1.2	1.5	2.0
Taylor	83	85	126	51.8	48.2	4.8	4.9	7.2
Union	9	11	12	33.3	9.1	0.8	0.9	0.9
Volusia	1,145	1,177	1,199	4.7	1.9	2.9	3.0	3.0
Wakulla	81	128	119	46.9	-7.0	5.4	7.8	7.2
Walton	76	56	86	13.2	53.6	2.6	1.8	2.7
Washington	26	35	40	53.8	14.3	1.5	2.0	2.2

(X) Not applicable.
1/ Average annual figures based on monthly data.
2/ Per 1,000 population based upon self-reports of county total population as well as county inmate population.
3/ Facility closed October 1993 and reopened June 1995.
Note: Data are collected monthly from the 67 county jail systems statewide from January 1, 1993 through December 31, 1995. The high increase in inmate population and incarceration rates in some of the counties is the result of holding a large portion of the inmate population for the U.S. Marshal and the contracting of bedspace.

Source: State of Florida, Department of Corrections, Bureau of Planning, Research, and Statistics, *Florida County Detention Facilities: 1995 Annual Report,* prepublication release and previous editions.

Table 22.16. COUNTY DETENTION FACILITIES: AVERAGE RATED INMATE CAPACITY IN THE STATE AND COUNTIES OF FLORIDA, 1995

County	Average rated capacity	Average over/under capacity Number	Per-centage	County	Average rated capacity	Average over/under capacity Number	Per-centage
Florida	44,520	-3,755	-8.4	Lafayette	15	-2	-13.3
				Lake	576	-107	-18.6
Alachua	874	-224	-25.6	Lee	851	36	4.2
Baker	81	-22	-27.2	Leon	908	-175	-19.3
Bay	547	-35	-6.4	Levy	124	-43	-34.7
Bradford	60	-18	-30.0	Liberty	15	-7	-46.7
Brevard	732	58	7.9	Madison	121	-46	-38.0
Broward	3,694	-148	-4.0	Manatee	900	-141	-15.7
Calhoun	24	-5	-20.8	Marion	1,144	-182	-15.9
Charlotte	186	-21	-11.3	Martin	456	-108	-23.7
Citrus	200	-43	-21.5	Monroe	655	-190	-29.0
Clay	125	17	13.6	Nassau	103	2	1.9
Collier	754	-242	-32.1	Okaloosa	396	-25	-6.3
Columbia	215	-18	-8.4	Okeechobee	168	-4	-2.4
Dade	6,272	514	8.2	Orange	3,234	-37	-1.1
De Soto	119	-30	-25.2	Osceola	389	133	34.2
Dixie	110	-56	-50.9	Palm Beach	2,450	-353	-14.4
Duval	3,100	-583	-18.8	Pasco	545	-65	-11.9
Escambia	1,280	-57	-4.5	Pinellas	1,829	-24	-1.3
Flagler	134	-76	-56.7	Polk	1,194	142	11.9
Franklin	76	-6	-7.9	Putnam	226	-37	-16.4
Gadsden	154	-15	-9.7	St. Johns	425	-186	-43.8
Gilchrist	44	-17	-38.6	St. Lucie	768	-66	-8.6
Glades	36	-10	-27.8	Santa Rosa	176	-27	-15.3
Gulf	40	-10	-25.0	Sarasota	717	-101	-14.1
Hamilton	102	-23	-22.5	Seminole	812	-145	-17.9
Hardee	161	-58	-36.0	Sumter	123	-27	-22.0
Hendry	110	10	9.1	Suwannee	127	-68	-53.5
Hernando	290	-32	-11.0	Taylor	180	-54	-30.0
Highlands	199	-1	-0.5	Union	26	-14	-53.8
Hillsborough	2,649	-129	-4.9	Volusia	1,494	-295	-19.7
Holmes	17	2	11.8	Wakulla	129	-10	-7.8
Indian River	413	-125	-30.3	Walton	101	-15	-14.9
Jackson	300	-122	-40.7	Washington	26	14	53.8
Jefferson 1/	20	-8	-40.0				

(X) Not applicable.
1/ Facility reopened June 1995.
Note: Includes jails, work release facilities, work camps, detention centers, and road prisons.
Source: State of Florida, Department of Corrections, Bureau of Planning, Research, and Statistics, *Florida County Detention Facilities: 1995 Annual Report*, prepublication release.

Table 22.20. JUVENILE DELINQUENCY: CASES AND YOUTHS REFERRED FOR DELINQUENCY BY MOST SERIOUS OFFENSE IN FLORIDA, 1993-94 THROUGH 1994-95

Offense	Cases received 1993-94	Cases received 1994-95	Cases received Percentage change	Youths referred 1993-94	Youths referred 1994-95	Youths referred Percentage change
Felonies	62,875	63,375	0.80	42,267	44,159	4.48
Murder/manslaughter	162	163	0.62	162	162	0.00
Attempted murder	277	237	-14.44	270	227	-15.93
Sex offense	1,618	1,497	-7.48	1,511	1,388	-8.14
Armed robbery	1,692	1,665	-1.60	1,450	1,500	3.45
Other robbery	2,195	2,506	14.17	1,921	2,202	14.63
Arson	612	643	5.07	574	593	3.31
Burglary	21,155	20,621	-2.52	15,474	15,358	-0.75
Auto theft	8,161	7,045	-13.67	4,282	3,899	-8.94
Grand larceny	4,074	4,359	7.00	2,652	2,912	9.80
Receiving stolen property	601	511	-14.98	350	297	-15.14
Concealed firearm	1,295	1,150	-11.20	903	829	-8.19
Aggravated assault/battery	8,063	8,605	6.72	5,740	6,315	10.02
Forgery	403	480	19.11	288	331	14.93
Felony nonmarijuana drug	3,619	4,200	16.05	1,939	2,505	29.19
Marijuana felony	931	1,154	23.95	612	774	26.47
Escape	1,895	1,562	-17.57	379	479	26.39
Resisting arrest with violence	528	518	-1.89	319	321	0.63
Shooting/throwing missile	1,020	1,083	6.18	693	748	7.94
Other felony	4,574	5,376	17.53	2,748	3,319	20.78
Misdemeanors	76,744	85,919	11.96	47,663	54,006	13.31
Assault/battery	15,836	17,857	12.76	10,149	11,615	14.44
Prostitution	95	80	-15.79	60	52	-13.33
Sex offense	133	176	32.33	97	112	15.46
Petty larceny	6,345	7,095	11.82	3,829	4,411	15.20
Shoplifting	22,194	26,419	19.04	16,690	20,140	20.67
Receiving stolen property	150	108	-28.00	60	45	-25.00
Concealed weapon	995	858	-13.77	603	503	-16.58
Disorderly conduct	2,625	2,737	4.27	1,441	1,423	-1.25
Vandalism	4,830	4,754	-1.57	2,829	2,704	-4.42
Trespassing	7,643	7,804	2.11	3,280	3,430	4.57
Loitering and prowling	2,771	2,818	1.70	1,124	1,113	-0.98
Misdemeanor nonmarijuana drug	1,137	1,849	62.62	719	1,158	61.06
Marijuana misdemeanor	3,250	4,095	26.00	1,829	2,335	27.67
Alcohol-related offenses	2,573	2,347	-8.78	1,967	1,653	-15.96
Violation of game laws	197	210	6.60	155	175	12.90
Resisting arrest without violence	1,940	2,227	14.79	703	801	13.94
Other misdemeanor	4,030	4,485	11.29	2,128	2,336	9.77
Other delinquency	17,095	19,702	15.25	3,200	4,110	28.44
Contempt	1,114	1,170	5.03	271	319	17.71
Violation of ordinance	82	20	-75.61	44	9	-79.55
Traffic	175	188	7.43	90	83	-7.78
Interstate compact	279	287	2.87	220	217	-1.36
Nonlaw violation of community control	5,983	7,111	18.85	951	1,239	30.28
Nonlaw violation of furlough	9	6	-33.33	2	2	0.00
Case reopened	3,556	4,555	28.09	751	1,172	56.06
Prosecution previously deferred	4,319	4,461	3.29	708	881	24.44
Transfer from other county	1,578	1,904	20.66	163	188	15.34

Note: 1993-94 data are revised. Percentage change from 1993-94.

Source: State of Florida, Department of Juvenile Justice, Bureau of Data and Research, *Profile of Delinquency Cases and Youths Referred at Each Stage of the Juvenile Justice System, 1990-91 Through 1994-95.*

Table 22.21. JUVENILE DELINQUENCY: CASES AT VARIOUS STAGES OF THE JUVENILE JUSTICE SYSTEM BY AGE, RACE, AND SEX IN FLORIDA, 1994-95

Item	Received	De-tained 1/	Disposition Non-judicial	Judicial
Total	168,996	31,019	87,513	92,228
0-9	2,210	84	1,677	509
10	1,869	131	1,304	686
11	3,696	374	2,342	1,527
12	8,633	1,119	5,014	3,965
13	16,886	2,731	9,271	8,531
14	26,585	4,876	13,707	14,916
15	33,399	7,033	16,672	19,526
16	36,373	7,236	18,203	20,849
17	36,020	6,828	18,085	19,651
18+	3,325	607	1,238	2,068
White male	73,703	12,260	38,635	39,904
Black male	55,059	13,540	26,083	34,042
Other male	626	129	301	394
White female	21,945	2,542	13,244	9,122
Black female	16,289	2,361	8,526	8,102
Other female	217	13	119	110
Unknown	1,157	174	605	554

Item	Disposition (Continued) Referred to JASP	Placed on community control	Commit-ments 2/	Trans-ferred to adult court
Total	24,121	36,418	9,309	7,019
0-9	638	155	2	2
10	508	264	10	2
11	888	637	57	0
12	1,858	1,805	218	8
13	3,014	3,785	763	34
14	4,020	6,237	1,640	238
15	4,219	7,788	2,517	571
16	4,575	7,976	2,270	2,414
17	4,202	7,154	1,603	3,422
18+	199	617	229	328
White male	11,077	17,066	3,946	2,848
Black male	5,920	11,938	4,144	3,658
Other male	111	148	36	34
White female	3,995	3,889	603	184
Black female	2,751	3,122	543	242
Other female	53	45	6	2
Unknown	214	210	31	51

JASP Juvenile Alternative Services Program.

1/ Placement in detention during the interim between arrest and case disposition.

2/ Placement in commitment programs ranging from day-treatment programs for less serious offenders to secure training schools and boot camps for more serious offenders.

Note: Since not all charges are always disposed in the same way, some duplication may exist.

Source: State of Florida, Department of Juvenile Justice, Bureau of Data and Research, *Profile of Delinquency Cases and Youths Referred at Each Stage of the Juvenile Justice System, 1990-91 Through 1994-95.*

Table 22.22. JUVENILE DELINQUENCY: YOUTHS REFERRED FOR DELINQUENCY TO THE JUVENILE JUSTICE SYSTEM BY AGE IN THE STATE AND COUNTIES OF FLORIDA, 1994-95

County	0-9	10	11	12	13	14	15	16	17	18 and over
Florida	1,894	1,480	2,699	5,696	10,356	15,070	18,654	21,236	22,979	2,211
Alachua	30	34	37	69	138	226	234	283	317	30
Baker	3	0	3	8	9	9	20	27	21	1
Bay	27	22	29	74	124	151	177	244	237	16
Bradford	3	2	5	13	13	23	32	38	42	2
Brevard	37	42	46	135	288	401	515	615	634	49
Broward	202	131	226	485	902	1,284	1,570	1,834	2,092	181
Calhoun	1	1	0	6	5	5	12	13	16	2
Charlotte	21	8	17	20	47	75	116	118	143	9
Citrus	10	6	17	37	46	84	109	91	113	6
Clay	13	20	28	68	103	154	190	187	215	16
Collier	16	19	25	73	118	156	191	237	213	12
Columbia	13	8	11	21	48	62	71	82	80	3
Dade	146	141	243	612	1,217	1,875	2,457	3,025	3,293	444
De Soto	3	10	4	15	25	32	29	42	31	2
Dixie	3	0	1	1	4	9	6	11	11	3
Duval	64	62	139	319	588	854	1,082	1,073	1,131	80
Escambia	36	33	46	123	262	339	433	503	469	39
Flagler	9	2	9	20	26	50	50	55	65	5
Franklin	0	1	0	3	6	10	15	12	21	0
Gadsden	4	2	3	11	40	66	91	78	89	6
Gilchrist	3	3	4	4	10	10	16	16	25	1
Glades	5	2	1	2	3	5	11	13	15	2
Gulf	2	2	4	8	12	21	13	17	16	3
Hamilton	0	4	1	4	7	15	19	24	22	2
Hardee	0	2	3	17	23	35	41	51	52	9
Hendry	9	2	4	20	26	37	47	54	63	3
Hernando	2	1	10	34	71	76	92	91	93	16
Highlands	14	10	20	41	54	81	80	105	98	9
Hillsborough	139	126	234	421	805	1,197	1,409	1,545	1,647	302
Holmes	0	0	1	3	6	10	10	11	13	1
Indian River	13	11	22	53	76	95	116	133	137	9
Jackson	5	4	8	12	26	34	48	56	53	8
Jefferson	1	0	0	5	8	10	19	28	21	1
Lafayette	0	0	1	0	2	3	5	6	5	1
Lake	44	25	46	77	123	157	205	219	237	10
Lee	19	17	50	98	209	327	447	510	574	41
Leon	23	28	47	73	185	220	258	334	329	20

See footnote at end of table. Continued . . .

Table 22.22. JUVENILE DELINQUENCY: YOUTHS REFERRED FOR DELINQUENCY TO THE JUVENILE JUSTICE SYSTEM BY AGE IN THE STATE AND COUNTIES OF FLORIDA, 1994-95 (Continued)

County	0-9	10	11	12	13	14	15	16	17	18 and over
Levy	3	1	2	8	14	23	41	42	40	8
Liberty	0	0	1	1	1	0	8	5	3	0
Madison	0	1	2	11	13	13	29	18	27	6
Manatee	75	45	60	142	221	342	392	384	397	32
Marion	48	27	55	121	193	245	310	305	312	30
Martin	20	14	15	46	73	90	115	139	132	7
Monroe	5	7	7	21	30	39	49	86	82	9
Nassau	7	12	10	19	25	45	72	68	79	3
Okaloosa	6	6	20	44	91	165	229	227	282	29
Okeechobee	4	5	16	19	28	39	55	58	53	6
Orange	114	76	199	362	651	978	1,237	1,340	1,379	106
Osceola	29	28	37	68	121	207	210	261	280	28
Palm Beach	130	70	134	286	542	750	955	1,054	1,172	150
Pasco	21	24	65	88	212	294	319	350	306	24
Pinellas	184	117	231	465	728	1,007	1,104	1,250	1,302	130
Polk	104	85	136	275	421	611	717	765	794	71
Putnam	15	11	31	35	67	112	123	148	172	8
St. Johns	20	5	18	24	49	93	101	124	157	7
St. Lucie	22	24	26	98	162	179	237	274	247	11
Santa Rosa	0	6	10	28	52	69	106	136	133	12
Sarasota	36	21	41	74	145	191	232	275	346	26
Seminole	31	25	64	127	220	349	411	532	578	43
Sumter	8	7	5	19	24	44	43	39	52	2
Suwannee	4	1	4	5	22	20	29	31	43	2
Taylor	1	5	5	18	16	24	24	27	28	0
Union	0	0	0	3	3	10	7	6	11	0
Volusia	73	61	134	218	374	567	676	712	795	70
Wakulla	2	3	4	6	16	24	33	24	26	1
Walton	0	0	1	4	17	19	36	47	48	6
Washington	0	1	3	2	8	12	16	16	24	2
Unknown	0	0	1	1	1	3	4	9	11	5
Out-of-state	12	11	17	73	161	308	498	703	1,035	33

Note: The number of youths referred is determined by counting only the most serious offense for which a youth is charged during the fiscal year. This differs from the number of cases received in that the most serious offense on any given date is counted as one case. Therefore, the same youth may be referred for additional offenses on different dates throughout the year, resulting in more than one case received.

Source: State of Florida, Department of Juvenile Justice, Bureau of Data and Research, *Profile of Delinquency Cases and Youths Referred at Each Stage of the Juvenile Justice System, 1990-91 Through 1994-95,* and unpublished data.

Table 22.23. JUVENILE DELINQUENCY: YOUTHS REFERRED FOR DELINQUENCY TO THE JUVENILE JUSTICE SYSTEM BY SEX AND RACE IN THE STATE AND COUNTIES OF FLORIDA, 1994-95

County	Total	Male			Female			Unknown
		White	Black	Other	White	Black	Other	
Florida	102,275	45,251	28,265	405	16,252	11,136	178	788
Alachua	1,398	433	558	4	153	245	2	3
Baker	101	68	15	0	12	6	0	0
Bay	1,101	620	185	14	197	71	11	3
Bradford	173	87	40	0	26	18	0	2
Brevard	2,762	1,421	538	18	566	208	7	4
Broward	8,907	3,167	3,543	17	989	1,061	6	124
Calhoun	61	35	12	1	9	4	0	0
Charlotte	574	364	66	0	125	19	0	0
Citrus	519	357	35	0	115	9	0	3
Clay	994	614	123	6	189	50	4	8
Collier	1,060	653	137	4	208	44	0	14
Columbia	399	188	110	0	54	47	0	0
Dade	13,453	4,792	5,206	7	1,458	1,912	7	71
De Soto	193	91	48	0	28	26	0	0
Dixie	49	32	4	0	10	3	0	0
Duval	5,392	1,804	1,996	53	720	759	25	35
Escambia	2,283	787	816	30	294	337	16	3
Flagler	291	152	44	1	70	21	1	2
Franklin	68	34	15	0	12	7	0	0
Gadsden	390	25	259	0	12	93	1	0
Gilchrist	92	60	8	0	21	3	0	0
Glades	59	27	15	8	6	1	1	1
Gulf	98	45	21	0	20	12	0	0
Hamilton	98	24	50	0	8	14	0	2
Hardee	233	163	14	0	46	9	0	1
Hendry	265	142	52	9	37	20	2	3
Hernando	486	305	57	0	93	29	0	2
Highlands	512	252	118	0	83	56	0	3
Hillsborough	7,825	3,177	2,221	27	1,152	1,031	3	214
Holmes	55	42	5	1	6	0	0	1
Indian River	665	354	138	0	125	46	0	2
Jackson	254	119	73	1	35	26	0	0
Jefferson	93	15	60	0	5	13	0	0
Lafayette	23	11	6	0	4	2	0	0
Lake	1,143	583	240	1	203	115	0	1
Lee	2,292	1,273	375	2	415	208	2	17
Leon	1,517	518	555	0	183	257	1	3

See footnote at end of table. Continued . . .

Table 22.23. JUVENILE DELINQUENCY: YOUTHS REFERRED FOR DELINQUENCY TO THE JUVENILE JUSTICE SYSTEM BY SEX AND RACE IN THE STATE AND COUNTIES OF FLORIDA, 1994-95 (Continued)

County	Total	Male			Female			Unknown
		White	Black	Other	White	Black	Other	
Levy	182	104	40	0	22	15	0	1
Liberty	19	10	3	0	5	1	0	0
Madison	120	20	84	0	6	10	0	0
Manatee	2,090	995	497	0	359	197	0	42
Marion	1,646	870	380	1	250	137	0	8
Martin	651	343	147	0	129	29	1	2
Monroe	335	216	41	0	62	14	1	1
Nassau	340	204	60	1	62	13	0	0
Okaloosa	1,099	599	162	13	253	59	5	8
Okeechobee	283	169	50	1	43	20	0	0
Orange	6,442	2,491	2,039	49	1,043	776	17	27
Osceola	1,269	733	156	6	293	55	6	20
Palm Beach	5,243	2,149	1,630	17	757	640	8	42
Pasco	1,703	1,119	83	1	439	55	2	4
Pinellas	6,518	3,128	1,440	79	1,116	685	17	53
Polk	3,979	1,854	975	5	660	477	1	7
Putnam	722	282	221	0	112	96	0	11
St. Johns	598	300	148	0	93	57	0	0
St. Lucie	1,280	527	409	1	173	166	0	4
Santa Rosa	552	396	21	2	126	5	2	0
Sarasota	1,387	792	239	2	243	104	4	3
Seminole	2,380	1,286	409	7	505	172	0	1
Sumter	243	107	86	0	27	22	0	1
Suwannee	161	83	43	0	23	12	0	0
Taylor	148	54	58	0	25	11	0	0
Union	40	18	12	0	5	5	0	0
Volusia	3,680	1,887	736	2	747	301	1	6
Wakulla	139	90	20	0	22	6	1	0
Walton	178	92	39	0	39	7	0	1
Washington	84	41	23	0	13	7	0	0
Unknown	35	19	5	0	5	1	1	4
Out-of-state	2,851	1,439	251	14	906	199	22	20

Note: The number of youths referred is determined by counting only the most serious offense for which a youth is charged during the fiscal year. This differs from the number of cases received in that the most serious offense on any given date is counted as one case. Therefore, the same youth may be referred for additional offenses on different dates throughout the year, resulting in more than one case received.

Source: State of Florida, Department of Juvenile Justice, Bureau of Data and Research, *Profile of Delinquency Cases and Youths Referred at Each Stage of the Juvenile Justice System, 1990-91 Through 1994-95,* and unpublished data.

Table 22.30. VICTIM SERVICES: CRIMES COMPENSATION TRUST FUNDS RECEIPTS IN THE STATE, JUDICIAL CIRCUITS, AND COUNTIES OF FLORIDA FISCAL YEAR 1994-95

(rounded to thousands of dollars)

Judicial circuit and county	Total	Court cost 1/	Other 2/
Florida	17,450	15,048	2,401
Circuit 1	669	568	101
Escambia	401	330	71
Okaloosa	147	135	13
Santa Rosa	91	80	11
Walton	29	23	6
Circuit 2	512	461	51
Franklin	22	17	5
Gadsden	66	62	4
Jefferson	24	23	2
Leon	367	331	36
Liberty	3	3	0
Wakulla	30	26	4
Circuit 3	178	149	29
Columbia	56	47	10
Dixie	8	6	2
Hamilton	33	32	0
Lafayette	5	3	1
Madison	20	14	6
Suwannee	28	24	4
Taylor	28	23	5
Circuit 4	1,722	1,529	193
Clay	211	198	13
Duval	1,403	1,240	163
Nassau	108	91	17
Circuit 5	896	736	159
Citrus	129	98	31
Hernando	107	92	15
Lake	201	179	22
Marion	429	344	85
Sumter	30	24	6
Circuit 6	1,773	1,540	232
Pasco	383	342	41
Pinellas	1,390	1,198	191
Circuit 7	758	668	90
Flagler	52	42	10
Putnam	78	70	8
St. Johns	37	10	28
Volusia	591	547	44
Circuit 8	312	266	46
Alachua	236	209	27
Baker	18	10	8
Bradford	25	21	4
Gilchrist	13	11	3
Circuit 8 (Cont.)			
Levy	18	13	4
Union	2	2	0
Circuit 9	1,602	1,390	212
Orange	1,450	1,248	202
Osceola	152	142	10
Circuit 10	708	623	85
Hardee	73	62	11
Highlands	43	29	14
Polk	592	532	60
Circuit 11	1,083	913	171
Dade	1,083	913	171
Circuit 12	681	585	96
De Soto	32	25	7
Manatee	256	224	33
Sarasota	392	336	56
Circuit 13	1,005	849	156
Hillsborough	1,005	849	156
Circuit 14	493	417	76
Bay	347	301	45
Calhoun	13	11	3
Gulf	17	15	2
Holmes	28	21	6
Jackson	61	46	16
Washington	27	23	4
Circuit 15	807	739	68
Palm Beach	807	739	68
Circuit 16	226	174	52
Monroe	226	174	52
Circuit 17	1,227	1,051	176
Broward	1,227	1,051	176
Circuit 18	1,029	897	132
Brevard	606	518	87
Seminole	424	379	45
Circuit 19	614	514	99
Indian River	136	113	24
Martin	176	149	27
Okeechobee	55	50	4
St. Lucie	246	202	44
Circuit 20	1,155	978	177
Charlotte	174	155	19
Collier	339	273	66
Glades	25	20	5
Hendry	70	62	8
Lee	547	468	79

1/ Mandatory court cost is $50 per conviction of which the court clerk retains $1. However, the average court cost collected per conviction is $24.69.

2/ Includes surcharges, offense, interest, restitution, subrogation, refunds, and other receipts.

Source: State of Florida, Office of the Attorney General, Division of Victim Services, *Annual Report, 1994-1995.*

Table 22.31. VICTIM SERVICES: VICTIM COMPENSATION AWARDS AND AMOUNT OF BENEFITS PAID IN THE STATE, JUDICIAL CIRCUITS, AND COUNTIES OF FLORIDA FISCAL YEAR 1994-95

Judicial circuit and county	Number of awards	Benefits awarded (dollars)
Florida	5,410	14,522,010
Circuit 1	164	471,841
Escambia	105	296,836
Okaloosa	27	94,646
Santa Rosa	22	69,379
Walton	10	10,980
Circuit 2	239	429,789
Franklin	16	32,315
Gadsden	42	94,791
Jefferson	10	20,901
Leon	159	253,161
Liberty	3	654
Wakulla	9	27,967
Circuit 3	91	167,184
Columbia	28	71,972
Dixie	3	7,500
Hamilton	1	9,500
Lafayette	1	9,999
Madison	11	10,003
Suwannee	12	13,338
Taylor	35	44,872
Circuit 4	635	1,579,684
Clay	18	40,150
Duval	609	1,498,822
Nassau	8	40,712
Circuit 5	146	384,494
Citrus	22	57,822
Hernando	13	60,608
Lake	26	84,994
Marion	77	161,913
Sumter	8	19,157
Circuit 6	560	1,452,120
Pasco	69	185,967
Pinellas	491	1,266,153
Circuit 7	217	590,981
Flagler	5	15,744
Putnam	34	92,440
St. Johns	39	116,334
Volusia	139	366,463
Circuit 8	123	344,309
Alachua	97	229,172
Baker	7	19,766
Bradford	9	50,171
Gilchrist	4	13,480
Circuit 8 (Continued)		
Levy	5	26,943
Union	1	4,777
Circuit 9	252	649,389
Orange	229	586,909
Osceola	23	62,480
Circuit 10	172	515,271
Hardee	8	23,066
Highlands	11	31,084
Polk	153	461,121
Circuit 11	689	2,586,447
Dade	689	2,586,447
Circuit 12	250	446,650
De Soto	14	35,874
Manatee	141	228,954
Sarasota	95	181,822
Circuit 13	532	1,390,504
Hillsborough	532	1,390,504
Circuit 14	144	345,766
Bay	83	218,162
Calhoun	4	10,991
Gulf	2	1,497
Holmes	3	1,224
Jackson	39	78,262
Washington	13	35,630
Circuit 15	276	862,245
Palm Beach	276	862,245
Circuit 16	40	122,241
Monroe	40	122,241
Circuit 17	319	789,686
Broward	319	789,686
Circuit 18	215	508,279
Brevard	153	387,266
Seminole	62	121,013
Circuit 19	111	311,023
Indian River	34	110,631
Martin	20	45,402
Okeechobee	12	31,153
St. Lucie	45	123,837
Circuit 20	235	574,107
Charlotte	24	35,200
Collier	46	93,782
Glades	1	1,242
Hendry	14	43,842
Lee	150	400,041

Note: Victim compensation claims are processed for financial assistance to crime victims for lost income (lost wages, disability, and loss of support), funeral expenses, and reimbursement of other out-of-pocket and treatment expenses directly related to a crime injury.

Source: State of Florida, Office of the Attorney General, Division of Victim Services, *Annual Report, 1993-1994*.

Table 22.50. CIVIL JUSTICE: TORT CASES AND PROCESSING TIME FOR CASES IN SELECTED COUNTIES OF FLORIDA, 1992

Item	Dade County	Orange County	Palm Beach County
Cases disposed, total	7,122	1,700	4,194
Auto	3,461	983	2,668
Premises liability	849	439	608
Product liability	216	33	136
Medical malpractice	216	62	149
Toxic substance	1,315	0	0
Cases per 100,000 population 1/	355	238	466
Processing time (percentage)			
Less than 1 year	56	50	51
1 year to less than 2 years	30	34	36
2 years to less than 3 years	9	10	9
3 years to less than 4 years	3	3	4
4 or more years	2	3	0
Mean (months)	13	15	14

1/ Based on 1992 U.S. Bureau of the Census population estimates.

Note: Tort cases are claims arising from personal injury or property damage caused by the negligent or intentional act of another person or business. Counties are from a sample of 45 of the 75 most populous counties in the U.S. It is estimated by the source that the nation's 75 largest counties comprise half of the nation's tort caseloads.

Source: U.S., Department of Justice, Bureau of Justice Statistics, *Bureau of Justice Statistics Special Report: Tort Cases in Large Counties, Civil Justice Survey of State Courts, 1992.*

Table 22.51. LAWYERS: NUMBER AND MEMBERS IN GOOD STANDING OF THE FLORIDA BAR BY SECTION IN FLORIDA, JULY 2, 1996

Section	Number of members
Members in good standing, total	54,751
Florida	44,150
Out-of-state	10,488
Foreign	113
Members in sections, total	24,734
Tax	1,810
Real property, probate	7,286
Trial	6,278
Business	3,867
General	1,598
Family	3,154
Local government	1,116
Workers' compensation	1,401
Criminal	2,213
Members in sections (Cont.)	
Environmental and land use	1,911
Administrative	919
Practice, management, and technology	840
Labor and employment	1,344
International	892
Entertainment, arts, and sports	802
Health	1,122
Public interest	350
Governmental	560
Elder	1,154
Out-of-state	1,436
Appellate practice	789

Source: The Florida Bar, release from the Records Department, July 2,1996.

Table 22.52. LAWYERS: MEMBERS IN GOOD STANDING OF THE FLORIDA BAR IN THE STATE AND COUNTIES OF FLORIDA, JULY 2, 1996

County	Number of members	County	Number of members
Total	54,751	Jefferson	19
Out-of-state	10,488	Lafayette	2
Foreign	113	Lake	201
Alachua	702	Lee	758
Baker	9	Leon	2,475
Bay	201	Levy	24
Bradford	16	Liberty	1
Brevard	727	Madison	11
Broward	5,449	Manatee	355
Calhoun	5	Marion	347
Charlotte	122	Martin	330
Citrus	75	Monroe	229
Clay	90	Nassau	29
Collier	568	Okaloosa	208
Columbia	74	Okeechobee	23
Dade	10,573	Orange	3,182
De Soto	24	Osceola	95
Dixie	2	Palm Beach	4,056
Duval	2,138	Pasco	261
Escambia	585	Pinellas	2,452
Flagler	35	Polk	651
Franklin	15	Putnam	66
Gadsden	48	St. Johns	153
Gilchrist	7	St. Lucie	233
Glades	3	Santa Rosa	59
Gulf	12	Sarasota	952
Hamilton	9	Seminole	499
Hardee	15	Sumter	22
Hendry	19	Suwannee	34
Hernando	99	Taylor	16
Highlands	70	Union	3
Hillsborough	3,604	Volusia	801
Holmes	11	Wakulla	22
Indian River	217	Walton	22
Jackson	24	Washington	11

Source: The Florida Bar, release from the Records Department, July 2, 1996.

Table 22.55. LEGAL SERVICES: AVERAGE MONTHLY PRIVATE REPORTING UNITS EMPLOYMENT, AND PAYROLL COVERED BY UNEMPLOYMENT COMPENSATION LAW IN THE STATE AND COUNTIES OF FLORIDA, 1995

County	Number of reporting units	Number of employees	Payroll ($1,000)	County	Number of reporting units	Number of employees	Payroll ($1,000)
			Legal services (SIC code 81)				
Florida	11,092	59,069	250,883	Lake	75	322	899
				Lee	203	1,192	4,217
Alachua	146	782	2,239	Leon	260	2,164	9,685
Baker	4	11	13	Levy	6	16	38
Bay	65	300	987	Madison	4	15	44
Bradford	9	20	29	Manatee	99	473	1,336
Brevard	215	923	3,462	Marion	112	523	1,944
Broward	1,452	6,510	27,435	Martin	93	483	1,669
Charlotte	33	230	714	Monroe	62	200	581
Citrus	27	131	339	Nassau	13	38	112
Clay	30	126	293	Okaloosa	93	312	751
Collier	162	791	3,054	Okeechobee	8	33	63
Columbia	22	83	263	Orange	726	5,507	24,688
Dade	2,753	14,018	67,974	Osceola	30	84	164
De Soto	5	20	48	Palm Beach	1,068	5,547	24,651
Dixie	3	4	6	Pasco	95	421	1,105
Duval	457	3,226	15,504	Pinellas	667	3,072	11,502
Escambia	156	977	3,790	Polk	177	1,031	3,736
Flagler	8	31	75	Putnam	21	76	126
Franklin	3	10	14	St. Johns	36	132	328
Gadsden	13	39	64	St. Lucie	71	331	1,280
Gilchrist	3	9	12	Santa Rosa	16	80	221
Gulf	5	17	34	Sarasota	268	1,392	5,359
Hardee	5	19	32	Seminole	137	483	1,277
Hendry	9	29	50	Sumter	8	22	42
Hernando	27	89	192	Suwannee	9	25	44
Highlands	32	124	315	Taylor	5	20	44
Hillsborough	743	5,094	23,641	Union	3	4	4
Holmes	4	7	8	Volusia	243	1,067	3,175
Indian River	60	287	1,050	Wakulla	3	8	11
Jackson	9	26	38	Walton	10	24	28
Jefferson	6	14	17	Multicounty 1/	7	11	35

1/ Reporting units without a fixed location within the state or of unknown county location.

Note: Private employment. These data include establishments which are engaged in offering legal advice or services and which are headed by a member of the Bar. Data are preliminary. Only counties for which data are disclosed are shown. Detail may not add to totals due to disclosure editing and/or rounding. See Tables 23.70, 23.71, 23.72, 23.73, and 23.74 for public employment data.

Source: State of Florida, Department of Labor and Employment Security, Bureau of Labor Market Information, "Employment and Wages" (ES-202), unpublished data.

GOVERNMENT FINANCE AND EMPLOYMENT

Tobacco Licenses, Fiscal Year 1994-95

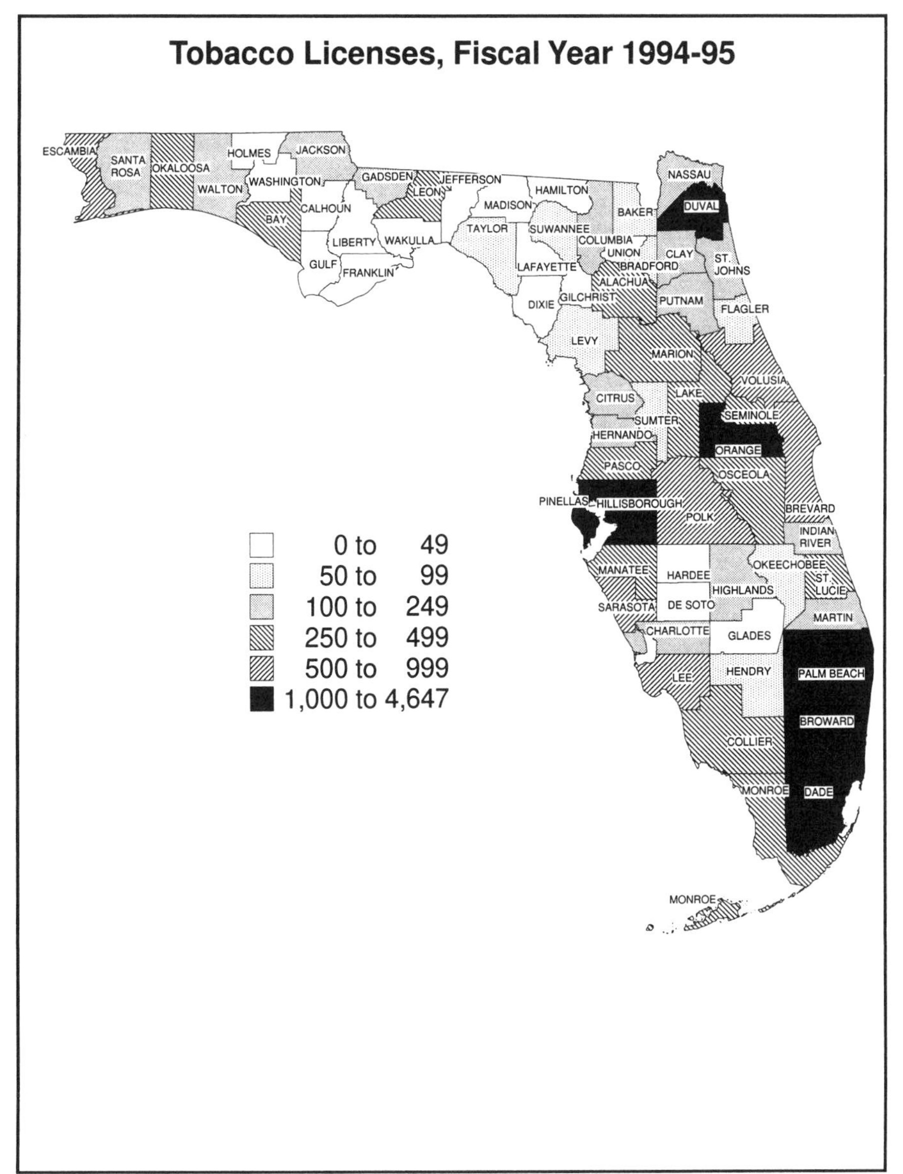

Source: Table 23.52

SECTION 23.00
GOVERNMENT FINANCE AND EMPLOYMENT

TABLES LISTED BY MAJOR HEADINGS

SECTION 23.00
GOVERNMENT FINANCE AND EMPLOYMENT
(Continued)

TABLES LISTED BY MAJOR HEADINGS

SECTION 23.00
GOVERNMENT FINANCE AND EMPLOYMENT
(Continued)

TABLES LISTED BY MAJOR HEADINGS

Table 23.07. FEDERAL GOVERNMENT FINANCE: EXPENDITURE BY AGENCY AND BY SPECIFIED PROGRAM IN FLORIDA AND THE UNITED STATES, FISCAL YEAR 1994-95

(in thousands of dollars)

Item	Florida	United States
Total (14)	74,992,000	1,363,511,000
Grants to state and local governments (46)	9,078,094	228,935,961
Department of Agriculture	690,531	16,089,507
Agricultural Marketing Service	11,123	381,059
Funds for strengthening markets	11,123	379,859
Cooperative projects in marketing	0	1,200
Cooperative State Research Service--agriculture experiment stations	9,022	413,825
Extension Service--extension activities	14,102	474,341
Farmers Home Administration	5,591	398,931
Food and Consumer Service	639,018	13,888,601
Child nutrition programs	379,797	7,251,368
Food stamp program	84,127	2,835,861
Special supplemental food program (WIC)	160,662	3,396,612
Food donations	12,124	324,992
Temporary emergency food assistance	2,172	63,311
Special milk program	136	16,457
Food Safety and Inspection Service--meat and poultry	2,474	41,302
Forest Service	8,597	403,528
Soil Conservation Service	604	87,920
Department of Commerce	30,754	557,151
Economic Development Administration--development assistance programs	21,937	305,419
National Oceanic and Atmospheric Administration	8,161	219,863
National Telecommunications and Information Administration--planning and construction	656	31,869
Corporation for Public Broadcasting--public broadcasting fund	10,750	292,467
Department of Defense 1/	2,309	244,824
Department of Education	703,587	15,955,128
Bilingual education and minority language affairs	23,568	311,039
Educational research and improvement-libraries	6,774	130,711
Office of Elementary and Secondary Education	354,306	8,824,691
Office of Postsecondary Education	3,297	92,492
Office of Special Education and Rehabilitative Services	254,370	5,232,889
Office of Vocational and Adult Education	61,216	1,359,024
Department of Energy	1,909	254,939
Environmental Protection Agency	79,741	3,352,726
Construction of wastewater treatment works	61,983	2,450,673
Abatement, control, and compliance	15,772	697,853
Hazardous substance response trust fund	1,986	204,200
Equal Employment Opportunity Commission	988	26,831
Federal Emergency Management Agency	87,208	1,488,606
Funds Appropriated to the President--Appalachian regional development programs	0	171,864
Department of Health and Human Services	4,903,388	126,077,340
Administration for Children and Families	1,204,777	33,155,949
Family support payments (AFDC)	621,867	17,150,696
Social services block grant	131,807	2,743,659

See footnotes at end of table.

Continued . . .

Table 23.07. FEDERAL GOVERNMENT FINANCE: EXPENDITURE BY AGENCY AND BY SPECIFIED PROGRAM IN FLORIDA AND THE UNITED STATES, FISCAL YEAR 1994-95 (Continued)

(in thousands of dollars)

Item	Florida	United States
Grants to state and local governments (Continued)		
Department of Health and Human Services (Continued)		
Administration for Children and Families (Continued)		
Children and family services	269,237	6,448,275
Foster care and adoption assistance	82,127	3,403,746
Low-income home energy assistance	17,124	1,419,143
Community services block grant	13,439	519,695
Refugee assistance	37,870	398,413
Assistance for legalized aliens	13,074	190,853
Other	18,232	881,469
Health Care Financing Administration--medical assistance (Medicaid)	3,515,912	89,070,431
Public Health Service	120,022	2,383,916
Health Resources and Services Administration	93,922	1,750,614
Centers for Disease Control	26,100	633,302
Substance Abuse, and Mental Health Administration	61,089	1,432,882
Social Security Administration supplemental security income	1,588	34,162
Department of Housing and Urban Development	978,461	25,607,288
Community development	173,101	4,339,223
Emergency shelters and homeless assistance	3,744	121,074
Low rent housing--operating assistance	81,586	2,853,549
Lower income housing assistance	603,721	15,943,462
Institute of Museum Services	257	14,153
Department of Interior	12,577	1,889,417
National Park Service	1,640	62,502
Department of Justice	116,971	1,889,861
Department of Labor	286,996	7,001,049
Employment and Training Administration	285,767	6,897,336
Job Training Partnership Act	172,299	3,589,599
State unemployment insurance and employment service operations	113,468	3,231,126
National Foundation on the Arts and the Humanities--National Endowment for the Arts	709	45,108
Tennessee Valley Authority-payments in lieu of taxes	0	251,723
Department of Transportation	1,161,650	26,311,190
Federal Aviation Administration--airport and airway trust fund	106,405	1,825,651
Federal Highway Administration	883,758	19,439,729
Federal Transit Administration	162,950	4,817,598
Department of the Treasury-Customs Bureau and IRS rebates	6,742	393,807
Department of Veterans Affairs	1,783	276,603
District of Columbia payment and Metro subsidy	0	714,070
Expenditure for salaries and wages (32)	7,206,268	168,150,613
Department of Defense 1/	3,339,996	71,192,209
Military	2,241,085	41,246,883
Active	2,062,537	35,463,190
Inactive	178,548	5,783,693
Civilian	1,098,911	29,945,326
Army	226,255	22,768,168
Navy	1,789,501	25,089,213

See footnotes at end of table.

Continued . . .

Table 23.07. FEDERAL GOVERNMENT FINANCE: EXPENDITURE BY AGENCY AND BY SPECIFIED PROGRAM IN FLORIDA AND THE UNITED STATES, FISCAL YEAR 1994-95 (Continued)

(in thousands of dollars)

Item	Florida	United States
Expenditure for salaries and wages (Continued)		
Department of Defense (Continued)		
Air Force	1,214,260	18,341,571
Other defense, civilian	109,980	4,993,257
Nondefense agencies 2/	3,866,272	96,958,404
Agriculture	67,649	4,167,972
Commerce	35,289	1,700,904
Education	181	261,265
Energy	1,687	1,194,607
Environmental Protection Agency	3,823	993,144
Federal Deposit Insurance Corporation 3/	6,173	975,765
Federal Emergency Management Agency	6,485	211,604
General Services Administration	5,203	783,302
Health and Human Services 4/	9,758	2,908,986
Housing and Urban Development	13,067	613,824
Interior	44,248	3,073,332
Justice 5/	243,786	5,023,081
Labor	16,423	843,809
Postal Service	2,161,301	41,931,298
Small Business Administration	4,837	261,376
Transportation	309,833	4,863,784
Treasury	255,217	7,012,619
Veterans Affairs	441,646	9,195,612
Other nondefense	239,666	10,942,120
Direct payments to individuals (1)	48,814,932	717,157,352
Social Security	22,894,881	330,832,323
Retirement insurance payments	16,629,298	221,557,642
Survivors insurance payments	3,931,529	66,135,695
Disability insurance payments	2,334,054	43,138,986
Medicare	13,080,213	180,108,577
Hospital insurance payments	6,952,663	114,894,038
Supplementary medical insurance payments	6,127,550	65,214,539
Federal retirement and disability payments	5,630,000	67,035,711
Civilian 6/	2,716,327	39,339,783
Military	2,913,673	27,695,928
Federal payments for unemployment compensation	889,246	28,730,907
Veterans compensation for service connected disability	899,019	11,554,516
Veterans pensions for nonservice connected disability	106,094	2,209,479
Veterans compensation for service connected death	252,692	3,007,229
Pensions to veterans' surviving spouses and children	34,164	815,375
Veterans educational assistance	59,021	913,290
Other veterans benefit programs	27,845	536,008
Supplemental security income payments	1,333,180	24,707,666
Food stamps	1,307,134	22,766,902
Social insurance payments for railroad workers	415,510	8,088,852
Housing assistance 7/	216,055	5,915,474
Pell grant program	253,531	5,288,231
Excess earned income tax credits	1,060,197	16,824,565
National guaranteed student loan interest subsidies	27,260	1,986,833
Federal workers compensation	125,050	1,858,906
Black lung payments	27,625	1,235,517

See footnotes at end of table. Continued . . .

Table 23.07. FEDERAL GOVERNMENT FINANCE: EXPENDITURE BY AGENCY AND BY SPECIFIED PROGRAM IN FLORIDA AND THE UNITED STATES, FISCAL YEAR 1994-95 (Continued)

(in thousands of dollars)

Item	Florida	United States
Procurement contracts 8/ (23)	8,697,586	202,209,187
Department of Defense	6,230,833	126,003,863
Army	1,336,853	25,068,183
Navy	1,615,754	36,750,112
Air Force	3,049,250	36,603,530
Other defense	228,976	27,582,038
Nondefense agencies	2,466,753	76,205,324
Agriculture	36,921	2,471,943
Commerce	5,241	799,024
Education	103	387,752
Energy	84,425	16,904,117
Environmental Protection Agency	12,094	927,060
Federal Emergency Management Agency	15,200	251,180
General Services Administration	143,078	5,353,672
Justice	37,448	1,857,195
Health and Human Services	14,621	2,941,955
Housing and Urban Development	113	213,185
Interior	17,697	1,492,115
Labor	15,179	800,718
National Aeronautics and Space Administration	1,259,041	11,537,989
Postal Service	453,529	8,798,898
State Department	22,783	564,309
Transportation	237,536	3,446,001
Treasury	28,778	1,788,061
Veterans	76,144	2,604,707
Other nondefense	6,822	13,065,443
Expenditure for other programs (50)	1,195,434	47,058,020
Grants	493,665	21,220,340
Department of Health and Human Services--research programs	143,082	9,344,302
National Science Foundation	51,022	1,416,211
Direct payments--other than for individuals	701,769	25,837,680
Department of Agriculture	60,290	8,443,855
Federal employees life and health insurance programs	430,736	10,731,577
Postal Service	103,546	2,008,898
National flood insurance claim payments	28,359	1,022,285

1/ Includes salaries, wages, and compensation, such as housing allowances; distribution based on duty station. 2/ Estimates based on place of employment. 3/ Includes Resolution Trust Corporation. 4/ Excludes Social Security Administration salaries, which are now included with "other nondefense" salaries figures. 5/ Includes FBI salaries. 6/ Includes retirement and disability payments to former postal employees. 7/ Includes Section 8 payments to nongovernment agencies and FEMA individual assistance payments under the Disaster Assistance Program. 8/ Value of annual contract actions; actual outlays for U.S. Postal Service only. Multiple year obligations of less than 3 years duration may be included.

Note: The number (after major expenditure categories) indicates Florida's rank among the states in per capita distribution of federal funds. Expenditures classified as "other" may not be specified in the table and are contained in the totals for major expenditure categories.

Source: U.S., Department of Commerce, Bureau of the Census, *Federal Expenditures by State for Fiscal Year 1995.*

Table 23.08. FEDERAL GOVERNMENT FINANCE: EXPENDITURE BY TYPE IN THE UNITED STATES AND IN THE STATE AND COUNTIES OF FLORIDA, FISCAL YEAR 1994-95

(in thousands of dollars, except where indicated)

County	Direct expenditure Total	Direct expenditure Department of Defense	Grants	Wages and salaries	Direct payment to individuals Total	Direct payment to individuals Retirement and disability
United States 1/	1,368,571	227,200	242,598	168,151	729,776	452,083
Florida	75,005,214	12,576,050	9,062,784	7,206,268	49,336,808	31,827,984
Alachua	879,057	67,982	228,715	131,898	462,429	312,458
Baker	67,011	4,405	18,793	2,265	31,317	14,239
Bay	945,096	461,958	73,172	282,931	471,707	359,767
Bradford	82,142	9,448	13,232	6,092	61,119	42,350
Brevard	4,849,766	1,737,463	161,869	392,729	1,651,374	1,271,965
Broward	5,767,233	155,759	501,248	329,153	4,757,579	2,837,394
Calhoun	67,361	1,681	35,186	1,344	28,931	19,074
Charlotte	645,003	31,855	32,709	11,034	595,871	426,024
Citrus	517,343	12,012	39,034	9,544	466,359	337,602
Clay	369,861	111,103	23,478	17,817	321,554	264,985
Collier	744,395	44,686	59,606	24,339	627,298	470,347
Columbia	238,892	11,284	57,319	37,956	139,186	102,375
Dade	8,620,505	303,275	1,678,907	877,923	5,704,919	2,878,743
De Soto	101,597	3,577	16,041	2,491	82,200	55,831
Dixie	53,961	12,230	6,252	884	45,970	36,435
Duval	4,193,156	1,616,075	397,972	1,359,441	1,985,458	1,320,308
Escambia	2,012,200	948,517	178,703	467,508	979,074	742,939
Flagler	181,693	6,229	13,760	3,867	157,467	128,984
Franklin	42,707	2,575	8,417	1,445	31,362	21,693
Gadsden	164,703	6,848	40,666	4,845	115,621	72,824
Gilchrist	37,906	1,469	6,747	948	28,934	20,951
Glades	17,805	666	3,105	500	13,929	9,944
Gulf	55,342	3,596	12,328	720	41,717	29,047
Hamilton	39,452	1,083	9,351	1,087	28,155	19,659
Hardee	71,118	1,621	15,075	2,350	52,835	35,312
Hendry	85,123	3,545	19,367	3,779	60,383	39,236
Hernando	650,814	14,998	42,963	12,887	591,234	427,063
Highlands	426,395	27,464	34,647	13,979	373,181	270,991
Hillsborough	3,904,520	627,907	581,191	615,374	2,355,359	1,626,393
Holmes	73,749	5,901	12,105	3,222	55,404	37,692
Indian River	524,881	24,108	27,791	16,118	473,683	341,657
Jackson	203,685	9,703	39,486	24,940	131,046	88,338
Jefferson	50,199	1,741	15,547	1,503	31,905	21,035
Lafayette	14,428	668	2,260	632	11,174	7,552

See footnote at end of table. Continued . . .

Table 23.08. FEDERAL GOVERNMENT FINANCE: EXPENDITURE BY TYPE IN THE UNITED STATES AND IN THE STATE AND COUNTIES OF FLORIDA, FISCAL YEAR 1994-95 (Continued)

(in thousands of dollars, except where indicated)

County	Direct expenditure Total	Direct expenditure Department of Defense	Grants	Wages and salaries	Direct payment to individuals Total	Direct payment to individuals Retirement and disability
Lake	863,213	46,033	56,986	23,177	774,569	574,577
Lee	1,745,467	59,438	158,963	81,067	1,484,612	1,056,084
Leon	2,287,757	239,557	1,552,148	82,246	446,312	312,387
Levy	117,682	5,948	16,106	2,937	95,760	69,601
Liberty	24,274	1,014	8,699	1,333	13,712	9,825
Madison	62,076	1,895	11,754	1,836	46,777	31,020
Manatee	1,063,954	65,239	95,304	58,864	877,590	617,280
Marion	1,005,973	30,707	110,435	27,502	855,279	637,143
Martin	538,044	18,729	30,910	13,005	485,782	344,498
Monroe	357,140	105,825	29,661	92,902	206,227	149,561
Nassau	227,347	51,034	22,867	45,834	150,006	121,043
Okaloosa	1,797,251	1,326,656	52,027	696,556	616,057	526,106
Okeechobee	134,040	7,718	17,216	3,058	108,435	69,546
Orange	3,987,163	1,708,594	365,368	453,061	1,849,121	1,307,632
Osceola	380,102	26,627	52,411	11,536	309,965	208,702
Palm Beach	5,411,697	986,553	406,968	233,445	3,756,522	2,456,419
Pasco	1,536,073	115,772	104,856	30,736	1,390,507	893,811
Pinellas	5,163,362	682,226	365,219	291,573	3,828,515	2,584,607
Polk	1,633,952	67,469	213,903	69,288	1,324,351	969,716
Putnam	275,066	11,896	43,404	6,490	222,847	153,224
St. Johns	423,451	70,469	50,128	22,630	313,490	235,217
St. Lucie	765,333	21,613	81,154	21,989	649,623	469,083
Santa Rosa	428,549	149,973	39,605	73,936	279,511	227,252
Sarasota	1,726,575	54,388	98,216	40,005	1,559,498	1,089,669
Seminole	834,934	89,917	81,856	67,339	654,017	486,177
Sumter	185,815	6,520	36,749	4,008	133,793	98,289
Suwannee	131,686	9,106	19,620	5,253	103,671	75,257
Taylor	83,351	17,271	13,048	2,071	53,433	36,448
Union	24,128	1,347	3,284	767	19,130	13,127
Volusia	1,953,145	222,403	187,933	63,928	1,530,778	1,086,256
Wakulla	121,932	74,007	9,117	2,513	37,982	26,212
Walton	132,136	20,803	19,474	8,971	98,965	74,374
Washington	82,847	5,870	16,142	2,868	62,384	42,149
Undistributed	2,800,599	0	284,208	0	2,017,619	67,406

1/ Rounded to millions of dollars.

Source: U.S., Department of Commerce, Bureau of the Census, the Internet at <http://www.census.gov/>.

Table 23.15. DEFENSE CONTRACTS: AWARDS AND PAYROLL IN FLORIDA, OTHER SUNBELT STATES, OTHER POPULOUS STATES, AND THE UNITED STATES, SPECIFIED FISCAL YEARS ENDING SEPTEMBER 30, 1990 THROUGH 1994

(in millions of dollars)

State	Contract awards 1/			Payroll 2/		
	1989-90	1991-92	1993-94	1989-90	1991-92	1993-94
	Sunbelt states					
Florida	4,880	4,995	5,910	5,702	6,277	6,164
Alabama	1,938	1,949	1,673	1,894	2,139	2,320
Arizona	3,400	1,946	1,975	1,473	1,658	1,642
Arkansas	314	288	374	680	703	701
California	22,312	23,843	22,573	13,580	14,202	13,467
Georgia	1,812	3,796	4,121	3,045	4,234	4,273
Louisiana	1,627	1,204	2,148	1,211	1,358	1,355
Mississippi	1,429	2,567	1,855	1,044	1,079	1,246
New Mexico	672	728	658	947	1,019	1,056
North Carolina	1,215	1,540	1,163	3,034	4,041	4,186
Oklahoma	622	759	759	1,794	2,035	2,015
South Carolina	699	756	998	2,437	2,699	2,529
Tennessee	1,191	1,262	1,173	920	984	1,068
Texas	9,132	8,672	8,145	6,709	7,016	7,201
Virginia	7,919	6,571	8,017	9,555	11,157	11,483
	Other populous states					
Illinois	1,339	1,354	1,256	1,879	1,775	1,810
Indiana	1,695	1,517	1,319	982	1,095	1,170
Massachusetts	8,166	5,686	5,106	964	993	1,081
Michigan	1,360	1,568	1,602	849	904	878
New Jersey	3,669	3,319	3,034	1,687	1,601	1,524
New York	6,835	5,430	3,629	1,756	1,810	1,894
Ohio	4,383	3,033	2,966	2,011	2,182	2,215
Pennsylvania	2,834	3,065	2,760	2,435	2,605	2,646
United States	121,254	112,285	110,316	88,650	99,250	99,822

1/ State data include net value of contracts over $25,000 for military awards for supplies, services, and construction.

2/ Data are estimates and cover active duty military and direct hire civilian personnel, including Army Corps of Engineers.

Note: Data refer to awards in year specified and to state in which prime contractor is located. Expenditure may extend over several years and work may be performed by a subcontractor in another state.

Source: U.S., Department of Commerce, Bureau of the Census, *Statistical Abstract of the United States, 1996,* and previous editions.

Table 23.29. STATE GOVERNMENT FINANCE: REVENUE, EXPENDITURE, DIRECT EXPENDITURE INDEBTEDNESS, AND CASH AND SECURITY HOLDINGS IN FLORIDA, 1994

Item	Total ($1,000)	Percentage change 1993 to 1994	Per capita 1/ (dollars)
Revenue, total	34,804,817	4.8	2,494
General revenue	29,483,899	6.6	2,113
Intergovernmental	7,406,684	2.4	531
Taxes	17,808,222	8.5	1,276
General sales	10,042,360	(NA)	720
Selective sales	3,509,427	(NA)	252
License	1,301,092	(NA)	93
Corporation net income	950,235	25.7	68
Other	2,005,108	-31.6	144
Current charges	1,609,710	13.8	115
Miscellaneous general	2,659,283	2.4	191
Utility	5,441	12.1	0
Insurance trust	5,315,477	-4.3	381
Expenditure, total	32,283,742	7.2	2,314
Intergovernmental	10,236,796	10.0	734
Direct	22,046,946	6.0	1,580
Current operation	14,751,388	6.3	1,057
Capital outlay	2,818,265	15.4	202
Insurance benefits and repayments	2,253,082	-5.5	161
Assistance and subsidies	1,360,237	3.9	97
Interest on debt	863,974	10.4	62
Exhibit: salaries and wages	5,622,214	4.1	403
Expenditure, total	32,283,742	7.2	2,314
General expenditure	29,991,369	8.3	2,149
Intergovernmental	10,236,796	10.0	734
Direct expenditure	19,754,573	7.4	1,416
General expenditure by function			
Education	10,231,108	9.3	733
Public welfare	6,725,033	9.6	482
Hospitals	486,832	6.3	35
Health	1,842,135	-6.4	132
Highways	2,710,990	14.4	194
Police protection	219,897	10.2	16
Correction	1,246,607	16.2	89
Natural resources	1,074,889	10.5	77
Parks and recreation	78,366	21.3	6
Governmental administration	1,158,193	7.0	83
Interest on general debt	863,974	10.4	62
Other and unallocable	3,353,345	6.2	240
Utility	39,291	24.9	3
Insurance trust	2,253,082	-5.5	161
Debt at end of fiscal year	14,565,270	6.8	1,044
Cash and security holdings	49,712,712	14.4	3,563

(NA) Not available.
1/ Based on U.S. Bureau of the Census population estimates.

Source: U.S., Department of Commerce, Bureau of the Census, the Internet at <http://www.census.gov/>.

Table 23.31. STATE TREASURER'S REPORT: RESOURCES AND LIABILITIES
FISCAL YEAR 1994-95

(in dollars)

Item	Balance sheet for fiscal year ending June 30, 1995	
	Resources	
Office cash		
Currency and coin		277,192.20
Fraudulent warrants receivable		0.00
Bank deposits		
U.C. benefit investment account 1/	1,816,912,475.60	
Demand accounts	A/ 176,688,083.46	
Time deposit account	863,100,000.00	
Total bank deposits		2,856,700,559.06
(The above does not include $11,633,229.75 held in clearing and/or revolving accounts outside the State Treasury.)		
Total all securities held by treasury		7,486,563,288.74
(The above does not include $643,976,773.66 invested for Treasurer's Special Purpose Investment Fund, merged October 1993.)		
Total state-owned resources in treasurer's custody		10,343,541,040.00
	Liabilities	
State Funds subject to Comptroller's warrants		
General revenue fund	1,300,039,912.56	
Trust fund	8,855,575,336.34	
Working capital fund 2/	0.00	
Infra-structure fund	120,590,000.00	
Total four funds		10,276,205,248.90
Fraudulent warrant reserve		0.00
Adjustments 3/		67,335,791.10
Total liabilities		10,343,541,040.00

A/ Includes per reconciled cash balance of $225,566,107.93, a difference of $48,878,024.47 which represents items that have cleared at the bank but have not been posted to the state ledger.
1/ Represents U.C. benefit funds held and invested by the federal government, administered by the Treasury.
2/ Working capital funds are invested within the Trust Fund Investment Program.
3/ Represents a $829.44 posting discrepancy within Comptroller's records, corrected in July 1995, and $67,336,620.54 interest not yet receipted to state accounts.
Note: Total market value of all securities held by Treasury $8,116,180,694.38.

Source: State of Florida, *Annual Report of the State Treasurer for the Fiscal Year Ending June 30, 1995.*

Table 23.40. STATE GOVERNMENT FINANCE: REVENUE, EXPENDITURE, AND CHANGE IN FUND BALANCE BY FUND TYPE IN FLORIDA, FISCAL YEAR 1994-95

(in thousands of dollars)

Item	Total 1/	Fund type: Governmental: General	Special revenue	Expendable trust
Beginning fund balance, July 1, 1994	8,538,312	1,389,521	4,369,702	1,839,252
Revenue, total	31,178,025	13,892,659	15,879,985	1,325,438
Taxes 2/	18,963,759	13,192,192	4,997,194	774,373
Licenses and permits	785,524	55,985	729,539	0
Fees and charges	2,480,990	361,253	1,832,278	252,369
Grants and donations	7,593,624	1	7,560,035	32,818
Investment earnings	559,159	113,592	220,161	182,295
Fines, forfeits, and judgments	196,434	273	137,442	58,719
Flexible benefits contributions	0	0	0	0
Refunds	598,459	169,363	403,260	24,864
Other	76	0	76	0
Expenditure, total	30,775,597	11,865,445	16,560,495	1,089,781
Current				
Economic opportunities, agriculture and employment	1,884,335	70,885	1,053,555	759,895
Public safety	2,125,187	1,643,001	482,186	0
Education	8,061,953	5,310,102	2,751,956	-105
Health and social concerns	10,748,975	3,971,806	6,777,155	14
Housing and community development	92,962	5,815	87,147	0
Natural resources and environmental management	643,128	140,419	502,709	0
Recreational and cultural opportunities	144,241	70,352	73,889	0
Transportation	633,121	0	632,880	241
Government direction and support services	3,349,160	583,983	2,419,687	329,687
Capital outlay	2,431,962	60,940	1,775,159	46
Debt service				
Principle retirement	228,868	7,019	3,262	0
Interest and fiscal charges	431,705	1,123	910	3
Excess (deficiency) of revenues over expenditures	402,428	2,027,214	-680,510	235,657
Other financing sources (uses)	-63,589	-1,637,857	547,155	-48,402
Excess (deficiency) of revenues and other financing sources over expenditures and other financing uses	338,839	389,357	-133,355	187,255
Change in reserve for inventories	-12,662	-17,021	4,359	0
Ending Fund Balance, June 30, 1995	8,864,489	1,761,857	4,240,706	2,026,507

1/ Total presented only to facilitate financial analyses. Includes fund types and account groups that use differing basis of accounting, restricted and unrestricted amounts, and interfund transactions which have not been eliminated. Excludes community water management districts, community college and university direct-support organizations, transportation/expressway authorities, and other component units.

2/ Florida levies neither a personal income tax nor an ad valorem tax on real or tangible personal property. Taxes are, however, the principal means of financing state operations.

Source: State of Florida, Office of the Comptroller, *Florida Comprehensive Annual Financial Report,* Fiscal Year Ended June 30, 1995.

Table 23.41. STATE GOVERNMENT FINANCE: EXPENDITURE BY SPECIFIED DEPARTMENT OR AGENCY AND BY FUND TYPE IN FLORIDA, FISCAL YEAR 1994-95

(in thousands of dollars)

Department or agency	Total all fund types	Governmental 2/ Special revenue	Governmental 2/ Capital projects	Proprietary 3/	Trust and agency funds 1/ Fiduciary expendable trust	Trust and agency funds 1/ State General revenue	Trust and agency funds 1/ State All trust funds	Other component units 4/
Expenditure, total	A/ 77,263,502	18,107,725	595,824	2,444,434	1,089,781	15,581,954	37,479,697	1,964,087
Departments of--								
Environmental Protection	1,965,925	542,509	163,892	0	0	56,573	803,214	399,737
Education	13,041,886	2,770,934	5,966	27,682	485	5,896,193	3,428,437	912,189
Community Affairs	346,523	286,231	17,693	42,599	0	0	0	0
Labor and Employment Security	3,743,386	737,762	0	14,911	743,281	0	2,247,432	0
Transportation	3,262,686	2,299,354	90,492	133,423	0	0	465,168	274,249
Health and Rehabilitative Services	6,752,180	2,308,861	25,231	73,280	0	1,777,634	2,567,174	0
Revenue	9,675,958	1,745,742	0	4,654	0	1,013,334	6,912,228	0
Agriculture and Consumer Services	200,159	86,519	24,406	0	0	89,234	0	0
State	60,418	55,777	0	732	0	0	0	3,909
Insurance	445,681	187,373	0	0	0	0	0	258,308
Commerce	44,795	37,404	0	0	0	0	0	7,391
Citrus	61,580	61,580	0	0	0	0	0	0
Law Enforcement	107,576	26,584	0	8,929	0	72,063	0	0
Management Services	6,109,454	75,904	3,753	618,752	0	0	5,411,045	0
Highway Safety and Motor Vehicles	1,265,409	179,996	0	18,204	0	96,654	970,555	0
Business and Professional Regulation	796,683	153,209	0	0	0	0	643,474	0
Corrections	1,477,641	0	251,310	23,313	0	1,129,366	0	73,652
Juvenile Justice	4,887	0	4,870	17	0	0	0	0
Lottery	2,428,116	0	0	1,377,407	0	0	1,050,709	0
Banking and Finance	6,500,585	0	0	153	16,614	851,227	5,632,591	0

See footnotes at end of table.

Continued . . .

Table 23.41. STATE GOVERNMENT FINANCE: EXPENDITURE BY SPECIFIED DEPARTMENT OR AGENCY AND BY FUND TYPE IN FLORIDA, FISCAL YEAR 1994-95 (Continued)

(in thousands of dollars)

Department or agency	Total all fund types	Governmental 2/ Special revenue	Governmental 2/ Capital projects	Proprietary 3/	Trust and agency funds 1/ Fiduciary expendable trust	Trust and agency funds 1/ State General revenue	Trust and agency funds 1/ State All trust funds	Other component units 4/
Departments of-- (Continued)								
Insurance	458,972	0	0	96,700	0	0	362,272	0
Other agencies								
Agency for Health Care Administration	10,548,291	4,172,946	0	0	0	2,344,230	4,026,333	4,782
State Board of Administration	478,050	148,926	0	0	329,124	0	0	0
Legislative Branch	139,578	0	0	0	0	139,578	0	0
Justice Administrative Commission	277,698	0	0	0	0	277,698	0	0
State Courts	170,527	0	0	0	0	170,527	0	0
State University System	2,715,763	0	0	0	0	1,058,486	1,657,277	0
Public Service Commission	10,875	0	0	0	0	0	0	10,875
Other agencies or departments	4,172,220	2,230,114	8,211	3,678	277	609,157	1,301,788	18,995

A/ Excludes $11,865,445,000 from the general fund, $664,052,000 in debt service funds, and $1,613,388,000 in pension trust funds not distributed by department or agency.

1/ Funds accounting for the assets held by the governmental unit in a trustee capacity and/or as an agent for individuals, private organizations, other governmental units and/or other funds are expendable, nonexpendable (including pension), and various agency funds not shown separately. Budgetary state fund types (or legal basis funds) include the general revenue fund, numerous trust funds, the budget stabilization fund, and the working capital (rainy day) fund. These are depicted on an actual budget basis reflecting the actual appropriation process.

2/ Governmental fund types also include the general fund and debt service fund.

3/ Enterprise and internal service funds.

4/ Other government, not-for-profit, and proprietary funds.

Source: State of Florida, Office of the Comptroller, *Florida Comprehensive Annual Report, Fiscal Year Ended June 30, 1995.*

Table 23.43. STATE GOVERNMENT FINANCE: SALES AND USE TAX COLLECTIONS BY TRADE CLASSIFICATION IN FLORIDA, FISCAL YEARS 1993-94 AND 1994-95

(amounts rounded to thousands of dollars)

Group	1993-94	1994-95	Per-centage change
All classifications, total	9,928,903	10,550,860	6.3
Food and beverage group	1,402,459	1,471,567	4.9
Grocery stores	469,065	482,906	3.0
Meat markets	782	894	14.2
Seafood dealers	1,110	1,030	-7.2
Vegetables and fruit markets	1,988	1,976	-0.6
Bakeries	4,492	4,719	5.1
Delicatessens	8,893	8,129	-8.6
Candy, confectionery, concession stands	22,635	23,549	4.0
Restaurants, lunchrooms, catering services	786,260	838,030	6.6
Taverns, night clubs, bars, liquor stores	107,235	110,334	2.9
Apparel group	323,638	332,837	2.8
Clothing stores	276,846	281,573	1.7
Shoe stores	45,140	48,580	7.6
Hat shops	1,652	2,684	62.4
General merchandise group	1,449,689	1,561,901	7.7
Department stores	502,220	545,728	8.7
Variety stores	374,947	409,666	9.3
Drug stores	129,786	127,094	-2.1
Jewelry, leather, and sporting goods	129,914	136,949	5.4
Feed, seed, fertilizer stores	6,316	6,269	-0.7
Hardware, paints, and machinery	108,430	110,326	1.7
Farm implements and supplies	17,001	19,696	15.8
General merchandise stores	144,896	169,413	16.9
Second-hand stores, antique shops, flea markets	18,076	20,001	10.6
Dry goods stores	18,103	16,759	-7.4
Automotive group	1,849,922	1,991,147	7.6
Motor vehicle dealers, trailers, campers	1,443,252	1,562,524	8.3
Auto accessories, tires, and parts	131,016	137,945	5.3
Filling and service stations, car wash	60,550	59,344	-2.0
Garage and repair shops	123,971	134,494	8.5
Aircraft dealers	14,351	16,355	14.0
Motorboat and yacht dealers	76,782	80,484	4.8
Furniture and appliances group	601,697	658,503	9.4
Furniture stores, new and used	204,654	214,375	4.8
Household appliances, dinnerware, etc.	77,884	76,425	-1.9
Store and office equipment	107,191	115,572	7.8
Music stores, radios, and televisions	211,969	252,131	18.9
Lumber, builders, and contractors group	563,762	595,112	5.6
Building contractors	23,599	27,880	18.1
Heating and air conditioning	31,384	32,697	4.2
Electrical and plumbing	64,459	70,588	9.5
Decorating, painting, and papering	36,158	35,585	-1.6
Roofing and sheet metal	10,941	10,827	-1.0
Lumber and building materials	397,221	417,535	5.1
General classification group	3,737,735	3,939,793	5.4
Hotels, apartment houses, etc.	433,640	458,357	5.7
Auctioneers and commission dealers	23,788	26,834	12.8
Barber and beauty shops	32,036	34,121	6.5
Book stores	32,525	35,894	10.4
Cigar stands and tobacco shops	1,674	1,899	13.4

Continued . . .

Table 23.43. STATE GOVERNMENT FINANCE: SALES AND USE TAX COLLECTIONS BY TRADE CLASSIFICATION IN FLORIDA, FISCAL YEARS 1993-94 AND 1994-95 (Continued)

(amounts rounded to thousands of dollars)

Group	1993-94	1994-95	Percentage change
General classification group (Continued)			
Florists	16,953	17,209	1.5
Fuel dealers, L.P. gas dealers	32,050	28,158	-12.1
Funeral directors monuments	4,434	5,904	33.2
Scrap metal and junk yards	2,506	2,822	12.6
Itinerant vendors	15,700	15,714	0.1
Laundry, cleaning services, alterations	11,275	11,809	4.7
Machine shops and foundries	10,853	11,637	7.2
Horse, cattle, and pet dealers	67,226	67,682	0.7
Photographers, photo supplies, art galleries	50,098	51,342	2.5
Shoe repair shops	1,006	1,019	1.3
Storage and warehousing	9,529	7,117	-25.3
Gift, card, and novelty stores, taxidermy	97,475	100,324	2.9
Newsstands	3,474	3,520	1.3
Social clubs and associations	25,850	25,827	-0.1
Industrial machinery equipment	109,161	120,969	10.8
Admissions	200,367	207,793	3.7
Holiday season vendors, Christmas trees	380	527	39.0
Rental of tangible property	165,901	178,111	7.4
Fabrication and sales of cabinets, etc.	45,743	47,511	3.9
Manufacturing and mining	282,075	316,600	12.2
Bottlers (beer and softdrinks)	6,548	5,770	-11.9
Pawn shops	4,744	5,427	14.4
Communications	414,251	449,540	8.5
Transportation	15,030	16,198	7.8
Graphic arts and printing	88,866	94,237	6.0
Insurance, banking, information services, etc.	20,825	25,763	23.7
Sanitary and industrial supplies	28,674	30,197	5.3
Packaging materials and paper boxes	7,911	8,915	12.7
Repair of tangible personal property	56,639	62,075	9.6
Advertising	15,734	17,875	13.6
Topsoil, clay, sand, and fill dirt	16,134	19,271	19.4
Trade stamp redemption centers	-1	9	-780.4
Nurseries and landscaping	24,652	24,955	1.2
Vending machines	18,318	21,465	17.2
Importing and exporting	9,993	10,694	7.0
Medical, dental, surgical, hospital supplies	27,584	33,658	22.0
Wholesale dealers	274,923	289,353	5.2
Schools and educational institutions	4,100	3,499	-14.7
Office space and commercial rentals	553,333	587,960	6.3
Parking lots, boat docking, and storage	16,289	16,767	2.9
Utilities, electric or gas	279,559	266,095	-4.8
Dual users of special fuels	1,070	1,132	5.8
Public works, government contractors	1,033	1,030	-0.3
Flea market vendors	7,588	7,862	3.6
Carnival concessions	416	468	12.6
Other professional services	1,937	1,975	1.9
Other personal services	65,806	71,222	8.2
Other industrial services	4,866	5,348	9.9
Commercial fisherman	122	128	4.8
Miscellaneous	95,072	82,207	-13.5

Source: State of Florida, Department of Revenue, unpublished data.

Table 23.45. STATE GOVERNMENT FINANCE: TAX COLLECTIONS BY OR WITHIN COUNTIES BY TYPE OF TAX COLLECTED IN THE STATE AND COUNTIES OF FLORIDA FISCAL YEAR 1994-95

(rounded to thousands of dollars)

County	Total 1/	Sales and use taxes	Motor vehicle tags	Pari-mutuel wagering taxes	Documentary stamp tax
Florida	11,641,664	10,550,860	387,250	93,536	610,018
Alachua	129,395	120,097	4,231	0	5,067
Baker	5,249	4,457	550	0	242
Bay	114,854	106,170	3,468	0	5,216
Bradford	9,187	8,194	620	0	373
Brevard	268,285	242,718	10,661	532	14,374
Broward	1,203,286	1,086,740	28,889	14,406	73,250
Calhoun	3,551	3,154	259	0	138
Charlotte	79,267	70,007	3,344	0	5,916
Citrus	49,098	43,314	2,744	0	3,039
Clay	70,409	58,696	3,013	4,023	4,677
Collier	208,391	181,562	5,588	0	21,241
Columbia	29,579	27,393	1,233	0	953
Dade	1,491,476	1,332,829	51,119	20,738	86,790
De Soto	10,623	9,130	766	0	727
Dixie	2,887	2,318	314	0	254
Duval	589,633	543,632	17,011	4,107	24,883
Escambia	187,627	172,263	6,257	2,076	7,031
Flagler	16,670	13,746	1,044	0	1,880
Franklin	5,045	3,744	217	0	1,084
Gadsden	12,665	11,388	783	0	494
Gilchrist	2,317	1,770	313	0	235
Glades	1,522	1,043	159	0	320
Gulf	5,281	4,555	322	0	404
Hamilton	5,816	5,441	220	0	154
Hardee	9,960	8,666	695	0	599
Hendry	13,894	11,658	1,075	0	1,161
Hernando	46,936	40,762	2,647	0	3,527
Highlands	41,064	36,845	2,193	0	2,027
Hillsborough	795,228	731,196	23,629	9,394	31,009
Holmes	4,474	3,899	391	0	184
Indian River	65,906	57,956	2,723	0	5,227
Jackson	20,132	18,574	1,024	0	534
Jefferson	5,195	2,912	293	1,792	197
Lafayette	954	701	140	0	112
Lake	96,532	85,204	4,879	0	6,449
Lee	331,171	292,305	10,198	4,534	24,134
Leon	161,519	148,905	4,857	0	7,757

See footnotes at end of table.

Continued . . .

Table 23.45. STATE GOVERNMENT FINANCE: TAX COLLECTIONS BY OR WITHIN COUNTIES BY TYPE OF TAX COLLECTED IN THE STATE AND COUNTIES OF FLORIDA FISCAL YEAR 1994-95 (Continued)

(rounded to thousands of dollars)

County	Total 1/	Sales and use taxes	Motor vehicle tags	Pari-mutuel wagering taxes	Documentary stamp tax
Levy	11,136	9,478	926	0	732
Liberty	1,262	1,014	182	0	65
Madison	4,378	3,796	386	0	196
Manatee	162,270	139,437	13,066	0	9,767
Marion	142,091	129,251	6,287	59	6,494
Martin	99,397	88,937	3,451	0	7,009
Monroe	99,268	90,240	2,175	0	6,853
Nassau	28,403	25,493	1,190	0	1,720
Okaloosa	116,409	106,031	4,011	0	6,367
Okeechobee	16,325	14,544	1,096	0	686
Orange	1,017,759	959,076	22,139	0	36,543
Osceola	114,800	103,401	3,208	0	8,191
Palm Beach	856,441	762,633	23,708	8,925	61,175
Pasco	141,107	124,033	8,043	0	9,031
Pinellas	611,877	552,060	19,282	8,691	31,844
Polk	289,122	266,677	12,658	0	9,787
Putnam	29,117	26,346	1,623	0	1,147
St. Johns	72,253	61,277	2,530	2,271	6,175
St. Lucie	92,295	81,916	4,184	112	6,083
Santa Rosa	36,050	29,738	2,265	0	4,047
Sarasota	243,702	215,481	7,924	1,225	19,072
Seminole	243,120	215,132	8,092	5,322	14,574
Sumter	13,959	11,584	992	0	1,383
Suwannee	12,210	10,797	835	0	578
Taylor	12,352	10,166	489	0	1,697
Union	2,394	2,018	285	0	91
Volusia	255,688	229,420	9,447	4,037	12,784
Wakulla	3,972	3,155	413	0	404
Walton	25,293	21,099	619	0	3,574
Washington	6,703	4,744	380	1,293	286
Out-of-state	738,081	738,081	0	0	0
Other	47,354	19,859	A/ 27,495	0	0

A/ Includes refunds.
1/ Does not include gasoline taxes; see Table 23.46 for gasoline tax collections.

Source: Columns 2, 5, State of Florida, Department of Revenue, unpublished data; Column 3, State of Florida, Department of Highway Safety and Motor Vehicles, Division of Motor Vehicles, *Revenue Report, July 1, 1994-June 30, 1995;* Column 4, State of Florida, Department of Business and Professional Regulation, Division of Pari-Mutuel Wagering, *64th Annual Report for the Fiscal Year Ending on June 30, 1995.*

Table 23.46. STATE GOVERNMENT FINANCE: GASOLINE AND GASOHOL TAX COLLECTIONS IN FLORIDA, FISCAL YEARS 1969-70 THROUGH 1994-95

Fiscal year	Gallons sold	Tax rate (cents)	Tax collected 1/ (dollars)
	Gasoline		
1969-70	3,054,891,901.3	7	213,842,433.12
1970-71	3,341,148,943.8	7	233,880,426.09
1971-72	3,685,131,310.5	7/8	291,484,318.30
1972-73	4,080,699,270.9	8	326,454,941.67
1973-74	4,157,754,572.7	8	332,617,165.82
1974-75	4,243,123,105.1	8	339,449,848.41
1975-76	4,326,195,422.0	8	346,095,633.76
1976-77	4,483,397,014.2	8	358,671,761.14
1977-78	4,721,812,693.4	8	377,745,015.47
1978-79	4,961,448,003.1	8	396,915,840.25
1979-80	4,765,935,970.1	8	381,274,877.61
1980-81	4,681,857,035.4	8	374,548,562.90
1981-82	4,746,090,470.3	8	379,687,237.63
1982-83	4,686,388,610.8	5.7/8/9.7	387,286,074.47
1983-84	4,709,246,332.0	5.7/8/9.7	455,678,899.26
1984-85	4,739,366,278.0	5.7/9.7	458,188,999.77
1985-86	5,003,004,954.0	5.7/9.7	483,953,518.77
1986-87	5,493,474,844.7	5.7/9.7	484,754,881.20
1987-88	5,869,584,946.8	5.7/9.7	569,328,353.84
1988-89	5,995,884,170.5	5.7/9.7	581,596,538.65
1989-90	6,087,306,071.0	5.7/9.7	590,082,229.69
1990-91	5,985,729,187.8	9.7/10.9/11.2	653,943,345.04
1991-92	6,065,182,815.5	9.7/10.9/11.2/11.6	689,690,791.78
1992-93	6,279,687,903.2	9.7/10.9/11.2/11.6/11.8	723,722,832.76
1993-94	6,451,928,258.1	10.9/11.2/11.6/12.1	765,014,400.64
1994-95	6,560,589,349.5	11.6/11.8/12.1/12.3	802,201,952.42
	Gasohol		
1980-81	40,041,320.0	3	1,201,239.60
1981-82	70,917,324.0	3	2,127,519.72
1982-83	174,716,609.0	3	5,241,498.27
1983-84	450,407,246.3	3/5.7	24,795,573.66
1984-85	580,254,644.0	5.7	32,540,874.16
1985-86	502,585,415.4	5.7/7.7	37,559,028.18
1986-87	216,061,242.3	7.7	16,636,263.27
1987-88	90,593,367.2	7.7/9.7	8,494,772.51
1988-89	83,299,691.4	9.7	8,081,088.78
1989-90	72,191,842.3	9.7	7,027,562.96
1990-91	84,213,028.6	9.7/10.9/11.2	9,177,965.47
1991-92	99,594,325.4	9.7/10.9/11.2/11.6	11,317,423.38
1992-93	104,007,445.0	11.6/11.8	12,162,419.87
1993-94	13,688,278.1	10.9/11.8/12.1	5,806,630.60
1994-95	20,384,143.0	12.1/12.3	2,791,240.05

1/ Includes collection fees.
Note: Some data may be revised.

Source: State of Florida, Department of Revenue, *Report of Fuel Tax Collections and Distributions, Fiscal Year 1994-95,* and unpublished data.

Table 23.48. STATE FUNDS TO LOCAL GOVERNMENT: DISTRIBUTION OF SHARED TAXES BY THE FLORIDA DEPARTMENT OF REVENUE TO COUNTY AND CITY GOVERNMENTS BY MAJOR SOURCE IN THE STATE AND COUNTIES OF FLORIDA FISCAL YEAR 1994-95

(rounded to thousands of dollars)

County	Total DOR distri-bution	Half-cent sales tax distributed to-- County govern-ments	City govern-ments	Emer-gency and supple-mental	Revenue sharing County	Munici-pal	County tax on motor fuel 1/
Florida	1,474,367	604,054	300,239	4,966	304,563	200,275	60,271
Alachua	18,885	6,611	4,547	0	3,773	3,094	860
Baker	1,426	326	91	300	364	121	223
Bay	15,811	5,654	4,228	0	2,806	2,405	718
Bradford	1,753	556	199	216	420	201	161
Brevard	38,308	12,607	9,902	0	7,959	6,098	1,742
Broward	156,631	45,380	54,971	0	23,200	28,536	4,544
Calhoun	940	230	69	132	221	99	190
Charlotte	10,386	5,854	591	0	3,135	206	600
Citrus	7,153	3,573	386	0	2,490	243	460
Clay	9,198	4,765	702	0	2,843	376	513
Collier	23,089	14,539	1,778	0	5,208	468	1,097
Columbia	4,382	2,062	483	0	1,111	273	454
Dade	232,178	79,122	44,317	0	44,268	58,033	6,438
De Soto	1,906	642	195	135	511	185	238
Dixie	956	180	42	175	226	95	240
Duval 2/	86,433	47,786	2,810	0	16,856	16,250	2,730
Escambia	25,526	12,839	3,175	0	6,716	1,665	1,131
Flagler	2,493	1,087	220	79	763	108	236
Franklin	979	241	117	83	186	123	229
Gadsden	3,397	723	312	623	779	684	275
Gilchrist	731	141	28	198	207	44	113
Glades	765	83	16	178	168	44	276
Gulf	1,140	272	175	146	218	125	204
Hamilton	1,164	378	142	63	230	130	221
Hardee	1,893	603	213	205	428	204	239
Hendry	2,379	770	292	121	568	210	418
Hernando	7,099	3,511	247	0	2,686	184	471
Highlands	6,090	2,630	723	0	1,688	509	540
Hillsborough	100,955	47,524	20,350	0	21,317	8,495	3,268
Holmes	1,264	301	82	256	316	118	190
Indian River	8,636	3,762	1,536	0	2,135	736	466
Jackson	3,656	1,236	491	72	878	515	465
Jefferson	1,015	213	51	178	259	72	242
Lafayette	480	55	11	118	104	37	156
Lake	13,910	5,181	2,806	0	3,347	1,758	819
Lee	40,435	19,155	8,072	0	8,749	2,987	1,473

See footnotes at end of table. Continued . . .

Table 23.48. STATE FUNDS TO LOCAL GOVERNMENT: DISTRIBUTION OF SHARED TAXES BY THE FLORIDA DEPARTMENT OF REVENUE TO COUNTY AND CITY GOVERNMENTS BY MAJOR SOURCE IN THE STATE AND COUNTIES OF FLORIDA FISCAL YEAR 1994-95 (Continued)

(rounded to thousands of dollars)

County	Total DOR distri-bution	Half-cent sales tax distributed to-- County govern-ments	Half-cent sales tax distributed to-- City govern-ments	Emer-gency and supple-mental	Revenue sharing County	Revenue sharing Munici-pal	County tax on motor fuel 1/
Leon	21,971	7,601	6,155	0	4,056	3,308	851
Levy	2,309	662	212	232	582	218	404
Liberty	570	78	16	102	103	37	234
Madison	1,383	248	100	249	325	156	305
Manatee	20,347	9,542	3,183	0	5,267	1,472	883
Marion	19,509	9,631	2,406	0	5,056	1,137	1,279
Martin	12,046	7,129	1,101	0	2,946	349	522
Monroe	12,079	5,975	2,249	0	2,346	703	805
Nassau	4,114	1,850	545	0	1,078	276	363
Okaloosa	15,613	6,531	3,203	0	3,414	1,669	796
Okeechobee	2,655	1,159	193	0	763	176	363
Orange	119,886	62,277	25,465	0	21,685	7,541	2,917
Osceola	14,516	6,570	2,846	0	3,041	1,201	858
Palm Beach	105,556	42,744	27,222	0	20,647	11,486	3,457
Pasco	20,236	10,102	1,175	0	7,149	761	1,048
Pinellas	84,312	26,974	24,379	0	15,966	14,401	2,592
Polk	40,758	16,994	7,692	0	9,477	4,506	2,089
Putnam	4,786	1,982	472	0	1,501	402	429
St. Johns	8,966	4,752	901	0	2,327	420	565
St. Lucie	13,460	4,192	3,367	0	2,912	2,286	703
Santa Rosa	5,733	2,401	392	0	2,026	327	587
Sarasota	30,010	14,866	4,878	0	7,273	1,977	1,015
Seminole	30,992	12,492	7,392	0	6,666	3,447	995
Sumter	2,689	850	239	198	709	261	433
Suwannee	2,318	784	215	172	620	223	303
Taylor	1,883	636	305	0	367	218	357
Union	783	139	48	228	165	104	101
Volusia	35,507	12,114	8,997	0	7,544	5,329	1,523
Wakulla	1,075	287	13	191	354	19	211
Walton	3,356	1,582	385	0	741	222	426
Washington	1,511	318	122	317	329	209	216

DOR Department of Revenue.

1/ State total includes the following distribution from oil and gas severance taxes: Florida, $762,832; Collier County, $93,932; Escambia County, $80,864; Hendry County, $3,058; Lee County, $32,315; and Santa Rosa County, $552,663.

2/ Duval County is the consolidated city of Jacksonville. See also disbursements to municipalities on Table 23.51.

Source: State of Florida, Department of Revenue, unpublished data.

Table 23.49. STATE FUNDS TO LOCAL GOVERNMENT: DISTRIBUTION FROM THE GENERAL REVENUE AND TRUST FUNDS TO SCHOOL DISTRICTS IN THE STATE AND COUNTIES OF FLORIDA, FISCAL YEAR 1993-94

(rounded to thousands of dollars)

County	Total disburse- ments	Distribution from-- General revenue funds	Trust funds
Florida	6,939,559	4,869,719	2,069,841
Alachua	107,830	77,677	30,152
Baker	20,033	14,907	5,126
Bay	89,383	66,654	22,729
Bradford	16,214	12,876	3,338
Brevard	192,585	138,907	53,677
Broward	704,503	492,985	211,517
Calhoun	9,344	7,061	2,282
Charlotte	29,108	16,567	12,541
Citrus	37,943	26,786	11,157
Clay	80,967	63,038	17,929
Collier	39,274	13,632	25,642
Columbia	39,950	26,092	13,859
Dade	1,284,946	923,223	361,723
De Soto	18,188	13,045	5,143
Dixie	12,329	6,734	5,595
Duval	413,956	301,028	112,929
Escambia	183,093	134,143	48,951
Flagler	13,632	8,257	5,375
Franklin	6,022	3,925	2,097
Gadsden	42,847	27,461	15,386
Gilchrist	9,900	7,552	2,348
Glades	2,795	1,556	1,239
Gulf	7,969	5,426	2,543
Hamilton	10,486	6,770	3,716
Hardee	19,606	13,600	6,006
Hendry	25,480	17,194	8,286
Hernando	41,119	31,466	9,653
Highlands	37,602	26,409	11,193
Hillsborough	496,937	370,984	125,953
Holmes	15,324	11,673	3,650
Indian River	26,106	14,187	11,919
Jackson	36,666	28,590	8,076
Jefferson	9,751	6,954	2,797

Continued . . .

Table 23.49. STATE FUNDS TO LOCAL GOVERNMENT: DISTRIBUTION FROM THE GENERAL REVENUE AND TRUST FUNDS TO SCHOOL DISTRICTS IN THE STATE AND COUNTIES OF FLORIDA, FISCAL YEAR 1993-94 (Continued)

(rounded to thousands of dollars)

County	Total disburse-ments	Distribution from-- General revenue funds	Trust funds
Lafayette	4,879	3,766	1,113
Lake	75,718	55,095	20,623
Lee	95,101	63,558	31,543
Leon	120,172	88,958	31,214
Levy	21,577	16,419	5,158
Liberty	5,351	3,932	1,420
Madison	13,777	10,535	3,241
Manatee	84,650	60,216	24,434
Marion	121,863	86,299	35,564
Martin	19,134	6,735	12,399
Monroe	28,924	22,305	6,619
Nassau	15,815	6,214	9,601
Okaloosa	96,001	74,454	21,547
Okeechobee	24,489	17,573	6,916
Orange	344,493	221,902	122,591
Osceola	73,970	53,727	20,243
Palm Beach	301,220	161,388	139,832
Pasco	135,820	97,681	38,140
Pinellas	286,007	207,615	78,391
Polk	256,880	180,068	76,811
Putnam	48,843	32,832	16,011
St. Johns	45,618	30,742	14,876
St. Lucie	72,603	47,806	24,798
Santa Rosa	67,544	49,139	18,405
Sarasota	61,620	35,426	26,194
Seminole	150,880	115,278	35,602
Sumter	21,599	16,539	5,060
Suwannee	22,326	17,004	5,322
Taylor	14,494	9,973	4,521
Union	9,347	6,897	2,450
Volusia	163,856	115,384	48,471
Wakulla	17,432	13,098	4,334
Walton	15,290	8,989	6,301
Washington	20,380	14,812	5,568

Source: State of Florida, *Annual Report of the Comptroller, Fiscal Year 1993-94.* Data from Department of Education.

Table 23.50. STATE LOTTERY: SALES IN THE STATE AND COUNTIES OF FLORIDA FISCAL YEARS 1990-91 THROUGH 1995-96

(rounded to thousands of dollars)

County	1990-91	1991-92	1992-93	1993-94	1994-95	1995-96
Florida	2,193,300	2,227,202	2,169,700	2,208,088	2,303,486	2,117,085
Alachua	21,065	22,207	22,922	23,428	25,103	23,734
Baker	2,289	2,310	2,255	2,504	2,501	2,303
Bay	26,392	26,498	24,721	23,504	24,939	21,866
Bradford	2,498	2,641	2,770	3,038	3,422	3,152
Brevard	66,827	69,147	67,290	69,882	71,821	68,880
Broward	229,216	227,822	225,594	228,624	231,817	209,958
Calhoun	1,088	1,166	1,140	1,159	1,312	1,227
Charlotte	16,700	17,795	17,661	18,222	19,528	17,900
Citrus	14,431	15,070	14,657	15,897	16,784	15,713
Clay	12,638	12,809	12,610	12,691	13,114	12,353
Collier	21,698	22,314	22,232	23,335	24,182	22,357
Columbia	7,754	8,127	8,371	8,268	8,790	8,424
Dade	374,815	378,322	362,759	374,679	375,442	354,696
De Soto	3,091	3,203	3,168	3,061	3,105	2,858
Dixie	1,003	1,015	895	1,120	1,305	1,348
Duval	105,271	107,895	108,200	109,681	115,885	106,516
Escambia	71,714	77,186	70,616	67,172	72,207	62,131
Flagler	4,762	5,136	5,175	5,724	6,397	6,234
Franklin	1,443	1,525	1,645	1,655	1,629	1,442
Gadsden	7,115	7,771	7,892	7,069	7,593	6,671
Gilchrist	709	821	961	950	932	1,152
Glades	978	1,098	1,223	901	953	907
Gulf	1,587	1,620	1,582	1,676	1,739	1,551
Hamilton	17,456	18,650	16,542	8,662	8,521	4,892
Hardee	1,976	2,088	1,967	1,998	2,238	1,982
Hendry	4,132	4,396	4,337	4,506	4,629	4,122
Hernando	15,978	17,112	17,765	19,443	20,285	19,531
Highlands	9,712	10,105	9,971	10,375	10,879	9,821
Hillsborough	120,834	120,136	117,110	120,124	128,350	117,034
Holmes	5,825	6,198	6,015	5,740	6,031	5,556
Indian River	14,074	13,596	13,226	14,718	15,783	14,626
Jackson	21,118	23,820	22,387	17,337	19,368	15,299
Jefferson	8,743	9,109	8,231	5,314	5,432	3,379
Lafayette	432	499	435	448	444	413
Lake	25,025	25,706	24,666	26,197	28,555	27,696
Lee	48,251	49,795	49,446	50,867	52,317	49,074

See footnote at end of table. Continued . . .

Table 23.50. STATE LOTTERY: SALES IN THE STATE AND COUNTIES OF FLORIDA FISCAL YEARS 1990-91 THROUGH 1995-96 (Continued)

(rounded to thousands of dollars)

County	1990-91	1991-92	1992-93	1993-94	1994-95	1995-96
Leon	25,469	25,505	24,074	23,366	25,641	21,986
Levy	4,140	4,521	4,679	4,697	5,191	5,024
Liberty	649	701	693	710	831	691
Madison	4,496	4,502	4,182	3,401	3,507	2,761
Manatee	30,065	30,324	29,701	31,558	33,011	29,786
Marion	31,340	33,229	33,466	35,926	38,014	35,354
Martin	16,453	16,659	17,112	17,589	18,486	17,284
Monroe	13,935	13,807	13,554	13,527	14,049	13,320
Nassau	25,656	26,051	24,298	16,554	16,425	11,390
Okaloosa	23,985	25,371	24,281	23,867	25,640	22,545
Okeechobee	4,659	5,008	5,132	5,494	5,644	5,136
Orange	113,388	111,963	107,891	110,261	118,085	110,784
Osceola	19,672	20,125	20,298	22,523	24,215	22,785
Palm Beach	141,993	142,399	138,584	144,989	151,562	140,687
Pasco	42,091	42,451	42,918	46,409	48,002	44,548
Pinellas	133,060	131,667	126,447	133,874	139,180	127,057
Polk	62,538	63,371	62,771	64,416	69,925	63,533
Putnam	9,944	10,239	10,334	10,763	11,468	10,675
St. Johns	11,502	11,988	12,043	12,574	13,397	12,391
St. Lucie	24,544	25,837	26,662	26,870	28,718	26,251
Santa Rosa	10,354	11,340	11,005	10,926	11,399	10,691
Sarasota	38,576	38,060	36,533	38,334	40,452	36,372
Seminole	35,050	33,633	32,073	33,491	35,889	33,927
Sumter	4,627	5,064	5,274	5,257	5,474	5,076
Suwannee	3,326	3,329	3,536	3,747	3,782	3,601
Taylor	2,490	2,506	2,402	2,563	2,751	2,463
Union	1,027	1,124	1,081	1,104	1,177	1,058
Volusia	60,108	61,749	60,556	63,699	67,907	63,640
Wakulla	1,738	1,750	1,856	1,931	2,112	1,895
Walton	5,773	6,173	5,935	5,841	6,267	5,712
Washington	2,013	2,047	1,888	1,861	1,950	1,867

Note: Data are unaudited gross sales amounts.

Source: State of Florida, Department of the Lottery, unpublished data.

Table 23.51. STATE FUNDS TO LOCAL GOVERNMENT: FUNDS DISTRIBUTED TO SELECTED CITY AND OTHER TYPES OF LOCAL GOVERNMENTS BY THE FLORIDA DEPARTMENT OF REVENUE, FISCAL YEAR 1994-95

(in thousands of dollars)

Government type	Total	2-cent cigarette tax	Revenue sharing trust fund	Half-cent sales tax
Florida 1/	521,665	22,814	200,275	298,576
City				
Jacksonville	8,770	1,209	7,561	0
Miami	27,332	424	9,660	17,248
Tampa	26,223	1,150	7,454	17,619
St. Petersburg	16,457	666	6,105	9,686
Hialeah	101,207	235	5,758	95,214
Orlando	22,612	897	4,970	16,745
Ft. Lauderdale	10,939	216	3,656	7,067
Tallahassee	9,645	278	3,308	6,059
Hollywood	9,319	180	3,245	5,894
Clearwater	6,606	280	2,261	4,065
Gainesville	6,685	260	2,653	3,772
Miami Beach	6,902	112	2,258	4,532
Coral Springs	6,354	129	2,019	4,206
Cape Coral	7,120	462	1,756	4,902
Pembroke Pines	5,445	108	1,833	3,504
Lakeland	5,531	354	1,856	3,321
Pompano Beach	5,284	107	1,699	3,478
Plantation	5,169	106	1,627	3,436
Sunrise	5,211	104	1,726	3,381
Palm Bay	4,343	187	1,595	2,561
West Palm Beach	5,732	208	1,687	3,837
Port St. Lucie	3,614	176	1,296	2,142
Largo	4,578	186	1,692	2,700
Boca Raton	5,145	199	1,305	3,641
Melbourne	4,072	174	1,520	2,378
Daytona Beach	4,172	232	1,514	2,426
Pensacola	5,098	468	1,577	3,053
Davie	3,766	76	1,222	2,468
Sarasota	4,427	334	1,213	2,880
North Miami	3,923	59	1,469	2,395
Lauderhill	3,722	72	1,290	2,360
Delray Beach	3,971	150	1,070	2,751
Boynton Beach	3,995	149	1,113	2,733
Deerfield Beach	3,400	69	1,066	2,265
Tamarac	3,410	68	1,122	2,220
Other				
Metro Dade 2/	34,641	1,203	33,438	0
Jacksonville/Duval 3/	7,777	0	7,777	0

1/ Includes amounts for municipalities not shown separately.
2/ Consolidated portion of Dade County and the city of Miami.
3/ The small portion of the city of Jacksonville and Duval County that is outside the consolidated area.

Note: Data are reported for the 35 most populous cities in Florida in 1995 and for other types of city/county governments. Cities are listed in population rank. Some data may not be comparable to earlier years.

Source: State of Florida, Department of Revenue, unpublished data.

Table 23.52. ALCOHOLIC BEVERAGE AND TOBACCO LICENSES: NUMBER OF LICENSES ISSUED IN THE STATE AND COUNTIES OF FLORIDA, FISCAL YEAR 1994-95

County	Alcoholic beverage licenses	Tobacco licenses	County	Alcoholic beverage licenses	Tobacco licenses
Florida	38,425	29,245	Lafayette	11	12
			Lake	466	333
Alachua	458	353	Lee	1,156	776
Baker	53	51	Leon	486	352
Bay	578	414	Levy	120	89
Bradford	66	60	Liberty	20	22
Brevard	1,248	867	Madison	50	46
Broward	3,663	2,557	Manatee	588	426
Calhoun	38	37	Marion	578	461
Charlotte	313	206	Martin	403	225
Citrus	295	205	Monroe	667	437
Clay	236	181	Nassau	153	125
Collier	752	428	Okaloosa	476	309
Columbia	148	131	Okeechobee	111	92
Dade	5,120	4,647	Orange	2,050	1,558
De Soto	62	50	Osceola	483	371
Dixie	48	39	Palm Beach	2,607	1,791
Duval	1,811	1,491	Pasco	642	489
Escambia	749	576	Pinellas	2,328	1,760
Flagler	135	88	Polk	1,054	863
Franklin	70	45	Putnam	183	160
Gadsden	142	127	St. Johns	381	232
Gilchrist	28	27	St. Lucie	440	341
Glades	46	34	Santa Rosa	164	146
Gulf	53	41	Sarasota	859	514
Hamilton	52	41	Seminole	710	492
Hardee	39	39	Sumter	104	93
Hendry	105	96	Suwannee	78	72
Hernando	269	174	Taylor	81	67
Highlands	212	148	Union	18	21
Hillsborough	2,087	1,819	Volusia	1,252	962
Holmes	52	49	Wakulla	61	49
Indian River	308	191	Walton	177	122
Jackson	133	133	Washington	47	49
Jefferson	52	43			

Source: State of Florida, Department of Business and Professional Regulation, *1994-1995 Annual Report.* Data from Division of Alcoholic Beverages and Tobacco.

Table 23.53. ALCOHOLIC BEVERAGE LICENSES: NUMBER OF LICENSES ISSUED BY TYPE OF LICENSE IN THE STATE AND COUNTIES OF FLORIDA, LICENSE YEAR OCTOBER 1, 1994 THROUGH SEPTEMBER 30, 1995

		Type of license						
County	Total	Clubs entertainment and tracks 1/	Package sales only 2/	Package and on-premises sales 3/	Distributors 4/	Manufacturers 5/	Import/ export 6/	Broker sales agent (BSA)
Florida	41,037	1,625	17,884	12,444	8,929	34	103	18
Alachua	494	8	245	124	117	0	0	0
Baker	58	2	42	10	4	0	0	0
Bay	618	19	227	230	142	0	0	0
Bradford	69	2	42	18	7	0	0	0
Brevard	1,329	66	533	430	293	3	4	0
Broward	3,927	104	1,668	1,197	944	2	9	3
Calhoun	41	0	28	13	0	0	0	0
Charlotte	335	27	125	85	98	0	0	0
Citrus	311	25	121	113	52	0	0	0
Clay	239	13	133	52	40	0	1	0
Collier	745	57	256	244	188	0	0	0
Columbia	164	6	104	29	25	0	0	0
Dade	5,662	105	2,532	1,980	991	1	52	1
De Soto	66	6	30	19	11	0	0	0
Dixie	53	0	28	20	5	0	0	0
Duval	1,904	61	954	551	330	3	4	1
Escambia	775	29	360	192	194	0	0	0
Flagler	144	11	41	66	26	0	0	0
Franklin	71	1	26	22	22	0	0	0
Gadsden	143	1	80	50	12	0	0	0
Gilchrist	30	0	18	5	7	0	0	0
Glades	46	1	22	13	10	0	0	0
Gulf	57	2	27	17	11	0	0	0
Hamilton	52	0	36	15	1	0	0	0
Hardee	43	0	29	14	0	0	0	0
Hendry	100	7	53	25	15	0	0	0
Hernando	279	20	121	89	49	0	0	0
Highlands	224	17	100	59	47	0	1	0
Hillsborough	2,244	81	1,059	558	537	3	5	1
Holmes	53	3	36	14	0	0	0	0
Indian River	320	30	134	84	72	0	0	0
Jackson	144	0	102	42	0	0	0	0
Jefferson	53	3	34	12	4	0	0	0
Lafayette	15	0	11	4	0	0	0	0
Lake	494	26	241	130	96	1	0	0
Lee	1,233	80	460	390	298	1	2	2
Leon	514	13	239	152	110	0	0	0
Levy	125	6	69	28	22	0	0	0
Liberty	20	0	16	4	0	0	0	0
Madison	50	0	38	12	0	0	0	0

See footnotes at end of table. Continued . . .

Table 23.53. ALCOHOLIC BEVERAGE LICENSES: NUMBER OF LICENSES ISSUED BY TYPE OF LICENSE IN THE STATE AND COUNTIES OF FLORIDA, LICENSE YEAR OCTOBER 1, 1994 THROUGH SEPTEMBER 30, 1995

County	Total	Type of license: Clubs entertainment and tracks 1/	Package sales only 2/	Package and on-premises sales 3/	Distributors 4/	Manufacturers 5/	Import/ export 6/	Broker sales agent (BSA)
Manatee	611	24	252	181	154	0	0	0
Marion	618	27	327	169	95	0	0	0
Martin	422	37	159	149	77	0	0	0
Monroe	734	30	230	257	216	1	0	0
Nassau	159	7	84	33	34	1	0	0
Okaloosa	506	26	180	157	143	0	0	0
Okeechobee	112	10	63	27	12	0	0	0
Orange	2,173	54	936	658	519	2	3	1
Osceola	510	12	219	169	109	0	1	0
Palm Beach	2,870	137	1,106	827	779	1	15	5
Pasco	706	58	300	202	146	0	0	0
Pinellas	2,519	98	1,001	759	654	1	2	4
Polk	1,099	45	591	270	180	13	0	0
Putnam	189	9	97	47	36	0	0	0
St. Johns	389	26	134	144	84	0	1	0
St. Lucie	492	28	263	123	77	0	1	0
Santa Rosa	160	0	106	54	0	0	0	0
Sarasota	888	58	275	298	257	0	0	0
Seminole	736	32	312	220	171	0	1	0
Sumter	105	6	67	19	13	0	0	0
Suwannee	84	1	58	25	0	0	0	0
Taylor	85	4	44	21	16	0	0	0
Union	19	0	12	2	5	0	0	0
Volusia	1,297	53	497	432	315	0	0	0
Wakulla	65	3	36	15	11	0	0	0
Walton	194	7	80	59	46	1	1	0
Washington	51	1	35	15	0	0	0	0

1/ Beer, wine, and/or all alcoholic beverages sold in clubs (including bottle clubs), civic and performing arts centers, at race tracks and from golf carts. Licenses included in this category are: 11C, 11CS, 11PA, 12RT, 14BC, and GC.

2/ Beer, wine, and/or all alcoholic beverages sold by the package only. Licenses included in this category are 1APS, 2APS, 3APS, 3BPS, 3CPS, and 3PS.

3/ Beer, wine, and/or all alcoholic beverages to consume on premises and by the package. Establishments with three are more bars (such as hotels) are included. Licenses included in this category are: 1COP, 2COP, COP, and 3M.

4/ Distributors of beer, wine, and/or liquor (including wine distributed to churches). Licenses included in this category are: 4COP, 5COP, 6COP, 7COP, 8COP, JDBW, and KLD.

5/ Manufacturers of beer, wine, and/or liquor. Licenses included in this category are: AMW, BMWC, CMB, CMBP, DD, and ERB.

6/ Licenses included in this category are: IMPR and MEXP.

Source: State of Florida, Department of Business and Professional Regulation, Division of Alcoholic Beverages and Tobacco, *Number and Series of Beverage Licenses Issued by County,* October 1995.

Table 23.54. PARI-MUTUEL WAGERING: PERFORMANCES, ATTENDANCE, AND REVENUE BY TYPE OF EVENT IN FLORIDA, FISCAL YEARS 1990-91 THROUGH 1994-95

Item	Number of-- Days	Per-form-ances	Paid attendance	Pari-mutuel handle (dollars)	Revenue to state (dollars)
All tracks and frontons					
1990-91	4,994	6,929	14,410,934	1,712,307,521	105,391,957
1991-92	5,321	7,282	14,109,252	1,734,102,853	100,647,639
1992-93	5,074	7,009	12,620,914	1,693,636,924	106,762,525
1993-94	5,169	7,121	11,428,607	1,639,598,007	102,137,962
1994-95	4,845	6,681	10,285,062	1,582,305,874	93,536,408
Thoroughbred tracks					
1990-91	365	365	2,139,748	453,042,131	11,740,085
1991-92	375	375	2,097,759	523,246,855	14,095,538
1992-93	372	372	1,908,066	521,495,616	14,004,011
1993-94	374	374	1,800,911	521,266,989	14,884,209
1994-95	379	379	1,789,908	516,739,403	14,503,157
Harness tracks					
1990-91	149	149	488,682	62,979,924	839,568
1991-92	161	161	481,854	71,574,323	1,035,561
1992-93	177	177	469,981	75,112,688	2,247,224
1993-94	196	196	451,965	76,342,577	1,221,611
1994-95	195	195	418,225	74,200,943	1,609,622
Quarter horse tracks					
1990-91	22	22	35,591	3,059,627	28,393
1991-92	20	20	35,755	2,654,959	25,576
1992-93	0	0	0	0	0
1993-94	0	0	0	0	0
1994-95	0	0	0	0	0
Greyhound tracks					
1990-91	2,862	4,055	8,255,669	919,075,892	73,590,913
1991-92	3,302	4,632	8,320,731	896,340,416	68,834,464
1992-93	3,223	4,487	7,371,852	862,232,223	71,945,550
1993-94	3,227	4,466	6,617,587	831,076,473	70,631,583
1994-95	3,045	4,240	5,897,749	800,744,617	67,797,851
Jai Alai frontons					
1990-91	1,596	2,338	3,491,244	274,149,947	19,192,998
1991-92	1,463	2,094	3,173,153	240,286,300	16,656,500
1992-93	1,302	1,973	2,871,015	234,796,397	18,565,740
1993-94	1,372	2,085	2,558,144	210,911,968	15,400,559

Note: These data represent the distribution of revenue derived from pari-mutuel performances and do not represent the total revenue received by the Division of Pari-Mutuel Wagering. Excluded are such items as licenses, fees, escheated tickets, charity, scholarship performances, and other miscellaneous items.

Source: State of Florida, Department of Business and Professional Regulation, Division of Pari-Mutuel Wagering, *64th Annual Report for the Fiscal Year Ending on June 30, 1995*.

Table 23.58. STATE RETIREMENT SYSTEM: MEMBERSHIP, PAYROLL, CONTRIBUTIONS ANNUITANTS, AND BENEFITS IN FLORIDA, JUNE 30, 1995

System	Active member-ship	Annual payroll ($1,000)	Accu-mulated contri-butions ($1,000)	Annu-itants	Annual benefits: Total paid ($1,000)	Annual benefits: Average (dol-lars)
Total	586,625	15,450,047	400,158	140,080	1,288,710	(X)
Average salary (dollars)	(X)	26,337	(X)	(X)	9,200	9,200
Florida retirement system	583,957	15,322,656	194,867	127,470	1,188,455	(X)
Regular members	526,414	13,470,799	172,652	119,896	1,077,983	8,991
Senior management members	1,195	90,698	3,084	144	4,565	31,701
Special risk members	52,327	1,603,201	14,320	6,407	79,870	12,466
Administrative support	247	8,825	280	49	824	16,823
Elected state officer class members	1,896	112,720	4,561	974	25,213	25,886
Renewed membership	1,878	36,413	0	(X)	(X)	(X)
Teachers retirement system	2,550	124,351	203,194	7,599	80,045	10,534
Survivors' benefits	(X)	(X)	(X)	1,123	2,112	1,881
State and county officers and employees retirement system	118	3,040	2,067	3,757	16,197	4,311
Highway patrol pension trust fund	0	0	0	104	1,331	12,800
Judicial retirement system	0	0	0	27	570	21,100

(X) Not applicable.

Table 23.59. STATE RETIREMENT SYSTEM: ANNUITANTS AND BENEFITS BY AGE OF RETIREMENT IN FLORIDA, JUNE 30, 1995

Retirement age	Retirees: Number	Retirees: Annualized benefits (dollars)	Joint annuitants: Number	Joint annuitants: Annualized benefits (dollars)
Total	125,815	1,195,119,397	13,142	91,478,102
Under age 50	3,892	24,383,957	1,020	6,228,571
50-54	9,863	97,942,014	1,474	9,707,440
55-59	24,574	257,723,437	2,665	19,506,943
60-64	51,620	491,004,003	4,277	31,545,997
65-69	29,424	268,704,180	2,813	18,625,393
70-74	5,104	45,956,352	660	4,659,567
75-79	1,073	7,796,210	167	932,395
Age 80 and over	265	1,609,243	66	271,795

Note: Annuitants include all retired persons or survivors of retired persons who are receiving monthly benefits. Does not include 1,123 persons receiving monthly benefits from the survivors' benefit trust fund or the 657 annuitants under various general revenue pensions.

Source for Tables 23.58 and 23.59: State of Florida, Department of Management Services, Division of Retirement, *Florida Retirement System: July 1, 1994-June 30, 1995 Annual Report.*

Table 23.60. STATE RETIREMENT SYSTEM: REVENUE, EXPENDITURE, AND BALANCES OF THE FLORIDA RETIREMENT SYSTEM, FISCAL YEARS 1993-94 AND 1994-95

Item	1993-94	1994-95
Revenue, total	5,224,681,077	5,907,568,360
Contributions	2,778,375,127	2,928,863,876
Investment earnings	1,617,138,732	1,954,815,363
Earnings from other trust funds 1/	213,838	253,999
Gain/loss on sale of investments	828,533,297	1,023,496,886
Other revenue	420,083	138,237
Expenditure, total	1,252,120,938	1,469,702,924
Benefit payments	1,144,595,924	1,266,903,642
Refund of contributions	2,242,334	2,508,704
Operating expenses	10,693,050	11,558,438
Contractual investment commissions and fees	35,959,398	32,955,086
Interest expense for repurchase agreements	58,252,800	155,424,015
Other expenses	93,148	353,039
Prior year adjustment	284,284	0
Excess of revenue over expenditure	3,972,560,139	4,437,865,436
Beginning fund balance	29,138,634,740	33,111,194,879
Year-end fund balance (June 30)	33,111,194,879	37,549,060,315

1/ Includes social security and savings bonds.

Table 23.61. STATE RETIREMENT SYSTEM: RETIREMENT TRUST FUND BALANCES OF THE FLORIDA RETIREMENT SYSTEM, FISCAL YEARS 1993-94 AND 1994-95

Trust fund	1993-94	1994-95
Total	33,134,353,512	37,580,419,615
Florida Retirement System	33,111,194,879	37,549,060,315
Health Insurance Subsidy	14,628,121	21,838,313
Institute of Food and Agricultural Sciences (IFAS) Supplemental Retirement Program	8,242,648	9,239,643
Optional Retirement Program	287,864	281,077

Source for Tables 23.60 and 23.61: State of Florida, Department of Management Services, Division of Retirement, *Florida Retirement System: July 1, 1994-June 30, 1995 Annual Report.*

Table 23.70. FEDERAL GOVERNMENT: AVERAGE MONTHLY EMPLOYMENT COVERED BY UNEMPLOYMENT COMPENSATION LAW BY INDUSTRY IN FLORIDA, 1995

SIC code	Industry	Number of employees
01-99	All industries	119,684
27	Printing, publishing, and allied industries	1
37	Transportation equipment	164
43	U.S. postal service	43,889
53	General merchandise stores	4,057
531	Department stores	4,045
539	Miscellaneous general merchandise stores	12
59	Miscellaneous retail	5
61	Nondeposit credit institutions	217
63	Insurance carriers	116
65	Real estate	38
70	Hotels, rooming houses, camps, and other lodging places	587
79	Amusement and recreation services	2,204
80	Health services	12,745
801	Offices and clinics of doctors of medicine	859
802	Offices and clinics of dentists	48
806	Hospitals	11,837
83	Social services	19
84	Museums, art galleries, and botanical and zoological gardens	7
87	Engineering, accounting, research, management, and related services	892
89	Services, NEC	548
91	Executive, legislative, and general government, except finance	1,956
92	Justice, public order, and safety	6,262
921	Courts	1,429
922	Public order and safety	4,833
93	Public finance, taxation, and monetary policy	5,374

See footnotes at end of table. Continued . . .

Table 23.70. FEDERAL GOVERNMENT: AVERAGE MONTHLY EMPLOYMENT COVERED BY UNEMPLOYMENT COMPENSATION LAW BY INDUSTRY IN FLORIDA, 1995 (Continued)

SIC code	Industry	Number of employees
94	Administration of human resource programs	2,875
941	Administration of educational programs	15
943	Administration of public health programs	70
944	Administration of social, human resource, and income maintenance programs	2,206
945	Administration of veterans' affairs, except health and insurance	585
95	Administration of environmental quality and housing programs	1,610
951	Administration of environmental quality programs	1,314
953	Administration of housing and urban development programs	296
96	Administration of economic programs	7,760
961	Administration of general economic programs	304
962	Regulation and administration of transportation programs	3,069
963	Regulation and administration of communications, electric, gas, and other utilities	51
964	Regulation of agricultural marketing and commodities	1,583
965	Regulation, licensing, and inspection of miscellaneous commercial sectors	410
966	Space research and technology	2,344
97	National security and international affairs	28,361
971	National security	27,299
972	International affairs	1,062

NEC Not elsewhere classified.
Note: Data are preliminary. Detail may not add to totals due to disclosure editing and/or rounding.

Table 23.71. INTERNATIONAL GOVERNMENT: AVERAGE MONTHLY EMPLOYMENT COVERED BY UNEMPLOYMENT COMPENSATION LAW BY INDUSTRY IN FLORIDA, 1995

SIC code	Industry	Number of employees
01-99	All industries	823
40-49	Transportation, communications, and public utilities	806
45	Transportation by air	803

Note: Data are preliminary.

Source for Tables 23.70 and 23.71: State of Florida, Department of Labor and Employment Security, Bureau of Labor Market Information, "Employment and Wages" (ES-202), unpublished data.

Table 23.72. STATE GOVERNMENT: AVERAGE MONTHLY EMPLOYMENT COVERED BY UNEMPLOYMENT COMPENSATION LAW BY INDUSTRY IN FLORIDA, 1995

SIC code	Industry	Number of employees
01-99	All industries	199,639
08	Forestry	1,129
16	Heavy construction other than building construction--contractors	7,280
61	Nondeposit credit institutions	63
73	Business services	328
79	Amusement and recreation services	1,241
80	Health services	6,983
82	Educational services	61,183
821	Elementary and secondary schools	733
822	Colleges, universities, professional schools, and junior colleges	60,309
823	Libraries	142
83	Social services	4,557
832	Individual and family social services	400
836	Residential care	4,157
84	Museums, art galleries, and botanical and zoological gardens	59
91	Executive, legislative, and general government, except finance	6,386
911	Executive offices	508
912	Legislative bodies	1,556
919	General government, NEC	4,322
92	Justice, public order, and safety	44,173
921	Courts	829
922	Public order and safety	43,343
93	Public finance, taxation, and monetary policy	4,921
94	Administration of human resource programs	41,180
941	Administration of educational programs	1,609
943	Administration of public health programs	31,030
944	Administration of social, human resource, and income maintenance programs	8,268
945	Administration of veterans' affairs, except health and insurance	272
95	Administration of environmental quality and housing programs	5,018
951	Administration of environmental quality programs	4,769
953	Administration of housing and urban development programs	249
96	Administration of economic programs	14,876
961	Administration of general economic programs	393
962	Regulation and administration of transportation programs	6,022
963	Regulation and administration of communications, electric, gas, and other utilities	406
964	Regulation of agricultural marketing and commodities	2,391
965	Regulation, licensing, and inspection of miscellaneous commercial sectors	5,664
97	National security and international affairs	263

NEC Not elsewhere classified.

Note: Data are preliminary. Detail may not add to totals due to disclosure editing and/or rounding.

Source: State of Florida, Department of Labor and Employment Security, Bureau of Labor Market Information, "Employment and Wages" (ES-202), unpublished data.

Table 23.73. LOCAL GOVERNMENT: AVERAGE MONTHLY EMPLOYMENT COVERED BY UNEMPLOYMENT COMPENSATION LAW BY INDUSTRY IN FLORIDA, 1994 AND 1995

SIC code	Industry	Number of employees 1994 A/	1995 B/
01-99	All industries	577,773	583,604
07	Agricultural services	1	1
16	Heavy construction other than building construction--contractors	26	10
41	Passenger transportation	1,063	1,167
44	Water transportation	32	30
45	Transportation by air	1,294	1,306
47	Transportation services	22	24
49	Electric, gas, and sanitary services	5,855	5,861
491	Electric services	2,472	2,377
492	Gas production and distribution	46	191
493	Combination electric and gas, and other utility services	1,641	1,601
494	Water supply	368	371
495	Sanitary services	1,329	1,321
58	Eating and drinking places	741	704
63	Insurance carriers	22	26
637	Pension, health, and welfare funds	3	2
639	Insurance carriers, NEC	19	24
65	Real estate	2,117	2,190
73	Business services	63	64
734	Services to dwellings and other buildings	34	35
737	Computer programming, data processing, and other computer-related services	28	30
75	Automotive repair services, and parking	174	196
79	Amusement and recreation services	848	790
792	Theatrical producers (except motion picture), bands, orchestras, and entertainers	62	60
794	Commercial sports	340	300
799	Miscellaneous amusement and recreation services	446	430
80	Health services	38,452	35,776
801	Offices and clinics of doctors of medicine	5	1
805	Nursing and personal care facilities	309	233
806	Hospitals	38,138	35,542
82	Educational services	300,850	307,893
821	Elementary and secondary schools	269,076	276,318
822	Colleges, universities, professional schools, and junior colleges	31,198	30,988
823	Libraries	576	587
83	Social services	126	92
832	Individual and family services	4	5
833	Job training and vocational rehabilitation services	69	73
839	Social services, NEC	54	14
86	Membership organizations	115	129
861	Business associations	4	2
864	Civic, social, and fraternal associations	105	126
865	Political organizations	1	0
869	Membership organizations, NEC	5	1
87	Engineering, accounting, research, management and related services	10	6

See footnotes at end of table.

Continued . . .

Table 23.73. LOCAL GOVERNMENT: AVERAGE MONTHLY EMPLOYMENT COVERED BY UNEMPLOYMENT COMPENSATION LAW BY INDUSTRY IN FLORIDA, 1994 AND 1995

SIC code	Industry	Number of employees 1994 A/	1995 B/
89	Services, NEC	50	49
91	Executive, legislative, and general government, except finance	178,556	178,959
911	Executive offices	1,131	429
912	Legislative bodies	55,625	56,204
913	Executive and legislative offices combined	121,419	121,934
919	General government, NEC	381	394
92	Justice, public order, and safety	35,307	36,569
921	Courts	6,808	7,002
922	Public order and safety	28,499	29,567
93	Public finance, taxation, and monetary policy	5,626	5,736
94	Administration of human resource programs	239	257
943	Administration of public health programs	10	14
944	Administration of social, human resource, and income maintenance programs	225	238
945	Administration of veterans' affairs, except health and insurance	5	5
95	Administration of environmental quality and housing programs	4,555	4,785
951	Administration of environmental quality programs	3,813	3,937
953	Administration of housing and urban development programs	742	848
96	Administration of economic programs	1,631	986
961	Administration of general economic programs	414	206
962	Regulation and administration of transportation programs	1,054	765
963	Regulation and administration of communications, electric, gas, and other utilities	143	(NA)
964	Regulation of agricultural marketing and commodities	8	11
965	Regulation, licensing, and inspection of miscellaneous commercial sectors	12	4

NEC Not elsewhere classified.
(NA) Not available.
A/ Revised.
B/ Preliminary.
Note: Detail may not add to totals due to disclosure editing and/or rounding.

Source: State of Florida, Department of Labor and Employment Security, Bureau of Labor Market Information, "Employment and Wages" (ES-202), unpublished data.

Table 23.74. GOVERNMENT EMPLOYMENT: AVERAGE MONTHLY EMPLOYMENT COVERED BY UNEMPLOYMENT COMPENSATION LAW BY LEVEL OF GOVERNMENT IN THE STATE AND COUNTIES OF FLORIDA, 1994 AND 1995

County	1994 A/			1995 B/		
	Federal	State	Local	Federal	State	Local
Florida	121,113	195,128	577,773	119,684	199,639	583,604
Alachua	3,180	25,446	9,125	2,961	25,667	9,779
Baker	69	1,645	787	71	1,694	787
Bay	3,569	1,080	7,045	3,460	1,130	7,073
Bradford	36	1,468	874	33	1,489	892
Brevard	6,221	2,101	16,246	5,913	2,162	16,279
Broward	6,625	7,778	60,176	6,804	7,752	61,415
Calhoun	37	419	429	33	442	448
Charlotte	232	698	3,633	234	723	3,683
Citrus	168	365	3,182	180	386	3,083
Clay	321	397	3,571	326	416	3,558
Collier	533	740	6,289	547	784	6,514
Columbia	1,029	1,475	2,158	1,118	1,537	2,196
Dade	18,007	16,771	95,469	17,667	16,910	95,715
De Soto	44	2,022	986	50	2,039	1,050
Dixie	22	459	448	20	462	547
Duval	15,732	6,842	28,338	16,355	7,095	27,957
Escambia	8,031	4,443	10,528	6,749	4,679	10,733
Flagler	72	131	1,411	74	137	1,479
Franklin	31	216	372	30	222	409
Gadsden	118	3,629	1,676	116	3,739	1,717
Gilchrist	24	470	416	24	482	491
Glades	12	32	309	12	36	304
Gulf	17	483	608	17	539	590
Hamilton	29	499	755	29	631	658
Hardee	45	549	1,075	48	597	1,101
Hendry	107	598	1,531	111	626	1,558
Hernando	257	582	3,698	264	588	3,829
Highlands	296	402	3,083	293	404	3,000
Hillsborough	10,822	14,509	39,784	10,615	14,754	40,316
Holmes	55	497	642	56	546	647
Indian River	343	519	3,735	348	521	3,736
Jackson	497	2,595	2,463	492	2,750	2,564
Jefferson	32	390	511	31	390	525
Lafayette	15	311	212	15	404	229
Lake	471	1,004	5,904	479	1,044	5,879
Lee	1,568	3,009	17,296	1,710	3,137	18,012
Leon	1,639	38,679	10,210	1,662	39,297	10,584
Levy	70	276	1,113	67	284	1,229
Liberty	53	385	240	53	419	254
Madison	46	488	849	45	527	870

See footnotes at end of table.

Continued . . .

Table 23.74. GOVERNMENT EMPLOYMENT: AVERAGE MONTHLY EMPLOYMENT COVERED BY UNEMPLOYMENT COMPENSATION LAW BY LEVEL OF GOVERNMENT IN THE STATE AND COUNTIES OF FLORIDA, 1994 AND 1995

County	1994 A/			1995 B/		
	Federal	State	Local	Federal	State	Local
Manatee	978	975	8,098	1,045	971	8,070
Marion	620	2,042	9,917	631	2,057	10,045
Martin	275	865	3,494	275	913	3,535
Monroe	1,273	736	3,373	1,283	765	3,472
Nassau	643	279	1,940	621	272	1,922
Okaloosa	6,659	923	5,745	6,269	975	5,765
Okeechobee	72	209	1,154	72	255	1,164
Orange	8,176	10,598	33,308	7,334	10,680	33,136
Osceola	241	459	5,072	244	485	5,363
Palm Beach	4,223	8,055	37,245	5,125	8,136	38,151
Pasco	557	1,217	8,928	612	1,253	9,212
Pinellas	5,990	4,436	31,055	5,879	4,546	31,322
Polk	1,357	4,328	18,875	1,396	4,427	18,915
Putnam	152	590	3,509	147	601	3,643
St. Johns	345	1,312	3,214	353	1,349	3,454
St. Lucie	473	1,206	6,613	473	1,280	6,721
Santa Rosa	695	518	3,192	706	542	3,433
Sarasota	849	1,683	11,471	852	1,704	10,838
Seminole	1,323	883	10,776	1,330	890	11,055
Sumter	99	657	1,113	303	780	1,213
Suwannee	105	290	1,054	107	295	1,104
Taylor	39	245	825	35	461	897
Union	19	1,787	360	19	1,834	422
Volusia	1,177	3,266	17,392	1,257	3,387	16,105
Wakulla	67	157	695	70	191	691
Walton	83	520	1,184	81	585	1,212
Washington	51	599	996	52	871	1,065
Multicounty 1/	3,735	1,537	(NA)	3,668	1,318	(NA)
Out-of-state 2/	366	358	(NA)	343	382	(NA)

A/ Revised.
B/ Preliminary.
1/ Reporting units without a fixed location within the state or of unknown county location.
2/ Employment based in Florida, but working out of the state or country.
Note: Not shown separately are public international government employment for the state and Dade County. Those figures are: 1994, Florida 804 and Dade County 576; 1995, Florida 823 and Dade County 589. Detail may not add to totals due to rounding.

Source: State of Florida, Department of Labor and Employment Security, Bureau of Labor Market Information, "Employment and Wages" (ES-202), unpublished data.

Table 23.75. STATE AND LOCAL GOVERNMENT: OPTIONAL GAS TAX RATES AND COLLECTIONS IN THE STATE AND COUNTIES OF FLORIDA, FISCAL YEAR 1994-95

(amounts in dollars)

County	Tax rate	Total collections	Service charge 1/
Florida	(X)	446,477,382	26,788,643
Alachua	0.06	6,067,203	364,032
Baker	0.06	830,963	49,858
Bay	0.06	4,972,503	298,350
Bradford	0.06	920,804	55,248
Brevard	0.06	13,994,000	839,640
Broward	0.06	41,926,298	2,515,578
Calhoun	0.06	484,902	29,094
Charlotte	0.06	4,419,219	265,153
Citrus	0.06	2,828,315	169,699
Clay	0.06	3,548,693	212,922
Collier	0.06	6,046,825	362,810
Columbia	0.06	3,108,378	186,503
Dade	0.06	53,100,075	3,186,005
De Soto	0.06	774,857	46,491
Dixie	0.06	511,434	30,686
Duval	0.06	24,917,335	1,495,040
Escambia	0.06	8,855,139	531,308
Flagler	0.06	1,161,885	69,713
Franklin	0.06	86,656	5,199
Gadsden	0.06	1,345,123	80,707
Gilchrist	0.06	249,552	14,973
Glades	0.06	293,539	17,612
Gulf	0.06	379,611	22,777
Hamilton	0.03	790,711	47,443
Hardee	0.06	805,439	48,326
Hendry	0.04	1,131,827	67,910
Hernando	0.06	3,538,763	212,326
Highlands	0.06	2,681,398	160,884
Hillsborough	0.06	29,196,501	1,751,790
Holmes	0.05	613,226	36,794
Indian River	0.06	3,617,687	217,061
Jackson	0.05	2,513,105	150,786
Jefferson	0.06	826,796	49,608
Lafayette	0.06	164,070	9,844
Lake	0.06	5,484,020	329,041
Lee	0.06	12,325,169	739,510
Leon	0.06	6,969,096	418,146
Levy	0.06	1,312,970	78,778
Liberty	0.05	320,573	19,234
Madison	0.03	1,255,763	75,346
Manatee	0.06	6,584,502	395,070
Marion	0.06	9,457,924	567,475
Martin	0.06	3,715,915	222,955
Monroe	0.06	3,237,386	194,243
Nassau	0.06	2,033,381	122,003
Okaloosa	0.05	4,615,855	276,951
Okeechobee	0.06	1,629,645	97,779
Orange	0.06	28,047,160	1,682,830
Osceola	0.06	5,450,835	327,050
Palm Beach	0.06	27,533,711	1,652,023
Pasco	0.06	8,028,808	481,728
Pinellas	0.06	21,969,645	1,318,179
Polk	0.06	17,202,917	1,032,175
Putnam	0.06	2,224,935	133,496
St. Johns	0.06	4,432,017	265,921
St. Lucie	0.06	5,715,896	342,954
Santa Rosa	0.06	3,283,948	197,037
Sarasota	0.06	8,306,075	498,365
Seminole	0.06	8,587,314	515,239
Sumter	0.04	2,920,619	175,237
Suwannee	0.06	1,457,521	87,451
Taylor	0.04	822,573	49,354
Union	0.05	354,106	21,246
Volusia	0.06	11,965,453	717,927
Wakulla	0.06	555,112	33,307
Walton	0.06	1,313,495	78,810
Washington	0.06	660211	39,613

(X) Not applicable.
1/ Six percent charge imposed on collections for state general revenue fund.
Note: Detail may not add to totals because of rounding.

Source: State of Florida, Department of Revenue, unpublished data.

Table 23.76. STATE AND LOCAL GOVERNMENT: EMPLOYMENT BY FUNCTION AND PAYROLL OF STATE AND LOCAL GOVERNMENTS IN FLORIDA AND THE UNITED STATES
OCTOBER 1993

Item	Florida		United States	
	State and local	State only	State and local	State only
Full-time employees only	619,685	150,216	12,022,718	3,410,079
Full-time equivalent employees, all functions	665,128	167,056	13,442,930	3,890,662
Government administration	51,542	18,548	868,109	315,581
Financial	20,119	7,547	333,288	155,147
Judicial and legal	19,336	9,118	307,477	114,264
Other	12,087	1,883	227,344	46,170
Police protection	46,006	3,717	722,412	85,856
Police officers only	30,776	2,120	542,534	53,003
Fire protection	16,956	B/	256,397	B/
Correction	41,387	29,069	550,061	362,689
Streets and highways	24,722	11,257	541,039	258,060
Air transportation and/or water transport and terminals	3,417	3	49,078	7,379
Public welfare	15,656	10,165	483,599	220,126
Health	19,161	12,909	352,038	162,832
Hospitals	42,577	16,153	1,039,418	509,815
Social insurance administration	A/	4,701	A/	108,182
Solid waste management	7,245	B/	109,497	1,145
Sewerage	7,375	B/	118,874	1,382
Parks and recreation	15,840	1,111	232,990	38,630
Housing and community development	3,341	B/	102,564	B/
Natural resources	10,323	7,036	180,124	149,156
Public utilities	20,870	450	431,860	27,426
Water supply	9,827	B/	146,690	936
Electric power	5,205	B/	82,140	5,810
Gas supply	542	B/	10,183	B/
Transit	5,296	450	192,847	20,680
Education	296,835	41,625	6,614,880	1,435,939
Elementary and secondary schools	237,680	B/	5,046,645	30,302
Higher education	59,155	38,419	1,568,235	1,306,350
Other education	A/	3,206	A/	99,287
Libraries 1/	4,283	B/	97,055	616
State liquor stores	A/	0	A/	8,722
Other and unallocable	29,685	10,312	476,744	197,126
October payroll, total ($1,000)	1,518,154	368,805	34,539,710	10,288,176

A/ State government only.
B/ Local government only.
1/ United States totals include state government amounts for some states.

Source: U.S., Department of Commerce, Bureau of the Census, the Internet at <http://www.census.gov/>.

Table 23.77. LOCAL GOVERNMENT: EMPLOYMENT BY FUNCTION, PAYROLL, AND AVERAGE EARNINGS OF COUNTY GOVERNMENTS IN SPECIFIED COUNTIES OF FLORIDA
OCTOBER 1992

Item	Alachua 1/	Bay	Brevard	Broward	Charlotte
Population, 1992	186,201	131,347	417,740	1,294,090	118,682
Total employees, all functions	1,241	681	3,378	9,148	1,380
Full-time only	1,207	664	3,136	8,681	1,286
Full-time equivalent	1,224	670	3,228	8,932	1,332
Public welfare	28	5	40	210	44
Hospitals	0	0	0	0	0
Health	97	11	147	999	86
Police protection	310	157	419	985	233
Police officers only	181	115	247	968	164
Correction	216	0	247	1,143	52
Highways	72	147	244	403	216
Parks and recreation	9	16	303	606	59
Government administration					
Judicial and legal	175	110	437	888	137
Financial and other	130	94	382	1,008	245
All other functions	187	130	1,009	2,690	260
October payroll, total ($1,000)	2,629	1,171	6,243	22,267	2,482
Average earnings 2/ (dollars)	2,160	1,743	1,949	2,527	1,881

Item	Clay 3/	Collier	Dade	Escambia	Hernando
Population, 1992	113,382	168,514	1,982,901	267,800	108,112
Total employees, all functions	735	1,963	36,734	2,027	745
Full-time only	690	1,867	33,835	1,961	737
Full-time equivalent	704	1,925	35,499	1,991	739
Public welfare	0	20	1,627	151	0
Hospitals	0	0	8,667	0	0
Health	5	131	556	143	24
Police protection	190	520	3,954	464	179
Police officers only	133	350	2,688	350	112
Correction	35	196	1,811	390	0
Highways	121	133	623	187	65
Parks and recreation	7	72	1,494	0	22
Government administration					
Judicial and legal	45	208	1,867	20	93
Financial and other	131	209	1,717	278	154
All other functions	170	436	13,183	358	202
October payroll, total ($1,000)	1,312	4,491	101,392	3,610	1,401
Average earnings 2/ (dollars)	1,880	2,362	2,938	1,815	1,897

See footnotes at end of table.

Continued . . .

Table 23.77. LOCAL GOVERNMENT: EMPLOYMENT BY FUNCTION, PAYROLL, AND AVERAGE EARNINGS OF COUNTY GOVERNMENTS IN SPECIFIED COUNTIES OF FLORIDA OCTOBER 1992 (Continued)

Item	Hills-borough	Lake	Lee	Leon	Manatee
Population, 1992	853,990	162,579	350,809	202,570	219,313
Total employees, all functions	12,867	914	2,770	1,306	2,282
Full-time only	11,297	883	2,579	1,211	2,140
Full-time equivalent	12,204	891	2,675	1,251	2,209
Public welfare	552	4	127	0	52
Hospitals	3,862	0	0	0	0
Health	607	30	189	171	172
Police protection	1,307	196	511	365	387
Police officers only	810	121	317	279	229
Correction	842	241	187	158	253
Highways	680	115	311	125	146
Parks and recreation	332	0	334	10	152
Government administration					
Judicial and legal	1,095	21	53	12	55
Financial and other	855	135	423	166	307
All other functions	2,072	149	540	244	685
October payroll, total ($1,000)	27,875	1,715	5,992	2,595	4,635
Average earnings 2/ (dollars)	2,288	1,928	2,272	2,093	2,122

Item	Marion	Martin	Oka-loosa	Orange	Osceola
Population, 1992	206,642	105,031	149,997	712,637	119,760
Total employees, all functions	1,234	1,231	786	8,060	1,120
Full-time only	1,214	1,189	757	7,311	1,070
Full-time equivalent	1,220	1,210	2,248	7,461	1,091
Public welfare	8	4	5	466	33
Hospitals	0	0	0	0	0
Health	19	79	78	147	15
Police protection	299	254	164	1,222	259
Police officers only	167	172	111	811	176
Correction	194	160	77	1,389	119
Highways	166	90	114	543	124
Parks and recreation	25	65	177	311	10
Government administration					
Judicial and legal	45	108	13	534	100
Financial and other	202	133	115	797	151
All other functions	262	317	201	2,052	280
October payroll, total ($1,000)	2,323	2,551	1,305	18,067	2,152
Average earnings 2/ (dollars)	1,905	2,126	1,699	2,439	1,983

See footnotes at end of table. Continued . . .

Table 23.77. LOCAL GOVERNMENT: EMPLOYMENT BY FUNCTION, PAYROLL, AND AVERAGE EARNINGS OF COUNTY GOVERNMENTS IN SPECIFIED COUNTIES OF FLORIDA OCTOBER 1992 (Continued)

Item	Palm Beach	Pasco	Pinellas	Polk	St. Lucie
Population, 1992	896,970	290,274	860,736	420,885	158,937
Total employees, all functions	8,793	2,514	5,294	3,856	2,195
Full-time only	8262	2407	5,221	3,504	1,910
Full-time equivalent	8,393	2,450	5,230	3,649	1,946
Public welfare	690	71	77	156	10
Hospitals	0	0	0	526	0
Health	164	24	122	349	0
Police protection	1,636	454	946	600	692
Police officers only	860	271	613	360	374
Correction	777	265	79	362	337
Highways	452	177	306	275	111
Parks and recreation	372	166	224	48	175
Government administration					
Judicial and legal	860	252	690	491	163
Financial and other	893	269	598	298	224
All other functions	2,549	772	1,558	544	234
October payroll, total ($1,000)	21,197	4,578	12,362	7,388	3,561
Average earnings 2/ (dollars)	2,543	1,880	2,362	2,053	1,842

Item	Sarasota	Seminole	Volusia
Population, 1992	287,203	305,872	383,983
Total employees, all functions	2,597	1,996	2,843
Full-time only	2,350	1,804	2,279
Full-time equivalent	2,486	1,891	2,449
Public welfare	9	6	28
Hospitals	0	0	0
Health	63	43	84
Police protection	434	382	461
Police officers only	277	204	245
Correction	214	210	332
Highways	227	184	267
Parks and recreation	215	43	228
Government administration			
Judicial and legal	53	236	123
Financial and other	361	236	398
All other functions	910	551	528
October payroll, total ($1,000)	5,285	4,151	4,945
Average earnings 2/ (dollars)	2,163	2,236	2,071

1/ Data are for October 1991.
2/ Of full-time employees.
3/ Data are for October 1990.
Note: Population estimates from University of Florida, Bureau of Economic and Business Research, Population Program, *Florida Estimates of Population, April 1, 1992.*

Source: U.S., Department of Commerce, Bureau of the Census, *County Government Employment in 1992.*

Table 23.78. LOCAL GOVERNMENT: EMPLOYMENT BY FUNCTION, PAYROLL, AND AVERAGE EARNINGS OF CITY GOVERNMENTS IN SPECIFIED MUNICIPALITIES OF FLORIDA OCTOBER 1992

Item	Clear-water	Coral Springs	Ft. Lauder-dale	Gaines-ville
Population, 1992	99,856	86,327	147,678	85,587
Total employees, all functions	1,533	647	3,271	1,795
Full-time only	1,450	600	2,264	1,718
Full-time equivalent	1,492	623	2,442	1,755
Highways	95	17	161	64
Police protection	345	266	734	363
Police officers only	274	134	464	267
Fire protection	139	10	276	149
Firefighters only	131	0	276	143
Solid waste management	153	28	0	0
Parks and recreation	166	111	417	92
Government administration				
Judicial and legal	8	8	21	15
Financial and other	147	67	283	100
Utilities	114	24	340	640
Water supply only	51	24	340	184
All other functions	325	92	210	332
October payrolls, total ($1,000)	4,093	1,705	6,617	4,905
Average earnings 1/ (dollars)	2,772	2,789	2,776	2,826

Item	Hialeah	Holly-wood	Jackson-ville
Population, 1992	195,579	123,296	653,206
Total employees, all functions	1,430	1,572	10,817
Full-time only	1,309	1,318	8,973
Full-time equivalent	1,337	1,470	9,886
Highways	34	72	573
Police protection	432	479	1,775
Police officers only	312	307	1,231
Fire protection	260	225	811
Firefighters only	228	200	748
Solid waste management	133	100	212
Parks and recreation	116	162	481
Government administration			
Judicial and legal	11	10	82
Financial and other	84	116	1,134
Utilities	133	74	1,882
Water supply only	133	74	382
All other functions	134	232	2,936
October payrolls, total ($1,000)	4,456	4,387	27,103
Average earnings 1/ (dollars)	3,341	3,153	2,888

See footnotes at end of table.

Continued . . .

Table 23.78. LOCAL GOVERNMENT: EMPLOYMENT BY FUNCTION, PAYROLL, AND AVERAGE EARNINGS OF CITY GOVERNMENTS IN SPECIFIED MUNICIPALITIES OF FLORIDA OCTOBER 1992 (Continued)

Item	Miami	Miami Beach	Orlando
Population, 1992	359,973	93,461	169,675
Total employees, all functions	3,757	1,314	4,115
Full-time only	3,491	1,274	4,107
Full-time equivalent	3,611	1,291	4,111
Highways	114	34	232
Police protection	1,379	414	771
Police officers only	980	297	527
Fire protection	661	197	355
Firefighters only	576	197	307
Solid waste management	402	44	122
Parks and recreation	237	179	305
Government administration			
Judicial and legal	70	20	32
Financial and other	528	97	283
Utilities	0	34	1,045
Water supply only	0	34	195
All other functions	220	272	966
October payrolls, total ($1,000)	14,097	4,177	10,668
Average earnings 1/ (dollars)	3,994	3,253	2,595

Item	St. Petersburg	Talla-hassee	Tampa
Population, 1992	239,132	129,258	281,837
Total employees, all functions	3,064	2,961	4,017
Full-time only	2,683	2,682	3,847
Full-time equivalent	2,887	2,792	3,935
Highways	77	249	301
Police protection	741	449	1,066
Police officers only	504	256	792
Fire protection	332	244	458
Firefighters only	301	230	413
Solid waste management	207	115	159
Parks and recreation	381	168	470
Government administration			
Judicial and legal	22	0	26
Financial and other	277	427	426
Utilities	192	612	245
Water supply only	192	98	245
All other functions	658	528	784
October payrolls, total ($1,000)	7,579	6,990	11,097
Average earnings 1/ (dollars)	2,715	2,540	2,861

1/ Of full-time employees.

Note: Population estimates from University of Florida, Bureau of Economic and Business Research, Population Program, *Florida Estimates of Population, April 1, 1992.*

Source: U.S., Department of Commerce, Bureau of the Census, *City Employment in 1992.*

Table 23.81. COUNTY FINANCE: REVENUE AND EXPENDITURE AND PER CAPITA AMOUNTS IN THE STATE AND COUNTIES OF FLORIDA, FISCAL YEAR ENDING SEPTEMBER 30, 1994

(amounts in dollars)

County	Revenue		Expenditure	
	Total	Per capita	Total	Per capita
Florida	17,563,541,176	1,265	17,229,082,953	1,241
Alachua	136,406,393	704	142,346,155	734
Baker	12,910,096	655	13,233,244	672
Bay	96,492,129	708	84,596,623	621
Bradford	26,968,294	1,114	18,661,698	771
Brevard	378,302,044	867	368,085,120	844
Broward	1,380,256,000	1,030	1,327,575,000	991
Calhoun	8,267,465	715	8,019,030	693
Charlotte	151,454,231	1,213	145,041,063	1,161
Citrus	76,914,423	748	72,467,982	705
Clay	93,279,645	792	103,013,239	875
Collier	285,083,588	1,579	258,118,116	1,430
Columbia	42,483,442	869	39,934,040	817
Dade	4,363,928,000	2,192	4,272,881,272	2,147
De Soto	24,618,809	938	25,100,944	956
Dixie	13,800,474	1,136	13,348,266	1,099
Duval 1/	1,336,740,707	1,881	1,233,054,437	1,735
Escambia	221,999,532	801	195,560,606	706
Flagler	32,821,587	930	32,967,434	934
Franklin	9,578,953	958	9,383,183	939
Gadsden	21,840,906	487	19,848,111	443
Gilchrist	8,791,478	763	9,201,941	798
Glades	11,548,139	1,380	10,731,272	1,283
Gulf	11,641,113	878	11,036,580	832
Hamilton	11,983,023	1,005	12,892,540	1,082
Hardee	33,198,193	1,478	32,002,223	1,425
Hendry	30,810,329	1,074	31,965,478	1,114
Hernando	106,548,602	928	98,309,294	856
Highlands	55,639,970	733	47,611,301	628
Hillsborough	1,197,406,240	1,362	1,219,241,594	1,387
Holmes	6,628,193	392	6,619,704	391
Indian River	117,936,552	1,211	117,295,939	1,204
Jackson	17,302,947	381	16,539,152	364
Jefferson	8,894,814	680	10,361,189	792
Lafayette	5,217,538	896	4,984,430	856

See footnotes at end of table.

Continued . . .

Table 23.81. COUNTY FINANCE: REVENUE AND EXPENDITURE AND PER CAPITA AMOUNTS IN THE STATE AND COUNTIES OF FLORIDA, FISCAL YEAR ENDING SEPTEMBER 30, 1994

(amounts in dollars)

County	Revenue		Expenditure	
	Total	Per capita	Total	Per capita
Lake	97,198,058	568	97,586,718	570
Lee	655,632,428	1,784	674,285,160	1,835
Leon	146,618,560	691	116,093,894	547
Levy	23,073,758	793	24,774,688	851
Liberty	7,906,012	1,209	6,043,827	924
Madison	14,506,648	816	15,437,632	869
Manatee	311,314,380	1,364	339,793,450	1,488
Marion	140,458,853	645	130,515,074	599
Martin	142,695,358	1,295	131,063,832	1,189
Monroe	167,998,106	2,042	175,010,648	2,128
Nassau	34,774,288	734	32,683,701	690
Okaloosa	101,919,346	644	100,043,707	632
Okeechobee	29,251,600	905	30,024,291	929
Orange	1,005,383,410	1,358	955,592,527	1,291
Osceola	180,148,247	1,374	240,322,562	1,833
Palm Beach	1,385,397,571	1,478	1,343,217,633	1,433
Pasco	215,128,791	720	225,059,099	753
Pinellas	847,613,094	973	852,915,106	980
Polk	314,007,174	718	357,750,874	818
Putnam	53,970,336	782	52,528,482	762
Santa Rosa	58,025,282	619	132,259,995	1,410
Sarasota	313,189,922	1,058	189,542,450	640
Seminole	225,837,463	713	52,291,542	165
St. Johns	122,881,187	1,297	306,207,851	3,231
St. Lucie	167,930,609	1,007	206,030,403	1,235
Sumter	53,284,649	1,514	42,424,775	1,206
Suwannee	24,211,118	826	23,962,330	818
Taylor	15,830,115	907	11,816,906	677
Union	5,469,712	436	5,437,011	434
Volusia	312,801,320	789	297,863,707	751
Wakulla	15,103,345	919	15,479,985	942
Walton	26,404,313	829	24,165,541	758
Washington	9,882,274	546	8,829,352	487

1/ Duval County is the consolidated city of Jacksonville.
Note: Per capita figures computed using Bureau of Economic and Business Research April 1, 1994 population estimates.

Source: State of Florida, Department of Banking and Finance, Office of the Comptroller, unpublished data.

Table 23.82. COUNTY FINANCE: REVENUE AND EXPENDITURE PER CAPITA, PERSONAL SERVICES EXPENDITURE, AND BONDED INDEBTEDNESS OF COUNTY GOVERNMENTS IN FLORIDA
FISCAL YEAR ENDING SEPTEMBER 30, 1993

County	Revenue per capita (dollars)	Expendi- ture per capita (dollars)	Personal services ex- penditure 1/	Bonded debt
Florida 2/	1,315	1,296	5,187,499,167	12,041,106,577
Alachua	709	786	46,363,445	71,775,000
Baker	547	572	3,998,337	0
Bay	769	718	19,607,630	83,543,000
Bradford	433	496	3,746,136	175,000
Brevard	825	814	99,022,865	205,355,307
Broward	824	838	430,028,000	1,664,385,193
Calhoun	562	556	2,277,606	475,000
Charlotte	1,109	1,222	39,964,480	121,860,000
Citrus	851	831	32,957,811	17,435,000
Clay	687	663	25,359,127	41,805,000
Collier	1,366	1,476	77,442,117	169,360,183
Columbia	664	639	9,488,975	11,245,000
Dade	2,206	2,168	1,533,089,000	2,545,511,596
De Soto	578	562	4,198,139	0
Dixie	1,461	1,584	3,664,449	3,027,061
Duval 3/	2,722	2,586	330,585,271	593,578,517
Escambia	848	810	69,762,536	91,600,000
Flagler	966	923	10,248,676	27,211,994
Franklin	1,052	998	3,450,669	1,525,000
Gadsden	469	441	6,332,586	7,695,000
Gilchrist	798	748	2,632,678	0
Glades	952	878	3,563,032	0
Gulf	790	727	3,033,307	4,449,300
Hamilton	945	957	3,935,323	5,870,000
Hardee	921	899	6,572,514	9,605,000
Hendry	977	994	8,435,902	5,875,000
Hernando	1,135	1,117	28,480,021	71,491,550
Highlands	617	584	19,355,582	640,000
Hillsborough	1,477	1,426	311,684,136	851,774,327
Holmes	403	367	2,379,017	1,783,000
Indian River	1,240	1,308	46,113,645	78,300,000
Jackson	363	408	5,003,975	8,745,000
Jefferson	639	665	3,039,013	0
Lafayette	1,088	862	1,586,058	0
Lake	521	520	34,639,411	33,545,000
Lee	2,294	2,576	120,398,109	678,742,745

See footnotes at end of table. Continued . . .

Table 23.82. COUNTY FINANCE: REVENUE AND EXPENDITURE PER CAPITA, PERSONAL SERVICES EXPENDITURE, AND BONDED INDEBTEDNESS OF COUNTY GOVERNMENTS IN FLORIDA FISCAL YEAR ENDING SEPTEMBER 30, 1993 (Continued)

County	Revenue per capita (dollars)	Expenditure per capita (dollars)	Personal services expenditure 1/	Bonded debt
Leon	801	832	42,781,972	97,168,942
Levy	793	738	7,275,962	8,130,000
Liberty	955	905	1,865,998	1,790,000
Madison	880	1,039	3,582,288	3,975,000
Manatee	1,229	1,217	84,992,252	227,923,809
Marion	504	457	44,757,238	78,389,718
Martin	1,581	1,565	47,690,162	105,904,497
Monroe	2,028	2,058	45,115,629	61,025,000
Nassau	693	659	10,994,076	98,139,000
Okaloosa	1,262	795	30,986,827	293,651,940
Okeechobee	1,045	1,045	9,278,427	7,275,000
Orange	1,574	1,346	302,812,561	925,052,245
Osceola	1,433	1,554	40,374,859	196,705,395
Palm Beach	1,602	1,680	355,407,616	751,910,000
Pasco	678	725	77,754,050	333,168,053
Pinellas	936	909	225,444,310	538,613,638
Polk	594	560	116,786,923	86,755,577
Putnam	738	742	15,596,949	26,052,094
St. Johns	996	1,120	31,447,753	104,255,398
St. Lucie	873	826	32,884,076	141,170,000
Santa Rosa	517	513	16,648,314	12,255,000
Sarasota	1,021	1,029	96,848,529	179,445,000
Seminole	762	778	70,337,005	174,770,000
Sumter	694	601	5,996,343	7,080,000
Suwannee	0	0	0	0
Taylor	748	719	5,202,934	0
Union	428	431	1,935,714	0
Volusia	726	730	95,167,814	164,099,335
Wakulla	945	1,103	4,267,869	5,463,163
Walton	780	763	9,608,346	2,555,000
Washington	371	347	1,216,793	0

1/ Amounts paid for salary and wages and employee benefits.
2/ Per capita figures computed using total revenue and expenditure from Tables 23.83 and 23.84 divided by April 1, 1993 population estimates.
3/ Duval County is the consolidated city of Jacksonville.
Note: Due to changes in the source, these data are not comparable with those shown in previous *Abstracts*.

Source: State of Florida, Department of Banking and Finance, *Local Government Financial Report, Fiscal Year 1992-93.*

Table 23.83. COUNTY FINANCE: REVENUE BY SOURCE OF COUNTY GOVERNMENTS IN FLORIDA FISCAL YEAR ENDING SEPTEMBER 30, 1993

(rounded to thousands of dollars)

County	Total	Taxes and impact fees	Federal grants	State and other govern-ments	Charges for services	Fines and forfeits	Other sources and transfers
Florida	17,896,053	5,391,485	631,315	1,413,049	4,842,867	137,925	5,479,412
Alachua	135,316	58,748	959	16,300	19,660	1,568	38,081
Baker	10,690	2,882	812	2,561	1,441	99	2,896
Bay	103,154	36,424	817	8,212	27,669	1,041	28,990
Bradford	10,098	3,203	27	2,451	984	382	3,052
Brevard	352,403	124,879	2,932	33,369	82,773	2,499	105,953
Broward	1,085,639	439,951	22,619	108,830	331,203	13,269	169,767
Calhoun	6,454	2,013	714	1,715	167	197	1,648
Charlotte	135,007	55,972	1,330	11,848	42,628	1,225	22,004
Citrus	85,844	36,079	2,289	9,926	11,373	663	25,514
Clay	79,010	30,104	334	11,582	13,604	1,114	22,272
Collier	238,649	88,759	3,069	23,550	65,321	3,769	54,182
Columbia	30,838	13,048	188	4,497	2,248	690	10,167
Dade	4,304,659	1,102,468	373,526	238,586	1,541,382	27,404	1,021,293
De Soto	14,739	8,489	97	3,103	1,050	306	1,694
Dixie	17,265	3,774	1,026	2,549	682	173	9,061
Duval 1/	1,910,010	330,220	71,848	138,163	927,718	9,858	432,203
Escambia	230,868	54,288	8,947	45,166	30,301	3,533	88,633
Flagler	32,411	14,779	158	3,736	2,643	296	10,799
Franklin	10,285	3,328	165	1,845	390	160	4,397
Gadsden	20,289	7,903	229	3,734	1,534	524	6,364
Gilchrist	8,556	2,641	597	1,642	904	150	2,623
Glades	7,879	3,713	453	1,985	444	388	896
Gulf	9,791	4,546	185	1,795	601	97	2,567
Hamilton	10,972	3,351	72	1,665	785	244	4,855
Hardee	20,296	7,884	112	3,253	1,607	299	7,140
Hendry	27,432	11,762	456	3,847	3,623	286	7,457
Hernando	126,835	36,317	64	7,764	19,505	571	62,615
Highlands	45,166	26,389	480	7,041	4,521	782	5,953
Hillsborough	1,279,394	362,605	32,506	85,464	169,631	2,306	626,882
Holmes	6,593	2,583	889	1,741	705	13	661
Indian River	118,599	52,227	1,222	8,731	27,554	850	28,014
Jackson	16,132	10,137	143	1,383	1,712	204	2,553
Jefferson	8,303	4,199	987	1,457	354	242	1,063
Lafayette	6,097	1,226	10	1,536	277	95	2,953

See footnotes at end of table. Continued . . .

Table 23.83. COUNTY FINANCE: REVENUE BY SOURCE OF COUNTY GOVERNMENTS IN FLORIDA FISCAL YEAR ENDING SEPTEMBER 30, 1993 (Continued)

(rounded to thousands of dollars)

County	Total	Taxes and impact fees	Federal grants	State and other govern- ments	Charges for services	Fines and forfeits	Other sources and transfers
Lake	87,230	38,151	4,124	11,856	18,873	1,415	12,811
Lee	820,470	145,370	8,398	37,578	152,094	2,911	474,118
Leon	165,424	61,670	2,508	15,278	14,842	1,332	69,794
Levy	22,416	8,395	2,234	3,321	2,087	364	6,015
Liberty	5,464	811	466	1,552	578	105	1,951
Madison	15,247	4,366	78	2,237	485	673	7,409
Manatee	274,725	84,029	3,035	23,110	85,655	1,746	77,150
Marion	107,027	62,062	650	18,253	14,877	2,442	8,742
Martin	168,863	60,175	887	12,552	27,771	2,232	65,246
Monroe	165,879	70,684	3,250	17,222	26,742	2,217	45,764
Nassau	32,194	15,432	315	4,561	3,900	461	7,525
Okaloosa	195,008	24,848	771	13,610	30,678	1,015	124,086
Okeechobee	33,199	9,347	546	4,344	1,816	436	16,712
Orange	1,146,082	395,412	12,708	100,702	196,075	10,515	430,671
Osceola	180,146	63,567	227	12,081	13,319	222	90,730
Palm Beach	1,471,791	394,262	15,902	77,244	330,662	8,646	645,075
Pasco	199,623	93,116	3,990	21,790	47,788	1,640	31,300
Pinellas	810,197	280,411	7,270	53,422	198,656	5,302	265,137
Polk	255,387	103,268	6,225	38,674	72,797	2,359	32,064
Putnam	49,972	21,304	18	5,686	8,326	614	14,023
St. Johns	90,892	36,540	201	9,249	18,784	762	25,355
St. Lucie	142,567	61,603	1,997	21,756	41,376	2,407	13,428
Santa Rosa	46,719	17,826	46	8,753	15,702	1,054	3,338
Sarasota	296,750	131,806	4,610	28,645	69,097	3,155	59,437
Seminole	237,124	110,710	3,935	22,122	40,515	2,650	57,191
Sumter	23,469	9,100	1,268	4,310	1,359	499	6,933
Suwannee	0	0	0	0	0	0	0
Taylor	13,013	6,942	2,333	1,456	1,736	269	276
Union	5,149	1,628	68	1,577	214	117	1,545
Volusia	283,418	110,940	7,755	30,849	64,932	4,212	64,730
Wakulla	14,560	4,583	3,122	2,514	2,061	152	2,129
Walton	23,850	12,729	1,444	4,172	1,954	564	2,988
Washington	6,523	3,508	673	1,547	122	140	533

1/ Duval County is the consolidated city of Jacksonville.
Note: Due to changes in the source, these data are not comparable with those shown in previous *Abstracts*.

Source: State of Florida, Department of Banking and Finance, *Local Government Financial Report, Fiscal Year 1992-93.*

Table 23.84. COUNTY FINANCE: EXPENDITURE BY FUNCTION OF COUNTY GOVERNMENTS IN FLORIDA, FISCAL YEAR ENDING SEPTEMBER 30, 1993

(rounded to thousands of dollars)

County	Total	General govern-ment	Public safety	Physical and eco-nomic environ-ment	Trans-porta-tion	Human services cultural and re-creation	Other uses and interfund transfers
Florida	17,651,448	3,409,572	3,015,942	3,059,040	2,206,913	2,033,809	3,926,262
Alachua	149,944	35,469	52,788	10,404	7,554	11,671	32,057
Baker	11,174	2,318	2,515	1,358	1,776	523	2,684
Bay	96,366	15,644	23,380	31,739	16,653	4,299	4,650
Bradford	11,577	3,200	2,674	859	1,516	918	2,409
Brevard	347,640	81,821	49,819	68,266	39,359	36,188	72,188
Broward	1,104,318	223,908	265,153	180,425	154,368	137,182	143,282
Calhoun	6,385	1,614	1,098	587	1,047	590	1,448
Charlotte	148,810	18,295	26,961	24,053	20,308	13,298	45,895
Citrus	83,857	18,297	36,173	6,062	15,858	7,467	0
Clay	76,209	14,039	17,976	8,465	9,675	5,154	20,899
Collier	257,894	72,567	54,597	44,907	22,042	17,025	46,757
Columbia	29,687	3,900	7,524	3,272	5,846	2,104	7,039
Dade	4,231,373	595,892	599,683	674,553	796,104	967,357	597,784
De Soto	14,329	3,469	2,090	1,366	2,923	747	3,734
Dixie	18,708	8,402	4,199	1,352	2,512	251	1,992
Duval 1/	1,814,792	355,159	211,983	727,340	173,231	102,209	244,869
Escambia	220,503	50,963	46,903	18,136	16,579	10,368	77,554
Flagler	30,988	8,994	6,405	2,049	4,593	1,556	7,391
Franklin	9,764	1,879	2,149	384	1,153	351	3,848
Gadsden	19,090	3,581	5,474	664	1,728	1,960	5,681
Gilchrist	8,024	2,041	1,757	968	865	209	2,183
Glades	7,267	3,069	2,042	760	933	434	29
Gulf	9,014	2,857	1,552	929	1,180	381	2,115
Hamilton	11,116	1,713	2,638	800	1,259	1,055	3,651
Hardee	19,820	9,615	5,313	881	2,380	981	651
Hendry	27,905	5,627	10,892	2,631	2,629	1,267	4,859
Hernando	124,843	59,623	30,304	12,217	12,041	6,433	4,224
Highlands	42,795	13,103	12,936	6,070	6,800	3,535	352
Hillsborough	1,235,791	202,133	172,282	183,618	60,531	129,066	488,161
Holmes	6,009	1,309	1,192	768	1,912	400	427
Indian River	125,129	29,189	28,099	21,755	11,891	12,244	21,951
Jackson	18,116	1,765	5,433	320	3,959	1,767	4,872
Jefferson	8,640	1,547	2,208	1,461	2,423	314	687
Lafayette	4,834	1,079	894	254	1,435	152	1,021
Lake	87,058	21,310	24,975	12,952	8,921	4,365	14,535

See footnotes at end of table. Continued . . .

Table 23.84. COUNTY FINANCE: EXPENDITURE BY FUNCTION OF COUNTY GOVERNMENTS IN FLORIDA, FISCAL YEAR ENDING SEPTEMBER 30, 1993 (Continued)

(rounded to thousands of dollars)

County	Total	General govern-ment	Public safety	Physical and eco-nomic environ-ment	Trans-porta-tion	Human services cultural and re-creation	Other uses and interfund transfers
Lee	921,224	104,825	56,048	166,526	99,138	51,782	442,906
Leon	171,663	55,046	36,581	13,498	9,365	7,584	49,588
Levy	20,853	4,301	5,142	2,724	2,491	1,053	5,141
Liberty	5,179	1,233	787	583	612	108	1,856
Madison	18,007	2,238	2,445	3,956	2,117	466	6,785
Manatee	272,048	53,244	48,441	61,337	27,191	22,197	59,639
Marion	96,910	29,246	34,091	6,764	15,057	9,895	1,857
Martin	167,156	34,152	31,383	19,201	13,312	11,881	57,226
Monroe	168,294	23,713	50,332	23,128	6,891	9,128	55,101
Nassau	30,563	6,818	8,183	2,977	5,891	1,494	5,291
Okaloosa	122,909	15,598	17,763	17,475	35,279	5,740	31,054
Okeechobee	33,202	4,610	7,627	889	2,572	2,163	15,341
Orange	980,182	254,882	212,756	108,160	82,808	75,115	246,461
Osceola	195,386	65,593	23,651	13,214	28,032	15,352	49,543
Palm Beach	1,542,981	316,071	229,222	196,846	114,074	94,730	592,038
Pasco	213,411	44,528	48,238	35,146	28,132	20,190	37,178
Pinellas	786,820	142,528	148,700	114,526	119,427	53,393	208,246
Polk	240,967	63,320	64,732	34,336	18,416	50,349	9,815
Putnam	50,196	12,249	11,197	5,923	5,587	2,833	12,408
St. Johns	102,153	27,516	21,966	14,560	7,096	9,590	21,426
St. Lucie	134,811	51,935	28,352	13,527	21,973	16,689	2,335
Santa Rosa	46,310	11,750	18,136	5,166	7,269	2,589	1,399
Sarasota	299,236	73,077	53,361	54,903	35,007	32,578	50,309
Seminole	241,884	47,064	48,221	45,577	49,547	14,026	37,447
Sumter	20,344	3,786	5,026	1,989	2,852	800	5,891
Suwannee	0	0	0	0	0	0	0
Taylor	12,496	3,117	5,252	1,440	2,046	640	0
Union	5,196	1,429	1,058	627	583	212	1,287
Volusia	284,880	67,636	63,596	33,584	41,828	35,219	43,017
Wakulla	16,989	5,185	6,389	2,420	1,373	181	1,442
Walton	23,329	5,754	4,868	4,839	5,670	1,228	970
Washington	6,099	1,739	334	570	1,291	781	1,386

1/ Duval County is the consolidated city of Jacksonville.

Note: See Table 23.82 for personal services expenditure, salaries and wages, and employee benefits included in the functional distribution. Due to changes in the source, these data are not comparable with those shown in previous *Abstracts*.

Source: State of Florida, Department of Banking and Finance, *Local Government Financial Report, Fiscal Year 1992-93*.

Table 23.85. MUNICIPAL FINANCE: REVENUE AND EXPENDITURE PER CAPITA, PERSONAL SERVICES EXPENDITURE, AND BONDED INDEBTEDNESS OF CITY GOVERNMENTS SERVING A 1993 POPULATION OF 45,000 OR MORE IN FLORIDA FISCAL YEAR ENDING SEPTEMBER 30, 1993

(in dollars)

City	Revenue per capita	Expendi-ture per capita	Personal services ex-penditure 1/	Bonded debt
Jacksonville (Duval) 2/	2,888	2,744	330,585,271	593,578,517
Miami	1,996	1,837	205,942,000	441,442,883
Tampa	2,950	2,862	182,048,591	651,785,007
St. Petersburg	1,764	1,595	127,849,228	291,905,753
Hialeah	813	699	80,875,625	5,865,000
Orlando	2,572	2,523	129,779,495	343,841,013
Ft. Lauderdale	2,185	1,947	112,687,395	132,595,000
Tallahassee	4,034	3,463	93,093,600	229,897,300
Hollywood	1,208	1,067	64,069,074	149,450,000
Clearwater	2,041	1,741	59,121,794	106,758,694
Miami Beach	3,465	2,773	69,044,338	132,965,000
Gainesville	3,068	2,859	70,829,952	405,795,000
Coral Springs	890	864	30,244,977	91,819,863
Cape Coral	1,321	1,380	33,885,385	279,160,279
Pembroke Pines	1,166	1,039	32,038,803	104,360,367
Pompano Beach	1,647	1,525	41,427,455	36,063,094
Lakeland	4,144	4,668	67,741,357	443,756,876
Plantation	1,128	1,076	20,884,763	37,592,811
Sunrise	1,706	1,486	32,393,744	175,838,764
Palm Bay	674	628	17,922,319	70,880,000
West Palm Beach	2,844	2,920	61,244,628	110,090,000
Largo	874	773	23,642,965	13,690,333
Port St. Lucie	499	570	14,792,881	25,122,021
Boca Raton	3,202	3,223	46,974,916	190,025,783
Melbourne	1,125	1,048	29,382,366	72,578,134
Daytona Beach	1,577	1,491	36,112,692	59,990,000
Pensacola	2,176	2,022	33,602,996	92,451,334
Davie	793	693	15,698,237	71,530,379
Sarasota	2,191	2,077	36,288,194	120,756,941
North Miami	1,354	1,148	21,375,873	19,150,000
Lauderhill	546	560	9,435,289	8,912,054
Delray Beach	1,929	1,874	28,244,626	92,159,475
Boynton Beach	1,956	1,791	29,987,956	93,195,000
Deerfield Beach	553	572	11,228,541	34,480,803
Tamarac	757	737	11,371,800	31,000,000
Bradenton	1,248	1,280	19,878,216	31,709,001
Margate	762	819	17,722,864	31,955,000
Ft. Myers	2,539	2,934	30,578,626	237,830,000

1/ Amounts paid for salary and wages and employee benefits. These amounts are included in the functional distribution on Table 23.87.
2/ Consolidated Duval County.
Note: Due to changes in the source, these data are not comparable with those shown in previous *Abstracts*.

Source: State of Florida, Department of Banking and Finance, *Local Government Financial Report, Fiscal Year 1992-93.*

Table 23.86. MUNICIPAL FINANCE: REVENUE BY SOURCE OF CITY GOVERNMENTS SERVING A 1993 POPULATION OF 45,000 OR MORE IN FLORIDA, FISCAL YEAR ENDING SEPTEMBER 30, 1993

(rounded to thousands of dollars)

City	Total	Taxes and impact fees	Federal grants	State and other govern-ments	Charges for services	Fines and for-feits	Other sources and transfers
Jacksonville (Duval) 1/	1,910,010	330,220	71,848	138,163	927,718	9,858	432,203
Miami	728,234	192,466	26,150	40,002	62,264	4,382	402,970
Tampa	834,677	126,844	33,921	46,692	139,749	3,619	483,852
St. Petersburg	422,879	92,627	3,628	35,053	142,101	2,255	147,215
Hialeah	162,588	65,824	9,867	6,331	37,230	0	43,337
Orlando	442,488	100,912	2,272	48,286	121,132	2,004	167,882
Ft. Lauderdale	325,151	83,766	11,882	18,769	93,765	3,698	113,270
Tallahassee	531,229	39,001	1,959	10,711	302,430	1,392	175,736
Hollywood	149,812	48,754	2,685	13,811	58,557	1,505	24,500
Clearwater	205,733	45,625	943	10,734	84,095	2,072	62,263
Miami Beach	329,800	91,350	3,687	13,579	44,656	3,054	173,474
Gainesville	285,612	20,255	10,702	6,573	186,133	1,057	60,892
Coral Springs	79,200	30,025	43	6,133	14,949	680	27,369
Cape Coral	107,514	27,562	724	9,554	25,920	462	43,292
Pembroke Pines	87,478	32,194	588	4,994	22,311	768	26,624
Pompano Beach	120,655	39,401	1,347	5,413	42,262	1,258	30,974
Lakeland	303,034	20,117	6,242	6,476	197,870	832	71,497
Plantation	82,017	22,739	0	6,139	26,729	780	25,630
Sunrise	122,119	32,134	631	9,271	36,620	370	43,092
Palm Bay	46,666	21,978	372	6,161	2,410	148	15,598
West Palm Beach	193,425	51,209	1,464	9,355	50,129	936	80,330
Largo	58,060	17,449	637	9,756	20,617	431	9,170
Port St. Lucie	32,817	14,675	231	3,591	8,602	348	5,370
Boca Raton	207,587	44,854	2,312	15,508	33,223	895	110,796
Melbourne	72,235	21,257	637	5,597	31,965	546	12,233
Daytona Beach	98,526	54,576	5,301	6,291	13,729	966	17,663
Pensacola	130,287	22,647	4,777	7,240	43,390	390	51,842
Davie	41,522	20,426	811	3,635	10,507	588	5,554
Sarasota	111,397	33,290	1,583	4,873	42,498	777	28,376
North Miami	68,042	15,370	807	4,888	22,739	381	23,856
Lauderhill	27,024	11,095	0	4,299	9,359	293	1,978
Delray Beach	93,838	27,230	3,636	6,034	29,837	397	26,703
Boynton Beach	94,769	23,920	244	5,773	26,090	160	38,582
Deerfield Beach	26,385	15,171	561	3,913	2,462	932	3,347
Tamarac	35,385	11,118	76	3,698	15,583	386	4,523
Bradenton	58,233	8,588	2,053	5,039	11,561	244	30,749
Margate	34,503	13,675	0	3,837	11,536	609	4,847
Ft. Myers	114,443	21,127	3,112	7,138	33,279	775	49,012

1/ Consolidated Duval County.

Note: Due to changes in the source, these data are not comparable with those show in previous *Abstracts*.

Source: State of Florida, Department of Banking and Finance, *Local Government Financial Report, Fiscal Year 1992-93.*

Table 23.87. MUNICIPAL FINANCE: EXPENDITURE BY FUNCTION OF CITY GOVERNMENTS SERVING A 1993 POPULATION OF 45,000 OR MORE IN FLORIDA, FISCAL YEAR ENDING SEPTEMBER 30, 1993

(rounded to thousands of dollars)

City	Total	General government	Public safety	Physical and economic environment	Transportation	Human services, cultural, and recreation	Other uses and interfund transfers
Jacksonville (Duval) 1/	1,814,792	355,159	211,983	727,340	173,231	102,209	244,869
Miami	669,991	315,974	159,038	73,629	27,917	40,771	52,662
Tampa	809,571	77,045	114,201	377,832	68,570	27,993	143,931
St. Petersburg	382,474	99,428	69,738	82,661	16,350	39,725	74,572
Hialeah	139,763	34,592	42,428	45,194	1,666	7,300	8,584
Orlando	434,124	85,824	65,915	104,215	41,862	39,118	97,190
Ft. Lauderdale	289,693	60,628	68,069	73,014	14,430	24,283	49,269
Tallahassee	456,122	25,341	39,149	246,297	36,738	15,248	93,350
Hollywood	132,309	28,784	50,694	41,217	5,066	4,455	2,093
Clearwater	175,500	15,395	29,648	68,800	10,054	18,853	32,750
Miami Beach	263,918	53,011	51,680	32,869	6,359	26,030	93,968
Gainesville	266,222	15,124	25,474	167,215	13,274	4,128	41,007
Coral Springs	76,876	36,088	16,513	9,538	5,509	9,063	165
Cape Coral	112,248	46,436	14,760	30,012	6,786	8,397	5,857
Pembroke Pines	78,010	27,197	23,409	14,957	3,101	7,824	1,521
Pompano Beach	111,730	58,257	0	45,957	0	6,691	824
Lakeland	341,388	22,464	28,524	207,320	18,663	12,691	51,726
Plantation	78,231	14,022	16,998	11,660	1,493	8,306	25,752
Sunrise	106,344	16,125	20,704	26,003	4,044	6,325	33,143
Palm Bay	43,498	4,012	14,096	3,601	7,963	1,723	12,103
West Palm Beach	198,633	26,815	34,380	53,656	15,103	11,978	56,701
Largo	51,353	11,223	13,138	18,291	1,344	5,573	1,786
Port St. Lucie	37,470	5,361	7,896	9,666	7,318	5,048	2,181
Boca Raton	208,928	50,317	24,758	32,573	9,503	15,892	75,885
Melbourne	67,327	10,132	16,068	20,622	9,911	5,522	5,073
Daytona Beach	93,168	16,211	21,679	32,780	4,347	8,835	9,315
Pensacola	121,050	18,668	17,756	39,361	20,132	6,810	18,323
Davie	36,275	9,650	12,940	7,799	2,672	2,617	596
Sarasota	105,589	33,601	25,622	28,211	6,488	11,667	0
North Miami	57,719	19,407	7,585	15,566	1,314	4,832	9,015
Lauderhill	27,717	7,079	8,914	7,700	916	3,109	0
Delray Beach	91,183	17,037	23,573	23,131	4,134	16,675	6,634
Boynton Beach	86,771	15,670	16,982	18,469	890	6,700	28,060
Deerfield Beach	27,271	10,092	10,720	1,965	1,226	2,824	443
Tamarac	34,446	7,919	9,373	14,989	1,072	927	166
Bradenton	59,693	4,916	8,035	11,344	1,474	2,630	31,294
Margate	37,088	6,512	8,721	12,503	1,000	1,247	7,105
Ft. Myers	132,261	26,047	15,067	27,332	4,893	23,657	35,264

1/ Consolidated Duval County.

Note: See Table 23.85 for personal services expenditure, salaries and wages, and employee benefits included in the functional distribution. Due to changes in the source, these data are not comparable with those shown in previous *Abstracts*.

Source: State of Florida, Department of Banking and Finance, *Local Government Financial Report, Fiscal Year 1992-93.*

Table 23.88. SPECIAL DISTRICTS: REVENUE AND EXPENDITURE OF SPECIAL DISTRICTS WITH REVENUE OF OVER $5,000,000 IN SPECIFIED COUNTIES OF FLORIDA FISCAL YEAR ENDING SEPTEMBER 30, 1993

(in dollars)

District	County	Revenue	Expenditure
Bay Medical Center	Bay	104,517,075	101,475,445
Baytree Community Development District	Brevard	11,169,158	5,751,205
Canaveral Port Authority	Brevard	15,773,185	12,341,080
Viera East Community Development District	Brevard	20,207,807	7,472,384
Broward County Housing Authority	Broward	33,439,890	20,113,712
Coral Springs Improvement District	Broward	10,562,003	7,707,553
Indian Trace Community Development District	Broward	14,802,855	23,847,168
North Broward Hospital District	Broward	492,750,951	489,524,174
North Springs Improvement District	Broward	18,335,084	14,335,071
Port Everglades Authority	Broward	43,915,551	41,085,768
South Broward Hospital District	Broward	272,137,000	285,598,000
Turtle Run Community Development District	Broward	9,897,463	10,155,107
Key Marco Community Development District	Collier	14,863,636	7,082,978
North Naples Fire Control & Rescue District	Collier	5,335,281	4,972,830
Escambia County Utilities Authority	Escambia	43,290,243	42,814,825
Hendry County Hospital Authority	Hendry	9,559,657	9,699,576
Children's Board of Hillsborough County	Hillsborough	8,849,804	8,656,097
Hillsborough County Aviation Authority	Hillsborough	235,856,430	283,288,451
Hillsborough Transit Authority	Hillsborough	23,474,089	23,603,397
Tampa Port Authority	Hillsborough	22,325,735	15,305,401
Tampa Sports Authority	Hillsborough	7,978,042	7,554,882
Tampa-Hillsborough County Expressway Authority	Hillsborough	16,108,810	15,818,929
Indian River Memorial Hospital	Indian River	6,875,068	7,726,710
Jackson County Hospital District	Jackson	21,722,414	21,836,901
Deer Island Community Development District	Lake	12,618,074	2,975,707
South Lake County Hospital District	Lake	12,171,425	11,287,788
Gateway Services District	Lee	5,692,611	4,503,769
Lee County Mosquito Control District	Lee	8,232,915	8,162,653
South Trail Fire Protection & Rescue Service District	Lee	5,645,032	5,463,105
Florida Keys Aqueduct Authority	Monroe	26,114,351	28,031,934
Nassau General Hospital	Nassau	12,472,946	12,460,884
Okaloosa County Gas District	Okaloosa	16,390,282	21,278,747
Greater Orlando Aviation Authority	Orange	181,860,000	199,539,000
Orange County Library District	Orange	18,766,756	16,520,917
Orlando-Orange County Expressway Authority	Orange	75,394,050	144,681,596
West Orange Healthcare District	Orange	38,826,106	38,321,996
Acme Improvement District	Palm Beach	12,551,174	13,067,311

Continued . . .

Table 23.88. SPECIAL DISTRICTS: REVENUE AND EXPENDITURE OF SPECIAL DISTRICTS WITH REVENUE OF OVER $5,000,000 IN SPECIFIED COUNTIES OF FLORIDA FISCAL YEAR ENDING SEPTEMBER 30, 1993 (Continued)

(in dollars)

District	County	Revenue	Expenditure
Children's Services Council of Palm Beach County	Palm Beach	15,188,693	15,125,262
East Central Regional Wastewater Facilities Board	Palm Beach	5,568,648	5,380,492
Greater Boca Raton Beach Tax District	Palm Beach	8,984,894	10,770,062
Indian Trail Water Control District	Palm Beach	5,974,842	6,308,004
Lake Worth Drainage District	Palm Beach	7,588,017	8,252,425
Northern Palm Beach County Water Control District	Palm Beach	39,931,632	38,537,413
Palm Beach County Health Care District	Palm Beach	109,686,124	84,706,017
Palm Beach County Housing Authority	Palm Beach	8,096,754	9,075,752
Port of Palm Beach District	Palm Beach	8,735,382	5,277,597
Seacoast Utility Authority	Palm Beach	19,850,444	18,616,986
South Indian River Water Control District	Palm Beach	14,101,526	5,521,991
Meadow Pointe Community Development District	Pasco	19,357,220	15,262,290
Board of Juvenile Welfare for Pinellas County	Pinellas	20,461,606	19,892,437
Pinellas Suncoast Transit Authority	Pinellas	25,733,110	29,235,756
Sarasota County Public Hospital District	Sarasota	239,616,857	220,927,349
St. Lucie County-Fort Pierce Fire District	St. Lucie	16,719,691	15,466,176
Halifax Hospital Medical Center	Volusia	176,703,422	165,175,723
Southeast Volusia Hospital District	Volusia	24,792,044	24,653,643
West Volusia Hospital Authority	Volusia	69,575,342	66,405,333
East County Water Control District	Multicounty	5,188,896	6,798,585
Florida Inland Navigation District	Multicounty	13,145,396	8,185,294
Lake Apopka Natural Gas District	Multicounty	7,679,194	6,974,290
Loxahatchee River Environmental Control District	Multicounty	5,944,532	7,219,913
Northwest Florida Water Management District	Multicounty	37,589,672	39,453,646
Reedy Creek Improvement District	Multicounty	165,560,475	170,707,549
Sarasota-Manatee Airport Authority	Multicounty	16,966,548	16,513,690
South Florida Water Management District	Multicounty	265,207,920	223,242,838
Southwest Florida Water Management District	Multicounty	81,594,730	76,718,827
St. Johns River Water Management District	Multicounty	70,139,750	74,391,983
Suwannee River Water Management District	Multicounty	17,661,169	8,090,040
Tri-County Transit Authority	Multicounty	22,007,310	27,515,294
West Coast Regional Water Supply Authority	Multicounty	24,400,400	24,420,368

Source: State of Florida, Department of Banking and Finance, *Local Government Financial Report, Fiscal Year 1992-93.*

Table 23.89. PROPERTY VALUATIONS: NET ASSESSED VALUES OF REAL, PERSONAL, AND RAILROAD PROPERTY IN FLORIDA, JANUARY 1, 1959 THROUGH 1995

(amounts rounded to thousands of dollars)

Year	Total		Real property		Personal property		Railroad and private car lines	
	Amount	Percentage change from previous year	Amount	Percentage of total	Amount	Percentage of total	Amount	Percentage of total
1959	12,167,304	11.49	10,706,612	88.00	1,319,246	10.84	141,447	1.16
1960	14,789,849	21.55	12,945,632	87.53	1,686,093	11.40	158,124	1.07
1961	16,678,864	12.77	14,659,588	87.89	1,855,228	11.12	164,049	0.99
1962	18,354,359	10.05	16,157,399	88.03	2,030,580	11.06	166,381	0.91
1963	19,210,827	4.67	16,890,665	87.92	2,152,967	11.21	167,195	0.87
1964	23,994,036	24.90	21,140,438	88.11	2,674,478	11.14	179,121	0.75
1965	29,760,016	24.03	26,233,082	88.15	3,321,356	11.16	205,578	0.69
1966	36,253,654	21.82	31,943,021	88.11	4,036,480	11.13	274,153	0.76
1967	40,606,927	12.01	35,154,260	86.57	5,162,026	12.71	290,640	0.72
1968	42,060,610	3.58	36,637,166	87.10	5,125,541	12.19	297,903	0.71
1969	45,180,722	7.42	39,697,479	87.86	5,187,897	11.48	295,346	0.66
1970	51,247,667	13.43	45,066,274	87.94	5,915,000	11.54	266,393	0.52
1971	59,967,320	17.01	51,822,900	86.42	7,845,286	13.08	299,134	0.50
1972	67,053,619	11.82	56,610,767	84.43	10,134,332	15.11	308,520	0.46
1973	82,146,275	22.51	69,936,535	85.14	11,870,966	14.45	338,774	0.41
1974	107,894,309	31.34	92,979,953	86.18	14,570,730	13.50	343,627	0.32
1975	120,558,360	11.74	103,460,245	85.82	16,690,698	13.84	407,417	0.34
1976	128,700,512	6.75	109,217,279	84.86	19,072,710	14.82	410,523	0.32
1977	139,650,757	8.51	118,232,881	84.66	20,925,041	14.98	492,835	0.35
1978	151,271,654	8.24	129,382,344	85.53	21,393,945	14.14	495,365	0.33
1979	159,642,320	5.53	135,705,468	84.38	24,422,967	15.30	513,884	0.32
1980	187,750,045	17.61	164,755,192	87.75	22,480,384	11.97	514,470	0.27
1981	237,140,341	26.31	211,148,696	89.04	25,579,874	10.79	411,772	0.17
1982	272,997,005	15.12	244,424,808	89.53	28,194,359	10.53	377,839	0.14
1983	298,583,050	9.37	266,304,607	89.19	31,858,923	10.67	419,519	0.14
1984	323,647,775	8.39	288,392,562	89.11	34,820,448	10.76	434,765	0.13
1985	356,061,973	10.02	317,508,051	89.17	38,100,514	10.70	453,408	0.13
1986	385,126,891	8.16	343,168,089	89.11	41,389,766	10.75	569,036	0.15
1987	417,508,830	8.41	372,504,470	89.22	44,326,033	10.62	678,327	0.16
1988	446,103,804	6.80	398,216,681	89.27	47,192,039	10.58	695,085	0.16
1989	485,766,305	8.90	434,583,860	89.46	50,554,052	10.41	628,394	0.13
1990	524,248,524	7.92	469,498,829	89.56	54,114,754	10.32	634,941	0.12
1991	553,456,777	5.57	496,581,168	89.72	56,260,942	10.17	614,667	0.11
1992	560,820,605	1.33	501,638,271	89.45	58,586,918	10.45	595,416	0.11
1993	570,341,544	1.70	509,360,697	89.31	60,380,135	10.59	600,712	0.11
1994	595,216,496	4.36	530,408,830	89.11	62,835,320	10.56	1,972,345	0.33
1995	625,223,806	5.04	557,384,382	89.15	67,174,474	10.74	664,950	0.11

Note: Net assessed value is total assessed or just value less nontaxable value of property having a classified use value. Classified use value is the value at which agricultural land and certain privately owned park and recreation land is assessed for tax purposes. The "highest and best" use principle is relaxed and assessment is based on current use only. Some data may be revised.

Source: State of Florida, Department of Revenue, *Florida Property Valuations and Tax Data, December 1995.*

Table 23.90. PROPERTY VALUATIONS: ASSESSED AND TAXABLE VALUES BY CATEGORY OF REAL PROPERTY IN FLORIDA, JANUARY 1, 1994 AND 1995

(rounded to thousands of dollars)

Category	Just value 1/		Taxable value 2/	
	1994	1995	1994	1995
Total 3/	640,871,083	657,498,950	449,465,795	468,232,996
Residential				
Vacant	25,981,377	25,713,955	25,639,269	25,325,758
Single-family	252,142,617	269,806,345	190,099,112	202,939,860
Mobile homes	10,164,497	10,527,464	5,633,716	5,803,069
Multifamily				
9 units or less	11,734,888	12,070,654	10,760,456	10,987,121
10 units or more	17,534,162	18,050,678	17,278,260	17,754,951
Condominiums	90,389,665	83,135,132	66,517,808	69,611,105
Cooperatives	3,034,861	3,007,595	2,236,804	2,205,351
Retirement homes	1,971,055	1,901,581	1,668,825	1,621,186
Commercial				
Vacant	7,773,357	7,701,612	7,646,439	7,588,992
Improved	79,658,234	81,499,670	78,382,526	80,091,183
Industrial				
Vacant	2,534,897	2,483,456	2,498,891	2,430,487
Improved	18,844,906	19,547,120	18,556,988	19,247,464
Agricultural	35,737,217	35,800,496	8,924,585	9,078,435
Institutional	16,208,722	17,166,367	3,675,928	4,005,866
Government	55,016,422	57,220,862	458,758	486,096
Leasehold	952,470	850,447	448,159	337,455
Miscellaneous	4,869,621	4,955,513	3,274,415	3,245,860
Nonagricultural	6,192,561	5,945,014	5,706,152	5,428,207

1/ The value of property for tax purposes as determined by the elected county property appraiser. Value is determined at the highest and best use of property, except for special classes provided for in Florida Statutes.

2/ The value against which millage rates are applied to compute the amount of tax levied. Total taxable value makes up the ad valorem tax base for units of government in Florida.

3/ Totals include centrally assessed values not shown elsewhere.

Source: State of Florida, Department of Revenue, *Florida Property Valuations and Tax Data, December 1995,* and previous edition.

Table 23.91. PROPERTY VALUATIONS: ASSESSED, EXEMPT, AND TAXABLE VALUES OF REAL PROPERTY IN THE STATE AND COUNTIES OF FLORIDA JANUARY 1, 1994 AND 1995

(rounded to thousands of dollars)

County	Just values 1/		Exempt and immune values		Taxable values 2/	
	1994	1995	1994	1995	1994	1995
Florida	628,787,710	658,369,664	180,308,773	185,482,280	448,165,222	468,933,559
Alachua	6,685,840	7,113,800	3,352,819	3,500,643	3,333,021	3,564,471
Baker	581,138	595,598	404,318	408,250	176,820	185,018
Bay	5,781,128	6,019,973	2,380,296	2,412,906	3,400,832	3,599,983
Bradford	627,567	647,262	359,037	363,525	268,530	281,906
Brevard	21,300,247	21,728,287	9,191,867	9,341,819	12,108,379	12,372,735
Broward	58,604,919	62,835,007	13,162,488	14,095,821	45,442,431	48,036,889
Calhoun	336,969	344,585	206,348	210,819	130,621	133,720
Charlotte	7,132,031	7,307,792	1,587,084	1,617,425	5,544,947	5,654,146
Citrus	4,181,459	4,289,215	1,347,747	1,395,649	2,833,712	2,887,865
Clay	3,812,252	3,989,575	1,368,709	1,422,154	2,443,543	2,564,500
Collier	18,268,555	19,283,826	3,138,371	3,201,953	15,130,184	16,038,210
Columbia	1,298,334	1,426,218	690,820	785,934	607,514	637,971
Dade	83,482,127	88,958,734	20,005,928	20,719,258	63,476,199	67,803,042
De Soto	1,217,722	1,251,313	706,011	707,184	511,711	543,646
Dixie	434,244	445,385	277,205	286,476	157,039	158,707
Duval	25,550,479	26,580,793	8,952,380	9,092,731	16,598,098	17,318,517
Escambia	8,491,440	8,753,827	4,344,270	4,384,311	4,147,169	4,339,301
Flagler	2,585,122	2,671,731	601,179	627,788	1,983,943	2,040,714
Franklin	1,204,864	1,270,749	828,997	831,824	375,867	436,490
Gadsden	857,674	901,492	467,408	484,125	390,266	412,704
Gilchrist	384,092	396,677	240,737	245,531	143,355	151,146
Glades	866,812	874,752	595,773	588,639	271,038	284,741
Gulf	612,129	636,522	306,951	314,809	305,178	321,713
Hamilton	392,268	426,397	204,226	219,774	188,042	206,315
Hardee	1,473,869	1,486,842	1,013,322	1,010,704	460,547	474,187
Hendry	2,288,659	2,398,657	1,497,244	1,515,352	791,415	883,252
Hernando	4,387,243	4,606,117	1,512,396	1,550,607	2,874,847	3,038,351
Highlands	3,008,023	3,127,874	1,101,292	1,146,997	1,906,731	1,979,732
Hillsborough	30,892,276	31,754,541	10,019,470	10,077,975	20,872,807	21,474,535
Holmes	446,177	452,966	292,135	297,211	154,042	155,755
Indian River	7,004,749	7,300,027	1,908,974	1,959,755	5,095,774	5,313,363
Jackson	1,240,244	1,274,202	762,359	774,540	477,884	499,631
Jefferson	408,043	421,233	247,497	256,111	160,545	164,864
Lafayette	240,870	227,459	164,413	148,340	76,457	79,087
Lake	5,988,518	6,363,572	1,890,543	1,919,268	4,097,975	4,423,650
Lee	23,218,244	24,122,483	4,807,577	4,923,580	18,410,668	19,085,834

See footnotes at end of table.

Continued . . .

Table 23.91. PROPERTY VALUATIONS: ASSESSED, EXEMPT, AND TAXABLE VALUES OF REAL PROPERTY IN THE STATE AND COUNTIES OF FLORIDA JANUARY 1, 1994 AND 1995 (Continued)

(rounded to thousands of dollars)

County	Just values 1/		Exempt and immune values		Taxable values 2/	
	1994	1995	1994	1995	1994	1995
Leon	9,741,542	10,250,111	4,778,277	4,801,928	4,963,265	5,328,947
Levy	978,442	1,029,429	395,244	438,180	583,198	591,035
Liberty	232,247	237,714	175,726	177,967	56,520	58,351
Madison	478,843	487,054	283,822	286,430	195,021	200,515
Manatee	10,137,413	10,667,348	2,605,458	2,678,686	7,521,237	7,914,378
Marion	7,850,265	8,028,659	3,253,140	3,323,265	4,597,125	4,694,574
Martin	9,173,700	9,315,256	2,280,550	2,317,525	6,893,150	6,965,860
Monroe	9,449,483	9,825,408	2,851,626	2,909,511	6,597,857	6,853,531
Nassau	2,097,985	2,169,794	620,038	636,456	1,477,946	1,532,838
Okaloosa	5,483,416	6,222,180	1,549,232	1,701,061	3,934,184	4,486,337
Okeechobee	1,330,697	1,353,922	625,155	645,284	705,543	707,224
Orange	38,611,246	39,905,552	9,796,951	10,107,654	28,814,294	29,701,996
Osceola	6,503,548	6,941,773	1,929,584	2,062,840	4,573,964	4,863,673
Palm Beach	61,350,205	64,079,053	12,981,462	13,265,879	48,368,742	50,329,078
Pasco	9,336,270	9,630,181	3,248,368	3,334,345	6,087,902	6,265,816
Pinellas	36,951,576	37,901,306	9,929,969	10,053,090	27,021,607	27,637,296
Polk	12,968,535	13,264,905	4,396,556	4,497,968	8,571,979	8,759,180
Putnam	2,069,363	2,122,863	872,302	888,871	1,197,061	1,226,884
St. Johns	5,187,377	5,694,627	1,187,321	1,278,800	4,000,056	4,336,130
St. Lucie	8,244,588	8,596,767	2,216,315	2,290,345	5,732,077	5,882,862
Santa Rosa	3,418,588	3,774,124	1,288,459	1,356,482	2,130,130	2,373,507
Sarasota	18,604,177	19,815,656	3,637,043	3,757,694	14,967,134	15,879,017
Seminole	12,407,002	12,831,323	2,702,296	2,781,584	9,704,706	10,033,515
Sumter	929,054	996,498	517,996	543,057	411,058	453,359
Suwannee	839,147	856,498	465,743	478,053	373,404	378,443
Taylor	772,678	791,433	430,518	436,991	342,160	353,843
Union	233,802	241,262	167,172	170,387	66,630	70,839
Volusia	15,039,902	15,598,653	4,055,011	4,242,458	10,978,091	11,267,736
Wakulla	555,034	585,101	342,685	344,535	212,350	232,622
Walton	2,017,771	2,330,403	495,207	546,660	1,522,564	1,768,503
Washington	507,488	539,327	291,354	288,507	216,134	238,978

1/ The value of property for tax purposes as determined by the elected county property appraiser before deduction of exemptions and immunities. Value is determined at the highest and best use of property, except for special cases provided for in Florida Statutes.

2/ The value against which millage rates are applied to compute the amount of tax levied. The tax base of a unit of local government also includes the taxable value of personal property and centrally assessed property.

Note: Data for 1994 are revised.

Source: State of Florida, Department of Revenue, *Florida Property Valuations and Tax Data, December 1995.*

Table 23.92. PROPERTY VALUATIONS AND TAXES: ASSESSED, EXEMPT, AND TAXABLE VALUES, MILLAGE RATES, AND TAXES ON MUNICIPAL REAL, PERSONAL, AND RAILROAD PROPERTY IN THE STATE, COUNTIES, AND SELECTED MUNICIPALITIES OF FLORIDA, 1995

(rounded to thousands of dollars, except where indicated)

County and municipality 1/	Total assessed value	Exemption value Homestead	Exemption value Other 2/	Taxable Value	Operating millage rate	Taxes
Florida TMP	342,718,829	35,078,670	53,119,116	254,521,044	5.0740	1,291,383
Alachua TMP	5,506,065	485,388	2,685,113	2,235,565	4.9880	11,151
Gainesville	4,987,070	391,992	2,647,394	1,947,684	4.9659	9,672
Baker TMP	113,056	22,966	19,670	70,421	3.5770	252
Bay TMP	3,174,052	442,198	510,372	2,221,483	2.4160	5,366
Panama City	1,439,712	184,060	343,614	912,037	5.0000	4,560
Bradford TMP	213,604	34,371	69,077	110,156	3.7460	413
Brevard TMP	11,305,246	1,725,723	1,344,524	8,134,998	3.6270	29,504
Cocoa	561,721	87,397	136,805	337,519	4.2000	1,418
Melbourne	2,925,621	378,364	568,423	1,978,834	3.9751	7,866
Palm Bay	2,375,822	459,719	185,129	1,730,974	3.2384	5,606
Rockledge	731,947	127,244	102,649	502,055	4.9900	2,505
Titusville	1,439,713	257,158	205,303	977,253	3.8146	3,728
Broward TMP	62,008,619	7,755,774	4,113,377	49,139,468	5.2420	257,590
Coconut Creek	1,460,101	266,719	134,608	1,058,774	4.2484	4,498
Cooper City	1,154,114	190,001	88,638	875,476	4.9570	4,340
Coral Springs	4,221,068	458,172	236,647	3,526,248	3.7563	13,246
Dania	1,036,103	91,695	146,778	797,630	6.2800	5,009
Davie	2,811,693	333,117	257,732	2,120,845	5.1086	10,835
Deerfield Beach	2,731,430	389,165	132,389	2,209,876	5.3230	11,763
Ft. Lauderdale	11,700,918	800,806	1,324,259	9,475,853	5.3907	51,081
Hallandale	1,590,507	223,168	53,164	1,314,176	6.9000	9,068
Hollywood	6,186,634	777,299	601,888	4,807,447	6.3685	30,616
Lauderdale Lakes	836,537	157,365	67,220	611,951	3.5000	2,142
Lauderhill	1,511,484	267,976	37,591	1,205,917	3.7500	4,522
Margate	1,665,962	355,484	66,632	1,243,847	6.4766	8,056
Miramar	1,582,554	286,950	148,932	1,146,671	6.5711	7,535
North Lauderdale	724,725	145,806	95,246	483,673	6.0367	2,920
Oakland Park	1,370,862	133,399	138,562	1,098,900	5.5395	6,087
Pembroke Pines	4,026,335	689,465	184,269	3,052,602	4.0882	12,480
Plantation	4,471,741	504,816	329,673	3,637,252	3.9300	14,294
Pompano Beach	4,766,675	432,764	348,263	3,985,648	6.1506	24,514
Sunrise	3,088,677	534,303	189,915	2,364,458	6.4500	15,251
Tamarac	2,009,841	448,105	65,550	1,496,187	5.2366	7,835
Calhoun TMP	68,131	14,992	14,749	38,391	1.3570	52
Charlotte TMP	1,221,823	105,466	85,116	1,031,240	3.2480	3,350
Citrus TMP	557,875	64,348	81,696	411,831	7.0420	2,900
Clay TMP	676,766	92,500	116,145	468,121	3.8220	1,789
Collier TMP	4,846,575	169,876	459,668	4,217,031	1.2120	5,111
Naples	4,814,535	167,639	454,855	4,192,041	1.1800	4,947
Columbia TMP	437,811	44,912	152,328	240,571	3.5570	856
Dade TMP	46,172,682	3,423,798	6,809,822	35,639,062	7.7180	275,046
Coral Gables	5,262,181	234,591	514,547	4,513,043	5.4580	24,632
Hialeah	5,734,869	774,800	590,119	4,369,949	8.2300	35,965

See footnotes at end of table.

Continued . . .

Table 23.92. PROPERTY VALUATIONS AND TAXES: ASSESSED, EXEMPT, AND TAXABLE VALUES, MILLAGE RATES, AND TAXES ON MUNICIPAL REAL, PERSONAL, AND RAILROAD PROPERTY IN THE STATE, COUNTIES, AND SELECTED MUNICIPALITIES OF FLORIDA, 1995 (Continued)

(rounded to thousands of dollars, except where indicated)

County and municipality 1/	Total assessed value	Exemption value: Homestead	Exemption value: Other 2/	Taxable Value	Operating millage rate	Taxes
Dade TMP (Continued)						
Homestead	723,811	67,083	158,033	498,695	8.6816	4,329
Miami	16,354,009	1,007,377	4,113,145	11,233,488	9.5995	107,836
Miami Beach	6,905,843	331,133	808,072	5,766,639	7.4990	43,244
North Miami	1,620,415	225,843	230,171	1,164,401	7.9620	9,271
North Miami Beach	1,368,542	193,978	140,182	1,034,383	7.8000	8,068
Opa-locka	478,200	38,104	61,746	378,350	9.8000	3,708
De Soto TMP	208,177	30,103	62,902	115,172	8.0820	931
Dixie TMP	54,649	10,948	22,277	21,423	0.8480	18
Duval TMP	7,843,907	756,231	2,088,240	4,999,436	1.3550	6,775
Jacksonville	6,012,359	505,774	1,955,819	3,550,766	0.4804	1,706
Jacksonville Beach	882,555	118,741	69,834	693,980	3.9071	2,711
Escambia TMP	2,323,499	363,382	452,287	1,507,830	5.0100	7,554
Pensacola	2,288,537	356,027	443,417	1,489,092	5.0570	7,530
Flagler TMP	400,798	43,527	56,327	300,945	3.1190	939
Franklin TMP	173,866	37,090	30,014	106,763	4.9900	533
Gadsden TMP	449,602	77,047	189,886	182,669	1.3810	252
Gilchrist TMP	48,008	10,999	10,041	26,969	0.3540	10
Glades TMP	38,080	6,791	10,991	20,298	4.5860	93
Gulf TMP	347,291	36,121	18,334	292,835	5.2450	1,536
Hamilton TMP	76,494	16,053	19,813	40,627	2.9590	120
Hardee TMP	176,721	36,838	50,175	89,708	5.8120	521
Hendry TMP	399,503	44,639	120,882	233,981	4.2090	985
Hernando TMP	354,148	26,910	110,410	216,828	7.5950	1,647
Highlands TMP	632,794	93,681	136,397	402,716	7.8780	3,173
Hillsborough TMP	16,940,675	1,729,826	3,741,741	11,269,107	6.2670	70,628
Plant City	1,066,865	133,232	170,220	763,412	4.7000	3,588
Tampa	14,920,703	1,483,354	3,509,695	9,727,654	6.5390	63,609
Temple Terrace	653,107	113,240	61,826	778,040	4.4100	3,431
Holmes TMP	106,437	19,896	28,101	58,439	0.0750	4
Indian River TMP	3,161,876	256,316	273,163	2,632,397	2.7000	7,108
Vero Beach	1,482,766	112,638	203,229	1,166,899	2.3041	2,689
Jackson TMP	364,088	66,097	119,157	178,833	2.0910	374
Jefferson TMP	71,353	13,799	14,637	42,917	9.5770	411
Lafayette TMP	16,270	3,976	4,398	7,896	2.0000	16
Lake TMP	3,094,170	494,785	422,921	2,176,464	4.5550	9,914
Leesburg	741,314	70,453	132,485	538,375	4.5000	2,423
Lee TMP	9,186,728	827,451	779,875	7,479,402	4.5960	34,373
Cape Coral	4,561,364	631,015	282,270	3,648,079	5.4298	19,808
Ft. Myers	2,459,025	149,112	435,642	1,774,271	5.7262	10,160
Leon TMP	8,749,066	584,240	4,139,018	4,025,808	3.2000	12,883
Tallahassee	8,749,066	584,240	4,139,018	4,025,808	3.2000	12,883
Levy TMP	310,122	49,395	37,982	222,744	3.5940	801
Liberty TMP	19,681	4,361	5,862	9,458	1.0000	9

See footnotes at end of table. Continued . . .

Table 23.92. PROPERTY VALUATIONS AND TAXES: ASSESSED, EXEMPT, AND TAXABLE VALUES, MILLAGE RATES, AND TAXES ON MUNICIPAL REAL, PERSONAL, AND RAILROAD PROPERTY IN THE STATE, COUNTIES, AND SELECTED MUNICIPALITIES OF FLORIDA, 1995 (Continued)

(rounded to thousands of dollars, except where indicated)

County and municipality 1/	Total assessed value	Exemption value Homestead	Exemption value Other 2/	Taxable Value	Operating millage rate	Taxes
Madison TMP	103,540	19,982	23,538	60,019	5.4310	326
Manatee TMP	3,730,361	389,043	415,114	2,926,204	2.3090	6,755
Bradenton	1,895,782	263,824	279,814	1,352,144	2.1901	2,961
Marion TMP	2,303,047	251,309	325,758	1,725,980	5.1130	8,825
Ocala	2,094,843	214,078	305,933	1,574,831	5.0881	8,013
Martin TMP	2,010,530	103,400	253,930	1,653,200	3.2560	5,383
Monroe TMP	3,827,578	100,200	1,690,245	2,037,133	3.9130	7,971
Key West	3,581,883	91,750	1,684,798	1,805,334	4.2172	7,613
Nassau TMP	953,289	74,967	256,101	622,221	6.4690	4,025
Okaloosa TMP	3,256,273	397,823	303,021	2,555,428	2.9400	7,512
Ft. Walton Beach	819,742	129,410	87,058	603,273	4.9700	2,998
Okeechobee TMP	208,077	26,216	30,018	151,844	3.9400	598
Orange TMP	22,394,925	1,246,787	4,406,515	16,441,623	3.9270	64,571
Apopka	814,106	115,004	90,575	608,527	3.7619	2,289
Ocoee	747,504	115,865	131,021	500,619	4.0000	2,002
Orlando	12,331,941	666,978	3,743,408	7,721,555	6.0666	46,844
Winter Park	2,224,509	154,510	289,288	1,780,710	3.6718	6,538
Osceola TMP	1,878,097	222,787	252,917	1,402,393	4.4480	6,238
Kissimmee	1,329,138	124,418	173,353	1,031,367	4.5453	4,688
St. Cloud	548,959	98,370	79,564	371,026	4.1790	1,551
Palm Beach TMP	40,843,322	3,266,045	3,697,926	33,279,351	5.2590	175,025
Belle Glade	289,018	40,322	82,233	166,462	9.2093	1,533
Boca Raton	8,838,314	497,997	823,050	7,417,267	3.2484	24,094
Boynton Beach	2,710,477	374,286	290,176	2,046,014	7.9251	16,215
Delray Beach	3,160,984	379,976	239,424	2,541,583	6.8700	17,461
Greenacres City	747,822	142,532	34,158	571,132	5.9000	3,370
Jupiter	2,935,186	224,254	318,717	2,392,215	2.1596	5,166
Lake Worth	956,557	153,395	158,749	644,413	8.2500	5,316
Palm Beach Gardens	3,385,457	221,567	298,281	2,765,609	3.9530	10,932
Riviera Beach	1,660,303	127,142	175,673	1,357,489	8.9997	12,217
Royal Palm Beach	742,384	134,206	62,704	545,474	7.0386	3,839
West Palm Beach	4,801,510	347,007	954,584	3,499,919	8.8747	31,061
Pasco TMP	1,353,909	191,513	253,276	909,120	5.7320	5,211
Pinellas TMP	28,800,475	3,885,999	3,316,833	21,397,643	5.1710	110,648
Clearwater	5,733,193	600,820	879,941	4,252,433	5.1158	21,755
Dunedin	1,562,526	256,093	297,165	1,009,268	4.8150	4,860
Largo	2,309,596	334,839	203,904	1,770,853	3.4000	6,021
Pinellas Park	1,854,967	293,793	146,513	1,414,661	4.3808	6,197
Safety Harbor	766,407	127,317	94,930	544,160	3.7527	2,042
St. Petersburg	9,597,162	1,515,958	1,345,422	6,735,782	7.7500	52,202
Tarpon Springs	923,191	129,711	109,608	683,872	5.4541	3,730
Polk TMP	6,455,858	820,482	1,559,235	4,076,141	4.2880	17,477
Lakeland	3,348,360	354,256	938,632	2,055,471	2.9950	6,156
Winter Haven	1,037,318	123,925	218,289	695,104	6.4000	4,449

See footnotes at end of table. Continued . . .

Table 23.92. PROPERTY VALUATIONS AND TAXES: ASSESSED, EXEMPT, AND TAXABLE VALUES, MILLAGE RATES, AND TAXES ON MUNICIPAL REAL, PERSONAL, AND RAILROAD PROPERTY IN THE STATE, COUNTIES, AND SELECTED MUNICIPALITIES OF FLORIDA, 1995 (Continued)

(rounded to thousands of dollars, except where indicated)

County and municipality 1/	Total assessed value	Exemption value Homestead	Exemption value Other 2/	Taxable Value	Operating millage rate	Taxes
Putnam TMP	561,830	69,998	203,191	288,642	7.5130	2,168
St. Johns TMP	854,778	91,685	161,945	601,148	5.3940	3,243
St. Lucie TMP	4,495,991	674,240	523,809	3,297,943	4.7870	15,787
Ft. Pierce	1,396,592	151,664	331,844	913,084	7.3305	6,693
Port St. Lucie	3,071,809	517,988	191,262	2,362,560	3.8400	9,072
Santa Rosa TMP	674,803	81,797	159,173	433,833	2.1680	940
Sarasota TMP	7,210,406	573,892	995,557	5,640,958	4.2040	23,713
North Port						
Sarasota	3,731,366	285,664	719,865	2,725,838	5.3390	14,553
Venice	1,372,963	124,506	203,595	1,044,861	3.4060	3,559
Seminole TMP	6,837,532	891,284	443,863	5,402,386	4.8520	26,214
Altamonte Springs	1,883,959	162,630	166,173	1,555,156	5.1858	8,065
Casselberry	765,065	124,456	24,596	616,013	3.4500	2,125
Oviedo	773,838	130,255	57,904	585,679	4.9950	2,925
Sanford	1,141,767	155,398	191,455	794,915	6.8759	5,466
Winter Springs	959,954	175,926	35,912	748,117	3.7023	2,770
Sumter TMP	173,930	32,276	19,281	122,373	4.0010	490
Suwannee TMP	181,763	32,713	47,971	101,080	4.7660	482
Taylor TMP	223,896	36,515	60,901	126,480	4.7900	606
Union TMP	50,155	8,024	18,806	23,325	2.1900	51
Volusia TMP	11,057,598	1,487,968	1,075,647	8,393,982	4.9160	41,265
Daytona Beach	2,897,667	285,694	524,824	2,087,149	6.5804	13,734
DeLand	773,076	83,470	177,415	512,191	6.2000	3,176
Edgewater	516,875	128,593	21,010	367,272	7.1010	2,608
New Smyrna Beach	1,231,515	141,126	86,493	1,003,896	5.5684	5,590
Ormond Beach	1,704,364	235,324	116,950	1,352,091	2.6250	3,549
Port Orange	1,321,486	267,760	101,661	952,065	4.5281	4,311
Wakulla TMP	95,714	14,387	46,953	34,374	0.9770	34
Walton TMP	175,433	35,620	34,630	105,184	4.2370	446
Washington TMP	155,408	28,903	35,473	91,032	4.3340	395

TMP Total municipal property.
1/ Only municipalities with a 1995 population of 15,000 or more are shown. Refer to the source for data for other municipalities.
2/ Includes governmental, institutional, and miscellaneous other exempt properties.

Source: State of Florida, Department of Revenue, *Florida Property Valuations and Tax Data, December 1995.*

Table 23.93. COUNTY MILLAGE: AD VALOREM MILLAGE RATES IN THE COUNTIES OF FLORIDA, JANUARY 1, 1995

County	Total county-wide millage	County government		District school board		Other mill-age 1/
		Oper-ating millage	Debt service millage	Oper-ating millage	Debt service millage	
Alachua	22.4314	9.2500	0.0310	9.1370	3.0400	0.9734
Baker	23.2464	9.3300	0.0000	9.5610	0.0000	4.3554
Bay	15.1800	5.6320	0.0000	9.4980	0.0000	0.0500
Bradford	17.0120	7.3770	0.0000	9.6350	0.0000	0.0000
Brevard	14.9865	4.2812	0.0000	9.1950	0.0000	1.5103
Broward	18.8401	7.3311	0.7854	9.4640	0.5726	0.6870
Calhoun	16.7090	10.0000	0.0000	6.6590	0.0000	0.0500
Charlotte	14.1785	4.4983	0.0000	9.1250	0.5552	0.0000
Citrus	18.0600	7.2390	0.0000	9.4800	0.0000	1.3410
Clay	17.8426	8.1796	0.0000	9.1810	0.0000	0.4820
Collier	12.5895	3.4889	0.0000	8.5930	0.0000	0.5076
Columbia	20.4204	8.7260	0.0000	9.5650	0.0000	2.1294
Dade	18.5930	6.8280	0.7890	9.3730	1.0160	0.5870
De Soto	17.8550	8.4800	0.0000	8.7580	0.0000	0.6170
Dixie	20.0124	10.0000	0.0000	9.5210	0.0000	0.4914
Duval	22.0448	11.1196	0.0962	9.4250	0.8820	0.5220
Escambia	18.7580	8.7890	0.0000	9.9190	0.0000	0.0500
Flagler	16.8500	4.6194	0.2726	9.7250	1.7110	0.5220
Franklin	16.5420	8.8380	0.0000	7.6540	0.0000	0.0500
Gadsden	19.2960	10.0000	0.0000	9.2460	0.0000	0.0500
Gilchrist	20.2434	10.0000	0.0000	9.7520	0.0000	0.4914
Glades	19.3380	10.0000	0.0000	8.6910	0.0000	0.6470
Gulf	15.8870	7.8190	0.0000	8.0180	0.0000	0.0500
Hamilton	19.7604	10.0000	0.0000	9.2690	0.0000	0.4914
Hardee	20.8800	10.0000	0.0000	9.5260	0.0000	1.3540
Hendry	22.2900	8.9000	0.0000	9.5960	0.0000	3.7940
Hernando	19.1730	7.8580	0.1000	9.3270	1.4660	0.4220
Highlands	17.7480	8.5000	0.0000	9.2480	0.0000	0.0000
Hillsborough	18.4572	7.9048	0.2642	9.4310	0.4362	0.4210
Holmes	15.0210	8.4900	0.0000	6.4810	0.0000	0.0500
Indian River	15.7458	4.2999	0.0000	9.1330	0.0000	2.3129
Jackson	15.5690	8.2740	0.0000	7.2450	0.0000	0.0500
Jefferson	18.7884	10.0000	0.0000	8.2470	0.0000	0.5414
Lafayette	19.7434	10.0000	0.0000	9.2520	0.0000	0.4914
Lake	14.9890	4.9270	0.0000	9.6780	0.0000	0.3840
Lee	14.7843	4.8471	0.0000	9.2710	0.0000	0.6662

See footnote at end of table.

Continued . . .

Table 23.93. COUNTY MILLAGE: AD VALOREM MILLAGE RATES IN THE COUNTIES OF FLORIDA, JANUARY 1, 1995 (Continued)

County	Total county-wide millage	County government		District school board		Other mill-age 1/
		Oper-ating millage	Debt service millage	Oper-ating millage	Debt service millage	
Leon	19.5510	8.6400	0.0000	9.4640	1.3970	0.0500
Levy	18.3590	9.0000	0.0000	9.3590	0.0000	0.0000
Liberty	17.8220	10.0000	0.0000	7.7720	0.0000	0.0500
Madison	17.7334	10.0000	0.0000	7.2420	0.0000	0.4914
Manatee	17.8804	7.1842	0.4770	9.2480	0.1615	0.8097
Marion	15.1480	5.2200	0.1800	8.5780	1.1700	0.0000
Martin	15.6000	5.1040	0.5560	9.1350	0.1180	0.6870
Monroe	13.8683	6.0983	0.0000	6.4330	0.0000	1.3370
Nassau	16.4891	6.8321	0.0000	9.1750	0.0000	0.4820
Okaloosa	13.1640	4.5280	0.0000	8.5860	0.0000	0.0500
Okeechobee	19.1367	8.7500	0.6717	9.7150	0.0000	0.0000
Orange	14.6639	5.2889	0.0000	9.3750	0.0000	0.0000
Osceola	16.1275	5.9945	0.0000	9.4320	0.7010	0.0000
Palm Beach	16.4997	4.2177	0.0000	9.2770	0.5200	2.4850
Pasco	20.2240	9.2340	0.1880	9.4180	0.9620	0.4220
Pinellas	18.2297	6.2660	0.0000	9.3290	0.0000	2.6347
Polk	17.3060	7.9770	0.0000	9.3290	0.0000	0.0000
Putnam	18.6860	8.4000	0.0000	9.2390	1.0470	0.0000
St. Johns	17.7280	6.3120	0.3500	9.5500	0.8560	0.6600
St. Lucie	20.0098	7.4795	0.0000	9.5560	0.0000	2.9743
Santa Rosa	16.0210	6.9720	0.0000	8.9990	0.0000	0.0500
Sarasota	23.0540	3.8424	0.1979	9.4630	0.0877	9.4630
Seminole	16.1962	5.1638	0.2134	9.2690	0.0000	1.5500
Sumter	20.0890	10.0000	0.0000	9.3690	0.0000	0.7200
Suwannee	18.9864	9.0500	0.0000	9.4450	0.0000	0.4914
Taylor	17.5594	8.0760	0.0000	8.9920	0.0000	0.4914
Union	20.6704	10.0000	0.0000	9.6790	0.0000	0.9914
Volusia	17.5810	6.1720	0.0000	9.5450	1.3420	0.5220
Wakulla	21.3140	9.2500	0.0000	9.6640	2.3500	0.0500
Walton	16.2720	6.8100	0.0000	9.4120	0.0000	0.0500
Washington	17.6710	10.0000	0.0000	7.6210	0.0000	0.0500

1/ Includes county government special service districts and independent special service districts.

Source: State of Florida, Department of Revenue, *Florida Property Valuations and Tax Data, December 1995.*

Table 23.94. LOCAL GOVERNMENT FINANCE: AD VALOREM TAXES IN THE STATE AND COUNTIES OF FLORIDA, JANUARY 1, 1995

(in millions, rounded to hundred thousands of dollars)

County	Total taxes levied: Amount	Total taxes levied: Percentage change 1994-1995	Municipal taxes	County taxes: County-wide: Total	County-wide: County government: Operating levy	County-wide: County government: Debt service	County-wide: District school board: Operating levy	County-wide: District school board: Debt service	County-wide: Special service districts	County-wide: Independent service districts	Less than county-wide: County government special services districts	Less than county-wide: Independent special services districts
Florida	11,691.3	5.90	1,287.3	9,286.2	3,386.9	151.3	4,981.1	258.2	44.6	464.0	128.7	376.0
Alachua	108.5	-1.06	1.5	98.1	38.9	0.1	38.5	12.8	0.0	7.7	0.0	2.0
Baker	6.3	3.48	0.3	6.0	2.5	0.0	2.5	0.0	A/	1.0	0.0	0.0
Bay	66.8	-0.61	5.4	59.5	23.9	0.0	32.1	3.3	0.0	0.2	1.6	0.0
Bradford	6.7	6.38	0.4	6.2	2.7	0.0	3.5	0.0	0.0	0.0	0.0	0.2
Brevard	272.6	1.46	34.7	216.4	59.9	0.0	128.6	0.0	20.6	7.3	1.0	0.9
Broward	1,428.7	5.76	257.6	1,029.3	400.5	42.9	517.0	31.3	0.0	37.5	9.3	132.6
Calhoun	2.9	5.34	0.1	2.9	1.7	0.0	1.1	0.0	0.0	A/	0.0	0.0
Charlotte	102.1	1.07	3.3	87.9	27.8	0.0	56.5	3.4	0.0	0.1	0.0	2.5
Citrus	80.9	1.61	2.9	74.9	30.0	0.0	39.3	0.0	1.4	4.2	1.8	1.3
Clay	55.2	6.41	1.8	53.4	24.9	0.0	27.0	0.0	0.0	1.4	0.0	0.0
Collier	242.9	4.59	0.0	213.3	59.1	0.0	145.6	0.0	0.9	7.7	0.0	17.4
Columbia	17.4	4.76	0.9	16.6	7.1	0.0	7.8	0.0	0.1	1.6	0.0	0.0
Dade	1,930.9	4.47	261.4	1,435.0	518.8	59.1	701.9	76.1	0.0	79.1	0.0	0.0
De Soto	9.4	-17.15	0.0	9.4	4.6	0.0	4.8	0.0	0.0	0.0	0.0	0.0
Dixie	4.3	3.27	A/	3.7	1.8	0.0	1.8	0.0	0.0	0.1	0.0	0.0
Duval	483.9	2.87	6.8	457.2	222.6	2.1	202.4	18.9	0.0	11.2	0.0	7.1
Escambia	116.4	2.52	7.6	106.9	49.3	0.0	57.3	0.0	0.0	0.3	0.0	0.0
Flagler	39.5	7.76	0.9	36.5	10.2	0.6	20.8	3.8	0.0	1.1	1.4	0.7
Franklin	8.3	9.87	0.5	7.7	4.1	0.0	3.6	0.0	0.0	A/	0.0	0.1
Gadsden	11.8	7.81	0.3	11.6	5.6	0.0	5.2	0.0	0.8	A/	0.0	0.0
Gilchrist	3.9	10.55	A/	3.8	1.9	0.0	1.8	0.0	0.0	0.1	0.1	0.0

See footnote at end of table.

Continued . . .

Table 23.94. LOCAL GOVERNMENT FINANCE: AD VALOREM TAXES IN THE STATE AND COUNTIES OF FLORIDA, JANUARY 1, 1995 (Continued)

(in millions, rounded to hundred thousands of dollars)

County	Total taxes levied: Amount	Total taxes levied: Percentage change 1994-1995	Municipal taxes	County taxes: County-wide: Total	County-wide: County government: Operating levy	County-wide: County government: Debt service	County-wide: District school board: Operating levy	County-wide: District school board: Debt service	County-wide: Special service districts	County-wide: Independent service districts	Less than county-wide: County government special services districts	Less than county-wide: Independent special services districts
Glades	6.5	5.77	0.0	6.5	3.3	0.0	2.9	0.0	0.0	0.3	0.0	0.1
Gulf	10.7	-1.61	1.5	9.1	4.5	0.0	4.6	0.0	0.0	A/	0.1	0.0
Hamilton	8.4	4.30	0.2	8.2	4.2	0.0	3.9	0.0	0.0	0.2	0.0	0.0
Hardee	15.2	5.73	0.5	14.7	6.5	0.0	7.1	0.0	0.0	1.0	0.0	0.0
Hendry	37.1	61.83	1.0	36.0	10.2	0.0	22.1	0.0	0.0	3.6	0.0	0.1
Hernando	74.8	6.28	1.6	67.8	27.8	0.4	38.2	0.0	0.0	1.5	0.0	5.1
Highlands	46.1	3.95	3.2	41.4	19.8	0.0	21.6	0.0	0.0	0.0	0.0	1.5
Hillsborough	691.3	2.11	71.3	507.0	208.6	7.0	248.9	11.5	0.0	31.0	16.0	20.9
Holmes	3.0	-2.39	A/	3.0	1.7	0.0	1.3	0.0	0.0	A/	0.0	0.0
Indian River	120.2	4.55	7.1	96.4	24.6	1.8	52.2	6.9	10.9	0.0	0.0	11.7
Jackson	10.6	1.79	0.4	9.9	5.3	0.0	4.6	0.0	0.0	A/	0.4	0.0
Jefferson	4.4	3.27	0.4	4.0	2.2	0.0	1.8	0.0	0.0	A/	0.0	0.0
Lafayette	2.0	9.90	A/	2.0	1.0	0.0	0.9	0.0	0.0	A/	0.0	0.0
Lake	98.3	13.04	9.9	78.6	25.8	0.0	50.8	0.0	0.0	2.0	0.9	8.9
Lee	392.3	-3.17	34.4	291.5	100.1	0.0	191.4	0.0	0.0	0.0	0.0	40.6
Leon	129.2	9.06	12.9	116.3	51.4	0.0	56.3	8.3	0.0	0.3	0.0	A/
Levy	13.9	2.49	0.8	12.7	6.2	0.0	6.5	0.0	0.0	0.0	0.0	0.5
Liberty	1.7	7.24	A/	1.7	1.0	0.0	0.8	0.0	0.0	A/	0.0	0.0
Madison	5.1	2.76	0.3	4.7	2.7	0.0	1.9	0.0	0.0	0.1	0.0	0.0
Manatee	169.3	-0.02	6.8	152.8	59.1	4.4	80.4	1.5	0.0	7.4	0.0	A/
Marion	109.0	0.09	8.8	82.5	28.4	1.0	46.7	6.4	0.0	0.0	1.4	3.2
Martin	142.1	3.68	5.4	126.7	40.9	4.5	73.2	0.9	0.0	7.2	0.0	0.0
Monroe	114.0	6.79	8.0	98.7	44.0	0.0	46.4	0.0	4.7	3.6	0.0	0.0

See footnote at end of table.

Continued . . .

Table 23.94. LOCAL GOVERNMENT FINANCE: AD VALOREM TAXES IN THE STATE AND COUNTIES OF FLORIDA, JANUARY 1, 1995 (Continued)

(in millions, rounded to hundred thousands of dollars)

County	Total taxes levied		Municipal taxes	County taxes								
				County-wide							Less than county-wide	
					County government		District school board		Special service districts	Independent service districts	County government special services districts	Independent special services districts
	Amount	Percentage change 1994-1995		Total	Operating levy	Debt service	Operating levy	Debt service				
Nassau	35.5	4.44	4.0	30.5	12.6	0.0	17.0	0.0	0.0	0.9	0.0	0.6
Okaloosa	76.0	10.87	7.5	64.5	22.2	0.0	42.1	0.0	0.0	0.2	0.0	4.0
Okeechobee	16.9	-0.01	0.6	15.8	7.2	0.6	7.8	0.0	0.0	0.2	0.0	0.5
Orange	713.9	3.92	64.9	516.9	186.4	0.0	330.5	0.0	0.0	0.0	0.8	26.3
Osceola	102.1	6.57	6.2	91.6	35.8	0.0	52.0	3.9	0.0	0.0	0.0	3.6
Palm Beach	1,182.8	1.93	175.0	921.0	231.2	16.5	508.6	28.5	0.0	136.2	74.8	11.9
Pasco	165.3	5.52	5.2	150.0	67.7	3.2	69.0	7.1	0.0	3.1	6.6	3.5
Pinellas	705.5	1.61	110.6	536.1	193.0	0.0	291.4	0.0	0.7	51.1	0.0	23.3
Polk	235.5	8.06	17.5	209.1	96.4	0.0	112.7	0.0	0.0	0.0	0.0	8.9
Putnam	43.1	7.23	2.2	38.9	17.5	0.0	21.4	0.0	0.0	0.0	0.0	1.0
St. Johns	90.2	7.98	3.2	83.1	29.6	1.6	44.8	4.0	0.0	3.1	2.1	1.4
St. Lucie	163.8	-0.32	15.8	146.6	53.6	0.0	68.6	0.0	3.1	21.3	1.5	0.0
Santa Rosa	45.3	12.73	0.9	44.1	19.1	0.0	24.9	0.0	0.0	0.1	0.0	0.3
Sarasota	272.6	4.83	23.7	248.1	65.9	3.4	162.3	0.0	1.5	15.0	0.0	0.0
Seminole	240.1	13.75	45.3	179.2	57.1	2.4	102.6	11.8	0.0	5.3	0.0	0.0
Sumter	12.7	9.20	0.5	11.8	6.1	0.0	5.7	0.0	0.0	0.0	0.0	0.4
Suwannee	11.2	11.44	0.5	10.7	4.7	0.0	4.9	0.0	0.0	1.0	0.0	0.0
Taylor	11.8	3.37	0.6	10.6	4.9	0.0	5.4	0.0	0.0	0.3	0.6	0.0
Union	2.1	6.43	0.1	2.1	1.0	0.0	1.0	0.0	A/	A/	0.0	0.0
Volusia	315.0	6.92	41.3	224.2	78.7	0.0	121.7	17.1	0.0	6.7	7.9	32.4
Wakulla	6.3	18.11	A/	6.3	2.7	0.0	2.9	0.7	0.0	A/	0.0	0.0
Walton	32.4	21.05	0.4	31.1	13.0	0.0	18.0	0.0	0.0	0.1	0.2	0.6
Washington	6.1	11.40	0.4	5.7	3.2	0.0	2.5	0.0	0.0	A/	0.0	0.0

A/ Less than $50,000.
Source: State of Florida, Department of Revenue, *Florida Property Valuations and Tax Data, December 1995.*

Table 23.95. LAND USE: ASSESSED VALUE AND PROPORTION OF LAND BY USE IN THE STATE AND COUNTIES OF FLORIDA, 1994 AND 1995

County	Residential Value (million dollars)	Residential Percentage of total value	Commercial Value (million dollars)	Commercial Percentage of total value	Industrial Value (million dollars)	Industrial Percentage of total value	Agricultural Value (million dollars)	Agricultural Percentage of total value	Institutional Value (million dollars)	Institutional Percentage of total value	Miscellaneous 1/ Value (million dollars)	Miscellaneous 1/ Percentage of total value
						1994						
Florida	389,619.30	66.2	86,148.25	14.6	21,226.71	3.6	10,076.77	1.7	15,992.94	2.7	65,598.35	11.1
Alachua	3,224.44	52.1	780.63	12.6	107.58	1.7	168.83	2.7	147.51	2.4	1,763.28	28.5
Baker	153.47	37.9	26.50	6.6	6.13	1.5	81.26	20.1	10.77	2.7	126.46	31.3
Bay	3,123.85	60.9	703.96	13.7	96.53	1.9	64.24	1.3	125.54	2.4	1,017.62	19.8
Bradford	259.94	58.5	43.72	9.8	8.07	1.8	65.24	14.7	17.72	4.0	49.61	11.2
Brevard	11,754.82	55.9	2,342.66	11.1	493.22	2.3	93.40	0.4	540.82	2.6	5,817.39	27.6
Broward	42,833.54	73.0	8,198.64	14.0	2,713.86	4.6	117.28	0.2	1,159.69	2.0	3,671.47	6.3
Calhoun	87.14	40.2	16.97	7.8	3.89	1.8	74.68	34.4	6.87	3.2	27.46	12.7
Charlotte	5,565.26	80.8	745.27	10.8	69.59	1.0	113.73	1.7	111.42	1.6	286.15	4.2
Citrus	2,753.57	68.2	446.19	11.1	26.99	0.7	48.70	1.2	97.01	2.4	664.82	16.5
Clay	2,488.97	70.3	461.45	13.0	64.37	1.8	67.42	1.9	114.65	3.2	343.85	9.7
Collier	810.46	27.2	565.39	19.0	189.05	6.3	245.58	8.2	88.72	3.0	1,082.44	36.3
Columbia	507.92	49.0	153.14	14.8	22.91	2.2	119.38	11.5	32.48	3.1	200.61	19.4
Dade	54,384.49	65.2	13,588.84	16.3	4,566.07	5.5	612.62	0.7	1,977.60	2.4	8,244.00	9.9
De Soto	326.16	44.1	72.89	9.9	8.51	1.2	217.94	29.5	23.50	3.2	89.93	12.2
Dixie	139.73	52.4	11.53	4.3	3.19	1.2	61.61	23.1	3.41	1.3	47.36	17.7
Duval	13,870.90	55.2	4,583.58	18.2	1,740.50	6.9	93.86	0.4	1,279.25	5.1	3,574.43	14.2
Escambia	4,316.41	52.2	954.28	11.5	246.69	3.0	81.17	1.0	307.52	3.7	2,364.41	28.6
Flagler	1,875.07	77.8	196.05	8.1	26.31	1.1	54.77	2.3	31.92	1.3	225.70	9.4
Franklin	376.89	37.9	32.77	3.3	6.01	0.6	25.05	2.5	11.63	1.2	542.06	54.5
Gadsden	387.06	52.4	46.21	6.3	38.93	5.3	107.70	14.6	29.04	3.9	129.16	17.5
Gilchrist	130.26	56.2	7.84	3.4	0.77	0.3	63.41	27.3	5.59	2.4	24.06	10.4

See footnote at end of table.

Continued . . .

Table 23.95. LAND USE: ASSESSED VALUE AND PROPORTION OF LAND BY USE IN THE STATE AND COUNTIES OF FLORIDA, 1994 AND 1995 (Continued)

County	Residential		Commercial		Industrial		Agricultural		Institutional		Miscellaneous 1/	
	Value (million dollars)	Percentage of total value	Value (million dollars)	Percentage of total value	Value (million dollars)	Percentage of total value	Value (million dollars)	Percentage of total value	Value (million dollars)	Percentage of total value	Value (million dollars)	Percentage of total value
					1994 (Continued)							
Glades	163.80	36.2	24.17	5.3	1.62	0.4	118.66	26.2	5.65	1.2	138.45	30.6
Gulf	280.71	57.3	21.00	4.3	20.93	4.3	28.64	5.8	9.23	1.9	129.23	26.4
Hamilton	100.27	37.0	15.19	5.6	54.30	20.0	57.32	21.1	5.46	2.0	38.57	14.2
Hardee	190.08	27.8	43.79	6.4	47.89	7.0	255.55	37.4	21.03	3.1	124.43	18.2
Hendry	432.00	38.7	97.63	8.7	34.34	3.1	330.55	29.6	23.22	2.1	199.24	17.8
Hernando	2,958.76	71.6	382.17	9.2	60.44	1.5	79.27	1.9	101.59	2.5	551.37	13.3
Highlands	1,663.29	60.2	385.33	13.9	51.12	1.8	246.26	8.9	119.98	4.3	297.42	10.8
Hillsborough	17,930.19	61.2	5,029.44	17.2	1,602.58	5.5	478.76	1.6	1,075.78	3.7	3,163.59	10.8
Holmes	116.47	37.2	22.39	7.2	2.66	0.9	102.03	32.6	15.31	4.9	54.10	17.3
Indian River	4,693.93	74.7	644.31	10.2	124.72	2.0	243.62	3.9	157.74	2.5	423.58	6.7
Jackson	493.52	52.5	97.04	10.3	25.40	2.7	59.15	6.3	45.25	4.8	219.29	23.3
Jefferson	73.24	28.3	20.96	8.1	2.11	0.8	114.93	44.4	10.84	4.2	37.01	14.3
Lafayette	37.62	31.5	2.97	2.5	0.70	0.6	60.80	51.0	2.87	2.4	14.33	12.0
Lake	3,983.31	69.3	590.84	10.3	130.76	2.3	196.32	3.4	168.17	2.9	676.61	11.8
Lee	17,026.65	76.4	2,810.15	12.6	536.90	2.4	117.44	0.5	472.29	2.1	1,323.41	5.9
Leon	4,561.41	48.4	1,182.00	12.5	157.16	1.7	93.37	1.0	228.18	2.4	3,203.29	34.0
Levy	468.44	54.2	72.97	8.4	6.38	0.7	148.64	17.2	21.35	2.5	147.25	17.0
Liberty	40.99	22.5	3.62	2.0	1.17	0.6	31.97	17.5	4.00	2.2	100.44	55.1
Madison	131.11	40.1	21.90	6.7	10.24	3.1	106.32	32.5	14.76	4.5	42.63	13.0
Manatee	6,653.86	69.1	1,310.72	13.6	384.21	4.0	257.63	2.7	285.12	3.0	731.56	7.6
Marion	4,168.68	60.0	821.65	11.8	279.75	4.0	378.80	5.4	172.51	2.5	1,131.59	16.3
Martin	5,519.19	74.1	746.25	10.0	181.28	2.4	316.68	4.3	106.80	1.4	575.06	7.7
Monroe	5,611.63	59.4	1,299.61	13.7	68.91	0.7	0.61	0.0	139.60	1.5	2,332.52	24.7
Nassau	1,327.74	67.1	246.53	12.5	64.83	3.3	122.47	6.2	39.27	2.0	176.64	8.9

Continued . . .

See footnote at end of table.

Table 23.95. LAND USE: ASSESSED VALUE AND PROPORTION OF LAND BY USE IN THE STATE AND COUNTIES OF FLORIDA, 1994 AND 1995 (Continued)

County	Residential		Commercial		Industrial		Agricultural		Institutional		Miscellaneous 1/	
	Value (million dollars)	Percentage of total value	Value (million dollars)	Percentage of total value	Value (million dollars)	Percentage of total value	Value (million dollars)	Percentage of total value	Value (million dollars)	Percentage of total value	Value (million dollars)	Percentage of total value
					1994 (Continued)							
Okaloosa	4,008.87	74.2	582.12	10.8	57.88	1.1	49.54	0.9	103.13	1.9	601.91	11.1
Okeechobee	556.97	58.2	100.80	10.5	12.55	1.3	158.24	16.5	23.39	2.4	105.45	11.0
Orange	19,818.89	52.8	10,104.60	26.9	1,714.96	4.6	454.05	1.2	1,343.08	3.6	4,133.16	11.0
Osceola	3,569.93	63.0	1,273.11	22.5	99.32	1.8	176.76	3.1	130.58	2.3	415.26	7.3
Palm Beach	45,035.67	75.7	7,410.55	12.5	1,433.82	2.4	752.84	1.3	1,073.30	1.8	3,762.97	6.3
Pasco	6,504.76	73.9	1,232.62	14.0	128.79	1.5	172.15	2.0	251.02	2.9	515.84	5.9
Pinellas	25,197.08	68.3	5,675.32	15.4	1,308.40	3.5	24.64	0.1	1,664.72	4.5	3,002.70	8.1
Polk	7,254.11	59.8	1,761.48	14.5	559.97	4.6	437.06	3.6	404.22	3.3	1,704.54	14.1
Putnam	1,221.71	64.4	144.23	7.6	74.19	3.9	52.08	2.7	69.08	3.6	334.49	17.6
St. Johns	3,849.56	76.7	530.83	10.6	60.79	1.2	73.30	1.5	151.51	3.0	353.36	7.0
St. Lucie	4,956.27	67.5	729.01	9.9	163.62	2.2	300.53	4.1	130.17	1.8	1,063.85	14.5
Santa Rosa	2,355.54	74.2	262.61	8.3	35.77	1.1	95.51	3.0	76.74	2.4	347.95	11.0
Sarasota	14,307.66	77.9	2,308.71	12.6	373.19	2.0	56.02	0.3	394.44	2.1	932.43	5.1
Seminole	9,260.06	75.8	1,786.37	14.6	432.90	3.5	26.70	0.2	228.93	1.9	479.15	3.9
Sumter	391.16	57.4	71.36	10.5	15.90	2.3	100.08	14.7	4.18	0.6	98.52	14.5
Suwannee	318.09	50.4	49.49	7.8	12.74	2.0	143.09	22.7	27.02	4.3	80.76	12.8
Taylor	239.68	46.7	49.79	9.7	57.14	11.1	85.43	16.6	17.49	3.4	63.96	12.5
Union	45.19	25.4	5.70	3.2	3.52	2.0	45.27	25.5	4.21	2.4	73.85	41.6
Volusia	10,888.75	73.4	2,062.21	13.9	362.65	2.4	131.11	0.9	476.92	3.2	921.61	6.2
Wakulla	241.92	48.2	16.32	3.3	8.34	1.7	34.57	6.9	6.52	1.3	194.49	38.7
Walton	1,472.45	75.7	99.84	5.1	11.57	0.6	93.02	4.8	28.10	1.4	240.99	12.4
Washington	127.73	41.1	20.06	6.5	9.06	2.9	91.11	29.3	15.56	5.0	47.24	15.2

See footnote at end of table.

Continued . . .

Table 23.95. LAND USE: ASSESSED VALUE AND PROPORTION OF LAND BY USE IN THE STATE AND COUNTIES OF FLORIDA, 1994 AND 1995 (Continued)

County	Residential		Commercial		Industrial		Agricultural		Institutional		Miscellaneous 1/	
	Value (million dollars)	Percentage of total value	Value (million dollars)	Percentage of total value	Value (million dollars)	Percentage of total value	Value (million dollars)	Percentage of total value	Value (million dollars)	Percentage of total value	Value (million dollars)	Percentage of total value
						1995						
Florida	421,462.66	67.0	89,453.28	14.2	22,062.75	3.5	11,358.31	1.8	17,105.29	2.7	67,987.92	10.8
Alachua	3,412.65	51.9	840.66	12.8	112.75	1.7	178.75	2.7	160.11	2.4	1,875.72	28.5
Baker	163.43	38.9	27.89	6.6	6.90	1.6	84.05	20.0	11.04	2.6	126.72	30.2
Bay	3,389.55	62.0	756.03	13.8	94.85	1.7	62.57	1.1	128.95	2.4	1,038.77	19.0
Bradford	271.62	58.8	45.95	10.0	8.96	1.9	66.53	14.4	19.15	4.1	49.53	10.7
Brevard	12,145.14	56.6	2,333.48	10.9	485.13	2.3	103.32	0.5	559.01	2.6	5,826.11	27.2
Broward	45,160.22	73.2	8,168.77	13.2	2,700.53	4.4	128.08	0.2	1,172.74	1.9	4,324.55	7.0
Calhoun	90.19	40.4	17.51	7.8	3.87	1.7	75.59	33.9	7.13	3.2	28.82	12.9
Charlotte	5,665.62	80.6	768.11	10.9	70.36	1.0	102.11	1.5	129.37	1.8	295.84	4.2
Citrus	2,825.54	68.1	454.49	10.9	28.26	0.7	41.11	1.0	107.71	2.6	693.86	16.7
Clay	2,622.69	70.5	480.16	12.9	64.85	1.7	68.99	1.9	127.62	3.4	354.31	9.5
Collier	14,367.76	77.6	1,885.91	10.2	285.26	1.5	233.68	1.3	345.14	1.9	1,386.72	7.5
Columbia	540.95	46.5	159.90	13.7	23.51	2.0	121.84	10.5	34.78	3.0	283.01	24.3
Dade	56,515.60	63.9	14,288.01	16.2	5,032.74	5.7	1,706.01	1.9	2,205.12	2.5	8,656.63	9.8
De Soto	334.82	42.7	73.73	9.4	9.69	1.2	246.43	31.4	24.40	3.1	95.70	12.2
Dixie	143.10	51.3	11.89	4.3	3.20	1.1	61.69	22.1	3.49	1.3	55.75	20.0
Duval	14,601.90	56.3	4,643.89	17.9	1,752.69	6.8	80.94	0.3	1,317.60	5.1	3,552.69	13.7
Escambia	4,510.88	53.1	996.70	11.7	251.23	3.0	67.49	0.8	315.92	3.7	2,360.03	27.8
Flagler	1,944.14	77.9	211.48	8.5	27.82	1.1	52.63	2.1	36.33	1.5	224.26	9.0
Franklin	435.81	41.2	36.50	3.4	6.33	0.6	25.09	2.4	12.00	1.1	542.80	51.3
Gadsden	411.95	53.1	48.20	6.2	40.16	5.2	111.45	14.4	31.80	4.1	132.44	17.1
Gilchrist	136.88	55.1	7.62	3.1	1.09	0.4	70.14	28.2	5.45	2.2	27.35	11.0
Glades	170.14	36.4	24.55	5.2	1.70	0.4	121.52	26.0	5.78	1.2	144.19	30.8

See footnote at end of table.

Continued . . .

Table 23.95. LAND USE: ASSESSED VALUE AND PROPORTION OF LAND BY USE IN THE STATE AND COUNTIES OF FLORIDA, 1994 AND 1995 (Continued)

County	Residential		Commercial		Industrial		Agricultural		Institutional		Miscellaneous 1/	
	Value (million dollars)	Per-cent-age of total value	Value (million dollars)	Per-cent-age of total value	Value (million dollars)	Per-cent-age of total value	Value (million dollars)	Per-cent-age of total value	Value (million dollars)	Per-cent-age of total value	Value (million dollars)	Per-cent-age of total value
					1995 (Continued)							
Gulf	298.98	58.3	21.46	4.2	21.02	4.1	27.70	5.4	10.68	2.1	132.84	25.9
Hamilton	104.52	35.7	15.21	5.2	67.11	22.9	59.79	20.4	5.84	2.0	40.47	13.8
Hardee	195.27	28.0	43.90	6.3	58.45	8.4	255.48	36.6	21.94	3.1	122.70	17.6
Hendry	432.06	38.7	97.63	8.7	34.34	3.1	330.55	29.6	23.22	2.1	199.24	17.8
Hernando	3,120.52	71.8	410.13	9.4	66.50	1.5	79.95	1.8	93.41	2.1	575.81	13.2
Highlands	1,720.80	60.3	390.41	13.7	54.62	1.9	271.78	9.5	125.59	4.4	289.02	10.1
Hillsborough	18,767.78	62.1	5,099.57	16.9	1,609.46	5.3	463.46	1.5	1,087.52	3.6	3,181.19	10.5
Holmes	120.72	37.1	22.51	6.9	2.80	0.9	100.58	30.9	17.64	5.4	61.53	18.9
Indian River	4,884.38	74.7	678.75	10.4	121.54	1.9	263.57	4.0	165.71	2.5	427.79	6.5
Jackson	518.38	53.3	101.21	10.4	26.73	2.7	58.72	6.0	47.80	4.9	220.63	22.7
Jefferson	77.15	29.0	20.66	7.8	2.15	0.8	117.97	44.4	10.67	4.0	37.20	14.0
Lafayette	39.29	31.7	2.94	2.4	0.69	0.6	63.38	51.2	3.10	2.5	14.49	11.7
Lake	4,319.69	70.6	628.85	10.3	134.77	2.2	201.66	3.3	174.35	2.9	655.52	10.7
Lee	17,714.22	76.8	2,901.43	12.6	530.65	2.3	149.93	0.7	488.05	2.1	1,280.06	5.5
Leon	4,840.72	49.2	1,287.80	13.1	173.20	1.8	92.41	0.9	232.55	2.4	3,208.31	32.6
Levy	468.44	54.2	72.97	8.4	6.38	0.7	148.64	17.2	21.35	2.5	147.25	17.0
Liberty	44.18	23.8	3.79	2.0	1.34	0.7	31.35	16.9	4.02	2.2	100.90	54.4
Madison	134.37	39.9	23.96	7.1	10.26	3.0	110.31	32.8	14.97	4.4	42.54	12.6
Manatee	7,088.12	70.4	1,315.24	13.1	375.21	3.7	273.68	2.7	293.11	2.9	727.46	7.2
Marion	4,335.65	60.8	807.82	11.3	288.73	4.1	387.71	5.4	177.38	2.5	1,131.42	15.9
Martin	6,409.97	76.1	803.62	9.5	176.38	2.1	166.50	2.0	119.46	1.4	748.12	8.9
Monroe	5,842.99	59.8	1,335.96	13.7	68.14	0.7	0.61	0.0	134.83	1.4	2,383.21	24.4
Nassau	1,396.61	68.2	240.48	11.8	65.24	3.2	124.64	6.1	44.38	2.2	174.99	8.6
Okaloosa	4,406.55	72.5	771.69	12.7	101.10	1.7	51.10	0.8	130.02	2.1	616.31	10.1

See footnote at end of table.

Continued . . .

Table 23.95. LAND USE: ASSESSED VALUE AND PROPORTION OF LAND BY USE IN THE STATE AND COUNTIES OF FLORIDA, 1994 AND 1995 (Continued)

County	Residential		Commercial		Industrial		Agricultural		Institutional		Miscellaneous 1/	
	Value (million dollars)	Percentage of total value	Value (million dollars)	Percentage of total value	Value (million dollars)	Percentage of total value	Value (million dollars)	Percentage of total value	Value (million dollars)	Percentage of total value	Value (million dollars)	Percentage of total value
1995 (Continued)												
Okeechobee	570.76	58.5	111.00	11.4	13.50	1.4	140.07	14.4	26.26	2.7	114.17	11.7
Orange	20,964.76	54.0	10,152.99	26.2	1,701.11	4.4	325.86	0.8	1,383.57	3.6	4,293.51	11.1
Osceola	3,803.32	62.6	1,351.58	22.2	100.84	1.7	189.68	3.1	136.18	2.2	494.01	8.1
Palm Beach	47,194.99	76.2	7,603.28	12.3	1,454.27	2.3	749.44	1.2	1,117.22	1.8	3,832.07	6.2
Pasco	6,747.23	74.4	1,234.71	13.6	126.85	1.4	173.44	1.9	249.96	2.8	536.53	5.9
Pinellas	25,915.84	68.9	5,588.80	14.9	1,373.30	3.7	15.66	0.0	1,676.04	4.5	3,049.22	8.1
Polk	7,487.08	60.3	1,710.96	13.8	615.16	5.0	460.99	3.7	415.14	3.3	1,719.37	13.9
Putnam	1,251.84	64.3	149.56	7.7	75.61	3.9	51.56	2.6	70.58	3.6	348.25	17.9
St. Johns	4,368.58	78.2	547.93	9.8	64.43	1.2	71.15	1.3	153.33	2.7	378.35	6.8
St. Lucie	4,396.43	65.0	690.57	10.2	165.80	2.5	331.42	4.9	137.53	2.0	1,038.87	15.4
Santa Rosa	2,613.49	75.2	281.60	8.1	36.96	1.1	99.83	2.9	82.16	2.4	361.38	10.4
Sarasota	15,032.34	77.6	2,336.78	12.1	418.47	2.2	55.62	0.3	589.84	3.0	950.51	4.9
Seminole	9,554.67	75.9	1,883.16	15.0	425.17	3.4	25.91	0.2	236.61	1.9	462.65	3.7
Sumter	442.11	59.4	79.54	10.7	16.78	2.3	102.59	13.8	4.99	0.7	98.45	13.2
Suwannee	331.86	51.1	49.43	7.6	12.75	2.0	148.45	22.9	27.13	4.2	79.38	12.2
Taylor	250.06	47.0	50.78	9.5	58.60	11.0	85.74	16.1	18.26	3.4	69.08	13.0
Union	48.49	26.3	5.86	3.2	3.52	1.9	48.09	26.1	4.26	2.3	74.10	40.2
Volusia	11,193.20	72.1	2,079.56	13.4	356.10	2.3	407.33	2.6	506.42	3.3	988.89	6.4
Wakulla	266.20	50.9	18.65	3.6	8.58	1.6	36.48	7.0	6.85	1.3	185.80	35.6
Walton	1,696.09	76.0	119.95	5.4	12.88	0.6	100.53	4.5	37.65	1.7	264.75	11.9
Washington	191.37	47.9	27.16	6.8	13.39	3.3	97.02	24.3	17.11	4.3	53.78	13.5

1/ Includes lease hold interests, utilities, mining, petroleum and gas lands, subsurface rights, right-of-ways, submerged lands, sewage disposal, borrow pits, wastelands, outdoor recreational/park lands, and governmental lands.

Source: State of Florida, Department of Revenue, unpublished data. Compiled by Armasi, Inc.

ECONOMIC INDICATORS AND PRICES

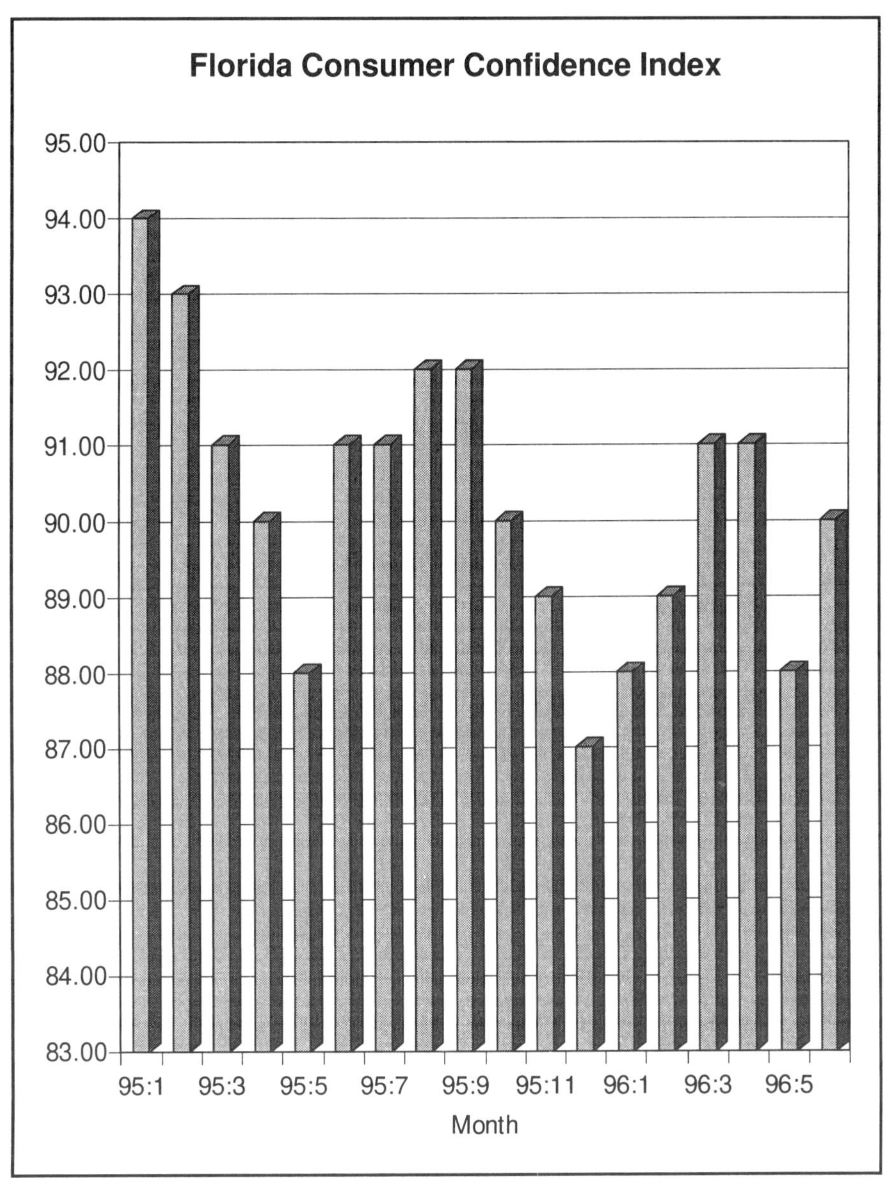

Source: Table 24.85

SECTION 24.00
ECONOMIC INDICATORS AND PRICES

TABLES LISTED BY MAJOR HEADINGS

HEADING PAGE

Table 24.12. ECONOMIC INDICATORS: SPECIFIED INDICATORS OF THE FLORIDA ECONOMY JANUARY 1990 THROUGH DECEMBER 1995

(not adjusted for seasonal variation)

Month and year	Unem- ploy- ment rate	Nonfarm wage and salary employ- ment 1/ (1,000)	Sales and use tax collec- tions 2/	Month and year	Unem- ploy- ment rate	Nonfarm wage and salary employ- ment 1/ (1,000)	Sales and use tax collec- tions 2/
1990				1993			
January	6.2	5,334.5	745.6	January	7.8	5,434.6	887.7
February	5.6	5,392.7	652.7	February	6.9	5,507.6	781.7
March	5.5	5,448.1	668.8	March	6.6	5,558.4	798.3
April	5.6	5,418.9	742.0	April	6.7	5,587.3	851.2
May	5.7	5,430.2	679.0	May	6.8	5,580.4	808.1
June	6.3	5,422.3	852.9	June	7.4	5,580.9	781.8
July	6.3	5,303.8	671.6	July	7.5	5,492.9	795.8
August	6.2	5,311.2	654.8	August	7.3	5,491.7	781.8
September	6.4	5,362.9	650.1	September	7.2	5,576.2	773.4
October	6.2	5,373.7	623.5	October	7.0	5,625.4	772.7
November	6.2	5,414.5	651.1	November	6.9	5,678.6	784.6
December	6.0	5,436.1	702.8	December	6.5	5,743.2	866.0
1991				1994			
January	6.9	5,301.7	729.8	January	7.3	5,657.6	915.6
February	6.8	5,323.2	651.5	February	6.5	5,724.8	796.5
March	6.8	5,355.3	676.0	March	6.4	5,788.3	841.4
April	7.0	5,316.8	719.4	April	6.4	5,799.2	931.2
May	7.1	5,318.0	676.9	May	6.5	5,801.7	845.3
June	7.8	5,294.5	663.7	June	7.1	5,806.5	825.0
July	7.9	5,193.2	644.7	July	7.1	5,708.6	832.8
August	7.7	5,207.1	651.7	August	6.9	5,713.7	813.0
September	7.8	5,260.0	654.8	September	6.7	5,828.0	825.8
October	7.6	5,271.6	628.8	October	6.3	5,836.3	822.1
November	7.6	5,332.6	655.8	November	6.0	5,947.6	841.7
December	7.7	5,357.5	717.7	December	5.5	5,979.9	913.8
1992				1995			
January	8.8	5,277.3	756.2	January	6.1	5,882.0	991.7
February	8.4	5,313.0	685.0	February	5.2	5,956.3	856.1
March	8.1	5,390.9	713.7	March	5.0	6,019.6	898.1
April	8.1	5,357.0	749.4	April	5.2	5,981.6	962.1
May	8.1	5,363.5	707.8	May	5.2	5,996.9	887.5
June	8.9	5,353.4	685.6	June	5.9	6,003.8	906.2
July	9.0	5,267.5	691.9	July	5.8	5,905.1	902.0
August	8.9	5,257.8	709.4	August	5.7	5,910.3	871.1
September	8.8	5,346.0	674.5	September	5.8	6,022.0	878.1
October	7.8	5,398.6	731.5	October	5.6	6,043.3	878.1
November	7.5	5,462.1	771.2	November	5.4	6,113.8	893.9
December	7.0	5,516.8	808.4	December	5.0	6,169.7	993.5

1/ Data are for employment covered by unemployment compensation.
2/ Data are in millions, rounded to thousands of dollars.
Note: 1990 unemployment rate and nonfarm wage and salary employment data from U.S. Department of Labor, Bureau of Labor Statistics. Some data are revised.
Source: State of Florida, Department of Labor and Employment Security, and State of Florida, Department of Revenue, unpublished data.

Table 24.15. GROSS STATE PRODUCT: ESTIMATES OF GROSS STATE PRODUCT (GSP) BY COMPONENT AND MAJOR INDUSTRIAL GROUP IN FLORIDA, SPECIFIED YEARS 1977 THROUGH 1992

(in millions of dollars)

Item	1977	1982	1987	1989	1990	1991	1992
Components of GSP							
Total	63,343	118,071	197,096	231,046	244,570	255,162	268,609
Compensation	38,059	72,439	116,223	136,177	146,264	150,886	159,886
Proprietors' income 1/	7,029	10,621	19,366	21,369	22,115	23,968	25,328
Capital charges	12,252	24,500	42,811	50,972	51,779	54,329	55,632
Indirect business taxes	6,003	10,511	18,697	22,527	24,412	25,978	27,764
GSP by major industry							
Farms	1,673	2,696	3,490	4,305	3,841	4,118	4,138
Agricultural services, forestry, and fisheries	581	899	1,710	1,825	2,066	2,224	2,343
Mining	546	1,827	740	774	771	748	696
Construction	3,446	7,314	12,156	13,159	13,049	11,562	11,457
Manufacturing	7,184	13,447	20,263	22,690	23,033	23,118	23,462
Durable goods	3,608	7,754	11,834	13,016	12,990	13,130	13,248
Nondurable goods	3,576	5,693	8,429	9,674	10,043	9,987	10,214
Transportation, communications, and public utilities	6,818	12,031	18,973	21,418	22,365	24,018	25,777
Wholesale trade	4,835	8,470	13,802	16,264	16,828	17,290	18,582
Retail trade	7,761	13,844	24,020	28,067	28,972	29,459	30,830
Finance, insurance, and real estate	10,611	20,842	38,050	44,747	47,731	50,753	53,439
Services	10,647	21,577	40,660	49,226	54,530	57,935	63,064
Government	9,240	15,124	23,233	28,570	31,385	33,938	34,820
Federal civilian	1,606	2,559	3,666	4,604	4,757	5,482	5,726
Federal military	1,620	2,704	3,552	3,943	4,264	4,540	4,825
State and local	6,015	9,860	16,015	20,023	22,364	23,916	24,269

1/ Includes inventory valuation adjustment and capital consumption allowances.
Note: Data for earlier years are revised. See Appendix for discussion of Gross State Product (GSP) estimates.

Source: U.S., Department of Commerce, Bureau of Economic Analysis, Regional Economic Information System, CD-ROM, June 1996.

Table 24.20. BUILDING PERMIT ACTIVITY: NUMBER OF PUBLIC AND PRIVATE RESIDENTIAL HOUSING UNITS AUTHORIZED BY BUILDING PERMITS IN FLORIDA AND THE UNITED STATES, 1983 THROUGH 1994

Month	1983	1984	1985	1986	1987	1988
Florida						
Annual total 1/	189,440	204,925	202,615	195,525	178,764	170,597
January	11,140	15,622	14,750	14,708	15,005	11,786
February	13,027	16,967	13,311	18,168	13,279	12,243
March	16,739	19,856	17,981	15,592	17,625	15,721
April	15,166	17,198	19,752	16,562	16,006	13,935
May	17,024	19,643	18,892	16,043	14,580	14,918
June	18,301	18,187	17,388	18,817	16,843	19,255
July	15,924	16,763	17,196	19,131	15,522	13,523
August	18,460	16,483	15,538	14,278	15,895	15,656
September	17,206	13,882	19,278	15,678	15,541	14,614
October	15,137	14,508	16,660	15,809	13,779	13,578
November	15,049	14,019	13,563	12,282	10,794	13,239
December	14,464	15,703	20,150	14,060	13,077	12,911
United States						
Annual total	1,613,254	1,664,663	1,733,266	1,769,443	1,534,772	1,455,623

Month	1989	1990	1991	1992	1993	1994
Florida						
Annual total 1/	164,985	126,347	95,308	102,022	115,103	128,264
January	13,582	14,982	7,141	7,103	7,438	11,166
February	13,404	9,318	7,025	6,974	8,604	9,962
March	14,163	12,228	7,485	9,707	9,810	12,164
April	14,593	12,314	8,697	8,870	10,226	11,766
May	17,165	11,836	9,986	8,093	10,893	11,658
June	17,454	12,078	9,773	9,776	11,052	12,077
July	11,756	11,113	9,372	9,853	10,118	11,825
August	13,657	10,667	8,063	8,009	10,119	13,369
September	12,393	8,700	7,246	8,689	11,517	12,136
October	12,754	8,622	7,440	8,972	8,940	11,002
November	11,483	8,592	6,378	7,337	9,333	10,284
December	11,279	6,933	8,458	8,887	12,875	10,483
United States						
Annual total	1,338,423	1,110,766	948,794	1,094,933	1,199,063	1,374,636

1/ Annual total reflects revisions not distributed to months.

Note: To arrive at state totals, data for metropolitan areas (MSAs and PMSAs) were taken from reports submitted by all places within these areas. Estimates of the data for nonmetropolitan areas in Florida and the United States were based on a sample of 16,000 places for 1983-1984, 17,000 places for 1985-1993, and 19,000 in 1994. Beginning with January 1986, data exclude public housing units. See Glossary for metropolitan area definitions and see map at the front of the book for area boundaries.

Source: U.S., Department of Commerce, International Trade Administration, *Construction Review, Spring 1995,* and previous editions.

Table 24.30. GROSS AND TAXABLE SALES: SALES REPORTED AND SALES AND USE TAXES COLLECTED BY THE DEPARTMENT OF REVENUE IN FLORIDA, 1962 THROUGH 1995

(sales and taxes rounded to dollars)

Year	Gross sales	Taxable sales	Net sales taxes paid	Number of reports
1962	15,320,661,116	7,090,619,990	187,473,059	(NA)
1963	16,103,205,516	7,470,457,359	207,577,878	1,375,162
1964	18,243,239,834	8,680,873,802	245,010,164	1,795,111
1965	20,159,138,762	9,306,446,815	270,654,499	1,822,855
1966	22,070,877,464	10,052,183,902	292,635,382	1,848,519
1967	23,523,783,328	10,738,028,301	314,139,054	1,868,644
1968	28,188,063,900	13,361,484,763	467,573,056	2,102,650
1969	33,441,677,220	16,246,816,932	616,919,658	2,324,350
1970	36,834,259,466	18,339,123,013	681,920,445	2,394,366
1971	41,255,223,174	20,272,358,516	784,708,762	2,528,429
1972	49,280,284,464	23,884,881,400	947,086,120	2,508,097
1973	59,294,867,904	28,264,125,745	1,136,864,712	2,495,557
1974	65,887,520,411	29,785,250,309	1,216,071,766	2,689,313
1975	66,764,958,864	29,329,230,180	1,197,020,925	2,845,986
1976	73,791,141,256	32,215,852,176	1,323,271,879	2,962,711
1977	82,783,600,922	36,274,024,296	1,500,074,880	2,788,578
1978	98,227,927,655	43,640,280,027	1,816,192,620	2,844,083
1979	114,373,759,327	50,555,056,774	2,074,119,153	3,005,717
1980	136,318,330,861	58,177,097,809	2,383,348,768	3,177,162
1981	156,619,282,052	66,750,301,522	2,691,772,260	3,214,217
1982	161,796,458,854	66,663,022,175	3,143,878,949	3,451,004
1983	168,492,566,327	73,906,494,761	4,035,324,107	3,632,967
1984	195,758,800,411	84,639,051,288	4,498,315,417	3,735,161
1985	210,089,814,330	89,673,013,371	4,874,199,447	3,887,677
1986	223,601,586,263	98,612,192,144	5,304,286,552	4,249,174
1987	259,753,403,821	113,379,458,921	6,053,620,606	5,054,411
1988	277,485,847,435	119,103,871,758	7,299,532,184	5,115,463
1989	289,076,440,275	122,788,168,387	7,834,635,188	5,101,085
1990	303,464,877,632	127,283,343,961	8,242,720,563	5,177,182
1991	310,147,685,581	126,648,591,209	8,181,744,259	5,505,665
1992	330,770,069,551	135,959,144,438	8,778,486,852	5,747,984
1993	360,267,713,516	150,592,943,893	9,582,751,878	6,091,241
1994	385,110,859,523	159,956,354,846	10,008,966,792	5,837,879
1995	423,309,073,509	171,551,704,651	10,975,746,043	(NA)

(NA) Not available.

Note: These sales were reported to the Department of Revenue for the 5 percent regular sales tax, the 5 percent use tax, and the 3 percent vehicle and farm equipment sales tax from January to December of each year. The sales occurred, for the most part, from December of the previous year through November of the posted year. In February 1988 the regular sales and use tax increased to 6 percent; this increase is reflected in the collections from March 1988. These data are not comparable with retail sales figures reported by the Bureau of the Census because of differences in definitions of retailers and retail sales. At various times, changes in the rate of the taxes or in the items to be taxed or excluded have been made. Data prior to 1993 are unaudited and are not comparable to later years.

Source: State of Florida, Department of Revenue, unpublished data. Data from 1987 to present are prepared by the University of Florida, Bureau of Economic and Business Research.

Table 24.72. CONSUMER AND PRODUCER PRICE INDEXES: ANNUAL AVERAGES AND PERCENTAGE CHANGES FOR ALL URBAN CONSUMERS INDEX AND PRODUCER PRICE INDEX IN THE UNITED STATES, 1979 THROUGH 1995

Year	Consumer prices 1/					
	All items		Commodities		Services	
	Index	Percentage change	Index	Percentage change	Index	Percentage change
1979	72.6	11.3	76.6	11.3	67.5	11.0
1980	82.4	13.5	86.0	12.3	77.9	15.4
1981	90.9	10.3	93.2	8.4	88.1	13.1
1982	96.5	6.2	97.0	4.1	96.0	9.0
1983	99.6	3.2	99.8	2.9	99.4	3.5
1984	103.9	4.3	103.2	3.4	104.6	5.2
1985	107.6	3.6	105.4	2.1	109.9	5.1
1986	109.6	1.9	104.4	-0.9	115.4	5.0
1987	113.6	3.6	107.7	3.2	120.2	4.2
1988	118.3	4.1	111.5	3.5	125.7	4.6
1989	124.0	4.8	116.7	4.7	131.9	4.9
1990	130.7	5.4	122.8	5.2	139.2	5.5
1991	136.2	4.2	126.6	3.1	146.3	5.1
1992	140.3	3.0	129.1	2.0	152.0	3.9
1993	144.5	3.0	131.5	1.9	157.9	3.9
1994	148.2	2.6	133.8	1.7	163.1	3.3
1995	152.4	2.8	136.4	1.9	168.7	3.4

Year	Producer prices 2/					
	All commodities		Farm products		Industrial commodities	
	Index	Percentage change	Index	Percentage change	Index	Percentage change
1979	78.7	12.6	99.6	13.6	75.7	12.8
1980	89.8	14.1	102.9	3.3	88.0	16.2
1981	98.0	9.1	105.2	2.2	97.4	10.7
1982	100.0	2.0	100.0	-4.9	100.0	2.7
1983	101.3	1.3	102.4	2.4	101.1	1.1
1984	103.7	2.4	105.5	3.0	103.3	2.2
1985	103.1	-0.6	95.1	-9.9	103.7	0.4
1986	100.2	-2.8	92.9	-2.3	99.9	-3.7
1987	102.8	2.6	95.5	2.8	102.6	2.7
1988	106.9	4.0	104.9	9.8	106.3	3.6
1989	112.2	5.0	110.9	5.7	111.6	5.0
1990	116.3	3.7	112.2	1.2	115.8	3.8
1991	116.5	0.2	105.7	-5.8	116.5	0.6
1992	117.2	0.6	103.6	-2.0	117.4	0.8
1993	118.9	1.5	107.1	3.4	119.0	1.4
1994	120.4	1.3	106.3	-0.7	120.7	1.4
1995	124.7	3.6	107.4	1.0	125.5	4.0

1/ 1982-84 = 100.
2/ 1982 = 100.
Note: See Appendix for discussion of consumer and producer price indexes.

Source: U.S., Department of Labor, Bureau of Labor Statistics, *CPI Detailed Report*, January 1996, and the Internet at <http://stats.bls.gov:80/>.

Table 24.73. CONSUMER PRICE INDEXES: INDEXES BY COMMODITY IN THE UNITED STATES 1994 AND 1995

(1982-84 = 100, except where indicated)

Index expenditure category and commodity	Relative importance December 1995	Annual average index 1994	Annual average index 1995	Percentage change 1994 to 1995
Wage earners and clerical workers index (CPI-W), all items	100.0	145.6	149.8	2.9
All urban consumers index (CPI-U), all items	100.0	148.2	152.4	2.8
Food and beverages	17.3	144.9	148.9	2.8
Food	15.8	144.3	148.4	2.8
Food at home	9.9	144.1	148.8	3.3
Cereals and bakery products	1.5	163.0	167.5	2.8
Meats, poultry, fish, and eggs	2.9	137.2	138.8	1.2
Dairy products	1.2	131.7	132.8	0.8
Fruits and vegetables	1.9	165.0	177.7	7.7
Other food at home	2.4	135.6	140.8	3.8
Sugar and sweets	0.3	135.2	137.5	1.7
Fats and oils	0.2	133.5	137.3	2.8
Nonalcoholic beverages	0.8	123.2	131.7	6.9
Other prepared food	1.0	147.5	151.1	2.4
Food away from home	5.9	145.7	149.0	2.3
Alcoholic beverages	1.6	151.5	153.9	1.6
Housing	41.3	144.8	148.5	2.6
Shelter	28.3	160.5	165.7	3.2
Renters' costs 1/	8.0	169.4	174.3	2.9
Rent, residential	5.8	154.0	157.8	2.5
Other renters' costs	2.2	196.3	204.3	4.1
Homeowners' costs 1/	20.1	165.5	171.0	3.3
Owners' equivalent rent 1/	19.7	165.8	171.3	3.3
Household insurance 1/	0.4	152.3	157.4	3.3
Maintenance and repairs	0.2	130.8	135.0	3.2
Maintenance and repair services	0.1	134.5	139.8	3.9
Maintenance and repair commodities	0.1	125.8	128.5	2.1
Fuel and other utilities	7.0	122.8	123.7	0.7
Fuels	3.8	111.7	111.5	-0.2
Fuel oil and other household fuel commodities	0.4	88.8	88.1	-0.8
Gas (piped) and electricity	3.4	119.2	119.2	0.0
Other utilities and public services	3.2	150.2	152.8	1.7
Household furnishings and operation	6.0	121.0	123.0	1.7
Housefurnishings	3.4	111.0	111.2	0.2
Housekeeping supplies	1.1	132.3	137.1	3.6
Housekeeping services 2/	1.5	138.5	143.7	3.8
Apparel and upkeep	5.5	133.4	132.0	-1.0
Apparel commodities	5.0	130.4	128.7	-1.3
Men's and boys' apparel	1.3	126.4	126.2	-0.2
Women's and girls' apparel	2.2	130.9	126.9	-3.1
Infants' and toddlers' apparel	0.2	128.1	127.2	-0.7
Footwear	0.7	126.0	125.4	-0.5
Other apparel commodities	0.5	149.5	152.4	1.9
Apparel services 3/	0.6	155.4	157.3	1.2

See footnotes at end of table. Continued . . .

Table 24.73. CONSUMER PRICE INDEXES: INDEXES BY COMMODITY IN THE UNITED STATES 1994 AND 1995 (Continued)

(1982-84 = 100, except where indicated)

Index expenditure category and commodity	Relative importance December 1995	Annual average index 1994	Annual average index 1995	Percentage change 1994 to 1995
All urban consumers index (CPI-U) (Continued)				
Transportation	17.0	134.3	139.1	3.6
Private transportation	15.4	131.4	136.3	3.7
New vehicles	5.0	137.6	141.0	2.5
New cars	4.0	136.0	139.0	2.2
Used Cars	1.3	141.7	156.5	10.4
Motor fuel	2.9	98.5	100.0	1.5
Gasoline	(NA)	98.2	99.8	1.6
Maintenance and repair	1.5	150.2	154.0	2.5
Other private transportation	4.6	162.1	170.6	5.2
Other private transportation commodities 4/	0.6	103.5	104.8	1.3
Other private transportation services 5/	4.0	175.8	186.0	5.8
Public transportation	1.5	172.0	175.9	2.3
Medical care	7.4	211.0	220.5	4.5
Medical care commodities	1.3	200.7	204.5	1.9
Medical care services 6/	6.1	213.4	224.2	5.1
Professional medical services	3.5	192.5	201.0	4.4
Entertainment 7/	4.4	150.1	153.9	2.5
Entertainment commodities	2.0	136.1	138.7	1.9
Entertainment services	2.4	166.8	172.0	3.1
Other goods and services	7.1	198.5	206.9	4.2
Tobacco and smoking products	1.6	220.0	225.7	2.6
Personal care	1.2	144.6	147.1	1.7
Toilet goods and personal care appliances	0.6	141.5	143.1	1.1
Personal care services	0.6	147.9	151.5	2.4
Personal and educational expenses	4.3	223.2	235.5	5.5
School books and supplies	0.3	205.5	214.4	4.3
Personal and educational services	4.1	224.8	237.3	5.6
Commodity and service group, all items	100.0	148.2	152.4	2.8
Commodities	42.9	133.8	136.4	1.9
Food and beverages	17.3	144.9	148.9	2.8
Commodities less food and beverages	25.6	126.9	128.9	1.6
Nondurables less food and beverages	15.1	128.4	129.5	0.9
Apparel commodities	5.0	130.4	128.7	-1.3
Nondurables less food, beverages, and apparel	10.1	130.3	132.9	2.0
Durables	10.5	124.8	128.0	2.6
Services	57.1	163.1	168.7	3.4
Rent of shelter 1/	27.7	167.0	172.4	3.2
Household services less rent of shelter 1/	8.7	136.3	138.3	1.5
Transportation services	7.1	168.6	175.9	4.3
Medical care services	6.1	213.4	224.2	5.1
Other services	7.6	185.4	193.3	4.3

See footnotes at end of table.

Continued . . .

Table 24.73. CONSUMER PRICE INDEXES: INDEXES BY COMMODITY IN THE UNITED STATES 1994 AND 1995 (Continued)

(1982-84 = 100, except where indicated)

Index expenditure category and commodity	Relative importance December 1995	Annual average index 1994	Annual average index 1995	Percentage change 1994 to 1995
Special indexes				
All items less food	84.2	149.0	153.1	2.8
All items less shelter	71.7	144.8	148.6	2.6
All items less homeowners' costs 1/	79.9	149.5	153.5	2.7
All items less medical care	92.6	144.7	148.6	2.7
Commodities less food	27.2	127.9	129.8	1.5
Nondurables less food	16.6	129.7	130.9	0.9
Nondurables less food and apparel	11.7	131.6	134.1	1.9
Nondurables	32.4	136.8	139.3	1.8
Services less rent of shelter 1/	29.4	170.7	176.8	3.6
Services less medical care	51.0	158.4	163.5	3.2
Energy	6.7	104.6	105.2	0.6
All items less energy	93.3	154.1	158.7	3.0
All items less food and energy	77.5	156.5	161.2	3.0
Commodities less food and energy	23.9	137.1	139.3	1.6
Energy commodities	3.3	97.6	98.8	1.2
Services less energy	53.6	167.6	173.7	3.6
Purchasing power of the consumer dollar (1982-84=$1.00; data in dollars)	(NA)	0.675	0.656	-2.8

(NA) Not available.

1/ Indexes on a December 1982 = 100 base.

2/ Includes postage, moving and storage, household laundry and dry cleaning services, and appliance and furniture repair.

3/ Apparel laundry and dry cleaning services.

4/ Includes motor oil, coolants, tires, and auto parts.

5/ Includes insurance, finance charges, registration and license fees, and auto rental.

6/ Includes professional services and hospital charges.

7/ Includes newspapers, magazines, books, sporting goods and equipment, toys, hobbies, music and photographic equipment, and pet supplies; also fees and admission to sporting events and other entertainment.

Note: See Appendix for explanation of CPI-W and CPI-U.

Source: U.S., Department of Labor, Bureau of Labor Statistics, *CPI Detailed Report,* January 1996.

Table 24.74. CONSUMER PRICE INDEXES: INDEXES FOR ALL URBAN CONSUMERS BY CATEGORY AND COMMODITY IN MIAMI-FT. LAUDERDALE AND TAMPA-ST. PETERSBURG-CLEARWATER FLORIDA, ANNUAL AVERAGE, 1995, AND MIAMI-FT. LAUDERDALE, FLORIDA JANUARY 1994, 1995, AND 1996

(1982-84 = 100, except where indicated)

Expenditure category and commodity	Annual average			
	Miami-Ft. Lauderdale		Tampa-St. Petersburg-Clearwater 1/	
	1995	Percentage change 1994 to 1995	1995	Percentage change 1994 to 1995
All items	148.9	3.7	129.7	2.5
Food and beverages	157.1	2.9	125.5	3.0
Food	157.2	2.9	125.0	3.0
Food at home	153.9	3.4	124.0	3.7
Cereals and bakery products	154.4	-0.3	136.2	4.6
Meats, poultry, fish, and eggs	136.1	3.4	122.6	3.6
Meats, poultry, and fish	137.9	3.2	122.7	3.4
Dairy products	136.6	0.9	116.7	0.6
Fruits and vegetables	227.6	6.6	137.9	2.9
Other foods at home	132.7	3.5	114.0	4.9
Food away from home	163.1	2.2	125.3	2.2
Alcoholic beverages	153.8	2.5	129.3	2.9
Housing	139.9	3.5	123.8	2.0
Shelter	148.8	4.3	130.5	2.8
Renters' costs 2/	151.7	4.2	118.3	2.2
Rent, residential	141.1	2.9	126.2	2.5
Other renters' costs	209.5	9.6	94.5	1.0
Homeowners' costs 2/	153.0	4.5	135.2	3.0
Owners' equivalent rent 2/	151.0	4.2	135.3	3.0
Fuel and other utilities	113.1	1.1	116.4	0.4
Fuels	105.2	1.1	110.7	-1.2
Fuel oil and other household fuel commodities	155.0	2.5	116.3	-6.4
Gas (piped) and electricity	104.4	1.1	110.5	-0.8
Household furnishings and operation	133.6	2.4	111.3	1.3
Apparel and upkeep	147.0	2.4	134.1	-6.6
Apparel commodities	139.8	2.3	133.6	-7.3
Men's and boys' apparel	141.0	3.4	119.2	7.9
Women's and girls' apparel	150.4	2.9	147.8	(NA)
Footwear	138.2	-2.7	92.1	-1.0
Transportation	139.8	3.3	124.9	5.1
Private transportation	139.3	3.5	125.6	5.5
Public transportation	144.2	1.8	115.8	1.5
Medical care	203.0	7.9	181.5	5.0
Entertainment	140.4	4.5	116.2	5.7
Other goods and services	169.7	4.2	147.6	4.4
Personal care	104.4	0.8	147.3	5.4

See footnotes at end of table.

Continued . . .

Table 24.74. CONSUMER PRICE INDEXES: INDEXES FOR ALL URBAN CONSUMERS BY CATEGORY AND COMMODITY IN MIAMI-FT. LAUDERDALE AND TAMPA-ST. PETERSBURG-CLEARWATER FLORIDA, ANNUAL AVERAGE, 1995, AND MIAMI-FT. LAUDERDALE, FLORIDA JANUARY 1994, 1995, AND 1996 (Continued)

(1982-84 = 100, except where indicated)

Expenditure category and commodity	Miami-Ft. Lauderdale January 1994	1995	1996	Percentage change 1995 to 1996
All items	141.0	147.3	152.0	3.2
Food and beverages	151.8	156.2	158.9	1.7
Food	151.7	156.2	158.8	1.7
Food at home	148.0	154.5	156.0	1.0
Cereals and bakery products	150.2	154.2	155.9	1.1
Meats, poultry, fish, and eggs	131.1	131.4	143.3	9.1
Meats, poultry, and fish	132.8	133.2	144.7	8.6
Dairy products	134.4	140.1	141.8	1.2
Fruits and vegetables	219.7	237.2	223.1	-5.9
Other foods at home	123.9	132.7	130.8	-1.4
Food away from home	158.3	160.9	164.7	2.4
Alcoholic beverages	149.3	153.6	157.2	2.3
Housing	133.0	138.5	143.8	3.8
Shelter	139.3	146.9	153.0	4.2
Renters' costs 2/	143.7	152.2	156.6	2.9
Rent, residential	133.2	139.4	143.8	3.2
Other renters' costs	201.4	223.1	227.4	1.9
Homeowners' costs 2/	142.4	150.0	157.2	4.8
Owners' equivalent rent 2/	141.4	148.3	154.8	4.4
Fuel and other utilities	113.7	112.6	116.8	3.7
Fuels	107.7	104.0	109.0	4.8
Fuel oil and other household fuel commodities	150.9	154.6	158.8	2.7
Gas (piped) and electricity	107.0	103.1	108.2	4.9
Household furnishings and operation	129.2	133.4	136.8	2.5
Apparel and upkeep	127.5	148.2	149.8	1.1
Apparel commodities	120.2	141.1	142.2	0.8
Men's and boys' apparel	119.2	141.6	141.5	-0.1
Women's and girls' apparel	119.3	150.9	155.0	2.7
Footwear	130.7	148.3	139.0	-6.3
Transportation	133.8	138.0	141.4	2.5
Private transportation	132.2	137.7	140.8	2.3
Public transportation	152.0	138.0	146.7	6.3
Medical care	184.7	196.6	212.8	8.2
Entertainment	132.1	140.5	142.5	1.4
Other goods and services	163.4	166.5	173.2	4.0
Personal care	105.6	104.5	101.0	-3.3

(NA) Not available.
(X) Not applicable.
1/ Indexes are on a 1987 = 100 base.
2/ Indexes on a November 1982 = 100 base for Miami-Ft. Lauderdale.
Note: The Miami-Ft. Lauderdale and Tampa-St. Petersburg-Clearwater areas are two of several metropolitan areas for which a consumer price index is issued bimonthly.
Source: U.S., Department of Labor, Bureau of Labor Statistics, *CPI Detailed Report,* January 1996.

Table 24.75. PRODUCER PRICE INDEXES: INDEXES BY STAGE OF PROCESSING, BY DURABILITY OF PRODUCT, AND BY COMMODITY IN THE UNITED STATES, ANNUAL AVERAGES 1993, 1994, AND 1995, AND JUNE 1996

(1982 = 100, not seasonally adjusted)

Item	Annual average 1993	Annual average 1994	Annual average 1995	June 1996
All commodities	118.9	120.4	124.7	127.9
By stage of processing				
Crude materials for further processing	102.4	101.8	102.7	113.1
Intermediate materials, supplies, etc.	116.2	118.5	124.9	126.2
Finished goods 1/	124.7	125.5	127.9	131.6
Finished consumer goods	123.0	123.3	125.6	130.0
Capital equipment	131.4	134.1	136.7	138.0
By durability of product				
Durable goods	126.8	130.0	133.9	133.8
Nondurable goods	113.2	113.6	118.1	123.4
Manufactures, total	121.8	123.8	128.9	130.5
Durable manufactures	126.7	129.6	133.2	133.3
Nondurable manufactures	117.0	118.2	124.6	127.5
Farm products, processed foods and feeds				
Farm products	107.1	106.3	107.4	128.9
Foods and feeds, processed	124.0	125.5	127.0	134.0
Industrial commodities				
Chemical and allied products	128.2	132.1	142.5	142.8
Fuels and related products and power	80.0	77.8	78.0	85.0
Furniture and household durables	123.7	126.1	128.2	130.4
Hides, skins, and leather products	143.7	148.5	153.7	149.3
Lumber and wood products	174.0	180.0	178.1	176.7
Machinery and equipment	124.0	125.1	126.6	126.4
Metals and metal products	119.2	124.8	134.5	131.9
Nonmetallic mineral products	120.0	124.2	129.0	130.9
Pulp, paper, and allied products	147.3	152.5	172.2	167.4
Rubber and plastics products	116.0	117.6	124.3	123.9
Textile products and apparel	118.0	118.3	120.8	122.0
Transportation equipment 1/	133.7	137.2	139.7	141.4
Motor vehicles and equipment	128.0	131.4	133.0	134.1

1/ Includes data for items not shown separately.
Note: See Appendix for discussion of producer price indexes.

Source: U.S., Department of Labor, Bureau of Labor Statistics, the Internet at <http://stats.bls.gov/>.

Table 24.76. ENERGY PRICES: NATURAL GAS, ELECTRICITY, FUEL OIL, AND GASOLINE PRICES, U.S. CITY AVERAGE AND MIAMI-FT. LAUDERDALE, FLORIDA JUNE 1995 THROUGH MAY 1996

(amounts in dollars)

Month and year	Piped gas per 40 therms		Electricity per 500 kilowatt-hours		#2 fuel oil per gallon-- U.S. city average	All types gasoline per gallon	
	U.S. city average	Miami-Ft. Lauderdale	U.S. city average	Miami-Ft. Lauderdale		U.S. city average	Miami-Ft. Lauderdale
1995							
June	28.980	41.326	50.448	42.269	0.895	1.281	1.398
July	28.980	40.746	50.552	42.269	0.885	1.252	1.368
August	28.799	39.996	50.395	42.269	0.879	1.222	1.295
September	28.907	39.996	49.735	42.269	0.870	1.206	1.227
October	28.573	39.987	49.472	44.047	0.873	1.185	1.212
November	27.982	44.374	49.209	44.047	0.879	1.161	1.172
December	29.280	44.871	48.571	44.047	0.905	1.160	1.160
1996							
January	29.570	45.972	48.538	44.047	1.007	1.186	1.203
February	29.645	46.781	48.542	44.047	1.001	1.181	1.209
March	28.604	47.919	49.137	44.047	1.020	1.219	1.246
April	28.858	46.319	49.221	43.886	1.065	1.305	1.336
May	30.486	46.116	49.232	43.886	1.038	1.378	1.393

Source: U.S., Department of Labor, Bureau of Labor Statistics, *CPI Detailed Report*, monthly releases.

Table 24.77. ELECTRICITY PRICES: COST PER KILOWATT-HOUR OF ELECTRICITY BY CLASS OF SERVICE OF THE FLORIDA ELECTRIC UTILITY INDUSTRY, 1982 THROUGH 1994

(in cents)

Year	Total	Residential	Commercial	Industrial	Street and highway lighting	Other public authorities	Interdepartmental
1982	6.60	7.07	6.45	5.38	9.81	5.97	6.64
1983	6.98	7.69	5.95	6.71	(NA)	7.37	(NA)
1984	7.91	8.81	7.00	6.79	(NA)	9.85	(NA)
1985	7.63	8.42	7.38	6.02	(NA)	7.22	(NA)
1986	7.23	7.98	6.83	5.74	(NA)	7.06	(NA)
1987	7.06	7.91	6.45	5.03	(NA)	10.34	(NA)
1988	7.04	7.80	6.71	5.31	(NA)	6.81	(NA)
1989	7.05	7.74	6.58	5.51	(NA)	8.20	(NA)
1990	7.03	7.77	6.82	5.10	(NA)	6.92	(NA)
1991	7.15	7.89	6.88	5.29	(NA)	6.95	(NA)
1992	6.90	7.75	6.41	5.36	(NA)	6.59	(NA)
1993	7.21	7.99	6.43	6.18	(NA)	7.37	(NA)
1994	6.90	7.78	6.33	5.56	(NA)	5.23	(NA)

(NA) Not available.

Note: Cost by class of service is defined as revenue by class of service/kilowatt-hour consumption by class of service. Some data are revised.

Source: State of Florida, Public Service Commission, Division of Research and Regulatory Review, *Statistics of the Florida Electric Utility Industry, 1994*.

Table 24.78. INDUSTRIAL AND COMMERCIAL FAILURES: NUMBER IN FLORIDA AND NUMBER AND LIABILITIES IN THE UNITED STATES, 1989 THROUGH 1994

Year	Florida		United States		
	New business incorpo-rations	Fail-ures 1/	New business incorpo-rations	Failures	
				Num-ber 1/	Current li-abilities 2/ $1,000,000)
1989	80,000	3,160	677,400	50,361	42,329
1990	82,172	3,655	647,366	60,747	56,130
1991	81,083	5,229	628,604	88,140	96,825
1992	86,037	5,375	666,800	97,069	94,318
1993	88,048	5,091	706,537	86,133	47,755
1994 A/	(NA)	3,605	(NA)	71,520	29,357

(NA) Not available.
A/ Preliminary.
1/ Includes firms discontinuing following assignment, voluntary or involuntary petition in bankruptcy, attachment, execution, foreclosure, etc.; voluntary withdrawals from business with known loss to creditors; also enterprises involved in court action, such as receivership and reorganization or arrangement which may or may not lead to discontinuance; and business making voluntary compromise with creditors out of court.
2/ Liabilities exclude long-term publicly held obligations; offsetting assets are not taken into account.
Note: Some data are revised.
Source: Dun & Bradstreet Corporation, New York, NY, *New Business Incorporations*, monthly, and *Business Failure Report*, annual, (copyright).

Table 24.79. PRICE LEVEL INDEX: RELATIVE WEIGHTS ASSIGNED TO SELECTED ITEMS PRICED FOR THE FLORIDA PRICE LEVEL INDEX, 1995

Item	Number of items	Weight	Item	Number of items	Weight
Apparel	17	6.440	Housing	28	37.888
Food	32	22.237	Apartment rent,		
Beer		1.631	monthly		4.208
Cup of coffee		1.425	Electricity		
Hamburger lunch		7.317	500 kilowatt-hours		1.518
Soft drink, served		1.425	1,000 kilowatt-hours		1.518
Wine		1.028	Hotel-motel rate 1/		1.315
Health, recreation, and			House purchase price		18.985
personal services	25	15.232	Transportation	14	18.203
College tuition 1/		2.311	Auto insurance		
Extraction		1.074	Liability		1.248
Dental filling		1.074	Physical damage		1.248
Movie rental		1.266	Auto repair charge		1.111
Safety deposit box			Chevrolet Cavalier 1/		4.024
fee		1.134	Ford Escort 1/		4.024
Semi-private room			Gasoline, unleaded		
rate		1.163	self-service		3.674
Hospital lab fee		1.098	Nonlocal travel 1/		1.015

1/ Constant price for all counties.
Note: Items weighted one percent or more are included. See also note on Table 24.80 and discussion under this section in the Appendix.
Source: State of Florida, Department of Education, Office of Education Budget and Management, *The 1995 Florida Price Level Index*.

Table 24.80. PRICE LEVEL INDEX: TOTAL INDEX AND INDEXES OF PRICES OF MAJOR ITEMS IN THE COUNTIES OF FLORIDA, 1995

(population-weighted state average = 100)

County	Florida Price Level Index: Index	Florida Price Level Index: Rank among counties	Food	Housing	Apparel	Transportation	Health recreation, and personal services
Alachua	96.72	20	101.60	91.62	108.82	99.00	93.28
Baker	90.29	61	95.51	81.96	94.71	98.42	90.27
Bay	95.40	30	101.86	89.78	97.73	97.57	95.27
Bradford	91.64	55	94.92	83.87	104.10	97.00	92.84
Brevard	98.04	16	103.31	93.62	98.05	98.12	100.30
Broward	104.93	3	102.25	109.16	96.33	101.68	106.68
Calhoun	89.15	65	93.13	79.42	94.52	97.02	93.99
Charlotte	96.68	21	99.70	90.57	92.97	96.73	107.74
Citrus	91.70	54	88.74	88.25	100.40	95.44	95.70
Clay	95.82	26	100.89	88.51	112.26	96.66	96.92
Collier	103.68	5	107.65	106.27	95.60	99.76	100.09
Columbia	90.92	60	95.62	84.80	91.14	96.87	91.00
Dade	106.78	2	103.32	112.60	100.00	105.88	102.61
De Soto	91.80	52	94.85	84.28	100.51	96.73	94.93
Dixie	91.91	51	94.33	85.13	103.62	97.03	92.78
Duval	98.13	15	99.49	94.86	102.70	97.79	101.97
Escambia	95.11	33	95.81	90.22	99.24	99.34	98.45
Flagler	96.32	24	103.32	92.31	95.11	97.72	94.19
Franklin	95.91	25	101.39	92.57	107.67	93.54	93.13
Gadsden	93.49	40	95.64	83.24	105.81	99.06	101.81
Gilchrist	92.00	48	94.10	87.87	96.06	96.82	91.00
Glades	97.83	17	103.60	92.23	94.26	100.95	100.05
Gulf	92.64	44	94.77	87.16	103.23	96.95	92.36
Hamilton	91.17	59	96.11	82.80	94.02	100.10	91.42
Hardee	91.29	57	93.88	85.14	90.01	97.85	94.44
Hendry	95.02	34	99.75	88.27	91.82	99.43	99.73
Hernando	92.82	43	95.37	87.01	96.27	96.44	96.63
Highlands	94.56	38	103.39	87.80	93.43	96.82	94.94
Hillsborough	100.32	8	99.76	103.28	101.87	99.34	94.90
Holmes	91.80	52	98.78	82.16	93.59	97.27	96.40
Indian River	98.42	14	99.32	96.01	96.86	99.97	101.47
Jackson	88.24	67	90.35	83.34	91.90	95.19	86.67
Jefferson	94.78	36	96.27	84.98	110.27	100.10	101.94
Lafayette	91.26	58	99.17	82.78	94.44	97.15	90.79
Lake	94.68	37	94.99	94.23	89.18	99.37	92.23
Lee	99.68	9	99.91	99.37	102.54	99.81	98.66
Leon	97.50	19	98.97	89.74	116.01	98.92	103.30
Levy	90.01	63	92.62	85.09	90.07	95.36	91.16

See footnote at end of table.

Continued . . .

Table 24.80. PRICE LEVEL INDEX: TOTAL INDEX AND INDEXES OF PRICES OF MAJOR ITEMS IN THE COUNTIES OF FLORIDA, 1995 (Continued)

(population-weighted state average = 100)

County	Florida Price Level Index: Index	Florida Price Level Index: Rank among counties	Food	Housing	Apparel	Transportation	Health recreation, and personal services
Liberty	93.10	41	97.95	82.64	108.89	96.44	99.05
Madison	90.20	62	97.05	79.76	93.87	100.19	90.77
Manatee	99.47	10	100.63	99.52	105.83	96.55	98.29
Marion	92.08	46	100.73	83.06	100.96	96.64	90.83
Martin	97.65	18	94.53	96.27	105.57	99.24	100.02
Monroe	109.30	1	104.14	124.19	96.12	100.30	99.18
Nassau	94.87	35	96.16	91.87	99.63	97.57	94.61
Okaloosa	95.33	31	93.94	91.25	104.02	99.45	98.07
Okeechobee	95.17	32	96.51	90.96	88.96	98.39	101.74
Orange	98.44	13	97.85	98.09	93.86	98.51	101.97
Osceola	96.45	23	102.55	92.79	96.36	96.68	95.67
Palm Beach	102.69	6	98.20	102.94	111.28	102.34	105.34
Pasco	93.79	39	94.47	87.40	96.74	98.82	100.17
Pinellas	101.48	7	99.44	105.99	100.91	98.43	97.99
Polk	95.59	27	95.79	94.11	95.64	97.82	96.06
Putnam	91.92	50	91.91	90.47	89.25	95.39	92.36
St. Johns	98.48	12	104.95	95.09	91.76	99.70	98.27
St. Lucie	95.55	29	102.32	88.39	95.77	98.78	98.12
Santa Rosa	91.98	49	91.40	85.73	93.09	97.54	100.09
Sarasota	104.71	4	106.36	106.88	120.07	97.99	98.52
Seminole	99.13	11	101.67	97.88	88.70	98.30	103.72
Sumter	91.31	56	95.09	88.36	77.91	94.84	94.23
Suwannee	89.19	64	94.19	81.80	90.90	95.78	90.35
Taylor	92.87	42	100.40	83.10	105.15	95.96	95.21
Union	92.22	45	97.02	81.96	109.31	98.70	93.58
Volusia	96.67	22	100.10	95.35	93.59	98.96	93.42
Wakulla	95.56	28	99.64	87.92	108.43	96.48	100.30
Walton	92.08	46	93.67	87.00	93.15	96.85	95.33
Washington	88.97	66	95.01	79.18	95.79	99.65	87.04

Note: The Florida Price Level Index is a set of numbers which reflects the price level in each county relative to population-weighted statewide average (100 for each category) for a particular point in time, 1995. It measures price level differences from place to place in contrast to the consumer price index prepared by the U.S. Bureau of Labor Statistics, which measures price level changes from month to month. The basis for these comparisons is one of fixed standard of living which represents the consumption pattern of a typical wage earner or clerical worker. The index measures in each county the relative cost of living by this standard. See Table 24.79 for relative weights of items priced.

Source: State of Florida, Department of Education, Office of Education Budget and Management, *The 1995 Florida Price Level Index.*

Table 24.85. CONSUMER CONFIDENCE INDEX: TOTAL INDEX AND COMPONENTS OF THE FLORIDA CONSUMER CONFIDENCE INDEX BY MONTH, JULY 1993 THROUGH JUNE 1996

(1966 = 100)

Year	Month	Index 1/	Index component: Current person- al 2/	Future person- al 3/	U.S. 1 year 4/	U.S. 5 years 5/	House- hold pur- chases 6/
1993	7	76.00	74.36	92.20	59.06	55.72	99.34
	8	77.50	78.36	88.06	63.05	60.51	97.60
	9	78.44	73.73	92.03	67.75	61.06	98.41
	11	83.00	78.00	94.00	75.00	67.00	101.00
	12	90.00	82.00	96.00	87.00	79.00	104.00
1994	1	94.00	85.00	104.00	94.00	77.00	107.00
	2	92.00	84.00	95.00	90.00	77.00	115.00
	3	90.00	82.00	96.00	87.00	73.00	114.00
	4	89.00	85.00	99.00	81.00	73.00	109.00
	5	91.00	88.00	100.00	87.00	71.00	112.00
	6	87.00	84.00	99.00	81.00	65.00	107.00
	7	87.00	85.00	100.00	79.00	67.00	105.00
	8	87.00	81.00	97.00	80.00	69.00	109.00
	9	88.00	84.00	98.00	81.00	67.00	111.00
	10	90.00	82.00	99.00	86.00	75.00	110.00
	11	93.00	84.00	100.00	92.00	77.00	110.00
	12	91.00	82.00	100.00	86.00	75.00	110.00
1995	1	94.00	85.00	102.00	93.00	79.00	110.00
	2	93.00	88.00	103.00	89.00	76.00	109.00
	3	91.00	86.00	103.00	85.00	72.00	109.00
	4	90.00	81.00	99.00	87.00	72.00	111.00
	5	88.00	87.00	96.00	79.00	66.00	111.00
	6	91.00	91.00	102.00	82.00	67.00	113.00
	7	91.00	88.00	101.00	89.00	68.00	111.00
	8	92.00	87.00	103.00	88.00	68.00	113.00
	9	92.00	88.00	99.00	88.00	70.00	114.00
	10	90.00	86.00	100.00	85.00	67.00	110.00
	11	89.00	86.00	99.00	87.00	70.00	105.00
	12	87.00	87.00	98.00	84.00	68.00	98.00
1996	1	88.00	91.00	102.00	81.00	68.00	100.00
	2	89.00	89.00	99.00	85.00	67.00	106.00
	3	91.00	87.00	99.00	86.00	71.00	112.00
	4	91.00	88.00	102.00	84.00	71.00	111.00
	5	88.00	86.00	100.00	84.00	71.00	102.00
	6	90.00	89.00	102.00	84.00	69.00	104.00

1/ Based on a monthly telephone survey of approximately 500 randomly selected Florida households through August 1993 and approximately 1,000 thereafter. Survey was not taken in October 1993. Compiled from survey responses giving views of personal financial and general business conditions.
2/ Personal financial conditions at time of survey as compared to previous year.
3/ Personal financial conditions anticipated a year from time of survey.
4/ U.S. business conditions anticipated a year from time of survey.
5/ U.S. business conditions anticipated five years from time of survey.
6/ Perception that the time of survey is a good time to buy major household items.
Source: University of Florida, Bureau of Economic and Business Research, Survey Program, *Florida Economic and Consumer Survey,* July 1996.

STATE COMPARISONS

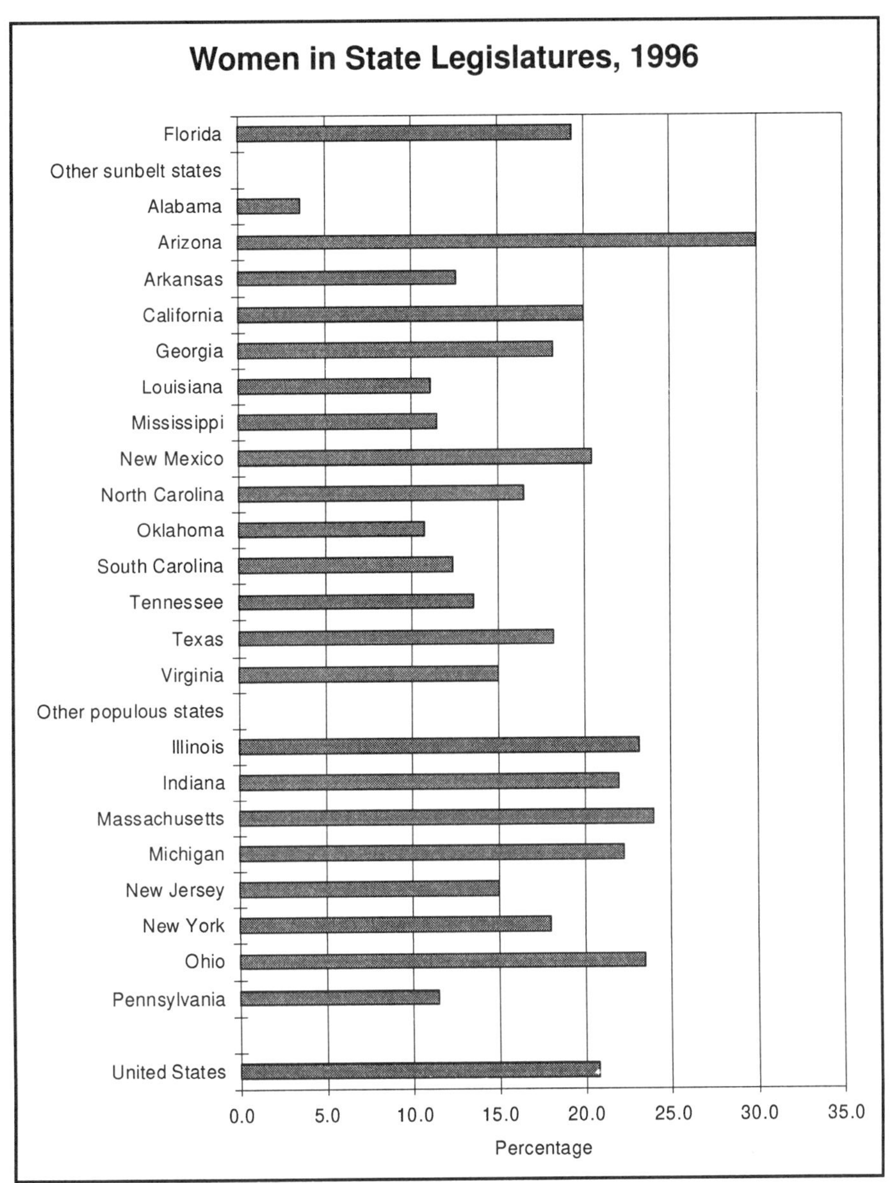
Women in State Legislatures, 1996
Florida
Other sunbelt states
Alabama
Arizona
Arkansas
California
Georgia
Louisiana
Mississippi
New Mexico
North Carolina
Oklahoma
South Carolina
Tennessee
Texas
Virginia
Other populous states
Illinois
Indiana
Massachusetts
Michigan
New Jersey
New York
Ohio
Pennsylvania
United States
0.0
5.0
10.0
15.0
20.0
25.0
30.0
35.0
Percentage

Source: Table 25.01

SECTION 25.00
STATE COMPARISONS

TABLES LISTED BY MAJOR HEADINGS

Table 25.01. SOCIAL STATISTICS AND INDICATORS: DEMOGRAPHIC, ECONOMIC, SOCIAL, AND PHYSICAL CHARACTERISTICS OF FLORIDA, OTHER SUNBELT STATES, OTHER POPULOUS STATES, AND THE UNITED STATES

State	Population					
		July 1, 1995 A/				
	Total April 1 1990 B/ (1,000)	Total (1,000)	Percent-age of population aged 65 and over	Rank among states	Persons per square mile of land area	Per-centage change 1990 to 1995
		Sunbelt states				
Florida	12,938	14,166	18.6	4	262.3	9.5
Alabama	4,040	4,253	13.0	22	83.8	5.3
Arizona	3,665	4,218	13.3	23	37.1	15.1
Arkansas	2,351	2,484	14.5	33	47.7	5.7
California	29,758	31,589	11.0	1	202.5	6.2
Georgia	6,478	7,201	10.0	10	124.3	11.2
Louisiana	4,220	4,342	11.4	21	99.7	2.9
Mississippi	2,575	2,697	12.3	31	57.5	4.7
New Mexico	1,515	1,685	10.9	36	13.9	11.2
North Carolina	6,632	7,195	12.5	11	147.7	8.5
Oklahoma	3,146	3,278	13.5	27	47.7	4.2
South Carolina	3,486	3,673	12.0	26	122.0	5.4
Tennessee	4,877	5,256	12.5	17	127.5	7.8
Texas	16,986	18,724	10.2	2	71.5	10.2
Virginia	6,189	6,618	11.1	12	167.1	6.9
		Other populous states				
Illinois	11,431	11,830	12.5	6	212.8	3.5
Indiana	5,544	5,803	12.6	14	161.8	4.7
Massachusetts	6,016	6,074	14.2	13	774.9	0.9
Michigan	9,295	9,549	12.4	8	168.1	2.7
New Jersey	7,730	7,945	13.7	9	1,070.9	2.8
New York	17,991	18,136	13.4	3	384.0	0.8
Ohio	10,847	11,151	13.4	7	272.3	2.8
Pennsylvania	11,883	12,072	15.9	5	269.3	1.6
United States	248,718	262,755	12.8	(X)	74.3	5.6

(X) Not applicable.
A/ Provisional.
B/ Some data may be revised.

Source: U.S., Department of Commerce, Bureau of the Census, the Internet at <http://www.census.gov/>.

Table 25.01. SOCIAL STATISTICS AND INDICATORS: DEMOGRAPHIC, ECONOMIC, SOCIAL, AND PHYSICAL CHARACTERISTICS OF FLORIDA, OTHER SUNBELT STATES, OTHER POPULOUS STATES, AND THE UNITED STATES (Continued)

State	Population (Continued)					
	July 1, 1995 A/ (Continued)					
	Age (1,000)					
	Under 5	5-17	18-24	25-44	45-64	65 and over
	Sunbelt states					
Florida	968	2,403	1,158	4,151	2,855	2,631
Alabama	301	779	442	1,293	886	552
Arizona	356	837	397	1,276	791	561
Arkansas	173	477	249	708	518	359
California	2,810	5,984	3,000	10,648	5,685	3,463
Georgia	551	1,372	728	2,417	1,414	718
Louisiana	336	903	458	1,303	847	494
Mississippi	209	553	302	781	520	331
New Mexico	138	362	167	505	330	183
North Carolina	514	1,285	715	2,301	1,481	899
Oklahoma	230	648	329	951	677	442
South Carolina	263	682	383	1,154	752	440
Tennessee	365	945	516	1,650	1,121	658
Texas	1,582	3,819	1,930	5,961	3,518	1,914
Virginia	464	1,149	658	2,252	1,359	737
	Other populous states					
Illinois	921	2,205	1,115	3,766	2,339	1,484
Indiana	408	1,079	582	1,815	1,186	733
Massachusetts	413	1,019	536	2,046	1,199	861
Michigan	683	1,837	918	3,017	1,913	1,182
New Jersey	577	1,386	672	2,556	1,663	1,090
New York	1,360	3,177	1,636	5,810	3,730	2,424
Ohio	773	2,087	1,063	3,458	2,280	1,490
Pennsylvania	784	2,125	1,070	3,675	2,501	1,916
United States	19,591	49,149	24,932	83,341	52,210	33,532

A/ Provisional.

Source: U.S., Department of Commerce, Bureau of the Census, the Internet at <http://www.census.gov/>.

Table 25.01. SOCIAL STATISTICS AND INDICATORS: DEMOGRAPHIC, ECONOMIC, SOCIAL, AND PHYSICAL CHARACTERISTICS OF FLORIDA, OTHER SUNBELT STATES, OTHER POPULOUS STATES, AND THE UNITED STATES (Continued)

State	Population (Continued)					
	Median age July 1 1995 B/	Projections, July 1, 2000 A/				Living in metro- politan areas 1992 C/
		Race				
		White	Black	Other races	Hispanic origin 1/	
		Sunbelt states				
Florida	37.6	82.4	15.4	2.2	15.2	93.0
Alabama	34.5	73.2	25.4	1.4	0.8	67.4
Arizona	33.1	87.8	3.0	9.3	23.0	84.7
Arkansas	35.3	83.0	15.3	1.7	1.3	44.7
California	32.3	77.4	7.8	14.9	30.3	96.7
Georgia	32.7	70.0	28.0	2.0	2.3	67.7
Louisiana	32.3	65.9	31.9	2.2	2.8	75.0
Mississippi	32.8	63.2	35.6	1.2	0.7	30.7
New Mexico	32.0	86.3	1.8	11.8	43.4	56.0
North Carolina	34.4	74.6	22.5	2.9	1.6	66.3
Oklahoma	34.5	81.9	7.4	10.7	3.7	60.1
South Carolina	33.4	68.1	30.7	1.2	1.2	69.8
Tennessee	34.9	82.4	16.3	1.3	0.9	67.7
Texas	31.6	84.6	12.2	3.3	30.8	83.9
Virginia	33.7	76.1	19.7	4.1	3.2	77.5
		Other populous states				
Illinois	34.1	79.8	16.1	4.1	10.4	84.0
Indiana	34.2	90.1	8.5	1.4	2.4	71.6
Massachusetts	34.9	90.3	5.9	3.8	6.6	96.2
Michigan	33.7	82.0	15.6	2.4	2.9	82.7
New Jersey	35.7	79.2	15.3	5.5	12.7	100.0
New York	35.2	75.8	18.6	5.6	13.7	91.7
Ohio	34.7	86.8	11.7	1.5	1.8	81.3
Pennsylvania	36.6	88.1	9.9	2.0	2.9	84.8
United States	34.0	6.7	34.2	87.9	0.0	79.7

A/ As a percentage of resident population.
B/ Provisional.
C/ Population in metropolitan statistical areas July 1, as defined through June 30, 1993, as a percentage of resident population. See Glossary for definition.
1/ Persons of Hispanic origin may be of any race.

Source: Column 1, U.S., Department of Commerce, Bureau of the Census, the Internet a <http://www.census.gov/>; Columns 2-5, U.S., Department of Commerce, Bureau of the Census, *Current Population Reports: Population Projections for States, by Age, Sex, Race, and Hispanic Origin, 1993 to 2020*. Series P25-1111; Column 6, U.S., Department of Commerce, Bureau of the Census, *Statistical Abstract of the United States, 1995*.

Table 25.01. SOCIAL STATISTICS AND INDICATORS: DEMOGRAPHIC, ECONOMIC, SOCIAL, AND PHYSICAL CHARACTERISTICS OF FLORIDA, OTHER SUNBELT STATES, OTHER POPULOUS STATES, AND THE UNITED STATES (Continued)

State	Housing					
	Households, July 1, 1994					New privately-owned units permitted 1995 A/ (1,000)
	Percentage change 1/	Persons per household	Age of householder			
			15-44	45-64	65 and over	
Sunbelt states						
Florida	6.3	2.50	2,307	1,568	1,581	122.9
Alabama	5.0	2.61	727	494	363	20.1
Arizona	9.8	2.66	732	430	340	52.7
Arkansas	4.0	2.58	408	284	235	11.7
California	4.5	2.83	5,622	3,186	2,042	83.9
Georgia	9.1	2.67	1,342	787	451	72.2
Louisiana	2.9	2.72	744	479	321	14.7
Mississippi	4.2	2.74	437	291	221	10.8
New Mexico	8.1	2.77	289	182	116	11.0
North Carolina	-4.9	2.55	1,293	820	566	60.9
Oklahoma	2.5	2.56	572	377	288	10.1
South Carolina	6.3	2.66	638	419	280	24.0
Tennessee	6.0	2.57	922	621	424	35.1
Texas	7.7	2.75	3,418	1,937	1,184	105.1
Virginia	6.4	2.60	1,229	757	453	43.1
Other populous states						
Illinois	-4.4	2.66	2,058	1,314	936	47.5
Indiana	-3.8	2.59	1,031	659	470	35.7
Massachusetts	0.8	2.57	1,067	671	528	16.4
Michigan	2.4	2.65	1,678	1,069	754	47.2
New Jersey	1.8	2.72	1,263	923	659	21.5
New York	0.5	2.64	3,041	2,133	1,494	28.1
Ohio	2.5	2.59	1,960	1,281	949	44.8
Pennsylvania	1.2	2.57	1,952	1,387	1,211	36.3
United States	4.4	2.64	46,020	29,049	20,876	1,332.5

A/ Based on a sample of 19,000 permit-issuing places. Data are unadjusted.
1/ April 1, 1990 to July 1, 1994.

Source: U.S., Department of Commerce, Bureau of the Census, the Internet at http://www.census.gov/>.

Table 25.01. SOCIAL STATISTICS AND INDICATORS: DEMOGRAPHIC, ECONOMIC, SOCIAL, AND PHYSICAL CHARACTERISTICS OF FLORIDA, OTHER SUNBELT STATES, OTHER POPULOUS STATES, AND THE UNITED STATES

State	Vital statistics					
	Rate per 1,000 persons				Suicides per 100,000 persons 1993 C/	Percentage of total births to teenage mothers 1993 D/
	Live births 1994 A/	Deaths 1994 A/	Marriages 1994 B/	Divorces 1994 B/		
	Sunbelt states					
Florida	13.7	10.6	10.4	5.9	15.5	13.4
Alabama	14.4	10.0	9.5	6.2	13.2	17.8
Arizona	16.2	8.5	9.0	5.8	18.4	15.1
Arkansas	14.1	10.9	15.6	7.1	13.1	19.4
California	18.5	7.1	6.5	(NA)	12.4	12.0
Georgia	15.4	8.0	8.9	5.2	12.4	16.1
Louisiana	15.9	9.4	9.7	(NA)	12.4	18.7
Mississippi	16.3	10.1	8.4	5.7	12.4	21.7
New Mexico	16.9	7.4	7.4	6.0	17.8	17.8
North Carolina	14.4	9.1	7.3	5.1	11.3	15.3
Oklahoma	14.0	10.0	9.0	6.7	15.2	17.2
South Carolina	13.9	8.6	13.9	4.2	13.5	16.2
Tennessee	14.6	9.6	15.5	6.6	13.2	16.9
Texas	17.5	7.5	10.4	5.4	12.6	16.1
Virginia	14.6	8.2	10.6	4.6	12.1	10.9
	Other populous states					
Illinois	16.1	9.2	7.9	3.7	9.9	12.8
Indiana	14.5	9.3	8.7	(NA)	12.8	14.1
Massachusetts	13.8	9.0	8.2	2.4	7.8	7.8
Michigan	14.7	8.8	7.5	4.1	11.5	12.6
New Jersey	14.8	9.2	6.7	3.0	7.1	7.9
New York	15.4	9.2	8.2	3.3	7.6	9.3
Ohio	14.6	9.5	8.4	4.5	10.4	13.6
Pennsylvania	13.0	10.6	6.3	3.3	11.7	10.5
United States	15.3	8.8	9.1	4.6	12.1	12.8

(NA) Not available.
A/ Preliminary. Birth and death rates are by place of residence and exclude nonresidents of the United States and members of the armed forces abroad.
B/ Preliminary. Marriage and divorce rates are by place of occurrence. Divorces include annulments.
C/ Place of residence and excludes nonresidents of the United States.
D/ Resident female population aged 15-19 years.

Source: Columns 1-4, U.S., Department of Health and Human Services, Centers for Disease Control and Prevention, *Monthly Vital Statistics Report,* Volume 43, No. 13, October 23, 1995; Columns 5, 6, U.S., Department of Commerce, Bureau of the Census, *Statistical Abstract of the United States, 1996.*

Table 25.01. SOCIAL STATISTICS AND INDICATORS: DEMOGRAPHIC, ECONOMIC, SOCIAL, AND PHYSICAL CHARACTERISTICS OF FLORIDA, OTHER SUNBELT STATES, OTHER POPULOUS STATES, AND THE UNITED STATES (Continued)

State	Health					Education
	Community hospital beds per 1,000 population 1993 A/	Hospital care expenditures, 1993 (million dollars)	Number of AIDS cases per 100,000 population 1995 B/	Active physicians per 100,000 population 1994 C/	Percentage of persons not covered by health insurance 1994 D/	Enrollment rate fall 1994 E/
			Sunbelt states			
Florida	3.8	17,131	67.21	219	17.2	91.7
Alabama	4.5	5,301	13.42	175	19.2	94.3
Arizona	2.5	3,999	13.72	201	20.2	99.6
Arkansas	4.5	2,723	11.74	166	17.4	92.3
California	2.5	34,827	34.96	241	21.1	91.4
Georgia	3.9	8,704	32.37	187	16.2	94.6
Louisiana	4.5	5,956	26.05	210	19.2	87.1
Mississippi	4.9	2,897	15.51	132	17.8	91.7
New Mexico	2.6	1,848	13.79	196	23.1	88.2
North Carolina	3.3	7,801	14.36	205	13.3	92.0
Oklahoma	3.7	3,329	8.16	155	17.8	95.1
South Carolina	3.2	4,221	27.16	179	14.2	94.6
Tennessee	4.5	7,208	17.06	218	10.2	93.0
Texas	3.3	21,592	28.04	183	24.2	98.3
Virginia	3.1	7,031	17.55	220	12.0	93.4
			Other populous states			
Illinois	3.8	15,621	23.70	235	11.4	88.5
Indiana	3.7	6,998	9.11	173	10.5	91.2
Massachusetts	3.5	10,034	23.11	373	12.5	89.7
Michigan	3.3	11,711	11.28	200	10.8	87.9
New Jersey	3.9	10,312	60.27	269	13.0	86.9
New York	4.3	28,001	69.23	343	16.0	89.2
Ohio	3.7	14,305	10.70	213	11.0	88.2
Pennsylvania	4.4	19,540	22.22	262	10.6	84.8
United States	3.6	323,919	28.48	230	15.2	91.2

AIDS Acquired Immunodeficiency Syndrome.

A/ Data are for civilian population based on reporting by facilities. B/ Data for the 12 months ending June 30, 1995, using 1994 resident population estimates. C/ Excludes federal physicians and the doctors of osteopathy. Rates are per 100,000 civilian population. D/ Based on civilian noninstitutional population benchmarks established by the 1990 census. E/ Public elementary and secondary school enrollment, fall 1994, as a percentage of persons 5-17 on July 1, 1994.

Source: Columns 1, 2, 3, National Center for Health Statistics, *Health United States, 1995*. Hyattsville, MD: Public Health Service, 1996; Column 4, American Medical Association, Chicago, IL, *Physician Characteristics and Distribution in the U.S.*, annual, (copyright); Column 5, U.S., Department of Commerce, Bureau of the Census, *Current Population Reports: Health Insurance Coverage, 1994*. Series P60-190; Column 6, U.S., Department of Commerce, Bureau of the Census, *Statistical Abstract of the United States, 1996*.

Table 25.01. SOCIAL STATISTICS AND INDICATORS: DEMOGRAPHIC, ECONOMIC, SOCIAL, AND PHYSICAL CHARACTERISTICS OF FLORIDA, OTHER SUNBELT STATES, OTHER POPULOUS STATES, AND THE UNITED STATES (Continued)

State	Education (Continued) Public elementary and secondary schools Average salary of teachers 1993-94 ($1,000)	Education (Continued) Public elementary and secondary schools Current expenditure per pupil in ADA 1992-93 (dollars)	Education (Continued) Number of higher education institutions 1994 A/	Climate Average annual days with rainfall .01 inch or more 1/	Climate Normal seasonal heating degree days 65 degrees base 2/	Personal finances Average revenue per KWH of electricity sold to residences 1994 (cents)
			Sunbelt states			
Florida	31.9	5,314	111	116	1,434	7.8
Alabama	28.7	3,830	80	122	1,702	6.7
Arizona	31.8	4,140	43	36	1,350	9.3
Arkansas	28.1	3,838	35	105	3,155	8.1
California	40.3	4,620	336	35	1,458	11.4
Georgia	30.7	4,730	119	115	2,991	7.7
Louisiana	26.3	4,330	35	114	1,513	7.6
Mississippi	25.2	3,390	46	109	2,467	7.1
New Mexico	27.9	4,643	35	61	4,425	9.1
North Carolina	29.7	4,894	123	112	3,457	8.2
Oklahoma	27.0	4,085	46	83	3,659	7.0
South Carolina	29.6	4,669	59	110	2,649	7.5
Tennessee	30.5	4,033	78	107	3,082	5.9
Texas	30.5	4,900	178	79	2,407	8.1
Virginia	33.0	5,326	93	113	3,963	7.8
			Other populous states			
Illinois	39.4	5,399	167	126	6,536	10.0
Indiana	35.7	5,439	78	126	5,615	6.8
Massachusetts	40.9	6,592	118	127	5,641	11.1
Michigan	45.2	6,402	109	136	6,569	8.3
New Jersey	44.7	9,491	61	112	5,169	11.5
New York	45.8	8,794	314	121	4,805	13.6
Ohio	35.7	5,260	157	137	5,708	8.6
Pennsylvania	42.4	6,914	218	117	4,954	9.6
United States	35.8	5,528	3,688	(X)	(X)	8.4

ADA Average daily attendance.
KWH Kilowatt-hour.
(X) Not applicable.
A/ Includes universities, colleges, professional schools, junior and teachers colleges, both public and private. Branch campuses count as separate institutions.
1/ Period of record through 1994.
2/ Sums of the negative departures of the average daily temperature from 65 degrees Fahrenheit. Period of record is 1961-90.
Note: Climate data are for a major city in each state.

Source: Columns 1-5, U.S., Department of Commerce, Bureau of the Census, *Statistica Abstract of the United States, 1996*; Column 6, U.S., Department of Energy, Energy Information Administration, *Electric Sales and Revenue, 1994*.

Table 25.01. SOCIAL STATISTICS AND INDICATORS: DEMOGRAPHIC, ECONOMIC, SOCIAL, AND PHYSICAL CHARACTERISTICS OF FLORIDA, OTHER SUNBELT STATES, OTHER POPULOUS STATES, AND THE UNITED STATES (Continued)

State	Personal finances (Continued)			Income and wealth		
	Average amount of life insurance in force per household 1994 A/ (dollars)	Automobile registrations per 1,000 persons 1994 C/	State gasoline tax rate December 31, 1994 (cents per gallon)	Median household income 1994 (dollars)	Persons in poverty 1994 (percentage)	Average adjusted gross income 1994 B/ (dollars)
			Sunbelt states			
Florida	94,800	539	12.1	29,294	14.9	31,951
Alabama	116,000	461,712	18.0	27,196	16.4	29,340
Arizona	91,700	453,986	18.0	31,293	15.9	31,166
Arkansas	89,200	315,998	18.7	25,565	15.3	27,037
California	112,300	469,045	18.0	35,331	17.9	35,254
Georgia	137,100	590,730	7.5	31,467	14.0	32,466
Louisiana	105,000	458,352	20.0	25,676	25.7	28,469
Mississippi	93,200	502,253	18.4	25,400	19.9	25,532
New Mexico	98,300	444,156	21.0	26,905	21.1	27,201
North Carolina	116,800	498,630	21.3	30,114	14.2	30,715
Oklahoma	89,000	478,608	17.0	26,991	16.7	28,090
South Carolina	111,400	495,799	16.0	29,846	13.8	28,655
Tennessee	112,100	717,329	20.0	28,639	14.6	30,362
Texas	111,200	473,312	20.0	30,755	19.1	31,245
Virginia	134,000	598,379	17.5	37,647	10.7	35,920
			Other populous states			
Illinois	136,300	529,783	19.0	35,081	12.4	36,818
Indiana	115,100	561,633	15.0	27,858	13.7	32,260
Massachusetts	136,300	507,925	21.0	40,500	9.7	38,035
Michigan	113,200	555,703	15.0	35,284	14.1	35,045
New Jersey	172,800	582,186	10.5	42,280	9.2	41,526
New York	130,700	435,190	22.6	31,899	17.0	38,195
Ohio	119,200	646,500	22.0	31,855	14.1	31,051
Pennsylvania	126,600	500,037	22.4	32,066	12.5	32,887
United States	118,700	514,439	18.4	32,264	14.5	33,472

A/ See Glossary for definition of "household."
B/ Preliminary data from a sample of individual income tax forms.
C/ Based on resident population as of July 1.

Source: Column 1, American Council of Life Insurance, *1995 Life Insurance Fact Book Update*; Columns 2, 3, U.S., Department of Transportation, Federal Highway Administration, *Highway Statistics, 1994;* Columns 4, 5, U.S., Department of Commerce, Bureau of the Census, the Internet at <http://www.census.gov>; Column 6, U.S., Department of the Treasury, Internal Revenue Service, Statistics of Income: *SOI Bulletin*, Spring 1996.

Table 25.01. SOCIAL STATISTICS AND INDICATORS: DEMOGRAPHIC, ECONOMIC, SOCIAL, AND PHYSICAL CHARACTERISTICS OF FLORIDA, OTHER SUNBELT STATES, OTHER POPULOUS STATES, AND THE UNITED STATES (Continued)

State	Income and wealth (Continued)	Business climate				Social insurance and welfare
	Average total income tax 1994 B/ (dollars)	Loan growth rates 1994-95 C/	Firms, 1992 A/ Total	Women-owned (percemtage)	Black-owned (percemtage)	Households in the federal food stamp program 1995 ($1,000)
Sunbelt states						
Florida	6,151	15.8	1,000,542	35.2	4.0	588
Alabama	5,053	12.7	227,119	31.5	6.5	209
Arizona	5,316	14.2	248,337	37.6	1.2	178
Arkansas	4,498	6.9	159,820	31.6	3.6	107
California	6,408	15.0	2,259,327	35.5	3.1	1,176
Georgia	26,754	12.0	425,118	33.6	9.0	329
Louisiana	5,191	19.5	236,589	32.5	8.6	267
Mississippi	4,293	10.8	135,497	30.2	10.4	185
New Mexico	4,533	10.3	107,377	37.8	0.9	87
North Carolina	4,947	14.4	439,301	32.4	6.7	258
Oklahoma	4,662	12.0	246,936	33.6	1.9	153
South Carolina	4,543	19.6	197,330	32.8	9.3	140
Tennessee	5,420	15.4	325,371	31.1	4.6	281
Texas	6,050	14.7	1,256,121	33.0	4.0	948
Virginia	5,939	21.4	391,451	35.4	6.7	235
Other populous states						
Illinois	6,900	14.0	726,974	34.5	3.9	488
Indiana	5,494	11.7	364,253	34.4	2.3	183
Massachusetts	6,822	11.8	442,848	33.3	1.6	178
Michigan	6,173	14.5	551,091	35.2	3.6	418
New Jersey	7,646	4.0	517,204	31.9	3.9	234
New York	7,074	11.7	1,159,700	34.1	4.4	1,027
Ohio	5,109	15.1	666,183	33.7	3.4	506
Pennsylvania	5,658	2.7	728,063	31.2	2.2	515
United States	5,930	12.3	17,253,143	34.1	3.6	10,870

A/ Data from the 1992 economic census.
B/ Preliminary data from a sample of individual income tax forms.
C/ Rates for commercial and industrial loans from December 31, 1994 through December 31, 1995.

Source: Column 1, U.S., Department of the Treasury, Internal Revenue Service, *Statistics of Income: SOI Bulletin,* Spring 1996; Column 2, Federal Deposit Insurance Corporation, *Quarterly Banking Profile,* Fourth Quarter 1995; Columns 3, 5, U.S., Department of Commerce, Bureau of the Census, *1992 Black-owned Businesses,* MB92-1; Column 4, U.S., Department of Commerce, Bureau of the Census, *1992 Women-owned Businesses,* WB92-1; Column 6, U.S., Department of Commerce, Bureau of the Census, *Statistical Abstract of the United States, 1996.*

Table 25.01. SOCIAL STATISTICS AND INDICATORS: DEMOGRAPHIC, ECONOMIC, SOCIAL, AND PHYSICAL CHARACTERISTICS OF FLORIDA, OTHER SUNBELT STATES, OTHER POPULOUS STATES, AND THE UNITED STATES (Continued)

	Social insurance and welfare (Continued)					
State	Average monthly social security benefits 1995 B/ (dollars)	Average weekly state unemployment benefits 1994 (dollars)	Public aid recipients 1994 A/ (percentage)	Average monthly AFDC payment per family 1994 (dollars)	Average Medicaid benefits per recipient 1994 (dollars)	Number of SSI recipients December 1993 (1,000)
	Sunbelt states					
Florida	662.06	168	6.8	279.31	2,470	293
Alabama	590.55	131	6.8	151.70	2,414	C/ 156
Arizona	662.27	148	6.5	309.53	390	C/ 63
Arkansas	581.03	161	6.6	183.12	3,687	91
California	663.50	154	11.7	560.35	1,995	994
Georgia	603.53	153	8.2	252.50	2,623	187
Louisiana	577.08	118	9.7	161.14	3,449	170
Mississippi	549.67	129	10.9	120.14	2,030	134
New Mexico	585.89	140	8.7	365.22	2,380	C/ 40
North Carolina	613.79	175	7.2	225.99	2,726	C/ 175
Oklahoma	527.35	168	6.2	291.03	2,494	C/ 70
South Carolina	608.35	154	6.7	184.80	2,871	C/ 104
Tennessee	604.16	142	9.0	161.10	2,093	168
Texas	617.81	185	6.3	159.63	2,443	D/ 371
Virginia	623.15	169	4.8	281.31	2,680	C/ 118
	Other populous states					
Illinois	692.94	199	8.3	323.06	3,349	C/ 245
Indiana	680.59	158	5.2	273.83	3,721	C/ 82
Massachusetts	666.29	237	7.5	542.40	4,296	149
Michigan	695.31	213	9.1	418.19	2,759	192
New Jersey	728.84	246	6.0	356.08	4,573	134
New York	699.30	203	10.0	544.05	6,441	536
Ohio	664.29	191	8.1	312.91	3,279	214
Pennsylvania	682.41	212	7.2	368.19	3,365	236
United States	648.76	182	7.7	377.78	3,167	5,984

AFDC Aid to Families with Dependent Children. SSI Supplemental Security Income.

A/ June recipients of AFDC and federal SSI as a percentage of resident population, July 1.

B/ Data are for December 1995 and include retired workers, disabled workers, survivors, and children.

C/ Data for persons with federal SSI payments only; state has state-administered supplementation.

D/ Data for persons with federal SSI payments only; state supplementary payments not made.

Source: Columns 1, 4, U.S., Department of Health and Human Services, Social Securit Administration, *Social Security Bulletin: Annual Statistical Supplement, 1996,* prepublication release; Columns 2, 3, 6, U.S., Department of Commerce, Bureau of the Census, *Statistical Abstract of the United States, 1996* and previous edition; Column 5, U.S., Department of Health and Human Services, *Medicaid Statistics: Program and Financial Statistics, Fiscal Year 1994.*

Table 25.01. SOCIAL STATISTICS AND INDICATORS: DEMOGRAPHIC, ECONOMIC, SOCIAL, AND PHYSICAL CHARACTERISTICS OF FLORIDA, OTHER SUNBELT STATES, OTHER POPULOUS STATES, AND THE UNITED STATES (Continued)

State	Employment					
	Labor force participation rate, 1995 A/		Average annual pay 1994 B/ (dollars)	Average weekly earnings for manufacturing 1995 C/ (dollars)	Annual average unemployment rate, 1995 A/	
	Male	Female			Male	Female
	Sunbelt states					
Florida	70.4	54.5	23,925	421.87	5.4	5.6
Alabama	72.4	55.3	23,616	464.54	6.4	6.1
Arizona	76.7	59.6	24,276	472.22	4.7	5.6
Arkansas	71.9	58.4	20,898	412.05	4.0	5.9
California	74.8	56.5	29,878	516.65	7.8	7.9
Georgia	75.8	59.2	25,306	453.03	4.3	5.5
Louisiana	69.8	53.6	23,176	580.18	7.0	6.8
Mississippi	71.4	55.8	20,382	399.34	6.1	6.2
New Mexico	71.9	55.6	22,351	428.00	6.3	6.2
North Carolina	74.7	59.8	23,449	429.14	3.6	5.2
Oklahoma	71.9	55.7	22,292	482.27	4.8	4.5
South Carolina	74.1	59.9	22,477	425.29	3.9	6.3
Tennessee	74.4	60.3	24,106	435.11	5.3	5.1
Texas	79.3	60.0	25,959	490.92	5.6	6.6
Virginia	78.0	63.0	26,031	489.14	4.0	5.0
	Other populous states					
Illinois	77.1	60.3	29,105	526.67	5.3	5.0
Indiana	78.8	64.2	24,908	587.42	4.3	5.1
Massachusetts	75.0	60.8	31,024	533.34	5.8	4.8
Michigan	74.5	57.9	29,541	722.53	5.4	5.3
New Jersey	75.1	58.7	33,439	566.81	6.6	6.2
New York	70.1	52.8	33,438	511.25	6.7	5.9
Ohio	74.5	58.3	26,133	625.83	4.8	4.7
Pennsylvania	71.5	55.0	26,950	529.05	6.0	5.7
United States	75.0	58.9	26,939	(NA)	5.6	5.6

(NA) Not available.
A/ Percentage of civilian noninstitutional population of each specified group in the civilian labor force. Includes persons 16 years old and over.
B/ Data are for workers covered by state and federal unemployment insurance programs.
C/ Average weekly earnings of production workers on manufacturing payrolls.

Source: Columns 1, 2, 5, 6, U.S., Department of Commerce, Bureau of the Census, *Statistical Abstract of the United States, 1996*; Column 3, U.S., Department of Labor, Bureau of Labor Statistics, *News: Average Annual Pay by State and Industry, 1994;* Column 4, U.S., Department of Labor, Bureau of Labor Statistics, *Employment and Earnings*, May 1996.

Table 25.01. SOCIAL STATISTICS AND INDICATORS: DEMOGRAPHIC, ECONOMIC, SOCIAL, AND PHYSICAL CHARACTERISTICS OF FLORIDA, OTHER SUNBELT STATES, OTHER POPULOUS STATES, AND THE UNITED STATES (Continued)

State	Employment (Continued) Percentage distribution of nonagricultural employment, 1995 A/					
	Construction	Manufacturing	Wholesale and retail trade	Finance insurance and real estate	Services	Government
	Sunbelt states					
Florida	5.1	8.0	25.8	6.3	34.3	15.4
Alabama	4.8	21.7	22.8	4.3	21.9	19.0
Arizona	6.6	10.8	25.2	6.0	29.2	16.7
Arkansas	4.1	24.2	22.7	3.9	22.2	16.6
California	3.9	14.4	23.5	5.9	30.0	16.9
Georgia	4.5	17.2	25.3	5.1	24.5	16.8
Louisiana	5.9	10.6	23.5	4.5	26.6	20.1
Mississippi	4.2	24.0	21.2	3.7	21.6	20.2
New Mexico	6.6	6.6	23.8	4.3	27.9	24.0
North Carolina	5.0	24.9	23.1	4.2	22.0	15.9
Oklahoma	3.6	12.9	23.7	5.0	26.2	20.5
South Carolina	5.3	22.9	23.3	4.2	22.0	17.9
Tennessee	4.3	21.7	23.5	4.4	25.4	15.0
Texas	5.1	12.8	24.3	5.4	26.4	18.1
Virginia	5.5	13.1	22.8	5.3	28.4	19.5
	Other populous states					
Illinois	3.9	17.3	23.5	6.9	28.2	14.3
Indiana	4.7	24.6	24.0	4.7	22.7	14.0
Massachusetts	3.0	15.0	23.1	6.9	34.4	13.2
Michigan	3.6	22.9	23.5	4.6	26.2	15.0
New Jersey	3.4	13.9	23.6	6.3	30.0	15.8
New York	3.2	12.0	20.5	9.2	32.2	17.7
Ohio	3.9	21.0	24.4	5.2	26.5	14.3
Pennsylvania	3.8	17.9	22.8	5.8	30.4	13.7
United States	4.5	15.8	23.3	6.0	28.1	16.5

A/ Does not include mining and transportation, communications, and public utilities.

Source: U.S., Department of Labor, Bureau of Labor Statistics, *Employment and Earnings*, May 1996.

Table 25.01. SOCIAL STATISTICS AND INDICATORS: DEMOGRAPHIC, ECONOMIC, SOCIAL, AND PHYSICAL CHARACTERISTICS OF FLORIDA, OTHER SUNBELT STATES, OTHER POPULOUS STATES, AND THE UNITED STATES (Continued)

State	Manufacturing: Jobs won/lost 1993 to 1995 (1,000)	Manufacturing: Rank among states in employment 1995	Manufacturing: As a percentage of gross state product 1992	Agriculture: Farm acreage 1995 B/ (1,000)	Agriculture: Farm cash receipt 1994 A/ Amount (million dollars)	Agriculture: Farm cash receipt 1994 A/ Rank among states
			Sunbelt states			
Florida	-2.8	14	8.7	10,300	5,978	9
Alabama	6.5	19	22.0	10,200	2,904	26
Arizona	16.2	28	12.6	35,400	1,869	32
Arkansas	14.6	24	23.6	15,000	5,276	11
California	-14.7	1	14.2	30,000	20,238	1
Georgia	30.2	11	18.2	12,000	4,716	14
Louisiana	3.0	31	19.4	8,500	2,013	31
Mississippi	2.3	25	24.4	12,900	2,916	25
New Mexico	2.6	43	12.3	44,000	1,524	34
North Carolina	12.9	8	30.8	9,200	6,369	8
Oklahoma	1.2	33	15.6	34,000	3,864	18
South Carolina	3.1	20	26.5	5,050	1,362	35
Tennessee	13.7	12	23.8	12,000	2,152	30
Texas	42.6	3	15.9	129,000	12,552	2
Virginia	-3.1	18	16.1	8,600	2,159	29
			Other populous states			
Illinois	33.6	5	18.6	28,100	8,223	5
Indiana	40.7	9	29.1	15,900	4,838	12
Massachusetts	-9.5	15	18.2	570	459	45
Michigan	66.6	4	27.2	10,700	3,419	20
New Jersey	-16.4	13	16.8	850	768	39
New York	-36.2	6	13.7	7,700	2,858	27
Ohio	51.6	2	26.3	15,200	4,475	16
Pennsylvania	-4.2	7	19.7	7,700	3,755	19
United States	328.0	(X)	17.7	972,253	179,669	(X)

(X) Not applicable.
A/ Includes net commodity credit loans.
B/ As of June 1.

Source: Columns 1, 2, U.S., Department of Labor, Bureau of Labor Statistics, *Employment and Earnings,* May 1996; Column 3, U.S., Department of Commerce, Bureau of Economic Analysis, *Survey of Current Business,* May 1995; Columns 4, 5, 6, U.S., Department of Agriculture, National Agricultural Statistics Service, the Internet at <http://www.usda.mannlib.cornell.edu:70/>.

Table 25.01. SOCIAL STATISTICS AND INDICATORS: DEMOGRAPHIC, ECONOMIC, SOCIAL, AND PHYSICAL CHARACTERISTICS OF FLORIDA, OTHER SUNBELT STATES, OTHER POPULOUS STATES, AND THE UNITED STATES (Continued)

State	Elections			Public safety		
	Percentage of voting-age population voting in 1994	Women in state legislatures, 1996 (percentage)	Hispanic elected officials 1994 A/	Adults on probation per 100,000 resident adults 1993	Inmates enrolled in education programs 1993 B/	Fatal motor vehicle accident rate 1994 C/
	Sunbelt states					
Florida	42.3	19.4	64	1,896	2,919	1.98
Alabama	45.8	3.6	0	1,084	2,500	1.95
Arizona	41.6	30.0	341	1,285	(NA)	2.05
Arkansas	41.6	12.6	2	980	(NA)	2.14
California	45.0	20.0	796	1,241	4,814	1.39
Georgia	35.4	18.2	0	2,861	2,928	1.55
Louisiana	34.2	11.1	12	1,063	1,155	1.99
Mississippi	44.3	11.5	0	527	350	2.41
New Mexico	46.8	20.5	716	676	456	1.89
North Carolina	35.7	16.5	0	1,645	2,598	1.74
Oklahoma	46.8	10.7	1	1,088	869	1.64
South Carolina	45.2	12.4	0	1,444	4,346	2.02
Tennessee	43.0	13.6	0	1,056	1,275	2.03
Texas	37.6	18.2	2,215	2,946	11,976	1.54
Virginia	45.7	15.0	0	482	951	1.22
	Other populous states					
Illinois	42.8	23.2	881	852	5,294	1.51
Indiana	38.7	22.0	8	1,951	(NA)	1.40
Massachusetts	51.6	24.0	1	1,021	2,981	0.86
Michigan	52.2	22.3	8	2,003	5,935	1.48
New Jersey	40.3	15.0	37	1,831	5,240	1.14
New York	44.6	18.0	83	1,141	10,007	1.34
Ohio	46.6	23.5	4	1,193	11,250	1.23
Pennsylvania	42.7	11.5	8	961	3,100	1.43
United States	44.6	20.8	5,459	1,490	9,036	1.53

(NA) Not available.

A/ Persons of Hispanic origin may be of any race.

B/ Enrollment in Adult Basic Education (A.B.E.) and/or General Education Development (G.E.D.) programs as reported by the Federal Bureau of Prisons.

C/ Rate per 100 million vehicle-miles of travel.

Source: Column 1, U.S., Department of Commerce, Bureau of the Census, *Statistical Abstract of the United States, 1995*; Column 2, Center for the American Woman and Politics (CAWP), National Information Bank on Women in Public Office, Eagleton Institute of Politics, Rutgers University, (copyright); Column 3, U.S., Department of Commerce, Bureau of the Census, *Statistical Abstract of the United States, 1996*; Columns 4, 5, U.S., Department of Justice, Bureau of Justice Statistics, *Sourcebook of Criminal Justice Statistics, 1994*; Column 6, U.S., Department of Transportation, Federal Highway Administration, *Highway Statistics, 1994*.

Table 25.01. SOCIAL STATISTICS AND INDICATORS: DEMOGRAPHIC, ECONOMIC, SOCIAL, AND PHYSICAL CHARACTERISTICS OF FLORIDA, OTHER SUNBELT STATES, OTHER POPULOUS STATES, AND THE UNITED STATES (Continued)

	Governmental expenditure					
	State and local government direct general expenditure, per capita, 1992-93 (dollars)					
State	Total	Education	Public welfare	Health and hospitals	Highways	Police protection
		Sunbelt states				
Florida	3,664.11	1,085.18	449.69	374.95	264.23	184.27
Alabama	3,283.06	1,065.81	491.18	599.27	252.03	96.43
Arizona	3,584.80	1,320.07	565.69	196.36	242.43	147.73
Arkansas	2,984.16	1,170.71	543.75	293.30	280.36	74.85
California	4,296.94	1,290.25	681.00	446.69	198.91	192.08
Georgia	3,538.23	1,153.65	542.61	555.75	226.48	117.52
Louisiana	3,845.46	1,140.61	719.69	520.69	264.23	136.75
Mississippi	3,057.37	1,095.61	481.02	451.11	273.85	73.34
New Mexico	4,034.90	1,402.69	496.56	374.46	595.67	138.28
North Carolina	3,320.90	1,234.56	479.03	422.93	239.63	109.81
Oklahoma	3,152.04	1,214.67	470.01	338.83	244.25	97.90
South Carolina	3,437.39	1,207.35	567.93	546.02	195.30	92.36
Tennessee	3,087.32	954.98	574.68	411.07	246.39	95.13
Texas	3,419.96	1,339.71	494.98	333.11	245.70	117.85
Virginia	3,403.08	1,290.47	419.32	293.38	249.99	124.69
		Other populous states				
Illinois	3,646.91	1,220.52	568.78	237.53	286.10	154.06
Indiana	3,486.61	1,310.05	620.58	349.86	236.46	83.84
Massachusetts	4,308.83	1,127.92	862.11	385.55	267.77	138.74
Michigan	3,955.21	1,572.76	654.64	380.99	211.05	127.03
New Jersey	4,588.04	1,618.95	681.99	224.05	286.39	179.46
New York	5,895.74	1,638.87	1,219.36	588.52	273.17	208.56
Ohio	3,598.01	1,304.22	677.03	302.60	232.48	122.18
Pennsylvania	3,747.58	1,340.71	729.25	224.98	227.96	103.80
United States	3,971.51	1,328.92	647.97	367.15	264.29	140.21

Note: Data are preliminary.

Source: U.S., Department of Commerce, Bureau of the Census, the Internet at <http://www.census.gov/>.

Table 25.01. SOCIAL STATISTICS AND INDICATORS: DEMOGRAPHIC, ECONOMIC, SOCIAL, AND PHYSICAL CHARACTERISTICS OF FLORIDA, OTHER SUNBELT STATES, OTHER POPULOUS STATES, AND THE UNITED STATES (Continued)

State	Governmental expenditure (Continued)					
	Federal government expenditure per capita, 1994-95 (dollars)					
	Total	Grants to state and local govern-ments	Salaries and wages	Direct payments to indivi-duals	Pro-cure-ments	Other
	Sunbelt states					
Florida	5,376.42	649.63	516.55	3,536.49	623.45	50.30
Alabama	5,403.53	878.06	701.65	3,034.98	725.20	63.63
Arizona	5,130.27	869.75	592.10	2,870.31	760.22	37.89
Arkansas	4,798.09	863.41	409.87	3,155.93	171.47	197.40
California	4,894.39	948.29	584.64	2,456.08	844.31	61.08
Georgia	4,736.14	835.91	822.16	2,408.29	611.56	58.21
Louisiana	5,220.50	1,276.88	477.08	2,762.62	486.24	217.69
Mississippi	5,338.94	1,036.38	582.04	2,910.67	725.27	84.59
New Mexico	7,151.84	1,235.79	980.82	2,611.82	2,231.50	91.90
North Carolina	4,342.23	834.17	641.19	2,550.43	284.23	32.22
Oklahoma	4,951.49	772.35	802.29	2,900.16	353.51	123.18
South Carolina	4,868.91	849.56	624.78	2,596.10	758.59	39.88
Tennessee	5,141.97	896.26	520.07	2,815.63	864.02	46.00
Texas	4,563.27	788.10	576.42	2,357.76	749.21	91.78
Virginia	7,860.11	598.90	1,834.31	2,741.75	2,533.74	151.43
	Other populous states					
Illinois	4,330.37	807.51	462.59	2,705.38	277.02	77.87
Indiana	4,003.34	634.66	353.11	2,553.60	291.78	170.18
Massachusetts	5,929.81	1,259.00	488.81	3,093.72	1,025.14	63.14
Michigan	4,166.62	855.77	301.95	2,753.68	212.11	43.11
New Jersey	4,797.72	859.61	449.04	2,916.66	539.36	33.05
New York	5,209.21	1,390.06	393.98	3,040.32	334.74	50.11
Ohio	4,550.09	819.74	415.72	2,866.04	403.10	45.49
Pennsylvania	5,360.74	930.98	491.34	3,427.83	444.76	65.84
United States 1/	5,180.29	918.28	636.48	2,762.33	765.40	97.80

1/ Average.

Source: U.S., Department of Commerce, Bureau of the Census, the Internet at <http://www.census.gov/>.

APPENDIX. EXPLANATORY NOTES AND SOURCES

SECTION 1.00. POPULATION

EXPLANATORY NOTES. The University of Florida Bureau of Economic and Business Research Population Program prepared a revised series of intercensal population estimates for the 1980s that appears in Table 1.20. Extreme caution must be exercised when deriving annual changes from successive estimates. Calculating such changes can lead to inaccurate conclusions regarding population growth, especially for small places. The best base of any estimate of population change is generally the most recent census enumeration.

Counties and municipalities are legal and political entities, but, from a sociological point of view the community of which a person considers himself or herself to be a part may not correspond to such an entity. Terms like "Greater Jacksonville" or "the Miami area" are used to indicate the real community. People do not hesitate to cross city or county limits or even state lines to work, to buy or sell, or to seek cultural, medical, recreational, or social services. For this reason, the U.S. Office of Management and Budget has designated areas known as Metropolitan Statistical Areas (MSAs). An MSA is a geographic area with a large population nucleus together with adjacent communities having a high degree of economic and social integration with that nucleus. These areas were designated as Standard Metropolitan Statistical Areas (SMSAs) before January 1983. New MSA designations were announced effective June 1983 and more recently, December 31, 1992.

Generally an area qualifies for recognition as an MSA in one of two ways: if there is a city of at least 50,000 population or an urbanized area of at least 50,000 with a total metropolitan population of at least 100,000. An MSA may include a single county or several counties that have close economic and social ties to a central city or urban area. In metropolitan complexes of one million or more population, separate component areas (previously MSAs or SMSAs) are defined if specified criteria are met. Such areas are designated Primary Metropolitan Statistical Areas (PMSAs) and any area containing PMSAs is designated as a Consolidated Metropolitan Statistical Area (CMSA).

In Florida, MSAs are defined in terms of entire counties. Population living in MSAs may be referred to as the metropolitan population. Nineteen MSAs were designated in Florida effective June 1983 and a twentieth was designated in June 1984. The two areas redefined as PMSAs together comprise the Miami-Ft. Lauderdale CMSA. On December 31, 1992, new MSA designations went into effect (see map on page vii). Florida's total remained twenty although several areas were redefined, two were combined and one was added. Table 1.65 contains population figures for Florida's current MSAs.

Agencies of the state government have grouped counties into different districts. There are eleven planning districts, each containing several counties that have common interests and needs for planning community development. A map on page 45 shows the counties by planning districts. Department of Health and Rehabilitative Services (HRS) districts are mapped on page 227, water management districts are on page 249, and crop-reporting-district boundaries are on page 303.

SOURCES. The Census of Population taken once every ten years by the U.S. Bureau of the Census provides basic statistics about population. Selected Florida data from the 1990 census are included in this *Abstract*. Table 1.19 contains a historical population series for counties beginning with the 1940 census.

At the back of this volume is an index of the most recent census information appearing in previous editions. In 1994, the Bureau of Economic and Business Research (BEBR), University of Florida, published a collection of county 1990 census data titled *1990 Census Handbook - Florida*. This volume also includes some 1980 data for comparison and information on how to use census data, primary census sources, and census definitions.

In addition to the decennial censuses, the Census Bureau issues a series of *Current Population Reports*, known as P-Series. These contain national, regional, and sometimes state population statistics resulting from periodic surveys, special censuses, and cooperative estimation and projection efforts between the individual states and the Census Bureau.

Between census years, estimates of the population of the state, counties, and municipalities of Florida are made by the BEBR Population Program. These are released annually in *Florida Estimates of Population.*

The *Abstract* contains estimates and projections of population by age, race, and sex. Benchmark data are from the 1990 census. The age, race, and sex estimates and projections are developed by BEBR and released in the *Florida Population Studies* series. New Table 1.36 highlights Hispanic population estimates by sex and age for Florida and its counties as published in a recent BEBR special population report. BEBR also provides unpublished data on total net migration and migration of persons aged 65 and over to Florida in new Table 1.73. Voting-age population estimates and projections are presented in Section 21.00.

Data on veterans come from the U.S. Department of Veterans Affairs in Washington, which releases reports on the age, location, and period of service of veterans. Data on immigrants are from the U.S. Immigration and Naturalization Services. Data on intercounty migration in Table 1.74 are from the Internal Revenue Service.

SECTION 2.00. HOUSING

SOURCES. The decennial Census of Housing is taken simultaneously with the Census of Population and provides basic information about people in their living arrangements. Tables from the 1990 census were not included in this volume to provide space for more timely statistics throughout the volume. However, extensive data from the 1990 Census of Housing can be found in previous *Abstracts* (refer to the census index at the back of this volume) and in the previously mentioned *1990 Census Handbook - Florida.*

The Census Bureau also issues the *Current Housing Reports* series, which provide statistics compiled on subjects from the decennial or special censuses and surveys such as the American Housing Survey (formerly Annual Housing Survey). Estimates of housing units and households in every state are now available as unpublished data on the Internet and appear in Table 2.01. Data on homeownership rates in new Table 2.02 are from the Census Bureau's *Housing Vacancy Survey* and are also available on the Internet.

The Bureau of Economic and Business Research (BEBR), University of Florida, makes annual estimates of the number of households and average household size for intercensal years. These are published in the series, *Florida Population Studies*.

Three agencies of the State of Florida provide information relating to housing. The Division of Motor Vehicles of the Department of Highway Safety and Motor Vehicles annually publishes the number of tags sold to owners of mobile homes and recreational vehicles. The Division of Hotels and Restaurants of the State Department of Business and Professional Regulation publishes statistics on apartment houses, rooming houses, and licensed lodgings. The Office of Education Budget and Management, Department of Education provides prices of average housing by county and the Florida Price Level Index, which includes a housing component.

The Florida Association of Homes for the Aging provides a list of homes with locations, number of units and beds in the annual *Directory of Members*. Data on home sales and median sales prices in metropolitan areas, are provided in unpublished form by the Florida Association of Realtors and the University of Florida's Real Estate Research Center.

SECTION 3.00. VITAL STATISTICS AND HEALTH

EXPLANATORY NOTES. Vital statistics usually include data on births, infant deaths, abortions, illegitimate births, marriages, divorces, annulments, and deaths by cause. For births and deaths, "resident" is the term indicating births or deaths among residents of a specified area regardless of where the event occurred. "Recorded" is the term used to identify births or deaths occurring in a specified area regardless of the usual residence of the person counted. The birth and death figures in this section are resident data. Marriages and dissolutions of marriage are reported by place of occurrence. Cases of Acquired Immunodeficiency Syndrome (AIDS) in Table 3.28 of this *Abstract* are diagnosed cases and reported cases. There is a time lag—occasionally as much as several years—between diagnosis of a case according to national Centers for Disease Control criteria and the case's entry into the Florida Department of Health and Rehabilitative Services (HRS) AIDS Reporting System.

SOURCES. The Public Health Statistics Section of HRS is the principal source of vital statistics data for Florida and its counties. Data are released monthly in *Vital News* and later accumulated in an annual report, *Florida Vital Statistics*.

Death rates by leading cause, as shown in new Table 3.15, are provided by the Florida Agency for Health Care Administration in cooperation with Local Health Councils of Florida. Their new publication, *Florida 1996 Health Data SourceBook,* profiles general health care in the state and counties. Other tables from this source can be found in Sections 7.00 and 20.00.

Statistics on AIDS are available from the State Health Office of the HRS. Data on child and teen deaths, maltreatments and runaways are used with permission from a copyrighted publication, Volume V of *The 1994 Florida Kids Count Data Book* produced by the University of South Florida, Florida Mental Health Institute, and the state Center for Children and Youth.

SECTION 4.00. EDUCATION

EXPLANATORY NOTES. In census counts and estimates of population, persons of Hispanic origin are considered to be of any race. Some duplication of data results when persons of Hispanic origin are summed with race data. The Florida Department of Education, on the other hand, reports persons of Hispanic origin as a separate entry. Therefore, totals are not complete unless persons of Hispanic origin are included. Every effort has been made to individually note the differences on the education tables where this occurs.

SOURCES. The principal sources of information on education in Florida include the annual *Profiles of Florida School Districts*, reports from the Bureau of Education Information and Accountability Services of the Division of Public Schools, other publications, and unpublished data from the Florida Department of Education.

Enrollment information about the State University System is available in the *Fact Book* published by the Florida Board of Regents. Accredited colleges and universities enrollment data are published by the Office of Educational Research and Improvement of the National Center for Education Data, U.S. Department of Education in the *Directory of Postsecondary Institutions*. Data on public community colleges come from reports of the State Board of Community Colleges, Florida Department of Education.

Data on the extent of public and private education, exceptional programs, the level achieved by the pupils, and the availability and enrollments of schools, colleges, and universities are all included in Section

4.00. Employment and finances of educational institutions and data on educational services are in Section 20.00. Additional information on the public funding of education is in Section 23.00.

SECTION 5.00. INCOME AND WEALTH

EXPLANATORY NOTES. The earnings components of personal income are allocated on a place-of-work basis. These earnings are converted to a place-of-residence basis by means of a residence adjustment factor. Property income and transfer payments are then added to earnings, resulting in total income on a place-of-residence basis. This conversion is illustrated in Table 5.14. The first basis, earnings by place of work, is useful in the analysis of the income structure of a given area in terms of industrial markets and purchasing power. Expressed per capita, the latter basis, earnings by place of residence, is an indicator of living standards and welfare level. See Section 9.00 for estimates of farm income.

Families and unrelated individuals are classified as being above or below the poverty level by comparing their calendar-year money income to an income cutoff or "poverty threshold." The income cutoffs vary by family size, number of children, and age of the family householder or unrelated individual. Poverty status is determined for all families (and, by implication, all family members). Poverty status is also determined for persons not in families, except for inmates of institutions, members of the Armed Forces living in barracks, college students living in dormitories, and unrelated individuals under 15 years old.

The poverty thresholds are revised annually to reflect changes in the Consumer Price Index. The poverty threshold for a family of four in 1995 was $15,570, as shown on Table 5.46. Poverty thresholds are computed on a national basis only. No attempt has been made to adjust these thresholds for regional, state, or other local variations in the cost of living.

The Statistics of Income series data published by the U.S. Internal Revenue Service are based on the tax-defined concept, adjusted gross income (AGI), which excludes certain types of income. Caution should be exercised in comparing these data over time as annual changes in tax law will continue to affect the definition of AGI.

State data showing distribution of income by income class are no longer published by the U.S. Internal Revenue Service. Table 5.03 presents percentage of income in the state distributed by household size and income class based on results from the Florida Consumer Attitude Survey, Bureau of Economic and Business Research (BEBR), University of Florida.

SOURCES. The source for statistics on personal income in Florida is the U.S. Department of Commerce, Bureau of Economic Analysis (BEA). The BEA has made comprehensive estimates of personal income, by type and industrial source, covering all metropolitan areas and counties in the nation for selected years from 1929 through 1994. Annual estimates are published in *Survey of Current Business*. Data in this *Abstract* are from the BEA's Regional Economic Information System (REIS) CD-ROM for June 1996.

Updated estimates of national poverty thresholds are published annually in the *Statistical Abstract of the United States* and can be found on the Internet. Poverty thresholds based on money income are published annually by the U.S. Bureau of the Census in *Current Population Reports*, Series P60 and are also on the Internet.

The income of military retirees appears in the Department of Defense publication *DOD Statistical Report on the Military Retirement System.*

A source for income data is the U.S. Internal Revenue Service. Data such as income sources, tax deductions, and credits are from statistical samplings of individual tax returns and are reported in the series *Statistics of Income.*

The data on income distribution for the state by income class are from the BEBR Florida Consumer Attitude Survey.

SECTION 6.00. LABOR FORCE, EMPLOYMENT, AND EARNINGS

EXPLANATORY NOTES. Tables of employment and payroll devoted to individual industries and nonprofit organizations are presented in this section and in other sections of *Abstract.* Data are defined by the State Unemployment Insurance Program and are often termed "covered employment" or "ES-202" data. Any firm or nonprofit establishment whose employees are covered by state and federal unemployment laws must submit monthly reports on the number of persons on its payroll and the amount employees were paid. The data generated from these reports provide useful measures of the impact of various industries, firms, or other organizations on the economies of the state and its counties. The Bureau of Labor Market Information of the Florida Department of Labor and Employment Security compiles these statistics. Many tables in this *Abstract* include revised data for 1994 as well as unpublished figures for 1995.

Covered employment data include most employed persons in Florida, but certain workers are specifically excluded from coverage. These are some agricultural and domestic employees, self-employed workers, and elected officials. Among the excluded self-employed are such occupations as insurance or real estate agents whose earnings are from commissions. Certain nonprofit organizations such as churches may elect to participate in the program.

Also missing from the tables are data for the state or counties in which there were so few units that the information for an individual establishment might be made public or estimated by competitors. In these instances and when one firm in a specific category or county has 80 percent of the employment of all the business in that category or county, no data are reported. Often data may be undisclosed at the level of the county or 3-digit SIC industry group but are reported in aggregate at the state level. Disclosure guidelines adopted by the Department of Labor and Employment Security in keeping with federal rules prevent publication of reporting units and employment ranges for undisclosed establishments.

The derivation and meaning of SIC codes are briefly discussed in the Preface and the Glossary, which lists the major industrial groups and codes. Table 6.03 presents data for all covered employees by industry and Tables 6.04 and 6.05 present employment data by county. Tables in various sections present state and county data by major industries and industry subgroupings, such as Tables 12.50, 12.51, 12.52, and 12.53, 13.36 and 13.37, etc.

Detailed employment data for governments appear in Section 23.00.

SOURCES. The basis of statistics on the employment status of the population is a monthly Current Population Survey (CPS) conducted by the U.S. Bureau of the Census and detailed data (e.g., employment by occupation, labor force status by age, race, sex) are available from the decennial censuses. The U.S. Bureau of Labor Statistics publishes monthly data from the CPS in *Employment and Earnings* and other related publications listed below. The Bureau of Labor Market Information (BLMI), Department of Labor and Employment Security of the State of Florida has the responsibility of preparing estimates of employment status following procedures developed in cooperation with the U.S. Bureau of Labor Statistics (BLS). The BLMI publishes information about Florida, its counties, metropolitan areas, and cities in *Florida Labor Force Summary*, and releases special reports on small counties. Different samples are used to prepare these sets of employment and unemployment estimates. Its *Florida Industry and Occupational Employment Projections* is published annually.

The U.S. BLS compiles statistics and publishes data on nonagricultural employment in Florida and its metropolitan areas. Its publications include monthly *Employment and Earnings* and *Geographic Profile of Employment and Unemployment.* It also publishes a series of bulletins or releases under the title *News.* Much of the BLS published data are also available on the Internet.

The U.S. Equal Opportunity Commission publishes the occupational distribution data shown in new Table 6.20 in *Job Patterns for Minorities and Women in Private Industry.*

The Florida Department of Commerce, Bureau of Economic Analysis publishes *Florida Facts: Florida's Fifty Largest Private Employers.*

The U.S. Bureau of Economic Analysis provides data on farm proprietors and wage and salary workers. Farm employment data appear in Section 9.00.

SECTION 7.00. SOCIAL INSURANCE AND WELFARE

EXPLANATORY NOTES. For purposes of managing state-administered public assistance programs, the state has been divided into fifteen Health and Rehabilitative Services districts; a map showing these districts appears on page 227.

SOURCES. The source of statistics on Social Security programs is the U.S. Department of Health and Human Services, Social Security Administration *Social Security Bulletin*, published monthly with an annual statistical supplement. The department also publishes data on state programs in *OASDI Beneficiaries by State and County* and *SSI Recipients by State and County*, and releases unpublished data.

Specified characteristics about unemployment insurance are published in the *Social Security Bulletin: Annual Statistical Supplement.* Historical average weekly wages and unemployment insurance contribution and disbursement data are provided by the Florida Department of Labor and Employment Security. Workers' compensation program data are published periodically in the *Social Security Bulletin*. County data on injuries and cost by industry are reported in the Florida Department of Labor and Employment Security, Division of Workers' Compensation *Report on Occupational Injuries*.

The Health Care Financing Administration in the U.S. Department of Health and Human Services provides unpublished data on Medicare.

Four public assistance programs—for the aged, the blind, the permanently and totally disabled, and dependent children—are administered by the state but are financed in part by the federal government in grants to states under the Social Security Act. The principal source of state and national data on these programs is the U.S. Department of Health and Human Services, Social Security Administration *Social Security Bulletin: Annual Statistical Supplement*.

The principal source of data on Florida and its counties is the Florida Agency for Health Care Administration. The agency also provides unpublished data on Medicaid recipients and expenditures by county. Published statistics on persons eligible for Medicaid are found in *Florida 1996 Health Data SourceBook* produced in cooperation with Local Health Councils of Florida. Food stamp data are provided in *Florida Food Stamp Program Participation Statistics* by the state Department of Health and Rehabilitative Services.

SECTION 8.00. PHYSICAL GEOGRAPHY AND ENVIRONMENT

SOURCES. Tables in this section containing information relating to temperature, precipitation, and other climatic phenomena present data supplied by the Environmental Satellite, Data, and Information Service of the National Oceanic and Atmospheric Administration (NOAA), U.S. Department of Commerce. Their publications are issued both annually and monthly under the title, *Climatological Data: Florida*. A map of National Weather Station Offices appearing on Table 8.70 is on page 255. Hurricane data are published in periodic NOAA technical memoranda.

The Geography Division of the Bureau of the Census, U.S. Department of Commerce provides revised data on the land and water area of the state and counties of Florida based on TIGER mapping files from the 1990 Census of Population and Housing.

The Division of Air Resources Management, Florida Department of Environmental Protection provides information on air pollution in the report *Comparison of Air Quality Data with the National Ambient Air Quality Standards*.

Data on water use are collected by the United States Geological Survey, five water management districts in the state, and the Florida Department of Environmental Regulation. A map of the water management districts with district headquarters is on page 249. Some water-use data are obtained from utilities and information on agricultural irrigation is collected by the Institute of Food and Agricultural Sciences at the University of Florida and the State of Florida Department of Agriculture and Consumer Services. The water-use data were compiled from these various sources by the United States Geological Survey, Florida District in cooperation with the Florida Department of Environmental Protection.

Solid waste data are published by the Bureau of Solid and Hazardous Waste, Florida Department of Environmental Protection in the annual report *Solid Waste Management in Florida*.

SECTION 9.00. AGRICULTURE

EXPLANATORY NOTES. Since 1840 a Census of Agriculture has been taken every five years. Congress authorized agricultural censuses to be taken in 1978 and 1982 to coincide with the quinquennial economic censuses. After 1982, the agricultural census again reverted to a five-year cycle to be taken in years ending in "2" and "7." Some parts of the 1992 Economic Census are included in this *Abstract*. An index at the back of this book lists recent census tables appearing in previous *Abstracts*. As defined since the 1978 census, a farm is "any place from which $1,000 or more of agricultural products were sold or normally would have been sold during the census year." Because data for selected items are collected from a sample of operators, the results are subject to sampling variability. Dollar values have not been adjusted for changes in price levels between census years.

When comparisons are made between Florida and other states, the other states selected either have a similar climate (the southern tier of Sunbelt states) or produce similar crops (citrus in Arizona and California, sugarcane in Hawaii and Louisiana, etc.).

SOURCES. Timely and detailed data on farm receipts, income, taxes, and value of farm marketings are provided in tables based on annual publications of the U.S. Department of Agriculture, *Agricultural Statistics* and *Economic Indicators of the Farm Sector*, as well as on the Internet. The U.S. Department of Commerce, Bureau of Economic Analysis provides additional farm-income data. Some data on farm income also appear in Section 5.00.

Data primarily covering characteristics of farms and farm operators are from the *1992 Census of Agriculture* published by the U.S. Department of Commerce, Bureau of the Census.

Agricultural employment information comes from the Bureau of Economic Analysis, U.S. Department of Commerce and from the Bureau of Labor Market Information, Florida Department of Labor and Employment Security. (See discussion under Section 6.00 of this Appendix.)

Information about citrus production, cash receipts, other crop cultivation, and livestock is from the Florida Agricultural Statistics Service, Florida Department of Agriculture and Consumer Services. A map of counties in crop-reporting districts appears on page 303. A complete series of crop estimates for the state dating back to 1919 is available from the reporting service upon request. The Florida Department of Citrus provides information on orange juice sales from A. C. Nielsen market research reports. The Florida Department of Business and Professional Regulation has data on veterinarians licensed in the state.

The Agricultural Stabilization and Conservation Service, U.S. Department of Agriculture provides state and county estimates of nonresident alien ownership of agricultural land.

SECTION 10.00 FORESTRY, FISHERIES, AND MINERALS

SOURCES. Forestry employment and payroll data come from the Bureau of Labor Market Information, Florida Department of Labor and Employment Security, as does similar information for fishing and mining. (See discussion under Section 6.00 of this Appendix.) The Division of Forestry of the Florida Department of Agriculture and Consumer Services provides data on the harvest of forest products. The

Forest Service, U.S. Department of Agriculture publishes data on national forests in *Land Areas of the National Forest System*.

The Marine Fisheries Information System, Florida Department of Natural Resources provides unpublished data on fish landings. The National Marine Fisheries Service of the National Oceanic and Atmospheric Administration, U.S. Department of Commerce publishes data on fishery products, plants, and co-operatives in its annual *Fisheries of the United States*. Table 19.45 in Section 19.00 gives information on the number of commercial boats registered in the state and counties of Florida.

Basic data on the production of minerals are from specific industry reports of the Bureau of Mines, U.S. Department of the Interior, and the *1992 Census of Mineral Industries*. The Bureau of Mines was disbanded in January 1996. Data may now be obtained from the U.S. Geological Survey.

SECTION 11.00. CONSTRUCTION

SOURCES. Statistics on building construction activity and characteristics of that industry (SIC codes 15-17) are in this section. The principal sources of building permit data for Florida are the Bureau of Economic and Business Research (BEBR), University of Florida, and the U.S. Bureau of the Census. The BEBR publishes monthly and annual summaries on the type and value of building permits for construction issued by local administrative offices throughout Florida in *Building Permit Activity in Florida*. The BEBR compiles, and makes available in unpublished form, data on construction starts appearing in new Table 11.05.

In December 1995, the Census Bureau discontinued the monthly publication *Current Construction Reports: Housing Units Authorized by Building Permits*. Some types of previously published data can now be found on the Internet. Building permit and housing starts data for states and producer prices of materials used in construction in the U.S. are from *Construction Review* published by the International Trade Administration of the U.S. Department of Commerce.

Data on employment and payrolls are supplied by the Bureau of Labor Market Information, Florida Department of Labor and Employment Security. (See discussion under Section 6.00 of this Appendix.)

SECTION 12.00. MANUFACTURING

SOURCES. Major industry divisions for manufacturing comprise SIC codes 20-39. Data on the number of units, employees, and payroll for these establishments were obtained from the Bureau of Labor Market Information, Florida Department of Labor and Employment Security. A number of industries are detailed in tables in this section and many include county breakdowns.

The U.S. Bureau of the Census conducts a complete count of manufactures every five years as part of its comprehensive economic census. Data from the *1992 Census of Manufactures* appears on new Table 12.06. The Bureau of the Census also conducts, in intervening years, a sample survey called the *Annual Survey of Manufactures*.

Unpublished data on the value of Florida products are made available by the Bureau of Economic Analysis, Florida Department of Commerce using the University of Massachusetts Institute for Social and Economic Research (MISER) program.

SECTION 13.00. TRANSPORTATION

SOURCES. The U.S. Department of Transportation provides data on roads and highways, tax receipts, bridges, and vehicles in *Highway Statistics*, a publication of the Federal Highway Administration.

Information about licenses, drivers of motor vehicles, and motor vehicle registrations comes from the Florida Department of Highway Safety and Motor Vehicles. The same department publishes accident data in *Florida Traffic Crash Facts* and automobile tag and revenue data in *Revenue Report.*

Every five years the Bureau of the Census conducts an economic census that includes a *Census of Transportation Industries*. Table 13.01 provides establishment, revenue, and annual payroll data for the transportation, communications, and public utilities industries in the state. An index at the back of the book lists tables from recent censuses appearing in previous editions of *Abstract*.

Employment and payroll figures for all modes of transportation except interstate railroads are supplied by the Bureau of Labor Market Information, Florida Department of Labor and Employment Security. A county-level aggregate of establishments in SIC codes 40-49 appears in new Table 13.36. Interstate railroads are not included because their employees are not covered by the same unemployment law as workers in other industries.

Data on miles of track in the state's rail system are from the Office of Planning, Florida Department of Transportation publication, *Florida Rail System Plan.*

Water transportation (SIC code 44) includes both the movement of vessels through Florida waterways and the volume of commodities shipped into and out of Florida ports. The authorities of the various ports in the state have supplied data on their activities.

Data on exports and imports through Florida customs are from a publication of the Bureau of Economic Analysis, Florida Department of Commerce, *Florida International Trade Update.*

Air traffic information comes from the Federal Aviation Administration of the U.S. Department of Transportation, *FAA Air Traffic Activity* and unpublished data. Air pilot data come from the publication *U.S. Civil Airmen Statistics*. Due to federal budget cut-backs, these publications are being discontinued. However, the data previously found in published form is expected to be on the Internet in the near future.

SECTION 14.00. COMMUNICATIONS

EXPLANATORY NOTES. Newspaper publishing and other print media (SIC code 27) are considered to be manufacturing by the U.S. Bureau of the Census as well as the Office of Management and Budget, which establishes the Standard Industrial Classification. Since newspapers, periodicals, and books compete with electronic media in providing communications, data are repeated in this section. Table 12.50 in Section 12.00 shows newspapers as a component of the manufacturing industry. Also included in Section 14.00 are data on telephones (SIC code 481), telegraph (SIC code 482), radio and television broad-casting (SIC code 483), and cable and other pay TV services (SIC code 484).

SOURCES. Postal revenue data are provided by the U.S. Postal Service. The Florida Public Service Commission supplies data on telephone companies servicing Florida, including the data on number of calls, billed minutes, and rates. Employment and payroll data are from the Bureau of Labor Market Information, Florida Department of Labor and Employment Security. (See discussion under Section 6.00 of this Appendix.)

SECTION 15.00. POWER AND ENERGY

SOURCES. Data in this section have been selected to describe the status of the electric, gas, and sanitary service industries, and the consumption and production of electricity, gas, gasoline, fuel oil, and nuclear power. Energy information is supplied in various publications by the Energy Information Administration, U.S. Department of Energy. Data on U.S. nuclear power plants in Table 15.50 are used with permission from *World Nuclear Performance*, a copyrighted publication of McGraw-Hill, Inc.

A major source of data on electrical energy in Florida is *Statistics of the Florida Electric Utility Industry* published by the Florida Public Service Commission.

The Florida Department of Community Affairs (DCA) publishes *Florida Energy Data Report, 1970-1992*, from which some historical data for Table 15.08 were obtained. The DCA also compiled and provided information from U.S. Department of Energy published and unpublished data on energy consumption, pricing, and production along with state and county data on motor fuel consumption. Another source of state motor fuel data is *Highway Statistics*, published by the Federal Highway Administration.

The Bureau of Labor Market Information of the State Department of Labor and Employment Security supplies information on employment and payroll in the utility industry. (See discussion under Section 6.00 of this Appendix.)

Information on consumer prices of energy as measured by the Consumer Price Index is reported in Section 24.00.

SECTION 16.00. WHOLESALE AND RETAIL TRADE

SOURCES. Covered employment and payroll information by kind of business and county comes from the Bureau of Labor Market Information (BLMI), Florida Department of Labor and Employment Security. (See the discussion under Section 6.00 of this Appendix.) Since there are some differences in coverage and classification, BLMI figures are not necessarily comparable with those from the economic censuses conducted by the Bureau of the Census every five years. Data from the *1992 Census of Wholesale Trade* and *1992 Census of Retail Trade* comprise several tables in this section (An index of recent census tables appearing in previous *Abstracts* is at the back of this edition.) Number of establishments, employment, payroll, and sales are presented both by kind of business and by county in which the establishments are located.

The Florida Department of Revenue is the source for information on sales reported by firms in connection with the sales and use tax laws. In addition to the data presented in this section, printouts of county gross and taxable sales by business category are available from the Bureau of Economic and Business Research (BEBR), University of Florida on a subscription basis. These business categories vary in coverage and classification from the Bureau of the Census and the Florida Department of Commerce figures. Data on retail sales tax collections may be found in Table 23.43. A time series of gross and taxable sales is in Table 24.30.

Health professionals who operate at the retail level and are required to have a license such as dispensing opticians or pharmacists are reported by the Florida Department of Business and Professional Regulation. These data are presented in Section 20.00.

SECTION 17.00. FINANCE, INSURANCE, AND REAL ESTATE

EXPLANATORY NOTES. Industries covered in this section are those SIC codes numbered 60 through 67, including banking and other credit agencies, establishments dealing in securities and commodities, insurance and real estate offices, and investment firms.

SOURCES. Historical and recent summaries of banking data for Florida may be found in the *Annual Report of the Division of Banking*, published by the state Office of the Comptroller. Another major source of banking data is the Federal Deposit Insurance Corporation, which issues *Statistics on Banking* and *Data Book: Operating Banks and Branches*.

Figures on number of establishments, employment, and payroll for banking and credit, insurance, real estate and investment industries come from the Florida Department of Labor and Employment Security, Bureau of Labor Market Information. (See the discussion in Section 6.00 of this Appendix.)

A source of information on savings institutions is *Summary of Deposits in SAIF-Insured OTS Regulated Associations*. The mortgage loan activity data are presented in Table 17.33 by permission of TRW

REDI Property Data, Inc. This firm collects loan activity data in forty counties and provides reports by subscription.

Data on homeowner and rental vacancy rates appearing in new Table 17.47 are from the Bureau of the Census, U.S. Department of Commerce publication *Housing Vacancy Survey*. These data may also be found on the Internet.

A basic source of information on activities of insurance companies in Florida is the *Annual Report* of the Florida Department of Insurance. Data on life insurance are from the American Council of Life Insurance in its *Life Insurance Fact Book Update*.

Information on licensed persons who handle real estate transactions is reported by the Florida Department of Business and Professional Regulation.

SECTION 18.00. PERSONAL AND BUSINESS SERVICES

EXPLANATORY NOTES. The Standard Industrial Classification System lists services from SIC code 70 to SIC code 89. A county-level aggregate of establishments with these codes appears in Table 18.28. Other tables in this section based on the establishments covered by the unemployment insurance law show data on personal services (SIC code 72), business services (SIC code 73), automotive repair, services, and parking (SIC code 75), miscellaneous repair services (SIC code 76), engineering, accounting, research, management and related services (SIC code 87), private household services (SIC code 88), and services not elsewhere classified (SIC code 89). Information about establishments with other service SIC codes are to be found in Sections 19.00, 20.00, and 22.00.

The U. S. Bureau of the Census has taken a Census of Services Industries as part of the economic census every five years since 1967. In 1977, coverage of service industries broadened from "selected services" to "all services except religious organizations and private households." Data on selected industries from the *1992 Census of Service Industries* are reported in Table 18.01. An index of recent census tables appearing in previous *Abstracts* is at the back of this edition.

SOURCES. Data on establishments, employment, and payroll of service establishments whose employees are covered by the unemployment insurance law are provided by the Bureau of Labor Market Information, Florida Department of Labor and Employment Security. (See the discussion under Section 6.00 of this Appendix.) Data for the same area and industry from the *Census of Service Industries* are not necessarily comparable because of differences in procedures, definitions, and establishments covered.

Many service establishments are operated by professional individuals who are licensed by the state. Data on these professionals have been supplied from the Florida Department of Business and Professional Regulation.

Information on health, educational, and cultural services is reported in Section 20.00.

SECTION 19.00. TOURISM AND RECREATION

EXPLANATORY NOTES. Estimates of the number of tourists entering Florida by automobile are made by the Florida Division of Tourism using traffic counts and information from welcome stations. Tourist arrivals by air are based on arrivals at major airports. Individual visitors are interviewed on a randomly selected basis about expenditures and length of stay. Sample results are expanded to the total visitor population.

SOURCES. The Office of Tourism Research, Florida Department of Commerce issues quarterly and county reports of tourist information and an annual report, *Florida Visitor Study*. The Transportation Statistics Office of the Florida Department of Transportation records traffic counts at strategic highway locations around the state. Data on tourist facilities (hotels, motels, and food service establishments) that are regulated by the Division of Hotels and Restaurants of the Florida Department of Business and Professional Regulation are available from the department's *Master File Statistics*. The Florida Department of Revenue provides information on the gross and taxable sales of businesses. Some businesses have been classified for purposes of presenting data in this section as "tourist- and recreation-related" businesses. The Department of Revenue also provides information on the tourist-development or local option tax collected in several counties.

Data on employment in tourist- and recreation-related industries come from the Bureau of Labor Market Information, Florida Department of Labor and Employment Security. (See discussion under Section 6.00 of this Appendix.)

Data on boats registered by county in Florida are provided by the Bureau of Vessel Titles and Registrations, Florida Department of Highway Safety and Motor Vehicles. Data on recreational boating and personal watercraft accidents appearing in new Tables 19.46-19.48 are from the Office of Waterway Management, Division of Law Enforcement, Florida Department of Environmental Protection. The Recreation and Parks Management Information System, Florida Department of Environmental Protection issues information on the nature, size, and popularity of state parks. Data on national parks in Florida were taken from the *National Park Service Statistical Abstract*, published by the National Park Service, U.S. Department of the Interior.

SECTION 20.00. HEALTH, EDUCATION, AND CULTURAL SERVICES

SOURCES. Data on establishments, receipts and payroll in Table 20.01 are from the *1992 Census of Service Industries* conducted by the U.S. Bureau of the Census. Data on employment are from the covered employment and payroll figures supplied by the Bureau of Labor Market Information, Florida Department of Labor and Employment Security. (See discussion under Section 6.00 of this Appendix.)

Information on physicians, dentists, nurses, opticians, pharmacists, and other licensed health service practitioners and professionals comes from the Florida Department of Business and Professional Regulation.

New data on general, short-term acute care hospitals from the Florida Agency for Health Care publication *Guide to Hospitals in Florida* appear in Tables 20.15, 20.16, and 20.17. A map of Community Health Purchasing Alliance (CHPA) regions is on page 535. The agency, in cooperation with Local Health Councils of Florida, also provided enrollment data for licensed Health Maintenance Organizations (HMOs) in new Table 20.25.

Library information is supplied by the Division of Library and Information Services, Florida Department of State in *Florida Library Directory with Statistics*.

Data on veterans hospitals come from the U.S. Department of Veterans Affairs, *Annual Report of the Secretary of Veterans Affairs*.

Church membership, Table 20.31, is from a copyrighted publication, *Churches and Church Membership*, issued by Glenmary Research Center in Atlanta.

Educational establishment information comes from the Florida Department of Education: *Profiles of Florida School Districts*; the Division of Public Schools, *Statistical Briefs*; and unpublished data sources.

Federal aid data are from the *Statistical Abstract of the United States.* Information on arts grants to Florida groups and individuals by county in Table 20.75 is from *Florida Funding for Culture and the Arts* issued by the Division of Cultural Affairs, Florida Department of State.

SECTION 21.00. GOVERNMENT AND ELECTIONS

SOURCES. Every five years since 1957, the U.S. Bureau of the Census has conducted a Census of Governments. This census covers four major subject areas: governmental organization, taxable property values, public employment, and governmental finances. Table 21.01 presents information from Volume 1 of the 1992 census about governmental units by type in Florida and the United States. Table 21.07 shows numbers of local governments and elected officials in Florida by county and by type of government. An index of recent census tables appearing in previous *Abstracts* is at the back of this edition.

The Division of Elections in the Florida Department of State provides information on registered voters and numbers of votes cast in given elections. The U.S. Bureau of the Census provides voting-age population estimates and November 1996 projections and electoral votes for other states and the United States on the Internet. These data appear in new Table 21.23 and Table 21.24. Estimates and projections on voting-age population, released annually by the Bureau of Economic and Business Research (BEBR), University of Florida, appear in tables 21.25 and 21.26.

Several private sources have granted permission to include data in this section. The Joint Center for Political and Economic Studies publishes the annual *Black Elected Officials: A National Roster*. The Council of State Governments publishes information on the composition of state legislatures in *State Elected Officials and the Legislature* and 1994 National Conference of State Legislatures unpublished data. Data on female officials may be found in copyrighted information releases from Rutgers University's Center for the American Woman and Politics.

SECTION 22.00. COURTS AND LAW ENFORCEMENT

EXPLANATORY NOTES. Data on criminal offenses are subject to certain limitations. Many crimes are not reported to law enforcement agencies and hence are not counted in preparing crime statistics. Victims may report crimes to prosecuting authorities rather than to law enforcement agencies or for various reasons may not report at all.

An additional factor to consider when studying crime rates in Florida is the presence of large numbers of tourists. The crime rates in this section are based on resident population. When adjustments are made for the tourist presence, the crime rate in Florida drops.

SOURCES. The principal source of data on crimes and criminals in Florida is *Crime in Florida*, the annual report of the state Department of Law Enforcement.

Other sources on the criminal justice system include publications of two divisions of the U.S. Department of Justice: the annual *Crime in the United States* from the Federal Bureau of Investigation, and reports and bulletins from the Bureau of Justice Statistics.

Data on county jails are from *Florida County Detention Facilities* issued by the Bureau of Planning, Research, and Statistics in the state Department of Corrections. Prison and prisoner information is made available by the Department of Corrections in its *Annual Report.*

Juvenile delinquency data are from the Bureau of Research and Data, Florida Department of Juvenile Justice.

Victim compensation data are from the *Annual Report* of the state Division of Victim Services, Office of the Attorney General.

Data on legal services come from the Florida Bar and the Bureau of Labor Market Information, Florida Department of Labor and Employment Security.

SECTION 23.00. GOVERNMENT FINANCE AND EMPLOYMENT

EXPLANATORY NOTES. A number of tables in the Health, Education, and Cultural Services section (20.00) contain data on property valuations, revenue, expenditure, and taxes for education by public agencies. In Section 19.00, Table 19.54 provides figures on the tourist-development/local option tax and Table 19.70 provides information about tax collections from tourist- and recreation-related businesses.

Although the official records of the Comptroller are used by the Bureau of the Census in its compilations on state and local government finances, the Bureau of the Census has found it necessary at times to classify and present the government financial statistics in terms of its own system of uniform concepts and categories rather than according to the diverse terminology and structure of individual governments. This procedure explains the differences that may be found between similar data from the two sources.

International government employment is shown in Table 23.71 and in a footnote on Table 23.74 in this *Abstract.*

SOURCES. The U.S. Bureau of the Census publishes a number of annual series and increasingly is providing data on the Internet. Users should contact the bureau for a list of current publications. It also conducts a Census of Governments every five years, coincident with the economic censuses. (An index of recent census tables in previous *Abstracts* appears at the end of this book).

Official records and reports of the Comptroller of the State of Florida comprise the basic source of information about government finances in Florida and are published in the *Florida Comprehensive Annual Financial Report* and *Annual Report of the Comptroller*. Other State of Florida sources of data on government finances and employment include the Department of Revenue, *Florida Property Valuations and Tax Data*; the Department of Business and Professional Regulation, data on pari-mutuel wagering and beverage and tobacco licenses; Department of the Lottery for ticket sales; the Department of Highway Safety and Motor Vehicles for motor vehicle licenses; *The Report of the State Treasurer*; the Bureau of Labor Market Information on employment and payroll; the Division of Retirement, *Annual Report*; and the Florida Department of Banking and Finance, *Local Government Financial Report*. Due to governmental reorganization and financial cut-backs, some state publications are no longer being produced. Included in a growing list of discontinued published resources are the *Annual Report of the Comptroller* and *Local Government Financial Report.* Some data from the most recently published editions of these sources have been repeated in this volume.

The Florida Department of Revenue annually reviews the ad valorem tax rolls submitted by county property appraisers and Armasi, Inc., compiles data from the tax rolls, making the data available with software that displays data geographically by county. Table 23.95 presents assessed land use values by county summarized by Armasi, Inc., from the Department of Revenue files.

SECTION 24.00. ECONOMIC INDICATORS AND PRICES

EXPLANATORY NOTES. Tables in the first twenty-three sections of the *Abstract* are primarily cross-sectional or "snapshot" portrayals of a set of circumstances or a situation existing at any one time. Because many readers are interested in charting trends over time, most tables in Section 24.00 contain data over several years.

Consumer price indexes are developed by the Bureau of Labor Statistics (BLS) of the U.S. Department of Labor and appear in the monthly *CPI Detailed Report*. The BLS publishes two indexes: one reflecting the buying habits of all urban households (CPI-U) and one reflecting the buying habits of urban wage earners and clerical workers (CPI-W). Both indexes are comparable with historical CPI figures; the index for all urban households is used in tables in this section (except for the entry of the CPI-W index in Table 24.73). The CPI-U is based on information reflecting the buying habits of about 80 percent of the U.S. population and represents all urban residents, including professional workers, the self-employed, the poor, the unemployed, and retired persons. Not included are persons living outside urban areas, farm families, persons in military services, and those in institutions. The Bureau of Labor Statistics issues a bimonthly CPI for the Miami-Ft. Lauderdale CMSA and Tampa-St. Petersburg-Clearwater MSA. (See Table 24.74.)

The BLS introduced a revised CPI with the release of the January 1987 index. Both the CPI-U and the CPI-W use updated expenditure weights based on data tabulated from the consumer expenditure surveys. Also, the rental equivalence measures of home ownership costs in both the CPI-U and the CPI-W were improved to better represent both owners' and renters' shelter costs.

The series of producer prices appears in Tables 24.72 and 24.75. According to the BLS, the series measures the average changes in prices received in primary markets of the United States by producers of commodities in all stages of processing. The sample used for calculating the indexes contains nearly 2,800 commodities and about 10,000 quotations selected to represent the movement of prices of all commodities produced in the agriculture, forestry, fishing, mining, manufacturing, gas, electric, and all public utilities sectors.

The *Florida Price Level Index* (FPLI) is prepared by the Office of Education Budget and Management, Florida Department of Education. The FPLI measures relative price levels across counties. Items representative of the expenditure categories used by the BLS in the CPI are surveyed in each county. Table 24.79 shows the relative weights of selected items in the survey; Table 24.80 compares the index and subindexes for major items across counties.

Data on price trends in construction are in Section 11.00. Section 15.00 contains additional information on energy prices.

The Bureau of Economic Analysis, U.S. Department of Commerce introduced estimates of Gross State Product (GSP) by component and by industry for each state for the period 1936-1986. GSP is the gross market value of goods and services attributable to labor and property located in the state. It is the state counterpart to national Gross Domestic Product (GDP). These estimates have been updated through 1992 (see Table 24.15), and are available on CD-ROM from the Regional Economic Information System.

SOURCES. Extensive series of economic indicators for the United States, Florida, and its counties are maintained in the BEBR Data Base, Bureau of Economic and Business Research, University of Florida. Data surveying consumer confidence is presented in the BEBR monthly publication, *Florida Economic and Consumer Survey.*

The Bureau of Labor Statistics, U.S. Department of Labor prepares consumer and producer price indexes and publishes them in detailed monthly reports and on the Internet.

The Department of Revenue of the State of Florida has data on sales and use tax collections. The Department of Labor and Employment Security provided employment data.

The International Trade Administration, U.S. Department of Commerce reports building permit activity in the states in *Construction Review*. Table 24.20 presents data from current and previous editions of this publication back to 1983.

Data on new incorporations and failures of industrial and commercial establishments shown in Table 24.78 are available by permission from the copyrighted reports, *New Business Incorporations* and *Business Failure Report*, published by Dun & Bradstreet.

The Florida Public Service Commission provides electricity price data in *Statistics of the Florida Electric Utility Industry.*

SECTION 25.00. STATE COMPARISONS

SOURCES. Both economic and noneconomic factors are listed in Table 25.01 to permit the reader to compare aspects of life in Florida to similar living conditions in other Sunbelt and populous states. There are numerous sources to this table, most of which have been discussed in previous sections. The *Statistical Abstract of the United States* published by the Bureau of the Census is a primary source as is census bureau information on the Internet. Sources not previously mentioned are the Federal Deposit Insurance Corporation, *Quarterly Banking Profile;* Bureau of the Census, *Black-owned Businesses* and *Women-owned Businesses;* U.S. Department of Health and Human Services, *Monthly Vital Statistics Report* and *Medicaid Statistics: Program and Financial Statistics*; National Center for Health Statistics, *Health United States;* U.S. Department of Energy, Energy Information Administration, *Electric Sales and Revenue; Sourcebook of Criminal Justice Statistics* from the U.S. Department of Justice, Bureau of Justice Statistics, and the copyrighted report *Physicians Characteristics and Distributions in the U.S.* published by the American Medical Association.

SUMMARY OF SOURCES

STATE SOURCES. Most of the state publications are available free of charge from the agency issuing the report. Supplies are frequently limited and sometimes requests cannot be honored unless they come from other state agencies. Increasingly, publication reproductions and/or unpublished data can be retrieved from the Internet. The state has a system of state depository libraries, coordinated by the Division of Library Services, Florida Department of State, R.A. Gray Building, Tallahassee. All state agency publications are supposed to be on file in depository libraries or available for interlibrary loan. The reference departments of most libraries are willing to answer questions about data in these publications if the requests are not too time-consuming. The Florida Division of State Library Services issues a monthly and annual summary of state agency publications called *Florida Public Documents*.

Depository libraries of the State of Florida include the public libraries of Bay, Broward, and Orange counties, Cocoa, Jacksonville, Miami Beach, Miami-Dade, Ocala, St. Petersburg, Tampa-Hillsborough, and West Palm Beach. University libraries designated as depositories are those at Central Florida, Florida Atlantic, Florida (Gainesville), Florida International, Florida State, Miami, North Florida, South Florida, West Florida, Jacksonville, and Stetson. The State Library of Florida in the R.A. Gray Building in Tallahassee also is a depository.

FEDERAL SOURCES. Some federal reports are available without charge from the agency issuing the information, but most federal publications must be purchased from the Superintendent of Documents, U.S. Government Printing Office (GPO), Washington, D.C. 20402 (phone 202/783-3238) or from a local Government Printing Office bookstore. Publications purchased from the GPO must be prepaid. As noted throughout this edition, agencies are making use of the Internet to provide easy access to publications and free data to users. The *Statistical Abstract of the United States* is similar in purpose to the *Florida Statistical Abstract* and much more comprehensive. Readers interested in information about the nation, its regions, and states are referred to it.

The federal government also maintains a system of depository libraries in all fifty states, usually the same libraries as state depositories. The University of Florida is designated as a regional depository library and is required to receive and retain one copy of all depository government publications made available to depository libraries either in print or on microfiche. Many of the libraries listed above as state depositories are also federal depositories and some are not listed. Refer to the annual directory printed by the University of Florida Libraries, *Federal Document Depositories and Resource Information for Florida and Puerto Rico*.

PRIVATE SOURCES. A number of private agencies and associations issue publications or reports which have been used in this and recent editions of *Abstract*. Some are copyrighted and have been used with permission. Several have additional information which can be obtained for a fee.

American Council of Life Insurance, Washington, D.C.
American Medical Association, Chicago, Illinois
Center for the American Woman and Politics (CAWP), National Information Bank on Women in Public Office, Eagleton Institute of Politics, Rutgers University
Council of State Governments, Lexington, Kentucky
Dun & Bradstreet Corporation, New York, New York
Federal Deposit Insurance Corporation, Washington, D.C.
Florida Association of Homes for the Aging, Tallahassee, Florida
Glenmary Research Center, Atlanta, Georgia
Joint Center for Political and Economic Studies, Washington, D.C.
McGraw-Hill, Inc., New York, New York
National Conference of State Legislatures, Denver, Colorado
TRW REDI Property Data, Inc., Walnut Creek, California

COMPUTER TAPES. The University of Florida Library in Gainesville maintains an extensive collection of information about Florida in books and files and on computer tapes. All the data from the population, housing and economic censuses can be accessed from their computer tapes. Data from the 1990 census and the Bureau of Labor Statistics are also available on CD-ROM. Many agencies make data available through the Internet worldwide computer network; this source may eventually replace many printed publications.

BUREAU PUBLICATIONS. The Bureau of Economic and Business Research (BEBR) at the University of Florida can supply a variety of detailed information about Florida:

Florida Estimates of Population. Intercensal estimates of the population of Florida, its counties, cities, and unincorporated areas. Also includes components of population change and density figures. Published annually. A summary of census results is published in census years.

Florida Population Studies. Bulletins providing information on age, race, and sex components of Florida's population, household numbers and average household size, projections of population, discussions of estimation and projection methodology, and other topics related to population. Published three times a year.

Special Population Reports. 1995 estimates of Hispanic population with age and sex detail is the most recent of these four releases. Also include revised 1980-90 population estimates by county, an evaluation of population projection errors for Florida counties and an evaluation of 1990 population estimation. Published periodically.

The Florida Long-term Economic Forecast. A two-volume long-range economic forecast of income, employment, construction, and population for the State of Florida, its metropolitan areas, and counties. Volume One focuses on the state and MSAs and Volume Two on the state and counties. Published annually.

Florida County Rankings. At-a-glance ranked data for more than 400 current data topics for all Florida counties, with a state comparison for each topic and pertinent data maps.

County Perspective. Individual ranking reports for each of Florida's 67 counties in the same categories used in *Florida County Rankings*, with historical data summaries.

Building Permit Activity in Florida. Monthly comparisons with year-to-date data, with an annual summary, of the value and number of units permitted in the state, counties, cities, and unincorporated areas of Florida.

The Economy of Florida. Twenty-three experts explore the many sectors of Florida's economy, including international trade, telecommunications, regions, health care, the labor market, housing, banking, military bases and defense manufacturing, and tourism.

1990 Census Handbook: Florida. Over 600 pages of census information for Florida, its counties, congressional districts and most populous cities and comparisons of Florida with the other forty-nine states.

Gross and taxable sales information. Printouts of sales information from the Florida Department of Revenue reports of gross and taxable sales for the sales and use taxes. Available by county and by kind-of-business category. Issued monthly and annually.

Florida Economic and Consumer Survey. Monthly survey data on Florida consumers' confidence in the national and local economies, buying plans, personal financial condition, and special topics.

BEBR Monographs. In-depth analyses of topics relevant to an understanding of the Florida economic and business climate. Issued periodically. Current titles include *Population Projections: What Do We Really Know?*; *Local Government Economic Analysis Using Microcomputers*; *Cuban Immigration and Immigrants in Florida and the United States: Implications for Immigration Policy*; *Urban Development Issues: What is Controversial in Urban Sprawl?*; *Preparing the Economic Element of the Comprehensive Plan*; *Concurrency Management Systems in Florida: A Catalog and Analysis*; and *The Economic Impact of Local Government Comprehensive Plans*.

BEBR Data Base. A computerized data management system containing extensive economic data for the United States, Florida, and all counties. Provides PC access to current and historical data for Florida, any of its counties and Metropolitan Statistical Areas, and for the United States. Continuously updated.

Migration releases. Based on data collected by the U.S. Bureau of the Census and Internal Revenue Service these BEBR-prepared reports include state and county migration flows with age, sex, and race detail. Updated as data becomes available.

For pricing and ordering information, please contact:

Bureau of Economic and Business Research
221 Matherly Hall
P. O. Box 117145
University of Florida
Gainesville, Florida 32611-7145
Phone: 352/392-0171 FAX: 352/392-4739
The Internet: http://www.cba.ufl.edu/bebr/
E-mail: bebr@bebr.cba.ufl.edu

GLOSSARY

ALIEN. Person who is not a citizen of the United States whether or not he/she is a resident, legally or illegally.

AMERICAN INDIAN, ESKIMO, OR ALEUT POPULATION. See Race.

ANCESTRY. A person's nationality group, lineage, or the country in which the person or the person's parents or ancestors were born before their arrival in the U.S. Different from other indicators of ethnicity, such as country of birth and language spoken in home and is a separate characteristic from race.

ASIAN OR PACIFIC ISLANDER POPULATION. See Race.

BLACK POPULATION. See Race.

BUSINESS ESTABLISHMENT. A commercial enterprise.

CHILDREN. Sons and daughters classified as "own child of householder," including stepchildren and adopted children, who have never been married and are under age 18.

CIVILIAN LABOR FORCE. See Labor Force.

CLASS OF WORKERS. Private wage and salary workers who work for a private employer for wages, salary, commission, tips, pay-in-kind, or at price rates. Private employers include churches and other nonprofit organizations. Also includes persons who consider themselves self-employed but who work for corporations where in most cases these persons own or are a part of a group that owns controlling interest in the corporation.

Government workers who work for a governmental unit, regardless of the activity of the particular agency.

Self-employed workers who work for profit or fees in their own unincorporated business, profession, or trade, or who operate a farm. Includes owner-operators of large stores and manufacturing establishments, as well as small merchants, independent craft-persons and professionals, farmers, peddlers, and other persons who conduct enterprises of their own.

Unpaid family workers who work without pay on a farm or in a business operated by a person to whom they are related by blood or marriage.

COLLEGE STUDENTS. See Residency.

COMMUNITY HEALTH PURCHASING ALLIANCE (CHPA). Authorized by the 1993 Florida legislature to assist members of the alliance in securing the highest quality health care at the lowest possible price. Membership is voluntary and available primarily to businesses that have 50 or fewer employees. CHPAs are state-chartered, not-for-profit, private purchasing organizations and have exclusive territories.

COMMUTE. Travel back and forth regularly, usually between place of residence and place of work.

CONSOLIDATED METROPOLITAN STATISTICAL AREA (CMSA). A large metropolitan complex with a population over one million in which individual metropolitan components, Primary Metropolitan Statistical Areas (PMSAs), have been defined.

CONSUMER PRICE INDEX (CPI). A measure of the average level of prices over time in a fixed market collection of goods and services. The index is intended to represent prices of most items and services that people purchase in daily living, and is calculated to represent purchases by urban wage earners and clerical workers or by all urban consumers.

CONTRACT RENT. See Rent.

COUNTY. An administrative subdivision of a state; a local government organization and political jurisdiction authorized and designated by a state's constitution or statutes.

DROPOUT. A student over the age of compulsory school attendance (16) who has voluntarily removed himself from the school system before graduation; or who has not met attendance requirements; or who has withdrawn from school but has not transferred to another public or private school or enrolled in any other educational program; or has withdrawn from school due to hardship without official granting of such withdrawal; or is not eligible to attend school because of reaching the maximum age for an exceptional student program.

EARNINGS. Sum of wage and salary income and net income from farm and nonfarm self-employment. Reported before deductions for personal income taxes, social security, bond purchases, union dues, and other deductions.

EDUCATIONAL ATTAINMENT. Years of school completed.

EMPLOYED PERSONS. All civilians 16 years of age and over that work at all as paid employees for an employer, or in their own business or profession, on their own farm, or who work 15 hours or more as unpaid workers in an enterprise operated by a family member and all those temporarily absent from their jobs due to such factors as illness or vacation (during a given reference week).

ENERGY. The ability to do work; can exist in many forms such as chemical, light, heat, etc.
Primary energy is energy available from conversion of original fuel rather than from a secondary form such as electricity.
Renewables are energy sources that can be used continuously or regenerated quickly such as wind, sunlight, wood, and solid waste.

FAMILY HOUSEHOLD. A householder and one or more other person(s) living in the same household who are related to the householder by birth, marriage, or adoption. All persons in a household who are related to the householder and are regarded as members of his or her family.

FAMILY HOUSEHOLD INCOME. See Income.

FARM. For the 1990 census, property of one acre or more where $1,000 or more of agricultural products were sold from the property in 1989.

FARM POPULATION. See Rural farm population.

FIRM. A business organization or entity consisting of one or more establishment(s) under common ownership or control; a commercial partnership of two or more persons.

GENERAL, SHORT-TERM ACUTE CARE HOSPITAL. Establishment that offers services more intensive than those required for room, board, personal services, and general nursing care. Offers facilities and beds for use beyond 24 hours by individuals requiring diagnosis, treatment, or care for illness, injury, deformity, infirmity, abnormality, disease, or pregnancy. Regularly makes available at least clinical laboratory services, diagnostic radiology services, and treatment facilities for surgery, medical, or obstetrical care, or other definitive medical treatment of similar extent.

GROSS STATE PRODUCT (GSP). The gross market value of the goods and services attributable to labor and property located in a state.

GROUP QUARTERS. All persons not living in households are classified by the Census Bureau as living in group quarters—institutional and noninstitutional. Institutional group quarters are all institutions offering care or custody, e.g., prisons, mental hospitals, nursing homes, juvenile institutions. Noninstitutional quarters include workers' dormitories, monasteries, convents, large rooming houses or boarding houses or communes having at least ten persons unrelated to the resident who maintains the living quarters. Noninstitutional quarters also cover certain living arrangements regardless of the number or relationship of the people in the unit such as military barracks, college dormitories, missions and emergency shelters for the homeless. Data on the homeless also include visible in street locations or predesignated street sites, (e.g., bridges, parks, bus depots) where the homeless congregate.

HISPANIC ORIGIN. Persons who classified themselves in one of the Hispanic-origin categories listed on the census questionnaire—Mexican, Puerto Rican, Cuban, or other Spanish/Hispanic origin. This latter category includes those whose origins are from Spain or the Spanish-speaking countries of Central or South America, or the Dominican Republic, or they are Hispanic-origin persons identifying themselves generally as Spanish, Spanish-American, Hispanic, Latino, etc. Origin can be viewed as the ancestry, nationality group, lineage or country in which the person or person's parents or ancestors were born before their arrival in the U.S. Persons of Hispanic origin may be of any race. Households and families are classified by the Hispanic origin of the householder.

HOMELESS POPULATION. See Group quarters.

HOMEOWNER VACANCY RATE. The proportion of the homeowner inventory which is vacant for sale. Rates are computed by dividing the vacant year-round units for sale only by the sum of the number of owner-occupied units, vacant year-round units sold but awaiting occupancy, and vacant year-round units for sale only.

HOMEOWNER VACANCY RATE. The proportion of the homeowner inventory which is vacant for sale. Rates are computed by dividing the vacant year-round units for sale only by the sum of the number of owner-occupied units, vacant year-round units sold but awaiting occupancy, and vacant year-round units for sale only.

HOUSEHOLD. The person or persons occupying a housing unit. Designation of a household as "family" or "nonfamily" is based on the householder. If the household has family members of the householder, then it is classified as a family household. If the householder is an individual unrelated to other household members, lives alone, or is living in group quarters (not institutionalized), then the household is classified as a nonfamily household.

HOUSEHOLD INCOME. See Income.

HOUSEHOLDER. Person, or one of the persons, in whose name the home is owned or rented and who is listed in column one of the census questionnaire. If there is no such person in the household, any adult household member could be designated as "householder."
Family householder is a householder living with one or more person(s) related to him or her by birth, marriage, or adoption.
Nonfamily householder is a householder living alone or with nonrelatives only.

HOUSING UNIT. A house, an apartment, a group of rooms, or a single room occupied as a separate living quarters, or if vacant, intended for occupancy as a separate living quarters.
Occupied housing unit is the usual place of residence of the person or group of persons living there at the time of the census enumeration, or the unit from which the occupants are only temporarily absent (away on vacation, etc.).
Owner-occupied housing unit is one in which the owner or co-owner lives, whether the unit is owned without lien or mortgaged.
Renter-occupied unit is any unit not classified as owner-occupied, including a unit rented for cash rent or one occupied without payment of cash rent.
Vacant housing unit has no one living in it at the time of census enumeration, unless the occupants are only temporarily absent. May be classified as "seasonal and migratory," or "year-round." Seasonal unit is intended for occupancy during only certain seasons of the year. Migratory unit is held for occupancy for migratory labor employed in farm work during crop season. Year-round vacant unit is available or intended for occupancy at any time of the year.

IMMIGRANTS. Aliens admitted for legal permanent residence in the United States, including persons who may have entered as nonimmigrants or refugees, but who subsequently changed their status to that of a permanent resident.

INCOME. The amount of money or monetary equivalent received during a specified time period in exchange for work performed, sale of goods or property, or from profits made on financial investments.
Adjusted gross income is a tax-defined concept of income. Certain kinds of income such as some portion of capital gains, social security, and in-kind transfer payments are excluded and certain types of expenses such as some trade and business expenses, alimony payments, and contributions to individual retirement plans are deducted.
Family household income and nonfamily household income are compiled by summing and treating as a single amount the money income of all family or nonfamily household members aged 15 and over.
Household income includes the money income of the householder and all other persons aged 15 and over in the household, whether related to the householder or not. Because many households consist of only one person, average household income is usually less than average family income.
Interest, dividend, or net rental income includes interest on savings or bonds, dividends from stockholdings or membership in associations, net royalties, and net income from rental of property to others and receipts from boarders or lodgers.
Labor income is an item generally used for various types of supplemental earnings in cash and in kind.
Mean income is the amount obtained by dividing the total income of a particular statistical universe by the number of units in that universe.
Median income is the amount that divides the income distribution into two equal groups, one having incomes above the median and the other having incomes below the median. For households, families, and unrelated individuals the median income is based on the distribution of the total number of units including those with no income. The median for persons is based on persons with income.

Money income is an income definition of the Census Bureau. It is the sum of amounts reported separately for wage and salary income; net nonfarm self-employment income; net farm self-employment income; interest, dividend, net royalty or rental income; social security or railroad retirement income; public assistance or welfare income; unemployment compensation; alimony; veterans' payments; and all other income. Not included are monies received from the sale of property owned by a recipient; the value of income "in-kind" from food stamps, public housing subsidies, medical care, employer contributions for pensions, etc.; withdrawal of bank deposits; money borrowed; tax refunds; exchanges of money between relatives living in the same household; gifts and lump-sum inheritances, insurance payments, and other types of lump-sum receipts.

Personal income is an income definition of the Bureau of Economic Analysis. It is the sum of current income received by persons from all sources and is measured before deduction of personal contributions to social insurance programs and income and other personal taxes. It is reported in current dollars and includes the following categories of earnings: private and governmental wages and salaries; labor income; farm and nonfarm proprietors' income; property income; and government and business transfer payments, but excludes transfers among persons. (Also, includes some nonmonetary income such as estimated net rental values—to owner—of owner-occupied homes, and the value of services furnished without payment, and food and fuel produced and consumed on farms.)

Disposable personal income is personal income less personal tax and nontax payments. Personal taxes include income, estate, gift, personal property and license taxes. Nontax payments include fines and penalties, tuition, and donations.

Property income is net rental income, dividends, and interest.

Proprietors' income is net income of owners of unincorporated businesses (farm and nonfarm, with the latter including the income of independent professionals).

Public assistance income includes three items: supplementary security income payments made by federal or state welfare agencies to low-income persons aged 65 or over, blind, or disabled; aid to families with dependent children; and general assistance. Separate payments received for hospital or other medical care are excluded.

Social security income includes social security pensions and survivors' benefits and permanent disability insurance payments made by the Social Security Administration prior to deductions. Medicare reimbursements are not included.

INDUSTRIAL CLASSIFICATION SYSTEM, STANDARD. Industrial classification system for classifying establishments by type of economic activity. Developed and published in a manual by the Executive Office of the President, Office of Management and Budget, and revised and published in 1987 (which supersedes the 1972/77 edition). Major industries are assigned two-digit SIC codes: 01 through 99; subdivisions are classified by three- and four-digit codes. The major industry groups and their SIC codes are as follows:

Agriculture (01, 02, 07)
Forestry and fisheries (08, 09)
Mining (10-14)
Construction (15-17)
Manufacturing (20-39)
Transportation, communications, and public utilities (40-49)
Wholesale trade (50-51)
Retail trade (52-59)
Finance, insurance, and real estate (60-67)
Services (70-89)
Public administration (91-97)
Nonclassifiable establishments (99)

An example of SIC coding is the construction industry, which is divided into major group SIC 15, "building construction—general contractors and operative builders"; group SIC 16, "heavy construction other than building construction"; and group SIC 17, "construction—special trade contractors." Group 15 is in turn divided into group 152, "general building contractors, residential buildings," group 153, "operative builders," and 154, "general building contractors, nonresidential buildings." Group 152 is subdivided into 1521, "general contractors, single-family houses," and 1522, "general contractors, residential buildings, other than single-family."

INMATES OF INSTITUTIONS. See Group quarters.

INTEREST, DIVIDEND, OR NET RENTAL INCOME. See Income.

LABOR FORCE. Includes the civilian labor force, which comprises all civilians in the noninstitutional population 16 years and over classified as "employed" or "unemployed" and members of the Armed Forces stationed in the United States.

MANUFACTURED HOUSING. Any prefabricated dwelling such as a mobile home or modular housing.

MANUFACTURING ESTABLISHMENT. An enterprise usually consisting of a single physical location where raw materials are transformed into new products.

MARITAL STATUS. Classification refers to the status of persons aged 15 and over at the time of census enumeration. Couples who live together (unmarried persons, common-law marriages) were allowed to report the marital status they considered the most appropriate. Persons reported as separated are those living apart because of marital discord, with or without a legal separation. Persons in common-law marriages are classified as now married, except separated if they consider this category most appropriate; persons whose only marriage has been annulled are classified as never married; persons married at the time of enumeration (including those separated), widowed, or divorced are classified as ever married. Persons whose current marriage has not ended by widowhood or divorce are classified as now married. This category includes married persons whose spouse may have been (1) temporarily absent for such reasons as travel or hospitalization; (2) absent, including all married persons living in group quarters, employed spouses living away from home or in an institution, or absent in the Armed Forces; and (3) those who are separated.

MARKET VALUE. Amount a seller reasonably expects to obtain in a market for commodities, merchandise, services, or whatever is being sold.

MEDICAID. A jointly funded state and federal health care program for low-income persons. States establish their own eligibility criteria and may set benefits above the minimum established by federal law.

MEDICARE. Federal health insurance program for people aged 65 and over. Also covers (since 1973) eligible disabled persons of any age and persons with chronic kidney disease.

METROPOLITAN POPULATION. Population living inside Metropolitan Statistical Areas (MSAs) or Consolidated Metropolitan Statistical Areas (CMSAs).

METROPOLITAN STATISTICAL AREA (MSA). A geographic area with a large population nucleus together with adjacent communities, which has a high degree of economic and social integration with the nucleus. An MSA may include entire counties and generally has a city of at least 50,000 population or an urbanized area of at least 50,000 with a total metropolitan population of at least 100,000. This term replaces the term Standard Metropolitan Statistical Area, which was used prior to January 1983. See map at front of the book for list of counties in MSAs.

MOBILE HOME. Movable dwelling, ten or more feet wide and thirty-five or more feet long (a movable dwelling of less than these dimensions is considered to be a travel trailer or a motor home), designed to be towed on its own chassis and without need of a permanent foundation. Does not include prefabricated or modular housing, travel trailers, and other self-propelled vehicles such as motor homes. Mobile homes or trailers to which one or more permanent rooms have been added or built are classified by the Census Bureau as single-unit, detached housing.

MILITARY PERSONNEL. See Labor force and Residency.

MILL. Unit of monetary value equal to 1/1000 of a U.S. dollar.

MILLAGE RATE. Tax rate stated in mills where one mill produces one dollar of tax for every $1,000 of taxable property.

MONEY INCOME. See Income.

MUNICIPALITY. Political subdivision within which a municipal corporation has been established to provide a general local government for a specific population concentration in a defined area. In Florida, municipalities may be called cities, towns, or villages and have been established either by special acts of the legislature or by general law.

NONFAMILY HOUSEHOLDER. See Householder.

NONMETROPOLITAN POPULATION. Population living outside of metropolitan areas (as defined by the U.S. Office of Management and Budget).

NONPUBLIC SCHOOL. See Private school.

NONRELATIVES. Any persons in the household not related to the householder by birth, marriage, or adoption. Includes roomers, boarders, partners, roommates, paid employees, wards, and foster children.

OCCUPATIONAL LICENSING. Required operational licenses for professional persons who operate at the retail level such as dispensing opticians or pharmacists.

OCCUPIED HOUSING UNIT. See Housing unit.

OWNER-OCCUPIED HOUSING UNIT. See Housing unit.

PER CAPITA. A per capita (per person) figure is defined by taking the total for some item (e.g., government expenditures, income) and dividing it by the number of persons in the specified population.

PERSONAL INCOME. See Income.

PERSONS PER FAMILY. Number of persons living in families divided by the number of families.

PERSONS PER HOUSEHOLD. Number of persons living in households divided by the number of households.

PLACE OF BIRTH. For census enumeration, the mother's usual state or country of residence at the time of birth. Native-born persons are those born in the U.S., Puerto Rico, or an outlying area of the U.S. Includes a small number of persons born at sea or in a foreign country but with at least one American parent. Foreign-born persons are those not classified as native born.

PLACE OF WORK. Geographic location at which workers carry out their occupational activities.

POVERTY STATUS. In census publications, based on a definition developed by the Social Security Administration in 1964 and revised by a federal interagency committee in 1969 and 1980. Defined by income levels that (depending on family or household size) describe a family or household as being in extreme want of necessities. Income cutoffs or poverty thresholds used by the Bureau of the Census to determine the poverty status of families and individuals are defined by family size and by presence and number of family members aged 18 and under. Unrelated individuals and two-person families are differentiated by age of householder. If total income of a family or individual is less than the corresponding threshold, the family or individual is classified as below the poverty level. Poverty thresholds are adjusted annually to allow for changes in the cost of living as reflected in the Consumer Price Index and are computed on a national basis only. The poverty index is based on money income and does not take into account noncash benefits, such as food stamps, Medicaid, and public housing. Differences in poverty thresholds based on farm-nonfarm residence have been eliminated. Nonfarm thresholds now apply to all families. Beginning in 1987, poverty thresholds are based on revised processing procedures and are not directly comparable with prior years.

POVERTY THRESHOLD. See Poverty status.

PRIMARY METROPOLITAN STATISTICAL AREA (PMSA). A Metropolitan Statistical Area which is part of a larger urban complex with a population over one million and is designated as a Consolidated Metropolitan Statistical Area (CMSA).

PRIVATE SCHOOL. Any individual, association, co-partnership, or corporation which designates itself an education center and which includes kindergarten or a higher grade below college level. Primarily supported by private funds.

PROPERTY INCOME. See Income.

PROPRIETORS' INCOME. See Income.

PUBLIC ASSISTANCE INCOME. See Income.

PUBLIC SCHOOL. Any school controlled and supported primarily by a local, state, or federal agency.

RACE. In census enumeration, reflects self-identification by respondents and does not necessarily denote a scientific definition of biological stock.

American Indian, Eskimo, or Aleut includes persons who are classified in one of these specific categories or who entered the name of a specific Indian tribe.

Asian or Pacific Islander includes persons who indicated their race as Japanese (also Nipponese and Japanese American), Chinese (also Cantonese, Tibetan, Chinese American, Taiwanese, and Formosan),

Cambodian, Hmong, Filipino, Korean, Thai, Vietnamese, Asian Indian, Hawaiian, Guamanian, Samoan, Laotian, or entered responses classified as other Asian or other Pacific Islander.
Black includes those who indicated their race as Black or Negro, or who classified themselves as African American, Afro-American, Jamaican, Black Puerto Rican, West Indian, Haitian, or Nigerian.
White includes those who indicated their race as "white," as well as persons who entered a response such as Canadian, German, Italian, Arab, Near Easterner, Lebanese, or Polish.
The other race category includes all persons not listed in the race categories described above. Persons reporting in the "other race" category and providing write-in entries such as multiracial, multiethnic, mixed, interracial, Wesort, or Spanish/Hispanic origin group (such as Mexican, Cuban, or Puerto Rican) are included here.

RENT. Contract (cash) rent is the monthly rent agreed to, or contracted for, regardless of any furnishings, utilities, fees, meals, or services that may be included. For vacant units, it is the monthly rent asked at the time of enumeration. In some tabulations, contract rent is presented for all renter-occupied housing units, as well as for "specified renter-occupied" housing units and for "specified vacant-for-rent" housing units which include renter units except one-family houses or mobile homes on 10 or more acres. Respondents were asked to exclude any rent paid for additional units or for business premises. Gross rent is the contract rent plus the estimated average monthly cost of utilities if these are paid by the renter. Renter units occupied without payment of cash rent are shown separately as no cash rent.

RENTAL VACANCY RATE. The proportion of the rental inventory which is vacant for rent. Rates are computed by dividing the vacant year-round units for rent by the sum of the number of renter-occupied units, vacant year-round units rented by awaiting occupancy, and vacant year-round units for rent.

RENTER-OCCUPIED HOUSING UNIT. See Housing unit.

RESIDENCY. The place where a person lives and sleeps most of the time is the usual residence. It may not be the person's legal or voting residence. College students are considered residents of the community in which they live while attending college. Military personnel (persons in the Armed Forces) are counted as residents of the area in which their installations are located. Persons staying only temporarily away from their usual residence (e.g., migrant workers, vacationers) are considered to have a usual home elsewhere in which they are counted for census purposes.

RETAIL TRADE. Businesses primarily engaged in selling merchandise for personal, household, or farm consumption.

RURAL FARM POPULATION. Only in rural areas and includes all persons living on places of one acre or more from which at least $1,000 worth of agricultural products were sold during 1989.

RURAL POPULATION. Population not classified as urban.

SCHOOL DISTRICT. A political organization and jurisdiction that supports and administers local public schools. There is an independent school district in each Florida county and there are 28 community college districts in the state.

SCHOOL MEMBERSHIP (ENROLLMENT). Cumulative number of students registered during a school year.

SERVICE INDUSTRIES. Establishments primarily engaged in rendering a wide variety of services to individuals and to business establishments.

SIC. Abbreviation of Standard Industrial Classification. See Industrial Classification System, Standard.

SOCIAL SECURITY INCOME. See Income.

SPANISH ORIGIN. See Hispanic origin.

SPECIAL DISTRICT. A local government entity established to provide one or more specific function(s) such as fire protection, public transit, water management, libraries, or hospitals. About one-third of Florida's special districts have taxing power.

TENURE OF HOUSING UNIT. See Housing unit.

TRANSFER PAYMENTS. General disbursements to persons for which they do not render current services. These include payments by government and business to individuals and nonprofit institutions.

UNEMPLOYED PERSONS. All civilians 16 years of age and over who do not work and who actively seek employment, and who are available to work except for temporary illness (during a given reference week).

UNRELATED INDIVIDUAL. Householder living alone or with nonrelatives or household member who is not related to the householder by blood, marriage, or adoption, or person living in group quarters who is not an inmate of an institution.

URBAN POPULATION. Comprises all persons living in urbanized areas and in places (incorporated and unincorporated) of 2,500 or more inhabitants outside urbanized areas.

URBANIZED AREA. Incorporated place and adjacent densely settled surrounding area that together have a minimum population of 50,000.

VACANT HOUSING UNIT. See Housing unit.

WHITE POPULATION. See Race.

WHOLESALE TRADE. Establishments primarily engaged in selling merchandise to retailers, to institutions, to industrial, commercial, and professional users, or to other wholesalers.

WORKERS. See Labor force and Class of workers.

WORKERS' COMPENSATION. State-administered medical care payments and income maintenance. Benefits are granted for work-caused disability, illness, injury, or death.

INDEX OF CENSUS TABLES

The U.S. Bureau of the Census conducts various censuses at regular intervals. This index lists tables that include data from the most recent of these censuses published in the 1990 through 1995 editions of the *Florida Statistical Abstract*. Only tables that cite Census publications and/or Census Summary Tape Files (STF) as the primary source are listed here. The Bureau of the Census is used frequently as a secondary source on tables throughout the *Abstract*. The user is encouraged to refer to the index at the back of the book for aid in locating additional census-related data. No tables from the 1996 edition are included here. A more complete index of census tables may be found in *Abstracts* from 1994 and earlier. Users are also directed to the *1990 Census Handbook - Florida* published in 1994 by the Bureau of Economic and Business Research. It contains the most-used state and county data from the decennial census.

CENSUS OF AGRICULTURE
(Conducted approximately every 5 years)

CENSUS OF GOVERNMENTS
(Conducted every 5 years)

CENSUS OF HOUSING
(Conducted every 10 years)

AREA AND DEMOGRAPHIC HARACTERISTIC INCLUDED	FLORIDA CENSUS YEAR	STATISTICAL ABSTRACT YEAR	STATISTICAL ABSTRACT TABLE
FLORIDA, SELECTED STATES, AND UNITED STATES			
UNITS IN STRUCTURE, PERCENTAGE AND MEDIAN VALUE OF OCCUPIED UNITS	1990*	1992-1994	25.01
STATE AND COUNTIES			
MOBILE HOMES BY HOUSING CHARACTERISTICS	1990	1992-1995	2.35
OCCUPIED HOUSING UNITS AND PERCENTAGE OWNER- AND RENTER-OCCUPIED	1990*	1992-1994	2.06
DITTO	1990*	1995	2.06
OCCUPIED HOUSING UNITS BY NUMBER OF UNITS IN STRUCTURE BY TENURE	1990	1992-1994	2.08
OCCUPIED HOUSING UNITS BY RACE AND HISPANIC ORIGIN OF HOUSEHOLDER	1990	1992-1994	2.07
BY TENURE	1990	1992-1994	2.07
OWNER-OCCUPIED HOUSING UNITS BY VALUE	1990*	1992-1995	2.09
RENTER-OCCUPIED HOUSING UNITS BY AMOUNT OF RENT	1990	1992-1994	2.10
DITTO	1990	1995	2.11
TOTAL, VACANT AND OCCUPIED HOUSING UNITS, AND VACANCY RATES	1990*	1991-1993	2.01
DITTO	1990*	1994-1995	2.02
TYPE AND PURPOSE OF FUEL USED	1990	1992-1994	15.05

CENSUS OF MANUFACTURES
(Conducted every 5 years)

AREA AND DEMOGRAPHIC CHARACTERISTIC INCLUDED	FLORIDA CENSUS YEAR	STATISTICAL ABSTRACT YEAR	STATISTICAL ABSTRACT TABLE
STATE AND SMSAS			
CHARACTERISTICS	1972-1982	1990	12.01
DITTO	1972-1987	1991-1995	12.01
ESTABLISHMENTS, EMPLOYMENT, VALUE ADDED BY MANUFACTURE, AND NEW CAPITAL EXPENDITURE	1972-1982	1990	12.01
DITTO	1972-1987	1991-1995	12.01
VALUE ADDED BY MANUFACTURE	1972-1982	1990	12.01
DITTO	1972-1987	1991-1995	12.01
STATE AND COUNTIES			
ESTABLISHMENTS, EMPLOYMENT, VALUE ADDED BY MANUFACTURE, VALUE OF SHIPMENTS, AND NEW CAPITAL EXPENDITURE	1987	1991-1994	12.06

*1990 Census of Population and Housing.

CENSUS OF POPULATION
(Conducted every 10 years)

AREA AND DEMOGRAPHIC CHARACTERISTIC INCLUDED	FLORIDA CENSUS YEAR	STATISTICAL ABSTRACT YEAR	STATISTICAL ABSTRACT TABLE
FLORIDA, SELECTED STATES, AND UNITED STATES			
EDUCATIONAL ATTAINMENT, HIGH SCHOOL AND COLLEGE GRADUATES	1990*	1992-1994	25.01
FAMILY HOUSEHOLD MEDIAN INCOME	1990	1992-1993	25.01
MOBILITY STATUS	1990*	1992-1994	25.01
PERCENTAGE OF PERSONS BELOW POVERTY LEVEL	1990*	1992-1993	25.01
FLORIDA AND UNITED STATES			
RACE AND HISPANIC ORIGIN	1990*	1992-1994	1.25
FLORIDA, STATE ONLY			
POPULATION, TOTAL	1830-1990	1991-1995	1.10
URBAN AND RURAL POPULATION	1830-1990	1991-1995	1.10
STATE AND COUNTIES			
AGE	1990*	1991	1.35
EDUCATIONAL ATTAINMENT	1990	1992-1995	4.01
EMPLOYMENT	1990	1992-1994	6.09
FAMILY HOUSEHOLD MEDIAN INCOME	1990	1992-1995	5.58
DITTO	1990	1992-1995	5.56
FAMILY HOUSEHOLDS BY SEX OF HOUSEHOLDER	1990	1992-1995	5.51
FAMILY HOUSEHOLDS BY INCOME LEVEL	1990	1992-1995	5.56
HIGH SCHOOL GRADUATES	1980-1990	1992-1995	4.01
HISPANIC ORIGIN	1990	1992-1995	1.26
HOUSEHOLD MEDIAN INCOME	1980-1990	1992-1994	5.58
DITTO	1990	1995	5.58
DITTO	1990	1992-1995	5.55
HOUSEHOLDS BY INCOME LEVEL	1990*	1992-1995	5.55
LABOR FORCE PARTICIPATION OF WOMEN AND WOMEN BY PRESENCE OF CHILDREN	1980-1990	1992-1995	6.13
LANGUAGE SPOKEN AT HOME	1990	1992-1995	1.92
MARITAL STATUS	1990	1992-1995	1.95
MEDIAN AGE	1970-1990	1995	1.38
NONFAMILY HOUSEHOLD MEDIAN INCOME	1990	1992-1995	5.58
DITTO	1990	1992-1995	5.57
NONFAMILY HOUSEHOLDS BY INCOME LEVEL	1990*	1992-1995	5.57
PERSONS BY OCCUPATION	1990*	1992-1994	6.24
PERSONS IN GROUP QUARTERS	1990*	1992-1995	2.16
POVERTY STATUS OF PERSONS, FAMILY HOUSEHOLDS, AND UNRELATED INDIVIDUALS	1990	1992-1995	5.50
POVERTY STATUS OF MALE HOUSEHOLDER FAMILIES AN FEMALE HOUSEHOLDER FAMILIES BY PRESENCE OF CHILDREN	1990	1992-1995	5.51
RACE	1990	1992-1995	1.26
RESIDENCE IN 1985 OF 1990 POPULATION	1990*	1992-1994	1.73
SEX	1990*	1991	1.35
TRANSPORTATION TO WORK	1990	1992-1995	13.01
URBAN AND RURAL POPULATION, AND RURAL FARM	1990*	1992-1995	1.11
STATE, COUNTIES, AND MUNICIPALITIES			
INCOME, PER CAPITA	1980-1990*	1992-1995	5.45

*1990 Census of Population and Housing.

CENSUS OF RETAIL TRADE
(Conducted approximately every 5 years)

AREA AND DEMOGRAPHIC CHARACTERISTIC INCLUDED	FLORIDA CENSUS YEAR	STATISTICAL ABSTRACT YEAR	STATISTICAL ABSTRACT TABLE
STATE AND COUNTIES			
WHOLESALE AND RETAIL TRADE, SALES	1987	1990-1992	16.06
DITTO	1992	1995	16.06
FLORIDA, STATE ONLY			
ESTABLISHMENTS, SALES, AND NUMBER OF UNINCORPORATED BUSINESSES BY KIND OF BUSINESS	1987	1990-1994	16.12
ESTABLISHMENTS, SALES, AND PAYROLL BY KIND OF BUSINESS	1992	1995	16.12
ESTABLISHMENTS, SALES, AND SALES PER ESTABLISHMENT	1939-1987	1990-1994	16.11
DITTO	1948-1992	1995	16.11

CENSUS OF SERVICE INDUSTRIES
(Conducted every 5 years)

AREA AND DEMOGRAPHIC CHARACTERISTIC INCLUDED	FLORIDA CENSUS YEAR	STATISTICAL ABSTRACT YEAR	STATISTICAL ABSTRACT TABLE
FLORIDA, STATE ONLY			
ESTABLISHMENTS AND RECEIPTS BY KIND OF BUSINESS	1982-1987	1991-1994	18.01
ESTABLISHMENTS, RECEIPTS, AND PAYROLL BY KIND OF BUSINESS	1987	1991-1994	18.02
DITTO	1987-1992	1995	18.01
HEALTH, EDUCATIONAL, AND SOCIAL SERVICES BY KIND OF BUSINESS, NUMBER OF ESTABLISHMENTS AND RECEIPTS	1982-1987	1991-1992	20.01
HEALTH, EDUCATIONAL, AND SOCIAL SERVICES BY KIND OF BUSINESS, NUMBER OF ESTABLISHMENTS, RECEIPTS, AND PAYROLL	1987-1992	1995	20.01
HEALTH, EDUCATIONAL, AND SOCIAL SERVICES, ESTABLISHMENTS AND RECEIPTS BY TAX STATUS	1987	1991-1992	20.02

CENSUS OF WHOLESALE TRADE
(Conducted approximately every 5 years)

AREA AND DEMOGRAPHIC CHARACTERISTIC INCLUDED	FLORIDA CENSUS YEAR	STATISTICAL ABSTRACT YEAR	STATISTICAL ABSTRACT TABLE
FLORIDA, STATE ONLY			
ESTABLISHMENTS, SALES, AND SALES PER ESTABLISHMENT	1948-1987	1990-1993	16.01
DITTO	1958-1987	1994	16.01
DITTO	1963-1992	1995	16.01
BY SIC CODE	1987	1990-1994	16.02
DITTO	1992	1995	16.02
STATE AND COUNTIES			
WHOLESALE AND RETAIL TRADE, SALES	1987	1990-1992	16.06
DITTO	1992	1995	16.06

Index of Tables

R

V

W

The *1990 Census Handbook: Florida* is a 'must have' for your reference shelf, providing easy access to the 1990 Census of Population and Housing. Most of these data will not be updated until after the year 2000 and there's no need to continue searching through volumes and volumes of books, tapes and CD-ROMS.

The *1990 Census Handbook: Florida* is one-stop-shopping for Census data. BEBR staff have compiled the most used and most requested data from the 1990 census in one book.

You will find U.S., state, county, city, and congressional district detail in the *Census Handbook.* We've included age, race, sex, ethnicity, language, education, income, employment, poverty, housing, disability and much, much more in a convenient, comprehensive and easy-to-use resource. $19.95 plus applicable sales tax. Diskette - $75.

Add applicable sales tax and send check made payable to University of Florida:
University of Florida
Bureau of Economic and Business Research
221 Matherly Hall
Post Office Box 117145
Gainesville, FL 32611-7145

or call (352) 392-0171 x219 to order.

If you don't have

order your copy today!